Russia
Sweden
Finland
Estonia
Latvia
Lithuania
Russia
Belarus
Germany
Poland
Czech
Slovakia
Ukraine
Switz.
Austria
Hungary
Moldova
Slovenia
Croatia
Romania
Italy
Serbia
Bulgaria
Georgia
Bosnia
Montenegro
Macedonia
Armenia
Albania
Greece
Turkey
Azerbaijan
Kazakhstan
Uzbekistan
Turkmenistan
Kyrgyzstan
Tajikistan
Mongolia
China
N. Korea
S. Korea
Japan
Tunisia
Cyprus
Lebanon
Israel
Syria
Iraq
Iran
Jordan
Afghanistan
Pakistan
Nepal
Bhutan
Libya
Egypt
Kuwait
Saudi Arabia
Qatar
U.A.E.
Oman
India
Bangladesh
Myanmar
Laos
Taiwan
Niger
Chad
Sudan
Eritrea
Yemen
Djibouti
Thailand
Vietnam
Philippines
Nigeria
Central African Rep.
Ethiopia
Somalia
Sri Lanka
Kampuchea
Cameroon
Brunei
Malaysia
Uganda
Kenya
Singapore
Gabon
Congo
Rwanda
Zaire
Burundi
Tanzania
Indonesia
Papua New Guinea
Angola
Zambia
Malawi
Zimbabwe
Mozambique
Madagascar
Namibia
Botswana
Fiji
New Caledonia
Australia
Swaziland
South Africa
Lesotho
New Zealand

Robinson Projection

Comparative Economic Systems

7TH EDITION

MARTIN C. SCHNITZER
Virginia Polytechnic Institute and State University

SOUTH-WESTERN College Publishing
An International Thomson Publishing Company

Acquisitions Editor: Jack C. Calhoun
Developmental Editor: Lois Boggs-Leavens
Production Editor: Sharon L. Smith
Production House: Lachina Publishing Services
Cover and Interior Designer: Craig LaGesse Ramsdell
Marketing Manager: Scott D. Person

Library of Congress Cataloging-in-Publication Data

Schnitzer, Martin.
Comparative economic systems / Martin C. Schnitzer.—7th ed.
p. cm.
Includes bibliographical references and index.
ISBN 0-538-85714-5
1. Comparative economics. I. Title.
HB90.S35 1996
330.12—dc20

96-20512
CIP

2 3 4 5 6 7 8 MT 3 2 1 0 9 8 7 6
Printed in the United States of America

International Thomson Publishing

South-Western College Publishing is an ITP Company. The ITP trademark is used under license.

Preface

The world continues to change since the sixth edition of this book appeared in 1994. The former Communist countries of central and eastern Europe continue to make progress in their conversion to market economies. It has not been easy for most of them. In some countries, the period of economic decline during the transition period is over; for other countries, it is not. In such countries as the Czech Republic, Hungary, and Poland, the process of privatization has dramatically altered the structure of ownership. There has also been a fundamental transition in the role of the state, in particular in the provision of the economic, financial, and legal institutions necessary to provide the underpinnings of a market economy. Nevertheless, challenges remain before the industrial and environmental legacy of decades of the Communist system can be overcome.

Capitalism and democracy now pretty much have the field to themselves, because there is no other competition for the allegiance of the minds of their citizens. However, powerful dynamics at work in the world can create instability. One dynamic, technology, has created a period that will be dominated by brainpower industries. Technology is transferable, which means that anything can be made anywhere in the world. Then there is the matter of an aging population in the rich industrial countries of the world, and an increasing population in the poor countries of the world. The aging population will strain the financial resources of the rich countries, and population growth in the poor countries will hinder their economic development and will cause millions of people to migrate to rich countries.

The three major economic areas of the world—the United States, Europe, and Japan—have developed serious problems. In the United States, real wages for the majority of American workers have fallen over the past twenty years, and income differences between rich and poor have increased. Unemployment has increased in Europe. High tax burdens and government regulation of business have had an adverse impact on entrepreneurship to the point that Europe has created no new jobs over the last three years. Japan, too, has its problems. Its "bubble economy" based on rising real estate prices has collapsed, and some of its giant banks have financial problems. But its main problem is the aging of its population, which will result in ever-increasing financial outlays on the part of the government.

The seventh edition of this book has several main purposes. The first is to compare three variants of capitalism, using the United States, Germany, and Japan as examples. The second is to examine the process of transition from communism to capitalism in four countries—Russia, Poland, the Czech Republic, and Hungary. Particular emphasis is placed on examining the present and the future of Russia. A third objective is to examine the development of the so-called Third World nations, which have the great bulk of the world's population but less than 20 percent of the world's GNP. The two largest countries in the world, China and India, will be compared in terms of their economic development. Other countries examined include Mexico, Nigeria, and South Africa.

As was true in previous editions, the author has relied on a variety of U.S. and international sources to provide the most current information. In some cases, the changes made in the book included data released as recently as April 1996. Where possible, primary sources were used, such as publications from the OECD, World Bank, International Monetary Fund, and United Nations. The publications of the European Bank for Reconstruction and Development provided the majority of the materials used in the chapters on Russia, Poland, the Czech Republic, and Hungary. The publications of the Inter-American Development Bank were used in the chapter on Mexico, and the monthly reports of the Deutsche Bundesbank provided current information on developments in Germany.

At the end of each chapter there is a summary, an number of discussion questions, and a list of recommended readings. The recommended readings provide the most current bibliography that is available on the subjects discussed in each chapter. A teacher's manual is also provided to aid course instructors. Answers are given for the discussion questions at the end of each chapter. A set of true-false and multiple choice questions are also provided for each chapter.

ACKNOWLDEGMENTS

Many people contributed to the development of this book. Comments received from professors and students over the years have influenced this edition as they did the earlier ones. In particular, I would like to thank my wife, Joan, for her invaluable assistance in typing and proofreading the chapters, and Christiane Bimberg, formerly of Martin Luther University in Halle, Germany, for her assistance in providing me with information concerning the status of East German women during the transition from Communism to capitalism. This edition was also influenced by the comments and suggestions of the following reviewers: Robert J. Jensen, Pacific Lutheran University, Robert T. Jerome, James Madison University, Kehar S. Sangha, Old Dominion University, William C. Schaniel, West Georgia College, Scot A. Stradley, University of North Dakota, and Irvin Weintraub, Towson State University. I also wish to thank Sharon Smith, Lois Boggs-Leavens, Craig Ramsdell, and the rest of the staff at South-Western College Publishing who provided the editorial support necessary to complete the manuscript.

About the Author

Martin C. Schnitzer received his Ph.D. in economics from the University of Florida. He teaches courses in government and business, and international business at Virginia Polytechnic Institute. Dr. Schnitzer is the author of ten books, including one on the Swedish economy and one concerning East and West Germany. He has lectured in Hungary and Poland and served on the U.S. East-West Trade Commission and the Virginia Export Council. He has served as an economic consultant to the U.S. Joint Economic Committee and has published a number of monographs on European economic policy.

Contents

CHAPTER 11
Poland, the Czech Republic, and Hungary 263

PART IV
Economies of the Less Developed and Developing Countries *299*

CHAPTER 12
Problems of the Less Developed Countries 301

PART I
The End of Isms

CHAPTER 1

The Triumph of Capitalism

In a book called *The End of History and the Last Man*,[1] the author, Francis Fukuyama, uses the term "the end of history" to mean that with the defeat of Communism an ideal social and political system is now in place, and there is nowhere else to go. He maintains that the free market has clearly emerged as the most efficient system for producing and distributing goods; the West and Western ideals have triumphed, and they are the endpoint of humankind's ideological revolution. According to Fukuyama, the human race now has one common destiny, a destiny that began with the French Revolution and its ideals of liberty and equality and has ended with the victory of the liberal democratic state. In his view, there will be minor problems here and there, such as the rise of religious fundamentalism and ethnic and nationalist tensions, but they will disappear over time.[2]

1. Francis Fukuyama, *The End of History and the Last Man* (New York: Basic Books, 1991).
2. According to Fukuyama, the end of history will be a sad time. In his view, the struggle for recognition, the willingness to risk one's life for a purely abstract goal, the ideological struggle that called forth daring, courage, and imagination are what made history interesting.

Another author, Robert B. Reich, in *The Work of Nations: Preparing Ourselves for 21st Century Capitalism,*[3] also discounts Communism as a thing of the past and maintains that a global economy dominated by capitalism will exist in the twenty-first century. The United States has led the way toward the attainment of global capitalism. After World War II, it channeled billions of dollars in aid to Western Europe and helped to create international financial institutions such as the International Monetary Fund and the World Bank. The scale and technological superiority of its core corporations extended the reach of U.S. capitalism throughout much of the world. Communism was contained as a political and military threat until its eventual collapse. However, times have also changed for the United States. Today, almost every factor of production—money, technology, factories, and equipment—moves effortlessly across national borders; the idea of a new world order dominated by the United States is meaningless. All that will remain within a nation's border are its people.

A COMPARISON OF CAPITALIST SYSTEMS: ONE APPROACH

Since capitalism has become the sine qua non of the world's present and future existence, what is left to compare? The answer is to compare various types of capitalism. One way in which capitalism can be compared is by distinguishing between individualistic Anglo-Saxon capitalism and communitarian European and Japanese capitalism. This two-pronged comparison, which is based on a distinction made by George C. Lodge,[4] forms part of the foundation of Lester Thurow's *Head to Head: The Coming Economic Battle Among Japan, Europe, and America.*[5] The Anglo-Saxon variant of capitalism dominated the last two centuries, with the United Kingdom dominant in the nineteenth century and the United States in the twentieth century. Who, then, will dominate the twenty-first century? According to Thurow, it will be the communitarian capitalism of Europe.

Individualistic Capitalism

Individualistic capitalism is associated with the writings of John Locke and Adam Smith. It was Locke who developed the argument that the right to govern rests in the hands of the governed, not the governor. Prior to Locke, it had been assumed that the king, not the people, had the right to rule. According to Locke, the individual is a fulcrum of society and has certain inalienable rights, including the right to own property.[6] According to Adam Smith, the individual, if permitted to pursue

3. Robert B. Reich, *The Work of Nations: Preparing Ourselves for 21st Century Capitalism* (New York: Alfred A. Knopf, 1991).
4. George C. Lodge, *The New American Ideology* (New York: Alfred A. Knopf, 1975).
5. Lester Thurow, *Head to Head: The Coming Economic Battle Among Japan, Europe, and America* (New York: Morrow, 1992).
6. John Locke, *Second Treatise on Civil Government, 1681.* Government comes into existence, said Locke, because of property. If there is no property, there is no need for government.

his or her self-interest, will promote the well-being of all. This will not result from charitable motives, but from the inexorable logic of the free market—the "invisible hand." Stated simply, if all people are motivated to work at full capacity, whether as laborers, artisans, or executives, the net supply of goods and services available for consumption by all will be increased.

According to Thurow, individualism in the United States and other Anglo-Saxon countries takes a number of forms: large income differentials, brilliant entrepreneurs such as Bill Gates, the founder of Microsoft and the richest man in America, and short-term profit maximization.[7] In the tradition of individualism each person is responsible for his or her own personal success. Life is a competitive struggle where the fit survive and those who are unfit do not. Individuals owe no particular loyalty to a company; they are free to leave for higher-paying jobs. Conversely, companies feel no loyalty to their employees; they can be laid off when times are bad, or for that matter when times are relatively good, as witnessed by the downsizing of many American corporations. Neither employers nor employees owe each other anything.

Communitarian Capitalism

The term *communitarian* has a number of connotations, but basically it means deriving satisfaction from being part of a group process as opposed to functioning as an individual. The role of the state is greatly expanded under communitarian ideology. It plays roles in stimulating economic growth and providing social welfare programs, and it also is involved in public investment expenditures for such things as job training. There is less job changing and more loyalty to the employer in communitarian capitalistic countries. Employers think more in terms of job retraining and teamwork. Companies think in terms of long-term strategies and often function as part of a group. Close cooperation between companies and the government can also exist. Communitarian capitalism is the result of different cultural and historical developments in Europe and Japan, where governments often as a matter of necessity played an important role in economic development.[8]

Germany and Japan are examples of communitarian capitalist countries. In Germany the state has played an important role since the time of Bismarck. There is codetermination between labor and management, with labor representatives sitting on the boards of directors of German companies. German banks are major shareholders in German companies. Job training is also the responsibility of companies and the government. In Japan the overwhelming emphasis is on the group and one's responsibility to it. Companies (including banks) are often part of a

7. The Anglo-Saxon common law doctrine of employment-at-will holds that the relationship between employer and employee is voluntary. Either one can terminate the relationship at any time. Employers are free to hire: employees are free to quit. Moreover, the private property concept under common law holds that an owner is free to do what he or she wants with it as long as no law is broken.

8. An example is Germany. Massive government intervention occurred in Germany in the period prior to World War I when it was trying to catch up with England as a major economic power. German capitalism had to have governmental help in order to achieve that goal.

group of companies. Employees are loyal to a company, and there is very little job switching. There is cooperation between business and government and between business and labor. Business thinks in terms of long-term objectives as opposed to short-term profit maximization.

A COMPARISON OF CAPITALIST SYSTEMS: AN ALTERNATIVE APPROACH

Although there is some validity to comparing capitalist systems according to the previously discussed two-pronged approach, the author prefers a second approach, which divides capitalist systems into three types. The first is the relatively free market system of the United States, where government intervention in the economy has been more regulatory than distributive.[9] The second is the social market capitalism of Europe, where governments play a major role in income distribution through elaborate social expenditure programs. The final type is the state-directed capitalism of Japan and other East Asian countries. The characteristics of each of these three types of capitalism are presented in the following sections.

U.S. Market Capitalism

Although there is no such thing as a completely free market economy, the United States comes closer than either Europe or Japan to this form of economy. The role of the federal government is smaller than in other capitalist countries. Taxes and government spending in relation to gross national product (GNP) are lower in the United States than in other countries. There is also very little state ownership of industry.[10] However, some government intervention is necessary in even the freest type of economic system. The very atmosphere for the conduct of business is created by the ability of the government to establish and maintain private property, freedom of enterprise, money and credit, and a system of civil laws for adjudicating the private disputes of individuals. Such institutions make possible an elaborate system of private planning in which individuals, rather than government, organize and direct the production of goods and services in response to the desires of consumers.

Social Market Capitalism

Social market capitalism, as represented in Germany and other Western European countries, includes an elaborate system of social welfare programs ranging from national health insurance to family allowances. In these countries a higher percentage of total government expenditures than in the United States go toward transfer

9. Examples are antitrust laws, environmental protection laws, and consumer protection laws.
10. However, privatization has reduced state ownership in many countries. Poland, Argentina, and Mexico are examples.

payments, which are payments such as unemployment compensation or retirement benefits to individuals who provide no goods or services in exchange. Corporations in these countries are far more circumscribed in their treatment of employees. In Germany codetermination gives workers the right to choose members who will sit on the boards of directors of many German companies. The role of government in Germany and other Western European countries is pervasive in several ways—through ownership of shares in private companies, subsidies to industries, and partial ownership of industries. There is also some reliance on economic planning of the indicative type.[11]

State-Directed Capitalism

This variant of capitalism exists in Japan and other East Asian countries. There is a far closer relationship between government and business in such countries as Japan and South Korea than in the United States and Europe, particularly in the allocation of capital and the role of industrial policy in the economy. Cultural differences between Japan and the United States and Europe make for a much more group-oriented form of capitalism based on consensus among various Japanese groups than in the more individualistic capitalism of the West. There is an absence of the welfare state in Japan; the function of social provider falls to business firms. There is indicative planning, but it is based in government consensus with other groups. Finally, there is an industrial policy in which industry representatives working with the Japanese Ministry of International Trade and Industry discuss strategies regarding where the economy should be going and key industries are targeted for capital allocation.

Public Sector Expenditures and Taxation

These three types of capitalism can be compared on the basis of the extent of government involvement in the economy. Two ways to compare this involvement are through the relationships of government expenditures to GNP and of taxes to GNP. The relationship of expenditures to GNP indicates the extent to which resources have been diverted from private to public use. These expenditures involve use of transfer payments as an instrument for the redistribution of income from one group to another. They include family allowances, old-age pensions, and unemployment compensation. Such expenditures also involve the provision of a broad array of goods, such as roads. On the other hand, the relationship of taxes to GNP indicates the extent to which governments have control over economic resources and the degree to which the cost of public activity is borne by the taxpayers of a nation.

11. Economic planning has been classified as indicative or imperative. Indicative planning applies to an economy in which a government indicates goals and stimulates compliance through tax and transfer policies. Imperative planning involves direct government control over resource allocation.

Table 1-1 presents government expenditures expressed as a percentage of GNP for countries representing each variant of capitalism. In 1993 Japan, Canada, and the United States had the lowest percentage of government expenditures to GNP, while the European countries had the highest.

Table 1-2 presents the relationship of taxes to GNP and compares various sources of revenue for the ten major countries. In 1993 taxes expressed as a percentage of GNP ranged from a high of 50.7 percent for the Netherlands to a low of 14.5 percent for Japan. Taxation can result in income redistribution, with various income groups having different proportions of national income after taxes than before. Income redistribution will occur particularly if the tax system is progressive. Income taxes accounted for 70 percent of central government revenues in Japan compared to 5.8 percent in Sweden.[12] Conversely, social security contributions accounted for 46.2 percent of government revenues in Germany compared to 0.0 percent in Japan. Indirect taxes expressed as a percentage of total central government expenditures ranged from a high of 32.7 percent in Sweden to a low of 3.8 percent in the United States.[13]

Governments in all of these countries have come to play a very important role in the attainment of such economic goals as employment, price stability, and economic growth. Gone are the days of laissez-faire, with its idea of limited government. Governments have come to serve as a powerful determinant of productive capacity through direct participation in the formation of capital. Government expenditures also have contributed to the health, education, and training of the labor force, and hence to productive capacity. Government has used income taxation and transfer payments to create a more equitable distribution of income. Many of these governments engage in regulation and control of business, for example, through antitrust laws, which are designed to protect consumers from such anticompetitive business practices as price fixing. Finally, these governments engage in social regulation, which involves occupational safety, environmental protection, and so forth.

CAPITALISM AND DEMOCRACY

Perhaps because various noncapitalistic economic systems have usually operated under dictatorial governments, there is a tendency to make capitalism synonymous with democracy. Actually the government of a capitalist economic system does not have to be democratic in the strict sense of the word. In a large and heavily populated capitalistic system like the United States, it would be impossible for all citizens to participate in the democratic process as they might have in the old New England town meetings.[14] It is also doubtful whether the citizens of a capitalist economy could participate in the government in any case since they dif-

12. The U.S. income tax is not really progressive. Its maximum rate is 39.6 percent.
13. It should be remembered that indirect taxes, such as sales taxes, are more widely used by state and local governments in the United States.
14. In fact, the majority of Americans do not vote in national, state, and local elections.

TABLE 1-1 *Central Government Expenditures by Types and as a Percentage of GNP, 1993*

	Percentage of Total Government Expenditures					
Country	*Education*	*Health*	*Social Security*	*Services*	*Percentage of GNP*	*Deficit as Percent*
United States	2.0	17.1	31.7	6.2	23.8	–4.0
Canada	2.7	4.6	41.9	8.7	25.8	–3.8
United Kingdom	3.3	14.0	32.5	6.6	43.4	–5.1
Italy	—	—	—	—	53.4	–10.1
Netherlands	10.2	13.7	41.5	5.6	53.9	–0.9
Sweden	7.3	0.4	53.3	16.2	53.9	–12.2
Spain	4.7	—	38.8	8.9	35.1	–3.7
France	7.0	16.1	45.5	5.0	45.5	–3.8
Germany	0.8	16.8	45.9	9.7	33.6	–2.4
Japan	—	—	—	—	15.8	—

Source: The World Bank, *World Development Report 1995* (New York: Oxford University Press, 1995), 181.

TABLE 1-2 *Central Government Revenues by Types and as a Percentage of GNP, 1993*

	Percentage of Government Revenue			
Country	*Income Taxes*	*Social Security*	*Indirect Taxes*	*Percent*
United States	50.7	34.2	3.8	19.7
Canada	52.7	16.7	17.7	22.1
United Kingdom	35.3	16.4	32.1	36.2
Italy	37.6	30.5	27.1	41.8
Netherlands	30.7	36.8	21.0	50.7
Sweden	5.8	36.7	32.7	40.1
Spain	32.2	37.9	21.7	31.4
France	17.3	44.5	27.0	40.7
Germany	15.0	46.2	24.5	31.6
Japan	70.0	0.0	16.9	14.5

Source: The World Bank, *World Development Report 1995* (New York: Oxford University Press, 1995), 183.

fer so much as individuals with respect to such matters as wealth and income, economic opportunities, education, and social status.

Is democracy consistent with economic efficiency? Lee Kuan Yew, Singapore's leader for many years, contends that it is not, because it leads to a lack of discipline that is inimical to economic development.[15] It is also argued that Taiwan and South Korea, two more of the East Asian state-directed economic powerhouses, have done well because they have been spared popular pressure to save jobs in unproductive industries, and thus were able to concentrate on policies likely to create new jobs and new wealth. However, one cannot conclude from the

15. Fareed Zakaria, "A Conversation with Lee Kuan Yew," *Foreign Affairs,* Vol. 73, No. 2 (March-April 1994), 109–126.

successes of these East Asian countries that nondemocratic governments are best for economic development. Were that the case, many other countries in Africa and South America would have achieved similar results. Cultural factors have played an important role in East Asian success.[16]

THE COLLAPSE OF COMMUNISM AND THE TRANSITION TO CAPITALISM

The collapse of Communism, although forecast by some Western experts,[17] was quite sudden. In a period of less than two years, Communism collapsed in the Soviet Union and in its Eastern European satellite countries. Political and economic structures that had been regarded as unchangeable have dissolved, and the generally accepted aim is the substitution of a market system for the old socialist system. The economies of the former Soviet Union and Eastern Europe lagged well behind those of Western industrial nations. Central economic planning was inefficient, and rejection of market prices, wages, and interest rates as indicators of scarcity resulted in production unrelated to the needs of consumers. State subsidies obscured high production costs and led to a waste of resources. State-imposed limitations on individual decision-making power crippled initiative and led to a decline in motivation. Reforms, when they finally came, were too little and too late to save the Soviet Union and Eastern Europe.

The economic performance of the Soviet Union and the Eastern-bloc countries was very much overrated by the West. It has cost East Germany, rated the star performer of all the former Communist countries, far more than anticipated to convert to the capitalist German system. Its productivity was less than half that of capitalist West Germany, and 70 percent of its giant state enterprises were obsolete and useless. It will cost at least $200 billion to modernize the East German transportation and communication systems, most of which were constructed before World War II. It will also cost billions of dollars to clean up the East German environment, considered to the most polluted in Europe. It will cost up to $1 trillion, or even more, to bring the East German economy up to West German levels.[18] But East Germany has been fortunate in that it has a wealthy West Germany willing to incur these costs in the interest of reunification.[19] Other former Communist countries, even though they have received foreign aid, are more on their own.

16. One factor is the so-called Confucian work ethic; another is the emphasis placed on responsibility to the family.

17. For example, Zbigniew Brzezinski, *The Grand Failure: The Birth and Death of Communism in the Twentieth Century* (New York: Charles Scribner's Sons, 1989); Judy Shelton, *The Coming Soviet Crash* (New York: Free Press, 1989).

18. Estimates made by the International Monetary Fund (IMF). The actual cost may be higher.

19. "Willing" is probably a major overstatement. The West German taxpayers, who have to bear the cost of reunification, are not happy. This has caused friction between West Germans and East Germans.

Table 1-3 presents per capita GNP for the Soviet Union, the Eastern European counties, and Yugoslavia for 1990, the year that transition to market economies started. East Germany was on its way to reunification, but its per capita GNP was about one-fourth that of West Germany.[20] The per capita GNP of the Soviet Union, which was very much overstated by some Western sources,[21] was $1,780, about one-third that of South Korea and less than those of Mexico, Panama, and Costa Rica.

The problems of conversion from centrally planned economies to market economies have been complex. The initial results have been serious economic disruptions and steep declines in output. National income has dropped in all of these countries, but particularly in the former Soviet Union. Fixed investment has also fallen, particularly in those industries where it is needed the most—energy, machine tools, chemicals, and housing. Foreign trade among the countries has collapsed, since the Council for Mutual Economic Assistance (CMEA) is no longer in existence. Table 1-4 presents changes in the growth of gross domestic product (GDP) in the Soviet Union and Eastern Europe from 1981 through 1992, highlighting the impact of the transition, which began in 1990.

Economic Problems of Transformation

Conversion from a centrally planned economy to a free market economy has not been easy, because a number of economic and social problems had to be overcome. The production systems of the Eastern European countries and the states that comprise the former Soviet Union had to be completely restructured and modernized, since they were obsolete and could not meet domestic needs or international standards. The division of labor under the old regimes did not reflect comparative cost advantages, being instead the result of state-imposed specialization oriented toward the needs of governmental economic plans. Attempts to achieve self-sufficiency led to governmental support of inefficient industries. Thus, the whole production system of each country had to be modernized and adapted to the needs of domestic and international markets, and infrastructures had to be modernized to facilitate both production and distribution.

Not only did production systems and physical infrastructures need to be changed; the human infrastructure also needed to change to overcome inexperience with capitalism and market institutions. Managers of state enterprises had to conform only to the dictates of the government's economic plan. Entrepreneurship and individual initiative are traits that have to be learned. Since workers were guaranteed employment, there was little incentive to work hard.[22] Income differences have widened as some people get ahead. This has created envy, because

20. "Grossly Exaggerated Product," *The Economist,* March 10, 1990, 71.

21. The CIA's *Handbook of Economic Statistics* for 1991 lists a per capita gross domestic product of $9,140 for the Soviet Union.

22. As one joke among Communist workers purportedly put it: "We pretend to work and they pretend to pay us."

TABLE 1-3 *Per Capita GNP for the Soviet Union, Eastern Europe, and Yugoslavia, 1990**

Country	*Per Capita GNP*
Soviet Union	$1,780
East Germany*	4,000
Bulgaria	2,210
Czechoslovakia	3,140
Hungary	2,780
Poland	1,700
Romania	1,640
Yugoslavia	3,060

**East German data from 1989.*

Sources: "Grossly Exaggerated Product," *The Economist,* March 10, 1990, 71; The World Bank, *The World Bank Atlas 1991,* 6–9; *The Economy of the USSR,* joint report by the World Bank, IMF, OECD, and EBRD.

TABLE 1-4 *Changes in Rates of Growth of GDP for the Soviet Union and Eastern Europe (annual average percentage change)*

Country	*1981–1987*	*1989*	*1990*	*1991**	*1992**
Soviet Union	3.2	3.3	–2.1	–15.0	–12.0
Eastern Europe					
Bulgaria	3.9	–1.4	–11.8	–22.0	–10.0
Czechoslovakia	1.4	1.3	–4.7	–12.0	–5.0
East Germany	4.1	2.4	–25.1		
Hungary	2.1	–0.2	–4.0	–6.0	–5.0
Poland	0.7	0.2	–12.0	–8.0	–3.0
Romania	4.5	–3.9	–8.2	–15.0	–5.0

**Estimates.*

Source: United Nations, Department of International Economic and Social Affairs, *The World Economy at the End of 1991: Short-Term Prospects and Issues,* December 1991, 6.

under Communism, no one, except for the members of the nomenklatura elite, had that much more money than the next person.[23]

Social Problems of Transformation

The social problems of transformation have been as difficult as the economic problems, if not more so. There has been a reconfiguration of the entire society of the former Communist countries into new social structures based on income. If there were not many winners under Communism, there also were not many losers. But times have changed, and there are some big winners and more big losers. Although safety-net measures have been taken, the social costs of economic transi-

23. Hedrick Smith, *The New Russians* (New York: Random House, 1990), Chapter 10, The Culture of Envy.

tion have been considerable. These costs have been borne by older people who depend on a state pension and who are faced with rising prices. The shift to the market economy has made people as well as industries obsolete. Gone are the certainties of a lifetime job, of subsidized holidays at company resorts, and of a certain stability based on a state-directed and controlled society where in exchange for security, obedience was expected in return.

Moscow, once the center of Communist rule, has become much like the Chicago of the 1920s when that city was dominated by Al Capone. Prostitution, protection rackets, murders, and other forms of crime have become common. But these forms of activities are not just limited to Moscow; they have spread to other Russian cities. The number of organized criminal groups more than quadrupled between 1990 and 1993. No longer can Russians walk through neighborhoods once thought safe. But it can be added that crime and corruption were well established in the Soviet planned economy, where bribery was a way of getting things done. Consumers could use bribes to get such things as automobiles and apartments. Bribery within the Communist Party apparatus was a way to get better jobs.[24]

Political Problems of Transformation

One thing that was supposed to happen after the collapse of Communism was the replacement of Communist Party leaders with democratically elected officials. For the most part, this has not happened.[25] In September 1993 parties led by former Communists and their allies won a majority of seats in Polish parliamentary elections. In Hungary in the spring of 1994 the former Communist Party, operating under a new name, won a majority of parliamentary seats. In Slovakia former Communists calling themselves Social Democrats replaced former Communists calling themselves Nationalists. In Romania the old status quo remains, even though the name of the party has been changed. Former dissidents and intellectuals who were largely instrumental in bringing about the collapse of Communism have been left out in the cold, replaced by politicians who were a part of the old power base and who had the contacts.

Does any of this matter? It is to be seriously doubted that there will be a return to the old-style Soviet Communism. For one thing, those who made out under Communism are now making out under capitalism.[26] A Polish study found that over half of the top leaders of the former Communist Party ended up as top busi-

24. Jim Leitzel, Clifford Gaddy, and Michael Alexeev, "Mafiosi and Matrioshki," *The Brookings Review*, Vol. 13, No. 1 (Winter 1995), 26–30.

25. Anne Applebaum, "The Fall and Rise of the Communists," *Foreign Affairs*, Vol. 73, No. 6 (November-December 1994), 7–13.

26. The author can cite three examples of persons he knows who have made the successful transformation from communism to capitalism. One, who was rector of a Polish university and a Communist, is now a member of the Polish parliament; a second, who was a professor at the same university and was Communist Party secretary for the city, is still a professor, has the same office, and is a business consultant; and a third, who was a professor and a party member, now works for the European Bank for Reconstruction and Development in London.

ness executives in the new economy.[27] With better connections, more money, and more property to begin with, they have benefited even more. Also, Poland, Hungary, the Czech Republic, and other Eastern-bloc countries want to join the European Union. On the downside, there is an adverse effect on democracy. Even when former Communists have a genuine interest in economic reforms, they can use their power to suppress the growth of rival political parties.

Approaches to a Market Economy

There are several approaches that can be used to convert a centrally planned economy into a market economy, but regardless of the approach, conversion does not come easily. One is called the "big bang" approach, which means that sweeping reforms are implemented immediately. Prices are freed from state control to seek their market-determined level, and the currency unit is devalued to reach a level more consistent with the values of international currencies. State subsidies of all types are eliminated, interest rates are allowed to rise, and state enterprises are turned loose to compete on their own. Wages are freed from state control and determined by market forces. Problems with the big bang approach include a high rate of unemployment and rising prices for goods and services.

A second approach is called the gradual approach, which means that changes will be spaced out over time to prevent economic disruptions such as inflation and unemployment. An example would be the gradual lifting of state price control over basic consumer goods and services, such as food and housing. Once one reform is consolidated and in place, another reform begins. The gradual approach protects many workers from the sharp shifts in income distribution that occur when the big bang is used. However, this approach also has its problems. One is the temptation not to go all the way to complete necessary reforms. The free market does not work if much of an economy remains centrally planned. For example, the price mechanism does not work when some prices are freed while others remain controlled, because production will gravitate toward areas in which prices are not controlled.

RICH COUNTRIES AND POOR COUNTRIES

Economic history shows that it is possible for countries to develop rapidly. For many countries, the pace of change has accelerated. For example, it took the United Kingdom fifty-eight years to double its output per worker, the United States forty-seven years, and Japan thirty-four years. However, it took South Korea only eleven years and China less than ten years.[28] The key is technological

27. Applebaum, 11. The numbers were higher in Hungary and Russia. In the former East Germany, former Communist officials were elected to office in both state and national elections held in the fall of 1994.

28. The World Bank, *World Development Report 1991* (Washington, D.C.: The World Bank, 1991), 12.

progress. Technology is far more transferable today than it was a hundred years ago, so developing countries have free access to technology introduced by industrial countries. Catching up is always easier than being the technological leader. Producers in poor countries can copy others' methods and technologies at relatively low cost, whereas rich countries have to devise new technologies to maintain rapid growth.

Today the industrialized economies dominate the world as they have for this century. However, it is possible that within a generation, several may be replaced by newly emerging economic powers. By 2020, China and India could rank among the world's five biggest economies. Many other nations could be rich by current standards. Score of countries, including those in the former Soviet bloc, have embraced market-friendly economic reforms and opened their borders to trade and investment. These policies are designed to promote rapid economic growth. But that does not mean that everybody will be a winner. For some parts of the world, notably Africa, the prospects for rapid economic development look grim, particularly if political instability continues and population growth outruns resources. Given the potential for political instability, the economic prospects of Russia are fragile.

Rich North, Poor South

The map in Figure 1-1 shows the division of the economies of the world based on income. High-income economies are located primarily in the Northern Hemisphere. Of the forty-four high-income economies, only two—Australia and New Zealand—are in the Southern Hemisphere. Of the sixty-four low-income economies, the great majority are located in Africa and Asia. In Asia, Bangladesh and Vietnam are among the world's poorest countries, with per capita incomes of less than $250 in 1994.[29] Africa is the poorest continent in the world. Of the sixty-four low-income countries with per capita incomes of $725 a year or less, thirty-one are in Africa. The real growth rate in per capital GNP for many African countries declined during the 1980s. Population increases that exceed growth compound the problems of most African countries. In Egypt, the population increased at an average rate of 2.0 percent for the period 1985–1994, while the real growth rate increased at an average of 1.0 percent.[30]

Table 1-5 presents a breakdown of the world economies on the basis of a division between low income, defined as a yearly income of $725 or less; lower-middle income, defined as $726 to $2,895; upper-middle income, defined as $2,896 to $8,955; and high income, defined as $8,956 or more.[31] The sixty-four low-income countries include China with a 1994 per capita income of $530 and India with a per capita income of $310. As the table indicates, approximately 60 percent of the

29. The World Bank, *The World Bank Atlas 1996* (Washington, D.C.: The World Bank, 1996), 20.
30. Three of the world's poorest countries are located in North America. Haiti has a per capita income of $220. In Central America, Honduras has a per capita income of $580 and Nicaragua a per capita income of $330.
31. The World Bank, *The World Bank Atlas 1996* (Washington, D.C.: The World Bank, 1996), 20.

FIGURE 1-1

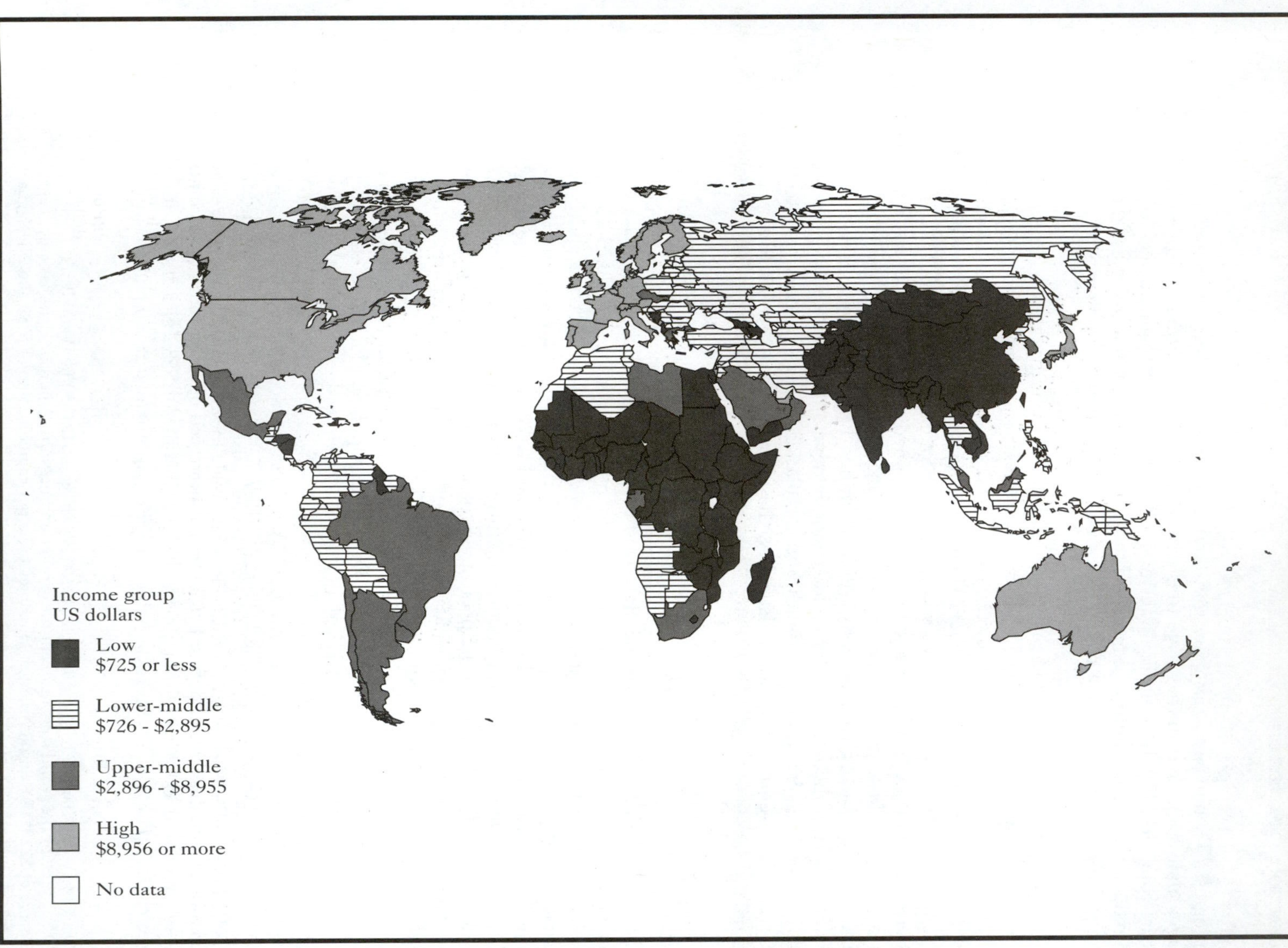

Source: The World Bank, *The World Bank Atlas 1996* (Washington, D.C.: The World Bank, 1996), 20.

TABLE 1-5 *A Comparison of the World's Economies Based on Income Distribution, 1993 GNP per Capita*

Income	*Number of Countries*	*GNP ($billions)*	*Population (millions)*	*Average per Capita GNP*
Low	64	$ 1,251	3,178	$ 390
Lower-middle	66	1,818	1,100	1,650
Upper-middle	35	2,207	476	4,640
High	44	20,517	849	24,170
Total	209	25,793	5,603	4,600

Source: The World Bank, *The World Bank Atlas 1996* (Washington, D.C.: The World Bank, 1996), 20.

world's population live in low-income economies, while approximately 16 percent live in the high-income economies. Conversely, the high-income economies account for around 80 percent of the world's GNP compared to around 4 percent for the poorest economies.

Purchasing Power Parity (PPP)

The concept of purchasing power parity (PPP) was developed by the Swedish economist Gustav Cassel, who used it as the basis for recommending a new set of exchange rates at the end of World War I that would allow for the resumption of normal trade relations between various countries.[32] It can be defined as the notion that a dollar should buy the same amount in all countries. In the long run the exchange rate between two currencies should move toward the rate that would equate the price of an identical basket of goods in the respective countries. Thus, purchasing power parity takes income comparison of countries one step farther. It enables us to compare what money will buy.[33] For example, the average Swiss annual income per capita in 1994 was $37,180, compared to the average American an-

32. Gustav Cassel, "Abnormal Deviations in International Exchanges," *Economic Journal* (December 1918), 413–415.
33. An interesting example of purchasing power parity is called the hamburger standard, in which the price of a McDonald's Big Mac, which is sold in sixty-eight countries, is compared by using a Big Mac PPP, which is the exchange rate that would leave hamburgers costing the same in Switzerland as in the United States. The average money cost of a Big Mac in the U.S. was $2.30 in 1994; in Switzerland it was SFr 5.70; and in Germany DM 4.60. Dividing both by the U.S. price of $2.30 gives a Big Mac PPP of $2.48 and $2.30 respectively compared to their actual money values of $3.96 and $2.69. This can be shown as follows:

	Big Mac prices in local currency	In dollars	$Exchange rate	PPP of dollar
United States	$2.30	$2.30	—	—
Switzerland	SFr 5.70	3.96	$1.44	$2.48
Germany	DM 4.60	2.69	1.71	2.00

nual income per capita of $25,860. However, when converted into real income, which measures purchasing power, the value of the Swiss income dropped to $24,390 for 1994 compared to the U.S. figure of $25,860.

Table 1-6 compares per capita money and real incomes for selected rich and poor countries for 1994. When money income is used as a comparison, the U.S. ranks sixth; when real income is used as a comparison, the U.S. ranks first among all nations. In 1993 Mozambique was the poorest country in the world, with an average annual money income of $80; when converted to real income, the amount increased to $380, reflecting its purchasing power but not changing its ranking.

Table 1-7 compares money GDP and real GDP for major countries.[34] When money GDP is used, Mexico would have a larger GDP than India, and Canada and China would have around the same GDP; when real GDP is used, China would rank far ahead of Canada, and India would rank ahead of Mexico. Purchasing power parity, which takes into account different price levels, is used to convert GDPs into dollars. Suddenly, the world takes on a different shape, as Asia increases in importance. Three of the top six countries as measured by real GDP are Asian countries.

Economic Rankings: Past, Present, and Future

History suggests that some of today's developing countries will one day overtake some of the rich countries, both in economic size and per capita GDP—just as Britain became richer than the Netherlands in the late eighteenth century, and the United States became richer than Britain in the late nineteenth century. The pace of economic development quickened in the twentieth century, particularly during the latter part. Thanks to better communications, technology is more diffused than in the past. Thus, it is easier for poorer nations to become richer than it was in the past. One day it seems likely that America's economic supremacy, just like Britain's in the last century, will gradually fade away. For example, if China's real per capita GDP increases by a rate of 6 to 7 percent a year, by the year 2020 it will have the highest real GDP.[35]

Table 1-8 ranks the top ten countries in the world for four time periods, starting at the beginning of this century. At that time the United States had recently become the productivity leader, based partly on its natural resources, but on high rates of investment and an educated and rapidly expanding labor force. The world in general was prosperous, but from 1913 to 1950, two world wars and a world de-

34. Gross domestic product (GDP) is the total value of production that takes place in a year in a country. Gross national product (GNP) is the total of all spending by consumers, businesses, government, and foreign trade, exports less imports, in a country.

35. China has had the world's largest economy for most of recorded history. It had the highest real per capita income until around 1500 and was still the world's largest until 1850, when it was overtaken by Britain. See Andrea Boltho, "China's Emergence: Prospects, Opportunities, and Challenges," *Policy Research Working Paper 1339*, The World Bank, August 1994.

TABLE 1-6 *Per Capita Income and Purchasing Power for Selected Rich and Poor Countries, 1993*

Rich			
Highest Average Money Income		*Highest Average Purchasing Power*	
Switzerland	$ 37,180	United States	$25,860
Japan	34,630	Switzerland	24,390
Denmark	28,110	Hong Kong	23,080
Norway	26,480	Japan	21,350
Sweden	23,630	Norway	21,120
United States	25,860	Denmark	20,800
Poor			
Lowest Average Money Income		*Lowest Average Purchasing Power*	
Mozambique	$ 80	Ethiopia	$ 410
Tanzania	90	Mali	520
Ethiopia	130	Mozambique	550
Malawi	140	Burundi	580
Sierra Leone	150	Malawi	600
Burundi	150	Madagascar	670

Source: The World Bank, *The World Bank Atlas 1996* (Washington, D.C.: The World Bank, 1996), 18–19.

TABLE 1-7 *Comparisons of Money GDP and Real GDP for Major Countries, 1993 (billions of U.S. dollars)*

Money GDP		*Real GDP*	
United States	$6,387	United States	$6,387
Japan	3,927	Japan	2,632
Germany	1,903	China	2,492
France	1,289	Germany	1,695
Italy	1,135	India	1,126
United Kingdom	1,043	France	1,221
China	581	Italy	1,045
Canada	574	United Kingdom	1,042
Spain	534	Brazil	856
Brazil	472	Russia	778

Source: The World Bank, *The World Bank Atlas 1996* (Washington, D.C.: The World Bank, 1996), 8–9, 18–19.

pression had a deleterious impact on the world economy.[36] The United States, which was not physically damaged during the world wars, retained its position at the top. After World War II the economic and political order changed, when the

36. Angus Maddison, *The World Economy in the 20th Century* (Paris: OECD, 1989), 13–18.

TABLE 1-8 *Ten Largest Economies, 1900, 1950, 1992, and 2020*

Real GDP			
1900	*1950*	*1992*	*2020*
United States	United States	United States	China
China	Russia	Japan	United States
United Kingdom	United Kingdom	China	Japan
Russia	China	Germany	India
India	India	France	Indonesia
France	Germany	India	Germany
Germany	France	Italy	South Korea
Italy	Italy	United Kingdom	Thailand
Japan	Japan	Russia	Brazil
Indonesia	Brazil	Brazil	Italy

Sources: Angus Maddison, *The World Economy in the 20th Century* (Paris: OECD, 1989), 112–113; The World Bank, *The World Bank Atlas 1995* (Washington, D.C.: The World Bank, 1995), 18–19; "The Global Economy," *The Economist*, October 1–7, 1994, 4.

United States and the Soviet Union became the two economic and political superpowers of the world. The period 1950 to 1973 was one of economic prosperity, with growth rates for many countries averaging around 5 percent a year. Since 1973, growth rates have been erratic for most countries.

GLOBALISM AND REGIONALISM

Globalism and regionalism are two main currents in the world today. Technological innovation is a driving force in the world economy and has no distinctive nationality. As technology has developed, it has become an increasingly internationally marketable commodity. A globalized market for goods and services has also resulted from rapid technological developments that have greatly diminished the costs of international transportation and communication, and international trade in manufacturing products has been boosted by the trend toward convergence in per capita incomes and demand patterns of industrial countries. There also has been a globalization of financial markets in that the pool of savings is worldwide, and financial intermediaries know no international boundaries.[37] Finally, companies manufacturing a particular product increasingly think in terms of the advantages of international locations rather than purely in terms of domestic production.

Moreover, skilled labor has become a part of a globalized marketplace. In the old days, products such as steel and automobiles were made in the United States, England, and Germany by American, British, and German workers. Today, both the products and the workers have changed, as knowledge has become readily

37. One trillion dollars a day changes hands in the world currency market, which is a high-tech global bazaar larger than all of the world's stock, bond, and commodities markets combined.

transferable through the operations of multinational corporations and through transnational licensing agreements. Engineers, accountants, economists, computer specialists, and other highly skilled workers can be produced anywhere. Indian or Malaysian engineers produced in the United States, in their home countries, or elsewhere can perform the same functions as American engineers, and are often paid far less. These engineers are connected with the rest of the world by fax machines and other forms of communication.

At the same time and as a counter to globalization, there are also trends toward regionalism. Three major economic spheres have been formed or are in the process of transformation. One is the North American Free Trade Agreement (NAFTA), which includes the United States, Canada, and Mexico. NAFTA has provided a common market of around 376 million people and a combined GNP of around $8 trillion.[38] Another is the European Union, consisting of twelve members at the time of its formation in 1993.[39] Its major objectives include the free movement of goods through the elimination of tariffs; the free movement of people, services, and capital from one country to another; and the creation of a common currency unit, the European Currency Unit (ECU).[40] Finally, there is the Asian Pacific Economic Cooperation (APEC), which was organized in 1995. Its purpose is to remove all trade and investment barriers in the Asia Pacific Area by 2020.

A world economy now exists as a result of technological change that is moving more rapidly than at any other time in history. As telecommunications and transportation have become more efficient, reducing time and space, firms of various nationalities are now able to combine their talents to provide goods and services to customers anywhere. Time has been compressed. Fax machines are able to disseminate information from the United States to other parts of the world, and vice versa, in a matter of minutes. Skilled labor and professional workers used to be concentrated in a few countries, but this is no longer true. At the same time there has been economic integration on a regional basis. There are several reasons why this has occurred. Consumer tastes are more likely to be similar, and distribution channels can be more easily established in adjacent economies.

SUMMARY

The sudden collapse of Communism as an economic and political system has left the world by default to capitalism. The transformation from communism to capi-

38. On December 11, 1994, President Clinton and the members of thirty-three other North and South American countries agreed to turn the entire region into the world's largest free trade zone, setting the year 2005 as the deadline for an agreement to remove barriers to trade and investment. The agreement, called the Free Trade of the Americas (FTAA), will create the world's largest free trade market.

39. The European Union was originally the European Community. In the fall of 1993, the EC gave way to the European Union to reflect the closer cooperation resulting from the Maastricht Treaty, which was adopted in 1993.

40. Sweden, Finland, and Austria have been added to the original twelve countries.

talism will be difficult and painful. The Soviet Union, which was the major military rival of the United States, is no more and has been replaced by independent nations and a loose federation called the Commonwealth of Independent States, which may or may not hold together. East Germany has been reunified with West Germany, and the other Eastern European countries are to varying degrees on the road to democracy and capitalism. It has been postulated that history has now come to an end and a new world order consisting of liberal democratic ideals and free market economies has arrived. But history is far from being over, and a new competitive phase is now under way.

There are several forms of capitalism in existence. One approach to distinguishing among its forms compares the individualistic form of capitalism as represented by the United States, Canada, and the United Kingdom with the communitarian form of capitalism as represented by Europe and Japan. Individualistic capitalism is competitive, a system in which individuals and companies strive for success and there is a certain element of the "survival of the fittest" philosophy of social Darwinism. Communitarian capitalism is more group-centered, a system where the individual or company succeeds as a member of the team. A second approach to distinguishing forms of capitalism postulates three types—the individual form of capitalism as represented by the United States, the social market capitalism as represented by Germany and Western Europe, and the state-directed form of capitalism as represented by Japan. This three-pronged approach will be used in this book.

QUESTIONS FOR DISCUSSION

1. What is the difference between individualistic capitalism and communitarian capitalism?
2. Discuss American market capitalism, social market capitalism, and state-directed capitalism.
3. What are some of the ways in which different types of capitalism can be compared?
4. How may the rich countries and the poor countries of the world be compared?
5. Trends toward globalism and regionalism are occurring at the same time. Discuss.
6. Economic history shows that it is possible for countries to develop rapidly. Discuss. Give examples.
7. How can a centrally planned economy be converted into a market economy?
8. What are some of the factors that have created a global economy?
9. What are some of the factors that have created regional economies?

RECOMMENDED READINGS

Applebaum, Anne. "The Fall and Rise of the Communists." *Foreign Affairs*, Vol. 73, No. 6 (November-December, 1994), 7–13.

Fukuyama, Francis. *The End of History and the Last Man*. New York: Basic Books, 1994.

Gati, Charles H. "Central and Eastern Europe: How Is Democracy Doing?" *Problems of Post-Communism,* Special Issue (Fall 1994), 44–49.

Hufbauer, Gary Clyde, and Jeffrey J. Schott. *Western Hemisphere Economic Integration.* Washington, D.C.: Institute for International Economics, 1994.

Maddison, Angus. *The World Economy in the 20th Century.* Paris: OECD, 1989.

Porter, Michael. *The Competitive Advantage of Nations.* New York: Free Press, 1990.

Reich, Robert B. *The Work of Nations: Preparing Ourselves for 21st Century Capitalism.* New York: Alfred A. Knopf, 1991.

Thurow, Lester. *Head to Head: The Coming Economic Battle Among Japan, Europe, and America.* New York: Morrow, 1992.

CHAPTER 2

Market Mechanisms and Capitalism

A fundamental dilemma of any economic system is a scarcity of resources relative to wants. Decisions are necessary to determine how a given volume of resources is to be allocated to production and how the income derived from production is to be distributed among the various factors—capital, labor, and land—that are responsible for it. Human wants, if not unlimited, are at least indefinitely expansible. But the commodities and services that can satisfy these wants are not, and neither are the factors of production that can produce the desired goods and services. These productive factors usually have alternative uses; that is, they can be used in the production of a number of different goods and services. The system must allocate limited productive resources, which have alternative uses, to the satisfaction of greater and growing human wants.

Large amounts of capital will not be available for use in production unless there is a process of saving and capital formation. This process is fundamentally the same in all types of economic systems. It cannot operate unless the available productive resources are more than adequate to provide a bare living for the people of the system. When it *is* able to operate, the process involves spending part of the money income of an economy, directly or indirectly, for capital goods rather than for consumer goods. In a nonmonetary sense, saving and capital formation require the allocation of a part of the productive resources of a country to producing capital goods rather than consumer goods. The cost of obtaining capital goods is the same in all economic systems: It means going without, for the present, the quantities of consumer goods and services that could have been produced by the factors of production.

In general, societies have endless ways of organizing and performing their production and distribution functions. In economic and political terms, the possible range is from laissez-faire capitalism through totalitarian communism. The economy of the United States today by no means represents a pure laissez-faire capitalist system. It is, rather, a mixed economic system. There are public enterprises, considerable government regulation and control, and various other elements that hinder the unrestrained functioning of market forces. However, to understand how a capitalist system works, it is necessary to know something about its institutional arrangements. For practical purposes, an *institutional arrangement* is a practice, convention, or custom that is a material and persistent element in the life or culture of an organized group. *Economic institutions* are ways of reacting to certain economic and social phenomena in certain economic situations. Some economic institutions rest on custom, while others are formally recognized through legislative enactment.

CAPITALISM AS AN ECONOMIC SYSTEM

A number of institutional arrangements characterize a capitalist economic system. These arrangements reflect a set of basic beliefs that define how a society should be organized, how goods and services should be produced, and how income should be distributed. In the United States these beliefs are incorporated into the institutional arrangements that typify a capitalist system—private property, the profit motive, the price system, freedom of enterprise, competition, individualism, consumer sovereignty, the Protestant work ethic, and limited government. Each of these institutions will be discussed in some detail.

Private Property

Under capitalism there is private ownership of the factors of production—land, labor, and capital. There are also certain rights concerning property. An individual has the right to acquire property, to consume or control it, to buy or sell it, to give it away as a gift, and to bequeath it at death. Private property ownership is supposed to encourage thrift and wealth accumulation and to serve as a stimulus to individual initiative and industry, both of which are considered essential to economic progress.

However, private ownership of property is subject to certain limitations. In practice, even under capitalism, property rights are often restricted by the actions of social groups or government units. Also, a good deal of the private wealth of capitalist systems, such as that of the United States, is owned not by individuals, but rather by business firms. There is actually a good deal of publicly owned property within a capitalistic system. Where public property exists, the exclusive control of wealth is exercised by a group of individuals through some political process.

The Profit Motive

The kinds of goods produced in an economy that relies on market arrangements are determined in the first instance by managers of business firms or by individual entrepreneurs. They are directly responsible for converting resources into products and determining what these products will be, guided by the actions of consumers in the marketplace. The profit motive is the lodestar that draws managers to produce goods that can be sold at prices that are higher than the costs of production. In private enterprise, profit is necessary for survival; it is the payment to owners of capital. Anybody who produces things that do not, directly or indirectly, yield a profit will sooner or later go bankrupt, lose the ownership of the means of production, and so cease to be an independent producer. There can be no other way. Capitalism, in other words, uses profitability as the test of whether any given item should or should not be produced, and if it should, how much of it should be produced.

The Price System

Individuals and businesses under capitalism are supposed to make most types of economic decisions on the basis of prices, price relationships, and price changes. The function of prices is to provide a coordinating mechanism for millions of decentralized private production and distribution units. The prices that prevail in the marketplace determine the kinds and quantities of goods and services that will be produced and how they will be distributed. Price changes are supposed to adjust the quantities of these goods and services available for the market.

The Price Mechanism. It is through the mechanism of prices that scarce resources are allocated to various uses. The interaction between the price system and the pursuit of profits is supposed to keep economic mistakes down to a reasonable level. Profit, which depends on the selling price of goods and the cost of making them, indicates to businesses what people are buying. An industry with a product that commands high prices relative to costs draws businesses, whereas low prices relative to costs check production by causing businesses to drop out.

Price Determination. In a free market economy, demand and supply determine the price at which a purchase or sale of a good is made. Demand originates with the consumer. It involves a desire for a good or service expressed through a willingness to pay money for it in the marketplace. Market demand is the sum of all individual consumers' demands for a particular good or service. There is an inverse relationship between market demand and the price of a good or a service. The higher the price, the lower the quantity of the good or service demanded.

Supply originates with the producer. It is the quantity of a good or service that a producer is willing to offer at any given price. Market supply is the sum of all the supplies that individual producers will offer in the marketplace at all possible prices over a given period. There is a direct relationship between market supply and price—the higher the price, the greater the supply of goods or services that will be provided.

The interaction of demand and supply determines the price for a good or service in the marketplace. The equilibrium price is the price that equates the quantity demanded with the quantity supplied in a market. It is the one price that will clear the market. At any price above the equilibrium price, supply is greater than demand, and the price must fall. At a price below the equilibrium price, demand is greater than supply, and the price must rise. In the following example, the equilibrium price is $3.00 per pound.

Market Demand	*Price per Pound*	*Market Supply*
180 pounds	$0.50	40 pounds
140	1.00	50
100	2.00	65
80	3.00	80
60	4.00	100
40	5.00	120

The forces of supply and demand acting through the price mechanism can send effective signals to the marketplace. For example, an increase in demand means that buyers will be willing to purchase more at any price than they were formerly. An increase in demand, with supply remaining constant, would result in an increase in price. The increased price would cause producers to supply more, so quantity would increase also. A decrease in demand would have the opposite effect.

Conversely, an increase in supply with demand remaining constant would result in a decrease in price. The lower price would lead to an increase in the quantity purchased. A decrease in supply would have the opposite effect. Consumers have to pay more for a smaller amount of a good or service.

Figure 2-1 illustrates the determination of prices and output in a free market. Both are determined at the intersection of the demand and supply curves. The equilibrium price is p_0, and q_0 is the quantity supplied. At any price above p_0, the quantity supplied is greater than the quantity demanded, and the price will fall. At any price below p_0, demand is greater than the quantity supplied, and prices will rise.

An increase in demand to D_1 with supply remaining constant will result in an increase in both price and quantity. The new equilibrium price will be p_1 and the quantity will increase to q_1. The increase in demand to D_1 will eventually result in an increase in supply (the supply curve shifts to the right) as producers react to the

FIGURE 2-1 *Determination of Equilibrium Price and Output*

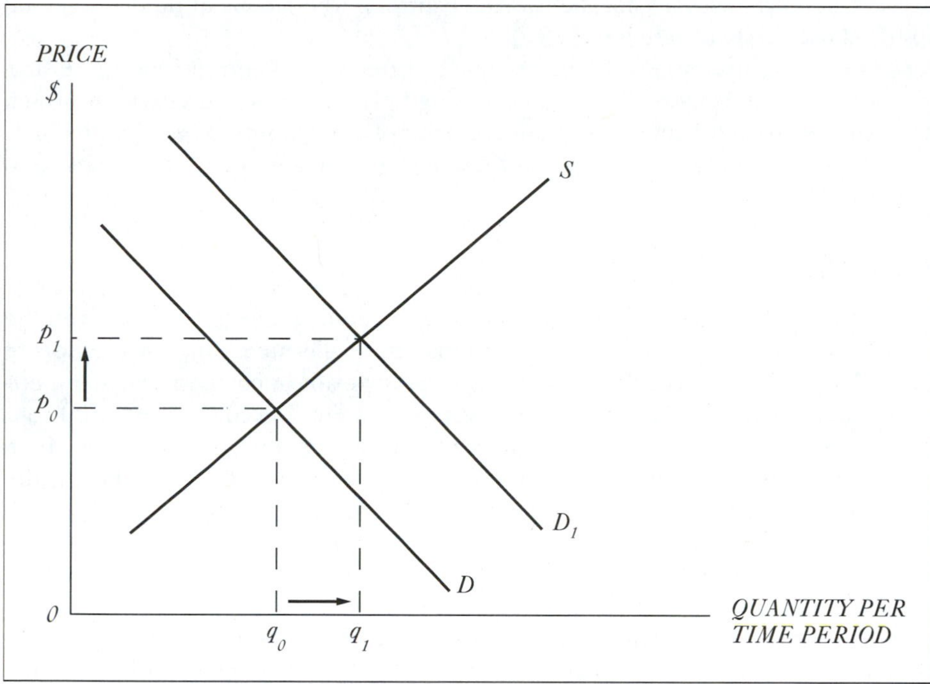

potential for higher profits. New producers will enter the market, and resources will be shifted from other areas into the market in anticipation of a greater rate of return.[1]

Freedom of Enterprise

Another basic institution of capitalism is freedom of enterprise. It refers to the general right of each individual to engage in any line of economic activity that appeals to that individual. However, there are limits placed on the choice of an activity. People cannot engage in activities that are deemed socially immoral (e.g., child pornography) or that may harm others (e.g., driving while intoxicated). As far as the government is concerned, the individual is free to move to any part of the country, work in any chosen occupation, and find and operate a business unit in virtually any field of lawful economic activity. By comparing market indicators—prices and costs—the individual is supposed to be able to select a field of activity

1. For example, as student enrollment in a college town increases, the demand for housing will increase. Townspeople will be willing to rent more rooms, and existing housing will be fully used. Rents will increase, and someone will decide to build apartments for students. The supply of housing will increase as available resources are shifted into housing construction.

that promises to be remunerative. The institution of private property furnishes the social sanctions necessary for the use and control of the factors of production vital to the chosen field of activity.

The theory used to justify the existence of freedom of enterprise is quite simply one of social welfare. That is, in choosing fields of economic activity in which they will be the most successful from the point of view of private gain, individuals will also be selecting fields in which they presumably will be most productive to society.

Competition

Given the institutions of private property and freedom of enterprise, and given the scarcity of resources and the reliance on a market to allocate them, the attempts of individuals to further their economic self-interest result in competition. Competition is an indispensable part of a free enterprise system. In economic life, self-reliant individuals must struggle and compete for economic rewards—good jobs, high pay, promotions, desirable goods and services, and security in old age. There is the element of social Darwinism in competition: Life is a competitive struggle in which only the fittest, in terms of resources, get to the top.

Certainly, *competition* is one of the "good" words in the American vocabulary. From a very early age, schoolchildren are told that the distinguishing characteristic of the historically successful U.S. economic system is competition and that other economic systems have inefficiencies because, to some degree, they lack that magic ingredient in the particular and unique context in which it exists in our economy. It is, therefore, not surprising that by statute and common law our legal system has been actively concerned with the maintenance of a competitive system.

Certain benefits are thought to be derived from competition in the marketplace. A competitive market will:

1. Allow the price mechanism to reflect actual demand and cost and thus maximize efficiency in the use of capital and other resources.
2. Encourage product innovation and long-run cost reduction.
3. Result in the equitable diffusion of real income.
4. Provide consumers with a wide variety of alternative sources of supply.

Individualism

Individualism is linked to a set of related institutional values of capitalism. Again there is social Darwinism—life seen as a competitive struggle where the fit survive and those who are unfit do not. Individualism also involves competition, which, when combined with social Darwinism, is supposed to provide some guarantee of progress through the inexorable process of evolution. Individualism is also related to equality of opportunity—the right of each person to succeed or fail on his or her own merit.

The institutions of private property ownership and individualism are related from two standpoints. First, private property ownership provides the spur for individual initiative, a reward to be gained through competition and hard work. Second, it provides some guarantee of individual rights against the encroachments of the state. It follows that a requisite for individualism is a limited state role. The rights of the individual would have precedence over those of the state, for the latter is a fictitious body composed of individual people who are considered to represent its members. The idea of individualism can therefore be a safeguard against the tyranny of the state.

Consumer Sovereignty

In a capitalistic market economy, consumer sovereignty is an important institution because consumption is supposed to be the basic rationale of economic activity. As Adam Smith said, "Consumption is the sole end and purpose of all production; and the interest of the producer ought to be attended to only as far as it is necessary for promoting that of the consumer."[2] Consumer sovereignty assumes, of course, that there is a competitive market economy. Consumers are able to vote with their money by offering more of it for products that are in greater demand and less of it for products that are not in demand. Shifts in supply and demand will occur in response to the way in which consumers spend their money.

In competing for consumers' dollars, producers will produce more of those products that are in demand, for the prices will be higher, and less of those products that are not in demand, for the prices will be lower. Production is the means; consumption is the end. Producers that effectively satisfy the wants of consumers are encouraged by large monetary returns, which enable them in turn to purchase the goods and services required for their operations. On the other hand, producers who do not respond to the wants of consumers will not remain in business very long.

Freedom of choice is linked to consumer sovereignty. In fact, one defense of the market mechanism is the freedom of choice it provides consumers in a capitalistic economy. Consumers are free to accept or reject whatever is produced in the marketplace. The consumer is king because production ultimately is oriented toward meeting the wants of consumers. Freedom of choice is consistent with a laissez-faire economy. It is assumed that consumers are capable of making rational decisions, and in an economy dominated by a large number of buyers and sellers this assumption has some merit. Since the role of the government is minimal, the principle of *caveat emptor,* "let the buyer beware," governs consumer decisions to buy.

The Protestant Work Ethic

The Protestant work ethic is an ideological principle stemming from the Protestant Reformation of the sixteenth century and is associated with the religious reformer John Calvin. Calvin preached a doctrine of salvation that later proved to be

2. Adam Smith, *An Inquiry into the Nature and Causes of the Wealth of Nations* (Indianapolis: Liberty Classics, 1981), 660.

consistent with the principles of a capitalist system.[3] According to Calvin and the Puritan ministers in early New England, hard work, diligence, and thrift are earthly signs that individuals are using fully the talents given to them by God for his overall purposes. Salvation is associated with achievement on this earth. Thus, work and economic gain have come to have a moral value. According to this view, it is good for the soul to work; rewards on this earth go to those who achieve the most. Moreover, salvation in the world to come is a reward that is in direct proportion to a person's contribution during life.

The Calvinist doctrine of work and salvation became an integral part of the ideology of capitalism. The hard work of merchants and traders often produced profits, and their thrift led to saving and investment. Saving is the heart of the Protestant work ethic. With Adam Smith's idea of parsimony (or frugality) and Nassau Senior's idea of abstinence, it was established that saving multiplied future production and earned its own reward through interest.

Carried into American society in the nineteenth century, the Protestant work ethic came to mean rewards for those who were economically competent and punishment for those who were incompetent or unambitious. Work was put at the center of American life. Most of the industrial capitalists of the last century belonged to fundamentalist Protestant churches. John D. Rockefeller, who became the richest man of his day, attributed his success to the "glory of God." (Skeptics, however, attributed his success to much more mundane factors than God's beneficence.[4])

Limited Government

For many years, the idea prevailed that the government in a capitalist system, however it might be organized, should follow a policy of *laissez-faire* with respect to economic activity. That is, activities of the government should be limited to the performance of a few general functions for the good of all citizens, and government should not attempt to control or interfere with the economic activities of private individuals. Laissez-faire assumes that individuals are rational and better judges of their own interests than any government could possibly be.[5] The interests of individuals are closely identified with those of society as a whole. It is only necessary for government to provide a setting or environment in which individuals can operate freely. This the government was supposed to do by performing only

3. Richard H. Tawney, *Religion and the Rise of Capitalism: A Historical Study* (New York: Harcourt, Brace, and World, 1926); and Max Weber, *The Protestant Ethic and the Spirit of Capitalism* (New York: Charles Scribner's Sons, 1930).
4. See, for example, Matthew Josephson, *The Robber Barons* (New York: Harcourt, Brace, and World, 1934); and Ida M. Tarbell, *The History of the Standard Oil Company* (New York: McClure, Phillips, 1904).
5. The term *laissez-faire* originated in France, possibly as early as the first half of the eighteenth century, and was later developed by Adam Smith as a rule of practical economic conduct. In particular, see Adam Smith, *The Wealth of Nations,* Book IV, especially p. 630. Laissez-faire was a reaction to the stringent government restrictions imposed on all phases of economic activity by mercantilism. Under mercantilism, the state controlled all businesses, and one could engage in a particular activity only by receiving a monopoly from the state.

those functions that individuals could not do for themselves: provide for national defense, maintain law and order, carry on diplomatic relations with other countries, and construct roads, schools, and public works.

In a free enterprise market economy, competition is regarded as a virtue rather than a vice. The proper use of resources in a free enterprise system is ensured by the fact that if a firm does not use resources efficiently, it goes broke. If the market is to function effectively, it must operate freely. If there is intervention in any form, then there is no effective mechanism for weeding out inefficient enterprises. Nevertheless, government has always participated to some extent in business activity of capitalist countries. From the very beginning, the government of the United States was interested in the promotion of manufacturing, and it passed tariff laws very early to protect American business interests. Subsidies were used to promote the development of canals, roads, and railroads. Business was a direct beneficiary of those subsidies.

INCOME DISTRIBUTION IN A CAPITALIST ECONOMY

Once goods and services have been produced, the next important question in any economic system is the manner in which these goods and services are to be divided or apportioned among the individual consumers of the economy. The distribution of income does not refer to the processes by which physical goods are brought from producers to consumers, but rather to the distribution of the national income, first in money and then in goods and services, among the owners of the factors of production—land, labor, and capital.

Income distribution in a market economy is based on institutional arrangements, such as the pricing mechanism, associated with this type of system. The demand for a factor of production is derived from the demand for the goods the factor helps to produce. High prices are set on scarce factors of production and low prices on plentiful factors. In terms of rewards to labor, workers whose skills are scarce relative to demand enjoy high income, while those whose skills are not scarce relative to demand do not. Professional football and baseball players receive high salaries because they possess a scarce talent and people are willing to pay to see them perform.

Measurements of Income Inequality

There are various measures of income inequality, including the Lorenz curve and the Pareto and Gini coefficients. Of these measures, the Lorenz curve is the most commonly used. The Lorenz curve involves the use of an arithmetic scale that begins with an assumption of income equality as a starting point. Equality in the distribution of income is found when every income-receiving unit receives its proportional share of the total income. If incomes were absolutely uniformly distributed, the lowest 20 percent of income earners would receive exactly 20 percent of the total income; the lowest 80 percent would get exactly 80 percent of the total income; and the highest 20 percent would get only 20 percent of the income. In using a Lorenz curve, the curve of absolute equality would actually be a straight line extending upward at a 45° angle from left to right, showing that 20 percent of income earners on the horizontal axis receive 20 percent of the income on the vertical axis, 40 percent of income earners receive 40 percent of the income, and so on. Any departure from this line is a departure from complete income equality.

Figure 2-2 illustrates the Lorenz curve. The straight line $0AF$ is the line of perfect equality. The line $0BF$—the Lorenz curve—shows a departure from equality. The farther $0BF$ is from $0AF$, the greater the inequality. There are certain weaknesses in the use of the Lorenz curve as a measure of income distribution. First, one cannot tell by inspecting a curve how unequal the distribution of income is. The use of percentages conceals the number of income-receiving units in the different income brackets. It is also true that the slope of a curve at various points gives no more information than the curve itself. On the other hand, the Lorenz curve is an excellent device for visual presentation of inequalities in the distribution of income. It can also illustrate the effects on the distribution of income of changes in taxes and government spending.

FIGURE 2-2 *The Lorenz Curve*

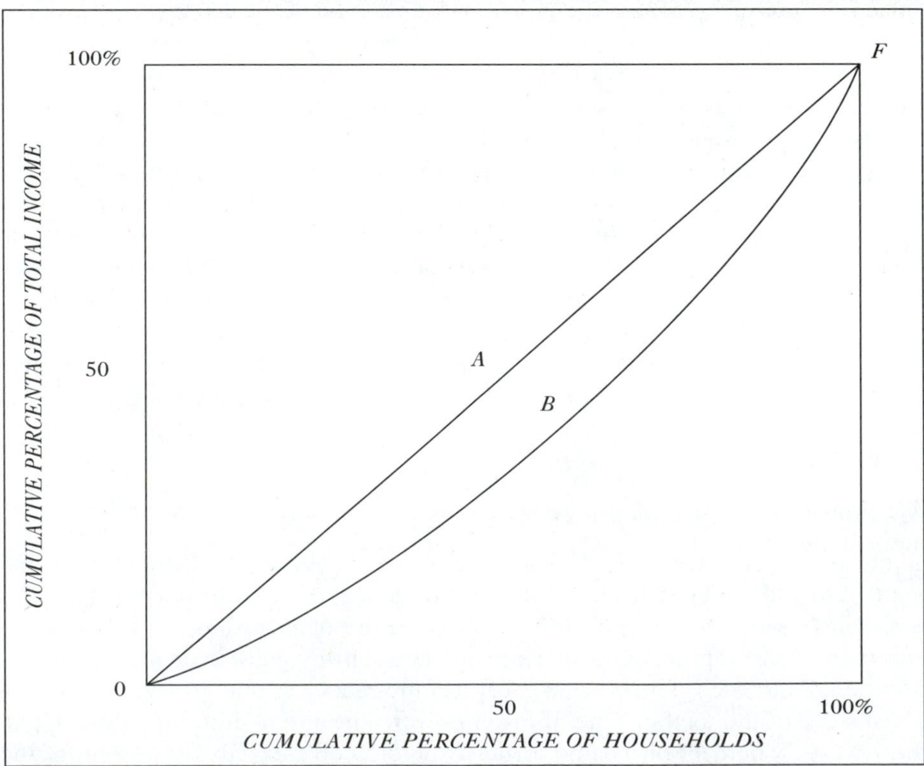

It is possible to avoid relying solely on visual comparisons of Lorenz curves to draw inferences about various income distributions. In a Lorenz diagram the Gini concentration coefficient is the ratio of the area between the diagonal and the Lorenz curve to the total area below the diagonal. For a perfectly equal distribution, the Gini coefficient is zero. The size of the Gini coefficient is tied to the concavity of the Lorenz curve—the greater the concavity, the greater the coefficient. The coefficient, however, is basically an average and does not tell anything about the extent to which inequality of distribution may be marked in various segments of the income distribution.

Another measure of income inequality is to compare the shares of total income earned by different quintiles in a country—the share received by the poorest 20 percent and that received by the top 20 percent. Perfect equality in the distribution of income would mean that each quintile would receive 20 percent of the income, and the quintile ratio between the top and bottom quintiles would be 1. The larger the ratio, the greater the amount of income inequality.

$$\text{Quintile Ratio} = \frac{\text{Percentage of income received by the highest 20 percent}}{\text{Percentage of income received by the bottom 20 percent}}$$

Table 2-1 compares quintile ratios for the major industrial countries and tends to confirm a point made by Lester Thurow that income distribution is more unequal in the individualistic capitalist countries than in the communitarian capitalistic countries.[6] However, it is important to point out that the data in the table are not current, and the ratios may not be totally accurate.

A recent report of income inequality in thirteen countries rated the United States as the country with the highest income inequality and Japan with the lowest.[7] Australia ranked second highest and Sweden second lowest. Moreover, the gap between the richest and poorest quintiles has widened in both the United States and the United Kingdom. In 1992 the top 20 percent of American households received 11 times as much as the bottom 20 percent, up from a multiple of 7.5 in 1969. In 1977 the income of the richest 20 percent of British households was four times as large as the bottom 20 percent; by 1991 the multiple had increased to around 8. The Gini coefficient for the United States increased from .34 in 1969 to .41 in 1993, and for the United Kingdom from .23 in 1977 to .34 in 1991.[8]

Rationale for Income Inequality

The primary rationale for income inequality in a capitalist economy is economic motivation, which means that individuals are usually motivated by the desire for monetary gain in their economic activities. That is, individuals attempt to follow

6. Lester Thurow, *Head to Head: The Coming Economic Battle among Japan, Europe, and America* (New York: Morrow, 1992).
7. *The Economist,* November 5–11, 1994, 20.
8. The Institute for Fiscal Studies, *For Richer or Poorer: The Changing Distribution of Income in the United Kingdom, 1961–1991* (London: IFS, 1994), 12–15.

TABLE 2-1 *Percentage Shares of Household Income by Quintiles for Selected Market Economies*

Country	*Year*	*Lowest Quintile*	*Highest Quintile*	*Quintile Ratio*
United States	1988	4.7	41.9	8.9
Japan	1979	8.2	37.5	4.6
United Kingdom	1988	4.6	44.3	9.6
Germany*	1988	7.0	40.3	5.7
France	1989	5.6	41.9	7.5
Sweden	1981	8.0	36.9	4.6
Netherlands	1988	8.2	36.9	4.5
Australia	1985	4.4	42.2	9.6

**West Germany before reunification.*

Source: The World Bank, *World Development Report 1995* (New York: Oxford University Press, 1995), 221.

their economic self-interest and try to acquire as many goods as possible for themselves, without much regard for the effects of their actions on other people. The desire for gain is supposed to make people work harder and longer than any other motive that could be substituted for it. Monetary gain also can be tied to such factors as the desire for power and prestige, which can be reflected in private property ownership and freedom of enterprise. Income inequality is also assumed to result in efficient resource allocation, in that people are pulled into those occupations for which the demand is the highest.

The famous baseball player Babe Ruth was once asked if he deserved a salary three times greater than that of the president of the United States. His answer was that people come to see him play baseball; they don't come to see him be president. Today, many athletes, movie stars, and musicians make at least ten times the amount paid to the president of the United States. The chief executives of many American firms make from forty to one hundred times as much as the average American worker. For whatever it is worth, the United States leads the world in the number of billionaires (it used to be millionaires) with Bill Gates, the founder of Microsoft, reportedly the world's richest person.[9]

The Luxembourg Income Study

A study of income distribution commissioned by the Organisation for Economic Co-Operation and Development (OECD) and published in 1995 indicated that the gap between rich and poor in the developed countries grew wider during the 1980s.[10] The largest increase in the income gap was in the United Kingdom, followed by the United States and Australia. There was a parallel increase in inequality of earnings in most countries due to the varying numbers of working women, the extent of self-employment, and increased early retirement. On the average, the poorest 20 percent of households paid less than 5 percent of all direct taxes in

9. *Forbes,* July 18, 1994, 154.
10. OECD, *Income Distribution in OECD Countries* (Paris: OECD, 1995).

the countries included in the study, while the richest 20 percent paid 50 percent of all direct taxes. Income transfers provided 30 percent of the median income to the poorest 20 percent in Belgium, the Netherlands, and Sweden compared to 14 percent of median income to the poorest 20 percent in the United States.[11] The United States had the most unequal distribution of income, while Finland had the most equal.[12]

Table 2-2 presents comparisons of income differences between rich and poor individuals in selected OECD countries. Income is disposable money income, which is of two types: primary income, which includes wages and salaries plus income from self-employment, and market income, which adds property income and other private cash income.[13] Government transfer payments, which include pensions, family allowances, unemployment compensation, and other welfare benefits, are also added to market income, and personal income taxes and social security contributions are deducted from it.

The most basic theory underlying income distribution in a market economy involves the concept of marginal productivity. This concept can be applied to the distribution of both labor and property income.[14] Under competitive market conditions, individuals, incomes are determined by (1) the amount of resources they can command, and (2) the market evaluation of these resources. Thus, the income received by a worker tends to be determined by supply and demand, so that the income received equals the contribution the worker is able to make to the value of goods and services. The contribution to total product made by the worker is known as the marginal physical product (*MPP*) of labor. The dollar value of the contribution is the marginal revenue product (*MRP*) of labor. It is found by multiplying the *MPP* by the selling price of the product. The same reasoning is also applied to the distribution of property income. Resource owners tend to be compensated according to the marginal revenue products of the resources they own.

Income Inequality and Economic Growth

The conventional wisdom has been that there is a correlation between income inequality and economic growth—the higher the amount of income inequality, the greater the rate of economic growth; the lower the amount of income inequality, the lower the rate of economic growth. Economic growth results from efficiency, and the mechanism of the free market promotes efficiency through competition. A competitive market transmits signals to producers of goods and services that re-

11. An earlier OECD study was done in 1976. France, with a Gini coefficient of 41.4, had the most unequal income distribution of the OECD countries, while Sweden, with a Gini coefficient of 30.2, had the most equal.
12. Thirty to 40 percent of total social welfare benefits went to the poorest 20 percent of the population in Canada, Norway, Switzerland, the United Kingdom, and the United States. France, Finland, Germany, Italy, the Netherlands, and Sweden do not target those with low incomes for proportionally greater income benefits.
13. Capital gains or losses are excluded from the computation of money income.
14. Income in a market economy emanates from two sources: (1) earned income from wages and salaries or self-employment and (2) property income.

TABLE 2-2
The Gap Between the Incomes of Rich and Poor Individuals (percentage of median income in each country)

Country	*Poor**	*Rich†*	*Ratio of Rich to Poor*
Finland, 1987	59	153	2.59
Sweden, 1987	56	152	2.72
Belgium, 1987	59	163	2.79
Netherlands, 1987	62	175	2.85
Norway, 1987	55	162	2.93
Germany, 1984	57	170	2.98
Switzerland, 1982	54	184	3.43
France, 1984	55	193	3.48
United Kingdom, 1986	51	194	3.79
Australia, 1985	47	187	4.01
Canada, 1987	46	184	4.02
Italy, 1986	49	198	4.05
Ireland, 1987	50	209	4.23
United States, 1986	35	206	5.94

**Relative income for individuals that are poorer than 90 percent of the individuals in the country and more affluent than 10 percent of the individuals, expressed as a percentage of national median income.*
†Relative income for individuals that are more affluent than 90 percent of the individuals in the country and poorer than 10 percent of the individuals, expressed as a percentage of national median income.

Source: OECD, *Income Distribution in OECD Countries* (Paris: OECD, 1995), 155.

flect the values, whether good or bad, of consumers. However, for every success, there are many failures; for every Michael Jordan, there are many thousands of basketball players who do not make the NBA. So efficiency is bought at the cost of unequal incomes, wealth, and power.

A recent study compared East Asian and Latin American countries in terms of the relationship between income inequality and economic growth by using their rates of economic growth for the period 1965–1989 and levels of income inequality in the 1980s as measured by the ratio of the income shares for the top and bottom quintiles for both regions.[15] The Latin American countries had a high degree of income inequality and a low or negative rate of economic growth; conversely, the East Asian countries had a low degree of income inequality and a high rate of economic growth.[16] The study suggests that, contrary to conventional wisdom, high income inequality in the distribution of income may have a significant and negative impact on the rate of economic growth. A prime factor in contributing to

15. The World Bank, *The East Asian Miracle* (New York: Oxford University Press, 1993), 1–31.
16. The East Asian countries were Korea, Taiwan, Singapore, Hong Kong, Japan, Indonesia, and Thailand; the Latin American countries were Brazil, Colombia, Mexico, Venezuela, Chile, Argentina, Bolivia, and Peru.

higher income inequality in Latin America was the unequal distribution of income in terms of both quality and quantity.

Figure 2-3 compares income inequality and growth in GDP in East Asian and Latin American countries for the period 1965–1989. Income inequality is measured by the ratio between the bottom 20 percent and the top 20 percent of income receivers. For example, the bottom 20 percent share of income in Brazil in 1988 was 2.1 percent compared to 67.5 percent for the top 20 percent, for a quintile ratio of around 32 (67.5 divided by 2.1). In South Korea the bottom 20 percent of income received 7.4 percent of total income in 1988 compared to 42.2 percent for the top 20 percent, for a quintile ratio of around 5.5 (42.2 divided by 7.4).

SAVING AND CAPITAL FORMATION UNDER CAPITALISM

In a capitalistic system, large amounts of savings are made by individuals on the basis of the relationship between interest rates and other prices. The necessary condition for such savings is that the interest rate be sufficient to overcome the time preference of the savers. Time preference is the desire to consume income in the present as opposed to sometime in the future. A certain amount of savings, however, is independent of the interest rate. Some savings are made to provide for

FIGURE 2-3 *Income Inequality and Growth of GDP, 1965–1989*

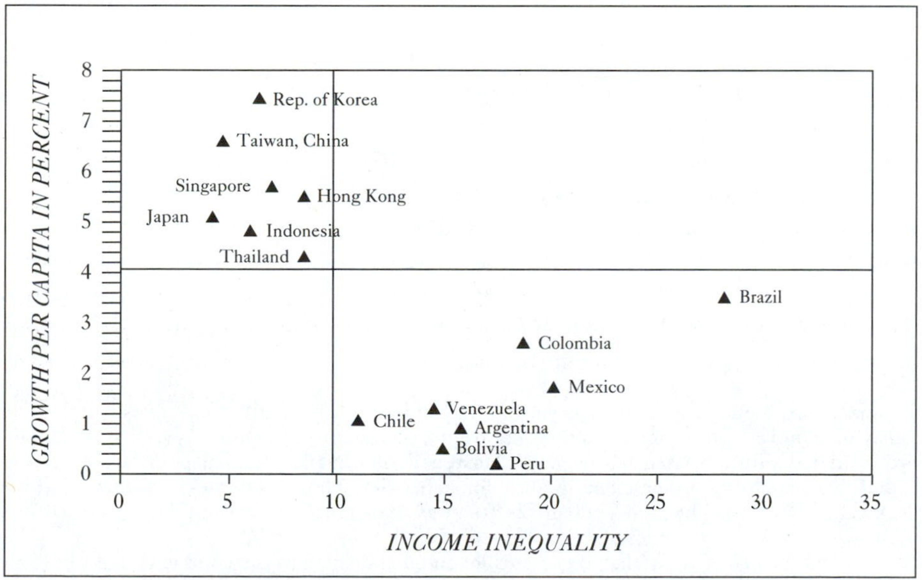

Source: World Bank, *The East Asian Miracle: Economic Growth and Public Policy* (Washington, D.C.: The World Bank, 1993).

certain financial emergencies or to obtain the power an accumulation of income can bring. People with very large incomes may save almost automatically because of the difficulties involved in finding enough consumption uses for their incomes.[17] Other savings, such as those that result when corporations retain their earnings instead of paying dividends to stockholders, do not depend on the voluntary decisions of the individuals (stockholders) whose earnings are being saved. Finally, there may be forced savings in the form of taxes that government may use directly or indirectly for capital purposes.

The use of capital goods in production clearly involves the existence of savings. Savings are translated into investment in a capitalist system through the market mechanism of supply and demand, with interest rates performing an allocative function. To be able to afford to pay interest on a loan and ultimately to repay the principal, the borrower must be able to put the funds to good use. This tends to exclude less productive uses and thus rations savings to more productive uses.

Under capitalism, saving and investment are carried out in large part by different sets of people for different reasons. Investment is the purchase of capital goods and as such is undertaken largely by businesses. The act of saving is undertaken by both individuals and businesses. With large numbers of scattered savers and borrowers who want to obtain funds for investment purposes, there is clearly a need for some type of intermediary or go-between to bring the savers and borrowers together. This function is performed to a large extent by commercial and investment banks that are privately owned and operated for a profit. These banks underwrite securities issues for governmental units as well as businesses. The investment bankers bring together the business and governmental units that desire short- and long-term funds and the individuals and institutions that have these funds to invest.

THE HISTORICAL DEVELOPMENT OF CAPITALISM

The roots of capitalism go back to the Middle Ages, when the search for profit was the dominant motive in the lives of many, especially the merchants of the Italian city-states of Genoa and Venice.[18] In fact, the discovery of America in 1492 can be attributed to the search for new markets. The Catholic church and other molders of public opinion came to accept the concept of profit in part because they, too, found good use for money. Earlier Catholic church thought had held that money

17. However, human psychology, as viewed by Hobbes, is an appetite that drives people ferociously to achieve their desires. In a modern society, the engine of appetite is an increased standard of living, with emphasis on display. Thorsten Veblen made a similar point when he contended that people are driven by an impulse for status. See Thomas Hobbes, *Leviathan* (Oxford: Blackwell, 1946); also Thorsten Veblen, *The Theory of the Leisure Class* (Boston: Houghton Mifflin, 1973).

18. The merchants of the Italian city-states invented almost all of the commercial devices that made a profit-seeking society possible. One such device was double-entry bookkeeping, which showed merchants that they were supposed to show a balance on the right side of the ledger.

was sterile in that it did not reproduce itself and that it was morally wrong to lend money to earn interest. However, there was nothing wrong in using money to buy something. But when it was seen that, if invested in productive enterprises, money could indeed make more money for the benefit of all, and that payment for the use of money (interest) would alone persuade the owners of money to invest it, the prohibition on lending at interest was abandoned.

No pronounced break can be discerned between the growing capitalistic practices of the later Middle Ages and those of modern times. The influx of gold and silver from the New World had major political and economic consequences in Europe, contributing to the rise of the nation-states. The new wealthy classes, who engaged in trade everywhere, needed a stable national government to guarantee commerce, protect sea routes, and ensure the arrival of merchant ships. Monarchs, who needed the financial support of wealthy merchants to pay for their wars, were expected to support home commerce. One method of supporting home commerce was to ensure that only ships of the home country could be used in transporting goods from, and sometimes even to, home ports.

Mercantilism

From the sixteenth to eighteenth centuries, it became accepted theory that a country was wealthy when it had a large reserve of gold and silver bullion.To obtain bullion, the country had to have what was known as a favorable balance of trade, gained by exporting more than was imported. Thus it was in the country's own interest to support home industry to enable it to export as many products as possible. This policy of supporting home industry came to be called *mercantilism.* It meant government intervention everywhere, but particularly in foreign trade. It also meant regulation of commercial relations between the mother country and her colonies; the colonies existed to furnish the mother country with raw materials and goods that could not be produced at home. The colonies were also expected to furnish the mother country with a favorable balance of trade, as represented by an inflow of precious metals into the country. It was against the policy of mercantilism that the thirteen colonies of North America arose and fought for their independence.

The Industrial Revolution

The Industrial Revolution changed national attitudes from the policy of mercantilism to a policy of laissez-faire. Scientific breakthroughs, inventions, and the factory system encouraged specialization and the concentration of production. These, in turn, encouraged a movement from national self-sufficiency to a doctrine of free trade, which was supported by classical economists Adam Smith and David Ricardo and the philosopher John Locke. During the nineteenth century, the amount of world trade increased rapidly while the pattern of world trade changed.

The Industrial Revolution consisted mainly of the application of machinery to manufacturing, mining, transportation, communication, and agriculture, and of the changes in economic organization that attended these applications.[19] Fundamental in the new industrial order was the development of a cheap, portable source of power. James Watt's invention of the condenser and of a practical method for converting the reciprocating motion of the piston into rotary motion made the steam engine a practical prime mover for all kinds of machinery.

The Industrial Revolution probably represented the hallmark of capitalism. The old method of small-scale production in the home with one's own tools could not meet the competition of machine production. The cost of machinery was prohibitive to individual workers. Hence, the factory system arose, with large-scale production in factories using machinery owned by the employer. The factory system stimulated the growth of division of labor and mass production through the standardization of processes and parts. Old industries began to produce on a much larger scale than previously, and new industries developed, offering new goods to satisfy new demands.

Industrial capitalists were created, and it was they who shaped the course of future industrialization by reinvesting their gains in new enterprises. The Industrial Revolution also enormously accentuated the movement toward international economic interdependence. As the people of Europe became more and more engaged in urban industry, they raised less food and became heavy importers of wheat, meat, and other food products. In exchange for food, Europe exported manufactured goods, and the entire world became a marketplace.

The doctrine of laissez-faire fit in with the development of capitalism. It carried with it a sense of independence, personal initiative, and self-responsibility. If individual initiative is respected, it gives free play to entrepreneurs to create products for those who want and will pay for them. A requisite for individualism is a limited state role. The individual's needs should have preference over those of the state, for the latter is, as pointed out earlier in this chapter, only a fictitious body composed of individual people who are considered to be its members. The ideas of individualism and laissez-faire were therefore regarded by Adam Smith and others as a safeguard against the tyranny of the state.

Finance Capitalism

Constant growth in the use of machinery, and especially mass production, made it increasingly necessary for individual entrepreneurs to raise large amounts of capital. As raising capital became more difficult, the control of industry passed more and more into the hands of a few large investment banking houses. This system became known as *finance capitalism.* Banks became professional accumulators of capital. Corporations, which by the latter part of the nineteenth century had be-

19. The Industrial Revolution began in England between 1770 and 1825 and in continental Europe after 1815. Some scholars contend that we are in a new period of postindustrial development. See, for example, Daniel Bell, *The Coming of Post-Industrial Society* (New York: Basic Books, 1976).

come the dominant form of business unit, were able to obtain large quantities of long-term capital funds by selling their securities with the assistance of investment banks. The banks underwrote and distributed the securities, eventually getting them in the hands of insurance companies, banks, investment trusts, and individual investors. These banking houses were able to acquire an inordinate amount of economic power through the ownership of securities and through the device of the interlocking directorate. An interlocking directorate occurred when officers of a bank served on the boards of directors of competing firms.

MODIFICATIONS OF PURE CAPITALISM

Various elements have combined over time to transform pure market capitalism into what might be called "state-guided" capitalism. In fact, the term *mixed economic system* is used in later chapters to describe countries that were at one time purely capitalistic. Part of this transformation has been the development of the welfare state, which resulted from the extremely unequal distribution of income that developed during the Industrial Revolution. A growing concentration of economic power in the hands of a few people created extremes of wealth and poverty. In the United States during the 1890s, for example, the department store magnate Marshall Field had an income calculated at $600 per hour; his sales clerks, earning salaries of $3 to $5 a week, had to work three to five years to earn that amount.[20] Working conditions for most workers in the Western industrial world were deplorable: The twelve-hour workday and seven-day workweek were not uncommon. There were no child labor laws; children of 8 and even younger worked in the coal mines and textile mills in the United States and England.

Government and the Decline of Laissez-Faire

Government has always played some role in Western society, even during the zenith of capitalism. In the historical development of the United States, government policy was primarily a mixture of measures that provided equality of opportunity for the common man, such as public education, and generous favors for those who knew how to help themselves, such as railroad and canal builders. Tariffs were enacted to protect American business firms from foreign competition. In France, where state participation in the economy had always been important, much of the railroad system was state owned by the 1850s, and the state also had a monopoly over the sale of such products as alcohol, tobacco, and tea. State ownership of certain industries also existed in Prussia.

20. Cited in Otto Bettman, *The Good Old Days—They Were Terrible* (New York: Random House, 1974), 67.

The Depression of the 1930s was probably the catalyst for increasing the role of government. On the basis of experience during the Depression, organized labor, farmers, business firms, and consumer groups turned to government for assistance in improving their incomes and ensuring economic security. The satisfaction of these demands made for a new concept of government. An increase in the power of the state has become the central fact of modern Western society. Crucial decisions about production and distribution have come to be made through the political process rather than through the marketplace.

Restrictions on Competition

Competition is one of the basic institutions of capitalism. Its justification, like that of other institutions, is found in the notion that it contributes to the social welfare. It is a regulator of economic activity and is thought to maximize productivity, prevent excessive concentration of economic power, and protect consumer interests. *Competition* may be used to describe the economic structure of a nation, applicable to all economic units—individuals, farmers, and business firms. Economic success goes to efficiently operated firms, and failure eliminates inefficiently and wastefully operated firms. The impersonal market system does not lock in products or skills that have become obsolete and therefore nonproductive.

But competition is a hard taskmaster, for there are losers as well as winners. Since losers don't think they should lose, they take action to prevent losing and thus the rules of the game are altered. The market system has been changed in many ways by government action to prevent or cushion the effects of losing. Through subsidies and restraints on foreign competition, uneconomic production methods and job skills have been maintained by governmental intervention.

Business firms have formed various combinations, cartels, trusts, and holding companies to prevent competition. Workers have joined labor unions to avoid individual competition, and obsolete job skills have been preserved. In the United States, obsolete jobs have been preserved in the construction industry and elsewhere through federal building codes, and inefficient firms, such as Chrysler, have received financial support from the government when otherwise they would have been eliminated by the forces of competition.

Antitrust Laws

Antitrust laws are based on two premises. The first is the English common law as it evolved through court decisions over a long time. In general, these decisions held that restraint on trade or commerce is not in the public interest. The second premise is the belief that competition is an effective regulator of most markets and, with a few exceptions, that monopolistic practices can be stopped by competition. This premise is based on the economic theory espousing pure or perfect competition as the ideal, since according to the theory competition forces firms to be efficient, cut costs, and receive no more than normal profits. The theory assumes that in a state of pure or perfect competition, economic decisions will be made by prices and price changes, both of which are determined by the market forces of supply and demand.

Social Regulation

Social regulation came into being because the market mechanism has not been effective in eliminating certain social problems. In a market economy, the price mechanism gives people no opportunity to bid against the production and sale of certain commodities and services that they regard as undesirable. Many people would be happier if they could prevent the production and sale of, for instance, tobacco products or the emission of noxious fumes from a chemical plant, and would pay the price if given the opportunity to do so. But there seems to be no way the market price mechanism can take these negative preferences into consideration, except through government controls on the output of goods deemed deleterious to the public interest. A prime example is government laws protecting the environment.

Social Security

In a laissez-faire type of economy, it is the responsibility of the individual to look out for himself or herself. This squares with the American concept of rugged individualism and explains why the United States was the last major country to adopt a system of social insurance. Rugged individualism, as epitomized by John Wayne in the movie *True Grit,* carried with it a sense of independence, personal initiative, and self-responsibility.[21] Life was a series of challenges to be met head on, as John Wayne did at the end of *True Grit* when he went charging into the four bad men. There was in individualism the idea of a "just meritocracy" where individuals should be left free to achieve what they could through their own abilities and efforts. An individual was responsible for himself or herself.

Perhaps as a reflection of this veneration for individual responsibility, the United States lagged well behind other countries in adopting a program of social insurance that would protect individuals against the misfortunes of life such as unemployment, illness, and old age. Germany, for example, had a comprehensive program of health insurance in place before the end of the last century. Insurance against unemployment in the United States was provided by the Social Security Act of 1935. It also provided for a system of annuities for workers over sixty-five years of age who had contributed regularly to the building up of a fund for this purpose. The reason for the passage of the Social Security Act was the Depression, which had no parallel in American history. Prolonged unemployment became the norm, and individual responsibility didn't mean much when there were no jobs to be had.

21. Henry Hathaway, director, *True Grit,* Paramount Pictures, 1969.

SUMMARY

Capitalism is an economic system characterized by a set of institutional arrangements. The centerpiece of capitalism is a freely competitive market where buyers satisfy their wants and sellers supply those wants in order to make a profit. The price mechanism determines resource allocation, and freedom of enterprise and private property ownership provide incentives to save and produce. Individualism is also at the core of the capitalist or free market ideology. It was assumed by Adam Smith and others that people were rational and would try at all times to promote their own personal welfare. The individual, in promoting his or her self-interest, was viewed as promoting the interest of society at the same time.

Competition is an indispensable part of a free enterprise system. In economic life, self-reliant individuals must compete for economic rewards (good jobs, high pay, and promotions), and business must compete for consumer incomes. The Protestant work ethic stressed rewards in this life, not in the hereafter. Hard work included thrift, which could provide the savings necessary for investment. The role of government is minimal in a capitalist economy.

The advanced capitalist countries of today have modified the institutions of capitalism. In the operation of capitalist economies, problems arose that seemed impossible for private individuals to solve. Their impact brought a demand for government intervention. As a result, government intervention and regulation are common features of life under capitalism. Consumers are not left to depend solely on competition to furnish them with foods and drugs of acceptable quality and purity; there are laws that provide certain standards in these matters. Capitalistic societies have never been willing to extend complete freedom of enterprise to any individual. That is, it has always been recognized that an individual, in selecting the most profitable field of activity, might well choose something that would be clearly antisocial. In such cases, government has not hesitated to step in with restrictions. But government has also altered the economic institutions of capitalism through, for example, subsidies to farmers and protection of inefficient business firms from competition.

QUESTIONS FOR DISCUSSION

1. What is meant by the term *institutions* as applied to an economic system?
2. Explain the concept of economic scarcity. Are there things that are not scarce?
3. Apply the concept of scarcity to life in the United States today. Is scarcity still present in the United States? How does scarcity affect an American's life?
4. What are the three factors of production? Why do economists classify resources in this way?
5. What is the function of profit in a market economy?
6. What is the function of the price mechanism in a market system?
7. How are incomes distributed in a market economy?

8. What are some of the factors responsible for the breakdown of a true market economy?
9. The United States economy has diverged from pure market capitalism. Why?

RECOMMENDED READINGS

Bell, Daniel. *The Coming of the Post-Industrial Society*. New York: Basic Books, 1976.

———. *The Cultural Contradictions of Capitalism*. New York: Basic Books, 1976.

Friedman, Milton, *Capitalism and Freedom*. Chicago: University of Chicago Press, 1962.

Hacker, Louis M. *The Triumph of American Capitalism*. New York: Simon & Schuster, 1940.

Heilbroner, Robert L. *The Making of Economic Society*. 4th ed. Englewood Cliffs, N.J.: Prentice Hall, 1962.

Hofstadtler, Richard. *Social Darwinism in American Thought*. Rev. ed. Boston: Beacon Press, 1955.

Okun, Arthur M. *Equality and Efficiency*. Washington, D.C.: The Brookings Institution, 1975.

Polanyi, Karl. *The Great Transformation*. New York: Rinehart, 1944.

Smith, Adam. *An Inquiry into the Nature and Causes of the Wealth of Nations*. Indianapolis: Liberty Classics, 1981.

Tawney, R. H. *Religion and the Rise of Capitalism*. New York: Harcourt, Brace, and World, 1926.

Toynbee, Arnold. *The Industrial Revolution*. Boston: Beacon Press, 1956.

Weber, Max. *The Protestant Ethic and the Spirit of Capitalism*. New York: Charles Scribner's Sons, 1930.

CHAPTER 3

Nonmarket Mechanisms: Socialism

The standard Marxist postulate was that communism was the inevitable concomitant of the crises of capitalism within industrialized society. The twentieth century was supposed to be the century of communism, during which there would be a continuous defection of countries from capitalism, with the instability and decay of the capitalist countries manifested in low rates of economic growth and chronic unemployment. World War I contributed to the advent of communism in Russia, and mass unemployment during the 1930s convinced many people that communism was the wave of the future. After World War II, the two major superpowers, the United States and the Soviet Union, ruled over a divided world, part capitalist and part communist. As late as 1989 countries ruled by the Communist Party accounted for around 34 percent of the world's population and 31 percent of the world's land area.[1] Included were two major countries, the Soviet Union and

1. Janos Kornai, *The Socialist System: The Political Economy of Communism* (Princeton, N.J.: Princeton University Press, 1992).

China. Of the twenty-six countries headed by the Communist Party, only four remain—China, Cuba, North Korea, and Vietnam—although the future status of Cuba is in doubt. The Soviet Union is gone and China, although still headed by the Communist Party, now has a dual economy, part state-owned and part privately owned. Czechoslovakia, Hungary, Poland, and other countries that were formerly a part of the Soviet bloc are now in the process of transforming their former socialist economies into capitalist economies. Communist parties are gone, and many of their former members have transferred their allegiance to a new political and economic system.

Before beginning a discussion of the political and economic systems of countries that were formerly Communist, it is necessary to distinguish between communism and socialism. To the West, the former Soviet Union was Communist, but that is not what it called itself. It called itself a socialist country (Union of Soviet Socialist Republics—USSR). In Marxist terminology there were two stages of communism. The first stage, socialism, was to be a transitional stage during which some elements of capitalism were to be maintained. The second stage, communism, was to be a higher stage marked by an age of plenty, distribution according to needs, the absence of money and the market mechanism, the disappearance of capitalism, and the withering away of the state. The political system of the former Soviet Union was Communist; the economic system was socialist.

In a non-Marxist form, socialism is an economic system that would modify, but not eliminate, many of the institutions of capitalism. The extent of modification is something that has never been completely delineated by socialists because there are many variations of socialism. Some socialists favor the complete elimination of private property, with replacement by public property ownership. Other socialists favor placing maximum reliance on the market mechanism while supplementing it with government direction and planning to achieve desired economic and social objectives.

Socialism today has also come to be associated with the concept of a welfare state, where the state, through a wide variety of transfer payments, assumes responsibility for protecting its citizens from all the vicissitudes of life. Private ownership of the agents of production is permitted, with state ownership of those facets of production and distribution considered vital to the interests of society. In reality Western society has incorporated many of the principles of both capitalism and socialism.

HISTORICAL DEVELOPMENT OF SOCIALISM

The terms *socialist* and *socialism* identify relatively new concepts. They first came into use in England and France in the early part of the last century and were applied to the doctrines of certain writers who were seeking a transformation of the economic and moral basis of society by the substitution of social for individual control of life and work.[2] The term *socialism* was popularized as the antithesis of *individualism*. However, precursors of socialism can be found among medieval writers and even going back as far as Plato. For example, Thomas Aquinas believed that property ownership should be private, but that the use of goods should be in common. Whatever goods a man possessed should be shared with the poor. He considered poverty undesirable because it led to sin, and he proposed that both church and state should help poor people bring healthy children into the world.

The Renaissance Utopias

During the Renaissance a number of scholars turned their attention to the construction of imaginary communities, or utopias, in which society was organized so as to remove all of the evils of the day. These utopias were primarily economic and social rather than religious. For the most part, they followed a definite pattern, the authors placing a group of regenerated people on an isolated land area where they could be free from contamination by the rest of the world. Rigid conditions would then be set up by means of which an ideal state would be attained. For example, in Sir Thomas More's *Utopia,* everything is owned in common and there is no money.[3] In the middle of each city is a marketplace to which each family takes the things it produces; from these central marketplaces products are distributed to central warehouses from which each family draws what it needs. Women and men have equal rights, and households are arranged so that women are relieved of some of their most time-consuming domestic duties.

French Utopian Socialists

French utopian socialism was associated with the French Revolution and later with the Industrial Revolution. The French Revolution created a great economic and political upheaval whose impact was felt all over Europe. In France every political and social division became rooted in the alignment of the revolution. Commercial business interests, as represented by a merchant class, replaced the aristocracy, who had gone to the guillotine. A large class of urban workers who had helped make the revolution found that their living conditions were largely unchanged. The fact that a great political revolution had taken place in France and that socially the results of this revolution were largely unsatisfactory set the stage for a new group of reformers, the French utopian socialists.

In general, the ideas of the utopian socialists were based on the theory that nature had ordained all things to serve the happiness of humankind and that every

2. *Socialist* seems to have been used first in England to describe the followers of Robert Owen. The word *socialism* was used in France to describe the writings of Saint-Simon and Fourier.
3. Lewis Mumford, *The Stories of Utopias* (New York: Boni and Liveright, 1992), 23–37.

person had natural rights due at birth.[4] Furthermore, it was believed that in the original state human beings were perfect. At various times in the past, however, people had tampered with the natural order of things by establishing customs and institutions that ran contrary to it. As a result, people in the existing state were not happy, enjoyed few if any rights, and certainly were far from being perfect. Having discovered the cause of human difficulties, the utopian socialists proceeded to the obvious solution of the problem of social regeneration. If people had lost their natural perfection through the establishment of unnatural customs and institutions, the thing to do was to discover the nature of the original state of goodness and then reorganize society so as to give nature's forces full play, unhampered by the conventions and institutions of the existing social environment.

However, the French utopian socialists could not agree on how to reorganize society. Some advocated the elimination of private property, considering it the main reason for human degeneracy. Others favored complete income equality. Babeuf proposed that production be carried out in common, distribution be shared in common, and children be brought up in such a way as to prevent the growth of individual differences. Saint-Simon, one of the better-known early French utopian socialists, rejected the whole idea of equality, arguing instead that people were naturally unequal and that any attempt to make them equal would involve greater injustices than actually existed at the time. However, differences were to be based on talent, rather than the inheritance of wealth. Saint-Simon favored an economic mechanism that would require each person to labor according to his or her capacity and would provide rewards on the basis of service. Charles Fourier worked out a plan for cooperative living in small communities that he hoped would lead to a transformation of society. These communities were called *phalanxes,* and each phalanx was to be self-sufficient. The highest pay would go to those performing the most necessary work, as determined by the members of the phalanx.

Socialism and the Industrial Revolution

The Industrial Revolution was in due course to revolutionize the economic life of the whole Western world. The availability of new technology encouraged the formation of real capital with which the technology might be put into widespread use. The availability of resources for use in capital formation encouraged the search for new technology that, once discovered, could be embodied in the real capital. The new technology enabled gross national product to be large enough to provide sufficient consumer goods to satisfy the minimum subsistence needs of the population and still have some resources left over. Population growth provided labor to use the enlarged amounts of real capital to increase total national output.

However, there was a darker side to the Industrial Revolution. Working conditions in factories were unpleasant. Equipment was sometimes dangerous and caused workers to have serious accidents. Average wages of industrial workers

4. Richard T. Fly, *French and German Socialists in Modern Times* (New York: Harper, 1883), 37–51.

were low, largely because the rapid expansion of population provided a large number of workers for the labor force. These workers concentrated in the industrial cities and competed with each other for jobs.

The cities that grew up or expanded to house the workers were unattractive and unpleasant. Many of them consisted of slums with houses of poor quality when constructed and in a constant state of disrepair thereafter. Charles Dickens, the great chronicler of English society in the nineteenth century, has a rather graphic description of the squalor of the London slums in his novel *Bleak House.*

Jo lives—that is to say that Jo has not yet died—in a ruinous place known to the like of him by the name of Tom-all-Alone's. It is a black, dilapidated street, avoided by all decent people, where the crazy houses were seized upon, when their decay was far advanced, by some bold vagrants who after establishing their own possession took to letting them out in lodgings. Now, these tumbling tenements contain by night, a swarm of misery. As on the ruined human wretch vermin parasites appear, so these ruinous shelters have bred a crowd of foul existence that crawls in and out of gaps in walls and boards; and rocks itself to sleep in maggot numbers, where the rain drips in; and comes and goes, fetching and carrying fever and sowing more evil in its every footprint.[5]

Modern Socialism

Modern socialism, as opposed to utopian socialism, had its genesis during the Industrial Revolution. It developed as a social reform movement to protest the seamy side of the Industrial Revolution. Robert Owen, an early English socialist, was considered a utopian socialist in that he developed a scheme for social regeneration: change society, you change the person. He believed that true happiness is found in making others happy.[6] Unlike many other social reformers, Owen had the money to carry out his plan of social regeneration. He crated a textile mill at New Lanark in Scotland in 1800, reducing the hours of work to 10 1/2 hours per day and raising wages.[7] He did not employ children under the age of 10. Education and playgrounds were provided for the children of mill workers. The experiment made money, and Owen was able to get a factory reform bill introduced in Parliament. However, other mill owners were not willing to adopt similar measures. Subsequent experiments by Owen were unsuccessful. Coming to the United States, he created a community called New Harmony in Indiana, but attempts to create a perfect community failed there as well.

Socialism coalesced into a political movement in England around the middle of the nineteenth century. A contributing factor in its development was mass unemployment created by business recessions. One of the basic defects of capitalism was the constant recurrence of recessions. In England and in other countries, un-

5. Charles Dickens, *Bleak House* (New York: Signet Books, 1964), 232–233.
6. Or, in the words of Paul, "remember the words of the Lord Jesus, how He said, it is more blessed to give than to receive" (Acts 20:35).
7. By the standards of those days, these provisions were not harsh.

employment and labor unrest began to occur more frequently, and a working-class movement developed in these countries.

The movement found its support in labor unions and among intellectuals who were not of the working class but felt that the political and economic structure of society had to be reformed for the benefit of the workers. A split developed between Marxist and non-Marxist socialists, with the former preaching class revolution and the overthrow of the existing political and social order, and the latter urging the attainment of economic, political, and social reforms by working within the existing system. Political parties representing both Marxist and non-Marxist points of view had been formed in France and Germany by 1900.

INSTITUTIONS OF SOCIALISM

Socialism developed into a viable political force in Western Europe around the latter part of the last century and continued to develop during this century. Socialist parties captured control of the governments of France and Greece in elections held in 1981. Socialism is no longer an important political force today. There are certain institutional arrangements that set socialism apart from capitalism and communism. These arrangements represent a modification in most of the institutions of capitalism, since socialism developed in opposition to some of the worst abuses of capitalism.

Private Property

Under ideal socialism, the rights of private property would be limited to consumption goods; productive wealth, land, and capital would in general be owned by society as a whole. Socialists today say that the social ownership of the means of production would be limited to the land and capital used in large-scale production. For example, the socialist government of former French President François Mitterrand proposed the nationalization of some French banks (the more important ones have already been nationalized) and some key industries, such as aluminum. In France, one car company (Renault) is state-owned, but another car company (Peugeot) is not.

Most socialists would permit private individuals to own and operate small farms, stores, and repair shops. Some even contend that certain industries, operating satisfactorily under private ownership and unsuited to government ownership and operation, be left alone to function in the hands of individuals. Modern socialists thus do not adhere to ideal socialism when it comes to the right of private property ownership.

The Price System

According to many socialists, the ideal socialist system would retain money and the price system, but it would not rely on price movements and price relationships in making important economic decisions to nearly as great an extent as a capitalist system does. Decisions as to the kinds and quantities of goods, particularly public goods, would be made by the government. A major socialist criticism of the price mechanism in a market economy is that prices do not reflect nonmarket wants of the people, such as the desire for economic security. Nor can negative wants be expressed through the price mechanism.[8] Also, individuals with large sums of money can express their wants through prices and thereby channel resources to the production of goods that the mass of consumers cannot afford. Socialism would divert productive resources to satisfy basic wants of all of the people before the relatively less important wants of the few with large incomes are satisfied.

Socialism and Government

Perhaps because various noncapitalistic economic systems have so often operated under dictatorial governments, there is a tendency in popular discussion to link capitalism with democracy and to link socialism and communism with dictatorship. However, this is not the case with socialism. European social democratic parties have operated within the framework of democracy. The 1981 elections of socialist governments in France and Greece illustrate the point.

By the early 1960s, many of the European social democratic parties severed completely whatever remaining ideological ties they had with Marx and communism. They abandoned their traditional opposition to private property and their goal of social ownership and turned their attention to improving the public mix of total goods and services. Thus, what have developed in Western Europe are mixed capitalist-socialist economies. When socialists come into power, the tilt is toward socialism; there is still reliance on a market economy, but also heavy governmental direction and planning to achieve desired social and economic objectives.

COMMUNISM

Early hints of communism can be found in Plato's *Republic.*[9] Plato's criticisms of the economic and social structure of his time led to his proposal for an ideal state. The state described in the *Republic* is a city-state, a type of political organization quite common in Greece at the time (431–351 B.C.). Among other things, Plato's ideal republic is a communist society in which all things are held in common, at least as far as the upper classes are concerned. The upper classes, or guardians of the state, eat in common dining rooms and live in common quarters, receiving

8. For example, there may be a number of people whose total satisfaction would be much increased if they could prevent the publication and sale of pornographic books or the production and sale of cigarettes. They might well be glad to pay a price to obtain that satisfaction of their negative preferences if the opportunity could be given them to do so. But there seems to be no way, short of government edict, in which the market mechanism can take these negative preferences into account.

9. In Irwin Edman, ed., *The Works of Plato* (New York: Modern Library, 1956), 397–481.

their support from contributions made by the citizens at large.[10] Members of the group never consider their own personal interests but always work for the good of the whole state. To ensure their disinterest, Plato does not make any provision for private interest, not even a private family life. However, Plato's communism was not for the masses, who were excluded from political life in his republic. Instead, it was communism of the select.

Karl Marx and Das Kapital

Both modern communism and socialism began in England as reactions against capitalism. As mentioned previously, unequal incomes, squalor, and poverty were characteristic of industrial life in England. The winds of revolution that had blown in from France had died away, and rank and privilege were firmly entrenched. The upper class was all-powerful over a tenantry for the most part unenfranchised.

Flattered, adulated, deferred to, the English aristocracy reigned supreme, with incomes enormously increased by the Industrial Revolution and as yet untaxed. The aristocracy was subject to no ordinary laws and held the government firmly in its hands. However, an entrepreneurial class had begun to emerge as a result of the Industrial Revolution, and the two classes clashed over government control. This conflict did very little to ameliorate the working conditions of the industrial masses.

This was the general economic and social milieu in which Karl Marx wrote *Das Kapital.* It is necessary to remember that Marx was a product of his time and that the activities of other persons in England, as well as in other countries, had attracted widespread attention to the problem of poverty. Marx is important because in *Das Kapital* he presented a dynamic theory of economics that still serves as the basis for much of communist dogma. The most important elements of the theory are summarized as follows.

The Marxist Theory of Income Distribution. According to Marx, the way in which people make a living at any given time is conditioned by the nature of the existing productive forces. There are three productive forces: natural resources, capital equipment, and human resources. Since people must use these productive forces in the process of making a living, some sort of relationship between people and the productive forces is necessary. Specifically, the property relation is involved. People may own certain productive forces individually, as in a capitalist society, or they may own them collectively, as in a socialist society. Under capitalism, there were people who owned property or capital and there were people who owned only their own labor. Marx called the former the capitalists or the *bourgeoisie* and the latter the workers, or the *proletariat.*

10. In Plato's republic there are three social classes—the rulers or guardians, the auxiliary guardians, and the artisans. The ruling class is selected from the auxiliary class and is composed of philosophers who have been selected after a long course of study. The artisans make up the largest group of the republic but have little status.

The Labor Theory of Value. Many economists of the eighteenth and nineteenth centuries, including Adam Smith and David Ricardo, believed that labor supplied the common denominator of value.[11] Marx adopted this idea and made it the basis for his own theory of income distribution. He stated that the one thing common to all commodities is labor and that the value of a commodity is determined by the amount of socially necessary labor required for its production. *Socially necessary labor,* as defined by Marx, is the amount of time necessary to produce a given product under existing average conditions of production and with the average degree of skill and intensity of labor.[12] The relative prices of two products will be in the same proportion as the amount of socially necessary labor required to produce them. If two hours of labor are required to make a pair of shoes and five hours of labor are required to build a cart, the price of shoes in the market will be two-fifths that of the cart.

The price of labor is the wage rate. The wage rate determines the income of those who own their own labor. Marx asserted that the wage rate itself is determined by the labor theory of value. How much a worker receives in income in return for working for an employer depends on how many labor hours are required to produce the necessities of life for that worker. If the necessities can be produced with five hours of labor per day, a worker can produce and be available to the employer for work if five hours' wages are paid to the worker each day. Even if the worker actually works twelve hours each day for an employer, the pay will be for only five hours because that is all it takes to sustain the worker. That is all the pay can be, under a labor theory of value. In effect, Marx believed in a subsistence theory of wages in a system of market capitalism.

Theory of Surplus Value. Although all value is created by the workers, it is expropriated by employers in the form of *surplus value,* which can be defined as the difference between the value created by the workers and the value of their labor power. When a worker sells labor power to an employer, the worker gives up all title and claim to the products of that labor. Income in the Marxist scheme is divided into two categories—surplus value, which is the source of all profit, and labor income. Value in the Marxist rubric can be expressed in the formula $C + V + S$, where C represents raw materials and capital consumption, V represents various outlays on wages, and S represents surplus value in the form of rent, interest, and profit. The C component, raw materials and capital, although clearly not labor, is explained away by Marx, who regarded it as stored-up labor from past periods. Thus the remainder, $V + S$, represents net output, which consists of the two basic income shares, wages and profit.

How much a worker gets as a wage is based on the amount of labor time socially necessary to produce subsistence or maintenance for the worker and the worker's family. Assume that this subsistence requires only five hours of socially

11. *Value* may be defined as the worth of a commodity or service as measured by its ability to command other goods and services in return. It is, in short, exchange value, which is the power to command exchange in the market.
12. Karl Marx, *Das Kapital* (New York: Modern Library, 1906), 198–331.

necessary labor time for its production. If the worker worked only five hours for the employer, the worker would be fully paid and there would be no surplus value. However, it is the employer's right to set the length of the working day, and it will normally be set at a number of hours greater than that required to produce the worker's subsistence. The difference between the actual hours worked and the labor time needed for subsistence is surplus value.

The Dynamic Weaknesses of Market Capitalism. Marx believed that the market distribution of income between workers and property owners was bound to be a source of increasing difficulty for capitalist economies.

Crises and Depressions. For one thing, it would sometimes be difficult to sell the output being produced. The workers received money income enough to buy only part of the total output. This part would necessarily take the form of subsistence or consumer goods. The capitalists received the rest, an amount sufficient to buy the remainder of the output of goods and services. But would they buy it? Of course they would buy some of it to satisfy their own consumption desires. The rest they might purchase in the form of capital goods with which to carry on production and to expand productive capacity if they found such a purchase profitable. However, from time to time there would be periods of months or even years when they would not find it profitable to expand capacity. These would be periods of crisis and depression. During these times there would be sharply increased financial losses for business, unsold output, business bankruptcies, falling prices, and unemployment.

Worsening Trends. Marx suggested that these crises and depressions would become increasingly severe. In each successive crisis, the weakest firms would disappear, being absorbed or replaced by a smaller number of larger firms. In the long run the number of firms and the number of capitalists would decline both absolutely and relative to the size of the economy and of the population. The proletariat would be absolutely and relatively enlarged.

The capitalist employers would be impelled by competition among themselves to substitute machinery or capital for labor, even though it was labor that provided surplus value and profits. The capitalists would be impelled to discover and introduce into use new technology because it would reduce the cost of subsistence needs for labor and thereby enlarge the amount of surplus value and profit. The increasingly severe crises, the substitution of capital for labor, and the introduction of new technology would create a larger and larger volume of unemployment among the workers. There would be an ever-increasing *industrial reserve army* of the unemployed.

Marx felt that the rate of profit on capital would fall continually lower, primarily because of the replacement of laborers with machines. The laborers were the source of all surplus and hence of all profits. Machines produced no surplus and, therefore, did not contribute to profits. The capitalists, desperately seeking to sustain profits, would seek ways to increase the surplus value by greater exploitation of the workers. They would resort to longer working hours, more intense work, and the employment of children.

There would be more and more severe crises, fewer and fewer capitalists, larger and larger unemployment, lower and lower profit rates, bigger and bigger amounts of unsold goods, and ever more outrageous exploitation of the workers by the capitalists. These trends would ultimately lead, in the Marxist view, to the end of market capitalism. It would be replaced with a new economic system, or rather, with a whole new society. In Marx's view, economic arrangements were causally determinant of all else in society, and capitalism's inevitable demise would mean a complete change of everything else in society.[13] Because Marx felt that the character of a society depended wholly upon its economic system, his philosophy is labeled *materialism*.

Economically Determined History. To reiterate, Marx contended that economic conditions were the basic causal forces shaping the nature of society. All other aspects of society—political, religious, and philosophical—depended upon the economic system of the society.

Materialism. For example, in a primitive nomadic society where horses might be of particular importance in enabling the people to gather food and to exist in general, the ownership of horses would be important to the people. Those persons who owned the horses would be able to control the others. That is, those who possessed the principal means of production would also possess the ability to rule. The religion and philosophy of the nomadic society would revolve about horses and those who owned them. The patterns of marriage and inheritance would be heavily influenced by considerations regarding the use and ownership of horses.

In a society that had amassed considerable real capital and technology, the capital would be the principal means of production. The society would be organized around the existence, ownership, control, and use of the capital. Political power would reside with the owners and controllers of capital, the capitalists. Religion and philosophy would sanctify the ownership and rationalize the social dominance of the owners.

In some advanced societies with great real capital, all ownership and control might be exercised by the government. It would act on behalf of all the people. Political power would rest with all the people. A philosophy of altruism would develop among them.

In the most advanced society, so much capital and such advanced technology would exist that enough goods and services would be produced to more than completely satisfy the desires of everyone. The ownership of the means of production would cease to matter. Political control over others would cease to have significance. Interpersonal animosity, based on the covetousness of each for the material goods and services of others, would disappear. Government, no longer necessary

13. A brief, clear and entertaining explanation of Marx's theories appears in Sir Alexander Gray, *The Development of Economic Doctrine: An Introductory Survey* (New York: John Wiley & Sons, 1931), Chap. 11. A more technically difficult account, which assumes more knowledge of economic analysis, can be found in Mark Blaug, *Economic Theory in Retrospect*, rev. ed. (Homewood, Ill.: Richard D. Irwin, 1968), Chap. 7.

as the instrument by which some controlled others or by which some were protected from others, would gradually wither away.

The Dialectic. Marx's view of philosophy and history is called a dialectic. From the philosopher Hegel, Marx adopted the notion that everything that happened in the world could be explained by the clash of opposites. In simple terms, Hegel claimed that a proper understanding of the world could be achieved if all change were viewed as a result of clashing ideas. First, there is an idea, such as a scarcity. Then there emerges an opposite idea, such as abundance. Finally, the two opposing ideas are combined into a new and superior idea, such as economy, which is a means to achieve abundance out of scarcity.

Marx adopted the notion of the clashing of opposites to produce a successor synthesis. However, he rejected the view that this clashing and synthesis took place basically and most significantly in the realm of ideas. Rather, according to Marx, the basic conflict and synthesis took place, as his philosophy of materialism suggests, in the real world of economic events, economic classes, and economic systems.

Dialectical Materialism. Marx welded together his views of the primacy of economic arrangements and of history as a progressive conflict into the doctrine of dialectical materialism. According to this doctrine, a society, such as that of Europe during the Middle Ages, is based on an economic system, such as manorial agriculture. A political structure, such as feudalism, and a philosophical and religious structure, such as medieval Catholicism, grow up in harmony with the economic base. There are three socioeconomic classes: landed nobility, clergy, and serfs. The economic system is successful in filling the material needs of the people. In fact, it is too successful for its own permanence.

The increasing productive ability of the manorial system makes it possible for some people to leave agriculture and become traders or craftsmen. Others have sufficient time to make economically useful discoveries and innovations. Gradually the techniques of production and other economic arrangements change. Local economic self-sufficiency decreases as trading increases. First guilds and then factory workers carry on production in place of the manorial serfs or craftsmen. There begins to grow up a new socioeconomic class made up of the shopkeeping proprietors, the factory managers and owners, and the merchant traders.

In the meantime, the political power remains, in an increasingly outmoded way, with the hereditary landed aristocracy. The religious rules grow more and more inappropriate for the economic system. For example, doctrines against usury and in favor of just prices become obsolete. Finally, the economic system and the seat of real power have changed enough that the new class, the bourgeoisie, is able to wrest political power from the landed nobility. They do so either by forceful revolution, by new laws, or by influence with the sovereign. They also reshape the religious code, perhaps by replacing Catholicism with Protestantism.

Capitalism thereby replaces feudalism. Then, because of its inherent nature, capitalism under the bourgeoisie unintentionally promotes its own replacement. Capitalism brings together the working proletariat and infuses in them a unity born of misery and exploitation. The class conflict between the proletariat and bourgeoisie sharpens with conditions increasingly favorable to a proletarian victory. The political superstructure of government is in the hands of the bourgeoisie, who use it to perpetuate their power. However, it fails to reflect the underlying economic reality of bourgeoisie weakness and proletarian strength. Religion has been used as a device for cowing the workers, for justifying their exploitation, and for drugging them with visions of heaven so that they will accept their earthly misery. However, religion becomes more and more obviously a sham.

Eventually, the workers topple the bourgeoisie government, seize the means of production, abolish private property, and set up a socialist state under the dictatorship of the proletariat. The economic system is thus converted to socialism. Then, because all else follows from economic change, the society becomes ultimately a communist one, without government, scarcity, conflict, or classes.[14]

The Weaknesses of Marxism

Each of Marx's main ideas can be disputed on a number of grounds.

The Labor Theory of Value. The labor theory of value, as an explanation of what determines relative prices of goods and services, is extremely vulnerable to criticism. Marx anticipated some of these criticisms and tried to deal with them.

Exceptions to the Theory. A piece of fertile land may exist and command a high price without any human labor at all having been expended on its creation. Such nonreproducible goods, Marx said, fall into a special category. The prices or values of this category are determined without reference to amounts of labor. Then what about a durable good that was produced some time ago and for whose production a technological improvement has been discovered in the meantime? The value of such a good will fall, Marx would say, in the meantime. It is not the amount of original labor expended but the amount necessary to replace a good that is the determining variable.

What about a unit of good much like many other units of the same good except that it embodies a much greater amount of labor because it was turned out by a very slow, inept worker? Will it on that account be much more valuable than the other units? No, it will not, because it is the actual amount of *socially necessary* labor that determines values and prices, Marx would answer. What about a good, like a hideous piece of sculpture, whose production required a great amount of labor but which cannot be sold for any price because no one wants it? Can it, all in all, be said to be of great value? No, Marx might answer, because labor expended on a useless product is not socially necessary labor. What about a good produced by a monopolist and sold at a high price? Is its price in proportion to the labor in it? Admittedly it is not, for monopoly may distort prices from true values.

14. A readable account of world history, including the Industrial Revolution, as seen by a modern Marxist, is Leo Huberman, *Man's Worldly Goods: The Story of the Wealth of Nations* (New York: Monthly Review Press, 1952).

The Problem of Diverse Kinds of Labor. What about two goods, one embodying four hours of unskilled labor and the other, four hours of skilled labor? Will the two goods sell at the same price? Do they have equal value? No, in creating and determining value, one hour of skilled labor counts for more than one hour of unskilled labor. To compute value, one must convert skilled labor into unskilled labor by multiplying the number of hours of skilled labor by an appropriate conversion number. How can the appropriate number be known? It is determined, in part, by the number of hours of labor socially necessary to produce the goods and services needed to sustain the skilled laborers through the period of training. It is also determined, in part, by the number of hours required for every laborer, skilled or unskilled, to produce the goods needed to rear that person from infancy and for subsistence during working years.

Unfortunately, too many qualifications and exceptions spoil the attraction of a generalization. The labor theory is of limited value after all the necessary modifications are taken into account. Furthermore, the modifications suggested above are incomplete. In the last case, for example, the number of labor hours necessary to sustain a worker consists itself of some hours of unskilled labor and some of skilled labor. To add the two together, a conversion number must be available. It is not available, however, for it is precisely what the whole procedure is set up to find.

Alternative Modern Theory. Modern economic theory, developed since Marx, explains values or prices in terms of degree of scarcity. According to this theory, the value of a thing in exchange for something else depends on how scarce it is. Its scarcity in turn depends on the state of its supply and the state of demand for it. Behind supply and demand lie a great many interdependent determinants. The scarcity theory is a complicated one, but it provides a more satisfactory explanation than the labor theory of value. The scarcity theory treats not only labor but also capital and natural resources as productive and value-creating.

Owing to the weaknesses of Marx's labor theory of value, his use of it as a basis for arguing against the capitalistic market society's distribution of income makes that argument weak. One might still question market capitalism or market capitalism's distribution of income. However, one would probably do so on grounds other than because one believed that only labor had the power to create value and that all value was in proportion to labor used.

The Subsistence Theory of Wages. Another element in Marx's theory of market capitalism is the subsistence theory of wages. Marx alternated between two explanations of this theory. One is that the wage rate will tend to fall until workers receive only enough income to provide a minimum physical existence for themselves. The other is that the wage rate will tend to fall until workers receive only enough to provide a psychologically or culturally determined minimum level of living for themselves.[15] The latter minimum might change as attitudes changed. It

15. See Thomas Sowell, *Marxism* (New York: William Morrow, 1985), 136–137.

might vary from place to place, depending upon the attitudes prevailing in the society of each place. Marx did not give a satisfactory causal explanation of why the wage rate under market capitalism tended toward a subsistence minimum, however defined.

The Malthusian Explanation. Marx rejected the explanation offered by such people as Thomas Malthus. Malthus had argued that any wage higher than subsistence would reduce the death rate or raise the birthrate. These changes would cause the population and the supply of labor to increase. The increase would depress the market for labor and force the wage rate down. Perhaps Marx rejected the Malthusian explanation because it seemed to place the blame on the workers or to suggest that any economic system, not just market capitalism, would produce the same undesirable result.

Lopsided Bargaining Power. Marx did contend that the bargaining power of each individual worker would be small relative to that of a capitalist employer in the negotiations on wage rates. A worker sometimes has no real alternative, other than unemployment, to accepting a job from one accessible employer. On the other hand, most employers either can offer work to any one of a number of different workers who are competing with each other for jobs or can withhold work entirely by shutting down operations.

Critics of Marx have pointed out that, at least sometimes, workers have considerable bargaining power. Their power arises because of their unusual skills, because they band together in labor unions, because there is competition among employers for their services, or because without their labor real capital is unprofitable. Even with weak bargaining power, there is no proof that the wage rate will fall to the subsistence level.

The Reserve Army of the Unemployed. Marx also contended that there usually would be substantial numbers of unemployed workers. They would always be ready to compete with those who had jobs. They would also furnish an inexhaustible supply of labor at a minimum subsistence wage rate, no matter how strong the demand for labor.

Critics of this argument emphasize that Marx never really convincingly demonstrated that capitalism creates unemployment. Indeed, if Marx were right that only labor creates surplus value and profits, capitalist employers would seek out and employ every available worker because, by so doing, profits could be maximized. Actually, real wages in countries heavily dependent upon market capitalism have risen substantially in the long run. A Marxist may choose to dismiss this evidence by claiming that it merely reflects a rising psychological minimum subsistence level. But one can reasonably rejoin that capitalism is performing well, not badly, in this respect. It has raised both aspirations and the means to fulfill them.

The Theory of Surplus Value. The theory of surplus value asserts that workers usually produce more goods and services than are needed for their subsistence. This assertion seems acceptable. It is probably equally acceptable, however, to assert that land is capable of producing more crop than that needed to reseed the land adequately in the next growing season. Likewise, a labor-saving machine may spare more labor hours than were required to make it. As the basis for an argument against market capitalism, the theory of surplus value is not a strong argument unless supplemented by a labor theory of value and a subsistence theory of wages.

Actually, land, labor, and capital cooperate in most production activities, regardless of the economic system. The complete removal of any one of these three factors would cause production to cease almost entirely. As long as they do cooperate, the productive output is usually more than enough to replace the worn equipment, maintain the natural resources, and provide for the subsistence needs of the workers. The excess may take the form either of suprasubsistence consumer goods or of capital goods that increase the society's stock of real capital.

The Theory of Crises and Trends. Another element in Marx's argument against market capitalism is the crisis or business cycle. These do occur in many forms of capitalistic economic systems. They had been the object of economists' inquiries and theories before Marx, and they have continued to be. Marx's explanation of them was incomplete and questionable, and we have not yet achieved a complete understanding of them. However, as a result of economic studies undertaken since the Great Depression, most economists believe that mixed economic systems can avoid severe crises and cycles by accepting rather modest government economic intervention. In any case, crises and cycles have not yet forced the complete collapse of market capitalism and its replacement by Marxist socialism or communism.

Many of the trends Marx predicted would bring the downfall of capitalism have not been corroborated by subsequent history. Most striking has been the failure of the capitalist owners to become a smaller and smaller percentage of the population and the proletariat a larger and larger percentage. An increasingly greater portion of the people of Western Europe and North America possess property in the form of savings accounts, shares of corporate stock, government bonds, houses, automobiles, and durable consumer goods. The proletarian proportion of the populace has diminished as skilled white-collar and service workers have come to outnumber unskilled, manual workers.

The percentage of the labor force unemployed has not increased in the long run, as Marx predicted it would. The quality of life of the majority of the population has not become increasingly miserable. Working conditions have improved, not deteriorated, on the average at least. In the long run, the rate of profit on capital has not fallen as much as Marx predicted. Technological and social changes have provided new, profitable opportunities for the use of machinery and other capital goods. The governments of most capitalist countries have not resolutely blocked every attempt by the majority of the people to obtain legislation to improve their lot. It is not the case that for most noncommunist, developed countries the government is used as the instrument by which an increasingly small number of capitalists keep subjugated an ever more preponderant working class.

The Theory of Economic Determinism and Dialectical Materialism. Marx's emphasis on the economic system of a society as determinant of all else about society can also be criticized.

Economics as Only One of Many Interdependent Forces. The economic system is as much a result as a cause of the general character of society. Religion and philosophy, for example, help to determine economic organization. A people's religion may emphasize the evil of the accumulation of material goods and the virtue of asceticism. In consequence, the economic system is likely to remain a traditional one, and economic growth will not occur. Alternatively, religion may lay stress upon individual responsibility and upon working hard, saving much, and investing productively. As a result, the economic system is likely to become a market one with rapid change. A people's philosophy may accord great prestige to those who are very successful in military, spiritual, or governmental affairs and little prestige to those who are economically successful. Then the economic system of the people is likely to remain organized around the principle of tradition, and what modern Westerners regard as economic progress will probably be slow.

The political system of a society may place and keep in power those who wish to maintain the status quo. Then economic change will probably occur only slowly. The cultural heritage of a people may include a great accumulated stock of technological knowledge. The economic system of that people will probably be very different from that of a people with little such knowledge. The physical environment of a people is also likely to shape their economic system. The tropics may offer no challenge to traditional economic organization, which remains underdeveloped. The arctic may offer too great a challenge, which prevents economic organization from being anything but traditional and underdeveloped.

Monocausal Theories of History. It is implausible that human history is simply a sequence of economic changes that bring about other changes. Such a theory of history is as questionable as every other monocausal explanation of history. For example, one other such theory is the *hero theory,* which claims that the shape of history is the result of the appearance from time to time of extremely influential people such as Plato, Jesus, Caesar, Charlemagne, Columbus, Luther, Marx, and Lenin. Another is the *idea theory,* which stresses the great historical influence of ideas such as monotheism, asceticism, altruism, capitalism, democracy, and communism. Another is the *war theory,* which claims that conflicts of arms provide the key to the understanding of history. There is also the *political theory,* which claims that history is the sequence of governments.[16]

The Merits of Marx

Marx's theory was not totally without merit. He did indicate some of the weaknesses of the market capitalism of his time and place. The inequality of income, wealth, and power of nineteenth-century European capitalism was too great to be permanently tolerated by the populace and too great by twentieth-century Western standards. Marx correctly predicted some of the trends in market capitalism.

16. A brief elaboration of this kind of criticism of Marx can be found in William Ebenstein, *Today's Isms: Communism, Fascism, Capitalism, and Socialism,* 7th ed. (Englewood Cliffs, N.J.: Prentice-Hall, 1973), Chap. 1.

Recurrent and sometimes severe business fluctuations have taken place. Unemployment has been a persistent problem. Inordinate political and social power has accrued to the economically most successful. Control, if not ownership, has been concentrated in the hands of those who guide the great private corporations.

Marx was perhaps the first to try to explain why history had occurred as it had rather than merely to describe what had occurred. He attempted to integrate economic theory with history. He was one of the few of his time to do so.

THE POLITICAL AND ECONOMIC SYSTEM OF THE SOVIET UNION AND EASTERN EUROPE

Control of the government machinery in the former Soviet Union and the former Communist countries of Eastern and Central Europe was in the hands of the Communist Party, the only political party permitted.[17] Membership in the Communist Party was limited to a small minority of the population, as Table 3-1 indicates. It maintained firm control over every aspect of life through its well-organized, disciplined organization. Communists held key positions in all institutions and enterprises in society. In factories, offices, schools, and villages, primary units called cells operated. Consisting of at least three party members, each cell was responsible for recruiting members and selecting delegates to local party conferences, which in turn selected delegates to conferences covering a somewhat wider geographic area. This process continued to the highest body of party authority.[18]

Organization

The organization of the Communist Party took the form of a pyramid. At the top of the pyramid was the Central Committee, which was elected at the meeting of the National Party Congress. It had no effective role as a decision-maker; its main function was to disseminate leadership aims and objectives of the leaders to officials in the various central government agencies, and downward to party officials at lower administrative levels. The Politburo was the supreme instrument of political power, responsible for all phases of national life—foreign policy, domestic economic policy, and military policy. The Secretariat of the Central Committee was responsible for the administration of the Communist Party. It was also responsible for providing leadership for the party organization, which consisted of a hierarchy of subordinate secretariats at lower administrative levels.

Party and Government Structure

The Communist Party was a part of the government bureaucracy, not independent from it as would be the case in the United States and other democracies. Party and

17. The Communist Party permitted minor parties to exist to provide token opposition.
18. This was called democratic centralism, which meant that all members of all legislative bodies from the lowest to the highest were elected. There were no opposition parties of any strength.

TABLE 3-1
Proportion of Party Members in Selected Countries, 1986

Country	*Party Members (thousands)*	*Party Members (percentage of population)*
Bulgaria	932	10.4
China	44,000	4.2
Czechoslovakia	1,675	10.8
East Germany	2,304	13.8
Hungary	871	8.2
Poland	2,126	5.7
Romania	3,557	15.6
Soviet Union	18,500	6.6
Yugoslavia	2,168	9.3

Source: Richard F. Staar, "Checklist of Communist Parties in 1986," *Problems of Communism*, Vol. 36, No. 2, March-April (Washington, D.C.: U.S. Government Printing Office, 1987), 45–47.

government structure paralleled each other. For example, in the former Soviet Union the basic party administrative units were the Central Committee, Politburo, and Secretariat; the basic governmental units were the Supreme Soviet and the Council of Ministers. Party leaders were members of both units. This interlocking relationship continued at all levels of government even down to rural areas. This interconnection of party and government provided unity of control and uniformity of ideological perspective. This did not mean, however, that party and government organs functioned as two perfectly synchronized parts of a smoothly working administrative machine. To the contrary, power rivalries and disputes were common.

The Nomenklatura System

All major appointments, promotions, and dismissals were the prerogative of the Communist Party. This prerogative of selection covered offices in government administration and all major managerial positions in the economy. There was an ideological imperative that party leaders had to maintain a monopoly of political, ideological, and economic power. This was done through the nomenklatura system, which was simply patronage designed to ensure party loyalty. Being a member of the nomenklatura elite carried with it a number of benefits—better apartments, access to the best schools, foreign travel, shopping at state stores that carried quality products from Western countries, and many other perquisites not available to the masses. Supposedly workers were "first among equals" in the former Soviet Union and the other socialist countries, but that was hardly the case.[19]

19. There is a famous quote in George Orwell's classic *Animal Farm*: "All animals are equal, but some are more equal than others." In the beginning when the animals took over the farm from its owner, all would run it and share equally, but the pigs took over. The Communist Party was very much like the pigs. It purported to rule in the name of the people.

THE ECONOMIC SYSTEM OF SOCIALISM

The socialist countries had the same type of economic system. One thing that immediately comes to mind is economic planning, which gave the state rather than the free market control over resource allocation. Under the socialist system, private firms employing hired labor either did not exist or were restricted to a small segment of the economy.[20] The almost total elimination of private property and other forms of capitalism was considered the main criterion of socialism. Control by the state over resource allocation was supposed to be more efficient and equitable than it was under capitalism. There would not be the waste of resources and conspicuous consumption that existed in the capitalist countries.

A major criticism of the capitalist market mechanism is that it produces too many things that have no social value. If there is a demand for a product, no matter how frivolous, then it is going to be produced. Socialism, by eliminating both private ownership of the means of production and the anarchy of the market, would allow organization on a national scale through economic planning. Such questions as what to produce, how to produce, and to whom goods would be distributed would be decided through economic planning. Saving and investment decisions, which would be determined by the supply of and demand for loanable funds in a market economy, would be determined by planning. With economic planning, the role of money and prices would become far narrower and more restricted than it was under capitalism.

Economic Planning

In the socialist economies, production and distribution were implemented through the use of economic plans. The plans represented an attempt to balance the supply of and demand for resources in order to achieve an equilibrium. Planning was not only concerned with every branch of economic activity, but embraced many other aspects of economic life. It was not content with merely making the socialist system operate; it also had such objectives as increasing national wealth or the industrialization of an economy. In other words, economic planning could have both short- and long-term goals. It relied on commands for its implementation; it was controlled by a central planning agency, by financial organizations such as the state bank, but above all by the political authorities. Economic planning was divided into several categories as follows:

Planning with a Time Horizon. Economic plans were divided into several time categories:

20. Some form of private enterprise existed in all of the socialist countries. In Poland most agriculture was privately owned. In East Germany, the most ideologically rigid of all of the socialist countries, small privately owned firms existed.

1. General plans laid down for a period of fifteen to twenty years were primarily concerned with long-term problems of structural changes on a national scale, technology, and the like.
2. Medium-term plans, usually covering a period of five years, were concerned mostly with changes in the capacity and rate of production of different industries and enterprises.
3. Annual plans within each five-year plan provided a detailed description of production plans for the year and served as a control mechanism by all state-owned enterprises.[21]

Physical Input-Output Planning and Financial Planning. The basic planning in the socialist economies was in real terms and involved physical output targets of the most important industrial and agricultural commodities and the allocation of labor at the national level, the balancing and transfers of important types of raw materials and equipment, and total national capital investment. Financial planning was used as a control mechanism. It was used to control the execution of the physical input-output plan, a control which was imposed by the banking system. It was also used to maintain a balance between consumer disposable income and the volume of consumer goods available. It consisted of three parts—the state budget, the credit plan, and the cash plan of the central bank. The credit and cash plans controlled the outlay of short-term credit and the cash and currency issued by the central bank.

The Use of Material Balances. Physical input-output planning relied on the use of material balances, which presented an intended relationship between supplies and their allocation for special commodities. Material balances were drawn up for all of the important types of industrial and agricultural products. An example of the use of material balances can be presented as follows:

Resources	*Distribution*
Physical stocks at the start of the planning period	Production and operating needs
Production	Capital construction
Imports	Replenishment of state inventories
Mobilization of internal resources	Exports
	Stocks at the end of the planning period
Total	Total

State Budget

In terms of the relationship of expenditures to gross domestic product, the state budgets of the socialist economies were much larger than the budgets of the major

21. There were also quarterly plans within each annual plan.

capitalist economies.[22] About half of the gross domestic product of the former Soviet Union, Poland, and other socialist countries flowed through their budgets. The reason for the size of the socialist state budget is obvious: many things financed by private enterprise in a capitalist economy were financed by the government. For example, investment expenditures, which in the United States would be financed by private enterprise, were financed to a considerable degree out of the state budget. Many other expenditures, such as expenditures on health and research that would be financed at least in part by private enterprise in a market economy, were financed out of the state budget.

The state budget was an integral part of economic planning, particularly the financial plan, which was the financial counterpart of the physical input-output plan. It involved cash, credit, and investment financing necessary to implement the attainment of the physical output goals spelled out in the national economic plan. It was through the state budget that taxes and other fiscal resources of the government were collected and distributed. The state budget was a prime vehicle for the allocation of resources for various purposes. In a market economy, the market is a device for the organization of economic activity by transmitting preferences to producers, who adjust output to direct resources into alternative uses.

Table 3-2 compares budgetary comparisons of selected socialist and capitalist countries in relationship to GDP. The major difference is the percentage of economic expenditures financed out of socialist budgets as compared to capitalist budgets. Economic expenditures include state investments in state-owned enterprises and state subsidies, which would include price supports to agricultural cooperatives and state-owned enterprises.

Money and Banking

Money in a socialist economy possessed many of the same functions as money in a capitalist economy. Within and outside the state sector, money served as a unit of account, that is, all goods and services that were bought and sold were valued in monetary units.

Money also functioned as a medium of exchange in that wages and salaries were paid in currency, and receivers of money could use it to buy goods and services. The ownership of money, however, did not give individuals command over the allocation of resources as it did in a capitalist economy, because resource allocation was determined by the economic plan and not by the price system.

Banking was centralized as a monopoly of the government in the socialist economies. Control over the money supply was vested in the state bank: in the Soviet Union, Gosbank, and in the German Democratic Republic, Staatsbank der DDR. Through the direct operation of the state bank, the government could control the volume of credit and hence the money supply. The state bank also played an integral part in the implementation of economic planning. It was responsible

22. The state budget is similar to the national budget of the United States, only far more comprehensive.

TABLE 3-2
Size and Economic Expenditures of Government Budgets, 1981 (in percentage of GDP)

	Total Budgetary Expenditures	*Economic Expenditures of the Budget*
Socialist Countries		
Czechoslovakia	53.1	22.8
Hungary	63.2	26.9
Poland	53.2	32.5
Soviet Union	47.1	25.8
Capitalist Countries		
Australia	33.6	2.8
France	46.4	4.6
United States	34.8	3.5
West Germany	49.8	4.8
Low-Income Capitalist		
India	21.3	6.8
Kenya	29.2	8.6

Source: Janos Kornai, *The Socialist System: The Political Economy of Communism* (Princeton, N.J.: Princeton University Press, 1992), 135–136.

for the implementation of the credit and cash plans. The credit plan regulated the granting of credit by the state bank to state-owned enterprises during a stipulated period of time; the cash plan controlled the amount of money the state bank could put into circulation. In addition to the state bank, there were banks that specialized by functions: foreign trade, agriculture, and savings.

Prices

The problem of pricing in a socialist economy was of a different nature from that under capitalism. For one thing, prices did not determine the allocation of resources to the extent that they do in a market economy. Moreover, pricing was a question not merely of economics but also of ideology and politics: the socialist rationale for prices was the law of value, the amount of labor time embodied in the creation of goods and services. Labor was the only factor of production credited with the capability of producing value. So the price or value of anything was determined by the amount of labor required to produce it. The relative value of two products would be in the same proportion as the amount of labor required to produce them.

A dual price system operated in the socialist economies: prices paid to producers and prices paid by consumers for retail goods. Producers' prices were those received by producing enterprises from other producing enterprises and from trading entities. Producer prices were normally based on an average cost for the entire branch of industry producing a product. Included in average costs were not only wage payments and material costs but also capital charges. In some cases producer prices were set by the state at levels below average cost, so that enterprises operated at a loss with the loss subsidized by state revenues.

Consumer retail prices consisted of all the components that made up the prices charged by the producer to the retailer plus a retail price markup. There was virtual isolation between producer and retail prices; what happened to the former had little to do with the latter. Retail prices were set by the state to keep supply and demand in balance within the guidelines of the economic plan. The setting of prices was based on the macrosocial preferences of the planners rather than on the true interaction of supply and demand affected by consumer preferences, but a certain amount of flexibility in retail prices was permitted within limits. For example, "free prices" set by supply and demand operated in the purchase and sale of certain agricultural products.

Income Distribution

The Communists deplored the great differences in the distribution of income and wealth in the capitalist system. The end result of communism was supposed to be a society in which income differentials would be eliminated, and social classes based on wealth distribution would disappear. This, of course, did not happen, and would not have happened in the former Soviet Union and the other socialist economies. Given the existence of the Communist Party and the nomenklatura elite, there was no such thing as a "classless" society. Moreover, the socialist system lagged behind numerous capitalist countries in the qualitative improvement of living standards. Economic security, including the guarantee of full employment, and a social security safety net that covered everyone was considered the major accomplishment of the socialist economies, but even here a price was paid in the curtailment of political, social, and economic liberties.

Table 3-3 compares income distribution in the former German Democratic Republic (DDR) and West Germany before reunification. In the socialist system of the DDR, income distribution was determined by the state rather than the marketplace. Income distribution had clear-cut aims within the scope of the state economic plan. Wages constituted almost all of the income distributed in the DDR and was determined by the government rather than by the forces of supply and demand. Wages were set within the framework of the state economic plan. In West Germany, a capitalist economy, wages were determined by supply and demand. Table 3-3 breaks down net household income by quintiles for the two countries for 1970 and 1983.[23]

23. There are a number of caveats regarding this table. First, only wage incomes are included. Excluded are incomes from property ownership, which would affect West German income but not East German income. Also it does not reflect the fact that West German income could buy a wider variety of goods and services at a lower price than East German income. However, housing, transportation, and food were subsidized in East Germany. The quality of social services was far better in West Germany.

TABLE 3-3
Comparison of Net Household Incomes in East Germany and West Germany by Quintiles (percent)

	1970 West Germany-	*1970* East Germany	*1983* West Germany-	*1983* East Germany
Quintile 1	8.3	9.7	9.8	10.9
Quintile 2	12.7	16.1	14.7	16.3
Quintile 3	16.8	19.7	18.3	19.7
Quintile 4	22.3	23.4	22.9	22.9
Quintile 5	39.9	31.1	34.3	30.2

Source: Deutscher Bundestag, *Materialien zum Bericht zur Lage der Nation im Getielten Deutschland, 1987* (Bonn: Bundesminister fur Innerdeutsche Beziehunger, February 1987), 503.

Organization of Industry and Agriculture in the Former Soviet Union and Eastern Europe

In a socialist economy most productive and distributive enterprises came under the jurisdiction of the state, which exercised virtually monopolistic control over all economic resources. It owned and operated large-scale industries, mines, power plants, railways, and other means of communication. It was a monopoly in banking and foreign trade, and it controlled the domestic channels of distribution in its role as manufacturer, farmer, merchant, and banker. It engaged in farming on its own account through the institution of the state farm, and it largely controlled agriculture through the institution of collective farming. In the field of labor relations, it was the sole employer of note and as such dominated bargaining between itself and its employees.

Organization of Industry. The organization of industry in the socialist economies was complex because an extensive bureaucratic structure was necessary to plan and administer production and distribution policies. To facilitate top-down planning, industrial organization was strongly skewed toward large state enterprises that were integrated both horizontally and vertically. Firms in a particular sector were grouped together in large industrial combines, which were national or regional. The extent of industrial concentration was much higher in the more developed socialist economies than in the United States. For example, in the former East Germany, which was the most developed country in the Eastern bloc, the largest 100 enterprises, or about 1 percent of all enterprises, produced half of industrial output in 1988.[24] Within industry, preferred treatment was given to producer or capital goods that would produce other producer goods.

Organization of Agriculture. The organization of agriculture was similar to that of industry in that it, too, was considered a basic part of the economic and political organization of the state, and there was a constant effort to combine agricultural

24. *Statistisehes Jahrbuch der DDR* (Berlin: Rudolf Haufe Verlag, 1990), 138.

enterprises into larger units to increase output. The two basic units of agricultural production were state farms and collective farms. State farms were owned and operated by the government and operated as regular industrial establishments with managers and hired workers. The budgets and operating plans of state farms were subject to government control. State farms were typically extremely large and received most of the capital investment allocated to the agricultural sector. Collective farms represented a form of agricultural organization in which individual farms pooled their resources and farmed on a collective basis.

SUMMARY

Socialism, as it existed in the former Soviet Union and the Soviet-bloc countries of Eastern and Central Europe, is a thing of the past even though it continues to exist in a diluted form in China. The development and the breakup and the decline of the socialist system amounted to the most important political and economic phenomena of the twentieth century. At the height of its power, more than a third of the world's population lived under it. But the system had a great impact on the rest of the world as well. For more than forty years the United States and the Soviet Union were the major superpowers of the world in direct ideological conflict with each other. Millions of people all over the world feared that if war broke out, they would have to encounter the military might of the Soviet Union.

So what then was the socialist system? It was the economic structure developed in the Soviet Union that was developed under Lenin and Stalin, but particularly by Stalin. It also emerged in China, in the countries that became a part of the Soviet bloc after the end of World War II, and in several Asian, African, and Latin American countries. The political system of these countries was run by the Communist Party, but the political and economic systems overlapped, with the party responsible for both. The main economic characteristic of socialism was state ownership of the means of production. Most natural resources and capital were state-owned, including land, manufacturing industries, finance, and domestic and foreign trade. A second characteristic was central economic planning, which was responsible for resource allocation. The third characteristic was the distribution of income by the state.

QUESTIONS FOR DISCUSSION

1. In the Marxist framework, what was the difference between socialism and communism?
2. What was Marx's labor theory of value? How can this theory be criticized?
3. What was Marx's theory of surplus value? Is it a valid theory?
4. What was the role of the Communist Party in a socialist system?
5. What was the function of economic planning in a socialist system?

6. Compare the allocation of resources in a market economy with that in a socialist economy.
7. Compare the distribution of income in a market economy with that in a socialist economy.
8. How were prices determined in a socialist system?

RECOMMENDED READINGS

Balinsky, Alexander. *Marx's Economics: Origin and Development.* Lexington, Mass.: Heath, 1970.

Kornai, Janos. *The Socialist System: The Political Economy of Communism.* Princeton, N.J.: Princeton University Press, 1992.

Lichtheim, George. *Marxism: A Historical and Critical Study.* New York: Praeger, 1961.

Marx, Karl. *Das Kapital.* New York: Modern Library, 1906.

Pryor, Frederic L. *A Guidebook to the Comparative Study of Economic Systems.* Englewood Cliffs, N.J.: Prentice-Hall, 1985.

Wilczynski, Joseph. *The Economics of Socialism.* London: George Allen and Unwin, 1970.

PART II

The New Role Model

CHAPTER 4
Comparative Capitalist Systems

The cold war is over, and trading and production have replaced military conquest as the preferred route to world influence. With Soviet socialism a thing of the past, the comparisons of capitalism and socialism that provided the framework for textbooks on comparative economic systems are no longer relevant. An alternative is to compare the various forms of capitalist systems in existence today. One approach is to compare individualistic capitalism to communitarian capitalism; a second approach is to compare market capitalism to social welfare capitalism and state-directed capitalism. The latter approach will be used in Chapters 4–7.[1]

1. A third way is to compare capitalism on the basis of culture. Charles Hampden-Turner and Alfons Trompenaars have written a book called *The Seven Cultures of Capitalism* (New York: Doubleday, 1993). They argue that capitalism has seven distinct cultures as reflected in the following seven countries: United States, Britain, France, Germany, Japan, Sweden, and the Netherlands. Culture influences economic practices. For example, German culture has determined the organization of German industry. It was late to industrialize, and development depended on a linkage between enterprise and the state. This tradition went back four hundred years.

It is important to note that some changes have taken place since the last edition of this book was published. One change is the general belief that social welfare benefits, particularly in some of the European countries, are no longer sustainable at their high levels. One problem is the aging population, and a second is high government budget deficits. As in the United States, welfare reform has proven to be an elusive goal, limited largely to quick fixes. In France, for example, the government has tried to reduce its pension burden by tying indexing to inflation rather than to wages. A second change is an increase in the rate of privatization. In Germany the government in December 1994 began to sell off the state-owned telephone monopoly, Deutsche Telekom, valued at $60 billion and the third-largest phone company in the world. The rationale for its privatization is that a new Deutsche Telekom, free from state ownership, will be better able to compete in the international communications market.

U.S. MARKET CAPITALISM

There never has been a purely free market economy in the United States. From its beginnings in 1787, the federal government has been involved in the promotion of manufacturing, and it passed tariff laws to protect U.S. business interests. Subsidies were used to build canals, roads, and various forms of transportation from which private enterprises benefited greatly. As industrialization and business concentration increased during the latter part of the last century, the federal government passed laws to regulate specific sectors of business—for example, railroads—or to control various forms of anticompetitive business practices, such as price fixing and division of markets. Government participation in the U.S. economy increased during the Depression of the 1930s, when minimum wage and social security legislation were passed, and regulatory agencies were created to regulate banks, communications, and the securities market. During the 1960s and early 1970s government regulation was extended to cover consumer product safety, the employment of women and minorities, the environment, and occupational safety.

U.S. Capitalism and Culture

U.S. capitalism is a reflection of U.S. culture, just as Japanese capitalism is a reflection of Japanese culture. In the United States, individualism is a carryover from the last century, when the West opened to settlement and large numbers of immigrants entered the United States. Most of these immigrants came from European countries, fleeing government oppression or economic hardship. The United States was viewed as a land of opportunity where an individual had an opportunity to get ahead through his or her own efforts, and each generation would have the opportunity to be better off financially.[2] The West provided opportunities for im-

2. This is called the American dream, but the current generation may be the first generation that is less well off than its predecessors.

migrants, particularly in agriculture, and this is where individualism flourished. It was the individual against the elements of nature, where the fittest survived and the weakest fell by the wayside.[3]

A second facet of U.S. capitalism is the emphasis placed on wealth and consumption. Role models for wealth accumulation date back as far as the last century, when the new industrial aristocracy was made up of wealthy entrepreneurs and business leaders whom some called "robber barons." The prototypical self-made capitalists were millionaires John D. Rockefeller and Andrew Carnegie. It was the wealthy who often set consumption standards that others tried to follow. It is interesting to note that the wealthy in the United States have never stirred up the class resentment that has existed in more-class-conscious societies such as England. Microsoft chairman and CEO Bill Gates, the richest billionaire in the United States, inspired admiration and the belief that anyone with a good idea can succeed in the United States.

Competition. Whether in business or sports, the United States is a competitive society. Its justification for this emphasis on competition is that it contributes to the welfare of society. When the industries and markets of an economy are organized competitively, certain supposedly desirable things will happen. First, competition is supposed to provide consumers with a wider variety of choices at lower prices. It is supposed to encourage innovation—the firm that builds a better mousetrap than its competitor succeeds. Finally, competition should bring about efficiency in the operation of business and industry by granting economic success to those firms efficiently operated and by relentlessly eliminating those inefficiently operated.

Government Intervention in the U.S. Economy

Government intervention in the U.S. economy has occurred for several reasons:

1. When there is a breakdown in competitive market forces, monopoly, oligopoly, and otherwise imperfectly competitive market structures cause inefficient resource allocation and socially undesirable market performances. Antitrust policies are designed to deal with industry conduct, such as price fixing, as well as aspects of industry structure that might foster monopolistic powers.
2. In a market economy, the price mechanism gives people no opportunity to bid against the production and the sale of commodities and services they regard as undesirable. Many people would be happier if they didn't have to breathe cigarette smoke in public places or noxious fumes from a chemical plant, but there is no way the marketplace can take these negative preferences into account, except through government control.

3. Willa Cather's novel *O Pioneers* is an excellent example. Set around the turn of the century, the novel is about a Scandinavian family that comes to Nebraska to find opportunity in farming. The father knows little about farming and fails like most of his neighbors. After his death, his daughter, who has far more business sense, becomes the family leader, buys the right property, farms the right crops, and enables the family to become prosperous.

3. Technological advances have created market externalities. The mass production of automobiles had an enormous impact on the development of the U.S. economy during the early part of this century. Thousands of jobs were created not only in the automobile industry but in related industries such as steel and rubber as well. However, the automobile become the prime source of air pollution. Air transportation also became an important form of transportation, but airplanes can create noise pollution.
4. Unemployment compensation and social security pensions were introduced into the United States later than in most other industrial countries. The rationale is to provide a measure of protection for persons who fall through the cracks through no fault of their own. It should be noted, however, that social welfare programs are by no means as comprehensive in the United States as in other countries. The provision of affordable health insurance has become a major domestic issue in the United States. Some 37 million Americans are without any form of health insurance.

Historical Background of Government Intervention

Government intervention in the U.S. economy can be divided into three time periods. The first lasted from 1870 to 1930. During this time, government intervention was essentially microeconomic and took the form of laws to regulate railroads and curb the power of monopolies. Only when the competitive, self-adjusting mechanism broke down did the government undertake to correct its most serious failings. The first laws to protect consumers were passed during this period. Laws regulating railroads and monopolies usually were initiated by state governments and only later adopted by the federal government. Laws were also passed to improve the lot of laborers with respect to working conditions, and taxes were imposed on income and wealth. But, for the most part, the laws directed against industrial concentration and the accumulation of wealth did not have much effect.

The second period, the Depression of the 1930s, marked the end of laissez-faire and the beginning of an increased role of government in the U.S. economy. During this time much legislation was passed to stimulate business recovery. Because people believed that certain defects in the business system were at least partly responsible for causing the Depression, laws were enacted regulating business in a number of areas, including banking, transportation, electric power, and the securities market. The Fair Labor Standards Act of 1938 enacted minimum wages and maximum hours for workers engaged in interstate commerce. The Social Security Act of 1935 provided for federal pensions for persons over 65 years of age. The federal debt, which was around $2 billion in 1929, had increased to $40 billion by 1939.[4] Mechanisms for the government's macrointervention began to be

4. *Economic Report of the President 1992* (Washington, D.C.: U.S. Government Printing Office, 1992), 385.

put in place during the 1930s and were consolidated with the passage of the Employment Act of 1946.

The third period of government intervention in the U.S. economy extended roughly from 1964 to 1975. This intervention was more broad-based in that it did not deal with specific economic issues such as monopoly power, pricing, industrial concentration, corporate economic power and its use and abuses, or unemployment. Instead, its focus was on the attainment of certain social goals such as environmental protection, consumer protection, employment of women and minorities, job safety, and so forth. These goals were associated with a change in societal values that has been characterized by such terms as *rising entitlements* and *quality of life*. Examples of government legislation during this period include the Civil Rights Act of 1964, the Clean Air Act of 1970, the Consumer Product Safety Act of 1972, and the Age Discrimination in Employment Act of 1967. These and similar laws created a new form of government regulation that has become comprehensive in its control over business activity.[5]

EUROCAPITALISM

Capitalism had its roots in Europe, and it was European thinkers who defined its institutions. The contributions of John Locke and Adam Smith have already been mentioned in Chapter 1. The concept of laissez-faire is associated with a school of thinkers in eighteenth-century France, the Physiocrats, whose main contribution to economic thought was their acceptance of a natural order. They believed that if society were left alone by government, it would work better than if government managed it. David Ricardo developed the principle of comparative advantage, which states that a country should export goods in which it has the greatest absolute advantage, and import goods in which it has the least comparative advantage.[6] The writings of Adam Smith, Ricardo, Jean Baptiste Say, John Stuart Mill, and others were incorporated into what is called the classical theory of economics, which provided the foundation for free market capitalism.[7]

However, the influence of these writers was greater in the United States than in Europe. The Industrial Revolution occurred earlier in Europe than in the United States and brought with it some unpleasant by-products. As discussed in Chapter 2, working conditions in factories and mines were deplorable. Men, women, and children were at work for long hours. The equipment was often dangerous and caused workers to have accidents that maimed or killed them. Intense

5. However, there has been considerable deregulation of business. The airline industry was deregulated in 1978, and the railroad and trucking industries were deregulated in 1980. The savings and loan and commercial banking industries were deregulated in 1981.
6. David Ricardo, *The Principles of Political Economy and Taxation* (New York: E. P. Dutton, 1948).
7. Later, classical theory of economics was expanded to include the writings of Alfred Marshall and A. C. Pigou.

market competition for jobs prevented workers from turning down employment even when it was unsafe. The cities that grew up or expanded to house the workers were unattractive and unpleasant.[8] Many of them consisted of slums, where thousands of people were crowded together without proper sanitation facilities.

Strong political movements developed in Europe around the middle of the last century. Socialist parties of both the Marxist and non-Marxist types were formed and gained considerable strength in European politics. Before the beginning of World War II, socialist political parties in France and Germany were second in importance only to the conservative parties. These parties were committed to raising the wages and improving the working conditions of workers. Government intervention increased in England, Germany, and other European countries in the latter part of the last century. This intervention took the form of child labor laws, unemployment compensation, social security, and laws mandating safer working conditions. During this century, Europe has experienced two major wars and a depression, all of which increased the role of government.

Characteristics of Eurocapitalism

The basic tenets of capitalism—the profit motive, private property ownership, private enterprise, and reliance on the market mechanism to allocate resources—exist in the three types of capitalism outlined in Chapter 1. However, there are differences among the three in that U.S. capitalism relies on individual action as opposed to collective action, and emphasis is placed on short-term rather than long-term gain. In Japan and other Pacific Rim countries, those priorities are reversed. Eurocapitalism is more diverse than either U.S. or Asian capitalism because Europe includes more countries and more diverse cultures. For instance, the Scandinavian countries have a history and culture different from the Western European countries. Nevertheless, the linchpin of Eurocapitalism is an elaborate system of social welfare benefits such as health care, pensions, and training for technical skills.[9] Every phase of economic activity carries with it some form of government involvement. For example, many European countries have strict laws against plant closures.[10]

The role of government in European economies is not limited to the provision of social welfare benefits, which is a relatively new phenomenon. Governments have been involved in other ways. In France, state intervention in the economy dates back to the time of Jean Baptiste Colbert, who was prime minister under Louis XIV. Believing that France could and should be the greatest industrial

8. See Charles Dickens, *Bleak House* (New York: Signet Books, 1964), 232–233.

9. The costs of this social overhead are considerable. German labor costs, half of which consist of government-mandated benefits, are the highest of the major industrial countries. There is concern over the ability of European firms to meet foreign competition.

10. In the United States, employers employing a certain number of workers have to give sixty days' notice of plant closings. There is no severance pay. In some European countries, a year's notice and up to a year's severance pay are required.

country of Europe, Colbert developed a policy of supporting national commercial and industrial interests by government means. To promote foreign trade, industries were created out of state funds. A canal was dug from the Bay of Biscay to the Mediterranean to improve the flow of trade between the different areas of France, while the highway system was made into the best in Europe. The greater part of the country became a customs-free area within which trade could flow freely.

There is current government support of industry. An example is Airbus Industrie, an aircraft manufacturer owned by the governments of France, Germany, Spain, and the United Kingdom that is designed to get Europe back into civilian aircraft manufacturing. Other joint government efforts designed to help European firms become more competitive include support of the European television industry, to which governments have provided some $6.3 billion, and Eurofighter, a program designed to build eight hundred new fighter aircraft. European governments have spent anywhere from 1.75 percent to 5.5 percent of their GNPs to help their industries.[11] Although privatization of state-owned firms has been occurring in all of the European countries, state-owned firms account for an important part of GNP in such countries as France, Italy, and Spain.[12]

France: Economic Planning

The principal difference between the economies of the United States and France is found in the area of industrial policy. The French have always been skeptical of the free market approach of the United States, believing instead that government must play a major role in the economy. Since post–World War II reconstruction, the French government has considered the development of certain domestic industries as critical to national economic development. Using a type of planning called indicative planning, it has involved a certain amount of French government intervention in the economy in the form of indirect control over credit and taxation.

Instruments of French Planning. French economic planning has relied on credit allocation, tax incentives, and public investment to accomplish its implementation, rather than on authoritarian direction or exhortation. The French treasury has been the major source of funds that have financed investment in the public and private sectors of the French economy. Most of these funds have been channeled through a special treasury account called the Fund for Economic and Social Development. Interest rates have often been lower than the borrower would have to pay in the market. Tax incentives have been used to promote activities that con-

11. Robert Ford and Wim Stryker, "Industrial Subsidies in the OECD countries," *OECD Economic Studies*, No. 15 (Autumn 1990), 37.

12. The pace of privatization has picked up in all three countries, but particularly in France, where several large formerly state-owned enterprises have been privatized. The French automobile company, Renault, which has been state-owned since the end of World War II, is set to be privatized, and increased privatization is a part of the current five-year plan.

form to the aims of the plan over those that do not. Public investment financed by the French government has accounted for more than half of all industrial investment in France.[13]

French Economic Plans. Altogether there have been eleven French economic plans, including the one that is currently in effect.[14] All have had different economic and social objectives. Some of the plans have been in effect for four years, others for five. The focus of the First Plan, which lasted from 1947 to 1953, was the reconstruction of the French economy after the damage inflicted by World War II.[15] It had as its basic objective the restructuring of the French steel and coal industries. The Sixth Plan (1971–1975) placed emphasis on the development of a computer industry that would achieve technological parity with the United States computer industry. The plan also gave priority to the development of the French aerospace industry. The Eighth Plan (1981–1985) channeled credit into regions removed from the Paris area to promote industrial decentralization. The French aerospace industry, which is one of the strongest in the world, was given increased access to credit. The Tenth Plan (1989–1992) stressed regional development in the Verdun area of northeastern France and increased government financial support to increase productivity in agriculture.

Political and Economic Change in France. The center-right coalition victory in the March 1993 national elections brought a major shift in French economic policy. The coalition is trying to reverse a centuries-old tradition of highly centralized administration and government control over the French economy. Prime Minister Edouard Balladur announced plans to privatize twenty-one state-owned industries, which in 1993 accounted for 30 percent of French GDP. Included were some of the largest companies and banks in the world: Rhône-Poulenc, Elf-Aquitaine, and Banque National de Paris.[16] The major rationale for privatization is to make French industries more competitive in international markets and in the European Union (EU). Subsidies have also been reduced for state-owned firms in all economic sectors to conform to multinational trade agreements and EU standards.

Sweden: The Role Model for the Welfare State

Although Sweden is a small country with a population of only 8.8 million people, its influence upon the world has been much greater than its size.[17] It was once

13. This has been facilitated by the fact that most banks are owned by the French government.
14. The French planning agency is called the Commissariat au Plan. Its inputs have been provided by representatives of agriculture, industry, and labor. It prepares the plan, submits it to the appropriate government authorities, and sees to its implementation once it has been approved.
15. This plan, called the Monnet Plan, eventually led to the creation of the European Community in 1956.
16. As of February 1995, four have been privatized and the remaining seventeen are in various stages of privatization.
17. Sweden was the foremost military power in central and eastern Europe in the seventeenth century.

called by Marquis Childs *The Middle Way*.[18] By this he meant that the economic system was halfway between the unbridled market capitalism of the United States and the state-planned economy of the Soviet Union. The goal of Swedish economic policy has been to modify the excesses of capitalism while avoiding the outright socialization of the agents of production as in the former Soviet Union. A goal has been to achieve a more equitable distribution of income through reliance on social welfare programs designed to redistribute income. Although Swedish social welfare programs are elaborate and comprehensive, the reverse side of the coin is that they are expensive.

Income transfers in Sweden take a number of forms:

1. Family allowances, which are regular cash payments to families with children, are paid in most industrial countries including Sweden. They are used as a means of redistributing income in such a way as to benefit the child-rearing portion of a nation's population.[19] This sum may be a flat amount per child or it may increase progressively based on the number of children. It is usually paid to the mother, whether she is single or married. Family allowances in Sweden are paid to families with children under the age of 16. The yearly amounts of these benefits range from around $1,500 for a family with one child to $11,000 to families with five children.[20] There is also an extended allowance for children aged 16 to 20 who are still in school. This allowance is around $2,000 annually.
2. Parental benefits are paid in connection with the birth or adoption of a child. Paid for a period of 450 days, these enable a parent to stay home with a child with compensation for the loss of income. For the first 360 days the amount received is 90 percent of the parent's income; for the final 90 days a standard amount of 60 kronor ($7) per day is allowed.
3. Old-age pensions are of two types: a basic pension that is paid to all Swedes and a supplementary pension that is payable to any Swede who has earned income from employment in excess of the base amount subject to the social security tax. Average income is calculated on the basis of a worker's fifteen highest-paid years.[21] In 1993 the average amount of the combined pensions was $8,300. A widow's pension is paid at the same rate as the basic pension and 40 percent of the supplementary pension. Those on disability can receive the full amount of both pensions.
4. National health insurance covers all Swedes. It includes paid family leave for up to 30 days. The average amount was $75 per day in 1993. A sickness cash benefit is paid to those who are sick and cannot work. A pregnancy cash benefit is payable for up to 50 days during the last stages of pregnancy. The national health insurance system covers medical and dental care.

18. Marquis Childs, *Sweden: The Middle Way* (New Haven: Yale University Press, 1961).
19. The family allowance was introduced in France in 1931 to spur an increase in the birthrate to compensate for enormous French losses in World War I.
20. The allowance increases to $3,500 for each additional child. However, birthrates are low in Sweden.
21. The retirement age in Sweden is 65; however, Swedes may retire earlier at a lower pension.

5. Unemployment compensation is paid for 300 days for workers under 55 and for 450 days for workers 55 and over. The benefit is 90 percent of a worker's gross wage.

Cost of the Swedish Welfare System. The total cost of the Swedish welfare system was 300 billion kronor ($42 billion) in 1994. In comparison to Swedish GDP, social insurance costs have increased in real terms from 7.0 percent in 1965 to 21.5 percent in 1994. These costs are financed by Swedish employers, the Swedish state budget, and county and municipal budgets. Contributions stipulated by law are only a part of the contributions paid by a Swedish employer. Apart from the mandatory social insurance system, employers are required to accept responsibility for certain measures over and above the legal benefits. All employers who have concluded collective agreements are obliged to take out other forms of insurance, including life insurance. When contributions from collective agreements are added, total employer contributions amount to 45 percent of average wages.

Sweden and Income Inequality. Large sums of money are redistributed through the medium of transfer payments in Sweden. As mentioned above, there are transfers, such as family allowances and old-age pensions, designed to benefit certain sectors of society. Then there are subsidies to certain sectors of the economy, such as agriculture, which result in lower prices for goods and services. Finally, there are some services provided by government that are in effect nonmonetary transfers, such as free education. On the other hand, personal income tax rates in Sweden are high, ranging from 20 to 51 percent at the national level and from 10 to 20 percent at the local level.[22]

Comparisons of income inequality among countries indicate that Sweden ranks very high when it comes to reducing the extent of income inequality between the highest and lowest income groups. Income distribution is more even in Sweden than it was in the Soviet Union and other former socialist countries.[23] When Swedish income distribution is compared to income distribution in the other high-income industrial countries of the world, only Japan has a more equal distribution of income. When you compare income distribution between Swedish men and women, Swedish women earn around 80 percent of what Swedish men make.[24]

The Swedish Model Reconsidered. The Swedish economy has run into major problems. Its unemployment rate at the beginning of 1995 was around 13 percent compared to an average of 2 percent for the 1970s and 1980s. A deficit in the Swedish government budget of 200 billion kronor ($30 billion), which amounted

22. The Swedish Institute, *Social Insurance in Sweden* (Stockholm: 1994), 5.
23. Janos Kornai, *The Socialist System* (Princeton, N.J.: Princeton University Press, 1992), 318; The World Bank, *World Development Report 1994* (New York: Oxford University Press, 1994), 221.
24. Ministry of Health and Social Affairs, *Social Welfare in Transition* (Stockholm, 1994), 12.

FIGURE 4-1 *Swedish Social Insurance and Other Benefits*

Health insurance

Allowances for medical expenses
- Out-patient services
- Hospital treatment
- Other treatment
- Dental care
- Birth control counseling
- Pharmaceutical preparations
- Travel expenses

Sickness benefits
- Sick pay
- Sickness benefit
- Rehabilitation allowance
- Grant for employment aids

Parental benefit
- In connection with the birth of a child and through the first eight years
- For temporary care of children

Maternity benefit

Pensions

Basic pension
- Old-age pension
- Disability pension
- Temporary disability pension
- Survivor's pensions
- Disability allowance

Special benefits
- Pension supplement
- Disability allowance
- Child care allowance
- Municipal housing allowance

Supplementary pension (ATP)
- Old-age pension
- Disability pension
- Survivor's pension

Partial pension

Other benefits

Other benefits
- Child allowance
- Child allowance supplement
- Maintenance advance
- Car allowance
- Training allowance
- Special adult study assistance
- Military and civil defence training allowance
- Social welfare allowance

Unemployment insurance

Allowances for medical expenses
- Daily unemployment benefit
- Cash labour market assistance
- Compensation pay when laid off

Work injuries insurance

Work injuries insurance
- Sickness benefit
- Life annuity
- Death benefit
- Allowance for medical expenses

Source: The Swedish Institute, *Facts on Sweden* (Stockholm, 1993), 6.

to 13 percent of Swedish GDP, is one of the highest in the industrial world.[25] The Swedish national debt corresponded to 90 percent of Swedish GDP,[26] and by 1996 interest payments on the debt will become the largest single item in the budget. The real rate of economic growth in Sweden increased by an average of 0.0 percent for the period 1985–1994, the second-lowest in Western Europe. In 1992 the government had to depreciate the kronor by 25 percent to make Swedish products more competitive in international markets. Sweden has also faced a financial crisis with a 25 percent decline in real estate values, increased bankruptcies, and the near collapse of the banking system. Finally, there is a lack of confidence in the Swedish political system.[27]

How much of Sweden's economic problems can be attributed to the ever-rising costs of the social insurance system, which have more than doubled since

25. The United States comparison is 3 percent.
26. The United States comparison is 60 percent, but the U.S. economy is growing and the Swedish economy is not.
27. The data on Sweden were taken from a report called *The Swedish Experience*, which was presented by the Director General of the National Insurance Board at the 7th Annual Conference of the National Academy of Social Insurance, Washington, D.C., January 26, 1995.

1975? The answer is that certainly rising welfare costs are part of the problem, a cause but not the only cause. The main problem with the system is that its cost is out of line with economic growth. There is no direct link between the state of the economy and benefit payments. Another problem is that the system provides wrong incentives. For example, a worker who is unemployed may draw unemployment compensation of up to 90 percent of his former income for a period of up to 450 days. He does not have to take any job that is unrelated to his previous occupation. Third, Sweden has been inundated by immigrants from the Middle East and Eastern Europe. These immigrants account for 10 percent of the Swedish population but over half of the children born each year. Even though 90 percent of these immigrants are not Swedish citizens, they are entitled to the same benefits that the Swedes receive.[28]

EAST-ASIAN STATE-DIRECTED CAPITALISM

The East Asian, or Pacific Rim, countries include Japan, South Korea, Taiwan, Hong Kong, and Singapore.[29] These countries have several things in common. All are resource-poor and, with the exception of Japan, all are countries created after World War II. (South Korea and Taiwan belonged to Japan before World War II, and Hong Kong and Singapore were part of the British empire.) All share the presumption that the state should promote industrial development and national prosperity; at the same time, all are committed to the development of a strong private sector and use an array of policy instruments, including protection and financial incentives, to promote that goal. They also share a commitment to free markets and to state assistance to industry.

Because Chapter 6 is devoted to a discussion of Japan, South Korea and Taiwan are used as examples of state-directed economies in this chapter. Both use economic planning that is linked to export development, and both are among the top fifteen exporting nations in the world. They have moved from an emphasis on the export of light, labor-intensive manufactured goods to competitive strength in higher-technology industries. South Korea is now the third-largest producer of large-capacity memory chips. In 1995 U.S. trade with South Korea and Taiwan amounted to $97.9 billion, an amount far greater than that with any European country. Moreover, the once inconceivable notion of unification of a divided Korea has now become a possibility with the decline of communism. North Korea's economy is on the verge of collapse due to withdrawal of the financial support it once received from China and Russia.[30]

28. There is a parallel to the immigration in California.
29. Hong Kong will become a part of China in 1997.
30. It is estimated that Korean reunification would cost at least $250 billion over a ten-year period.

South Korea and Taiwan: Industrial Policy

One example of the interplay between government policy and industrial development is the history of the South Korean automobile industry. It began in 1962 when a public enterprise created an auto assembly plant in a joint venture with Nissan of Japan.[31] The Korean government instituted import restrictions on finished products, but exempted component parts for assembly from payment of duty. In 1965 the government transferred the assembly plant to a private Korean firm and entered into a technology agreement with Japan. The government set a target of 50 percent domestic content in five years, while imposing import restrictions on foreign automobiles. The Heavy and Chemical Industries Plan of 1973 identified autos as a priority industry, and in 1974 a ten-year industry-specific plan for automobiles was published with the goal of making the industry a major exporter by the early 1980s.

Three *chaebol* (conglomerates) were picked to produce cars for export, and export targets were set for each of them.[32] Export prices for cars were set low, often below cost, and the government made up the difference. For example, one Hyundai model that cost $3,700 to produce was sold for $5,000 in Korea and $2,200 overseas.[33] Three target markets were selected in stages: Southeast Asia, then Latin America and the Middle East, and then Canada and the United States. In the early 1980s Hyundai, picked by the government to be the sole producer of cars, was given low-interest loans to increase its investment in plants and equipment. In 1988 Hyundai produced 650,000 cars, 63 percent of which were exported.[34] The success of Hyundai prompted the government to allow the two other companies to reenter the auto market.

Taiwan's industrial policy has followed several strategies. From 1945 to the late 1950s, it followed a policy of import substitution to develop light manufacturing industries.[35] From 1960 to around 1975, import substitution controls were dropped, and the emphasis was placed on the export of light manufactured products. From the 1970s into the 1980s, the government increased its efforts to develop heavy industries. The government is able to influence industrial policy through its state-owned banks, which allocate credit on the basis of priorities the government establishes for industries. The government has also taken direct responsibility for accelerating technology development and its application to industry. It maintains four research institutes that conduct research in such fields as electronics, software technology, and food processing. (These institutes are under

31. Congress of the United States, Office of Technology Assessment, *Competing Economies: America, Europe, and the Pacific Rim* (Washington, D.C.: U.S. Government Printing Office, October 1991), 313–317.
32. The chaebol are discussed in the following section.
33. *Competing Economies,* 314–317.
34. *Competing Economies,* 329–331.
35. Import substitution refers to a government policy of developing local industries while maintaining high tariffs and import controls on competing foreign production.

the jurisdiction of the National Science Council, which is responsible for coordinating research efforts.)

Electronics is Taiwan's most important industrial category, and the government was crucial to its development. It began by encouraging foreign firms to set up offshore assembly operations, which were located in export-processing zones. Then the government made plans to acquire semiconductor design and production capabilities. One way this was done was to recruit a foreign partner to set up a demonstration facility, with the aim of transferring technology to Taiwanese business firms. A series of joint venture arrangements were made with U.S. firms to fabricate customized computer chips in a state-of-the-art production facility built by the Taiwanese government. Joint ventures typically have involved the Taiwanese government, Taiwanese private enterprises, and foreign firms. Today, the semiconductor industry in Taiwan is dominated by foreign firms, mostly American, which account for two-thirds of production.

South Korea: The Chaebol[36]

South Korea provides an excellent example of state-directed capitalism. The Korean War left South Korea with an economy devoid of resources, technology, and managerial know-how. To survive and grow, the country developed a policy of rapid economic growth through industrialization in export areas. This was accomplished through a linkage between the Korean government, the Korean banks, which were owned by the government, and the chaebol, which are family-owned conglomerates similar to the zaibatsu that dominated Japan before World War II. The chaebol developed during the immediate postwar period as small enterprises milling rice or repairing automobiles and expanded into conglomerates by using the technique of cross-investment. Member companies of a chaebol would invest in stocks to acquire a new company. Then they would use the increase in group capital to borrow from banks at low interest rates.

There are around fifty chaebol in South Korea. The big four are Hyundai, Samsung, Daewoo, and Lucky-Goldstar, accounting for 50 percent of South Korea's GNP. Unlike the Japanese keiretsu, which will be discussed in detail in Chapter 6, they do not have a bank at their core, but instead a general trading company. For example, Hyundai Trading Company is the core of the Hyundai chaebol. The trading companies are responsible for exporting the manufactured products of the chaebol and are subsidized at low interest rates by the Korean government. Control over a chaebol is in the hands of the chairman, often the original founder, who appoints directors to each company in the chaebol.[37] The chaebol have been subsidized by government-supported bank loans that have carried low

36. The information on the chaebol was provided by Sook-kyong Lee, an employee of the Mitsui Bank of Seoul, Korea, and a former student of the author.
37. The directors of the other companies may be brothers, sons, or sons-in-law of the chairman.

interest rates with long maturity and are nondefaultible because of government backing.[38] Export loans have carried the lowest interest rates.[39]

South Korea and Taiwan: Economic Planning

Economic development in South Korea and Taiwan has to be understood in the context of Japanese colonialism, for both were former colonies of Japan. Although Japanese rule over the two colonies was at best a mixed blessing, the Japanese did promote industrial development, particularly in Taiwan. During the 1930s, the Japanese began to develop in Taiwan such industries as food processing, textiles, shipbuilding, aluminum and copper refining, cement, and chemical fertilizers. Agricultural development was also a part of Japanese economic policy, and a communications infrastructure was laid down, designed to increase production of rice and sugar, both needed in Japan. The Japanese maintained complete control over economic development in both colonies, but they did leave a developed infrastructure, modern business institutions, and commercial centers.[40]

After the end of World War II, Taiwan became a part of China, and Korea was divided into two parts, North Korea and South Korea. The former was under the sphere of influence of the Soviet Union, the latter under the influence of the United States. In 1949, the Chinese government was defeated by the Chinese Communists, and its leader, Chiang Kai-shek, went to Taiwan, followed by millions of Chinese soldiers and civilians. South Korea was destroyed during the Korean War and had to rebuild itself from scratch. Both South Korea and Taiwan based their economic development policies on import substitution to develop their home industries. This involved the use of import controls and multiple exchange rates. Government intervention took the form of industrial policies and the promotion of exports.

Economic Planning: South Korea. Both South Korea and Taiwan are undergoing a fundamental structural shift from labor-intensive to technology- and capital-intensive production and from export-driven to demand-driven growth. Both have had to move out of labor-intensive industries to more technologically advanced sectors. Korea's Seventh Five-Year Plan (1992–1996) sets forth government goals for speeding the development of its technological capabilities as well as improving market liberalization. The South Korean plan has the following objectives:

38. The banks were state-owned until the early 1970s. Now they are privately owned, but the Korean government still controls lending policies.
39. The chaebol are criticized on the grounds that they are large and inefficient, absorb vast amounts of capital, and produce goods at a relatively high cost. See Brian Kelly and Mark London, *The Four Little Dragons* (New York: Simon and Schuster, 1989), 53–55.
40. Robert Wade, *Governing the Market: The Role of Government in East Asian Industrialization* (Princeton, N.J.: Princeton University Press, 1990), 73–75.

1. A nationwide computer network will be created to integrate all systems into one digital network by the end of the century.
2. Major projects are planned to upgrade South Korea's road network, establish a high-speed rail system, and expand seaport facilities in Pusan and Inchon.
3. Environmental standards are to be improved through investment on the part of the Korean government, which will cost $11.7 billion over the five-year planning period.
4. Korea's energy needs are to be more adequately met by the construction of eighty-five new power plants to be started during the planning period and completed over a fifteen-year period.

Economic Planning: Taiwan. The Taiwanese Six-Year Plan involves $303 billion in state expenditures, the bulk of which will be spent on infrastructure. The plan will do the following:[41]

1. Harbor, highway, and railroad facilities are to be integrated into an island-wide transportation system at a cost of $104 billion.
2. Telecommunications systems, particularly long-distance and international communications, are to be improved at a cost of $7 billion.
3. Taiwan's state-owned power company is to construct several nuclear and thermal power plants at a cost of $11 billion.
4. More attention is to be placed on environmental problems. Projects associated with the plan include the construction of 60 new waste water treatment plants, 157 new sewage disposal plants, and 34 sanitary landfills.

The East Asian Miracle

South Korea and Taiwan are a part of what has been called "The East Asian Miracle," which means that they and other East Asian countries have achieved a higher rate of economic growth than other regions of the world.[42] A global competitiveness report placed Hong Kong and Singapore among the world's top four economies, along with Japan and the United States.[43] Taiwan was ranked 18th and South Korea 24th, ahead of Spain, Portugal, and Italy. Since 1960 the economies of these countries, excluding Japan, have grown more than twice as fast as the rest of East Asia, three times faster than Latin America, and twenty-five times faster than sub-Saharan Africa. Income inequality and poverty are also lower and life expectancy and the level of education are higher in the East Asian countries than in other regions of comparison. In 1960 South Korea and Taiwan had a lower per capita GDP than Nigeria; in 1993 their per capita GDPs were twenty-five times

41. *Business America*, "Korea and Taiwan" (Washington, D.C.: U.S. Department of Commerce, August 24, 1992), 3–5.
42. The World Bank, *The East Asian Miracle* (New York: Oxford University Press, 1990). The countries are Japan, Taiwan, South Korea, Hong Kong, Malaysia, Indonesia, and Thailand.
43. "Asia's Four Tigers Spring into the First World," *Wall Street Journal*, February 28, 1995, A-17. The four tigers are South Korea, Taiwan, Hong Kong, and Singapore.

higher. Table 4-1 compares the real annual rate of growth in per capita GNP for selected countries from East Asia, South Asia, sub-Saharan Africa, and Latin America for two time periods, 1965–1984 and 1985–1993.

The same countries can be compared in terms of a human development index, which uses life expectancy, adult literacy, average years of schooling, and real per capita GDP as measurements (see Table 4-2). Most of the countries in the table were a part of a colonial empire, and most achieved their independence at about the same time. However, it is important to point out that there are major cultural and historical differences between the East Asian countries and some of the other countries included in the table. For example, the East Asian countries have not had the religious problems that have plagued India or the tribal conflicts that led to a bloody civil war in Nigeria.

Market-Friendly Development Policies

East Asian economic development strategy has been called the market-friendly strategy.[44] This means that government plays a distinct role in market guidance in several ways, as follows:[45]

1. It maintains a high investment in human capital through the reduction of illiteracy and the education of a skilled labor force.
2. It controls the financial system, either directly or indirectly, and makes private capital subordinate to industrial capital.
3. It promotes exports through financial incentives such as tax breaks for exporters.
4. It modulates the impact of foreign competition in the domestic economy through import restrictions.
5. It promotes technology acquisitions from multinational corporations and builds a national technology system.
6. It maintains strong macroeconomic stability through the use of fiscal and monetary policies in order to maintain stable foreign exchange and interest rates.
7. It provides a competitive environment for private enterprise.

It should be emphasized that some East Asian countries fit this model better than others. Japan, Korea, and Taiwan have intervened extensively in markets to guide private sector resource allocation, whereas in Malaysia and Thailand government has taken a less interventionist approach.[46] Some countries, notably Japan and Korea, have combined competition with the benefits of cooperation among firms and between government and the private sector. In comparing East Asia to Latin America, one reason for East Asian success is that governments such as Korea and Taiwan have had better macroeconomic policies. With limited budget def-

44. *The East Asian Miracle*, 27.
45. Wade, *Governing the Market*, 26–27.
46. *The East Asian Miracle*, 10.

TABLE 4-1
Comparisons of Changes in Real GNP for East Asia and Other Regions (percent)

	Real per Capita GNP	
	1965–1984	*1985–1994*
East Asia		
South Korea	6.6	7.8
Singapore	7.8	6.9
Malaysia	4.5	5.7
South Asia		
India	1.6	2.9
Pakistan	2.5	1.6
Sub-Saharan Africa		
Nigeria	2.8	1.2
Kenya	2.1	0.0
Zambia	–1.5	–1.3
Latin America		
Mexico	2.9	0.6
Brazil	4.6	–0.4
Argentina	0.3	1.9

Sources: The World Bank, *World Development Report 1986* (New York: Oxford University Press, 1986), 180–181; The World Bank, *World Bank Atlas 1996* (Washington, D.C.: The World Bank 1996), 18–19.

icits to reduce inflation, real interest rates are much more stable than in Latin America, thus increasing the rate of saving.

THE ECONOMIES OF THE UNITED STATES, JAPAN, AND GERMANY

The United States, Japan, and Germany are the three economic superpowers of the world. They account for around 50 percent of the world's GNP, even though they have only 8 percent of the world's population. They are also the three largest trading countries in the world, with a combined 31 percent of world exports and imports. The United States and Japan are the two wealthiest countries in the world, Germany is fourth, and combined they have over half of the world's wealth. Most of the largest banks and multinational corporations of the world are either American, Japanese or German, and the three most important currency units are the dollar, the yen, and the deutsche mark. Even though Germany is supposed to become a part of a united Europe, it will remain the most important entity and the engine for economic growth in the European Community.

The United States, Japan, and Germany developed during different time periods and under a different set of circumstances. The United States experienced a rapid rate of industrialization during the period following the Civil War. This in-

TABLE 4-2 *Human Development Index (HDI) for East Asia and Other Regions, 1992*

	Life Expectancy at Birth (years)	*Adult Literacy Rate (percent)*	*Mean Years of Schooling*	*Real Per Capita GDP (dollars)*	*HDI Rank**
East Asia					
South Korea	71.1	97.4	9.3	9,250	31
Singapore	74.8	89.9	4.0	18,330	35
Malaysia	70.8	81.5	5.6	7,790	59
South Asia					
India	60.4	49.9	2.4	1,230	134
Pakistan	61.5	35.7	1.9	2,890	128
Sub-Saharan Africa					
Nigeria	50.4	52.5	1.2	1,560	141
Kenya	55.7	74.5	2.3	1,400	130
Zambia	48.9	75.2	2.7	1,230	136
Latin America					
Mexico	70.8	88.6	4.9	7,300	53
Brazil	66.3	81.9	4.0	5,250	63
Argentina	72.1	95.9	9.2	8,860	30

**Out of 174 countries.*

Source: United Nations Development Program, *Human Development Report 1995* (New York: Oxford University Press, 1995), 155–157.

dustrialization was facilitated by three factors—immigration, the construction of a transcontinental railroad system that opened up the western part of the country for economic development, and an inflow of foreign capital for investment. There was little state intervention in the economy; railroad and antitrust regulation came toward the latter part of the century. New forms of transportation and communication not only brought about a revolution in distribution; they also created a greater revolution in production.[47] New technologies transformed the processing of grains, sugar, vegetable oils, and other foods, and revolutionized the refining of oil and the making of steel.

Germany was the second country to develop as an industrial nation. Prior to the Franco-Prussian War of 1870, Germany was a collection of states dominated by Prussia and united into one country by Bismarck. State economic intervention in one form or another existed. Railroads were owned by individual states and eventually became part of a national railroad system. A social security system was introduced into Germany in the 1880s. Germany developed rapidly after the end of the Franco-Prussian War. It became particularly strong in the chemical and electrical

47. Alfred D. Chandler, *Scale and Scope: Dynamics of Industrial Capitalism* (Cambridge: Harvard University Press, 1990).

TABLE 4-3 *Economic Performance of the United States, Germany, and Japan, 1900–1994*

	Real GDP per Capita (dollars)					
	1900	*1913*	*1929*	*1950*	*1973*	*1994*
United States	2,911	3,772	4,909	6,697	10,977	25,860
Germany	1,558	1,907	2,153	2,508	7,595	19,890
Japan	677	705	1,162	1,116	6,623	21,350

	Real Growth Rates (average annual rate increase in percent)				
	1900–1913	*1913–1950*	*1950–1973*	*1973–1985*	*1985–1994*
United States	4.0	2.8	3.7	2.5	1.3
Germany	3.0	1.3	5.9	1.8	1.9
Japan	2.5	2.2	9.3	3.7	3.2

	Value of Exports[1] ($billions)					
	1900	*1929*	*1950*	*1973*	*1986*	*1994*
United States	1.4	5.2	10.3	71.4	217.3	505.1
Germany	1.1	1.3	2.0	67.6	243.3	410.2
Japan	.1	.5	.8	37.0	210.8	336.4

[1]*Merchandise exports.*

Sources: Angus Maddison, *The World Economy in the 20th Century* (Paris: OECD, 1989), 19, 36, 138; The World Bank, *The World Bank Atlas 1996* (Washington, D.C.: The World Bank, 1996), 18, 19; U.S. Department of Commerce, International Trade Administration, *Business America*, Vol. 116, No. 9 (September 1995), 23–24.

equipment industries. The German firm Siemens built the world's largest industrial complex, producing a wide variety of products, including telecommunication equipment, large machinery, motors, dynamos, and cables.

Japan was the last of the three to industrialize. Historically, it had been an isolated country insulated from foreign influence by the natural barriers of its surrounding seas and run by feudal warlords. When the Meiji Restoration of 1868 opened up Japan to the West, the country realized it had a long way to go before it could compete industrially. State direction and guidance were factors from the start in influencing economic development. Japan's defeat of Russia in the Russo-Japanese War of 1904 made Japan a first-class world power. It became prominent in the shipbuilding industry. Government support for business developed early to lessen dependence on foreigners. The government supplied part of the capital needed by business either directly or through the medium of special banks that continue to exist today.

Table 4-3 presents an economic comparison of the performance of the United States, German, and Japanese economies from the beginning of this century to the present using real per capita GDP as a measurement. In 1900 German real per capita GDP was about half that of the United States, and Japanese real per capita

GDP was around one-fifth of U.S. income. The United Kingdom ranked second to the United States in 1900 and eleventh in 1994.[48]

SUMMARY

The end of communism has completely changed the world economic and political order. The "isms" that once dominated the world are gone, with the exception of capitalism. The point has been made in Chapters 1 and 4 that there are three variants of capitalism—the U.S. variant, the European variant, and the East Asian variant. Comparisons can be made on the basis of market freedom, which is relative to begin with. The markets of a number of economies are thought of as free because large segments of the economy are shaped by market forces. In all of these economies, both government and markets are instruments of economic and social policies. Most of the restraints that governments have placed on markets exist because the market does certain things poorly, such as providing social goods or a clean environment.

Chapters 5, 6, and 7 will compare three countries that represent the three variants of capitalism. Chapter 5 discusses the United States, which likes to think of itself as being the most free market economy in the world and probably is. Chapter 6 discusses Japan, the third major economic power, which exemplifies state-directed capitalism. Japan and the fast-development countries of South Korea and Taiwan have placed restraints on free markets or have shaped them in ways that help achieve economic development. They have restrained imports in order to develop domestic industries and have permitted the formation of cartels. They have relied on industrial policy to target certain industries for economic development and have provided large-scale investments for basic research in technology. Chapter 7 covers Germany, the most powerful country in Europe, which represents Eurocapitalism. Eurocapitalism is social market capitalism, with much state involvement in the provision of social overhead capital.

QUESTIONS FOR DISCUSSION

1. What is Eurocapitalism? How does it differ from U.S. capitalism?
2. In what way has the U.S. government intervened in the American economy?
3. What is industrial targeting? How was it used in South Korea to develop the Korean automobile industry?
4. What is the role of economic planning in France, South Korea, and Taiwan?
5. Sweden provides an excellent model of social market capitalism. Discuss.
6. What are some of the problems confronting the Swedish economy?
7. What is a chaebol?

48. G. C. Allen, *A Short Economic History of Japan* (London: Unwin University Books, 1964).

RECOMMENDED READINGS

Cetron, Marvin, and Owen Davies. *Crystal Globe: The Haves and Have-Nots of the New World Order.* New York: St. Martin's Press, 1992.

Congress of the United States, Office of Technology Assessment, *Competing Economies: America, Europe, and the Pacific Rim.* Washington, D.C.: U.S. Government Printing Office, 1992.

Marshall, Ray, and Mark Tucker. *Thinking for a Living: Education and the Wealth of Nations.* New York: Basic Books, 1992.

National Social Insurance Board. *Social Insurance Statistics Facts 1993.* Stockholm, 1994.

"The Swedish Model Reconsidered," *The Economist*, Vol. 334, No. 7902 (February 18–25), 49–50.

The World Bank. *The East Asian Miracle.* New York: Oxford University Press, 1994.

United Nations Development Programme. *Human Development Report 1995.* New York: Oxford University Press, 1995.

Wade, Robert. *Governing the Market: Theory and Role of Government in East Asian Industrialization.* Princeton, N.J.: Princeton University Press, 1990.

CHAPTER 5

The Economic System of the United States

The United States is the best example of a capitalist market economy. However, although there is heavy reliance on the market mechanism to allocate resources, it cannot be said that the United States conforms to the model of a pure free enterprise market economy. Instead, "the rules of the game" have been changed over time as various groups have sought to change the results that a free market can give. Farmers have sought protection against fluctuations in farm prices by demanding subsidies. Textile companies want tariffs and import quotas placed on the import of textile products made by foreign competitors. Workers want financial protection against unemployment. Many changes have occurred over time as government has sought to modify the workings of the free market.

PRIVATE ENTERPRISE

Private enterprise is one of the basic institutions of the U.S. economy. There is very little government ownership of industry. There is freedom of ingress and egress in the marketplace. Anyone with an idea and capital is free to start his or her own business. There is the right to succeed and the right to fail. The United States consists of some very large corporations and hundreds of thousands of smaller ones.

Large Corporations

The concentration of many industries in the hands of a few firms is a fact of life in the United States and other industrial nations. The trend toward industrial concentration in this country began in the last century, when many industries came to be dominated by large firms. In the 1920s corporate largeness was stimulated by changes that were occurring in the economy, in particular the mass production of automobiles. Size came to have an advantage from the standpoint of using modern marketing and production methods. World War II also contributed to the trend toward largeness. Large corporations produced the airplanes and tanks used by the United States and its allies in the war. During the 1960s and 1970s the trend increased, facilitated by a new type of merger called the conglomerate merger, which represented a union of disparate companies.

Table 5-1 presents a comparison of the assets of large corporations to the total assets of the industries they represent. In the table, corporations with assets of $250 million or more are considered to be large corporations.

Large corporations may also be global corporations. As modern technology has increased, it has become an internationally marketable commodity because it is readily transferable through the operations of global corporations. This has resulted in the globalization of production. Coupled with the globalization of production is the globalization of financial markets. The pool of saving is worldwide, and intermediaries that mobilize savings for investment know no international boundaries because they have the technological sophistication to access markets

TABLE 5-1 *A Comparison of the Assets of Large Corporations to Total Corporate Assets by Industries, 1992 ($millions)*

Industry	*Total*	*Asset-Sized Class ($250 million and over)*
Agriculture, forestry, and fishing	67,757	4,744
Mining	212,963	160,525
Construction	243,036	50,860
Manufacturing	4,028,360	3,401,427
Transportation and public utilities	1,573,824	1,433,578
Wholesale and retail trade	1,483,428	785,368
Finance, insurance	10,780,681	9,317,284
Services	636,752	305,406

Source: U.S. Department of Commerce, Bureau of the Census, *Statistical Abstract of the United States* (Washington, D.C.: U.S. Government Printing Office, 1995), 549.

worldwide. Finally, there has been a globalization of markets for goods and services. Thus, the global corporation—United States and foreign—does business all over the world and has no particular allegiance to a given country.

Small Enterprises

There are also thousands of small and medium-sized business firms that provide employment for the majority of U.S. workers as well as much of the innovation necessary for international competitiveness. The number of small companies is increasing,[1] in part as a result of executive downsizing by many large corporations. Former executives create new companies that find a niche in areas once dominated by corporate giants. In addition, small family-owned companies use new technology to carve out market niches in many industries, exploiting the latest technology, employing highly skilled workers, and utilizing sophisticated managerial and financial techniques. Moreover, as the United States becomes a more service-oriented economy, opportunities have increased for consulting firms. More people are also self-employed. A breakdown of employees and payrolls by employment size is presented in Table 5-2.

GOVERNMENT

For many years, the idea persisted that the government of a capitalistic system should follow a policy of laissez-faire. This idea was based on the concept of natural liberty. Each individual was assumed to be a more or less rational human being and a better judge of his or her own interest than any government could be. In the natural order of things, people's pursuit of their own interests would inadvertently benefit others as well. Government had a limited role to play in society. Its activities should be limited to the performance of a few general functions. Examples of those functions would be the administration of justice, the construction of public works, and the protection of citizens from foreign invasion.

It has been realized, however, that the institutions of capitalism are manmade, not the product of some natural order. In the operation of a capitalist economy, economic and social problems arise that do not lend themselves to ready solutions by private individuals. U.S. government intervention in the American economy increased the most during the Depression of the 1930s and World War II. Some of the types of government expenditures listed later in Table 5-3 reflect this point. Social security, which accounts for the single largest expenditure in the federal budget, is a product of the Depression. It was designed to provide some form of income security for older persons when millions of Americans were out of work. Probably the bulk of veterans' benefits applies to those persons who served during World War II.

1. In 1993 706,537 new businesses were incorporated in the United States.

TABLE 5-2
Employees and Payrolls by Employment-Size Firms, 1992

Employment-Size Employers	(thousands)
Employees, total	92,801
Under 20 employees	25,000
20 to 99 employees	27,030
100 to 499 employees	22,227
500 to 999 employees	6,275
1,000 or more employees	12,275
Annual Payroll	($billions)
Total	2,272
Under 20 employees	536
20 to 99 employees	586
100 to 499 employees	550
500 to 999 employees	186
1,000 or more employees	413

Source: U.S. Department of Commerce, Bureau of the Census, *Statistical Abstract of the United States 1995* (Washington, D.C.: U.S. Government Printing Office, 1995), 540.

The appropriate role of government in the American economy has become an important subject. In November 1994, the Republicans won majority control in both the U.S. House of Representatives and the U.S. Senate and have pushed to reduce the amount of government intervention in the economy on the grounds that it is inefficient, unfair, and expensive. Another Republican objective is to pass an amendment that would require the federal budget to be balanced. A third objective is to cut income taxes, assuming that individuals can spend their incomes more wisely than government. Still another objective is to eliminate or combine certain government agencies to reduce bureaucracy and promote efficiency.

Public Finance

Public finance is an indicator of the extent of government participation in a modified market economy. Taxes serve two purposes: they provide government with a source of revenue, and they can be used to effect a redistribution of income and wealth. The personal income tax is the most important source of income to the federal government, the sales tax is the most important source of income to the states, and local governments rely on property taxation. Government expenditures for goods and services account for around 20 percent of the U.S. GNP and provide a source of demand for many business products, and government transfer payments redistribute income from one economic group to another. Table 5-3 presents the budget of the U.S. government for the 1994 fiscal year.

The Composition of Taxes and Expenditures. The three main sources of revenue to the federal government are individual income taxes, social insurance receipts, and borrowing. The three most important types of government expenditures are direct benefit payments to individuals, national defense, and interest payments on the national debt. As previously noted, the largest component of total federal government payments is social security, which accounts for around 40 percent of total government expenditures.

Economic Stabilization Policies. Government intervention includes fiscal and monetary policies that are implemented by its use of taxation and transfer payments, by its purchases of goods and services, and by the Federal Reserve's control of the money supply and interest rates. Fiscal policy refers to the tax and expenditure policies of the federal government. Its objective is to increase or decrease the level of aggregate demand through changes in the level of government expenditures and taxation. The federal budget is the fulcrum of fiscal policy. It provides a system of planning and control over government activities by the executive and legislative branches of government. Monetary policy is used by the Federal Reserve to control the level of national income and the price level through variations in the money supply.

Government Regulation and Control of Business

The regulation and control of business is a second area in which the U.S. government has become firmly entrenched. This became necessary for several reasons, all of which are associated with some failure of the market system. One failure is its inability to furnish individuals or society with a satisfactory means for achieving certain wants, for example, the desire for a clean environment. Initiative for a

TABLE 5-3
U.S. Government Expenditures for the Fiscal Year 1994 (billions of dollars)

Defense	281.6
International affairs	17.1
Space, science, technology	16.2
Energy, environment	26.3
Agriculture	15.1
Transportation	38.1
Education	46.3
Medicare, medicaid	223.9
Health, income security	241.9
Social security	319.6
Justice	15.3
Veterans	37.6
Net interest	203.0
Other	16.8
Offsetting receipts	–37.8
Total outlays	1,460.9
Total revenues	1,257.7
Total deficit	–203.2

Source: Office of Manpower and Budget, *Budget of the United States Government* (Washington, D.C.: U.S. Government Printing Office, 1995), 3.

clean environment therefore falls to public agencies, which use controls that inevitably have a major impact on the operation of business firms. The distribution of income and wealth can be considered a second flaw in the market system. It became apparent that large incomes often accrue to some people not on the basis of their contribution to output but through inherited wealth or the exercise of special privilege.

Antitrust Laws. The rationale for antitrust laws is to promote market competition by preventing the formation of business combinations, such as trusts, that could work against the public welfare. American antitrust laws are encapsulated in the Sherman and Clayton Acts. The Sherman Act prohibits the formation of monopolies and other business combinations that restrain interstate or foreign trade. It also prohibits various anticompetitive business practices such as group boycotts and price fixing. The Clayton Act prohibits mergers whose end result is to substantially lessen competition and prohibits price discrimination whose intent is to ruin competitors. The Clayton Act also restricts the arrangement of interlocking directorates: it provides that no person shall be a director in two or more corporations if they are competitors.[2]

Social Regulation. The government also engages in social regulation of business in such matters as hiring the disabled, occupational safety, consumer protection, environmental protection, and affirmative action. The rationale for social regulation is that the market system does not work to solve such problems as sex and race discrimination, or negative externalities created by rising living standards. For example, as quality-of-life demands increase, there is public pressure for government regulation to provide clean air, clean water, and safe disposal of toxic waste. Expanded definitions of equality give rise to new entitlements, which in turn result in government regulations to provide them. An example is equal employment opportunity.

Government Ownership of Industry

Government ownership of industry is quite limited in the United States, but all levels of government do own and operate government facilities of many kinds. One example is the Tennessee Valley Authority (TVA), a major public enterprise for the production and distribution of public power in the southeastern part of the United States. The TVA was created to erect dams and hydroelectric power plants, to provide electric power, to improve navigation on the Tennessee River, to promote flood control, and to prevent soil erosion. Other government units own local transportation systems and own and operate water, gas, and electricity plants. Government also produces directly or indirectly atomic power and other goods and carries out projects connected with slum clearance and housing.

2. Neither Japan nor Germany restricts the use of interlocking directorates.

Government credit programs constitute a gray area in that they do not involve outright state ownership of industry. However, federal credit programs have an impact on private industry. For example, the housing industry relies on the various federal mortgage credit programs for a good portion of its funding. Exporters may obtain financial assistance through the Export-Import Bank, and farmers may get credit assistance from the Farmers Home Administration. The Small Business Administration makes direct loans to small business firms, and loans are available for the construction of educational and housing facilities. Many loans made by banks are insured or guaranteed by the federal government. Loan insurance is particularly important to the housing market; without it most people probably could not afford to build homes.

UNIONS

Unions provide the third part of the business, government, and union triumvirate. Workers in the United States and other capitalist countries have not been content to rely solely on market forces to determine their economic status. Instead, they have banded together to form labor unions for the purpose of bargaining collectively with employers. The worker's need for a job is not reduced, but under collective bargaining an employer must deal with labor as a unit, not as separate individuals. Labor unions vary in strength and importance in the world's major industrial nations. In Germany they participate in their employer's decision-making process through the policy of codetermination; in England they are directly involved in the political process through membership in the British Labor Party.

Unions in the United States hit their peak in terms of membership during the 1940s and 1950s and then began a slow decline as the country shifted from a goods-producing to a service society. This shift represents a change in the type of work people do, from physically intensive labor to knowledge-intensive labor. In 1945 almost half the American labor force was employed in manufacturing jobs; in 1990 the number of manufacturing jobs was around 20 percent. Conversely, the number of persons employed in service-producing jobs has doubled since 1945. The majority of jobs today are knowledge-based white-collar jobs, not blue-collar jobs, and white-collar workers tend to identify more with management than with labor. Many union jobs were lost in the auto and steel industries, which laid off more than a million blue-collar workers during the 1980s as foreign competition began to erode U.S. markets. This downsizing of employment has continued into the 1990s.

AN EVALUATION OF THE U.S. ECONOMY

The U.S. economy has its strengths and weaknesses. It has the highest standard of living in the world. As of March 1996 its unemployment rate was 5.6 percent, less than half of the unemployment rate in France, Italy, Spain, and Belgium. Its rate of inflation has been relatively low compared to that of other industrialized countries, and its growth rate during the 1990s has exceeded that of Japan, its main economic rival. But there is also a downside to the U.S. economy. It is the world's leading debtor nation. In March 1995 the dollar declined to historic lows against the German mark and the Japanese yen. The United States has also run a deficit in its current account, which has contributed to higher interest rates. Many Americans have experienced a decline in living standards because their real wages have fallen or remained constant since the 1970s.

The United States as a Debtor Nation

The United States is the world's leading debtor nation, a position it last held in the nineteenth century and up to 1914. As Table 5-4 indicates, foreign investment in the United States, which takes the form of both direct and portfolio investment, amounted to around $3.3 trillion in 1994, while U.S. direct and portfolio investment abroad amounted to around $2.5 trillion. A resulting debt of approximately $800 billion reflects the difference between what foreigners own in the United States and what Americans own overseas. The United States was the world's leading creditor nation after 1914 and continuing into the 1980s, when it relinquished its position to Japan. As its merchandise trade deficit grew, larger amounts of dollars were shifted overseas as payments for such items as foreign-made cars and television sets. Many of these dollars came back to the United States in the form of foreign investment in real estate, stocks and bonds, plant construction, and the purchase of U.S. companies.

Foreign debt is not necessarily deleterious to a country's national interests. When the United States was a debtor nation prior to World War I, foreign capital helped provide the investments necessary to build American railroads, steel mills, meat-packing plants, and other industries. These industries in turn created wealth and employment and made the United States an industrial power. However, during the 1980s, the U.S. borrowed to finance its defense buildup, which had no lasting value. Foreign direct investment in the United States provided jobs for U.S. workers, new management techniques, new technology, and new capital formation, which otherwise would have come from U.S. savings. Conversely, it can be argued that foreign debt makes the United States vulnerable to the actions of for-

TABLE 5-4 *U.S. Assets Abroad and Foreign Assets in the U.S., 1993 (millions of dollars)*

U.S. Assets Abroad		*Foreign Assets in the U.S.*	
Direct investment abroad	760,980	Direct investment in U.S.	545,266
Portfolio investment	1,759,490	Portfolio investment	2,803,900
Total	2,520,470	Total	3,349,166

Source: U.S. Department of Commerce, Bureau of Economic Analysis, "U.S. Net International Investment Position, 1994," June 28, 1995, 6.

eign investors and that outflows of income represent a loss of income to the United States. The foreign debt has also resulted in a deterioration in the U.S. balance of payments. Related to the external or foreign debt is the national debt.

The National Debt. Former President Ronald Reagan will probably be regarded as one of the most popular and charismatic presidents of this century, but there is much controversy over what he accomplished. Those who think he was an outstanding president point to the economic prosperity of the 1980s and improved political relations with the then Soviet Union. His critics point to the massive increase in the federal debt, the excesses of Wall Street, the Iran-Contra scandal, and increased inequality of income and wealth. Budget deficits, which were financed in part by foreign borrowers, helped to stimulate prosperity, but the federal debt, which was less than a trillion dollars in 1980, was $4.9 trillion by the end of 1995. Table 5-5 presents federal budget deficits and the federal debt for the period 1980–1995.

Merchandise Trade Account Deficit. The merchandise trade account measures the trade deficit or surplus. Its balance is derived by subtracting merchandise imports from merchandise exports. An export is considered positive because it results in a flow of income from abroad; an import is considered negative because it results in outflow of money paid abroad. The merchandise trade account is part of a country's current account, which consists of three other accounts: services ac-

TABLE 5-5
Federal Government Deficit and Debt, 1981–1995 (billions of dollars)

Year	*Deficit*	*Debt*	*Debt as Percentage of GDP*
1981	–79.0	994.8	32.8
1982	–128.0	1,137.3	36.1
1983	–207.8	1,371.7	40.3
1984	–185.4	1,564.7	41.4
1985	–212.3	1,817.5	45.0
1986	–221.2	2,120.6	49.7
1987	–149.8	2,346.1	51.7
1988	–155.2	2,601.3	57.8
1989	–152.5	2,868.0	54.7
1990	–221.4	3,206.0	58.1
1991	–269.2	3,598.5	63.4
1992	–255.1	4,002.1	67.6
1993	–203.2	4,351.4	69.5
1994	–192.5	4,643.7	70.0
1995	–196.7	4,921.0	70.6

Source: *Economic Report of the President 1995* (Washington, D.C.: U.S. Government Printing Office, 1996), 367.

count,[3] income receipts and payments on assets account,[4] and unilateral transfers. The current account and the capital account, which reflects the flow of assets between countries, are the major components of a country's balance of payments, a summary of all transactions between residents of the home country and residents of all other countries.

Table 5-6 presents the U.S. current account for 1994. It had a negative balance of around $118 billion. The major contributing factor to the deficit is the deficit in the merchandise trade account, which amounted to $164 billion. Half of this trade deficit was with two countries, China and Japan.

Table 5-7 presents the balance in the U.S. merchandise trade account and the current account for the period 1983–1994. Imports of goods have exceeded exports of goods by around $1.5 trillion during the period, while the deficit in the current account has amounted to around $1.0 trillion during the period. This deficit is a contributing factor to the status of the United States as the leading international debtor. Its debt in 1994 was $556 billion, which amounted to around 12.0 percent of U.S. GDP.

The debtor status of the United States can be linked to the U.S. budget and trade deficits. The budget deficit is a primary catalyst for the trade deficit and also impacts on savings and investment. It also increases the national debt, which has more than quadrupled since 1980. The budget deficit has created several problems. First, interest payments on the national debt are a fixed cost that must be covered out of government expenditures. For the fiscal year 1995, interest payments accounted for 16 percent of total federal government expenditures.[5] Second, to finance the deficit and to refinance that part of the national debt that comes due, the U.S. Treasury must constantly borrow money in competition with private investors. Since the savings rate in this country is low, some of Treasury's borrowing must come from other countries, which has increased U.S. international indebtedness. Net investment payments added to the current account deficit in 1994.

The collapse of the dollar in early 1995 is related to U.S. budget and trade deficits. The dollar has been the world's major reserve currency since World War II, meaning that other countries use it as a means of payment and hold it in their treasuries as a store of value. The U.S. dollar has been the linchpin of international finance, and the most important component of the Eurocurrency market.[6] At one time, it accounted for over 70 percent of the world's currency holdings, but by March 1995 it accounted for only 58 percent.[7] U.S. budget and trade deficits have flooded the world with dollars. Foreign governments and currency traders have

3. Examples are consulting fees, banking services, and transportation services.
4. Examples are dividends and interest from U.S. ownership of foreign assets and vice versa.
5. Executive Office of the President, Office of Manpower and Budget, *Budget of the United States Government, Fiscal Year 1995*, 3–4.
6. The Eurocurrency market consists of currencies deposited outside the country of issue. Sixty-five percent of Eurocurrencies consist of Eurodollars. The Eurocurrency market is an important source of short-term debt.
7. *The Economist*, March 11–17, 1995, 15.

TABLE 5-6
U.S. Current Account, 1994 (billions of dollars)

Exports	+
Merchandise trade account	+ 502,485
Services	+ 196,716
Income from U.S. assets abroad	+ 137,619
Total	836,820
Imports	–
Merchandise imports	–666,584
Services	–138,829
Income from foreign assets in U.S.	–146,891
Unilateral transfers	–35,766
Total	–954,304
Current account deficit	–117,484

Source: U.S. Department of Commerce, Bureau of Economic Analysis, "U.S. International Transactions, 1994," June 28, 1995.

TABLE 5-7
U.S. Merchandise Trade and Current Account Deficits, 1983–1994 (billions of dollars)

Year	*Merchandise Trade Deficit*	*Current Account Deficit*
1983	–67,102	–44,460
1984	–112,492	–99,773
1985	–122,173	–125,372
1986	–145,081	–151,201
1987	–159,557	–167,097
1988	–126,959	–128,194
1989	–115,249	–102,820
1990	–109,033	–91,748
1991	–74,068	–6,952
1992	–96,097	–67,886
1993	–132,575	–103,896
1994	–166,098	–151,245

Source: *Economic Report of the President 1995* (Washington, D.C.: U.S. Government Printing Office, 1996), 392.

exchanged dollars to buy yen and deutsche marks, thus driving up their values against the dollar.

International Comparisons of Living Standards

According to many measures, such as consumer comforts, U.S. citizens enjoy the world's highest living standards. They enjoy more choices of goods and services at better prices than residents of most other countries.[8] It leads the world in the number of automobiles, the number of telephones, and the number of television

8. As of March 1995, for example, a large box of Cheerios cost $12 and apples were $5 a pound in Japan.

sets. U.S. houses generally are more affordable and offer more amenities than housing in other countries. In the United States the average price of a home is around 3 times the average annual salary of a U.S. worker compared to multiples of 8.6 in Japan, 6.4 in Italy, 6.1 in the United Kingdom, and 4.9 in Canada. Japan has a higher money per capita income than the United States, but its real standard of living is lower.

However, the United States does not measure up well in other areas. Its divorce rate is the highest of all of the industrial countries and so are the homicide rate, the rate of serious assaults, the number of drug offenses, and the rate of AIDS. Despite the amount of money it spends on health care, it does a poorer job of providing its citizens with adequate health care than any other industrial country in the world. Around one-fifth of all U.S. citizens have no health insurance coverage, and the increased cost of health insurance is getting beyond the reach of many others.[9] It has higher health expenditures than any of the other major industrial countries but also the highest infant mortality rate and the shortest life expectancy. Table 5-8 presents a comparison of living and health standards for the G-7 countries.[10] The United States had the highest real GDP but lagged in other areas.

An Uncompetitive Society: Education

No country in the world spends more money on education and has so little to show for it as the United States. In 1992, for example, the U.S. spent $6,291 per secondary student compared to $3,547 for Japan, yet has a high school dropout rate ten times higher than Japan's. One-fifth of U.S. adults are functionally illiterate. In international achievement comparisons, U.S. students do poorly in math, science, geography, and other subjects.[11] Although test scores of U.S. students have generally risen in recent years, the United States still lags behind most industrial nations, particularly in math and science. College-bound students in Europe and Japan usually have had two more years of science and math than their American counterparts.

Moreover, there has been a shift in the demand for labor in the American workplace in favor of more highly skilled, educated workers.[12] At the same time there has been a shift in employment away from the goods-producing sectors that once provided high-paying jobs for blue-collar workers, most of whom were men. Millions of jobs have been lost in such sectors as coal mining, steel, aluminum, and

9. A comprehensive national health insurance program developed by the Clinton administration was rejected on the grounds that it was too bureaucratic and expensive. The problem still remains, but there is no push in Congress to reform the health system.

10. The G-7 countries are the United States, Canada, the United Kingdom, Germany, France, Italy, and Japan.

11. It was reported in *USA Today* that 25 percent of American high school students couldn't find the United States on a world map.

12. It is forecast that by the year 2000, 50 percent of all jobs in the United States will require education beyond high school and 30 percent will require a college degree.

TABLE 5-8 *A Comparison of Living and Health Standards in the G-7 Countries*

Country	*Real per Capita GDP*	*Per Capita Health Expenditures*	*Life Expectancy at Birth*	*Infant Mortality Rate per 1,000 Live Births*
United States	$25,860	$2,867	76.0	9
Canada	21,320	1,917	77.4	7
Germany	19,890	1,663	76.0	6
Japan	21,350	1,307	79.5	5
France	19,820	1,656	76.9	7
United Kingdom	18,170	1,033	76.2	7
Italy	18,610	1,408	77.5	8

Sources: United Nations Development Program, *Human Development Report 1995* (New York: Oxford University Press, 1995), 129; The World Bank, *World Development Report 1995* (New York: Oxford University Press, 1995), 215; U.S. Department of Commerce, Bureau of the Census, *Statistical Abstract of the United States 1995* (Washington, D.C.: U.S. Government Printing Office, 1995), 859.

automobile production. These jobs have been replaced by lower-paying jobs in the service sector. McDonald's, for example, provides more jobs than U.S. Steel or Chrysler.[13] Immigration has increased the relative supply of less-skilled labor and has contributed to the increasing inequality of income. Inner cities have experienced poor job opportunities, more concentrated poverty, and low-quality schools.

However, the U.S. educational system is not all bad. U.S. universities are considered to be among the best in the world. The Japanese classroom, which produces some of the world's highest test scores, is also among the world's most crowded. Moreover, it is necessary to point out that the philosophy of the American educational system is different from that of other countries. It does not have the two-track system that exists in Europe. The two-track system separates students into two categories, those who are college-bound and those who are not. The latter, for the most part, are funneled into vocational training programs. There is an advantage to this approach because it provides countries such as Germany with a highly skilled labor force. There is an advantage to the American approach in that it does not penalize late bloomers and offers more Americans of all ages an opportunity to go to college.

Income Inequality

Income inequality is greater in the United States than in any other major industrial country and has increased. From 1979 to 1993 the top 40 percent of American families saw their incomes, measured in terms of purchasing power, increase while the bottom 60 percent of families saw a decrease. From 1950 to 1978 all income groups gained as the American economy grew. It was a time when unskilled as-

13. In 1994 McDonald's employed 168,000 workers compared to 122,000 for Chrysler and 28,000 for U.S. Steel.

sembly-line workers with little, if any, education beyond a high school diploma were able to achieve a middle-class standard of living. U.S. firms had very little competition from abroad and an expanding consumer market at home. Foreign wages were not a factor that impacted on U.S. wages. But all of this changed during the 1970s as foreign competition began to catch up with U.S. companies, providing quality goods at lower costs to U.S. consumers.

Faced with this new competition, U.S. manufacturers turned to technology to increase productivity, substituting machines for people wherever possible. Companies began to eliminate thousands of workers from their payrolls, sometimes more than half of the permanent labor force. As manufacturing employment decreased, employment in the service industries was growing faster than in any other sector, often providing lower-paying jobs, many without benefits such as health insurance. Moreover, the competition for jobs increased, particularly in the 1980s, as those who were born during the post–World War II era began entering the labor force. Women, too, also entered the labor force in large numbers. In 1969 the civilian labor force in the United States was 81 million; by 1993 that number had increased nearly 60 percent to 128 million. The technological revolution that hit the manufacturing sector then reached the service sector, replacing bank tellers with automatic teller machines and telephone operators with automated switching equipment.[14]

Table 5-9 presents the distribution of money income of U.S. families by quintiles and income at selected positions in constant 1993 dollars for 1980 and 1993. As the table indicates, there was a decline in income received by the bottom 80 percent of the families and a gain for the top 20 percent. During the same period the top 5 percent of families increased their share of income from 15.3 percent in 1980 to 19.1 percent in 1993. The lowest one-fifth of families had their share of income reduced from 5.2 percent in 1980 to 4.2 percent in 1993. The trend toward greater inequality in the distribution of income continued into 1994 and 1995. In 1994 the median income of families declined to $35,407 from $36,959 in 1993 and $36,573 in 1992.

Table 5-10 presents changes in the median income of U.S. households by race and Hispanic origin as measured by constant 1993 dollars for the period 1970–1993. As the table indicates, all households made little gain in purchasing power. The gains that were made occurred during the period 1985–1990, with white households showing the greatest gain. In 1994 the bottom one-fifth of households living on incomes of $13,426 or less received 3.6 percent of personal income compared to 4.3 percent in 1984. The three-fifths in the middle received 47.3 percent of total income compared to 50.8 percent in 1984 and 52.2 percent in 1974, while

14. It is also necessary to mention that tax rates were reduced during the 1980s. The Economic Recovery Tax Act of 1981 provided a cut in the top income tax bracket from 70 to 50 percent. The corporate income tax was reduced from 48 to 46 percent. The Tax Reform Act of 1986 reduced personal and corporate income taxes still further. Personal tax brackets were simplified from four to three rates: 15, 28, and 31 percent. The rates are currently 15, 28, 36, and 39 percent.

TABLE 5-9 *Money Income of U.S. Families—Percentage Distribution of Aggregate Income Received by Quintile and Income at Selected Positions, 1980 and 1993 (1993 dollars)*

	All Families in 1980	*All Families in 1993*
Number (1000)	60,309	68,506
Percentage Distribution		
Lowest fifth	5.2%	4.2%
Second fifth	11.5	10.1
Third fifth	17.5	15.9
Fourth fifth	24.3	23.6
Highest fifth	41.5	46.2
Top 5 percent	15.3	19.1
Upper Income at Selected Positions (dollars)		
Lowest	$17,535	$16,952
Second	29,645	30,000
Third	41,988	45,020
Fourth	58,871	66,794
Lower limit of top 5 percent	92,158	113,182

Source: U.S. Department of Commerce, Bureau of the Census, *Statistical Abstract of the United States, 1995* (Washington, D.C.: U.S. Government Printing Office, 1995), 475.

the top one-fifth living on more than $62,681 received 49.1 percent of the income, up from 45.2 percent in 1984 and 43.5 percent in 1974.[15]

Who Gained and Who Lost. Certain groups have gained and certain groups have lost as a result of the increased inequality in the distribution of real income. Those who had either not finished high school or not had any education beyond high school saw their real incomes decline the most because they were more likely to hold low-paying, unskilled jobs. Men generally did worse than women. Average earnings for men who had not finished high school declined by 23 percent from 1979 to 1992 compared to a decline of 7 percent for women.[16] During the same period, the average earnings for men who were high school graduates declined by 17 percent compared to a 1 percent increase for women. Average earnings for male college graduates increased by 5 percent compared to an increase of 19 percent for female college graduates. The average weekly earnings for women increased from 59 percent of those for men to 71 percent.

Other income gainers were the CEOs of major U.S. companies. The difference between the average CEO's income and the income of the average worker increased from a ratio of 41 to 1 in 1973 to 225 to 1 in 1994. The richest 1 percent and 5 percent of income earners have gained, and the bottom 60 percent of in-

15. *Roanoke Times*, October 6, 1995, A3.
16. *U.S. News and World Report*, January 22, 1996, 48.

TABLE 5-10
Median Income of U.S. Households by Race and Hispanic Origin, 1970–1993 (in constant 1993 dollars)

Year	*All Households*	*White*	*Black*	*Hispanic*
1970	30,558	31,828	19,373	—
1975	30,340	31,728	19,047	22,793
1980	31,095	32,805	18,899	23,968
1985	31,717	33,450	19,901	23,454
1986	32,825	34,510	19,881	24,196
1987	33,150	34,927	19,935	24,596
1988	33,255	35,155	20,041	24,868
1989	33,685	35,433	21,073	25,545
1990	33,105	34,529	20,648	24,688
1991	31,962	33,493	19,953	24,074
1992	31,553	33,173	19,316	23,273
1993	31,241	32,460	19,533	22,886

Source: U.S. Department of Commerce, Bureau of the Census, *Statistical Abstract of the United States, 1995* (Washington, D.C.; U.S. Government Printing Office, 1995), 469.

come earners have lost in terms of real income. In 1973 the richest 5 percent of households received an average income of $83,271 measured in 1993 dollars and an average income of $105,945 in 1994.[17] The poorest one-fifth of households received an average income of $7,981 in 1994 dollars in 1973, and an average of $7,762 in 1994, while the respective income figures for the next-poorest fifth were $19,988 and $19,224. There has also been an increase in the number of families making more than $100,000 a year. In 1994, 8.4 percent of all families made over $100,000 a year; however, two-thirds of those families had two income earners.

The Winner-Take-All Society. One explanation of rising income inequality in the United States has been provided in a book written by Robert H. Frank and Philip J. Cook called *The Winner-Take-All Society.*[18] The authors contend that a growing number of markets have come to resemble the entertainment industry, where a few superstars command very high incomes. It is relative, not absolute, performance that is rewarded. A tiny difference in talent or skill, or just plain luck, can result in vastly greater rewards for a few people. Although the competition for top positions in winner-take-all markets attracts talented workers, it generates two kinds of waste. First, it attracts too many contestants. Second, it gives rise to unproductive patterns of consumption and investment.

The growth of the winner-take-all society can be attributed to the development of communication technologies, in particular electronic communication and data processing. This has had two mutually reinforcing effects. One is that a huge increase in the demand for the works of a particular author or singer can be satis-

17. Ibid., 42.
18. Robert H. Frank and Philip J. Cook, *The Winner-Take-All Society* (New York: Free Press, 1995).

fied without any corresponding increase in supply. The other is called the "network" effect: the value to people throughout the world of listening to a particular singer or watching a particular movie is reinforced by the thought that all their friends are watching the same programs. This helps to explain why a limited number of actors, authors, movie directors, and sport stars do very well. Coupled with the development of communications technology is the emergence of English as the universal language, which furthers the expansion of winner-take-all markets.

But winner-take-all markets are not limited to entertainment; they are also applicable to the high rewards received by some doctors, lawyers, and management consultants. The explanation used to explain income differentials in these fields is based on the concept of rank ordering. For example, if two companies are rivals in a takeover bid, both will consider it more important to buy the best legal talent available than to save money by buying the second best, knowing that their rival will make the same calculation. Both companies will spend much more on legal advice than is necessary to hire a good lawyer. A similar analogy would hold true for consulting and medicine, where incomes would be bid up through competition to get the best.

Wealth

Inequality in the distribution of wealth has also increased over the past twenty years. In 1989 the top 1 percent of wealthholders received 39 percent of total wealth as measured by net worth, while the bottom 80 percent of wealthholders received 15 percent. The distribution of wealth in that year was the most unequal since the 1920s, when the top 1 percent of wealthholders received 45 percent of total wealth. Over the next fifty years, inequality in the distribution of wealth began to decline, and by 1970 the top 1 percent of wealthholders owned 20 percent of total wealth. Then inequality in wealth distribution began to grow rapidly, particularly during the period 1983–1989. During this time, financial assets, bank deposits, and equities began to increase in importance as a part of wealth holdings. By 1982 the top 1 percent of wealthholders owned 30 percent of total wealth, and by 1989 their ownership had increased to 39 percent. Their share has continued to increase in the 1990s.

Table 5-11 presents a distribution of wealth based on total assets and net worth for 1989. The net worth of wealthholders with assets of $10 million or more was three times that of wealthholders of $600,000 or less. Also presented is the percentage of total assets and net worth held by wealthholders.

Comparisons of Wealth Inequality by Countries. Wealth inequality was greater in the United Kingdom than in the United States. In 1920, the top 1 percent of wealthholders as measured by marketable net worth owned 60 percent of the wealth in the United Kingdom compared to around 45 percent in the United States.[19] This lasted until after World War II, when the Labour government of

19. Edward N. Wolff, *Top Heavy: A Study of the Increasing Inequality of Wealth in America* (New York: The Twentieth Century Fund Press, 1995), 30.

TABLE 5-11 *Top Wealthholders with Gross Assets of $600,000 or More, 1989**

	All Wealthholders				
Size of Net Worth (dollars)	*Number (thousands)*	*Assets ($billions)*	*Net Worth ($billions)*	*Assets (%)*	*Net Worth (%)*
Under $600,000	812	483	298	8.9	6.2
600,000–900,000	1,344	1,118	1,024	20.7	21.3
1,000,000–2,499,999	945	1,539	1,404	28.6	29.2
2,500,000–4,999,999	206	707	696	14.3	14.5
5,000,000–9,999,999	73	530	492	9.8	10.3
10,000,000 or more	36	956	890	17.7	18.5
Total	3,116	5,396	4,805	100.0	100.0

**Estimates based on estate tax returns.*
†Net worth equals assets minus debt and mortgages.

Source: U.S. Department of Commerce, Bureau of the Census, *Statistical Abstract of the United States* (Washington, D.C.: U.S. Government Printing Office, 1995), 469.

Clement Attlee raised the rates of income and inheritance taxes. By 1960 the top 1 percent of wealthholders in the United States had a greater percentage of total wealth than the top 1 percent in the United Kingdom. There was also a greater concentration of wealth in the hands of the few in Sweden and other European countries than in the United States in the early part of this century.

However, all of this has changed. There is now greater equality in the distribution of both wealth and income in Europe than in the United States. This is a direct result of government tax policies designed to reduce income inequality, which was held to be responsible for the mass unemployment that existed in Europe during the 1930s.[20] Income taxes in such countries as the United Kingdom and Sweden became far more progressive than in the United States. It should be emphasized, however, that differences in wealth taxation systems and in definitions of wealth exist among countries and cannot account entirely for changes in wealth inequality.

Poverty

At the opposite end of the income and wealth scale is poverty, which has increased as income and wealth inequalities have increased. From 1960 to 1973 the national poverty rate decreased from 22 percent of the population to 11 percent; it then

20. The writings of John Maynard Keynes had an enormous impact on the economic policy of European countries after World War II. Keynes argued that unemployment was a result of a lack of aggregate demand. Since the European countries had experienced mass unemployment prior to World War II, their postwar objective was to maintain full employment. Consumption was the key to maintaining a high level of aggregate demand. Since the rich spent less and saved more (their marginal propensity to consume was low), and the poor spent more and saved less (their marginal propensity to consume was high), tax the rich and redistribute the income.

rose to 15 percent by 1993.[21] The poverty rate for children, which decreased from 27 percent in 1960 to 14 percent by 1973, had risen to 23 percent by 1993. One major cause of the increase in poverty is the increase in the number of female-headed households. The proportion of children under 18 who live with one parent has tripled, from 9 percent in 1960 to 27 percent in 1993. The poverty rate in households headed by a single female is 46 percent. Many females raising children alone are high school dropouts and lack the skills necessary to compete in a workplace that demands ever-increasing skills.

Other factors have also contributed to an increase in poverty. One, already mentioned, is the fall in the real income of workers. Most of the higher-paying jobs in manufacturing are gone, and those that are left require more skills. Racial and ethnic discrimination contribute to poverty because they set up barriers to employment. Poverty is higher for blacks and Hispanics than for whites.[22] Table 5-12 presents a breakdown of poverty based on various social characteristics. The poverty level in 1993 was $14,763 for a family of four.

Comparisons with Other Industrial Countries. Americans have long been willing to tolerate greater income inequality than other nations. It is simply accepted as a part of America's individualistic culture, where many sports stars and musicians have been catapulted into the ranks of multimillionaires. Probably one reason why Americans feel less resentment toward income inequality than Europeans is that upward mobility has been higher in the United States than in Europe. Americans have always been attracted to rags-to-riches stories of poor people rising to the top of the heap through their own initiative. Many Americans still view poverty as the result of individual failures in character rather than the operation of market forces. The response has been different in Europe where reduction in poverty is addressed through the government tax-transfer payment mechanism.

There is an overlap between income inequality and poverty. If poverty is defined as the condition of families with less than half of median family income, then countries with wider income inequalities will tend to have more poverty. The United States has one of the most unequal income distributions of all industrial countries, so comparisons with the European countries may exaggerate the extent of its absolute poverty. The author of a paper published by the Luxembourg Income Study, an international project designed to study income inequality and poverty, took the figure of half of median income in the United States and converted it into other countries' currencies using purchasing power parity. He found that the U.S. poverty rate was lower than that for all Western European countries.[23]

21. *Economic Report of the President 1995* (Washington, D.C.: U.S. Government Printing Office, 1995), 178.
22. In 1993 Hispanic males earned 65 percent of what white males earned; black males earned 74 percent of what white males earned.
23. "Inequality: For Richer or Poorer," *The Economist*, November 5–11, 1994, 20.

TABLE 5-12
Characteristics of Poverty in the United States, 1992

	Percent Below Poverty Level			
Year	*All Races*	*White*	*Black*	*Hispanic*
1970	12.6	9.9	33.5	—
1975	12.3	9.7	31.3	26.9
1980	13.0	10.2	32.5	25.7
1985	14.0	11.4	31.3	29.0
1986	13.6	11.0	31.1	27.3
1987	13.4	10.4	32.4	28.0
1988	13.0	10.1	31.3	26.7
1989	12.8	10.0	30.7	26.2
1990	13.5	10.7	31.9	28.1
1991	14.2	11.3	32.7	28.7
1992	14.8	11.9	33.3	29.3
1993	15.1	12.2	33.1	30.6
	Children Below Poverty Level			
	All Races	*White*	*Black*	*Hispanic*
1970	14.9	10.5	41.5	—
1975	16.8	12.5	41.4	33.1
1980	17.9	13.4	42.1	33.0
1985	20.1	15.6	43.1	39.6
1986	19.8	15.3	42.7	37.1
1987	19.7	14.7	44.4	38.9
1988	19.0	14.0	42.8	37.3
1989	19.0	14.1	43.2	35.5
1990	19.9	15.1	44.2	37.7
1991	21.1	16.1	45.6	39.8
1992	21.6	16.5	46.3	38.9
1993	22.0	17.0	45.9	39.9

Source: U.S. Department of Commerce, Bureau of the Census, *Statistical Abstract of the United States, 1995* (Washington, D.C.: U.S. Government Printing Office, 1995), 480.

IS THE UNITED STATES IN THE PROCESS OF DECLINE?

Headlines in the newspapers and on television would tend to make people believe that the United States is in the process of decline. The dollar hit a historic low against the German mark and the Japanese yen in the spring of 1995, the merchandise trade deficit for 1994 was the highest in history, and so was the deficit in the current account.[24] The O. J. Simpson trial has been called the consummate ex-

24. However, the dollar has gained in value against the yen and the deutsche mark since the spring of 1995. Merchandise exports for the United States for 1995 were $583.9 billion and merchandise imports were $770.8 billion, for a deficit of $186.9 billion. The current account deficit for 1995 was approximately $152 billion.

ample of American culture, reflecting our preoccupation with the rank and the sordid.[25] American moral values have been compared to those in Rome that led to the decline and fall of the Roman empire. The U.S. divorce rate is high, more families are fragmented, and teenage pregnancies are higher in the United States than in other developed countries.

Moreover, scholars of various persuasions have expressed pessimism about America's future. Paul Kennedy, a Yale historian, stated in a 1987 book that the United States was in the process of decline.[26] Clyde V. Prestowitz and others were a part of what can be called "the Japanese will win" group. In his 1988 book *Trading Places* Prestowitz saw Japan taking over first place from the United States.[27] Mancur Olsen observed that mature societies start to decline when layers of special-interest groups impede the normal functions of capitalism.[28] Lester Thurow contends that we have lost the competitive game to the Europeans and Japanese.[29] Robert B. Reich argues that we are unprepared to compete in the twenty-first century in part because schools are not providing U.S. students with the requisite knowledge.[30]

Despite these gloomy predictions, however, the United States is not in the process of decline. The once vaunted Japanese economy has developed serious economic and social problems. A united Europe that would present a serious challenge to the American economy has not developed and may never develop. Over 10 percent of the Western European labor force is unemployed. The income of a nation depends on its know-how, and the U.S. nation has plenty of that. There remains a creative dynamism[31] about the American economy that may be lacking elsewhere, particularly in Europe. There are thousands of U.S. entrepreneurs who move society and get things done. Examples are Bill Gates, the founder of Microsoft, and Dave Thomas, the founder of Wendy's.[32]

Strengths of the U.S. Economy

The United States has many strengths. Its standard of living, as measured by real per capita GDP, is the highest in the world. Its unemployment rate, as of the spring of 1996, is the lowest of all major countries, with the exception of Japan. The average productivity of U.S. industries and workers as a whole is at the top or near the top compared to other nations. We are getting back to a leading position in industries once considered lost to the Japanese, including the car industry. An-

25. The O. J. Simpson case has been called the Super Bowl of murder trials.
26. Paul Kennedy, *The Rise and Fall of the Great Powers* (New York: Random House, 1987).
27. Clyde V. Prestowitz, *Trading Places* (New York: Basic Books, 1988).
28. Mancur Olsen, *The Rise and Fall of Nations* (New Haven: Yale University Press, 1983).
29. Lester Thurow, *Head to Head: The Coming Economic Battle Among Japan, Europe, and America* (New York: Morrow, 1992).
30. Robert B. Reich, *The Work of Nations* (New York: Alfred A. Knopf, 1991).
31. Joseph Schumpeter used the term *creative destruction*. To him, the entrepreneur was the one who was responsible for change, with the new replacing the old.
32. Dave Thomas is a high school dropout.

TABLE 5-13 *Unemployment Rate in the Major Industrial Countries, 1985–1994 (percent)*

Year	*United States*	*Canada*	*Japan*	*France*	*Germany**	*Italy*	*United Kingdom*
1985	7.2	10.5	2.6	10.5	7.2	6.0	11.2
1986	7.0	9.5	2.8	10.6	6.6	7.5	11.2
1987	6.2	8.8	2.9	10.8	6.3	7.9	10.3
1988	5.5	7.8	2.5	10.3	6.3	7.9	8.6
1989	5.3	7.5	2.3	9.6	5.7	7.9	7.3
1990	5.5	8.1	2.1	9.1	5.0	7.0	6.9
1991	6.7	10.3	2.2	9.6	4.3	6.9	8.8
1992	7.4	11.3	2.2	10.4	4.6	7.3	10.0
1993	6.8	11.2	2.5	11.8	5.8	10.5	10.0
1994	6.1	10.3	2.5	11.9	6.4	11.6	9.5
1995	5.6	9.5	3.4	11.7	10.8	12.1	8.8

**West Germany.*

Source: *Economic Report of the President 1996* (Washington, D.C.: U.S. Government Printing Office, 1996), 399.

other point worth considering is that the U.S. position as a provider of services, such as consulting, is by far the strongest of any country and will increase in the future. Finally, it has a resiliency matched by few countries.

Tables 5-13 and 5-14 compare unemployment rates and real economic growth for the United States and other major industrial countries.

Weaknesses of the U.S. Economy

There is fairly unanimous agreement that one major problem confronting the U.S. economy is a low rate of savings. The United States used to be a nation of savers. From the period after the Civil War and up to World War II, the U.S. savings rate was the highest in the world and far higher than Japan's.[33] But the savings rate began to decline after World War II as Americans became more consumer oriented.[34] The lack of savings has contributed to problems in the American economy in that it has reduced the amount of money available for capital formation, increased the cost of borrowing, and made the United States more dependent on outside income sources to finance the deficit in the federal budget. Table 5-15 presents the rate of savings for the United States and other major industrial countries.

Economic insecurity among American workers at present is probably the highest since the Depression of the 1930s. Virtually every sector of the American economy is in a vise because of unremitting foreign competition. The result is a contin-

33. Competitiveness Policy Council, First Annual Report to the President and Congress, *Building a Competitive America*, March 1, 1992, 9.
34. In 1960–1969 the net savings rate was around 8 percent; for 1990–1993 it was around 4 percent.

TABLE 5-14 *Growth Rates in Real GDP for the Major Industrial Countries (percent)*

Country	*1976–1985*	*1986*	*1987*	*1988*	*1989*	*1990*	*1991*	*1992*	*1993*	*1994*	*1995*
United States	2.9	2.9	3.1	3.9	2.5	1.2	-.6	2.3	3.1	4.1	2.9
Canada	3.4	3.3	4.2	5.0	2.4	–.2	–1.8	.6	2.2	4.1	2.2
Japan	4.2	2.6	4.1	6.2	4.7	4.8	4.3	1.1	–.2	.5	.5
France	2.3	2.5	2.3	4.4	4.2	2.5	.8	1.2	–1.5	2.9	2.9
Germany	2.2	2.3	1.5	3.7	3.6	5.7	2.9	2.2	–1.2	2.9	2.6
Italy	3.1	2.9	3.1	4.1	2.9	2.1	1.2	.7	–1.2	2.2	3.0
United Kingdom	2.9	4.3	4.8	5.0	2.2	.4	–2.0	–.5	2.2	3.8	2.7

Source: *Economic Report of the President 1996* (Washington, D.C.: U.S. Government Printing Office, 1996), 402.

TABLE 5-15
Gross Savings Rates for Major Industrial Countries

Country	*Percentage of GDP*
Canada	12.8
France	19.8
Germany	22.1
Italy	17.2
Japan	33.9
United Kingdom	12.8
United States	14.5

Source: OECD Economic Surveys, *United States* (Paris: OECD, November 1995), Appendix, Basic Statistics, International Comparisons.

uous wave of downsizing that has persisted even though the American economy has been in a period of expansion for the past four years. In 1995 U.S. corporations announced a million layoffs. Many of those who were laid off were middle-level managers. Bank mergers have eliminated some 70,000 jobs, and it is estimated that 450,000 more bank employees will lose their jobs by the end of the decade. Downsizing in the communications industry has resulted in the loss of 140,000 jobs since 1993, and more layoffs are expected in the future. Where downsizing is the norm, wages rise slowly, in part because workers are fearful of losing their jobs. Moreover, the real incomes of the great mass of workers have been declining, and income inequality has been rising. Real wages of the median-income worker have fallen 4.6 percent since 1979, and more than half of that decrease has come since 1992. This comes at a time when the U.S. economy is slowing down. Even though the value of the U.S. dollar has improved against other currencies, particularly the mark and the yen, U.S. exports are feeling the effects of reduced buyer demand throughout the world. So, as the United States enters the 1996 election year, it has problems that defy easy solutions. What all of this could lead to is class warfare of the type that existed during the 1930s.

SUMMARY

In his 1996 State of the Union message, President Clinton declared that the U.S. economy was the healthiest it had been in three decades. He cited the misery index, which is a combination of inflation and unemployment rates, as being the lowest in twenty years. The stock market reached an all-time high in 1995 and continued its advance in 1996. He also claimed credit for the economic recovery, which started before he became president but continued afterward. Business profit also increased, and the deficits in the merchandise trade and current accounts began to show a decline toward the end of 1995. To some extent, these gains were attributable to factors over which the president had little control. The stock market did gain in 1995, but that had more to do with a shift in investment preference from foreign stocks to domestic stock.

Nevertheless, the United States has its share of problems. The savings rate continues to be lower than those of other industrial nations. Income inequality and wealth inequality continue to increase. All sorts of social problems exist. A majority of families have experienced either little change or a decline in their real incomes over a period of time. There has been a shift in demand in favor of more-educated workers and away from the traditional blue-collar jobs that paid high wages for less-educated workers. There is a Darwinian global economic competition that is the most powerful force affecting the United States since the end of the cold war. This has resulted in increased job insecurity in the United States as downsizing by American firms has increased.

QUESTIONS FOR DISCUSSION

1. What is meant by a trade deficit? A current account deficit?
2. Why is the role of education of increasing importance in competition with other nations?
3. What are some of the factors responsible for poverty in the United States?
4. Income and wealth inequality increased in the United States during the 1980s. Discuss some of the reasons this happened.
5. What are the strengths of the U.S. economy?
6. What are the weaknesses of the U.S. economy?
7. To what extent can the development of large corporations be regarded as a departure from a free market system?
8. What are some of the factors responsible for the increased role of government in the United States?

RECOMMENDED READINGS

Economic Report of the President 1996. Washington, D.C.: U.S. Government Printing Office, 1996.

Frank, Robert H., and Philip J. Cook. *The Winner-Take-All Society.* New York: Free Press, 1995.

"Inequality: For Richer or Poorer." *The Economist,* November 5–11, 1994, 79–81.

Madrick, Jeffrey. *The End of Affluence: The Causes and Consequences of America's Economic Dilemma.* New York: Random House, 1995.

McRae, Hamish. *The World in 2020.* Cambridge, Mass: Harvard University Press, 1995.

Nau, Henry. *The Myth of America's Decline.* New York: Oxford University Press, 1992.

OECD Economic Surveys. *United States.* Paris: OECD, 1995.

The Conference Board. *The Great Income Shuffle.* New York, 1992.

Wolff, Edward N. *Top Heavy: A Study of the Increasing Inequality of Wealth in America.* New York: The Twentieth Century Fund Press, 1995.

CHAPTER 6

Japan

To much of the world, Japan has appeared to be an economic colossus that would eventually replace the United States as the world's leading economic superpower. Even in the United States there were writers who belonged to the Japan-will-win school.[1] They cited Japanese feats in the area of high technology, once considered the exclusive domain of the United States. They also cited the Japanese real economic growth rate, which was much higher than the rates in the United States and in Europe. Japan had transformed itself in a relatively short period of time into a world superpower through hard work and a social organization so cohesive and well managed that it was the envy of much of the world. Moreover, during the 1980s Japan became the leading creditor country in the world and the United States became the leading debtor nation, and Japan was buying up assets in the United States and the rest of the world.

1. They cited among other things Japanese technology, the Japanese educational system, Japanese culture, the strength of the Japanese yen against other currencies, and the financial resources of Japanese banks.

Now all of this has changed. Even though Japan is still a world superpower, it has developed a number of economic, political, and social problems. There have been political and stock market scandals that would have overturned most governments. The large Japanese banks have seen their assets lose much of their value as investments in real estate at home and abroad declined in value. In 1992–1993, the Japanese economy experienced its deepest recession since the first oil crisis of 1973, with real GDP growing an average of 0.6 percent. The slowdown was caused in part by corporate restructuring occasioned by declining profits and increased world competition. The earthquake in Kobe in January 1995 caused billions of dollars of damage to the economy.

When one considers the economic base from which the country has had to operate, however, the performance of the Japanese economy has been remarkable. The land area is small, the natural resources are limited, and the population is large. Its economy was virtually destroyed during World War II. It was very much a feudal society until the middle of the nineteenth century and had to build a new set of institutions upon which to create a modern economy. It remains vulnerable to world economic and political upheavals because it has to import a high percentage of its resources. Dependence on exports and imports is a fact of life for the Japanese. But Japan has shown that competitive advantage can be created by a resource-poor nation.[2]

THE ECONOMIC SYSTEM

Japan has an economic philosophy that embraces the basic concepts of a modern capitalist economy. This philosophy was grafted onto a country that had almost no outside contact with the Western world before 1853, when Commodore Matthew C. Perry and his U.S. naval squadron forced Japan against its will to open itself to the West.[3] With the shock of exposure to the outside world, it became apparent to the Japanese that they had to make a choice: Either create a modern industrial state or become another market for Western goods. They chose the former, and in a relatively short period Japan was transformed from an underdeveloped country into a world economic power. It did this by emulating the industrial powers of the West in every possible way; it cast aside centuries-old behavioral patterns in favor of anything Western. By the beginning of this century, Japan had achieved sufficient industrial and military might to inflict a military defeat upon the forces of the Russian empire.

The economic development of Japan can be divided into two major time periods: The Meiji Period from 1868 to 1913 and the period following the end of

2. Michael Porter, *The Competitive Advantage of Nations* (New York: Free Press, 1990), 17–25.
3. Actually, Christian missionaries had reached Japan by the middle of the fifteenth century. The Dutch established a trading post at Nagasaki in 1638 and maintained it for several centuries. Dutch became the language of Western learning in Japan, and through books brought in from the Netherlands, Japanese scholars managed to keep at least partially abreast of intellectual and scientific progress in the West.

World War II from 1948 to 1960. Each period is significant in understanding how Japan has transformed itself into a major world power. A common denominator in both periods is the role the Japanese government played in stimulating economic development. Human capital was also important in aiding economic growth, for Japan has had few natural resources, and land was far from abundant relative to the size of the population.

The Meiji Period, 1868–1913

The Meiji Restoration of 1868 marks the beginning of the development of Japan as a modern industrial nation.[4] In the first years after the Restoration, the most important development in Japan was the creation of an environment conducive to economic growth. In order to survive the economic encroachments of Western powers, Japan, by national policy, had to master the secret of industry. To gain the necessary knowledge, Japanese students were sent to study the technology of Western nations. Also, Western engineers and technicians were temporarily employed in Japan to teach the Japanese the techniques of production. The Japanese learned to adapt the technology of the West for their own purposes.

The Role of Government. The government became a major operator of key industries. The modernization of Japan during the latter part of the last century included the nationalization of key sectors of the economy such as the postal service, telephone and telegraph communications, and railways. The government also built and operated iron foundries, shipyards, machine shops, and factories. Tobacco, salt, and camphor became government monopolies.[5] The government provided technical and financial assistance to private interests in other industries.

The financial and monetary base for the economy was established in 1882 when the Bank of Japan was formed. Tax policies were designed to stimulate capital formation. Taxes were levied on agricultural land and the sale of farm products. The proceeds provided for public capital formation, which went into the development of roads and educational facilities. Expenditures on arsenals, navy yards, warships, and the like provided a military underpinning for the process of economic development.

The Role of Private Enterprise. While the government was involved in producing the conditions requisite to economic growth and industrial development, private enterprise also flourished and developed during the Meiji period. An important development during the Meiji period was the displacement of the samurai, or warrior caste, which had dominated Japan for centuries. The samurai were inte-

4. The Meiji Restoration was called a "restoration" because the powers of the government that the Tokugawa Shogunate had usurped were restored to the emperor of Japan, who came to be known posthumously as the Emperor Meiji.
5. The government also financed the development of experimental or pilot plants to train Japanese workers and to adapt Western production techniques to Japanese conditions. These plants became models for private industry to follow.

grated into Japanese society, and some went into business. Therefore, in Japan businesspeople were drawn from the upper classes of society and enjoyed immediate respect and prestige. In this regard, Japan started at an advantage, for in most developing countries, the business class is composed largely of people in lower social classes or from racial and religious minorities not respected by the population. In addition, by building up export industries based on low-cost labor, Japan was able to obtain foreign exchange to purchase food and raw materials needed by the economy.

Japanese capitalism was characterized by the development of concentrated economic power in the form of business combines called *zaibatsu*. Each combine consisted of twenty to thirty major firms, all concentrated around a large bank. These major firms represented each of the important industrial sectors in the economy, so that a group would typically include a shipping company, a steel company, an insurance company, and so forth. Zaibatsu combines were larger than any U.S. corporation and were under the control and management of a few family dynasties. The Mitsui combine, for example, employed 1,800,000 workers prior to World War II, and Mitsubishi employed 1,000,000 workers.[6] There was a working relationship between the zaibatsu and the Japanese government in that the latter, through military force or otherwise, provided penetration of new markets.

Post–World War II Development of Japan

With Japan's defeat in World War II and its subsequent occupation by the United States came problems of reform and reorganization for the economy. A new constitution, which incorporated Western principles of democratic parliamentary government, was promulgated by the United States for Japan in November 1946.[7] The dissolution of the zaibatsu into a number of independent business enterprises was another part of U.S. occupation policy. Antitrust laws molded after the U.S. Sherman and Clayton Acts were imposed on the Japanese. Later, however, the Japanese government enacted various laws to exempt certain industries from antitrust legislation. These exemptions were designed to improve Japan's position as a world exporter by allowing certain types of export cartels.[8] The U.S. occupation of Japan also resulted in the introduction of consumer technology, which the Japanese readily assimilated. The Japanese became wards of the United States and received gifts, low-interest loans, and machinery that restored productive capacity in a number of industries, especially textiles.[9]

6. Corwin Edwards, "The Dissolution of Zaibatsu Continues," *Pacific Affairs* (September 1946), 8–24.
7. The U.S. military occupation of Japan ended in 1952.
8. Japanese antimonopoly laws permitted the development of cartels and other forms of business combinations to a far greater extent than is permitted by U.S. antitrust laws.
9. Jean-Jacques Servan-Schreiber. *The World Challenge* (New York: Simon and Schuster, 1981), 178–184.

However, Japanese economic development policy could not depend on U.S. largesse alone. Local needs had to be satisfied first. The shipbuilding industry had been destroyed during the war and, as a small island country, Japan needed ships of every type for survival. With government aid, the shipbuilding industry developed rapidly; by 1956 the Japanese had become the world's largest producer of ships.

Japan also developed an export strategy to achieve industrial development. For exports, the country's leaders recognized that they would have to depend on handicrafts, textiles, and other small-scale industries in which Japan enjoyed the advantage of low-cost labor. Human capital was an important factor in the early postwar period. Veterans were absorbed in the labor-intensive industries. Earnings from exports were used to finance the acquisition of machine tools that would help Japan produce modern machinery. This led to the development of other industries, notably Honda, which developed from a one-man operation in 1951 to the largest motorcycle company in the world.

The Role of the Japanese Government. The Japanese government has played and continues to play an important role in the development of the Japanese economy. The postwar development of Japanese industry was facilitated through government grants and low-interest loans. There has also been extensive use of fiscal and monetary policies to stimulate economic growth. Special tax incentives are used to promote high rates of saving, investment, and capital formation as well as the introduction of new products and technology.

Probably most important to the success of the Japanese economy has been the development of a close working relationship between government and business. This relationship is based to some extent on the realization that because Japan has few natural resources, it is necessary to reach some consensus about resource allocation. Government and business leaders attempt to decide jointly on policy objectives that will promote the national interest rather than special-interest groups.[10]

ORGANIZATION OF INDUSTRY

Japanese industry is a product of the culture and the unique economic development of the country. Its industrial groups have no parallel in other countries. Although it is half the size of the United States in population, it ranks second only to the United States in the number of large corporations,[11] and its banks are the largest in the world.

10. Peter F. Drucker, "Behind Japan's Success," *Harvard Business Review,* Vol. 59, No. 1 (January-February 1981), 83–90.
11. Of the 500 largest corporations in the world, 151 are American, 149 are Japanese, and 44 are German. See *Fortune,* August 7, 1995, F-33, F-34, and F-37.

Japan can be characterized as having a dual economy—very efficient in some industries and very inefficient in others. Existing on the periphery of large corporations are a number of family-owned companies employing from two to one hundred workers. They typically manufacture a subassembly or provide a service sold only to their major customers.

The Keiretsu

Industrial groups called the *keiretsu* are of two types, horizontal and vertical.[12] The horizontal group consists of a family of corporations spanning numerous industries and centered around a bank. There are six horizontal keiretsu in Japan—Sumitomo, Mitsui, Mitsubishi, Sanwa, Dai-Ichi Kangyo, and Fuyo. The first three were part of the former zaibatsu before World War II. The keiretsu are enormous in size. The Sumitomo keiretsu (Figure 6-1), for example, consists of firms in banking, electronics, glass, oil, and metals, and a trading company. The total value of its assets and the volume of its sales amount to hundreds of billions of dollars. Table 6-1 presents the value of its assets for 1993 for its banks, major industries, and trading company. There are interlocking directorates in each keiretsu, and companies affiliated with one can own stock in one another. Loans by banks to each member can be made at low interest rates, and presidents of each company meet to conduct business strategy.

The vertical keiretsu is formed of an industrial group and its subsidiaries. There are thirty-nine vertical keiretsu, many of which are in such industries as automobiles and electrical equipment. Toyota affords an excellent example of this type of keiretsu. It has financial ties with all of its suppliers. For example, it owns 34 percent of the company that makes its clocks, 21 percent of the company that makes its body frames, 41 percent of the company that makes its tires, 22 percent of the company that manufactures its disc brakes, and 33 percent of the company that manufactures its upholstery.[13] Members of a vertical keiretsu own shares in one another's companies, exchange information, and cooperate in new ventures. When Toyota opened plants in the United States, its suppliers followed, and they continue to deliver components to its U.S. plants just as they do in Japan.

The Sogo Shoshas

Another important form of business organization in Japan is the trading company, or *sogo shosha*.[14] There are a half dozen trading companies, and they are among the largest enterprises in the world. Most of Japan's foreign trade is done through trad-

12. Dick K. Nanto, "Japan's Industrial Groups: The Keiretsu," *Japan's Economic Challenge*, Joint Economic Committee, Congress of the United States (Washington, D.C.: U.S. Government Printing Office), 72–88. This provides an excellent discussion of the keiretsu.

13. "Japan: All in the Family," *Newsweek*, June 10, 1991, 38–39.

14. See Kiyoshi Kojima, *Japan's General Trading Companies: Merchants of Economic Development* (Paris: OECD, 1984).

FIGURE 6-1 *Sumitomo Group*

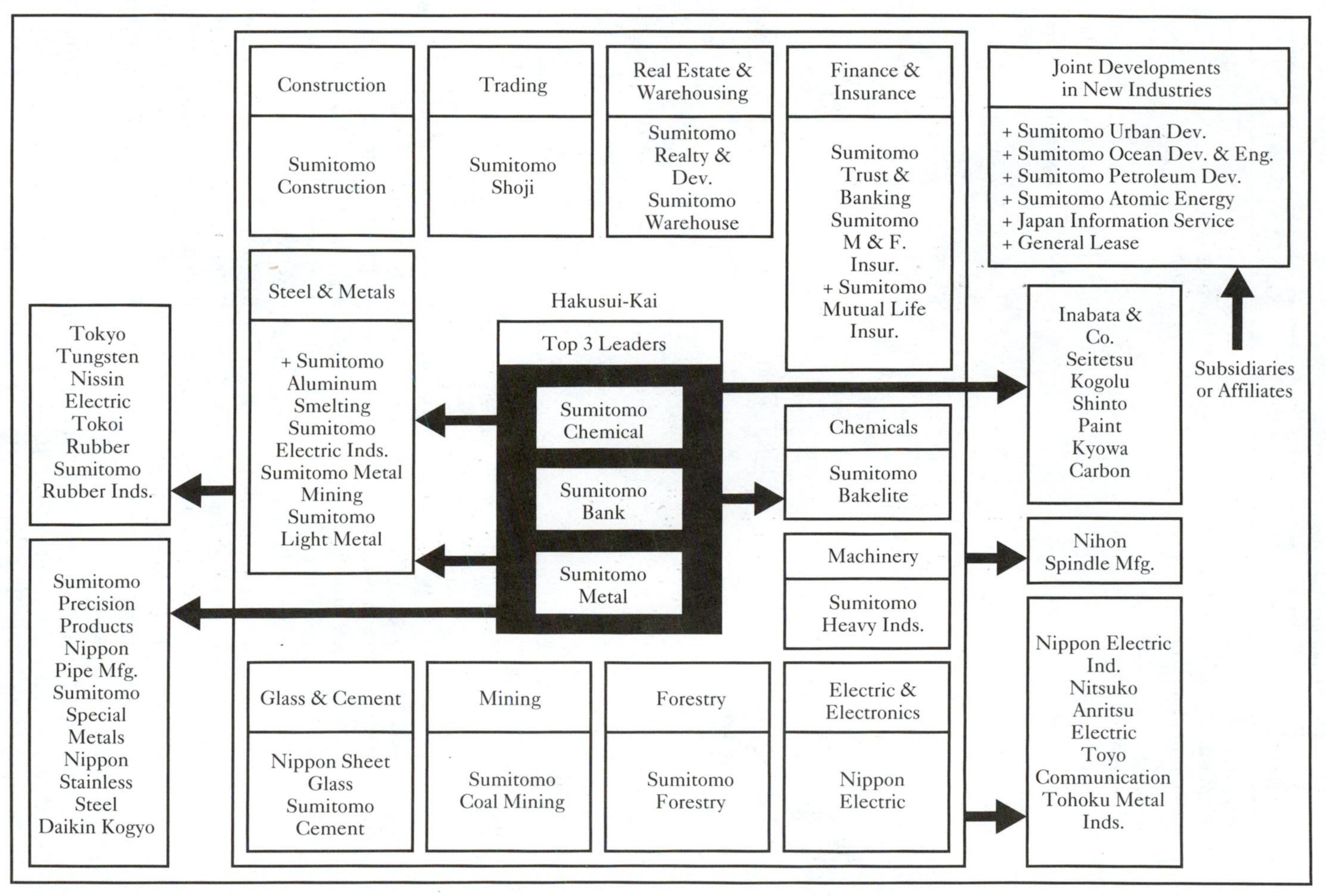

Source: Clyde V. Prestowitz Jr., *Trading Places: How We Allowed Japan to Take the Lead* (New York: Basic Books, 1988), 158.

TABLE 6-1 *The Sumitomo Keiretsu ($billions)*

Sumitomo	*Assets*	*Sales*	*Deposits*	*Loans*
Trading				
Sumitomo Trading Co.	48.9	155.2		
Sumitomo Forestry	3.6	6.0		
Banking				
Sumitomo Bank	531.8		435.4	352.0
Sumitomo Trust	305.3		277.5	133.0
Insurance			**Insurance in Force**	
Sumitomo Life	209.0			2,764.8
Industry				
Sumitomo Electric	11.2	10.2		
Sumitomo Marine	15.3	3.8		
Sumitomo Chemical	11.8	8.4		
Sumitomo Heavy Industry	6.7	4.5		
Sumitomo Metal	23.4	13.5		
Sumitomo Mining	5.8	4.1		
Sumitomo Rubber	4.8	4.5		
Total	1,177.6	210.2		485.0
Frame of reference				
Banking				
Sumitomo Bank	531.8		435.4	
Citicorp	216.6		145.1	
Insurance				
Sumitomo	209.1			2,764.1
Prudential	165.7			913.8

Source: *Forbes*, July 18, 1994, 235–242.

ing companies, each of which is represented in every country in the world. A trading company may be part of a keiretsu (Sumitomo is an example). Trading companies operate diverse businesses on their own while providing many services to member firms. They procure raw materials, distribute products, and finance some activities of member firms. They are involved in both exporting and importing and can absorb foreign exchange risks for their groups. Moreover, they engage in overseas transactions for Japanese firms as well as for buyers and sellers in other countries. Handling most of Japan's exports and imports, sogo shoshas serve as screening mechanisms to filter out any imports that might be damaging to members of a keiretsu. For example, if soda ash can be imported more cheaply than it could be made in Japan, a trading company could limit its importation to protect the Japanese company.

Table 6-2 presents the six major trading companies in Japan as measured by total revenue in 1994. Three of the six—Mitsui, Sumitomo, and Mitsubishi—are members of keiretsus. The top four trading companies had higher revenues than General Motors, which is the largest manufacturing firm in the world.

TABLE 6-2
The Six Major Japanese Trading Companies (millions of dollars)

Companies	*Revenues*
Mitsubishi	175,836
Mitsui	173,490
Itochu	167,825
Sumitomo	162,476
Marubini	150,187
Nissho Iwai	100,875
General Motors	154,951
Ford Motor	129,439

Source: *Fortune*, August 7, 1995, F-1.

The existence of the keiretsu has been a bone of contention between the United States and Japan to the point that the U.S. Federal Trade Commission started a probe of Japanese companies and their parts suppliers in the United States. The Japan-U.S. Structural Impediments Initiative involves the request by the United States that the Japan Fair Trade Commission enforce the antimonopoly provisions of Japanese antitrust laws.[15] The existence of the keiretsu does not mean that competition does not exist. There is much competition among the keiretsu companies, but they compete much more on quality than on price. The end result is speedy technological innovation and a rapid decline in the cost of production in Japan's manufacturing sector. They are world-class competitors in technology, manufacturing processes, and product development.

PUBLIC FINANCE

The public sector in Japan consists of the national government, local governments, and public enterprises. Unlike the United States and Germany, local governments in Japan have little fiscal autonomy and depend on transfers of income from the national government. Japan has followed a trend common in many countries around the world, privatizing certain state-owned industries, such as the telecommunications and railroad industries. But the role of the public sector in Japan is different from that in other countries. It is characterized by a small share of government consumption, a large share of government investment, and significant control over private sector funds through the use of government financial intermediaries.[16] The two major taxes in Japan are personal and corporate income taxes.[17] In 1992 Japan added a value-added tax to broaden its tax base.

15. After the Japanese defeat in 1945, the United States wrote a new constitution for Japan, changed its political system, and used its own antitrust laws to draft a set of Japanese laws, including antitrust. The Japanese Fair Trade Commissions is the equivalent of the U.S. Federal Trade Commission.
16. An example is the Ministry of Posts and Communications.
17. They accounted for 64 percent of total revenue in the 1991 Japanese budget.

Taxation in Japan

A characteristic of both Japanese personal and corporate income taxes is that the government changes the rates and exemptions each year. Annual changes in the tax laws constitute an important part of the government budgetary policy and are used to achieve certain economic and social objectives. For example, to stimulate savings, provisions of the personal income tax provide for tax exemption of interest income from deposits in postal savings accounts. Considerable use has been made of accelerated depreciation provisions to stimulate business investment. Some tax provisions promote the introduction of new products and technology. Provisions designed to stimulate exports and foreign investment exempt a certain part of income from exports and investments from taxes.[18]

Fiscal Policy

Japan has pursued relatively tight fiscal policies since 1982 to restrain growth in the national debt, which is around 70 percent of the Japanese GNP.[19] However, its trade surplus with the rest of the world caused other G-7 nations to pressure Japan to reduce its debt to them and to spend more money on internal growth. The government responded with a $35 billion ten-year plan to improve the Japanese infrastructure. Japanese fiscal policy has come to place more priority on stimulating internal growth. Priority in the 1991 budget was given to the improvement of social overhead capital, such as urban infrastructure and transportation. Japanese infrastructure is inferior to that in the West, particularly as measured by the percentage of the population served with water and sewer mains. Another fiscal policy measure is to reduce reliance on bonds to finance government expenditures in order to reduce interest payments on the national debt.

Social Security

Most workers in Japan are covered by any of six social security programs. The National Pension plan covers all workers and their spouses. Employees, both public and private, are covered by an additional plan. Most private employees participate in the employees' pension insurance program, which provides an earnings-related retirement benefit, and four other programs referred to as mutual aid associations cover public workers and some private workers. Basic benefits depend on the program. Retirement benefits are usually a flat amount per month based on years of contribution. Contributions come from employers, employees, and the government. Medical benefits are provided by employers and are retained by employees after retirement. Population aging has created a serious financial problem in Japan as it has in the other advanced countries.

18. Price Waterhouse, *Corporate Taxes: A Worldwide Survey*, 1990, 432.
19. OECD Economic Surveys, *Japan* (Paris: OECD, 1994), 50. Half of the debt is owned by the government.

The Banking System

The banking system of Japan can be divided into a number of institutions, with the Bank of Japan providing the connecting link. Japanese banks are classified as commercial banks, long-term credit banks, and foreign exchange banks. Some private financial institutions specialize in financing small and medium-sized enterprises and investment in agricultural equipment. In addition are government-owned financial institutions that supplement the functions of the private financial institutions. Included among the government financial institutions are the Japan Development Bank, Postal Savings, Export-Import Bank of Japan, Housing Loan Corporation, and Small Business Finance Corporation. Most of these government financial institutions were created after the end of World War II and currently play an important role in the financial operations of the nation.

The largest borrowers of funds in Japan are corporate business concerns, which dominate investment activities in the country. The biggest source of savings is private individuals who invest their money in postal savings accounts. This money, along with government trust and pension funds, is funneled into the government-owned lending institutions mentioned above. Large and medium-sized Japanese corporations borrow from private Japanese banks or issue stocks and bonds to raise money; small companies (usually subcontractors to the larger ones) get most of their loans from the government through the Small Business Finance Corporation.

The Central Bank. The Bank of Japan was established in 1882. Since its establishment, it has always served as the fiscal agent for the government. It provides the government with borrowing facilities and over the years has assumed a wide range of activities, including handling public receipts and payments, Treasury accounts, and government debt, and buying and selling foreign exchange.

The Bank of Japan also carries out a wide variety of activities with commercial banks and other institutions. These include receiving deposits, making loans, discounting bills and notes, and buying and selling Treasury bills. Commercial banks turn to the Bank of Japan as a source of funds the way U.S. banks borrow from the Federal Reserve. Since commercial banks depend on the central bank for credit, discount policy has played an important and effective role in maintaining general economic stability. A restriction of central bank credit has an immediate and significant impact on commercial bank policy.

Commercial Banks. Japan has become banker to the world. As Table 6-3 indicates, the seven largest banks in the world are Japanese; all are much larger than Citicorp, the largest U.S. banking institution. But it is not only the Japanese banks that are large. Nomura, the giant Japanese securities firm, has a global equity trading volume greater than Merrill Lynch, the leading American firm. The resources of the Japanese financial system give Japan unprecedented influence over how global resources are allocated. They also provide significant financial resources to Japanese industrial firms.

Government Financial Institutions. The government itself is engaged in substantial financial activities through its ownership of a number of specialized credit institutions. Loans are provided for long-term industrial development, export financing, and agriculture as part of government policy for stimulating economic growth in an economy where capital is scarce. These institutions obtain loanable funds from the special counterpart fund in the national budget and from individual savings in the form of postal savings, postal annuities, and postal life insurance. These savings and the surplus funds from special budgetary accounts are deposited in a trust fund bureau, which can use the funds for loans to public enterprises and financial institutions. Loans are also made to the private sector, particularly to industries that are export related. However, as a rule, private sector financing is undertaken in cooperation with private lending institutions.

The Export-Import Bank. The Japan Export-Import Bank provides long-term loans at subsidized interest rates to exporters of Japanese products. For example, loans have been provided for the construction of tankers, textile machinery, and railroad cars. Loans have also been provided to finance projects such as the development of iron ore mines in India and the construction of textile mills in South America. In addition, the bank provides financing and debt guarantees to attract foreign capital into Japan. To stimulate economic development in Southeast Asia, the government set up a special account with the bank called the Southeast Asia Development Corporation Fund. Funds were provided out of the national budget. The fund was eventually transformed into an independent corporation and currently finances long-term investment in Southeast Asia.

Japan Development Bank. Another important government-owned financial institution is the Japan Development Bank. The bank provides long-term loans at low interest rates to basic domestic industries. Through its control over loanable funds that are in the hands of official financial agencies like the Japan Development Bank, the government is able to exercise some control over national investment. It can thereby exert some influence with respect to its national economic plans.

TABLE 6-3
The Largest Banks in Japan (millions of dollars)

Bank	*Assets*
Sanwa	$624,393
Dai-Ichi Kangyo	622,927
Fuji	615,189
Sumitomo	613,856
Sakura	600,514
Mitsubishi	592,447
Norinchuken	513,341
Citicorp	250,489

Source: *Fortune*, August 7, 1995, F-2, F-3.

Another financial institution directly owned and operated by the government is the Small Business Finance Corporation, which provides long-term loans to small businesses when financing by ordinary financial institutions proves difficult. The government-owned Agriculture, Forestry, and Fisheries Finance Corporation provides long-term, low-interest loans for investment in agricultural equipment by agricultural cooperatives and individual farming enterprises. Loanable funds for both corporations are obtained from the national budget and from earnings on investments in securities and call loans.

The Ministry of Posts and Communications (MPT). This is the prime savings institution in Japan, with total savings of over one trillion dollars. Every housewife in Japan saves through the postal service, giving her savings to the mail carrier in her district for deposit in the post office. This money then goes to finance such government agencies as the Japan Development Bank. But the MPT does more than collect savings; it also regulates and structures the Japanese telecommunications industry.

Monetary Policy. The Bank of Japan has three instruments used to control the volume of credit and money—bank rate policy, open market operations, and reserve requirements. Bank rate policy involves the lowering or raising of discount rates and interest rates. The alteration of these rates is the most important monetary policy instrument in Japan because city banks rely heavily on loans from the Bank of Japan, and industries, in turn, rely heavily on bank loans. Costs in general and the availability of bank funds are highly responsive to changes in the discount and interest rates on commercial and export trade bills, overdrafts, and general secured loans. In addition, the Bank of Japan can place a ceiling on borrowing for each bank above which it can impose a penalty rate or refuse to make loans.

Open market operations are inhibited by the lack of a well-developed capital market and are not important as an instrument of monetary policy. Legal reserve requirements are far below the standard of reserve requirements in other major countries, and manipulation of these requirements by the Bank of Japan is a supplementary instrument of monetary control.

Labor-Management Relations

The distinctive feature of Japanese trade unions is that they are usually company unions. The typical Japanese labor union is made up of employees of a single company or of a single operational unit within a company, regardless of their occupation. Approximately one-fourth of the Japanese labor force belong to trade unions, with each union loosely tied to one of four central labor organizations. However, the central organizations have little authority over the company unions, which carry on the bargaining with employers. Negotiations between labor and management are conducted within each enterprise; however, the negotiations are conducted within the context of certain Japanese labor practices that differ from those in many other countries.

Many Japanese firms, in particular the larger ones, provide lifetime employment for their employees, which makes for a very different balance of power between union and management in Japanese firms. Employees know that their future depends on their company's future and that labor work stoppages could hurt their company's competitive position. Since it is difficult to obtain employment by leaving one company for another, the union will rarely press its demands so far as to seriously damage the company. Forcing a company into bankruptcy, for example, would put workers at the mercy of the labor market.

Positions within a company are determined largely on the basis of age and length of service, and Japanese companies routinely provide a number of fringe benefits for their employees. As a result, negotiations between labor and management in Japan are limited primarily to wages. During February through April each year, unions begin what is called the *shunto,* "spring wage struggle," with their respective companies. If agreement is not reached, the union may go out on strike, but since there is one union for each company, industry-wide strike efforts are rare. Unions may also resort to public demonstrations to make the community aware of their demands.

This is not to say that Japanese labor-management relations are perfect. There is industrial conflict, as evidenced by frequent wildcat strikes on the government-owned national railways. Worker-days lost through strikes, though much lower than in the United States, are higher than in Sweden or former West Germany. The number of work stoppages is also high in comparison to former West Germany and France. With the current emphasis on automation, the potential for labor conflict may well increase in Japan during the next few years. The failure of successive conservative governments to develop labor-oriented social welfare programs also provides a potential for labor unrest.

Japanese employers are also organized into several confederations, the largest of which is the Federation of Economic Organizations (*Keidanran*). It is made up of financial, industrial, and trading associations that include almost all of Japan's largest business firms. Membership in the federation is institutional, and its work is carried out by standing committees. Keidanran wields considerable influence in government economic policies because many business and political leaders share a common educational background and family ties. The federation provides the Japanese with a mechanism for reconciling industrial policy objectives with political and social goals.

Government and Business Relations

The combination of free enterprise and government control in Japan dates back to the Meiji Restoration in 1868. As previously mentioned, the government was active during the Meiji era in introducing Western industrial methods into Japan and also took the lead in promoting the development of industries of strategic importance. Fundamental shifts in government policy took place during the 1930s. To counteract the effects of the worldwide depression, state intervention in the economy increased. The electric power industry was nationalized in 1938, and other strategic industries were brought under government control.

After World War II, the government continued its role in the economy as an expediter of business development. Policies to increase exports encouraged mergers that resulted in large-scale business operations and the revival of the zaibatsu combines. Special tax privileges, subsidies, and low-interest loans were used to strengthen certain industries and certain types of economic activity. The Japanese government continues to exercise an important role in the nurturing of Japanese industry.

Ministry of International Trade and Industry (MITI). MITI is probably the most important and powerful government agency in Japan, at least as far as Japanese business is concerned. Created in the late 1940s to guide industrial modernization and promote exports, its mandate was to determine a basic course of action to improve Japan's future comparative advantage and to mobilize each sector to contribute to the whole. Building a steel industry was one of Japan's most important postwar priorities. MITI encouraged Japanese banks to supply the capital that purchased steel-producing equipment and technology from the West, mostly from the United States. Tax incentives, low-interest loans, and other financial incentives were also given to the steel industry. MITI has continued to restructure industry by concentrating resources in areas where it thinks Japan needs to be competitive in the future.[20]

MITI has a number of functions.[21] Its primary function is to offer guidance to Japanese industry. Providing the "big picture," so to speak, of where it thinks Japan as a nation should be heading, it develops an industrial policy for Japan and formulates and guides its implementation. It serves in a consultative capacity to other government agencies and is responsible for the flow of funds to favored industries. It has the power to grant licenses and patents and to determine which firms will get them. No plant, supermarket, or department store in Japan can be built without notification to and authorization from MITI. It has the power to suspend the antitrust laws and create cartels, either to aid industries in recession or to develop particular target industries. It has authority over electric power rates and other energy prices in Japan.[22]

Agency of Industrial Science and Technology (AIST). AIST is a semi-independent agency under the jurisdiction of MITI that is responsible for the promotion of technology. It monitors scientific and technical developments abroad and identifies new technology that will be important to Japanese industries. One of the strengths of Japanese industry is that it is well informed about worldwide scientific and technological developments. AIST consults with Japanese industry to encourage the use of new technologies that will further the national interest; it sponsors

20. The U.S. equivalent of MITI would include the Departments of Commerce and Energy, the Office of the U.S. Trade Administration, the Export-Import Bank, the Small Business Administration, the National Science Foundation, the Overseas Private Investment Corporation, the Environmental Protection Agency, and parts of the Departments of Commerce and Justice.
21. Prestowitz, *Trading Places*, 115.
22. Ibid., 117.

research that will make the needed technology available. It is also responsible for the development of patents.

INDUSTRIAL POLICY IN JAPAN

Industrial policy is a form of strategic planning. It outlines the basic strategy a nation intends to follow to achieve economic growth and meet foreign competition. There is nothing particularly unique about industrial policy. The former Soviet Union always incorporated such policy in its five-year economic plans, and the French have used it in their economic plans. Industrial policy involves choosing an industry or industries to emphasize at a particular point in time. For Japan, that time began after the end of World War II. The economy had been destroyed during the war, and it was necessary to devise a strategy for economic redevelopment. In the immediate postwar period, preferential financial treatment was given to developing coal and steel. Import restrictions were used to protect local industries, and exports were subsidized. Attention was also focused on developing the infrastructure, which had been destroyed during the war.[23]

The Ministry of International Trade and Industry (MITI) was given the responsibility for developing Japanese industrial policy. Priority was given to the attainment of economic growth through exports. In the 1950s tax incentives and subsidies were used to favor certain industries that would add to export earnings, which would then be used to modernize Japanese industries. Earnings from shipbuilding were used to modernize the steel industry. MITI believed that individual Japanese companies could not compete against foreign competitors, so it relaxed Japanese antitrust laws to permit megamergers between Japanese firms. It also coordinated investment to avoid overcapacity. In the 1960s priority was given to the production of automobiles for export to the rest of the world, and Japan eventually became a world leader. Recently there has been a shift in Japanese industrial policy to pursue objectives other than growth through exporting.[24]

Would Industrial Policy Work in the United States? During the late 1980s, industrial policy was in vogue in some academic circles because of its role in Japan's economic success. But what worked well in Japan would not work well in the United States, which has a far more decentralized form of government. Japan is not as large as California. Moreover, in Japan there is a close linkage between business and government; in the United States, to the contrary, the relationship between the two is quite adversarial. The institutional arrangements in the two countries also are totally different. Japanese society is based on group cooperation; U.S. society is not. Industrial policy in Japan was a result of the need to rebuild its economy after World War II. The best way to do this was to develop industries

23. The World Bank, *The East Asian Miracle* (New York: Oxford University Press, 1994), 101.
24. More emphasis is being placed on energy conservation and environmental protection.

that would export goods to obtain the money necessary to rebuild the economy.[25] Also, Japan, like South Korea and Taiwan, has few natural resources and had to make the best use of what it has.

AN EVALUATION OF THE JAPANESE ECONOMY

The Japanese economy developed a number of problems in the early 1990s. An economic slowdown was driven by restructuring in the corporate sector as a result of declining productivity and international competitiveness associated with an appreciation in the value of the yen relative to other currencies. Japanese direct investment abroad declined from $67.5 billion in 1989 to $34.1 billion in 1992.[26] Land values declined by one-third of their peak values in 1991, and Japanese banks, which had much of their assets tied up in land, lost money. Japanese business firms began to lose their international competitive position as a result of increasing labor costs and companies for the first time in years had to lay off workers.[27]

Appreciation of the Japanese Yen

The appreciation of the yen against other world currencies, but particularly against the U.S. dollar, has had a major impact on the Japanese economy. Table 6-4 presents a comparison of the yen-dollar exchange rate for selected time periods. As the table indicates, the yen has gained in value against the dollar. The increased value of the yen has increased labor and materials costs in Japan, thus increasing the cost of Japanese exports.[28] On the other hand, foreign producers were able to increase their share of the domestic market as the cost of imports in Japan decreased.[29]

Japanese Economic Indicators

Table 6-5 presents key economic indicators for Japan and the United States. Japanese money GDP is second only to that of the United States; unlike the United States, it has a positive balance in its merchandise trade and current accounts[30] and

25. South Korea used the same strategy to rebuild its economy, which was destroyed by the Korean War.
26. OECD Economic Surveys, *Japan* (Paris: OECD, 1994), 21.
27. This meant that Japanese companies that had a policy of guaranteed job employment had to lay off middle-level managers to reduce labor costs.
28. However, the strong yen has stimulated Japanese investment in other countries where labor costs are lower than in Japan. China and Malaysia are where Japanese investment is going.
29. Trade agreements with the United States have opened up Japanese markets to U.S. exporters. Nevertheless, in 1995 the United States imported around $59 billion more in goods from Japan than it exported to Japan.
30. The current account is the most important part of a country's balance of payments. It consists of four components: the merchandise trade account, which is the value of exports and imports of goods; the service account, which is the value of exports and imports of services; investment income from assets abroad and investment income going to other countries; and unilateral transfers.

TABLE 6-4
A Comparison of the U.S. Dollar and Japanese Yen Exchange Rates (yen per U.S. dollar)

Period	*Yen*
1969	358.36
1975	296.78
1980	226.63
1985	238.47
1990	145.00
1991	134.59
1992	126.78
1993	111.08
1994	102.18
1995 (April)	88.22
1995 (October)	99.04
1996 (May)	104.70

Source: *Economic Report of the President 1996* (Washington, D. C.: U.S. Government Printing Office, 1996), 400; *Wall Street Journal*, May 9, 1996, C17.

a deficit in its service account. Its real rate of economic growth, although erratic in the 1990s, was the highest for all major industrial countries during the 1980s. The rate of inflation as measured by the consumer price index has been the lowest for all industrial countries, and the unemployment rate for 1995 was just over one-half of the U.S. unemployment rate and one-third of the unemployment rate in the United Kingdom.

Strengths of the Japanese Economy

Lester Thurow posed the question of who, in economic terms, would own the twenty-first century—Japan, Europe, or America.[31] He listed various strengths the Japanese possess that will make them a serious contender. Among these strengths are cohesion and homogeneity, which give Japan an ability to focus its economic might that few other countries possess. Japanese culture is its major strength. Also, Japan is the world's largest creditor nation, with a trade surplus that has been averaging around $120 billion a year.[32] This surplus adds to the amount of Japanese savings that can be used to finance investment to secure future economic success. In head-to-head competition against U.S. and European firms, its companies have proved to be hard to beat. Japanese high school students score well in any international achievement test, and its ability to train workers in the labor force is unmatched. Moreover, Japan has the most equal distribution of income of all of the world's high-income economies. There is a far smaller gap between haves and have-nots in Japan than there is in the United States. The Japanese government has undertaken measures to promote more efficiency. Efforts have been made to

31. Lester Thurow, *Head to Head: The Coming Economic Battle Among Japan, Europe, and America* (New York: Morrow, 1992).
32. It was $135 in 1995.

TABLE 6-5 *A Comparison of Key Economic Indicators for Japan and the United States, 1994 and 1995**

	Japan	*United States*
Real GDP, 1994 ($ billions)	2,668.8	6,749.5
Real GDP growth, 1985–1994 (percent)	3.2	1.3
Merchandise exports ($ billions)	372.1	495.0
Merchandise imports ($ billions)	224.9	660.0
Merchandise trade balance ($ billions)	147.2	–165.0
Services ($ billions)	–4.0	50.0
Current account ($ billions)	136.0	–155.7
Industrial production (1987=100 percent)	115.8	121.9
Consumer price index (1982–1984=100 percent)	119.2	152.4
Unemployment rate, 1995	3.2	5.6

**1995 data are preliminary.*

Sources: The World Bank, *World Bank Atlas 1996* (Washington, D.C.: The World Bank, 1996), 18, 19; *Economic Report of the President 1996* (Washington, D.C.: U.S. Government Printing Office, 1996), 398, 399, 402; OECD Economic Surveys, *Japan* (Paris: OECD, 1994), 29–45.

deregulate the economy to promote competition. In particular, the inefficient distribution system, which has added as much as 20 percent to the cost of food, is being deregulated.[33] To improve access to the Japanese domestic market, active measures have been taken to lower barriers to imports and foreign direct investment. The former will lower food prices, and the latter will provide Japan access to new technology.

Weaknesses of the Japanese Economy

On March 29, 1995, Mitsubishi Bank and Bank of Tokyo announced a merger that, if consummated, would create the largest bank in the world with assets of $820 billion.[34] This merger reflects the problems that have existed in the Japanese banking system, in particular property loans that turned bad when Japanese real-estate values declined by as much as 30 percent in the early 1990s. In 1994 Japan's major banks disclosed that they had lost $134 billion in property loans. However, despite the decline in land values, land still remains an expensive proposition in Japan. Real land prices in Japan have risen by more than 6 percent a year on average during the period 1955–1994, an overall increase of twelve times.[35] This has made the distribution of property wealth in Japan more unequal. Table 6-6 presents an international comparison of housing prices.

The Japanese economy also faces other weaknesses. Demographics is probably its most serious problem. Nowhere in the industrial world is the phenomenon of population aging occurring more rapidly than in Japan. By the year 2025, it is

33. OECD Economic Surveys, *Japan* (Paris: OECD, 1994), 29.
34. *Wall Street Journal*, March 29, 1995, 1.
35. OECD, *Japan*, 73.

TABLE 6-6 *International Comparison of Housing Prices, 1990 or 1991 (dollars)*

Housing	*Japan*	*France*	*Germany*	*United Kingdom*	*United States*
Detached house, nationwide					
Price	442,000		262,000	168,800	100,300
Ratio to average earnings	15.5		9.8	7.5	3.9
Detached house, capital city					
Price	660,100		436,800	244,100	
Ratio to average earnings	20.6		16.4	10.8	
Apartment, capital city					
Price	457,000	263,600	156,100	140,200	
Ratio to average earnings	13.5	11.4	5.8	6.2	

Source: OECD Economic Surveys, *Japan* (Paris: OECD, 1994), 80.

predicted that it will have the oldest population in the world.[36] This will have a major impact on the Japanese economy in that it will increase the demand for government social services. Financing new and expanding government services will required revisions in the Japanese fiscal system as the number of persons 65 and older is projected to hit 42 percent by the year 2020. The size of the Japanese labor force will decline relative to the number of retirees.

SUMMARY

At one time, Japan was supposed to be the heir apparent to the United States as the world's leading economic superpower. It had grown faster and invested more in future growth than any other country. It became the world's largest creditor nation, with the world's largest trade surplus. Its market share of world exports increased steadily, and its manufacturing firms often dominated competition against American and European firms. But times have changed, and although Japan is still a major economic power, there is little likelihood that it will catch up with the United States. Its success has been driven by an export-led economy, and domestic industries have often been inefficient by world standards. Japan will find it increasingly difficult to use exports as the leading edge for its domestic economy. To grow faster than the rest of the world, Japan's export industries will have to capture larger and larger foreign market share, and this is not likely to happen.

But Japan also has other problems. The use of poison gas by religious extremists in the Tokyo subway system illustrates how vulnerable Japan can be to terrorism. The earthquake that destroyed much of Kobe illustrates another problem, the ever present possibility of natural disasters. Life expectancy in Japan is the highest in the world, which means that the Japanese will live longer and will cost

36. "The Economics of Ageing," *The Economist,* January 27, 1996, Survey, 1–16.

more in terms of the provision of social services. The birthrate has been declining, so fewer Japanese will enter the labor force. Japan's strength is its cohesive internal culture based on history, tradition, and language, but this can also become a weakness. Its culture, which is very difficult to join, may not absorb workers from other societies.

QUESTIONS FOR DISCUSSION

1. Discuss the relationship between government and business in Japan.
2. What are some of the problems confronting the Japanese economy?
3. What is a keiretsu? What is a sogo shosha?
4. What is industrial policy? How does it work in Japan?
5. Should the United States have an industrial policy?
6. Discuss the role of the Ministry of International Trade and Industry (MITI) in the Japanese economy.
7. Discuss some of the ways in which Japanese government provides financial support to business.
8. Explain some of the factors that have been responsible for a high rate of personal saving in Japan.
9. Will the next century be known as the Japanese century?

RECOMMENDED READINGS

Bergsten, C. Fred, and Marcus Noland, *Reconcilable Differences?* Washington, D.C.: Institute for International Economics, 1993.

Cutts, Robert. "Capitalism in Japan: Cartels and Keiretsus." *Harvard Business Review*, Vol. 70, No. 4 (July-August 1992), 48–55.

Ito, Takatoshi. *The Japanese Economy*. Cambridge, Mass.: MIT Press, 1991.

Lincoln, Edward J. *Japan's New Global Role*. Washington, D.C.: The Brookings Institution, 1993.

OECD Economic Surveys. *Japan*. Paris: OECD, 1994.

Porter, Michael. *The Competitive Advantage of Nations*. New York: Free Press, 1990, 384–421.

The World Bank. *The East Asian Miracle*. New York: Oxford University Press, 1993.

Tsuru, Shigeto. *Japan's Capitalism: Creative Defeat and Beyond*. New York: Cambridge University Press, 1992.

Wood, Christopher. *The Bubble Economy*. London: Sidgwick and Jackson, 1992.

Woronoff, Jan. *Japan as Anything but Number One*. Armonk, N.Y.: M. E. Sharpe, 1991.

Yoshihara, Kunco. *Japanese Economic Development*. New York: Oxford University Press, 1994.

FORMER EAST AND WEST GERMANY

CHAPTER 7

Germany

The former West Germany and East Germany have reunited after forty years of separation. Germany is a world economic superpower, ranking behind only the United States and Japan in total GNP. It is one of the leading export countries in the world,[1] and many of its industries are world-class competitors. Nevertheless, it is not free of economic and social problems. The cost of absorbing East Germany has proved to be much greater than expected and probably will add up to a trillion dollars by the end of the century. This has already put a strain on the German budget and on the capital market. Social strain is also evident, as thousands of Eastern Europeans have poured into Germany in search of better jobs.[2]

There are similarities between Germany and Japan and between Germany and the United States. Germany and Japan started the process of industrialization

1. It ranked second only to the United States in 1994 and 1995, but was first in 1993.
2. Russians and Ukrainians have moved to Poland in search of jobs, while Poles have moved to Germany.

at about the same time. In both countries, government became a supporter of industrial development. This continues to hold true today. The German political system is similar to that of the United States. Both are federal republics, with three levels of government—federal, state, and local. The political structure reflects the fact that Germany was once a federation of states. Both federal governments have a bicameral legislature.[3] In Germany there are sixteen state governments (*Lander*), including five that were formerly part of East Germany. The basic unit of German government is the *Gemeinde*, or township. There is also the *Landkreise*, which corresponds to a U.S. county.

After World War II, that part of a divided Germany that eventually became West Germany relied on a free market policy instead of state controls to accomplish recovery from the devastation brought about by the war. The guiding concept that governed this policy was called *Soziale Marktwirtschaft*, or social market economy, which had been formulated by a group of economists at the University of Freiburg during the war. They believed that political freedom and maximization of welfare could be ensured only by the creation and maintenance of free market competition.[4] Competition would be enforced by the government through the banning of restrictive business practices, the creation of a monopoly office designed to reduce the power of cartels, and encouragement of competition by various instruments of economic policy. Soziale Marktwirtschaft today has come to mean a combination of a market economy coupled with an elaborate and expensive social welfare system.

East Germany was a part of the *Zuzammenbruch* (breakup) that occurred after Hitler's Third Reich was defeated in World War II. It was created out of the provinces of Prussia, Thuringia, Pomerania, Brandenburg, and Saxony and was occupied by the Russian army. Its industrial base was partially destroyed by the war, and what machinery and rail transportation remained were carted away to the Soviet Union. Much of East Germany was agricultural, made up of large estates owned by the Junkers, the land-owning aristocracy of Prussia. Walter Ulbricht, a German Communist who had fled Germany when Hitler came to power, became the first president. Agriculture was collectivized, and a Stalinist economic model was introduced into the country, which formally became the German Democratic Republic in 1949. After millions of Germans had fled to the West, the Wall was built in 1961.

GERMAN REUNIFICATION

It was said that if a socialist system wouldn't work in East Germany, it couldn't work anywhere. The East Germans possessed the famous Prussian self-discipline, the Protestant work ethic,[5] and other socioeconomic factors necessary to build a

3. The German legislative bodies are the Bundestag and Bundesrat. The Bundesrat, which is the upper house, is appointed by the states but does not propose legislation.
4. Germany was controlled by the Nazis and before them by the Kaisers.
5. The Protestant Reformation began in East Germany. Most East Germans were Lutheran.

successful economy. Also, East Germany boasted the highest living standard of any socialist country. It had implemented Stalin's model of democratic centralism and its application to economic organization more rigorously than its Eastern European neighbors, and its leaders were slavish in their devotion to the Soviet Union. Moreover, its efficient secret police (*Stasi*) made the Soviet KGB look like amateurs when it came to controlling the population.[6] Finally, the Wall,[7] built to separate East Germany from West Germany, created a closed society in which the state had complete control over resource allocation.

The collapse of East Germany was sudden and unexpected. It began in the summer and fall of 1989 when thousands of East Germans literally beat down the doors to get out of East Germany and into West Germany.[8] There were several reasons for the collapse, not least of which was exposure to West German television that revealed the differences in living standards between East Germans and West Germans, differences that widened during the 1980s. Outdated production techniques at the plant level were combined with sectoral monopolies for final products, eliminating competition and stifling innovation and efficiency. Moreover, a newer generation of East Germans simply did not share the devotion to socialism of many of their elders. They were more concerned about such issues as human rights, peace, and the environment. However, many wanted to reform East German society rather than integrate with West Germany, while still others wanted economic reunification and the benefits it would bring.[9]

A COMPARISON OF WEST GERMANY AND EAST GERMANY

West Germany and East Germany afford an excellent comparison between a capitalist country and a Communist country, because they existed side by side for forty years and had a common heritage. The Federal Republic of Germany (FRG), or West Germany, was created out of the Western portion of the German Reich and was divided into a British, an American, and a French zone of occupation. East Germany, as mentioned above, fell under the Soviet sphere of influence, and from it the German Democratic Republic (DDR) was created. Silesia, a third part of Hitler's Reich, was given to Poland and is now a part of that country.

6. The Stasi (Staatsicherheitsdienst) was the East German equivalent of the Gestapo, which was the control mechanism used by the Nazis. Altogether, it had 200,000 full-time and part-time members in a country of 17 million. Its activities were based on the assumption that every person was a security risk, and state security took precedence over the law. Virtually every public and private assembly included a Stasi agent to report on what was said.

7. The Wall is commonly referred to as the Berlin Wall. Newspaper and television carried pictures of demonstrators on top of the Berlin Wall, which was only a part of the Wall.

8. To add insult to injury, it came at a time when East Germany was in the process of celebrating the fortieth anniversary of its creation.

9. Peter H. Merkl, *German Reunification in the European Context* (University Park, Pa.: Penn State University Press, 1993), 48–49.

Almost from the beginning, the development of the two Germanies was different. Marshall Plan aid played an important role in the revival of West Germany. Some $4.5 billion was spent to help it recover from war losses. This aid supported the modernization of plants and equipment by supplying foreign exchange and investment funds. A contrary approach was taken by the Soviets in East Germany. The Soviet economy, including much of its industrial base, had been severely damaged by the Germans during World War II.[10] To compensate for their losses, the Soviets dismantled and hauled off to plants in the Soviet Union East German machinery, trains, railroad ties, and vast amounts of other items.

As the two Germanies went their separate ways, the West German economy relied on market forces and incentives to recover from the devastation brought about by World War II. This reliance, coupled with extensive social welfare programs, became German economic and social policy to today.[11] An opposite approach was taken in East Germany. At first, private enterprise was permitted and existed side by side with a socialized sector. However, as East German Communists, who were under the direction of Moscow, were able to gain more control over the economy, industry and agriculture were placed under state control, and the first formal economic plan was introduced in 1949.

A Comparison of West Germany and East Germany Before World War II

It cannot be said that East Germany was an underdeveloped region upon which a Stalinist growth model imposed a policy of forced economic development. Before World War II, it was the agricultural breadbasket of Germany; moreover, it had a well-defined industrial base. It was the locus of much of Germany's chemical industry and produced office, textile, and precision machinery and a wide line of automobiles. All of Germany's production of electrical goods was centered in East Germany. World leadership in the production of optical goods was held by the Carl Zeiss firm of Jena, which became part of East Germany. In terms of living standards and level of income, there was little difference between East and West Germany before World War II.[12] In fact, per capita industrial output was 16 percent higher and per capita income 6 percent higher in East Germany than in West Germany.[13]

East Germany was the clear leader in agricultural production before the war. It was the food base for Germany, and it produced products for export including grain, sugar beets, and potatoes. After the war the area became a perennial grain importer and a major food-deficit region. East Germany also had advantages in

10. The Soviet Union lost 20 million people during World War II.

11. Henry Wallich, *Mainsprings of the German Revival* (Princeton: Van Nostrand, 1963).

12. The investment policies of Hitler's Third Reich concentrated on increasing industrial output in eastern Germany to prepare for the eventual war with Russia.

13. Bruno Gleitze, *Ostdeutschland Wirtschaft* (West Berlin: Duncker and Humblot, 1956), 191–193.

land fertility. Table 7-1 presents comparisons of agricultural productivity in the pre–World War II areas of East and West Germany and during more recent years. As the table indicates, agricultural productivity was in general higher in East Germany than in West Germany before the war.

During the period from 1945 to 1960, East German economic growth lagged behind that of West Germany. It was not until 1959 that East Germany regained the level of economic development its area had achieved in 1939, while the West German economy had attained this level by 1952.[14] Per capita East German GNP ran consistently about 75 percent of the West German level during the same period. Using 1936 as a base year of 100 percent for both East and West Germany, East German GNP was 77 percent of the base in 1950, compared to 117 percent of the base for West Germany. In 1955 the respective percentages were 108 and 184, and in 1960, 137 and 249. To some extent circumstances had worked against the East German economy in that its recovery had been delayed by Soviet dismantling policies. On the other hand, it had the advantage of a command economy and could force resources into the production of capital goods.

The Wall was erected in 1961 to prevent the continuing exodus of East Germans to West Germany. East Germany was walled in from the West for twenty-eight years. It failed to narrow the gap in productivity and living standards with West Germany; on the contrary, productivity began to lag far behind that of West Germany as the system became more and more inflexible. The pursuit of economic self-sufficiency isolated it from technological developments that were happening in the world. Investment was concentrated in a few selected industries, while other industries were ignored. Energy use was inefficient and wasteful. Above all, the hard-line leaders refused to consider any form of economic and social reform.

East Germany and West Germany Compared on the Eve of Reunification

As reunification began, the East German economy was far worse off than anyone had supposed. Its standard of living was well below that of West Germany, and its GNP was about one-tenth that of West Germany.[15] Its average gross wage was about one-third and its net take-home pay about 40 percent of that of West Germany. It had enormous environmental problems, particularly in the chemical and energy sectors. More than half of its foreign trade was with other CMEA[16] countries, and it had a net foreign debt in convertible currencies of some $16 billion

14. Edward M. Snell and Marilyn Harper, "Postwar Economic Growth in East Germany: A Comparison with West Germany," Joint Economic Committee, 91st Cong., 2nd Sess., 1970.
15. Leslie Lipschitz, "The Two Economies on the Eve of Reunification," in *German Reunification: Economic Issues,* Leslie Lipschitz and Donogh McDonald, eds. (Washington, D.C.: International Monetary Fund, 1990), 1–5.
16. CMEA, or Council for Mutual Economic Assistance, was a trading bloc consisting of the Soviet Union, Poland, East Germany, Czechoslovakia, Romania, and Bulgaria. Most of these countries' foreign aid was with each other.

TABLE 7-1
Agricultural Production in East and West Germany for Selected Years

Year	*FRG*	*DDR*
	*All Grains**	
1935–1938	22.4	23.9
1970	33.4	28.2
1984	53.6	45.1
	*Potatoes**	
1935–1938	185.0	194.3
1970	272.3	195.7
1984	331.5	224.0
	*Sugar Beets**	
1935–1938	327.2	301.2
1970	444.2	320.1
1984	494.7	325.3
	*Milk***	
1935–1938	2,436.0	2,549.0
1970	4,126.0	3,314.0
1984	5,120.0	4,187.0

**Doppelzentners: 1 doppelzentner = 100 kilograms*
***Kilograms*

Source: Deutscher Bundestag. *Materialien zum Bericht zur Lage der Nation im geteilten Deutschland 1967* (Bonn: Verlag Dr. Hans Heger, 1967), 412; *Materialien zum Bericht zur Lage der Nation im geteilten Deutschland 1987* (Bonn: Verlag Dr. Hans Heger, 1987), 441–442.

(more than one-tenth of its GNP) at the end of April 1990. Its industrial system was obsolete in the structure of both capital and products, and its level of labor productivity was about 35 percent that of West Germany. The range of consumer products was limited, and luxury goods were unavailable.

Industry. East German industry was overrated by Western experts. It may have been the best of the East European bloc countries, but it was uncompetitive by Western standards. Industrial production amounted to around a fourth of that of West Germany. Because the service sector was weak, the industrial sector accounted for two-thirds of national output, compared to 40 percent in West Germany.[17] Even the elite industries, those into which the state poured the most money, were outmoded by Western standards. Particularly weak was the transportation system, most of which was built before World War II. Only 16 percent of

17. Deutsche Bank, Economics Department, *Special: East Germany* (Frankfurt, December 1989), 5.

the railroad system was electrified, compared to 98 percent in West Germany, and the rolling stock (locomotives and freight and passenger cars) was old.[18]

East German industries had a number of problems that will take time and money to correct, including the following.[19]

1. *Chemicals.* Although the East German chemical industry was the country's elite industry and many plants, particularly those producing petrochemicals, were modern, other plants dated back to before World War II. Very few products fit into the West German chemical mix because of their inferior quality.
2. *Steel.* The East German steel industry was outmoded and uncompetitive by Western standards. An estimated 40 percent of steel was produced by the open-hearth method, a process not used in West Germany for at least twenty years. Many plants dated back to before World War II. In contrast to the West German steel industry, the steel industry employed too many workers.
3. *Mechanical engineering and motor vehicles.* This was East Germany's most important export industry, with its products going to the other CMEA members. It was the main supplier of agricultural machinery to the Soviet Union and also provided railroads, machine tools, and earthmoving equipment. However, there were problems of adaptation in the West German economy. The proportion of computer-controlled machinery in these East German industries was one-third that of West Germany, and technology used in automobile production was outdated by at least twenty years.
4. *Electronics, data processing, precision engineering, and optical equipment.* Much money was invested in these areas. Optical equipment made by the Carl Zeiss company was of world-class quality before World War II and remained of good quality.[20] The area of telecommunications was woefully weak and the expense of converting it into a first-class system will be around $70 billion. As for data processing, a single combine (*Kombinat*) made all of the parts and the finished product, which created numerous problems, because if one section broke down, everything broke down.
5. *Food.* Food products were of poor quality and limited in supply and variety. The quality of supply had worsened over the preceding twenty years. The negative effect of striving for self-sufficiency was felt here.
6. *Housing.* Housing was of poor quality. Two-thirds of all housing in East Germany was built before World War II. Building materials were of low quality. Rents were subsidized, and there was little incentive to build houses.

Organization of East German Industry. The economic plan was the be-all and end-all of the East German economic system, and thus everything had to be cen-

18. Deutsche Bank, *Special: East Germany*, 1989, 11.
19. Deutsche Bank, *Special: East Germany*, 1989, 8–10.
20. The Zeiss family has now reclaimed its former ownership.

tralized and implemented from the top down.[21] East German industrial production was concentrated in large state enterprises, which were integrated both horizontally and vertically. Enterprises in a particular sector and their suppliers were formed into industrial combines (*Kombinate*). Each combine was responsible for developing its long-range and annual production plans and coordinating all of the plans of its member enterprises. In 1988 there were 126 national combines, 95 regional combines, and 3,408 state enterprises.[22] The combines accounted for 98 percent of industrial employment, production, and exports, but they and the firms they represented became top-heavy with managers and bureaucrats and thus inflexible.

East German and West German industry can be compared in two ways. First, East German industry was far more concentrated and labor-intensive. The typical state enterprise in East Germany employed on the average ten times as many workers. This can be attributed in part to the guarantee of full employment in the East German system, which made it virtually impossible to lay off unneeded workers. In East Germany industrial production and employment were dominated by large state enterprises. In 1988 state enterprises with fewer than 500 workers provided 12 percent of industrial jobs and production; in West Germany more than two million firms with fewer than 500 workers accounted for two-thirds of the industrial jobs and 40 percent of production. Table 7-2 compares number of employees per enterprise in East and West Germany in 1988 in selected industries.

Labor Productivity. Productivity in East and West German industry can also be compared. For each branch of industry, production is divided by employment to obtain comparable productivity values for the two countries. The results of the comparison for three time periods are shown in Table 7-3. They are as follows:

1. Labor productivity was lower in East German industry than in West German industry. This can be attributed in part to the fact that relatively more workers were employed in East German industry than in West German industry, causing diseconomies of scale. Differences in labor productivity varied considerably from industry to industry.
2. Those industries that were given priority in terms of allocation of investment funds did not achieve productivity anywhere near the West German level. This can be attributed in part to the fact that the degree of automation was far greater in the FRG than in the DDR.
3. The East German economic plans contributed to a lack of flexibility in production. Production bottlenecks in certain industries occurred on numerous occasions.

21. East German planning was the same as in other socialist countries, but even more centrally controlled. It had three sets of plans—a long-term plan of fifteen years, a five-year plan, and an annual operating plan.
22. *Statistisches Jahrbuch der DDR* (Berlin: Staatsverlag der DDR, 1989), 138–139.

Agriculture. Organization of agriculture in East Germany was very similar to that of industry. Agriculture was controlled by the state through economic planning. The supply and price of inputs, the share of output marketed, the prices paid for agricultural products, and farm income and expenditures were regulated by the plan. Overall procurement goals were established for agricultural products that were to be delivered to state procurement agencies. Given the procurement goals that were supplemented by local requirements, each agricultural unit had to formulate a production plan. Planning was from the top down, with control flowing from the Ministry of Agriculture to the regional and local levels.

TABLE 7-2 *Industrial Employment Structures in East Germany and West Germany, 1988*

	East Germany	*West Germany*
	(Employees per Enterprise)	*(Employees per Enterprise)*
Chemical industry	1,419	296
Metal industry	3,209	474
Construction materials	712	71
Electronics, electrical engineering	1,554	333
Automotive industry	838	217
Textile industry	1,301	169
Food industry	480	125

Source: Gerhart Fels and Claus Schnabel, *The Economic Transformation of East Germany: Some Preliminary Lessons* (Washington, D.C.: Group of Thirty, 1991), 13.

TABLE 7-3 *Industrial Worker Productivity in East and West Germany (DDR as percentage of FRG = 100)*

Industry	*1970*	*1980*	*1988*
Power and fuels	61	37	45
Chemicals, synthetic fiber, rubber	34	44	55
Metallurgy	41	39	—
Construction	44	44	40
Water production and use	62	56	—
Steel, machinery, vehicles	44	46	45
Electronics, precision, and optics	38	43	50
Textiles	53	57	55
Consumer goods	55	58	56
Food, beverages, and tobacco (average)	60	43	40
Average	48	44	48

Source: Deutscher Bundestag, *Materialin zur Lage der Nation im geteilten Deutschland 1987* (Bonn: Verlag Dr. Hans Heger, 1987), 392; Deutsche Bank, Economics Department, *Special: East Germany* (Frankfurt, December 1989), 8–11.

The two basic agricultural units were the state farms and the collective farms. The state farms were owned by the government and operated as regular industrial entities with managers and hired workers. The state farms were large; in 1988 there were 465 state farms, 311 of which were in animal production. The average state farm contained 24,000 acres.[23] State farms were subsidized out of the state budget, and output, as mentioned previously, was determined by a production plan. The collective farm was socially owned; that is, the land was farmed by individual farmers who pooled their talents and resources and operated on a collective basis. In 1988 there were 3,855 collective farms.[24] The average collective farm was around 3,000 acres in size. There were very few private farms, but ownership of private plots was permitted. As much as 40 percent of all fruit, eggs, and poultry were produced on private plots.

Table 7-4 compares agricultural productivity in East and West Germany for two time periods (1970 and 1984). There are different farm entities involved: private farms in West Germany and state and collective farms in East Germany. The average size of the West German farm was much smaller, averaging around 44 acres, compared to 24,000 acres for the average East German state farm and 3,000 for the average collective farm. In 1988 around 10 percent of the East German labor force was employed in agriculture, compared to 3 percent in West Germany. East German agricultural productivity left much to be desired. Labor productivity was 40 percent of the level in West Germany; productivity as measured by land area was around 75 percent.[25]

Living Standards

Although East Germany had the highest living standard of all of the Soviet bloc economies, it was well below that of West Germany. Moreover, the living standards of the two countries grew farther apart during the 1980s. When money wages are translated into real wages (which represent the purchasing power of money wages) some goods cost less in East Germany than in West Germany while other goods cost more. However, it is necessary to remember that basic necessities, particularly food, rent, and transportation, were subsidized by the East German government. The prices charged by the state to consumers bore little or no resemblance to production costs or procurement costs paid to farms. Many consumer goods were priced well below cost, but prices for such items as coffee and fruit were maintained at high levels.

Moreover, differences in quality between East and West German goods were pronounced. For example, West German automobiles were far superior to East German automobiles. When reunification occurred, the first thing many East Germans did was to get rid of their automobiles and purchase West German cars. The

23. *Statistisches Jahrbuch der DDR, 1989*, 181.
24. Ibid.
25. West German agriculture is not as productive as it is in some other European countries.

TABLE 7-4 *A Comparison of Agricultural Productivity in East and West Germany for 1970 and 1984*

Produce	*Year*	*FRG*	*DDR*	*DDR as percent of FRG*
All grains[a]	1970	33.4	28.2	84.4
	1984	53.6	45.1	84.1
Wheat	1970	37.5	35.6	93.9
	1984	62.6	52.3	82.5
Rye	1970	30.8	26.8	70.8
	1984	43.9	35.0	79.7
Barley	1970	32.2	30.1	93.5
	1984	51.3	47.8	93.2
Potatoes	1970	272.3	195.7	71.9
	1984	331.5	244.0	73.6
Sugar beets	1970	444.2	320.1	72.1
	1984	494.7	325.3	65.8
Clover	1970	78.1	72.8	93.2
	1984	84.5	115.1	136.2
Corn	1970	444.9	348.0	78.2
	1984	435.5	300.6	69.0
Milk[b]	1970	4,126.0	3,314.0	80.3
	1984	5,120.0	4,187.0	82.0
Meat (beef)[c]	1970	171.0	116.0	67.8
	1984	180.0	1130	60.1
Meat (pork)	1970	146.0	94.0	64.4
	1984	160.0	107.0	66.9
Chicken (eggs)[d]	1970	220.0	168.0	76.4
	1984	265.0	217.0	81.9

[a]*Kilos per hectare: A kilo is 2.2 pounds; a hectare is 2.47 acres.* [b]*Kilos per milk cow.* [c]*Kilos in beef and pork.* [d]*Number of eggs per laying hen.*

Source: Deutscher Bundestag, *Materialin zum Bericht zur Lage der Nation im geteilten Deutschland, 1987* (Bonn:

quality of East German housing was also inferior. Living area per person in East Germany was smaller than in West Germany, and 40 percent of all housing in East Germany had been constructed before World War II. In 1987 over half of all East German housing units were without central heating and a bathroom. Although a West German family unit got more housing in terms of size and quality than an East German family unit, rent was much higher and constituted a much larger proportion of total expenditures.

Table 7-5 compares the amount of work time in East Germany and West Germany required to earn enough money to buy consumer goods such as television sets and cars. As the table indicates, the West German worker clearly had superior purchasing power in terms of time invested. Moreover, the time difference widened over time. For example, it took approximately 32 hours for a West German

TABLE 7-5
Purchasing Power in East and West Germany as Measured by Work Time Necessary to Earn Money to Purchase (hours and minutes)

Type of Purchase	*West Germany*	*East Germany*
Men's shirt	1.22	7.19
Men's shoes	5.20	24.01
Men's suit	10.49	59.30
Women's pantyhose	0.12	2.40
Women's dress	4.44	21.30
Children's shoes	2.35	7.21
Radio-cassette	13.36	207.09
Color TV	81.34	1,008.56
Washing machine	59.09	491.04
Refrigerator	29.54	272.19
Vacuum cleaner	13.32	82.09
Car	694.33	4,375.00
Railroad fare, 15 kilometers	1.46	0.27
Dark bread, 1 kg.	0.12	0.07
Sugar, 1 kg.	0.07	0.17
Butter, 1 kg.	0.36	1.39
Eggs, dozen	0.10	0.36
Milk, litre	0.05	0.07
Cheese, 1 kg	0.52	1.43
Pork cutlets, 1 kg.	1.01	1.47
Apples, 1 kg.	0.09	0.15
Lemon, 1 kg.	0.16	0.54
Coffee, 250 g.	0.21	4.20

Source: Bundesministerium für Innerdeutsche Beziehungen, *Zahlenspiegel Bundesrepublik Deutschland/Deutsche Demokratische Republik*, Ein Vergleich, Bonn, 1989, 77–78.

worker to earn enough to buy a suit in 1969, compared to about 49 hours for the East German worker. The respective times in 1987 were about 11 hours and 60 hours.[26]

The Environment

Pollution has a direct impact on quality of life because it subtracts from real income. East and West Germany can be compared according to the extent to which each country polluted its environment. East German industry was not only far more inefficient than West German industry, but it was also a greater contributor to pollution of the environment. Four-fifths of energy requirements were met by

26. Bundesministerium für Innerdeutsche Beziehungen, *Zahlenspiegel Bundesrepublik Deutschland/Deutsche Demokratische Republik*, Ein Vergleich, Bonn, 1989, 77–78; Deutschland Archiv, Vergleich der Deutschen Lebenstandarte, May 1970, 5–7.

the use of brown (lignite) coal. The poor quality of the coal and the low level of efficiency of outdated plants meant that there was a high amount of energy waste and also a high level of pollution. East German power plants were not equipped with desulphurization/denitrification systems. Although its land area was one-half and its population one-fourth that of West Germany, East Germany emitted 4.7 million tons of sulfur dioxide in 1982 compared to 3.0 million tons for West Germany.[27] Pollution has had a negative effect on the East German ecosystem, particularly in the destruction of fish and wildlife.[28]

Income Distribution

It can be assumed that incomes are more evenly distributed in a socialist economy than in a capitalist economy. This is certainly true when East and West Germany are compared. Food, housing, and transportation were subsidized in East Germany, and its wage structure was compressed to narrow income differentials among occupation groups and blue-collar, white-collar, and professional workers. A truck driver or construction worker would make as much or perhaps more than a college professor or a doctor. In comparing average monthly wages in similar occupational categories in East and West Germany, there was a differential of 270 marks a month between the highest-paying occupation (transportation) and the lowest-paying occupation (construction) in East Germany and a difference of 2,336 deutsche marks (DM) between the highest-paying occupation (banking and financial services) and the lowest-paying occupation (retailing) in West Germany.[29]

A comparison of average industrial wages in East Germany and West Germany for January 1990—before economic and political reunification occurred—is shown in Table 7-6. The monthly average industrial wage of the East German worker was around 40 percent that of the West German worker. Labor productivity per East German worker was less than one-third of the West German level. Also included in Table 7-6 are the average taxes and social security contributions paid. East German workers paid no income tax, and rent was subsidized by the state. The West German currency unit is used.

Role of Women in East and West Germany

Kaiser Wilhelm was the original male chauvinist. His view of the role of women in pre–World War I German society was summarized in three words: *Kinder, Kirche,*

27. "Luftverunreinigung in der DDR: Die Emission von Schwefeldioxid und Stickoxiden," Deutsches Institut für Wirtschaftsforschung, Berlin, July 25, 1985, 337–341.
28. West Germany is not free of pollution problems. Nitrous oxide pollution in West Germany during the 1980s was far worse than in East Germany because West Germany had far more cars.
29. *Statistisches Jahrbuch der DDR 1989*, 151; "Frauenpolitische Aspekt der Arbeitsmarktentwicklung in Ost and Westdeutschland," Deutsches Institut für Wirtschaftsforschung, July 25, 1991, 428.

TABLE 7-6
Average Monthly Earnings in Industry in East and West Germany, January 1990

	East Germany (DM)	*West Germany (DM)*
Average gross earnings	1,609	4,021
Taxes	0	–348
Social security contribution	288	–720
Average net income	1,321	2,953
Rent	–110	–925
Average net income after rent	1,211	2,028

Source: Gerhard Fels and Calus Schnabel, *The Economic Transformation of East Germany: Some Preliminary Lessons* (Washington, D.C.: Group of Thirty, 1991), 26.

Kuche (children, church, and kitchen). A woman was supposed to have children, preferably six or seven, because more children, particularly if they were males, meant more soldiers for the German army

But times changed in both East and West Germany; after World War II both countries had among the lowest birthrates in the world. East Germany was not reproducing itself and West Germany was only barely maintaining the size of its population. Moreover, the role of women in society had changed dramatically, but far more so in East Germany than in West Germany. In 1990, 64 percent of East German women between the ages of 16 and 60 were in the labor force, compared to 39 percent of West German women.[30] Moreover, three-fourths of all East German married women worked, compared to 40 percent of West German married women. East German women had far greater access to professional jobs than West German women; there was far less inequality in pay between men and women in East Germany; and East German women had far greater access to child-care centers subsidized by the state. Nevertheless, East German women worked on the average nine more hours a week than their West German counterparts, and very few of them were part of the political and economic power structure of East Germany. Moreover, East German men were not noted for their willingness to help around the house. The women had to stand in line to shop for food, and the East German divorce rate was the highest in the world.[31]

Table 7-7 compares men's and women's average monthly earnings in West Germany for various occupations, with women's earnings expressed as a percentage of men's earnings. Percentages are shown for both blue-collar and white-collar

30. "Frauenpolitische Aspekt der Arbeitsmarktentwicklung," 422.
31. Heide Pfarr, "Policy on Women in the German Process of Reunification," unpublished paper. Pfarr is a member of the Berlin city council.

TABLE 7-7
Average Monthly Earnings of West German Male and Female Workers (males = 100 percent)

Industries	*Blue-Collar*	*White-Collar*
Mining	75	74
Energy	72	80
Processing	66	64
Manufacturing	70	64
Trade	77	66
Transportation	67	81
Banking and finance	77	74
Services	76	67
Self-employed	66	60

Source: "Frauenpolitische Aspekt der Arbeitsmarktentwicklung in Ost und Westdeutschland," Deutsches Institut für Wirtschaftsforschung, July 25, 1991, 428.

workers. There were smaller differences between men's and women's earnings in East Germany, because income was determined by the state for each occupation. For East German women as a whole, their earnings were 75 percent of men's earnings, compared to 67 percent for West German women.[32]

PROBLEMS OF REUNIFICATION

One thing that can be said about German reunification is that West Germany seriously underestimated its cost. The productivity and competitiveness of East German state enterprises turned out to be far worse than expected, and the restructuring process will take far longer than expected. Forty years of a command economy had led to an unacceptable and inadequate capital stock and totally different management and work practices, and entrepreneurship had virtually disappeared. Only one-third of East German machinery and equipment was less than five years old as of reunification, while 21 percent was more than twenty years old. Agriculture possessed many of the same characteristics as industry. It was labor-intensive and not competitive with other European producers. Like the large state industrial enterprises, the majority of agricultural enterprises operated at a loss and were supported by state subsidies.

There were other costs as well. The environment needed to be cleaned up, and the infrastructure needed to be modernized. The East German educational system, from the university level all the way down to grade school, had to be changed, and the East German legal system had to be converted to the West German legal system, which involved the training of more lawyers and judges. The East German social security system had to be converted to the West German sys-

32. Pfarr, 5.

tem, and the East German banking system had to be scrapped and remade into the two-tiered West German banking system. There was also the matter of property ownership, which will tie up the legal system for years to come. Widespread corruption in the former East Germany has also created problems. Former high-ranking Communist officials have stashed hundreds of millions of dollars abroad.

Political Reunification

The East German political system was very centralized, with a monolithic political leadership. Former West Germany is a federal republic with three levels of government—federal, state and local. East Germany was divided into five administrative divisions—Mecklenburg, Brandenburg, Saxony, Saxony-Anhalt, and Thuringia—fourteen regions, and the capital at East Berlin. The Lander Act of July 22, 1990, created the states of Mecklenburg-Western Pomerania, Brandenburg, Saxony-Anhalt, Saxony, and Thuringia, with much shifting of territories that had been parts of the original administrative divisions, giving the new Germany a total of sixteen states. The new capital of Germany eventually will be Berlin, and each of the five new states has a capital. Elections are national, state, and local, and so is the division of taxes. The first free elections since 1946 were held on May 6, 1990.

Economic and Monetary Union

The German Economic, Monetary, and Social Union (GEMSU) went into effect in July 1990.) With the ratification of the German Unity Treaty in September of that year, East Germany ceased to exist as a country and became part of a united Germany. Economic integration involved the wholesale adoption of the West German social market economy, in which there would be a free play of market forces, within an elaborate social system that provides medical services, unemployment benefits, vacation pay, paid maternity leave, family allowances, and old-age pensions.

The adoption of East Germany by West Germany was similar to buying an old house. In buying an old house, there are several alternatives—leave the house as it is, remodel it, or gut it and build again, using what you can salvage. The East German economic system was worse off than anticipated, particularly its industry. This meant that West Germany has had to start basically from scratch in redoing the economic and social structure. This has led to the creation of a new banking system, a new tax and social security system, and a decentralized and competitive market structure through the introduction of private property rights, by privatizing state-owned firms, and through the creation of a new educational and legal system.

Monetary Union. On July 1, 1990, the West German DM became the legal tender for the united Germany and the West German Deutsche Bundesbank became the only monetary authority. Wages, salaries, rent, and other current payments were converted from the East German mark (M) to the West German DM (deutsche mark) at a ratio of 1M = 1DM. East German residents could convert their marks into DM at a 1-to-1 ratio for amounts of up to 2,000 marks for those persons under 14 years of age; up to 4,000 marks for those between the ages of 14 to 59; and up to 6,000 marks for those 59 years and over. Other East German financial assets and liabilities were convertible at a ratio of 2M = 1DM.[33]

The banking system of East Germany was similar to that of the other socialist economies. There was no money and credit market, and loans and interest exercised no allocative function. Loan allocation was an instrument of economic planning. The State Bank (*Staatsbank*) was both an issuing bank and a commercial bank; it was responsible for the preparation of the cash and credit plans and held the accounts of all state enterprises. As there were no tax offices, the bank and its branches served as a collection agency for the state budget. As a commercial bank, it was responsible for loans to industry. It had control over specialized banks—the Foreign Trade Bank, the German Trade Bank, and the Bank for Agriculture and the Food Industry. In addition, there were savings banks (*Sparkassen*), cooperative banks, and people's banks, all of which were under the control of the State Bank.

The former East German banking system was converted to the two-tiered West German system. The East German State Bank was replaced by the West German Deutsche Bundesbank, which is now the central bank for the united Germany.[34] The West German commercial banks, such as the Deutsche Bank and Dresdner Bank, now operate as commercial banks in East Germany, having absorbed the former branch offices of the State Bank, and perform their commercial functions. The West German Deutsche Landsbank absorbed the East German Foreign Trade Bank. The other specialized East German banks were absorbed by various West German banks. The East German savings banks were restructured to match their counterparts in West Germany.[35] The same was true of the East German cooperative banks. Conversion losses, which occurred when East German bank assets were converted into West German assets, were handled by an equalization fund administered by a West German–created Deutsche Kreditbank.[36] The total amount of the fund was DM57 billion ($35 billion).

Industry

East German industry as well as agriculture, which was run like an industry, are being privatized along the lines of the West German social market model. To facilitate the process of privatization, in July 1990 the West German government

33. *Monthly Report of the Deutsche Bundesbank* (Frankfurt, July 1990), 16–19.
34. For more thorough details on the East German banking system and its conversion to the West German system, see *Monetary Report of the Deutsche Bundesbank for July 1990*, 16–24; also "Monetary and Financial Issues in German Reunification," in Lipschitz and McDonald, *German Unification: Economic Issues*, 144–154.
35. In West Germany savings banks are run by the communities.
36. East German bank assets were converted into West German deutsche marks at a lower rate than East German bank liabilities because of the low valuation placed on their holdings.

created a trust agency, Treuhandanstalt (Treuhand for short), which was given legal title to all companies that had previously belonged to the East German state. It assumed responsibility for the privatization of 12,500 companies comprising 35,000 individual economic units, plus 20,000 restaurants and retail stores.[37] It was also given responsibility for the sale of 25 billion square meters of real estate (80 billion square feet) and 9.6 billion square meters of forest land (30 billion square feet).[38] Treuhand was supported by budgetary revenues from the German government and provided credit or loan guarantees to potential investors. Before an East German company could be sold, its assets had to be revalued in terms of West German accounting methods, and a company's assets and liabilities were carried at their estimated market value.

Several approaches were used to privatize East German industry:

1. Small companies and stores were privatized through manager or worker buyouts, leasehold arrangements, and public auctions. Virtually all of the small commercial establishments were privatized by the end of 1991.
2. Large state enterprises were privatized through direct sale to West German or foreign investors. A few were bought by former East German Communist Party members who had stashed away money.[39] Many state enterprises were broken up and sold separately. Some enterprises were so obsolete that their properties were sold as scrap.
3. State farms and collective farms were difficult to sell. First, they had to be broken up into smaller land components. Second, there was the matter of affordability, for German farmers like American farmers have to purchase mechanized equipment. Third and most important, there was and remains the question of who owns the land. Most of the land was expropriated by the East German government in 1951, and prior to that some of it had been seized by the Nazis during the period 1933 to 1945.[40]

Results of Privatization

When Treuhand started the privatization of East German industry and agriculture, the total market value of these assets was DM600 billion ($370 billion), and some seven million East Germans were employed in some 12,500 state enterprises. At the end of 1994 the true value of these assets was DM60 billion, and the debt of

37. Paul Dodds and Dr. Gerald Wachter, "Privatization Contracts with the German Treuhandanstalt: An Insider's Guide," *The International Lawyer,* Spring 1993, 1–5.
38. Dodds and Wachter, "Privatization Contracts," 5.
39. For example, leaders of the Stasi, the East German police, had stashed away some $150 million in Swiss banks at the time of reunification.
40. The West German courts will be tied up for years to come trying to resolve property disputes.

Treuhand was DM270 billion ($150 billion). There were several reasons for this outcome:[41]

1. The properties were overvalued, in part because reliance was placed on East German statistical data that were inaccurate.
2. Falsified East German statistics claimed an industrial output far larger than it actually was.
3. Most projections of enterprise values were based on the assumption of East German industry's remaining an integral part of CMEA, which still existed at the time of reunification. Approximately 50 percent of East German exports were with CMEA.
4. Often the selling price of East German enterprises was helped by the assumption of enterprise debts by Treuhand. This was used as leverage to encourage investors to preserve jobs in East Germany.[42]

Economic Cost of Reunification

Contrary to what the West German politicians promised the voters in 1990 on the eve of reunification, the cost has been high. Between 1990 and 1994, West Germany transferred about 5 percent of its assets to East Germany each year. About one-third of this cost, or 1.5 percent of West German GNP, was financed by government deficits; the remaining two-thirds was financed by tax increases and increases in social security contributions.[43] The public share of West German GNP rose from 46 percent of GNP in 1990 to 51.5 percent in 1994, and the share of taxes and social security contributions increased from 40.4 percent to 44.5 percent. Government debt increased to 51.5 percent of GNP by 1994, the highest level since 1945. There was some counterbalance in that West German GNP increased by an average of 1.5 to 2.0 percent a year as a result of increased West German sales in East Germany. Interest rates increased in West Germany, which impacted on European interest rates in general. Table 7-8 presents the cost of German reunification from 1991 to 1994 and projected to 1997.

Although the financial cost of reunification was borne by the West Germans, the East Germans also paid a price, particularly in the area of unemployment. At the time of reunification in 1990, there were around 8.7 million workers in the East German economy. Everyone was guaranteed a job, and the rate of unemployment was minimal. Conversion to a market economy changed all that. In the second quarter of 1990, for example, 85,300 East Germans were unemployed. One year later the number had grown to 834,900 and in the second quarter of 1992 to

41. Gerlinde Sinn and Hans-Werner Sinn, *Jumpstart: The Economic Reunification of Germany* (Cambridge, Mass.: MIT Press, 1992), 96–111.

42. "Farewell, Sweet Treuhand," *The Economist,* December 24–January 6, 1995, 82–84.

43. Ullrich Heilemann and Wolfgang H. Reinicke, *Welcome to Hard Times: The Fiscal Consequences of German Unity* (Washington, D.C.: The Brookings Institution, 1995), 1–2.

TABLE 7-8

Year	*Cost of German Reunification (billions of dollars)**
1991	85.6
1992	103.7
1993	109.0
1994	107.4
1995	130.3
1996	134.4
1997	136.7
Total	700.1

**Converted at an average exchange rate of $1 = DM 1.5.*

Source: Ullrich Heilemann and Wolfgang H. Reinicke, *Welcome to Hard Times: The Fiscal Consequences of German Unity* (Washington, D.C.: The Brookings Institution, 1995), 26.

1,290,400.[44] In January 1996, six years after reunification, there were 1.1 million East Germans unemployed, or around 15.2 percent of the East German workforce, and another 500,000 were participating in job-creation programs.[45] Almost three million jobs have been lost in East Germany since 1990.

Social Costs of Reunification

Little attention has been paid to the social costs of reunification, but they have been considerable. No one group was affected more than East German women. Before reunification the rate of female participation in the East German economy was much higher than it was in the West Germany economy.[46] They were guaranteed job equality, which, however, did not mean they got the better-paying jobs. They were entitled to abortion on demand, and they were provided with day-care centers for their children. All of this changed as a result of reunification. Women are the main victims of the downsizing of the labor force. The unemployment rate for women is twice that of men, as Table 7-9 indicates, and remains so more than five years after reunification. Jobs of comparable status are usually unavailable to East German women.[47] Abortion is no longer free on demand, and divorces are harder to come by.[48]

Another group adversely affected by reunification was older people, many of whom believed in communism. Helga Fanger had spent most of her life as an ar-

44. *Monthly Report of the Deutsche Bundesbank* (Frankfurt, February 1993), 58.
45. *Monthly Report of the Deutsche Bundesbank* (Frankfurt, January 1996), 13.
46. East German women constituted 50 percent of the workforce, compared to 37 percent for West German women.
47. However, the author knows three East German women who improved their positions.
48. The divorce rate in East Germany was 50 percent compared to 15 percent in West Germany.

TABLE 7-9
Unemployment Rates for Men and Women in the Former East Germany (percent)

State, City	*Men*	*Women*
Mecklenbrug—West Pomerania	10.8	19.8
Brandenburg	9.0	18.2
East Berlin—City	10.7	12.9
Saxony	8.3	18.9
Saxony—Anhalt	11.3	20.2
Thuringia	8.9	18.8
East Germany	9.4	18.6

Source: Bundesministerium für Arbeit und Socialordnung, *Beschaftigungssituation und Arbeitsmarktchancen von Frauen in Ostdeutschland* (Bonn, November 1995).

dent Communist.[49] She had been employed more than thirty years at a light-bulb plant, and was the party secretary in her apartment block. It was alleged that she was a spy for the state security apparatus, the Stasi. After reunification, her factory was shut down, she lost her job, became an alcoholic, and was eventually murdered. Many other people who had also spent their entire working life under socialism expected the state to take care of them as it had for so long. There is the sense of loss of community that existed in East Germany, a stability that was state-enforced, but stability nevertheless.

THE GERMAN ECONOMY

A united Germany now has a population of 81 million and a land area not much smaller than it was before World War II. It has the strongest economy in Europe and its currency unit, the D-mark (deutsche mark), not only dominates the currency systems of Europe but is also one of the strongest currencies in the world. Germany is one of the leading export countries in the world, and many of its industries are world-class competitors. But it also has its problems, not the least of which has been the cost of German reunification, which has placed a strain on the German financial system. Moreover, German labor costs are the highest in Europe, if not the world, and are affecting the competitive position of German firms in world trade.

Germany is a very good example of social market capitalism in which government plays a very important role, particularly in the area of social welfare. German programs are among the most comprehensive and expensive in the world. In 1993 one-third of German disposable income came from social welfare expenditures.[50] Almost 40 percent of a German worker's wages are represented by government-

49. "To Live and Die in Berlin," *U.S. News and World Report*, February 6, 1995, 48–50.
50. Annual Report of the Deutsche Bundesbank, 1993.

mandated benefits that employers have to pay workers. Then there are government expenditures on vocational training programs that are more comprehensive than those in any other industrial country. A considerable part of German direct investment is financed out of tax revenues, and the German tax structure, unlike that of the United States, is weighted more toward investment than consumption. The tax system also provides incentives that are designed to increase savings. In 1993, the German household saving rate was 12.4 percent of disposable income compared to 4.1 percent for the United States.[51]

Banking

The German banking system differs from the U.S. banking system. German banks provide most of the investment capital to industry because of the high savings rate in Germany and because Germans tend to prefer bank savings to investments in stocks and bonds. The major commercial banks are far more powerful than their counterparts in the United States because they are major shareholders in German corporations and their executives sit on the boards of directors of these same corporations.[52] It is estimated that German banks directly or indirectly own one-fourth of the voting stock in a quarter of Germany's largest corporations and are the source of 28 percent of the members of their supervisory boards.[53] In 1993 the Deutsche Bank, the largest bank in Germany, with assets of $321 billion, owned 29 percent of the stock in Daimler-Benz, the largest German industrial firm with sales of $59 billion.[54]

There are three nationwide banks—the Deutsche Bank, the Dresdner Bank, and the Commerzbank, all privately owned—which have a national and international network of branch banks. They are more important to the German economy than their counterpart banks in the United States are to the U.S. economy because through credit and interlocking directorships, they control a large part of the German economy.[55] Then there are state and regional commercial banks, also privately owned, that also own shares in German corporations. In addition, German corporations own stock in other German corporations. German corporations obtain 12.8 percent of their financing from bank borrowing compared to 1.9 percent for

51. Ibid.

52. This would be illegal in the United States.

53. W. R. Smyser, *The Economy of United Germany: Colossus at the Crossroads* (New York: St. Martin's Press, 1992), 84.

54. *Forbes*, July 18, 1994, 232.

55. In the United States the Clayton Act of 1914 was passed in part because the American banker J. P. Morgan and his associates in J. P. Morgan and Company held directorates in sixty-three corporations with assets of $74 billion. Altogether this bank controlled one-fourth of the corporate assets in the United States. Section 8 of the Clayton Act states that no person shall be a director in two or more corporations if they are competitors. The Glass-Steagall Act of 1933 prohibits U.S. banks from owning U.S. corporate securities.

U.S. corporations and own about 60 percent of the stocks and bonds of German companies.

There are also savings banks and special-purpose banks. Savings banks are municipally owned. The savings banks are oriented toward local needs such as housing, small business loans, and municipal government projects. They, too, provide a major source of capital for the German bond and stock markets. Some savings banks rank among the largest credit institutions in Germany, but most are small local banks. Special-purpose banks are also important. They derive their income from government savings from budgetary surpluses and accumulations by the social security system, and lend the savings to private industry. An example of a special-purpose bank is the Reconstruction Loan Corporation, which is responsible for the provision of long-term credits to finance exports.

Labor Unions

The trade union movement in Germany is dominated by one major labor confederation, the Deutsche Gewerkschaftsbund (DGB), which was established in 1949 as a federation of sixteen industrial unions comprising every economic sector of the West German economy. For example, office and production employees in the textile industry are organized into the textile union. The DGB represents about one-fourth of the workers in the West German labor force and, following reunification with East Germany, has included East German workers. The principal unions within the DGB are the metalworkers, the public service and transportation workers, who went on strike in May 1992, and the chemical, paper, and ceramics workers. There are also other German unions. White-collar workers and higher-ranking civil servants, reflecting class divisions and higher social status, have their own unions. Even the German armed forces have their trade union, called the Deutscher Bundeswehr-Verband, but membership is not obligatory. Around 45 percent of all German workers are in unions compared to 17 percent in the United States.

Employers Associations

Employers in the European countries, including Germany, are far better organized than they are in the United States. The most important employers federation is the German Federation of Employers Association, which combines thirty-four associations made up of local and regional associations representing different parts of German industry. National associations are responsible for collective bargaining with unions represented by the DGB.

In addition, there are the German chambers of commerce and their trade association, the Deutsche Industrie und Handelstag (DIHT). Membership is obligatory for all German firms, regardless of their size. A major responsibility of the chambers of commerce is involvement in vocational training programs. As public law bodies, they set store hours, issue business licenses and work permits, resolve disputes between business firms, and interact with government institutions at all levels. Thus, their functions are central to the operation of the German economy.

Codetermination (Mitbestimmung)

As already noted, a unique feature of labor-management relations in German industries is codetermination of business policies on the part of labor and management. Its purpose is to give workers a voice in determining public policy, and as a principle it dates back to the development of trade unionism in the last century. It was tied into the idea of a just social order, which permeated German trade unions at that time. The first relevant legislation was passed in World War I, when the Law on Auxiliary Services for the Fatherland made workers' committees obligatory in all enterprises with fifty or more workers engaged in war contracts. However, after Germany lost the war, codetermination did not become a labor-management issue again until the passage of the Works Constitution Act of 1952, which was applied to workers in the iron, steel, and coal industries. Subsequent acts have broadened the application of codetermination to cover all German firms with five or more workers.[56]

Codetermination takes place through two structures—supervisory boards and works councils.[57] The supervisory board must have one-third worker representation in firms between 500 and 2,000 employees and one-half worker representation for firms with 2,000 workers or more. For public corporations, there must be equal representation of labor and management; for private corporations, there must be equal representation between labor and management, plus one representative who is supposed to be neutral. This neutral representative, who is elected by both groups, is supposed to serve as a tiebreaker. Supervisory boards make investment and other long-term decisions for companies. Membership on a supervisory board gives employees a voice in personnel policy matters but not operational issues, which are the domain of management.

Functioning at the factory level, the works council exists in most German firms and covers all aspects of job conditions. All individual worker dismissals must be brought to the works council before notice can be given, and it may intervene by filing suit in a labor court against the dismissal. It deals with other issues of immediate concern to workers, such as plant closings or new production processes. It cannot block major investment decisions by employers or interfere with large-scale capital transfers; it is basically restricted to making the best out of general working conditions. In some respects, works councils are more important than supervisory boards in that they involve greater worker participation in issues of more immediate concern.

56. There have been five laws on the subject, the last passed in 1976.
57. Firms can have both structures depending on their size.

Vocational Education

The educational system of Germany is one of its major strengths in that it has created a skilled labor force capable of handling new industrial technologies. This may be contrasted with the United States, where the high school dropout rate is eight times higher than that of Germany, and where in international student achievement comparisons, U.S. students usually rank near the bottom in math and sciences. This means that many U.S. workers are unable to compete for jobs that require technical skills. The German labor force, on the other hand, annually receives vocational training in some 400 occupations. Training, often with a preselected employer, will usually last for two or three years. There are also a number of short, or refresher, courses available to workers.

Each year around one-half of German teenagers between the ages of 15 and 19 receive vocational training within a range of 400 occupational specialties, including crafts, carpentry, car repair, electronics, sales, office or banking work, medical technician work, and secretarial work. Vocational training is administered by the German state governments,[58] trade unions, and business firms in conjunction with the German school system. The trainee normally is assigned to a company and then works for it two or three days a week. The remainder of the week is spent at a state vocational school.[59] Vocational training programs cost industry an estimated DM35 billion ($22 billion) annually, but the end result is that the labor force is well trained and unemployment among teenagers is low. Germany has the highest share of world trade in goods with a high skill content.

Social Security and Other Welfare Measures

Social security programs in Germany date back to Bismarck's opposition to socialism and his dislike of trade unions, which led him to sponsor the health insurance law of 1883. By 1911, when the Insurance Consolidation Act brought all German insurance systems under one statute, the majority of German workers were insured against sickness and invalidism. Unemployment insurance, which had originated in the United Kingdom in 1911, was introduced into Germany in 1927. War and war-related pensions and financial assistance comprise an important component of German social welfare pensions. Included are various measures for the creation and maintenance of transit and reception camps for refugees.[60] Then there is the family allowance, or children's allowance (*Kindergeld*) as it is commonly called, which is separate from the social insurance system and is financed out of general government revenues.

58. John Ardagh, *Germany and the Germans* (London: Hamish Hamilton, 1989), 112–115; also Michael E. Porter, *The Competitive Advantage of Nations* (New York: Free Press, 1989), 355–382.
59. According to Porter, this is one of Germany's major competitive advantages and one of the United States' weakest.
60. This is a cause for unrest on the part of many Germans who see no need to pay for foreigners—Vietnamese, Poles, or any refugees.

TABLE 7-10
Total Income Component and Direct and Social Security Taxes in West Germany, before Reunification (billion DM)

Gross wages and salaries	742.3
Income tax	–126.8
Social security contributions	–107.2
Net wages and salaries	508.3
Gross income of self-employed	262.8
Income tax	–30.3
Social security contributions	–13.9
Net income	218.6
Income transfers (pensions and other)	217.5
Income tax	–4.5
Social security contributions	–0.6
Net transfers	266.3

Source: Deutscher Bundestag, *Materialien zum Bericht zur Lage der Nation im geteilten Deutschland,* February 1987, Bonn, 720.

The bulk of social security expenditures are kept in the social budget *(Sozialbudget)*, which is administered by the federal government but separately from the federal budget. The bulk of the German social security system is financed by payroll taxes levied on both employers and employees, other contributions, and the general revenues from the federal budget. The revenues from payroll taxes are never adequate to cover all expenditures by the system. Thus, some proportion of all taxes paid by individual taxpayers is used to help finance the social security system. In 1990 total social security payments amounted to DM658 billion ($348 billion), which represented about 24 percent of the German GNP. There was a deficit of around DM24 billion ($11 billion) in the social security budget.[61]

Table 7-10 shows the tax and transfer effect of social security on the West German economy for 1983. The income-transfer effect is greater on wage and salary earners. Direct taxes and social security contributions amounted to 31.5 percent of average monthly wages of wage and salary earners compared to 22.5 percent in 1970.[62] The average is probably 40 percent today given changing demographics and the absorption of the former East German social security system.

AN EVALUATION OF THE GERMAN ECONOMY

Particularly during the period immediately after the end of World War II and continuing up to 1960, the performance of the West German economy was very good.

61. OECD Economic Surveys, *Germany* (Paris: OECD, 1994), 57, 150–153.
62. Deutscher Bundestag, *Materialien zum Bericht zur Lage der Nation im geteilten Deutschland,* Bonn, 1987, 720.

The economy was helped to some extent by Marshall Plan aid from the United States and by the Korean War, which stimulated U.S. demand for German manufactured products. However, as Table 7-11 indicates, the performance of the German economy after 1960 has not been outstanding. The Japanese growth rate was highest for all of the time periods, with the exception of the projected increase from 1991 to 2000.

Strengths of the German Economy

The German economy possesses many strengths, including an educational system whose emphasis on vocational education has provided a highly skilled labor force. Its currency unit, the D-mark, is one of the strongest in the world, it has a positive merchandise trade account, and the Deutsche Bundesbank, the central bank of Germany, has kept the inflation rate low. With respect to German reunification, the long-term effect is likely to be positive because it will strengthen Germany's economic position as the center of Europe. Its high rate of savings, necessary for capital formation, is channeled through the banking system into industry. It also has a reputation for producing quality products that dates back to the last century, and it has a reputation for world-class research in such fields as chemistry, metallurgy, and medicine.

Weaknesses in the German Economy

The German economy also has its share of weaknesses. The cost of German reunification has proved to be far more than was expected and has increased the deficits in the budgets of the federal, state, and local governments as well as in the special reunification funds. Another problem is the general decline in the competitive po-

TABLE 7-11 *Real GNP Growth Rates for the G-7 Countries for Various Time Periods (percent)*

Country	*1950–1955*	*1960–1973*	*1974–1979*	*1980–1991*	*1992–2000*
Germany	8.2	4.4	2.4	2.3	1.7
France	4.6	5.6	2.8	2.2	2.3
Italy	5.6	5.3	3.7	2.3	2.0
United Kingdom	2.8	3.3	1.5	1.9	2.2
United States	3.3	3.9	2.6	2.1	2.6
Japan	8.8	9.6	3.6	4.1	2.6
Canada	4.0	5.3	4.2	2.4	3.3

Note: Figures for 1992–2000 include East Germany.

Source: OECD Economic Surveys, *Germany* (Paris: OECD, 1994), 70.

TABLE 7-12
Comparisons of Value Added per Hour Worked Germany/U.S. and Germany/Japan

Germany/U.S.	*U.S. = 100 Percent*	
Industry	**1979**	**1990**
Food, beverages, tobacco	74.1	75.8
Textiles, apparel, leather	85.9	88.2
Chemicals, allied products	106.0	76.7
Basic, fabricated metals	90.1	98.8
Machinery, equipment	110.7	87.6
Other manufacturing	80.1	79.3
Total manufacturing	95.8	85.9
Germany/Japan	*Japan = 100 percent*	
Food, beverages, tobacco	186.2	204.9
Textiles, apparel, leather	156.5	183.8
Chemicals, allied products	135.9	91.5
Basic, fabricated metals	106.9	103.3
Machinery, equipment	139.1	76.6
Other manufacturing	201.3	144.4
Total manufacturing	153.0	110.3

Source: Bart van Ark and Dirk Pilat, "Productivity Levels in Germany, Japan, and the United States: Differences and Causes," *Microeconomics*, Vol. 2, 1993.

sition of Germany in the world markets, attributable to a number of factors including a decline in German labor productivity compared to other countries. There is also a lag in technological innovation, reflecting government regulatory barriers and the lack of risk capital, which inhibit the establishment of new firms that could provide needed new technologies. There are also deficiencies in human capital, especially managerial skills. Moreover, Germany is lacking in entrepreneurship. Finally, demographics works against Germany in that the population is aging and the number of new entrants into the labor force is in the process of decline.

Tables 7-12 and 7-13 present a comparison of the German, Japanese, and U.S. economies. The three economies account for close to half of the world's GDP. Table 7-12 illustrates a problem confronting the German economy, namely that German manufacturing productivity disadvantage relative to the United States has widened in recent years. The decline in Germany's relative productivity was particularly large in chemicals, which has been Germany's premier industry dating back to the last century. There has also been a significant decline in productivity in the German machinery and transport equipment industries. This decline has been in those industries in which Germany had been a clear world leader up to 1979. Japan has also taken a productivity lead over Germany in the same industries.

TABLE 7-13 *A Comparison of Germany, Japan, and the United States, 1994*

	Germany[a]	*Japan*	*United States*
Human Development			
Mean years of schooling	11.6	10.8	12.4
Life expectancy, years	76.0	79.5	76.0
Infant mortality rate[b]	6.0	7.0	9.0
Human development index	0.927	0.937	0.937
Economic Indicators			
Real per capita GDP	$19,890	$21,350	$25,860
Real GDP growth rate, 1985–1994	1.9%	3.2%	3.3%
Exports	380,154	362,224	464,773
Imports	348,631	241,624	603,438
Merchandise trade balance	31,523	120,600	–138,665
Current account balance	–25,563	131,510	–103,925
Gross fixed capital formation[c]	20.9%	30.8%	15.6%
Gross savings rate[c]	22.1%	33.9%	14.5%
Inflation rate, 1985–1994	2.9%	1.3%	3.3%

[a]*Includes East Germany.* [b]*Per 1,000 live births.* [c]*Percent of GDP.*

Source: The World Bank, *The World Bank Atlas 1996* (Washington, D.C.: The World Bank, 1996), 8–9, 18–19; The World Bank, *World Development Report 1995* (New York: Oxford University Press, 1995), 187, 195; United Nations Development Program, *Human Development Report 1995* (New York: Oxford University Press, 1995), 155; OECD Economic Surveys, *United States* (Paris: OECD, November 1995), Basic Statistics International Comparisons.

SUMMARY

East Germany and West Germany have been reunited after forty years of separation. The cost of reunification has been far more than was originally anticipated, and many problems still remain. Nevertheless, the new Germany has emerged as the economic colossus of Europe, and the D-mark along with the Japanese yen are the two strongest world currencies. Germany, Japan, and the United States are the world's leading economies, each dominating their parts of the world as they did before World War II. Each represents a different form of capitalism: Germany, social welfare capitalism; Japan, state-directed capitalism; and the United States, free market capitalism. In the competitive scheme of things, it was once believed that Japan would be the dominant economic power in the twenty-first century, but Japan developed internal problems that have yet to be resolved. Europe too, including Germany, may not live up to the expectations of the Economic Union.

QUESTIONS FOR DISCUSSION

1. Compare the living standards of West Germany and East Germany before reunification.
2. What were some of the problems that have been encountered in the privatization of East German agriculture and industry?
3. Who has borne the cost of German reunification?
4. What groups in the former East Germany have gained or lost as a result of reunification?
5. The German system of vocational training is regarded by many as the best in the world. Would it work in the United States?
6. What is codetermination? Would it work in the United States?
7. What is the relationship between banking and industry in Germany? Would this relationship be illegal in the United States? Why?
8. Why is Germany called a social market economy?
9. In what ways is the German economy superior to that of the United States? In what ways is the economy inferior?

RECOMMENDED READINGS

German Reunification

Borneman, John. *After the Wall.* New York: Basic Books, 1990.

Deutsche Bundesbank, Economics Department. *Special: East Germany.* Frankfurt, 1990.

Dodds, Paul, and Gerald Wachter. "Privatization Contracts with the German Treuhandanstalt." *The International Lawyer*, Spring 1993, 1–5.

"Farewell, Sweet Treuhand." *The Economist*, December 24, 1994–January 6, 1995, 82–84.

Fels, Gerhart, and Claus Schnabel. *The Economic Transformation of East Germany: Some Preliminary Lessons.* Washington, D.C.: Group of Thirty, 1991.

Fisher, Marc. *After the Wall.* New York: Simon & Schuster, 1995.

Hancock, M. Donald, and Helga A. Welsh. *German Reunification.* Boulder, Colo.: Westview Press, 1993.

Heilemann, Ullrich, and Wolfgang H. Reinicke. *Welcome to Hard Times: The Fiscal Consequences of German Unity.* Washington, D.C.: The Brookings Institution, 1995.

Merkl, Peter H. *German Reunification in the European Context.* University Park, Pa.: Penn State University Press, 1993.

Sinn, Gerlinde, and Hans-Werner Sinn. *Jumpstart: The Economic Reunification of Germany.* Cambridge, Mass.: MIT Press, 1993.

The German Economy

"Can the German Social Market System Survive?" *The Economist,* May 4th, 1996, 17–19.

Edwards, Jeremy. *Banks, Finance, and Investment in Germany.* Cambridge, Eng.: Cambridge University Press, 1994.

Giersch, H., Karl-Heinz Paque, and Holger Schmieding. *The Fading Miracle: Four Decades of Market Economy in Germany.* Cambridge, Eng.: Cambridge University Press, 1993.

OECD Economic Surveys. *Germany.* Paris: OECD, 1994.

Pond, Elizabeth. "Germany in the New Europe." *Foreign Affairs*, Vol. 71, No. 2, Spring 1992, 114–130.

Smyser, W. R. *The Economy of United Germany: Colossus at the Crossroads.* New York: St. Martin's Press, 1992.

van Ark, Bart, and Dirk Pilat. "Productivity Levels in Germany, Japan, and the United States: Differences and Causes." Washington, D.C.: Brookings Papers, *Microeconomics*, Vol. 2, 1993, 1–69.

PART III

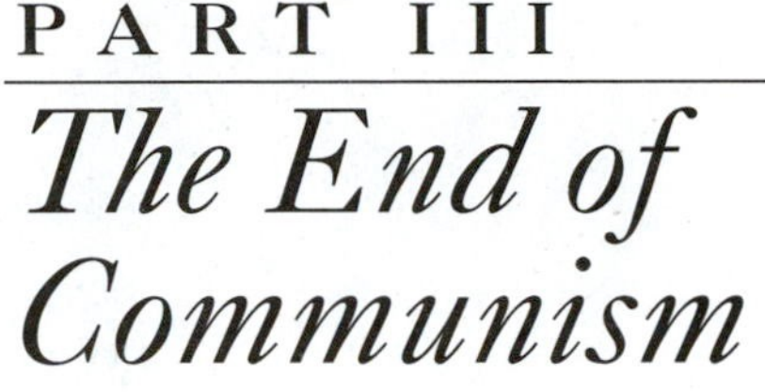

The End of Communism

CHAPTER 8
The Rise and Fall of Communism

Decades of Communist rule left a complex economic and social legacy in the former Soviet Union and the Eastern European countries that were a part of the Soviet bloc. One legacy is the extent to which environmental pollution, a by-product of an emphasis on industrial development, has become a costly expense that now has to be dealt with. Communist rule destroyed traditional institutions of civil society and inhibited open exchange on ethnic group rights and aspirations. Ethnic strife has now become a serious problem in the former Soviet Union, which was a multinational empire put together and ruled by the czars and then, after the Revolution of 1917, by a centralized Communist government. With the Communists came centralized control of economic planning and production, ambitious plans for rapid industrialization, the neglect of agriculture and the consumer sector, isolation from the world, and a lack of concern over the social impact of economic policies.

The Soviet Union imploded from within, and the promise of the creation of a utopian society that once appealed to many people never materialized. At the end it was hard to remember that for most of the seven decades of its existence, it was far from a foregone conclusion that Soviet Communism would perish while American capitalism survived and not the other way around.

It is also hard to believe that the Soviet Union, to a considerable degree, shaped American politics for most of this century, beginning with U.S. and Allied intervention in the Russian civil war of 1919–1920, continuing with the alliance with the Soviet Union to defeat Hitler in World War II, and ending with the cold war.

THE RISE OF COMMUNISM IN RUSSIA

The Russian Revolution of 1917 is often thought of as the work of a small group of radicals called Bolsheviks who took advantage of Russia's defeat in World War I, murdered the czar, and seized power.[1] The Bolsheviks had very little to do with the making of the revolution; their leaders, including Lenin, were not in the country when it occurred. Like the French and American Revolutions, the Russian Revolution was in the making for many years before it actually broke out. No one can understand the success of communism in Russia, which was a backward country compared to industrialized England and Germany, without some knowledge of the factors that made the revolution and the eventual seizure of power by the Communists possible. These factors were as follows:

1. First among the causes of the revolution was the existence of an autocratic government in which one person, the czar, was the supreme ruler—a dictatorship as complete as that of its successor, the Communists. Although from time to time some reforms were made, the czars were complete autocrats, and as a result the condition of the Russian people was the most backward in Europe. The last czar, Nicholas II, simply did not have the ability or the inclination to implement reforms that might have prevented the revolution.

2. The second factor that caused the revolution was the condition of the Russian peasants, who constituted 70 percent of the population and lived in poverty. Even though serfdom had been abolished in Russia in 1861, the majority of peasants had no land and had to hire themselves out as farm laborers. Other peasants who owned land found it too small to cultivate and sold it to the large landowners.

3. Poor labor conditions also contributed to the revolution. Wages were low and paid irregularly, hours were long, the employment of women and children common, and factory conditions unsafe. Attempts to use strikes to improve working conditions were put down by the cossacks, and strikers were sent to Siberia.[2] Labor unions were illegal, and legislation designed to protect workers was not enforced.

1. John Reed, *Ten Days That Shook the World* (London: Boni and Liveright, 1919).
2. Lenin, Stalin, and other Communist leaders continued the practice of sending political and other opponents to Siberia.

4. Another factor that contributed to revolution was a very complicated racial problem that has flared up today. Much of Russia was populated by non-Russians: Poles, Ukrainians, other Europeans, and a wide variety of Asiatics. Non-Russians made up over half of the total population of the Russian empire. Efforts were made to make them Russian by forbidding the use of other languages than Russian. Resistors of Russification were shot or sent to Siberia.

World War I

World War I was the catalyst that brought about the Russian Revolution. Russia had already lost a major war, the Russo-Japanese War of 1904. This defeat was followed by the Russian Revolution of 1905, which began when workers demonstrated for safer working conditions. This demonstration was put down by the Russian army, and many lives were lost. A wave of strikes eventually forced the czar to make political concessions. A constitutional monarchy was created, and freedom of speech and assembly were granted to the people. However, the reforms were too little and too late. Discontent was further exacerbated by Russian defeat during World War I, and in 1917 the revolution occurred, bringing about a complete economic, social, and political change.

The Russian Revolution

The first phase of the revolution began in March 1917, when a series of riots over food shortages led to strikes in Petrograd.[3] Soldiers sent in to suppress the strikes joined the strikers. Czar Nicholas then abdicated, and a provisional government was created. At the same time workers and soldiers who had participated in overthrowing the czar formed the Soviet (council) of Workers and Soldiers Deputies. The provisional government proved to be ineffectual in implementing needed economic and social reforms, while the Petrograd soviet grew in influence and became a model for similar organizations that sprang up all over Russia. A reform program was developed that included labor legislation and land distribution.

In October 1917 the second and final phase of the Russian Revolution began. The Bolshevik[4] faction, led by Lenin, had played only a minor role in the March revolution but was able to take advantage of the chaos in Russia. They came out with a radical program calling for worker ownership of the factories and distribution of land to the peasants. In what could be called a coup d'état, the Bolsheviks seized control of power by persuading elements of the Russian army and navy to revolt.[5] Then they seized control of the Petrograd soviet and forced the provi-

3. Petrograd (St. Petersburg) was the capital of Russia. In 1924 its name was changed to Leningrad. In 1991 the name again became St. Petersburg.
4. There were two factions: the Mensheviks, who favored a gradual change to socialism, and the Bolsheviks, who were for immediate change.
5. As Lenin said: "We found power lying in the streets and picked it up." The actions of a few persons coupled with luck accomplished the greatest revolution of this century.

sional government to surrender. The revolution was over and the Communists were in power.

LENIN AND COMMUNISM

In 1918 the Bolsheviks formally formed the Communist Party and the machinery that was to run the Soviet Union for seventy-four years was put in place. A decree declared all land to be the property of the state, and industrial and commercial enterprises were given to committees selected by workers. The expectation of the Bolshevik leadership in October 1917 was that the Russian Revolution would trigger a revolution that would bring about the collapse of capitalism throughout Europe. A corollary to this belief was that once capitalism collapsed, socialism would automatically appear. In Lenin's view the total organization required to wage World War I represented that rational organization of economic life that was the essence of socialism.[6] However, capitalism did not collapse, and socialism did not automatically appear once the war was over.

The Creation of a Party State

One characteristic of the former Soviet Union was a dual Communist Party and government administrative structure. Lenin said the proletariat should be led only by a small, dedicated core of Communists who would direct society like an orchestra, dictating who should play each violin and hearing if someone played a false note. One way to ensure complete control over the machinery of government was to put it in the hands of the Communist Party. This system of dual administration, first developed in the army[7] to ensure loyalty, was eventually applied to any function in Soviet society, including government. The function of the party was to realize a political and economic vision; its vocation was not to exercise techniques and professional competence but to see that everything conformed to the vision. The functional government bureaucracy was monitored by a parallel party administration.

The New Economic Policy, 1921–1928

A state of chaos existed in Russia after the Russian Revolution was over. A civil war broke out between the Communists and their opponents. This war, which was eventually won by the Communists, lasted until 1920 and did much property damage. One outcome of the war was the creation of the Red Army, which became the mainstay of Soviet military power up to the time of the collapse of the Soviet Union. The Communists encountered a number of problems after the war was over. The whole economy was on the verge of collapse. To feed factory workers

6. Martin Malia, *The Soviet Tragedy: A History of Socialism in Russia, 1917–1991* (New York: Free Press, 1994), 111.
7. Ibid., 115.

the government ordered the peasants to hand over their grain above a certain minimum for feed and seed. When peasants refused to do this, their produce was requisitioned by military force. This led to a decline in agricultural production, food shortages in the cities, and a decline in industrial production.

Lenin introduced the New Economic Policy (NEP) in March 1921. The government kept its control over such areas of economic activity as large-scale industry, transportation, banking, and foreign trade. Many other sectors were opened to private enterprise. Markets were restored, and peasants were allowed to sell their surplus grain at market prices. Small business firms were returned to their former owners. Forced labor was abolished, and money wages were generally adopted as a medium of exchange. To attract foreign capital the government offered foreign companies concessions for trade and manufacturing and for the exploitation of natural resources. The NEP was generally quite successful. Industrial production regained its 1913 level by 1927 and agricultural production also increased. The NEP saved the Soviet economy from collapse and enabled the Communists to maintain and consolidate their power. However, after Lenin's death in 1924, Joseph Stalin assumed power. In 1928 a decision was made to industrialize rapidly and to convert workers and peasants into the proletariat. Stalin was able to achieve the complete socialization of industry and agriculture.

Stalin and the Development of Communism

Stalin's main objective was to industrialize the Soviet Union as soon as possible. To do this, he collectivized agriculture, killed off the more prosperous farmers who resisted, and inaugurated a series of five-year plans. The First Five-Year Plan (1928–1932) marked an attempt to convert all available resources into industrial development, with targets of production set for every sector. Priority was given to the production of steel, which was supported at the expense of agriculture. By collectivizing agriculture into state farms and collective farms, Stalin was able to siphon off what otherwise would have gone into consumption and divert it to industry. The Soviet Union was able to attain a rapid rate of industrial growth during the 1930s, but it came at a high price, particularly in the neglect of agriculture.

A Second Five-Year Plan (1933–1937) followed the first, and a third, intended for the years 1938–1942, was greatly modified with the approach of World War II. Both plans continued the emphasis on development of capital goods industries, particularly steel. The three plans strengthened Soviet industry and set the nation on the road to modernity, but at a price. Consumers and peasants paid for progress—the former in terms of the capital that was withheld from their standard of living, and the latter in terms of loss of freedom to own land and produce crops. There was always a shortage of consumer goods, but they were regarded as expendable at a time when it was considered necessary to build the Soviet Union into an industrial power.

Party Purges. It is estimated that some 20 million Russians lost their lives during Stalin's purges of the 1930s. Among those executed were most of the generals in the Soviet army, many leading Communist Party members, and millions of ordinary citizens. It was officially stated that the accused had either plotted with foreign powers for an invasion of the Soviet Union or had in some other way conspired against the welfare of the state. Any disagreement within the party became a challenge to Stalin and ultimately a crime. A system of terror, implemented by the secret police, left no individual secure during Stalin's long reign as the dictator of the Soviet Union. No one, not even Politburo members, was free from the possibility of death or deportation to Siberia.

The Party Elite. Any pretense of creating a classless society vanished with Stalin. Instead, the state became highly bureaucratized, and those who were part of the bureaucracy gained power and privilege. It was Stalin who created this class of persons, the nomenklatura elite, who were absolutely subservient to him and would carry out his orders. Once a person became part of the nomenklatura elite, his or her position was assured for life. The elite was self-perpetuating in that members' privileges were extended to their children, who also eventually became part of the system. This vast structure of overlapping privileges, controls, rewards, and vested interests remained in place until 1990.

The Soviet Union After World War II

The Soviet Union became one of the two major military superpowers after the end of World War II, a position it maintained until 1991. It extended its economic and political control over the Eastern and Central European countries of Poland, Romania, Bulgaria, Hungary, Czechoslovakia, and Yugoslavia,[8] and a part of the defeated Germany, which became the German Democratic Republic (East Germany). Since these countries became miniature versions of the Soviet Union, economic planning also became a way of life for them. In successive stages, each country moved toward the nationalization of industry, banking, trade, and agriculture. After 1948 each government launched long-term economic plans, consciously modeled after the Soviet five-year plans, with emphasis placed on rapid industrial expansion, especially in the production of steel. As industry and agriculture were almost completely nationalized by this time, planning represented the final step toward developing a command economy designed to direct the productive effort of each country.

The Post-Stalin Period

Joseph Stalin was the leader of the Soviet Union from 1924 until his death in 1953. He left a mixed legacy in that he made the Soviet Union into an industrial nation but at a high cost to society. During the 1930s industrial output rose rapidly and exceeded 10 percent growth annually.[9] For example, the production of pig iron in-

8. Yugoslavia split from the Soviet bloc in 1948.
9. E. J. Simmons, *U.S.S.R.—A Concise Handbook* (Ithaca: Cornell University Press, 1946), 20.

creased from 13.0 million tons in 1932 to 48.2 millions tons in 1940, the production of steel from 6.2 million tons in 1932 to 14.9 million tons in 1940, and the production of tractors from 23,900 in 1932 to 147,100 in 1940. The Soviet economy continued to grow after World War II, maintaining its emphasis on industrial production, which came at the expense of agriculture and consumer living standards. Moreover, Stalin's rule continued to be based on a system of terror after World War II.

Nikita Khrushchev. Stalin was replaced by Nikita Khrushchev, who introduced a number of policy changes. In an effort to improve efficiency in production, more-decentralized responsibilities for ministries, administrators, and plant managers were introduced through the creation of *sovnarkhozy*, which were administrative units generally based on the territorial and economic significance of an area. Economic plans continued to favor investment in producer goods and heavy industry at the expense of the consumer. Nevertheless, economic life in the Soviet Union during the Khrushchev period improved, with shorter lines for foods and increased availability of consumer goods. However, Khrushchev was deposed as party leader and premier in 1964[10] and replaced by Leonid Brezhnev, who remained in power until his death in 1982.

Leonid Brezhnev. Under Brezhnev's regime, Soviet troops invaded Czechoslovakia and Afghanistan, and the concept of the Brezhnev doctrine was born. This doctrine held that the Soviet Union would fight to keep its Eastern European satellites within its sphere of influence. Living standards improved during the Brezhnev years, particularly for the nomenklatura and for Brezhnev himself, but even the masses benefited to a certain extent. More emphasis was placed on the development of agriculture, particularly in the area of livestock production. This commitment extended to the use of grain imports to help cover shortfalls in livestock feed output and to an acceptance of external debts to make possible such imports. Soviet imports of grain increased from a low of 600,000 tons in 1969 to around 46 million tons by 1981. The process of economic and social decay began during the Brezhnev era and accelerated during the latter part of it.[11]

Brezhnev was followed into office by Yuri Andropov, who died in 1984 and was replaced by Konstantin Chernenko, who died in 1985. The 1980s witnessed a decline in economic growth in the Soviet Union. It began to lag farther behind the West in technology, particularly in the production of computers and software. For example, in 1987 the Soviet Union possessed around 200,000 microcomputers, compared to over 225 million in the United States.[12] It also lagged far behind in

10. His handling of agriculture was probably the main reason for his deposal. He raised retail prices on agricultural products and reduced the size of private garden plots.
11. The Brezhnev period is noted for corruption in high places and the generally poor performance of agriculture.
12. Anders Aslund, *Gorbachev's Struggle for Economic Reform* (Ithaca, N.Y.: Cornell University Press, 1989), 12–13.

fields that required large and sophisticated supplies of laboratory equipment. The quality of nearly all Soviet products was poor by world standards and declining. Because of low quality, few Soviet manufactured goods could be exported to the West. The Soviet Union was losing out to the newly industrialized countries in manufacturing exports to the West. The same was also true of the Eastern European countries.

GORBACHEV, PERESTROIKA, AND GLASNOST

General Secretary Mikhail Gorbachev was named *Time* magazine's "Man of the 1980s" and rightfully so, because no man had a greater impact on the decade than he. He was responsible for the developments in Eastern Europe; no Eastern European country would have dared to break away from his predecessors, particularly Leonid Brezhnev because of the Brezhnev Doctrine, which justified Soviet intervention in the internal affairs of the Eastern European countries, beginning with the Soviet invasion of Czechoslovakia in 1968. Relations between the United States and the Soviet Union improved immensely; armaments were reduced; and the prospect of a third world war was virtually eliminated. When Gorbachev replaced Chernenko in 1985, the Soviet economy was in a mess, so he initiated broad economic and political reforms in an effort to revitalize the Soviet economy. However, they failed to produce economic gains for the population. Food and other goods remained in short supply, and social unrest increased. In 1989 the Communist governments in Eastern Europe fell, and in 1990 Lithuania, Latvia, and Estonia declared their independence from the Soviet Union.[13] A coup attempt in August 1991 to depose Gorbachev failed, but his time in office was drawing to an end. He resigned as leader of the Soviet Union in December 1991.

Perestroika

The Russian word *perestroika* means restructuring. The concept did not begin with Gorbachev; rather, it was first put forth before the revolution of 1917 by some political groups that wanted a restructuring of Russian society. It was also a concept used in the early Stalinist period, when it meant some form of reorganization in culture, education, and economics. Under Gorbachev, it represented an attempt to modernize Soviet society, which meant less bureaucracy, central planning, and coercion in the economic field; more reliance on private initiative and incentive; and an attempt to rekindle the spirit of the masses to build a better and more energetic socialist society within the Marxist-Leninist framework.[14] The old economic system—where only quantity of output counted and where payment was made ac-

13. Lithuania, Latvia, and Estonia were created as separate countries after World War I, but were absorbed into the Soviet Union in 1939 when Hitler and Stalin divided up Poland.
14. Walter Laquer, *The Long Road to Freedom: Russia and Glasnost* (New York: Charles Scribner's Sons, 1989), 52.

cording to whether the plan was fulfilled, not whether the products were needed by anyone—was simply inefficient.

Perestroika, 1985–1987. Perestroika consisted of three major elements—tighter economic discipline, industrial modernization, and economic reform. It was first used to improve rather than to change the economic system.[15] Efforts were made to improve quality control by setting higher standards for Soviet industrial products. Also, a major effort was made to modernize and retool Soviet industry by providing more investment funds from the state budget and from foreign loans. There was also what was called the "human factor" campaign, an effort to increase personal accountability and productivity. Gorbachev replaced party chairmen and head officials of many government ministries to improve discipline and initiated an anti-alcohol campaign to reduce worker absenteeism. To do this, he either shut down or curtailed the hours of the state liquor stores. To improve the productivity of workers, he increased the wage base by 20 percent for blue-collar workers and 30 percent for specialists.

The effects of the first stage of perestroika were mixed at best. The anti-alcohol campaign, although well-intentioned, did not work because drinkers simply made their own "bathtub" vodka. In addition, the state lost money from declining sales of alcohol, thus increasing the deficit in the state budget.[16] The quality control program worked well in that some 18 percent of output was rejected on first inspection, but output stalled, production targets were missed, and bonuses were reduced. Restrictions on the power of state ministries led to a reduction in their bureaucracies from 1.6 million employees in 1986 to 871,000 by 1989, but the result was an increase in the bureaucratic power of the fifteen union republics and autonomous regions.[17] Finally, measures designed to increase the role of private activity in the Soviet economy largely failed.

Perestroika, 1987–1989. New reforms were implemented, the cornerstone of which was the Law on State Enterprises announced on July 1, 1987. It abolished the traditional mandatory output targets, it allowed enterprises to contract directly with their suppliers and customers, and it gave them greater latitude in decisions concerning investments and the distribution of profit. Enterprises were given centrally determined profit norms and were subject to rules determining prices, but were free to produce and trade as they wished. The Law on State Enterprises also affected wages, in that enterprises were given more latitude to increase wages and bonuses out of their wage funds. Workers were allowed to form councils to elect managers. In 1988 prices were reformed, permitting enterprises to negotiate con-

15. *A Study of the Soviet Economy*, vol. 1, International Monetary Fund (Washington, D.C.: The World Bank, 1991), 21–24.
16. Anders Aslund, "Gorbachev, Perestroika, and Economic Crisis," *Problems of Communism*, January-April 1991, 26–28
17. Ibid., 27.

tract prices for new goods, within limits that varied by industry and time period.[18] Private enterprise activities were liberalized in March 1988, permitting collective farms and family cooperatives to engage in private selling and buying. Joint venture legislation was passed to attract foreign capital.

Failure of Perestroika. The major reason perestroika failed was that it encompassed too many reforms that were uncoordinated and came too late to save the Soviet economy. There was a multiplicity of economic decision-making centers. Many of the administrative methods traditionally used to direct the Soviet economy from the center were abandoned without waiting for the mechanisms needed to guide decentralized decision making to be put in place. Even though enterprises were given more latitude in production, they produced goods with high profit margins that, in the absence of market competition, were often not what consumers wanted. Although wages were raised, the production of consumer goods did not increase; black marketeering, on the other hand, did. Consumer discontent increased, and strikes and ethnic unrest occurred.[19]

Glasnost

Glasnost means openness about public affairs in every sphere of life.[20] When the concept was introduced by Gorbachev in 1985, it involved an exposé of bureaucratic inefficiencies and waste and mismanagement in the economic system. Glasnost encouraged perestroika because, through popular support, Gorbachev was able to initiate a series of changes that focused on restructuring the Soviet economy. Glasnost was considered an effective form of public control over the activities of all public entities and a lever in correcting shortcomings. It marked an enormous step forward in comparison with the dismal state of affairs that prevailed before Gorbachev. If nothing else, it allowed Soviets to let off steam and give vent to their frustrations. But in the end, it was the catalyst that brought about the collapse of Communism.

Glasnost and the Soviet Economy. Glasnost had a direct impact on the Soviet economy. It revealed much about the state of the economy, particularly its shortcomings. For example, glasnost attacked official statistics, which had been notoriously untrustworthy. Some attempts were made to supply more valid statistical data, such as grain harvest data, but other data on crime and alcoholism were not published.[21] There was also more openness when it came to discussing the Soviet

18. However, all but a few prices continued to be set by the authorities either at the central, republic, or local level.
19. *The Soviet Economy Stumbles Badly in 1989*, paper presented by the Central Intelligence Agency and the Defense Intelligence Agency to the Technology and National Security Subcommittee, Joint Economic Committee, Congress of the United States, April 1990, 16–22.
20. Glasnost was not a new concept in Russian history. Gorbachev quoted Lenin as saying: "More light! Let the party know everything!" However, glasnost went back long before Lenin. The term was used in the Russian periodicals of the nineteenth century.
21. Laquer (1989), 197–205.

supply system. Seventy years after the 1917 revolution, the Soviet Union had not created the good life; in fact, conditions had gotten worse. Cars made in the 1950s were better-made than cars made in the 1980s. Shoddy goods and the absence of services became a topic for discussion under glasnost.

Glasnost and Soviet Society. Glasnost revealed the bad side of Soviet society, from alcohol to pollution, failings that the Soviet Union had refused to admit when it held itself up as a country that had solved all social problems. Glasnost was used by Gorbachev as a moral crusade to cut down on alcoholism, corruption, drugs, and prostitution. However, it was expanded to include subjects that were previously considered sacrosanct, including a full airing of the mistakes of the past. Soviet censorship was relaxed, and books, articles, authors, and ideas that were formerly banned began to flood the mass media. The public trial of Stalinism and its excesses was an important part of glasnost. The whole sordid history of Stalin's rule was unveiled in the Soviet press, with the disclosure that between 1935 and 1941 7 million people were shot and 13 million others were sent to forced labor camps, where most of them died.[22]

Glasnost and Nationalism. Glasnost and perestroika were linked in that free, public discussion of problems and events and the restructuring of the Soviet economy were compatible ideas and either one led to the other. However, glasnost also led to ethnic nationalism in the Soviet Union. Nowhere was this more apparent than in the Baltic republics of Latvia, Lithuania, and Estonia, which took "openness" literally and demanded independence from Moscow. But nationalism was not limited to the Baltic republics; it had spread to other areas of the Soviet Union as well. By the end of 1990, all of the remaining Soviet republics had declared some form of independence. Gorbachev proposed the Union Treaty to give them more autonomy, but it was too late. The year 1991 marked the end of the Soviet Union and its replacement by the Commonwealth of Independent States.

Democratization

Democratization (*demokratizatsiya*) was the third prong in Gorbachev's approach to reform the Soviet economy. Perestroika was to be reinforced and driven by glasnost, which would in turn be stimulated by democratization. This was designed to encourage pressure from the bottom up to spur reforms, as opposed to traditional Leninist emphasis on total control from above.[23] Gorbachev felt that continued reliance on the traditional approach would doom his reforms for the simple reason that he would be opposed by a party structure of power and privilege. Even limited democratization from above meant concessions that were bound to be repug-

22. Stephen F. Cohen and Katrina vanden Heuvel, *Voices of Glasnost* (New York: W. W. Norton, 1989), 27–28.
23. This was called democratic centralism. It was predicated on the belief that the Communist Party was the chosen representative of the proletariat; therefore, no elections were necessary, so the leaders were free to choose their own successors and subordinates.

nant to a ruling elite steeped in the Marxist-Leninist notion that it alone was the repository of tradition and power.

THE PERFORMANCE OF THE SOVIET ECONOMY IN THE 1980s

When Gorbachev took over the leadership of the Communist Party, he stated that his goal would be to reform Soviet economic and political life. While his efforts at political liberalization were enormously successful, probably much to his political regret his attempts to revitalize and reform the Soviet economy were largely ineffectual. Economic reform was supposed to make the Soviet Union more competitive in the production of conventional products, such as machine tools, as well as high-technology products. He also promised to raise the living standards of the Soviet people. He failed on both counts, particularly the latter. The per capita real standard of living showed a decline during the five years (1985–1989) that he was in power. Many goods were in short supply because he did little to stimulate the production of consumer goods.

Economic Growth

Table 8-1 presents the performance of the Soviet economy for the 1980s. In fairness to Gorbachev, he inherited a rather poor economic situation. From 1979 through the early 1980s, there was a drop in the real rate of economic growth and a decline in the production of many industrial goods. But there was little improvement after he was in office, and he had to assume a major share of the responsibility for the poor performance. Investment policies led to a failure of industrial modernization and did not increase the rate of economic growth. Even more important

TABLE 8-1
Soviet Economic Performance for Selected Years (annual rate of growth in percent)

Year	*Real per Capita GNP*	*Industry*	*Agriculture*
1981–1985	1.0	2.0	1.2
1984	0.5	2.5	–0.5
1985	0.0	2.0	–3.9
1986	3.1	2.7	10.3
1987	0.2	2.9	–4.0
1988	1.5	2.4	–3.2
1989	0.5	0.2	3.1

Source: Central Intelligence Agency, *Handbook of Economic Statistics 1989* (Springfield, Va.: NTIS, 1990), 34, 58; Central Intelligence Agency and the Defense Intelligence Agency, *The Soviet Economy Stumbles Badly in 1989* (Report to the Technology and National Security Subcommittee, Joint Economic Committee, Congress of the United States, 1990), 4, C11.

was the Soviet lag in key technologies, such as computers and electronic components and instruments, that offered the promise of future economic growth. Increased international competition using new technologies left the Soviet Union far behind the West.

Foreign Trade

The Soviet Union's lack of export competitiveness was an important impediment to the success of perestroika. Its inability to increase export earnings from manufactured goods was reflected in the commodity composition of exports, which basically consisted of military hardware, crude and refined oil, and natural gas. Import strategy was directed toward running a surplus in the merchandise trade account, which was accomplished through cutbacks in imports from the developed countries. This adversely affected Soviet industry because imports were cut in Western machinery and equipment, impairing Soviet ability to improve the quality and assortment of its manufactured products and to compete in world markets, where it had to earn more hard currency to service the interest on its foreign debt and to purchase advanced technology. The net hard currency debt of the Soviet Union to the West, as indicated in Table 8-2, almost tripled during the 1980s.

Defense and the Economy

The Soviet Union met its Vietnam in Afghanistan and eventually had to withdraw after a useless expenditure of money and human resources. These expenditures as well as those made in response to the military buildup of the Reagan administration drained resources that could have been applied to Gorbachev's economic reforms. Military expenditures increased the deficit in the Soviet state budget from around 2 percent of Soviet GNP in 1983 to around 10 percent in 1989. However, it was more than the military buildup that contributed to the deficit in the state budget. One factor was an increase in consumer subsidies of some 43 billion rubles from 1985 to 1989, which made this the fastest-growing expenditure item in the

TABLE 8-2 *Hard Currency Debt of the Soviet Union to the West (billions of dollars)*

	1980	*1984*	*1985*	*1986*	*1987*	*1988*	*1989*
Gross debt	20.5	22.2	29.0	36.0	40.8	41.7	47.0
Less assets in Western banks	10.0	11.5	13.3	14.9	14.4	14.4	15.0
Net debt	10.5	10.7	15.7	21.1	26.4	27.3	31.0
Net interest	–1.2	–1.2	–1.5	–1.7	–2.2	–2.4	–3.0
Gold sales	1.6	1.0	1.8	4.0	3.5	3.8	3.6

Source: Central Intelligence Agency and the Defense Intelligence Agency, *The Soviet Economy Stumbles Badly in 1989* (Report to the Technology and National Security Subcommittee, Joint Economic Committee, Congress of the United States, 1990), Table C8.

state budget. State revenues were adversely affected by falling oil prices and a loss of revenue from the sale of alcohol. Table 8-3 presents expenditures and revenues, the deficit, and the deficit expressed as a percentage of GNP for the period from 1985 to 1989.

Food and Other Goods and Services

An abundance of food and other goods and services is the most important measure of living standards. Gorbachev failed to deliver in this area despite his promises to increase availability, especially of food. A Soviet survey in 1988 showed that only 23 out of 211 varieties of foodstuffs were readily available in state stores.[24] Even bread was in short supply, and rationing was imposed on products such as meat. Real per capita living standards decreased, and the rate of inflation increased. Even including imports of grain and meat, the availability of consumer goods fell far short of consumer demand, and goods produced in the Soviet Union were of inferior quality. Meanwhile, enterprise reforms allowed for an increase in wages, while shortages of consumer goods increased.

THE END OF THE SOVIET UNION

Communism is Dead[25]

The Soviet Union lasted two years after the 1980s had ended. By 1991 trying to save it was like rearranging the deck chairs on the *Titanic,* because no matter what was tried, it didn't work. Most of the economic and political institutions that had held the country together in the past were discredited. Six years after Gorbachev launched his program of economic reforms, much of the economic and political system that had been put together by Lenin and Stalin had been undermined. A struggle began between the central government and its constituent republics over the control of resources. There was also a growing fiscal and monetary crisis that contributed to inflation, as the deficit in the Soviet state budget increased to over 100 billion rubles, or 12 percent of the Soviet GNP.[26] Bank credit had to be expanded to support financially troubled enterprises. Decades of mismanagement left many industrial sectors with an aged capital stock that was unable to cope with changing demand.

The Soviet economy continued to decline, but at an accelerated rate in 1991. Real gross domestic product declined by 2 percent in 1990 and 17 percent in 1991.[27] Retail prices, which had increased by 5.6 percent in 1990, increased by 86

24. Marshall I. Goldman, "Gorbachev the Economist," *Foreign Affairs,* Vol. 69, No. 2 (Spring 1990), 26.
25. Boris Yeltsin in a speech before a joint session of Congress, Wednesday, June 17, 1992.
26. *A Study of the Soviet Economy,* 282–283.
27. International Monetary Fund, *The Economy of the Former U.S.S.R. in 1991* (Washington, D.C., April 1992), 41.

TABLE 8-3 *Revenues and Expenditures of the Soviet State Budget (billions of rubles)*

Year	*Revenues*	*Expenditures*	*Deficit*	*GNP*	*Deficit as a percent of GNP*
1985	367.7	386.0	18.3	770.0	2.3
1986	366.0	415.6	49.6	798.5	6.0
1987	360.1	429.3	69.3	825.0	8.4
1988	365.5	445.9	80.4	875.0	9.2
1989	384.9	480.1	96.8	924.1	10.4

Source: International Monetary Fund, The World Bank, Organization for Economic Cooperation and Development, European Bank for Reconstruction and Development, *A Study of the Soviet Economy*, Vol. 1 (February 1991) 53, 54, 280, 281.

percent in 1991.[28] Industrial output fell by 7 percent, and a shortage of imported parts adversely affected food processing, chemical, and light industries. Agricultural output also showed a decline in 1991, as grain production fell from 211.5 million tons in 1990 to 154.7 million tons in 1991. The energy sector declined in both 1990 and 1991, in part because of equipment shortages, and coal production was lower in 1991 than it was in 1980. There was an increase in social and ethnic unrest, including a coal strike and a civil war in Georgia. The growing decentralization of political power and the regionalization of markets also contributed to a decline in output.

The year 1991 marked the end for Gorbachev, who had lost most of his power as the republics broke away to form either separate countries or independent states. Reforms were still being made, but to little avail. An effort was made to change the banking system by creating central banks at the republic level. The December 1990 Law on Banks and Banking permitted commercial banks to carry on a broad range of banking.[29] Gosbank, which had been the monobank under central planning, became part of a three-tiered banking system that included republic central banks and commercial banks. The foreign exchange system underwent some changes in 1991, with commercial banks given a more prominent role in foreign exchange transactions, and the ruble was given multiple exchange rates against foreign currencies.

Prices were liberalized in 1991, with many prices shifted from a state-determined to a contractual basis where buyers and sellers could set prices within limits. Retail prices were reformed in April 1991, which reduced the share of state fixed prices in favor of regulated prices and contractual prices between the producer and the retailer. Fixed prices on certain goods, such as meat and bread, were raised with the objective of reducing state subsidies. The April price reforms resulted in an increase in the retail price level of about 55 percent. Also, before the April price reforms took effect, much hoarding took place, with the result that re-

28. International Monetary Fund, *The Economy of the Former U.S.S.R. in 1991*, 58.
29. The former specialized banks of the Soviet Union were reorganized into commercial banks.

tail stores were short of consumer goods. Also in 1991, agricultural procurement prices were increased substantially, with the intent of improving production incentives. The price reforms were followed by an announcement on the part of the national, or union, government rejecting the old command system in favor of a commitment to privatization.

Radical changes were made in the area of public finance, which had been centralized in the Soviet state budget and used to enforce plan objectives. Revenue sharing with republic and local government units served only as an administrative device to simplify central resource allocation, and expenditures were guided by the state planning agency called Gosplan. By 1990, however, this began to change because of pressure from the republic and local levels of government for regional fiscal decentralization. In 1990 the fiscal relationship was changed, with the republics and lower-level governments given much more control over the preparation of their own budgets. For the first time since the creation of a centrally planned economy, there were separate budgets. The central government retained primacy in determining the tax system, but by mid-1991 the republics began to demand the right to levy their own taxes.

The second half of 1991 witnessed the end of the Soviet Union. In August an abortive attempt was made to overthrow the leadership of President Gorbachev. After the failed coup by Communist Party hard-liners, Gorbachev resigned as Communist Party general secretary, and the whole party apparatus collapsed. The flow of power to the republics that had already started accelerated after the coup, and Boris Yeltsin, president of the Russian Federation, who had opposed the coup, replaced Gorbachev as the leader of the country. Those republics that had not left the Soviet Union declared their independence, including Russia and Kazakhstan. The power of the union, or national government, slipped away, and the republics began the takeover of properties that had formerly belonged to the union but were located in their territories. On December 8, 1991, three major republics—the Russian Federation, Ukraine, and Belarus—agreed to form a Commonwealth of Independent States (C.I.S.). On December 21, 1991, eight other republics joined the C.I.S. and signed the Alma-Ata Agreement. The Soviet Union was left on the dustbin of history.[30]

REORGANIZATION OF THE SOVIET UNION

The former Soviet Union consisted of fifteen separate republics, three of which—Estonia, Latvia, and Lithuania—declared their independence in 1990 and were formally recognized as independent nations by the U.S.S.R. The Soviet Union before its breakup was one of the most ethnically diverse countries in the world, in-

30. There are eleven members of the Commonwealth of Independent States—the Russian Federation, Ukraine, Belarus, Armenia, Azerbaijan, Kazakhstan, the Kyrgyz Republic, Moldova, Tajikistan, Turkmenistan, and Uzbekistan. Georgia did not join, and Estonia, Latvia, and Lithuania were independent states.

cluding some ninety nationalities among its 290 million people. The largest nationality group was Russian, comprising around half of the population. The Ukrainians and Belorussians made up another 20 percent, and a number of non-Slavic groups, formed by Turkish Moslem people, accounted for around 15 percent. There were also non-Slavic Christians, including Armenians and Georgians; Moldavians, who were once aligned with Romania; and Estonians, Latvians, and Lithuanians. Other nationalities were interspersed in the mountains and valleys of the Caucasus where they had lived for centuries; still others lived in Siberia and the Arctic Circle. Although Russian was the most common language, some two hundred different languages and dialects were spoken, and racial and religious animosities had existed for centuries.

Table 8-4 presents the population and per capita incomes of the fifteen republics in the year of the dissolution of the Soviet Union. The republics very enormously in natural resource wealth. Estonia, Latvia, and Lithuania, which are now independent countries, were among the wealthiest republics. The Ukraine has rich farmland, which made it an important source of food for the former U.S.S.R.; it provided more than a fifth of the U.S.S.R.'s meat and dairy output and around one-quarter of total grain, potato, and vegetable production. Kazakhstan is rich in minerals. The poor republics of Central Asia—Uzbekistan, Turkmenistan, Tajikistan, and Kirghizia (now called the Kyrgyz Republic)—are agrarian, and that region also faces a challenge in meeting its water needs. The Russian Federation encompasses over half of the population, 75 percent of the land area, and 60 percent of net material product and possesses industry and natural resources.

TABLE 8-4 *Land Area, Population, and per Capita Incomes for the Republics of the Former U.S.S.R., 1991*

Republics	*Land Area (square miles)*	*Population (thousands)*	*Per Capita Income (dollars)*
Armenia	11,490	3,360	$2,150
Azerbaijan	33,340	7.219	1,670
Belarus	80,137	10,328	3,110
Estonia	17,413	1,591	3,830
Georgia	27,000	5,478	1,640
Kazakhstan	1,049,155	16,899	2,470
Kirghizia	76,460	4,448	1,550
Latvia	24,595	2,693	3,410
Lithuania	25,170	3,765	2,710
Moldova	13,000	4,384	2,170
Russian Federation	6,600,000	148,930	3,220
Tajikistan	55,240	5,412	1,050
Turkmenistan	186,400	3,748	1,700
Ukraine	231,990	51,999	2,340
Uzbekistan	172,241	20,955	1,350

Source: The World Bank, *The World Bank Atlas 1992* (Washington, D.C.: World Bank, 1992), 8–9, 18–19

The Commonwealth of Independent States

In a way the Commonwealth of Independent States is like the European Community. The eleven members are independent republics, and for all practical purposes they are independent nations. Several have applied for membership in the International Monetary Fund and other world financial and political organizations. They have agreed to promote interrepublic trade by eliminating quotas and other forms of trade restrictions. The ruble will remain the common monetary unit, but any republic is free to issue its own currency. The republics also plan to have a uniform tax system and will take measures to preserve interindustry ties that existed in the Soviet Union. They have agreed to create a new legal base to regulate business relations between the different states. Balance of payment settlements between the republics will be handled by mutual agreement, but each state can impose restrictions on payment.

The Russian Federation

The first republic to be formed after the Bolshevik Revolution was the Russian Soviet Federated Socialist Republic. In 1922 it joined the Ukraine and Belarus to form the Soviet Union. The Russian Federation was the wealthiest part of the former U.S.S.R., accounting for 91 percent of industrial output. Table 8-5 presents its share in various economic indices of the Soviet economy.

In June 1991 the Russian Federation became a sovereign country, and in December joined the Ukraine and Belarus (Belorussia) to form the Commonwealth of Independent States (C.I.S.). The C.I.S. claimed successor status to the former

TABLE 8-5
Share of the Russian Federation in the Economy of the former U.S.S.R. for 1990 (percent)

Population	51
Employment	57
Industry	59
Agriculture	57
Gross Domestic Product	62
Industrial output	90
Oil	90
Coal	56
Trucks	86
Consumer goods	56
Timber	92
Natural gas	79
Freight	54
Housing investment	53
Retail trade turnover	57
Services	58

Source: International Monetary Fund, Economic Review, *Russian Federation* (Washington, D.C., April 1992), 53.

U.S.S.R. and occupied the seat at the United Nations formerly held by the U.S.S.R., including its permanent seat on the U.N. Security Council. The C.I.S. also occupies the embassies of the former U.S.S.R. all over the world, including the one in Washington.

WHY DID COMMUNISM FAIL?

The collapse of the Soviet Union represented the greatest social disaster of this century. In its beginning, it offered hope for the creation of a utopian society, but that never came close to reality. Constant coercion held the country together, but coercion could not last forever. Still, no one could have predicted that the Soviet Union would collapse when it did. There was a mystique of invincibility about the country that carried over from World War II after the Red Army defeated the Germans and captured Berlin. It was this army that went into Hungary in 1956 and Czechoslovakia in 1968 to put down uprisings. But the war in Afghanistan destroyed the myth of invincibility. Even though economic sclerosis had set in during the 1980s, there were still no signs that the country was in any imminent danger of collapsing.

But this does not explain why communism collapsed so suddenly. Disproving Marxist predictions that countries would defect from capitalism during the twentieth century, capitalist countries have instead turned out to be more adaptable than communist countries in a rapidly changing world.

Failure of the Economic System

Centrally planned economies could function reasonably well in the age of coal, steel, and manufacturing, but they could not compete in the highly complex and dynamic postindustrial world. The pace of international technological innovation is a driving force in the world economy, and the world's body of scientific technology doubles every decade. The Communist world was pretty much isolated from the rest of the world, and its insularity cost it dearly. At the time of its demise, the Soviet Union was not competitive even with such developing countries as South Korea. Moreover, direct comparisons between the Eastern and Western European countries over two different time periods show the Eastern European countries lost ground. Table 8-6 provides these comparisons.

Economic Planning. Weaknesses in economic planning in Communist countries included the following:

1. State enterprises placed emphasis on plan fulfillment rather than profitability. Product markets were distorted by production, price, and trade controls that insulated domestic prices from international ones. Asset and capital markets were practically nonexistent, with financial flows responding passively to plan demands.

TABLE 8-6 *An Income Comparison of Eastern and Western European Countries for 1937 and 1988 (dollars)*

National Income per Capita, 1937		*Gross Domestic Product per Capita, 1988*	
Western Europe		Western Europe	
United Kingdom	440	United Kingdom	12,810
Germany	340	West Germany	18,480
France	265	France	16,090
Austria	190	Austria	15,470
Eastern Europe		Eastern Europe	
Czechoslovakia	170	Czechoslovakia	3,300
Hungary	120	Hungary	2,460
Poland	100	Poland	1,860
Yugoslavia	80	Yugoslavia	2,520

Source: Andres Solimano, *On Economic Transformation in East-Central Europe,* Working Paper 677 (Washington, D.C.: The World Bank, May 1991), 16, 33.

2. Central planning did not promote efficiency and productivity growth. Distorted input and output prices divorced resource use from resource costs. Plans emphasized the heavy industry and resource sectors of the economy at the expense of consumer goods and services. Compressed and arbitrary wage structures and job security were poorly linked to productivity and inhibited worker motivation.
3. Economic planning undervalued natural resources and placed little emphasis on environmental safeguards, which created serious environmental problems. The emphasis on heavy industry and low energy prices resulted in a level of energy use two to three times that of market economies.
4. An important part of the planning legacy common to all socialist countries was the absence or weakness of core market-oriented institutions. Legal and accounting standards were weak, and there was no tradition of independent audit. State enterprises lacked marketing and strategic planning capabilities and inventory control, and they had little information about the profitability of the various products they were ordered to produce.

Burden of Defense Expenditures

It can be argued that one thing that caused the collapse of the Soviet Union was an inability to continue matching defense expenditures with the United States, particularly when it came to spending on more sophisticated technology. In 1990 national defense expenditures in the United States amounted to $300 billion, or 6 percent of the U.S. GNP.[31] In the Soviet Union total defense expenditures

31. Office of Manpower and Budget, *Budget of the United States Government, Fiscal Year 1991* (Washington, D.C.: U.S. Government Printing Office, 1990), 153.

amounted to around 20 percent of the state budget and around 14 to 18 percent of the Soviet GNP, which was one-third that of the United States.[32] Soviet defense expenditures placed a burden on the economy. For one thing, the best human and material resources were channeled into defense-related activities. The huge amounts of human and material resources claimed by the military and space establishment were particularly detrimental to agriculture. The resources forgone for defense could have resulted in a higher standard of living for the Soviet consumer. The most apparent tradeoff was between defense weapons and producer or durable goods, with decreases in the latter resulting in smaller capital stock, one of the primary ingredients in economic growth.

The Bureaucracy

The bureaucracy and the nomenklatura elite of the Soviet Union and Eastern Europe were obstructions to change.[33] Like bureaucrats all over the world, Communist bureaucrats resist change, particularly when they feel threatened. However, Communist bureaucrats may be more likely than other bureaucrats to resist change, because reforms reduce their power by definition. Therefore, to be successful, reforms must break the power of the bureaucracy, and that is easier said than done. Bureaucratic conservatism and dogmatic orthodoxy tend to reinforce each other, with dogma legitimizing established power and power protecting the established dogma. Coupled with that was the system of nomenklatura, with its vast structure of overlapping privileges, controls, rewards, and vested interests. Since reforms threatened the privileges of the nomenklatura elite, they fought against them. Thus, reformers such as Gorbachev encountered obstacles because to implement reforms they had to rely on the very people they wanted to get rid of.

Glasnost

Glasnost provided the eventual undoing of the Communist system.[34] It meant openness in every sphere of life, something that never would have been possible in the days of Stalin or Brezhnev. Glasnost released the genie from the bottle by reducing fear, the one element that had held Soviet society in check for seventy years. When Soviet coal miners went on strike, it was reported on both Soviet and foreign television, and the miners were interviewed by reporters. In the old days, the miners would have been shot or sent to Siberia. Glasnost contributed to ethnic nationalism in the Soviet Union. Nowhere was this more apparent than in the Bal-

32. Central Intelligence Agency, National Foreign Assessment Center, *Handbook of Economic Statistics* (Washington, D.C.: U.S. Government Printing Office, 1985), 64.
33. In former East Germany there were 2.2 million bureaucrats in a country of 17 million people.
34. Seweryn Bailer, "The Death of Soviet Communism," *Foreign Affairs*, Vol. 70, No. 5 (Winter, 1991/92), 172–173.

tic republics of Latvia, Lithuania, and Estonia, which took "openness" literally and demanded independence from Moscow.

LEGACIES OF COMMUNISM

The attractiveness of communism as an ideology was based on the belief that it could create a society free from exploitation and want. It failed to do this. It proclaimed the building of God's kingdom on earth and the happiness of mankind, but it couldn't deliver on its promises. Instead of the withering away of the state and the emancipation of the proletariat, the state, as represented by the Communist Party, ran a tightly controlled economic and political system. Communism had its successes in the Soviet Union—industrialization, the defeat of Nazi Germany, postwar reconstruction, the space race, and the achievement of military parity with the United States, but a high price was paid for them. It left behind several legacies that are by-products of an emphasis on industrialization at all costs and the achievement of economic self-sufficiency.

Environmental Pollution

Communism left an environmental disaster in the Soviet Union and Eastern Europe. Production at all costs, without regard for the environment, was the basic objective of the economic plans. A major source of pollution involved the burning of soft brown high-sulfur coal, called lignite, which emits a yellow-brown smog that was often so thick that drivers had to turn on their headlights during the day. Air pollution was particularly bad in East Germany, Czechoslovakia, and Poland. The area around the Lenin steel mill on the outskirts of Krakow in southern Poland and the coal-mining area around Katowice were and remain among the most polluted areas in the world.[35] Katowice is a grimy, soot-laden city where coal dust turns everything brown. In the northern area of the former Czechoslovakia, sulfur dioxide, a by-product of burning brown coal, is often fifty times the maximum safety limit.[36]

Eastern Europe's waterways are fouled by sewage, chemicals, and acid rain. The Vistula River, which runs through Poland, is so laden with poisons and chemicals that its waters are unfit for drinking or even for factory coolants. Acid rain has damaged the forests of Eastern Europe. In former Czechoslovakia groundwater contamination has rendered 50 percent of the water supply undrinkable; twenty-five tons of pollution gas fall on each kilometer of the area each year.[37] Moreover, there is the possibility of a nuclear disaster similar to that at Chernobyl. The

35. When the author was in Katowice in October 1991, the guard rails on bridges were corroded. The only thing that had changed since he was there in 1985 was that the steel mill no longer bears Lenin's name.
36. *MacNeil/Lehrer News Hour*, January 2, 1992.
37. *MacNeil/Lehrer News Hour*, January 2, 1992.

Czech and Slovak Republics operate eight Soviet-made nuclear reactors that can and have cracked under pressure. Two nuclear meltdown accidents in 1976 caused several deaths and injuries that were kept a secret until recently.

Efforts to clean up the environment in Eastern Europe have inevitably clashed with the desire to raise living standards by increasing the production and consumption of food and manufactured products. The revolution against the communist system was in part a reaction against a system that could not deliver the goods. However, transformation from a centrally planned economy to a market economy has created unemployment. At least for the time being, employment is more important than the environment. In Poland, rather than risk massive unemployment, the government has kept the steel mills open and still mines lignite, both of which are major causes of pollution. Little has changed in former Czechoslovakia, where steel mills and strip mining continue to pollute the environment.

Poor Infrastructure

The infrastructure in Eastern Europe and the former Soviet Union is a disaster. In Poland most of the major roads were built by Hitler before World War II or by the German army during World War II, and the railroad system was developed by the Germans before World War I. The transportation system in the former East Germany is also outdated; its network of roads was built by Hitler during the 1930s. Because the road system was inadequate, East German railroads had to take on the major share of the transportation of goods; this resulted in considerable cost disadvantages in the use of energy. Telecommunication facilities in East Germany were even less developed than transportation, because the East German government cut telephone communication to the West in order to keep its people isolated.[38]

Uncompetitive Trade

The Council for Mutual Economic Assistance (CMEA, sometimes referred to as Comecon) was created in 1949. Its European members were the Soviet Union, Poland, East Germany, Czechoslovakia, Hungary, Romania, and Bulgaria. It developed an elaborate institutional framework for planning and implementing bilateral trade between member countries, denominated in transferable rubles. An integral part of each country's five-year plan, CMEA trade was managed by a few foreign trade organizations (FTOs) that operated directly under ministries in charge of foreign trade. The FTOs had a trading monopoly on a wide variety of products. The principal advantage of CMEA to each member was access to low-cost raw materials and assured exports regardless of production costs.

38. It was still very difficult to get through to East Germany on the phone two years after the Berlin Wall came down.

However, CMEA had distinct disadvantages that carry over today to Eastern Europe and the former Soviet Union.[39] The ease of disposing of output in each member country meant that it was not necessary to upgrade output mix and process technologies in line with world market standards. The separation of the domestic economy from changes in world relative prices and from technological innovation over time ossified the industrial structure of each member country, making industries increasingly uncompetitive. The result was that the monopolistic domestic and regional seller's market reduced incentives for producers to keep up with international standards of production and process technology and to develop effective marketing know-how. As a result, CMEA's world export shares declined during the 1980s, while world export share of the Asian newly developed countries (NDCs) increased.[40] Table 8-7 presents shares of Soviet bloc countries in CMEA exports for 1989.

THE SOCIAL LEGACY OF COMMUNISM

The Soviet Interview Project (SIP) of the University of Illinois interviewed thousands of emigrants from the Soviet Union, most of whom had left during the Brezhnev era, about the desirable and undesirable aspects of living in their former country.[41] The desirable aspects included free comprehensive health care, free public education, control of crime in the streets, job security, subsidized housing, and inexpensive food. These were the main components of a social contract that existed between the Soviet Union and its citizens. Although there were some flaws in the contract—housing was usually substandard, people had to wait in line for goods that were often unavailable, and medical care was often of poor quality—most respondents were generally satisfied. So the Soviet Union did not collapse because of dissatisfaction with living standards. There had to be other causes.

The social contract also had a negative side. Communist Party members and the nomenklatura elite received a superentitlement program that provided special medical care, trips abroad, vacation homes, better-quality food and clothing available at special state stores, and access to the best universities. There was also large-scale corruption, the inevitable by-product of a one-party state. Although the public was aware of special privileges that contradicted the claim of a classless society, special privileges and corruption were not sufficient in themselves to cause the overthrow of the system. There were more important factors, some of which have already been mentioned. One factor was the potential for conflict on the part of diverse nationalities. Some of these nationalities had been acquired by the So-

39. Martin Schrenk, "The CMEA System of Trade and Payments: The Legacy and Aftermath of Its Termination," *Working Paper 753* (Washington, D.C.: The World Bank, August 1991).

40. In 1970 Eastern Europe's share in world exports was 6.8 percent compared to 1.0 percent for the Asian NDCs. In 1987 the Eastern European share had dropped to 4.7 percent, compared to 6.8 percent for the East Asian NDCs.

41. James R. Millar, ed., *Politics, Work, and Daily Life in the USSR: A Survey of Former Soviet Citizens* (Cambridge, Eng.: Cambridge University Press, 1987).

TABLE 8-7
Shares of Soviet Bloc Countries in CMEA Exports for 1989 (percent)

Country	*Exports of CMEA*	*U.S.S.R. Share*
Bulgaria	83	76
Czechoslovakia	54	62
DDR (East Germany)	42	62
Hungary	39	64
Poland	35	61
Romania	38	59
U.S.S.R.	46	—

Source: Allen H. Gelb and Cheryl W. Gray, "The Transformation of Economies in Central and Eastern Europe," *Policy and Research Series 17*, Policy, Research, and External Affairs (Washington, D.C.: The World Bank, June 1991), 16.

viet Union after World War II.[42] Other nationalities had been a part of a diaspora that forced minority groups to migrate to different regions.[43]

Attitudes and Behavior

A system that rigidly controlled the lives of people would certainly have had an impact on their attitudes and behavior. One thing that comes to mind is individual initiative. When one has been guaranteed a job for life, it would be difficult for him or her to adjust to a market economy with its sink-or-swim philosophy. Adaptation would often depend on the age of the person; the older the person, the more difficult it is to adjust.[44] Also lost are social identities that were once anchored in secure occupations. For example, in former East Germany after its merger with West Germany entire university and research institutes were shut down, and many professors who taught Marxist-Leninist economics or the Russian language were suddenly without jobs. Since college professors are held in high esteem in Germany, the blow to their self-esteem must have been enormous. Students also had their college degrees completely eliminated.

Then there is the matter of trust. The Soviet Union and also East Germany, Czechoslovakia, Romania, and Bulgaria were tightly controlled by the police and informers. In East Germany, for example, one out of every three persons in a country of 17 million either worked for the secret police in a full-time or part-time capacity or was an informant.[45] Each apartment complex had a person who would

42. Examples were Estonia, Latvia, and Lithuania.
43. Scattering nationalities throughout the country began with Lenin. The purpose was to reduce their potential for troublemaking.
44. It is necessary to mention that a second economy, often underground, existed in all of the socialist countries. People provided goods and services that were unavailable in state stores, so many people had some business experience.
45. Priests were also informers. One woman told the author that her minister told on her to the secret police. After reunification, the informed-on became informers on those they had a grudge against.

check on the comings and goings of the occupants, and any strange activity was reported to the police. Each block or place of employment had a person or persons who would do the same thing. Distrust that had built up over many years is bound to carry over even though the system has changed.

Loss of Identity

While many groups have gained a sense of identity they didn't have when they were a part of the Soviet Union, other groups have lost a sense of identity. The Russian ethnic group is an example. In a poll, nearly three-quarters of Russians supported the idea of the restoration of the Soviet Union as a union of sovereign states linked together at least economically and politically.[46] Missing is the sense of what the Soviet Union once was, a superpower to be reckoned with. The Russian ethnic group was the core of the Soviet Union. One can also wonder about the loss of such symbols of past Soviet might as the national anthem (the "Internationale") and the hammer and sickle flag, both of which are no more.[47]

Women

It has already been pointed out that the one group that lost the most in the reunification of East Germany and West Germany were the East German women. Under communism there was a professed commitment to gender equality because both sexes should contribute to the building of socialism. Women were educated and entered the labor force in large numbers. They were provided various forms of social assistance: guaranteed maternity leaves, guaranteed job security, and child-care facilities.[48] However, women were far from equal in the socialist economies. They had the double burden of income earner and family work at home. There was not equal pay for equal work; women's salaries were lower than men's. They were also concentrated in the service occupations—medicine, law, and teaching—that paid less than occupations dominated by men. The core sectors of socialism—the bureaucracy and heavy industry—were dominated by men. They were in positions of authority, but those positions were largely symbolic.

So the question is, has the position of women improved now that socialism is a thing of the past and capitalism is in? The answer is, probably not. In the political sphere, women have been increasingly marginalized in that they participate far less in the democratically elected parliaments of the post-Communist countries of Central and Eastern Europe. The role of women in society is also being redefined,

46. Peter Juviler, "Making Up for Lost Choice: The Shaping of Ethnic Identity in Post-Soviet States," in James R. Millar and Sharon L. Wolchik, eds., *The Social Legacy of Communism* (New York: Cambridge University Press, 1994), 50.
47. The U.S. national anthem is difficult to sing, but efforts to change it have been futile.
48. Gail Kligman, "The Social Legacy of Communism: Women, Children, and the Feminization of Poverty," in James R. Millar and Sharon L. Wolchik, eds., *The Social Legacy of Communism* (New York: Cambridge University Press, 1994), 253–257.

meaning that their proper role is supposed to be in the home. Social assistance such as child-care centers, once provided under socialism, has been reduced or eliminated. Personal choice with regard to reproduction, which was legal under socialism, has been withdrawn in some countries. There has also been an increase in prostitution. In Moscow and elsewhere, prostitution, pornography, and striptease shows are common.[49]

SUMMARY

The once-monolithic totalitarian system of the Soviet Union that had existed for seventy-five years is now a thing of the past, brought down by internal problems, not military defeat. Now comes the hard part, because converting to stable societies, particularly in the former Soviet Union, will not be easy. Civil wars between ethnic groups will continue. It is entirely possible that the existing republics created out of the former Soviet Union will fragment into many enclaves based on ethnic or religious differences. Also, the conversion from a centrally planned socialist economy to a free market capitalist economy has been anything but easy. Conversion will take years. Societal conditions, particularly for women, have also deteriorated. Conversion has resulted in an enormous increase in crime and other forms of social deviance.

QUESTIONS FOR DISCUSSION

1. What are the social legacies of communism?
2. Discuss Lenin's New Economic Policy.
3. Discuss some of the factors that caused the Russian Revolution of 1917.
4. Stalin was responsible for the creation of a socialist economy in the Soviet Union. Do you agree?
5. What were some of the reasons for the collapse of the Soviet Union?
6. There was in essence a social contract between the leaders of the Soviet Union and the people. What was it?
7. Why was environmental pollution a legacy of the Soviet economy?
8. In what ways were the leaders of the Soviet Union able to handle ethnic problems that exist today?
9. What was the purpose of perestroika and glasnost?
10. It is alleged that women were better off under communism, which guaranteed equality of the sexes, than they are in the United States or Western Europe. Do you agree or disagree?

49. This is not to say that prostitution or pornography did not exist in one form or another in the former Soviet Union. However, it was far less overt. The Communists were very puritanical. Even beauty pageants were forbidden.

RECOMMENDED READINGS

Dunlop, John B. *The Rise of Russia and the Fall of the Soviet Empire.* Princeton: Princeton University Press, 1993.

Ellman, Michael, and Vladimir Kontorovich, eds. *The Disintegration of the Soviet Economic System.* London: Routledge, 1992.

Goldman, Marshall I. *What Went Wrong with Perestroika.* New York: Norton, 1992.

Kaiser, Robert. *Why Gorbachev Happened: His Triumphs, His Failure, His Fall.* New York: Touchstone Press, 1992.

Kapinski, Ryszard. *Imperium.* New York: Alfred A. Knopf, 1994.

Kligman, Gail. "The Social Legacy of Communism: Women, Children, and the Feminization of Poverty," in James R. Millar and Sharon L. Wolchik, eds., *The Social Legacy of Communism.* New York: Cambridge University Press, 1994, 252–271.

Malia, Martin. *The Soviet Tragedy: A History of Socialism in Russia, 1917–1991.* New York: Free Press, 1994.

Millar, James R., ed. *Politics, Work, and Daily Life in the USSR.* Cambridge, Eng.: Cambridge University Press, 1987.

Millar, James R., and Sharon L. Wolchik. "The Social Legacies and the Aftermath of Communism," in James R. Millar and Sharon L. Wolchik, eds., *The Social Legacy of Communism.* New York: Cambridge University Press, 1994, 1–31.

Prybyla, Jan. "The Road to Socialism, Why, Where, and How." *Problems of Communism,* Vol. XL (January-April 1991). Washington, D.C.: U.S. Government Printing Office, 1991), 1–17.

Reed, John. *Ten Days That Shook the World.* London: Boni and Liveright, 1919. This is a chronicle of the October 1917 revolution.

Rennick, David. *Lenin's Tomb: The Last Days of the Soviet Empire.* New York: Random House, 1993.

Roxburgh, Angus. *The Second Russian Revolution.* London: BBC Books, 1991.

Smith, Hedrick. *The New Russians.* New York: Random House, 1991.

THE FORMER SOVIET UNION

CHAPTER 9

Russia

Revolutions can be divided into three stages. The first stage involves the destruction of the old system. In the French Revolution it meant the destruction of the *ancien régime,* which consisted of the king, the aristocracy, and the large landowners; in the United States it meant getting rid of British rule; and in Russia it meant getting rid of the czar and the institutions associated with czarist rule. The second stage involves the transition from the old to the new order. There is no set time period in which the transition takes place. It took about ten years after the Bolshevik Revolution of 1917 before the Communists were finally able to consolidate their power. The third stage involves the creation of a new economic and social order. In the United States it began with the adoption of a constitution and the election of a president.

The Russian Revolution of 1991 has been called the silent revolution. Although the old order is gone, no king lost his head, no czar was shot, and no bloody battles were fought. To a considerable extent, the old order has become the new order. As is true in the former East Germany and elsewhere, those who were once in power remain in power. This includes the former nomenklatura elite, bureaucrats, police, and the military, all of whom are still around in one capacity or another. Some of them, with the help of American business schools, are learning how to become good capitalists, while others have become Russian versions of Al Capone. There is still a military-industrial complex employing thousands of workers in production and research. Nevertheless, after seventy-four years of Communist rule, "economic man" is alive and well in Russia.

TRANSITION TO A MARKET ECONOMY

Russia was the core of the Soviet and czarist empires. The first republic to be formed after the Bolshevik Revolution, it was called the Russian Soviet Federated Socialist Republic.[1] In 1922 it joined the Ukraine and Belarus to form the Soviet Union. As Table 8-5 indicated, the Russian Federation was the wealthiest part of the former Soviet Union, accounting for 91 percent of industrial output. From a natural resource standpoint it is the richest country in the world. Large-scale enterprises in the highly monopolized Soviet industrial sectors were based in Russia, and Moscow was the center of government. Moreover, Russia was and is the dominant market for all of the newly independent states that were formerly a part of the Soviet Union. Most scientists and their facilities were and are located in Russia.[2]

A legacy of the Soviet Union was consumer neglect, a poor infrastructure, and environmental negligence. The medical infrastructure lacked basic equipment and medicines, and medical staffs were often inadequately trained. Housing was of poor quality, and living quarters were crowded. Agriculture was inefficient because it lacked storage, transport, distribution, and processing facilities. The end result was food shortages and food of low quality. Services of all types were generally poor. The transportation system provided poor passenger service and inefficient freight service. It also suffered from a deteriorating infrastructure of railways, a declining stock of usable tractors and trucks, roads that were often unusable, and a merchant marine that was obsolete by Western standards. Shortages of inputs for the transportation sector, such as steel and spare parts, were also problems.

However, the greatest legacy was environmental degradation. As has been mentioned previously, the Soviet Union and other centrally planned economies placed emphasis on the development of heavy industry. Success was based on the increased physical production of steel and other products. Emphasis was also placed on the development of nuclear power plants, which were often poorly designed. One result was the Chernobyl disaster, which spread radioactive contami-

1. Russia is also called the Russian Federation.
2. Some areas of science in Russia such as fundamental science, military science and space research are considered world-class.

nants throughout much of Europe.[3] Soil contaminated by excessive use of pesticides, herbicides, and fertilization has been exposed to erosion and runoff into the water supply. Air pollution from industry and transportation was unrestrained by environmental laws. Oil and chemical spillage was common.[4] The end result was an unhealthy population with lower life expectancy, increased birth defects, and the possibility of damage to the gene pool.

The remainder of this chapter will examine the process of the change in Russia from a socialist economy to a market economy. However, other changes have to be noted as well, which are shown in Table 9-1. For example, there is the matter of property rights. Who owns property, the state or the individual? The basis of property rights in a market economy is that the individual will put this asset to its best use by comparing its cost to its expected rate of return. This argument provides the ultimate rationale for relying on private property as the basis for an efficient organization of economic activity in an economy.

TRANSFORMATION OF THE POLITICAL AND LEGAL SYSTEMS

The political system of the former Soviet Union was based on the principle of democratic centralism,which was predicated on the assumption that victory in the Bolshevik Revolution of October 1917 meant that the people had spoken through their representative, the Communist Party. Consequently, party leaders assumed the right to choose their own successors and subordinates. Thus, rule was by the selected, not by the elected. Western democratic ideals based on the American and French Revolutions had no carryover to the Soviet Union. The right of a people to freely rule themselves through the choice of elected representatives was absent. Freedom of religion and freedom of speech, both of which are part of the democratic ideal, were also not permitted.[5]

The Communist Party was the only party permitted in the Soviet Union, and of course this gave its candidates for elected positions an obvious advantage. Only candidates belonging to the party would be considered. Legislative machinery exercised no real power in the political process, but it did serve a public relations

3. A friend of the author's who lives in Slovenia, which is about 1,500 miles from Chernobyl, said that they were not allowed to drink milk and were not allowed outside on certain days when radioactive fallout in the atmosphere was high.

4. The domestic oil pipeline, built by the Communists, had 700 leaks in 1994 and a 100,000-ton oil spill in 1994. It was three times the size of the *Exxon Valdez* disaster.

5. A constitution was adopted in 1936. In its final form it provided for the creation of a popular legislative body, direct elections, universal suffrage, the equality of the sexes, a secret ballot, and a supposed guarantee of freedom of speech, press, assembly, worship, and other personal liberties. It is ironic that this constitution was adopted during the time when the Stalinist purges were going on. Millions of people were executed; other millions were sent to concentration camps in Siberia. State prosecutors enforced the will of Stalin. There were show trials at which persons were judged guilty before any defense. There was no freedom of the press.

TABLE 9-1 *A Comparison of Centrally Planned and Market Institutional Arrangements*

Type of Institution	*Centrally Planned*	*Market*
	Economic Institutions	
Resource allocation	Central planning	Free market
Resource ownership	State	Private
Pricing	State	Free market
Income distribution	State	Free market
Profit determination	State guidelines	Free market
	Related Institutions	
Money and banking	State owned	Primarily private
Public finance	State budget	More decentralized
Industrial organization	Large combines	Large private companies
Agriculture	State and collective farms	Privately owned farms
	Political Institutions	
Government structure	Centralized	Federal (U.S.) or centralized
Political parties	Communist Party	Two or more parties
	Legal Institutions	
Laws	Centralized legal system, no business laws or private property laws	Contract law Tort law Bankruptcy law
	Social Institutions	
Individual	Cooperation	Competition
Social contract	Extreme paternalism	Varies by country
Labor unions	Controlled by government	Independent of government
Education	Curriculum state-controlled and ideological	Curriculum less ideological and far broader

purpose in that it gave Soviet citizens a sense of participation in the process of election. If nothing else, the process did permit some feedback pertaining to economic and social conditions. The Soviet Union could also claim to the rest of the world that it permitted free elections despite the fact that there were no opposition parties. However, criticism of the principles of the Communist Party was not permitted.

The Political Transformation

Boris Yeltsin formally abolished the Communist Party in 1991 after a coup attempt to restore the old regime failed. The drafting of a new constitution, which had begun in 1989 when Mikhail Gorbachev still presided over the Soviet Union, continued under Boris Yeltsin and was ratified in December 1993. Unlike the American

Constitution, which separates power among the executive, legislative, and judicial branches of government, the new Russian constitution is one-sidedly in favor of the president, or executive branch, and grants less power to the legislative and judicial branches.

One of the objectives of the Russian legal reforms is the creation of a constitutional court to resolve disputes between the executive and legislative branches of government. The constitution provides for freedom of speech, assembly, religion, and the press. It also guarantees free elections and the formation of political parties.

The first free parliamentary elections were held in December 1993. The State Duma—the lower house of parliament—was to be elected by two systems: proportional for large regions and by plurality for small regions. A number of political parties ran candidates. These parties were grouped into three categories: those parties that were pro-democracy and economic reform; those parties that were pro-democracy and gradual economic reform; and those parties that were generally pro-democracy but anti-economic reform.[6] Included in the last category was the Russian Communist Party, the successor to the Communist Party of the Soviet Union, which favored a continuance of economic planning and a large state sector. Also included was the Liberal Democratic Party, which is neither liberal nor democratic. It is led by Vladimir Zhirinovsky, who wants to restore Russian greatness and reclaim lost territory. The pro-democracy and economic reform group won 111 seats; the gradual economic reform group won 42 seats; and the anti-reform group won 146 seats.[7]

Legal Framework

It would be impossible to transform a socialist, centrally planned economy into a market economy without changing the legal system. Laws in the former Soviet Union and other socialist countries were circumscribed in their use and involved criminal law and family law. There was no need for property, contract, and bankruptcy laws because the state owned everything and state-owned enterprises were not allowed to go bankrupt. Most civil complaints were heard by a judge with a lawyer representing the plaintiff and another the defendant. Law was held in low esteem, and lawyers were considered to be nonproductive, one of the parasitic classes so despised by Marx. Consequently, lawyers were poorly paid and most, like doctors, were women. Thus, the legal system had no applicability to a market economy.

Conversion of Laws to a Market Economy. Several major areas of law have to be constructed from scratch during the transition period from socialism to capitalism. They are as follows:

6. Andrei P. Tsygankov, "Choices for Russian Democrats," *Problems of Post-Communism*, Vol. 42, No. 2 (March-April 1995), 50.
7. Parliamentary elections were held in late 1995 and presidential elections in 1996.

1. Contract law lies at the heart of any business or individual transaction involving performance. The law has to provide remedies for breach of contract. It sets the framework within which parties can legally contract, and it protects vulnerable parties to contracts, such as consumers and tenants.
2. Bankruptcy law involves a decision to close an operation and distribute its assets. The possibility of bankruptcy in a market economy enforces fiscal discipline in an enterprise, something that was not necessary in the socialist economies.
3. The role of property law in a market economy is all-important because ownership has many dimensions, including the right of sale, control, and access. It facilitates title to property and the identification of assets and liabilities necessary to any transaction.
4. Competition law, referred to as antitrust law, is necessary to prevent such anticompetitive business practices as price fixing, division of markets, and group boycotts.[8] It is also designed to prevent the creation of anticompetitive business structures such as monopolies.
5. Securities law is necessary to regulate the sale of stocks and bonds to the public. It involves the creation of a regulatory body to protect buyers of securities against fraud and to require some form of disclosure of information from companies issuing stock.[9]
6. Intellectual property law, which covers patents, trademarks, and copyrights, is necessary to protect owners from any form of legal infringement in both domestic and international commerce.[10]

Choice of Law. A legal system can be based on one of two major types of law: common law or code law. Common law is a product of the Anglo-Saxon heritage. It was developed around A.D. 1150 in England during the reign of Henry II. It is the legal system of the United States, the United Kingdom, Canada, and other countries that were formerly a part of the British empire. It uses the jury system and relies on judicial precedent to resolve disputes. It has very little historical relevance to Russia and Eastern Europe.

Code law, on the other hand, has been used in Europe dating back to A.D. 450, when Rome adopted a code of laws that was applicable to all Romans. Formalized into writing by the Emperor Justinian in A.D. 534, these laws were called the *Corpus Juris Civilis*. There is no jury system under code law because decisions are based on law, not judicial precedent. Code law is less complex than common law. There are two kinds of code law: the French civil code (*Code Napoléon*) and the

8. The major laws regulating competition in the United States are the Sherman Act of 1890 and the Clayton Act of 1914.
9. The Securities and Exchange Commission is the regulatory body in the United States.
10. The use of trademarks illustrates the difference between common law and code law. Common law would hold that the right of property would depend on its use in a dispute between two parties. Code law would hold that property ownership would be based on which party registered the trademark.

German civil code (*Burgerliches Gesetzbuch*). The Napoleonic Code was used in Russia during the time of the czars; it was also used in Poland and Romania before they became Communist. The German civil code was used in Czechoslovakia, Hungary, and Bulgaria before they too became Communist.

The New Legal System of the Russian Federation. The Russian legal system is in a state of flux. There are two competing legal systems, American common law and German code law, reflecting two types of capitalism: America's winner-take-all capitalism and Germany's staid boardroom capitalism. The U.S. legal system employs 850,000 lawyers; the German legal system employs 32,000 lawyers. The legal competition involves corporate laws, particularly as they involve the issuance of common stock. In the United States, corporate finance comes from shareholders; in Germany, it comes from banks rather than shareholders.[11] The Russian privatization program created 45 million shareholders and gave U.S. securities firms leverage over the choice of corporate law. Other forms of law in Russia follow code law. The new Russian civil code approved in June 1994 will apply to property and contracts. Bankruptcy law will also follow the civil code.[12]

ECONOMIC TRANSITION

The 1980s represented a period of slow economic growth and stagnation in the Soviet Union, a process that began during the 1960s. Annual growth for the period 1980–1991 averaged around 2 percent.[13] Despite Gorbachev's attempts at economic reform, there was a drop in both industry and agriculture.[14] Shortages of supplies increased and living standards worsened. Inflationary pressures intensified along with large increases in budget deficits and the money supply. In 1991 the budget deficit had increased to around 20 percent, and by the end of the year both the Soviet Union and Russia had defaulted on payments on their foreign debt obligations. At the end of 1991 Boris Yeltsin, the first president of Russia, proposed a program of change to a market economy and was given the power by Russia's congress to do so. He outlawed the Communist Party, dismantled the bureaucratically directed economy, and began economic reform.

11. German banks, unlike American banks, can trade and sell securities and other financial products.
12. The discussion of the Russian legal system is based on several sources: the law office of Hunton and Williams of Washington, D.C., which has a branch office in Warsaw, Poland; the Commercial Law Development Program of the U.S. Department of Commerce; and the European Bank for Reconstruction and Development, *Transition Report 1995*.
13. The World Bank, *The World Bank Atlas 1993* (Washington, D.C.: The World Bank, 1993), 19.
14. Mention should be made of the Shatalin Plan of 1990, which, in a period of 500 days, would have eliminated the socialist economic system. It was rejected by Gorbachev as being too radical.

Shock Therapy Versus Gradualism

There are two main approaches to economic reform of a centrally planned economy, shock therapy and gradualism. Shock therapy involves an immediate scrapping of the old system in order to build a completely new one. A basic rationale for junking the old system is to lessen the opportunities for the nomenklatura elite to get their hands on the new system. One way to do this is to create a democracy.[15] At the core of shock therapy is a set of short-term policies designed to create a free market and to achieve macroeconomic stabilization and control through government fiscal and monetary policies. Shock therapy would simultaneously do the following:

1. Prices would be freed to achieve market-clearing prices determined by supply and demand, and to eliminate hoarding by transforming an economy from a seller's market to a buyer's market. This would induce a supply response.
2. Money wages and income would be frozen to cause real wages and incomes to fall. This is designed to prevent a wage-price spiral and to reduce real production costs.
3. Government expenditures would be reduced by cutting subsidies and entitlements and reducing defense expenditures.
4. Aggregate demand would be reduced by reducing deficit spending and raising taxes, in particular a value-added tax, which is a tax on consumption. This would cause unemployment to rise and induce employers to make a more rational choice in their use of labor.
5. Bank credit would be tightened, the money supply would be controlled, and a two-tiered banking system headed by a new central bank would be created.
6. The economy would be opened up to world markets by replacing the exchange rate mechanism, in which the ruble was inconvertible into foreign currencies and the supply of foreign currencies was held by the state, with a floating exchange rate in which the ruble is convertible into other currencies.

A more gradual approach would take into consideration that American-style monetarist macroeconomic stabilization policies are not particularly applicable to a socialist economy having different institutional, social, and cultural variables. For example, after the American and French Revolutions were over, the legal systems of common law and code law remained in place as a part of the new building blocks. Seventy years of the communist ideal, based on abstract nineteenth-century ideas, were imposed on the economic and political system of the Soviet Union. Critics of shock therapy claim that it too is based on abstract monetarist principles. Gradualists would argue that it is better to use a more pragmatic approach that would, for example, rely on experience gained from the use of the Marshall Plan after the end of World War II. It was designed to achieve political stabilization in postwar Europe by achieving economic stability. Grants were made

15. James R. Millar, "The Failure of Shock Therapy," *Problems of Post-Communism*, Vol. 41 (Fall 1994), 22.

to specific countries, including Germany, to be used to develop their own development strategies.[16]

In January 1992 the Russian government embarked on a shock therapy policy of economic reform. Prices were decontrolled on most producer and consumer goods. Steps were made to reduce the deficit through cuts in government spending, including defense spending and subsidies to industry and agriculture, and to impose a new tax system. Foreign trade was liberalized although certain restrictions were retained, such as export and import licensing and a requirement that a large portion of foreign exchange earnings be sold to the government. The initial impact of shock therapy was an increase in unemployment and a fall in living standards. Tight fiscal and monetary policies were relaxed, and easy credit and subsidies to industry were introduced. A continuous struggle occurred in Moscow over the pace of reform.

Privatization

By far the most important problem in converting a socialist centrally planned economy to a market economy is privatization of state-owned enterprises. Privatization can be defined as the general process of involving the private sector in the ownership or operation of a state-owned enterprise. It can refer to the purchase of all or part of a state-owned company; it also covers the privatization of management. State-owned enterprises occupied all areas of economic activity in the socialist economies, and for the most part they never achieved the efficiency, productivity, and related performance levels expected of them. Despite efforts to reform them, their performance level deteriorated during the 1980s.[17] Despite massive government investment in science and technology, state enterprises operated far below existing Western technological standards. To some extent, this resulted from undefined property rights that inhibited those enterprises from acting in an entrepreneurial fashion.

Sequencing of Privatization. Privatization does not take place in a vacuum. Before property can be privatized, certain preconditions must exist.[18] First, there must be macroeconomic adjustments. There must be a price system that gives correct signals not only about the real value of the assets and companies to be privatized, but also about their chances of survival in an open market exposed to international competition. Second, there must be a proper legal framework that establishes ownership rights, titling procedures, and arrangements for the transfer of property. In addition, labor and social security laws are needed to establish em-

16. For a comparison of the shock therapy and gradual approach arguments see Anders Aslund, "Prospects of the New Russian Market Economy" in *Problems of Post-Communism*, Special Issue, Vol. 41 (Fall 1994), 16–20; and James R. Millar, "The Failure of Shock Therapy," 21–25.
17. Barbara Lee and John Nellis, "Enterprise Reform and Privatization in Socialist Economies," *World Bank Discussion Paper 104* (Washington, D.C.: The World Bank, 1991), 3–7.
18. Guillermo de la Dehesa, *Privatization in Eastern and Central Europe*, Occasional Paper 34 (Washington, D.C.: Group of Thirty, 1991), 4–10.

ployer and worker rights and labor contracts. Third, there is the matter of asset valuation. In principle, the value of a state-owned enterprise is the price it fetches in the marketplace. One way to value enterprise assets is to use foreign auditors.[19] Fourth, restructuring is necessary. This refers to the breakup of former state monopolies into more salable forms. Also, removal of any large or open-ended liability for an enterprise may be necessary before it can be sold.

Methods of Privatization. There are a number of ways in which state enterprises can be privatized.[20] One way is to distribute to every person a share of equity in the enterprises being privatized. This is called the voucher method, referring to the vouchers, or certificates, that each person receives, giving him or her an entitlement in equity shares. A second method has been through the use of public auctions. This is typically used in the sale of small enterprises, such as restaurants and dry cleaning establishments. The problem has been that those who have the money to buy them were usually part of the nomenklatura elite of the old communist system. A third way is to give away state-owned enterprises to workers and managers. This is the easiest and quickest way to privatize, but there is a problem in that workers and managers were often the cause of inefficiency in those state enterprises. A fourth way is to sell state enterprises to workers and managers. A fifth way is to sell state enterprises to foreign companies.[21]

Privatization of Industry. In the former Soviet Union each sector of industry was managed by its own ministry in Moscow, whose bureaucrats picked the managers to run the state-owned enterprises. People were picked who could be relied on to meet the objectives of the economic plan that each ministry was responsible for implementing. Emphasis was placed on physical output planning, and success for a manager was based on fulfilling or overfulfilling the output target specified by the plan. The reforms of the 1980s were designed in part to give managers more latitude in the choice of inputs used in the production process and in the choice of products to be produced and sold within the framework of the economic plan.

The first part of privatization proved to be easy. Small enterprises, such as shops and cafes, were usually bought by their workers. However, it was decided to use a voucher system for larger firms. By the autumn of 1992, every Russian citizen was given a free voucher having a face value of 10,000 rubles, worth about $25 at that time.[22] The voucher holder had three options: to sell it for cash; to put it into an investment fund that would pool vouchers and invest them in large blocks;

19. Western accounting firms, such as Price Waterhouse, are used in Russia to revalue state assets in terms of market value.

20. Eduardo Borenstein and Manmohan S. Kumar, "Proposals for Privatization in Eastern Europe," *International Monetary Fund Staff Papers*, Vol. 38, No. 2 (June 1991), 300–326.

21. For example, General Electric bought the Hungarian firm Tungsram, and PepsiCo bought the leading candy manufacturer in Poland.

22. Without mass privatization, the nomenklatura elite would have bought up all the enterprises.

or to invest it directly at auction in an enterprise. The first auction was held in December 1992. By June 1994, when all vouchers were set to expire, shares in 2,621 medium-sized and large enterprises had been auctioned off.[23] By the end of that month, 86 percent of the Russian industrial labor force was working in the private sector.

The Bolshevik Biscuit Factory. The Bolshevik Biscuit Factory was the first Russian state enterprise to be auctioned off. Originally established in 1855, it was nationalized in 1918 by the Bolsheviks. The factory is located in Moscow and produces cakes, biscuits, and waffles. Its output at the time of privatization was 250 tons daily and 62,500 tons a year.[24] It employed 2,320 workers and was one of the few state-owned enterprises to have operated successfully on its own. As of January 1, 1992, its current assets exceeded its current liabilities by a ratio of 2.8 to 1. Its reputation was based on its name and product and, as one investor said, "My younger son is in commerce, and he said Bolshevik was certain to make large profits."[25] The auction was opened on December 9, 1992, and was closed on December 24, 1992. Approximately 20,000 bids were accepted at the price of one share per voucher. Those who worked for Bolshevik got 25 percent of the enterprise free.[26] Figure 9-1 presents an example of a privatization voucher.

The voucher was a liquid security. It was actively traded on organized exchanges throughout Russia. On the Russian Commodity and Raw Material Exchange, the largest exchange in Moscow, around 100,000 vouchers changed hands each day. By the end of 1994, some 8.8 million employees worked for more than 10,000 firms that had been privatized in voucher auctions. These workers represented 45 percent of the manufacturing workforce in Russia.[27] This can be considered good for the reason that the voucher program was conceived in a hostile political environment. It was opposed by the bureaucrats and workers and managers for state firms. One way to get around these constraints was to give local government control over small-scale privatization and the revenues derived from the sale of small shops and enterprises.[28]

Table 9-2 presents the ten largest privately owned industrial enterprises in Russia as of January 1, 1995. The largest company, Autovaz, produced 580,000 cars in 1994 and exported 198,000 of them. It was valued at $45 million at the time of privatization. It should be noted that it takes nearly one worker to produce a car compared to one worker to produce twenty-six cars in Japan.

23. "Russia's Emerging Market," *The Economist*, April 8–14, 1995, Survey, 6.
24. European Bank for Reconstruction and Development, *Bolshevik Biscuit Factory* (London: EBRD, April 1993), Appendix 1.
25. Ibid., 26.
26. Russian enterprises slated for privatization could register either as joint-stock companies or as corporations. The majority of enterprises chose the corporate form because workers and managers concluded it gave them better control over the enterprise.
27. OECD, Center for Cooperation with the Economies in Transition, *Mass Privatization: An Original Assessment* (Paris: OECD, 1995), 164.
28. As of January 1995, 95 percent of all shops in Russia were privately owned.

FIGURE 9-1

TABLE 9-2 *Ten Largest Privatized Enterprises in Russia*

Companies	*Employees*	*Industry*	*Dollar Value at Auction ($ millions)*
Avtovaz	551,817	Motor vehicles	45
United Energy System	216,278	Electricity generation	647
Norilsk Nickel	161,520	Nonferrous metals	466
Gaz	109,036	Motor vehicles	27
Magnitogorsk-Metallurgical	108,526	Metallurgy	47
Zil	103,000	Motor vehicles	16
Lukoil	102,700	Oil	293
Surgutneftegaz	80,200	Oil and gas	81
Nizhnevartovskneftegaz	65,780	Oil and gas	168
Yuganskneftegaz	60,823	Oil and gas	72

Source: "Russia's Emerging Market," *The Economist,* April 8–14, 1995, Survey, 16.

Privatization of Agriculture. Agriculture was also privatized in Russia. It too had been controlled by the government through economic planning. The supply and price of inputs, the shares of output marketed, and the prices paid for agricultural output, as well as farm income and expenditures, were regulated by the plan. Overall output goals were established for agricultural products that were to be delivered to the government. There were three main types of agricultural production units:

1. *State farms.* The state farm was the highest form of socialized production unit and enjoyed a favorable status in Soviet agriculture. State farms were intended to increase agricultural production through economies of scale by utilizing modern agricultural techniques. State farms accounted for one-fourth of total agricultural output in the Soviet Union. They were mostly inefficient.
2. *Collective farms.* Unlike workers on state farms, collective farmworkers were not paid wages but shared in the income of the collective farm. Also, unlike state farms, collective farms were not financed out of the state budget but from the income of the collective farm. However, there was an attempt to shift to a regular cash wage paid on a monthly basis.
3. *Private plots.* Private plots represented the third form of agriculture in the Soviet Union. They were divided into three categories: plots operated by state farmworkers, plots operated by collective farmworkers, and plots operated by workers in urban areas. Although they accounted for less than 3 percent of the land under cultivation, they accounted for approximately one-third of the total Soviet Union production of meat and milk and two-thirds of the eggs and potatoes.

Most of Russian agriculture has experienced the same legal transformation as Russian industry. Collective farms were transformed into closed partnerships owned by their workers. However, subsidies to the agricultural sector have continued, as has bureaucratic control.[29] State farms were broken up and sold at auction. Many were simply unsalable because of their geographic location or because their equipment was obsolete. Moreover, since politicians have retained control, the result has been corruption in the sale of land. There has been an increase in the quality and quantity of agricultural products available to Russian consumers, at a higher cost.

Table 9-3 presents the change that has occurred in the Russian private sector in agriculture. The portion of private agricultural production out of total production nearly doubled from 22 to 38 percent from 1989 to 1993. A quarter to one-half of livestock inventories were privately owned by the end of 1993. Nevertheless, substantial limitations remain in the private sector in Russian agriculture. Private farms still represent a small portion of agricultural production in Russia. Most important, marketing of agricultural production is still predominantly in the hands of the government through government procurement.

July 1994 Privatization Edict. In July 1994 President Yeltsin issued an edict that changed the process of privatization. First, shares in privatizing companies that had previously been sold for vouchers now could be sold for cash. Second, workers in an enterprise about to be privatized retained their priority rights to acquire shares in the privatized enterprise. Three options were carried over from the voucher privatization process. They are as follows:[30]

29. American farmers have political clout, but there are many more Russian farmers than American farmers.
30. Edward H. Lieberman, Sally J. March, and Svetlana Almakaeva, "New Russian Civil Code Bodes Well for Business," *National Law Journal*, November 14, 1994, C10–11.

TABLE 9-3
Private Agricultural Production and Livestock Herds as Share of Russian Total (percentage of production)

	1989	*1993*
Gross agricultural output	22.0	38.0
Meat	23.9	40.0
Milk	23.2	35.6
Eggs	21.2	27.3
Wool	22.2	36.6
Grain	0.0	5.2
Sugarbeets	0.0	3.9
Potatoes	58.6	80.0
Vegetables	29.2	65.0
Cattle	16.2	26.1
Hogs	15.5	28.7
Sheep and goats	25.1	41.9

Source: U.S. Department of Agriculture, International Agriculture and Trade Reports, *Former USSR* (Washington, D.C., May 19, 1994), 12.

1. Workers can buy up to 51 percent of the common stock at par value.
2. If the enterprise is insolvent, workers can acquire control by initially buying 30 percent of the common stock at a discount with an option to obtain the shares that remain in state ownership.
3. Members of a labor collective can receive preferred nonvoting stock equal to 25 percent of the authorized capital free of charge and can buy up to 10 percent of the voting stock at a discount. Management can buy up to 5 percent.

Foreign investors were given several options for acquiring stock in privatized companies. After shares have been distributed to workers and management on the basis of one of the above three options, the remainder can be sold through an authorized state or municipal property fund, through commercial competition, or at auction. These auctions deal in cash rather than investment vouchers.

On March 7, 1996, Boris Yeltsin signed a decree stating that owners of farmland, including those who own it indirectly through shares in collective farms, can buy, sell, or mortgage their land, provided it stays in agricultural use and in Russian hands. The decree also allows a free market in the small landholdings of some 40 million people, formerly passed on only through inheritance.[31]

As of March 1996 more than nine-tenths of Russian agriculture is controlled by large, inefficient, undercapitalized collective farms, which are run pretty much as they were in the old Soviet Union. Most often, they are run by managers who are indifferent to free market forces.

31. "Russian Land Reform: The Earth Moves," *The Economist,* March 16–23, 1996, 76.

Financial Markets

The development of a financial market is also important in the transition from a centrally planned economy to a market economy. Financial markets have two fundamental functions. The first is to mobilize savings, and the second is to allocate them to the most efficient uses. The role of financial markets in a centrally planned economy was very limited. Individuals had very little influence on the allocation of resources, on the rate of saving, on the level and allocation of investment, or on the rate of interest. The distribution of income was determined directly through the control of prices and wages and by government-imposed obstacles to saving and wealth accumulation. Credit was rarely extended to individuals, and when available was directed toward socially approved purchases. Interest served no allocative function as it would in a market economy.

Banking. The monetary system of the Soviet Union was a tool of the annual plan, which was conceived in physical terms. The plan determined the shares of the total physical resources of the country that would go into consumption and investment. A corollary of the physical plan was the financial plan, divided into the state budget, a credit plan, and a cash plan. Monetary policy, which was exercised by the state bank (Gosbank), was used to control the volume of credit to state enterprises and make available the growth of cash in line with the planned gap between receipts and outlays in the household sector. The state bank monitored the observance of the plan by guaranteeing enterprises credit necessary to carry out planning transactions and seeing that credit was used for these transactions.

Gosbank performed the functions of the central bank and commercial banks and was the repository of funds from the state budget. It was also the collector of taxes.[32] There were also special-purpose banks, one of which was Sberbank, the savings bank in the Soviet Union. It acted as the conduit of household saving to finance the fiscal debt of the Soviet Union. Another bank was Vneshtorgbank, created in 1924. It was responsible for financing Soviet foreign trade and for carrying out a large part of Soviet international financial settlements. It also held the official foreign reserves of the Soviet Union. Another special bank was the Agroprombank, which was responsible for the provision of credit to state and collective farms.

Creation of a Two-Tiered Banking System. A two-tiered banking system was created in the Soviet Union in 1988 as a result of the perestroika reforms. Gosbank was broken up into two separate entities, a central bank and a group of commercial banks. The central bank assumed some of the functions of a Western central bank, such as the conduct of monetary policy, which involves regulating overall

32. Since producers and retailers had accounts with branches of Gosbank, it was relatively easy for bank representatives to monitor sales. Each enterprise had an account with only one branch and had to make all payments, except cash wages, on checks drawn from that branch. Both producer and consumer prices were controlled by the state.

credit and interest rates. Russian commercial banks have not been an important source of private capital for business enterprises.[33] They have made most of their money by taking in ruble deposits, selling the rubles for dollars, watching the ruble depreciate, and then taking the foreign exchange profit when the depositors ask for their rubles back. The safest way of lending money is to confine loans to companies in which a bank has an equity stake, and hence some control over management.[34]

Table 9-4 lists the ten largest commercial banks in Russia as of January 1, 1995, measured by the value of their assets. The three largest banks were formerly a part of the Soviet banking system. Sberbank was the savings bank, Vneshtorg the foreign trade bank, and Agroprom the bank that made agricultural loans. A similarity has developed between these banks and the major German commercial banks in that they are buying equity stakes in Russia's large industrial firms. In April 1995 the Russian government announced that it planned to allow equity ownership in Russia's most profitable companies, including oil and gas enterprises, for a $2-billion line of credit.[35]

Securities Market. The development of a securities market is also important in the transition from socialism to capitalism. Financial institutions, including a securities market, mobilize domestic savings by providing a range of instruments (in the case of securities markets, debt and equity instruments) that enhance the efficiency of investment and return to capital. Securities markets also facilitate trading in government debt obligations. In the United States, government debt obligations, ranging from short-term Treasury bills to long-term Treasury bonds, are bought and sold in various U.S. and foreign securities markets.

Government Capital. Much of the capital of Russian enterprise still comes from government subsidies and directed credit from the central bank.[36] Subsidies take several forms: import subsidies, energy subsidies, and subsidies for making interest payments on already subsidized credits. Agriculture and energy have been the major beneficiaries of the government and central bank's subsidies and credit policies, as are very large manufacturing firms. Firms that get credit from the central bank usually get it at negative real interest rates. In addition, the government often subsidizes the interest payments to the central bank made by enterprises out of the budget. Thus, the combination of subsidies and loans reallocates massive resources to some sectors of the economy, in particular agriculture, which has been hard to privatize. In the allocation of credits and subsidies, no discrimination is made between state-owned and privatized enterprises.

The first Russian stock exchanges were opened in the summer of 1991, and as of November 1995, there were around seventy exchanges.[37] The securities market

33. Maxim Boyko, Andrei Shleifer, and Robert Vishny, *Privatizing Russia* (Cambridge, Mass.: MIT Press, 1995), 134.
34. *The Economist,* Survey, 14.
35. "Russia Taking Privatization to the Bank," *Wall Street Journal*, April 20, 1995, A-8.
36. OECD, *Mass Privatization: An Initial Assessment*, 182–183.
37. European Bank for Reconstruction and Development, *Transition Report*, November 1995, 56.

Table 9-4
Ten Largest Commercial Banks in Russia as of January 1, 1995 ($ billions)

Bank	*Assets*
Sberbank	14.77
Vneshtorg	6.26
Agroprom	6.10
Inkombank	3.06
Rossissky	2.58
Unexim	2.35
Moscow Industrial	2.06
Imperial	1.95
International Company for Finance and Investment	1.93
Stolichny	1.78

Source: "Russia's Emerging Market," *The Economist,* April 8–14, 1995, Survey, 14.

is still unregulated and segmented. The main volume of business has been the purchase and sale of privatization vouchers, gold certificates, and short-term debt obligations. Russian securities markets also deal in commercial paper, promissory notes, currency futures, and hard currency certificates of deposit. Privatization of industry has resulted in an increase in the purchase and sale of stocks and bonds. Outside the securities markets there is also over-the-counter trading in stocks and bonds. Portfolio investment by foreigners is normally done this way. But there are problems that have affected the securities markets, not the least of which was the crash of the Mexican stock market in December 1994, which dampened the enthusiasm foreign investors had for emerging markets.

Public Finance

The operation of any modern state requires the collection of large sums of money to finance public services and pay for the general administrative expenses of government. This was as true of the Soviet Union as it is of any capitalist country. However, there were great differences in the ways in which the two forms of economic system acquired and disposed of their revenues. The most important difference was the role that the national, or state, budget played in resource allocation in the Soviet Union. It was a consolidated budget that provided for the revenues and expenditures of the national, republic, and local units of government. It was also closely related in terms of revenues and expenditures to the national economic plan. It was the major instrument for financing most types of investment and for controlling the use of investment in accordance with planning goals.

Taxation. The role of taxation in the centrally planned economy of the Soviet Union was nominal, because planning determined resource allocation. It was simply the difference between output and what the state chose to release to private households and firms. The turnover tax was the most important source of tax revenue. The basic role of the turnover tax, which has the impact of a sales or excise tax, was to siphon off the excess purchasing power of consumers. It varied in response to supply and demand conditions.

A second important tax was the profits tax levied on state enterprises. It was a mechanism by which the state extracted the financial surplus of enterprises. Since the state was the sole owner of enterprises, there was no need to distinguish between dividends and taxes. Since all pricing and production decisions were made by the state, different taxes had neutral effects on both efficiency and incentives. Moreover, both turnover and profits taxes could be adjusted ex post, making statutory tax rates irrelevant.

Expenditures. State expenditures were divided into four major categories: expenditures to finance the national economy, social-cultural measures, defense, and administration. Financing the national economy accounted for over half of expenditures in the Soviet state budget. Included were allocations to state enterprises for capital investments and financial capital. Capital goods and construction industries were the major recipients of budget funds for investment purposes. Appropriations from the state budget were used to finance the construction of transportation facilities, investment in state farms, and housing construction.

Expenditures on social and cultural measures were divided into three major categories as follows:

1. Expenditures on education, science, and culture, including the support of schools, museums, expositions, and the performing arts.[38] Scientific research included research designed to support national defense.
2. Expenditures on health and physical education covered outlays for medical and hospital facilities, training of medical personnel, and medical research. Physical culture expenditures included outlays for athletic programs carried out throughout the Soviet Union.
3. Social security and social insurance represented expenditures for old-age, disability, and sickness and maternity benefits.

National defense expenditures included outlays for research and development for complex military equipment, armed forces personnel, maintenance of military facilities, and military construction. It was estimated that Soviet military expenditures amounted to around 14 to 18 percent of the Soviet GNP compared to around 6 percent of United States GNP for U.S. defense expenditures. National defense expenditures placed a burden on the Soviet economy, absorbing huge amounts of human and material resources that could have been used to produce consumer goods.

Conversion of the Public Financial Systems. Changes in the fiscal system were necessary to transform Russia from a centrally planned economy to a market economy. The administration of the tax system of the former Soviet Union had been

38. The Soviet Union did a far better job of supporting culture than most capitalist countries. When left to the free market, cultural support has low priority. The Bolshoi Ballet, once the crowning cultural jewel of the Soviet Union, is now broke.

relatively simple. Planning dominated resource allocation, and the role of taxation was nominal. It performed no redistributive function. The vast majority of funds were channeled through the state bank and the state budget, so there was no need for a collection agency such as the IRS. Any change in the tax system was made by the central planners to conform with planning objectives, not by law as is required in the U.S. political system. So the challenge of tax reform in the transition to a market economy was to assure that adequate revenue could be raised and that the tax environment was conducive to private sector development and effective resource allocation.

Changes in the Russian tax system have been rather piecemeal. Some tax changes were made in 1991 and 1992 when value-added and excise taxes were introduced, and a legal base for taxation was created by the passage in the Duma of the Law on the Basic Principles of Taxation.[39] A three-tiered tax system was created, consisting of federal, regional, and local taxes, but revenue sharing among the three levels of government was not clearly defined. In 1992 and 1993 the Russian government operated without a budget. The first formal budget was passed by the Duma in June 1994, and in January 1995 a law was passed making it illegal for the national government to finance its deficit by printing money.[40] It, too, will have to borrow at market rates of interest.

Table 9-5 presents a breakdown of Russian tax revenues expressed as a percentage of GDP for 1993. The most important taxes are the value-added tax, the rate of which was 21.5 percent; the enterprise profits tax, whose rate is 35 percent; a progressive personal income tax, with rates from 12 to 30 percent; excise taxes, ranging as high as 90 percent; and export taxes.[41]

Expenditures. Expenditures came from three sources: consolidated federal, state, and local budgets; extrabudgetary funds; and unbudgeted import subsidies granted by the federal government. Expenditures reflect the view that the function of the state is to support production, regardless of whether anyone needs or wants the production. This is a carryover from the past. Subsidies are an important component of federal budget expenditures, particularly agriculture, which was the black hole of the Soviet economy. Even though Russia now has some 350,000 private farmers, and some attempts have been made to break up state and collective farms, one-fifth of the population is still employed in farming.[42] Import subsidies are also important. In 1993 budgeted and unbudgeted import subsidies amounted to 2.8 percent of Russian GDP.[43] Subsidies are also important at the local level of

39. The value-added tax is one of the more commonly used taxes in the world. It is a tax levied on the amount of value added to products at each stage of the production process. It is an excellent source of revenue and is difficult to avoid. An excise tax is a tax based on the sale of specific commodities such as liquor. The Soviet Union used a personal income tax, but it was of minimal importance and was not used to redistribute income.
40. *The Economist*, April 8–14, 1995, Survey, 19.
41. European Bank for Reconstruction and Development, 56.
42. "Russia's Emerging Market," 19.
43. *Russian Federation 1994*, 18–19.

Table 9-5
Russian Tax Revenues Expressed as a Percentage of Russian GDP, 1993

	Level of Government		
Tax	*National*	*State*	*Local*
Value-added tax	4.5	6.9	2.5
Excise tax	0.4	0.9	0.5
Profits tax	3.4	10.3	7.0
Household income tax	—	2.7	2.7
Foreign revenues	3.3	3.4	0.1
Total all sources	13.7	28.5	17.5

Source: International Monetary Fund, IMF Economic Reviews, *Russian Federation 1994* (Washington, D.C.: International Monetary Fund, 1994), 91.

government. Subsidies granted by local governments amounted to 4.0 percent of Russian GDP in 1993.

Table 9-6 presents federal government expenditures expressed as a percentage of Russian GDP for 1995. The 1995 budget set a cap on the federal deficit of 5.6 percent of GDP, in part to qualify for a $6.4-billion loan from the IMF. The budget was passed in March 1995.

Foreign Trade

The former Soviet Union was largely isolated from international markets. The government controlled international financial and trade flows to ensure that foreign economic transactions were carried out in accordance with the economic plan. Government control of prices and exchange rates led to the inconvertibility of the ruble, thus inhibiting trade and capital flows. Hard currency allocations for Soviet imports were based on the relative importance of the imports to the economic plan. Trade was managed by foreign trade organizations (FTOs) that operated directly under the jurisdiction of various ministries. The FTOs had a trading monopoly on a wide variety of products. This led to the isolation of Soviet industries from foreign competition and from the technological advances of Western industries. It fostered manufacturing industries that were not competitive in world markets and lacked incentives to export.

The Ruble. The ruble is convertible into other currencies within Russia; it is not convertible outside of Russia. However, the U.S. dollar is more important than the ruble as a medium of exchange in Russia, and as of March 30, 1996, the exchange rate was $1 = 4,873 rubles.[44] A formal dollar-ruble exchange rate was set in 1992. The use of the ruble in foreign trade and investment is circumscribed by regula-

44. *Wall Street Journal*, March 30, 1996. The ruble is pegged within a band of 4,300–4,900 rubles per dollar.

Table 9-6
The Russian Federal Budget for 1995 (percentage of GDP)

Expenditures for	*Percent*
National economy	3.5
Conversion	0.1
Foreign economic activity	1.9
Education	0.9
Culture	0.3
Health and sport	0.5
Science	0.6
Law and order	1.7
Administration	0.5
National defense	4.9
Other*	7.6
Total	22.5

**Mainly subsidies and credits.*

Source: "Russia's Emerging Market," *The Economist*, April 8–14, 1995, Survey, 19.

tions set by the Russian government. As of April 1995, the regulations were as follows:[45]

1. Nonresident foreign companies are not permitted to trade in rubles in Russia, and can set up ruble accounts only to cover their day-to-day expenses. They are also not permitted to exchange rubles for dollars through authorized Russian banks or participate in currency exchanges..
2. Resident companies, which includes 100 percent wholly owned subsidiaries and joint ventures, are permitted to have a ruble account and a hard currency account. They may also convert rubles to dollars through authorized banks and currency exchanges.
3. Nonresident foreign companies may exchange hard currency for rubles through the Central Bank of Russia and place the proceeds in a special account. Ruble profits can be converted into hard currency through banks and currency exchanges.

Ordinary Russians can exchange rubles into dollars, yen, D-marks, and other currencies through banks authorized by the central bank or foreign exchange markets. They may have foreign currency accounts at authorized Russian banks. The ruble market rate is determined by the buying and selling of rubles at weekly auctions held by the Moscow Interbank Currency Exchange.[46] Trading sessions in

45. U.S. Department of Commerce, International Trade Administration, *Commercial Overview of Russia* (Washington, D.C.: International Trade Administration, April 19, 1995), 16.
46. The Moscow Interbank Currency Exchange (MICE) is the largest currency exchange in Russia, in terms of both volume of currency traded and number of financial institutions.

hard currencies also take place on the Moscow Central Stock and Currency Exchange.

Foreign Trade. Russian exports in 1993 amounted to $43 billion while Russian imports amounted to $27 billion, for a favorable merchandise trade account of $16 billion.[47] There has been a major shift away from trade with other republics that were formerly a part of the Soviet Union, with the exception of the Ukraine. The bulk of this increased trade has been with Western Europe. In 1993 $24.6 billion in trade was with Western Europe.[48] Energy exports accounted for 40 percent of the value of all Russian exports, while consumer goods and light industrial products accounted for over half of the value of Russian imports. However, export quotas was placed on the export of most energy and raw material products.[49] Tariffs averaging 12.7 percent of the price of the import and excise taxes ranging from 10 to 400 percent are levied on most imports.

SUMMARY

Russia has begun the transition from a centrally planned economy to a market economy. Much has been done in a short period of time, but there is still more to do. Most of the institutions of the former Soviet Union have been restructured to fit into a market environment. Russia has private enterprise, a democratic form of government, a commercial banking system, and a new system of public finance. It enjoys advantages denied to most countries. It has immense national wealth in the form of oil, gas, and precious metals as well as strong human resources, a literate workforce, and an abundance of scientists and engineers. There is also freedom from fear—fear being the one thing that made the Stalinist system work for so many years.

QUESTIONS FOR DISCUSSION

1. Why is the Russian Revolution of 1991 called the silent revolution?
2. Discuss some of the legacies that the Soviet Union left to the Russian Federation and the other former Soviet republics.
3. What was the principle of democratic centralism?
4. The establishment of a framework of laws is probably the most important step in the conversion of a socialist economy to a market economy. Discuss.
5. What is shock therapy? How was it applied to Russia?

47. *Commercial Overview of Russia*, 7.
48. *Russian Federation*, 107.
49. They were eliminated in 1995.

6. Compare the Russian banking system when Russia was a part of the Soviet Union to the Russian banking system today.
7. What is a privatization voucher? How did it work? Was privatization successful?
8. Why is an organized financial market important to the creation of a market economy?
9. What role does the Russian government play in the provision of capital?
10. How has the system of public finance been changed in Russia?
11. Discuss the status of the Russian ruble. Is it convertible?

RECOMMENDED READINGS

Aslund, Anders. *How Russia Became a Market Economy.* Washington, D.C.: The Brookings Institution, 1995.

Berliner, Joseph S. "The Gains from Privatization," in *The Former Soviet Union in Transition,* Vol. 1. Joint Economic Committee, Congress of the United States, 103d Cong., 1st. Sess. Washington, D.C.: U.S. Government Printing Office, 1993, 240–254.

Boycko, Maxim, Andrei Shleifer, and Robert Vishny. *Privatizing Russia.* Cambridge, Mass.: MIT Press, 1995.

Center for Cooperation with the Economies in Transition. *Mass Privatization: An Original Assessment.* Paris: OECD, 1995.

European Bank for Deconstruction and Development. *Transition Report 1995.* London: EBRD, 1995.

Holtzman, Franklyn D. "The Soviet-Russian Ruble: The Past, Present, and Future of Convertibility." In *The Former Soviet Union in Transition,* Vol. 1. Joint Economic Committee, Congress of the United States, 103d Cong., 1st. Sess. Washington, D.C.: U.S. Government Printing Office, 1993, 405–421.

International Monetary Fund. *IMF Economic Reviews, Russian Federation 1994.* Washington, D.C., 1994.

Kornai, Janos. *The Socialist System.* Princeton, N.J.: Princeton University Press, 1992.

Lieberman, Edward H., Sally J. March, and Svetlana Almakaeva. "New Russian Civil Code Bodes Well for Business." *National Law Journal,* November 14, 1994, 10–11.

Millar, James R. "The Failure of Shock Therapy." *Problems of Post-Communism,* Vol. 41, Special Issue, Fall 1994, 21–25.

Modiselt, Lawrence E. "The Cultural Dimension: Is There a Basis for Free Enterprise?" In *The Former Soviet Union in Transition,* Vol. 1, Joint Economic Committee, Congress of the United States, 103d Cong., 1st Sess. Washington, D.C.: U.S. Government Printing Office, 1993, 330–340.

"Russia's Emerging Market." *The Economist,* April 8–14, 1995, Survey, 3–22.

World Bank. "Subsidies and Directed Credits to Enterprises in Russia: A Strategy for Reform." Working paper. Washington, D.C.: World Bank, 1994.

World Bank. "Russia: The Banking System in Transition." Working paper. Washington, D.C.: World Bank, 1993.

THE RUSSIAN FEDERATION

CHAPTER 10

The Future of Russia

"Today Russia does not change every year, it changes every month."[1]

May 8, 1995, marked the fiftieth anniversary of the end of World War II. In no country that had participated in the war was that date more celebrated than in Russia. To honor the event President Clinton went to Moscow to pay his respects to those who fought in what the Russians still refer to as "The Great Patriotic War." It is an indisputable fact that the army of the Soviet Union did more to defeat the German army than any other Allied country, including the United States. Casualties were very high, and much of the country was destroyed by the war.[2] The Soviet Union finished the war as a world superpower, but fifty years later that

1. Anonymous Russian.
2. The Soviet Union lost eight million soldiers, ten times as many as the combined total for the other Allies. Roughly three-fourths of the German soldiers who died during the war did so fighting the Russians. In addition, some twenty million civilians were killed, and such cities as Leningrad, Kiev, and Rostov were completely destroyed.

power was gone, with only a reminder of past glories as Russian war veterans passed the reviewing stand in Red Square as others had passed before Stalin fifty years earlier.

Today Russia's leaders are mostly half-reformed creatures of Soviet upbringing, trying to build a democracy and a market economy on the undestroyed remains of communism. And this condition makes Russia highly unreliable.[3] It is going to take a long period of time before a definite judgment can be made concerning the results of Russian market reforms. Another problem is political instability, both within Russia and in the other republics that were formerly a part of the Soviet Union. Russia has no democratic past to go back to, no cultural and political tradition upon which to build a democratic society. Many older and poorer people still think of normality as the stagnation years of the Brezhnev regime when most Russians were about equal in living standards. Now Russia is going through a revolution that has brought about one of the biggest redistributions of income any modern nation has ever seen.

In their book *Russia 2010* Daniel Yergin and Thane Gustafson use scenario planning in an attempt to predict what Russia will be like in the year 2010.[4] There are three difficult transitions that Russia faces. The first is from dictatorship to democracy; the second is from a centrally planned economy to a free market; and the third, which may be the most difficult to make, is the abandonment of an empire four centuries old. Will Russia be a cooperative partner in world affairs, or will it be driven by imperialism? Yergin and Gustafson present four possible scenarios for Russia:[5]

1. The first scenario is one of a society and an economy that are running down. Lawlessness is on the increase, and nostalgia for the old political and economic order has created the politics of resentment and humiliation.[6]
2. Another scenario involves the emergence of a strong political middle that stabilizes a weak central government. An alliance of defense and industrial managers formed with the army and police aims to restore self-respect and reimposes the state on the economy.
3. Chaos is the third scenario, involving several possibilities. First, Russia could move toward two spheres of influence. The eastern part of Russia, including Siberia, could come under the influence of Japan or China, while the western part would orient itself toward Germany and Scandinavia. The central government would be weak. However, this could be followed by a reaction leading to the centralization of power and development of an authoritarian and aggressive

3. The Economist Intelligence Unit gave Russia a country risk assessment of 90 in the first quarter of 1996. This rating was based on economic and political factors. Only Iraq had a higher risk assessment, and that was the maximum of 100.
4. Daniel Yergin and Thane Gustafson, *Russia 2010,* The Cera Report (New York: Random House, 1993).
5. Ibid., 13–15.
6. These are precisely the conditions that existed in Germany after the end of World War I and that gave rise to Adolf Hitler.

nationalistic state, with Russia reimposing its dominance on the other states of the former Soviet Union.

4. The final scenario is called the *chudo*, or miracle, in which Russia becomes an economic miracle on the order of Germany and Japan after the end of World War II. Unlike those two countries, Russia does not have a commercial tradition or a preexisting base of private property; like those two countries, it has an educated workforce and a pent-up demand for goods and services. Moreover, unlike Germany and Japan, Russia has enormous mineral resources.

RUSSIA'S HISTORY

The noted dissident Andrei Sakharov made the statement: "We know too little about the laws of history." If history has laws, they are unfavorable to the development of democratic institutions in Russia. It is impossible to turn a four-century-old empire, ruled at the center by despots, into a nation-state overnight. Resentment over the breakup of the Soviet Union and a decline in living standards could bring about a repeat of what happened in Germany in 1923. If there is a total collapse of the economy, and that is a possibility, there could be internal chaos and even war, both on and within Russia's borders. Upheaval within Russia could spread to the rest of the former Soviet Union, and from there to Europe, Asia, and the Middle East.

The Mongol Period, 1236–1462

Russia was created out of blood and chaos. In the early thirteenth century, the Mongols, united under Genghis Khan, moved from the Asiatic steppes, poured into southern Russia, and defeated the feudal lords of Russia. Later they crossed the Volga River, destroyed northern and central Russia, and burned Moscow to the ground. The Mongols ruled Russia for almost two hundred years,[7] with Kiev as their capital. The Mongols were responsible for one important contribution to the eventual development of the Russian state: they compelled a loose group of feudal lords to pull together in order to survive. Their power was based in Moscow, and under single leadership an army was trained that could fight the Mongols on an even basis. They defeated the Mongols and the power passed to Moscow, which has retained it to the present.[8]

After the expulsion of the Mongols, Moscow, or Muscovy as it was called, expanded under the leadership of Ivan the Great, who united most of European Russia under his rule. Muscovy expanded eastward to the Ural Mountains and along the Volga River valley. It also expanded south to the Black Sea. A wide vari-

7. Peter I. Liashchenko, *A History of the National Economy of Russia to the 1917 Revolution* (New York: Macmillan, 1949), 235–237.

8. The Mongols eventually settled in southeastern Russia and introduced the Muslim religion into that area.

ety of nationalities were assimilated into what was eventually to become Russia. The economy of Muscovy was essentially based on agriculture and trade. The peasants who farmed the lands were personally free, could own land, and owed only specified taxes, paid in kind to the local feudal lord for his protection. In this respect their position in medieval times was superior to that of their counterparts in the West.

The Czarist Period, 1547–1917

Personal power and the formal assumption of the title of czar occurred in 1547 under the reign of Ivan the Terrible. The feudal lords were largely replaced by a new class of landed gentry who received their land directly from the czar in return for the provision of financial support. In the process the peasants lost their freedom and became serfs through legislation by the czar, who needed them not only for taxes but for service in the army. Thus, for some three hundred years peasants were the backbone of the economy, and attempts to improve their lot usually failed.[9] The czars, beginning with Ivan, held their power through strict heredity.[10]

A succession of czars, beginning with Peter the Great, expanded the Russian empire. Peter recognized the need to modernize Russian technology, so he imported technicians from Western Europe to aid in this process. In this way, he built himself an army and a navy that defeated Sweden and enabled him to gain the Baltic regions. He created the town of St. Petersburg, which became the capital of Russia.[11] Succeeding czars acquired much of Poland and the Crimea and other areas from Turkey by the end of the eighteenth century. In the nineteenth century, Russia expanded eastward in an imperialist rivalry with Great Britain to see which country could grab the most territory. Russia acquired northern Persia and the area of Turkestan. By the end of the century the Russian empire in Asia embraced over six million square miles. It was composed of many groups of peoples who spoke different languages and had different cultures.

Industrial Capitalism in Russia

Industrial capitalism came late to Russia. The machines and inventions upon which industrial capitalism is based could not find application within the feudal economy of Russia. Czarist rule and serfdom suppressed all manifestations of personal initiative and invention, and did not prepare and create the technical culture necessary for capitalism. Thus a capitalist machine-factory technology could not

9. The serfs were freed in 1861. Many went to the cities to work in the factories, but the majority of the peasants continued to work on the farms.

10. This is not quite true. Ivan was a brutal despot, and a period of anarchy lasting for some thirty years occurred until 1613, when Michael Romanov became czar. The Romanov dynasty lasted until 1917. Russian rule was based on the Byzantine, or Eastern, tradition, which meant that the czar had complete authority over church and state.

11. St. Petersburg was renamed Leningrad by the Bolsheviks and the capital was moved to Moscow. Leningrad has now been renamed St. Petersburg.

be created in its full form within the framework of what was basically a feudal agrarian economy. In most Russian industries, handwork still predominated. The serf-manned iron industry of Russia was unfamiliar with the steam engine, worked in primitive refineries, and displayed complete technical backwardness. By 1850 Russia was the most backward industrial country in Europe.

The cotton industry, helped by foreign capital, was the first to begin its transition to capitalist machine technology, although all of the machinery was imported from England. The freeing of the serfs in 1861 provided a source of cheap labor. A marked increase in industrial development began to occur in the latter part of the nineteenth century, primarily as a result of the investment of foreign capital. By 1890 foreign capital represented 70 percent of all the capital invested in Russia and was particularly important in the development of heavy industry and railroads.[12] Most industrial development took place in four regions: the Moscow industrial region, where textiles were produced; the St. Petersburg region, which concentrated on the metal-processing and machine-building industries; the region that is now eastern Poland, which had the iron, coal, and chemical industries; and the Ukrainian region, which had coal, iron, and basic chemical industries.[13]

Czarist economic policy pertaining to the development of industry had an adverse effect on the economic development of Russia that continues to exist today. First, most of the industrial development took place in the Moscow and St. Petersburg regions. Czarist national policy blocked economic development of the non-Russian areas that constituted most of Russia. The areas of Russia that were richest in resources were off limits to foreign investors. These regions were ostensibly reserved for Russian capital. These regions were non-Russian, so czarist policy opposed their development. The base that could have contributed to the development of Russian industry remained undeveloped. Heavy industry lacked a fuel base, and light industry lacked a raw material base.

Russia at the Beginning of World War I

Before the beginning of World War I in 1914 Russia was basically an agricultural country. Russian industry had begun a process of industrial concentration similar to what had been going on in the United States and Germany. In 1910, for example, 53.5 percent of Russian industrial workers were employed by firms with five hundred or more workers.[14] There were a large number of small companies employing fifty or fewer workers whose technology was not comparable to Western standards. These firms employed 11.6 percent of all industrial workers in 1910. Along with industrial concentration came an increase in productivity. The growth of productivity in the iron and steel industry increased by 50 percent during the

12. Liashchenko, 323.
13. When Germany invaded Russia in 1941 it destroyed 80 percent of the Russian industrial base within a year. Russia had to transport its industry beyond the Ural Mountains to keep producing.
14. Liashchenko, 670.

period 1900–1909 and by 400 percent in comparison to 1890.[15] Productivity was also increased by the substitution of improved internal combustion and electric engines for steam engines.

Nevertheless, Russian industry was far behind American and German industry in terms of development and productivity. Total power sources, computed on a per capita basis, showed Russia to be at one-fifteenth of the level prevailing in the United States and one-eighth of that in Germany. In terms of the absolute total of mechanical power per 100 Americans, Germans, and Russians, the United States had a figure of 25 horsepower, Germany 13, and Russia 1.6.[16] Although Russia had attained some success in the production of iron and steel, many major industries were either completely or almost completely nonexistent in Russia in 1913. There was no automobile industry, most machinery had to be purchased from abroad, and basic chemical production was poorly developed. In 1913 the volume of industrial production in Germany was 6 times and in the United 14.3 times as much as Russia. Table 10-1 presents a breakdown of the Russian economy in 1913 based on types of economic activity.

Russia in 1914 already had some of the basic ingredients of a market economy. It had an industrial working class, although small in number. It also had a commercial, technical, and professional middle class. It had a banking system and a securities market.[17] Some effort toward political reforms had been made, and had the war not started in 1914, it is entirely possible that a constitutional monarchy with some sort of political democracy would have been created. But the war did occur, and Russia was not industrially prepared for it and lost. Seventy-four years after the Bolshevik Revolution of 1917, it had to create a political democracy and a myriad of institutions that are necessary for the development of a market economy. It is far from certain that it will be successful.

The Legacy of Russian History

Russian culture is a product of seven centuries of Mongol, czarist, and Communist rule. It can be argued that Russia cannot transform itself from a statist to a free market economy because there are too many cultural forces at work to prevent it, including the influence of collectivist institutions such as the peasant communes and the lack of a native capitalist tradition. There is also what is referred to by Hedrick Smith as the culture of envy.[18] Anyone who becomes too successful is subject to personal attacks by his or her neighbors. On the other hand, it can be argued that there has always been capitalism in one form or another, dating back to Mongol times when there were traders, merchants, small farmers, and money lenders.

15. Ibid., 671.
16. Ibid., 672.
17. The Russian banking system was controlled by French banking interests. Russian banks were privately owned and had a controlling interest in most large industrial enterprises in Russia.
18. Hedrick Smith, *The New Russians* (New York: Random House, 1994), 179–205.

RUSSIA IN ECONOMIC TRANSITION, 1990–1994

Even after separating from the fourteen republics that were also a part of the former Soviet Union, Russia is still the largest nation in the world, comprising eleven time zones. Yet it is far from being an economic power. Its money GDP in 1993 was not much larger than that of Australia, whose population is about one-eighth the size of Russia's. It would be better to consider Russia as an emerging market economy in the same category as Argentina, Malaysia, and Mexico, but it has one thing that other emerging market economies lack—immense natural resources in the form of oil, gas, and precious metals. Tables 10-2 and 10-3 compare Russia and other emerging market economies on the basis of various economic and social factors.

Tables 10-4 and 10-5 present indications of economic activity through the period 1990 through January–June 1994. Real gross domestic product has shown a

TABLE 10-1
The Russian Economy in 1913

	Millions of rubles	*Percent*
Agriculture	8,792	51.4
Industry	4,793	28.0
Construction	699	4.1
Transportation	1,356	7.9
Trade and communications	1,468	8.6

Source: Peter I. Lyaschenko, *History of the National Economy of Russia to the 1917 Revolution* (New York: Macmillan, 1949), 697.

TABLE 10-2 *Economic Comparisons of Russia and Other Emerging Market Economies, 1993*

		Share of GDP in Percent		
Country	*Real per Capita GDP*	*Agriculture*	*Exports*	*Investment*
Czech Republic	7,910	6	57	18
Poland	5,380	6	24	15
Brazil	5,630	12	7	16
Argentina	8,920	6	7	20
Mexico	7,050	8	13	24
Venezuela	7,890	2	29	9
Thailand	6,870	10	39	40
Malaysia	8,610	14	90	39
Turkey	4,610	16	21	22
Russia	5,260	7	27	28

Source: The World Bank, *The World Bank Atlas 1996* (Washington, D.C.: The World Bank, 1996), 18–19.

TABLE 10-3 *Human Development Index for Russia and Other Emerging Market Economies*

Country	*Life Expectancy at Birth*	*Adult Literacy Rate*	*Human Development Index*	*Rank*
Czech Republic	71.3	99.0	.872	38
Poland	71.1	99.0	.855	51
Brazil	66.3	81.9	.804	63
Argentina	72.1	95.9	.882	30
Mexico	70.8	88.6	.841	53
Venezuela	71.7	90.4	.859	47
Thailand	69.0	93.5	.827	58
Malaysia	70.8	81.5	.822	59
Turkey	66.5	80.5	.792	66
Russia	67.6	98.7	.849	52

Source: United Nations Development Programme, *Human Development Report 1995* (New York: Oxford University Press, 1995), 155.

TABLE 10-4 *Selected Indicators of Economic Activity for Russia, 1989–January–June 1994 (real percentage change from one year earlier)*

	1990	*1991*	*1992*	*1993*	*Jan.–June 1994*
Gross domestic product	–3	–13	–19	–12	–17
Industrial production	—	–8	–18	–16	–26
Extraction industries	—	–4	–11	–15	–14
Processing industries	—	–8	–19	–16	–30
Consumer goods	7	–1	–15	–11	–28
Agricultural products	–4	–5	–8	–4	—
Freight	–4	–8	–24	–25	–27

Source: International Monetary Fund, Economic Reviews, *Russian Federation 1994* (Washington, D.C.: IMF, March 1995), 65.

cumulative decline of around 50 percent since the pretransition peak of 1989. There has been more of a real decline in the industrial sector than in the agricultural sector, and some industrial sectors have declined more than others. Gross agricultural output declined by 4 percent in 1993 compared to a 16 percent decline for industrial production.

Income and Wealth Inequality

The economy of Russia today can be compared to that of the United States of the 1880s. The 1880s in the United States were the era of the robber barons, when cutthroat competition prevailed in the marketplace and vast fortunes were made

TABLE 10-5 *Real Gross Industrial Output by Sectors, 1989– January–June 1994 (percentage change from one year earlier)*

	1990	*1991*	*1992*	*1993*	*Jan.–June 1994*
Electric power generation	2.0	0.3	–4.7	–5.3	–7
Fuel	–3.3	–6.0	–7.0	–15.0	–14
Chemicals	–3.3	–8.3	–22.6	–19.9	–35
Machinery	1.0	–10.0	–16.2	–16.6	–42
Construction materials	–0.9	–2.4	–20.4	–17.6	–32
Light industry	–0.1	–9.0	–30.0	–23.4	–46
Food processing	0.4	–9.5	–16.4	–9.2	–24
Ferrous metallurgy	–1.9	–7.4	–16.4	–16.6	–24

Source: International Monetary Fund, Economic Reviews, *Russian Federation 1994* (Washington, D.C.: IMF, March 1995), 65.

by such entrepreneurs as John D. Rockefeller and Andrew Carnegie.[19] This was done in a society whose philosophy was based on the Darwinist application of survival of the fittest to the business world. At the same time that Rockefeller, Carnegie, and others were making millions, legally or illegally, the average worker in the United States was making around $1,000 a year. Today, while billionaire ruble capitalists are riding around in Rolls-Royces and Mercedes-Benzes, the average Russian worker makes around $1,000 a year.[20] This income difference is a source of resentment for some people and a motivation for others.

Although income inequality existed in the Soviet Union before its dissolution, it has increased in Russia during the period 1990–1994. The Gini coefficient, which is a major measure of income inequality, increased from 27 percent in 1989 to 35 percent in early 1994.[21] The decile ratio, which is the ratio between the top and bottom 10 percent of income recipients, increased from around 5 to around 10 for the same time period. This differential is reflected in part by a widening of wage differentials among occupations (see Table 10-6). It is unlikely that income inequality in the Russian Federation comes close to equaling that of the Latin American countries, where the extent of income inequality is the highest in the world.

19. Matthew Josephson, *The Robber Barons* (New York: Harcourt, Brace, and World, 1934).
20. A Russian professor told the author she was paid $100 a month, which she said was about average for Russia. Her husband was a banker/entrepreneur.
21. International Monetary Fund, Economic Reviews, *Russian Federation 1995* (Washington, D.C., March 1995), 192. The Gini coefficient is defined as twice the area between the 45-degree line and the Lorenz curve of income distribution. If the latter were perfectly uniform, the Gini coefficient would equal zero, whereas if all income were to be received by a single individual, it would equal one.

TABLE 10-6 *Russian Wages for Various Economic Sectors, 1987–1994 (rates of average monthly sectoral wage to average monthly wage in the economy)*

Sector	*1987*	*1988*	*1989*	*1990*	*1991*	*1992*	*1993*[a]	*1994*[a]
Industry	1.08	1.07	1.06	1.05	1.09	1.17	1.05	1.06
Agriculture	0.99	1.02	1.00	1.04	0.88	0.67	0.55	0.48
Construction	1.23	1.25	1.31	1.27	1.26	1.38	1.41	1.34
Trade	0.79	0.77	0.78	0.87	0.85	0.87	0.82	0.84
Communication	0.85	0.87	0.88	0.86	0.90	0.93	0.92	1.35
Information processing	0.76	0.82	0.92	0.97	0.93	0.88	0.94	1.03
Science	1.04	1.04	1.22	1.19	0.93	0.75	0.66	0.77
Education	0.77	0.79	0.71	0.68	0.70	0.62	0.89	0.76
Health	0.70	0.71	0.69	0.68	0.75	0.65	0.87	0.79
Public administration	0.89	0.93	0.98	1.23	0.98	0.94	1.26	1.31
Minimum wage	0.36	0.37	0.31	0.27	0.24	0.11	0.09	0.08
Wage dispersion[b]	1.90	2.10	2.30	2.10	2.80	3.90	3.60	3.80

[a]*December 1993 and May 1994.* [b]*Ratio between the highest and lowest sector wage.*

Source: International Monetary Fund, Economic Reviews, *Russian Federation 1994* (Washington, D.C.: IMF, March 1995), 79.

Real Wages and Pensions

Real wages and real pensions have shown a marked decline during the transition period, although there was some leveling off between 1992 and early 1994. As Table 10-6 indicates, wage dispersion among various sectors of the Russian economy has increased rather dramatically since 1989. For example, in 1989 the difference in the average monthly wage in industry and agriculture was a ratio of 1.06 to 1.00; in May 1994 the ratio was 1.06 to 0.48. The difference between the minimum monthly wage and the average monthly wage in industry was a ratio of 1.06 to 0.31; in May 1994 the ratio was 1.06 to 0.08. The minimum monthly wage is approximately 8 percent of the average monthly wage for all industries.[22] Table 10-7 presents average real wages and real pensions and relative money wages for economic sectors, using 1987 as a base period.

Labor

Unemployment was something that officially did not exist in the former Soviet Union. Anyone who wanted to work was entitled to a job.[23] The factory worker was supposed to be first among equals and the true representative of the proletariat. It was an article of faith among the Communists that mass unemployment

22. The dollar-ruble exchange rate on May 24, 1995, was $1 = 5,039 rubles. The monthly minimum wage as of May 1995 was approximately 30,000 rubles, which is around $6 a month. The average monthly wage is about $80.
23. Those who could work but didn't were branded as social parasites and received no benefits.

TABLE 10-7 *Average Monthly Real Wages and Real Pensions (1987=100 percent)*

	Real Wages		*Real Pensions*	
	Average	*Minimum*	*Average*	*Minimum*
1987	100	100	100	100
1988	109	100	102	100
1989	117	97	105	97
1990	127	92	—	115–138
1991	119	76	—	78
1992	86	30	54	48
1993	90	27	—	45
1994 (Jan.)	81	24	58	43
1994 (July)	88	22	—	41

Source: International Monetary Fund, Economic Reviews, *Russian Federation 1994* (Washington, D.C.: IMF, March 1995), 78.

would be responsible for the collapse of capitalism. A socialist planned economy would be able to utilize labor and other resources more efficiently.

However, it did not turn out that way. An overuse of labor contributed to an inefficient combination of labor and capital, which was a factor in the declining performance of the Soviet economy.[24] There was no motivation for enterprise managers to be efficient; they were judged by their ability to meet the physical output quotas specified in the economic plan.

Wages were low and were distorted in favor of manual labor. Based on a complex wage structure, the system resulted in the average wage being close to the minimum wage, and in narrow and distorted wage differentials between sectors and occupations. Workers remained in jobs well past the retirement age, largely because pensions were so low they made continuing to work a must. State-owned enterprises were largely responsible for the welfare of their workers, providing subsidized food, consumer goods, housing, holiday facilities, and health services. Labor unions existed in the Soviet Union but did not enjoy much autonomy. They did not have the right to strike, and decisions on wage rates, output norms, hours of labor, and similar matters were prerogatives of the government. Union leaders were simply state functionaries acting as transmission belts for Communist Party commands.

Transition to a Market Economy. The Employment Act passed in 1991 recognized open unemployment as legitimate for the first time since 1920. However, the mass unemployment that occurred in East Germany after German reunification and in Poland during its transition to a market economy has not happened.

24. For many years, there was a contrived labor shortage in which there were artificially created jobs because an enterprise manager could receive a higher wage fund from a ministry. The manager could use the money for other purposes, including self-enrichment.

One factor is that many large state-owned enterprises have been left intact because the political consequences of their dissolution would be great. Another factor is that bankruptcy remains a taboo because the government does not want social chaos. In the first two years of price liberalization in January 1992, not a single enterprise was allowed to go bankrupt. It was not until 1993 that a Federal Bankruptcy Agency was created. By January 1995, it had taken action against four hundred state-owned enterprises that had defaulted on their debts, and courts had placed over five hundred firms in receivership.[25]

In 1990 there were approximately 75.3 million workers in Russia, most of whom were employed by state- and city-owned enterprises and collective farms. Very few were employed by the public enterprises. As Table 10-8 indicates, the employment breakdown had changed dramatically by the first half of 1994. There was a decrease in the number of workers employed by the public sector and an increase in the number of workers who worked for private enterprise and mixed public-private enterprise.

Table 10-9 presents the number of unemployed workers in Russia as of September 30, 1994. However, the unemployment rate is considerably understated. Registered unemployment refers to those workers who have filed for unemployment benefits or job training. If this is used by itself, the unemployment rate would be around 2 percent of the Russian labor force. However, there are two other types of unemployment. The first is hidden unemployment, which involves shorter working hours, and the second is forced leave, which is involuntary leave without pay.[26] Total unemployment in Russia as of September 30, 1994, was estimated at 10 percent of the labor force, and this may be understated.[27]

Poverty, Women, and the Safety Net

The Soviet Union always denied the possibility that poverty could exist under socialism, proclaiming it an evil of capitalism. However, poverty was a reality in the Soviet Union, and Soviet authorities admitted that at least 20 percent of the population lived in poverty.[28] As is also true in the United States, there was the feminization of poverty in the Soviet Union. Single women and mothers with children were much more likely to be found among the urban poor. In the Soviet Union women earned between 18 to 29 percent less than men, in part because of occupational segregation, which also exists in the United States. The three lowest-paid occupations were education, health, and trade, all dominated by women. Women

25. "Russia's Emerging Market," *The Economist,* Survey, April 8–14, 1995, 13.
26. For a discussion and criticisms of the computation of Russian unemployment statistics, see Guy Standing, "Enterprise Restructuring in Russian Industry and Mass Unemployment," *Labour Market Papers I* (Geneva, Switzerland: International Labour Office, 1995), 4.
27. According to Standing, the death rates of young and middle-aged men have risen sharply, and this phenomenon has been associated with stress and insecurity linked to the radical economic changes that have occurred in Russia.
28. *New York Times,* January 22, 1989, 11.

TABLE 10-8 *Distribution of Employment by Property Forms in Russia, 1990–1994*

	1990	*1991*	*1992*	*1993*	*1st half 1994*
Total (in millions)	75.3	73.3	72.0	71.0	70.3
Percent					
Public sector	82.6	75.5	68.9	52.1	49.2
Mixed property forms	4.0	10.1	11.7	20.6	26.3
Private	12.5	13.3	18.3	26.2	33.4
Funds, social institutions	0.8	0.9	0.8	0.7	0.7
Joint ventures	0.1	0.2	0.3	0.4	0.4

Source: Guy Standing, "Enterprise Restructuring in Russian Industry and Mass Unemployment," *Labour Market Papers I* (Geneva, Switzerland: International Labour Office, 1995), 6.

TABLE 10-9 *Registered Unemployment in Russia, 1993–1994*

	Sept. 30, 1993	*July 1, 1994*	*Sept. 30, 1994*
Nonemployed job seekers	968,645	1,516,102	1,687,895
Of whom percent unemployed	72.9	83.1	84.5
Of whom percent receiving unemployment comp.	63.6	68.6	84.1
percent in training programs	3.0	3.1	3.2
percent in public works	2.2	2.3	1.5

Source: Guy Standing, "Enterprise Restructuring in Russian Industry and Mass Unemployment," *Labour Market Papers I* (Geneva, Switzerland: International Labour Office, 1995), 4.

were also paid less than men, even when both had similar education, experience, and responsibility.[29] Single women with children and pensioners living alone were the most likely to be poor.

As Table 10-10 indicates, poverty continues to exist in Russia. Income inequality and the level of poverty have increased during the transition. About one-tenth of the total Russian population was estimated to be very poor in 1993, in the sense of suffering from malnutrition. In the table, trends in poverty in Russia from 1980 to 1993 are presented. Prior to 1992, the poverty line was based on a minimum consumption basket based on per capita consumption of meat, fish, and milk. Although the prices of these items were subsidized, they were often unavailable. For 1992–1993 the poverty line was based on a minimum subsistence level that varied from month to month depending on fluctuations in the value of the ruble. The use of the price mechanism to ration goods has worsened the access to them for many people.

29. Jeanine Braithwaite, "The Old and the New Poor in Russia: Trends in Poverty," *Russia, Poverty Policy and Responses* (Washington, D.C.: The World Bank, forthcoming).

TABLE 10-10
Poverty Trends in Russia, 1980–1993

	Poverty Line (rubles per capita per month)	*Percent Below Poverty Line*
1980	64.6	11
1985	76.7	13
1990	93.3	10
1991	190.0	11
1992		
January	635.0	30
March	1,031.0	23
June	1,639.0	19
December	4,282.0	19
1993		
March	8,069.0	35
June	16,527.0	25
October	32,400.0	29
December	42,800.0	23

Source: Jeanine Braithwaite, "The Old and New Poor in Russia: Trends in Poverty," *Russia, Poverty Policy and Responses*, Vol. 2 (Washington, D.C.: The World Bank, forthcoming).

The Safety Net. One aspect of the wage system of the former Soviet Union was that wages were a relatively small part of total remuneration. State-owned enterprises were responsible for the provision of a wide variety of social services, including vacations and medical care. In 1994, as Table 10-11 indicates, a very high percentage of workers were covered by entitlements to a wide variety of social benefits, showing that many enterprises, state-owned or otherwise, retained a commitment to the provision of social benefits. Local governments continue to provide rent subsidies that are far below the market price, and subsidies for the consumption of bread, meat, and milk are also provided.

Inflation and the Public Debt

Inflation has been a major problem in Russia. During the first five months of 1995, consumer prices appreciated at a rate of 4 percent a month.[30] Moreover, the consumer price index has been very volatile, appreciating and depreciating by as much as 30 percent in one month. Inflation has been driven by the deficit in the budget of the Russian government. Until 1994 that deficit was financed by borrowing money from the central bank at a nominal rate of interest. One cause of the deficit was the cost of a common currency, the ruble, in the Commonwealth of Independent States, whose members were able to borrow rubles from Russia's central bank. These rubles then flowed back into the Russian economy, increasing

30. *The Economist,* May 20–26, 1995, 107. In March 1996 the consumer price index showed a 78 percent increase over March 1995.

TABLE 10-11 *Benefit Entitlements for Russian Workers, Mid-1994 (percentage of workers)*

Benefits	*Administrative Workers*	*Regular Workers*	*Non–Regular Workers*
Paid vacations	99.7	99.5	48.6
Rest houses	44.8	44.5	20.7
Sickness benefits	93.0	93.5	55.9
Paid health services	51.0	51.3	28.1
Subsidized rent	15.6	16.4	5.8
Bonuses	72.1	72.7	41.5
Profit sharing	66.1	65.6	27.8
Retirement benefits	73.2	73.4	24.4
Subsidized food	18.5	18.8	11.1
Subsidized meals at work	51.3	53.1	31.5
Subsidized consumer goods	9.9	9.9	7.6
Transportation subsidies	30.2	31.8	14.4

Source: Guy Standing, "Enterprise Restructuring in Russian Industry," *Study Paper I* (Geneva, Switzerland: International Labour Office, 1995), 55.

the money supply and government spending. A second source of inflation was government subsidy payments to coal, agriculture, and the military-industrial complex. The third cause of inflation was that the Russian government operated without a budget in 1992 and 1993.

The 1994 budget was passed by the Russian parliament in 1994. The 1995 budget cleared the lower house (Duma) of parliament in the spring of 1995. A new law was passed at the beginning of 1995 making it illegal for the government to finance its deficit by printing money. In the future it will have to borrow at market-determined interest rates. The 1995 budget is supposed to set a cap on the national deficit of 5.6 percent of Russian GDP.[31] A major problem is that there has been a carryover of the traditional socialist view that the function of the state is to support production, regardless of whether or not anyone needs the product. This view has to be discarded in the market economy.

Table 10-12 presents the overall inflation rate in Russia from 1992 to January 1995 as measured by the consumer price index. January 1992 marked a turning point in the government's effort to control inflation. For one thing, the tools of monetary policy, particularly as applied to the control over interest rates, had no application in the former Soviet Union. The whole concept of business borrowing through the interest rate mechanism was foreign to socialism. Interest rates were allowed to fluctuate and the ruble exchange rate was devalued to the point where by December 1992, the ruble/dollar exchange rate was 414.6 rubles to $1.[32] Inflation began to fall in 1992 after a January high of 245 percent. Excluding January,

31. The International Monetary Fund lent $6.4 billion to Russia in March 1995 to finance two-fifths of the budget deficit.
32. *Russian Federation*, 122.

TABLE 10-12
Consumer Price Inflation (average monthly changes in percent)

Year	*CPI*
1992	
January	245
April	22
July	11
October	23
1993	
January	26
April	19
July	22
October	20
1994	
January	18
April	8
July	5
October	15
1995	
January	11
February 1995–February 1996	89

Sources: Anders Aslund, *How Russia Became a Market Economy* (Washington, D.C.: The Brookings Institution, 1995), 184; International Monetary Fund, IMF Economic Reviews, *Russian Federation 1994* (Washington, D.C.: IMF, March 1995), 73; *The Economist*, March 30–April 6, 1996, 100.

inflation increased at an average rate of 20 percent during the rest of 1992. The 1993 average monthly inflation rate was a little higher than the 1992 rate, while the average monthly inflation rate in 1994 showed a marked decline.

Foreign Trade

Much of Russia's trade was with other members of CMEA, and when CMEA collapsed in 1991 there was a sharp decline of some $20 billion in Russian exports. In December 1991 the Soviet Union defaulted on its external debt, and as a consequence, Russia's imports declined by some $37 billion between 1990 and 1991.[33] One major problem in reforming foreign trade was that the system that had existed under the Soviet Union was so controlled and regulated. There were a multitude of individual exchange rates for various commodities with completely different domestic and foreign exchange rates. In December 1991 imports were controlled through the allocation of hard currency at an exchange rate of 1.6 rubles per dollar or 1 percent of the true market rate of rubles for dollars. This caused import subsidies to increase to 20 percent of GDP.

33. European Bank for Reconstruction and Development, *Quarterly Economic Review* (London: EBRD, September 1992), 105.

Exchange Rates. One foreign trade objective of the government was to make the ruble convertible, which means that the ruble could be bought and sold outside of Russia. In 1993 there were still several exchange rates, all set by the government. The official exchange rate was 0.6 rubles to the dollar. Two special exchange rates applied to imports by Russians who held hard currency. A separate market rate set for tourists was allowed to float within a 10 percent limit. However, the ruble's inconvertibility outside Russia discouraged Western firms from doing business in Russia because it was difficult to repatriate profits. Many firms had to resort to barter arrangements for such exports as oil and lumber.

The official ruble exchange rate is quoted by the central bank of Russia based on market exchange rates determined in daily auctions held at the Moscow Interbank Foreign Currency Exchange (MICEX) and in St. Petersburg, Rostov, and other major Russian cities. The dollar is the intervention currency of the central bank, which participates as a net buyer and seller of the dollar to smooth out exchange rate fluctuations. A reference exchange rate is announced by the bank twice a week and is equal to the closing rate at the Tuesday and Thursday auctions at the MICEX. The central bank quotes exchange rates of the ruble for the European Currency Unit (ECU)[34] and twenty-six convertible currencies on the basis of the MICEX ruble/dollar rate and the cross-rate relationship between the dollar and other major international currencies.

Russian Foreign Trade. Table 10-13 presents Russian exports and imports for the period 1990–1994. In 1990 over half of Russian exports and imports were to and from countries that belonged to the Council for Mutual Economic Assistance (CMEA). When CMEA was dissolved in 1991, Russian foreign trade was adversely affected. Exports fell by 40 percent between 1990 and 1992, and imports by 55 percent. Former CMEA countries such as Poland and Czechoslovakia began to trade more with the West. Moreover, trade with other republics that were formerly a part of the Soviet Union also began to decline. Russia decreased its exports to some of these republics because they lacked export financing. In 1993 Russia's three most important trading partners in order were the Ukraine, Germany, and China. Since 1991 Russia has run a surplus in its merchandise trade and current accounts.

Has Russia Become a Market Economy?

Janos Kornai, a professor of economics at Harvard, listed five major characteristics of a socialist system of the type that prevailed in the Soviet Union. They were as follows:[35]

34. The ECU is a market basket of currencies of countries belonging to the European Union.
35. Janos Kornai, *The Socialist System: The Political Economy of Communism* (Princeton: Princeton University Press, 1992), 360–365.

TABLE 10-13 *Russian Exports and Imports, 1990–1994 (billions of dollars)*

	1990	*1991*	*1992*	*1993*	*1994*
Exports, excluding other republics	71.1	50.9	42.4	43.0	48.0
Imports, excluding other republics	81.8	44.5	37.0	27.0	35.7
Trade balance	–10.7	6.4	5.4	16.0	12.3

Source: Anders Aslund, *How Russia Became a Market Economy* (Washington, D.C.: The Brookings Institution, 1995), 281.

1. There was one ruling party, the Communist Party, and it and the state were one and the same. There was no organized opposition, and both party and state adhered to Marxist-Leninist ideology.
2. There was state ownership of the means of production. State-owned enterprises were dominant in the production process. Private enterprise was very limited. Quasi-state ownership took the form of collective farming.
3. Resource allocation was done through central economic planning. This required top-down bureaucratic coordination. Physical output goals were emphasized, and there was state control over production and resource flows.
4. Money played no useful purpose in the socialist economy. It could not be used in international commerce as a medium of exchange.
5. There were no budgetary constraints placed on state enterprises. They were not allowed to fail; instead they were subsidized by the state.

It is argued that Russia is now a market economy because the economic transition from socialism to capitalism has been accomplished.[36] Markets instead of economic planning now exist to allocate resources. Privatization of property is in the process of being accomplished, and enterprises now have to compete on their own. The economy has been monetized, interest rates now serve as a resource allocator, and the Russian ruble has become a convertible currency within limits, its exchange rate market determined. The command structure between the state and enterprises has been eliminated, the Communist Party is no longer in power, there are political parties, and free elections have been held. Fixed and arbitrary prices and administrative controls have disappeared altogether. Prices have been liberalized and wages are, for the most part, market determined. Export and import restrictions have also been liberalized.

As in any social upheaval, however, there are winners and losers. In Russia the winners are very conspicuous, and the losers for the most part are inconspicuous. Although Russia has developed a large, educated urban middle class, it is poor, owns little or no property, has no savings, and has little identity with capitalism. Add to the middle class a working class, and they too have few resources. Both groups feel vulnerable and economically and physically exposed, particularly to

36. Anders Aslund, *How Russia Became a Market Economy* (Washington, D.C.: The Brookings Institution, 1995), 4–5.

the disorder and decadence they see in everyday life. There is a lack of class identity, as well as a lack of social "transmission belts" such as trade unions and strong political parties. But it is the order of the past to which many people remain attached, and their fear of the anarchy of the present in Russia is political tinder.[37]

Any prediction about the next few years in Russia begins with the economy. Some predictions are optimistic, others pessimistic. *The Economist* in its April 1995 survey of the Russian economy is for the most part quite optimistic.[38] So is Anders Aslund, who states that Russia is a market economy and has been at least since the end of 1993.[39] On the other hand, there are those who take a bleak view of Russian economic reforms and the future. One forecast is for a semidemocratic Russia allied with the West and with an economic policy based on the Chinese model.[40] The argument is that production has declined and few people are living better. Serious reforms have not been undertaken in agriculture, and little reduction has occurred in the industrial labor force employed by the large state enterprises.

RUSSIAN SOCIAL AND POLITICAL PROBLEMS

Although communism as an ideology is gone, it has not been replaced by any new ideal that commands allegiance. Moreover, there are a number of problems besetting Russia that threaten to create social and political instability. Russia suffers from a high crime rate that can cause political instability as it already has in Italy. There is little likelihood that crime will be controlled anytime in the immediate future. To keep some semblance of order, a large police force will be needed to cope with and control crime, and this will take money. Given the continued existence of nuclear missiles, there is always the possibility that organized crime will get involved in some form of nuclear blackmail. Increases in drug and alcohol abuse are direct concomitants of the increase in crime.

Communism papered over ethnic problems that had existed for centuries, but as Yugoslavia has proved, once strong centralized control is ended, animosities are quick to surface. Russia has its ethnic problems, as witnessed by what has happened in Chechnya. There are many ethnic groups in Russia, most of whom have grievances against the government or each other. Since the dissolution of the Soviet Union, there have been disputes and violence between Georgians and the mi-

37. Again, there is a parallel between Germany after World War I and the current situation in Russia. Kaiser Wilhelm abdicated in 1918, ending a strong monarchy. This was replaced by a weak, democratic Weimar Republic. The 1922–1923 German inflation destroyed the middle class. Conflicts between various armed groups were common, and there was a breakdown in social values. The decadence of Berlin in the 1920s can be compared to the decadence of Moscow in the 1990s.

38. *The Economist,* April 1995.

39. Anders Aslund, *How Russia Became a Market Economy* (Washington, D.C.: The Brookings Institution, 1995), 5.

40. Jerry F. Hough, "Russia—On the Road to Thermidor," *Problems of Post-Communism,* Vol. 41, Special Issue (Fall 1994), 26–31.

nority Abkhazy and South Ossetians over their autonomy. Armenia and Azerbaijan have also been involved in a bloody war over Armenian enclaves in Azerbaijan. Some twenty-five million Russians live as minorities in the fourteen other republics that were also a part of the Soviet Union. They may well want closer identity with Russia, which could provide some future Russian leader with an excuse for aggression.[41]

Crime and Corruption

Russia in the 1990s, particularly in the big cities, can be compared to Chicago and New York during the 1920s, an era well known for such illegal activities as bootlegging, racketeering, and prostitution. Al Capone, who called himself a businessman, was into all three, creating jobs and providing services for a clientele ranging from the rich to the poor. His organization penetrated and controlled all levels of Chicago municipal government from the mayor's office to judges to the cop on the beat. Just as in Chicago, organized crime has penetrated to all levels of government in the large Russian cities and to the country. As Al Capone demonstrated in Chicago, once organized crime becomes intertwined with government, it cannot be easily separated.

It should be pointed out that corruption existed in the former Soviet Union. Bribery was the most common type of corruption and it took many forms, ranging from payments for better food and apartments to kickbacks from enterprise managers to state ministry officials for needed resources. But organized crime in Russia is now all-pervasive. It has hindered elections, limited human rights, and compromised freedom of the press. It undermines foreign investment and trade by increasing the risks of capital investment. It encourages trade in contraband rather than legitimately traded goods. It dominates much of export activity not only in Russia but in other republics that were formerly a part of the Soviet Union. It also dominates the tourist industry, controlling hotels such as the Intourist in Moscow. As Table 10-14 points out, various forms of crime are on the increase in Russia.

Ethnic Problems

The former Soviet Union, despite the variety of its people, was predominantly a Slavic nation.[42] The Slavic population was divided into three main groups: Russians, who accounted for around half of the total population of the country; the Ukrainians, who accounted for around 20 percent; and the Belorussians, who accounted for less than 5 percent of the population. Ethnic differences among these three main Slavic groups go back over many centuries, with each group being a

41. Hitler used a similar situation in 1938 to occupy the Sudetenland, which was a majority German enclave within Czechoslovakia. The area had been a part of Germany before World War I, but was taken from Germany to form a part of the newly created country of Czechoslovakia.

42. There were three main Slavic groups: the East Slavic group, which includes the Russians, Ukrainians, and Belorussians; the West Slavic group, which includes the Poles, Czechs, and Slovaks; and the South Slavic group, which includes Bulgarians, Slovenians, and Serbo-Croatians.

TABLE 10-14
Russian Crime Statistics, 1993

Crime	*Total*	*Percent Increase over 1992*
Homicide	29,213	27
Assault	66,902	24
Narcotics trafficking	53,200	80
Organized crime groups	5,700	33
Bribery	4,500	35

Source: Louise I. Shelley, "Organized Crime in the Former Soviet Union," *Problems of Post-Communism,* Vol. 42, No. 1 (January–February 1995), 59.

separate political entity for a good three hundred years. Then there were a wide variety of non-Slavic groups, which constituted about one-fourth of the total population of the Soviet Union. Most of these groups are located chiefly along the western and southern borders of the country. All of the territories of Russia were conquered and colonized by the Russians, who first under the czars and then under the Communists ran the country.

Although friction between the Russians and various minorities goes back for hundreds of years, Joseph Stalin provides an excellent example of how minorities were treated. When the collectivization of agriculture occurred in the late 1920s, it fell the heaviest on the Ukraine, which was heavily agricultural. Stalin sent the army in to enforce collectivization, and thousands of Ukrainians were executed.[43] A similar situation occurred in Belorus, where every prominent Belorussian Communist was purged by Stalin. Stalin's policies also encountered resistance among the non-Slavic groups, and the result was the same. An attempt was also made by Stalin to collectivize culture by rewriting history to prove that cultural differences between Russians and non-Russians that went back for many centuries really did not exist.[44]

Nationalism in Russia

Nationalism, which had been suppressed in the Soviet Union, has reemerged in Russia[45] and in many of the other republics. It is expressed in the violence that has recently taken place in Chechnya, which has tried to declare its independence from Russia. Chechnya is totally different from Russia in culture.[46] In the nineteenth century it had fought to maintain its independence from Russia. In the civil

43. When Hitler invaded Russia in 1942, the Ukrainians looked on him as a liberator.
44. No minority in the Soviet Union was treated worse than the Jews. The government broke up their communities, banned their religion, and attacked their culture as being antiproletarian. However, Russia was notoriously anti-Semitic. There were many pogroms during czarist rule.
45. Russians constitute 80 percent of the Russian population, with the remaining 20 percent representing diverse ethnic groups. There are fourteen ethnic-based regions in Russia.
46. Chechnya, or the Chechen Republic as it is called, has a population of around 1.3 million, over half of whom are Chechen. Chechnya has its own language, and its religion is Moslem. It formally seceded from Russia in 1992.

war of 1919–1921 it had fought on the side of the Russian forces that were opposing Lenin and the Bolsheviks, and in 1928 it had opposed collectivization. During World War II the Chechens were uprooted and deported en masse to East Asia because Stalin thought they were collaborating with the Germans. When they returned to their homeland after the war, much of their former territory had been given away to other nationalities.[47] In 1994 the Russian army invaded Chechnya to bring it under state control.

However, Chechnya is not the only republic that would like to assert its independence from Russia. There is also Tatarstan, a Russian republic with a multiethnic population of around 3.6 million. Approximately half of its population are Tatars, which are a product of the Mongol invasion of Russia during the thirteenth century, a mixture of many nationalities. Many of the Tatars are Islamic, and that can pose a problem in terms of Islamic fundamentalism. Like the Chechens, the Tatars were deported from their homeland by Stalin during World War II on the grounds that they had conspired with the Germans. Unlike Chechnya, however, a very large minority of Russians live in Tatarstan, which makes a complete separation from Russia less likely.

Democracy

Russia is in the process of transformation from a one-party state and a centrally planned economy to a democracy and a market economy. It can be argued that democracy and free markets need each other in order to achieve success. A free market cannot exist without a legal system that provides property rights and establishes the rules of the game for business to follow. Without a free market, there cannot be a true democracy or a functioning economy. Both democracy and a free market are necessary to create a culture of entrepreneurship. Whether or not both will succeed in Russia depends on their acceptance by the Russian public. The economic performance so far has been uneven, and democratic institutions have not been in place long enough to arrive at any conclusion about their success.

There is little precedent upon which a democracy in Russia can be based. Russia has never lived under a democracy. No other country has had so elaborate a political ideology in existence for such an extended period of time. Its institutions were inherited from the Soviet system. Too much of the status quo remains, in that Russian politicians were a part of the old regime and the nomenklatura elite maintains control over much of the economic apparatus of the country. The political system is weak. It has little authority, and it has no social consensus behind it. Democracy cannot be created overnight; it is a long, drawn-out process that will take many years to accomplish.

47. It might be added that the same thing happened in the United States during World War II when Japanese-Americans were deported to concentration camps and their properties were seized by the U.S. government. After the war was over, most of the Japanese did not get their properties back, and restitution was not paid until recently.

TABLE 10-15
Performance of the Russian Economy, 1990–1998 (real percentage change in GDP from one year earlier)

Year	*Real GDP*
1990	–3.0
1991	–13.0
1992	–19.0
1993	–12.0
1994	–15.0
1995	–4.0
1996 estimate	2.3
1997 projected	3.5
1998 projected	5.1

Sources: International Monetary Fund, Economic Reviews, *Russian Federation 1995* (Washington, D.C.: IMF, March 1995), 65; International Monetary Fund, *IMF Survey*, Vol. 25, No. 7 (April 1, 1996), 119.

Performance of the Russian Economy

The performance of the Russian economy has been uneven. The restructuring of the banking system has been slow, and the pace and scale of the privatization program have been below expectations. Land reforms have also been slow. However, as Table 10-15 indicates, real GDP for 1995 showed an improvement and is expected to be positive in 1996. A reduction in the rate of inflation has also occurred, which is regarded as an essential condition for economic recovery. The current account increased from $3.4 billion in 1994 to $4.7 billion in 1995, and the merchandise trade account was $22 billion for 1995.

SUMMARY

Scenarios envisioning Russia's future range from optimistic to pessimistic. There are those who feel that Russia is well on its way to becoming a market economy thanks to the shock therapy approach. The old Soviet economic system had collapsed and had to be replaced by a new economic order as quickly as possible. A new democratic state had to be built and a market economy created to free the country from the past. On the other hand, there are those who feel that the process of creating democratic institutions and a market economy will be a long and laborious process with many possible pitfalls. There is no real experience with democracy in Russian history. The Russian economy has many problems. There has been a marked decline in the production of a wide variety of goods ranging from oil and steel to farm products. Differences in the distribution of wealth and income have widened, and there has been an increase in the poverty rate.

QUESTIONS FOR DISCUSSION

1. Scenarios of the future of Russia range from optimistic to pessimistic. Discuss. In your opinion, which scenario is most likely?
2. Income and wealth differentials probably have increased considerably during Russia's transition to a market economy. Why has this happened?
3. Crime has become a significant social and economic problem in Russia. What are some of its consequences that would affect the future?
4. Were crime and corruption nonexistent in the former Soviet Union?
5. What are some of the problems involved in the creation of democratic institutions in Russia?
6. Does Russian history have any application to the economic and social development of the country today?
7. Discuss the development of the Russian economy before the beginning of World War I. Is there a parallel between Russian and American economic development in the nineteenth century?
8. One of the claims made by the Soviet Union was that unemployment did not exist. Was this true? Were workers better off in the Soviet Union than they are in Russia today?
9. Communist propaganda glorified the role of women. Were women better off under communism than they are in Russia today?
10. Could Russia become another Yugoslavia, with various ethnic groups battling for control over areas of the country?

RECOMMENDED READINGS

Aslund, Anders. *How Russia Became a Market Economy*. Washington, D.C.: The Brookings Institution, 1995.

Balzar, Marjorie Mandelstam. "From Ethnicity to Nationalism: Turmoil in the Russian Mini-Empire." In James R. Millar and Sharon L. Wolchik, eds. *The Social Legacy of Communism*. New York: Cambridge University Press, 1994, 56–88.

Bush, Keith. "Political-Economic Assessments: Russia." In *The Former Soviet Union in Transition*, Vol. 2. Joint Economic Committee, Congress of the United States, 103d Cong., 1st. Sess. Washington, D.C.: U.S. Government Printing Office, 1993, 950–960.

"Can Russia Escape Its Past?" *Time*, December 7, 1992, 32–66.

Connor, Walter D. "Labor Unions in the New Russia: Four Years On." *Problems of Post-Communism*. Vol. 42, No. 2 (March-April 1995), 8–12.

Feshbach, Murray. "Environmental Calamities: Widespread and Costly." In *The Former Soviet Union in Transition*, Vol. 2. Joint Economic Committee, Congress of the United States, 103d Cong., 1st Sess. Washington, D.C.: U.S. Government Printing Office, 1993, 686–703.

Hough, Jerry F. "Perilous Ties? Economic Reform and Russian Imperialism." *The Brookings Review*, Vol. 12, No. 3 (Summer 1994), 5–9.

International Monetary Fund, Economic Reviews, *Russian Federation 1994.* Washington, D.C.: IMF, 1995.

Koen, Vincent. "How Large Was the Output Collapse in Russia? Alternative Estimates and Welfare Implications." IMF Staff Papers. Washington, D.C.: IMF, November 1994.

Mahlia, Martin. "Russia's Democratic Future—Hope Against Hope." *Problems of Post-Communism.* Vol. 42, No. 2 (March-April 1995), 54–61.

McFaul, Michael. "Why Russia's Politics Matter." *Foreign Affairs.* Vol. 74, No. 1 (January-February 1995), 87–99.

Moskoff, William. "Unemployment in the Former Soviet Union." In James R. Millar and Sharon L. Wolchik, eds., *The Social Legacy of Communism.* New York: Cambridge University Press, 1994, 354–378.

Popper, Steven W. "A Note on the Emigration of Russia's Technical Intelligentsia." In *The Former Soviet Union in Transition,* Vol. 2, Joint Economic Committee, Congress of the United States, 103d Cong., 1st Sess. Washington, D.C.: U.S. Government Printing Office, 1993, 767–782.

Yergin, Daniel, and Thane Gustafson. *Russia 2010,* The CERA Report. New York: Random House, 1993.

EASTERN EUROPE

CHAPTER 11

Poland, the Czech Republic, and Hungary

The collapse of Communism in the Soviet Union and the countries that formed the Soviet bloc has resulted in the creation of a number of new countries. The former Soviet Union now consists of fifteen countries, including Russia. The German Democratic Republic (East Germany) has been reunited with West Germany. Czechoslovakia has split into two countries, the Czech and Slovak Republics, and Poland, Hungary, Romania, and Bulgaria have retained their identities. When Yugoslavia, which was Communist but not a member of the Soviet bloc, is added, there are the new countries of Slovenia, Croatia, and Macedonia. Finally, there is Albania, which was isolated from the world and was the most committed to Communism of all of the countries. Altogether, there are twenty-five countries now in the process of conversion to market economies.

The fastest-reforming economies are to be found in Central Europe. They include Poland, the Czech Republic, Slovakia, Hungary, and the Baltic Republics of Estonia, Latvia, and Lithuania. Their economic performance relative to the region can be seen in Table 11-1. For these countries, the end of Communism was the end of Russian domination and the start of their return to the Western European fold, an aspiration to which economic reforms were central. Most of the countries would like to join the European Union, and new laws are being written that are comparable to European Union legislation. New institutions are being shaped that look like continental European ones. Banks, for example, are being patterned on the banks of Germany. The Warsaw Stock Exchange is modeled on the stock market of Lyons, France. Hungary's agricultural support system is becoming like the common agricultural policy of the European Union.

In one way, these countries have not changed. Although democratic institutions have been introduced, most are run by former Communists who call themselves socialists. In Poland and Hungary they have returned to power in free elections, while in Romania they have never left power. In part they are back in power because there was a gap between expectations and reality on the part of the populace. Democracy and economic reforms were expected to create the good life immediately. This did not occur; living standards fell for many people, and unemployment increased. So former Communists have been able to get elected by pledging to continue moving toward the creation of market economies while reducing the pain of transition.

HISTORY OF CENTRAL AND EASTERN EUROPE

With two exceptions, Hungary and Romania, the countries of Eastern and Central Europe are Slavic in their ethnic makeup. This has proved to be no guarantee of harmony, as events in Bosnia have demonstrated. Sarajevo, the capital of Bosnia, has played an inordinately prominent role in the history of this century. On June 28, 1914, the Archduke Franz Ferdinand, heir to the throne of the Austro-Hungarian Empire, and his wife were assassinated at Sarajevo by a Serb nationalist. That incident led to a crisis between Austria-Hungary and Serbia that led to World War I. The assassination was linked to a movement called Pan-Slavism, which was at work among the peoples of the Balkans and the subject nationalities of the Austro-

TABLE 11–1
Population and Real per Capita GDP for Countries of Central and Eastern Europe, 1994

	Population (in thousands)	*Real per Capita GDP*
Bulgaria	8,818	$4,230
Czech Republic	10,295	7,910
Hungary	10,161	6,310
Poland	38,341	5,380
Romania	22,736	2,920
Slovak Republic	5,333	6,600

Source: The World Bank, *The World Bank Atlas 1996* (Washington, D.C.: The World Bank, 1996), 8–9, 18–19.

Hungarian Empire. Pan-Slavism preached the cultural and political solidarity of the Slavic people.

The Mongol and Turkish Conquests

Two events have had an enormous impact on the history of Central and Eastern Europe. The first event was the invasions by the Mongols and later the Turks. The Mongols, led by Genghis Khan, conquered Poland and most of Central Europe. Even though the Mongols left no civilization, their policy of playing one group off against another created animosities that exist to this day. The Turks under Suleiman conquered much of Eastern and Central Europe in the sixteenth century and created the Ottoman Empire, which lasted until World War I. Serbia, Romania, Greece, and Bulgaria were all part of the Ottoman Empire for more than three hundred years until they won their independence in various wars of liberation. Religious friction between Moslems and Christians dates back for centuries. The strife in Bosnia is regarded by many Serbian Christians as payback time against Bosnian Moslems.

POLAND, THE CZECH REPUBLIC, AND HUNGARY

Czechoslovakia, Poland, and Hungary were the three most important Eastern European Communist countries. All were created by the Treaty of Versailles, which ended World War I, and all were once part of the Austro-Hungarian Empire. Czechoslovakia was created in 1918 by combining two different ethnic groups—the Czechs and the Slovaks. Hungary, which lost more than two-thirds of its territory, became an independent nation in 1919. Poland was created out of territory that had been claimed over a period of time by Germany, Russia, and the Austro-Hungarian Empire. Historically, it had suffered the misfortune of being the common battleground for invaders ranging from the Mongol hordes of Genghis Khan to the Magyars and Swedes to the Germans and Russians—a misfortune which was to continue in World War II.

Economic Development

Of the three countries, Czechoslovakia, with its steel mills and munitions factories, was the most industrially developed region before World War II. Hungary and Poland were primarily agrarian, dominated by large landowners. Czechoslovakia continued to develop industrially during the period between World Wars I and II and by the 1930s had the highest living standard in Eastern Europe. Its industry was concentrated in the capital-goods–producing sector and in chemicals. It was a net exporter of manufacturing goods and a net importer of raw materials and food. The reverse was true in Hungary and Poland, because they were more agrarian and less industrialized. Their manufacturing sectors focused on the processing of food, textiles, and other light industries. Differences in the economic development of the three countries are exemplified in the structure of their exports for 1938 (see Table 11-2).

Economic and Political Development After World War II

All three countries were adversely affected by World War II. Prior to the war, a part of Czechoslovakia was annexed and integrated into the German economy under a system of centralized state control.[1] The remainder of the country became part of the Third Reich when Germany invaded Poland in 1939. Poland, which was an independent country from 1918 to 1939, was divided into two parts, one part going to Germany and the other to the Soviet Union.[2] Germany invaded the Soviet Union in 1941, and much of the fighting took place in Poland.[3] After the war was over, the territory of Poland shifted westward to include about one-third of German territory, while half of prewar Poland was given to the Soviet Union. Hungary supported Germany and helped it by providing men and materials. It was invaded by the Russians toward the end of the war, and much of its industrial base was destroyed.

After the war, the economies of the three countries were organized along the lines of the Soviet economic system. The first and most important move was the nationalization of industry, banking, and trade. The nationalization of agriculture followed later. Political parties were tolerated at first under the guise of a popular front, but the Communists soon seized control. During the period from the early 1950s to the collapse of Communism in the late 1980s, the three countries developed in different ways. Czechoslovakia was the most ideologically rigid[4] and the most industrialized, a carryover from the period between the two world wars. Hungary, the most reform-minded, experimented with a number of economic reforms from 1968 to the collapse of Communism in 1989. Poland was the least committed to Communism, and most of its agriculture remained in private hands.

The End of Communism

The collapse of the Soviet-bloc countries occurred in 1989, two years before the end of the Soviet Union. It was sudden and swift and inevitable because their economies were almost all bankrupt. Some governments, including those of Poland and Bulgaria, had borrowed heavily from the West to shore up their declining economies. Others printed more money, which in a system of fixed prices meant queues, shortages, and more corruption. In Poland the rate of inflation as mea-

1. This began with the German occupation of the Sudetenland in 1938.
2. The Molotov-Ribbentrop agreement secretly divided Poland up between the Soviet Union and Germany even before the Germans invaded Poland in September 1939.
3. This was particularly true toward the end of the war. Warsaw was 95 percent destroyed by the Germans.
4. This was particularly true after the "Prague Spring" of 1968, which caused the Soviet Union to send tanks in to put down reform attempts.

sured by a 1985 base year of 100 percent increased to 828 percent by 1989. There was a slowdown in the Hungarian economy during the 1980s, with real economic growth in GNP increasing at an average rate of 1 percent a year. Serious attempts at economic reforms in the bloc countries were never fully implemented and inevitably would clash with centralized economic control.

The performance of the Soviet-bloc countries can be compared to that of the Western European countries by using per capita GNP before World War II and 1990. In 1990 all of the countries had somewhat similar economic systems. As Table 11-3 indicates, the Western European countries performed better.

The Legacy of Communism

The legacy of Communism was rather uneven among the Soviet-bloc countries of Central and Eastern Europe. Czechoslovakia, Romania, and the former East Germany were the most ideologically rigid. Poland and Hungary were more flexible. In Poland the majority of the population never really accepted Communism, in part because of their resentment of Russia and in part because of the opposition of

TABLE 11-2 *Structure of Exports in Czechoslovakia, Hungary, and Poland for 1938 (percent)*

	Czechoslovakia	*Hungary*	*Poland*
Manufactured goods	71.8	13.0	6.4
Raw materials and intermediate goods	19.8	31.7	65.1
Foodstuffs	8.4	55.3	28.5
	100.0	100.0	100.0

Source: Excerpted from Nicholas Spulber, *The Economics of Communist Eastern Europe* (New York: John Wiley & Sons, 1957), 115.

TABLE 11-3
Per Capita GNP for 1938 and 1990 for Western and Eastern European Countries (in 1990 U.S. dollars)

Country	*1938*	*1990*
Western Europe		
Austria	1,800	19,200
Italy	1,300	16,800
Spain	900	10,900
Portugal	800	4,900
Eastern Europe		
Czechoslovakia	1,800	3,100
Hungary	1,100	2,800
Poland	1,000	1,700
Romania	700	1,600

Source: Bartlomiej Kaminski, "The Legacy of Communism," in *East-Central European Economies in Transition*, Joint Economic Committee, Congress of the United States, 103d Cong., 2nd Sess. (Washington, D.C.: U.S. Government Printing Office, November 1994), 17.

the Catholic Church to Communism. Unlike that in the other countries, most of Polish agriculture remained in private hands. Hungary was the first country to experiment with economic reforms beginning in 1968 with what was called the New Economic Mechanism. These reforms were of three types: allowing greater scope for the private sector; giving increased autonomy to managers of state enterprises to determine prices and production; and liberalizing certain economic policies. These reforms established institutions that a market economy would later require.

When Communism collapsed, the Soviet-bloc countries were faced with the same transition problems that faced Russia. They had to adopt the institutions of a market economy. When the process of transition began in the late 1980s, the experience and theory to guide it were largely lacking. All of these countries had certain distinctive institutional features that set them apart from market economies. No matter how reformed the economic system, the core institutions were the same. There was reliance on economic planning, and the Communist Party was the sole political party. The invisible hand of the market was supplanted by the visible hand of the party-state apparatus. Their production structures overemphasized the development of heavy industries, particularly steel, and underemphasized the development of the service sector. The export sector was poorly developed since all of the countries were members of the Council for Mutual Economic Assistance (CMEA).[5]

The Process of Transition

The transition process involved privatizing former state enterprises. As outlined previously, there are several approaches to privatization, including the use of vouchers. Privatized enterprises, however, need access to investable funds through the development of a domestic financial sector that has to be completely restructured. Moreover, financial discipline has to be created through the ultimate sanction of bankruptcy. This requires the development of a new legal framework. All of the countries have now embarked on the creation of a new legal system. Taxation is also fundamental in the transition to a market economy because of the changing role of government responsibilities. Finally, there has to be an integration of the transition economies into world trade, particularly after the collapse of CMEA. Their integration requires major adjustments in the direction and composition of foreign trade. Their openness allows them to import relative price structures from world markets.

Table 11-4 presents the extent of private sector activity in the Soviet-bloc countries as of 1989, the last year before the transition process began. Private sector shares of GDP ranged from a high of 28.6 percent of GDP in Poland to a low of

5. The economic development of the Soviet-bloc countries was predicated upon access to cheap natural resources in the Soviet Union, particularly oil. Trade usually involved a barter arrangement in which Hungarian consumer goods or Czech machine tools were exchanged for Russian oil.

TABLE 11-4 *Private Sector Activity in the Soviet-Bloc Countries Before Transition*

Country	*Private Sector Share in GDP in 1989 (percent)*	*Private Sector Share Total Employment, 1989 (percent)*
Bulgaria	6.2	5.9
Czechoslovakia	4.1	1.2
Hungary	13.0	—
Poland	28.6	44.3
Romania	13.0	5.9

Source: Philippe Aghion, Oliver Blanchard, and Robin Burgess, *The Behavior of State Firms in Eastern Europe, Pre-Privatization*, Working Paper No. 12 (London: European Bank for Reconstruction and Development, October 1993).

4.1 percent of GDP in Czechoslovakia. Private enterprise was particularly well developed in trade and construction as well as in agriculture.

POLAND

Joseph Stalin, not noted for his sense of humor, once said that it was easier to saddle a bull than it was to impose Communism on the Poles. Subsequent events proved him right. Communism did not have the hold it had in other Eastern European countries for several reasons. First, Poland had no tradition of communism before World War II. Second, there is a resentment of any outside power, particularly Germany and the Soviet Union, both of which had made Poland a battleground for centuries. Third, the Catholic church has always been a viable part of the life of Poland and a bulwark against change. Finally, an aspect of the Polish national character is a romantic fatalism created by many centuries of being a common battleground for Swedes, Germans, Russians, and Austrians. Poles have revolted countless times against their oppressors, usually with disastrous results.

Communism was used by many Poles as a way to advance their causes; few were ideologically committed. For this reason there were few reprisals after communism collapsed. Most Poles went about their business as if nothing had changed.[6] Party members simply held on to the jobs they had or used their positions to be first in line to buy state enterprises or acquire private property. This stands in contrast to the hard-line attitude taken in Czechoslovakia toward the Communists once Communism had collapsed, and to Romania, where the Communist dictator, Nikolae Ceaucescu, was executed along with his wife.

6. The former head of the Communist Party in the city of Wroclaw still is president of a university, and a member of Solidarity who was jailed by the Communists is vice president.

Problems of the Polish Economy

The problems of the Polish economy began in the 1970s. Prior to that time, Communist economic policies were based on the Soviet industrial model. Resources were directed to such industries as iron and steel, heavy machinery, and chemicals. This development strategy was not effective for Poland, because it was so different from the Soviet Union in resources and size. Profitable industries had to subsidize unprofitable ones, and high operating costs made many plants and industries unprofitable. The consumer and agricultural sectors, whose resources went into the development of heavy industry, suffered accordingly. A high level of consumer unrest, which was attributed to chronic shortages of meat and consumer goods, led to food riots and a shake-up in the Communist Party.

During the 1970s Edward Gierek, the new party secretary, promised an increase in consumer living standards. To achieve this, large amounts of new capital goods were imported from the West to modernize Polish industry. These goods were paid for through borrowing from Western financial sources. The Poles expected to pay off the debt with expanded exports to the West in the form of goods produced by their new technology. However, this did not occur, and much of the money was wasted by Gierek and other party leaders on other projects. Moreover, the growth of exports to the West did not keep pace with the hard-currency debt from abroad. Problems worsened in the 1980s, beginning with the military crackdown on the Solidarity movement and ending with the collapse of the Polish economy.

Agricultural Problems. Poland was the only centrally planned economy in Eastern Europe that relied principally on private farming for the bulk of agricultural production,[7] although there were some state and collective farms. Prior to World War II Poland was one of the premier agricultural countries in Europe and a net exporter of agricultural goods; by the 1970s and 1980s agriculture was so inefficient that food products had to be imported.[8] There were several reasons for agricultural inefficiency. First, most Polish farms were too small to achieve economies of scale, and farmers could not invest in equipment for mechanizing farm tasks. Second, processing facilities such as slaughterhouses and meat-processing plants were run by inefficient state monopolies. Third, the distribution system was inefficient, with much waste and spoilage before farm products reached consumers. Finally, state investment in agriculture was very low.

Low Industrial Productivity. The index of Poland's industrial production, as Table 11-5 indicates, was lower in 1989 than in 1985. Both capital and labor productivity declined, and there was a lack of economic motivation and pressure to economize on the use of fuels and raw materials. Technology was obsolete, and

7. The Communists tried to institute collective farming but were met with armed opposition by farmers, and there were many deaths.
8. When the author was in Poland in 1985, there was a food shortage.

many industries were uncompetitive even by Eastern European standards. The whole industrial structure had been created during the time of Stalin, with priority given to the development of the iron and steel industry, heavy machinery, and other producer goods. The two largest state enterprises in Poland, the Lenin shipyard in Gdansk and the Lenin steel mill in Katowice, were bankrupt even with government support. Efforts to restructure these industries with the aid of Western capital and technology failed.

Table 11-5 provides some indices of Polish economic performance during the 1980s. Industrial production showed a decline for the decade, and consumer prices increased rapidly at the end of the decade. The foreign debt increased in relation to GNP, as exports failed to increase at a rate necessary to reduce debt service payments. Real per capita GNP increased at an average annual rate of less than 1 percent for the decade.

Economic Reforms

Economic reform in Poland has involved measures designed to dismantle government control over the economy. These reforms have included privatization of state enterprises, liberalization of prices, currency reforms, and legal, political, and administrative reforms. The Polish economy prior to the downfall of Communism was similar to the East German economy. Central planning had placed emphasis on capital formation and was not guided by a coherent price structure. High levels of subsidies accounted for around half of Polish government budgetary expenditures. Prices to consumers were based on social considerations, and consumer goods and housing were provided at prices well below their cost. The principal role of the Polish banking system was to prepare the financial plan and to monitor the success of state enterprises in achieving plan targets. Ownership of enterprises

TABLE 11-5 *Polish Economic Performance During the 1980s (percent)*

Year	*Foreign Debt/ GNP*	*Industrial Production*	*Growth in Real GNP*	*Consumer Prices*
1980	30.1	100	1.1	100
1981	32.2	97	–0.9	147
1982	39.1	94	1.2	220
1983	40.8	91	1.4	285
1984	43.2	93	1.8	330
1985	47.4	95	2.6	377
1986	50.3	96	2.5	451
1987	66.0	94	–2.3	584
1988	62.3	96	2.0	968
1989	58.0	91	–2.0	3,388

Sources: The World Bank, *World Debt Tables 1988–1989* (Washington, D.C.: The World Bank, 1989), 49; Central Intelligence Agency, *Handbook of Economic Statistics, 1991* (Springfield, Va.: National Technical Information Service, 1991), 38, 40, 42.

was in the hands of the state, and few people had the incentive to concern themselves with managing them successfully.

During the 1980s the Polish government progressively relaxed bureaucratic controls. By the end of the decade only the key sectors (mining, transport, communications, steel, and coal) remained under centralized control. In other sectors enterprises were permitted to choose their sources of supply, market their products, change their assortment of products, and decide within limits on the volume and direction of investments made out of retained earnings. However, despite the loosening of some controls, most of the bureaucratic-administrative structure remained in place until 1989. Most major state enterprises continued to have a single source of inputs. Enterprise managers continued to face the possibility of arbitrary bureaucratic interference. If an enterprise had a loss, it could receive a subsidy, particularly if the enterprise mined coal or produced steel.

The Solidarity-led government took office on September 12, 1989, and moved toward a market economy. In 1989 the state-owned sector in Poland generated around 75 percent of GNP and consisted of 21,000 state enterprises. Of these, 9,000 were funded by central or local authorities, and 12,000 were cooperatives.[9] There were 5,486 industrial enterprises, including 2,463 cooperatives, most of them small units. Large and medium-sized enterprises were, with few exceptions, state-owned. In December 1989 public sector enterprises employed 8.6 million workers, of whom just over 4 million were employed in industry. State enterprises had no legal standing and could not be sold. Their budgetary allocation was administered through a state ministry or local authority.

Shock Therapy

Poland was the first of the Soviet-bloc countries to use shock therapy, which involves a transformation from communism to capitalism as quickly as possible. There were several reasons for using this approach as opposed to a more gradual one. First, a country that moves quickly toward capitalism and democracy will get there sooner than a country that does not. Second, a sharp break with the political past is necessary because it puts into power forces that want to end communism, not prolong it. Third, the greater the reform, the faster the number of people who will benefit from it and who will provide support for further reform. Fourth, rapid reform tends to make it difficult for groups opposing it to coalesce. Finally, a rapid transition disperses economic resources and creates a propertied class, two steps necessary for the creation of a democratic society.

Shock therapy in Poland involved the following approaches:[10]

9. *Maly Rocznik Statystyczny 1991* (Warsaw: Glowny Urzad Statystyczny), 125.

10. Jeffrey Sacks, *Poland's Jump to the Market Economy* (Cambridge, Mass.: MIT Press, 1994), 35–78.

1. It freed most of its prices from central control and eliminated most subsidies.[11] Prices were allowed to increase, which reduced purchasing power but increased incentives for farmers and factories to produce and thus increased supply.[12]
2. The central government balanced its budget to eliminate deficit spending, which had contributed to a rapid increase in inflation in the economy during 1988 and 1989.
3. Poland devalued its currency unit, the zloty, made it convertible, and allowed it to float, that is, to attain an international market-determined level. Devaluation was supposed to encourage foreign investment and make Poland's own goods more competitive in world markets.
4. State enterprises were privatized in order to create an ownership group. A Ministry of Ownership was created to oversee the privatization process, and specialized institutions were set up to facilitate it.

The Privatization Process

When Poland began the privatization process, it had a distinct advantage over Russia and most of the other countries involved in the transition to a market economy in that private enterprise had existed under Communist rule. Poland had some people who had already had entrepreneurial experience, particularly in the service industries. Poles were allowed to travel to other countries, and many spent time in Western Europe and the United States. They were able to save hard currency, make business contacts, and learn Western business techniques. They were able to exploit Poland's shortage of goods by bringing back items that were in scarce supply. With the hard currency that many had accumulated by working abroad, they created their own businesses.

The State Enterprise Privatization Law, which was adopted in July 1990, permitted four separate approaches to the privatization of state property:

1. Sales of entire firms to Polish or foreign investors.
2. Liquidation of firm assets and their sale to private investors.
3. Free distribution of stock shares to investors.
4. Establishment of holding companies.

Like East Germany and other Communist countries, the Polish economy was dominated by large state enterprises. Firms with more than 500 workers numbered around 2,000 and accounted for 80 percent of industrial employment in Poland. Firms with more than 1,000 workers numbered 1,000 and accounted for 66 percent of employment in industry.[13] As was the case in Russia and other coun-

11. Subsidies were maintained on housing.
12. The increase in the supply of food and clothing was very evident when the author was in Poland in 1991.
13. *Maly Rocznik Statystyczny 1991*, 170–171.

tries, Polish industrial firms were obsolete by Western standards and have proved to be difficult to dispose of. An example is the Lenin steelworks in the industrial city of Nowa Huta, which employed some 36,000 workers in 1990. Its products were not competitive in world markets. Six years later, the steelworks, now renamed Huta Sendzimira to shed the association with Lenin,[14] is still operating and still losing money, even though the workforce has been reduced by 11,000 workers. Yet the mill is too politically important to close down, and it continues to be subsidized.

Nevertheless, privatization has had notable success. By 1992 the private sector share in GDP had increased from 28.6 percent in 1989 to 47.5 percent, and the private sector share in total employment increased from 44.3 percent to 51.1 percent.[15] Small pieces of the economy were converted rather quickly into the free market. Nearly 80 percent of retail and wholesale outlets were privatized by October 1991.[16] Half of the nation's trucking industry was in private hands, and more than 1.2 million new private companies were created in the sixteen months after privatization started. Privatization has worked particularly well in the service sector. Restaurants and small grocery stores have sprung up everywhere. Banks have been privatized, as have department stores. But the industrial base of Poland remains a problem because many Polish industries cannot compete in world markets.

The Legal System

The point has been made before that a system of laws has to be in place to facilitate the transition from a centrally planned economy to a market economy. First, there has to be the choice of a legal system—common law or code law. Second, there are laws that govern the use of property, for example, intellectual property. One of the more important laws is bankruptcy law, which serves several related functions in a market economy. First, the threat of bankruptcy imposes a degree of financial discipline on business managers. Second, it provides a mechanism to liquidate enterprises that fail and to repay creditors' claims according to agreed-upon priorities. In a transition economy there are two groups that would use bankruptcy law. The first group is state enterprises that need restructuring or liquidation; the second group is the private sector, for which bankruptcy law provides debt-collection procedures.

14. Lenin has had a rather ignominious end, not only in Poland, but elsewhere. Universities named for Lenin have been renamed, as have streets. The unkindest cut of all occurred in Leipzig, Germany, when a statue of Lenin was pulled down and sold to a buyer who wanted to use it in a theme park.

15. Philippe Aghion, Oliver Blanchard, and Robin Burgess. *The Behavior of State Firms in Eastern Europe: Pre-Privatization* (London: EBRD, 1993), 2.

16. "Against the Grain: A Survey of Poland," *The Economist*, April 16–22, 1994, 14.

The Polish legal system is based on the French and German code systems.[17] A new bankruptcy law provides for the reorganization as well as the liquidation of property. Procedures may be initiated by either the creditor or the debtor. However, there has been a reluctance on the part of the government to enforce bankruptcy against state-owned enterprises. Protection of intellectual property has been improved through the passage of two laws in 1994.[18] The first law is a trademark law that provides up to a year's imprisonment for those persons who sell goods with counterfeit trademarks, and the second is a copyright law that protects not only literary and musical works, but also computer software and industrial designs. An antimonopoly law patterned on the antitrust laws of the European Union was introduced in 1993.[19]

Public Finance

In Soviet-type economies, including Poland, resource allocation was regulated by central planning. The state budget was a key part of planning in that it represented the administration of the entire payment system. Virtually all payments were made through the state financial sector. The two most important taxes were the turnover tax and the tax on enterprise profits. The most important expenditure in the state budget was subsidies, which accounted for 16 percent of the Polish GDP in 1988.[20] The bulk of these subsidies went to support state-owned enterprises. When transition began in 1990, Poland was faced with two fiscal problems. The first was to create incentives for private initiative by reducing state intervention in the economy. Second, the budget deficit, which had increased to 8 percent of Polish GDP by 1989, had to be kept within limits to reduce the potential for inflation.

Tax Reforms. Four major changes were made in the Polish tax system.[21] In 1989 an enterprise income tax was introduced with a uniform tax rate of 40 percent. In 1990 a 2 percent payroll tax was levied to finance the newly established unemployment insurance fund. A personal income tax was introduced in 1992. The tax is levied on a pay-as-you-earn basis with withholding at the source. Marginal tax rates in 1995 ranged from 21 percent to 45 percent. In 1993 a value-added tax was

17. The French civil code is the Napoleonic Code, which was introduced in 1804. The German civil code was introduced in 1896. The two codes are somewhat similar. The French code system is used in France, Italy, Belgium, Portugal, and the Netherlands. The German civil code is used in Germany, Austria, and Hungary and in Czechoslovakia before World War II.

18. Pirating of intellectual property has been a serious problem in Poland. According to estimates, 80 percent of clothing and 50 percent of coffee on the Polish market are sold by Polish entrepreneurs under pirated trademarks.

19. Poland hopes to become a member of the European Union.

20. Sacks, 66.

21. Gerd Schwartz, "Public Finances," in Liam P. Ebrill, Ajai Chopra, Charalambos Christofides, Paul Mylonas, Inci Otker, and Gerd Schwartz, *Poland: The Path to a Market Economy* (Washington, D.C.: International Monetary Fund, October 1994), 7.

introduced at a standard rate of 22 percent and a minimum rate of 7 percent. The tax administration was also changed. Local and regional tax officers were created, and the main administration was integrated into the Ministry of Finance. In 1993 about 10 million personal income tax returns had to be processed manually.

Expenditures. The two main objectives of expenditure reforms were to reduce subsidies and to reduce the deficit in the budget. Subsidies to enterprises and consumers were reduced, but expenditures on social welfare had to be increased as the rate of unemployment increased. When prices were liberalized in 1990, it was no longer feasible to provide subsidies on goods and services. Budgetary subsidies to state farms were phased out. Military expenditures were also reduced as the troop strength of the Polish army was reduced from 400,000 in 1988 to 290,000 in 1993. Table 11-6 compares revenues and expenditures of the Polish government for 1989 and 1993. The deficit in the federal budget has shown a decline from 7.3 percent of GDP in 1989 to 2.9 percent in 1993.

Banking

Prior to transition, the National Bank of Poland was the central bank. It had a monopoly of traditional banking functions as well as commercial bank activities. Its

TABLE 11-6
Major Revenues and Expenditures of the Polish Government, 1989–1993 (percentage of GDP)

	1989	*1993*
Revenues	41.5	45.5
Tax revenues	33.8	39.1
Enterprise income tax	9.7	5.3
Personal income tax	3.4	9.1
Turnover taxes and excises	8.9	10.6
Social security contributions	7.4	9.9
Other	4.4	—
Capital revenue	—	0.5
Other	7.7	5.9
Expenditures	48.8	48.4
State budget expenditures	41.8	46.0
Factor income payments	6.9	11.8
Direct government demand	6.7	6.0
Producer subsidies	4.5	—
Income transfers	19.6	20.4
Consumer subsidies	8.4	—
Social security benefits	11.2	20.4
Other	4.1	—
Outside the state budget	7.0	2.4
Deficit	–7.3	–2.9

Source: Liam P. Ebrill, Ajai Chopra, Charalambos Christofides, Paul Mylonas, Inci Otker, and Gerd Schwartz, *Poland: The Path to a Market Economy,* Occasional Paper 113 (Washington, D.C.: International Monetary Fund, October 1994), 13.

operations were linked to the national economic plan, and monetary policy played a passive role. It was also responsible for the formation of the annual cash and credit plans. In 1989 its functions were changed by two new laws, the Act on the National Bank of Poland and the Banking Law. Nine state-owned commercial banks took over the commercial functions of the National Bank of Poland. In October 1991 the legal status of these commercial banks was transformed into that of joint-stock companies 100 percent owned by the Polish Treasury. The National Bank of Poland was given the responsibility for the implementation of monetary policy.[22]

There are four different groups of banks in Poland: state-owned commercial banks, state-owned specialized banks, private banks, and cooperative banks. The state-owned commercial and specialized banks dominate the Polish financial system, accounting for over three-quarters of total banking assets. The functions of each type of bank may be summarized as follows:

1. *The nine state-owned commercial banks.* These banks perform the same functions as commercial banks in Western countries. However, they are less regulated and as a consequence have made some bad loans, particularly to large state enterprises.[23] They are free, as are private banks, to set their own interest rates on deposits and loans. The eventual intent of the Polish government is the privatization of these banks. As of mid-1995 three of them have been privatized.
2. *State-owned specialized banks.* There are four state-owned specialized banks in Poland: Bank Handlowy, which deals with foreign trade; PKO-SA, which deals with consumer foreign currency deposits and transactions; the Bank for Food Economy, which deals with lending to agriculture and cooperative banks; and PKO, which deals with consumer deposits and housing loans. They, too, have had problems with bad debts and have had to be recapitalized by being provided Treasury-issued recapitalization bonds.
3. *Private banks.* The Banking Law of 1989 authorized the creation of private banks, and by the end of 1992 some ninety banks had been created.[24] Several private banks have been created with foreign capital, and foreign banks have opened up branch banks in Poland. However, private banks are small in comparison to their state-owned counterparts, and many are undercapitalized. They are also at a competitive disadvantage against state-owned banks in that the latter have open-end deposit insurance from the Polish Treasury.

22. The president of the National Bank of Poland is appointed by the Parliament at the request of the president of Poland. Each year the NBP must submit to Parliament a draft of monetary policy guidelines.

23. In 1991, 62 percent of outstanding loans for seven of the nine commercial banks were either a total loss, doubtful, or substandard, primarily because of loans to state enterprises. Little effort was made to seek other customers.

24. Ajai Chopra, "Monetary Policy and Financial Sector Reforms," in Liam P. Ebrill, Ajai Chopra, Charalambos Christofides, Paul Mylonas, Inci Otker, and Gerd Schwartz, *Poland: The Path to a Market Economy*, Occasional Paper 113 (Washington, D.C.: International Monetary Fund, October 1994), 39.

4. *Cooperative banks.* There are over 1,600 cooperative banks in Poland, accounting for 6 percent of total bank assets. Their primary function is to make housing loans. Deposits in these banks are guaranteed by the Polish Treasury.

Capital Markets

Capital markets are necessary to the privatization process because they set the market value of privatized companies on an ongoing basis. They also force the banking system to become more competitive. Capital markets are in their infancy in Poland. The Warsaw Stock Exchange, which was in existence before World War II, was reopened in 1991. In addition to being the only venue in Poland for the public trading of stocks, the exchange also conducts trading in Polish Treasury bills. In 1993 the exchange was the strongest-performing exchange in the world, appreciating 1,000 percent.[25] Only a small number of companies have access to the stock exchange,[26] however, and the majority of Polish firms don't borrow because of high interest rates. Most private investment is financed from retained earnings. Corporate bonds are not a viable option because of high interest rates and the lack of investment banks.

Exchange Rates

The Polish currency unit, the zloty (zl), was an inconvertible currency prior to the transition from a socialist economy to a capitalist economy. The official exchange rate was set by the government at an artificially low rate with the intent of making Polish exports profitable in world markets. In addition to the government-determined exchange rate, there was a black market for foreign exchange where the value of the zloty was determined by market forces. The dollar, for example, which would be set at a fixed dollar/zloty exchange rate by the government, would have a totally different black market rate. Artificial trade barriers of various sorts were used, including export and import licenses, the use of import quotas, and the need for approval to export or import specific commodities. The end result was that Poland was isolated from competition in world markets.

One of the first things that had to be done during the transition period was to devalue the zloty in relation to world currencies. In January 1990 the exchange rate of the zloty was fixed at a rate of 9,500 zl = $1.26.[27] The main reason for fixing the exchange rate was to reduce inflation, which had been averaging an increase of 30 percent a month, by reducing the excess demand for foreign goods. Another reason for devaluing the zloty was to reduce the deficit in the balance of payments. Successive devaluations of the zloty were used to reverse the outflow of

25. On October 22, 1994, the Polish stock market index was 9,444; on March 27, 1996, it was 11,414.
26. Chopra, 40.
27. The zloty was pegged to the U.S. dollar. In 1992 it was pegged to a basket of currencies including the U.S. dollar, the German mark, and the Japanese yen.

foreign currency reserves that had resulted from inflation and a decline in Polish export competitiveness in world markets. The official exchange rate increased to 13,360 zl = $1 by February 1992. By July 1994 subsequent devaluations of the zloty had changed the Polish-U.S. exchange rate to 22,300 zl = $1. In January 1995 the zloty was revalued by the Polish government at a rate of 2.4 zl = $1.[28]

The great bulk of Polish foreign trade before the demise of Communism was with other CMEA countries including the Soviet Union. Since the collapse of CMEA there has been a radical shift in trade toward the European Union countries and away from former CMEA partners. During the period 1990–1991 Polish exports to the CMEA countries declined by over 70 percent, while Polish exports to Western Europe increased by 61 percent.[29] During the period 1989–1993 Polish foreign trade doubled, with most of the increase going to the United States, Japan, and Western Europe. The share of the private sector in foreign trade has more than doubled during transition, with private sector exports increasing from 21.9 percent of total exports in 1991 to 57.6 percent in 1993. Foreign investment is permitted in Poland, and many state-owned firms have been sold to foreign buyers.

Evaluation of the Polish Economy

Poland is well on its way toward becoming a market economy. The number of private enterprises has more than doubled during the period of transition. In July 1995 it was 2.2 million. In addition to the increase in local enterprises, the transition has made it possible for foreign investors to set up companies in Poland, particularly through the use of joint ventures. The entry of foreign firms into Poland and other former Soviet-bloc countries has contributed to improvements in productivity and the transfer of technical skills. Consumer choice of products and services has increased. Because of the fall in relative prices, households have been able to reduce the share of their budgets spent on food. As Table 11-8 indicates, inflation has declined and the real growth rate has started to increase.

However, privatization of state-owned enterprises has created some problems. State authorities have been reluctant for political reasons to sell some large state-owned enterprises. The program to privatize Poland's largest state enterprises was only beginning to take effect by mid-1994. The privatization of Poland's 1,494 state farms has also been slow to develop. Many are bankrupt, but they are often the only employer in the areas in which they are located. Another problem of transition is the high unemployment rate that continues to exist in Poland. Income differentials have increased, and real wages for many workers have declined. As the following section indicates, there have been winners and losers during the transition period, with the losers concentrated heavily among industrial workers.

28. The zloty is now convertible and subject to what is called managed float, meaning that it is allowed to fluctuate within a band ± 7 percentage points around a central exchange rate. On April 1, 1996, the zloty–dollar exchange rate was 2.63 zl = $1.

29. Paul Mylonas, "Integration in the World Economy," in *Poland: The Transition to a Market Economy*, 73.

Tables 11-7 and 11-8 present the performance of the Polish economy during the transition period. It should be noticed that private employment in the agricultural sector accounts for more than 20 percent of the employment in the Polish economy compared to less than 3 percent in the U.S. economy.

Winners and Losers in Poland's Transition to a Market Economy

Who has gained from Poland's jump to a market economy and who has lost? The winners have a stake in the free market; the losers get nostalgic for the past. The shift from a centrally planned economy has made many workers as well as industries obsolete, as an unemployment rate around 16 percent in 1995 can testify. Materially, the majority of Poles are better off as a result of the shift from a centrally planned to a market economy. Ownership of such consumer goods as cars, color television sets, and washing machines has doubled during transition. Home ownership has also shown an increase. However, a new socioeconomic class structure has emerged that was not there when it was Communist. Poland had an elite group, the nomenklatura, but it drew its members from all segments of society. Now everything has changed and winners and losers can now be sorted out.

Winners:

1. English teachers and anyone who has business and social contacts with the West. English is a language that is of prime importance because it is the language of international business.
2. Entrepreneurs who are able to identify a consumer need and satisfy it. There is also a black market in which money has been made.
3. State enterprise managers and members of the nomenklatura elite who have the money to buy state enterprises.

TABLE 11-7 *Employment by Sector in Poland, 1988–1992 (thousands)*

Total Employment	*1988*	*1989*	*1990*	*1991*	*1992*
	17,203	16,854	16,511	15,601	15,096
Socialized sector	12,215	11,779	8,942	7,633	6,800
Industry	4,320	4,177	3,250	2,745	2,413
Construction	1,071	964	792	546	347
Agriculture	996	963	594	458	329
Transportation, communications	998	933	820	715	629
Trade	1,388	1,342	322	212	172
Services	3,288	3,260	3,039	2,850	3,138
Private sector					
Private agriculture	3,620	3,560	3,831	3,806	3,708
Other private sectors	1,188	1,515	3,738	4,162	4,588

Source: Liam P. Ebrill, Ajai Chopra, Charlambos Christofides, Paul Mylonas, Inci Otker, and Gerd Schwartz, *Poland: The Path to a Market Economy,* Occasional Paper 113 (Washington, D.C.: International Monetary Fund, October 1994), 92

TABLE 11-8 *Inflation, Unemployment, and Economic Growth in Poland, 1990–1995 (percent)*

	1990	*1991*	*1992*	*1993*	*1994*	*1995*
GDP real growth rate	–11.7	–7.8	–1.5	4.0	4.5	7.0
Unemployment	6.3	11.8	13.6	15.7	16.0	16.0
Consumer price inflation	585.8	70.3	44.3	37.6	27.5	20.4
Real per capita GDP ($U.S.)	1,690	1,830	1,950	2,227	2,238	2,470

Sources: The World Bank, *The World Bank Atlas*, 1995, 1994, and 1993, and the Central Office of Statistics, Warsaw, Poland; *The Economist*, March 30-April 6, 1996, 100.

4. Those persons who are educated, because education has become the leading determinant of income, a relationship that did not exist before transition. Under Communism, coal miners were paid more than doctors and college professors. It was a matter of Marxist ideology. Fewer than 10 percent of Poles have attended a university. Now graduates are in great demand, particularly if they speak English.

Losers:

1. Farmers. Making up about one-fourth of the Polish labor force, they have seen their incomes reduced as economic reform has reduced subsidies to agriculture. Inefficient state farms have been closed. Most private farms were too small to be profitable. Modernization will reduce the agricultural labor force by more than 50 percent by the end of the century.
2. Industrial workers, particularly steelworkers and coal miners. Coal miners were the elite of the Polish labor force during Communism. Their salaries were two to three times the average wage. Steelworkers were also well paid. Neither industry is competitive in world markets. The end of CMEA also affected Polish industries that were heavily involved in trade with the Soviet Union and other Soviet-bloc countries.
3. People who depend on government financial assistance. Approximately 30 percent of Poles receive some form of financial assistance from the government. This assistance amounts to 15 percent of Polish GDP. More than a third of Poles who draw pensions also have jobs. Cutbacks have been made in welfare assistance.

Democratic Institutions

In Poland popular dissatisfaction with the costs of transition has led to the election of governments that have included ex-Communists. In fact, ex-Communists have gained power, and the current leader is a former Communist. Parties that were once popular, including Solidarity, are out of power. Several elections have been held, and there are many political parties, including the Democratic Left Alliance, which is the successor to the old Communist Party.[30] Two pillars of democracy are missing: stable political parties and a constitution. Most parties, including the Democratic Left Alliance, profess support for economic reforms, but they want to make adjustments in the process. Many Poles are not identified with any political party, so there are weak ties between Poles and their leaders. Polish politics will continue to be affected by the transition from socialism to capitalism, but a return to the past is highly unlikely.[31]

THE CZECH REPUBLIC

Czechoslovakia, now the Czech and Slovak Republics, had the highest living standard of all of the East-Central European countries before World War II. It was created by the Treaty of Versailles and included much of the industrial base of the former Austro-Hungarian Empire. It developed both capitalistic and democratic institutions during the period 1919–1939. When it was occupied by the Soviet Union after World War II, it was reorganized along the lines of the Soviet economic system. With the exception of East Germany, it became the most ideologically rigid of the Soviet-bloc countries, and any attempt at economic reform was rigidly suppressed. Under Communism 98 percent of the means of production were owned by the state. Prices were set by the state, and wages were tightly controlled. Economic planning stressed the development of heavy industry, and most foreign trade was done with the other CMEA countries.

In 1989 the authoritarian rule of Gustav Husak was toppled by the peaceful "velvet revolution," and Czechoslovakia became an independent country. It had a very small service sector, and production of consumer goods was relatively small. It was industrialized with an emphasis on military and heavy industry and collectivized in agriculture. Production facilities were located and developed, not according to domestic needs or comparative advantage in regional markets, but to the needs of the Soviet Union. The end result was an overemphasis on heavy industry[32] and military industry, subsidized energy inputs resulting in inefficient energy use, and environmental problems of the highest order. In addition, marketing and management skills necessary for the transition to a market economy did not exist.

Privatization

Privatization in Czechoslovakia took several forms. One was restitution, which involved the return of property to those who owned it prior to its confiscation or na-

30. Six elections have been held. In the 1995 election Lech Walesa was voted out of office.
31. Zoltan Barany, "The Return of the Left in East-Central Europe," *Problems of Post-Communism*, Vol. 42, No. 1 (January-February 1995), 41–45.
32. Heavy industry accounted for 17.5 percent of total employment in Czechoslovakia compared to 3 percent in developed Western countries.

tionalization when the Communists took power in 1948. Property was returned to the original owners or to their heirs except in cases where buildings had been constructed on the land after it was nationalized. About 30,000 industrial and administrative buildings, forest properties, and agricultural properties that had been nationalized by the Communists during the period 1948–1955, as well as 70,000 residential properties nationalized during the period 1955–1959, were returned to their original owners.[33] The value of the assets returned was around $5 billion.

Auctions. Small-scale privatization of small shops and businesses began on November 1, 1990, and was accomplished mainly through public auction. However, few persons could afford to bid on these businesses. Those who could generally fell into two categories. The first category included those who were a part of the nomenklatura elite and anyone who had the opportunity under Communist rule to make money illegally. This included those persons who sold any commodity by weight or volume, such as butchers and gas station operators. Also included in this category were persons who exchanged money on the black market for foreign currency. The second category included persons who had financial backing from people in other countries who, by law, could not purchase a business in Czechoslovakia. Auctions were held as often as four times a week, and by November 1992 over 20,000 small-scale enterprises had been sold.[34]

Vouchers. On May 18, 1992, Czechoslovakia decided to sell 1,200 of its larger state enterprises by distributing shares in them to millions of its citizens through the issuance of vouchers. Every citizen over the age of 18 was entitled to a voucher book with 1,000 investment points that could be bid at auction. Every share in each of the 1,200 companies was priced at the same fixed number of points. Individuals could bid themselves or give all or some of their points to privately run investment funds in exchange for shares in the fund. The managers of the funds would bid the points they collected. The voucher books cost 1,000 koruna ($33), which represented a week's pay for the average citizen. The rationale for the voucher system was to achieve privatization as soon as possible. The scheme also had political advantages in that it spread private property ownership widely.

The privatization process was to occur in three waves, with each wave divided into several rounds. The first wave began in May 1992 and was completed by July 1993. The businesses selected for that wave were those that were most prepared for privatization and had little strategic importance. During that period, 25 percent of the country's assets were privatized. The second wave began in 1993 and was completed in December 1994 after six rounds of share offers. Of the shares offered, 96.3 percent were allocated to individuals and investment funds.[35] The

33. However, former owners of houses or apartments were not allowed to evict current tenants.
34. Joshua Charap and Alena Zemplinerova, *Restructuring in the Czech Economy*, Working Paper No. 2 (London: European Bank for Reconstruction and Development, March 1993), 6.
35. Data are for the Czech Republic only. It is necessary to remember that the Czech and Slovak Republics separated into two separate countries in January 1993.

third wave, which began in 1995, included many heavy industries, such as refineries, telecommunications, and utilities. In late June 1995 a partnership of the Dutch and Swiss phone companies were given a 27 percent stake in the Czech phone company, SPT Communications, with a bid of $1.45 billion.[36]

Table 11-9 presents the privatization measures used, the privatized units, and the privatized property in percent for the period 1992. The data are for Czechoslovakia before the split. Included in the table are transfers of state-owned properties to local governments, pension funds and the like, and direct sales to a designated owner.

Table 11-10 presents the change in the size structure of Czech industrial enterprises resulting from privatization. Prior to the transition to a market economy, the Czech economy had been dominated by large state enterprises. In 1989, 430 state industrial enterprises existed in Czechoslovakia, 123 of which employed 2,500 or more workers, and none of which employed fewer than 300 workers. By August 1992, 16,852 enterprises had been created of which 2,258 had more than 25 employees.

Banking

The banking system of Czechoslovakia was in every way similar to the banking system of other Communist countries. There was a central bank—the Czechoslovak State Bank—which issued money and handled all financial transactions between state-owned enterprises. Three banks, each with limited functions, were directly under the control of the central bank. Two of these were commercial banks with specialized functions, and the other was a national savings bank that collected the savings of the population and transferred them to the central bank. As in other Communist countries, the central bank was responsible for the implementation of the national financial plan, the purpose of which was to adjust the supply of money to the real output goals of the national physical output plan.

Banking reforms in Czechoslovakia were somewhat easier to undertake during the transition period than in Poland and Hungary because it was in better financial shape. It had a low foreign debt and a government deficit of less than 1 percent of GDP.[37] Poland and Hungary had foreign debts amounting to over half of their GDPs and large budget deficits. A problem that confronted banking reform in the three countries was what to do with the bad debt of state enterprises. In 1991 a special bank, the Consolidated Bank, was set up to manage the debt by providing credit to indebted enterprises.[38] Major banking reforms were initiated in the same year with the passage of the Banking Act and the State Bank Act. A new banking

36. *Wall Street Journal*, June 29, 1995, A12.
37. Michael Marrese, "Banking Sector Reform in Central and Eastern Europe," in *East-Central European Economies in Transition*, Joint Economic Committee, Congress of the United States, 103d Cong., 2d Sess. (Washington, D.C.: U.S. Government Printing Office, November 1994), 118.
38. Ibid., 120.

TABLE 11-9 *Privatization in Czechoslovakia According to Method Used*

Privatization Method	*Privatization Units in Percent*	*Book Value of Units in Percent*
Auction	8.62	0.8
Voucher	31.23	89.2
Public tender	7.90	2.2
Direct sale	25.28	5.7
Restitution	26.97	2.0
	100.00	100.00

Source: Joshua Charap and Alena Zemplinerova, *Restructuring in the Czech Economy*, Working Paper No. 2 (London: European Bank for Reconstruction and Development, March 1993), 12.

TABLE 11-10 *Industrial Enterprises by Employment in Czechoslovakia, 1989–1992*

Number of Employees	*1989*	*1992*
25–99	—	549
100–149	—	216
150–299	—	522
300–599	48	409
600–1,199	84	260
1,200–2,499	175	195
2,500–4,999	74	78
5,000 and over	49	29
Total	430	2,258

Source: Joshua Charap and Alena Zemplinerova, *Restructuring the Czech Economy*, Working Paper No. 2 (London: European Bank for Reconstruction and Development, March 1993), 6.

system was created and was largely in place when Czechoslovakia split into the Czech Republic and the Slovak Republic in January 1993.[39]

Other Reforms

The point has already been made that it is no simple task to convert a centrally planned economy into a market economy because two entirely different sets of institutions are involved. Privatization of state-owned enterprises and conversion of a one-tiered to a two-tiered banking system are two parts of the process. The legal system has to be changed, particularly in the areas of property, contract, and bankruptcy law. Changes in taxation are also fundamental to transition because the government has to finance the purchase of resources, whereas under central plan-

39. At the end of 1994 there were 57 privately owned commercial banks and one state-owned commercial bank. The Czech government has a substantial minority interest in many commercial banks. Of the 57 private commercial banks, 20 are partly owned foreign banks and 21 are foreign-owned banks.

ning the government commanded the resources. A securities exchange is necessary to facilitate equity financing. The new economies have to be open to foreign trade, particularly with the collapse of CMEA. The reforms in Czechoslovakia may be summarized as follows:

1. A securities market was created in 1992. Currently there is the Prague Stock Exchange and an over-the-counter exchange.
2. Contract, bankruptcy, property, and intellectual property laws are in effect. The Czech legal system is based on the German civil code.
3. The Czech currency unit, the koruna, is convertible within the country and will be convertible outside by 1996.[40]
4. Foreign trade has been opened up to the rest of the world, and foreign investors have the same access to credit as Czech investors.

An Evaluation of the Czech Republic

The Czech Republic has the highest standard of living of all of the countries in Eastern and Central Europe. It has also had the smoothest transition to a market economy. Its labor force was the most technically skilled and best educated, and it had the heritage of democracy and an industrialized market economy from 1919 to 1948. It was relatively free from foreign debt when the transition to a market economy began in 1990. The split from Slovakia also benefited the Czech Republic in that it did not have as many of the large, inefficient industrial enterprises that are difficult to privatize as did Slovakia. However, it is dependent on external factors such as foreign investment and the growth of the Western European economy.

Table 11-11 presents the performance of the Czech economy during the transition period 1990–1995. The unemployment rate is much lower than in Poland and Hungary, largely because government policy has kept wages low and promoted early retirement programs. Another factor that has kept unemployment low is the lack of an effective bankruptcy law. The Czech Republic has also run a budgetary surplus, thus reducing the potential for inflation.

HUNGARY

Hungary was a major part of the old Austro-Hungarian Empire. The Treaty of Versailles created three independent nations—Austria, Czechoslovakia, and Hungary—and Hungary for a brief period was ruled by the Communists. Prior to and after World War I, Hungary was an agricultural country dominated by large landed estates, but it also had an industrial base.[41] Hungary had a per capita income of

40. The exchange rate of the dollar and koruna on April 2, 1996, was $1 = 30.14 korunas. The koruna is pegged to a basket comprising the deutsche mark and the dollar, with the deutsche mark weighted 65 percent.
41. Thirty-six percent of total Hungarian output was from industry, and 35 percent from agriculture.

TABLE 11-11 *Selected Czech Economic Indicators, 1990–1995 (percent)*

	1990	*1991*	*1992*	*1993*	*1994*	*1995*
GDP growth rate	–1.2	–14.2	–6.6	–0.9	2.6	4.0
Inflation	9.7	56.7	11.1	20.8	10.0	9.0
Unemployment	0.8	4.1	2.6	3.5	3.2	4.0

Sources: OECD, *OECD Economic Outlook* (Paris: OECD, June 1995), 111–114; The World Bank, *The World Bank Atlas*, 1992, 1993, 1994, 1995, and 1996.

$120 in 1937, which was second only to Czechoslovakia among the Eastern European countries.[42] After World War II, Hungary was ruled by a coalition of political parties, but by 1949 the Communists were firmly in control, and industry and banking had been nationalized. In 1956 an uprising against the rigid controls of the Communist government occurred, and the Soviet Union sent in troops and tanks to put it down. Janos Kadar, who became the leader of Hungary, proved more flexible and willing to experiment with reforms than leaders in the other Eastern European countries.[43]

The New Economic Mechanism (NEM), 1968

The New Economic Mechanism (NEM) introduced the Hungarian reforms. Its objective was to reduce central government intervention in the economy at the enterprise level. Enterprises were made independent economic units with the right to determine the structure of their production and sales. This policy conformed to one basic objective of the reforms, namely, to relieve the planning authorities of the task of preparing intricate economic plans. Instead, broad guidelines were provided for enterprises to follow. They were given latitude with respect to quality, styling, and pricing. They were then given the right to determine their own production mix on the basis of their preferences. A modified market economy was permitted in which enterprises could react to consumer preferences. Nevertheless, the central planning authorities were able to exercise some control over enterprise production through the use of economic levers designed to induce cooperation by making it more profitable to produce certain items.

Later Reforms

Reforms introduced in 1984 and 1985 were aimed at increasing the efficiency of state enterprises. A compulsory reserve fund, introduced in 1968, was eliminated. In its place, reserves held from pretax profits were allowed, based on the decisions of enterprise managers. Bonds could be issued by state enterprises and sold to the general public to raise capital. A new form of management was introduced in 1985.

42. Poland, Romania, Bulgaria, and Yugoslavia had lower per capita incomes.
43. Janos Kadar ruled Hungary for thirty-two years.

Rather than being chosen by the Communist Party, managers and staff of small and medium-sized enterprises were to be selected by the workers, who were also given the right to recall them. Enterprise councils were introduced in the same year as a new form of management for large state enterprises. They were given the following responsibilities:

1. Approval of capital budgets, major resource allocation decisions, and financial statements of enterprises.
2. Approval of mergers, acquisitions, or any other major reorganization decisions.
3. Election and evaluation of the performance of the managing director.

Stocks, Bonds, and Foreign Investment

It can be said that Hungary was much farther on the road to a market economy than the other Eastern European countries when Communism collapsed in late 1989. In January 1989 any company in Hungary was given the right to issue and sell stock to the public. The rationale for the sale of stocks and bonds was to end dependence on state subsidies. In 1988 the Hungarian government passed laws to encourage more foreign investment in Hungary, including the formation of joint ventures with Hungarian enterprises. A 1989 law permitted the setting up of 100 percent foreign-owned firms. Restrictions were reduced on the amount of earnings that could be repatriated out of Hungary.

By 1989 in terms of asset values, about half of the Hungarian state-owned enterprises were managed by enterprise councils, and the other half, mainly transportation and utilities, were managed by the state ministries. However, the privatization process was under way. In June 1989 a law was passed that allowed enterprise managers and workers to initiate the privatization process. The result was a number of spontaneous privatizations, whereby managers and councils more or less confiscated enterprise assets and either became the new owners or arranged sales to foreign investors. This enabled Hungarian managers to become owners without having to pay a fair price. Often the new managers and owners were former members of the Hungarian nomenklatura elite.

Problems of the Hungarian Economy

Despite efforts to convert the Hungarian economy into an efficient market-oriented socialist economy, problems developed, particularly during the 1980s. There was persistent economic stagnation, particularly during the second half of the decade, and the foreign debt almost doubled. The rate of economic growth in Hungary during the 1980s was lower than that in most of the other Eastern European countries, and its current account balance was negative for each year.[44] There

44. The World Bank, *World Debt Tables, 1988–1989* (Washington, D.C.: The World Bank, 1989), 29.

was a need to make the Hungarian industrial sector more efficient because, despite reforms, subsidies continued to be paid to state enterprises. Hungary became poorer relative to the OECD market economies. From 1975 to 1989 Hungarian real GDP was estimated to have grown by about 35 percent, compared to 54 percent for the OECD countries, and its per capita income was 50 percent lower than that of Portugal, the poorest OECD country.[45]

Low Productivity. There was a slowdown in Hungarian economic growth during the 1980s, with real per capita growth in GNP averaging about 1 percent a year. A fall in factor productivity and a misallocation of investment resulted in resource wastage. Modernization attempts were hindered by the fact that an increasing share of resources was allocated to inefficient enterprises in the heavy industry sector. Productivity increases were also retarded by the declining health of the population, which contributed to increased absenteeism and prolonged illnesses. Finally, slow productivity growth was attributed to financial constraints imposed by the large foreign debt, which imposed limitations on the import of investment goods into Hungary.

Foreign Trade. Although the bulk of Hungarian foreign trade was with its fellow CMEA members, it was more involved with trade to the West than any other Eastern European country. All of the Eastern European countries have lost world market shares to the developing countries of East Asia. This reduced hard currency earnings in many Hungarian export sectors. The bulk of Hungarian exports were raw materials whose prices declined in world markets, and imports consisted in part of manufactured goods whose prices went up in world markets. Hungary had a negative balance of trade during the 1980s. It also lost a major source of hard currency, namely, its reexporting of Soviet oil. Also, lower world prices for oil during the 1980s meant less hard currency for Soviet purchase of Hungarian products. Hungarian foreign debt also increased in the 1980s, as Table 11-12 indicates.

Hungary After 1989

Hungary was much farther along toward the creation of a market system than either Poland or former Czechoslovakia, so shock therapy was not needed. A two-tiered banking system had already been created, and some enterprises had already been privatized. It also had far more experience in attracting foreign investment than the other two countries, and it had already begun to shift its foreign trade away from dependence on CMEA markets. It had fewer pollution problems than either of the other countries, and its infrastructure was in reasonably good shape.[46]

45. OECD Economic Surveys, *Hungary* (Paris: OECD, 1991), 11–12.
46. This goes back to the old Austro-Hungarian Empire, when Budapest and Vienna were co-capitals and were linked by rail and the Danube.

TABLE 11-12 *Hungarian Economic Performance During the 1980s (percent)*

Year	*Foreign Debt/ GNP*	*Industrial Production*	*Growth in Real GNP*	*Consumer Prices*
1980	47.3	100	1.5	100
1981	46.4	98	0.8	105
1982	40.0	102	0.6	112
1983	46.8	104	0.5	128
1984	51.1	106	1.1	133
1985	65.5	107	2.0	144
1986	71.2	109	2.1	150
1987	75.5	110	0.6	163
1988	70.2	109	2.1	184
1989	65.5	106	–2.3	218

Sources: The World Bank, *World Development Tables, 1988–1989* (Washington, D.C.: The World Bank, 1989), 49; Central Intelligence Agency, *Handbook of Economic Statistics, 1991* (Springfield, Va.: National Technical Information Service, 1991), 38, 40, 42.

Privatization

The major initial attempt to privatize industry and agriculture began in 1989, when state-owned enterprises were given the right to transform themselves into either mixed or privately owned companies. However, some state enterprise managers used this opportunity to sell assets to themselves or their friends at bargain prices and without competitive bidding. As a result of public dissatisfaction with this behavior, a government agency called the State Property Agency was created, and state-owned property was transferred to it. It was given authority to value property assets and to handle the process of privatization. It was to select those state companies that would be most attractive to Hungarian and foreign investors. It hired consulting firms to value the assets of state enterprises that were to be sold, usually through bids. In March 1991 the agency started a second round of privatization by selling off state holding companies.

Hungarian privatization has taken several forms. One is restitution for property seized by the Communists after 1949. About 1.2 million Hungarians were given compensation coupons that could be used to purchase land, apartments, businesses, or other property that had been expropriated by the Communists. The coupons were tradable on the Hungarian Stock Exchange. The most important method of privatization, however, was through direct sale to foreign investors.[47] Small-scale privatization, which involved the sale of stores and restaurants, occurred through direct sales to buyers. Large state enterprises have proved more difficult to privatize. Some have been liquidated, while others were sold to foreign

47. In 1989 General Electric bought the Hungarian state enterprise Tungsram for $150 million. Tungsram was one of the very few Hungarian state enterprises that was competitive in world markets.

or Hungarian investors. Privatization of agricultural cooperatives involved the giving of coupons that could be used to purchase the land.[48]

Taxation and Expenditures

The major tax reform in Hungary was the adoption of a value-added tax in 1988 to make the Hungarian tax system similar to those of the Western European countries. The tax applies to most goods and services. A corporate income tax was introduced in 1989, and the rates of the personal income tax were changed.[49] On the government expenditure side, the aging of the population and unemployment have created fiscal problems. The retirement age for women and men was lowered to reduce unemployment, but this increased pension expenditures. Increased unemployment and widespread tax evasion increased the deficit in the national budget, which in turn increased the national debt. The government also had to assume the debt of a number of state enterprises to make them more salable.

Price Reforms

The most basic and critical requirement in changing from a centrally planned economy to a market economy is the establishment of market-based relative prices for commodities and factors of production. Such prices are essential to create the right signals for resource allocation. Pricing reforms occurred earlier in Hungary than in Poland and Czechoslovakia. The process of price reform in Hungary was gradual, extending back to the New Economic Mechanism of 1968, but consumer price controls were used in 1979. This interfered with free market determination of relative prices and prevented profits from reflecting enterprise performance. Many prices were freed during the 1980s to reach market-determined levels, and by 1990 the price of 90 percent of Hungarian goods and services was market determined. This meant that in many cases prices required realignment and that inflation increased.

Banking Reforms

A two-tiered banking system was created in 1987. Three commercial banks were created to assume the commercial banking activities of the former National Bank of Hungary. These banks were set up as joint stock companies, with 80 percent state ownership and the remainder owned by state enterprises. In 1989 the banks were allowed to compete against each other for customer accounts and business and consumer loans. Generally, the loans were of poor quality and the banks had to be recapitalized by the government. As of May 1995 the Hungarian banking

48. This did not work well because buyers and sellers would cut deals in order to undervalue property.
49. The rate is progressive up to a high of 45 percent. Tax collection is inefficient and evasion is easy.

system consisted of two distinct groups of institutions—five large state-owned banks consisting of four commercial banks and one savings bank and thirty small and medium-sized private banks, many of which are foreign-owned. It is this group of banks that form the dynamic element in the Hungarian banking system.[50]

Exchange Rates

The forint, like the Polish zloty and the Czech koruna, is not fully convertible. It is pegged to a currency basket consisting of the U.S. dollar (30 percent) and the ECU[51] (70 percent). The value of the peg to the basket of currencies has been adjusted periodically, mainly on the basis of the difference between domestic and foreign rates of inflation. The forint has been devalued frequently. The state monopoly for foreign exchange operations, which was a product of Communism, has been eliminated, and commercial banks now handle that function.

An Evaluation of the Hungarian Economy

Hungary was well on its way to market reforms when Communism finally collapsed, and by 1990 it was one-third of the way to a market economy. It had another advantage over other East-Central European countries in that it had established a democratic structure. In May 1990 major free elections were held that resulted in the amendment of the Hungarian constitution to promote political stability.[52] Hungary also was far more involved in promoting foreign investments than any of the other countries. Laws had been passed to allow for direct foreign investment of capital in Hungary. In 1989 the American firm General Electric bought the Hungarian state enterprise Tungsram for $150 million. Finally, Western goodwill toward Hungary gave the country a major advantage over the other East-Central European countries when it came to attracting foreign loans.[53]

Various institutional changes were made during the transition period. A two-tiered banking system was created in 1992. It has developed rapidly and consists of the Central Bank of Hungary, 37 commercial banks of which 17 are fully or partially privately owned, 6 specialized financial institutions, and 260 savings cooperatives.[54] The foreign exchange system is largely free of restrictions on current ac-

50. International Monetary Fund, *Hungary—Recent Economic Developments and Background Issues*, IMF Staff Study Report No. 95/35 (Washington, D.C.: IMF, May 1995), 157–158.

51. The dollar–forint exchange rate on April 1, 1996, was $1 = 142 forints.

52. The results of free elections are similar to those that have been held in Poland. In the initial elections, reformers and those who were not members of the Communist Party were elected to run the government. When unemployment and inflation occurred, former Communists ran as members of the Socialist Party, which now rules Hungary.

53. Paul Marer, "Hungary During 1988–1994: A Political Economy Assessment," in *East-Central European Economies in Transition*, Joint Economic Committee, Congress of the United States, 103rd Cong., 2nd Sess. (Washington, D.C.: U.S. Government Printing Office, November 1994), 482–483.

54. European Bank for Reconstruction and Development, *Transition Report 1995* (London: EBRD, November, 1995), 45.

TABLE 11-13 *Performance of the Hungarian Economy, 1990–1995 (percent)*

	1990	*1991*	*1992*	*1993*	*1994**	*1995**
GDP real growth rate	–4.0	–10.2	–5.0	–2.3	1.0	1.5
Unemployment	2.5	8.0	13.0	12.1	9.8	9.5
Consumer price inflation	33.4	32.2	25.0	22.5	23.0	20.0
Real per capita GDP	2,780	2,750	3,190	3,300	3,800	4,000

**Estimates.*

Sources: The World Bank, *The World Bank Atlas*, 1993, 1994, 1995; U.S. Embassy in Budapest.

count transactions, but not on capital transactions. The forint is pegged to a currency basket including the U.S. dollar, and is not fully convertible.

Table 11-13 presents the performance of the Hungarian economy from 1990 to 1995. Its performance has been somewhat similar to that of Poland in that inflation and unemployment have created problems. Both countries also have a large foreign debt.

A COMPARISON OF THE POLISH, CZECH REPUBLIC, AND HUNGARIAN ECONOMIES DURING TRANSITION

Poland, Czechoslovakia, and Hungary were the most important of the Soviet-bloc countries before the transition from socialism to capitalism began.[55] Although all were a part of the Austro-Hungarian Empire, each had developed its own different historical, cultural, political, and economic characteristics over a period of many centuries. Historical and cultural differences eventually resulted in the creation of the Czech and Slovak Republics in January 1993. Each country was dependent on CMEA for the bulk of its foreign trade. During the transition to a market economy, each country has pursued a different path of change, and each has experienced a period of recession, unemployment, and recession. The Czech Republic has done the best job in the transition process, but it had certain advantages that Poland and Hungary did not have—the lack of a foreign debt burden and an industrial base created before World War II.

There is a mixed record of success and failure. Living standards for many people have declined and income inequality has widened. On the other hand, goods that were once in short supply are now in abundance, and there is a closer fit between consumer preferences and purchases. There has also been a change in direction in foreign trade away from CMEA to trade with the West. Also, much of the breakdown in production can be attributed to the legacy of Communism, which also includes a decaying infrastructure, environmental pollution, and Soviet Union political-military control and transfer of resources. In all three countries

55. East Germany was the most important, but had no separate identity before World War II.

TABLE 11-14 *Comparison of Privatization Methods Used in Russia, Poland, the Czech Republic, and Hungary*

Country	*Privatization Method*	*Major Participants*	*Private Sector Share as Percentage of GDP*
Russia	Mass voucher privatization	Workers and managers	55
Poland	Liquidation mass voucher privatization from fall 95	Workers and managers	60
Czech Republic	Mass voucher privatization	Investment privatization funds	70
Hungary	Direct sales to domestic and foreign investors	Domestic private companies, managers, and foreigners	60

Source: European Bank for Reconstruction and Development, *Transition Report 1995* (London: EBRD, November 1995), 129.

large state enterprises need to be restructured and broken up, and an efficient commercial banking system also has to be developed.

Table 11-14 presents a comparison of the privatization methods used in Russia, Poland, the Czech Republic, and Hungary during the transition period. Table 11-15 compares the progress in transition from communism to capitalism as of August 1995 for selected former Communist countries including several republics of the former Soviet Union. As the table indicates, Belarus and Ukraine have made the least progress. The Czech Republic has made the most progress, particularly in privatization. Table 11-15 compares changes in real GDP, inflation, and unemployment for the three countries, using the period 1988–1993.

SUMMARY

Poland, the former Czechoslovakia, and Hungary have entered the post-Communist world and are in the process of conversion to market economies. Hungary was always the most reform-oriented of the three countries and was the first to attempt to reform its economy on a broad scale and begin the transformation to a market economy. Czechoslovakia was the most industrialized of the countries and had the highest living standards. However, it was rigidly controlled by the Communist Party, and no attempt at economic or political reform was made until the government was overthrown in December 1989. Poland was the poorest of the three countries, but also began to initiate economic and political reforms before the final collapse of Communism. It was also the first of the three countries to bite the bullet of free market austerity by introducing shock therapy.

Except in the Czech Republic, high unemployment rates continue to characterize the economic transition taking place in Poland, Hungary, and other East-Central European countries. This has complicated the transition process and has resulted in the election of political parties promising both slower reforms and an improved social security safety net. Small service enterprises have proven to be far

TABLE 11-15 *Progress in Transition from Communism to Capitalism—1995*

		Enterprises		*Markets and Trade*		*Financial Institutions*		*Legal Reforms*
	Countries' Private Sector Share of GDP	*Large-Scale Privatization*	*Small-Scale Privatization*	*Price Liberalization*	*Trade and Foreign Exchange*	*Banking Reforms*	*Securities Market*	*Effectiveness on Investment*
Belarus	15	2	2	3	2	2	2	3
Bulgaria	45	2	3	3	4	2	2	3
Czech Republic	70	4	4*	3	4*	3	3	4
Georgia	30	2	3	3	2	2	1	2
Hungary	60	4	4*	3	4*	3	3	4
Latvia	60	2	4	3	4	3	2	2
Poland	60	3	4*	3	4*	3	3	4
Romania	40	2	3	3	4*	3	2	2
Russia	55	3	4	3	3	2	2	2
Slovakia	45	3	4*	3	4*	3	3	3
Slovenia	45	3	4*	3	4*	3	3	3
Ukraine	35	2	2	3	2	2	2	2

1. Means little or no progress has been made toward becoming a market economy.
2. Means that some changes have occurred. At least plans to privatize are either in motion or partially implemented. Some prices have been liberalized, while others are state controlled. Most exports and imports are subject to some form of state control.
3. Means that at least 25 percent of large-scale enterprises have privatized, and there is complete privatization of small companies. Most prices have been freed from state control. Most exchange controls have been lifted on export and imports, and a legal system is in place.
4. Means that more than 40 percent of state enterprises have been privatized, and everything else is in place.

4*. Means that the country is most advanced toward a market economy.

Source: European Bank for Reconstruction and Development, *Transition Report 1995* (London: EBRD, November 1995), 11.

easier to privatize than many large state enterprises. A new legal system has been introduced in the three countries and free elections have been held. Former Communists now head the governments of Poland and Hungary, but are committed to the continuation of the transition process to market economies. The financial system has proven to be somewhat of a problem in the three countries.

QUESTIONS FOR DISCUSSION

1. Compare the approaches to privatization used in Poland, the Czech Republic, and Hungary.
2. How has privatization proceeded in the three countries? What problems still remain?
3. It would appear that of the three countries the Czech Republic has had the greatest success in converting to a market economy. Discuss.
4. Discuss the use of the voucher system in the Czech Republic.
5. What was the "shock therapy" approach that was used in Poland?
6. Even though there has been rapid change in Poland, the Czech Republic, and Hungary, in some areas there has been little change. Discuss.
7. What was the role of CMEA in East-Central European Trade?
8. Even though the banking systems of Poland, the Czech Republic, and Hungary have been privatized, many problems still remain. Discuss.
9. Who has gained and who has lost in the transition from communism to a market economy?
10. There is an enormous increase in income inequality in Poland, the Czech Republic, and Hungary during transition. Why has this occurred? Is it good or bad?

RECOMMENDED READINGS

"Against the Grain: A Survey of Poland." *The Economist*, April 16–22, 1994, 1–22.

Aghevli, Bijan B., Eduardo Borensztein, and Tessa van der Willigen. *Stabilization and Structural Reform in the Czech and Slovak Federal Republic: First Stage.* Occasional Paper 92. Washington, D.C.: International Monetary Fund, March 1992.

Aghion, Philippe, and Oliver Jean Blanchard. *On the Speed of Transition in Central Europe.* Working Paper No. 6. London: European Bank for Reconstruction and Development, July 1993.

Borish, Michael, Millar F. Long, and Michael Noel. *Restructuring Banks and Enterprises: Recent Lessons from Transition Economies.* Discussion Paper 279. Washington, D.C.: The World Bank, 1995.

Carlin, Wendy, John Van Reenen, and Toby Wolfe. *Enterprise Restructuring in the Transition: An Analytical Survey of the Case Study Evidence from Central and Eastern Europe.* Working Paper No. 14. London: European Bank for Reconstruction and Development, July 1994.

Charap, Joshua, and Alena Zemplinerova. *Restructuring in the Czech Economy*. Working Paper No. 2. London: European Bank for Reconstruction and Development, March 1993.

Crane, Keith. "The Costs and Benefits of Transition." In *East-Central European Economies in Transition*. Joint Economic Committee, Congress of the United States, 103d Cong. 2d Sess. Washington, D.C.: U.S. Government Printing Office, November 1994, 25–48.

Ebrill, Liam P., Ajai Chopra, Charalambos Christofides, Paul Mylonas, Inci Otker, and Gerd Schwartz. *Poland: The Path to a Market Economy*. Occasional Paper 113. Washington, D.C.: International Monetary Fund, October 1994.

European Bank for Reconstruction and Development. *Economic Transition in Eastern Europe and the Former Soviet Union*. London: EBRD, November 1995.

Gati, Charles. "Central and Eastern Europe: How Is Democracy Doing." *Problems of Post-Communism*, Vol. 41, Fall 1994, 42–45.

International Monetary Fund, Economic Reviews. *Czech Republic*. Washington, D.C.: IMF, 1995.

——— Staff Country Report. *Hungary*. Washington, D.C.: IMF, 1995.

Kaiser, Phillip. "The Czech Republic: An Assessment of the Transition." In *East-Central European Economies in Transition*. Joint Economic Committee, Congress of the United States, 103d Cong. 2d Sess. Washington, D.C.: U.S. Government Printing Office, November 1994, 506–507.

Sacks, Jeffrey. *Poland's Jump to the Market Economy*. Cambridge, Mass.: MIT Press, 1994.

Slay, Ben. *The Polish Economy*. Princeton, N.J.: Princeton University Press, 1994.

Wolchick, Sharon L., Foltan Baranyi, and Jane Curry. "Post-Communist Politics in East Central Europe." *Problems of Post-Communism*, Vol. 42, No. 1, January-February 1995, 35–41.

World Bank. *Poland: Policies for Growth with Equity*. Washington, D.C.: The World Bank, 1995.

PART IV

Economies of the Less Developed and Developing Countries

CHAPTER 12

Problems of the Less Developed Countries

The countries of the world can be generally classified as more developed and less developed, or as haves and have-nots, and a few are somewhere in between. Unfortunately, a majority of countries can be classified as less developed—including China and India, which have more than a third of the world's population between them. Mass poverty exists in the less developed countries and basic consumption needs remain unfulfilled. The magnitude of poverty is all too apparent. We read about it in newspapers and see it on television. A drought in Ethiopia and other parts of Africa was responsible for the death by starvation of thousands of people. Anyone who has been to a less developed country is struck by the squalor and the number of beggars in the large cities. The enormous gap between more and less developed nations increases the potential for social conflict in the world.

This chapter is divided into several parts, the first of which examines the subject of economic development. The second part discusses the characteristics of the less developed countries. It looks at population—the causes and consequences of population growth and its link to economic development and performance. The third part explores some theories of economic development. Many economists are concerned with the conditions necessary for economic development confronting the less developed countries, and there are many. Possible solutions to the problems of economic development make up the last part of the chapter—but solutions will not come easily. The problems of the less developed countries can be attributed in part to the economic and financial policies of the developed countries.

ECONOMIC DEVELOPMENT

Although the terms economic growth and economic development are often used interchangeably, they have different meanings. *Economic growth* can be defined most simply as the ability of a nation to expand its capacity to produce the goods and services its people want. It represents an increase in the real output of goods and services. *Economic development* means not only more real output but different kinds of output than were produced in the past.[1] It includes changes in the technological and institutional arrangements by which output is produced and distributed. There can be economic growth without economic development. For example, a country that relies on the production of oil for export can have its growth rate increase as greater inputs lead to greater output of oil, while its economic development may be minimal. However, the process of economic development almost necessarily depends on some degree of simultaneous economic growth.

A number of factors must exist before economic development can take place in any country. Most of the developed countries in the world have at least several of them, as explained below:

1. The quantity and quality of a country's labor force have an impact on its economic development. However, the existence of a large labor force does not guarantee economic development. India is an excellent case in point. A labor force has to have education and job skills, both of which are lacking in India because it is a poor country.
2. The quantity and quality of real capital are important for economic development. Real capital is capital goods or inventories in the form of raw materials, machines, and equipment used for the ultimate purpose of producing consumer goods. The supply of real capital depends upon the level of savings in a country, which is the difference between its income and its consumption. In countries at a subsistence level, there is little difference between income and consumption.
3. The level of technological attainment in a country must be considered. Technology as a concept deals more with the productive process than with the introduction of new goods. It involves the relationship among inputs of economic resources of land, labor, and capital. The combination of these inputs will determine both the level and type of technology.

1. Bruce Herrick and Charles F. Kindleberger, *Economic Development,* 4th ed. (New York: McGraw-Hill Book Co., 1983), 21–23.

4. The quantity and quality of a country's natural resources are also important. Great natural resources contributed to the economic development of the United States. However, it is possible for a country to develop without adequate natural resources. Japan has attained a high level of economic development by importing what it needs.
5. Sociocultural forces also affect economic development. Religion is an example. The role of religion as an economic force can vary considerably among countries. The theocratic society of Iran offers a case in point, where modern ways are resisted. Other sociocultural forces are the underlying competitive nature of an economy, the distribution of income and wealth, the pattern of consumer tastes, the dominant forms of business organization, and the organization of society.

CHARACTERISTICS OF THE LESS DEVELOPED COUNTRIES

Three-fourths of the world's population live in the less developed countries. Most of the nations of Latin America, Africa, and Asia fall into this category.[2] However, the less developed countries are by no means all alike; some countries are in different stages of economic development from others. There is a vast degree of difference between the lives of, say, the typical slum dweller of Mexico City and an average peasant in Bangladesh or Ethiopia. Although Mexico's per capita income is one-sixth that of the United States, it is twenty times that of Bangladesh or Ethiopia. Nevertheless, the less developed countries possess some common characteristics, and a discussion of each is in order.[3]

Per Capita Income

Whether a country can be classified as developed or less developed is often determined by the size of its per capita gross national product (GNP), a rough measure of the value of goods and services produced and available on the average to each country. Among the poorest countries of the world are China, India, Bangladesh, and Pakistan, which account for 40 percent of the world's population but less than 2 percent of the world's gross national product. The per capita GNP for each of these countries is less than 5 percent of the annual U.S. figure, which was $25,860 for 1994, and the average of $24,170 for the developed countries.[4] Bangladesh had a per capita income of $230 in 1994, which was less than 1 percent of the per capita income for the United States. The poverty this figure represents shows up in nu-

2. The United Nations classifies countries on the basis of more developed and less developed. More developed regions comprise all of Europe and North America, plus Australia, Japan, New Zealand, and the former U.S.S.R. All other regions are classified as less developed.
3. See Harvey Leibenstein, *Economic Backwardness and Economic Growth* (New York: Macmillan, 1957), 40–41.
4. The World Bank, *The World Bank Atlas 1996* (Washington, D.C.: The World Bank, 1996), 20.

tritionally inadequate diets, primitive and crowded housing, an absence of medical service, and a general lack of educational facilities.

In 1994 there were 64 countries with a per capita income of less than $725.[5] These countries accounted for around 60 percent of the world's population, but their total GNP was less than 2 percent of that for the developed countries. Conversely, there were 44 high-income developed countries, which had around 16 percent of the world's population, but more than 80 percent of the world's gross national product. The in-between countries range from countries considered poor (as opposed to poorest) to countries in various stages of economic development.

Table 12-1 presents a breakdown by categories of GNP for selected countries, ranging from those that are poor to those that are in the high-income category. India and China, with almost 40 percent of the world's population, are poor. Lower-middle income countries would include Poland and Russia. Countries that are considered upper-middle range from Brazil to South Korea. However, it is important to note that Brazil and Mexico have high rates of poverty. High-income countries range from Spain to the United States.

Overpopulation

Although the overall rate of population growth in the world has been declining since the late 1970s, annual world population figures have increased each year. In 1995 the world population increased by 100 million persons, bringing the total to 5.7 billion, or twice the level of twenty years ago.[6] Given current projections of population increase, the world population is estimated to be around 6.3 billion by the end of this century, with almost all the increase taking place in Latin America, Africa, and Asia, where birthrates are high and mortality rates are declining. Moreover, the bulk of the population increase will take place in the countries that can afford it the least. For example, the populations of China and India, two of the poorest countries in the world, are projected to increase by 420 million persons each by the year 2010, and the populations of Bangladesh and Pakistan are projected to increase by 50 million each.

Table 12-2 presents the population, birth, and death rates for selected less developed countries that together have over half of the world's population. Remember that for these countries the more people there are, the less will be the real capital and natural resources per capita. India, one of the poorest countries in the world, had a 1995 population of 931 million and will double its population in 36 years. Mexico, with a birthrate of 27 per 1,000 persons and a death rate of 5 per 1,000 persons, will double its population in 34 years. China will double its population in 62 years, while Nigeria, with one of the highest birthrates in the world, will double its population in only 22 years. Conversely, the United States, with a birthrate of 15 per 1,000 persons and a death rate of 9 per 1,000 persons, will double its

5. See Chapter 1 map, page 16.
6. Carl Haub and Machiko Yanagishita, *1995 World Population Data Sheet* (Washington, D.C.: Population Reference Bureau, 1995).

TABLE 12-1
Money Per Capita GNP and Real Per Capita GNP for Countries, 1994

Income Groups	*Money per Capita GNP*	*Real per Capita GNP*
Low Income		
Kenya	$260	$1,350
India	310	1,290
Nigeria	280	1,430
China	530	2,510
Lower-Middle		
Bulgaria	1,160	4,230
Colombia	1,620	5,970
Poland	2,470	5,380
Russian Federation	2,650	5,260
Upper-Middle		
Brazil	3,370	5,630
Malaysia	3,520	8,610
Hungary	3,840	6,310
Mexico	4,010	7,050
South Korea	8,220	10,540
High		
Spain	13,280	14,040
United Kingdom	18,410	18,170
Germany	25,580	19,890
United States	25,860	25,860
Japan	34,630	21,350

Source: The World Bank, *The World Bank Atlas 1996* (Washington, D.C.: The World Bank, 1996), 18–19.

population in 105 years. Germany, with a zero rate of population growth, will never double its population.

Agriculture

One of the most fundamental characteristics of the less developed countries is that a very high percentage of the population is employed in agriculture. There is absolute overemployment in agriculture; that is, it would be possible to reduce the number of workers and still retain the same total output. The level of agrarian technology is low; tools and equipment are limited and primitive. Opportunities for sale of agricultural products are limited by transportation difficulties and the absence of local demand. Agricultural output in the less developed countries is made up mostly of cereals and primary raw materials, with relatively low output of protein foods. The reason for this is the conversion ratio between cereals and meat production; that is, if one acre of cereals produces a certain number of calories, it would take more than one acre to produce the same number of calories from meat products.

TABLE 12-2 *Population Data for Mid-1995*

Country	*Population (millions)*	*Birthrate (per thousand)*	*Death Rate (per thousand)*	*Population Doubling Time (years)*
Bangladesh	119	36	12	29
Pakistan	129	39	10	24
India	931	29	9	36
China	1,219	18	6	62
Indonesia	198	24	8	43
Nigeria	101	43	12	22
Kenya	28	41	12	23
Egypt	62	30	8	31
Sudan	28	41	12	23
Algeria	28	30	6	29
Haiti	7	35	12	30
Guatemala	11	39	8	22
Bolivia	7	36	10	27
Mexico	94	27	5	34
Brazil	158	25	8	41
United States	263	15	9	105
Germany	82	10	11	—

Source: Carl Haub and Machiko Yanagishita, *1995 World Population Report* (Washington, D.C.: Population Reference Bureau, 1995).

Table 12-3 presents the percentage of the labor force employed in agriculture, industry, and services for less developed countries with a per capita gross national product of less than $725 a year, other less developed countries, and, as a frame of reference, developed countries such as the United States and former West Germany. In Malawi, one of the poorest countries in the world, 85 percent of the population of working age is employed in agriculture (compared to 2 percent in the United States and 4 percent in former West Germany). Note also that as countries develop industrially they eventually reach a point where employment in the service industries exceeds employment in manufacturing. The United States is an example of what is called a *postindustrial country*, with employment in services far exceeding employment in industry and agriculture.[7]

The Status of Women

Table 12-4 presents the life expectancy, mortality rate at childbirth, and educational attainment of women in the less developed and developed countries.

7. Daniel Bell, *The Coming of Post-Industrial Society* (New York: Basic Books, 1976). An industrial society is defined by the quantity of goods as marking a standard of living; a postindustrial society is defined by the quality of life as measured by the services and amenities—health, education, and the arts—deemed desirable for everyone.

TABLE 12-3 *Labor Force Participation in Agriculture, Industry, and Services for Selected Countries, 1993 (percent)*

Country	*Per Capita Income*	*Agriculture*	*Industry*	*Services*
China	$490	61	18	21
Indonesia	740	50	16	34
India	300	63	14	23
Bangladesh	220	65	15	20
Nigeria	300	45	7	48
Malawi	200	86	5	9
Thailand	2,100	66	12	22
Pakistan	430	48	20	32
Brazil	2,930	23	23	54
Mexico	3,610	23	28	49
Japan	31,490	7	34	59
Germany	23,560	4	44	52
United States	24,740	3	26	71

Source: The World Bank, *World Development Report 1995* (Washington, D.C.: The World Bank, 1995), 147–148, 162–163.

TABLE 12-4 *A Comparison of Life Expectancy, Maternal Mortality Rates, and Educational Levels of Women in Less Developed Countries*

Country	*Life Expectancy (years)*	*Mortality Rates (per 100,000 live births)*	*Adult Literacy (females per 100 males)*
Ethiopia	52	560	53
Kenya	57	170	78
Niger	58	700	30
Sudan	56	550	56
Zaire	50	800	75
Congo	48	900	
Bangladesh	55	600	47
India	60	460	55
Pakistan	61	500	47
China	70	95	79
Haiti	58	600	87
Guatemala	67	200	77
Mexico	76	110	95
Japan	83	11	100
United States	79	8	100

Sources: Carl Haub and Machiko Yanagishita, *1995 World Population Data Sheet* (Washington, D.C.: Population Reference Bureau, 1995); United Nations Development Programme, *Human Development Report 1995* (New York: Oxford University Press, 1995), 51–53, 168–169.

Women who live in the poorest countries of the world have a life expectancy lower than that of men. Their mortality rate at childbirth is much higher than for women in the developed countries, and their level of education is lower than for males in the poorer countries. A number of factors contribute to the lower status of women in the less developed countries. Religion is one factor, in that there may be proscriptions against the use of birth control measures. A large family is considered an asset in many countries because there are more breadwinners. Also, more importance is attached to educating males, even in industrially advanced countries such as Japan.

Income Distribution

Incomes are distributed far more unequally in the less developed and developing countries than in the developed countries. Several factors are responsible for this income inequality. In the poorest countries, there is generally no middle class, and the majority of workers are employed in agriculture. Rapid population growth and other factors make economic development extremely difficult. Table 12-5 compares income distribution for selected less developed and developing countries. It should be noticed that the degree of income inequality is very high in the Latin American countries. In Mexico and Brazil the top 20 percent of households receive over 50 percent of total household income, and the top 10 percent receive over a third of household income. The Gini coefficient for these countries is much higher than for the advanced industrial countries. The statistics do not reflect the enormous difference in living standards between haves and have-nots.

Table 12-6 presents real rates of economic growth for selected less developed and developing countries. During the 1980s the Latin American and African countries had very low growth rates. During the 1980s 61 nations had a negative real per capita growth rate and another 13 countries had a real per capita growth rate of less than 1 percent. The majority of countries with a per capita income of less than $500 had a decline in their real per capita growth rates. Conversely, the developed countries had real per capita growth rates of 2 to 3 percent during the decade. Japan had a real per capita growth rate of 3.5 percent, and the United States had a real per capita growth rate of 2.2 percent.

Technological Dualism

Technological dualism is a prominent feature of many less developed countries. It is the coexistence in a society of two modes of production. One is generally categorized as modern, capital intensive, export oriented, and often foreign owned and managed; the other is traditional, labor intensive, dedicated to producing for the home market or for the family itself, and domestically owned. The second mode may involve small cottage industries where each worker performs all of the production operations. The first mode of production operates in a sector of the economy that is technologically well advanced and highly productive, while the second

TABLE 12-5 *Income Distribution for Selected Countries (percent)*

Country	*Lowest Quintile*	*Highest Quintile*	*Ratio Between Highest and Lowest*
Tanzania	2.4	62.7	26.1 to 1
Bangladesh	9.5	38.6	4.1 to 1
India	8.8	41.3	4.7 to 1
Pakistan	8.4	39.7	4.7 to 1
Peru	4.9	51.4	10.5 to 1
China	6.4	41.8	6.5 to 1
Kenya	3.4	61.8	18.2 to 1
Botswana	2.5	59.0	23.6 to 1
Guatemala	2.1	63.0	30.0 to 1
Venezuela	4.8	49.5	10.3 to 1
Brazil	2.1	67.5	32.1 to 1
Mexico	4.1	55.9	13.6 to 1

Source: The World Bank, *World Development Report 1995* (New York: Oxford University Press, 1995), 220–221.

TABLE 12-6
Real per Capita Growth Rates for Selected Countries, 1980–1990, 1985–1994 (percent)

Country	*Real Growth Rate (1980–1990)*	*Real Growth Rate (1985–1994)*
Argentina	–1.8	1.9
Bangladesh	0.7	2.1
Brazil	–2.7	–0.4
Greece	0.8	1.3
Haiti	–2.3	–5.0
Kenya	0.3	0.0
Mexico	–0.9	0.6
Nigeria	–3.0	1.2
Peru	–2.0	–2.5
Philippines	1.2	1.8
Senegal	0.0	–0.5
Tanzania	–0.7	1.1
Uganda	0.8	3.0
Venezuela	–2.0	0.6
Zaire	–1.5	–0.8
Zambia	–1.9	1.3

Source: The World Bank, *The World Bank Atlas 1991, 1996* (Washington, D.C.: The World Bank, 1991, 1996), 6–9, 18–19.

mode of production involves a sector that has old technology and low productivity. Technological dualism can lead to social dualism because new products and production methods often cause people to change their beliefs and ways of living. In countries where the two different modes of production exist, workers in the two sectors will have different and often conflicting social values.

THEORIES OF ECONOMIC DEVELOPMENT

Economic development involves changes in the composition of a country's outputs and inputs. Economists have long been concerned with the conditions necessary for economic development, and over time a considerable number of economic development theories have evolved.[8] The "big push" theory is seen as a way to break the circle of low income resulting from low productivity, which is caused by a low rate of capital formation, which in turn comes from a low rate of saving resulting from low income. According to this theory, a large, balanced wave of investment in different industries will enlarge markets, create support industries, increase growth because the industries will buy from each other, and lead to increases in income and saving. Thus the circle will be broken

The "dependency" theory of economic development is in a way related to colonialism and imperialism. Most less developed countries were at one time possessions of Spain, England, France, or other European countries. These countries hindered the development of their colonies by exploiting their natural resources and denying them access to technological development. When independence was achieved, these former colonial possessions remained economically and psychologically dependent on their former owners.

Marxist Theory of Economic Development

One approach to explaining economic development is the Marxist theory. Marx contended that economic conditions were the basic causal forces shaping society, with economic development occurring in stages beginning with the evolution of medieval feudalism into industrial capitalism as a result of technological change. But Marx viewed capitalism as merely a stage in the evolution of society toward the communist state, which is the inevitable final form of economic and social organization. According to Marx, economic development under capitalism results from technological progress, which depends on investment. The latter depends on profit, which, in turn, is affected by wages. The key proposition in Marxian economics is that all value comes from labor; for that reason, the profits of capitalists arise from the exploitation of labor. Capitalists pay a subsistence wage to the workers and claim the surplus value, that is, the value created by the workers less their wages. This eventually causes consumption to decline and economic crisis to develop

The buying power of the home markets decreases because the workers are earning subsistence wages and their purchasing power is insufficient to take all of the goods that the capitalists produce. Inventory accumulates, which causes the rate of profit to fall for the amount of money invested. The capitalists must turn to foreign markets to absorb their excess goods. But foreign markets are limited in

8. Herrick and Kindleberger, *Economic Development*, Chapter 2.

number, and imperialist wars result. Eventually, within the colonies, liberation movements will occur that are directed against the mother country. India, Kenya, and Rhodesia (now Zimbabwe) are examples of former British colonies that have achieved their independence.

The result of imperialist wars and liberation movements, the Marxists say, will be the downfall of capitalism. Then the less developed countries will develop along Marxist lines. In the Marxist scheme of things, the less developed countries are simply precapitalist and would have to go through the capitalist phase before they could enter the optimum state of communism.

Rostow's Theory of Economic Development

Probably the most recent prominent theory of economic development is Walt Rostow's "takeoff" theory.[9] According to Rostow, in the process of economic development nations pass through five stages:

1. *The traditional society.* In the first stage, the nation's society is traditional (or feudal). All societies before the Renaissance were traditional societies with little upward social mobility. Most resources were concentrated in agriculture. A crucial attribute is the absence of any cumulative, self-reinforcing process of material improvement.
2. *Prerequisites for takeoff.* In the second stage, the prerequisites for sustained and systematic change are created. Chief among the prerequisites is an abandonment by at least part of the population of the philosophy of fatalism and determinism. There must be entrepreneurs in finance and manufacturing who are willing to take risks. Other changes in attitude and philosophical values must take place, including a respect for the individual, not on the basis of inherited status, but because of economic efficiency. Finally, a leading sector (e.g., mining, petroleum) is necessary for the takeoff.
3. *The takeoff.* In this stage, which lasts for twenty to thirty years, the pace of social and economic change suddenly accelerates. An important part of this acceleration is an increase in the percentage of the gross national product that is saved and invested in capital goods. Another important step is the establishment of manufacturing. There is also continued change in such things as customs of the people, governmental forms and practices, and kinds of economic units of existence.
4. *Drive to maturity.* This stage is a period of self-sustaining increases in both total and per capita gross national product. During this stage of some sixty years, industry comes to employ the most advanced technology available anywhere and becomes capable of producing whatever it wishes, being constrained only by market conditions and availability of resources.

9. Walt Whitman Rostow, *The Stages of Economic Growth: A Non-Communist Manifesto* (New York: Cambridge University Press, 1971).

5. *Mass consumption.* The last stage is mass consumption of consumer durable goods and services. The production of these goods and services enables the majority of the population to attain high living standards.

Rostow's theory of the stages of economic growth has been criticized on a number of counts. Included among these is the charge that it fails to fit with historical fact. Some countries did not have a takeoff at all; rather, they developed steadily over a long period. The theory is also criticized because it fails to specify what makes each of the stages peculiarly distinctive relative to the others. It is further criticized for its failure to include forces that may be important in causing growth. However, Rostow's theory does indicate that important changes must occur before a nation in the traditional stage can advance in its development.

The Dependencia Theory

Another explanation of economic development is the dependencia theory. Although the dependencia theory has been applied to Latin America, it can be applied to the African countries as well. Some of Latin America's problems began with colonial exploitation by Spain and Portugal under the economic system known as mercantilism. The Latin American colonies were expected to provide Spain and Portugal with gold, silver, and other resources and to serve as markets for Spanish and Portuguese manufactured goods. Because trade between the home countries and the colonies was tightly regulated, a sustainable economic base was not developed in the colonies after they became independent in the last century. But even after independence, dependencia theorists claim that exploitation did not end because American and British firms invested in such export sectors as oil, mining, and agriculture and repatriated the profits from their sale back to the United States and England. The growing importance of this investment in Latin America, it is argued, led to the dominance of the capital-rich countries over the capital-poor countries, and created the basis for the dependencia theory.

Dependencia theory covers a wide range of interpretations. Some theorists argue that the economic development of Latin America was not in the best interest of the developed capitalist countries. As a result, the developed countries formed alliances with the elites of Latin America to inhibit economic development that could undermine the economic and social position of the elites. Elites are unlikely to act against their own self-interest to give the poor more power. Another version of the theory holds that the dynamism of the Latin American economies lies outside their own countries, but their options are limited by the development of capitalism at the center. Dependencia theorists place most of the blame for the low economic growth in Latin America on foreign investment and on multinational corporations that promote the interest of the few at the expense of the many.[10]

10. Eliana Cardoso and Ann Helwege, *Latin America's Economy* (Cambridge, Mass.: MIT Press, 1995), 56–61.

OBSTACLES TO ECONOMIC DEVELOPMENT

Economic growth and development have been occurring slowly or not at all in many of the less developed countries. In Malawi, for instance, the average annual economic growth rate was negative for the period from 1960 to 1982; for Bangladesh, the average annual economic growth rate was 0.3 percent. Per capita income is not only very low, it is not increasing very much. The people of the less developed countries want higher living standards. Given the communications revolution that has been developing throughout the world, people in even the remotest villages in Latin America and Africa have some idea of what the good life is. However, it turns out that economic development is an extremely elusive objective. The obstacles to its achievement are many, and the task of converting backward, poor people into at best moderately well-off ones is far from easy. There are many obstacles to economic development, and a review of some of them is in order.

Population

In 1798 the English clergyman Thomas Malthus published his book *An Essay in the Principles of Population.*[11] His world outlook was pessimistic; it suggested that population grows faster than the food supply. Based on scattered empirical evidence, including the colonizing of North America, Malthus calculated that population tended to double every twenty-five years in a geometric progression, whereas food supplies tended to increase in an arithmetic progression. An example is shown in Table 12-7.

His proposition was based on two assumptions: Technological change could not increase food supply faster than population, and population growth would not be limited by fewer births, only by more deaths. Although both assumptions have proved to be wrong, there is an element of truth in his predictions. It took more than 4,000 years of recorded history for China to have its first 500 million people, but only a little more than three decades to increase the population to one billion. Regardless of a country's size, natural resources, or level of development, countries with large populations and high birthrates face increasing problems. At current rates of population increase, the population of developed countries will double in 432 years and the population of less developed countries will double in 36 years.[12]

Population Growth and an Ever-Increasing Labor Force. In 1965 there were 1.3 billion workers in the world. Twenty-one percent of this labor force lived in high-income countries, 27 percent in middle-income countries, and 52 percent in low-income countries.[13] Twenty-five percent of the world's labor force lived in

11. Thomas Malthus, *An Essay in the Principles of Population* (London: J. M. Dent & Sons, 1951).
12. Carl Haub and Machiko Yanagishita, *1995 World Population Data Sheet* (Washington, D.C.: Population Reference Bureau, 1995).
13. The World Bank, *World Development Report 1995*, 9.

TABLE 12-7 *Malthusian Progressions for Population and Food Supply*

Year	0	25	50	75	100	125	150	175	200
Population size	1	2	4	8	16	32	64	128	256
Food supply	1	2	3	4	5	6	7	8	9

sub-Saharan Africa and South Asia, the two poorest regions in the world. By 1995 the world labor force had almost doubled, but the percentage of the labor force living in the high-income countries had decreased from 21 percent in 1965 to 15 percent in 1995. Conversely, the percentage of the labor force living in the low-income countries increased from 52 percent in 1965 to 58 percent in 1995. By 2025, the world labor force is projected to be 3.7 billion, of which 61 percent will be in the low-income countries and 11 percent in the high-income countries. The greatest gains will be in sub-Saharan Africa and South Asia. Table 12-8 presents average annual growth rate projections in percent for selected countries for the period 1995–2025.

Urbanization. Urbanization and congestion are population-related problems. Often peasants are driven off the land into the cities by poverty or takeovers of the land by rich landowners or foreigners. Overcrowding can lead to increased population, unemployment, stress, and a demand for human services that can be greater than the capacity of the urban area to provide. Overcrowding can lead to an increase in health costs, not only from communicable disease, but also from heart disease, cancer, and other ailments caused by a stress-related breakdown in the body's immunity. Urbanization problems are particularly acute in less developed countries because they lack the financial resources to provide the necessary services to cope with their problems. By the end of the century, at least 22 cities in the world will have a population of more than 10 million; 60 will have more than 5 million. Most are located in the less developed countries. See Table 12-9.

Food Shortages. The larger the population of a country, the greater the demand for adequate food. Both a rural overpopulation and a rising tide of urban consumers compete for a limited agricultural output. In most less developed countries the need to satisfy the demand for food has prevented the allocation of resources to economic development. As a result, the inability to industrialize reduces the potential to earn money from exports to pay for the import of food products. It is a vicious cycle of hunger.

Food shortages can also have a deleterious effect on the health of a country's workers. A case in point is Ethiopia, where famine has resulted in the death of countless thousands of persons. Other African countries have also been affected by famine. Nutritional deficiencies in the less developed countries lead to a lower level of worker productivity, with subsequent lower agricultural and industrial output as a result.

TABLE 12-8
Population and Increase in Labor Force Participation, 1995–2025 (average annual percentage growth rate)

High-Income Countries	
Canada	0.65
Germany	–0.31
France	–0.07
United States	0.44
Japan	–0.41
Latin America	
Argentina	1.25
Brazil	2.90
Mexico	1.83
Peru	2.16
East Asia	
Korea	0.55
China	0.41
Malaysia	2.01
Thailand	2.66
South Asia	
Bangladesh	2.75
India	1.60
Africa	
Kenya	3.45
Ivory Coast	3.91
Nigeria	3.19
Egypt	2.35
Zaire	3.54

Source: The World Bank, *World Development Report 1995* (New York: Oxford University Press, 1995), 144–146.

Although food production in the less developed countries has increased in recent decades, it has just kept pace with the population growth in some countries and has failed to do so in others, including thirty African countries. In Nigeria, the largest country in Africa, the average annual rate of agricultural production declined during the period from 1970 to 1980.[14] The output of food in China and India has exceeded population growth, but only by a narrow margin.

Moreover, in the less developed countries, increases in agricultural acreage have been relatively small. In the main, further growth of the land frontier is constrained in many countries. In Africa, for example, the expansion of farmland is limited by the Sahara Desert, rivers, jungles, and mountains and also by diseases that destroy livestock and farm products. Insecticides used to try to control the

14. The World Bank, *World Development Report 1988,* 84–88.

TABLE 12-9
Most Populous Cities in the World in 1994 and 2015

1994	*2015*
Tokyo	Tokyo
New York	Bombay
Sao Paulo	Lagos
Mexico City	Shanghai
Shanghai	Jakarta
Bombay	Sao Paulo
Los Angeles	Karachi
Beijing	Beijing
Calcutta	Dhaka
Seoul	Mexico City
Jakarta	Calcutta
Buenos Aires	Delhi

Source: "A Survey of Cities," *The Economist,* July 29-August 4, 1995, 5.

diseases have had undesirable effects on the environment. In India the number of rural households and people trying to earn a living in agriculture has increased at a rate far in excess of cultivated land.

Infrastructure

Capital can be classified in two ways—social overhead capital and physical capital. The former includes the structures and equipment required for shelter, public health, and education, and the latter consists of plants and equipment used in industry and agriculture. Poor countries are deficient in both forms of capital because savings and incomes are low. They cannot afford the medical services and education facilities necessary to improve the quality of the labor force. This fact becomes evident in Table 12-10. In Bangladesh, for example, there is one physician for every 5,220 persons; in the United States there is one physician for 470 persons.[15] In Malawi, only 4 percent of people of secondary school age are in school and only 1 percent of those in the college age group are in some form of higher education. In Japan, the corresponding statistics are 97 percent and 20 percent. Only 2 percent of the relevant age group attends college in China; however, this is a legacy of the Cultural Revolution, when universities were closed down.[16]

Infrastructure, or social overhead capital, is a descriptive economic concept that refers to the existence of highways, railways, airports, sewage facilities, housing, schools, and other social amenities that indicate the development or lack of development of an area or region. Once an infrastructure is in place, it encourages both economic and social development. Developed countries have developed in-

15. In Malawi there is one physician for every 50,000 persons.
16. The colleges were closed during the Cultural Revolution for ideological reasons, and professors and students were put to work in the fields with the peasants to learn humility and to ponder socialist ideals. Working side by side in a manure pile was considered a good way to eliminate class distinctions.

TABLE 12-10 *Health- and Education-Related Indictors for Selected Countries*

	Population per Physician	*Percentage of Age Group in Secondary Schools*	*Percentage of Age Group in Higher Education*
Burundi	17,240	6	1
Nepal	16,110	36	7
Malawi	50,360	4	1
Chad	29,410	7	1
Bangladesh	5,220	19	4
Niger	35,140	6	1
Zambia	11,430	31	2
China	1,060	51	2
Myanmar	12,900	21	5
Paraguay	1,260	30	8
Brazil	2,430	39	12
Thailand	4,420	33	19
Japan	660	97	20
United States	470	99	25

Source: The World Bank, *World Development Report 1995* (New York: Oxford University Press, 1995), 214–217.

frastructures; less developed countries generally do not. This creates a problem for economic development, because industry will not normally locate plants in areas where there is a poor infrastructure. In particular, mass consumption products require the existence of skilled labor, sewage disposal facilities, transportation and communication facilities, and other amenities for their marketing.

Education. Educational facilities are a key component in the infrastructure of any area or region. Education itself is directly related to the quality of life and constitutes a form of human capital. Literacy, or rather the lack of it, is not as directly related to a country's population as it is to the country's stage of economic development. There is a positive correlation between a lower standard of living and a higher rate of illiteracy. It has been estimated that one-third of the world is illiterate. Most of this illiteracy is concentrated in countries with high birthrates, large populations, and the least to spend on education. A lack of educational opportunities maintains the distinction between the haves and have-nots in society and perpetuates class differences. It also reduces the base of educated labor upon which the economic development of the country depends.

Roads. A requisite for the economic and social development of a country is an adequate system of roads. Few countries can depend exclusively on other forms of transportation. Air transportation is too expensive for most products, and railroads are limited to specific routes between main access points. Poor countries do not usually have the resources to maintain an adequate road system. Physiography also works against the development of an adequate highway system. Most of the less developed countries are located in geographic areas of the world with barriers to transportation. For example, the Sierra Madre and Andes mountains have inhibited the east-west development of Mexico, Bolivia, and Peru. Transportation is also hard to develop in countries dominated by tropical jungles, because vegetation overtakes roads in only a short time.

Other Facilities. Dams, bridges, sewage disposal, and other facilities are a vital part of a region's infrastructure but are usually inadequate in the less developed countries. Dams control flooding and provide the water supply and electric power necessary for economic and social development. Bridges create more efficient transportation by linking areas that are separated by bodies of water. Inadequate sanitary facilities can result in the spread of communicable diseases such as cholera and typhoid fever. Garbage and waste materials dumped in city streets attract rats and other animals, which increase the possibility of epidemics. Communication facilities must be adequate to handle the needs of a region. The cost and efficiency of service must be considered. Government-owned telephone and postal services are notoriously inefficient in less developed countries.

Low Savings Rate

As mentioned above, there is an extreme imbalance in the distribution of income in less developed countries, exacerbated in part by the existence of a large component of unskilled labor. The vast majority of workers do not earn enough to do any saving; moreover, a minority of households get most of the income. In Mexico, for example, in 1984 the top 10 percent of income earners received 39.5 percent of national income; in Brazil in 1989 the top 10 percent received 51.3 percent of national income. This group should provide much of the saving necessary for capital formation. However, savings are usually invested out of the country or in real estate, where there is a quick and high rate of return. Political instability provides a good reason to invest one's income in, say, Swiss bonds, which will be safe from possible expropriation by a new government.

Savings are a requisite for capital formation, for without it investment for capital formation cannot take place. Inadequate amounts of capital and the inability to increase the capital are obstacles to economic development. It can be said that less developed countries are caught in a vicious circle. Because savings are small, investment is low and the capital stock is small, and the real gross national product is small. Nations that save little grow slowly and are locked into a cycle of poverty.[17]

Limited Range of Exports

Less developed countries usually depend on the export of agricultural products, fuels, minerals, or metals such as copper. Many depend on the export of a single product for the bulk of national income. Nigeria depends on the export of oil for around 80 percent of its total export earnings. Thus the drop in the world market

17. Ragnar Nurkse, *Problems of Capital Formation in Underdeveloped Countries* (New York: Oxford University Press, 1953).

price of oil has created problems for the Nigerian economy. When oil prices were high during the early 1970s, Nigeria benefited. It ran a surplus in its balance of payments, and it could use foreign earnings to improve living standards. Government spending increased to improve the infrastructure of the Nigerian economy. However, during the early 1980s, the world demand for oil declined, and oil prices fell from a peak of $35 a barrel in 1980. Revenues from oil exports declined, Nigeria had a deficit in its balance of payments, and it now has the problem of a large foreign debt incurred when oil prices were high and earnings were good.

Countries that depend on exports of agricultural products and minerals are usually at a disadvantage in trade with the developed countries. The terms of trade, the real quantity of exports required to pay for a given amount of real imports, favor the developed countries. Brazilian coffee and Mexican oil are much more subject to shifts in world prices than are American computers and Japanese cars. When prices decline for coffee or oil, Brazil and Mexico will have to give up more income to import computers and cars. Conversely, the United States and Japan will have to give up less income to acquire coffee and oil. There is an inelastic demand for many products exported by the less developed countries. When prices for a product fall, there is no offsetting increase in revenue resulting from a more than proportionate increase in demand.

Foreign Debt

About forty of the world's poorest countries are classified by the World Bank as having an unsustainably high foreign debt burden. This means that the value of their total debts is more than 220 percent of their export earnings. Compounding the problem is the fact that in many poor countries, export earnings fluctuate wildly because raw material prices are subject to greater changes than prices of manufactured goods. For many countries, their foreign debt has set back their economic development. Moreover, the world financial system has been disrupted by the prospect of widespread default on the foreign debts of the developing world. Many debtor countries are unable to borrow in the international financial markets on normal credit terms. Table 12-11 presents the debt ratios for selected countries. As the table indicates, the foreign debt of some countries is as much as ten times export earnings.

Sociocultural Factors

Sociocultural factors can also provide an obstacle to economic development.[18] Culture involves interaction between individuals and groups. It consists of behavioral patterns and values of a social group. It is culture that influences individual and group behavior and determines how things will be done, at least in theory if not in practice. It includes a number of features such as the status distinction, based on

18. For a discussion of sociocultural factors and their impact on development see Edmund Leach, *Social Anthropology* (New York: Oxford University Press, 1982).

TABLE 12-11 *External Debt Ratios for Selected Countries, 1993*

Country	*Percentage of Exports*	*Percentage of GNP*	*Interest Payments as Percentage of Exports*
Uganda	844.5	55.7	25.6
Tanzania	726.5	20.6	9.5
Zambia	518.5	160.8	14.8
Ivory Coast	533.3	224.0	15.1
Kenya	228.7	103.0	11.3
Bangladesh	188.9	31.1	4.3
India	225.0	29.1	14.8
China	83.8	18.0	3.7
Nicaragua	2,397.4	695.4	15.9
Argentina	417.3	28.6	25.3
Brazil	296.0	26.3	9.2
Mexico	175.6	32.8	10.5
Bulgaria	231.1	119.4	4.8
Poland	228.9	49.7	5.5
United States (est.)	125.2	12.2	6.2

Sources: The World Bank, *World Development Report 1995* (New York: Oxford University Press, 1995), 200–201; *Economic Report of the President 1994* (Washington, D.C.: U.S. Government Printing Office, 1994), 268, 292.

education, caste, politics, religion, or sex, between members of a social group. Culture may also assume the form of language differences identifying a group or region. It also may extend to production, with the use of machinery and equipment in an industrial society creating a culture that is alien to agrarian societies. Cultures need a certain amount of conformity to keep groups of people working together, but they also need new ideas to promote progress.

Religion. Religion can provide the spiritual foundation for a culture. It can also exacerbate the problems of economic development. Cultural conflicts in the area of religion can be serious, as anyone familiar with the Middle East can testify. Conflicts between Hindus and Moslems created such severe problems in governing India after it gained its independence from the United Kingdom that Pakistan was made a separate Moslem country. The assassination of Indian Prime Minister Indira Gandhi involved a religious conflict between Hindus and Sikhs over the alleged defiling of the latter's holy temple at Amritsar by Indian troops. Several days of rioting resulted in threats and destruction of property. The revolt against the shah of Iran was led primarily by fundamentalist Islamic clergy who felt that traditional religious values were being replaced by Western values of materialism. Religion can establish moral and economic norms in a culture by prescribing limits, particularly the subordination of impulse, on acceptable conduct.

Fate. A fatalistic view of life is one of the differences between Western and Eastern culture. Fate is called *karma* in the Hindu and Buddhist religions and *kismet* in the Moslem religion. Karma holds that every action carries with it a reward or punishment. One literally has little control over one's life; it is controlled by destiny. Good fortune is the result of some action in the past, even in a previous life, that was good. Conversely, bad fortune is also the result of some bad act committed at some time in the past. A person is unaware of past actions, good or bad; it is simply his or her karma at work.

Social Organization. The social organization of a society refers to the roles of men, women, and children within a system. Employment, manners, dress, and expectations are virtually dictated by each culture to its members. Certain actions may be permitted or denied through a legal process, but the majority of actions are learned through interaction in the culture or from the training by those familiar with the culture. A social organization functions within the cultural system of the society in which it is located. The component parts—that is, the people—function and work together through patterns of interaction that develop among the members. These interactions take many forms of interpersonal relationships that can have an effect on economic development.

Classes. Each social system has a demarcated class system. Class distinction may be based on religion. An example is the Hindu religion, with its caste system. At the top are the Brahmins, who are members of the priestly class; at the bottom are the untouchables. Social classes may achieve distinctiveness based on hereditary titles or through being arbiters of taste and refinement. Class may be based on educational attainment, particularly in societies where education is limited to the select few. Class systems can inhibit economic development; in some societies, business is regarded as a lowly occupation, something done by the lower classes or foreigners.

Family. In all cultures, men, women, and children live together in families. The family is the one basic institution found everywhere. It represents a sort of social insurance and insulation against the trials and tribulations of life. However, the role of the family varies in different countries. In Japan it represents stability in a country that prizes consensus. It is probable that the group ethic, including family solidarity, has contributed to the economic development of Japan. The role of the family can also work against economic development. In many parts of the world large families are regarded as an economic asset. The children can be put to work in the fields when they are young and contribute to family income. They are also expected to take care of their elderly parents. Birth control methods designed to limit family size are often resisted in the less developed countries, even though the population is greater than the food resources available to feed it.

Physiography

The physiography of a country can have an impact on its economic and social development for better or worse. Flat, fertile soil, supported by water and suitable climate, provides the basis for agriculture. Dense forests provide a renewable resource—wood—and also furnish a refuge and habitat for wildlife as well as a root base that prevents soil erosion. Fast-running rivers and streams offer a potential for hydroelectric development. Water is vital to the support of life and forms a primary source of transportation. Given the state of world technology, deserts, once a barrier to economic development, are now less formidable. In many of the less developed countries, a combination of physical forces has had an adverse effect on economic and social development.

Soil. Because humans must eat in order to survive and because nearly all of our food is either directly or indirectly a product of the soil, agriculture is probably the most important activity on earth. A shortage of productive land is one of the major problems facing the world and its rapidly growing population. Although this problem hardly exists in the United States, it is endemic in most of the less developed countries. The ratio of arable lands to people is basic to agricultural productivity and consumption rates. As the maximum productivity per unit of agricultural land is achieved, the per capita amount of food available must decrease as the population continues to increase. Maintenance of soil fertility, vital to productivity, is a growing problem as soils are becoming more and more exhausted throughout the world.

Less than 5 percent of the total land area of Latin America and Africa has the combination of climate and physiographic conditions necessary for agricultural production.[19] The mountainous nature of Bolivia and Peru makes cultivation of most of the land impossible. In most of Latin America, climatic variations run to the extremes of either too much or too little rain; the Amazon basin of Brazil, for example, receives too much rainfall, resulting in the rapid leaching of nutrients from the soil. The tropical lands of Africa have sufficient moisture and are very fertile, but the presence of human and botanical tropical diseases results in low agricultural productivity. The remaining lands, which occupy an enormous expanse, are semidesert or desert and can produce little without irrigation.

Mountains. While mountains provide a basis for tourism and winter sports, they are a barrier to economic development. Mountainous terrain makes farming difficult if not impossible, makes mining expensive and hazardous, and inhibits the construction of transportation facilities. The forests that cover many mountain slopes are a valuable resource, but harvesting is difficult. Transportation is hard to develop in countries such as Guatemala, Bolivia, and Peru, which are dominated by mountain ranges. In Asia, the Himalaya range makes a large land area inaccessible and unavailable for development. In China, economic development of the whole country is difficult because much of the land area is isolated from the main population centers by insurmountable mountains.

19. Bernard Gilland, "Considerations on World Population and Food Supply," *Population and Development Review* (July 1983), 203–211.

SOLUTIONS FOR ECONOMIC DEVELOPMENT

There are no easy solutions that will enable less developed countries to become developed. Many have nothing of value to export and little potential for industrial development. They are hamstrung by hostile social, cultural, and political institutions. The average annual growth rate of the poorest countries in the world, those with over half of the world's population and with a per capita income of $695 or less, was 1.7 percent over the period from 1965 to 1990.[20] The average annual growth rate of India was 1.9 percent, and its per capita income for 1990 was $350. At that rate of growth, it would take more than fifty years for India's per capita income to double. The rate of investment in India and other of the poorest countries is constrained in three ways: the capacity of the country to absorb additional capital, the level of domestic savings, and foreign exchange rates that affect trade with other countries. Even so, India was far better off than Bangladesh, which had an average annual growth rate of 0.7 percent for 1965 to 1990, or Malawi, which had a negative rate of growth and a negative rate of investment for the same period.

Foreign Aid

Foreign aid involves a transfer between the more developed nations and less developed nations for the purpose of promoting economic development. The transfer may be in the form of grants that do not have to be repaid or loans that carry lower rates of interest and longer periods of repayment than normally would prevail for the borrowing country. Foreign aid may also come in a variety of physical forms. Technical assistance and supplies of foods are examples of physical aid.[21] However, foreign aid cannot be considered a panacea for economic development. It may concentrate benefits in a few hands and may fail to change incentives and responses needed for broad economic development. Foreign aid can be used for consumption purposes, generating a one-time increase in well-being for those lucky to get it but leaving no lasting benefits. Many foreign aid projects have long gestation lags before their output is directly marketable. This can conflict with public expectations of immediate success.

Internal Policies

Certain development policies that do not involve assistance have been used with varying degrees of success by a number of countries. These policies rely on the notion that a less developed country can pull itself up by its bootstraps. The Com-

20. World Bank, *World Development Report 1992*, 218.
21. The World Bank makes loans to less developed countries to improve their economic and social infrastructures. The United States and other developed countries have their own programs of capital and technical assistance for the less developed countries.

munist countries followed a policy of unbalanced growth, where resources are channeled away from the production of agriculture and consumer goods and into the development of heavy industry. By following this policy, the Soviet Union was able to transform itself from an agricultural to an industrial country, although at considerable cost.[22] Then there are policies based on trade to achieve development. The inward-looking or import-substitution policy promotes the development of home industries by restricting the import of outside products.[23] Though this policy has its drawbacks, it has been used by come countries, notably Mexico and Brazil, to achieve some economic development. There is also an outward-looking trade policy that relies on exports of products to achieve development. Internal resources are used to develop export industries, and exports are subsidized by the government.

Government Monetary and Fiscal Policies. Government monetary and fiscal policies are also used to promote economic development. Central banks use monetary policy to control the level of national output and the price level through changes in the money supply. Increasing the money supply can have a stimulative effect on an economy, as witnessed by the development of Spain as the world's leading country during the sixteenth century. The flow of gold and silver from the New World stimulated the economic development of Spain and provided the base for "easy money" policies in the Dutch and German banking houses of Western Europe.[24] The problem with an "easy money" policy, however, is that less developed countries are inflation prone. Shortages of goods develop as a result of bottlenecks in production, and prices rise. Investment on the part of the rich is directed toward speculative holdings, such as real estate, rather than toward the creation or expansion of productive enterprises. A constantly rising price level tends to aggravate this tendency by making speculation all the more profitable.[25]

Fiscal policy affects aggregate demand through changes in government spending and the level of taxation. An expansionary fiscal policy can stimulate economic growth and development through an increase in government spending, various tax breaks, or both. The problem with fiscal policy is that it is far more adaptable to the developed countries, where income, output, consumer spending, taxation, and investment are high enough to be manipulated. Many less developed countries rely on sales taxes as a major source of revenue. Income taxes are often not feasi-

22. The industrialization was achieved in its early stages largely at the expense of the landowners and the peasants. The former were liquidated and the latter were literally starved to provide a surplus of foodstuffs for the support of workers in the factories.

23. For example, to build a domestic automobile industry one could restrict the import of automobiles.

24. It might be added that gold and silver proved to be the ruination of Spain. The Spanish kings spent the wealth on military conquests. Gold and silver increased the money supply in Spain, creating inflation that eventually destroyed the economy.

25. Inflation also worsens income inequality between rich and poor and increases the potential for social unrest.

ble because there is little income to tax or tax avoidance is easy. Countries may also resort to deficit financing—expenditures that are greater than revenues—to stimulate the economy. The deficit is financed by borrowing from the central bank or through the sale of debt to the public. However, in the less developed countries, there are no money markets for the sale of the debt, and the public does not have the money. Thus, borrowing is done primarily through the central bank.

Market Mechanisms. Some economists feel that the problems of the less developed countries can be solved by market forces coupled with a nineteenth-century government policy of laissez faire. All developed countries began by being underdeveloped; they developed naturally without state intervention through the market application of capital, entrepreneurial and technical skills, and labor. Essentially, market mechanisms consist of permitting individual buyers and sellers to make economic decisions for themselves and letting things be as they are or will be. Market mechanisms can play an important role in the conversion of a less developed country into a developed one. The ideas of how they can do so have been formulated from the British experience and from other developed countries such as the United States and Japan. But it is unlikely that market mechanisms alone will achieve economic development for the less developed countries. Moreover, there are tremendous differences between the situations of England and the United States over the past two centuries and the less developed countries of today. Some of them may summarized as follows:

1. Sociological forces favored development of the United States and other Western countries. The Protestant work ethic emphasized thrift.[26] This attitude helped produce a flow of savings sufficient to finance the introduction of new commodities and new techniques brought on by the Industrial Revolution.
2. Technological factors were more favorable to development in the Western world than they are to the less developed countries of today. The simplest of these factors is the extent of resource endowment. If one compares the resource endowment of the United States to that of Bangladesh or Pakistan, the contrast is apparent. The proportions in which land, labor, and capital are available are a drag on development in the latter two countries. The proportions favor agriculture against industry: labor is abundant; land is relatively limited; and capital is very scarce.[27]
3. Political factors also favored economic development of the Western countries. In the United States, for example, nationalism did not manifest itself in a hostility toward the inflow of foreign capital. There was a large and continuous flow of foreign capital into the country during the period from 1865 to 1900 when the United States became a world industrial power. In many of the less

26. R. H. Tawney, *Religion and the Rise of Capitalism* (New York: Harcourt, Brace and World, 1926), Chapters 1 and 2.
27. Colin Clark, *The Conditions of Economic Progress* (London: Macmillan Co., 1951).

developed countries today, foreign investment may be threatened with outright expropriation. Foreign investment is limited because risks of unpredictable government action, often based on nationalistic sentiment, are added to the normal risks attendant in investment abroad.

SUCCESS IN EAST ASIA

The East Asian countries, which include the "Four Tigers"—Hong Kong, South Korea, Singapore, and Taiwan—and the three newly industrializing countries—Indonesia, Malaysia, and Thailand—comprise what is called the East Asian miracle. Since 1960 these countries have grown three times faster than Latin America and South Asia, including India, and twenty-five times faster than the sub-Saharan African countries.[28] These countries have done a far better job of reducing poverty than the Latin American and African countries. For example, the number of people in poverty in India during the period 1972–1983 increased; in Malaysia for a similar period, the number of people in poverty was cut in half.[29] The East Asian countries have accomplished a high rate of economic growth by promoting a high rate of savings, developing an educated labor force, attracting foreign technology, creating a business-friendly environment, and promoting the development of specific industries. Exports have been promoted by keeping exchange rates competitive. High real interest rates have been maintained to ensure that investment is directed into the areas of highest returns.

Can East Asian success be transferable to other areas of the world, including Africa and Latin America? The answer is that it would be very difficult. For one thing, the countries mentioned above have had stable political leadership. Cultural differences also have to be considered. These countries predicated their success on an export-based strategy that included the sale of manufactured goods. This took a number of years to develop, but it was successful. Manufacturing wages in these countries rose 170 percent in real terms between 1970 and 1990, while at the same time they grew by only 12 percent in Latin America and fell in many African countries. Moreover, the global economy is in a period of rapid economic change that will affect rich and poor countries alike by threatening jobs and wages.[30]

28. The sub-Saharan region would include the great majority of African countries and would exclude Algeria, Egypt, Tunisia, and a few other countries.

29. The World Bank, *The East Asian Miracle* (New York: Oxford University Press, 1994), 33.

30. The unemployment rate as of April 1996 among the countries of Western Europe averaged 10.4 percent. It is to be doubted that there will be any increase in foreign aid to the poorer regions of the world.

SUMMARY

More than half of the world's population live in countries with a per capita GNP of $725 a year or less; another 1.1 billion live in countries with a per capita income between $726 and $2,895 a year. Moreover, the population growth rates in these countries are much higher than in richer countries. The average number of births per woman are four or more in eighty-three countries with a combined GNP of one-sixth of that of the United States. Many countries with higher per capita incomes, such as Brazil and Mexico, can hardly be called modern industrial economies. The poorer countries of the world are committed to economic development as a way to raise living standards, but they face many obstacles in achieving a rate of investment that will provide a satisfactory rate of economic growth. One major obstacle is the lack of an adequate infrastructure to provide the services necessary for industrial development. Sociocultural factors can also inhibit development. Probably the most important obstacle to economic development is an ever-increasing population in the poor countries.

QUESTIONS FOR DISCUSSION

1. What are some examples of sociocultural factors that block economic development?
2. What is the dependencia theory of economic development? Apply it to Latin America and Africa.
3. What is Rostow's theory of the stages of economic development?
4. What are the typical economic and social features of a less developed country?
5. Distinguish between economic growth and economic development.
6. Why do less developed countries have a disadvantage in terms of trade with developed countries?
7. Many poorer countries have a large external debt. How does this impact on their economic development?
8. Why is the savings rate low in the poor countries of the world? How does this impact on their economic development?

RECOMMENDED READINGS

Davidian, Zaven. *Economic Disparities Among Nations: A Threat to Survival in a Globalized World.* New York: Oxford University Press, 1995.

Haggard, Stephen. *Developing Nations and the Politics of Global Integration.* Washington, D.C.: The Brookings Institution, 1995.

Harrison, Lawrence E. *Who Prospers: How Cultural Values Shape Economic and Political Success.* New York: Basic Books, 1992.

Haub, Carl, and Machiko Yanagishita. *1995 World Population Data Sheet.* Washington, D.C.: Population Reference Bureau, 1995.

Jacobson, Jode L. *Gender Bias: Roadblock to Sustainable Development.* World Watch Paper No. 110. Washington, D.C.: World Watch, 1992.

Leach, Edmund. *Social Anthropology.* New York: Oxford University Press, 1982.

Razin, Assaf, and Efraim Sadka. *Population Economics.* Cambridge, Mass.: MIT Press, 1995.

"War of the Worlds." *The Economist,* October 1–7, 1994, 1–38.

The World Bank. *Toward Gender Equality: The Role of Public Policy.* Washington, D.C.: The World Bank, 1995.

———.*The East Asian Miracle.* 1993.

———. *World Development Report 1995.*

United Nations Development Programme. *Human Development Report 1995.* New York: Oxford University Press, 1995.

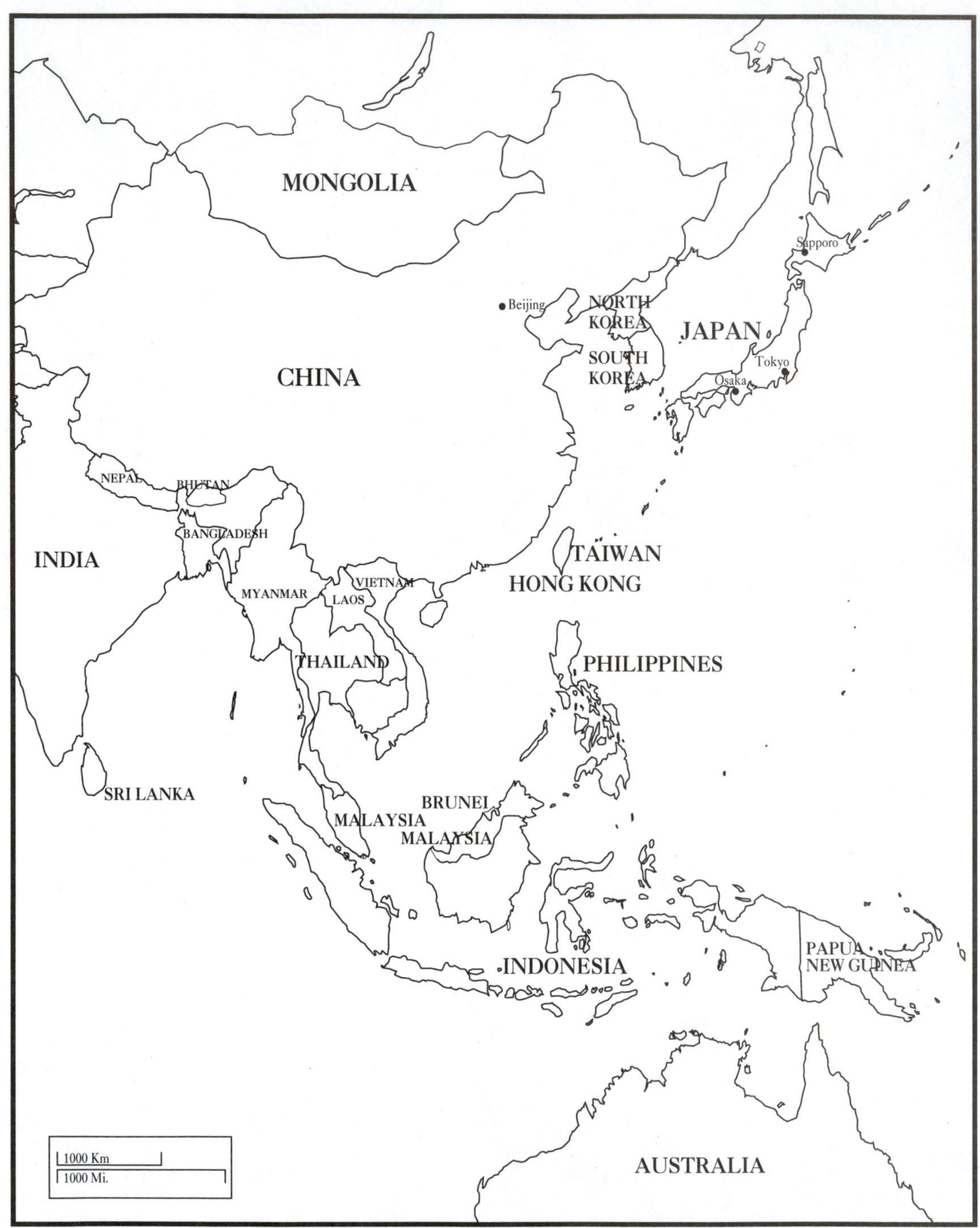
MONGOLIA
Beijing
NORTH KOREA
JAPAN
Sapporo
SOUTH KOREA
Tokyo
Osaka
CHINA
NEPAL
BHUTAN
BANGLADESH
INDIA
TAIWAN
HONG KONG
VIETNAM
MYANMAR
LAOS
PHILIPPINES
THAILAND
SRI LANKA
BRUNEI
MALAYSIA
MALAYSIA
INDONESIA
PAPUA NEW GUINEA
AUSTRALIA
1000 Km
1000 Mi.

CHINA

CHAPTER 13

The People's Republic of China

China remains the last great bastion of Communism in the world, but it stands at the edge of an uncertain future. Already the Communist Party has been obliged to jettison so much of its ideology that its rule has become arbitrary and more fragile. Its bureaucratic ways have become the biggest obstacle to the further development of a truly free enterprise economy, and corruption is endemic. The Chinese leaders, particularly Deng Xiaoping, are getting old. China is at a crossroads. What will happen when its current leaders are gone? Will the next generation of leaders move toward greater market reforms and a greater relaxation of state control over the economy? The concern about who will run China next can have an adverse effect on China's economic and political development in the future.

China is a country of economic contrasts. Its rate of economic growth has been among the highest in the world over the past fifteen years. The number of its people living in poverty, unable to feed themselves adequately, has fallen to below 100 million in a population of 1.2 billion, or 1 in 12; in 1978 the proportion was 1 in 4.[1] Workers' real incomes have doubled and tripled. Many Chinese are able to af-

1. By contrast, close to one-half of India's population of 900 million live in poverty.

ford such things as telephones, television sets, cars, and other consumer goods. But there are also many problems, beginning with a high rate of inflation. The infrastructure has to be modernized, and new jobs must be created for an ever-expanding population. The government's legitimacy now rests on keeping ahead of a rising tide of material demands, but as corruption increases, economic efficiency is reduced.

Hong Kong will become a part of China in 1997. Hong Kong, mainland China, and Taiwan, which is considered by China to be another Chinese province, constitute what is called the Chinese Economic Area, bound together by a common culture. The combined GDPs of these three parts would be around $1 trillion. The combined foreign trade of the area in 1994 was around $700 billion, making it the third most important trading area in the world. Moreover, overseas Chinese in such countries as the United States, Malaysia, and Singapore have furnished some $2 trillion in investment assets to the area. It has been suggested that China itself could become one of the world's largest economies, if not the largest, by the year 2020. This forecast is predicated on the assumption that the Chinese output will continue to increase at an average annual rate of 8.5 percent a year and that there will be no major political disruptions.

THE HISTORY OF CHINA

China was a country when Russia was a collection of duchies and principalities. It was involved in domestic and foreign trade on a major scale. Chinese goods were traded all over Asia and as far as Western Europe.[2] For most of the world's recorded history, China was almost certainly the world's largest economy. It had the highest per capita income in 1500 and remained the world's largest economy until 1850, when it was replaced by England.[3] As late as 1830 China was responsible for 30 percent of world manufacturing output. The Chinese political system helped facilitate economic development of the country. China developed under a succession of dynasties that preserved a central core of tradition and authority while permitting considerable self-rule at the village level. Although the emperor in theory had absolute power, an efficient civil service ran the country. The Confucian system of beliefs provided the basis for comprehensive exams for all civil service positions.

China was exposed to Western economic influence long before Japan was. Western trade with China expanded in the latter part of the eighteenth century. Military intervention in China occurred during the Opium War of 1839–1842 when England sent a military expedition to the country to compel continuation of

2. Chinese goods, including spices, were sold in Venice, Florence, and other Italian city-states as early as the twelfth century. Marco Polo visited China, or Cathay as it was called, to secure trading concessions. He found China more advanced in many ways than Venice and Florence.
3. Andrea Boltho, Uri Dadush, Dong He, and Shigeru Otsubo, *China's Emergence: Prospects, Opportunities and Challenges* (Washington, D.C.: The World Bank, August 1994), 3.

the sale of opium.[4] It received a number of concessions from China, including claim to Hong Kong. Other countries, including the United States, also staked out a succession of economic claims in China, and by the end of the century, foreign business interests dominated much of the Chinese economy. At the same time that Western economic penetration of China was increasing, the internal political system was collapsing. The end result was a series of events which, in the course of less than a year, swept away the Manchu dynasty and spawned Communist China. Still, at the beginning of this century, China was second only to the United States in the size of its real GDP.[5]

China 1900–1945

During the first part of the twentieth century, China experienced wars, famines, and internal political problems. Chinese resentment over foreign control of the economy led to the Boxer Rebellion of 1990.[6] The Manchu dynasty ended in 1912, and China then declared itself a republic. Under the leadership of Sun Yat-sen some effort was made to modernize the Chinese economy and to improve the educational system. After his death Chinese warlords ran most of the country. Eventually some order was restored during the 1920s when the regime of Chiang Kai-shek was established. The Chinese Communist Party was also created during this period. During the 1930s China experienced war, floods, and famine. When Japan invaded China in 1937, the Communists, led by Mao Tse-tung, cooperated with the Chiang Kai-shek government to fight the Japanese.

DEVELOPMENT OF THE ECONOMIC SYSTEM

At the end of World War II, China was split into two factions, the Nationalists and the Communists, both of which had resisted Japanese incursions since the beginning of the Sino-Japanese War in 1937. Japan's defeat set up a struggle for control of occupied China extending from Manchuria in the north to Canton in the south. Mediation was attempted by the United States, and a tripartite committee consisting of Nationalists, Communists, and the United States was set up to work out conditions for a coalition government. These efforts proved short-lived, and a civil war broke out in 1946. The Nationalists' initial advantage in territory and logistics were lost, and the Nationalist government was driven from the Chinese mainland to Taiwan by the Communists in 1949.

4. Opium was England's leading export for a period from 1790 to 1840. It was cultivated by the British in Asia and sold in Asian markets, including China.

5. Angus Maddison, *The World Economy in the 20th Century* (Paris: OECD, 1992), 112.

6. The Chinese lost and had to pay reparations to the victorious Western powers, thus adding insult to injury. The United States demanded equal economic access to China, and U.S. trade flourished, increasing from $16.7 million in 1900 to $138.4 million in 1920. U.S. banks entered the Chinese financial market and floated many Chinese loans.

The Period of Consolidation, 1949–1952

When the Communists formally announced the creation of the Chinese People's Republic on October 1, 1949, they were able to begin the consolidation of power and the development of a new type of economic system. Certainly the task was not easy. Years of fighting and inflation had debilitated the economy. Widespread corruption had been rampant under the Nationalist government. The masses of the people were illiterate and had to be trained and educated to fit into an industrial base that was to be the fountainhead for the development of the Communist economic system.

During this period, Chinese industry was also placed under the control of the government. In 1949, the Communist government took over those state organizations it identified as bureaucratic capital. During 1951 and 1952, the government took over all foreign-owned businesses. In 1952 and 1953, private enterprises were placed under government control.[7]

The First Five-Year Plan, 1953–1957

The First Five-Year Plan marked the second stage in the economic development of the People's Republic of China. To implement the plan, the Chinese relied heavily on Russian expertise. Soviet technicians were imported to develop the plan and to run the factories. Agreements were reached providing for Soviet aid in building or expanding electric power plants and supplying agricultural, mining, and chemical equipment. Soviet financial aid took the form of low-interest loans. The Soviets also contracted for the construction of factories producing a wide variety of products, including chemicals, synthetic fibers and plastics, liquid fuel, and machine tools. The Soviets also built modern iron and steel complexes, nonferrous metallurgical plants, refineries, and power stations and trained Chinese technicians to operate them. Sets of blueprints and related materials giving directions for plant layouts were also provided for the Chinese.

The land reforms of 1949 to 1952 were followed by a series of organizational reforms beginning with the simplest form of social enterprise, the *mutual aid team,* and progressing through successive stages of producer cooperatives to complete collectivization of the farms in 1957. At that time the peasants lost all title to the land. This same organizational pattern was followed for craftspersons and small retailers. By 1957, practically all industrial enterprises were state owned or collectives.

The Great Leap Forward, 1958–1960

In 1958 the Chinese departed from the pattern of economic development set by the First Five-Year Plan and moved to a new approach that relied on the idealistic fervor of the masses of workers and peasants to drive the economy ahead much

7. Gregory Chow, *The Chinese Economy* (New York: Harper & Row, 1985).

more quickly. This approach was called the *Great Leap Forward.* It is an example of idealistic extremism that substituted zeal for the material incentives developed under the First Five-Year Plan. China's enormous population was regarded as an economic asset and not a liability—the more people, the more hands to build communism. Emphasis was placed on indigenous methods of production and the development of labor-intensive investment projects. To put the basic objective of the Great Leap Forward simply, the population was to be harnessed to increase production and make China a world power.

Agriculture. In agriculture, economic policy involved the formation of communes. The communes marked the final stage in the transition of agriculture away from private enterprise, which had existed during the first years of Communist rule. Under communal organization, all vestiges of private property were eliminated. The peasants were not only deprived of the private plots, livestock, and implements that had been left to them through previous collectivization; they also had to surrender their homes. The purpose was to turn the peasants into mobile workers ready for any task in any area to which they might be assigned.

Industry. In industry, economic policy emphasized the use of labor to create thousands of tiny industrial units throughout the country. Again, the Communists planned to capitalize on the presence of a large labor surplus to accomplish rapid industrialization, particularly in rural areas. During that part of the year when the rural population was underemployed, labor could be employed for useful output. Small, indigenous industrial plants were created to harness the energies of the labor force. These plants included handicraft workshops, iron and steel foundries, fertilizer plants, oil extraction, machine shops, cement manufacture, coal and iron ore mining, and food processing. The capital used to build the small plants came from the local communes and from taxes on state enterprises. Labor, however, was the key factor employed in the development of local industry.

Top priority was given to the iron and steel industry. Lack of technology and equipment was replaced by mass fervor. This has been called facetiously "the steel mill in every backyard" policy. Some 80 million people were involved in an attempt to create a do-it-yourself steel industry. Two million backyard furnaces were developed throughout China. Many millions of Chinese worked day and night turning out steel, while millions of others labored in the extraction of iron ore and coal. The result was the development of labor-intensive, small-scale steel production with a low capital-output ratio. Although the output of iron and steel was increased by the backyard furnace method, much of it was of poor and often unusable quality, reflecting the absence of quality control standards and necessary technical expertise. Production in other areas suffered as well because more than one-tenth of the population was diverted from other pursuits into the production of steel.

Failure of the Great Leap Forward. The Great Leap Forward was not a success. Although industrial and agricultural output rose sharply in 1958, much of the gain was spurious. The output was often of such poor quality that most of it had to be scrapped. Production costs were high, reflecting an indiscriminate development of small plants in almost all industries. There was also a disregard for cost considerations at the level of the local plant because the most important success indicator was the degree to which the local cadre (leaders) could fulfill or overfill physical quotas. Output was maximized at the expense of quality and cost, and inputs of labor and raw materials could have been more effectively employed elsewhere. A shortage of fuel and raw materials caused by the waste involved in the backyard furnace method of production and a lack of adequate transportation facilities were responsible for the demise of many plants.

Sino-Russian Relations. The Great Leap Forward also caused a rift in the relationship between the Chinese and the Soviet advisers and technicians that had been sent to help them. In essence, the Soviet blueprints for making China a self-sufficient world power were set aside in favor of a development program that made little economic sense. The Chinese persisted in ignoring the advice of their Soviet technicians despite the fact that the USSR intimated that support would be withdrawn unless the Great Leap Forward was discontinued. In 1960 the Soviet technicians were withdrawn from China. With them went the equipment, financial aid, and blueprints that had played a paramount role in the development of the Chinese economy during the First Five-Year Plan. This departure en masse of the technicians had a negative effect on China because it could not replace their expertise.

Proletarian Cultural Revolution, 1966–1969

The Third Five-Year Plan, which began in 1965, was eclipsed by a political aberration of the first magnitude called the *Proletarian Cultural Revolution*. This was an attempt by Mao Tse-tung to mold Chinese society into his prescribed pattern. It placed primacy on ideological cant over scientific expertise and reverted to the Great Leap Forward period in its attempt to replace material incentives with political ideology and to denigrate any emphasis on technical excellence.[8] It aimed at annihilating, throughout China and particularly in the universities, any tendency toward a moderate or revisionist viewpoint concerning the role of Communism in world affairs. Intransigence toward the Western countries in general and the United States in particular was to be maintained until Western influence was eliminated from Asia. The Soviets did not escape the general opprobrium that the Chinese engendered toward the West, because Mao was furious with them for drawing back from war and subversion with the West in the interest of coexistence.

The rationale of the Cultural Revolution was political as well as economic. It involved Mao's attempt to develop a new socialist morality that would place pub-

8. A poster in a Beijing park proclaimed, "We do not need brains! Our heads are armed with the ideas of Mao Tse-tung."

lic interest above individualism. He believed that Stalin had permitted the development of a new class structure in the form of a state bureaucracy that differed little from a capitalist class structure. Soviet claims of egalitarianism ignored the special privileges for this small bureaucratic and technical elite. Moreover, Mao believed that the Soviet Union and other socialist countries had moved away from the utopian idea of an egalitarian society by introducing material incentives and bonuses, which tended to differentiate among workers. An ethical revolution was needed, for people had to be changed in order to create a new order of society.

The Cultural Revolution represented a step backward in terms of economic growth. The average annual rate of growth of gross national product during the period from 1966 to 1968 was –2.5 percent, reflecting a general decline in industrial output of around 15 to 20 percent in 1967. More important, the Cultural Revolution encouraged an ideological polarization within the regime and weakened consensus on the nation's fundamental values and priorities. The regime faced the task of rebuilding a stable institutional structure and working out a new pattern of relationships among various groups.

The Post–Cultural Revolution Period, 1970–1976

The end of the Cultural Revolution ushered in another stage of Chinese economic development. For one thing, central economic planning in the form of a Fourth Five-Year Plan was reintroduced. Both the Second and Third Five-Year Plans were largely shunted aside by sudden shifts in Chinese ideological policies—the former by the Great Leap Forward and the latter by the Cultural Revolution.

However, there were additional political interruptions during this period. The leaders began jockeying for power as it became evident that both Chairman Mao and Premier Chou En-lai were in failing health. Radical elements in the Communist Party wanted to continue the Cultural Revolution. Denouncing material incentives, orderly economic planning, and reliance on foreign technology, they brought disorder into production by opposing rules and regulations. Toward the end of 1975 and the beginning of 1976, the radicals increased their attacks on government bureaucrats and party leaders who were in favor of economic modernization. Serious riots occurred in some of the largest Chinese cities.

The year 1976 was a momentous one for China. Premier Chou died in February, and Chairman Mao died in September. With the death of the two major political leaders, a struggle for succession developed between those who wanted to maintain a rigid ideological status quo, with collective behavior and control and a closed door to the outside world, and those who wanted to modernize the economy and increase the rate of economic growth. The latter faction won out, and Deng Xiaoping was elected party leader.[9]

9. The so-called Gang of Four, including Mao's widow, wanted to continue the Cultural Revolution. In a showcase trial in 1978, they were found guilty and imprisoned.

In December 1978, the Central Committee of the Communist Party convened in Beijing (Peking). The session declared that if China were to develop successfully, it must turn from class struggle to modernization and completely restructure its economy. *The Four Modernizations Program,* originally started by Premier Chou in 1975, was incorporated into a Ten-Year Plan that called for increases in grain output, steel production, and capital construction through the purchase of foreign plants and technology. The program emphasized the development of four major economic sectors—agriculture, industry, science and technology—and national defense. The centerpiece of the program was to be the creation of the massive Baoshan steel complex, which would turn out 6.7 million tons of steel a year with the most advanced technology imported from Japan, West Germany, and the United States. Baoshan was an expensive failure, however, caused in part by China's inability to assimilate foreign technology and in part by an unrealistic emphasis on the role of heavy industry in developing the Chinese economy. A period of retrenchment and reappraisal of Chinese economic goals set in.

The 1980s

The early 1980s marked a liberalization of the Chinese economy as the ambitious goals of the Four Modernizations Program were scaled down and the government turned its attention to more immediate objectives, such as improving productivity and increasing output. It introduced more competition into the economy, not only by permitting private businesses to exist, but also by turning over small, unprofitable state-owned enterprises to private collectives. In 1984 a number of reforms were introduced that were aimed at improving the structure of the Chinese economy. There was a separation of government from state enterprise functions. The purpose was to give state enterprises more autonomy over their operations. Prices were restructured away from uniform prices set by the state and toward a floating price system for some products and free prices for others. In enterprises, differences in wages among various trades and jobs were widened so as to apply fully the principle of awarding the diligent and punishing the indolent.

These and other measures promoted rapid economic growth during the 1980s, but they also created some problems. The gap in living standards between the richer coastal areas and the poorer areas of the interior grew wider. The rate of inflation increased to around 30 percent, and in 1988 the government initiated a series of austerity measures, which included cutbacks in investment projects, reimposition of price controls on industrial projects, and a cessation of further experiments with market reforms.[10] It also tightened credit ceilings for domestic banks and raised interest rates on bank loans. Unemployment increased, and con-

10. Barry Naughton, "Inflation: Patterns, Causes, and Cures," in *China's Economic Dilemmas in the 1990s: The Problems of Reforms, Modernization, and Interdependence,* Vol. 1, Joint Economic Committee, Congress of the United States (Washington, D.C.: U.S. Government Printing Office, 1991), 135–144.

sumer living standards declined. Worker unrest increased as thousands of factories were closed or operated below capacity. The decline in revenues contributed to an increase in the deficit in the Chinese state budget for 1988 and 1989. The government also increased its state control over the economy by giving more power over industrial enterprises to the State Planning Commission.

Table 13-1 presents the performance of the Chinese economy in the 1980s as measured by the average annual increase in real industrial output and retail prices. Foreign trade and investment from abroad during the 1980s made an important contribution to Chinese economic development, and by the end of the decade its foreign trade had almost tripled.

THE COMMUNIST PARTY

The Communist Party is the official political party of China, and its leaders function as the ruling class. A self-selected group beholden to no one, they oversee government and industry. The party delegates much of the running of the country to a government bureaucracy organized separately but subordinate to it. It exercises its control over government by a system of parallel rule. A party committee keeps watch within every institution of government at every level. This results in an enormous duplication of work. The bureaucracy is closely controlled. The main instrument of the party's power over the bureaucracy is the nomenklatura system, which specifies the thousands of official posts and public offices that can be filled only by personnel whom the party has selected and approved.

A new power elite has also developed in China, where family ties have always mattered. As the nation has prospered, so have the children of the revolutionaries who founded the Communist Party. Members of these families lead lives of privi-

TABLE 13-1
Performance of the Chinese Economy in the 1980s (percent)

	Real GNP	*Real Gross Industrial Output*	*Retail Prices*
1980	7.9	9.3	6.0
1981	4.4	4.3	2.4
1982	8.8	7.8	1.9
1983	10.4	11.2	1.5
1984	14.7	16.3	2.8
1985	12.8	21.4	8.8
1986	8.1	11.7	6.0
1987	10.9	17.7	7.3
1988	11.3	20.8	18.6
1989	4.4	8.5	17.8

Source: Michael W. Bell, Hoe Ee Khor, and Kalpana Kochhar, *China at the Threshold of a Market Economy,* Occasional Paper 107 (Washington, D.C.: International Monetary Fund, November 1993), 66.

lege, attend the best schools, and make the right contacts.[11] Political rule and economic rule overlap, with the latter involving increased control of the Chinese economy by an oligarchy of powerful families. They are becoming similar to the Chinese family clans that dominate business in much of East Asia. To maintain their power and privilege, members of the new family elites also hold high party, government, and military positions.[12] In the so-called classless society of the past, one leader, Mao, reigned supreme; almost everybody else lived in relative equality, which usually meant poverty. But times have changed, and the Communists are no longer shooting landlords; they have become landlords themselves.

Because the Communist Party will not tolerate free speech, or a free press, or political opposition, let alone submit itself to the test of free and fair elections, there are no checks and balances such as exist in democratic countries. And because the Communist Party needs a large state sector to exercise its power, this will place limits on how far the private sector can expand. It will not tolerate the growth of any political organization that could challenge its monopoly on political power. This became quite evident in May 1989, when Chinese troops massacred Chinese students and their supporters who had demonstrated for democracy in Tiananmen Square in Beijíng. The massacre, which was shown on Western television, caused an initial loss of international goodwill but had little impact on foreign investment in China.[13]

The big question that has to be answered is what will happen to the Communist Party after the death of Deng Xiaoping. Will the new leader be capable of exerting strong central control? Will the country fragment along economic lines, with the rich coastal regions going their own way and discarding Communist rule? Will China unite behind a strong, army-backed leader who would promote a Nationalist agenda that includes the absorption of Taiwan? It is likely that the Communist Party will remain in power for at least the immediate future, but given what happened in the Soviet Union, nothing is certain.

THE ECONOMIC SYSTEM

The Chinese economy can be called a mixed economy[14] in that to some extent resource allocation is carried out by market-determined prices, although many markets are imperfect in that they are regulated. There is a mixture of private, collective, and state enterprises. Large inflows of foreign and Chinese overseas capital

11. Kathy Chen, "As China Prospers, So Do the Children of Communist Leaders," *Wall Street Journal*, July 17, 1995, A1, A12.

12. Deng Xiaoping's family includes a vice-minister and two heads of corporations. His daughter is his personal secretary and his son is a real estate developer.

13. In July 1995 Harry Wu, a Chinese dissident now living in the United States, was arrested by the Chinese government when he entered China.

14. Jan S. Prybyla, "Mainland China's Economic System: A Study in Contradictions," in *Issues and Studies*, Vol. 30, No. 8 (Taipei, Taiwan: Institute of International Relations, August, 1994), 13–18.

have contributed to the diversification of property forms outside the state-owned sector. Many millions of Chinese work in private enterprise activities. Changes in the ownership structure of agricultural land have occurred. The land remains state-owned, but households now have extensive rights of use to their assigned land plots, including the right to transfer their use. The spread of consumerism has been facilitated by the information revolution, which has served to break down the belief system promoted by Communism.

Economic Planning

The Chinese have developed eight five-year plans, the latest of which runs from the period 1991 to 1995. There is also a ten-year development program for the 1990s that has as its major goal the development of new energy sources and the continued development of agriculture. The Eighth Five-Year Plan also places priority on agriculture, particularly in the area of distribution. Focus has been placed on the proper handling of meat, poultry, eggs, milk, fish, vegetables, and fruit to eliminate spoilage. The purpose is to improve the living standards of consumers by increasing the quantity of food. Another priority of the plan has been the development of export markets.

Formulation of Economic Plans. The State Planning Commission has overall responsibility for economic planning, including the drafting of the five-year plans and the annual operating plan. An economic commission reviews the fulfillment of the annual economic plans and institutes economic reforms. Both are responsible to the State Council, which is the executive branch of the government. It, in turn, is responsible to the National People's Congress, the highest elected organ of the Communist Party.

The five-year and annual operating plans can be broken down into sectoral plans that indicate what and how much individual enterprises should produce. In agriculture, specific goals are set for consumption within the agricultural sector and for distribution to other sectors. In transportation, the plan covers the construction of facilities, with particular emphasis on the development of the railroad system. Then there is a plan that covers capital formation for individual economic sectors and is concerned with resource allocation. A labor plan covers the allocation of labor inputs to the various sectors of the economy. Plans for foreign trade, social and cultural development, and regional development are also used. The foreign trade plan covers export and import commodity targets and the use of foreign exchange. Finally a set of financial plans controls government income and expenditures. The objectives are to regulate resource allocation between consumption and investment and to regulate the flow of credit from the banking system.

Implementation of the Plans. The State Council, through its various ministries, is responsible for implementation of the economic plans. There are forty ministries, each dealing with the different segments of the economy. These ministries also operate at the intermediate levels of Chinese government. The central government prepares its economic plans through the administrative units at the different levels. Directions pass downward through the various administrative levels to the factories and enterprises.

Public Finance

The function of taxes in China is to ensure control through the state budget over a part of the incomes of state enterprises as well as over the financial and economic activities of those engaged in private enterprise. As in the other socialist countries, the state budget is very important to the Chinese economy because a large part of all investment is undertaken with funds allocated through it. In addition, normal government expenditures such as national defense and social welfare are financed through it. Tax reforms have been a component part of economic reform in that more reliance has been placed on taxes as a source of government revenue and less on profit remittances from state enterprises.[15] The purpose of this change is to reward state enterprises by allowing them to keep after-tax profits earned as a result of better management.[16]

Tax Reforms of 1994

A major reform of the Chinese tax system occurred in 1994. Its objective was to give the Chinese government more control over the tax system, reversing the erosion of its taxing power by local governments.[17] A value-added tax (VAT), imposed at a standard rate of 17 percent, has replaced the turnover tax.[18] Revenues from the tax are to be split 75–25 between the national government and local governments. The tax on state-owned enterprise profits was standardized at 33 percent.[19] A new Chinese personal income tax applies to Chinese and foreign individuals. The tax rate on wage and salary income ranges between 5 percent and 45 percent, and the rate on private business owners varies from 5 percent to 40 percent.[20] A network of national tax offices is being set up to supplement a system that relied on local government tax collection.

15. Penelope B. Prime, "Taxation Reform in China's Public Finance," in *China's Economic Dilemmas in the 1990s: The Problems of Reforms, Modernization, and Interdependence,* Vol. 1, Joint Economic Committee, Congress of the United States (Washington, D.C.: U.S. Government Printing Office, 1990), 167–168.

16. Another reason for the change was that collective enterprises were taxed differently, in that they always paid taxes on profits and were responsible for losses when they occurred, whereas the state budget subsidized the losses of the state enterprises. Cutting loose state enterprises from the budget would put them into competition with collectives for profits and customers.

17. The share of central government revenue dropped from 60 percent in 1978 to 40 percent by 1993. The purpose of the tax reform is to increase the central government's share of total tax revenue to 50 percent by the year 2000.

18. The turnover tax, as used in the socialist economies, was levied primarily on consumer goods and was applied at every stage of production. It was a highly differentiated tax that varied from product to product.

19. This rate applies to state-owned enterprises, joint ventures, foreign-funded enterprises, and private Chinese companies.

20. The previous rate was as high as 60 percent.

Expenditures

Central state budget expenditures include subsidies to loss-making state-owned enterprises. These subsidies have often offset income taxes on state enterprises. In addition to subsidies to state-owned enterprises, there are budgetary allocations to them for capital expenditures and working capital. Other appropriations from the state budget are used to finance the construction of transportation facilities, investments in state farms, housing construction, and defense. However, the role of the state budget in fixed capital asset investment has declined in importance. Table 13-2 presents total revenues and total expenditures for the Chinese state budget for the period 1988–1994. The budget has shown a deficit for each year. This deficit, which has averaged around 4 to 5 percent of Chinese GDP, has contributed to inflation. Most of the deficits are financed by the People's Bank of China.

Banking

The banking system in the People's Republic of China represents a financial control mechanism for carrying out economic planning. All state enterprises and cooperatives have accounts with the central bank, and control can be exercised because most transactions are in terms of money through bank transfers. Purchases and sales of goods by each enterprise can be matched against authorized payments and receipts. Government control over income and expenditures is also expedited through the credit and cash plans of the banking system.

The People's Bank of China. The People's Bank of China (PBC) was formed in 1959 as the central bank of the country. It is under the jurisdiction of the Staff Office for Finance and Trade and is responsible for the supervision of financial trans-

TABLE 13-2
Total Revenues, Expenditures, and Deficits in the Chinese State Budget (billions of yuan)

Year	*Revenues*	*Expenditures*	*Deficits*
1985	228.4	232.4	-4.0
1986	244.6	263.2	–18.6
1987	257.5	282.6	–25.1
1988	280.3	313.7	–33.4
1989	326.4	363.8	–37.3
1990	355.0	391.7	–36.7
1991	367.2	415.2	-48.0
1992	392.8	453.9	-61.1
1993	476.2	549.1	-72.9
1994*	511.9	610.8	-98.8

**Budget for 1994.*

Source: Wanda Tseng, Hoe Ee Khor, Kalpana Kochhar, Dupravko Mihaljek, and David Burton, *Economic Reform in China: A New Phase*, Occasional Paper 114 (Washington, D.C.: International Monetary Fund, November 1994), 23.

actions that correspond to the physical production plans. All state enterprises have accounts in branch banks under its direct jurisdiction. In this way, the People's Bank can exercise control because all expenditures and transfers made by the enterprises come under its scrutiny.

As the central bank of China, the People's Bank has the following responsibilities:

1. Issuing Chinese currency.
2. Financing credit to state enterprises. Funds to support credit expansion are obtained from the national budget, from retained profits, and from customer deposits.
3. Supervising expenditures of state enterprises to see that they conform to national planning objectives.
4. Developing the credit plan and the cash plan, which are financial counterparts of the physical economic plans.
5. Monitoring the performance of state enterprises.

The credit plan is concerned with the amount of short- and medium-term credit that is to be provided to state enterprises and agricultural communes by the People's Bank. Funds can be allocated only for purposes that conform to the national plan. The cash plan consists of a set of cash inflows and cash outflows essentially in the form of a balance sheet. Cash inflows include retail sales receipts, savings deposit receipts, repayment of agricultural loans, deposits of communes, and public utility receipts. Cash outflows consist of wage payments by state enterprises and communes, government purchases of industrial and agricultural products, government administrative expenses, transfer payments by the state to individuals, management expenditures of state enterprises, new loans to agriculture, and withdrawals of savings deposits.

The credit and cash plans are coordinated with the physical production plans to provide financing for expenditures required by the production plans. This means that the People's Bank can supervise the operations of state enterprises to enforce conformance to production plans because purchase and sales of goods can be matched against authorized payments and receipts.

Cash Plan. The Chinese economy is largely cash-based. Cash remains the only payment instrument for the household and consumer sectors, and it is the preferred medium of exchange for most of the industrial enterprise sector. Thus, the currency management practices of the People's Bank of China have not changed much since before the reforms period. The cash plan continues to function as a central planning instrument in determining the supply of currency. The annual cash plan is prepared by the PBC based on estimates of growth, inflation, fixed asset investment, cash requirements in the agricultural sector, and growth in the consumption fund, which covers wages, salaries, and pensions paid by state enterprises. The State Council approves the cash plan, with inputs from various ministries and the State Planning Commission. These procedures tend to introduce an inflationary bias to the plan.

Other Financial Institutions. A two-tiered banking system was created in China in 1994 when the People's Bank of China became a central bank, responsible for monetary policy, and four specialized state-owned banks were established to handle commercial lending operations. The four specialized banks are the Agricultural Bank of China, the Bank of China, which is responsible for financing both domestic and foreign trade, the Industrial and Commercial Bank of China, and the People's Construction Bank of China. The Agricultural Bank, for example, provides agricultural loans. It also controls the allocation of rural savings to rural credit cooperatives that provide credit to individual cooperatives and to individual undertakings involving private plots of land. Each specialized bank is under the jurisdiction of a government ministry.

In addition to the four state-owned specialized banks, there are state-owned national or regional universal or comprehensive banks and three major development banks. The regional development banks, responsible for loans to both state and private enterprises, are located in the fastest-growing regions of China. Then there is a network of rural and urban credit cooperatives. The rural credit cooperatives are under the jurisdiction of the Agricultural Bank of China and collect deposits from and extend credit to rural households and enterprises. The urban cooperatives provide the same functions in urban areas. There are foreign and joint-venture banks in China, and a large network of financial intermediaries that are also affiliated with the four specialized state-owned banks. The structure of the Chinese financial system is presented in Table 13-3. The banking system is under the jurisdiction of the State Council.

Securities Markets. Two stock exchanges were opened in Shanghai and Shenzhen in 1994.[21] Initially, only Chinese citizens were allowed to buy and sell shares of stock, but in 1992 foreigners were also allowed to buy and sell stock in Chinese companies.[22] State-owned enterprises can form joint-stock companies and sell stock. The emergence of joint-stock companies and equity markets represents a major change in the ideological framework of Chinese reforms. They are no longer considered to be at odds with the institutional underpinnings of a socialist economy because stock ownership is seen as being compatible with public ownership of enterprises. Some of the stocks of private and state-owned enterprises are traded not only on the two Chinese stock exchanges, but also on the Hong Kong and New York stock exchanges.

Weaknesses of the Chinese Banking System. The four state banks that are directly under the control of the People's Bank of China control around 80 percent of the financial assets in the country. They have to support the some 100,000

21. Before the Communist takeover of China in 1949, Shanghai was the financial center of East Asia and it had an international stock exchange.

22. There are three types of common stock: A shares, which are owned and traded only by Chinese citizens; B shares, which are special issues available for purchase only by foreigners; and H shares, which are listed on the Hong Kong Stock Exchange.

TABLE 13-3
Structure of the Chinese Financial System

Central Bank
- People's Bank of China

Specialized Banks
- Industrial and Commercial Bank of China
- Agricultural Bank of China
- Bank of China (domestic and foreign)
- People's Construction Bank of China

Universal Banks
- China Merchants Bank
- Bank of Communications
- China International Trust and Investment Bank
- Fujean Industrial Bank

Development Banks
- China Investment Bank
- Guangdong Development Bank
- Shenzhen Development Bank

Savings Banks
- Yantai Savings Banks and others

Cooperatives
- Rural Credit Cooperatives
- Urban Credit Cooperatives

Others
- People's Insurance Company (domestic and foreign)
- Foreign Deposit-Taking Banks

Source: Wanda Tseng et al., *Economic Reform in China: A New Phase*, Occasional Paper 114 (Washington, D.C.: International Monetary Fund, November 1994), 13.

state-owned enterprises that are the backbone of the socialist economy. Most of the loans are never paid back because many state enterprises lose money. Meanwhile, the most profitable part of the economic sector, private enterprises and cooperatives, find it difficult to obtain loans. Many private enterprises must rely on personal loans to get started and then can expand only with retained earnings. Instead of operating on the basis of commercial banking principles and rejecting customers who are a poor credit risk, the state banks simply do what the government tells them to do. Local governments, which own 80 percent of state enterprises, pressure banks for favorable treatment.

Organization of Industry

Chinese industry may be divided into three categories—state-owned enterprises, collective enterprises, and private enterprises. As Tables 13-4 and 13-5 indicate,

TABLE 13-4
The Changing Role of the State in Industrial Production (percent)

Year	*State-Owned Sector*	*Privately Owned Sector*
1978	77.6	22.4
1979	78.5	21.5
1980	76.0	24.0
1981	74.8	25.2
1982	74.4	25.6
1983	73.3	26.7
1984	60.1	30.9
1985	64.9	35.1
1986	62.3	37.7
1987	59.7	40.3
1988	56.8	43.2
1989	56.1	43.9
1990	54.6	45.4
1991	52.9	47.1
1992	48.1	51.9

Source: Zu-liu Hu, *Social Protection, Labor Market Rigidity, and Enterprise Restructuring in China* (Washington, D.C.: International Monetary Fund, October 1994).

the share of state-owned enterprises in industrial output and employment has been steadily declining, while the share of cooperatives and private enterprises has steadily increased. In 1978 state-owned enterprises accounted for 78 percent of China's industrial output; by 1994 that figure had fallen to 43 percent.[23] Ironically, the number of workers in the state-owned enterprises has increased as farmers from rural areas have moved to the cities.[24] But it is the private sector that has injected the dynamism into the Chinese economy. There are some 25 million private enterprises ranging from joint ventures to one-person shops.[25]

State-Owned Enterprises. As of 1995 there were around 100,000 state-owned enterprises, including 11,000 medium-sized and large ones.[26] Control over state-owned enterprises has changed. They were formerly under the control of central government ministries, financed by central government expenditures out of the state budget and subject to central economic planning. During the 1980s the central government decentralized supervisory and central planning control over most state enterprises. These responsibilities passed to provincial and municipal governments, with the latter allowed to contract out management of these enterprises to local managers and workers. Large state enterprises in key fields such as oil and

23. "Shrinking the Chinese State," *The Economist*, June 10–16, 1995, 33.
24. Zu-liu Hu, *Social Protection, Labor Market Rigidity, and Enterprise Restructuring in China* (Washington, D.C.: International Monetary Fund, October 1994), 1–2.
25. Joseph Kahn, "New Entrepreneurs Are Remaking China," *Wall Street Journal*, July 26, 1995, A1.
26. "A Survey of China," *The Economist*, March 18–24, 1995, 6.

TABLE 13-5
The Changing Distribution of the Chinese Industrial Labor Force in the State and Non-State Sectors (percent)

Year	*State-Owned Sector*	*Private Sector*
1978	51.5	48.5
1979	50.9	49.1
1980	49.7	50.3
1981	50.0	50.0
1982	49.7	50.3
1983	49.1	50.9
1984	46.3	53.7
1985	45.2	54.8
1986	44.0	56.0
1987	43.7	56.3
1988	43.8	56.2
1989	44.7	55.3
1990	45.0	55.0
1991	44.9	55.1
1992	44.2	55.8

Source: Zu-liu Hu, *Social Protection, Labor Market Rigidity, and Enterprise Restructuring in China* (Washington, D.C.: International Monetary Fund, October 1994), 4.

steel production continue to remain under the jurisdiction of central government ministries. Table 13-6 shows the dominance of state enterprises in certain industries.

The performance of most state-owned enterprises has generally been poor. Waste and inefficiency are problems. Many state enterprises lose money because they carry surplus workers who otherwise would be unemployed; they also provide workers with housing and health care. The quality of Chinese industrial output lags behind that of the developed countries by ten to twenty years. In 1990 state-owned enterprises lost around $20 billion, which amounted to 5.3 percent of Chinese GDP; in 1993 they lost around $12 billion, or 2.4 percent of Chinese GDP.[27] Although some are efficient, state-owned enterprises absorb a large share of the country's resources, contributing to a deficit in the state budget because of the subsidies that have to be paid. These subsidies have averaged around 10 percent of state budget expenditures over the past fifteen years. A bankruptcy law passed in 1986 has been rarely used.

Reforms enacted in 1993 and 1994 are designed to make state-owned enterprises more efficient, while still emphasizing the maintenance of state ownership as the cornerstone of the Chinese economy.[28] One reform is designed to relieve state-owned enterprises of the responsibility of providing social services to their workers. The government is to increase its responsibility for providing these services. Another reform is designed to create market-based relationships between

27. "Shrinking the Chinese State," 33.
28. Wanda Tseng et al., *Economic Reform in China: A New Phase* (Washington, D.C.: International Monetary Fund, November 1994), 42–45.

TABLE 13-6
Output of Chinese State-Owned Enterprises as Percentage of Total Output, 1993 (percent)

Industry	
Petroleum	100
Tobacco	98
Power	95
Iron and steel	90
Electronics	80
Food processing	75
Chemicals	70
Machinery	70
Textiles	65
Coal	60

Source: "A Survey of China," *The Economist*, March 18–24, 1995, 6.

enterprises to reduce the accumulation of interenterprise debt. Government control over wage and employment policies is to be reduced, and more financial autonomy from state ministries will be allowed. As mentioned previously, state-owned enterprises are free to form joint-stock companies and issue stock. Mergers of enterprises to improve efficiency is also permitted. Nevertheless, the state still maintains some control over enterprise pricing.

Collectives. What distinguishes collectives from state-owned enterprises is that they are under the jurisdiction not of the central government and provincial governments, but of lower-level governments.[29] Collectives affiliated with a municipality or county are called urban cooperatives; those affiliated with townships and villages are called rural collectives. Although they are supposed to be collectively owned, they operate largely in a market-based environment. A group of citizens can take the initiative in establishing a collectively owned enterprise. The means of production are neither private property nor state property, but the property of the collective. The collective has the exclusive right to own, control, and handle its means of production and products. It keeps its own accounts and is responsible for its profits and losses. Thus, the line dividing collectives from private enterprises has become increasingly blurred.

Private Enterprise. The Chinese Communist leaders have an ambivalent position on the role of private enterprise. Its existence was justified on the grounds that it served an economic purpose in certain areas of economic activity where state control was not feasible. It could be easily constrained by government regulation and by dependence on the socialist economy. During the 1980s, however, re-

29. China has five levels of government: (1) The central government with its capital at Beijing; (2) 22 provinces, 5 autonomous regions, and 3 municipalities under the control of the central government; (3) 336 prefectures and municipalities at the prefectural level; (4) 2,182 counties, autonomous counties, and cities at the county level; and (5) tens of thousands of townships, towns, and city districts. This makes ruling from the top rather difficult, so many government units are pretty much free to do what they want to do without much interference from the top. Many towns and villages have their own enterprises.

forms that decentralized economic power and increased the role of the profit motive weakened central government control. While private enterprise remained dependent on goodwill and informal relationships, it grew rapidly and became a significant feature of the Chinese economy that was under local government, rather than central government, control. As the Chinese economy moves toward capitalism, there are those in power that would like to bring back socialism as it once existed. But the private sector has grown so fast that any serious effort to suppress it would cause economic collapse.

Joint Ventures. The Chinese government has made an active effort to attract foreign investment. One approach that has been used since 1980 involves joint ventures between Chinese and Western firms. An example is Occidental Petroleum, which signed an agreement with China to develop and jointly operate what could eventually become the world's largest open-pit coal mine. Licensing and franchising agreements have also been reached with foreign firms. An example is Coca-Cola, which has been given the exclusive right to produce and sell Coca-Cola in China. Coca-Cola provides the syrup and the authorized use of its trademark, and the drink is bottled for sale in China.

Special Enterprise Zones (SEZs). Special enterprise zones were created by the Chinese government during the early 1980s to attract foreign investment. They are specifically delineated areas created to achieve several economic objectives. The first is to attract foreign investment, particularly in plans and equipment. A second objective is the creation of hard-currency export industries, and a third objective is to import modern industrial technology. Foreign investors are offered a wide variety of inducements such as preferential tax rates, flexible wage and labor policies, more modern infrastructure, and less bureaucratic interference than anywhere else in China. Manufacturing, heavy industry, and infrastructure development are particularly favored because they create markets for Chinese raw materials. Foreign investment has been attracted to these zones, which are located in eastern China along the seacoast. Profits from these investments can be transferred out of China.

Organization of Agriculture

Agriculture is the most important sector in the Chinese economy, accounting for around one-third of Chinese GNP and two-thirds of the labor force. It has gone through a number of phases since the Communists came to power in 1949. Producers' cooperatives created in 1955 were incorporated into collective farms in 1956. Land was no longer privately owned; it was collective property, with the peasants allowed to own farm animals and small plots of land. In 1958 communes replaced the collective farms. A commune was a multipurpose unit that was supposed to perform administrative as well as economic functions. All vestiges of private property were removed, the peasants ate in mess halls, and the distribution of food was based in part on the needs of individuals and in part on work performed. The communes remained the highest level of collective organization in China until the end of the 1970s.

A series of agricultural reforms were initiated in the 1980s. Recollectivization of farmland and reform in production planning were designed to encourage production incentives. The self-responsibility system (*baochan dasho*) was introduced. Although still owned by the state, land was divided into small plots and contracted out to be farmed privately. Each farm family was given the necessary inputs, including land, cattle, farm machinery, and equipment. The only obligation of a farmer besides paying rent and a small agricultural tax was to deliver a fixed amount of produce, which was sold to the state at a fixed price. Any amount produced in excess of the fixed amount belonged to the farm family to consume, to sell to the state at a higher price, or to sell in the free market.

Agricultural reforms continued during the 1980s. In 1988 purchase prices for grain production under state contract were raised. The dual-track pricing system was changed by reducing the share of grain produced under state contracts and increasing free-market transactions. Compulsory contract procurement quotas for grains and cotton were replaced by contract purchases. In 1988 the government raised the price it paid for contract grain and instituted price differences based on grain quality. Peasants were given permission to purchase and transfer land-lease rights, a system designed to permit more efficient, larger-scale operations. The government also strengthened the land-leasing period for rural land from fifteen to thirty years to provide greater incentives for farmers to adopt land-use measures. Finally, the government increased investment in fertilizer and pesticide production, transportation, and distribution networks, and agricultural infrastructure projects such as irrigation.

Until 1979 the Chinese government followed a policy of food self-sufficiency, particularly in the production of grain, irrespective of the difference in regional comparative advantages. It also kept producer prices of agricultural goods at levels far below what they would have been if market factors had been used to provide consumers with low-cost food. Consumer prices, too, were administratively set. Producers' sales quotas were fixed. State purchase prices and state selling prices bore little relationship to each other. Prices were irrelevant to distribution, since farm products were allocated in a planned way through the administrative process. Finally, prices did not affect consumer behavior because supplies of most goods were rationed by state economic planning.

The trend toward liberalization of the state procurement and pricing systems led to a situation where by 1991, about 50 percent of all agricultural purchases took place at market-determined prices, 20 percent were subject to state-guided prices, where maximum and minimum prices were set, and the remaining 30 percent were sold at state-determined prices.[30] Price and procurement reforms had an impact on the Chinese agricultural and rural economy in several ways. Production and productivity of grain crops and livestock products showed a substantial increase, and rural incomes, savings, and investment also increased. Regional comparative advantages have been exploited more fully, and interregional markets

30. Mahmood H. Khan and Mohsin S. Khan, *Agricultural Growth in Sub-Saharan African Countries and China* (Washington, D.C.: International Monetary Fund, April 1995), 17.

have developed. On the other hand, rising farm productivity has left about 100 million rural workers without work, causing a migration to the cities. Farm income continues to lag behind urban income, in part because the price of some consumer staples is still controlled by the government.

Table 13-7 presents the performance of Chinese agriculture during the period 1975–1992. It is important to note that as late as 1992, two-thirds of the Chinese labor force was still employed in agriculture, although there has been a decline in the share of agriculture in GNP. The arable land per capita has also shown a decline.

Foreign Trade

Until 1978 China's foreign trade was carried out through twelve state-owned foreign trade corporations (FTCs) organized along product lines. They procured and traded the quantities directed by the central economic plan, and all profits and losses were absorbed by the state budget. As a result of the economic reforms, the degree of economic planning was reduced, and there has been much more reliance on market mechanisms for determining the prices of exports and imports. Foreign trade corporations have been given more autonomy, and most now come under the jurisdiction of provincial authorities. By 1991 exports and imports subject to mandatory central economic planning were 30 percent and 20 percent, respectively; by 1994 both figures were less than 20 percent.[31] Some imports are subject to import licensing, which is used to implement the economic plan and to protect certain sectors of the economy. Some exports are also subject to government licensing.

Foreign exchange in China is handled in several ways. There is a swap market covering foreign exchange earnings that is retained by foreign trade corporations and other exporters.[32] In the swap market, holders of foreign exchange can sell any excess to enterprises that offer the best price.[33] This allows the exchange to be allocated in accordance with market-oriented criteria. Access to swap centers to purchase foreign exchange is subject to authorization by the State Administration of Exchange Control and is restricted to enterprises that need foreign exchange either to service their foreign currency debt or to import goods that are consistent with the economic objectives of the state. Actual purchase of foreign exchange outside the swap markets is usually limited to foreign funded enterprises (FFEs). Subject to the approval of the Ministry of Foreign Trade and Economic Cooperation, FFEs can use foreign exchange for operating needs and debt repayment.

31. *Economic Reform in China: A New Phase*, 5.

32. China has a two-tiered currency system in use: foreign exchange certificates (FECs) and *renminbis* (RMBs). The RMB is not convertible into foreign currency, and is used for internal commerce but not for the purchase of imported goods. The FECs are converted into foreign currencies at government-controlled rates and are designed to be used for the purchase of imported goods. The State General Administration of Exchange Control is responsible for currency exchange, while the Bank of China is the only bank authorized to conduct foreign exchange business.

33. Hoe Ee Khor, *China's Foreign Currency Swap Market* (Washington, D.C.: International Monetary Fund, 1994).

TABLE 13-7 *Performance of Chinese Agriculture, 1975–1992*

	1975	*1980*	*1985*	*1990*	*1992*
Share of Agriculture (percent)					
GNP	36	35	33	28	27
Labor force	76	74	71	67	66
Trade	—	74	44	33	28
Agriculture Value Added (dollars)					
Per worker	213	228	318	358	385
Per hectare*	800	949	1,477	1,759	1,906
Indices of Output (1980=100 percent)					
Food	84.7	98.8	127.4	157.6	175.8
Food per capita	90.8	98.7	118.6	136.1	145.2
Cereal Output (kilograms)					
Per capita	258	283	321	340	350
Per hectare*	2,074	2,923	3,837	4,199	4,587
Arable Land per Capita					
Hectares*	0.106	0.099	0.089	0.081	0.075

**1 hectare = 2.471 acres.*

Source: Mahmood H. Khan and Mohsin S. Khan, *Agricultural Growth in Sub-Saharan African Countries and China* (Washington, D.C.: International Monetary Fund, April 1995), 3.

The swap market can be viewed as a transitional mechanism for an economy that is in the process of change from a system of central planning to one that is more market oriented. Under central planning the volume and composition of external trade and the allocation of foreign exchange were handled administratively. The structure of relative prices in the economy bore no relation to international prices; the exchange rate was merely an accounting unit and did not play a role in linking international prices to domestic prices.[34] Thus, it was difficult to determine the appropriate level of the exchange rate. The swap market provides a mechanism by which greater latitude is given to market forces in exchange rate determination as the price system is undergoing reform. It contributes to China's strong export performance by raising the profitability of the export sector.

AN EVALUATION OF THE CHINESE ECONOMY

It is necessary to remember two things about China. First, it is a developing country with a money per capita income of $530 in 1993. Translated into purchasing-power parity in international dollars, the per capita income is $2,510, or about one-twelfth of purchasing-power parity of U.S. per capita income.[35] Multiplied by its

34. Ibid., 16.
35. The World Bank, *The World Bank Atlas* (Washington, D.C.: The World Bank, 1996), 18–19.

population of around 1.2 billion,[36] this would give China a real GDP greater than Germany's.

When ranked by money per capita income, it is in the bottom one-fourth of the world's countries. Second, despite all of its economic reforms, China remains a country dominated by the Communist Party. It is governed by top-down politics, with each official's career dependent on the favor of higher-level officials.

Economic Growth

As Table 13-8 indicates, the growth rate of the Chinese economy has been spectacular. It has expanded at an average annual growth rate of 10 percent for the past fifteen years, and the volume of its foreign trade has expanded at an even faster rate of 15 percent. In 1994 China, along with Hong Kong and Taiwan, became the third-largest exporter-importer in the world.[37] Its average annual growth rate for the period 1980–2010 is projected at 8.1 percent.[38] If this trend were to continue, it is possible, as Table 13-9 indicates, that China's GDP as measured by purchasing-power parity could become the largest in the world sometime in the next century. This is based on the assumptions that the process of reform will continue and that the economy's infrastructure will be improved to the extent that it can cope with the continued increase in economic growth.

Strengths of the Chinese Economy

There are factors that favor the continued expansion of the Chinese economy. China has had a current account surplus over the past decade, and it, Hong Kong, and Taiwan have a foreign exchange reserve of $165 billion. These reserves supplement domestic investment. The degree to which the trade and investment of these three economies are integrated means they are close to being a single economic unit today and will be even more so tomorrow. As Table 13-9 indicates, the rise in China's share of world output between 1980 and 2010 is somewhat comparable to the one recorded by the United States during the three decades prior to the end of the nineteenth century, and larger than the Japanese increase in world output during the period 1950–1980. The likelihood is that China will follow the American and Japanese patterns, with a rapid rise in its importance in international trade.

China's manufactured exports have primarily been light manufactured products of a labor-intensive nature. This pattern of specialization is expected to continue in the future, with emphasis on the production of textiles and clothing. These are the products that drive the exports of Japan, South Korea, and Taiwan.

36. Depending on the methodology used, there is considerable variation in the size of Chinese per capita GDP and total GDP. The author has typically relied on World Bank data that include the concept of purchasing-power parity. When this is used, Chinese per capita GDP would be about the same as that of Bolivia and El Salvador, two of the poorer countries in Latin America.

37. U.S. Department of Commerce, International Trade Administration, *Business America* (Washington, D.C.: U.S. Government Printing Office, May 1995), 18.

38. *China's Emergence: Prospects, Opportunities, and Challenges,* 11–15.

TABLE 13-8
Growth in Real Chinese GNP, 1980–1995 (percent)

1980	7.9
1981	4.4
1982	8.8
1983	10.4
1984	14.7
1985	12.8
1986	8.1
1987	10.9
1988	11.3
1989	4.4
1990	4.1
1991	7.7
1992	13.0
1993	13.4
1994	11.8
1995	10.2
1996	10.0

Sources: Wanda Tseng et al., *Economic Reform in China: A New Phase,* Occasional Paper 114 (Washington, D.C.: International Monetary Fund, November 1994), 2; OECD, *OECD Economic Outlook* (Paris: OECD, June 1995), 116; International Monetary Fund, *World Economic Outlook, May 1996* (Washington, D.C.: IMF, May 1996), 24.

There are certain complementaries between China and Japan, once the bitterest of enemies. China has some of the natural resources that Japan needs, as well as a huge labor supply, while Japan has many of the technologies and the management expertise that China needs for modernization. Direct foreign investment in China, particularly from Taiwan and Singapore, has increased more rapidly than in any other country in the world.[39]

Weaknesses of the Chinese Economy

The Chinese economy also has some major weaknesses that may very well have an adverse effect on its future rate of economic development. Internal political stability is at real risk in China.[40] The issue of political succession will eventually have to be resolved. Corruption is rampant and exists at all levels of government, eroding respect for the Communist Party and for the legal system. Foreign investors have discovered they have no legal recourse when their businesses are blackmailed or their revenues extorted by corrupt government officials. Chinese pirating of intellectual property rights is common and has become a bone of contention with the United States. There is a reluctance to play by international legal rules, commercial and political. But there are also a number of other problems.

39. In 1993, 20 percent of total world investment flows went to China.
40. *The Economist* assigns a risk factor of 80 percent to China, which is high.

TABLE 13-9 *Major Countries' Emergence into the World Economy (annual average percentage change)*

	U.S. 1870–1900	*Japan* 1950–1980	*China* 1980–2010	*Chinese Economic Area* 1980–2010
Growth of GDP	3.9	7.7	8.2	7.9
Share of world output at start	15.4	3.2	3.6	4.2
Share of world output at end	25.7	10.1	15.4	17.1
Change in share	10.3	6.9	11.8	12.9
Share of world manufacturing exports at start	3.8	3.4	0.8	3.3
Share of world manufacturing exports at end	14.7	11.2	6.4	10.3
Change in share	10.9	7.8	5.6	7.0

Source: Andrea Boltho, Uri Dadush, Dong He, and Shigeru Otsubo, *China's Emergence: Prospects, Opportunities, and Challenges,* Policy Research Working Paper 1339 (Washington, D.C.: The World Bank, August 1994), 3.

Inflation. Over the past five years, the average rate of inflation in China has risen at a rate of 20 percent. There are several reasons for this. First, there has been a high rate of capital inflow from other countries. Almost $30 billion of foreign direct investment entered China in 1994, roughly half of the total for all developing countries. The swapping of foreign exchange into yuan caused the domestic money supply to grow, and increased Chinese foreign exchange reserves up to $51 billion by the end of 1994. Second, government-owned state banks have to support a large number of unprofitable state-owned enterprises. This lends an inflationary bias to the annual cash plan that is administered by the People's Bank of China.[41] Political pressure forces the PBC to print more money.[42] Money supply growth in China was 34 percent in 1994 compared to a real growth rate of 10 percent.[43]

Agriculture. Although agricultural production has been high in recent years, gains in the future may have difficulty keeping up with population growth. Virtually all arable land is cultivated, and increase in per-unit output will be limited because China's yields are already first-class by world standards.[44] Rising farm productivity has caused a migration of millions of farmworkers to the cities, thus increasing the unemployment rate. There are major problems. One is the regional disparity in farm incomes. In the more prosperous farming areas of China, farmers make three

41. It is a feature of China's banking system that when both borrower and lender are state-owned, discretion goes out of the window when it comes to loans and repayments. China's banks, including the PBC, do what the central and local government tell them to do.
42. Marc Quintyn, "Currency Management and Monetary Programming in China," *IMF Survey*, Vol. 24, No. 15 (Washington, D.C.: International Monetary Fund, July 31, 1995), 237–238.
43. The money supply referred to is M2, which consists of M1, coins, currencies, and checking account balances, plus small time deposits, savings balances, and Eurodollars.
44. For example, in wheat as measured by tons per hectare, China has performed better than the United States.

to four times more income than farmers in the less prosperous farming areas. Another problem is that an estimated one-third of China's cropland has been lost over time to soil erosion, energy projects, and industrial and housing development. If the trend continues, another 15 percent of cropland could be lost by the year 2020.

Population. China's population in mid-1995 was 1.2 trillion. Despite efforts by the government to enforce birth control, the population is expected to increase to around 1.4 trillion by the year 2010 and to 1.5 trillion by the year 2025.[45] This will put pressure on China's agriculture because production gains will have difficulty keeping up with population increases. As was true in the former Soviet Union, China's grain storage and transportation facilities are inadequate, causing the loss of anywhere from 10 to 20 million tons of grain annually because of poor storage facilities. China will have to raise its reliance on imported food to meet the demands of an ever-increasing population over the next decades.[46] The Chinese population is aging and its life expectancy is increasing. Eventually this will increase the cost of the Chinese social security system.

SUMMARY

China is the only major Communist country left in the world, and it is likely, barring some major domestic upheaval, that it will remain so for the remainder of the century. Chinese leaders have initiated a number of reform measures designed to raise living standards and have given a greater role to market forces. However, the Chinese leaders maintain control over the economy. Inefficiency in the state sector remains, and many state enterprises continue to perform poorly, increasing the deficit in the state budget. China's growth rate during the 1980s and 1990s has been quite high, and China has become a major trading nation, running a surplus in its current account and accumulating a large foreign exchange that has added to its supply of savings. Foreign direct investment has also poured into China. The country also has a small external debt.

China also has its share of problems. Inflation continues to be high. If the Communist Party, after the death of Deng Xiaoping, has run out of leaders capable of exerting strong central control, some form of internal fragmentation may occur. China lags far behind other developing countries in terms of infrastructure, technology, environmental protection, and international affairs. Corruption is also a major problem. The banking system is in need of drastic reforms. If the state banks had been operating on the basis of Western commercial operating principles, most lending to inefficient state-owned enterprises would have been stopped. The central bank, the People's Bank of China, has little operating autonomy and can do little to stop inflation. Population growth threatens to outrun agricultural supplies, as the best land is already in use.

45. Population Reference Bureau, 1995 World Population Data Sheet (Washington, D.C.: PRB, 1995).
46. *A Survey of China*, 20.

QUESTIONS FOR DISCUSSION

1. What is the Chinese Economic Area? Why is it important?
2. China calls itself a socialist market economy. Do you agree?
3. How has the role of state-owned enterprises, cooperatives, and private enterprises changed over the past ten years?
4. Why are state-owned enterprises generally inefficient?
5. What are some of the general problems that face private enterprise in China?
6. Evaluate the performance of the Chinese economy in terms of living standards and economic growth.
7. What impact will the acquisition of Hong Kong in 1997 have on the Chinese economy?
8. China needs to greatly modernize its infrastructure during the 1990s. Discuss.

RECOMMENDED READINGS

"A Survey of China." *The Economist,* March 18–24, 1995, 1–21.

Bell, Michael W., Hoe Ee Khor, and Kalpana Kochhar. *China at the Threshold of a Market Economy.* Washington, D.C.: International Monetary Fund, September 1993.

Boltho, Andrea, Uri Dadush, Dong He, and Shigeru Otsubo. *China's Emergence: Prospects, Opportunities, and Challenges.* Policy Research Working Paper 1339. Washington, D.C.: The World Bank, August 1994.

Chen, Kathy. "As China Prospers, So Do the Children of Communist Leaders." *Wall Street Journal,* July 17, 1995, A1, A12.

Hornik, Richard. "Bursting China's Bubble." *Foreign Affairs,* Vol. 73, No. 3 (May-June 1994), 28-42.

Hu, Zu-liu. *Social Protection, Labor Market Rigidity, and Enterprise Restructuring in China.* Washington, D.C.: International Monetary Fund, October 1994.

Kahn, Joseph. "New Enterprises Are Remaking China." *Wall Street Journal,* July 26, 1995, A1, A8.

Khan, Mahmood H., and Mohsin S. Khan. *Agricultural Growth in Sub-Saharan African Countries and China.* Washington, D.C.: International Monetary Fund, April 1995.

Prybyla, Jan S. "Mainland China's Economic System: A Study in Contradictions." In *Issues and Studies.* Vol. 30, No. 8 (August 1994), Taipei, Taiwan: Institute of International Relations, August 1994.

Segal, Gerald, "China's Changing Shape." *Foreign Affairs,* Vol. 73, No. 3 (May-June 1994), 43–58.

"Shrinking the Chinese State." *The Economist,* June 10–16, 1995, 33–34.

Tseng, Wanda, et al. *Economic Reform in China: A New Phase.* Occasional Paper 114. Washington, D.C.: International Monetary Fund. November 1994.

Young, Susan. *Private Business and Economic Reform in China.* Armonk, N.Y.: M. E. Sharp, 1995.

CHAPTER 14
India

India has the second-largest population in the world, some 900 million people. When China and India are combined, they have around 40 percent of the world's population. They are also among the poorest countries in the world, with per capita incomes of less than $725 a year, but both have achieved a measure of industrial development. India was created as an independent country in 1947, and the People's Republic of China was created in 1949. Both had in the past been occupied by foreign powers. For almost two hundred years India was a part of the British Empire, while China was controlled variously by the Americans, British, Germans, Russians, and Japanese. China's economic development was predicated along the lines of the standard Leninist model, which placed emphasis on the creation of heavy industry, and it was run by the Communist Party. India also followed a state-directed approach to economic development, but it maintained the institutions of a democratic society.

However, China and India are much more dissimilar than they are similar. China has a much more homogeneous population and a common language, while

India has a very heterogeneous population and a number of languages.[1] China's culture is linked to the teachings of Confucius, who stressed hard work and thrift, while India has many cultures and religions.[2] India is a country marked by religious and ethnic rivalries where Hindus fight Moslems and Sikh and Kashmiri separatists fight for independence.[3] China has no such problems. India runs some risk of being fragmented into a number of different parts, but that possibility is far less likely in China. On the other hand, democratic institutions in India facilitate much smoother political transitions than China will face after the death of Deng Xiaoping.[4] Moreover, India is a society in which private property and profit have existed uninterrupted for centuries. Table 14-1 presents a comparison of China and India and Table 14-2 contrasts the two nations' GPDs throughout the twentieth century.

A HISTORY OF INDIA

The British influence on India, which lasted for some two hundred years, cannot be minimized. India's legal system is based on the British-based common law, which dates back to the Norman Conquest of England in 1066. Precedents in common law countries, including India, provide the stability necessary for people and businesses to plan future actions. Second, there is the English language, which is used extensively in India and is the common business language of the world. Third, India's educational system is patterned after the British educational system, even to the inclusion of the elite public schools, which are models of Eton and Harrow. The great majority of Indian students who study abroad attend universities in England and the United States. Their culture is oriented toward the West. India's political system is also a product of British rule. It is a democracy, with free elections and the active participation of major political parties.

England and Mercantilism

Mercantilism was a trade theory that formed the foundation of economic thought from about 1500 to 1800. According to mercantilist theory, countries should export

1. English is the most important language for business communication. Hindi is spoken by 30 percent of the population. Other languages include Bengali, Urdu, Punjabi, Kashmiri, Sindhi, Sanskrit, and others. Altogether, India has ninety-eight different languages and dialects.
2. India has most of the world's major religions. There are Hindus, Moslems, Buddhists, Jains, and Christians, plus many religious offshoots. Hindus and Moslems have clashed for centuries, and refuse to drink water from the same glass. India is also the most culturally diverse country in the world.
3. Prime Minister Indira Gandhi was assassinated by Sikh separatists, and her son Rajiv Gandhi, who had also served as prime minister, was assassinated by a Tamalese separatist when he was running for reelection. The bombing of the Bombay stock exchange in 1994 was also attributed to separatist movements.
4. Arthur Walton, "After Deng the Deluge," *Foreign Affairs*, Vol. 74, No. 5 (September-October, 1995).

TABLE 14-1 *A Comparison of China and India*

	China	*India*
Population in 1995 (millions)	1,218.8	930.6
Per capita income 1994 (dollars)	530	310
GNP 1994 (billions of dollars)	630.2	278.7
Real per capita growth rate, 1985–1994 (percent)	6.9	2.9
Life expectancy (years)	69	60
Birthrate (per 1,000 people)	18	29
Death rate (per 1,000 people)	6	9
Population-doubling time (years)	62	36
Infant mortality rate (per 1,000 births)	44	74
Illiteracy rate (percent of population)	14	50
Human Development Index (174 countries)	111	134

Sources: Carl Haub and Machiko Yanagishita, *1995 World Population Data Sheet* (Washington, D.C.: Population Reference Bureau, 1995); The World Bank, *The World Bank Atlas 1996* (Washington, D.C.: The World Bank, 1996), 18; United Nations Development Programme, *Human Development Report 1995* (New York: Oxford University Press, 1995), 94.

more than they import, and if successful, would receive the value of their trade surpluses in the form of gold from the country or countries that ran deficits. In order to export more than they imported, governments established monopolies over their countries' trade. Colonial possessions were used to support this trade objective. First, the colonies supplied many commodities that the mother country would otherwise have to purchase from another country, thus having to expend gold. Second, the colonial powers sought to run trade surpluses with their colonies as a way to obtain revenue. They did this not only by monopolizing colonial trade but also by preventing the colonies from engaging in manufacturing. Thus the colonies had to export less highly valued raw materials and import more highly valued manufacturing products.

Countries that embraced mercantilist policies were Portugal, Spain, England, France, and the Netherlands. All were sea powers. The Portuguese were the first to develop contact with India, establishing possession in the western part of the country in 1511.[5] The Portuguese were followed into India by the Dutch East India Company, which established control over ports in the southern part of the country around 1600. However, the two major protagonists in India, as in North America, were the British and the French, with the British establishing possession at Bombay and the French at Calcutta in the early part of the seventeenth century. The two countries controlled most of India's foreign trade for 150 years through chartered monopolies. In England, the British East India Company was chartered by Queen Elizabeth and became a joint-stock company. It controlled trade with

5. They remained there until India declared its independence in 1947.

TABLE 14-2
GDP Indices for China and India, 1900–1987 (1913 = 100 percent)

	China	*India*
1900	90.0	88.3
1913	100.0	100.0
1929	120.9	109.0
1932	126.8	110.2
1950	103.7	128.4
1955	159.4	155.4
1960	186.7	189.1
1964	210.7	231.6
1965	230.0	222.3
1970	311.1	280.3
1975	418.9	325.9
1980	547.7	384.9
1981	572.6	408.7
1982	626.6	421.5
1983	692.4	454.8
1984	793.7	469.2
1985	891.2	491.5
1986	958.8	511.3
1987	1,049.0	518.9

Source: Angus Maddison, *The World Economy in the 20th Century* (Paris: OECD Development Centre Studies, 1989), 124.

India until it was dissolved in 1833. The French had an equivalent company,[6] which had a monopoly of trade between France and India.

British Ascendancy in India

The French controlled much more territory in India than did the British, but they lost India, like Canada, to the British primarily because England had become the leading maritime power in Europe. France was engaged in wars in Europe and did not have the resources to pour into Canada and India. British control over India was also made easier by the breakup of the Mogul Empire into a number of different principalities with no central control. It was easy for the British to divide and conquer, and by 1750 they were de facto rulers of much of the country. In successive wars, the British conquered the rest of India, and it became part of the British Empire. The concept of empire was confined to the establishment of law, the foundation of an administrative system, the dispensing of justice, and the creation of a tax system. India served as a market for British manufactured products, and sent cotton and other raw materials to England.

6. In the latter part of the 1700s, the British East India Company began to sell opium grown in India to China. It was the company's most important export.

Independence of India, 1947

The movement for Indian independence from England dates back to the nineteenth century. Certain reforms made by the British to provide India with more autonomy did not go far enough, and various separatist groups formed in India around the end of the last century. It was not until after the end of World War I that the British were willing to give India some voice in its government, but the British maintained executive control. After the end of World War II it was only a matter of time before India would receive its independence. A campaign of civil disobedience to British authority, which had begun with Mohandas Gandhi and others during the 1920s, was initiated against England after the end of the war. In 1947 the British relinquished control of India. Eventually, India became two countries based on religion, Hindu India and Muslim Pakistan.

THE ECONOMIC AND POLITICAL DEVELOPMENT OF INDIA

India was the center of British imperial rule in Asia, so when it achieved its independence in 1947, certain economic and political institutions were a carryover from British rule. The cities of Bombay, Calcutta, and Madras were the business and financial centers of India, and were also the centers of politics and government administration. There was an infrastructure consisting of good railroads, trunk roads, and a modern communications system, plus a centralized administrative system. The medium of the English language provided the means for the political and cultural unification of the country. Education facilities were in place. In the cities, education in high schools, colleges, and universities had expanded rapidly since the founding of universities in the cities of Bombay, Calcutta, and Madras in 1857. An engineering school was also established in 1886.

However, there was also a downside to freedom and independence, for a number of problems still remained. When India drafted its constitution in 1950, 80 percent of the wealth of the country was held by 2 percent of the population. The great majority of Indians lived in rural areas, and most were poor and illiterate. They lived and worked on small farms, using antiquated farm implements that hadn't changed in centuries. The infrastructure in the rural areas was poor. Medical facilities were inadequate, so there was a high rate of infant mortality. Even so, the high birthrate in the rural areas contributed to the ever-increasing rate of population growth. The lot of women was particularly bad. More were likely to be illiterate than men, and they had few rights.[7]

7. Even today in rural areas of India, women are killed because they committed adultery or because their dowry was not large enough.

Government

The government established by the Constitution of 1950 follows a federal pattern, with specific powers divided between state governments and the central government. India consists of twenty-four states, each with its own language and culture. The Indian Constitution is based on the British Magna Carta and on the French and American Constitutions. The ideals of liberty, equality, and fraternity are taken from the French Constitution, while the notion of a secular state and a federal republic of states is taken from the American Constitution. The legislature in India is just like the British system, with the prime minister as the head of the government and the source of executive power. There is a Parliament headed by a president who presides over a bicameral legislature. There are also a Cabinet and a Supreme Court, which is the highest judicial body in India.

Executive Power. The executive power of government in India technically is held by the president in New Delhi, the capital of India, and by state governors. These ceremonial heads of state have the power to assent to bills passed by the legislature and brought to them for consideration, and they also have the right to return to the legislature bills they feel should be reconsidered. The president and the governors also summon the legislatures into session, and they address the legislatures on problems facing their respective governments. But they have no real executive strength. That is held by the prime minister of India and the heads of the cabinets of the national and state governments. The prime minister has authority until such time as he or she recommends to the president that Parliament be dissolved and new elections be held.

Legislative Power. Legislative power in the central government and in the state governments follows the British form of government. The Indian Parliament is made up of two houses similar to the British House of Commons and House of Lords. The lower house, the Lok Sabha (House of the People), is made up of 520 members, and the upper house, the Rajya Sabha (Council of States), of no more than 250 members. The upper house is by no means as important as the lower house for purposes of legislation. Like the British House of Lords, it is not subject to dissolution and functions as a continuous body. It serves as a repository for a large number of India's elder statesmen. Members of the lower house are elected by direct vote; members of the upper house are elected by state legislatures.

Judicial Power. The Indian judicial system is somewhat similar to that of the United States. The Supreme Court is the highest court in India. It is headed by a Chief Justice, who is joined by no more than seven associates. Judges of the Supreme Court are appointed by the president after consultation with such of the judges of the state supreme courts and the high courts as the president deems necessary. The Supreme Court is the final interpreter of the Constitution and is the final court of civil appeals. At the state level, there are high courts that hold full legal powers within their particular states, with the exception of those cases where the Supreme Court has jurisdiction. The governor in each state, in consultation with the high court, appoints district judges within the state.

Bureaucracy. India inherited from England an efficient administrative system. The old Indian civil service was a model to the world because it selected intelligent persons who were expected to be competent.[8] They were also expected to assume responsibility for administration over any level of operation in government. Indian civil service personnel moved in their careers from a subordinate office in a district up to district and divisional administration in the states, then up to positions of responsibility at the central government level. For many years, civil service positions were held only by the British, except for minor positions at the local level, which were held by Indians. This began to change after World War I, when more Indians began to enjoy positions of authority. After independence from England, a new Indian civil service simply followed an established administrative framework.

ECONOMIC DEVELOPMENT AFTER INDEPENDENCE

After India became an independent nation, the leaders of the country beginning with Jawaharlal Nehru were faced with a number of problems. The first was to create a new economic order that would lessen India's dependent relationship with England, where it had continued to send raw materials in return for manufactured goods. The Indian economy was underdeveloped, with resulting low standards of living for the great majority of the population. Eight percent of the people were illiterate. The riots and destruction that accompanied the partition of India and Pakistan were costly in lives and in property damage and had brought the country to an economic standstill.[9] So something had to be done to develop a new economic order. The result was the development of a state-directed economy based on economic planning.

Economic Planning

Contrary to what some people may have thought, India was not a Communist country even though it had close ties with the former Soviet Union. It preferred to call itself a democratic socialist country, with emphasis placed on the welfare state.

8. The British civil service has had far more prestige than the United States civil service. It attracted many capable people from the best British schools. People from the British aristocracy went into the civil service, but particularly the army. Many British people of note served in the Indian civil service. Rudyard Kipling and George Orwell come to mind.
9. During the first three days of Indian independence 750,000 people were killed in riots between Hindus and Moslems.

There were both a public sector and a private sector. Many Indian industries were state-owned. There was reliance on broad-scale economic and social planning. Economic planning was more similar to the French indicative form of planning[10] than to the Soviet imperative type of economic planning, and like France, India is a capitalist country with a considerable amount of state ownership of industry. Control over credit allocation gave the planners control over the direction of planning objectives. India relied on the use of five-year plans.[11] A planning commission was responsible for developing plan objectives. Reliance was placed on input-output tables to determine the consistency of the plan.[12]

The First Five-Year Plan (1951–1956). Under this plan, priority was given to increasing agricultural production, rehabilitating the railroad system, and starting river valley developments to increase irrigation and the supply of electric power. Some attention was given to the revitalization of rural Indian life through a community development program. The development of such industries as cement, paper, chemicals, and light engineering was emphasized. Government monetary policy was aimed at maintaining price stability. Financial support for the development of agriculture and industry came from both the government and private sectors of the economy and from foreign aid, mostly provided by the United States.

The Second Five-Year Plan (1956–1961). The government announced in 1956 that its objective was to create a mixed economy in which government enterprise would carry out activities essential to the state. Private enterprise would carry out the rest. However, a greater emphasis was placed on the public sector than on the private sector. The Second Five-Year Plan was more ambitious than the first, giving much greater emphasis to the improvement of transportation and communications and the development of electric power. Another goal was to increase the production of iron and steel through the construction of new steel mills, with technical assistance provided by West Germany and the Soviet Union.

The Third Five-Year Plan (1961–1966). The major objective of this plan was to increase the production of food grains, cotton, oil seeds, jute, and sugar cane. A second objective was to increase the generation of electric power. A third objective was to increase the production of such industrial products as steel, aluminum,

10. French indicative planning can be viewed as a set of directives that are used to guide the direction of the private sector as well as the public sector of the economy. France was able to use a whole range of measures to direct economic activity. An example would be access to bank credit and favorable interest rates to guide investment.

11. An annual plan was also published for each year by the state planning commission. It was released at the beginning of each fiscal year, which for India was July.

12. Economic planning in the Soviet Union consisted of physical input-output planning and financial planning. Input-output planning meant that the economy was divided up into a number of branches, each of which was assigned inputs and outputs. These branches were presented on a grid showing how much each economic sector bought and sold from other sectors.

cement, and pig iron. Target goals were set. For example, food grains were to be increased from 75 million tons in 1961 to 105 million tons in 1966, and the output of cotton was to increase from 5.4 million bales in 1961 to 7.2 million bales in 1966.[13] Finished steel was to be increased from 2.6 million tons in 1961 to 6.9 million tons in 1966. In the social welfare area, an objective was to introduce health care into the rural areas of India, along with the improvement of education facilities.

The Fourth Five-Year Plan (1966–1971). The third plan met with some reversals. Even though agricultural harvests showed some improvement, India's population continued to grow at a rate of more than 2 percent a year, well above plan estimates.[14] There were also wars with China and Pakistan. Industrial construction proceeded at a lower rate than called for in the plan. The Fourth Five-Year Plan and the annual plans stressed agriculture because India had experienced a broad-scale famine for the first time in twenty years. Emphasis was placed on the output of such industrial products as fertilizer and equipment meant for agricultural use. Efforts were to be intensified to complete factories in the process of construction and to improve export potential.

The objective of the four five-year plans was to convert a poor, primarily agricultural and traditional economy to a richer, dynamic, industrial and modern nation—and to do so in a generation or two. Growth was to expand employment, reduce the unevenness in the distribution of income and wealth, and provide more equality of opportunity. Public investment was supposed to increase total investment, which would increase growth and employment. Public enterprises would replace some private enterprises and would replace profit with social gains. Changes in people's activities and in their motivation and attitudes were assumed to be logical derivatives of planning programs, but as in the Soviet Union, it didn't work out that way.[15]

In 1967 the government decided to end the fourth plan because India's development record did not match what had been expected in the plans even though much outside assistance had been received. The United States had provided development loans and grants to the extent of $6.5 billion over the period 1951–1969, most of which was in agricultural commodities. The World Bank was also a major participant in providing loans to India during the four plans, providing loans to the extent of $2 billion. The Soviet Union also was associated with the Indian growth effort, providing loans and technical assistance. Altogether, some $13 billion was poured into India during the period 1951–1967, but the end result was average growth rates well below expectations.[16] India's food deficit also exceeded

13. Wilfred Malenbaum, *Modern India's Economy* (Columbus, Ohio: Charles E. Merrill, 1971), 91–102.
14. The projected growth was 1.3 percent a year.
15. Malenbaum, 62–63.
16. Ibid., 57.

expectations, and its dependence on foreign assistance, particularly the provision of food grains, had increased.

Nationalization of Industry

A major wave of nationalization occurred in India after India's national elections of 1971. Jawaharlal Nehru, leader of the Congress Party of India, envisioned the creation of a socialist economy, which he held to be compatible with a democratic society.[17] He rejected capitalism along with its underlying principles of private property, private profit, and income inequality. He recognized that class conflict was inherent in society, but he did not agree with the Marxist view that violence should be used to achieve the overthrow of capitalism. Instead, he wanted to achieve a transition through democratic means to a mixed economy where economic planning would allocate resources. As Nehru and the Congress Party became the dominant political leader and party in India, nationalization of industry became the instrument of state control over the Indian economy.

The government had nationalized life insurance companies in 1956 and the major commercial banks in 1969, with the stated objective of creating a socialist society.[18] In 1971 the government nationalized general insurance companies, but more important was the nationalization of the coal industry. In October 1971, some two hundred coal mines and coking ovens were taken over by the state; in May 1972, the coal mines were nationalized. The rationale for nationalization of the coal industry was to integrate its output to the production of iron and steel, which was also put under state control, as was copper. The cotton textile industry, India's oldest and largest industry, contributing some one-fifth of the country's national income, was also nationalized. The industry had experienced serious financial problems during the 1960s, and many factories had closed by the end of the decade. In agriculture, the wholesale wheat trade was nationalized with the objective of socializing the distribution of grain.

The Government Dominance in Industry. By 1975 the Indian government was dominant in key sectors of the economy. As Table 14-3 indicates, it had a 95 percent or larger share in many industries. In terms of employment in 1977, 70 percent of all Indian workers were employed in the public sector, while 30 percent were employed in the private sector. In only three areas—agriculture, manufacturing, and wholesale/retail trade—did private employment exceed public employment. Public employment in the coal industry amounted to 97 percent of its labor force; it was 100 percent in insurance, 75 percent in banking, 90 percent in construction, and 95 percent in the public utilities. In terms of gross domestic capital formation during the 1970s, the public sector share ranged from a high of 52 per-

17. Nehru had studied in England and observed the class divisiveness that existed in the country. He was influenced by the teachings of Beatrice and Sidney Webb, leaders of the Fabian Socialist movement. They advocated a democratic approach to socialism.

18. Baldev Raj Nayar, *India's Mixed Economy* (Bombay, India: Popular Prakashan, 1989), 297.

TABLE 14-3
Industries in Which the Indian Government Accounted for 95 Percent or More of Production

Manufacturing
Paper
Chemicals and chemical products
Drugs and pharmaceuticals
Petroleum products
Electrical equipment and machinery
Basic and nonferrous metals
Transportation equipment
Fertilizers
Minerals
Fuels
Metallic minerals
Nonmetallic minerals
Other Areas
Banking and insurance
Transportation and communications
Commercial energy

Source: Baldev Raj Nayar, *India's Mixed Economy* (Bombay, India: Popular Prakashan, 1989), 378.

cent in 1976 to a low of 41 percent in 1970. However, the bulk of gross domestic savings for the private sector averaged 80 percent of total saving for the period 1950–1980.

The major wave of nationalization took place during the period 1969–1973. It had a generally deleterious effect on the economy.[19] Inflation and food shortages caused industrial unrest. Business was alienated by nationalization and restrictions placed on the private sector. The rich and middle-class peasants turned against the government because it had nationalized the wheat trade. Strikes occurred in the public sector and were put down by the police and the Indian army. A state of emergency was declared by Prime Minister Indira Gandhi in June 1975.[20] Making an effort to appeal to every disaffected group in India, she stated that the government had no intent of continuing its nationalization policies. Nevertheless, the government nationalized the oil industry by acquiring Esso and Shell, thus gaining control over 95 percent of the industry in India.[21]

India in the 1980s

The process of nationalization was finished by 1975. State control over key sectors of the Indian economy, particularly heavy industry and banking and insurance,

19. Ibid., 330–331.
20. Indira Gandhi was the daughter of Prime Minister Nehru.
21. The government also ran Coca-Cola out of India because it refused to give the government its formula.

had been established. Prime Minister Gandhi and her Congress Party were voted out of office in 1976, but the reason was political, not economic. When she returned to power in 1980, her ideological approach had changed. The country experienced a balance of payments crisis that demonstrated that it could not finance its energy needs without increasing its exports.[22] Foreign trade been largely ignored during the process of economic development, and foreign investment in India was made unwelcome. Its production apparatus had been denied technological modernization through a restrictive policy on the import of technology. Thus, it had to provide a more outward bias to its largely inward-based economy.

Nevertheless, no real change in the structure of the Indian economy occurred. In terms of investment, the public sector was favored over the private sector. Moreover, the economic infrastructure, which was a monopoly of the public sector, had reached a state of crisis. The Sixth Five-Year Plan (1980–1985) placed emphasis on the development of energy, improvement of transportation facilities, and irrigation and flood control. What change did occur was a relaxation on investment by the private sector in certain areas of industry. Although still under bureaucratic control and monitoring, the private sector was allowed to increase its investments in core industries, such as chemicals, drugs, ceramics, and cement. The government also opened to the private sector areas of industrial activity, such as oil exploration and power development, that were previously closed to it.[23]

After Mrs. Gandhi's assassination in 1984, her son, succeeding her as prime minister,[24] continued the policies implemented by his mother and the Congress Party in the early 1980s. These involved a relaxation of controls placed on private enterprise in the area of investment and the setting of performance-based standards. However, not much changed and government control over the economy continued. At the same time there was a pronounced shift in Chinese economic strategy that began in 1978 and continued during the 1980s. This strategy involved a greater reliance on market-driven forces, with more freedom for private enterprise to function. Moreover, India had fallen out of favor with the West, but particularly with the United States, while China gained in favor and attracted the foreign investments that India needed for its economic development.

22. OPEC increased the price of oil, and oil imports as a percentage of export exchange earnings increased from 30 percent in 1978 to 90 percent by 1980.

23. It is necessary to point out that state-owned banks owned equity shares in the major private firms. For example, banks owned 40 percent of the largest private firm in India and 42.5 percent of the common stock of the second-largest firm. In some firms bank ownership was more than 50 percent.

24. This means that since independence in 1947 India was ruled for most of the time by a family dynasty beginning with Nehru, continuing with his daughter, and then continuing with her son, who might still be prime minister of India today had he not been assassinated while campaigning for reelection.

An Evaluation of the Indian Economy

It has been said that the reason the Indian hybrid system of capitalism and socialism failed was that it combined the worst of both systems, failing to deliver either economic growth or social welfare. It constrained the growth of the private sector by allowing it to expand only with government permission. Government control was omnipresent. Foreign trade was controlled by import quotas and high tariffs, access to foreign exchange was limited, controls were placed on land use and on trade in farm products, and heavy industry was owned by the public sector. The Indian bureaucracy increased in size and power and became more corrupt. During the 1980s the government began to push for higher economic growth by increasing its borrowing from abroad. The end result was little gain in the growth rate but an increase in the foreign debt to double what it was in 1980.[25]

India's economic plans failed to promote high rates of economic growth and an increase in per capita income. A goal was to double per capita income beginning with the start of the First Five-Year Plan in 1950 and ending by 1975. To the contrary, increases in per capita income were small. Meanwhile, Taiwan and South Korea had passed India by 1960, and China by 1963. While Indian per capita income remained flat during the 1980s, the per capita incomes of Taiwan and South Korea tripled.[26] India did poorly even when compared to other low-income South and East Asian countries. During the period 1965–1986 Indian per capita income increased at an average annual rate of 1.8 percent compared to 4.0 percent for Thailand, 4.6 percent for Indonesia, and 4.3 percent for Malaysia.[27] The average annual growth rate for China was 5.1 percent.

It has been argued that India has done far better than it did when it was a part of the British Empire.[28] This is true. Living standards have improved, and people live longer. But other countries that were colonies of England or other countries have done better. Examples are Malaysia, Thailand, and Indonesia. It is also argued that these countries succeeded because they were much smaller than India and could grow at higher rates. The counterargument is that China is larger than India and its growth rate was more than twice that of India's. Poverty was reduced in India to some extent, but in 1990, more than forty years after India became a country, 48 percent of the population lived in poverty and 52 percent of adults were illiterate.[29] In China the corresponding rates were 12 percent and 22 percent.

25. The World Bank, *World Development Report 1995* (New York: Oxford University Press, 1995), 200.

26. Jagdish Bhagwati, *India in Transition*, (Oxford: Clarendon Press, 1993), 23.

27. The World Bank, *World Development Report 1988* (New York: Oxford University Press, 1988), 222–223. The average annual growth rate in per capita income for all low-income countries was 3.1 percent.

28. Bhagwati, 24–25.

29. United Nations Development Programme, *Human Development Report 1992* (New York: Oxford University Press, 1992), 132–133.

Why, then, did India's economy not perform well between the period 1950–1990? Efficiency and growth were stultified for three main reasons:[30]

1. Industry and trade were controlled by an all-powerful state bureaucracy that regulated market entry and import competition. It penalized unauthorized expansion of capacity; it required licenses to perform many types of business activity; and it controlled most aspects of investment and production.
2. While other countries were expanding their foreign trade, Indian development policy was doing just the opposite. It did not use the exchange rate mechanism to promote exports, and it protected home markets through the use of high tariffs and import quotas. Countries with a much smaller industrial base than India's exported far more manufactured goods and eventually passed India in the size of their manufacturing sectors. India's share of world exports fell from 2.1 percent in 1950 to 0.4 percent in 1980.
3. A large public sector reduced overall efficiency and productivity. The central government controlled 244 enterprises, most of them overstaffed for political reasons. Few budget constraints, and few incentives to make these enterprises profitable, contributed to a fiscal and foreign exchange crisis in the 1980s that forced India into near bankruptcy and required loan assistance from the IMF.

Since 1951 India's industrial development has been, and still is, promoted within a planning framework. While government-controlled monopolies were responsible for supplying inputs to the infrastructure and heavy industry, the activities of the private sector were controlled by the government through the use of industrial and import licensing. In accordance with national priorities as set forth in the economic plan, the government issued industrial licenses for installing equipment in different production units. The import licensing system was used as a mechanism to control the allocation of foreign exchange to different sectors of the economy. The importer had to present to the relevant government authority an industrial license for the good produced and, based on the category of the good to be imported, was issued an import license.

Operating within a highly regulated economic environment the Indian private sector often obtained its supply of essential inputs from the public sector, either directly from state-owned enterprises or indirectly, as in the case of imported inputs from foreign trade organizations. For reasons that are now well established, the supply of these inputs was not fully responsive to demand conditions. Administered pricing and lack of economic incentives to managers and workers hindered the appropriate responses of state-owned enterprises to market signals. In addition, restrictive trade policies in the guise of protecting infant industries and economizing on foreign exchange involved the imposition of quantitative restrictions on imported inputs. Shortages in government-regulated inputs occurred at the same time that high rates of capacity underutilization in manufacturing industries occurred.

30. Bhagwati, 46–67.

Table 14-4 presents a comparison of the capacity utilization rates in U.S. and Indian manufacturing industries for the period 1972–1985, with 100 percent used as the base for full capacity. As the table indicates, the average for India was 20 percent lower than for the United States. Supply limitations rather than demand limitations were the main reason for capacity underutilization in India.

INDIAN REFORMS IN THE 1990s

The world changed dramatically in the early 1990s, leaving India more of a backwater country. Several major developments occurred, the most important of which was the collapse of Communism. The Soviet Union, which had maintained close economic and political ties with India, was no more. A number of new countries, including Russia, were created out of it and wanted foreign aid from various international lending institutions to implement their conversion to market economies. Many claimants were in line for limited loanable funds. A second development was the collapse of India's international credit rating. Borrowing from private or public lending sources was impossible without an effort to reform the Indian economy. A third development was a decline in the inflow of income from Indian guest workers in the Middle East oil fields, which was caused by the crisis in Kuwait.[31]

Economic Reforms

Emergency reforms were introduced in October 1990 in an attempt to resolve the financial crisis. Increased taxes were placed on petroleum products, corporations, and imports to reduce the deficit in the Indian government budget, which amounted to 8.4 percent of Indian GDP. The rupee was devalued to make imports more expensive, and restraints were placed on commercial credit for imports. By early 1991, however, with only two weeks' worth of foreign exchange left, the government had to go to the IMF for a loan, which became contingent on further economic reforms. Prime Minister Narasimha Rao, who took office in June 1991 after the collapse of the previous government, initiated a number of economic reforms.[32] Export subsidies were reduced, much of the industrial licensing system was dismantled, and areas once closed to private industry were opened up. Foreign investment, which had been unwelcome in India, was pursued through the use of various tax breaks.[33]

Other reforms included the devaluation of the rupee by 24 percent in 1991. The maximum tariff rate was reduced from 400 percent to 65 percent, and raw materials and capital goods can now be freely imported. Most exchange controls have been lifted, and the rupee is convertible within limits. The highest rate of the per-

31. Remittances from Indian workers abroad are a major source of income to India, just as remittances of Mexican workers in the United States would be a major source of income to Mexico.
32. Some piecemeal reforms were introduced in the 1980s but had accomplished little.
33. Nevertheless, foreign investment is limited to priority areas and requires government approval.

TABLE 14-4
Capacity Utilization Rates in U.S. and Indian Manufacturing Industries, 1972–1985 (percent)

Year	*United States*	*India*	*Difference*
1972	82.8	63.4	–19.4
1973	87.0	61.4	–25.6
1974	82.6	57.6	–25.0
1975	72.3	58.5	–13.8
1976	77.4	58.0	–19.4
1977	81.4	56.9	–24.5
1978	84.2	60.1	–24.1
1979	84.6	60.3	–24.3
1980	79.3	58.6	–20.7
1981	78.2	60.4	–17.8
1982	70.3	59.4	–10.9
1983	73.9	58.4	–15.5
1984	80.5	60.2	–20.3
1985	80.1	61.3	–18.8
Average	79.6	59.6	–20.0

Source: Ratna Sahay, *Input Shortages in Mixed Economies: An Application to Indian Manufacturing Industries* (Washington, D.C.: International Monetary Fund, 1991), 12.

sonal income tax was reduced from 56 percent to 40 percent and of the corporate income tax from 57.5 percent to 46 percent. Reforms were also made in the area of public enterprises, which have dominated the Indian economy. In particular, the scope of the public sector is to be reduced. However, there has been no great willingness on the part of the government to privatize the public sector, even though it is inefficient. It is allowing the purchase of shares in some of the more profitable public enterprises. Short of privatization, the government plans to reduce the scope of the public sector to eight rather than eighteen areas.[34]

Prior to 1991 foreign firms were allowed to enter the Indian market only if they possessed technology unavailable in India. Almost every aspect of production and marketing was tightly controlled, and many foreign companies in India abandoned their investments. The reforms changed the laws on foreign investment. The new laws approve foreign equity investment of up to 51 percent so long as they are made in one of thirty-four government-designated priority areas that account for the bulk of industrial production. However, foreign equity investment in excess of 51 percent must be negotiated with the government.[35] Export earnings for foreign corporations are exempt from the Indian corporate income tax, and there are no restrictions on dividend remittances on authorized foreign investment. Foreign brokerage firms are also permitted to function in India.

34. U.S. Department of Commerce, *Country Commercial Guide: India* (Springfield, Va.: National Technical Information Service, 1995), 44.
35. Ibid., 63.

The Indian reforms have been in effect for too short a period to judge whether or not they have been successful. No major privatization of government-owned industries has occurred. For example, the major government-owned airline, Air India, remains a monopoly; private airlines are only permitted to fly routes not served by Air India. On the other hand, the private sector has broken the public postal monopoly in high-value areas. The reforms have opened up new business opportunities helped by an increased flow of funds into the Indian stock market. The opening of the economy to both domestic and foreign competition has required old Indian business firms, once favored by the government, to compete in order to survive. Probably more important is that increased business opportunities may curtail the outflow of India's best-trained businesspeople, engineers, and scientists.

As Table 14-5 indicates, India has a long way to go before it can achieve higher living standards for its people. It is a country in the low state of human development, ranking 134 out of 174 countries in 1993, behind such countries as Pakistan, Kenya, and Lesotho, which are not exactly role models for economic development. China, by comparison, ranked 111, which put it in the medium development category. As Table 14-6 indicates, India's poverty and illiteracy rates are high, and it has few of the amenities that many countries, including some of the poorer ones in Latin America, enjoy. Even those persons who might be con-

TABLE 14-5
Human Development Index for India, 1992

Ranking among 174 countries	134
People without access to sanitation (millions)	646
Illiterate males (millions)	102
Illiterate females (millions)	169
Malnourished children under five (millions)	69
Life expectancy at birth, males (years)*	60
Life expectancy at birth, females (years)*	60
Infant mortality rate per 1,000 births*	74
Mean years of schooling, males	3.5
Mean years of schooling, females	1.2
Telephones per 1,000	2
Women in labor force (percent)	29
Percentage of labor force in agriculture	62
Percentage of GNP received by highest 20 percent of population	41.3
Percentage of GNP received by lowest 20 percent of population	8.8
Ratio of highest to lowest	4.7

**Data are for 1995.*

Sources: United Nations Development Programme, *Human Development Report, 1995* (New York: Oxford University Press, 1995), 129–175; The World Bank, *World Development Report 1995* (Washington, D.C.: The World Bank, 1995), 220; Carl Haub and Machiko Yanagishita, *World Population Data Sheet 1995* (Washington, D.C.: World Population Reference Bureau,

TABLE 14-6 *Human Development Index for India and Other Asian Countries, 1993*

	Life Expectancy at Birth (years)	*Adult Literacy Rate (percent)*	*Human Development Index (rank out of 174 countries)*
High Human Development	72.9	95.8	
Japan	79.5	99.0	3
South Korea	71.1	97.4	31
Singapore	74.8	89.8	35
Thailand	69.0	93.5	58
Malaysia	70.8	81.5	59
Medium Human Development	66.8	79.3	
Philippines	66.3	94.0	100
Indonesia	62.7	82.5	103
China	68.5	79.3	111
Low Human Development	55.8	48.3	
Pakistan	61.5	35.7	128
India	60.4	49.9	134
Bangladesh	55.6	36.4	146
Afghanistan	43.5	28.9	170

Source: United Nations Development Programme, *Human Development Report 1995* (New York: Oxford University Press, 1995), 155–157.

sidered well off by Indian standards would be considered poor by most standards. One study indicates that only 2.3 percent of the population has a household income of more than $2,484 a year.[36]

Moreover, there is a certain amount of antagonism toward Western investment in India that is probably a carryover from the British dominance of the country. A chauvinistic pride manifested itself in September 1995, when Indians demonstrated against the presence of such American firms as PepsiCo, Coca-Cola, and McDonald's, wanting them to leave the country.[37] Admittedly, the three companies produce and sell products that don't add much to the value of output of the Indian economy, but they do provide capital and create employment. But more important, such demonstrations may send the wrong signal to Western investors at a time when India needs more foreign investments.

Population

In 1900 the population of India was 235.5 million. By 1950 it had increased to 356.9 million, and by the end of this century, it will have increased to one billion.

36. "A Survey of India," *The Economist*, January 21–27, 1995, 1.

37. Just to prove there was nothing personal, the demonstrators also wanted to kick out Wimpy's, the British hamburger chain. Coca-Cola has already been kicked out once.

It increased by 120 million during the first half of this century; it increased by that much during the 1980s alone. The rate of population growth in India for the first half of the century was less than one-half of 1 percent a year; in one decade it was negative.[38] However, the rate of population increase in India during the 1980s averaged 2.1 percent a year, an increase that can be attributed mostly to lower death rates. In 1900 life expectancy at birth in India was 22.6 years; by 1950 it had increased to 32.5 years. By 1995 life expectancy in India had almost doubled, to 60 years. Although birthrates have declined, they have not declined nearly as much as death rates.

Population growth has had a deleterious effect on the economic development of India in several ways. First, it means that a large amount of new capital equipment is needed each year to provide for the addition to the population. Second, the population increase puts a new strain on the Indian infrastructure because more money has to be spent each year on building new schools to cope with the growing number of children. Third, the amount of saving necessary for capital formation is lower in India than it is in China and other East Asian countries. Fourth, with the growth in population the amount of natural resources, particularly land, is beginning to decrease. This is in a country where agricultural output accounted for 30 percent of Indian GNP in 1993.

Poverty and Illiteracy

In 1993, India accounted for one out of every four persons in poverty in the world—350 million people, or almost 40 percent of the Indian population, lived in absolute poverty, 280 million in rural areas.[39] Approximately half of the Indian population is illiterate, and more than half of these are women. The greatest concentration of poverty is in such states as Behar, West Bengal, Uttar Pradesh, and Maharashtra, which have 40 percent of India's population and a per capita GDP of less than $200 a year. A factor contributing to poverty is that almost two-thirds of the Indian labor force is employed in agriculture.[40] As India's farmworkers move to the cities, they contribute to an increase in urban poverty and place an ever-increasing strain on the infrastructure in such major cities as Bombay, Calcutta, and New Delhi, which have become among the largest cities in the world. Coupled with poverty is the high rate of malnutrition that exists among Indian children.

Bureaucracy

For all practical purposes, it is the Indian bureaucracy that has run the country. It is the bureaucrats who have set the prices for many goods and services, regulated

38. Robert E. Ward and Roy C. Macridis, *Modern Political Systems: Asia* (Englewood Cliffs, N.J.: Prentice-Hall, 1963), 247.
39. United Nations Development Programme, *Human Development Report 1995* (New York: Oxford University Press, 1995), 135.
40. Ibid., 177.

market entry and the expansion of industry, and substituted their wishes for the individual choices of consumers and manufacturers. The move on the part of the government to reduce its role in the economy is a threat to their power. Like bureaucrats in the former Soviet Union, or in any society, they will resist any change that would affect their prerogatives. Government jobs are often given to friends and relatives of politicians, and the end result is inefficiency. An example is state electricity boards, which set the cost of most of the electricity provided in India. One electricity board has 80,000 employees to provide the same amount of power that a U.S. utility could provide with 500 workers.[41]

Corruption

Corruption is endemic in India. It involves both politicians and bureaucrats who have exploited the state control system, and it has a corrosive impact on the moral ethos of the country. Business firms bribe bureaucrats in order to get export subsidies or import licenses, and politicians take bribes for doing favors. Electoral roles are rigged in favor of certain political parties, which helps to explain why the Congress Party has remained in office for forty-three out of the forty-eight years since India became independent. In both national and state elections violence has become common.[42] To some extent it is a result of gang warfare, and to some extent it is the result of the divisiveness that exists in Indian society. Indians are divided on the basis of caste and on regional and religious grounds.

State Control over the Economy

Despite the economic reforms of the 1990s that were supposed to reduce the extent of government intervention in the Indian economy, the change is far from complete. Despite moves to reduce tariffs and quantitative restrictions on imports, India still has a ban on the importation of most consumer goods. Although import licensing has been liberalized, the system is still in place. Many imports have to be channeled through state-owned enterprises. Nearly all apparel, fabrics, and yarn are banned to protect India's textile industry. Government procurement practices are designed to favor local manufacturers and to discriminate against foreign manufacturers. Despite efforts made to attract foreign investment, there is a lack of intellectual property protection, particularly in the area of patents and trademarks.[43] All insurance companies and most banks are state-owned. Foreign investment, where allowed, has to conform to planning goals.

41. *A Survey of India,* 20.

42. There is some parallel to the national election in Mexico in 1994, where a presidential candidate was assassinated.

43. This has been a major bone of contention between the United States and India, and also China.

PERFORMANCE OF THE INDIAN ECONOMY

A point made earlier in this chapter is that much was expected from India after it became independent in 1947. Its economic development drew financial support from various international lending institutions throughout the 1950s and continuing to the middle of the 1960s. China, on the other hand, received very little financial support except from the Soviet Union. As China moved away from the Soviet Union, India moved closer to it. Spurred by President Nixon's visit to China in 1972, U.S.-Chinese relations began to move into high gear while U.S. relations with India were turning sour. While China was moving toward market reforms, India was moving away from reliance on the market by nationalizing industries. Chinese economic growth was spectacular, while Indian economic growth was lackluster. Over a thirty-year period, life expectancy in China increased by 26 years; in India it was 11 years.[44]

Moreover, during the period 1960–1988 the growth rate in per capita GDP was flat, which had a deleterious impact on the reduction of poverty in India. Low growth rates impinge upon the provision of social assistance necessary to ameliorate poverty. The low growth rate has also impaired the development of the Indian infrastructure. An example is the lack of an adequate transportation system, an absolute necessity for economic development. Another factor working against economic development is that primary education in India is not mandatory; the national government leaves it to the states to decide whether it is important for children to attend school. Some do not. In rural India a quarter of the boys and half of the girls have never been to school.[45] Educational inequalities reflect social inequalities exacerbated by a caste system that serves to promote income inequality.[46]

Table 14-7 presents measurements of the performance of the Indian economy for the period 1991–1995. In some respects the Indian economy has shown improvement; in other respects it has not. Foreign direct investment increased from $155 million for the period 1991/92 to $1 billion for the period 1994/95, and during the same period foreign exchange reserves increased from $5.7 billion to $18.0 billion. The inflation rate is down, and there has been an increase in real per capita GDP. However, the unemployment rate has remained steady at around 22 percent of the Indian labor force, and the population continues to increase at an average

44. The World Bank, *The East Asian Miracle* (New York: Oxford University Press, 1993), 33. In 1960 the life expectancy at birth in China was 43 years, in 1990 it was 69 years; in India, life expectancy in 1960 was 47 years, in 1990 it was 58 years.
45. United Nations Development Programme, *Human Development Report 1995*, 53.
46. Hinduism is the dominant religion in India, and the caste system is part of it. It is a fourfold order. At the top are the Brahmins (priests) followed by warriors, merchants, and workers. Then there are the outcastes. The recognition of caste implies a belief in karma (fate). Karma is based on the principle of transmigration of the soul. Status acquired upon rebirth is awarded on the basis of good and evil acts of the previous existence, weighed on the scales of moral merit.

TABLE 14-7 *Performance of the Indian Economy*

	1991/92	*1992/93*	*1993/94*	*1994/95*
Domestic Economy				
Population (millions)	857	872	890	908
Population growth (percent)	2.0	1.9	2.0	2.0
GDP ($billions)	251.1	244.1	252.4	285.5
GDP per capita (dollars)	293.4	279.9	283.6	314.4
Real GDP (percent change)	1.0	4.6	3.8	5.0
Consumer price index (percent change)	13.5	9.6	8.0	11.0
Production and Employment				
Unemployment (percent)	22.0	22.0	22.5	22.5
Agricultural production (percent change)	–1.9	3.9	1.0	3.0
Industrial production (percent change)	0.0	1.8	2.5	6.0
Balance of Payments				
Exports ($billions)	18.2	18.8	22.7	26.0
Imports ($billions)	20.3	22.9	24.1	27.5
Trade balance ($billions)	–2.1	–4.1	–1.4	–1.5
Current account balance ($billions)	–2.5	–5.3	–2.2	–1.7
Foreign direct investment ($millions)	155.0	261.0	600.0	1,000.0
Foreign debt ($billions) as a percentage of GDP	74.5	79.2	80.0	81.0
Foreign exchange reserves ($billions)	5.7	6.7	15.5	18.0

Note: Figures are for fiscal years. The Indian fiscal year is April 1 to March 31.

Source: U.S. Department of Commerce, *Country Commercial Guide, India* (Springfield, Va.: National Technical Information Service, 1995), 79–80.

annual rate of 2 percent. In two of the four years, agricultural production was less than the increase in the rate of population, and 70 percent of the population lives on farms.

SUMMARY

India was a part of the British Empire for two hundred years. It achieved its independence in 1947 and adopted a state-directed approach to developing the economy. Although a private sector existed, it was allowed to expand only with the permission of the government. Heavy industry became a part of the public sector. Quotas and high protective tariffs were used to protect home industries. Access to foreign exchange was limited because there was no reliance on an export-driven growth strategy. There were controls on land use and on trade in farm products. Resource allocation was determined by the government through the use of five-year plans and annual plans that established output priorities for the country. The performance of the Indian economy was at best average, but certainly not as good as that of many other Asian countries. In the 1980s India tried to increase its growth rate by borrowing from foreign sources, but the end result was a near bankruptcy of the economy.

A number of economic reforms have been made in the 1990s. More of the Indian economy has been opened up to the private sector, tax rates have been lowered, and the system of industrial and import licensing has largely been abandoned. Restrictions against foreign investments in India have been relaxed. Nevertheless, there is still considerable state intervention in the economy. Reliance is still placed on economic planning, and there has been almost no privatization of state-owned industries. In some respects the Indian economy has shown improvement since the economic reforms have been implemented; in other respects it has not. In terms of economic and social development, India has not performed as well as China. Its economic growth rate is lower and its standard of living as measured by such standards as longevity, literacy, malnutrition, and poverty is also lower.

QUESTIONS FOR DISCUSSION

1. What legacy did British rule leave India?
2. Compare Indian economic planning to Chinese economic planning.
3. It can be said that the Indian government after independence pursued an inward-oriented strategy of economic development instead of an outward-oriented strategy. Discuss.
4. What were some of the reasons for the generally poor performance of the Indian economy during the period 1950–1990?
5. How was Indian economic development similar to that of the Soviet Union?
6. What were some of the factors that contributed to a virtual collapse of the Indian economy in 1990?
7. Which country, India or China, has done a better job of economic and social development in the past forty years? Why did one develop faster than the other?
8. Discuss the economic and social problems that continue to retard economic development in India.

RECOMMENDED READINGS

"A Survey of India." *The Economist,* January 21–27, 1995, 1–24.

Bhagwati, Jagdish. *India in Transition.* Oxford: Clarendon Press, 1993.

Eshvaran, Mukesh, and Ashok Kotwal. *Why Poverty Continues to Exist in India.* New York: Oxford University Press, 1993.

———. *India: Background Papers.* IMF Staff Country Report No. 95/87. Washington, D.C.: IMF, September 1995.

International Monetary Fund. *India: Recent Economic Developments.* IMF Staff Country Report No. 95/86. Washington, D.C.: IMF, September 1995.

Jalan, Bimal. *India's Economic Crisis: The Way Ahead.* New York: Oxford University Press, 1995.

Joshi, Vijay, and Ian M. D. Little. *India: Macroeconomic and Political Economy 1964–1991*. Washington, D.C.: The World Bank, 1991.

Lewis, John P. *India's Political Economy: Governance and Reform*. New York: Oxford University Press, 1995.

Nayar, Baldev Raj. *India's Mixed Economy*. Bombay, India: Popular Prakashan, 1989.

Parker, Karen, and Steffen Kastner. *A Framework for Assessing Fiscal Sustainability and External Viability, with an Application to India*. Washington, D.C.: International Monetary Fund, October 1993.

Sahay, Ratna. *Input Shortages in Mixed Economies: An Application to Indian Manufacturing Industries*. IMF Working Paper. Washington, D.C.: International Monetary Fund, June 1991.

World Bank. *India: Recent Economic Developments Prospects*. Washington, D.C.: The World Bank, 1995.

UNITED STATES
Nogales
Gulf of Mexico
MEXICO
North
Pacific
Ocean
Mexico City
Acapulco
BELIZE
GUATEMALA
HONDURAS
EL
SALVADOR
Mexico
National Capital
Leon
City
International Boundary
0
Miles
300

MEXICO

CHAPTER 15
Mexico

Mexico is one of twenty-six Latin American countries occupying half of the land area of North and South America.[1] Most of them have a number of economic, political, and social characteristics in common. First, with the exception of Brazil,[2] all are former colonies of Spain and achieved their independence from her.[3] Second, with the exception of Brazil, Spanish is the common language. Third, Catholicism is the common religion of all of these countries. Fourth, political instability has been characteristic of Latin America, with military dictators in power through much of this century. Democratic governments, for the most part, have been unstable. Fifth, the economic development of the Latin American countries has

1. The Caribbean countries are included in this number, although some do not have a common heritage with Latin America.
2. Brazil was a colony of Portugal and Portuguese is its language.
3. Their independence from Spain was accomplished by revolutions similar to the American Revolution.

been very uneven during this century, and they have lagged well behind the East Asian countries in their rate of economic growth. Finally, the countries have followed the wave of privatization that has occurred throughout the world, and they are privatizing their own state-owned industries.

Mexico is of major importance to the United States for several reasons. First, for better or for worse, usually the latter, its history has been inextricably linked to that of the United States. Much of the United States was formerly a part of Mexico, and was taken from Mexico after the U.S.-Mexican War of 1847.[4] The Latin culture, including the language, is an import from Mexico. Second, Mexico is one of the United States' most important trading partners. In 1995 U.S.-Mexican trade amounted to $118 billion, an amount exceeded only by U.S. trade with Canada and Japan. The signing of the North American Free Trade Agreement (NAFTA) will increase U.S. trade with Mexico, and from Mexico to the rest of Latin America.[5] Finally, U.S. direct and portfolio investment in Mexico has increased since the signing of NAFTA. However, it has introduced an element of vulnerability into the economies of both countries, as witnessed by the Mexican financial crisis in December 1994.

THE ECONOMY OF LATIN AMERICA

The decade of the 1980s was a time period that the Latin American countries would like to forget. The economic gains made during the 1960s were largely canceled out by the poor performance of the Latin American countries during the 1980s. Inflation was rampant in many of the countries. In Argentina, for example, inflation was running at a rate of 1,000 percent a year or better, the economy collapsed, and a new currency unit was introduced. During the good times of the 1970s when world prices were high for such products as coffee and petroleum, Mexico, Brazil, and other Latin American countries borrowed heavily in the world capital markets, pledging future revenue from coffee and petroleum for debt repayment. However, world market prices for these and other products plummeted during the 1980s, leaving the Latin American countries with a debt they could not repay. The rate of economic growth for most of the Latin American countries was negative during the 1980s, and unemployment and social unrest increased.

Table 15-1 presents per capita GDP and real per capita growth rates in GDP for the major Latin American countries for the past twenty-five years. As the table indicates, most of the Latin American countries had a higher real per capita GDP in 1980 than they did at the end of the decade.

4. The Treaty of Guadalupe-Hidalgo gave New Mexico, Arizona, and California to the United States.

5. Chile is supposed to become a member, and by the year 2020 all of the Latin American countries will become members.

Inflation

In addition to stagnant economic growth, inflation was a problem during the 1980s for the Latin American economies. Argentina, once the dominant economic power in Latin America, is a case in point. It experienced a high inflation rate. The political pendulum swung between government conservatives and reformers, with the result that much of the national wealth was exported abroad. Political instability was exacerbated by Argentina's loss of the Falkland Islands war with Great Britain. However, as Table 15-2 indicates, the inflation was not limited to Argentina; it was even worse in Brazil and Peru.

TABLE 15-1 *Gross Domestic Product per Capita, 1994*

	GDP per Capita (1994 dollars)	*Average Annual Real Growth Rates (percent)*		
		1970–1980	*1980–1990*	*1990–1994*
Argentina	6,081	0.9	–2.2	6.4
Boliva	934	0.0	2.2	1.7
Brazil	2,596	6.9	–0.6	0.6
Chile	2,870	1.0	1.4	5.5
Colombia	1,545	3.2	1.7	2.2
Mexico	3,041	3.6	–0.6	0.6
Peru	1,885	0.9	–3.4	3.1
Venezuela	2,923	0.1	–1.4	0.8
Latin America	2,619	3.4	–1.2	1.8

Source: Inter-American Development Bank, *Economic and Social Progress in Latin America* (Baltimore: Johns Hopkins University Press, 1995), 263.

TABLE 15-2 *Changes in the Consumer Price Index for Selected Latin American Countries (percent)*

Country	*1988*	*1989*	*1990*	*1991*	*1992*	*1993*	*1994*
Argentina	343.0	3,079.8	2,314.0	171.7	24.9	10.6	3.9
Bolivia	16.0	15.2	17.1	21.4	12.1	8.5	8.3
Brazil	682.3	1,287.0	2,937.8	440.9	1,009.7	2,148.4	2.668.7
Colombia	28.1	25.8	29.1	30.4	27.0	22.6	23.8
Mexico	114.2	20.0	26.7	22.7	15.5	9.7	7.0
Peru	667.0	3,398.7	7,481.7	409.5	73.5	48.6	13.7
Uruguay	62.2	80.5	112.5	102.0	68.4	54.1	44.7
Venezuela	29.5	84.2	40.8	34.2	31.4	38.1	60.8

Source: Inter-American Development Bank, *Economic and Social Progress in Latin America* (Baltimore: Johns Hopkins University Press, 1995), 308.

Foreign Trade

Latin American trade is similar to African foreign trade in that the bulk of exports consists of fuels, minerals, and agricultural products and the bulk of imports consists of manufactured products. Both Mexico and Venezuela derive over half of their export income from petroleum, while for Colombia, the leading export is coffee. When oil and coffee prices are high in world markets, the terms of trade are favorable for many of the Latin American countries. However, as Table 15-3 indicates, that was not the case during the 1980s. As the world price of oil declined, the terms of trade for Mexico and Venezuela fell drastically to a point where they were around half of what they were in 1980.

Population

Although the birthrates of most of the Latin American countries have declined dramatically over the past twenty years, birthrates still are high and create major problems. First, the rate of economic growth has to continue to expand in order to provide more jobs for an ever-increasing labor force. Second, the infrastructure of the major Latin American cities is not adequate to support urban migration. In most large cities, the water supply and educational and health facilities are becoming more inadequate as urbanization continues. Urbanization also places a burden on both national and municipal governments' social welfare expenditures. In Mexico, for example, over 65 percent of municipal government revenues comes from transfers from the budget of the Mexican government. Third, an ever-increasing population compounds the problem of unemployment and underemployment in both urban and rural areas.

Table 15-4 presents the birthrates and death rates and population-doubling time for selected Latin American countries. The data are for 1995.

Foreign Debt

Foreign debt became the number-one problem for most of the Latin American countries during the 1980s and threatened their economic and political stability.

TABLE 15-3 *Terms of Trade for Selected Years for Major Latin American Countries (percent)*

Country	*1980*	*1985*	*1988*	*1991*	*1993*	*1994*
Argentina	100	81	67	60	63	63
Brazil	100	82	102	87	84	87
Chile	100	83	106	88	73	79
Colombia	100	90	107	84	71	81
Mexico	100	87	63	62	62	64
Venezuela	100	111	57	66	58	57

Source: Inter-American Development Bank, *Economic and Social Progress in Latin America 1995* (Baltimore: Johns Hopkins University Press, October 1995), 25, 57, 65, 77, 133, 183.

TABLE 15-4 *Birthrates and Death Rates and Population-Doubling Time for Selected Latin American Countries and the United States*

Country	*Population*	*Birthrate per 1,000*	*Death Rate per 1,000*	*Doubling Time in Years*
Brazil	157.8	25	8	41
Argentina	34.6	21	8	55
Colombia	37.7	24	6	39
Venezuela	21.8	30	5	27
Bolivia	7.4	36	10	27
Chile	14.3	22	6	41
Mexico	93.7	27	5	34
Peru	24.0	29	7	33
Guatemala	10.6	39	8	22
U.S.	263.2	15	9	105

Source: Carl Haub and Machiko Yanagishita, *1995 World Population Reference Sheet* (Washington, D.C.: Population Reference Bureau, May 1995).

The foundation of the problem was laid during the 1970s when Latin American governments, including those of Brazil and Mexico, buoyed by optimistic forecasts for the prices of their commodity exports, borrowed heavily from foreign banks, usually at floating interest rates.[6] The total Latin American debt to foreign banks increased from $115 billion in 1978 to $280 billion by 1984.[7] The optimistic forecasts on commodity prices proved wrong, and the burden of the foreign debt increased as exports declined. In August 1982 Mexico declared its inability to service its debt, and in November 1982 Brazil found itself in the same position. Costa Rica declared a moratorium on its debt payment.

By 1986, Brazil's foreign debt was one-third of its GNP and three times larger than its exports. In Mexico, foreign debt was larger than GNP. As export values fell in world trade, the Latin American countries had to reduce social welfare expenditures for the poor in order to meet interest payments on the foreign debt. However, interest arrears had increased from $100 million in 1980 to $8.1 billion in 1987 and $10.6 billion by 1989.[8] Meanwhile, social unrest increased in Latin America. Several international plans were developed to help the Latin American debt problems. The Baker Plan of 1985 involved the use of International Monetary Fund (IMF) loans to foster economic growth. IMF credit increased from $3.0 billion in 1982 to $18.2 billion in 1987. The countries had to make structural changes in their economies; Argentina, for example, changed its whole monetary system. In 1989 the Brady Plan was designed to ease the debt burden of the Latin

6. Floating interest rates are determined by supply and demand. Interest rates charged by U.S. and other foreign banks more than doubled from 1978 to 1983.
7. Inter-American Development Bank, *Economic and Social Progress in Latin America* (Baltimore: Johns Hopkins University Press, 1990), 16.
8. Inter-American Development Bank, *Economic and Social Progress*, 17.

American countries by direct debt reduction and stretching out the remainder over a longer period of time.[9]

Income Inequality

The thing is, there is no equality here. Everything is disproportional. The rich are very rich, and the poor are very poor. The poor stick to the poor, and the rich, well, they go to the Hilton. The day I go to the Hilton Hotel, I'll know there has been another revolution.[10]

This statement was made by one of the people quoted in Oscar Lewis's book *The Children of Sanchez,* written more than thirty years ago about a Mexican family. Little has changed in Mexico or the rest of Latin America since then. The rich live in a style that puts all but a few American billionaires to shame, while the majority of its population live in various degrees of poverty. Mexico and Brazil, the two largest and wealthiest countries in Latin America, have the most skewed distribution of income and wealth in Latin America. In Brazil, the top 20 percent of the population receive 32 times the income of the bottom 20 percent.[11] The *favelas* (slums) of Rio de Janeiro possess some of the worst poverty in the world. In Mexico, the top 10 percent of households received 39 percent of total household income, compared to 45 percent for the bottom 80 percent.[12] About 45 percent of Mexican families have an income that is less than half the national average. The Gini coefficients for Brazil and Mexico are around 0.6, which is far higher than the coefficients for the developed countries.[13]

Table 15-5 presents income distribution for selected Latin American countries. Comparisons can be made with Sweden, which is supposed to have the least income inequality of the industrialized Western countries.

Income Inequality and Economic Development. The point was made in Chapter 2 that income inequality has been a constraint on economic development in Latin America. There is no question that the Latin American countries have underperformed in comparison to other economic areas of the world, but particularly East Asia, where income is more evenly distributed. Argentina was the most important country in Latin America at the beginning of this century,[14] while the East Asian countries were British, Dutch, and Japanese colonies. This colonial status was not ended until World War II was over. In 1950 South Korea was completely destroyed by the Korean War, and Taiwan, which had been a colony of Japan, was

9. Inter-American Development Bank, *Economic and Social Progress,* 19.

10. Oscar Lewis, *The Children of Sanchez* (New York: Random House, 1961), 339–340.

11. The World Bank, *World Development Report 1995* (New York: Oxford University Press, 1993), 292–293.

12. Ibid., 221.

13. As mentioned previously, the Gini coefficient measures income inequality, with 0 being perfect equality and 1 being perfect inequality.

14. Culturally Argentina is somewhat similar to the United States and Canada. It, too, is a nation of immigrants. It was colonized in the last century by people from southern Europe.

TABLE 15-5 *Income Inequality for Selected Latin American Countries (percent)*

Country	*Lowest Quintile*	*Highest Quintile*	*Highest 10 Percent*	*Ratio of Quintiles*
Guatemala	2.1	63.0	46.6	30 to 1
Peru	4.9	51.4	35.4	10.4 to 1
Honduras	2.7	63.5	47.9	17.7 to 1
Nicaragua	4.2	55.3	39.8	13.2 to 1
Costa Rica	4.0	50.8	34.1	12.7 to 1
Panama	2.0	49.8	42.1	29.9 to 1
Mexico	4.1	55.0	39.5	13.6 to 1
Brazil	2.1	67.5	51.3	32.1 to 1
Chile	3.3	60.4	45.8	18.3 to 1
Venezuela	4.8	49.5	33.2	10.3 to 1
Colombia	3.6	55.8	39.5	11.0 to 1
Sweden	8.0	36.9	20.8	4.6 to 1
Japan	8.7	27.5	22.4	4.3 to 1

Source: The World Bank, *World Development Report 1995* (Washington, D.C.: The World Bank, 1995), 220–221.

occupied by the defeated Chinese armies of Chiang Kai-shek, while Argentina continued to be the economic power of Latin America. But as Table 15-6 indicates, this has changed in the past twenty years. South Korea, Taiwan, Singapore, and Malaysia have outperformed the major Latin American countries in terms of living standards and economic development.

Income inequality has had a deleterious effect on Latin America in several ways.[15] First, the wealthy have invested little of their money in the development of their countries, instead preferring to invest it in the United States and Europe. Fortunes have often been made in real estate speculation. Second, the import substitution, capital-intensive strategies that Mexico and other countries have followed primarily benefited the rich. By contrast, the export-oriented strategy followed by the East Asian countries put them on a labor-demand growth path. Third, investment in human capital has been greater in East Asia than in Latin America because the demand for educated workers is greater. A stronger demand for educated workers elicits a greater supply, thus reducing income inequality.

Corruption

I don't know about political things. The first time I voted was in the last election, but I don't think there is much hope there. The men in the government always end up rich and the poor are just as badly off.[16]

15. Nancy Birdsall and Richard Sabot, "Inequality as a Constraint on Economic Growth in Latin America," *Development Policy* (Washington, D.C.: Inter-American Development Bank, November 1994), 3.
16. Lewis, *Children of Sanchez*, 342.

TABLE 15-6 *A Comparison of per Capita Income and Inflation Rates for Latin American and East Asian Countries, 1994 (dollars and percent)*

	Per Capita Income		*Average Inflation Rate*	
Countries	*Real GNP*	*Real Growth Rate, 1985–1994*	*PPP*	*1985–1994*
Latin America				
Argentina	$8,060	1.9%	$8,920	317.2%
Brazil	3,370	–0.4	5,630	913.0
Mexico	4,010	0.6	7,050	39.9
Venezuela	2,760	0.6	7,890	36.6
East Asia				
Korea	8,220	7.8	10,540	6.8
Malaysia	3,520	5.7	8,610	3.1
Singapore	23,360	6.9	21,430	3.9
Thailand	2,210	8.2	6,870	5.1

Source: The World Bank, *The World Bank Atlas, 1996* (Washington, D.C.: The World Bank, 1996), 18–19.

That statement, too, was made thirty years ago, but conditions have not changed. In Brazil, President Fernando Collor de Mello resigned following charges of corruption. Like many Latin American politicians, he was elected on a platform of cleaning up corruption, but, like most of them, he succumbed to the temptations that high office presents. Scandals led to rioting and street demonstrations in the major Brazilian cities. It is almost an article of faith that any Latin American politician worth his, and sometimes her[17] salt will amass at least a small fortune before leaving office. It can be argued that at least in part it is the Latin American cultural heritage that is responsible for corruption. The conquistadores came to Latin America to strike it rich by finding gold and silver, and they returned to Spain as rich men. The Latin American countries were governed for three hundred years by viceroys sent by Spain, usually as a reward for some favor done the Spanish king.

The problem is that corruption often permeates all strata of Latin American society, from presidents to ministers to civil servants to garbage collectors. The average minister or director may amass a small fortune during a term in office. Nepotism is a fact of life in Latin American politics. For example, Eva Peron, who was once president of Argentina, appointed her brother to the job of minister of defense, a brother-in-law to the position of ambassador to Spain, and a sister to head the ministry of social welfare. A former president of Mexico appointed his son, his mistress, two cousins, and his sister to ministerial jobs, and his wife was appointed head of cultural affairs. All enjoyed extravagant lifestyles, and the president him-

17. Eva Peron, former president of Argentina, was born in poverty, married a general who was also a president of Argentina, and was partial to diamonds, which she stored in Swiss banks along with gold and silver bracelets.

self constructed a five-mansion complex, with tennis courts, swimming pools, stables, and a gymnasium. It is estimated that the president and his family amassed a fortune of around $7 billion.[18]

Latin America Enters the 1990s

A renaissance of sorts began to take place in many of the Latin American countries in the late 1980s and has continued into the 1990s. An example is Argentina, which, despite its economic potential, had one of Latin America's worst performing economies for years. Its real growth rate for the 1980s was –1.8 percent.[19] For half a century, state intervention in the Argentine economy had channeled resources into unproductive sectors, while high import barriers made Argentine industry inefficient by shielding it from foreign competition. In 1950 Argentina had a per capita income larger than that of Spain and five times that of South Korea. By 1980, Spain's per capita income was twice that of Argentina, and South Korea's per capita income was equal.[20] Inflation averaged 450 percent during the 1980s and peaked at 20,266 percent in March 1990. Government budget deficits contributed to this inflation.

Argentine President Carlos Menem introduced a number of economic reforms including the introduction of a new currency unit, the austral, which was made fully convertible at a fixed rate of 10,000 australs = $1 and 100 percent backed by gold and foreign currency reserves.[21] The country was opened up to foreign investors, thus exposing Argentine business firms to foreign competition. Import tariffs were reduced from an average of 50 percent to around 10 percent. Finally, Menem privatized a number of state-owned enterprises that used to cost the government billions of dollars to run. The Argentine airline Aerolineas Argentina and the telephone system were privatized. These reforms have improved the performance of the Argentine economy during the 1990s. The inflation rate is down to around 40 percent a year, and the growth in real GDP has averaged better than 5 percent during the period 1990–1995.[22] By 1993 the ratio of investment to real GNP increased to 21 percent compared to 14 percent in 1990.

The other Latin American countries have had problems similar to those of Argentina. The state was dominant in many sectors of their economies, inflation was a major problem, and their growth rates were negative during most of the 1980s. Import substitution policies were used to protect home markets, and budget deficits were incurred to finance social welfare spending. Deficits in their current accounts and balance of payments contributed to inflation. These countries have instituted reforms similar to those followed by Argentina. Many state-owned

18. Alan Riding, *Distant Neighbors* (New York: Alfred A. Knopf, Inc., 1985), 117–119.

19. The World Bank, *The World Bank Atlas 1991* (Washington, D.C.: The World Bank, 1991), 6.

20. "A Survey of Argentina," *The Economist*, November 26–December 2, 1994, 6.

21. Soon afterward Argentina adopted a new currency, the peso, which was fixed at $1. The peso must be backed by the central bank's gold and foreign currency reserves.

22. OECD, *OECD Economic Outlook* (Paris: OECD, June 1995), 120.

enterprises were privatized in order to bring in more money to government treasuries. Currencies were revalued and pegged to the dollar. Foreign investment was encouraged and import restrictions were lowered against foreign goods.

Despite the increase in economic growth and a decrease in inflation, the Latin American countries still have a number of economic and social problems to be resolved. To sustain higher growth rates, the low domestic saving rates in the Latin American countries will have to increase. They are much lower than the saving rates of the East Asian countries. Latin America's economic growth depends to a major extent on external financing, which has made it vulnerable to changes in the international financial markets. Another problem is low productivity, attributable in part to protectionist policies that have been used to protect home industries, labor codes that hinder worker productivity, inadequate infrastructure, and poor educational facilities. Still another problem is the extent of poverty that continues to exist in Latin America (see Table 15-7). Almost half of its population is poor, and the rate of economic growth has not been enough to reduce the extent of poverty.

MEXICO: THE ECONOMIC SYSTEM

Mexico is of increased importance to the United States for several reasons. First, the United States, Canada, and Mexico have signed and ratified the North American Free Trade Agreement (NAFTA), which has created a new trading bloc. Second, Mexico is one of our three most important trading partners, the others being Canada and Japan. In 1995 Mexico's trade with the United States amounted to $118 billion.[23] It has become a major market for U.S. goods; around 70 percent of its imports come from the United States. Third, it has become an important location for U.S. direct and portfolio investments. But this has proved to be a mixed blessing for both countries, as witnessed by the spectacular crash of the Mexican peso in December 1994, which caused the withdrawal of foreign capital and led Mexico to devalue the peso.[24] Fourth, the two countries have a common border, which facilitates increased trade.

As a result of Mexico's import substitution policy, the overall incentive structure favored production in the domestic market. Although some direct incentives for exports were provided, there was a distinct bias against exports. The external competitiveness of most exportable goods declined. Trade and exchange restrictions limited trade flows and severely distorted the relationship between international and domestic prices. The import substitution policy promoted and protected an industrial sector that was generally inefficient and was unable to compete in international markets. Only oil was readily tradable in world markets and came to be of increasing importance to the Mexican economy. Certain Mexican industries were favored over others when it came to import substitution,

23. Mexico's trade with the United States in 1995 was equal to the combined U.S. trade with Germany and the United Kingdom.
24. The crash also had a deleterious effect on the U.S. financial markets.

TABLE 15-7
People in Absolute Poverty in Selected Latin American Countries (percent of population)

Country	*Urban*	*Rural*
Argentina	15	20
Colombia	40	45
Brazil	38	66
Mexico	23	43
Peru	52	72
Venezuela	30	42
Bolivia	—	86
Haiti	65	80
Costa Rica	24	30
Panama	36	52
Guatemala	60	80
Honduras	74	80

Source: United Nations Development Programme, *Human Development Report 1995* (New York: Oxford University Press, 1995), 178–179.

which meant that resource allocation was distorted. Economic inefficiencies became prevalent, with industrial growth mostly a result of capacity expansion with little productivity gains.

Oil

Mexico has a characteristic common to many less developed and developing countries—reliance on one major export product. In Mexico's case it is oil. In 1991 oil exports amounted to over half the total exports of the Mexican economy. Since its discovery in 1863, oil has been both a blessing and a curse to the Mexican economy. Wide swings in world oil prices have brought Mexico boom and bust. Oil has figured prominently in Mexican politics, particularly in its relations with the United States. On more than one occasion, the United States has intervened militarily and behind the scenes to protect U.S. oil interests in Mexico. The oil industry, which is a state-owned monopoly, Petroleos Mexicanos (PEMEX), is the largest expense item in the Mexican state budget, but its revenues, particularly from exports, are also the single most important contributor to total government revenues.

Agriculture

Agriculture has been called the Achilles heel of the Mexican economy, and with good reason. Mexico is highly unsuited for agriculture. Much of the northern part of the country is desert; two mountain ranges run the length of the country; tropical jungles cover the southern region; and much of the topsoil of the country is so thin that little can grow. Only 15 percent of the total land area of Mexico is cultivable. Most of Mexico's agriculture depends on rainfall for moisture, and during most of the 1980s rainfall was significantly below the national average. Agriculture employs one-fourth of the Mexican labor force, while accounting for less than 9 percent of Mexico's GNP. There has been a steady outmigration of Mexican farmworkers to such Mexican cities as Mexico City and Monterrey and illegal entry into the United States. There is also an imbalance between cultivable land, population centers, and water resources in that water resources are in the underpopulated areas, as are the larger, more productive land holdings.

The organization of agriculture has long been a factor that has worked against the development of a viable agricultural sector. Mexican agriculture is typified by three types of land holdings: communal, public, and private. The communal, or *ejido,* land holding is unique to Mexico, dating back to the time of the Aztecs. The land is held by the ejidos and is farmed by *ejidatarios,* or farm laborers, who share in the proceeds. The ejidos are considered to be very inefficient and are criticized on the grounds that not allowing private property ownership weakens the attachment to the soil and separates ownership from rewards. The bulk of Mexican agricultural output comes from the private farms, 4 percent of which produce more than 50 percent of total agricultural output.[25]

Economic Development

In terms of international comparisons of economic development, Mexico is at the same stage, or middle level of development, as such countries as Brazil, Hungary, and Venezuela, which have similar per capita incomes.[26] It is at a higher stage of economic development than the former Soviet Union and Poland and is far more developed than either China or Nigeria. Its economy is less autonomous and more vulnerable to external economic forces than the economies of subsistence level and single export countries. When world oil prices were high during the 1970s, the oil wealth of Mexico generated the foreign exchange necessary to finance internal economic development, but it also enhanced the country's attractiveness to foreign lenders. When oil prices dropped in the 1980s, Mexico was stuck with a large foreign debt.

Economic Development Strategies. Several economic growth strategies have been used by various countries to achieve economic and social development. The first approach is to rely on the export of a primary product, such as copper or oil, to raise living standards. This approach may not involve an attempt to achieve industrialization. For example, the Arab countries have used revenue from oil exports to raise living standards, but there has been very little attempt to achieve widespread industrial development. Oil revenues have been used to improve the infrastructures of these countries through the construction of educational facilities, roads,

25. Most of the more profitable Mexican farms are located near the Mexican-U.S. border, which is a bone of contention with U.S. farmers in the lower Rio Grande valley of Texas.

26. Hungary had a 1994 per capita income of $3,840, Venezuela $2,760, Brazil $3,370, and Mexico $4,010. Other countries with per capita incomes similar to that of Mexico are the Russian Federation, with a per capita income of $2,650, and Malaysia, with a per capita income of $3,520.

and hospitals. Venezuela, on the other hand, has used revenues from its oil exports to accomplish more broadly based industrial development.

A second approach to economic development is to achieve inward industrialization through import substitution. This has been the development strategy of Mexico, Brazil, Argentina, and several other Latin American countries. Restrictions on imports are supposed to increase the demand for local consumer goods and encourage the development of domestic industries. Both Mexico and Brazil have established consumer and capital goods industries that provide for local consumption. This strategy is not without its costs; protection from import competition often raises the prices of local goods to consumers, limits selection, and creates inefficiency on the part of producers because there is no competition.

The third approach has been followed by Japan, Singapore, South Korea, and other East Asian countries since the end of World War II. This is outward industrialization and involves the export of manufactured goods ranging from clothing to automobiles. Measures to increase exports are for the most part likely to develop rather slowly; it is a matter of improving production techniques, labor skills, and managerial methods, and introducing new industries. An export surplus is a form of saving that can be used to finance the development of new export-related industries. However, it involves internal sacrifices because the emphasis is placed on production for sale abroad and using the proceeds from exports to develop more exports instead of concentrating on the development of local consumer-based industries.

Mexico's Development Strategy. Mexico began to pursue economic development in the early 1950s through a policy of import substitution. It relied heavily on state intervention in the economy. Exchange controls, import quotas, and other restrictions designed to limit imports were used by the Mexican government to promote the development of home industries by making imports more expensive. This compelled Mexican consumers either to pay higher prices for imported goods or to buy domestic products. In effect, consumers were forced to subsidize the development of Mexican industry through the substitution of domestic products for imported products.

Capital investment was stimulated through tax policies and government subsidies to aid industry. The government intervened directly to promote the development of certain industries. For example, the Automobile Manufacturing Law of 1963 required foreign automobile companies operating in Mexico to increase the share of locally manufactured components to 60 percent of each car produced. The law was designed to stimulate local manufacturing through import substitution and to make the auto industry a primary source of employment.

The world oil shortage of the 1970s caused a rebirth of the Mexican oil industry and a change in development strategy away from import substitution toward the use of oil for export expansion. New oil discoveries returned Mexico to the status it had enjoyed earlier in the century as a major world oil producer. Two important government development policy decisions were made. The first was to push for increased oil production, and the second was to base export policies on the sale of oil to the United States and other oil-importing countries. Earnings from oil exports were supposed to be used to improve the infrastructure of the Mexican economy and to increase social welfare expenditures to the lower income groups of the population. All too often, however, export earnings were wasted on pet projects of Mexican politicians or in some form of graft (which has been endemic in Mexican politics).[27]

Government Ownership of Enterprise. The Mexican government has intervened both directly and indirectly to promote expansion in all sectors of the Mexican economy. Since the 1930s, when foreign oil properties were nationalized,[28] the state has been involved in the economy to a greater extent than in most Latin American countries. In 1982, the government nationalized the banking system. It owned the oil industry, most of the electric power industry, and established and subsidized government enterprises that were in direct competition with private ones in the same industry, such as steel production. It exercised considerable control over access to credit through state-owned financial institutions and constructed social-overhead facilities, such as ports and roads, with the intent of influencing the geographic location of private investment. The government also placed restrictions on the type of foreign investment that would be permitted in Mexico and on the extent of foreign ownership. It emphasized economic nationalism through legislation designed to encourage industrial imports, through exchange controls, and through import licensing.

Banking. Banking is another area in which the Mexican government has exercised an important role in the Mexican economy. The monetary policy of the Central Bank of Mexico (Banco de Mexico), which is a government entity, has been used as part of economic development policy. The Nacional Financiera is the second most important government-owned bank. Its function is to promote industrial development by allocating credit to industries, both public and private, that are a part of the government's program for economic development. Nacional Financiera has financial interests in such industries as steel, pulp and paper, fertilizers, electric equipment, sugar, textiles, beverages, cement, and hotels. Its revenues come primarily from the government budget and interest on loans.

MEXICO IN THE 1980s

The prelude to the 1980s was set in the 1970s. Mexico became more of a state-directed economy during the 1970s when the Mexican government adopted a policy of growth through public expenditure. Laws were passed restricting foreign investment in Mexico, and the government increased its control over such strategic economic sectors as energy and coal. The government based its policies on the assumption that more state control over the market price mechanism would result in

27. Francisco Carrada-Bravo, *Oil, Money, and the Mexican Economy* (Boulder, Colo.: Westview Press, 1982), 37–38.
28. The Mexican oil industry at that time was controlled by U.S. and British oil companies.

more efficient resource allocation and make the country more prosperous. It also would reduce social tensions by increasing the amount of money spent on pension and health benefits, and by building more education and health facilities. The increase in government spending was enhanced by the discovery of major oil reserves in Mexico in 1976. As a tradable good owned by PEMEX, the state-owned oil monopoly, oil generated revenues that were used to further finance state expenditures. The deficit in the government budget doubled and the inflation rate tripled during the decade.[29]

The 1982 Debt Crisis

High government expectations of ever-increasing revenues from oil sales continued into the 1980s. Increases in government spending led to borrowing from abroad by using projected increases in oil revenues as collateral. This increased the external foreign debt from around $28 billion in 1975 to $88 billion in 1982.[30] The peso exchange rate depreciated by 2.0 percent in 1980, 12.9 percent in 1981, and 465.7 percent in 1982.[31] Unfortunately oil prices began to decline as world supplies of oil began to increase, and the deficit in Mexico's balance of payments increased as oil revenue decreased. In August 1982 the government announced that it could not meet foreign debt payments, even though the peso was devalued from 26.35 to the dollar in January to more than 45.46 pesos to the dollar by March.

The government had to obtain a rescheduling of its foreign debt from international banks and from the International Monetary Fund. In September 1982, during the height of the debt crisis, the Mexican banking system was nationalized by the government. The rationale for the nationalization was to give the government control over credit allocation. The peso was devalued, and exchange controls were imposed on imports. However, the price of oil continued to drop, from $25 a barrel in 1985 to an average price of $12 a barrel in 1986. As a result, the internal and external conditions of the Mexican economy continued to worsen, with public sector revenues and export receipts declining by the equivalent of 6 percent of the Mexican GDP.[32] By July 1986 the Mexican government had to refinance its foreign debt, which by that time was more than half the Mexican GDP. The economy sta-

29. Eliot Kalter, "The Mexican Strategy to Achievable Sustainable Economic Growth," in *Mexico: The Strategy to Achieve Sustained Economic Growth*, Occasional Paper 99 (Washington, D.C.: International Monetary Fund, September 1992), 5.
30. Ibid., 4.
31. Liliana Rojas-Suarez, "An Analysis of the Linkages of Macroeconomic Policies in Mexico," *Mexico: The Strategy to Achieve Sustained Economic Growth*, Occasional Paper 99 (Washington, D.C.: International Monetary Fund, September 1992), 18.
32. The Mexico City earthquake of 1985 had an adverse effect on the peso. The government's handling of the crisis by expropriating private property caused people to sell off their Mexican assets. Economic policies pursued by the U.S. government also had an adverse effect on the Mexican economy. A combination of an expansionary fiscal policy and a tight monetary policy caused real interest rates to rise in the United States and in the Euromarket, where most international loans are funded.

bilized in 1987, but inflation and interest rates continued to increase, and the Mexican stock market collapsed in October.

Even though the economy began to stabilize toward the end of the 1980s, the foreign debt continued to be a problem. Payment on the debt had to be rescheduled on several occasions. By 1988 there was a net income transfer abroad equivalent to 3.5 percent of the Mexican GDP. However, the debt crisis was not just limited to Mexico; a number of other countries were involved. The Brady Plan, announced by the United States in 1989,[33] emphasized debt forgiveness by major U.S. banks, which held much of the Mexican debt, rather than new bank lending. Banks were given a choice. They could either make new loans or they could write off portions of existing loans in exchange for new government securities whose interest rates were backed with money from the International Monetary Fund. Mexico, for example, could issue bonds as substitutes for the bank loans.[34]

Privatization

During the latter part of the last century and the early part of this century, most of Mexico's resources fell under the control of foreign business interests, particularly American and British. Oil resources were controlled by American and British oil companies. Tin, lead, zinc, and silver resources were controlled primarily by American companies, as was the Mexican railroad system. Such public utilities as electric power and gas companies were owned by the British, while the Germans owned the sugar plantations. At the time of the Mexican Revolution of 1910, around 90 percent of the wealth of Mexico belonged to foreign investors or to the Catholic Church. The purpose of the revolution was to change this, and it did. The Constitution of 1917 gave the state the right to exercise control over the assets of the country. This right was exercised in 1938 when American and British oil companies were nationalized by the Mexican government.

Government Involvement in the Economy. State involvement in the economy has occurred to a greater extent in Mexico than in other Latin American countries. It has exercised considerable control over access to credit through state-owned financial facilities. It has placed restrictions on the type of foreign investment that would be permitted in Mexico and on the extent of foreign investment. It was involved in production activities that did not attract private investment, such as shipyards and fertilizer plants, in which return on investment was long term or the initial outlay was too large. It owned the oil industry, most of the electric power industry, and established and subsidized government enterprises that were in direct competition with private enterprises in the same sector, such as steel production.

33. The Baker Plan, which preceded the Brady Plan, involved debt rescheduling and new loans to Mexico and other countries.

34. As a part of debt restructuring, the U.S. government sold Mexico thirty-year zero-coupon Treasury bonds that could be used as collateral for the bonds it planned to issue as a substitute for the bank loans.

TABLE 15-8
Number of State-Owned Enterprises in Mexico, 1982–1990

Year	*Total*
1982	1,155
1983	1,074
1984	1,049
1985	945
1986	737
1987	617
1988	412
1989	379
1990	280
1991	239

Source: Nora Lustig, *Mexico: The Remaking of an Economy* (Washington, D.C.: The Brookings Institution, 1992), 105.

In 1982 it nationalized the banking system, which marked the highest point of state intervention.

Reasons for Privatization. Privatization of state-owned entities began in the 1980s. There were several reasons for this divestiture of state-owned assets.[35] One reason was to raise public revenues through the sale of the assets. A second was to reduce subsidies, which had contributed to a deficit in the budget. A third was to improve allocative and managerial efficiency, and a fourth was to restore private sector confidence in the Mexican economy. Beginning in 1983 the privatization process began in earnest, as Table 15-8 indicates. The number of state-owned entities was reduced from over 1,100 in 1982 to fewer than 250 by the end of 1991. The large communication company, Telefonos de Mexico, was privatized, as were the previously nationalized commercial banks. Two airlines, a truck manufacturing company, and two steel companies were also nationalized. Restrictions were lifted on foreign investment in Mexico.

Performance of the Mexican Economy During the 1980s

As Tables 15-9, 15-10, and 15-11 indicate, the performance of the Mexican economy in the 1980s was not good. Mexico had a severe economic crisis in 1982, which was compounded by the decline in the world price of oil. Its foreign debt, which was supported by revenues from oil exports, increased at a time when world interest rates were also increasing. There was an increase in the rate of inflation, and real-wage rates declined during the decade. The Mexican peso, which had begun the decade at an exchange rate of 23 pesos = $1, was devalued many times, and by the end of the decade the exchange rate was 2,461 pesos = $1. Great hard-

35. Nora Lustig, *Mexico: The Remaking of an Economy* (Washington, D.C.: The Brookings Institution, 1992), 104.

TABLE 15-9 *Mexican Public Sector Budgetary Revenues, Expenditures, Interest Payments, and Deficits, 1980–1990 (percentage of GDP)*

Year	*Expenditures*	*Revenues*	*Interest Payments*	*Deficits*
1980	31.1	25.5	3.2	–7.5
1981	38.7	26.3	4.9	–14.1
1982	41.8	27.8	8.0	–16.9
1983	39.0	31.7	12.1	–8.6
1984	37.7	31.3	11.7	–8.5
1985	37.5	30.4	11.3	–9.6
1986	42.5	29.4	16.4	–15.9
1987	43.7	29.5	19.6	–16.0
1988	38.4	28.7	16.5	–12.4
1989	34.1	27.6	12.9	–5.5
1990	33.4	25.5	9.9	–3.5

Source: Eliot Kalter, "The Mexican Strategy to Achieve Sustainable Economic Growth," in *Mexico: The Strategy to Achieve Sustained Economic Growth*, Occasional Paper 99 (Washington, D.C.: International Monetary Fund, September 1992), 4–5.

TABLE 15-10
Inflation Rates in Mexico in the 1980s (percent)

Year	*Inflation Rate*
1978	17.5
1979	18.2
1980	26.3
1981	27.9
1982	58.9
1983	101.9
1984	65.5
1985	57.7
1986	86.2
1987	131.8
1988	114.2
1989	20.0

Source: Liliana Rojas-Suarez, "An Analysis of the Linkages of Macroeconomic Policies in Mexico," in *Mexico: The Strategy to Achieve Sustained Economic Growth*, Occasional Paper 99 (Washington, D.C.: International Monetary Fund, September 1992), 16.

ships were imposed on the Mexican people, as the Mexican government had to reduce the deficit in the national budget by cutting social spending.

The Mexican economy underwent a profound economic change after the debt crisis of 1982. Foreign trade was liberalized as import licensing, exchange controls, and other forms of trade restraints were relaxed. To encourage capital inflows into Mexico, restraints on foreign investments were lifted. By the end of 1982 the government had determined that the size of the public sector affected adversely both economic productivity and efficiency. The overall deficits of the state-owned en-

TABLE 15-11
Real GDP and Real Wages in Mexico During the 1980s (average annual growth in percent)

Year	*Real GDP*	*Real Wages*
1980	8.3	–6.8
1981	8.8	1.6
1982	–0.6	0.7
1983	–4.2	–22.8
1984	3.6	–7.1
1985	2.6	–2.7
1986	–3.8	–5.9
1987	1.7	–1.9
1988	1.2	–1.3
1989	3.3	9.0

Source: International Development Bank, *Economic and Social Progress in Latin America, 1992 Report* (Washington, D.C.: International Development Bank, 1992), 133.

terprises had accounted for about one-fourth of the government's borrowing requirements. The deficits, financed mainly from the national budget, were attributed to nonmarket pricing policies and increased inefficiency. The number of state-owned enterprises was reduced from over 1,100 in 1982 to fewer than 250 by 1991 through a process of mergers, liquidations, and sales.

AN EVALUATION OF THE MEXICAN ECONOMY

The improvement in the Mexican economy that had begun in the latter part of the 1980s continued into the early 1990s. Real GDP increased by 3.3 percent in 1989, 4.4 percent in 1990, and 2.8 percent in 1991.[36] Consumer prices stabilized at an increase of around 20 percent a year, and then declined in 1991 and 1992. The peso was stabilized and was eventually pegged to the dollar at a rate of approximately 3.2 pesos = $1. Real wages showed increases from 1989 to 1993 at an average of better than 6 percent a year. The merchandise trade account and current account remained negative, however, and the terms of trade, with 1980 as an index of 100, declined from 63.2 in 1988 to 56.0 in 1993.

NORTH AMERICAN FREE TRADE AGREEMENT (NAFTA)

In August 1992 the United States, Canada, and Mexico concluded the North American Free Trade Agreement (NAFTA). Under the agreement, which has been ratified by the legislatures of the three countries, all duties, tariffs, and other

36. Inter-American Development Bank, *Economic and Social Progress in Latin America 1994* (Washington, D.C.: Inter-American Development Bank, October 1994), 121.

trade barriers will be eliminated within fifteen years. It will create a free trade area similar to that of the European Union, except there will be no common currency unit. For most goods, existing customs duties will either be eliminated when the agreement takes effect or phased out in ten years. In the agreement, Mexico retains full government control over the Mexican oil, gas, refining, basic petrochemicals, nuclear, and electricity sectors. The agreement also removes investment barriers among the three countries. Each country will have to treat NAFTA investors no less favorably than its own investors. All nontariff barriers to agricultural trade between the United States and Mexico have been eliminated.

The agreement is regarded as a plus factor for U.S. direct investment, which began in Canada and Mexico in the last century, when U.S. firms invested in the forest industries of Canada and the transportation and mineral industries of Mexico. U.S. capital built the Mexican railroad system, and the Rockefeller and Guggenheim interests developed the Mexican oil, silver, and copper industries. By the end of the last century all of Latin America became the preserve of American business interests. All of this changed in this century, however, as Mexican and Latin American nationalism increased. Table 15-12 presents a summary of U.S. direct investment in Canada and Mexico and of Canadian and Mexican direct investment in the United States for 1994.

The Exchange Rate Crisis—December 1994

Less than a year after the ratification of NAFTA by the U.S. Congress, Mexico experienced a currency crisis of the first order that led to the devaluation of the peso. In part it was attributable to the social unrest in Chiapas, a poor state in southern Mexico. An uprising over the subject of land distribution that had occurred in 1993 recurred in late 1994, shaking foreign investors' faith in the Mexican economy. Probably more important was the fact that Mexico had a massive deficit in its current account. Between 1987 and 1993, while exports grew by roughly one-half, imports increased by 100 percent. In 1993 Mexican exports amounted to roughly $50

TABLE 15-12 *U.S. Direct Investment in Canada and Mexico and Canadian and Mexican Direct Investment in the U.S., 1994 ($ billions)*

U.S. Direct Investment in	*All Industries*	*Petroleum*	*Manufacturing*	*Finance*	*Other*
Canada	72.8	8.6	35.0	12.2	17.0
Mexico	16.4	—	10.7	2.0	3.7
Canadian and Mexican Investment in U.S.					
Canada	43.2	2.6	16.9	3.4	20.3
Mexico					

Source: U.S. Department of Commerce, Bureau of Economic Analysis, *Survey of Current Business* (Washington, D.C.: U.S. Government Printing Office, June 1995), Tables 1, 2.

billion, while Mexican imports amounted to $65 billion. This resulted in a loss of foreign financial reserves held by the Mexican government. Finally, interest rates around the world, but particularly in Mexico, were rising, making it a less attractive place for foreign investment.

In December 1994, at a time when foreign exchange reserves held by the government had dropped from $26 billion to $7 billion, the peso, which had been tied to the dollar at an exchange rate of approximately 3.4 pesos to $1, was let free to float against the dollar. The purpose was to stimulate Mexican exports in order to reduce the deficit in the current account. By the end of December, the peso had dropped to a rate of around 5.8 to $1. The impact of the currency devaluation on the Mexican economy was enormous. It shook foreign investors' confidence, which was reflected in a drop in the value of Mexican stocks on the Bolsa and NYSE.[37] The stock values of such American companies as PepsiCo, which had a sizable market in Mexico, also declined. The paper value of American investment in Mexico declined by some $8 billion.[38]

To shore up confidence in the Mexican financial system, the Clinton administration provided a $40-billion assistance package to guarantee the sale of Mexican government dollar-denominated Treasury bonds to foreign investors. Mexican finances depend on capital flows from abroad, particularly the United States. Low Mexican savings rates create a trap. When Mexico's economy grows at a rate of 4.5 percent or more—levels considered necessary to alleviate widespread poverty—it imports more goods and builds up a deficit in its current account that only foreign capital inflows can finance. But inflows of foreign capital are based on foreign confidence in the stability of the exchange rate of the peso and short-term interest rates.[39] The U.S. bailout requires Mexico to raise short-term interest rates to attract capital and to pledge oil revenues as collateral for the loan.

The Political System

Mexico has had a one-party political system since 1929, when the Partido Revolucianario Institutional (PRI) was created. With few exceptions, the PRI governed unopposed until the 1988 presidential election, when it was challenged by parties from both the right and the left and won with a bare majority of the votes. The PRI was charged with election fraud, but that has become routine for Mexican elections.[40] The major cause of fraud is that the PRI has been in office for so long. Having some 45,000 patronage jobs it can dispense to the party faithful after each election has provided a golden opportunity for politicians and their friends to en-

37. For example, Telefonos de Mexico stock fell from $65 a share in early December to $38 a share by early January 1995.

38. This involved the dollar-denominated, short-term tesebono bonds.

39. According to an IMF report, Mexican, not foreign, investors caused the crash of the peso by staging a run on their currency.

40. The opposition, according to exit polls, won a majority of the votes. PRI-appointed election officials claimed that atmospheric conditions caused the computers to malfunction, and the PRI candidate was declared the victor.

rich themselves.[41] There is also an interplay between business and government in Mexico in that business contributors to the PRI have been given special treatment when it comes to purchasing former state-owned enterprises.[42]

The Presidential Election of 1994. The presidential election of 1994 provided rather dramatic testimony on what is wrong with the Mexican political system. Luis Donaldo Colosio was nominated as the candidate of the PRI. He promised to reform the whole political process, but he was assassinated in Tijuana in March 1994. The PRI then had to nominate a second candidate, Ernesto Zedillo, for president. The PRI won the national election in August, and Zedillo was elected president. In September, another political assassination occurred: Jose Francisco Masseau, secretary general of the PRI, was shot in Mexico City. The brother of the former president of Mexico, Carlos Salinas de Gortari, was charged with masterminding the assassination, and Carlos Salinas had to seek asylum in the United States.[43]

Performance of the Mexican Economy

Compared to its performance during the 1980s, the Mexican economy has shown considerable improvement during the 1990s. The inflation rate continued to decline and reached single-digit levels in 1993 and 1994.[44] Real wages, which had decreased during the 1980s, increased at an average annual rate of 5.9 percent during the period 1990–1994.[45] Interest payments due on the foreign debt decreased from 39.2 percent of Mexican exports in 1984 to 17.4 percent of Mexican exports in 1994. The foreign exchange rate was stabilized at 3.1 pesos = $1. On the other hand, the deficit in the Mexican current account increased from $3.9 billion in 1989 to $22.8 billion in 1993, and the merchandise trade account, which was positive during most of the 1980s, was negative during the period 1990–1994. There was a turndown in economic activity in 1993, but the economy rebounded strongly in 1994. Then the currency crisis occurred in December. Table 15-13 presents the performance of the economy for the period 1990–1996.

Living Standards

Mexico continues to have its share of economic and social problems. Although the population growth rate has slowed in recent years, the Mexican labor force continues to increase at a faster rate than the capacity of the economy to create jobs. Many Mexican workers who emigrate to the United States are impoverished rural

41. As a Mexican politician said: "*El politico quien es pobre, es un pobre politico*" ("The person who is poor is a poor politician").
42. Harry Hurt III, "It's Time to Get Real About Mexico," *Fortune*, September 5, 1995, 108.
43. He is alleged to have absconded with $20 million.
44. The inflation rate in 1993 was the lowest for twenty years.
45. Inter-American Development Bank, 121.

TABLE 15-13 *The Performance of the Mexican Economy, 1990–1996 (yearly percentage changes)*

	1990	*1991*	*1992*	*1993*	*1994*	*1995*	*1996*
Real GDP	4.4	3.6	2.8	0.4	3.5	–2.9	3.0
Real private consumption	6.1	4.9	3.9	0.2	3.7	–7.5	1.0
Real public consumption	2.3	3.9	2.3	2.0	2.5	–9.5	–1.0
Real gross fixed capital formation	13.1	8.3	7.0	–0.1	8.1	–20.8	5.1
Real domestic demand	6.5	5.3	5.1	–0.1	4.5	–11.3	1.9
Exports of goods and services	3.6	4.6	1.7	7.3	3.7	18.0	11.0
Imports of goods and services	19.7	16.8	20.9	–1.3	12.9	–25.0	9.0
Consumer prices	114.2	20.0	26.7	22.5	15.5	9.8	7.0

Source: OECD, *OECD Economic Outlook* (Paris: OECD, June 1995), A1–A19.

workers from the poorest agricultural areas of Mexico. The rate of inflation, although it continues to decline, remains higher in Mexico than in the United States, and depresses the level of real wages for the average Mexican worker. The rate of illiteracy remains high in Mexico, particularly in rural areas where educational facilities are poor. Even though the role of women in Mexico has improved, both economically and socially, they are generally less educated and receive far lower wages than men. Urbanization has created a combustible mixture of poverty, unemployment, crime, and disease.

Table 15-14 presents various measures of Mexican living standards. For example, in 1994 Mexico's ranking in the Human Development Index was 53 out of 174 countries,[46] considered a high stage of human development. It ranked lower than Argentina, Colombia, and several other Latin American countries. It ranked 41 out of 209 countries in money per capita income in 1994, well ahead of the African countries and most of the Asian countries.[47]

Income Distribution

The income gap between rich and poor widened during the 1980s, when inflation was a major problem. Capital mobility and higher interest rates worked to the advantage of wealthy Mexicans. Mexico's move to dismantle trade barriers benefited businesses large enough to compete at home and in foreign markets. Privatizing state-owned industries also worked to the advantage of Mexican and foreign investors. By contrast, wage and salary earners during the 1980s were adversely affected by the fall in real wages and a higher tax burden, while the poor who relied

46. United Nations Development Programme, *Human Development Report 1995* (New York: Oxford University Press, 1995), 155.
47. *The World Bank Atlas 1996*, 18–19.

on agricultural output and prices suffered from falling agricultural prices during the latter part of the 1980s. Table 15-15 presents Mexican income distribution for 1984 and 1989. The percentage of household income received by the top 10 percent of Mexican households increased from 32.8 percent in 1984 to 37.9 percent in 1989. Much of this gain can be attributed to a rise in the Mexican financial markets.

TABLE 15-14
Measures of Mexican Living Standards

Life expectancy, years	
Men	70
Women	76
Birthrate per 1,000 persons	27
Death rate per 1,000 persons	5
Doubling time, years	34
Annual national increase, percent	2.2
Infant mortality rate per 1,000 live births	34
Percent attending secondary schools	
Males	67
Females	56
Percent attending college	
Males	23
Females	16
Human development index	
Population access to sanitation (percent)	55
Population access to safe drinking water (percent)	77
People in poverty (millions)	26.4

Sources: Carl Haub and Machiko Yanagishita, *1995 World Population Data Sheet* (Washington, D.C.: Population Reference Bureau, 1995); United Nations, *Human Development Report 1995* (New York: Oxford University Press, 1995).

TABLE 15-15
Distribution of Household Income in Mexico by Quintiles 1984, 1989, and 1992 (percent)

	1984	*1989*	*1992*
First quintile	4.8	4.4	4.3
Second quintile	9.5	8.4	8.4
Third quintile	14.2	13.2	12.8
Fourth quintile	21.9	20.4	20.3
Fifth quintile	49.5	53.5	54.2
Upper 10 percent	32.8	37.9	38.2
Gini coefficient			
Monetary income	0.456	0.489	0.509
Real income	0.551	0.592	0.540
Upper 10 percent	0.594	0.600	0.590

Source: OECD Economic Surveys, *Mexico* (Paris: OECD), 1992, 101; 1995, 110.

Reasons for Income Inequality. There are a number of reasons for income inequality in Mexico, some of which are common to other less developed countries and some of which are the results of conditions particular to Mexico.

1. The economic growth policies of the 1960s and 1970s benefited the wealthy and the upper-middle class the most. Import substitution kept imports out and stimulated Mexican business. Emphasis was placed on industrialization, which did create jobs but particularly benefited a small number of large Mexican firms that were capital intensive.
2. The Mexican tax system is probably more regressive than progressive. The personal income tax, though progressive, is evaded by many persons, and social welfare benefits are low.
3. Much Mexican wealth is concentrated in real estate or in investments abroad.
4. Income inequality is another carryover from the latifundio system of the nineteenth century, when a few families controlled much of the land of Mexico. Even though the Revolution of 1910 broke up the latifundio system, most of those families retained their wealth.[48]
5. Corruption still remains endemic in Mexico. *La mordida* (the bite) ranges from payments to patrolmen for fixing traffic tickets to bribes of high-level government officials. It includes the business and political elites. Compounding the problem is the rise of drug trafficking in Mexico. Like Colombia, Mexico is dominated by a few families of enormous wealth who can influence politicians. Some of the drug money allegedly has been used to buy companies that were privatized during the Salinas de Gortari administration.

Poverty

The collapse of the peso in December 1994 widened the gap between rich and poor by increasing the price of imports. Most of the wealth in Mexico is concentrated in the hands of thirty families; despite the slow growth of a middle class, 20 percent of Mexicans still live on less than $10 a week. Mexico is a country with huge class and racial divisions. Middle-class businesspersons as well as consumers were hurt by the devaluation of the peso. The cost of imports from the United States increased, as did interest rates on business loans.[49] The all too frequent scenario of economic instability repeated itself in 1994, adversely affecting the poor and the middle class, but having very little impact on the rich.

Estimates of the extent of poverty vary considerably.[50] In 1984 around 20 percent of Mexican households had incomes below the Mexican minimum wage, which was the equivalent of $3.31 a day and was considered an income sufficient

48. Land reforms initiated by the government in January 1993 distributed more land from the ejitarios to the peasants. However, some of them sold their land to large landholders.
49. "Mexico Drops Efforts to Prop Up Peso," *Wall Street Journal*, December 23, 1994, A3.
50. A PBS program on Mexico that aired on January 5, 1993, stated that 60 million Mexicans out of a population of 85 million lived in poverty. Other estimates place the rate of poverty at 50 percent of the population or as low as 20 percent.

to cover the basic essentials for an average household. By 1989 real living standards had declined, and an income equivalent of two minimum wages was used to define poverty.[51] When a delineation is made between moderate poverty and extreme poverty, one estimate had 17 million persons, or over 20 percent of the population, living in extreme poverty in 1987. Even a minimal decline in the income of the poor can have a devastating effect on their welfare. Even those in the middle quintile in income distribution are not well off by U.S. standards and are adversely affected by rising prices of rent and consumer goods.

Nevertheless, there has been an increase in Mexican living standards. Birthrates and death rates have shown a steady decline. Life expectancy at birth has increased, and the infant mortality rate has decreased. The fertility rate for women has declined from 6.7 in 1960 to 3.1 in 1994. The life expectancy of women in 1994 was 76 years and for men, 70 years. Sanitation facilities have improved, and the illiteracy rate has dropped. But there are still problems of an excess population relative to the resource base of the country. There are still too many people employed in agriculture. Millions of Mexicans have emigrated to the United States in search of better jobs. Underemployment of much of the Mexican labor force exists, and the economy is not growing fast enough to absorb new entrants into the labor force.

SUMMARY

NAFTA was supposed to be the making of a new, vitalized Mexican economy that would be propelled to a higher level of economic development. The Mexican currency crisis of 1994 has, at least for the present, postponed this development. It may be a long time before the country can achieve the sustained growth that South Korea and other East Asian countries have used to create jobs and improve living standards. Corruption still remains a major problem, and the living standards of many people have not improved. The population is still increasing at a rate faster than the country can absorb new entrants into the labor market. Political unrest, punctuated by two major political assassinations in 1994 and a peasant uprising in Chiapas, has introduced an element of political uncertainty into the economy that could discourage needed foreign investment. Extreme poverty and income inequality impede social progress.

QUESTIONS FOR DISCUSSION

1. Why have the East Asian countries achieved a higher rate of economic development and living standards than the Latin American countries?

51. OECD Economic Surveys, *Mexico* (Paris: OECD, 1992), 111–112. The minimum wage in 1989 was approximately $4.14 a day.

2. Mexico based its economic development in the 1950s and 1960s on a policy of import substitution. Discuss.
3. What are some of the factors responsible for the extreme income inequality that exists in Mexico and the other Latin American countries?
4. What caused the Mexican currency crisis of 1994? What impact did it have on the Mexican and American economies?
5. What impact did the 1980s have on the Mexican economy?
6. Discuss the relationship of population growth to economic development in Mexico and Latin America.
7. Discuss the importance of oil to the Mexican economy.
8. In what ways has Mexico changed in the 1990s? In what ways hasn't it changed?

RECOMMENDED READINGS

"Argentina: Survey." *The Economist,* November 26-December 2, 1994, 1–18.

Birdsall, Nancy, and Richard Sabot. "Inequality as a Constraint on Economic Growth in Latin America." *Development Policy.* Washington, D.C.: Inter-American Development Bank, November 1994, 1–5.

Hurt, Harry, III. "It's Time to Get Real About Mexico." *Fortune,* September 5, 1995, 98–108.

Inter-American Development Bank. *Economic and Social Progress in Latin America.* 1995 Report. Baltimore: Johns Hopkins University Press, 1995.

Loser, Caludio, and Eliot Kalter, eds. *Mexico: The Strategy to Achieve Sustained Economic Growth.* Occasional Paper 99. Washington, D.C.: International Monetary Fund, September 1992.

Lustig, Nora. "Mexico: The Slippery Road to Stability." *The Brookings Review,* Vol. 14, No. 2 (Spring 1996), 4–9.

Maddison, Angus. *The Political Economy of Poverty, Equity, and Growth: Brazil and Mexico.* New York: Oxford University Press, 1992.

"Mexico: The Long Haul." *The Economist,* August 26-September 1, 1995, 11–19.

Naim, Moises. "Latin America the Morning After." *Foreign Affairs,* Vol. 74, No. 4 (July-August 1995), 45–61.

Torres, Craig, and Paul B. Carroll. "Mexico's Mantra for Salvation: Export, Export, Export." *Wall Street Journal,* March 17, 1995, A6.

U.S. General Accounting Office. *Mexico's Financial Crisis: Origins, Awareness, Assistance, and Initial Efforts to Recover.* Washington, D.C.: USGAO, February 1996.

NIGERIA AND SOUTH AFRICA

CHAPTER 16

Nigeria and South Africa

Africa is the poorest continent in the world. In 1994, twenty-eight of the sixty-four poorest countries in the world were located in Africa. The African countries have had lower growth rates than other countries, their birthrates are the highest in the world, and their populations are expected to double in twenty-four years. Their economic development has been held back by a number of factors, not the least of which have been political corruption and tribal wars. A case in point was Rwanda in 1994, where the Hutu and Tutsi tribes took turns slaughtering each other. Nigeria, which at one time appeared to be the African country most likely to achieve economic development, has squandered its opportunities. What most African countries need is a stable political environment that would help establish credibility and stability in government policy.

Nigeria, which has the largest population of all of the African countries, and South Africa, which has the largest GNP, will be compared and examined in this chapter. Although both countries were formerly a part of the British Empire, they are totally different in many ways. Nigeria depends on the export of one major product—oil—while South Africa has a diversified economy. Now that the problem of apartheid has been resolved, South Africa is regarded as one of the big emerging markets of the future and a role model for other African nations. Nigeria, at least for the present, appears to be going nowhere.

CHARACTERISTICS OF AFRICA

The majority of African countries have three things in common. First, with few exceptions, they were once colonies of a European country; second, they are poor; and third, uncontrolled population growth limits their potential economic development and creates enormous social problems.

Colonialism

For centuries, Africa was called the "dark continent," unknown to all outsiders except a few explorers. All of this changed when European powers decided at the Berlin Conference of 1885 to divide up Africa into enclaves or spheres of influence. Five countries shared in the division of African territory—Belgium, England, France, Germany, and Portugal. Belgium got that area of Africa known as the Congo, which became one of the largest copper-producing areas in the world. England, which was already established in Egypt and the Cape of Africa, acquired the Sudan, southern Africa, and part of southwest Africa. France, which had already conquered Algeria, was given West Africa. Germany was given the right to parts of East Africa and southwest Africa, including the area known as the Tanganyika territory.[1] Portugal, the smallest of the five European countries, was given what was left in southern East and West Africa, including the areas that are now the countries of Angola and Mozambique.

The African colonies served two purposes. First, they provided a source of wealth for their owners in the ruling countries. Private companies were given monopoly rights by their governments to operate in the colonies and became the general media of commerce. The South Africa Chartered Company, owned by Cecil Rhodes, was given the right to develop the resources of southern Africa. The discovery of gold in the South African Rand and diamonds at Kimberley made Rhodes one of the richest men in the world.[2] Second, the African colonies served as markets for the products of the ruling countries. Until 1870, British manufactured goods found a market in other European countries. After 1870, Germany, France, Belgium, and other countries were able to satisfy their home markets and began to produce a surplus for sale abroad. With increasing saturation of the European markets, all looked for more markets overseas, and for this purpose, Africa served admirably. Thus, the race to acquire colonies began.

1. Germany lost its colonies after the end of World War I.
2. Cecil Rhodes is the man who established the Rhodes scholarship.

The colonies were governed by administrators sent from London, Paris, Berlin, Brussels, and Lisbon. The colonial civil service and military were run by the ruling countries, and the middle-class merchants were either European nationals, Indians, or Chinese. Native Africans were given little opportunity for self-government and were given no positions of authority in the colonial governments. As a result, when the colonies achieved their independence and became self-governing nations, there was a leadership vacuum. Most of the foreign civil servants, engineers, and merchants who had made up the backbone of government and commerce returned to their home countries. Their positions were filled by persons with little training in government or no technical experience. Animosity toward anything foreign also resulted in the forced departure of Indian and Chinese merchants from some African countries. Unfortunately, the locals did not have the entrepreneurial skills to run the businesses vacated by the Europeans and Asians.

Poverty

Africa is by far the poorest of the world's continents. Its per capita income of around $660 is 3 percent of that of the United States. Mozambique, the poorest country in the world, had a per capita income of $80 in 1994, and Tanzania, the second poorest, had a per capita income of $90.[3] Only South Africa would qualify as being in the same stage of economic development as Brazil and Mexico. Libya, which has the highest per capita income of all of the African countries, derives its income from oil exports. Moreover, the average annual rate of economic growth of many African countries was negative for the period 1980–1993, with the Ivory Coast having a negative growth rate of 4.6 percent.

Table 16-1 presents per capita GNP and average rate of growth per capita for fifteen African countries, and Table 16-2 compares real per capita GDP for nineteen African countries in 1960 and 1991. (The Asian nations included in these tables may be compared as former colonies of European empires not located in Africa.) Most of the poorer countries are located in the sub-Saharan region of Africa.[4] With the exception of Ethiopia, all were former colonies of Belgium, England, France, Germany, or Portugal. It is in these low-income countries that slow economic growth has done the most to perpetuate poverty. The rate of savings for many African countries is low—in some cases negative. This reduces capital formation. For example, Nigeria, the largest African country, had an average annual decrease in gross domestic investment of 10.2 percent during the period 1980–1990. Income distribution is far more unequal than it is in developed countries. In Kenya, for example, the highest 10 percent of the population received 47.9 percent of household income in 1992, compared to 38.1 percent for the lowest 80 percent.[5]

3. The World Bank, *The World Bank Atlas 1996* (Washington, D.C.: The World Bank, 1996), 18–19.
4. The sub-Saharan region includes Central Africa. Twenty-five of Africa's twenty-seven countries are in the sub-Saharan region.
5. The World Bank, *World Development Report 1995* (New York: Oxford University Press, 1995), 220.

TABLE 16-1 *Per Capita GNP and Average Annual Growth Rates for Selected African Countries*

	Per Capita GNP (dollars)	*Average Annual Real Growth in GNP in Percent, 1980–1993*
Mozambique	90	–1.5
Tanzania	90	0.1
Ethiopia	100	–1.8
Malawi	200	–1.2
Rwanda	210	–1.2
Niger	270	–4.1
Kenya	270	0.3
Nigeria	300	–0.1
Zambia	380	–3.1
Ivory Coast	630	–4.6
Egypt	660	2.8
Senegal	750	0.0
Morocco	1,040	1.2
Algeria	1,780	–0.8
South Africa	2,980	–0.2
Indonesia	740	4.2
Malaysia	3,140	3.5

Source: The World Bank, *World Development Report 1995* (Washington, D.C.: The World Bank, 1995), 162–163.

Population Growth

Africa's population is growing faster than the population of the other continents. In addition, its population is outstripping food production. Famines in Somalia and Ethiopia have been publicized on national television, but other African countries have also had famines. The number of hungry and malnourished Africans has increased to almost one-fifth of the continent's population. Moreover, the population increase has put pressure on medical care, housing, and the overall infrastructure of the African countries. Infant mortality rates are much higher than those for other developing and developed countries, but birthrates are the highest in the world. The average African woman has 5.8 children; the average American woman has 2.1 children; and the average German woman has 1.3 children. Africa's total population will double in twenty-four years. Western Europe's will double in 741 years.

Their large populations create a burden for most African countries in terms of resource allocation. Most resources must be used for consumption. Incomes are low, so human and physical capital is less developed.[6] The population growth af-

6. Human capital represents the skills that people use in combination with their labor effort. These skills are the result of education or training carried out some time in the past and used for future production. A long period of schooling lowers a society's quantity of labor resources, but the lost working time is offset by the greater productivity that results from the knowledge and skill gained from the education. Physical capital, such as factories and machines, makes it possible for countries to produce more efficiently than they can without them.

TABLE 16-2
A Comparison of Real per Capita GDP for African Countries, 1960–1991 (PPP $)

Country	*1960*	*1991*
Kenya	635	1,350
Congo	1,092	2,800
Madagascar	1,013	710
Zambia	1,172	1,010
Nigeria	1,133	1,360
Niger	604	542
Botswana	474	4,690
Egypt	557	3,600
Chad	785	447
Rwanda	538	680
Ghana	1,049	930
Angola	880	1,000
Algeria	1,676	2,870
Morocco	854	3,300
Sudan	975	1,162
Zaire	379	469
Ethiopia	262	370
South Africa	2,984	3,885
Sierra Leone	871	1,020
South Korea	690	8,320
Malaysia	1,783	7,400

Source: United Nations Development Programme, *Human Development Report, 1994* (New York: Oxford University Press, 1994), 136–137.

fects both the demand for and the supply of savings. Household savings—usually the largest component of domestic savings—are reduced by the high dependency burdens associated with rapid population growth. At any given level of per capita income, greater numbers of dependents cause consumption to rise, so savings per capita will fall. Governments can, within limits, use fiscal and monetary policies to change a country's rate of savings, irrespective of demographic conditions. However, the effectiveness of fiscal and monetary policies is predicated on the existence of a well-developed system of public finance and banking, which most African countries do not have.

Table 16-3 presents population, birth and death rates, and population-doubling time for selected African countries, many of which can be expected to double their population in less than twenty-five years. The implication is clear, particularly from the standpoint of education. Increases in the number of school-age children require increased spending on education, even if the objective is just to maintain current enrollments and standards. In a world of rapid technological change, these countries need to improve their schools both quantitatively and qualitatively. They will have to generate more national savings, or curtail other investments in, for example, power and transport. But the latter are also an important part of a country's infrastructure and are necessary for economic development. If a country is unwilling or, more likely, unable to make these sacrifices, spending

TABLE 16-3 *Population Data for Selected African Countries, 1995*

	Population (millions)	*Birthrate (per 1,000)*	*Death Rate (per 1,000)*	*Population-Doubling Time (years)*
Chad	6.4	44	18	27
Ethiopia	56.0	46	16	23
Mali	9.4	51	20	22
Zaire	44.1	48	16	22
Uganda	21.3	52	19	21
Tanzania	28.5	45	15	22
Niger	9.2	53	19	21
Ghana	17.5	42	12	23
Kenya	28.3	45	12	21
Sudan	28.6	41	12	23
Zambia	9.1	47	17	23
Nigeria	101.2	43	12	22
Cameroon	13.5	40	11	24
Egypt	61.9	30	8	31
Algeria	28.4	30	6	29
South Africa	43.5	31	8	30
Africa	720.0	41	13	24
Developed countries	1,169	12	10	432

Source: Carl Haub and Machiko Yanagishita, *World Population Data Sheet 1995* (Washington, D.C.: Population Reference Bureau, 1995).

must be spread over a large group of schoolchildren to the detriment of the quality of their education; otherwise, a growing number of children have to be excluded.

Political and Social Instability

Political and social instability are common problems in many of the African countries and inhibit their economic development. In 1994 Rwanda was wracked by a civil war that resulted in tribal genocide. A civil war continues in the Sudan, and in Algeria there is friction between Islamic fundamentalists and the government. All too frequently, the African countries have become hostage to leaders who are solely intent on gaining and holding political power and enriching themselves in the process. An example is General Mobutu of Zaire, Africa's longest-serving dictator, who has used the economy for his personal gain.[7] But he is not alone; most African countries are run either by the military or by one political party that permits only token opposition. Genuine political democracy exists in only a handful of the African countries.

7. The most infamous leader was Idi Amin, dictator of Uganda, who practiced tribal genocide, systematically killing people who were members of tribes other than his own. He patterned himself after Adolf Hitler, whom he greatly admired.

A number of factors contribute to the political and social instability of Africa. Poverty is obviously a very important factor, and uncontrolled population growth is another. Corruption is still another. Politicians and bureaucrats line their pockets at the expense of the public. Even in countries as poor as Chad, ownership of a Mercedes-Benz by a government official is very common.[8] As often as not, large amounts of foreign food, cash, and equipment aid never reach their intended destinations.[9] Tribal conflicts are another major factor inhibiting political stability. In all but a handful of African countries, tribal loyalties still predominate, especially in rural areas where nationalist sentiment has not penetrated.[10] Savage warfare between tribes is common. The bloodiest war in postcolonial Africa was fought in Nigeria from 1967 to 1970, when the predominantly Ibo region of southeastern Nigeria seceded and formed the independent state of Biafra. The civil war cost a million lives before Biafra was brought under control.[11]

Foreign Trade

The composition of foreign trade is a factor that has worked against the economic development of most of the African countries. Their exports, based on raw materials, have included such products as oil, cotton, and copper, while their imports have included manufactured goods. Nigeria is an excellent example. In 1993, oil accounted for 94 percent of Nigerian export earnings; conversely, machinery and other manufactured goods accounted for 85 percent of its expenditure on imports.[12] The price of oil and other minerals usually fluctuates more in world markets than the prices of manufactured goods. The end result is that the terms of trade for most of the African nations have been unfavorable and, as Table 16-4 indicates, has had an adverse effect on the current accounts and balance of payments of the African countries. However, the world prices of oil improved in the 1990s and created a surplus in the Nigerian current account.

Human Development

The great majority of African countries are in a low state of human development. Of the fifty-four countries ranked in the low state, forty-three are African countries; of the twenty lowest countries ranked, eighteen are African countries.[13] They are at the bottom of such human development indicators as life expectancy at birth, adult literacy rates, and mean years of schooling.[14] But the problems do

8. A Mercedes-Benz costs around $50,000. The per capita GNP of Chad is $190.
9. This is true for Somalia, a country that is literally starving to death. Food reaches Somalia but is stolen by gangs of thugs.
10. Zaire has two hundred tribes speaking some seventy-five languages, from the Pygmies to the Baluba. Tribal conflicts may be the reason for the emergence of one-party states in Africa. The ruling tribe simply exterminates other tribes.
11. The civil war in Rwanda in 1994 may be bloodier.
12. The World Bank, *World Development Report 1995*, 190–192.
13. There are fifty-four African countries.
14. For example, in Guinea the adult illiteracy rate is 75 percent, and in Burkina Faso it is 80 percent.

TABLE 16-4
Current Account Balance and Terms of Trade for Selected African Countries, 1993

	Current Account ($ millions)	*Terms of Trade (1987 = 100 percent)*
Tanzania	–935	85
Ethiopia	–433	67
Sierra Leone	–128	76
Burundi	–190	52
Malawi	–221	86
Uganda	–369	49
Madagascar	–326	68
Nigeria	1,537	99
Kenya		81
Gambia	–35	95
Zambia	–471	98
Zimbabwe	–295	89
Ivory Coast	–1,402	79
Rwanda	–360	73
Cameroon	–794	77
Algeria	361	95
South Africa	1,743	105

Source: The World Bank, *World Development Report 1995* (Washington, D.C.: The World Bank, 1995), 186, 187, 194, 195.

not stop there. The majority of the population in many of these countries do not have adequate access to health services, safe water, or sanitation facilities. A majority of children under the age of five are malnourished, and infant mortality rates are the highest in the world. In most African countries, the great majority of women are illiterate; their birthrates are the highest in the world; and more of them die in childbirth.

Table 16-5 presents measures of human development for the African countries. The countries are ranked by the human development index, and most rank very low. Niger, which ranked at the bottom of 174 countries, had a human development index of 0.207 compared to a human development index of 0.578 for Honduras, which ranked 116. Haiti, the poorest country in Latin America and the Caribbean, had a human development index of 0.362, which ranked it 148, which was higher than twenty-three African countries.[15] Eighteen of the twenty countries that were the lowest in the index were African countries.

THE DEVELOPMENT OF NIGERIA

At the beginning of the twentieth century, Nigeria did not exist as a national entity, and it was notable in world commerce chiefly as a supplier of a few tropical

15. Haiti ranked higher than twenty-three of the fifty-four African countries, yet it is considered a basket case when it comes to economic development.

TABLE 16-5
Human Development Index and Rankings for Selected Countries (rank out of 173 countries)

	Human Development	*Rank*
High Human Development		
Canada	0.950	1
United States	0.937	2
Mexico	0.842	53
Medium Human Development		
Turkey	0.792	66
South Africa	0.705	95
China	0.594	111
Nicaragua	0.611	109
Low Human Development		
Kenya	0.481	130
India	0.439	134
Nigeria	0.406	141
Haiti	0.362	148
Rwanda	0.332	156
Ethiopia	0.227	171
Mali	0.222	172
Sierra Leone	0.221	173
Niger	0.207	174
Sub-Saharan Africa	0.389	

Source: United Nations Development Programme, *Human Development Report 1995* (New York: Oxford University Press, 1995), 155–157.

products, such as palm oil and spices. During earlier centuries, its commercial history was very largely dominated by the slave trade. It became a formal British colony in 1860 and was recognized by other European powers as a British enclave at the Berlin Conference of 1885.

British colonial rule proved a mixed blessing for Nigeria. Its main direct contributions were building railroads and developing harbor facilities. Administrative measures were also used to encourage and regulate the production of cotton and other crops for export.[16] Trade and banking were run by companies chartered in England. Barclay's Bank ran the banking system, and the Royal Niger Company was responsible for the development of crops for export. Rules, attitudes, and monopolistic practices by the British colonial administration, churches, and firms excluded Nigerians from any participation in government and commerce.

The economic and social orientation of the British colonial government in Nigeria changed dramatically after World War II. It moved from maintaining the existing colonial economy to a new approach that allowed more Nigerian participation in the economy. Priority was placed on the development of industry and trade that would be run by Nigerians. An increasing degree of local self-government was embodied in successive constitutions of 1951, 1954, and 1957; by then, Nigerian

16. Gavin Williams, *Nigeria Economy and Society* (London: Rex Collings, 1976), 18–19.

control over the government apparatus was substantial. A capitalism nurtured by colonialism developed, particularly in the areas of trade and light industry. The British-Nigerian colonial relationship came to mean planned economic development, the spread of industrialization, and better social services for the Nigerian people. England systematically extended the rights of self-government, so when Nigeria achieved its independence in 1960, it had a bureaucracy that had some experience with government and a small but expanding business class. The British had also spent money on developing agriculture and transportation systems and on extending medical and educational services.[17]

The Nigerian Economy

In 1994 Nigeria had a per capita GNP of $280, down from a per capita income high of $860 in 1981. It is the largest country in Africa, and its fertility rate of 6.3 percent is above the average for all African countries.[18] Its population-doubling time is twenty-two years, compared to an average of twenty-four years for all African countries and 432 years for the developed countries. Despite the fact that Nigeria is more industrialized than most of the other African countries, over half of the labor force is employed in agriculture. In 1993 agriculture accounted for 34 percent of Nigerian GDP compared to 2 percent in the United States.[19] In terms of value added by manufacturing, Nigeria ranked sixth among all African nations in 1992, behind Egypt, Morocco, Algeria, Tunisia, and South Africa.[20] It is a country in the lower state of transition.

Oil

Oil, especially in a developing country, can be a decisive factor in economic growth. It is an easily negotiable source of wealth for the producer, an efficient source of energy for the user, and a good base for industrialization because of the variety of products needed by the petrochemical industry. However, oil can be a mixed blessing. It fueled the prosperity of the Nigerian economy from 1965 to 1980, but it was also responsible for the economic slump during the 1980s. The worldwide oil glut of the 1980s had a disastrous effect on the Nigerian economy. Earnings from exports of Nigerian oil declined from a high of $26 billion in 1980 to $6.2 billion in 1988.[21] The spot price per barrel of Nigerian crude ranged from a high of $18.80 to a low of $13.70 during 1987 and 1988. As oil prices declined, the

17. It should be pointed out that the post–World War II England was far different from the England that was the dominant world power of the last century. Imperialism led to the development of the British Empire. However, by the end of World War II, the empire was a thing of the past, and the colonies no longer served the purpose of providing markets and raw materials.
18. Carl Haub and Machiko Yanagishita, *World Population Data Sheet 1995* (Washington, D.C.: World Population Reference Bureau, 1995.)
19. The World Bank, *World Development Report 1995*, 166.
20. Ibid., 172–173. It ranked second behind South Africa in 1981.
21. Economic Intelligence Unit, *The Economist* (Nigeria: Author, 1989–90), 26.

terms of trade became more unfavorable. Imports increased in price at the same time oil prices were falling. To illustrate the value of oil exports to the Nigerian economy, the GNP fell from $76 billion in 1980 to $29.9 billion in1994.[22]

The Role of the Government

Nigeria is a federal republic consisting of nineteen states. Although the states have a certain amount of autonomy, they receive most of their money from the federal government, which derives its revenue from taxes and oil exports. The most important taxes are a petroleum profits tax and excise taxes. A personal income tax is used, but the rate of avoidance is high.

There are three ways in which a government can intervene in a mixed economy. First, intervention can occur through fiscal and monetary policies. Second, there can be a more direct intervention through economic planning, with government policies designed to affect resource allocation and business conduct and performance. Third, there can be government ownership and control of the means of production. All are used by the Nigerian government, which plays a dominant role in the economic development of the country. It is the largest single employer, and it is the principal exporter and importer. It is responsible for the development of the national economic plans and the setting of planning priorities. It grants subsidies and makes loans to various sectors of the economy and implements foreign trade policy.

Economic Planning. Economic planing represents an effort to facilitate the process of economic and social development through the creation of national goals and priorities. Financing for projects that have planning priority comes from the federal budget and from credit provided by the banking system. Some projects are financed by various international lending institutions, including the World Bank.

Since it became independent in 1960, Nigeria has formulated several economic plans, the last of which was the Fourth National Development Plan. The purpose of the plan was to provide a general guideline for Nigeria's economic and social priorities. The basic goals of the Fourth Plan were to develop Nigeria's physical and social structure and agricultural and industrial bases, so that the country would become less vulnerable to the fluctuations of the world oil market. Some eight thousand development projects were listed in the plan, with an estimated investment of $125 billion during its duration. Most of these projects were canceled in 1984 when the military government that deposed the civilian government of President Shagari in the 1983 military coup imposed austerity measures on the Nigerian economy.

A key policy in Nigerian economic planning has been import substitution. Manufactured goods constitute the main targets of Nigeria's import substitution policy. The policy has been implemented in three ways. First, Nigerian industries,

22. The World Bank, *The World Bank Atlas 1996* (Washington, D.C.: The World Bank, 1996), 19.

including textiles, furniture, motor vehicles, glass products, and consumer appliances, are heavily protected by tariffs. Successive increases in tariffs have produced a sharp decline in the absolute level and in the rate of increase of imports of such goods. Second, these and other manufacturing industries have been favored by tax policies including accelerated depreciation and special relief from taxes for a period of from three to five years depending upon the amount of local capital invested. Third, many businesses are exclusively reserved for Nigerians. This restricts the amount of foreign involvement in local activity.

Much of the growth in Nigerian manufacturing is a result of the planned policy of import substitution. However, the process of import substitution has not helped the foreign debt problem, because it has resulted in an increase in imports of raw materials. To produce at home the goods previously imported, many of the basic raw materials that have not been available locally have had to be imported.

Private Enterprise

Economic activity in most sectors of the Nigerian economy is primarily the function of private enterprise. To some extent, British colonial rule facilitated the development of a local entrepreneurial class in Nigeria. The British financed the development of railroads and port facilities. They abolished the trading monopolies of coastal tribal kingdoms, internal tolls, and the arbitrary interference of African tribal rulers with the free conduct of commerce. The British pound was introduced as the common medium of exchange. The increase in world demand for export crops in the early years of the twentieth century encouraged British firms to advance credit for the production of cash crops. This credit in turn facilitated the sale of imported goods. The expansion of export production and the increase in the money supply in the form of produce advances increased local opportunities in retailing and in handicraft and food production for the domestic market. The initial expansion of British colonial rule encouraged competition in the distributive trades.

In order to develop new export crops, traders and farmers adapted existing social institutions to regulate land ownership or use, mobilize savings and credit facilities, and recruit labor to clear, weed, plant, and harvest crops. The successful creation of export production by Nigerian traders and planters contrasted with the failure of British government and foreign company plantations. Thus, in Nigeria, colonialism enabled Africans to develop agricultural production and generally stimulated the domestic production of other goods.

British ownership and operation were limited primarily to railroad investments, banking, and mineral resources. A dual economy developed, with the Nigerians controlling farm production, trading, and small business enterprises. Nevertheless, the British controlled the economy, and Nigerian private enterprise was not allowed to compete with British commercial interests. British investments in railways led them to prevent the development of any form of local transportation system that might provide competition.

The economic orientation of British colonial rule changed after World War II from maintaining the dual colonial economy to increasing the extent of Nigerian participation in all sectors.[23] This goal was to be accomplished through government financial support of private enterprise, which the Nigerians themselves would run but the British would control. However, increasing nationalism sharply increased the Nigerian desire for more participation and control in the development of the economy. Control by Nigerians over private enterprises increased. This participation was limited primarily to the trade and services sectors of the economy. Very few Nigerians possessed the expertise or the capital to own and manage a modern production enterprise. Publicly owned Nigerian corporations began a growing number of enterprises intended to be run as profitable business ventures. At the time of Nigerian independence in 1960, state capitalism existed side by side with private capitalism. Political abuses of public corporations made them largely unsuccessful, and Nigeria relied increasingly on foreign-owned enterprises for the development of a modern economy.

Postcolonial Development. The private sector of Nigerian economy increased in importance during the period following independence. Gross private fixed investment increased from less than half of the total fixed investment in 1960 to 65 percent by 1975. Most of this increase took the form of foreign direct investment. The reliance on private investment in general and foreign direct investment in particular has encouraged foreign and private domestic investment by offering financial incentives to invest in those sectors that contribute most to economic development.

Results of Private Enterprise. Nigerian entrepreneurs have established a large variety of very small enterprises. Such undertakings are easy to start, even by men and women with little education, training, or business experience, and barriers to entry are negligible. The technical knowledge is simple, and many have acquired it as workers or apprentices in other small firms or through experience with large firms or in government. Capital requirements are usually minimal, and individual entrepreneurs can often operate with virtually no capital of their own, relying instead on advances from their suppliers. Requirements for skilled labor are usually negligible, and there is an abundance of semiskilled and unskilled labor. What all of this means is that there are a very large number of small enterprises in Nigeria producing and distributing in local markets. However, it is difficult for any of these enterprises to acquire the capital and technological know-how to make the transition to large-scale operations.

THE PERFORMANCE OF THE NIGERIAN ECONOMY

The Nigerian economy has very serious problems. It deteriorated badly during the 1980s. From 1980 through 1989 real per capita GNP declined at an average annual rate of 0.3 percent. GNP fell from $99 billion in 1980 to $28 billion in 1989, and

23. Sayre P. Schatz, *Nigerian Capitalism* (Berkeley: University of California Press, 1977), 4–7, 22–27.

per capita GNP fell from $860 to $250 in the same time period.[24] This decline can be attributed to one factor—the drop in the world price of oil from $40 a barrel in 1980 to a low of $14 a barrel in 1987.[25] In 1980 Nigeria's per capita income was $500 less than South Korea's; however, by the end of the decade its per capita income was $5,000 less. In 1980 the Nigerian GNP was larger than the South Korean GNP; by the end of the decade, the South Korean GNP was seven times larger.[26] Both Malaysia and Thailand, which had lower GNPs than Nigeria in 1980, had larger GNPs in 1988. Nigeria can be compared to Indonesia—large, diverse, and oil-rich, but Indonesia has diversified away from its dependence on oil and Nigeria has not, and that is one of its major problems.[27]

Population Growth

Owing to a high fertility rate and a declining death rate, the population of Nigeria is growing rapidly. The size and composition of the population are affected by several factors. First, given the high birthrate and declining mortality rate, the population is young, with 49 percent 15 years of age or younger. A young population tends to have an adverse effect on the size and productivity of the labor force. Also, population growth will increase as female children reach childbearing years. Second, there is enormous ethnic diversity: more than 250 groups with different languages and customs. Active tribal rivalries compound the problems of government. Third, the population is unequally distributed geographically. The areas of greatest population density are either the cities, which do not have an adequate infrastructure, or areas that are remote from transportation facilities. Fourth, less than 25 percent of the relevant age group (persons 15 to 22 years old) are attending secondary schools or college. Table 16-6 presents some of the demographic characteristics of Nigeria.

Corruption

Corruption is a fact of life in Nigeria and assumes many forms. There is the standard low-level bribe, called *dash* or *chai*, which is payment for services rendered or anticipated. This payment may take the form of a package of razor blades, a case of Scotch, or a digital watch. Higher-level bribes include payment of money or a very expensive gift. Then there is political corruption, including bribery, inflated results, fake voter rolls, reversal of election results, and under-age voters. State-owned corporations are often run by political hacks rather than trained civil servants. Public projects are often not completed because politicians and contractors have appropriated the funds.[28] The tax system of the country is so inefficient that

24. The World Bank, *World Development Report 1991* (Washington, D.C.: The World Bank, 1991), 204–205.
25. The world price of oil in 1995 and early 1996 ranged from $14 to $18 a barrel.
26. In 1993 it was ten times larger.
27. In 1994 Indonesia had a per capita GNP of $880 compared to $280 for Nigeria.
28. An example is the construction of the new capital of Abuja, where waste and corruption resulted in a cost ten times the original estimate.

TABLE 16-6 *Human Development Characteristics of Nigeria*

Birthrate (per 1,000)	43
Death rate (per 1,000)	12
Natural increase (percent)	3.1
Population-doubling time (years)	22
Infant mortality rate per 1,000 live births	72
Fertility rate per women of childbearing years	6.3
Life expectancy (years)	
Male	48
Female	50
Daily calorie intake per person	2,200
Students enrolled in secondary schools (percent)	20
Adult illiteracy (percent of population)	48
Students enrolled in college (percent)	2
Percent of workers employed in agriculture (percent)	46
Rank among 174 countries in human development	141

Sources: Carl Haub and Machiko Yanagashita, *1995 World Population Data Sheet* (Washington, D.C.: Population Reference Bureau, 1995); The World Bank, *World Development Report 1995* (New York: Oxford University Press, 1995), 212–213; United Nations Development Programme, *Human Development Report 1995* (New York: Oxford University Press, 1995), 161, 163, 165.

much of the revenue potential is not realized because tax evasion is widespread and tax officials are often corrupt.

Political Instability

Nigeria has been ruled by a military government for most of the time since it gained its formal independence from England in 1960. The latest military coup occurred in 1982, and that faction has run the country ever since. A proposed handover of the government to civilian rule was delayed in the summer of 1992 because of ethnic and religious unrest, and poverty riots created the worst disturbances in Nigeria in a decade. Political instability is caused by a number of factors, including poverty, which has been exacerbated by both the decline in oil earnings and by the adverse effect of droughts on food supply. Approximately 40 percent of Nigerians live in poverty.[29] Imbalances between urban and rural areas, between the employed and unemployed, and between rich and poor are the prime causes of political instability. Nigeria also has had a very limited experience with democracy.[30]

29. United Nations Development Programme, *Human Development Report 1994* (New York: Oxford University Press, 1994), 165. Depending on estimates, the rate of poverty in Nigeria ranges from 40 to 80 percent of the population. The *Human Development Report* uses the term "absolute poverty."

30. The current military leader of Nigeria is General Sani Abacha, who has declared that Nigeria is not ready for democracy. He achieved worldwide attention in early 1996 when he had a number of political dissidents, including a well-known writer, hanged despite international protests.

SOUTH AFRICA

South Africa is regarded as the country with the greatest economic development potential of all of the African countries, particularly since it has become a democracy.[31] It has the most advanced, broadly based, and productive economy in Africa. It possesses a modern infrastructure supporting the distribution of goods to major urban centers, and it has well-developed financial, legal, communications, energy, and transport sectors. Its stock exchange ranks among the top ten in the world in the value of transactions. Its average per capita income of $3,010 is the highest of all of the African countries.[32] Although mining is still South Africa's single most important source of export revenue, the economy has become more diversified, with manufacturing and services accounting for around 70 percent of GDP.

Conversely, there are also problems. South Africa has one of the most unequal distributions of income in the world. In 1993 the top 20 percent of the population received 63.3 percent of the income, while the bottom 80 percent of the population received 36.7 percent.[33] There are extremes of wealth and poverty in South Africa, with whites making an average income nine times that of blacks. If whites and blacks were separated into two countries, the white 12 percent of the population would receive a much larger income than the black 88 percent of the population. If the human development index is used, the white population would rank 24th among all nations, behind Italy and Spain, and the black population would rank 123d, behind Lesotho and ahead of the Congo. South Africa's actual rating of 95th puts it in the category of medium human development.[34]

THE HISTORY OF SOUTH AFRICA

South Africa was a product of the mercantilist policies of England and the Netherlands. The Dutch East India Company established the first permanent colony in South Africa in 1652 and used it as a way station to its possessions in East Asia. Gradually, the Dutch began to push inward from its colony at Cape Town and began to colonize the interior of South Africa. The Dutch maintained control over South Africa for some 140 years. It was regarded as a source of raw materials for the Netherlands and as a market for Dutch manufactured goods. Dutch seapower began to decline, however, and by the end of the eighteenth century England had become the leading seapower in Europe. South Africa became important to the British because it controlled their trade routes to India. Emigration from England

31. It is the only African country listed by the U.S. Department of Commerce as one of the ten emerging markets of the future.

32. Libya has a higher per capita income, but is wholly dependent on oil exports.

33. The World Bank, *World Development Report 1995*, 221.

34. "Survey of South Africa," *The Economist*, May 20–26, 1995, 1–2; United Nations Development Programme, *Human Development Report 1995*, 156.

to South Africa began in 1820, and the Dutch settlers moved inward to create their own enclaves.[35]

The British began to expand northward from Cape Town and other seaports during the 1830s, and expansion continued throughout the century. A colonial rivalry had begun between England and Germany, with each country out to claim more African territory. Eventually the dispute was resolved, and the British were able to lay claim to most of what is now South Africa. The British East Africa Company was given a royal charter to conduct business in South Africa. However, the catalyst in the economic development of the colony was the discovery of gold and diamonds, creating a mining boom that lasted for more than fifty years. It also led to the Boer War between the British and the Boers, the first of the many wars of this century.[36] In 1910 the British created the Union of South Africa. It became a country in 1966.

Gold and diamonds became to South Africa what oil became to Mexico and Nigeria. For the first fifty years of this century, the South African economy was based on the mining of these products for export. They accounted for 90 percent or more of the value of South African exports during the period 1911–1961, and the real per capita income of the population more than doubled during that period. In the 1960s South African GDP increased at an average annual rate of 6 percent, but then an economic downturn occurred as the world prices for gold and diamonds began to fall. New sources of gold were discovered in other countries, and platinum became more valuable. The real growth rate for the period 1980–1993 was negative, and failed to keep up with the increase in population.

South Africa has many problems to overcome before it can become the South Korea of the future. Its industries have been protected by tariffs and, for the most part, are not competitive by world standards. Shielded from foreign competition, many companies function in oligopolistic markets. Two companies control 75 percent of the sugar market; three companies control 75 percent of the fertilizer market; and three companies control 90 percent of the market in chemical fibers used to weave textiles.[37] South African manufacturers have charged 20 percent more for metal bolts they sell in their own country than identical ones they export. It costs three times more to produce a yard of cloth in South Africa than it does in India. Moreover, productivity in South Africa is lower than it is in comparable countries. In Mexico, which has about the same per capita income as South Africa, each Mexican worker takes about one-third of the time a South African worker takes to build a car.[38]

But there are other problems as well. Who will replace President Nelson Mandela, now 76? Who has the stature to hold the country together as Mandela has? Will the current political arrangement, which allows shared power among several political parties, end up like Zimbabwe, the former Rhodesia, which has one political party

35. The Dutch settlers were called Boers. They created the Orange Free State.
36. The Boer War lasted from 1899 to 1901.
37. "A Survey of South Africa," *The Economist*, May 20–26, 1995, 1–26.
38. Ibid., 10.

with one leader? There is also the potential for tribal warfare between the Zulus and other tribes.[39] Political stability is necessary to attract foreign investment. In 1994 U.S. direct investment in South Africa was less than $300 million, compared to $16.4 billion for Mexico; for Africa as a whole, U.S. direct investment in Africa amounted to $2.7 billion, compared to $5.7 billion for Argentina and $2.4 billion for Malaysia.[40] The investment in South Africa is primarily in the form of portfolio investment (stocks and bonds) that could be readily sold if a political crisis developed.

THE FUTURE OF AFRICA

The next 25 years may well bring the greatest shift in economic power the world has seen over the past 150 years. Today, the industrial economies dominate the world as they have done since the middle of the nineteenth century, but the power base seems to be shifting from West to East. The average annual growth rate in real GDP for the period 1974–1993 increased by 2.6 for the industrial countries of the West compared to 7.6 percent for East Asia and 4.8 percent for South Asia; projected annual average growth for the period 1994–2003 is 2.7 percent for the industrial countries, 7.6 percent for East Asia, and 5.3 percent for South Asia.[41] It is not just Taiwan, Singapore, and South Korea that have become world-class competitors; other countries, such as Malaysia and Thailand, are aggressively pursuing economic development. Then there are India and China, which, in terms of real GDP, are projected to be among the top five economies in the world by 2025.[42]

Africa is the world's poorest continent. Its people, unlike those of any other continent, were poorer at the end of the 1980s than they were at the start. While the rest of the world is getting more prosperous, Africa is not. It has no model of homegrown success, a second South Korea. Moreover, growth projections for the future do not look all that optimistic. The real GDP growth rate for sub-Saharan Africa, where much of the poverty is located, is projected to be 3.9 percent a year for the period 1994–2003. This projection is based on much lower incomes in the countries in this area, so most will probably be little better off in 2004 than they are now unless some radical changes are made.

The East Asia Role Model

It is postulated that there is a lot Africa can learn from the East Asian experience with economic development.[43] Twenty-five years ago the East Asian countries

39. The Zulus are the largest tribe in South Africa, accounting for 22 percent of the population. They conquered the other tribes in the last century and even defeated the British army.
40. U.S. Department of Commerce, Bureau of Economic Analyses, *A Survey of Current Business, June 1995*, Table 2.
41. "A Survey of the Global Economy," *The Economist*, October 1–7, 1994, 1.
42. See Chapter 1.
43. International Monetary Fund, "IMF Survey," March 6, 1995, 68–75.

had many of the problems Africa is experiencing today—widespread poverty, low domestic savings, a narrow production base, and extensive government involvement in their economies. What would be necessary for Africa to follow the East Asian model would be, first, a stable political environment now absent in most African countries. The second requisite is sound monetary and fiscal policies to prevent inflation or deflation and stabilize foreign exchange rates. Third, there must be human investment in health, education, and the infrastructure. Fourth, there have to be market-based policies that promote saving and investment. Losses generated by public enterprises in some African countries are larger than expenditures on health and education. Not only is this a poor allocation of scarce resources, but it sends the wrong signals to investors about government priorities.

SUMMARY

Most of Africa is in a state of crisis. The growth rate is negative, population is increasing more rapidly than the resource base, and fewer than one-third of the nations have anything resembling multiparty politics. A state of civil war exists in some countries and could expand to other countries. The destruction that began in Rwanda in April 1994 resulted in racial genocide. Any attempt to redraw borders on ethnic lines would seem certain to accelerate political disintegration and inspire new conflicts. Most of Africa lacks the crucial educated middle and professional classes and the mediating private and public institutions that would make democracy possible. Instead, corruption is rampant, and rule by military dictatorship or warlords is common. The stability necessary to attract investment is not there; the whole continent receives less U.S. direct investment than Brazil or Argentina. It is hoped that South Africa will become an economic role model for the rest of Africa, but this may not occur.

QUESTIONS FOR DISCUSSION

1. Discuss some of the factors that have held back the economic development of Africa.
2. What was the impact of British colonialism on the development of Nigeria and South Africa?
3. What are some of the problems that confront the future development of South Africa?
4. Why has democracy failed to take hold in most African countries?
5. Discuss the influence of oil on the Nigerian economy.
6. Twenty years ago such East Asian countries as South Korea, Malaysia, and Thailand were behind Nigeria and other African countries in terms of per capita income and GNP. Now they are well ahead. Why has this happened?
7. Compare the South African economy to the economies of Mexico and Brazil.
8. In your opinion, will the economies of the African countries improve in the future?

RECOMMENDED READINGS

"A Survey of South Africa." *The Economist,* May 20–26, 1995, 1–26.

"Achieving Growth in South Africa: Lessons from East Asia." *IMF Survey,* International Monetary Fund, July 17, 1995, 217–220.

"Closer Integration in Global Economy Vital for Africa." *IMF Survey,* International Monetary Fund, July 17, 1995, 217–220.

Haub, Carl, and Machiko Yanagishita, *1995 World Population Data Sheet.* Washington, D.C.: Population Reference Bureau, 1995.

McCarthy, F. Desmond, ed. *Problems of Developing Countries in the 1990's.* Vol. 1, World Bank Discussion Paper No. 97. Washington, D.C.: The World Bank, 1991.

Michaels, Marguerite. "Retreat from Africa." *Foreign Affairs,* Vol. 72, No. 1 (January-February 1993), 93–108.

Pfaff, William. "A New Colonialism." *Foreign Affairs,* Vol. 74, No. 1 (January-February 1995), 2–6

United Nations Development Programme. *Human Development Report 1995.* New York: Oxford University Press, 1995.

The World Bank. *World Development Report 1995.* Washington, D.C.: The World Bank, 1995.

PART V

Toward a Multipolar World

CHAPTER 17
A Changing World

CHAPTER 18
The New World Order

CHAPTER 17
A Changing World

Technological change and continually falling transportation and communications costs have been a major force contributing to global integration. Advances in information technology have created a service revolution. Technological innovation has expanded the opportunities for all sorts of services. An example is international finance, where flows of money know no boundaries. Interest rate changes in one economy affect investments in other economies. Global markets determine resource allocation. The impact of technological change on the world will be enormous. In the United States, for example, almost 75 percent of the jobs that are being created are in the service fields, which will require greater educational skills for workers to compete. Since 1987, only workers with postgraduate and professional degrees have enjoyed increasing incomes in the United States.

About 99 percent of the approximately one billion workers who will enter the labor force in the next thirty years will live in the low- and middle-income countries.[1] Will these workers lag farther behind workers in rich countries in terms of

1. The World Bank, *World Development Report 1995* (Washington, D.C.: The World Bank, 1995), 7.

income differences because of lower investment and educational attainment levels? Economic growth and integration into world markets have not solved the problem of poverty; on the contrary, poverty may increase as millions more workers enter the labor force of the future. In this increasingly competitive world dominated by knowledge-intensive technology, the key to economic success has become human resources, not natural resources, and this favors the rich countries. Moreover, unemployment problems in the rich countries as well as the poor countries have been exacerbated by the absence of an engine of economic growth, a role played by the United States in the three decades following the end of World War II.[2]

At the same time that technological change has been going on, the role of the state has been changing. Its role is shrinking throughout the world as more countries have adopted the free market approach to resource allocation. Will the rich countries, many of whom have financial problems of their own, created in part by an aging population, continue to give financial aid and other forms of assistance to poor countries so the latter can upgrade the educational level of their workers? The skilled workers of the rich industrial countries now earn more than sixty times the income of unskilled African or Indian workers, so the key, in part, is to improve their educational skills and opportunities for employment. But this requires money, and this is what the poor countries lack.

The remainder of this chapter will be devoted to some of the problems the poor nations of the world are facing. The problems to be examined are population growth, gender inequality, and unfavorable trade balances. The rate of population growth is increasing the most in the poor countries. The poorer the country, the greater the gender bias. Gender bias lowers productivity. This exists at a time when human resources are replacing natural resources in importance. In the poor countries, women perform the lion's share of work, working longer hours and contributing more to family income than men. International trade will be the main vehicle for economic growth in the future. World merchandise trade is expected to increase at a rate of 6 percent a year, and trade in services will increase even faster.[3] Will this help the poor countries of the world?

POPULATION GROWTH

In 1994, 56 percent of the world's population lived in low-income countries, with an average per capita GNP of $390 a year. By contrast, 15 percent of the world's population lived in rich countries, with an average per capita income of $24,170 a year.[4] The difference between the average per capita income of the rich and poor countries is 62 to 1.[5] Moreover, as Tables 17-1 and 17-2 indicate, the gap between rich nations and poor nations has widened over the years. For example, it has been

2. The engine for economic growth today comes from East Asia, excluding Japan.
3. *World Development Report 1995*, 9.
4. The World Bank, *The World Bank Atlas 1995* (Washington, D.C.: The World Bank, 1995), 20.
5. In 1988 the difference was 53 to 1.

TABLE 17-1 *Economic Differences Between Rich and Poor Nations (percent of activity)*

	Global GNP	*Trade*	*Commercial Bank Lending*	*Domestic Investment*	*Domestic Saving*	*Foreign Private Investment*
1960–1970						
Richest 20%	70.2	80.8	72.3	70.4	70.4	73.3
Poorest 20%	2.3	1.3	0.3	3.5	3.5	3.4
Ratio, richest to poorest	30/1	62/1	326/1	20/1	20/1	21/1
1989						
Richest 20%	82.7	81.2	94.6	80.6	80.5	58.4
Poorest 20%	1.4	1.0	0.2	1.3	1.0	2.7
Ratio, richest to poorest	59/1	86/1	485/1	64/1	62/1	21/1

Source: United Nations Development Programme, *Human Development Report 1992* (New York: Oxford University Press, 1992), 36.

TABLE 17-2 *Global Income Disparity Between Rich and Poor Nations, 1960–1989 (percent)*

	Richest 20 percent	*Poorest 20 percent*	*Ratio of Richest to Poorest*	*Gini Coefficient*
1960	70.2	2.3	30 to 1	0.69
1970	73.9	2.3	32 to 1	0.71
1980	76.3	1.7	45 to 1	0.79
1989	82.7	1.4	59 to 1	0.87

Source: United Nations Development Programme, *Human Development Report 1992* (New York: Oxford University Press, 1992), 36.

estimated that the average per capita income of the richest nations was 11 times greater than the average per capita income of the poorest countries in 1870. This is in sharp contrast to the ratio of 62 to 1 that exists today.

One-fifth of the world's population live in countries where the population growth rate is increasing by less than 1 percent a year. These countries account for 77 percent of the world's GNP. Included are the United States, Canada, Europe, Japan, Australia, and New Zealand. Conversely, another one-fifth of the world's population live in countries where the population growth rate is increasing by 2.2 percent a year or more. These countries account for around 1.6 percent of the world's GNP.[6] As Figure 17-1 indicates, these countries are mostly located in Africa and southern Asia. Table 17-3 indicates that future increases in the world's la-

6. Ibid., 8.

FIGURE 17-1

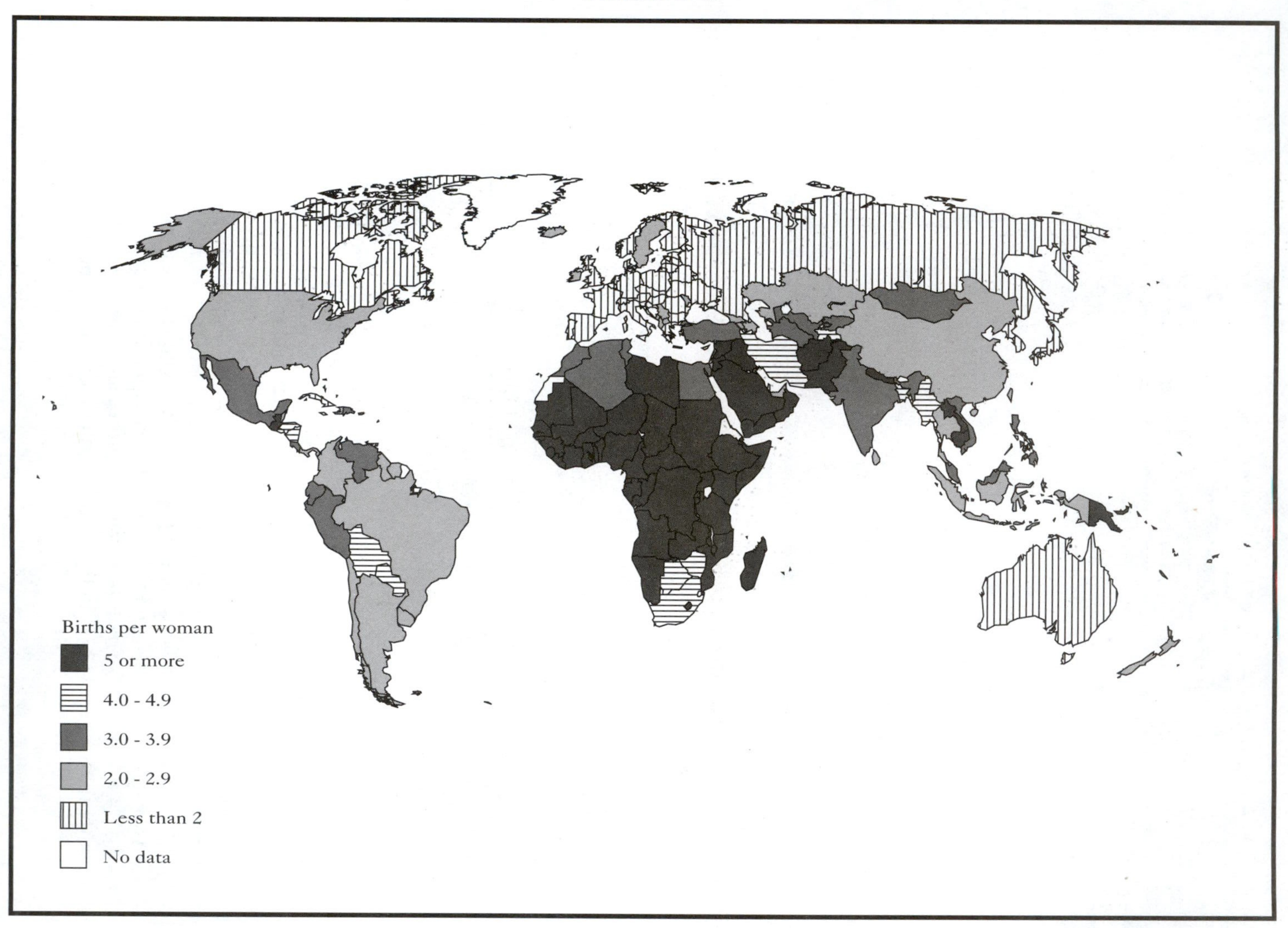

Births per woman
5 or more
4.0 - 4.9
3.0 - 3.9
2.0 - 2.9
Less than 2
No data

bor force will be in these countries. This will make the task of raising the living standards of the world's poor next to impossible. Despite an increase in world living standards over the past thirty years, much of the world's population has been left out.

Table 17-3 presents a comparison of population growth and projections of population growth for rich industrial countries and poor developing countries. These countries have two-thirds of the world's population. The extent of the demographic divide between the rich countries and the poor countries is very clear. With the exception of the United States, the population of the other rich countries has stabilized, and in the future will decline for some countries. The opposite holds true for the developing countries. An example is Pakistan, which had a population of 39 million in 1950, but which is projected to have a population of 312 million by 2030. Ethiopia, which recently experienced a severe famine, is projected to have its population increase by 106 million during the period 1990–2030. In comparison to such countries as India and Pakistan, the United States has far more natural resources and capital for investment and a much more skilled labor force. Raw numbers for the world's labor force are presented in Table 17-4.

TABLE 17-3 *Population Growth for the Most-Populated Countries 1950–2030 (millions)*

				Amount of Increase	
Countries	*1950*	*1990*	*2030*	*1950–1990*	*1990–2030*
Slow-Growth Countries					
France	42	57	62	15	5
Germany	68	80	81	12	1
Italy	47	58	56	11	–2
Japan	84	124	123	40	–1
Russia	114	148	161	34	13
United Kingdom	50	58	60	8	2
United States	152	250	345	98	95
Rapid-Growth Countries					
Bangladesh	46	114	243	68	129
Brazil	53	153	252	100	99
China	563	1,134	1,624	571	490
Ethiopia	21	51	157	30	106
India	369	853	1,443	484	590
Indonesia	83	189	307	106	118
Iran	16	57	183	46	126
Nigeria	32	87	278	55	191
Pakistan	39	115	312	76	197

Source: Lester R. Brown and Hal Kane, *Full House: Reassessing the Earth's Population Carrying Capacity* (New York: W. W. Norton, 1994), 59.

TABLE 17-4 *The World's Labor Force by Income Groups and Regions of the World*

	Millions of Workers			*Percentage of Total*		
	1965	*1945*	*2025*	*1965*	*1995*	*2025*
World	1,329	2,476	3,656	100	100	100
Income Group						
High	272	382	395	21	15	11
Middle	363	658	1,020	27	27	28
Low	694	1,436	1,241	52	58	61
Region						
Sub-Saharan Africa	102	214	537	8	9	15
East Asia and Pacific	448	964	1,201	34	39	33
South Asia	228	440	779	17	18	21
Europe and Central Asia	180	239	281	14	10	8
Middle East and North Asia	29	80	204	2	3	6
Latin America and Caribbean	73	166	270	5	6	7
High-income OECD*	269	273	384	20	15	10

* *Includes the United States, Canada, Germany, France, United Kingdom, and other rich countries.*

Source: The World Bank, *World Development Report 1995* (Washington, D.C.: The World Bank, 1995), 9.

Unemployment and Underemployment

In 1995 almost one-third of the world's labor force were either unemployed or underemployed, and many of those who were employed were working for low wages with little prospect for financial advancement.[7] Unemployment is by no means limited to the poor countries of the world. Western Europe has experienced some of the highest unemployment rates since the Depression of the 1930s. In March 1996 the unemployment rate in Spain was 22.8 percent, Belgium 13.7 percent, France 11.8 percent, and Germany 11.8 percent.[8] In the transition economies of Eastern Europe, unemployment is high in some countries and the rate of poverty has increased. In Hungary, the unemployment rate was close to 20 percent in March 1996, and a majority of those who were unemployed had been out of work for more than six months.[9] Almost every country, with the exception of those that are a part of the East Asian Pacific Rim group, suffered from a combination of insufficient employment growth and a lack of jobs sufficient to enable workers to maintain and improve their incomes.

Poverty

Most of the poor and underemployed live in Africa and southern Asia. India is a good example. Despite a large and varied resource base and a rich endowment of

7. Ray Marshall, "One-Third of the World Is Out of Work," *Foreign Policy Magazine*, 1995.
8. *The Economist*, October 19–26, 1995, 119.
9. Ibid., 119.

skilled workers, it remains one of the poorest countries in the world, with a per capita income of $310 in 1994. It has a large industrial sector, accounting for over one-fourth of its GDP, but 70 percent of its labor force are still employed in agriculture. In India, as in other poor countries, the majority of the poor live in rural areas with far less access to educational opportunities than city dwellers have. There is a bias in most poor countries in favor of the cities in the allocation of physical and human resources. Land policies that make it difficult for the poor to acquire land have led to a migration of workers to the cities before the cities are able to provide employment.[10]

Population and the Environment

The impact of population growth is probably felt the most in sub-Saharan Africa. During the past fifty years an average of 1.3 million hectares per year of productive land has turned into desert. Probably the most important environmental problem the world faces is deforestation, because trees provide oxygen and prevent soil erosion. The rain forests of equatorial Africa are disappearing at an alarming rate.[11] Again, the problem is that deforestation occurs in the poorest areas of the world, where people eke out a marginal existence. The end result is a food supply reduced by the leaching of the soil, polluted water supplies, and land that has become less arable.

An ever-increasing population can also have an impact on the world's capacity to continue to feed it. One-third of the population of sub-Saharan Africa does not get enough to eat. In South Asia some 300 million people do not get enough to eat; in Latin America it is 100 million.[12] Altogether some one billion people in the world are malnourished. Unquestionably, the food supply in the world has been increasing as new farming techniques have increased agricultural productivity, but it remains to be seen whether or not the food supply can keep up with population growth. One solution is family planning, but the countries that need it the most are those that practice it the least. For example, Tanzania is one of the poorest countries in the world, yet its fertility rate is among the highest in the world, and only 21 percent of adult women use contraceptives.[13]

Employment in the Future

Technological change has been a major driving force of this century. In the United States and other major countries at the beginning of this century, the majority of the labor force was employed in agriculture. Increased improvement in land utili-

10. Mexico is an excellent example. Its population has quintupled over the past forty years as workers have migrated from the rural areas to find employment. Many are unemployed or underemployed because of lack of educational opportunities in the rural areas.
11. One estimate predicts that half of the world's rain forests will be gone by the year 2000. Other estimates are more optimistic.
12. *Human Development Report 1995*, 26–28.
13. Population Reference Bureau, *1995 World Population Data Sheet.*

zation and farming technology increased agricultural productivity to the point where less than 3 percent of the U.S. labor force is currently employed in agriculture. During most of this century the automobile industry was the driving force behind job creation. It was labor-intensive because millions of American workers were employed on the assembly lines to mass-produce automobiles. Raw materials, such as iron ore, were used to produce steel for automobile manufacture. The seminal product of the 1990s, however, is the computer chip, compounded of 2 percent energy and raw materials and 98 percent ideas, skills, and knowledge.

So the question is, "Are poor countries likely to catch up with rich countries in the future?" It has been pointed out that divergence in per capita incomes of the rich countries and the poor countries increased from 11-to-1 in 1870 to 38-to-1 in 1960 to 52-to-1 in 1985.[14] Since 1985 the divergence has increased to 62-to-1. Countries that are initially poor tend to grow more slowly than richer countries and to have less-educated populations. This comes at a time when job skills continually require more-educated workers. The Uruguay Round agreement holds out the promise of freer international trade, which should benefit more workers to become more productive as the goods they produce increase in value. But this will increase competition, and competition will create winners and losers. Even though the world has become integrated as a result of the transportation and communications revolution, a new golden age of reduced inequality between rich nations and poor nations is unlikely.

GENDER INEQUALITY

In August 1995 the United Nation's Fourth World Conference on Women was held in Beijing, China. The choice of Beijing was based on the UN belief that China had done more for women than most other developing countries. Besides, it was felt that the international influx of women would be good for China by shaming it into changing its position on human rights. It didn't exactly work out the way the UN intended. On the contrary, women of all nationalities were harassed one way or another by the Chinese security police, and the conference site was sealed off from Chinese onlookers. Security officers with video cameras deterred Chinese delegates from attending the discussions on such controversial subjects as human rights and legal equity. The Chinese press, which is controlled by the government, railed against the spiritual pollution brought in by the visiting women.[15] The delegation from Iran argued that Islam as practiced in Iran is best for all women—a proposition that had few takers.

14. *World Development Report 1995*, 53.
15. On the *CBS Nightly News* coverage of the women's convention in Beijing, some footage was devoted to showing a Chinese woman whose face was permanently scarred because her husband had thrown acid at her. She said her husband had the right to do this because she disobeyed him. So much for spiritual pollution!

Reasons for Inequality

These events do, however, illustrate how cultural factors, including religion, are responsible for differences in the treatment of men and women. Certainly, the Moslem religion is a male-dominated religion if there ever was one. Even in Turkey, probably the most enlightened of the Moslem countries, women have generally been shut out of the political process.[16] The Moslem priests and mullahs who call the faithful to prayer are invariably men. The legal system, which is based on interpretation of the Koran, is the domain of legal scholars who are male. The chador, a cloth covering the head and shoulders, has to be worn by women in many Moslem countries. Their participation in many forms of business activity is also very restricted.

In the poor countries, most of the activities of women take place in the nonwage sector of the economy for the purpose of household consumption. For example, women in rural Kenya work on average 56 hours a week compared to 42 hours for men. This also carries over to girls, who work an average of 41 hours a week compared to 35 hours for boys. In household work, including firewood and water collection, women put in 10 times the hours of men, and girls 3.7 times the hours of boys.[17] Almost 80 percent of men's work but only 41 percent of women's involves earning income. Girls spend 10 times the hours of boys in income-related activities outside the household. Self-employed urban women are the worst off of all Kenyan women, working more than 75 hours a week. Kenyan men are more likely to earn cash wages for their work, and they are less likely than women to spend it on food and consumption.

The low valuation of women is further reinforced by women's institutionally enforced lack of control over physical resources. In most countries, females have few legal rights regarding marital relations, the division of property, or land tenure.[18] In some countries, men can divorce their wives, but not the other way around; also, it is difficult for the woman to get any form of alimony. Inheritance of property in many countries is limited to male relatives. What this does is to institutionalize poverty for women because they have no control over resources. Control over property conveys power, but it is usually the males who control it. There is also a carryover into such areas as education and health. As Figure 17-1 shows, working against women is their high fertility rate in the poor countries. Fertility rates offer one of the strongest clues to the status of women.

Two-thirds of the world's illiterate are women, and two-thirds of those who live in poverty are also women. The main factor in causing the high rates of illiteracy and poverty among women is the lack of equal educational opportunities, particularly in the poor countries. The smaller the percentage of females attending school, the greater the female/male gap; the closer the female percent is to the

16. However, women head the governments of Turkey, Pakistan, and Sri Lanka.
17. United Nations Development Programme, *Human Development Report 1995*, 92.
18. Jodi L. Jacobson, *Gender Bias: Roadblock to Sustained Development*, Worldwatch Paper 110 (Washington, D.C.: Worldwatch, 1992.)

male percent, the smaller the gender gap. Moreover, in the poor countries females are more likely to suffer from malnutrition than males, and more girls than boys die at an early age. In rural India in the Punjab 21 percent of the girls suffer from malnutrition compared to 3 percent of the boys. Low-income boys fared better in nutritional requirements than upper-income girls.

Income Differences

Regardless of the country, rich or poor, women earn less money than men. It does not always follow that the poorer the country, the greater the difference in income inequality between the sexes. For example, there is less income inequality between the sexes in Tanzania and Vietnam, two of the poorest countries in the world, than in Sweden, one of the richest.[19]

Table 17-5 presents a comparison of women's average wages expressed as a percentage of men's average wages for selected countries. Of the fifty-five countries used in the comparison, the United States ranked in the middle, above Belgium, Switzerland, the United Kingdom, and Canada, and below the Scandinavian countries. China was almost at the bottom and so was South Korea. Japan was not included, but the difference between average earnings of the sexes is far greater in Japan than in the United States.

Table 17-6 presents a gender-related development index (GDI) for selected countries. Included in the index are such factors as the share of earned income received by men and women, the adult literacy rate for men and women, and the percentage of males and females attending primary, secondary, and tertiary schools. Another factor that went into the compilation of the index was the life expectancy of men and women. For most of the 130 countries used in the index, the life expectancy of females is higher than for males, but the poorer the country, the lower the life expectancy for both sexes. The combined primary, secondary, and tertiary enrollment is lower for females than for males in the poorer countries, but equal or even higher for the richer countries. The greatest disparity in income earned by each sex was in Saudi Arabia, where men received 94.7 percent of earned income and women 5.7 percent.

Four Scandinavian countries and the United States constitute the first five countries in the table.[20] But regardless of the rankings, no country treats its women as well as its men. In many countries, including India, the gender disparity is greater than 50 percent; in most of the African countries, the disparity is greater than 65 percent. Also, gender disparity does not depend on the level of income of

19. In 1994 Tanzania had a per capita GNP of $90, the lowest of all countries, and Vietnam had a per capita income of $190.

20. Scandinavian women have always played a prominent role in society. Of the eight women who have won the Nobel Prize for Literature since it was first given in 1901, two were from Scandinavia. The first woman to win the prize was Selma Lagerlof from Sweden in 1908. The Norwegian author Sigrid Undset won it in 1928. Alva Myrdal, a Swede, was co-winner of the Nobel Peace Prize in 1982.

TABLE 17-5
Women's Average Wages as a Percentage of Men's Average Wages

Country	*Rank*	*Women's Wage as Percentage of Men's*
Tanzania	1	92.0
Australia	3	90.8
Sweden	6	89.0
Norway	7	86.0
Kenya	9	84.7
Denmark	14	82.6
France	17	81.0
Italy	19	80.0
Germany	30	75.8
United States	31	75.0
Mexico	32	75.0
Spain	38	70.0
United Kingdom	39	69.7
Switzerland	43	67.6
Canada	47	63.0
China	53	59.4
South Korea	54	53.5
Bangladesh	55	42.0
Average for all countries		74.9

Source: United Nations Development Programme, *Human Development Report 1995* (New York: Oxford University Press, 1995), 36.

a country. For example, Saudi Arabia, which has a much higher per capita income than the majority of the countries used in the index, ranked 81 with a gender-related index of 0.514, which was below such low-income countries as China and Nicaragua. However, there has been an improvement in the gender-related index for all countries since 1970. The average value then for the index was 0.434; in 1992 the average value was 0.638.[21]

Table 17-7 presents a gender empowerment measure (GEM) of the economic, professional, and political participation of women. The percentage of income earned by women presented in Table 17-6 can be used as a source of economic power that allows the earner to exercise a wider range of options. Participation in professional jobs gives women greater access to the decision-making process and provides opportunities for career development. Access to political opportunities also gives women the opportunity to participate in the political decision-making process. All measurements comprising the index are weighted equally. As Table 17-7 indicates, the four Scandinavian countries rank at the top, with the United States ranking 8, Japan 27, and France 31. Those countries at the bottom of the index are mostly the African countries, but India ranked 101 and Pakistan ranked 114. The rich industrial countries are making better use of the productivity of

21. *Human Development Report 1995*, 79.

TABLE 17-6 *Gender-Related Development Index for Selected Countries*

Country	GRI Rank	GRI Index	Share of Earned Income (percent)		Adult Literacy Rate (percent)		Combined Primary, Secondary, and Tertiary Enrollment (percent)	
			Female	Male	Female	Male	Female	Male
Sweden	1	0.919	41.6	58.4	99.0	99.0	79.3	76.7
Finland	2	0.918	40.6	59.4	99.0	99.0	100.0	90.6
United States	5	0.901	34.6	65.4	99.0	99.0	98.1	91.9
Japan	8	0.896	33.5	66.5	99.0	99.0	76.3	78.4
Canada	9	0.891	29.3	70.7	99.0	99.0	100.0	100.0
Switzerland	19	0.852	27.1	72.9	99.0	99.0	70.8	76.8
Poland	22	0.838	39.3	60.7	99.0	99.0	76.4	74.4
Russia	29	0.822	38.4	61.6	98.7	98.7	69.7	67.3
Mexico	46	0.741	22.3	77.7	86.0	90.7	64.0	66.0
China	71	0.578	31.2	68.8	70.0	88.2	51.8	58.0
India	99	0.401	19.2	80.8	35.2	63.7	45.8	63.8
Nigeria	100	0.383	28.5	71.5	42.1	63.4	47.3	55.5
Zaire	102	0.372	29.0	71.0	63.5	84.3	31.5	45.7
Pakistan	103	0.360	10.1	89.9	22.3	47.8	16.3	32.6
Ethiopia	124	0.217	29.4	70.6	22.6	42.7	11.8	15.6
Afghanistan	130	0.169	7.1	92.9	12.7	44.1	9.6	18.7

Note: Germany was not included among the 130 countries ranked.

Source: United Nations Development Programme, *Human Development Report 1995* (New York: Oxford University Press, 1995), 76–77.

their women than are the poorer countries. The latter cannot hope to improve their economic status until they train their women.

FOREIGN TRADE

Foreign trade has become a prime engine of economic growth and is projected to grow at a rate of more than 6 percent a year for the next ten years.[22] Trade in services will increase even faster, particularly as advances in information and telecommunications technology expand trade in long-distance services. World merchandise exports have risen from 11 to 18 percent of world GDP in the past two decades. Services have increased from 15 percent of world trade to over 22 percent since 1980, and world sales of foreign affiliates of multinational corporations may exceed the value of the world's total exports. These changes have transformed the world economy. They are driven by a push toward trade and capital liberalization, an increased globalization of corporate production and distribution, and the inter-

22. The World Bank, *Global Economic Prospects and the Developing Countries* (Washington, D.C.: The World Bank, 1995), 5–6.

TABLE 17-7 *Gender Empowerment Measure for Selected Countries*

Country	*GEM Rank*	*GEM Measure*	*Seats Held in Parliament (percent women)*	*Administrators and Managers (percent women)*	*Professional and Technical Workers (percent women)*
Sweden	1	0.757	33.5	38.9	63.3
Norway	2	0.752	39.4	25.4	56.5
Canada	5	0.655	17.3	40.7	56.0
United States	8	0.623	10.3	40.2	50.8
Switzerland	17	0.513	15.9	5.3	39.0
China	23	0.474	21.0	11.6	45.1
Japan	27	0.442	6.7	8.0	42.0
France	31	0.433	5.7	9.4	41.4
Poland	32	0.432	13.0	15.6	60.4
Mexico	42	0.399	7.3	19.4	43.2
Brazil	58	0.361	5.5	17.3	57.2
Greece	67	0.343	6.0	10.1	43.1
Bangladesh	80	0.287	10.3	5.1	23.1
Turkey*	98	0.234	1.8	4.3	31.9
India	101	0.226	7.3	2.3	20.5
Nigeria	108	0.198	2.1	5.5	26.0
Pakistan*	114	0.153	1.6	2.9	18.4
Afghanistan	116	0.118	1.9	0.7	13.5

Note: Germany was not included among the 116 countries ranked.

**The heads of government in Turkey and Pakistan are women.*

Source: United Nations Development Programme, *Human Development Report 1995* (New York: Oxford University Press, 1995), 84–85.

national mobility of capital, which is flowing in increasingly diverse ways across countries and regions in search of new, profitable opportunities.

The Uruguay Round

The conclusion of the Uruguay Round is expected to provide a stimulus to world trade. This trade agreement, the most extensive ever signed, is expected to have a bearing on the economic prospects of industrialized and developing countries alike. The Uruguay Round will push for the reduction of various trade barriers, including tariffs and import quotas. Trade dispute resolution will be handled by the new World Trade Organization (WTO). The Round agreement also plans for the elimination of nontrade barriers, such as export subsidies and licensing of imports, and for the increased protection of intellectual property rights. In the United States alone, it is estimated that the Uruguay Round will increase national income between $100 billion and $200 billion in the tenth year after it has been ratified, for an increase of from 1.5 percent to 3 percent of GDP.[23]

23. *Economic Report of the President 1995* (Washington, D.C.: U.S. Government Printing Office, 1995), 205.

TABLE 17-8 *Effects of Uruguay Round Tariff Changes on Exports of Least-Developed Countries*

Least-Developed Countries in the Region	*Millions of Dollars*			*Percentage of Total Exports*		
	U.S.	*Eur. Union*	*Japan*	*U.S.*	*Eur. Union*	*Japan*
Asia	36.41	–0.82	2.84	6.41	–0.10	1.40
Africa	4.21	–5.47	–6.45	0.38	–0.10	–0.64
Other	11.40	0.02	0.17	2.79	0.02	0.51
Total	52.03	–6.28	–3.44	2.51	–0.10	–0.28

Source: The World Bank, *Global Economic Prospects and the Developing Countries* (Washington, D.C.: The World Bank, 1995), 38.

However, there will be winners and losers throughout the world. The winners will be those that are already winning, and the losers will be those that are already losing. It is necessary to remember that five countries—the United States, Germany, Japan, France, and the United Kingdom—accounted for 45 percent of the world's merchandise trade in 1994 and close to 50 percent of trade in services.[24] As for the effect of the Uruguay Round on the least-developed countries of the world, the impact would appear to be minimal. These countries get some preferential treatment anyway, particularly if they were former colonies of England or France. Table 17-8 presents the effects of the Uruguay Round on the less-developed areas of the world.

World Merchandise Trade

Table 17-9 presents a breakdown by regions of the world of total merchandise exports for 1993. As the table indicates, the high-income industrial countries account for around 70 percent of total world exports. The two leading export nations, Germany and the United States, export more than the combined totals of the other regions of the world. Among the poorer countries of the world, China's exports were four times those of India, but exports for both countries increased at a faster rate than the world average. Africa and South Asia, with a combined population of around two billion, are the poorest regions of the world, accounting for around 2 percent of world exports. Since world trade is expected to be the main engine of economic growth over the next decade, some areas of the world may be left behind.

World Resource Flows to Developing Countries

Table 17-10 presents the flow of private and public resources from the rich developed countries of the world to the developing regions of the world in 1993. Private resources consist of two main categories, direct investment and portfolio invest-

24. *The Economist,* April 6–13, 1995, 109.

TABLE 17-9 *Distribution of World Exports by Regions of the World for 1993 ($millions)*

Region		*Percentage Growth 1981–1993*
High-Income	2,885,291	5.5
Industrial	2,545,315	5.0
G-7	1,907,647	4.9
Germany	380,154	4.2
Japan	362,244	4.0
U.S.	464.773	6.1
Asia	341,653	10.5
East Asia	307,853	10.9
China	91,744	11.3
South Asia	33,780	7.5
India	21,553	7.1
Latin America and the Caribbean	132,128	3.2
Europe and Central Asia	153,827	4.4
Russian Federation	43,900	—
Turkey	15,343	6.8
Middle East and North Africa	91,807	0.7
Saudi Arabia	40,858	–2.0
Sub-Saharan Africa	56,068	3.4
South Africa	22,873	5.7
World	3,660,773	5.4

Source: The World Bank, *Global Economic Prospects and the Developing Countries* (Washington, D.C.: The World Bank, 1995), 83.

ment. Direct investment includes the acquisition of tangible assets such as real estate and factories, and portfolio investment involves the acquisition of stocks, bonds, and other securities. Public investment involves loans and other forms of financial assistance from governments and international lending agencies such as the World Bank and the International Monetary Fund. As the table indicates, the great bulk of income flows to the Middle East, North Africa, and sub-Saharan Africa comes from public development assistance. Forty percent of total income flows went to Asia and China in particular, which received more income than all of South Asia. Most of the investment in Asia and in Latin America and the Caribbean was from private sources.

It is necessary to remember that free trade produces winners and losers as a result of international price changes both within countries and between them. Those countries that are more raw materials oriented and that have less-skilled workers will probably be hurt more than countries that are more manufacturing or service oriented and have skilled workers. The relative scarcity of workers whose skills are in demand in international markets will cause their wages to rise and will hurt those countries with an abundance of workers whose skills are not in demand. Increased

TABLE 17-10 *Long-Term Resource Flow to Developing Countries, 1993 ($millions)*

All Developing Countries	*Total*	*Private*	*Public*
	209,400	157.656	51,744
Asia	84,940	68,426	16,515
East Asia	73,569	62,783	10,787
China	41,235	36,261	4,975
South Asia	11,371	5,643	5,728
India	6,567	4,559	2,008
Latin America and Caribbean	63,126	57,709	5,417
Argentina	18,127	15,109	3,017
Mexico	22,283	22,241	42
Europe and Central Asia	37,854	27,759	10,095
Russia	6,878	3,207	3,671
Turkey	6,761	7,077	–316
Middle East and North Africa	5,301	1,618	3,883
Sub-Saharan Africa	18,177	2,145	16,033
Ethiopia	1,049	4	1,045
Nigeria	1,005	890	115

Source: *Global Economic Prospects and the Developing Countries* (Washington, D.C.: The World Bank, 1995), 84–85.

export competition means that unless countries are able to match the productivity gains of their competitors, the wages of their workers will be eroded. In some parts of the world entire regions could be adversely affected, and no region of the world is more vulnerable than Africa, which was the subject of Chapter 16.

SUMMARY

The world is changing rapidly. Technological change, particularly in the area of communications, has resulted in the integration of world financial markets, and international economic integration has been helped by the conclusion of the Uruguay Round. But the world still can be divided into rich nations and poor nations, the haves and the have-nots. It is the poorest nations that cause the greatest concern because they constitute one-half of the world's population. Some will succeed in improving their living standards, and others will not. There are three major problems that will continue to inhibit the economic development of many of the poor countries. The first is population growth, which pours millions of workers into the labor force where no jobs are available. The second problem is gender disparity, causing millions of women who could add to productivity to be underpaid or underemployed. The final problem is that foreign trade, particularly in the area of service, will fuel the growth of the future but requires a skilled labor force that the poorer countries may not be able to supply.

QUESTIONS FOR DISCUSSION

1. Income inequality between rich nations and poor nations has widened during this century. Why is this true?
2. Economic growth by itself has not lifted many parts of the world out of poverty. Discuss.
3. Economic and social disparities can vary widely between regions on the same continent. Discuss.
4. What is meant by the internationalization of services?
5. What can be done to improve the living standards of poor nations?
6. How does the role of women vary in the rich nations and poor nations?
7. What is GEM? How does it differ from GDI?
8. How has gender inequality worked against the economic development of poor nations?
9. What impact will the Uruguay Round have on the world economy?

RECOMMENDED READINGS

Brown, Lester R. and Hal Kane. *Full House: Reassessing the Earth's Population Carrying Capacity.* New York: W. W. Norton, 1994.

Harrison, Lawrence E. *Who Prospers: How Cultural Values Shape Economic and Political Success.* New York: Basic Books, 1992.

Haub, Carl, and Machiko Yanagishita. *1995 World Population Data Sheet.* Washington, D.C.: Population Reference Service, 1995.

International Monetary Fund. *International Capital Markets: Developments, Prospects, and Policy Issues.* Washington, D.C.: IMF, August 1995.

Jacobson, Jodi L. *Gender Bias: Roadblock to Sustainable Development.* Working Paper 110. Washington, D.C.: World Watch, 1992.

Krugman, Paul, and Robert Lawrence. *Trade, Jobs, and Wages.* Working Paper 4478. Cambridge, Mass.: National Bureau of Economic Research, 1993.

Page, Sheila, and Michael Davenport. *World Trade Reform: Do Developing Countries Win or Lose?* London: Overseas Development Institute, 1994.

Tinker, Irene. *Persistent Inequalities: Women and World Development.* New York: Oxford University Press, 1992.

United Nations Development Programme. *Human Development Report 1995.* New York: Oxford University Press, 1995. The report deals with gender equality.

"War of the Worlds." *The Economist,* October 1–7, 1995, 1–38.

World Bank. *Global Economic Prospects and the Developing Countries.* Washington, D.C.: The World Bank, 1995.

World Bank. *World Development Report 1995.* Washington, D.C.: The World Bank, 1995.

CHAPTER 18
The New World Order

The world has changed more rapidly since 1990 than at any time since the end of World War II in 1945. The older world order, which provided a stability of sorts, is gone. Economic and political conflicts among the United States, Europe, and Japan were held in check by common concerns about the military threat of the Soviet Union. Bitter ethnic divisions, both within the Soviet Union and in Eastern and Central Europe, were kept under tight rein by the Soviet army. Now the Soviet Union has become a thing of the past, a relic of the cold war, and nationalism has become a contending force in the new world order. As leader of the West during the cold war, the United States has attained an international military preeminence beyond challenge. It also remains the world economic leader at a time when Japan is having major economic problems and the European Union has encountered friction over a common currency unit.

A communications revolution has also occurred that has resulted in the demise of distance. This may well be the most significant economic force shaping the next half century, just as the mass production of the automobile was the most significant force in shaping the first half of the twentieth century. Many services will become internationally tradable and easier to ship from one country to another than goods are today. Countries thousands of miles apart will be able to offer services that up to now required proximity. The farther a country or an area is from the main centers of economic activity, the more it can gain as a result. The developing countries will be able to keep skilled and educated workers who otherwise might have migrated to where the jobs are.

This final chapter will first recapitulate what has happened during the century that will soon come to an end. Empires have come and gone, and fascism and communism, two alternative political and economic systems that controlled much of the world, have been consigned to the dustbin of history. During this century the United States has been the leading country in terms of living standards and level of performance. It began the century and will finish it with the world's largest economy. Unless something happens, it will continue to be the leader in the twenty-first century. Political instability and the threat of regional wars continue to be on the rise. Moreover, nationalism has become a force in the new world order at the same time that transnational technological change has made the world smaller.

THE WORLD OF THE TWENTIETH CENTURY

In 1900 the population of the world was around 1.6 billion, one-third of which lived in China and India. The leading world powers were the United States, England, France, Italy, the Austro-Hungarian Empire, Russia, and Japan. With the exception of the United States and France, all were ruled by monarchs. The total GDP of the world was around $1.6 trillion. There were around sixty countries in existence, and international currency exchange was governed by the gold standard. Most of the world was a part of the British, Dutch, French, and German Empires. The leading export nations were the United States, England, and Germany. Foreign direct investment by the major world powers amounted to $108 billion and was most heavily concentrated in the mineral resources of Latin America. Three-fourths of the investment was made by England, the United States, Germany, and France. The average per capita income difference between the Western and Asiatic countries was 5 to 1, and for the Western and Latin American countries, 3 to 1.[1]

Table 18-1 presents a ranking of the ten major countries of the world in 1900 in terms of real GDP, population, and exports. Japan, which eventually became one of the world's leading exporters, ranked 23d among all nations in 1900. In 1994 the United States ranked first, Germany second, Japan third, and the United Kingdom fourth in the value of world exports. The population of the United States has tripled since 1900, while the population of France has increased by only

1. Angus Maddison, *The World Economy in the 20th Century* (Paris: OECD, 1989), 15.

TABLE 18-1 *Rankings of the Top Ten Countries of the World in 1900*

	GDP ($billions in 1980 prices)	*Rank*	*Population*	*Rank*	*Exports ($billions in 1980 prices)*	*Rank*
United States	221,714	1	76,094	4	12,368	3
China	160,434	2	400,000	1	1,967	12
United Kingdom	111,586	3	41,135	7	20,545	1
India*	107,072	4	284,400	2	4,418	5
Russia	98,029	5	128,687	3	3,193	7
Germany	89,678	6	56,046	5	12,404	2
France	62,288	7	38,940	9	5,657	4
Italy	43,981	8	32,416	10	2,101	9
Japan	29,840	9	44,100	6	346	23
Indonesia†	20,060	10	40,209	8	1,005	18

**India was a part of the British Empire in 1900.*

†Indonesia was a part of the Dutch Empire in 1900.

Source: Angus Maddison, *The World Economy in the 20th Century* (Paris: OECD, 1989), 29.

16 million, the United Kingdom by 17 million, and Germany by 24 million.[2] The greatest gains in population were made by China, India, and Indonesia. Japan has jumped from ninth to second in real GDP ranking, and China is third.

1900–1913

The years prior to the beginning of World War I in 1914 were years of high prosperity. Among the developed countries of the world, economic growth was the highest in the United States and Canada and the lowest in England. The United States had recently become the world economic leader, a position held by England during most of the nineteenth century. This leadership was based in part on its natural resources, and in part on high rates of investment and an ever-expanding labor force.[3] European countries had lower rates of investment, but the growth of exports increased economic growth because it facilitated specialization and economies of scale.[4] However, Latin America achieved a faster rate of economic growth than either North America or Europe during the pre–World War I years. Argentina's huge natural resource base, coupled with high rates of investment and

2. British, French, and German war losses during World War I were enormous. Some five million men were killed. In World War II four million German soldiers were killed.

3. Most of the investment in the United States came from Europe. European capital financed the development of the railroad and steel industries in the United States. By the end of the last century, the United States had become the world's leading debtor country. Europe also supplied most of the immigrants who became an integral part of the U.s. labor force.

4. A good example was the development of the German chemical industry, which became the largest in the world.

increased immigration from Europe, created the fastest rate of economic growth in North and South America.[5]

1913–1950

The world changed drastically during the period 1913–1950. Two world wars and the Depression of the 1930s were responsible for most of the change. World War I destroyed the old political order. The Austro-Hungarian Empire disappeared and with it the Hapsburg monarchy. In Russia, the Bolshevik Revolution of 1917 deposed the czar and ushered in a Communist regime. In Germany the monarchy collapsed when Kaiser Wilhelm fled to the Netherlands, and the Weimar Republic was created. The Treaty of Versailles terminating World War I imposed harsh measures on Germany, including the loss of much of its territory and the payment of war damages to the victors, measures that led to the rise of fascism and to World War II. The United States was the main winner. It began the war as the world's leading debtor nation and ended up as the world's leading creditor nation.

The Depression of the 1930s was the prelude to World War II. Mass unemployment created serious economic problems and threatened the survival of the capitalist countries. In Germany, Adolf Hitler and the National Socialist Party gained control of the government, and the democratic Weimar Republic was no more. In Japan, the military gained government control. Fascism became the new economic and political order, joining communism as an alternative to capitalism, which many people began to see as incapable of dealing with the problems created by the Depression.[6] The gold standard, which had been in existence for some 110 years, went out during the Depression, and each country imposed its own form of international currency exchange control.[7] In England, the writings of John Maynard Keynes led to the creation of a new school of economic theory called Keynesian economics. This theory, which purported to explain the causes of unemployment and its cure, became a standard part of economic policy in Europe after World War II.

World War II reshaped Europe and destroyed fascism as an economic and political system. It also created two world superpowers that were to dominate the world for most of the remainder of the century—the United States and the Soviet Union. Western Europe, helped in part by Marshall Plan aid from the United

5. During the period 1900–1913, Argentine per capita exports exceeded in value per capita exports from the United States and Germany.

6. Fascist Germany and Communist Russia were admired by many Americans during the 1930s. Ambassador Joseph Kennedy, father of President John F. Kennedy, was one admirer, as was Charles Lindbergh, the famous aviator. Hitler was admired because he brought order out of chaos. American intellectuals thought communism was to be the wave of the future.

7. The gold standard involved the setting of international exchange rates between countries by pegging various currencies to gold. For example, in the United States one ounce of gold was worth $20.67 and in England one ounce of gold was worth 4.25 pounds. The exchange rate of dollars into pounds was $20.67 divided by 4.25, or $4.86 exchanged for one pound, and vice versa. Both the dollar and the pound were backed by gold.

States, was in the process of recovering from the devastation caused by World War II. The Bretton Woods agreement of 1944 created a new international currency exchange system in which the U.S. dollar became the major world currency unit and other world currencies were pegged to it.[8] The World Bank was created to provide financial assistance to member countries with balance of payments problems. The General Agreement on Tariffs and Trade (GATT) was created to promote free trade between nations by removing trade restrictions, such as import quotas, which had contributed to prolonging the Depression of the 1930s.

1950–1973

The 1950–1973 period has been referred to as the golden age of the twentieth century.[9] Western Europe and Japan had recovered from the damage caused by World War II, and a number of new nations were created. The dollar was the world's strongest currency unit. Real economic growth rates were high for many countries, and inflation and unemployment rates were low. The Marxist claim that unemployment would prove to be the undoing of capitalism did not materialize, as governments adopted Keynesian fiscal policies aimed at the attainment of full employment. The role of government increased significantly during this period through the provision of a wide variety of social welfare programs.[10] There was greater access to technology, and foreign direct investment increased. The United States and the Soviet Union maintained a status quo arrangement that created a certain element of stability in the world.

Probably the most important aspect of this time period was a rapid rate of economic growth based on exports. The rate of economic growth was higher during this period than in any other period. It was facilitated by an acceleration in the growth rate of capital stock, a rate four times higher than the rate for 1913–1950. Export growth, too, was higher during this period than at any other time in the century. The highest rates of growth were achieved by South Korea and Taiwan, two former colonies of Japan.

1973–1987

During the 1973–1987 period, the growth of the world economy slowed dramatically. The average annual growth rate for Africa declined from 5.1 percent for the period 1950–1973 to 2.2 percent for the period 1973–1987, and the average annual growth rates for the Soviet-bloc countries declined from 5.0 percent for 1950–1973 to 1.8 percent for 1973–1987. The decline was not limited to Africa and the Soviet-

8. The Bretton Woods agreement fixed the dollar-gold relationship at $35 = 1 ounce of gold. All other currencies were pegged to the dollar, e.g., 4 marks = $1.

9. Maddison, 65.

10. In the United States, government expenditures increased from 21.4 percent of GDP in 1950 to 30.7 percent of GDP in 1973. In Germany, the increase was from 30.4 percent to 41.2 percent.

bloc countries. The average annual rate of economic growth in Japan decreased from 9.3 percent for 1950–1973 to 3.7 percent for 1973–1987. During the same two periods, the average annual growth rate in the United States declined from 3.7 percent to 2.5 percent, and in Germany, from 5.9 percent to 1.8 percent. Tables 18-2 and 18-3 present real average annual growth rates and export growth rates for selected countries for the four time periods—the pre–World War I period, the period including both world wars and the Depression, the so-called golden age period, and the period of decline.

There were several reasons for the slowdown of the world economy. The first and probably the most important reason was the oil shock of 1973, when OPEC increased world oil prices. As the export price of oil increased, oil-importing nations including the United States had to pay more, and the price of products and services dependent on oil increased. The result was inflation. The U.S. dollar became overvalued as dollars flooded the world markets. Germany revalued the mark against the dollar. These factors caused the breakdown of the dollar-based

TABLE 18-2 *Real GDP Growth Rates for Selected Countries, 1900–1987 (average annual rate in percent)*

Country	*1900–1913*	*1913–1950*	*1950–1973*	*1973–1987*
Canada	2.4	1.0	4.1	1.8
France	2.9	2.7	4.9	2.8
Germany	3.0	1.3	5.9	1.8
Italy	2.8	1.4	5.5	2.4
Japan	2.5	2.2	9.3	3.7
United Kingdom	1.5	1.3	3.0	1.6
United States	4.0	2.8	3.7	2.5
OECD average	2.9	2.0	4.9	2.4
China	1.0	0.1	5.8	7.5
India	0.8	0.7	3.7	4.1
Indonesia	1.8	0.9	4.5	5.4
Pakistan	1.0	1.4	4.4	6.1
South Korea	–2.0	1.7	7.5	7.9
Taiwan	1.8	2.7	9.3	7.8
Thailand	1.7	2.2	6.4	6.2
Asian average	1.7	1.3	5.4	5.9
Argentina	6.4	3.0	3.8	0.8
Brazil	3.5	4.2	6.7	4.8
Chile	–3.4	3.3	3.7	1.9
Colombia	–4.2	3.8	5.2	3.9
Mexico	2.6	2.6	6.4	3.6
Peru	–3.5	2.8	5.4	2.6
Latin American average	3.9	3.3	5.2	2.9
USSR	3.5	2.7	5.0	2.1

Source: Angus Maddison, *The World Economy in the 20th Century* (Paris: OECD, 1989), 36.

TABLE 18-3 *Export Growth Rates (average annual compound growth rate in export volume)*

Country	*1913–1950*	*Growth Rate*	*1973–1986*
Canada	3.1	5.8	4.2
France	1.1	8.2	3.3
Germany	–2.8	12.4	4.4
Italy	0.6	11.7	4.9
Japan	2.0	15.4	7.6
United Kingdom	0.0	3.9	3.7
United States	2.2	8.3	1.7
OECD average	1.0	8.6	4.2
China	1.1	2.7	10.4
India	–1.5	2.5	2.5
Indonesia	2.3	6.5	3.3
Pakistan	–1.5	3.6	6.7
South Korea	–1.3	20.3	14.0
Taiwan	2.6	16.3	11.6
Thailand	2.3	4.4	9.4
Asian average	0.7	7.1	7.6
Argentina	1.6	3.1	4.4
Brazil	1.7	4.7	6.8
Chile	1.4	2.4	9.1
Colombia	3.9	3.8	6.0
Mexico	–0.5	4.3	11.1
Peru	2.7	5.8	–2.2
Latin American average	1.8	4.0	5.9
USSR	–0.1	10.0	4.7

Source: Angus Maddison, *The World Economy in the 20th Century* (Paris: OECD, 1989), 67.

international monetary system created by the Bretton Woods agreement of 1994. The linkage between gold and the dollar and currencies pegged to the dollar was broken, and currencies were allowed to float. Oil-importing countries encountered balance of payments problems, which led to their use of economic policies designed to stop inflation and reduce deficits.

1987–2000

The world has continued to change rapidly. Probably the seminal event of this century has been the collapse of Communism, which had once held out the hope of creating a utopian society where all needs would be provided for. There were many inefficiencies in the Soviet-type of command economy called socialism. The quality of consumer goods was poor, and waste and corruption were endemic. Work incentives were poor, alcoholism was widespread, and life expectancy declined, in part because little attention was given to maintaining a safe environment. The nuclear disaster at Chernobyl is one example. An ever-increasing flow of resources was committed to the military and to the support of such client countries as Cuba and Vietnam. Soviet military expenditures increased to the point where they were consuming around 16 percent of the GDP. Foreign trade was regulated by CMEA and was uncompetitive by world standards. Direct action to improve the Soviet economy was too little and came too late.

The only countries of the world showing continued improvement are the East Asian countries. For the period 1985–1994, China's real per capita growth rate grew by 6.9 percent, South Korea's by 7.8 percent, Malaysia's by 5.7 percent, and Singapore's by 6.9 percent.[11] Conversely, the growth rate for Japan averaged 3.2 percent and was less than 1 percent for the period 1992–1994.[12] One reason for the East Asian success has been prudent monetary and fiscal policy management, which has kept foreign indebtedness low. The ratio of debt service to exports for the East Asian countries is about half what it is in Latin America and Africa. Interest rates are also more stable, making interest payments on foreign debt less of a burden. The East Asian countries have also put more reliance on an export-oriented strategy to keep their exchange rates competitive. As Table 18-4 indicates, the East Asian countries are projected to have a growth in real per capita income over three times the world average for the period 1995–2004.

The Future

In his 1988 bestseller *The Rise and Fall of the Great Powers*, Paul Kennedy states: "The only answer to the question increasingly debated by the public of whether it can preserve its competitive position is no, because it simply has not been given to any one society to remain permanently ahead of the other."[13] He cites examples of some of the great empires of Europe that have come and gone, beginning with Spain, the dominant power for some two hundred years. Spain was followed by the Netherlands, which became the financial center of Europe and the leading seapower. The Netherlands was followed by England, which dominated the last century and created the largest empire ever known. Who, then, would replace the United States? The answer, according to Kennedy, was Japan.[14]

Another view of changes in economic dominance among the world's powers is expressed by Lester Thurow. Thurow considers Communitarian capitalism as practiced by Europe to be superior to individualistic capitalism as practiced by the Anglo-Saxon countries because cooperation wins out over individualism.[15] In the

11. The World Bank, *The World Bank Atlas 1996* (Washington, D.C.: The World Bank, 1996), 18–19.

12. The growth rates for the five countries in 1995 were China 10.9 percent, South Korea 6.8 percent, Malaysia 8.8 percent, Singapore 9.1 percent, and Japan 2.2 percent.

13. Paul Kennedy, *The Rise and Fall of the Great Powers* (New York: Random House, 1988), 533.

14. Kennedy was not alone. Some authors felt that Japan would become the leading world power because of its vast financial resources, while others pointed to the Japanese educational system or to the industrial structure of Japan as reasons for Japanese superiority to the United States.

15. Lester Thurow, *Head to Head: The Coming Economic Battle Among Japan, Europe, and America* (New York: Morrow, 1992).

TABLE 18-4
Growth of Real per Capita GDP for the Period 1995–2004 (average annual percentage growth)

World	1.9
High-Income Countries	2.4
G-7 countries	2.3
Low- and Middle-Income Countries	3.3
East Asia and Pacific	6.6
Latin America and the Caribbean	1.9
Europe and Central Asia	2.9
Middle East and North Africa	0.6
Sub-Saharan Africa	0.9

Source: The World Bank, *Global Economic Prospects and the Developing Countries* (Washington, D.C.: The World Bank, 1995), 79.

twenty-first century, Thurow believes, communitarian Europe will prevail. Among the strengths he cites is the emphasis that European companies place on long-term goals as opposed to the short-term goals of American companies. He also points out that European countries, particularly Germany, upgrade labor skills through the provision of vocational education programs.

The European Union is supposed to create economic advantage by merging the resources of many countries, but, contrary to Thurow's initial theories, one-tenth of the European labor force was unemployed as of April 1996. Opportunities have been missed in areas where the European Union is supposed to be strong. An example is biotechnology, one of Europe's strengths, but many European companies plan to relocate elsewhere because of government regulations and high taxes. And Germany still has to pay for the cost of reunification.

It is simply not in the cards for either Japan or Europe to overtake the United States in the future. Both Kennedy and Thurow are wrong. One thing that will work to the advantage of the United States is the service revolution, which has been facilitated by advances in technology. Services now account for close to one-fourth of world trade and three-fifths of foreign direct investment flows. Services represent the only positive in the U.S. current account by reducing the deficit incurred in the merchandise trade account. Telecommunications technology is an area in which the United States excels. As computer and communications technology transforms services, their continued development can be regarded as a precondition for economic growth in the future. Table 18-5 presents the increase in world service trade for the period 1980–1993.[16]

Service trade works to the future advantage of the United States. For one thing, it has made the transition from an industry-based economy to a service-based economy. Services accounted for around 70 percent of U.S. employment in 1995. In Europe, the percentage is lower because rules and regulations make it

16. The OECD countries include the Western European countries, Turkey, Canada, the United States, and Japan. The U.S. service trade amounted to about 30 percent of the total for the OECD countries.

TABLE 18-5 *World Trade in Services, 1980–1993 (billions of dollars)*

	1980	*1985*	*1990*	*1992*	*1993*
Trade in Commercial Services	358.0	379.6	790.8	936.1	933.7
OECD	283.3	298.5	648.2	764.9	752.0
Rest of the world	74.6	81.1	142.6	171.1	181.8
Share of Services in Total Trade in Percent	17.0	18.2	20.4	21.9	22.2
OECD	18.8	19.3	21.2	22.7	23.1
Rest of the world	12.7	15.3	17.5	19.0	19.1

Source: The World Bank, *Global Economic Prospects and the Developing Countries* (Washington, D.C.: The World Bank, 1995), 47.

difficult to get rid of excess industrial labor in the steel mills, automobile industry, and coal mining.[17] The service revolution has created the development of a supportive physical and human infrastructure. In the physical infrastructure, the United States has a highly developed telecommunication system. The United States also has a trained labor force to use the information technology in the service industries. As an economy becomes more service-intensive, workers have to be trained more intensively over their employment lifecycles, and their performance becomes more dependent on access to information technology. Michael E. Porter, author of *The Competitive Advantage of Nations,* lists services as a key area in which the United States has a competitive advantage over other nations.[18] Table 18-6 presents the service areas in which the United States has the advantage. The data are for 1990.

Impact on Poverty and Unemployment

Technological change involves the substitution of ideas, skills, and knowledge for physical resources. The most important product of the first half of this century was the automobile, which required 60 percent raw materials and 40 percent labor. The most important product of the 1990s is the computer chip, which requires 2 percent raw materials and 98 percent labor.[19] The labor involved in producing the automobile was primarily unskilled and semiskilled and required little education; the labor involved in producing the chip requires skill and education. The economies most likely to succeed in technological change are the East Asian economies; their high investment in basic education prepares a workforce that can develop and use technology to improve productivity. The United States, Canada, and Europe also will benefit.

A premium is now placed on human capital, and people fortunate enough to have an education followed by job experience are going to become more valuable.

17. In November 1995, Bethlehem Steel, once the second-largest steel producer in the United States, closed its main plant. In 1965, it employed 31,000 workers.
18. Michael E. Porter, *The Competitive Advantage of Nations* (New York: Free Press, 1990), 255.
19. Ray Marshall, "The Global Job Crisis," *Foreign Policy*, No. 100 (Fall 1995), 19.

TABLE 18-6
Areas in Which the United States Has Competitive Advantage in the Provision of Services

Areas	*U.S. Position*
Fast foods and food services	1
Education	
University	1
Graduate	1
Leisure	
Entertainment	1
Medical	
Health care services	1
Hospital management	1
Travel Related	
Hotels	1
Car rentals	1
Business	
Accounting	1
Legal services	1
Advertising	1
Engineering	1
Financial	
Consumer finance	1
Commercial banking	1
Investment banking	1
Information	
Information processing	1
Information-data	1

Source: Michael E. Porter, *The Competitive Advantage of Nations* (New York: Free Press, 1990), 255.

This works to the disadvantage of the poor countries, where illiteracy rates are high, few people finish secondary schools, and even fewer go on to college. The poor countries do not have the money to spend on education, and their economies often depend on the export of natural resources such as oil. It is to be doubted that technological change will have much of an impact on their economies, for the great mass of their population lacks the skills necessary to compete in an increasingly competitive world. The gap in incomes between rich countries and poor countries, which has widened considerably during this century, will continue to widen in the future.

TOWARD A NEW WORLD ORDER

Another author, Robert B. Reich, in *The Work of Nations: Preparing Ourselves for 21st Century Capitalism,*[20] also discounts Communism as a thing of the past and main-

20. Robert B. Reich, *The Work of Nations: Preparing Ourselves for 21st Century Capitalism* (New York: Alfred A. Knopf, 1991).

tains that a global economy dominated by capitalism will exist in the twenty-first century. The United States has led the way to the attainment of global capitalism. The scale and technology of its core corporations extended the reach of U.S. capitalism throughout much of the world. However, times have changed even for the United States. Today, almost every factor of production—money, technology, factories, and equipment—moves effortlessly across national boundaries, and jobs go where they can be performed most efficiently; the ideal of a new world order dominated by the United States is meaningless because the relentless forces of world capitalism are causing corporations to lose their natural identities.

The European Union

The most important regional trading bloc in the world is the European Union (EU). It consists of fifteen member countries with a combined population of 370.2 million and a total GNP of $7.6 trillion. Table 18-7 provides these data for each member country. The purpose of the EU is to create a United States of Europe by eliminating trade barriers between countries and creating a common currency called the European Currency Unit (ECU).[21] Physical barriers to the free flow of goods, services, and people are being removed. Uniform technical standards are in the process of adoption, and the tax systems of the member countries are being harmonized. People are granted the right to live, work, vote, and run for office anywhere within the EU.[22] There is an agreement among the member nations to create a common foreign and defense policy.

North American Free Trade Agreement (NAFTA)

A second major world trading bloc consists of the United States, Canada, and Mexico, which were linked together by the ratification of the North American Free Trade Agreement (NAFTA) in 1994. Bilateral trade between the United States and Canada in 1995 amounted to $272 billion and between the United States and Mexico to $118 billion. Canada ranked first as the United States' most important trading partner and Mexico ranked third. U.S. trade with Canada and Mexico was greater in value than U.S. trade with Europe. As a comparison of Table 18-7 and Table 18-8 indicates, the combined GNP and population of the three countries in 1994 was about equal to those for the European Union. NAFTA differs from the EU in that one of its members, the United States, is by far the domi-

21. The ECU currently serves as a unit of account in the European Union. Its value is a weighted balance of the currency units of the member EU countries, with the German mark and the French franc accounting for over half of the weight. It can be used as a denomination for bonds and bank loans.

22. The Maastricht Treaty of December 1991 created the European Union. It called for the creation of a supranational government with a common currency unit that would replace the existing currencies.

TABLE 18-7
Population and GNP for European Union Countries, 1994

Members	*Population (millions)*	*GNP ($billions)*
Original Six		
Belgium	10.2	231.1
France	57.7	1,355.0
Luxembourg	0.4	16.0
Germany	81.1	2,075.5
Italy	57.1	1,101.3
Netherlands	15.4	338.1
Later Entrants		
Denmark	5.2	145.4
Greece	10.4	80.2
Ireland	3.5	48.3
Portugal	9.8	92.1
Spain	39.6	525.3
United Kingdom	58.1	1,069.5
New Members		
Austria	7.9	197.5
Finland	5.1	95.8
Sweden	8.7	206.4
	370.2	7,577.5

Source: The World Bank, *The World Bank Atlas 1995* (Washington, D.C.: The World Bank, 1996), 8, 9, 18, 19.

TABLE 18-8
Population and GNP for the NAFTA Countries, 1994

Members	*Population (millions)*	*GNP ($ billions)*
United States	260.1	6,737.3
Canada	29.1	569.9
Mexico	91.9	368.7
	381.1	7,675.9

Source: The World Bank, *The World Bank Atlas, 1996* (Washington, D.C.: The World Bank, 1996), 8, 9, 18, 19.

nant country, and the living standards of another member, Mexico, are lower than those of any EU member.

The purpose of NAFTA is to promote freer trade among the member countries by reducing trade barriers.[23] Tariffs on goods flowing among the countries are

23. NAFTA is not really comparable to the European Union in terms of its objectives. There will be no standard currency unit for the three countries, nor will there be a supranational government like the European Parliament and the European Court of Justice. Citizens of the United States, Canada, and Mexico will not have the right to live, work, vote, or run for office in each other's country.

to be reduced over a fifteen-year period.[24] Investment restrictions in each country have been lifted in most sectors.[25] Tariffs and import quotas on cars are to be eliminated over a ten-year period, and Mexico will gradually open up its financial service sector to U.S. and Canadian investments. Environmental laws are to be enforced by a panel representing the three countries. The treaty will also eliminate tariffs on the import of textiles in ten years. Eventually NAFTA is supposed to expand to include virtually every country in Latin America.

WHITHER SOCIALISM?

Russia will hold a presidential election on June 16, 1996, and former Communists and their allies are favored to win. Economic conditions have not improved for the majority of Russians since the collapse of Communism. Living standards have declined, the rule of law is weak, and a solid middle class has not emerged.[26] The privatization of state assets has improved the efficiency of the Russian economy, but the main winners have been the nomenklatura elite. The creators of the richest private firms in Russia are former staff members from various Communist Party organizations.[27] The Russian army does not appear to be reliably under civilian control, and the war in Chechnya has divided the country. Even though the constitution of 1993 gave Russia the outward form of a democracy, there are forty-three political parties, most of which are built around a single leader who wants to turn Russia back to some form of authoritarianism.

There is also nostalgia for the past when Russia was a part of the Soviet Union, and the latter was a world superpower. Many Russians feel that in the old days, everyone at least had a job and living costs were low. The worst political excesses of Stalin have been forgotten; he is remembered as a leader when the Soviet Union defeated Germany in World War II. Russian politicians have been able to capitalize on the desire of many voters to recapture the past glory of the country.[28] Nostalgia and the poor performance of the Russian economy could work to the advantage of the revived Communist Party, which did well in elections in 1995. But this does not mean that there will be a full reversal of economic reforms and a return to the old-style Communism of the Soviet Union. One reason is that too many Russian politicians have a stake in maintaining the economy as it is.

Short of the use of force, which is highly unlikely, Russia will not get its old empire back. The military is in disarray and has had too much trouble with Chech-

24. Most tariffs between the United States and Mexico on agricultural products have already been removed. Tariffs on cars are to be removed over a ten-year period.

25. The state-owned Mexican oil monopoly Pemex is off limits to foreign investors.

26. "Russia's Rich and Poor," *The Economist*, April 29-May 6, 1995, 63–64. At the end of 1994, 21 percent of Russians were recorded as below the official poverty line, then equal to monthly income of 145,500 rubles ($44).

27. Leonid Khotin, "Old and New Entrepreneurs in Today's Russia," *Problems of Post-Communism*, Vol. 43, No. 1 (January-February 1996), 49–57.

28. An example is Vladimir Zhirinovsky.

nya to warrant any future incursions. The former Eastern and Central European satellite countries of the Soviet Union are lost forever. Czechoslovakia, Hungary, and Poland are now democracies. Their market economies are oriented toward Western Europe, and they hope eventually to become a part of the European Union. Bulgaria and Romania have also gone their separate ways and have no inclination to return to the past. That leaves only those republics that were once a part of the Soviet Union but are now independent countries, and they too would resist any attempt by Russia to take them back into the old regime.

Reinventing Socialism

It is argued that the reason the Soviet Union collapsed is that its leaders misapplied the principles of Marxism to the country. The Russian Revolution of 1917 abolished capitalism and proclaimed that the new system would be democratic and socialist. Neither happened; instead, the revolution spawned a dictatorial political regime and an overcentralized economy. The former froze class relationships into a repressive political environment, and the latter engendered an inefficient allocation of resources. There were a lack of innovation and a lack of motivation on the part of workers and managers because central planning emphasized plan targets in terms of quantity. The political dictatorship stultified economic development by prohibiting the free development of science and technology, a crucial mistake in an ever-changing world. Thus, by the 1980s, the Soviet economy was no longer viable.

What, then, would bring about a revival of Marxist socialism? Some observers point out that capitalism continues to show the same symptoms of crisis, exploitation, discrimination, pollution, and war.[29] It is also argued that the degree of democracy for most people is low in democracies where there is extensive capitalist ownership of property. To make a democracy work effectively, there must be a high degree of equality of income, wealth, and economic power—and the United States is offered as an example of a country with a high degree of inequality in these areas. Control of an enterprise by capitalists subverts democracy, it is argued, because they can hire and fire people at will regardless of the wishes of the workers and the community. Supporters of this point of view believe that the way to create a fairer and more just world is to reinvent socialism to eliminate the flaws of the United States and the former Soviet Union. As applied to the United States, this would be done as follows:[30]

1. Political democracy would be promoted by the automatic voting registration of all citizens at birth, effective at 18 years old. Rights of minorities and women would be increased, the latter through the passage of the Equal Rights Amendment. There would only be public financing of elections.

29. Howard J. Sherman, *Reinventing Marxism* (Baltimore: Johns Hopkins University Press, 1995).
30. Ibid, 327–337.

2. Economic democracy would be provided by the guarantee of full employment. This would be done through the use of monetary and fiscal policy to promote jobs in the private sector and public sector jobs. Public investment would be increased on roads, bridges, education, health care, and transportation. Expenditures would be increased on public housing, and there would be free health care and education for all. Workers would control many enterprises, and income taxes would be made strongly progressive.

WHITHER CAPITALISM?

After the fall of the Berlin Wall in 1989 and the collapse of Communism in the Soviet Union in 1991, there were those persons who proclaimed that capitalism is here to stay.[31] But times have changed during the 1990s, and a highly competitive global capitalism has emerged that has transcended national borders. The triumph of capitalism pushed a number of countries toward becoming market economies. This had the effect of flooding the world with low-skilled labor, prompting mass migration and a fight for jobs. Above all, shifts in technology, transportation, and communication are in the process of creating a world where anything can be made or sold anyplace on the face of the earth. One result is that whole regions, even continents, can be bypassed as brainpower, not natural resources, has become the major source of national competitive advantage.

There are many world problems. The income gap between rich countries and poor countries is widening, and in the United States and some other countries the gap between rich people and poor people has also widened. Europe has several serious problems. Unemployment has increased, and rising labor costs have caused European firms to move to other countries, including the United States.[32] The financial burden of the welfare state has increased in Europe, particularly as the population has grown older.[33] Rising public expenditures have had an adverse effect on economic performance.[34] But in the end, it is politics that matters most because reductions in public spending, as the French government found out, will be fiercely resisted by those who have something to lose.[35] Finally, with Mexico as an object lesson, the financial markets stand ready to punish those countries that can't keep their finances in order.

31. Francis Fukuyama, *The End of History and the Last Man* (New York: Basic Books, 1991).
32. German labor costs, which are around $32 an hour including fringe benefits, are the highest in the world. Labor costs in Czechoslovakia, Germany's next-door neighbor, were $6 an hour. Major German automakers have moved to Alabama and South Carolina. Since 1990 the United States has created 8,600,000 net new jobs; Europe has created zero.
33. "A Survey of the Economics of Ageing," *The Economist*, January 17–February 2, 1996, 1–16. Old-age pensions expressed as a percentage of GPD will triple in Germany, France, and Italy by the year 2025.
34. Vito Tanzi and Ludger Schuknecht, "The Growth of Government and the Reform of the State in Industrial Countries," *IMF Working Paper*, December 1995.
35. Government attempts to cut entitlements caused rioting throughout France in early 1996.

It is argued that capitalism provides no sustaining ideology, no set of principles for which voters in democratic societies would be willing to make sacrifices.[36] Other civilizations, including those of Egypt and Rome, were able to survive for an extended period of time because they focused on the community and not on the individual. Rome succeeded because its social organization was cohesive and disciplined, and was able to build an empire. The Romans condemned the vulgar and ignoble commercial values that lie at the heart of capitalism.[37] By contrast, five hundred years ago the Chinese led the world in technology, but with no uniting vision of where that technology should lead them, they declined. The same thing could happen to the capitalist countries of today because of the number of problems that exist. An example is the trade imbalance between the United States and Japan, China, and other East Asian nations that could cause a financial collapse similar to that which occurred in the 1930s.[38]

SUMMARY

The American century, far from being over, is on its way into the next century. The information revolution has altered the balance of national power, and the United States leads the world in the new technologies. Not only does it lead in military power and economic production, but it has a comparative advantage in its ability to collect, process, and disseminate information. In the information age, the importance of technology and education has increased, while that of geography, population, and raw materials has decreased. The information edge that the United States possesses cuts in many directions. It increases its military capability in the areas of collection, intelligence, and surveillance, and enhances its diplomacy because its information edge can help prevent regional conflicts. It is better able to project its ideals, institutions, and culture throughout the world.

The world labor force is projected to increase at a rapid rate in the future. Most of this growth is projected to occur in the poor countries of the word, which makes the task of raising living standards very difficult. The major shift in the economy of the United States is also affecting the world economies. This shift has been driven by breakthroughs in transportation, communications, and industrial technology, placing a greater emphasis on education. There has to be an enormous improvement in human capital if poor countries of the world can expect to benefit from technology. Currently 44 percent of the labor force in poor countries is employed in agriculture compared to 3 percent in the high-income countries. But greater investment in human capital has to occur in an environment conducive to economic growth, and that environment is lacking in many countries.

36. Lester C. Thurow, *The Future of Capitalism* (New York: William Morrow and Company 1996).
37. Ibid., 14.
38. The world banking system collapsed. In the United States some 7,000 commercial banks went broke during the period 1929–1932.

QUESTIONS FOR DISCUSSION

1. The world has witnessed some dramatic changes during this century. Discuss some of the changes that have occurred.
2. In what ways has the technological revolution of the latter part of this century changed the world?
3. The United States is expected to continue its dominance as the world's leading economic power into the next century. Discuss the reasons why.
4. What are some of the factors that could lead to a revival of socialism throughout the world in the twenty-first century?
5. At least for the present, neither a united Europe nor Japan appears to provide the United States the challenge that was once expected of them. Discuss.
6. Political instability has been on the increase since the end of the cold war. Why has this happened?

RECOMMENDED READINGS

Economic Report of the President 1996. Washington, D.C.: US Government Printing Office, 1996.

Maddison, Angus. *The World Economy in the 20th Century*. Paris: OECD, 1989.

Marshall, Ray. "The Global Job Crisis." *Foreign Policy*, No. 100 (Fall 1995), 19–26.

Nye, Joseph S., Jr., and William A. Owens. "America's Information Edge." *Foreign Affairs*, Vol. 75, No. 2 (March-April 1996), 20–36.

Porter, Michael E. *The Competitive Advantage of Nations*. New York: Free Press, 1990.

Reich, Robert B. *The Work of Nations: Preparing Ourselves for 21st-Century Capitalism*. New York: Alfred A. Knopf, 1991.

Sherman, Howard J. Reinventing Marxism. Baltimore: Johns Hopkins University Press, 1995.

Stiglitz, Joseph. *Whither Socialism?* Cambridge, Mass.: MIT Press, 1995.

"A Survey of the Economics of Ageing." *The Economist*, January 27–February 6, 1996, 1–16.

Tanzi, Vito, and Ludger Schuknecht. *The Growth of Government and the Reform of the State in Industrial Countries*, IMF Working Paper, Washington, D.C.: International Monetary Fund, December 1995.

Thurow, Lester C. *The Future of Capitalism*, New York: William Morrow and Company, 1996.

Yunker, James A. *Socialism Revised and Modified: The Case for Pragmatic Market Socialism*. New York: Praeger, 1992.

Index

A

B

C

H

I

J

K

L

M

N

R

S

U

V

W

Y

Z

Health Care Food Service Systems Management

Catherine F. Sullivan, PhD, RD
Sullivan Associates
Detroit, Michigan

Courtney Atlas, MPH, RD
Wayne County Community College
Detroit, Michigan

An Aspen Publication®
Aspen Publishers, Inc.
Gaithersburg, Maryland
1998

The authors have made every effort to ensure the accuracy of the information herein. However, appropriate information sources should be consulted, especially for new or unfamiliar procedures. It is the responsibility of every practitioner to evaluate the appropriateness of a particular opinion in the context of actual clinical situations and with due considerations to new developments. Authors, editors, and the publisher cannot be held responsible for any typographical or other errors found in this book.

Aspen Publishers, Inc., is not affiliated with the American Society of Parenteral and Enteral Nutrition.

Library of Congress Cataloging-in-Publication Data

Sullivan, Catherine F.
Health care food service systems management /
Catherine F. Sullivan, Courtney Atlas.—3rd ed.
p. cm.
Rev. ed. of: Management of medical foodservice/
Catherine F. Sullivan. 2nd ed. c1990.
Includes bibliographical references and index.
ISBN 0-8342-0921-7
1. Health facilities—Food service—Management.
2. Hospitals—Food service—Management.
I. Atlas, Courtney. II. Sullivan, Catherine F.
Management of medical foodservice. III. Title
[DNLM: 1. Food Service, Hospital—organization & administration.
2. Task Performance and Analysis. 3. Personnel Management—methods.
WX 168 S949h 1998]
RA975.5.D5S847 1998
362.1′76′068—dc21
DNLM/DLC
for Library of Congress
97–26951
CIP

Orders: (800) 638-8437
Customer Service: (800) 234-1660

Editorial Resources: Jane Colilla
Library of Congress Catalog Card Number: 97-26951
ISBN: 0-8342-0921-7

Printed in the United States of America

1 2 3 4 5

Table of Contents

Foreword

It is a great pleasure to write the foreword to the third edition of *Health Care Food Service Systems Management*. The first edition, entitled *Management of Medical Foodservice*, was published in 1983. This edition provides updates in both management and food service issues, including leadership principles, dietetics guidelines, and federal and state rules and regulations.

This edition brings up to date the service operation and requirements for licensure and certification. Despite the progress made in dietetics, foodborne illness continues to be a major public health problem. An update in sanitation issues and the inclusion of a discussion of hazard analysis critical control points should enable readers to reduce the incidence of such illness in their facilities.

As a nutrition and food management consultant for many years, I conducted surveys throughout the state of Michigan. It is with this background that I know how helpful this book will be in promoting desired outcomes: this book is the answer to challenging food service problems.

The systems approach to management allows the staff of a health care food service facility to recognize that a plan of operation is necessary to provide an intended level of service on a consistent and continuous basis. In health care facilities, it is necessary for a registered dietitian, with the support of qualified staff, to coordinate functions of the department, to attain the intended level of health care and outcomes, and to provide for efficiency of operation.

The reader will be pleased with the contents of this edition, which represents the commitment and dedication of Dr. Sullivan and Mrs. Atlas to the profession of dietetics in promoting practical guidelines and standards of practice to ensure positive outcomes for patients and residents.

Carlean Williams, MS, RD
Dietitian (Retired)

Preface

The third edition of *Health Care Food Service Systems Management* is designed, as was the previous edition, entitled *Management of Medical Foodservice*, as a text for students in dietetics and as a reference for practitioners and administrators in health care facilities. Both groups need technical knowledge and practical management skills if they are to understand and utilize available resources fully. The objectives of this book are to present information in a systematic and pragmatic manner so that the reader can get a broad view of management of health care food service, to emphasize the intra- and interdepartmental milieu in which a health care food service manager must work, to concentrate on activities, functions, and problems unique to health care food service operations, and to provide essentials of health care food service management in a single book with an emphasis on practical application.

The authors believe that the menu is the hub of the health care food service system, and all subsystems revolve around it. The presentation of management principles prior to discussing food service systems provides a practical approach to systems management, emphasizing that management is paramount to the food service system.

Chapter 1 presents a comprehensive overview of the systems approach: how systems and subsystems interrelate and how systems theory applies to the management of health care food service. Chapters 2 through 8 provide a basis for understanding management concepts, from how to develop objectives and goals to a discussion of time management. Chapter 3 gives an update of problems in role delineation, the health care team, patient care plans, and patient and organizational ethics. Chapter 5 provides the latest information about changing leadership patterns and how they affect the employee.

Chapters 9 through 15 discuss the following subsystems as an integral part of a food service system: menu planning, equipment, food purchasing, food production, distribution and service, personnel, and finance. New topics include the Food Guide Pyramid, recommended dietary allowances, food labeling, sulfites, vegetarian diets, the Family and Medical Leave Act, and the minimum wage increase. Discussions of computer technology and hazard analysis critical control points are an integral part of Chapters 9 through 15.

New material in the Appendixes includes an update of Omnibus Budget Reconciliation Act (OBRA) guidelines for both clinical and management issues, patient rights, forms relating to the OBRA minimum data set, resident assessment protocol, and hazard analysis critical control points, and recommended dietary allowance information.

Charts, graphs, and photographs are used to illustrate and clarify the theory and practical applications. All subject matter is treated in a manner that can be easily understood by students and practitioners.

Acknowledgments

Many people have contributed to the third edition of this book. Although the title has changed from *Management of Medical Foodservice*, the principles are the same. Special thanks to Louise Jones, MS, RD, Nutrition and Food Management Consultant, Michigan Department of Public Health, for expert guidance on new regulations about the OBRA guidelines; to Willie Atlas, BS, Human Resource Consultant, Michigan Consolidated Gas Company, for helpful insights on current trends in human resources; to Cubie Watson, MS, RD, Director of Dietary Services, Marriott Management Services; to Barbara Saulter, MA, RD, Director of Dietetics at Hawthorn Center; and to Cedric Marks, BS, Instructor in Sanitation, Wayne State University, for providing input from a practical viewpoint. Catherine Sullivan thanks her daughter, Kimberly, and her son, John, for assisting with word processing, and her husband, Claude, for his enduring patience.

Chapter 1

A Systems Approach

Conceptualizing the diverse, complex nature of health care food service management can best be accomplished through the use of the systems approach. As defined by Johnson et al. (1967), a systems approach is "a way of thinking." It is not a set of rules on how to organize and manage, but is a way of looking at the various parts as they integrate to make an organized whole. The practitioner, functioning in an environment of different parts, must be able to analyze the inherent interrelationships. An understanding of how the various parts of the food service system are related and how effective outcome in one part is affected by outcome in another part is of paramount importance. Systems theory, as a frame of reference, facilitates this comprehension.

COMPLEXITY OF MEDICAL FOOD SERVICE

There are certain commonalities among various types of food service operations, such as health care, industrial, hotel, and school food service, but there are also distinct differences. These differences are complex enough to warrant special attention. The uniqueness of medical food service begins with its primary objective, which is to provide direct, individualized, total nutritional care for patients on both regular and modified diets. This is not the mission of any other type of food service operation. In addition to the primary objective, meals are provided for personnel and guests, and for special activities in a variety of settings. For example, in non–health care food service operations, the nutritional component may be subordinate to other objectives, such as profit and marketing of goods and/or services. The exception may be in the case of school food service, where partial nutritional care is provided by meeting one third of the daily dietary allowance in the school lunch.

In most medical facilities of 300 beds or more, the food service manager may be involved in all forms of production and service found in other types of operations, as well as the following:

- patient food service (personalized diet, room service)
- cafeteria (employee and guest meals)
- vending (contract or independent)
- short order (coffee shop, snack bars)
- table service (special luncheons and dinners)
- banquet (special activities)
- tea service (retirement, promotion parties)
- carryout service

Another reason why management of health care food service requires special attention is the nature of the client. Most patients are not hospitalized by choice. Therefore, managers of medical food service must be able to deal with the psychological effects of providing nutritious meals to individuals in an unfamiliar atmosphere with consideration to other factors that may be associated with their state of health.

Special attention is also required because much of the information required for effective and efficient operation is scattered in a number of resources with little attempt to organize available knowledge into a cohesive, understandable whole. With the use of the systems approach to management, order can be brought to what often may be characterized as a frustrating, chaotic situation.

SYSTEMS DEFINED

The difficulty associated with defining a system is attributed to the broad use of the term and the manner in which it is used in the various disciplines. Early use of systems theory related primarily to the physical sciences and engineering. As applied in disciplines such as physics, biology, and engineering, the parts of the system were considered to be static, concrete, or mechanical. As all practitioners can attest, management of a health care food service operation is far from static as subsystems interface inside and outside the systems' boundaries. A theoretical base, applicable to management, must recognize the difference in terms of parts or subsystems. Additionally, the systems approach as applied to management is concerned with people as well as machines and materials.

As defined by Barnhart and Barnhart in *The World Book Dictionary* (1983), a system is "a set of things or parts forming a whole: a mountain system, a railroad system." According to this definition, many man-made and natural units, such as automobiles, rivers, planets, electrical units, plumbing units, and organizations, can be classified as systems. One of the earlier investigators and founders of general systems theory emphasizes interaction with the environment and defines system as "a set of elements standing in interrelation among themselves and with the environment" (Von Bertalanffy 1972, 417). The key word in this definition and one that is useful to our discussion is *environment*. For our purposes, a combination of the two definitions is used to define a system as the integration of parts into an organized whole that functions within a larger environment for a specific purpose. In this definition, the parts are considered subsystems and the larger environment is the medical facility in which the system (food service) operates.

CLOSED AND OPEN SYSTEMS

Systems may be classified as closed or open. In a closed system, there is little or no interaction with the environment. This type of system is primarily physical in nature. The reverse is true of an open system, which is characterized primarily as social. Systems, as related to management of a medical food service, are open because there is constant output into and input from the environment. An open system does not operate in isolation; it is interrelated and interdependent.

INPUT-OUTPUT RELATIONSHIP

How inputs and outputs are viewed depends on the vantage point. Outputs from one system may be the inputs for another (Berrien 1968). This concept is discussed later in this chapter under Suprasystems. The input-output relationship for a health care food service system is illustrated in Figure 1–1. The inputs are the resources and the outputs are the finished products. In health care food service, the raw products are processed into acceptable meals for patients. For the system to survive, the outputs must be useful and acceptable to the larger environment (medical facility). When the output is unsatisfactory, the finished product is rejected and eventually the system will fail unless corrective action based on feedback is taken (Bertrand 1972).

The feedback loop provides control and is an important part of the system. Feedback, as shown in Figure 1–1, can be directed to input or process, and may be of a negative or positive nature. When the output is unsatisfactory, there will be a flow of complaints from the environment. In health care food service, the complaint may refer to an unacceptable entree ("The meat is tough"). The feedback loop for corrective action may go to input, such as purchasing, or to process, such as preparation technique, to determine the problem area. The manager uses negative feedback as a point of corrective action and positive feedback as an opportunity to praise, encourage, and motivate employees. In a successful operation, it is desirable to have more positive than negative feedback.

SUBSYSTEMS

A subsystem is a component of a system and has a specific purpose of its own. It is designed to operate within a system in an integrated manner in order to realize the pri-

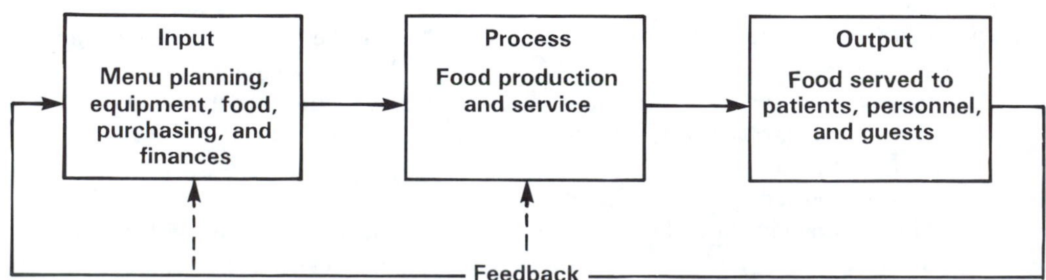

Figure 1–1 Input-Output Relationship

mary purpose of the total system. In health care food service, the subsystems are identified as follows:

- menu planning
- equipment selection and design
- food purchasing
- food production
- food service
- personnel
- finances

Other components of a food service system, such as sanitation, safety, quality control, and computer application, are not considered subsystems and therefore are not presented as a separate entity. The conceptual view is that these components are an integral part of all subsystems.

SYSTEM-SUBSYSTEM RELATIONSHIP

The relationship between systems and subsystems is shown in Figure 1–2. The importance is placed on how effectively and efficiently the subsystems interact and are integrated into the system for the purpose of achieving the goals of the system and the environment.

The menu is considered the hub of the system, with subsystems interrelated and interdependent on its purpose, process, and content. The view of menu planning as the hub of the system is based on the concept that all the activities taking place in the other subsystems are dependent on the purpose, process, and content of the menu. Examples of how the subsystems overlap in their relationships and dependence are described in the following:

- Equipment is selected and designed according to the types and volumes of food items on the menu. If baked potatoes are to be served with roast beef, then ovens (conventional, convection, or microwave) must be available for timely preparation of both items. The number of ovens required will depend on the volume needed for a given time. Because the purchasing of equipment is based on need, some pieces of equipment could be eliminated completely. For example, if no fried-food items appeared on the menu, there would be no need to purchase a deep fat fryer.
- Food is purchased according to dictates of the menu. Depending on the use of the food item, it may be desirable to vary the quality or grade of food purchased. For

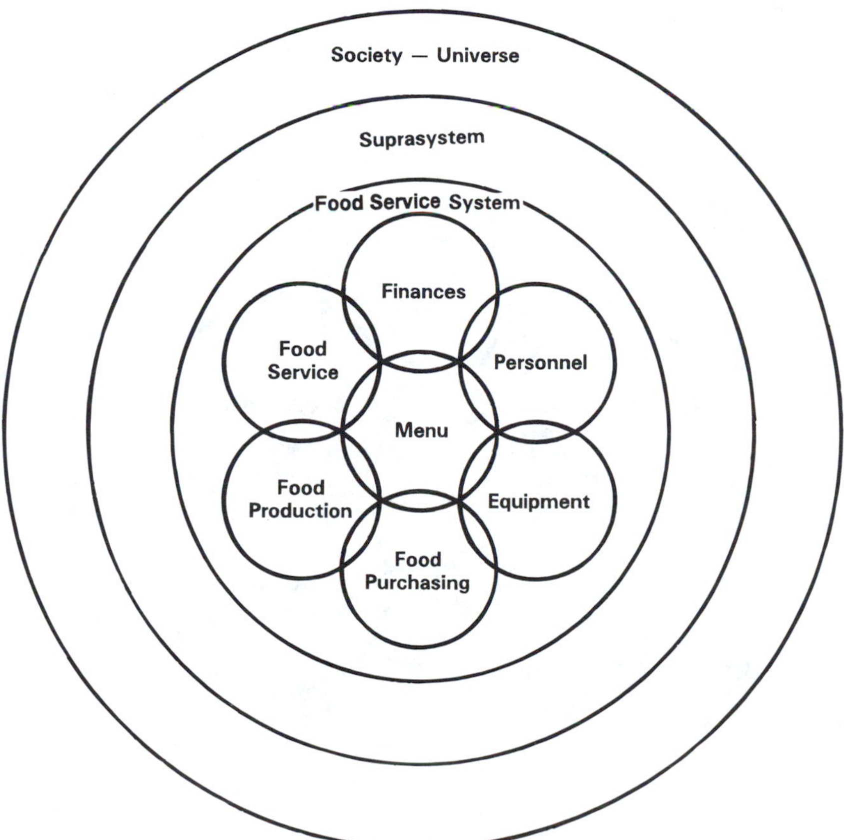

Figure 1–2 Conceptual Model of the System-Subsystem Relationship

example, if canned peaches were served as a dessert, a higher quality would be required than if they were served in a jellied form as a salad.

- The production of a food item is directly related to the intended use as indicated on the menu. Whether to fry, bake, broil, peel, or trim a food item will depend on the nature of the food and for whom it is intended. Food for patients on modified diets is prepared differently from food for patients on regular diets.
- The service of food with reference to portion size, holding, and serving temperatures is directly related to menu planning. For example, the portion sizes for stews, casseroles, and sliced meats are all different. In addition, there are some controlled-intake diets in which specific portions (by ounce) are prescribed. Holding and serving temperatures vary from frozen to the very hot, depending on the menu item and the production system.
- Personnel skills required to prepare and serve food depend on the type and complexity of the food item. For example, if gourmet foods appear on the menu, more highly skilled employees are required.
- Finances are related to menu planning in a number of ways. For example, the food cost will vary depending on menu offerings of seasonal foods, low versus high quality, the portion size, and so forth.

When the menu is accepted as the hub of the food service system, it is considered to be a catalyst that sets into motion the functions to be performed in other systems. It is important for managers to understand interrelationships that are dependent on effective menu planning.

SUPRASYSTEMS

A suprasystem is the environment in which systems function. The relationship between a suprasystem and a system is similar to that between a system and a subsystem. This is evident because the outputs from a system serve as inputs for the suprasystem. Expressed another way, the food service system may be considered to be a system or a subsystem, depending on how it is viewed. For example when the food service system receives input from its subsystems, it is regarded as a system; when the food service system provides inputs for the larger system (medical facility), it may be considered a subsystem. As shown in Figure 1–3, the food service system is just one item in the partial list of interrelated parts. As noted, the patient is the hub of the suprasystem and the other systems interact to provide support.

The suprasystem is also part of a larger environment, with inputs from systems (food service) and outputs (healthy individuals) into the community. The outputs must be

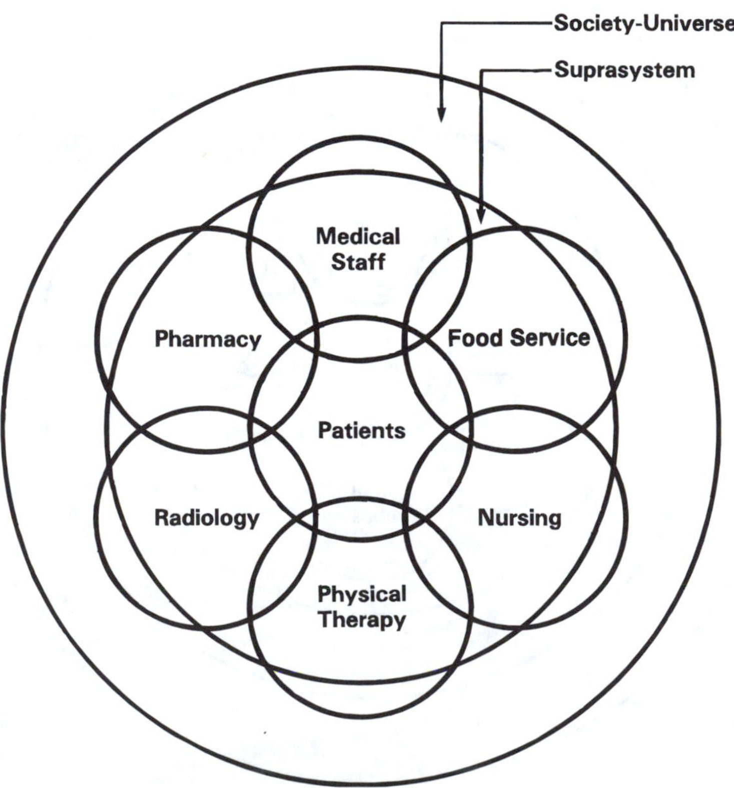

Figure 1–3 Conceptual Model of the Suprasystem-System Relationship

acceptable to the larger environment if the suprasystem is to survive. To use the illustration in Figure 1–1, the feedback loop may return to any one of the inputs, such as food service, nursing, or medical, or to the processing of the inputs.

Health care facilities are complex organizations. Their degree of complexity depends on purposes, objectives, and goals, as is discussed in Chapter 2. The more complex the organization, the greater the need for a systems approach. Some of the advantages of approaching the management of a medical food service from a systems viewpoint are as follows:

- It provides the manager with an understanding of the basics necessary to operate in a milieu of dynamic interrelationships.
- It requires the manager to look at all parts and discern the interdependence of each as a part of the whole.
- It provides a conceptual framework for viewing the interrelationships of parts in a complex operation and how they overlap in meeting organizational goals.
- It forces the manager to synthesize rather than isolate the various parts within the food service system.

REFERENCES

Barnhart, C.L., and R.K. Barnhart, eds. 1983. *The world book dictionary.* Vol. 2: L–Z. Chicago: Doubleday.

Berrien, F.K. 1968. *General and social systems.* New Brunswick, NJ: Rutgers University Press.

Bertrand, A.L. 1972. *Social organizations.* Philadelphia: F.A. Davis.

Johnson, R.A. et al. 1967. *The theory and management of systems.* New York: McGraw-Hill.

Von Bertalanffy, L. 1972. The history and status of general systems theory. *Academy of Management Journal* 15, no. 4: 407–426.

CHAPTER 2

Developing Objectives and Goals

It is appropriate that objectives and goals precede theory pertaining to organization, because the structure and functions of an organization are based on its purpose. Additionally, when objectives and goals are defined, there are indications for functional levels and relationships within the organization. Not only must objectives and goals be defined, but they must be communicated in such a way that they will serve to direct action, motivate members of the organization, provide standards for measurable performance, and evaluate organizational effectiveness. At a time when accountability is most prominent for those in managerial positions, statements in terms of what is to be achieved are most important.

OBJECTIVES AND GOALS DEFINED

Some writers prefer not to distinguish between objectives and goals (Terry 1978; Albanese 1975; Huse and Bodwitch 1977) and thus use the terms interchangeably. Other writers make a distinction not only between objectives and goals, but also between related terms such as *purpose, mission*, and *target* (Koontz and O'Donnell 1974). *Purpose* is considered the highest aim and relates to reasons why an organization exists. Statements at this level are broad and general in nature. *Mission* is also a broad term and similar to purpose, except that it is usually applied to nonprofit organizations such as military operations, churches, government, and medical facilities. *Goals* or *targets* are more specific and are usually stated in terms of quality or quantity, whereas *objectives* are used to indicate the end point of a management program. Objectives may be stated as long range, intermediate, or short range.

According to Carlisle (1976), objectives are a desired condition and refer in a general way to the results or conditions that an individual or organization wishes to attain in the future. His thesis is that the hierarchy of organizational aims, in descending order, is as follows:

1. purpose
2. objective
3. strategy
4. organizational goal
5. subunit goal
6. individual goal

It is believed that aims should be established in this order to ensure goal compatibility. Application of this theory, as applied to health care facilities, is illustrated in Exhibit 2–1.

As noted in Exhibit 2–1, purpose and objectives are more general in nature than goals, and refer to the philosophy and ideals of the organization. You might expect to find statements of purpose and objectives posted in the lobby of an institution or included in annual reports issued by the organization.

Because objectives start at the top and filter down through the organization, the question may be asked, "Who is involved in the formulation of objectives?" Generally, the purpose and objectives are formulated by top administration with input from vested interest groups. For health care facilities, the interest groups may include federal, state, and local governments; foundations or other private funding groups; owners; and the community in which the facility operates.

Strategy refers to the method or schemes used to achieve the objectives. Although financing is frequently part of the strategy, other resources such as personnel, equipment, and materials may well be included in the method stated for achieving the purpose of the organization. For example, in the use of methods, the strategy may be to promote organizational efficiency.

Exhibit 2–1 Carlisle's (1976) Theory of Organizational Aims as Applied to Medical Facilities

- Purpose: to be responsive to the needs of the community.
- Objective: to meet health care needs by providing quality health care to individuals and groups.
- Strategy: to gain support from both private and public sources.
- Organizational goal (health care facility): to provide personalized and professional health care treatment for patients.
- Subunit goal (food service): to provide total nutritional care for patients.
- Individual goal: to perform challenging and creative work in health care setting.

Goals, in contrast to objectives, are concrete statements that contain a certain amount of specificity for obtaining objectives. Put another way, goals are tools for translating the general statements pertaining to purpose, objectives, and strategy into meaningful guidelines for organizational activity. Therefore, organizational, subunit, and individual goals must be based on aims at the top of the hierarchy. Because the organization is made up of individuals, each with his or her own set of personal goals, conflict is more likely to occur at the individual level. How the organization and individuals adapt to goal conflict is discussed later in this chapter.

GOAL CLASSIFICATION

Seldom will an organization have only one goal. To illustrate the variety of goals organizations seek, Perrow (1970) distinguishes five categories, as follows:

1. *Social goals*—Social goals refer to society in general, such as cultural values, maintaining order, and producing goods and services.
2. *Output goals*—Output goals refer to the consumer toward whom the product is directed. The importance placed on this category is an understanding of the organization's relationship to the environment. Examples of how conglomerates may add new products or services are discussed in detail. These include such actions as the diversification of products by Ford Motor Company when it took over Philco Appliances, provision of Job Corps training to the unskilled or unemployed worker, and the attack on the Tennessee Valley Authority because it interfered with local competition.
3. *System goals*—System goals refer to the manner in which the organization functions, independent of the goods and services it produces or its derived goals. Some typical system goals are profit for the organization, high rate of growth, and emphasis on a particular type of organization structure.
4. *Product goals*—Product goals refer to the characteristics of goods or services produced, such as quality or quantity, variety, styling, availability, uniqueness, or innovativeness.
5. *Derived goals*—Derived goals refer to how organizations use power in pursuit of other goals, independent of product or system goals. The power generated by organizations may be in the form of political aims, community services, employment development, investment, and plant location and relocation policies. For example, organizations can decide to move from one community and select a relocation site, thus affecting the lives of individuals in both areas.

Perrow used the case of the National Foundation for Infantile Paralysis to illustrate his goal classification. Polio had been practically eliminated as a result of research, thus leaving the foundation without concrete goals. The foundation considered several alternatives and finally decided to concentrate on childhood diseases in general. Although the shift was from polio to all childhood diseases, there was no change in output goals: to finance research and to treat human diseases. The system goals in support of health causes were not changed, nor was the highly centralized structure at the national level or the decentralized local leadership. In terms of derived goals, the new arrangement served as a means to an end, generating power and prestige in the health field.

Organizational goals, as well as those for individuals, are generally multiple in nature and may be pursued simultaneously or in sequential order. One of the problems associated with formulating objectives and goals is that often the stated goal is quite different from the goal pursued. According to Huse and Bodwitch (1977), the official goals are for public view, whereas the actual goals toward which the organization exerts its energy or effort are used as operating guidelines. On a lower level, the food service department may have as its objective to provide optimum nutritional care, yet resources may be provided for only minimal care.

GOAL CRITERIA

Because goals are more specific than objectives, it may be desirable to understand guidelines for ensuring goal validity. As proposed by Carlisle (1976), eight guidelines (Exhibit 2–2) apply to establishing goals.

The most controversial of the guidelines set forth in Exhibit 2–2 is the one related to restriction of the number of goals. Carlisle suggests limiting organizational goals to six or fewer. The number may be realistic when we consider that goals relate to major areas and not to the activities and tasks involved in attaining the goal. Furthermore, because goals are likely to be multiple at all levels of the organization, it is realistic for managers to pursue a number of goals simultaneously. According to Koontz and O'Donnell (1974), the number of goals established and pursued by a manager will depend on how much is delegated, thereby limiting the manager's role primarily to assigning, supervising, and controlling.

An example of a subunit goal and the associated tasks and activities is shown in Exhibit 2–3. The objective relating to this goal may be to lower food costs, which is a very broad and general statement, but the goal is specific in both quantity and time.

GOAL CONGRUENCY

Organizations have goals. Individual members of the organization have goals. The optimal relationship is achieved when organizational and individual goals harmonize in such a fashion that both are met. Frequently, this harmonizing calls for adjustment of goals of both parties.

Exhibit 2–2 Carlisle's (1976) Eight Guidelines for Establishing Goals

1. Make goals specific:
   - Do goals provide direction?
   - Do goals imply action?
2. Make goals verifiable:
   - Are quantitative controls set?
   - Are qualitative controls set?
   - Are time limits set?
   - Are cost controls set?
3. Make goals action-oriented and result-oriented:
   - Do goals focus on results?
   - Do goals imply action?
   - Do goals serve to motivate?
4. Make goals realistic:
   - Are areas for improvement included?
   - Are goals reachable?
5. Make goals problem-oriented:
   - Do goals focus on poor performance?
   - Are goals ranked according to priority?
6. Make goals restricted in number:
   - Are goals limited for each unit?
   - Are goals limited for each individual?
7. Make goals participative:
   - Do participants have input in setting goals?
   - Do participants have authority comparable to assigned responsibility?
8. Make goals balanced and integrated:
   - Are goals consistent at all organizational levels?
   - Do goals cover all major activities?

Exhibit 2–3 Sample of a Subunit Goal for a Food Service Unit

Subunit:	Patient tray service
Objective:	To reduce food costs
Goal:	To reduce the number of unused trays delivered to wards by 90% from present level of 45 trays per day within a 30-day period.
Tasks:	Consult with patient service personnel. Monitor unused trays left after each meal. Review census sheets. Review standard operating procedures for diet changes (admissions, discharges, surgery, other). Determine cause for excessive number of unused trays. Communicate with nursing personnel. Reinforce or rewrite standard operating procedure. Train food service personnel, if needed.

A new employee who enters the organization brings his or her own set of values, goals, and needs. The primary reason for joining the organization may be monetary gain or security, but not necessarily. The employee may seek prestige, social interaction with others, and challenging and creative work, or there may be other reasons that may not be stated during the interview or written on job application forms. Attempts to integrate personal and organizational goals can result in situations varying from no conflict to workable conflict and cooperation (Albanese 1975).

No Conflict

Although it is uncommon to have no conflict, mutual goals are more likely to be found between top executives and the organization than with employees at the lower level of the hierarchy. In such cases, one can say that the executive's life and work are identical. It is further theorized that, for most employees, there is no conflict between some of the personal goals and the goals of the organization. For example, an employee who cannot satisfy any of his or her personal goals while meeting the goals of the organization probably should leave.

Destructive Conflict

Destructive conflict develops when there is incongruence between the needs of the mature personality and the goals of the formal organization. Organizational interference may be in the form of rules, policies, controls, authority, and methods of supervision. Employees cope with this type of conflict in a number of ways: some may leave the organization; some will work toward higher positions in the organization with the hope that the higher position will be less restrictive; others will increase absenteeism, decrease productivity, and withdraw from active involvement in organizational activities; and some may cope by committing acts of sabotage and violence.

Workable Conflict and Cooperation

There is recognition on the part of the organization and the part of the employee that they need each other. Therefore, there is enough give and take on both sides to permit sufficient organizational survival and growth. The degree of conflict may be related to whether the individual views work as a central life interest. For individuals who value work as a part of but not the total or central life interest, the restrictions placed on behavior are not too upsetting. These employees simply find outside activities to fulfill their needs.

As practitioners, managers can probably cite a number of job-related incidents that reflect goal congruence or conflict. For example, when an employee talks about the organization in terms of *we*, there is inference of goal congruence. On the other hand, when an employee says, "This is not part of my job," the inference is that goal conflict is taking place. In the latter example, the employee either does not know or understand the organizational goal or may have lost interest or a sense of direction because of the growing complexity and bureaucracy of medical facilities. If the primary reason for existence of a medical facility is to promote patient wellbeing, this fundamental justification must be communicated to the lowest level of the organization.

MANAGEMENT BY OBJECTIVES

One of the most effective systems that can be used to foster goal congruency is management by objectives (MBO). The concept of MBO was introduced by Drucker (1954) during the early 1950s and was further developed by Odiorne (1965) a decade later. The system, which deals with individual and organizational goal setting, is widely used in both public and private organizations.

In practice, both the employee and the supervisor are involved in the assessment of the employee's job responsibilities and the ranking of tasks in the order of importance. If there are discrepancies—and there usually are—differences are discussed until mutual agreement is reached. The second phase is similar to a job performance appraisal in which both parties indicate strengths and weaknesses of job performance. Again, discussion follows to reinforce the employee's strengths and to suggest ways to improve in areas of weakness. After agreement has been reached in job improvement, performance standards are established for all major duties. During the final stage, when goals are agreed upon, resources required for implementing tasks are provided. Frequent feedback is an important part of the system and should be an integral part of the evaluation.

No system is perfect. Although the advantages far outweigh the disadvantages, there are some shortcomings. MBO, as does any other system, requires adequate time for planning. The system cannot be put into effect overnight. In large organizations, it may take several years before the program is integrated throughout the organization. All participants involved in goal setting should be thoroughly indoctrinated in the philosophy of the system and how to avoid pitfalls, such as inflexibility and exclusive concentration on short-term goals. With adequate consideration to the above, benefits of using MBO may be the following:

- The system can be implemented and used throughout the organization.
- MBO improves role clarification for both managers and subordinates.
- MBO elicits commitment with concepts of participative management.
- MBO encourages initiative and creativity on the part of the participants.
- With its open environment, MBO improves communication.
- The goal-setting process improves morale.
- The system improves coordination and planning of short- and long-range goals.
- MBO promotes effective performance appraisals based on results.
- MBO improves productivity.
- The system provides feedback through frequent progress reports.

There have been successes and failures in attempts to apply MBO in various organizations. The application of MBO has the greatest potential for success if there is proper atmosphere, organizational clarity, and an effective management information system (McConkey 1972). The importance of adequate preparation cannot be overemphasized, because the basic premise is that of accomplishing goals of the organization and the individual in a more efficient and effective manner. This can best be realized if there is good structure, goal congruency, goal clarity, and goal commitment (Villarreal 1974).

POLICIES, PROCEDURES, AND RULES

Policies, procedures, and rules are part of the decision-making process that determines how the organization will function in meeting overall aims and objectives. The policy-making process for the business-for-profit type of operation is considerably less complicated than that for organizations such as complex medical facilities. One of the reasons for the complexity of decision making in medical facilities is the presence of multiple lines of authority: board of governors, medical boards and chiefs, and administrators. Rakich and Darr (1978) delineate policy-making responsibilities in hospitals as follows:

1. Governing boards make overall policy.
2. Medical boards and chiefs recommend and implement policies related to medical service.
3. Administrators recommend and implement policies dealing with financial and support services and with the relationship of these services to medical service and other units within the organization.

In addition, policies are influenced by external sources, such as the American Hospital Association; the Joint Commission on Accreditation of Healthcare Organizations (Joint Commission); employee unions; and local, state, and federal agencies.

In practice, the terms *policy, procedure*, and *rule* are frequently grouped together and issued as the organizational or departmental policy manual. This grouping is due, in part, to the nature of some policy statements. Policy statements tend to limit or establish parameters for decision making. The degree to which alternatives are limited depends on whether the policy statement contains elements of a rule. In the following discussion, a distinction is made between the terms.

Policy

A policy is a broad statement used as a guide for managerial decision making. The individual responsible for carrying out a policy has some discretion in its implementation. A sample policy statement is illustrated in Exhibit 2–4.

This policy has elements of a rule, but the manager of the food service unit has discretion in terms of the number of meals offered per day (three, four, or more) and the hours of meal service. The rule element is that the manager must

Exhibit 2–4 Sample Policy for a Food Service Unit

DATE: __________

POLICY NO.: __________

Unit: Food Service Department

Subunit: Patient tray service

Policy: Not more than 14 hours shall elapse between the serving of the evening meal and the next substantial meal for patients who are on oral intake and do not have specific requirements.

Effective: Immediately

APPROVED BY:

Director, Food Service	Administrator
Chief, Medical Staff	Chief, Nursing

Review dates: __________ __________

__________ __________

conform to the time span as specified in the policy. Policies and procedures are often interdepartmental, with application to more than one department. In the example given in Exhibit 2–4, the policy must be adhered to by the medical staff and the nursing staff, as well as the dietary department.

Procedure

A procedure is a step-by-step sequence of how an activity is to be performed. The procedure may include prescribed standards for time, quality, and quantity. A sample procedure with reference to the above policy is shown in Exhibit 2–5.

In compliance with the policy for time span between evening and morning meals, the procedure is specific in terms of meal hours. As in most procedures, there is a call for action rather than thinking on the part of those responsible for carrying it out.

Rule

A rule is specific action to take or not to take in a given situation. A rule leaves no discretion on the part of an individual responsible for carrying it out. It is a simple, straightforward, and explicit statement. A rule is able to

Exhibit 2–5 Sample Procedure for a Food Service Unit

DATE: ____________
PROCEDURE NO.: ________

Unit: Food Service Department

Subunit: Patient tray service

Reference: Policy No. FS 26

Purpose: To ensure that patient meals are served at proper intervals.

Procedure:

1. Meals will be served to patients at the following hours:

   Breakfast 7:00 AM
   Lunch 11:30 AM
   Dinner 5:00 PM

2. Observe the following rotation for tray service:

   East Wing
   South Wing
   West Wing
   North Wing

Effective: Immediately

APPROVED BY:

________________________	________________________
Director, Food Service	Administrator
________________________	________________________
Chief, Medical Staff	Chief, Nursing

Review dates: ____________ ____________
____________ ____________

stand alone without further explanation. An example of a rule is as follows:

Rule: There shall be no smoking in the food preparation and service areas.

To summarize, a distinction is made between the terms *policy, procedure*, and *rule:* a *policy* tells you what to do, with discretion; a *procedure* tells you how to do it, with no discretion; and a *rule* tells you what you can or cannot do, with no discretion.

Oral versus Written Policies, Procedures, and Rules

The decision to use oral or written forms of communicating policies, procedures, and rules is no longer left entirely to the discretion of the organization. The need to defend against possible lawsuits from employees and clients and the need to comply with standards posed by outside agencies make it imperative that written forms of communication are in use.

Advantages of Written Policies

In addition to making sure that major areas are covered, other advantages are that written policies do the following:

- Improve the communication process.
- Can be checked for consistency with overall objectives and goals.
- Can be used to orient and train new employees.
- Can be used for objective performance rating.
- Reduce confusion on the part of employees.
- Can be used to measure standards of performance.
- Aid in delegation of authority.

It may be impossible to establish policies for all potential problem areas, but when problems continually arise in an area without policy guidelines, managerial attention is needed.

REFERENCES

Albanese, R. 1975. *Management: Toward accountability for performance*. Homewood, IL: Richard D. Irwin.

Carlisle, H.M. 1976. *Management: Concepts and situations*. Chicago: Science Research Association.

Drucker, P. 1954. *The practice of management*. New York: Harper & Row.

Huse, E.F., and J.L. Bodwitch. 1977. *Behavior in organizations: A systems approach to managing*. Reading, MA: Addison-Wesley.

Joint Commission on Accreditation of Hospitals. 1988. *Accreditation manual for hospitals*. Chicago.

Koontz, H., and C. O'Donnell. 1974. *Essentials of management*. New York: McGraw-Hill.

McConkey, D.D. 1972. Implementation: The guts of MBO. *Advanced Management Journal* 37, no. 2: 13–18.

Odiorne, G. 1965. *Management by objectives*. New York: Pitman.

Perrow, C. 1970. *Organizational analysis: A sociological view*. Belmont, CA: Wadsworth.

Rakich, J.S., and K. Darr. 1978. *Hospital organization and management*. New York: Halsted.

Terry, G. 1978. *Principles of management*. Homewood, IL: Richard D. Irwin.

Villarreal, J.J. 1974. Management by objectives revisited. *Advanced Management Journal* 39, no. 2: 28–33.

CHAPTER 3

Organization Theory and Design

The starting point for organization design is to examine and understand why an organization exists. Concern should center around the following:

- the stated objectives
- the work to be accomplished
- the individuals in the workplace
- the environment in which the organization operates

An organization is formed when it is necessary to combine the efforts of two or more individuals in the process of meeting stated objectives. The primary purpose for organizing is to divide the work that must be accomplished; this can be done only after one has defined and examined the objectives and has thorough understanding of them. According to Barnes et al. (1970), when objectives are defined, a framework is provided within which the detailed organization structure can be built. In the process of dividing the work, determination is made on internal interactions such as lines of communication, authority, responsibility, control, and other patterns of human relationships necessary to accomplish objectives and goals. The approach to organization design varies from one organization to another. This text supports the open system theory of organization, as is discussed later.

At this time, it is appropriate to provide an overview of traditional theories of organization for a better understanding of modern concepts. The principles of traditional management, developed during the early part of the twentieth century, were sound, valid, and applicable to their time. Many of these principles can be found in organizations today, in varying degrees. The following discussion presents a brief description of three theoretical approaches to organization: classical theory, human relations theory, and open system theory.

CLASSICAL THEORY

Classical theory developed in three streams: bureaucracy, administrative theory, and scientific management (Hicks and Gullett 1975). The three theories were developed by different theorists, about the same time, and with essentially the same practical effects on management. Because of the similarity of basic assumptions, the theories are grouped as one approach.

Bureaucracy

The bureaucracy theory is characterized by extensive rules and procedures, rigid hierarchical structure of authority and responsibility, systematic division of labor, impersonal relationships, and centralized authority from top to bottom. To some individuals, the word *bureaucracy* is synonymous with red tape, which is the direct opposite of its intended purpose—to promote rational, competent, and efficient organization (Albanese 1975). As the major contributor to the bureaucracy theory, Weber (1967) concentrated on the internal workings of the organization and the efficiency therein. The main features of bureaucratic structure, as proposed by Weber, are systematic division of labor, hierarchy of authority, system of rules, system of procedures, impersonality, and technical competence.

The extent to which the above characteristics are found in an organization will depend on the degree of bureaucratization. In studying the concepts of bureaucracy, Hall (1972) concluded that the degree of bureaucratization depends on the type of organizational activity. For example, in the ideal bureaucracy, all of the factors would be present, whereas nonbureaucratic or simple organizations would have a low degree of all of the features present.

Administrative Theory

Administrative theory focuses on the upper levels of the organization with emphasis on principles of management. According to Hicks and Gullett (1975), a bureaucratic theorist proposes what an organization should be, and an administrative theorist proposes how to accomplish or implement an effective organization.

The principles and functions of management, as proposed by Foyal (1949), Mooney and Reiley (1939), Urwick (1944), Gulick (1937), and others, were all centered on efficiency. Division of work is considered the foundation of organization by administrative theorists. If work is divided, then it must be coordinated. The *principle of coordination* means that the subdivision of work should be allotted to persons in a structure of authority so that orders can flow from superior to subordinate, reaching the bottom of the organization (Gulick 1937). Because persons in authority give orders, the principle relating to a structure of authority is known as the *scalar chain*. This principle implies that a hierarchy of authority exists in a series of steps from the very top to all subordinate positions and is necessary to promote effective communication and control.

In addition to defining the hierarchy of authority, a major principle also relates to whom an individual is responsible. To avoid confusion and inefficiency, *the principle of unity of command* dictates that each individual should receive orders and be responsible to only one superior. This principle is interpreted to mean that each individual should know exactly to whom he or she is accountable for particular responsibilities (Albanese 1975). This generality is a particular problem because of the dual line of authority found in many complex organizations today, especially medical facilities.

Administrative theorists believe that there is a limit to the number of persons an individual can manage effectively. The principle that deals with this managerial problem is called *span of control*. Vytautas A. Graicunas (1937) used a mathematical formula to show the possible numbers of relationships between an individual and his or her subordinates. As subordinates increase in numbers, potential relationships increase geometrically. For example, for 4 subordinates there are 11 relationships with any one individual. A 5th subordinate will bring 20 new relationships, plus 9 more relationships to each colleague, for a possible 100 relationships in the unit. Although there are no absolute numbers of subordinates that a superior should manage, the number generally varies from 3 to 6 for upper levels of management, and up to 15 for lower levels. Factors affecting the optimum number relate to the level of training of subordinates; the nature of the job; the complexity of the job; location of jobs, such as widely dispersed or all in same location; the difficulty of the job; and the knowledge of the superior.

The *principle of line and staff* relates to the authority of individuals in the respective positions. The main difference between line and staff is that line personnel have the authority to give orders, whereas staff personnel tend to serve in an advisory or consultative capacity. In addition to line and staff, most organizations have individuals in positions with functional authority. In this capacity, the position holder may serve as both line and staff. For example, a personnel director may have direct supervision of an assistant personnel director, a secretary, and others in the personnel area, and at the same time have limited authority over all departments in the organization in terms of personnel action.

Scientific Management

Scientific management marked the beginning of the scientific method as applied to organization. It was in direct contrast to bureaucracy and administrative theories, which used good judgment as a basis for arriving at managerial principles. Frederick Taylor is considered the father of scientific management because of his contributions to the theory. Taylor, along with other theorists such as Henry Gantt, Harrington Emerson, and Frank and Lillian Gilbreth, focused on the improvement of individual work performance. Based on his work experience at Bethlehem Steel, Taylor's research to improve work efficiency centered around four main principles (Filey and House 1969):

1. *The development of the best method to perform a job.* This involves analyzing each task in detail. In modern organizations today, this principle is known as work simplification.
2. *The selection and development of workmen.* Select the right worker using scientific methods and train him or her in the proper method of performing the job.
3. *The bringing together of proper method and the properly selected and trained person.*
4. *The close cooperation of managers and workers.*

Taylor's emphasis on breaking down components of the job and specialized training at the lower level as well as the managerial level was his greatest contribution to the scientific management theory.

Henry Gantt is noted for developing the Gantt chart, a device used to measure actual versus planned performance. The straight-line chart is used to measure the activity by the time it takes to perform it (George 1968). In addition, Gantt is known for his task and bonus plans for remunerating workers. According to his plan, a day's wages were paid for output less than standard, a bonus for achieving standard, and rewards for production above standard. His concern for efficiency was not at the expense of the human factors of management.

Harrington Emerson's work centered on efficiency, and he was the first to use the term *efficiency engineering*

(George 1968). Emerson was an advocate of a strong staff, and of counsel, as reflected in 2 of his 12 principles of management. For example, on the principle of common sense, he urged managers to strive for knowledge and seek advice from every quarter. On the principle of competent counsel, he states that managers should actively seek advice of competent individuals. He used the military as an example of strong staff and counsel. As one of America's first consultants, he served as the expert witness for Brandeis in 1910 and stated that the U.S. railroads could save a million dollars a day by adopting scientific management principles.

Frank and Lillian Gilbreth were also concerned with efficiency, as evidenced by studies centered on motion economy that laid the foundation for application of job simplification as we know it today. Frank Gilbreth's interest was aroused during his work as an apprentice bricklayer, where he observed various work methods used by the bricklayers. His research led to the invention of a number of instruments and techniques relating to motion economy (George 1968), including the following:

- Used motion picture film to observe and analyze work motions.
- Invented the microchronometer, a clock with a sweeping hand, which was used with motion picture film to determine how long it took to perform various motions. The instrument was capable of recording time to $^1/_{2000}$ second.
- Devised the cyclegraph, which showed the motion patterns involved in performing a task, by placing a small lighted electric bulb near the employee's hand.
- Used a chronocyclegraph to determine the acceleration, deceleration, and direction of movement; the device was added to the circuit to determine the speed and direction of movement.
- Used the technique of consolidating hand motions into 17 basic motions known as therbligs (Gilbreth spelled backward with the *th* transposed).
- Invented the process chart and flow diagram to record patterns used in performing a task.

In their quest for the "one best method," the Gilbreths provided practical application of the science of management.

HUMAN RELATIONS

Early organization and management thought centered around efficiency, high productivity, and low labor cost. The feelings, needs, and attitudes of the worker were practically ignored. It was not until the middle of the 1930s that significant attention was given to the people in the organization. During this period, major contributions were made by Elton Mayo and his associates. These contributions are commonly referred to as the Hawthorne studies.

THE HAWTHORNE STUDIES

As reported by Henderson et al. (1937), studies conducted at the Hawthorne plant of the Western Electric Company were initiated and influenced by two main factors: there was interest in the problems of fatigue and monotony in factory work, and the researchers were aware that there were no satisfactory criteria for dealing with people, compared with the carefully contrived experiments for materials and machines. The studies, conducted between 1927 and 1932, were in three phases.

Relay Assembly Test Room Experiment

In this experiment, five women were transferred from their usual work surroundings to an experimental room in which their work was supervised by an appointed observer. During the entire period of five years, continuous and accurate records were maintained on quantity of output, quality of output, room temperature, lighting, conversations, reasons for temporary stops, amount of time spent in bed, and number of developed human relationships. From time to time, experimental changes were arbitrarily introduced, such as change in hours of work, introduction of rest periods, and change in illumination. The workers were informed about the nature of the experiments, and they agreed to cooperate. They were instructed to work at a comfortable pace and were warned against attempts to increase output. Nevertheless, the rate of output increased throughout the study, regardless of changes in work conditions. The average increase in speed of about 30 percent was not attributed to skills development, because all of the women were experts at relay assembly. The increase in productivity can be attributed to changes in the social environment, which is made up of sentiments and routine. The results also suggest that the achievements were largely due to an equilibrium between plant authority and the spontaneous social organization of the women.

Bank-Wiring Room Experiment

This experiment consisted of two investigations simultaneously. One method was an indirect conversational interview; the other was by direct observation. Both the interviewers and the observers were studying the same group of workers. The interviewer conducted interviews by appointment, whereas the observer was placed with the group to record performance, conversations, and other significant events. The spontaneous social organization of this group centered on fear and mistrust because they were not sure of management's intentions. This was quite different from the previous experiment with women in the relay assembly room. In that experiment the women were told about the experiment, and they agreed to cooperate. This resulted in a high degree of accord between workers and management.

Employees in the bank-wiring experiment defeated the official plan of the company through formation of an informal organization. For example, individual differences in performance were related to the individual's position in the group rather than to his or her actual capacity. The employees established group norms for output levels, striking a medium between producing too much and producing too little.

The supervisory controls established by management failed. It was assumed that the worker was primarily moved by economic interests and that he or she would act to optimize the economic rewards.

OPEN SYSTEM THEORY

In the open system approach to organization, one of the key determinants is the degree of interaction with the environment. This approach is in direct contrast to the bureaucracy theory, which considered the external environmental pressure as a threat, and to scientific and administrative management theories, which generally ignored the environment (Albanese 1975). During the period of classical theory, the organization was functioning in a more stable, predictable environment in terms of economics, energy (personnel, materials, machines, and information), and uniformity of individual value system. Support for an open system theory is offered below by the succinct description of the milieu in which a complex organization must function.

Characteristics of an Open System

Organizations, as open systems, have characteristics in common with other open systems, such as input, process, and output, but they also have distinct characteristics. According to Mink et al. (1979), an open organization is characterized as follows.

It Is an Integrated Whole

In an open system, unity of organizational mission or purpose is fostered through the sharing of information, with credibility of leadership based on the ability to use a systemwide perspective for problem solving through persuasion rather than relying on legal authority.

It Has Interdependent Components

An open system discourages empire building, because all parts of the system are responsive to each other. In the human body, for example, the various organs are interdependent subsystems that exchange nutrients, oxygen, nitrogen, and other biological elements. When the free flow or exchange of elements is blocked, disease results. In human organizations, blockage occurs with closed, belligerent members or defensive departments. In an open organization, internal responsiveness is fostered through collaboration of managers and staff, rather than through authority.

It Has Interchange with the Environment

An open organization continually interfaces with the environment that it serves or on which it depends for survival. The interchange of activities, data, and energy with other systems in the environment that may affect decisions and goals of the organization makes for a proactive, rather than a reactive, relationship. An open organization anticipates new data and the possible changes that may come with them. Thus it is prepared for decision making before a crisis develops.

It Interrelates at the Individual, Group, and Organization Levels

Three characteristics (unity, internal responsiveness, and external responsiveness) are used to describe openness of the individual, group, and organization. Openness is increased at the individual level in terms of unity when there is a positive self-concept. For internal responsiveness, an awareness of one's feelings, wants, and needs increases openness, and positive interaction with others increases openness in external responsiveness. At the group level, unity is fostered when one can identify with the team goals and objectives, realizing that group output is greater than the sum of individual output. For internal responsiveness, the group exhibits positive interpersonal skills, facilitating interaction among team members; for external responsiveness, openness is increased when the group cooperates in gathering and relating external information relevant to the task of the group. At the organization level, unity is increased when there is development of common goals of organization and the managerial process is in accord with purpose and mission. For internal responsiveness, unity is increased when there is positive reaction to and impact on components within the organization. For external responsiveness, the organization is socially relevant and responsive to the larger community, and it is profitable and productive.

In addition to the foregoing, open systems share the characteristics of negative entrophy, feedback, homeostasis, differentiation, and equifinality (Katz and Kahn 1966). Negative entropy means that, to survive and maintain internal order, the system must import more energy from the environment than it expends. Feedback refers to information input that describes the environmental condition, thus providing a signal to the system on its functioning in relation to the environment. The use of information input enables the system to correct malfunctions within the organization or to adapt to changes in the environment, thus creating a steady state of homeostasis. Because organizations exist in a changing and demanding environment, they must be able to adapt to environmental demands as a means of survival. Open systems have a tendency toward differentiation or specialization among their subsystems because of both dynamics and the relationship between growth and survival. Finally, the principle of equifinality suggests that there is no one best way to achieve an objective. Put another way, a system can use a variety of inputs and transform them in a number of ways, yet achieve the same final state. This principle suggests the flexibility associated with an open system rather than the rigidity found in classical theory.

Imperfections of an Open System

Open system theory is considered the most appropriate for organizations in today's environmental climate, but it also suffers from imperfection, as do most other theories of organization. According to Albanese (1975), open system theory has two main problems: lack of clearly defined boundaries and overemphasis on synergism. The boundary problem stems from the inability to establish defined limits, because all elements within a system are interrelated to some degree among themselves and with the environment. Establishing criteria to determine what is relevant as an entity into the system is somewhat arbitrary; therefore, different managers will define the system in different ways. The differences in system definition can be important in determining managerial effectiveness.

The second problem associated with the open system is that of synergism. The idea of synergism reflects the systems view because the emphasis of the theory is on relationships and synthesis. Synergism means that the whole is greater than its parts. In terms of the organization, this means that the combined efforts of the various systems produce a greater total than would the individual systems acting independently. There is the possibility of deemphasizing the importance of individual members and relying too much on relationships as a source of understanding systems parts.

ORGANIZATION DESIGN

The design of an organization structure is analogous to the skeleton of the human body. Put another way, the structure provides a framework for the efficient flow of the many processes that are constantly going on. The structural design is static in nature and therefore cannot reflect all of the relationships and interrelations that exist. Although the formal organization is not realistic in some respects, it is a valuable tool for controlling and coordinating the network of activities.

Formal Organization

Formal organization is usually represented by a chart that is a graphic display of the organization structure. The chart attempts to describe the formal relationships found in an organization in the performance of activities. A typical chart, with its lines and boxes, is designed to show some control over communication, authority, power, responsibility, and accountability (Hicks and Gullett 1975).

Communication

The chart depicts communication lines in all directions: downward, upward, and horizontal. For example, downward communication may take the form of management decision making, which flows down to systems and subsystems within the organization. Upward communication refers to reports to supervisors on results achieved, questions concerning policies, employee complaints, and other matters that need to be considered at a higher level. Horizontal communication is across departmental or unit lines, such as the communication between the dietary and nursing departments.

Authority

Authority may be viewed as the right to do something. It has also been referred to as institutional power, inasmuch as it is formally sanctioned by the organization of which the person who possesses the authority is a member. Authority typically gives an individual the right to issue instructions to others and to see that they are carried out. Authority may be centralized or decentralized. When authority is widely dispersed or delegated throughout the organization, decentralization of authority exists. When authority is in the hands of a few persons, centralized authority is found. Span of control, as discussed earlier, is also a form of authority and is typically depicted on organization charts. Line, staff, and functional authority are also defined through the organization chart, which shows that line personnel have the right to give orders, whereas staff personnel are limited to giving advice and consultation. For example, staff personnel may consult with the personnel director on matters of hiring, grievances, and other personnel activities. Functional authority allows a position holder to issue instructions in a limited area, such as the approval of expenditures over $100 by the purchasing manager.

Power

Power is a broader concept than authority. It can be defined as the ability to do something. An individual may possess power over activities or personnel without having legal or institutional authority. Power may stem from technical competence, seniority, and friendship with other powerful people inside or outside the formal organization.

Responsibility

The obligation a position holder feels for his or her actions is called responsibility. Unlike authority, responsibility cannot be delegated.

Accountability

When results are measured with predetermined standards, accountability is said to exist. Accountability may be thought of as flowing upward through the formal organization structure. Each level is accountable to the next.

Some problems associated with a formal organization are as follows:

- Organizational status is associated with the placement of boxes.
- The chart does not show the relationship of external influences.
- The chart is static and therefore ignores dynamic interrelationships.
- The chart does not depict the informal relationships that are present in all organizations.

Informal Organization

The informal organization operates outside the formal organization. It arises out of the need for employees to interact socially, to establish cohesiveness with coworkers, and to satisfy individual motives. The informal organization facilitates communication in ways not open to the formal organization and therefore can foster the purpose of the formal organization or work against it.

The grapevine is a prime example of the informal organization, which can be both helpful and detrimental if not used for organizational purposes. The manager has an excellent opportunity to use the grapevine to communicate information that will assist in his or her coordination of subordinate efforts. If recognized and used properly, the informal organization can supplement the formal organization in its goals and objectives.

DESIGN OF HEALTH CARE FACILITIES

The level of care in health care facilities ranges from minimal care in health-related facilities to acute care in hospitals. In between the two types, we find skilled nursing care in long-term care facilities and other facilities offering care for the mentally ill, homes for the aged, and homes for children and other adults that provide lodging, meals, social activities, and a minimum of health care. The organization design for the various facilities depends on the respective goals, objectives, and services rendered.

Long-Term Care Facilities

Long-term care is a broad term and includes a number of facilities that provide custodial, basic, and skilled nursing care. Confusion surrounding the nomenclature used to describe the various facilities is widespread, with most facilities lumped under the heading of nursing homes. Schneeweiss and Davis (1974) use the following classification for long-term care facilities:

- Domiciliary care facilities. This category includes homes for the aged, public and private homes for adults, and residence for adults.
  1. Residency for adults. This type of facility provides lodging, food, housekeeping services, and activity programs for adults who require such services on a continuous basis.
  2. Proprietary home for adults. This type of facility is operated for profit and provides lodging, food, and the services of attendants to ensure safety and comfort in bathing, dressing, feeding, and moving about. Medical and nursing services are not provided.
  3. Public home. This type of facility is a residence for adults and typically is operated without an infirmary.
  4. Home for the aged. This is a proprietary or nonprofit facility with services similar to those for residency for adults.
- Health-related facilities. These are intermediate-care facilities providing lodging, food, social activities, social services, and minimal physical care. Nonambulatory patients usually are not admitted.
- Extended-care facility or nursing home. This type of facility provides 24-hour skilled nursing care, rehabilitative or restorative services, and other health services under the supervision of a physician.
- Senior citizen hotel. A senior citizen hotel is a facility for the elderly who do not suffer from chronic illness.

The classification fails to differentiate types of nursing homes, such as those providing skilled nursing care, intermediate care, and minimal care. There are distinct differences, as noted by the Michigan Department of Public Health (1985). In Michigan, nursing homes are classified as follows:

- skilled nursing facility (SNF)
- nursing facility (NF)
- facility for the care of mentally ill patients
- facility for the care of mentally retarded patients
- facility for the care of patients with tuberculosis

This classification is based on the intensity of care provided, with the skilled nursing care facility providing the most intensive care. States may differ in their classifications of care provided; therefore, the practitioner is advised to become familiar with local health codes.

Skilled nursing facilities participating in Medicare must meet certain specified requirements as provided in Section 1819 of 54 FR 5359 (February 2, 1989) and additional requirements if they are necessary for the health and safety of individuals to whom services are furnished in the facility.

Nursing facilities for Medicare, as amended in 57 FR 43924 (September 23, 1992), may not be an institution for mental diseases (U.S. Department of Health and Human Services 1992). For Medicare and Medicaid purposes (including eligibility, coverage, certification, and payment) the "facility" is always the entity that participates in the program, whether that entity comprises all of, or a distinct part of, a larger institution.

The level of care in long-term care facilities improved considerably with passage of federal laws that governed both the physical facility and the quality of care provided. Prior to 1935, care for the institutionalized elderly and the chronically ill individual was left entirely to the discretion of the various states, with different rules and regulations for licensure, level of care, and funding. The passage of federal legislation had a major impact on the growth and standards of operation for long-term care, as follows (Moschetto 1981):

- The Social Security Act (1935) provided monthly assistance to the disabled and to persons over 65 years of age. With the available funds, indigent individuals were able to pay for the improved quality of care.
- The Hill-Burton Act (1946) contributed to improved facilities and care by providing grants and loans for the construction and equipment for facilities.
- Amendments to the Social Security Act (1950) were the beginning of vendor payments to nursing home owners.
- The Small Business Act and Small Business Investment Act (1958) made loans available to nursing homes.
- The National Housing Act (1959) encouraged construction and renovation of nursing homes with the provision of mortgage insurance.
- The Kerr-Mills program (1960) encouraged expansion of medical care for the elderly by increasing federally matched funds to states using medical vendor payments.
- The Mental Health and Retardation Acts (1963 and 1965) shifted the focus of care for mentally ill patients by promoting the transfer of mentally ill elderly from psychiatric hospitals to nursing homes.
- Medicare and Medicaid Amendments (1965) were added to the Social Security Act. Medicare provided medical insurance for persons aged 65 years and older; Medicaid provided a federal-state grant program for the indigent. Medicare is funded and administrated by the federal government, whereas Medicaid is administered by the state with matching federal funds.

With the use of outside funding, long-term care facilities also had to comply with outside rules and regulations for licensure, certification, quality of care, and organization. In the state of Michigan, concerted effort has been made to unify standards of operation for food service, with recommended standards formulated for all state-owned and state-operated food service operations.

The organization of long-term care facilities depends on the intensity and nature of care provided. In a basic nursing care facility, the organization may appear as shown in Figure 3–1.

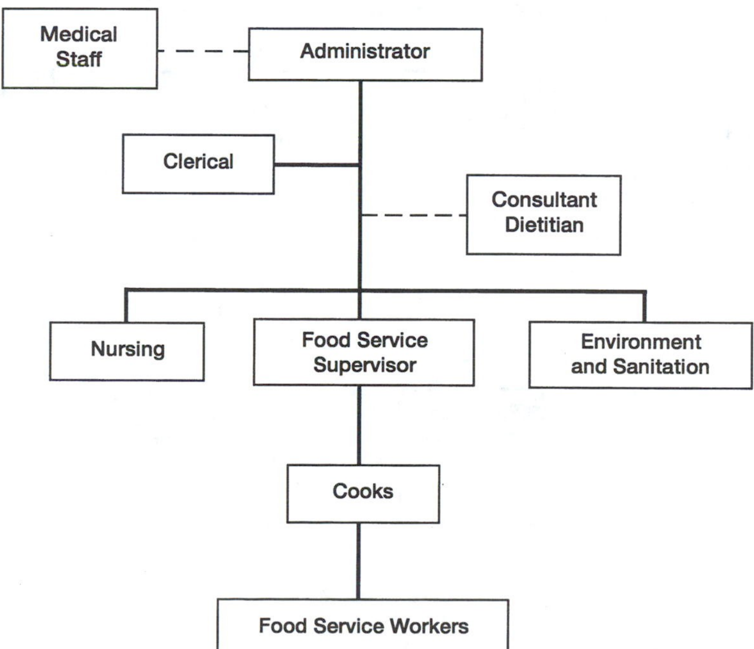

Figure 3–1 Organization Chart for a Basic Nursing Care Facility. *Note:* Broken lines indicate communication, not direct supervision.

The dietary department is usually supervised by a food service supervisor, with the advice and consultation of a registered dietitian. As a result of diagnosis-related groups (DRGs) with shorter lengths of stay in acute care facilities, patients are admitted to nursing homes in a more critical state of illness. In efforts to provide adequate nutritional care, registered dietitians are staffed on a full-time basis in large SNFs. As indicated by the broken lines in Figure 3–1, the consultant dietitian holds a staff position and reports directly to the nursing home administrator. The food service supervisor reports directly to the nursing home administrator and is responsible for production and service of food to both patients and personnel. The food service supervisor is a member of all mandated committees that concern patient food service, as required by the accrediting agency.

The SNF offers the most intensive care among the long-term care facilities. The facility, as all nursing home facilities in the state of Michigan, must be licensed. The facility may meet qualifications and request certification under guidelines for extended care facilities. Under these circumstances, organizations of skilled nursing care and extended care facilities are similar, as shown in Figure 3–2.

Nursing homes, along with other categories of medical care facilities, became eligible for accreditation by the Joint Commission on Accreditation of Healthcare Organizations (Joint Commission) in 1967, as follows (American Medical Association 1967):

- Category I: Hospitals
- Category II: Extended care facilities—establishments with medical staff and continuous nursing service to provide comprehensive post–acute hospital care for a relative short duration
- Category III: Extended care facilities—establishments with medical staff or medical staff equivalent and continuous nursing care to provide long-term inpatient care (not necessarily post–hospital care) for a variety of medical conditions
- Category IV: Resident care facilities—establishments that furnish regular and frequent, but not continuous, medical and nursing service for the safe, hygienic, and sheltered living of residents not capable of or desiring independent living

The extended care facility is an establishment or a designated part of an establishment that provides highly

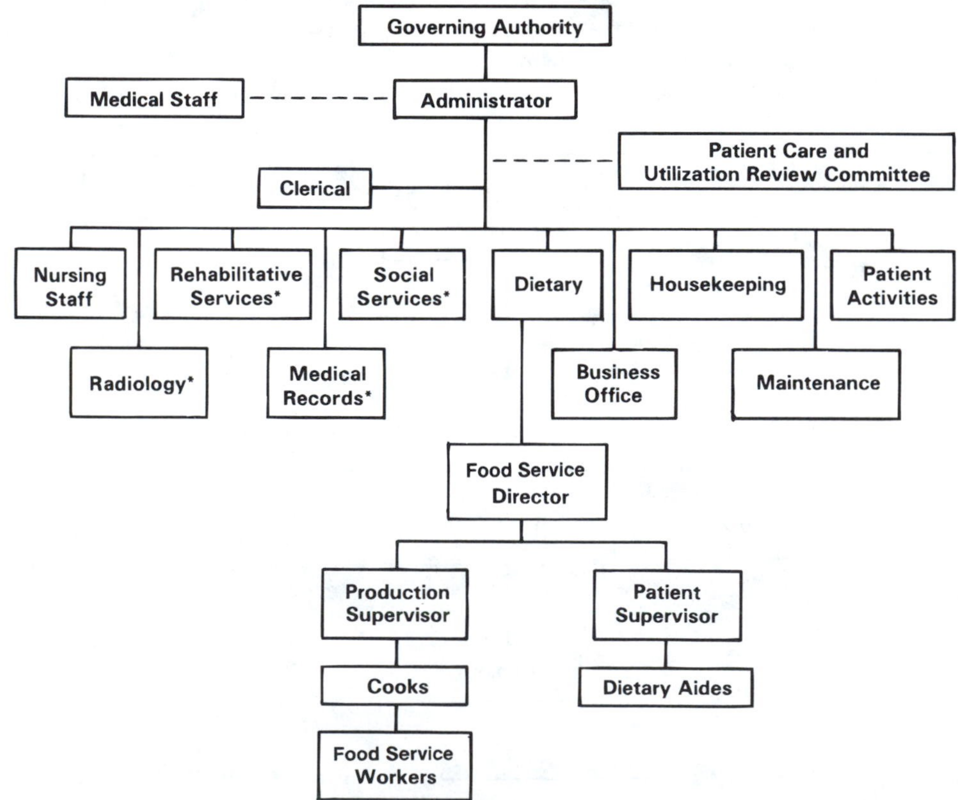

Figure 3–2 Organization Chart for Skilled Nursing Care and Extended Care Facilities. *Note:* Broken lines indicate communication, not direct supervision. An asterisk indicates that part-time or consultant services may be provided.

skilled nursing care and rehabilitative care to patients post–hospital stay. Emphasis is on restorative care, such as physical, occupational, and speech therapy. The extended care may be provided in a facility separate from the hospital or it may occupy a distinct part of a hospital, such as a designated floor or unit. To qualify as an extended care facility under the Medicare Program, the provider of service must comply with the Conditions of Participation as specified in Pub. L. No. 89-97, an amendment to the Social Security Act (U.S. Department of Health and Human Services 1966).

Long-Term Care Survey

The laws and regulations governing conditions and standards of participation in Medicare-Medicaid for long-term care facilities have remained constant, but major changes have occurred in the process used to compile information on compliance. The purpose to implementing a new survey process is to ensure that the quality of life and resident rights, as intended by law and required by residents, is actually being provided in nursing homes.

The old survey process focused on structural requirements, such as written policies and procedures, staffing, and physical plant characteristics. The new Long-Term Care Survey process (formerly referred to as Patient Care and Services [PACS]), known as the Omnibus Budget Reconciliation Act (OBRA), is patient-outcome oriented. For example, in ascertaining whether menus are planned and followed to meet the nutritional needs of each resident, surveyors will no longer routinely evaluate the written menu. Instead, surveyors will observe residents for physiological, psychological, and social factors that may affect food intake. In addition, surveyors will confirm through interviews with residents and staff that nutritional needs are met on a regular basis.

The Long-Term Care Survey process was implemented nationwide in April 1986. Final procedural guidelines, as published in the Federal Register (U.S. Department of Health and Human Services 1988), list the following components for a complete SNF/NF survey:

- Life Safety Code requirements
- administrative and structural requirements
- direct resident care requirements, using the following worksheets (amended 1991):

  HCFA-677—Medication Pass Worksheet
  HCFA-804—Kitchen/Food Service Observations
  HCFA-805—Resident Review Worksheet
  HCFA-807—Surveyor Notes Worksheet

The Long-Term Care Survey process is used for all surveys of SNFs and NFs, whether free-standing, distinct parts, or dually certified. Advance notice to a facility that a survey is scheduled on a certain date is not provided. The surveyors enter an SNF/NF unannounced. During the survey, the following tasks are performed (U.S. Department of Health and Human Services 1991):

- task 1: off-site survey preparation
- task 2: entrance conference/on-site preparatory activities
- task 3: initial tour
- task 4: sample selection
- task 5: information gathering
  1. general observation of the facility
  2. kitchen/food service observation
  3. resident review
  4. quality-of-life assessment
  5. medication pass
  6. quality assessment and assurance review
- task 6: information analysis for deficiency determination
- task 7: exit conference

The procedural guidelines provide surveyors with cross-references (Conditions of Participation) for the survey area; suggest what to observe in patient outcome; suggest questions for interviews with staff and residents; suggest what to look for in the medical records; and indicate how each factor is to be evaluated. (For details of the survey process relating directly to dietetic services see Appendixes A and B.)

Hospitals

The acute care hospital provides the highest level of medical care and is the most complex of all medical facilities (see Figure 3–3).

Complex Organization

The complex organization found in hospitals is due to a number of factors (Rakich and Darr 1978), as follows:

- There is a wide diversity of objectives and goals for the various personnel and subsystems within a complex facility. Conflict is likely to arise as subsystems carry out responsibilities involving complex medical and surgical cases, research, education, hotel-type accommodations, and other duties associated with patient care.
- The diversity of personnel ranges from the most highly skilled and educated to the unskilled and uneducated. The task of the organization and of management is to find ways to coordinate the efforts of the different groups so that they are able to work together.
- The hospital is in continuous operation 7 days a week, 24 hours a day. The scheduling of personnel so that there will be adequate coverage is a monumental task.
- In most hospital operations there are dual lines of authority. The duality refers to the board of governors,

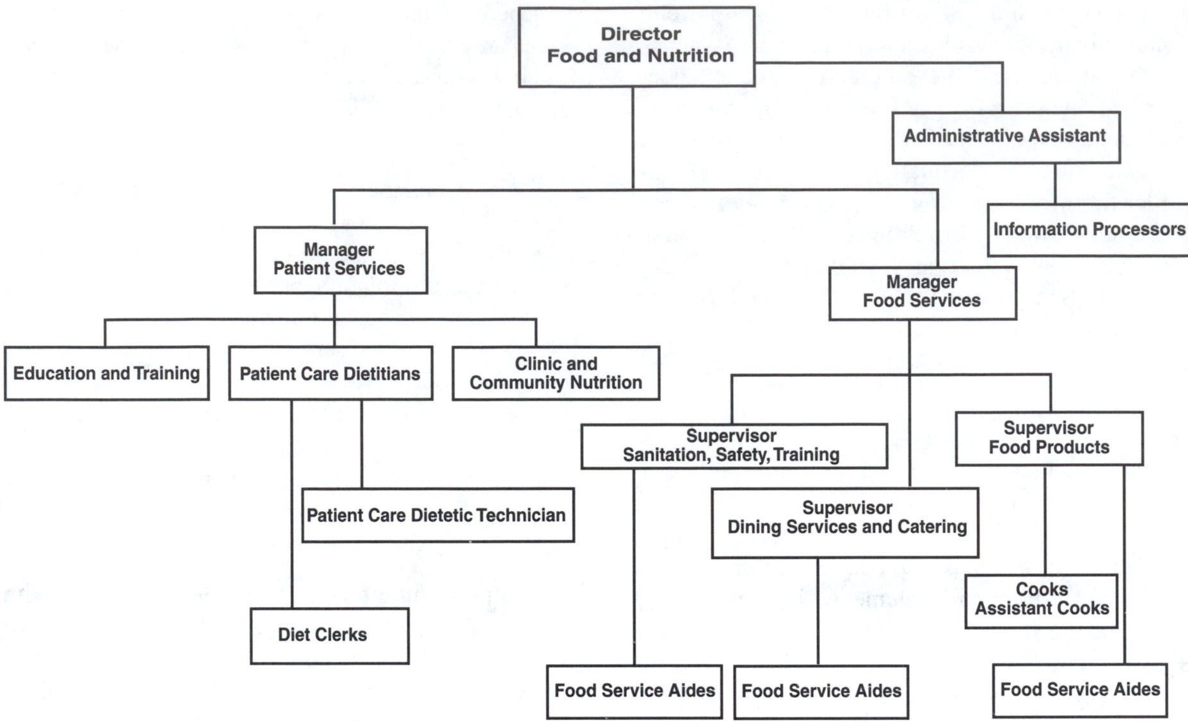

Figure 3–3 Organization Chart for Department of Dietetics

medical staff, and administrators, as discussed earlier. In addition, there is the legal authority of administrators and the functional authority of the medical staff, which often overlap and may create conflict.

- Hospitals deal with problems of life and death. The nonroutine activities associated with complex hospitals often put undue psychological and physical stress on personnel at all levels. The consumer of hospital services cannot possibly understand the full thrust of ongoing activities and often becomes confused and hypercritical of the setting and results.
- There is a problem in measuring the major product. Although there are accrediting agencies with mandated patient care policies, the patient care has eluded precise measurement.

Because of the complexity of hospitals, it is evident that mechanistic, bureaucratic, formal authority principles of organization are not sufficient and cannot be applied across the board. Consideration must be given to the dynamics of sociopsychological forces at work within the organization. According to Georgopoulos (1972), organizational efficiency, as well as high-level performance by members of the organization, depends to a great extent on social efficiency. His theory is that social efficiency may be a more critical determinant of organization effectiveness than economic and technical efficiency because hospitals provide solutions to major problems. Considerations should center on the following:

- organizational adaptation—the ability for continuous adjustment to external conditions and the ability for successful response to relevant changes
- organizational allocation—the ability to procure, deploy, allocate, and utilize human resources and materials; to resolve problems of access to and distribution of authority, rewards, and information; to apply work specialization and allocation of tasks; and to enact participative decision making
- organizational coordination—the ability to articulate and interrelate the diverse roles and interdependent activities; to regulate and synchronize different functions so that all time and effort are expended toward solution of systems problems and goal attainment
- organizational integration—the ability of the system to integrate all members into the organization in such a manner as to enhance cooperation and compliance in achieving overall sociopsychological unity and coherence
- organizational strain—the ability to minimize tension as a result of friction and confrontation among key groups, unequal status participants, and highly independent groups and members of the organization

- organizational output—the ability to maximize efficient and reliable performance by all departments and members; to maximize opportunities for personal growth and satisfaction in efforts to reach and maintain high levels of patient care or health services to the community
- organizational maintenance—the ability to stabilize an organization's identity and integrity in the face of constant external changes and the potentially disruptive and threatening situations that may develop internally

An understanding of open system concepts, characteristics of complex human organizations, and the inherent problems associated with a dynamic, adaptive, and problem-solving social-technical system is a prerequisite for organizational design of a medical facility. The typical voluntary not-for-profit hospital is usually organized with the sharing of power in a triad: governing body, administrator, and medical staff. The trend, according to Rakich and Darr (1978), is changing to one of corporate structure in which the governing authority delegates power to a chief executive officer, who is responsible for all activities, including medical care. This type of structure is prevalent in hospitals where physicians are employed by the organization, such as the Veterans Administration and the military.

According to White (1963), many companies omit broken lines, which indicate communication, because they tend to clutter the chart. Furthermore, persons in a modern operation are free to communicate, for legitimate reasons, with almost anyone else in the organization. The solid lines are necessary to show relationships based on the power to discharge, discipline, issue orders, and communicate formal instructions and reports. Put another way, broken lines may or may not be used at the discretion of the parties at either end of the chart, whereas solid lines must be used regardless of the interest or convenience of individuals involved.

The use of charts with vertical and horizontal lines is not universally accepted for all types of organizations. Two other modes frequently referred to are the concentric and the matrix organization.

Concentric Organization

The concentric organization chart has been used in business and industry for more than 30 years. The most distinguishing feature of the chart is the use of circles to indicate echelon levels. An illustration of organization charts for a hospital dietetics department, using both the traditional and concentric models, is shown in Figures 3–4 and 3–5.

According to Browne (1950), the concentric organization chart offers a more satisfactory presentation for the following reasons:

- The chart improves representation of the dynamics of personal relationships because functions are centered around individuals, not below them. The schematic design, using circles rather than a horizontal plane, surrounds the director with contacts, influences, and relationships that stimulate from all directions.
- The chart eliminates the *above* and *below* concept. Various echelons of authority are represented by the distance of the circle from the center or focal point, thus avoiding the emotional concepts of above or below, higher or lower, superior or inferior, top or bottom.
- The chart presents an organization without loose ends. With the circular presentation, there is no left or right drop-off or vacuum of existing functions or relationships.
- The chart eliminates the upside-down organization structure because there is no top or bottom. The perspective is the same regardless of the angle or specific position from which the chart is viewed.
- The chart simplifies designing and understanding. The problem associated with space in designing the tradi-

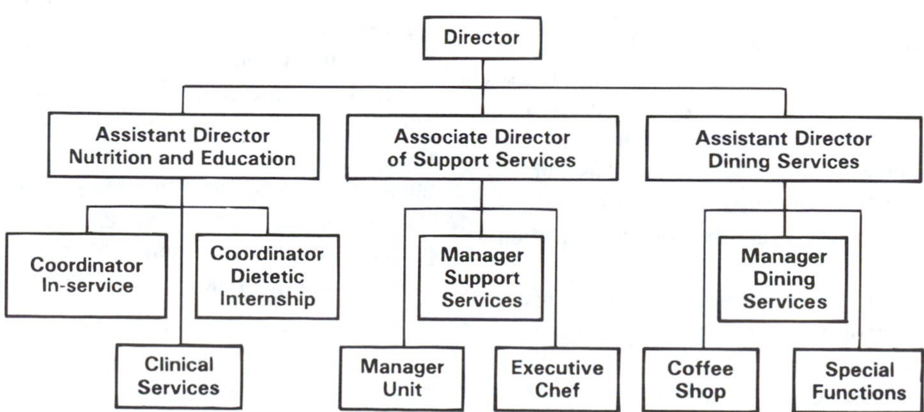

Figure 3–4 Organization Chart: Traditional Model

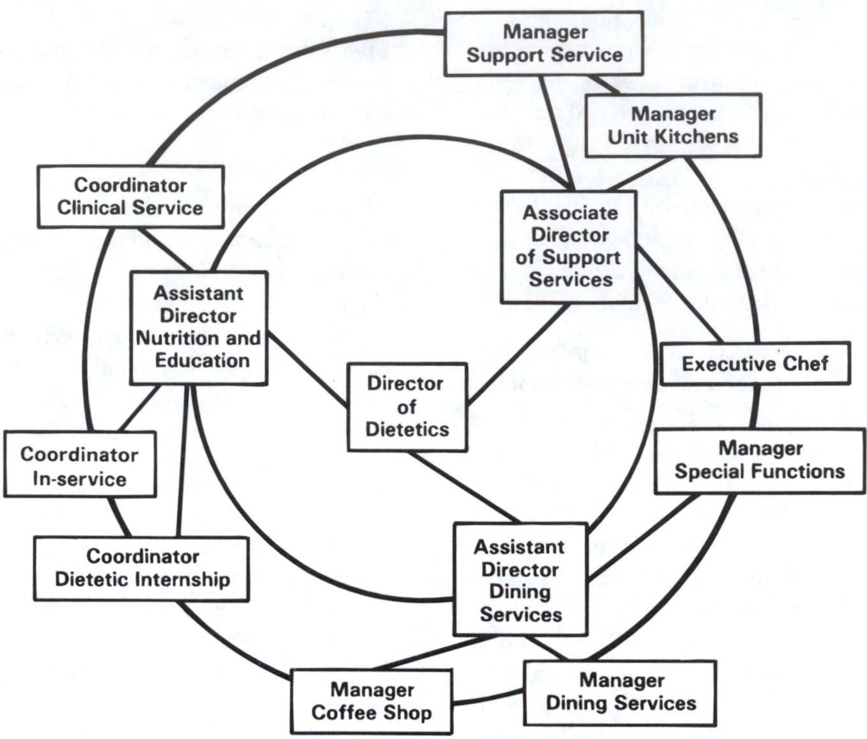

Figure 3–5 Organization Chart: Concentric Model

tional chart is eliminated with the use of circles. When the traditional model is used, there are physical limitations to designing the fourth or fifth echelon level without decreasing the size of the boxes. This may cause confusion in interpretation of status.

Matrix Organization

The concept of matrix organization, introduced over two decades ago, was initially used for special projects only. Today, the matrix form of organizing is found in a variety of contexts: product management, task force management, production teams, and new business development teams. It is used by business and industry, government agencies, professional organizations, and hospitals. When the matrix form of management is introduced into an organization, there are changes in traditional management practices, such as authority and responsibility, span of control, department specialization, resource allocation patterns, and personnel evaluation (Cleland 1981).

As shown in Figure 3–6, there is a dual chain of command that departs from the traditional principle of reporting to only one supervisor. Because personnel in medical facilities frequently perform under dual lines of authority, the introduction of matrix management would not constitute a dramatic change in established procedures. The essentials necessary for effective teamwork are also required for effective matrix management. In matrix management, as in the team approach to patient care, there must be integration and coordination of individual and group efforts because authority, responsibility, accountability, and power shift and cut across functional lines. The matrix organization is used in hospitals to generate a number of reports to assist management in the decision-making process (Sinioris et al. 1982). In hospitals, the matrix formation is centered on the patient as the product line and is closely related to physician specialty. In such cases, the specialty or programs form the horizontal lines (cardiology, obstetrics, and the like), whereas the vertical axis is represented by support services (such as nursing and physical therapy).

Matrix organization is complex and requires considerable attention to the organizational climate prior to its implementation. Because matrix organization involves sharing of authority and responsibility, the struggle for power by individual managers can be one of the biggest problems. Other problems encountered with matrix organization, according to Davis and Lawrence (1978), include the following:

- There is a tendency toward anarchy resulting from dual command, as people become confused over who is really the boss.
- There is the misconception that matrix management is the same as group decision making, thus wasting an enormous amount of time.

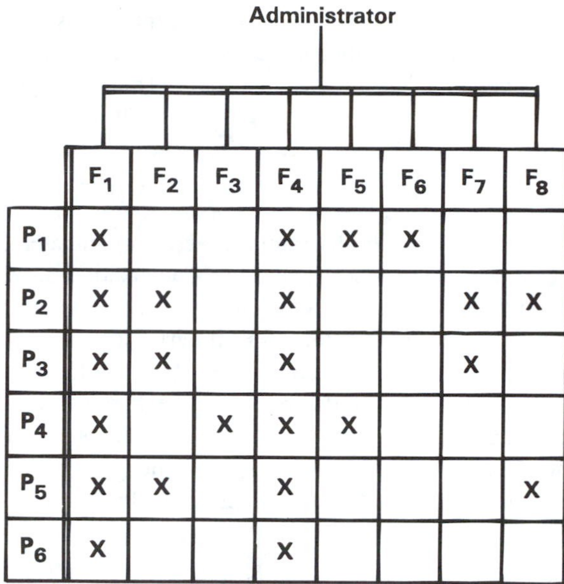

Figure 3–6 Conceptual Model of Matrix Organization

- During an economic crisis when business is slow, the matrix is used as a scapegoat for poor management practices and is discarded in favor of more direct action.
- There is the fear that management cost will double because of the dual chain of command.
- There is a tendency for the matrix to sink to lower levels in the corporate structure.
- There is the fear of decision strangulation as a result of endless debate and the clearing of all decisions by higher administration.

The matrix organization will most likely be used to a greater extent by open organizations such as medical facilities simply because it lends legitimacy to what is now accomplished in an informal manner.

Multihospital Systems

A major trend in hospital organization is the advent of multihospital systems. The single hospital is gradually disappearing as hospitals band together in efforts to maintain quality patient care during a period of adverse economic conditions. The major systems currently in use are as follows:

- Merger—A merger takes place when the assets of two or more institutions are consolidated or when one institution acquires another (usually smaller) institution. When assets are consolidated, a new corporate structure is formed and may be housed in a new facility, or one facility may be closed and only one facility used. Legally, the merged hospitals must be under single ownership and have one governing body; one medical staff; one set of bylaws, rules, and regulations; and all mandated medical staff committees (Baydin and Sheldon 1978).
- Joint venture—This system differs from the merger in how it is organized and controlled. The distinguishing feature is that each institution maintains its identity. This arrangement is possible when two or more institutions with powerful identities agree to combine resources in order to deliver improved patient care at lower cost. In a joint venture of hospitals in Boston (Baydin and Sheldon 1978), a new physical structure was built to house the three hospitals. The corporate structure, Affiliated Hospital Center, Inc., was organized with a vice president as chief operating officer, with members from each institution constituting the governing board. Each hospital is responsible for its own financing, budget, medical staff appointments, teaching, research, and other components. Ambulatory care is to be run by all three. Cost of shared services is prorated to all three hospitals.
- Holding company—A holding company owns and controls all stock of the other facilities and derives its income from interest and dividends. When facilities are nonprofit and without stock, all property, assets, and income as well as debts, liabilities, and obligations of the facilities become those of the holding company (Baydin and Sheldon 1978). The holding company concept permits the small nonprofit hospital to maintain viable patient care by providing a broad economic base.
- Investor-owned system—The system is owned and managed by national hospital chains that are proprietary and public. The largest of these national hospital companies is the Hospital Corporation of America (HCA). At the end of 1980, HCA operated 188 hospitals, with more than 80 new sites under development. Operating revenues increased 37 percent from 1979 to 1980 to more than $1.4 billion; income was up about 50 percent to approximately $81 million (Tinsley 1981). Ownership of facilities means total control and the ability to provide unlimited managerial resources at the corporate level.
- Contract department management—In this arrangement, there is a legal agreement between a health facility and an outside management company for the management of a specified department. The degree of control granted to the management company is spelled out in the contract. During 1981, a total of 4,951 departments in medical facilities were managed full-time by 138 outside contractors (Punch 1982a). Housekeeping,

among 33 different departments managed by outside companies, is the most frequently contracted service. Food service has the largest number of contract management providers, followed by housekeeping, respiratory therapy, and physical therapy.

- Contract shared-consultant service—This system provides services beyond departmental boundaries and is available to medical facilities in more than 50 different areas. One company, which limits its services to medical records abstracting, had the largest number of clients (2,777) during 1981 (Punch 1982b). Other services offered by providers include financial consulting, management engineering, strategic planning, risk management, and others.
- Shared services—These are cooperative ventures by two or more hospitals. Services can be classified as referred service, purchased service, multisponsored service, or regional service (American Hospital Association 1976). A referred service is maintained by one member of the group, and other institutions refer patients who need the service. Patients receive direct billing by the provider. A purchased service is a patient service provided by another institution. The institution requesting the service pays the provider directly and then bills the patient. A multisponsored service is jointly operated and controlled by a group of institutions. There is a legal arrangement, with controls established through mutual agreement or through a separate corporation, to include board representation from each institution. A regional service, such as computerized information service, is sponsored by an association of institutions. The service is financed through association funds, assessment of members, direct charges to member institutions, or a combination of these. Shared food services include group purchasing, prepared food purchasing, sharing of preparation, and shared management and personnel.

All types of multihospital systems have proliferated and expect to continue in the same direction for years to come. The primary reason for the various types of networking is financial. A survey of 668 chief executive officers nationwide revealed that nearly as many hospitals are considering mergers as have already done so (Moore 1987). The survey also showed that hospitals in the Southwest have the highest level of merger activity (29.8 percent), whereas only 14.7 percent of hospitals in the Southeast have merged. A large percentage of hospitals have established referral networks instead of merging. Referral activity was highest in the Midwest (32.1 percent), compared with 17.6 percent in the Southeast. The same regions that displayed the most and least activity in mergers also displayed the most and least interest in managed care contracting.

The trend of mergers and acquisitions continues, with hospitals leading in the health care sector. In 1994, a total of 504 business combinations was announced: hospitals, long-term care facilities, physician medical groups, health maintenance organizations (HMOs), laboratories, psychiatric facilities, and rehabilitation facilities (Meredith and Steever 1995). The largest transactions in 1994 in terms of dollar volume were all for-profit hospitals. The five largest were Columbia/HCA's acquisition of HTI; Tenet Healthcare's acquisition of AMI; HTI's acquisition of WPIC Holdings, Inc.; Community Health Systems' acquisition of Hallmark Healthcare; and OrNda's acquisition of Fountain Valley Regional Hospital.

The growth of managed care during the 1980s and 1990s became the driving force behind physician alliances, hospital mergers, and national and regional hospital alliances (Brown 1996). Several trends seem likely in the next five years or more.

- Physicians will continue to form networks for managed care. More group practices will form.
- Dramatic changes will continue in the insurance side of the business. Blue Cross and Blue Shield are experimenting with all kinds of integrative moves by converting their business from service and indemnity contracts to managed care.
- Academic medical centers will fill the void for regional providers in offering a full-service package of services.
- Community hospitals will continue to merge with regional players rather than remain outside and independent of networks.
- Regional multihospital health systems will continue to push for more physicians, especially in managed care. More single hospitals will merge with systems, systems will merge, and a growing number will either merge or sell to insurers.

How is the increase in mergers affecting personnel? What thought is given to human resources and when? How is administration assisting employees with the trauma involved when one or more facilities merge? According to Marks and Cutcliffe (1988), during the premerger phase, the chief executive officers are surrounded by bankers and lawyers until the deal is consummated. Little consideration is given to critical management components such as communication, integration, organizational design, and staffing until the merger is in place. In fact, key managers who will lead the postmerger and human resource personnel are usually absent from the initial planning.

A merger is a change. Employees approach change differently, depending on the nature and magnitude. When employees must rely on the grapevine for information, the result may be stress, anxiety, and lower productivity; some may even quit the job in fear of what might happen. Fear and insecurity may have merit, because downsizing is usually a consequence of a merger. Steps that managers can take to alleviate the trauma associated with mergers are offered by Davy et al. (1988) and Fink (1988), as follows:

- Communicate with employees in a timely manner. If legally possible, make announcement to employees before the news media break the story. Maintain channels of communication throughout the transition period. Conduct honest, frequent meetings to enhance a feeling of security and to assist in reducing rumors.
- Reduce uncertainty and ambiguity. Create transition committees to serve as information conduits between top management and the work force. Consider establishing a telephone merger hotline so that employees can express concerns and ask questions anonymously. Administer an open-ended survey to obtain information about employee expectations. Clarify any incorrect expectations.
- Address the issue of job security. Provide honest information about the possibility of layoffs. Consider providing an outplacement program. Provide an employee and family counseling program. Conduct seminars on how to cope with stress.

Contract Food Management

The organization of a food service department can be affected in a number of ways when the medical facility decides to contract food service (Zaccarelli and Ninemeier 1982). Staffing becomes the number one concern for employees currently working at the facility. The food management company may bring in a completely new staff, or staffing may be divided, with some employees paid by the facility and others by the food management company. It is often the director of the dietary department and other members of the in-house management team who are in competition with the outside company. As shown by asterisks in Figure 3–7, managerial positions held by employees of the food management company are the director of dietetics, the food service director, and the cafeteria supervisor. The organization structure is typical, with high-level managerial positions staffed by the

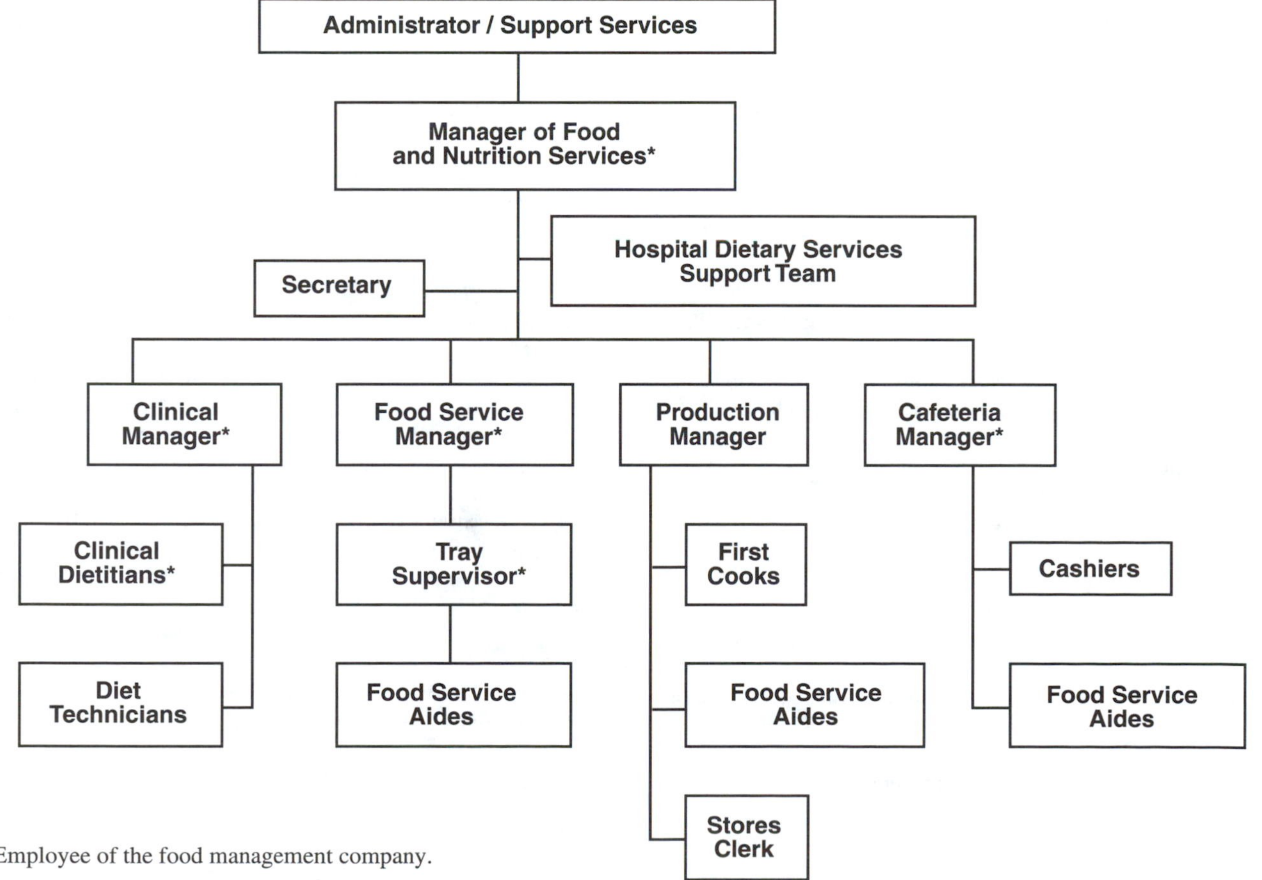

Figure 3–7 Organization Chart for Hospital Food Service Operated by a Food Management Company. Courtesy of HDS Services, Farmington Hills, Michigan.

food management company, and clinical service staffed by health care facility employees. In this structure, the director of dietetics is considered a department head and is responsible to both the health care facility administrator and the food management company. In some organizational structures, the director of clinical services reports directly to an administrator at the health care facility, rather than to the food management company director as indicated in Figure 3–7. This type of organization further emphasizes the need to understand concepts of the matrix organization.

REFERENCES

Albanese, R. 1975. *Management toward accountability for performance.* Homewood, IL: Richard D. Irwin.

American Hospital Association. 1976. *Shared food services in health care institutions.* Chicago.

American Medical Association. 1967. *The extended care facility: A handbook for the medical society.* Chicago.

Barnes, M.C. et al. 1970. *Company organization: Theory and practice.* Beverly Hills, CA: Davlin Publishing.

Baydin, D., and A. Sheldon. 1978. Corporate models in health care delivery. In *Hospital organization and management*, ed. J.S. Rakich and K. Darr. New York: Halsted Press.

Brown, M. 1996. Mergers, networking, and vertical integration: Managed care and investor-owned hospitals. *Health Care Management Review* 21:29–37.

Browne, C.G. 1950. The concentric organization chart. *Journal of Applied Psychology* 34, no. 6:375–377.

Cleland, D.I. 1981. The cultural ambience of matrix organization. *Management Review* 70, no. 11:25–39.

Davis, S.M., and P.R. Lawrence. 1978. Problems of matrix organizations. *Harvard Business Review* 56, no. 3:131–142.

Davy, J.A. et al. 1988. After the merger: Dealing with people's uncertainty. *Training Development Journal* 42, no. 2:56–61.

Filey, A.C., and R.J. House. 1969. *Managerial process and organizational behavior*. Glenview: IL: Scott, Foresman.

Fink, C.A. 1988. The impact of mergers on employees. *Health Care Supervisor* 7, no. 1:59–67.

Foyal, H. 1949. *Industrial and general administration.* London: Pitman.

George, C.S. 1968. *The history of management thought.* Englewood Cliffs, NJ: Prentice Hall.

Georgopoulos, B.S., ed. 1972. *Organization research on health institutions.* Ann Arbor, MI: Institute for Social Research, University of Michigan.

Graicunas, V.A. 1937. Relationships in organization. In *Papers on the science of administration*, ed. L. Gulick and L. Urwick. New York: Institute of Public Administration.

Gulick, L. 1937. Notes on the theory of organization. In *Papers on the science of administration*, ed. L. Gulick and L. Urwick. New York: Institute of Public Administration.

Hall, R.H. 1972. The concept of bureaucracy: An empirical assessment. In *Organizational systems*, ed. K. Azumi and J. Hage. Lexington, MA: D. C. Heath.

Henderson, L.J. et al. 1937. The effects of social environment. In *Papers on the science of administration*, ed. L. Gulick and L. Urwick. New York: Institute of Public Administration.

Hicks, H.G., and C.R. Gullett. 1975. *Organization theory and behavior.* New York: McGraw-Hill.

Katz, D., and R.L. Kahn. 1966. *The social psychology of organizations.* New York: John Wiley & Sons.

Marks, M.L., and J.G. Cutcliffe. 1988. Making mergers work. *Training and Development Journal* 42, no. 4:30–36.

Meredith, E.B., and S.B. Steever. 1995. Mergers and acquisitions: What's going on. *Healthcare Financial Management* 49 (December '95 suppl HFM Resource Guide): 12–26.

Michigan Department of Public Health, Bureau of Health Care Facilities. 1985. *Nursing homes and nursing care facilities.* Lansing, MI.

Mink, O.G. et al. 1979. *Developing and managing open organizations.* Austin, TX: Learning Concepts.

Mooney, J.D., and A.C. Reiley. 1939. *The principles of organization.* New York: Harper Brothers.

Moore, B. 1987. What's driving upcoming mergers? *Hospitals*, 5 January.

Moschetto, C.A. 1981. Predictions about the future of LTC (long term care). *Nursing Homes* 30, no. 5:42–50.

Punch, L. 1982a. Leading firms boost contract business 18.2%. *Modern Healthcare* 12, no. 7:116–122.

Punch, L. 1982b. Shared services pacts up 22%. *Modern Healthcare* 12, no. 7:124–134.

Rakich, J.S., and K. Darr. 1978. *Hospital organization and management.* New York: Halsted Press.

Schneeweiss, S.M., and S.W. Davis. 1974. *Nursing home administration.* Baltimore: University Park Press.

Sinioris, M.E. et al. 1982. Planning: Program matrix aids planning process. *Hospitals* 56, no. 8:75–77.

Tinsley, E. 1981. Health-care chains: Big business' niche in a $billion industry. *Restaurants and Institutions* 89, no. 10:81–88.

Urwick, L. 1944. *The elements of administration.* New York: Harper Brothers.

U.S. Department of Health and Human Services. 1966. *Conditions of participation for extended care facilities: Social Security Administration HIM-3.* Washington, DC: U.S. Government Printing Office.

U.S. Department of Health and Human Services, Health Care Financing Administration. 1988. *Medicare and Medicaid; long term care process; final rule.* Federal Register 53 (117), 22850–23100.

U.S. Department of Health and Human Services, Health Care Financing Administration. 1991. *Requirements for long term care facilities: Final rule.* Federal Register 56 (187), September 26, part 483. Effective April 1, 1992.

U.S. Department of Health and Human Services. 1992. *Long-term care facilities.* 57 Federal Register 43924, September 23.

Weber, M. 1967. The ideal bureaucracy. In *Organization and human behavior*, ed. G.D. Bell. Englewood Cliffs, NJ: Prentice Hall.

White, K.K. 1963. *Understanding the company organization chart.* New York: American Management Association.

Zaccarelli, H., and J.D. Ninemeier. 1982. *Cost effective contract food service: An institutional guide.* Gaithersburg, MD: Aspen Publishers, Inc.

Chapter 4

Managerial Roles and Responsibilities

The concept of roles relates to organizational expectations, such as the work required, the tasks to be performed, and the situations and processes the individuals must deal with, as implicated by position, status, and relationships (Newman 1973). All individuals within an organization have roles, whether they are explicit or implied. To avoid misunderstanding, the person in the role should be fully informed about what he or she is expected to achieve, what objectives are involved, and what activities are required or permitted. A managerial role implies that the individual has other resources, including human resources, for which he or she is accountable.

MANAGERIAL ROLES

In medical food service, the diverse, complex managerial roles and responsibilities are subject to both external and internal influences. In Michigan, the director of a medical food service must meet qualifications and guidelines established by the state department of health, federal guidelines for participation in Medicare and Medicaid programs, and standards of the Joint Commission on Accreditation of Healthcare Organizations (Joint Commission).

Director of Medical Food Service

The director of a medical food service operation affects nutritional care through the direction of all aspects of dietetic services, including the following responsibilities:

- Organizes department as appropriate to the scope and complexity of services offered in meeting objectives of the organization.
- Plans, organizes, controls, and evaluates components of food service systems (menu, equipment, food and materials, finances, and human resources).
- Develops policies and procedures for provision of optimal nutritional care in a safe and sanitary environment.
- Adheres to established guidelines, both internal and external, in exercising managerial functions.
- Participates in committee activities with reference to the nutritional care of patients.
- Coordinates and integrates administrative and therapeutic services interdepartmentally and intradepartmentally.
- Develops, implements, and evaluates quality assurance standards for all aspects of the food service system.
- Plans and controls fiscal resources through effective budget and cost measures.
- Uses effective written and verbal communication techniques interdepartmentally and intradepartmentally.
- Maintains effective public relations interdepartmentally and intradepartmentally.
- Ensures adequate staffing for optimal level of nutritional care.
- Plans, implements, and evaluates appropriate training and educational programs for personnel.
- Utilizes current research on standards of practice relating to a medical food service operation.

The organization of a medical food service operation reflects both administrative and therapeutic duties, with personnel assigned according to level of care and complexity. The administrative and therapeutic services, in most instances, are assigned to registered dietitians (RDs). To assist in the delineation of roles and responsibilities for certain classifications of dietitians, a position paper was issued by the

American Dietetic Association (ADA; 1981) with descriptions as paraphrased below.

Administrative Dietitian, RD

The administrative dietitian is a member of the management team and affects the nutritional care of groups through the management of food service systems that provide optimal nutrition and quality food. Responsibilities include the following:

- Plans, develops, controls, and evaluates food service systems.
- Develops short- and long-range department plans and programs consistent with departmental and organizational policies.
- Manages and controls fiscal resources and recommends budget programs.
- Utilizes human effort and facilitating resources efficiently and effectively.
- Coordinates and integrates clinical and administrative aspects of dietetics to provide quality nutritional care.
- Establishes and maintains standards of food production and service, sanitation, safety, and security.
- Maintains effective written and verbal communications and public relations interdepartmentally and intradepartmentally.
- Compiles and utilizes pertinent operational data to improve efficiency and quality of food service systems.
- Plans, conducts, and evaluates orientation and in-service educational programs.
- Interprets, evaluates, and utilizes pertinent current research relating to nutritional care.
- Develops menu patterns and evaluates client acceptance.
- Develops specifications for procurement of food, equipment, and supplies.
- Plans or participates in the development of program proposals for funding.
- Plans layout design and determines equipment requirements for food service facilities.
- Administers personnel policies as established by the department and the organization.

Clinical Dietitian, RD

The clinical dietitian is a member of the health care team and affects the nutritional care of individuals and groups through the assessment, development, implementation, and evaluation of nutritional care plans. The clinical dietitian cooperates and coordinates activities with members of the management team. Responsibilities include the following:

- Develops and implements a plan of care based on assessment of nutritional needs and correlated with other health care plans.
- Counsels individuals and families in nutritional principles, dietary plans, food selection, and economics, adapting plans to the individual.
- Utilizes appropriate tools in the provision of nutritional care.
- Evaluates nutritional care and provides follow-up for continuity of care.
- Communicates appropriate dietary and nutritional care data through record systems.
- Participates in health team rounds and serves as a consultant on nutritional care.
- Utilizes human effort and facilitating resources efficiently and effectively.
- Evaluates food served for conformance to quality standards and dietary prescriptions.
- Compiles and develops educational materials and uses them as aids in nutrition education.
- Compiles and utilizes pertinent operational data to ensure provision of quality nutrition care.
- Interprets, evaluates, and utilizes pertinent current research related to nutritional care.
- Provides nutrition education to students and personnel.
- Plans and organizes resources to achieve effective nutritional care.
- Plans or participates in the development of program proposals for funding.
- Maintains effective written and verbal communications and public relations interdepartmentally and intradepartmentally.
- Administers personnel policies as established by the department and the organization.

Teaching Dietitian, RD

In large and/or teaching hospitals, managerial roles may include those in teaching and research. The teaching dietitian, with advanced preparation in dietetics or education, plans, conducts, and evaluates educational programs in one or more dietetic subject matter areas. Responsibilities include the following:

- Develops the dietetic curriculum, including courses to meet the needs of the students.
- Plans, conducts, and evaluates the educational experiences for dietetic, medical, dental, nursing, and other allied health students and clients.
- Guides and evaluates students' performance.
- Plans and conducts orientation and in-service educational programs for the organization's personnel.
- Prepares, evaluates, and utilizes current educational methodology and instructional media to enhance learning experiences of students.

- Maintains accurate, detailed records of data.
- Contributes expertise as a member of the organization's teams for planning and evaluating, and participates in committee and other organizational activities.

Research Dietitian, RD

The research dietitian, with advanced preparation in dietetics and research techniques, plans, investigates, interprets, evaluates, applies, and expands knowledge in phases of dietetics and communicates findings through reports and publications. Responsibilities include the following:

- Plans, organizes, and conducts or participates in programs in nutrition, foods, or food service systems research.
- Evaluates and utilizes appropriate methodology and tools to carry out program plans.
- Maintains accurate and detailed records.
- Evaluates and communicates findings.
- Utilizes human effort and facilitating resources efficiently and effectively.
- Interprets, evaluates, and utilizes pertinent current research related to program needs.
- Maintains effective verbal and written communications and public relations interdepartmentally and intradepartmentally.
- Plans, conducts, and evaluates dietary studies and participates in epidemiologic studies with a nutritional component.
- Studies and analyzes recent scientific findings in dietetics for application in current research, for development of tools for future research, and for interpretation to the public.
- Plans or participates in the development of program proposals for funding.

Consultant Dietitian, RD

The consultant dietitian, with experience in administrative and clinical dietetic practice, assists in the management of human effort and facilitating resources by advice or services in nutritional care. The consultant does not assume responsibility for the day-to-day operation of the food service facility; that role is assigned to the dietetic service supervisor. The role of the consultant is to advise, observe, evaluate, instruct, and recommend. Responsibilities include the following:

- Evaluates and monitors food service systems, making recommendations for a conformance level that will provide nutritionally adequate, quality food.
- Develops budget proposals and recommends procedures for cost controls.
- Plans, organizes, and conducts orientation and in-service educational programs for food service personnel.
- Plans layout design and determines equipment requirements for food service facilities.
- Recommends and monitors standards for sanitation, safety, and security in food service.
- Develops menu patterns.
- Assesses, develops, implements, and evaluates nutritional care plans and provides for follow-up, including written reports.
- Consults and counsels with clients regarding selection and procurement of food to meet optimal nutrition.
- Develops, maintains, and uses pertinent record systems related to the needs of the organization.
- Develops, uses, and evaluates educational materials related to services provided.
- Consults with the health care team concerning the nutritional care of clients.
- Provides guidance and evaluation of the job performance of dietetic personnel.
- Interprets, evaluates, and utilizes pertinent current research relating to nutritional care.
- Maintains effective verbal and written communications and public relations interdepartmentally and intradepartmentally.

For optimal performance of the above tasks, the consultant should have a minimum of three years' experience with varied responsibilities such as therapeutic services, administrative supervision, and staff education. In addition, the qualified consultant should be aware of pertinent legal codes including state nursing home licensing law; federal regulations for Medicare and Medicaid; Occupational Safety and Health Administration (OSHA) standards; city and local codes, including fire, safety, and sanitation; and labor laws such as compensation, unemployment, disability, and union contract (American Dietetic Association 1977a).

Federal guidelines specify that there must be a qualified dietitian as consultant but do not specify the frequency and time required. The amount of time spent by consultant dietitians varies from one visit every six months to four hours per week (Consultant Dietitians in Health Care Facilities 1987). The state of Maine requires four hours per week for a single unit (40 beds), plus an additional two hours per week for each additional unit. A survey of the Illinois consultant dietitian's role and functions revealed that 74 percent of the 43 respondents reported insufficient time at nursing homes to perform in an efficient and effective manner (Welch et al. 1988).

The amount of time spent by consultant dietitians has an impact on the outcome of resident care in a number of ways. In addition to direct resident care the consultant dietitians, with expertise in both management and clinical services, need ample time to monitor production and service, train staff (including nursing personnel), and promote interdepartmental communication.

Dietetic Technician–Dietary Manager

A dietetic technician is a technically skilled individual who has successfully completed an associate degree program in general dietetics that meets the approval of the ADA. A dietary manager is an individual who has completed a 90-hour classroom program plus 6 months of supervised work experience that meets certification standards of the Dietary Managers Association (DMA). Both the dietetic technician and the dietary manager may work in administrative or clinical areas, with appropriate responsibilities, and under the directions of a registered dietitian. The dietary manager is eligible for membership in the DMA. The dietetic technician is also eligible for membership in the DMA and the ADA.

In long-term care facilities, the dietetic technician or dietary manager may have total responsibility for the food service operation, under the direction of a consultant dietitian. Depending on the level of services offered, duties and responsibilities may be as follows:

- Plans menus on the basis of established guidelines.
- Standardizes recipes and tests new products for use in the facility.
- Procures and receives supplies and equipment following established procedures.
- Supervises production and service.
- Monitors food service for conformance with quality standards.
- Maintains and improves standards of sanitation, safety, and security.
- Selects, schedules, and conducts orientation and in-service educational programs for personnel.
- Participates in determining staffing needs, in selecting personnel, and in on-the-job training.
- Develops job specifications, job descriptions, and work schedules.
- Plans master schedules for personnel.
- Maintains a routine personnel evaluation system.
- Understands and supports personnel policies and union contracts.
- Assists in the implementation of established cost-control procedures.
- Gathers data according to prescribed methods for use in evaluating food service systems.
- Makes recommendations that may be incorporated into policies and develops written procedures to conform to established policies.
- Recommends improvements for the facility and for equipment.
- Submits recommendations and information for use in budget development.
- Compiles and uses operational data.
- Obtains, evaluates, and utilizes dietary history information for planning nutritional care.
- Guides individuals and families in food selection, food preparation, and menu planning based on nutritional needs.
- Calculates nutrient intakes and dietary patterns.
- Assists in referrals for continuity of patient care.
- Utilizes appropriate verbal and written communication and public relations interdepartmentally and intradepartmentally.

A nursing care facility may recognize the role of a part-time or full-time dietitian, a dietetic technician, or a dietary manager. In Michigan, rules and regulations for nursing homes (Michigan Department of Public Health 1985) specify the following qualifications for the supervisor of dietary or food service:

- Dietary or food service in a home shall be supervised by an individual who meets any of the following qualifications:
  1. Is registered by the Commission on Dietetic Registration of the ADA.
  2. Is qualified to take the registration examination required for registered dietitian status.
  3. Is a graduate of a dietetic technician program approved by the ADA.
  4. Is a graduate of an approved dietary managers' training program that qualifies such person for certification by the DMA.
  5. Is a graduate of a dietary managers' program granted approval status by the Michigan Department of Public Health before July 6, 1979.

In Mississippi, regulations require that the dietary department shall be directed by a registered dietitian or a certified dietary manager with frequent and regularly scheduled consultations with an RD, and must earn 15 hours of continuing education each year, approved by the ADA or the DMA (Consultant Dietitians in Health Care Facilities 1987). The functions and responsibilities of the consultant dietitian and the dietetic service supervisor in patient nutritional care for long-term care facilities have been defined by the ADA (1977b) and are presented in Table 4–1.

PROBLEMS OF ROLE DELINEATION

There are problems associated with listing tasks for managerial roles simply because no list is all-inclusive. The roles and responsibilities of health care professionals in dietetics are constantly under review. A study on how practitioners view future roles of the dietetic professional (Parks and Kris-Etherton 1982) concluded that the practitioner must have an awareness of cost containment in the health care setting, professional fees for dietary services, shifts from therapeutic to normal nutrition as the importance of preventive health care is recognized, technological

Table 4–1 Comparison of Duties of Consultant Dietitian and Dietetic Service Supervisor

Consultant Dietitian	*Dietetic Service Supervisor*
1. *Policy development*	
a. Reviews and participates in the development of the facility's patient care policies to ensure the inclusion and support of nutritional care.	a. Provides operational information needed for determining patient care policies related to nutritional care.
b. Suggests revisions in these policies where necessary.	b. Understands policies and their impact on the daily operation of the dietetic service.
c. Consults with nursing, medical, dietetic, and other services on procedures to implement policies affecting nutritional care.	c. Assists in developing dietetic service procedures related to nutritional care.
d. Evaluates the effectiveness of nutritional care procedures and adjusts when necessary.	d. Provides feedback on the effectiveness of procedures.
2. *Setting priorities and goals*	
a. Evaluates the capability of dietetic service to deliver nutritional care, based on staffing, support systems, and responsibilities of other services.	a. Provides operational information needed to determine priorities.
b. Assists in setting realistic goals and priorities for establishing a system to ensure that each patient has adequate daily intake.	b. Participates in the selection of priorities and goals affecting dietetic services.
c. Confers with the administrator, dietetic service supervisor, director of nursing, and other appropriate heads of service to secure their concurrence in these priorities and goals.	
3. *Development of service to meet patient nutritional needs*	
A. *Nutritional assessment*	
a. Identifies the information needed for a nutritional assessment and the sources from which it can be obtained.	a. Participates in the development of forms and procedures for gathering information about the patients' food needs.
b. Ensures that suitable forms are developed and that procedures are appropriate for collecting and recording information.	b. Collects information according to established methods and procedures. Some sources of information are (i) patient (foods liked and disliked); (ii) nurse (allergies, self-feeding ability, appetite and food intake, weight); (iii) patient's family; and (iv) observation of the patient at mealtimes.
c. Clarifies the responsibilities of the dietetic, nursing, and social services in collection of assessment data. Offers training when necessary.	
d. Reviews information collected on individual patients to identify those needing further assessment by the dietitian. Identifies individual problems requiring nutritional intervention.	
B. *Nutritional planning and implementation*	
a. Develops the nutritional component of the patient's plan of care, including preparation for discharge.	a. Contributes nutritional assessment information to care planning conferences.
b. Reviews with dietetic supervisor, nursing service, physician, and others as appropriate.	b. Ensures that the menu served to the total population is nutritionally adequate and well received.
c. Participates in patient care planning conferences or shares information with the dietetic service supervisor to be taken to the planning conference.	c. Ensures that each patient's menu is modified according to the plan of care.

continues

Table 4–1 continued

Consultant Dietitian	Dietetic Service Supervisor
3. *Development of service to meet patient nutritional needs (continued)*	
d. Plans for periodic review.	d. Identifies and reports to the consultant dietitian any problems in the implementation of the plan of care.
e. Identifies responsibilities of the dietetic service in implementing nutritional care and provides appropriate guidance.	e. Reinforces diet counseling with patients and provides follow-up information to families.
f. Provides diet counseling to patients and families where necessary.	
C. *Evaluation*	
a. Ensures that there is a method for identifying patients who are not eating, not responding to the plan as anticipated, or whose condition has changed (e.g., food and fluid intake, weight survey, patient visitation).	a. Maintains the system to monitor the total facility population.
b. When a problem is identified, evaluates and changes plan when indicated.	b. Follows through on individual review of plans.
c. Suggests useful studies to the facility's committee on patient care evaluation.	c. Participates in the evaluation of the plan's effectiveness.
D. *Documentation*	
a. Enters nutritional assessment and plan in the dietary and medical records and reports the patient's response, changes in plans, and preparation for discharge.	a. After training, records information about each patient's food intake or implementation of plan of care in the appropriate records as designated by the policy of the facility.
4. *Staff training*	
a. Develops a relevant plan for in-service training for all facility staff. Helps conduct some sessions. Reviews objectives and methods of nutritional care.	a. Assists in the development of a plan of in-service and participates in training sessions.
b. With the assistance of the dietetic service supervisor, provides appropriate training to the dietetic staff.	b. Conducts training sessions for the dietetic staff.
c. Ensures the maintenance of records for orientation and training.	c. Keeps training attendance reports and updates personnel files as necessary.
5. *Provision of current information to facility staff*	
a. Recommends suitable references on basic nutrition, therapeutic nutrition, medical terminology, food preparation, feeding techniques and aids, regulations, safety and sanitation, and others.	a. Refers to resources as necessary and identifies additional needs.
b. Interprets current research findings.	

Source: Reprinted with permission from *Patient Nutritional Care in Long-Term Care Facilities*, © 1977, American Dietetic Association.

advances in health care, and legislation that relates to the application of quality care. As reported by Neville and Tower (1988), the ADA Role Delineation Steering Committee has appointed members to five resource committees to participate in a logical analysis to determine job responsibilities of entry-level dietitians, dietetic technicians, and registered dietitians practicing beyond entry level. As noted in a later discussion of diagnosis-related groups (DRGs), dietetic professionals have responded to future implications of cost containment, community outreach, and documentation of services rendered.

The process of downsizing results in a reduction in human and material resources available for providing services for patients. One of the effects of downsizing on medical food service has been the realignment of dietary personnel with other department personnel, and the emergence of the multiskilled employee. Examples of this phenomenon include changes in job responsibilities at various levels of organization within the department, including management and other employees.

Department Directors

The department director may have duties extended to include management responsibilities for other departments, such as housekeeping.

Supervisors

Many employees in supervisory positions who were previously responsible for specific dietary areas, such as education and training, have found their roles expanded. To better utilize their skills, these supervisors are given additional training to enable them to provide education and training for several related departments.

Clinical Dietitians

Dietitians who were trained under the guidelines of the ADA have been and still are multiskilled. Extensive training in both nutrition and food service management prepares the dietitian to assume various roles. For this reason a multiskilled classification for the dietitian refers to expanded roles and responsibilities rather than new training. Expanded roles include purchasing agent, manager of patient care teams, nutrition support coordinator, employee wellness coordinator, administrator for contract management services, and many more.

Dietetic Technicians

Those who function under titles such as patient care associate are responsible for coordinating, with other team members, specific areas of patient care. The responsibility for coordination of patient care shifts from one team member to another as the patient's needs dictate. Each patient care team is responsible for a group of patients. This approach takes the dietetic technician out of the diet office and places him or her in the patient care area. Duties may include nutrition screening, ascertaining patient preferences, menu distribution, meal rounds, diet instruction, and other services.

Food Service Workers

Food service workers are referred to as food service assistants (FSAs). Food service assistants are trained to be multiskilled, along with nurses' aides and housekeeping aides. They perform common duties that are patient focused. These employees operate in a matrix organization setting. This means that FSAs may be responsible to both management in the food service department and the nursing personnel in charge of the patient care team to which they are assigned. Duties performed may include those duties traditionally thought of as housekeeping and nurses' aides functions.

With the emergence of these new roles, it becomes imperative to provide training. Focused training is the key to success in implementing the multiskilled worker concept. This requires the combined planning efforts of management in the food service, nursing, and housekeeping departments.

Diagnosis-Related Groups

The most recent federal law that affects the roles and responsibilities of medical food service personnel is the Social Security Amendment of 1983 (Pub. L. No. 98-21, 98th Congress, first session). Changes have occurred in the method of payment for inpatient hospital services from a cost-based, retrospective reimbursement system to a prospective payment system (PPS) based on categories of 470 DRGs. The system is composed of major diagnostic categories organized by organ systems and disease etiology, and the 470 DRGs. In the September 1 Federal Register (U.S. Department of Health and Human Services 1983), there is a complete listing of the DRGs, relative weighing factors, geometric mean length of stay, and length-of-stay outlier points used in the PPS. The length-of-stay outlier points used in the PPS refer to supplemental payment to hospitals for atypical cases. Five percent to six percent of the total DRG expenditure is used as a basis for calculating such additional payments. These cases include patients whose length of stay exceeds the average for the DRG.

To ease transition, the PPS was phased in over a three-year period. All Medicare payments were based on a combination of specific hospital rates and national and regional DRG rates, as shown in Table 4–2.

Table 4–2 Phase-In Periods for Diagnosis-Related Groups

Federal Fiscal Year Beginning October 1	*Hospital-Specific Rate Percentage*	*Federal Rate Percentage*	
		National	*Regional*
1983	75	—	25
1984	50	12 ½	37 ½
1985	25	37 ½	37 ½
1986	—	100	—

Source: Reprinted from Health Care Financing Administration Medicare Program: Prospective Payment for Medicare Inpatient Hospital Services, *Federal Register*, Vol. 49, No. 1, pp. 234–340, 1984.

Rules governing DRG implementation are another form of accountability imposed on the hospital system in an effort to control the cost of health care. As a subsystem of the hospital, the medical food service department is also affected. The degree to which DRGs affect departmental functions and services depends on previous administrative practices, roles and responsibilities, and involvement in professional activities such as the professional standards review organization, utilization review, and other committees that demonstrate contributions to the health care team.

To counteract the financial effects of DRGs, the following activities have been initiated at the departmental level:

- communicating the possible roles and responsibilities of administrative and clinical personnel to top administration; participating in hospital-based home health care; supporting community outreach programs relating to follow-up patient care; increasing outpatient services, such as diet clinics; involving administrative and clinical staff in a corporate consulting program, with appropriate consultant fee schedules
- documenting cost of service based on each of the DRGs; conducting time studies; emphasizing record keeping; establishing fees for services
- increasing marketing efforts with emphasis on revenue-generating activities; enhancing food quality and customer satisfaction by balancing high- and low-cost foods on selective menus; reducing the menu cycle to correspond with length of patient stay; expanding catering services to the larger community with carryout menus; promoting competitive merchandising in the cafeteria; reducing hours of operation; increasing self-service; participating in mobile home meal plans

Since implementation of DRGs, two questions are frequently asked: (1) Did the new method of payment system for hospital inpatient care meet its objective to control cost? (2) How did the new method of payment affect the financial status of hospitals? According to McCarthy (1988), the goals of the DRG system were met, but there has been an increase in hospital closings, creating a fragile hospital system. In addition, the DRG system does not recognize new labor costs (salary raises), differences in costs based on severity of illness, differences in costs to hospitals for nonlabor resources, differences in the availability of non–acute care services, and new technology. McCarthy believes that reform of the payment system is essential, but the reform does not require abandoning the DRG system. One of the latest reforms (U.S. Department of Health and Human Services 1987) is a rule that changes Medicare prospective payment regulation for inpatient hospital services to allow an adjustment for sole community hospitals that experience a significant increase in inpatient operating costs attributable to the addition of new inpatient services or facilities.

Medicare's DRG-based PPS has been successful in controlling expenditures for inpatient hospital services because it introduced incentives for hospitals to control costs by aggregating payments into all-inclusive packages (Averill et al. 1996). Prospective payment has been limited to hospital payment for inpatient care. There still remains the opportunity to introduce competition into the PPS and to extend the PPS to cover physician fees for inpatient care and payment for segments of outpatient services.

According to Bailis (1996), the Medicare program is ailing in the delivery and cost effectiveness of its service. Skilled nursing facilities (SNFs) can offer the best quality at costs far below those in comparable acute care settings—even though the patients are older and sicker than the population of acute care–based SNFs. Managed care has recognized the benefit of substituting SNF days for more expensive hospital days. Fee-for-service Medicare, too, is making more use of post–acute care. Since 1989, acute care lengths of stay have declined by 31 percent in 62 DRGs with substantial subacute care utilization. Traditional Medicare does not maximize potential savings because the DRG payments have not been properly adjusted to reflect the reduced length of acute care stays.

The PPS, to be fully effective, needs to incorporate the following:

- fixed payments for episodes of care covering all services provided during a Part A Medicare SNF stay
- payment covering all SNF costs (routine, ancillary, and property costs)
- reimbursement specific to the individual patient's diagnosis, acuity, or case mix, and covering the full continuum of postacute, subacute, and rehabilitation classifications
- payments based on diagnosis rather than location of delivered services (other than geographic region)
- payments adjusted for local market and facility construction costs

- policies that encourage SNFs to offer higher acuity services and that include sound outlier payment structures addressing cases of extraordinary costs
- full recognition of the high costs for the highest-acuity SNF patients, including any interim system considered
- reports on patient outcomes and outlier policies, with a move toward an outcome-based quality system instead of the rigid and nearly unworkable Omnibus Budget Reconciliation Act (OBRA) standards in effect at present
- policies to reflect intra-SNF transfers during covered stays and to ensure that payments are made on the patient classification most accurately reflecting the care provided during the illness at the end of a covered stay
- recognition of the need for a continuation of the current low-volume SNF PPS

Multiple Roles

Another problem associated with the listing of tasks is that the role occupant frequently functions in multiple roles, with high dependence on other human resources. For example, as a specialist in administrative or therapeutic dietetics, the professional may also serve as consultant in nutritional care to other units within the organization or as a member of the health care team. Effective interaction as a member of the team will depend on the level of decision making and the amount of authority on the part of the individual professional.

HEALTH CARE TEAM

The quality and effectiveness of care provided by an individual health care professional is limited by his or her own range of expertise. A team approach to health care combines the skills, knowledge, and experience of several professionals. Because the team approach emphasizes multiple input, a coordinated treatment plan for each patient may be achieved. The passage of federal legislation, with a primary objective of protecting invested funds, made the concept of health care teams a reality.

Professional Standards Review Organizations

Mandated under section 294F of Pub. L. No. 92-603 in 1972, professional standards review organizations (PSROs) are required to involve local practicing physicians in the review and evaluation of health care services provided by Medicare, Medicaid, and Title V (maternal and child health) of the Social Security Act (American Dietetic Association 1976). The objective of the PSRO program is to ensure quality of health care. The primary emphasis, as prescribed by law, is to determine whether health care services delivered to Medicare, Medicaid, and maternal and child health patients are medically necessary, meet professionally recognized standards of health care, and are provided in the most appropriate setting to meet the patient's needs. The PSRO must specify its procedure for review of health care to include the following:

- concurrent review of the necessity of admission and continued stay in the hospital
- medical care evaluation studies
- retrospective analysis of health care practitioner, institutional, and patient profiles

Screening criteria are established as part of the review process to determine whether there is medical necessity for admission, whether there is a need for continued hospitalization after a specified time period, whether the services meet established standards, and whether there is discrepancy between method of treatment and acceptable standards of treatment for a particular diagnostic category. The last condition would indicate the need for continuing education programs for practitioners. Health care practitioners must develop norms, standards, and criteria in order to have an effective review and screening process. Norms are the numerical or statistical variations from a norm or criterion. Criteria are predetermined elements against which the quality of services may be measured and developed and based on professional expertise and professional literature.

Role of the Registered Dietitian in PSROs

The most appropriate level of involvement for the registered dietitian is in the form of peer review, as part of the patient care audit committee (American Dietetic Association 1976). This role is supported by laws governing PSROs, which require the involvement of non–physician health care practitioners in the review of care provided by their peers. The director of the department of dietetics or a qualified dietitian designee must participate in the activities of one or more committees that must be established by the hospital as part of the review mechanism process. As a member of the committee, the registered dietitian should be involved as follows:

- Provide dietary input by developing criteria, norms, and standards regarding the dietary management of problems or diagnoses chosen for review or audit.
- Modify criteria, norms, and standards as new data and scientific evidence become available to ensure improved care as opposed to endorsing current practices.
- Use the review process in the department of dietetics for the peer assessment of dietetic services alone.
- Identify areas of deficit in dietary care and services and develop policies and/or educational programs to correct deficits.
- Use the findings of the review system to plan continuing education for practicing dietitians and for input into the educational system for dietetic students.

There should be an effective working relationship between the patient care audit committee, the utilization review committee, and the continuing education committee if quality assessment of patient care is to be accomplished. The findings of the patient care audit committee can assist the utilization review committee in developing criteria for admission and continued-stay reviews, and assist the continuing education program by defining educational needs of health care practitioners.

Developing a Nutrition Care Plan

The purpose of a nutrition care plan for patients is to return the individual to a state of wellness as soon as possible and in the most effective manner. Components of a patient care plan involve four basic steps: assessment, planning, implementation, and evaluation.

Nutritional assessment involves the screening process to collect facts and to identify problems and needs of the patient. The collection of data, based on both subjective and objective observations, should include the following:

- interviews with patient to determine food intake patterns, food restrictions and preferences based on cultural or religious factors, recent significant changes in weight or appetite, observed emotional or physical limitations
- reviews of medical histories from patients' medical records to include laboratory test results, anthropometric measures, and clinical findings from the admitting examination

Data collected during the assessment phase should be analyzed for nutritional deficiencies. If it is determined that a nutritional deficit exists, immediate steps should be planned to restore the patient to a state of well-being. The planning process should include the following actions:

- Draft statements of short- and long-term goals for the patient in behavioral terms.
- Develop specific dietary interventions, such as calculated diets and supplements.
- Outline a system for communicating the nutritional care plan to other members of the health care team, stating the required support for accomplishing goals. The format of the system should be consistent with that used by other team members in a particular facility.
- Develop a method for checking response and/or progress toward goals, such as diet acceptance and total intake.
- Make plans for discharge with consideration to factors such as ability or willingness to adhere to dietary regimen, living conditions, and need for general assistance.

Implementation of a health care plan requires that the dietitian communicate with the health care team and with members of the production and service units within the dietary department. In order to ensure that patients will receive the nutritional care as planned, dietary personnel must be informed of special needs, including between-meal nourishments. Members of the health care team are informed through documentations in the patient's medical record. The recording of nutritional information in medical records may take the traditional form of entries in chronological sequence or a format of the problem-oriented medical record (POMR). Regardless of the method used, the documented information should support the dietary assessment, the care provided, and the results obtained (American Hospital Association 1976).

In acute care, screening is completed on all patients, but nutrition assessment is not completed on all patients; assessment is completed only if indicated from the initial nutrition screening. One of the reasons for this procedure in hospitals is the short length of stay, which is approximately three days for most patients.

The Joint Commission's standards for patient assessment and nutrition care (Joint Commission 1997) are set forth in Exhibit 4–1. Such assessment should be made in accordance with the Joint Commission's guidelines for patient rights and organization ethics (Joint Commission 1997; Exhibit 4–2).

OBRA Guidelines for Nutrition Assessment

The Omnibus Budget Reconciliation Act of 1987 was mandated and became law as a result of major concerns related to the care and treatment of nursing home residents. The act emphasizes resident assessment, quality of care, and quality of life and resident rights (see Appendixes B and C). The OBRA of 1987 was amended in 1988 and 1989, and became final in 1991. The act has undergone several changes from 1992 to the latest amendment in 1995, which became effective in January 1996.

In nursing facilities, guidelines for the assessment of resident care are quite comprehensive and detailed, and promote the interdisciplinary team in resident care planning. The role of the dietitian or dietetic technician, trained to translate the science of nutrition into the art of feeding and caring for the nutritional needs of residents, is a major part of the interdisciplinary team.

The OBRA directed the Health Care Financing Administration (HCFA) to develop a standardized resident assessment instrument (RAI) for assessing residents' needs. The RAI includes two components: the minimum data set (MDS) and resident assessment protocols (RAPs) to provide guidance for assessment in major areas of health concerns. The HCFA also developed a process in which the assessment would be used for an individualized care plan for the resident.

Exhibit 4–1 Joint Commission Standards for Assessment and Nutrition Care of Patients

The goal of the patient assessment function, as proposed by the *Comprehensive Accreditation Manual for Hospitals* (CAMH), is to determine what kind of care is required to meet a patient's initial needs as well as his or her needs as they change in response to care (1997). To provide patients with the right care at the time it is needed, qualified individuals in a hospital assess each patient's care needs throughout the patient's contact with the hospital. Major standards relating to nutrition care are as follows.

ASSESSMENT OF PATIENTS

PE 1.2 Nutritional status is assessed when warranted by the patient's needs or condition.

PE 1.3 Functional status is assessed when warranted by the patient's needs or condition.

PE 1.3.1 All patients referred for rehabilitation services receive a functional assessment.

Intent of PE 1.2 through PE 1.3.1

In its initial assessment, the hospital identifies patients at risk for nutritional problems, according to criteria developed by dietitians and other qualified professionals. The hospital refers such patients to a dietitian for further assessment.

During the initial assessment, the hospital also identifies patients who require a functional assessment, using criteria developed by rehabilitation specialists and other qualified professionals. This functional assessment, in turn, identifies any patients who will need rehabilitation services. Any patients who are currently receiving rehabilitation services at the hospital have had a functional assessment.

Some patients coming into the hospital setting may need special nutritional care, and some patients may need rehabilitation services or other services addressing their ability to function. These patients will require specialized assessments. Therefore, it is important for the hospital to identify patients with special needs.

CARE OF PATIENTS

The *goal* of the care of patients is to provide individualized care in settings responsive to specific patient needs. Patients deserve care that respects their choices, supports their participation in the care provided, and recognizes their right to experience achievement of their personal health goals. Major Joint Commission standards include the following.

TX.4 Each patient's nutrition care is planned.

Intent of TX.4

Based on the results of the nutrition screen and, when appropriate, nutrition assessment and reassessment, the nutrition therapy plan is implemented for all patients determined to be at nutritional risk. Patients at nutritional risk include the following:

- patients with actual or potential malnutrition
- patients on altered diets or diet schedules
- patients with inadequate nutrition
- lactating and pregnant women
- geriatric surgical patients

Organization criteria guide development of the nutrition therapy plan. A nutrition therapy plan is not ordinarily developed for patients receiving only a regular diet by mouth.

All patients, regardless of their nutritional status or need, receive a prescription or order for food or other nutrients. The food or other nutrients ordered can range from nothing by mouth (NPO orders) to regular diets, to parenteral or enteral tube nutrition.

TX.4.1 An interdisciplinary nutrition therapy plan is developed and periodically updated for patients at nutritional risk.

Intent of TX.4.1

A more intensive plan for nutrition therapy may be indicated for patients at high nutritional risk. The plan identifies measurable goals and actions to achieve them. The patient's physician, the registered dietitian, nursing, and pharmaceutical services staff participate in developing the plan, and their roles in implementation are clearly defined.

TX.4.1.1 When appropriate to the patient group served by a unit, meals and snacks support program goals.

Intent of TX.4.1.1

Depending on the types or ages of patients served, some units may provide snacks or meals for special occasions or recreational activities. For example, on a child or adolescent service, the child learns to select appropriate snacks according to a plan for nutrition care. When appropriate, facilities that permit patient involvement are available for preparing and serving meals and snacks. Staff members assist patients when necessary and ensure that each patient receives an adequate amount and variety of food.

TX.4.2 Authorized individuals prescribe or order food and nutrition products in a timely manner.

Intent of TX.4.2

Food and nutrition products are administered only when prescribed or ordered by medical staff, authorized house staff, or other individuals with appropriate clinical privileges. Consistent with medical staff rules and regulations, verbal prescriptions or orders for food and nutrition products are accepted by designated personnel. Verbal prescriptions and orders are authenticated by the initiator within a defined time frame. All prescription orders

continues

Exhibit 4–1 continued

are documented in the patient's medical record before any food or other nutrient is administered to the patient. A prescription or order for food or other nutrients is accepted by designated personnel. Such orders are documented in the patient's medical record before any food or other nutrient is administered to the patient.

TX.4.3 Responsibilities are assigned for all activities involved in safe and accurate provision of food and nutrition products.

Intent of TX.4.3

Staff responsibilities for preparation, storage, distribution, and administration of food and nutrition products are clearly defined to ensure safety and accuracy.

TX.4.4 Food and nutrition products are distributed and administered in a safe, accurate, timely, and acceptable manner.

Intent of TX.4.4

Food is distributed in a timely manner to preserve nutrient value and serving temperature and provide nutrition that is appetizing and palatable. Food and nutrition products are distributed and administered to the patients for whom they were prescribed or ordered.

TX.4.5 Each patient's response to nutrition care is monitored.

Intent of TX.4.5

Ongoing patient monitoring is essential to effective, appropriate, and continuous nutrition care. Nutrition care monitoring is a collaborative process that may include the following:

- a formal nutrition care team
- representatives from multiple disciplines conducting patient care rounds
- communication among the various disciplines
- integration of nutrition care with the patient care team

TX.4.6 The nutrition care service meets patients' needs for special diets and accommodates altered diet schedules.

Intent of TX.4.6

Food and nutrition services include processes for

- meeting special diet or diet schedule needs
- providing food or nutrition products at times other than the regular delivery schedule
- accommodating personal dietary requests
- storing, handling, and controlling food or nutrition products obtained from outside sources

TX.4.7 Nutrition care practices are standardized throughout the organization.

Intent of TX.4.7

The medical staff, the nutrition care service or department, and other disciplines (for example, nursing) collaborate in developing and maintaining standardized approaches to nutrition care. Approaches are communicated and used throughout the organization (Joint Commission 1997).

All hospital staff should have access to the entire manual to get a full understanding of all components, including standards, intent, examples of implementation, and evidence of performance. The scoring section aids in understanding compliance level with standards and aggregation rules that apply to departments and disciplines or professionals across the hospital.

The *Manual* also includes an interpretation of terms and cross-referenced information that may be helpful. In addition to the *Comprehensive Accreditation Manual for Hospitals* and the Joint Commission *Standards Manual*, nursing homes seeking Joint Commission accreditation should find the following publications helpful:

- *Comprehensive Accreditation Manual for Long-Term Care*
- *Accreditation Manual for Long-Term Care*
- *Standards for Long-Term Care*
- *Accreditation Protocol for Subacute Programs*

Copies of all of the above manuals are available from the Joint Commission at a specified fee or free to already accredited organizations.

Source: © *Comprehensive Accreditation Manual for Hospitals.* Oakbrook Terrace, IL: Joint Commission on Accreditation of Healthcare Organizations, 1997. Reprinted with permission.

The MDS (amended 1995; amendment effective January 1996) is divided into several parts (see Appendix D):

- background information at intake—admission
- background information at return—readmission
- customary routine (only at first admission)

The facility must conduct initially and periodically a comprehensive, accurate, standardized, reproducible assessment of each resident's functional capacity. This assessment must be conducted no less than 14 days after the date of admission and includes the following:

- Section A. Identification and background information
- Section B. Cognitive patterns
- Section C. Communication/hearing patterns
- Section D. Vision patterns
- Section E. Mood and behavior patterns

Exhibit 4–2 Joint Commission Patient Rights and Organization Ethics

The goal of the patient rights and organization ethics function is to help improve patient outcomes by respecting each patient's rights and conducting business relationships with patients and the public in an ethical manner. Following is a list of all standards for this function:

RI.1	The hospital addresses ethical issues in providing patient care.
RI.1.1	The patient's right to treatment or service is respected and supported.
RI.1.2	Patients are involved in all aspects of their care.
RI.1.2.1	Informed consent is obtained.
RI.1.2.1.1	All patients asked to participate in a research project are given a description of the expected benefits.
RI.1.2.1.2	All patients asked to participate in a research project are given a description of the potential discomforts and risks.
RI.1.2.1.3	All patients asked to participate in a research project are given a description of alternative services that might also prove advantageous to them.
RI.1.2.1.4	All patients asked to participate in a research project are given a full explanation of the procedures to be followed, especially those that are experimental in nature.
RI.1.2.1.5	All patients asked to participate in a research project are told that they may refuse to participate, and that their refusal will not compromise their access to service.
RI.1.2.2	The family participates in care decisions.
RI.1.2.3	Patients are involved in resolving dilemmas about care decisions.
RI.1.2.4	The hospital addresses advance directives.
RI.1.2.5	The hospital addresses withholding resuscitative services.
RI.1.2.6	The hospital addresses forgoing or withdrawing life-sustaining treatment.
RI.1.2.7	The hospital addresses care at the end of life.
RI.1.3	The hospital demonstrates respect for the following patient needs:
RI.1.3.1	confidentiality;
RI.1.3.2	privacy;
RI.1.3.3	security;
RI.1.3.4	resolution of complaints;
RI.1.3.5	pastoral counseling;
RI.1.3.6	communication.
RI.1.3.6.1	When the hospital restricts a patient's visitors, mail, telephone calls, or other forms of communication, the restrictions are evaluated for their therapeutic effectiveness.
RI.1.3.6.1.1	Any restrictions on communication are fully explained to the patient and family and are determined with their participation.
RI.1.4	Each patient receives a written statement of his or her rights.
RI.1.5	The hospital supports the patient's right to access protective services.
RI.2	The hospital has a policy and procedure, developed with the medical staff's participation, for the procuring and donation of organs and other tissues.
RI.3	The hospital protects patients and respects their rights during research, investigation, and clinical trials involving human subjects.
RI.3.1	All consent forms that address the information specified in RI.1.2.1.1 through RI.1.2.1.5 indicate the name of the person who provided the information and the date the form was signed, and address the participant's right to privacy, confidentiality, and safety.
RI.4	The hospital operates according to a code of ethical behavior.
RI.4.1	The code addresses marketing, admission, transfer and discharge, and billing practices.
RI.4.2	The code addresses the relationship of the hospital and its staff members to other health care providers, educational institutions, and payers.
RI.4.3	In hospitals with longer lengths of stay, the code addresses a patient's rights to perform or refuse to perform tasks in or for the hospital.

Source: © *Comprehensive Accreditation Manual for Hospitals.* Oakbrook Terrace, IL: Joint Commission on Accreditation of Healthcare Organizations, 1997. Reprinted with permission.

- Section F. Psychosocial well-being
- Section G. Physical functioning and structural problems
- Section H. Continence in last 14 days
- Section I. Disease diagnoses
- Section J. Health conditions
- Section K. Oral/nutritional status
- Section L. Oral/dental status
- Section M. Skin condition
- Section N. Activity pursuit patterns
- Section O. Medications
- Section P. Special treatments and procedures
- Section Q. Discharge potential and overall status
- Section R. Assessment information

The RAPs are used to assist clinical decision making and serve as a link between assessment and plan of care (see Appendix D for an example of a RAP for feeding tubes). All sections of the MDS require scrutiny to determine whether nutrition intervention is needed. There are 18 RAPs in the RAI, version 2.02. However, there are five RAPs that specifically address nutrition concerns.

The names of the RAPs in version 2.0 are unchanged from the original version, as are the RAP guidelines. The triggers in almost all of the RAPs have been revised, especially the following:

- nutrition status
- feeding tubes
- dehydration/fluid maintenance
- dental care
- pressure ulcers

The RAP process includes the following five steps:

1. The interdisciplinary team uses the RAI triggering mechanism to determine which RAP problem areas require review and additional assessment. The triggered conditions are indicated in the appropriate column on the RAP summary form (see Appendix D).
2. The interdisciplinary team members review the triggered conditions (specific to their area of knowledge as designated by the registered nurse coordinator), and are guided by the RAPs and other assessment information as needed to determine the nature of the problem and understand the causes specific to the resident.
3. Based on the review of assessment information, the interdisciplinary team decides whether the triggered condition affects the resident's functional status or well-being and warrants a care plan intervention.
4. The interdisciplinary team documents key findings of the resident's status based on the RAP review and description of the team's rationale in making a care planning decision. The decision to proceed to care planning is also indicated in the appropriate column on the RAP summary form.
5. The interdisciplinary team, in conjunction with the wishes of the resident, resident's family, and attending physician develop, revise, or continue the care plan based on this assessment.

A RAP may have several MDS items or sets of items that are defined as triggers. Only one of the trigger definitions must be present for a RAP to be triggered. Note that the concept of "automatic" and "potential" triggers used in the original version of the RAI has been eliminated. In the current version of 2.0, there are no "potential" triggers or situations in which a symbol on the trigger legend does not require RAP review.

The trigger definitions can be found in

- section II of each RAP
- the RAP key found at the end of each RAP
- RAP trigger legend (see Appendix D)

The trigger legend is a two-page form that summarizes all of the triggers for the 18 RAPs. It is not a required form that must be maintained in the resident's medical record; rather, it is a worksheet that may be used by the interdisciplinary team members to determine which RAPs are triggered from a completed MDS form.

Many facilities use automated systems instead of the trigger legend form to trigger RAPs. Software programs used for automated triggering should be matched against the trigger definitions to make sure that they are correctly identifying triggered RAPs. The HCFA has also developed test files for facility validation of a software program's triggering logic. It is the facility's responsibility to ensure that the software is triggering correctly. At a minimum, ask whether the triggered RAPs are what you would have expected. Did the software miss some RAPs you thought should have been triggered? Are others triggered that you did not expect?

There are four different types of triggers that can change the focus of the RAPs review:

1. *Potential problems*—These are factors that suggest the presence of a problem that warrants additional assessment and consideration of a care plan intervention. They are usually narrowly defined as factors that warrant additional assessment. They include clinical factors commonly seen as indicative of possible underlying problems and consequently have generally been well understood by facility staff members.
2. *Broad screening triggers*—These are factors that assist staff to identify hard-to-diagnose problems. Because some problems are often difficult to assess in the elderly nursing home population, certain triggers have been broadly defined and consequently may have a fair number of false positives (i.e., the resident may trigger a RAP that is not automatically representative of a problem for the resident).
3. *Prevention of problems*—These are factors that assist staff to identify residents at risk of developing particular problems. Examples include risk factors for falling or developing a pressure ulcer.
4. *Rehabilitation potential*—These are factors that are aimed at identifying candidates with rehabilitation potential. Not all triggers identify deficits or problems. Some triggers indicate areas of resident strengths. In general, these factors suggest consideration of programs to improve a resident's functioning or minimize decline.

The interdisciplinary team members who are assessing a resident whose condition triggers a RAP should know what responses on the MDS triggered the RAP. This step is often missed, especially if someone other than the person who completes the MDS reviews the trigger legend or the triggering is automated. Referring to the triggers section of the RAP to identify relevant triggers can help to steer the assessment to factors particular to the individual resident. For example, if a staff member assigned to assess a resident who has fallen or is at risk for falls knows that the fall RAP was triggered because the resident had been dizzy during the MDS assessment period (MDS item J1f—dizziness was checked), the RAP review would include a focus on causal factors and interventions for dizziness. While reviewing the RAP, other factors may come to light regarding the resident's risk for falls, but knowing the trigger clarifies or possibly rules out certain avenues of approach to the resident's problem.

At the same time, there can also be a tendency to believe that the RAP review is limited only to those MDS items that triggered the RAP. Such a view is false and can lead to key causal factors going unnoticed and a less-than-appropriate plan of care being initated. Many of the trigger conditions serve to initiate a more comprehensive review process, including specific causal factors (as referenced in the guidelines) that are to be considered relative to the resident's status.

Assessment of the Triggered RAPs

Reviewing a triggered RAP means doing an in-depth assessment of a particular clinical condition in terms of the potential need for care plan interventions. The RAP is used to organize or guide the assessment process so that information helpful in the understanding of the resident's condition is not overlooked.

The triggered RAPs are used to glean information that pertains to the resident's condition. While reviewing the RAP, the team considers what MDS items caused the RAP to trigger and what type of trigger it is (i.e., potential problem, broad screen, prevention of problems, or rehabilitation potential). This focuses the review on information that will be helpful in deciding whether a care plan intervention is necessary.

The utilization guidelines are instructions concerning when and how to use the RAI. The individual resident's care plan must be evaluated and revised, if appropriate, each time an RAI comprehensive assessment is completed. Facilities may either make changes on the original care plan or develop a new care plan.

According to Gallagher-Allred (1992), the federally developed MDS does not provide all the information that is necessary to assess completely the resident's nutritional status or identify dietary needs. Therefore, an additional assessment form such as the one in Appendix D is usually needed. The following areas are covered:

- resident identification information
- ability to provide food preference, opinions about mealtimes, and diet
- ability to self-feed
- ability to eat as desired
- usual food intake
- diseases or conditions that decrease nutrient intake
- diseases or conditions that increase nutrient requirements
- diseases or conditions that may suggest need for therapeutic diet or food texture modification
- diseases or conditions that may suggest need for supplementation
- medications and treatments or procedures that affect nutritional status or diet order
- laboratory data indicative of nutritional status
- presence of symptoms potentially indicative of poor nutritional status
- summary of nutritional care level
- estimated daily nutrient needs
- summary of resident and family input into nutrition care
- discharge potential
- plan of care

Prior to the comprehensive interdisciplinary resident care conference, the resident assessment protocol summary is completed in order to present a brief verbal report on the problems, strengths, and goals for the resident (see Appendix D).

The resident's care plan is a comprehensive assessment of the problems and the approach to follow in meeting needs. The conference involves the resident in developing his or her care plans, attending physician, registered nurse, registered dietitian or dietetic technician, and other disciplines as determined by the resident's needs. To minimize the time required for each assessment, all team members should examine each resident's medical record prior to the conference and come prepared to discuss problems, measurable goals, and approaches.

All members of the team attending the conference will sign the care plan at the time of review. The dietitian or dietetic technician will document problems, strengths, measurable goals, and approaches in the progress notes, indicating progress or lack of progress.

OBRA Summary

To fulfill federal requirements each time a comprehensive assessment is required, long-term care facilities must complete the following:

- the MDS, plus any additional core items that make up the state RAI

- the RAP summary form, on which facilities must indicate which RAPs have been triggered, the location of information gathered during the RAP review process, and the final care planning decision
- documentation of clinical information (e.g., assessment information) from the RAP review to assist in care planning and follow-up

The following is a schematic of the overall RAI framework:

MDS + TRIGGERS + RAPs ⟶ COMPREHENSIVE (UTILIZATION GUIDELINES)

The MDS consists of a core set of screening and assessment elements, including common definitions and coding categories, that forms the foundation of the comprehensive assessment.

The triggers are specific resident responses for one or a combination of MDS elements. The triggers identify residents who either have or are at risk for developing specific functional problems and require further evaluation using RAPs designated within the state-specified RAI. MDS item responses that define triggers are specified in each RAP. Turn to the RAPs for tube feeding (in Appendix D) to review these items and the accompanying RAP guidelines. The trigger legend form serves as a useful summary of all RAP triggers. Note that the symbols have been changed and the process streamlined. The trigger legend summarizes which MDS item responses trigger individual RAPs and has been designed as a helpful tool for facilities if they choose to use it. It is a worksheet, not a required form, and does not need to be maintained in each resident's record.

The RAPs provide structured, problem-oriented frameworks for organizing MDS information and additional clinically relevant information about an individual's health problem or functional status. What are the problems that require immediate attention? What risk factors are important? Are there issues that might cause you to proceed in an unconventional manner for the RAP in question? Clinical staff are responsible for answering questions such as these. The information from the MDS and RAPs forms the basis for individualized care planning.

The requirements for resident assessment are applicable to all residents in certified long-term care facilities. The requirements are applicable regardless of age, diagnosis, length of stay, or payment category. An RAI must be completed for any resident residing in the facility longer than 14 days. Assessments are made as follows:

- Complete MDS assessment for background information upon admission.
- Complete full MDS within 14 days of admission.
- Review MDS for nutrition screening within 14 days of admission.
- Perform nutrition assessment from evaluation of MDS. Information from the MDS is used to develop a comprehensive care plan. Each assessment must be conducted or coordinated with appropriate participation of health professionals. Therefore, it is recommended that the registered dietitian or dietetic technician perform the nutrition component.
- Convene an interdisciplinary team care plan conference to conduct a comprehensive assessment 14 days after admission.
- Perform a complete reassessment if the resident was discharged then readmitted to the facility and a permanent change in condition occurred.
- Perform a quarterly review of the MDS for each resident to identify any physical or mental changes. The nursing facility must examine each resident no less than once every three months, and as appropriate revise the resident's assessment to ensure the continual accuracy of the assessment (see Appendix D).
- Perform an annual reassessment, or after a significant change in physical or mental condition.

Using the POMR Method of Documentation

Nutritional care information based on the POMR is organized in three specific areas: database, problem list, and progress notes. The database includes information from the physical examination, complaints at admission, results of laboratory tests, dietary history, patient's attitude toward and knowledge of food and nutrition, and resources of home and family.

The problem list may include medical, physical, emotional, and religious problems, or any other problem affecting the patient that requires additional information, treatment, or education. The list is maintained and updated as often as new problems arise. The advantage of having a problem list in the patient's medical record is that all team members can supervise and share in the solution.

Progress notes, recorded by the appropriate team member, indicate the actions taken for a particular problem. The progress notes may be recorded by using the SOAP—an acronym for *subjective* (information derived from the patient during interviews), *objective* (clinical findings from initial physical examination, laboratory tests, and anthropometric measures), *assessment* (interpretation and analysis of objective data, with emphasis on consistency), and *planning* (recommendations and plans to obtain more information, treat, and educate, including follow-up care)—format.

Medical Records

The recording of information, consistent with policies of the organization, should be sufficient to support the dietary assessment, justify the nutritional care, and document results accurately (American Hospital Association 1976). Progress notes should be brief, without sacrificing essential facts. Avoid professional jargon and any remarks that may be critical of treatment provided by other members of the team. Keep in mind that the patient has a right to see his or her medical record. Effective communication dictates that progress notes should be comprehensible by all members of the health care team.

Authorized Personnel

All entries in medical records should be signed and dated by the person making the entry. This person may be a dietitian, a dietetic technician, or the dietary manager, depending on the policies of the institution. In long-term care facilities where services of a full-time dietitian are not available, responsibilities for recording inpatient medical records may be assigned to the dietetic technician or the dietary manager. The consultant dietitian is responsible for training the dietetic service supervisor and for determining whether the supervisor has the ability to document in medical records. In acute care facilities, where the nutritional care is more complex, registered dietitians should do the charting.

What To Record

Guidelines for recording in the patient's medical record by the qualified dietitian or authorized alternate are as follows (American Hospital Association 1976):

- Confirmation of diet order. Make a notation that the prescribed diet is being fulfilled; this should be done within 24 hours of admission.
- Summary of dietary history. Summarize the patient's daily diet pattern, nutrient deficiencies, food allergies, lifestyle, and socioeconomic resources; include an assessment of the diet-disease relationship.
- Nutritional care therapy. Describe the type of diet and any restrictions, the patient's daily nutrient intake, diet acceptance, and changes in diet order or diet instruction; note referral of the patient for assistance with diet at home.
- Nutritional care discharge plan. Describe the diet instruction given and place a copy of the instruction in the patient's medical record; forward the description or a copy of the diet to the referral agency or nursing home, along with plans for nutritional care follow-up.
- Dietetic consultation. Acknowledge physician's written request for consultation. Consultation reports reflect assessment of the patient's dietary history, examination of the patient's medical record for previous dietary history, and recommendations for a normal or modified diet. Record subsequent counseling of the patient or family in the patient's medical record.

COMMITTEE RESPONSIBILITIES

The role of the registered dietitian does not diminish the responsibilities of the food service director in ensuring optimal nutritional care. To understand the diverse and complex nature of patient care, the director must have an understanding of food and nutrition principles and their relationship to patient well-being. In addition, the director or an authorized designee must participate in the following committees concerned with patient care, as mandated by federal or state law.

Infection Control Committee

The purposes of the infection control committee are to establish preventive measures by developing policies and procedures for sanitation and aseptic techniques; to develop isolation procedures; to maintain records of all incidents of infection involving patients and personnel; to establish a system for evaluation and reporting infections; and to develop a system for in-service education on preventive and control measures.

Administrative Staff Meeting

Regularly scheduled meetings are held to allow participation by department heads in the decision-making process; to provide for input and open communication; and to keep administrative personnel abreast of all changes affecting the organization and their respective departments.

Budget Committee

The purposes of the budget committee are to include all department heads in the operational budget planning; to ensure appropriate input; and to ensure congruence with organizational goals and objectives.

Quality Control Committee

The primary purpose of the quality control committee is to develop policies and procedures for optimal quality of patient care through ongoing quality assurance audits.

Safety Committee

The safety committee is responsible for ensuring a safe environment for patients and a safe place of work for employees as mandated by OSHA and other regulations.

Effective teams within the health care setting, both administrative and clinical, are those that encourage and recognize contributions from members who possess various skills, knowledge, and experience. This cooperative effort is necessary for consistently high-quality nutritional care.

PROFESSIONAL ETHICS

A health care professional needs a combination of both technical competence and ethical competence. Technical competence involves possession of adequate knowledge and skills to care for patients.

All professionals have written and unwritten codes of ethics to follow. To behave in an ethical manner is simply to do the most good and the least harm to others and to perform the proper professional dos and don'ts. Morality is a combination of judgment, actions, attitudes, and other behaviors of an individual that can be judged right or wrong (Tancredi 1974). In many situations, it is not always obvious which decision or approach is the morally or ethically correct one. Even when specific written ethical codes and guidelines exist, ethical dilemmas may emerge. An ethical dilemma exists when helping one patient may result in harm to another patient (Purtilo and Cassel 1981). A dietitian may be faced continually with the dilemma of how to delegate time spent with various patients. The health care professional must weigh alternatives to determine which option will be the most beneficial and the least harmful. Extreme examples of unethical conduct that compromises patient well-being for personal gain are situations in which the clinical dietitian accepts gifts or other favors from patients for services rendered or the director of food services accepts kickbacks from vendors. The practice of professional ethics in the health care environment requires that personal prejudices, preferences, and personal gains be set aside for the good of the patient.

The current ethical issue for dietetic professionals revolves around nutrition support for patients in varying states of illness. It joins the debate regarding use of artificial respirators, ventilators, kidney dialysis, and other forms of medical support. As societal values change with reference to death, dying, suffering, pain, and patient rights, dietetic professionals must face the ethical dilemma of whether to withhold or withdraw nutrition support. The question of who has the right to deny basic biological needs of nutrition and fluids has both legal and moral ramifications. According to Studebaker (1988), nutrition and hydration are different from other forms of medical therapy. All people, regardless of their state of health, require food and water. Denial of these essentials is, de facto, a death sentence.

The position of the American Dietetic Association (1987) is that the dietitian should take an active role in developing criteria for feeding the terminally ill adult within the practice setting and collaborate with the health care team in making recommendations on each case. The position paper presents a comprehensive view of issues related to feeding the terminally ill from an ethical, legal, medical, and nutrition perspective, concluding with guidelines that dietitians can use in deciding the appropriateness of providing or withholding nutrition support.

In addition to terminally ill adults, there are other patients who may be of ethical concern for the dietitian in the practice setting, such as malnourished patients, competent patients who refuse food, cancer patients, and incompetent patients in a permanent vegetative state (Schiller 1988). In addition to developing criteria through collaboration with health team members, Schiller recommends that the dietitian prepare for committee participation as follows:

- Be familiar with basic legal and ethical principles.
- Clarify personal values with regard to food and feeding, euthanasia, use of life-sustaining treatments, pain, living wills, artificial feeding, terminal disease, and prolongation of life.
- Recognize bases for conflicting legal judgments in nutrition support cases.
- Review published guidelines, such as the ADA position paper, as a basis for decision making.

Because all health care professionals are individuals with various personal ethics, and all patients have differing needs, it is crucial for all professionals to be familiar with the code of ethics of their profession and the ethical guidelines of the institution by which they are employed. General guidelines for dietitians require a commitment from the dietitian (American Dietetic Association 1988) to do the following:

- Provide professional services with objectivity and with respect for the unique needs of individuals.
- Avoid discrimination against other individuals on the basis of race, creed, religion, sex, age, and national origin.
- Fulfill professional commitments in good faith.
- Conduct himself or herself with honesty, integrity, and fairness.
- Remain free of conflict of interest while fulfilling the objectives and maintaining the integrity of the dietetic profession.
- Maintain confidentiality of information.
- Practice dietetics based on scientific principles and current information.
- Assume responsibility and accountability for personal competence in practice.
- Recognize and exercise professional judgment within the limits of his or her qualifications and seek counsel or make referrals as appropriate.
- Provide sufficient information to enable clients to make their own informed decisions.
- Inform the public and colleagues of his or her services by using factual information. Refrain from advertising in a false or misleading manner.

- Promote and endorse products in a manner that is neither false nor misleading.
- Permit use of his or her name for the purpose of certifying that dietetic services have been rendered only if he or she has provided or supervised the provisions of those services.
- Accurately present professional qualifications and credentials.
  1. Use "RD" or "registered dietitian" or "DTR" or "dietetic technician registered" only when registration is current and authorized by the Commission of Dietetic Registration.
  2. Provide accurate information and comply with all requirements of the Commission of Dietetic Registration program in which he or she is seeking initial or continued credentials from the Commission on Dietetic Registration.
  3. Refrain from aiding other persons in violation of any requirements of the Commission on Dietetic Registration or aiding other persons in representing themselves as an RD or a DTR when they are not, thus avoiding disciplinary action.
- Present substantiated information and interpret controversial information without personal bias, recognizing that legitimate differences of opinion exist.
- Make all reasonable effort to avoid bias in any kind of professional evaluation. Provide objective evaluation of candidates for professional association memberships, awards, scholarships, and job advancements.
- Voluntarily withdraw from professional practice under the following circumstances:
  1. The professional has engaged in any substance abuse that could affect his or her practice.
  2. The professional has been adjudged by a court to be mentally incompetent.
  3. The professional has an emotional or mental disability that affects his or her practice in a manner that could harm the client.
- Comply with all applicable laws and regulations concerning the profession and is subject to disciplinary action under the following circumstances:
  1. The professional has been convicted of a crime under the laws of the United States that is a felony or a misdemeanor, an essential element of which is related to the practice of the profession.
  2. The professional has been disciplined by a state, and at least one of the grounds for the discipline is violation of one or more of these or substantially equivalent principles.
  3. The professional has committed an act of misfeasance or malfeasance that is directly related to the practice of the profession as determined by a court of competent jurisdiction, a licensing board, or an agency of a governmental body.
- Accept the obligation to protect society and the profession by upholding the code of ethics for the profession of dietetics and by reporting alleged violations of the code through the defined review process of the American Dietetic Association and its credentialing agency, the Commission on Dietetic Registration.

The American Dietetic Association (1988) has defined steps in the procedure for the review process when a member has allegedly violated the code of ethics for the profession of dietetics, as follows:

1. Complaint to the ethics committee
2. Preliminary review of the complaint
3. Response by the person against whom the complaint is made
4. Disposition of the complaint
5. Remedial action
6. Preparation for a hearing and notice of hearing date
7. Hearing—right of concerned parties
8. Cost responsibility
9. Decision of ethics committee
10. Appeal—right of the respondent
11. Notification of adverse action

MALPRACTICE

The director of a medical food service operation has total responsibility for the quality of nutritional care provided to patients. In small medical facilities where only one dietitian is employed, the director of food service has responsibility for providing both administrativve and clinical nutritional care. In large facilities, the responsibility for nutritional care of patients is delegated to clinical dietitians. Because the patient is entitled to services from the dietitian, any dissatisfaction with the service provided may result in a malpractice suit (Baird and Jacobs 1981). Areas of obvious neglect would involve failure to carry out the diet order prescribed by the physician, incorrect assessment of the nutritional status of the patient, or incorrect or inadequate instruction to the patient. To protect against such liability, the dietitian should consider the following:

- Follow the code of ethics of the ADA and the individual institution where he or she is employed.
- Avoid statements that contradict the diagnosis given by the attending physician.
- Explain all instructions carefully and clearly and support them with written literature, if possible.
- Encourage the patient to contact the dietitian by phone in case of future questions or concerns regarding dietary regimen and instructions.
- Assess, treat, and instruct the patient only in a manner appropriate to his or her professional training and background.

- Consult another dietitian or professional if in doubt regarding method of assessment, treatment, or instruction of any patient.

In addition to these general guidelines, a precise documentation by the dietitian in the patient's medical record is necessary. Besides being a tool for communication among health care professionals, the written record is the dietitian's best defense against potential malpractice suits.

Because of the current climate of changing moral and ethical thinking and patient rights, dietitians are joining physicians and other health care professionals in their concern with the legal aspects of their practice. The dietitian needs to review the full trial transcripts of judicial decisions in order to gain a perspective of the arguments for and against the decision. Brief summaries of four judicial decisions involving nutrition and hydration follow.

Decision One

Barber v. Superior Court, 147 Cal. App. 3d 1006, 195 Cal. Rptr. 484, (1983). Two physicians charged with murder and conspiracy to commit murder petitioned the California Court of Appeals for a writ of prohibition after a magistrate ordered the complaint dismissed and the trial court ordered it reinstated. The prosecution arose after life-support measures were terminated for a deeply comatose patient in accordance with the wishes of the patient's immediate family.

Clarence Herbert had undergone surgery for closure of an ileostomy. Petitioner Robert Nejdl, MD, was Herbert's surgeon, and petitioner Neil Barber, MD, was his attending internist. Shortly after the successful surgery, and while in the recovery room, Herbert suffered cardiorespiratory arrest. He was revived and placed on life-support equipment. Within the following three days, it was determined that Herbert was in a deeply comatose state from which he was not likely to recover. Tests and examinations indicated that Herbert had suffered severe brain damage, leaving him in a vegetative state that was likely to be permanent. The physicians informed family members of his condition and chances for recovery. The family convened and drafted a written request to hospital personnel stating that they wanted "all machines taken off that are sustaining life." As a result, petitioners ordered removal of the respirator and other life-sustaining equipment, but the patient showed no signs of change. After two more days and after consulting with family, petitioners ordered removal of the intravenous tubes that provided hydration and nutrition.

The court held that cessation of heroic life-support measures was not an affirmative act, but rather a withdrawal or omission of further treatment, and that the physicians' omission to continue life-support measures, although intentional and with knowledge that the patient would die, was not an unlawful failure to perform a legal duty, given the fact that the patient had virtually no chance of recovery, and given the wishes of the family. The court further held that the failure to institute formal guardianship proceedings did not render the physicians' conduct unlawful, because there was no such statutory requirement, and that, under the circumstances, the wife was the proper person to act as surrogate for the patient. In addition, the court held that there was no legal requirement for prior judicial approval of a decision to withdraw treatment.

Decision Two

In the matter of Claire C. Conroy, 464 A. 2d 303 (N.J. Super. Ct.), (1983). The guardian of an 84-year-old nursing home patient suffering from severe organic brain syndrome and a variety of other serious ailments sought removal of a nasogastric tube from the patient, who was totally dependent on the tube for nutrients and fluids. The New Jersey Superior Court held that the nasogastric tube could be removed from the patient. The guardian *ad litem* of the patient appealed. Conroy died while the appeal was pending.

From her teen-aged years until her retirement at age 62 or 63, Conroy was employed by a cosmetic company. She was never married but was devoted to her three sisters. The last of her sisters died in 1975, leaving her nephew as her only living relative. In 1979, he petitioned for and was granted guardianship of Conroy, whom he then placed in a nursing home. Conroy was ambulatory upon admission but was somewhat confused because of her organic brain syndrome. In 1982, she developed necrotic ulcers on her left foot as a complication of diabetes. She was unable to maintain a conversation because of her extreme confusion, but she was aware of and could respond to commands. It was observed that Conroy was not eating, and thus a nasogastric tube was inserted. Except for a two-week period, during which time she was fed puréed food but with poor results, this tube remained in place until her death. Her physician testified at trial that Conroy was not brain dead, not comatose, and not in a chronic vegetative state. The physician who testified for the guardian described Conroy's mental state as "severely demented." Severe contractions of her lower legs kept her in a semifetal position. According to her physician's testimony, if the nasogastric tube had been removed, Conroy would have died of dehydration and starvation in about a week. Her physician described this as a painful death.

The New Jersey Superior Court, Appellate Division, held that because the patient was not in a chronic vegetative state but was simply very confused, the bodily invasion the patient suffered as result of her treatment was small and death by dehydration and starvation would be painful; and that the state's interest in preserving life outweighs the patient's privacy interest, and thus removal of the nasogastric tube, upon which the patient was totally dependent for nutriment and fluids, would have been improper.

Decision Three

In the matter of Shirley Dinnerstein, 380 N.E. 2d 134 (Mass. Ct. App.), (1979). The plaintiffs in this case sought appeal on the question of whether a physician attending an incompetent, terminally ill patient may lawfully direct that resuscitation be withheld in the event of cardiac or respiratory arrest where such has not been approved in advance by a probate court.

The patient was a 67-year-old woman who suffered from Alzheimer's disease, first diagnosed in 1975. She suffered a stroke in 1978 that left her totally paralyzed on her left side. She was confined to a hospital bed, in an essentially vegetative state, immobile, speechless, unable to swallow without choking, and barely able to cough. She was fed through a nasogastric tube (intravenous feeding had been discontinued because it caused her pain). She also had high blood pressure, which was difficult to control; there was risk in lowering it because of a constriction in an artery leading to kidney. She had a serious, life-threatening coronary artery disease resulting from arteriosclerosis. Her life expectancy was no more than a year, but she could have gone into cardiac or respiratory arrest at any time. In this situation her attending physician recommended that if cardiac or respiratory arrest occurred, resuscitation efforts should not be undertaken.

The patient's family, consisting of a son who was a practicing physician, and a daughter, with whom the patient lived prior to her admission to a nursing home, concurred in the doctor's recommendation. The family joined with the doctor and the hospital in bringing action for declaratory relief. The probate judge appointed a guardian *ad litem*, who opposed.

A judgment was entered in accordance with the prayers of the complaint for declaratory relief, declaring that, on the findings, the law does not prohibit a course of medical treatment that excludes attempts at resuscitation in the event of cardiac or respiratory arrest and that the validity of an order to that effect does not depend on prior judicial approval.

Decision Four

In the matter of Mary Hier, 464 N.E. 2d 959 (Mass. Ct. App.), (1984). Prior to transfer to a nursing home, Mary Hier, 92 years old, spent 55 years at a psychiatric hospital. At both the hospital and the nursing home, she received thorazine to relieve her delusions and extreme agitation without suffering adverse side effects. Mrs. Hier resisted administration of the medication because of an aversion to being injected with needles. She also suffered for many years from a hiatal hernia and a large cervical diverticulum in her esophagus. The combined effect impeded her ability to ingest food orally. In 1974, she underwent a gastrotomy for placement of a gastric feeding tube, but repeatedly pulled out the tube. Difficulty in replacing the tube at the nursing home prompted transfer to a hospital. Upon examination, the physician determined that the stoma was almost completely closed and that replacement of the tube would require surgery. Mrs. Hier refused to have any surgery performed. A petition was filed for appointment of a guardian with consent authority. The probate court ordered appointment of a temporary guardian with authority to consent to administration of antipsychotic drugs but without authority to consent to surgical procedures necessary to provide her with adequate nutritional support. The guardian appealed. Physicians explored a number of alternative feeding methods, but decided that all were medically contraindicated because of the complexity of the patient's medical problems and her lack of cooperation.

The judge, in applying the substitute judgment analysis, took into consideration the facts that the proposed operation was intrusive and burdensome; that Mrs. Hier had repeatedly and clearly opposed procedures necessary to introduce tube feeding (both gastric and nasogastric); that benefits of a gastrotomy were diminished by her repeated history of dislodgment; that dislodgment could not be prevented except by physical restraints; and that physicians who had evaluated her condition were making thoughtful recommendations that the surgery was inappropriate. Judgment was affirmed.

Dietitians' activities in institutions where they are employed are not the only places where they may be held accountable for dietary advice given. Talking at a group meeting or even talking to a friend can carry the possibility of a malpractice suit. It is crucial to avoid statements that may be interpreted as treatment, prescription, or diagnosis. Preventive measures instrumental for the dietitian include choosing words carefully, provision of brief but clear documentation in patients' records, strict adherence to the code of ethics, and continual demonstration of high professional standards.

REFERENCES

American Dietetic Association. 1976. *Professional standards review procedure manual*. Chicago.

American Dietetic Association. 1977a. *Guidelines for consultant dietitians in long-term care facilities*. Chicago.

American Dietetic Association. 1977b. *Patient nutritional care in long-term care facilities*. Chicago.

American Dietetic Association. 1981. Position paper on recommended salaries and employment practices for members of the American Dietetic Association. *Journal of the American Dietetic Association* 78, no. 1:62–78.

American Dietetic Association. 1987. Position of the American Dietetic Association: Issues in feeding the terminally ill adult. *Journal of the American Dietetic Association* 87, no. 1:78–85.

American Dietetic Association. 1988. Code of ethics for the profession of dietetics. *Journal of the American Dietetic Association* 88, no. 12:1592–1596.

American Hospital Association. 1976. *Recording nutritional information in medical records*. Chicago.

Averill R.F. et al. 1996. Achieving short-term Medicare savings through the expansion of the prospective payment system. *Health Care Management Review* 21, no. 4:18–25.

Bailis, S.S. 1996. Prospective payment for skilled nursing care. *Nursing Home Journal* 46, no. 10:22–24.

Baird, P.M., and B. Jacobs. 1981. Malpractice: Your day in court. *Food Management* 16, no. 2:41–43.

Consultant Dietitians in Health Care Facilities: ADA Practice Group. 1987. *Dietary regulations for skilled nursing facilities: A comparison of the state regulations and the federal conditions of participation*. Pensacola, FL: Ross Laboratories.

Gallagher-Allred, C.R. 1992. *OBRA: A challenge and an opportunity for nutrition care*. Columbus, OH: Ross Products Division, Abbott Laboratories.

Joint Commission on Accreditation of Healthcare Organizations. 1997. *Comprehensive accreditation manual for hospitals*. Oak Brook Terrace, IL.

McCarthy, C.M. 1988. DRGs: Five years later. *New England Journal of Medicine* 318:1683–1686.

Michigan Department of Public Health. 1985. *Rules and regulations for nursing homes*. Lansing, MI.

Neville, J.N., and J.B. Tower. 1988. President's page: Plans for update of the role delineation studies. *Journal of the American Dietetic Association* 88, no. 3:356–357.

Newman, D. 1973. *Organization design: An analytical approach to the structuring of organization*. London: Edward Arnold.

Parks, S.C., and P.M. Kris-Etherton. 1982. Practitioners view dietetic roles for the 1980s. *Journal of the American Dietetic Association* 80:574–576.

Purtilo, R.B., and C.K. Cassel. 1981. *Ethical dimensions in the health care profession*. Philadelphia: W.B. Saunders.

Schiller, M.R. 1988. Ethical issues in nutrition care. *Journal of the American Dietetic Association* 88, no. 1:13–15.

Studebaker, M.E. 1988. The ethics of artificial feeding. *New England Journal of Medicine* 319:306.

Tancredi, L.R. 1974. *Ethics of health care*. Washington, DC: National Academy of Science.

U.S. Department of Health and Human Services, Health Care Financing Administration. 1983. *Medicare program: Prospective payment for Medicare inpatient hospital services*. Federal Register 48(171), 39752–39886.

U.S. Department of Health and Human Services, Health Care Financing Administration. 1987. *Medicare program: Payment adjustment for sole community hospitals*. Federal Register 52 (157), 30362-30368.

Welch, P. et al. 1988. Consulting dietitians in nursing homes: Time in role functions and perceived problems. *Journal of the American Dietetic Association* 88, no. 1:29–34.

CHAPTER 5

Functions of Management

Management functions are discussed throughout the text as applied to specific areas in the management of a medical food service operation. The purpose of this chapter is to provide a sense of cohesiveness to what is conceptualized as the functions of management and to promote managerial responsibility for implementation of functions through leadership and employee motivation.

CLASSIFICATION OF MANAGERIAL FUNCTIONS

Management scholars have not reached agreement on what functions are fundamental to the management process. As illustrated in Figure 5–1, fundamental functions leading to goal achievement are classified into five categories (Terry 1978). Note in particular the four functions of management that are included in each of the five combinations: planning, organizing, directing, and controlling. Staffing, listed in two combinations, is considered a part of organizing because management allocates human resources. Actuating and coordinating are involved in carrying out the planning and organizing functions through the efforts of subordinates. Representing and motivating are accomplished through leadership because managerial practices have an impact on human behavior.

Planning

Planning involves identifying future activities that will promote the objectives and goals of the department. There are short-range and long-range goals. Plans for the next day, the next week, the next month, or every year are considered short-range. The food service manager should promote short-range planning to the lowest possible level. For example, the chef or head cook must plan for production and service (using a production worksheet) at least one day in advance. Long-range planning may involve periods of time up to 10 years or more. Plans should be in writing and reflected on the capital budget if large sums of funding are required. Long-range plans must be flexible enough to accommodate any technological and economic changes and other external conditions that may develop over a period of time.

Organizing

Organizing is the dividing of work activity for the purpose of meeting objectives and goals of the department and the organization. The result of organization is an orderly structuring of roles and responsibilities necessary to perform the various work activities. To perform the organizing function, the food service director must know what resources are available and the necessary interrelationships required in getting the job done. (See Chapter 3 for organization and design of food service departments.)

The most valuable resource, and the one requiring a large portion of the manager's attention, is the human resource. In organizing the various tasks and activities, consideration is given to the type of employee required to perform the function, based on experience, skills, and interest. Smooth organization depends on the relationship of the employee to the assigned job, the interrelationship of employees in a designated unit, and the relationship of one unit to another within the food service department.

As a result of organizing efforts, lines of communication, decision making, and authority emerge. Organization charts are used to provide visual displays of the levels within the department, divisions, units, sections, and titles associated with each.

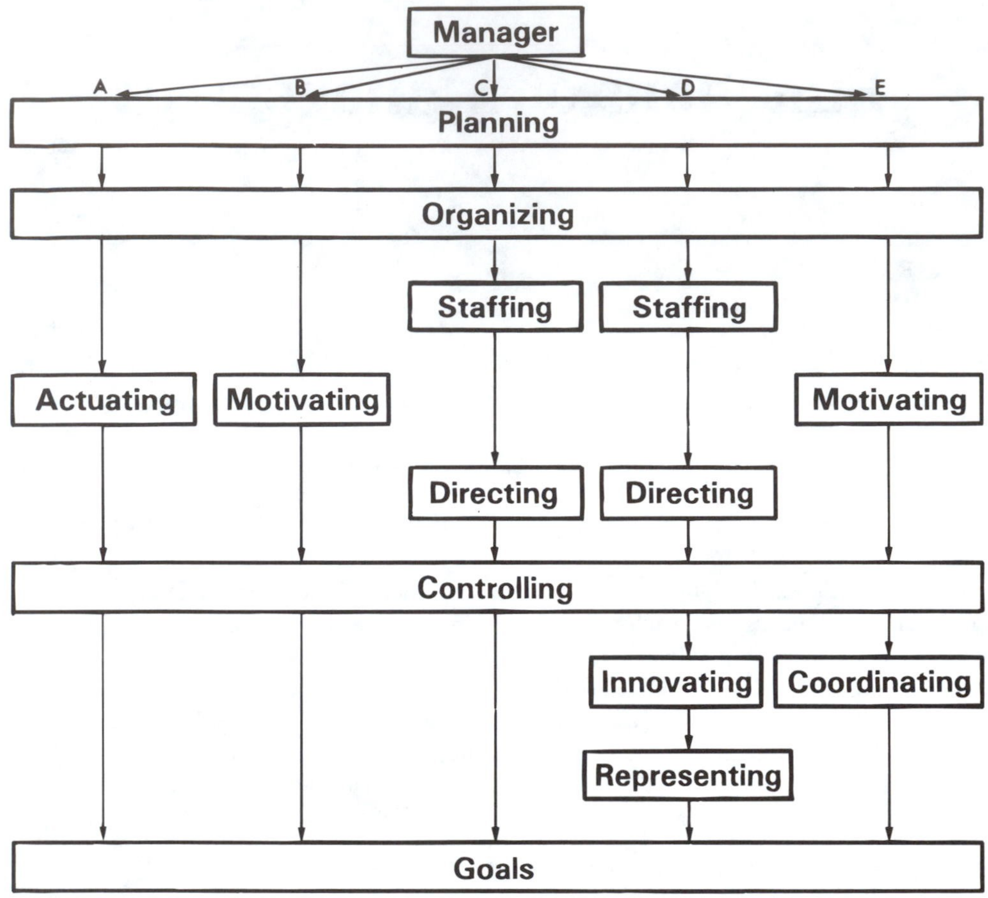

Figure 5–1 Five Combinations of Fundamental Functions Making Up the Management Process. From top to bottom, category **A** consists of planning, organizing, actuating, and controlling; **B**, planning, organizing, motivating, and controlling; **C**, planning, organizing, staffing, directing, and controlling; **D**, planning, organizing, staffing, directing, controlling, innovating, and representing; **E**, planning, organizing, motivating, controlling, and coordinating. *Source:* Data from G. Terry, *Principles of Management*, © 1960, Richard D. Irwin.

Directing

Directing is the coordinating, integrating, guiding, and initialing of subordinates' efforts in such a way that objectives and goals of both the department and the employee are met. In carrying out the directing functions, the manager must assign tasks, give orders, train, and supervise work activity. In directing the work of others, the manager must provide all necessary information and the proper tools and equipment to get the job done effectively. Some of the managerial tools that are helpful in carrying out this function are job descriptions and job standards. Good direction is important if employees are to know what is expected of them. It is also important to realize that the work is done through human effort and that the methods used in directing may have a negative effect on employee morale. The manager must determine the most appropriate leadership approach to use.

Controlling

Controlling is a process of determining whether planned activities are carried out. In carrying out the control functions, a manager must know what was planned and the goals and standards that the plan must meet. To determine whether results are in line with plans, measurable standards must be in use. With an established criteria (job standards), comparison of performance against standards can be made. When a discrepancy is found between the expected and actual performance, it will be necessary to assess the significance of the differential. If the difference proves significant, corrective action must be taken. The corrective action taken should not be of a punitive nature but aimed at improving performance and promoting good human relations.

Hypothetical Example of Management Functions

Susan Doe is director of dietetics at a 350-bed hospital. In view of the current economic climate, the hospital administrator asked Susan to develop ideas for generating revenue. She conducted a feasibility study and submitted a proposal for operating a moderately expensive commercial restaurant, accessible to all visitors entering the hospital. The employee/visitor cafeteria, located in a remote area, would continue operation. The projected revenue and potential public relations were primary incentives for administrative approval. Susan used the four principles of management discussed previously to carry out the project.

Planning

Susan used key personnel in the department to assist with details of planning and major decision making. Objectives and goals were clarified to ensure congruence with those of the department and the hospital. Tasks to be completed prior to the opening date were determined and assigned, such as remodeling of the proposed area, writing policies and procedures, purchasing equipment, and menu planning (the hub of the operation). Susan used the PERT technique (see Chapter 8) to ensure timely completion of the project.

Organizing

During this phase, Susan analyzed all functions to be performed, and divided work according to positions. She developed job specifications, job descriptions, and job standards. Staffing decisions were made regarding whether to hire new employees or train and use current staff. Salary scales were determined based on experience and skills required for each position. Lines of communication (in an organization chart) were established based on position and responsibility. The necessary equipment and tools to support functions were purchased, and printed menus were ordered.

Directing

The project was completed within the allotted time. Employees were hired or transferred from main production and service areas. Susan spent time coordinating all activities, such as orientation, training, and supervision of work. The restaurant opened for business.

Controlling

Susan used measurable tools (job standards) to monitor quality and quantity of work. Susan remained flexible during the initial phase and took corrective action when necessary, using the feedback loop (see Chapter 1) to ensure customer satisfaction.

LEADERSHIP

Leading and managing are not synonymous, although the terms are used interchangeably. Simply being a manager, even a good manager, does not necessarily make someone a leader. The distinction, clearly drawn by Albanese (1975), implies that people follow managers because their job description requires them to follow; people follow leaders voluntarily and for reasons of their own choosing. The following discussion attempts to distinguish the types of behavior exhibited by managers and leaders within organizations.

Management Defined

Management is the accountability to formulate and achieve the objectives of the organization. A manager has legal authority, within the organization, to plan, organize, direct, and control.

Leadership Defined

Leadership is the responsibility to represent the needs and goals of employees and to help them achieve what they want. A leader deals in emotions, excites camaraderie and unity, and guides vague notions into concrete actions. Leadership is generally recognized as the art of influencing and directing people in a manner that wins their obedience, confidence, respect, and enthusiastic cooperation in achieving a common objective. According to Lester (1981), leaders are self-starters, seeking out opportunity for making a change in the organization, rather than waiting for opportunity to come knocking at the office door.

The term *leader* is never found on the organization chart, except maybe as group leader. No one is officially known as the leader of one department or the other. But the term *manager* is frequently used to describe a position on an organization chart. The reason may be that there is more consensus of what a manager is or does, such as planning, organizing, directing, and controlling. A leader is not officially appointed by an organization; a leader asserts herself or himself despite organizational constraints. One becomes a leader through recognition by superiors, peers, and subordinates.

Formal and Informal Leaders

In every organization there is the formal manager, designated on the organization chart, with legal authority. Then there is the informal leader with no legal authority, but one who has a great deal of power and influence within the organization. For the individual who wants to be effective as a manager and leader, one must be aware of where organization leaders are, both formal and informal. When support is needed for introducing change, one must make sure that the change is accepted by the informal leader, and that he or she will persuade others to cooperate.

Characteristics of Managers and Leaders

Managers have the potential for becoming leaders. The degree to which an individual functions as both a manager and a leader depends on the personal attitudes toward goals, and the organizational climate. According to Zaleznik (1977), managers are basically different types of people, and the work conditions favorable to the growth of one may be inimical to the other. Some of the major characteristics of managers and leaders are discussed below.

Attitude Toward Goals

Managers tend to adopt impersonal, if not passive, attitudes toward goals. Leaders are active instead of reactive; they shape ideas rather than respond to them. In essence, leaders adopt a personal and active attitude toward goals.

Conception of Work

Where managers act to limit choices, leaders develop fresh approaches to long-standing problems and open issues for new options. Consequently, leaders create excitement in work. Leaders work from high-risk positions, often seeking out danger, especially when opportunity and reward appear high. In other words, they are not afraid to rock the boat. For managers, the instinct for survival dominates their need for risk and their ability to tolerate mundane, practical work to assist their survival.

Relations with Others

Managers prefer to work with people; they avoid solitary work because it makes them anxious. The need to seek out others with whom to work and collaborate stands out as an important characteristic of managers. The manager communicates with his or her subordinates by using signals instead of messages. One reason the manager does this is that signals are inclusive and subject to reinterpretation should people become angry or upset, whereas messages involve the direct consequences that some people will not like. Messages are often referred to in less emotional terms, such as unscrupulous or detached. In contrast, leaders attract strong feelings of identity, such as love or hate.

The satisfaction of leadership comes from helping others get things done and changed, and not from getting personal credit for doing and changing things. Have you ever worked for someone who took credit for your creative and innovative ideas? Are you guilty of this kind of relationship with your subordinates? An affirmative answer to either question indicates poor leadership.

Self-Image

Managers see themselves as conservators and regulators of the existing state of affairs within the organization. Perpetuating and strengthening the existing organization enhances a manager's sense of worth. Leaders tend to feel a separation from their environment. They may work in environments, but they never belong to them. Their sense of who they are does not depend on membership, work roles, or social indicators of identity.

Leadership Styles

The style of leadership has a direct influence on productivity and human relations, making the difference between an effective and an ineffective organization.

Theory X and Theory Y

The theories developed by Douglas McGregor (1960) are basic assumptions to guide a manager's strategy in managing employees. Management practices that are consistent with theory X are commonly classified as those of an autocratic leader; those that are consistent with theory Y are classified as belonging to a democratic leader.

The autocratic leader uses force and position of authority to get others to do as he or she directs. The subordinate has no part or very little part in influencing decisions. This leader often takes credit for accomplishments and puts blame for failure on others. This style of management tends to lose its effectiveness after the physiological needs of mankind have been met, because the manager is not concerned with the human elements involved.

The democratic leader seeks to lead mainly by persuasion and example, rather than by force, fear, or power. He or she encourages participation in decision making and seeks to meet the objectives of the worker as well as those of the organization. The style encourages the use of certain factors such as responsibility, delegation of work, and self-control in the work environment.

McGregor felt that the attitude of the manager was likely to have an effect on the attitudes and behavior of the employees. A manager with theory X assumptions believes the following:

- Work is inherently distasteful to most people.
- Most people lack ambition and have little desire for responsibility, and thus prefer to be directed.
- Most people have little capacity for creativity in solving work-related problems.
- Most people must be closely controlled and often coerced to achieve organizational objectives.

In contrast, a manager with theory Y assumptions has the following beliefs:

- Work is as natural as play, if conditions are favorable.
- Self-control is often indispensable in achieving organizational goals.
- The capacity for creativity in solving organizational problems is widely distributed in the population.
- People can be self-directed and creative at work if properly motivated.

The manager with theory X assumptions generally ends up with theory X employees. Those same employees are likely to become theory Y employees when placed in an environment with theory Y assumptions in practice. Put another way, employees live up to their expectations.

Boss-Centered and Subordinate-Centered Leadership

The autocratic-democratic dichotomy presents problems for the manager who wants to be democratic in his or her relations with subordinates and at the same time maintain the necessary authority and control in the organization. To assist managers faced with this dilemma, Tannenbaum and Schmidt (1973) developed a leadership pattern featuring a continuum of possible leadership behavior. Each type of action is related to the degree of authority used by the boss and to the amount of freedom available to his or her subordinates in reaching decisions. The actions at one extreme characterize the manager who maintains a high degree of control, whereas those at the other extreme characterize the manager who releases a high degree of control. Neither extreme is absolute; authority and freedom are never without their limitations.

The basic thesis is that the successful leader is one who is aware of those forces that are most relevant to his or her behavior at any one time and is able to behave accordingly.

Regardless of the leadership style employed, it should be based on sensitivity and understanding for human relations and the tasks to be performed.

BEYOND TRADITIONAL LEADERSHIP: EMPLOYEE EMPOWERMENT

The organization of medical facilities, as we know it, is undergoing drastic changes. The status quo of layers and layers of management is no longer in existence. Organizations have been flattened by eliminating midlevel managers and requiring managers to expand their areas of responsibility. For example, the food service director may also direct the department of housekeeping, or vice versa. Other areas, such as security, have also come under the direction of food service.

If these changes are taking place on the management level, it would be prudent for the food service director to take a look at positions in his or her own department. Currently in food service the jobs and job titles have become specialized to the point that employees are quick to say, "That's not my job." Why not consider job rotation or cross-training on all levels so that flexibility is available to managers in getting the work done?

Employees must accept cross-training as beneficial to them, such as letting management know that they are qualified for more responsible tasks, that it allows employees to express their creativity, or that it may lead to promotions and extra pay. If committed employees are to become a reality, they must understand the rationale of the process and how it will benefit them.

Management Insecurity

Food service directors and other members of the management team must first deal with their own feelings, values, and behaviors before they attempt to change the work climate within the department. They must be willing to examine their thought patterns, analyze their behavior toward employees, and become committed to being a facilitator rather than a "boss." Some directors may fear a loss of power if management tools such as employee work schedules are not completed by them. According to Zoglio (1994), if you can mentally define power as the ability to influence others to join you in accomplishing goals, you will be able to embrace participative leadership with less fear of diminished power. A good beginning is an ability to answer in a positive manner the following questions:

- Are you firmly committed to employee empowerment by allowing employees to participate fully in decisions that affect them?
- Are you willing to be open with employees by telling them the truth; by telling them exactly what is going on within the organization?
- Are you willing to give up old practices that you are comfortable with and take on new strategies that may present risks for you?
- Are you willing to "take a back seat" and allow employees an opportunity to excel on their own or to make an occasional mistake?
- Are you willing to allow employees to take over tasks that have been in your domain (e.g., making out work schedules for other workers in the department)?
- Are you willing to listen to employees rather than making all decisions on your own?
- Are you willing to be patient and allow employees an opportunity to solve problems on their own?
- Are you willing to give up punitive measures when employees make a mistake in favor of coaching to facilitate problem solving?

In addition to the above questions, you might also ask all managerial personnel to respond to the questionnaire on motivating the contemporary worker (see Exhibit 5–1 later in this chapter). You have probably noticed that the work ethics and values of the contemporary employee are quite different from those of the older employee. In addition, you may have a number of temporary or contingent employees on staff who require a different managerial approach.

After convincing yourself that change is needed, you must convince employees that change is necessary. Do they trust you? Will they listen to what you are saying and then wait to observe your actions? Have employees been surprised by past organizational behavior, such as downsizing or massive layoff without any prior notice? Keep in mind that unless employees are given an opportunity to participate in decision making, they are likely to resist the change.

Your efforts to change the organizational climate may or may not be accepted by the employees. You must build trust before employees commit themselves to the process. Be candid with employees. Tell them why changes are taking place. After all, employees may be more concerned with their own personal needs than with organizational needs. Employees need to understand how the change will be beneficial to both the organization and to them. Therefore, your first order of business is to seek goal congruency (see detailed discussion in Chapter 2).

Start by developing a departmental purpose statement. Let the employees know that the bottom line is patient/resident outcome and how commitment to that purpose is beneficial to them as well as the organization. If your department is well organized, standards have also been developed. This will be most important when the process of employee empowerment is introduced. Allow your employees to share in the vision that you have for the department, share standards of operation, and seek acceptance and congruency.

Employee Involvement

Communicate with employees, and allow them to have an input in your plans for change. One effective means of communication is to meet with all employees in a unit or department at the same time. This is possible if work schedules are planned so that on at least one day of the week all employees are on duty. At some facilities, this day is used for meetings, training, and any other special activities, such as special assignments.

If one wishes to create a department that is committed to employee empowerment, one must be able to influence employees' thinking processes. This ability allows employees to share the same vision that you have. A meeting of all employees at the same time can serve this purpose. Find out how and what your employees are thinking and feeling about the organization and the work environment by asking the following questions:

- How do you feel about working at this facility? (List the good and bad features.)
- Would you describe your work as "working for" or "working with" the company?
- How would you feel if this facility was reported as one of the worst health care facilities in the state or one of the best health care facilities in the state?
- How do you feel when we pass all external inspections, such as sanitation inspections, inspections by the Joint Commission, or others?
- How do you feel when we fail to pass all external inspections?
- Are you proud to tell friends and acquaintances where you are employed?
- What are some of the good features about the working conditions at this facility?
- What conditions would you change about the work environment if you had the power?
- How would you feel about having more authority to make decisions about your work?

Throughout the text, emphasis has been placed on the human resources within the organization. For example, in Chapter 2 there is a discussion of goal congruency that purports that individual and organization goals should strive for a harmonous relationship. Also, management by objectives stresses the need for input from both the employee and management on the assessment of performance in efforts to reach goal congruency.

In Chapter 3, Frederick Taylor's "economic man" theory is no longer applicable in terms of employee motivation. The theme throughout the chapter promotes the theory that the most valuable resource in the organization is the human resource. Role delineation, as discussed in Chapter 4, emphasizes the dual or multiple roles that are prevalent in health care facilities.

Leaders are moving toward theory Y in the workplace instead of the close supervision expressed by theory X. The contemporary leader relates more closely to theory Y and believes that it is possible to create an environment in which people work because they want to rather than need to; where rewards, rather than punishments, get the job done. As Carlisle (1995) reports in an interview with McGregor, he continues to operate as plant manager in a "superorganized" manner. McGregor practices what he proposes in theory Y. This chapter continues by promoting the need for understanding what factors affect employee motivation, and how to effectively communicate both organizational and individual thought patterns as related to the work environment.

The movement toward employee empowerment is a continuous process. It will not happen overnight. The process requires employee involvement, listening to employee ideas and opinions, communicating the goals and objectives of the organization and seeking congruency, and communicating standards relating to continuous quality improvement of patient/resident outcome.

Executives want to know how long it takes to change a company and its culture. The textbook answer is clear. Most companies say five to seven years (Jick 1995). The Michigan Consolidated Gas Company (MichCon) strategy for change began in 1989 and is an ongoing process of continuous improvement (Atlas et al. 1996). The change strategy used at MichCon was to create an atmosphere for total participation, choice, and continual organizational leasing; to create, communicate, and focus energy on a compelling vision; and to develop self-awareness and positive self-regard for all employees. To increase organizationwide business literacy, a necessary prerequisite to empowered, customer-focused decision making, MichCon introduced interactive learning maps covering the competitive environment, the financial side of the business, customer expectations, and the company's growth plan. As of 1995, two thirds of the employees had experienced the maps. Ongoing process improvement, through various tools, continues to be a key focus of the change effort. Current focus is on the development of work units to operationalize the company's strategic plans further.

Again, the optimum method of strategic planning is to involve the entire company in order to make effective, significant changes in the environment. Financial resources are required for some changes, but there is no financial cost involved in treating employees as human resources. Why wait if you can see changes coming in your organization? At least you can be somewhat prepared for the change.

MOTIVATION AND THE EMPLOYEE

Motivation refers to the way external forces (managerial practices, organizational climate, and the like) affect human behavior on the job. Because motives are an internal state, motivation is inherent in the individual when he or she first enters the workplace. It is management's responsibility to elicit, rather than instill, motivation. An understanding of what motivated the individual to seek work is the first step to understanding employee motivation. Attempts are made during the selection process, by using sophisticated tools such as psychological tests, to screen individuals so that the employee fits the position. Yet employees with identical skills and abilities will perform at different levels of quantity and quality. The problem is not new, but the approaches to motivation have changed over the years.

Approaches to Motivation

Traditional Theory of Motivation

Frederick Taylor's approach to motivation, as discussed in Chapter 3, was that of the classic "economic man." He believed that wage incentives were enough to offset any other employee motives and that high productivity would continue as long as output was associated with the amount of earnings. The theory worked for a while because it met the needs of the employees at that time. The evaluation of management theory, however, has proven the economic theory to be a less viable form of motivating employees. For example, federal law now mandates a minimum wage for each employee, regardless of production level. As long as the employee remains on the job, a certain degree of economic security is guaranteed. In addition, the employee is further protected with unemployment benefits should he or she be dismissed.

The Hawthorne Studies

The Hawthorne studies, discussed in Chapter 3, proved to be a major breakthrough in terms of employee motivation. It was concluded that productivity increased for the women in the relay assembly room as a result of the social relationships and improved work conditions. Men in the test room, however, established work norms to which they all conformed. Despite wage incentives for piecework, productivity was not increased. The Hawthorne studies were the beginning of the human relations era in management. They proved that work incentives were not primarily based on economics.

Maslow's Need Hierarchy

Maslow theorized that the needs of humans exist in a hierarchical order and that one need must be met before another emerges. According to Maslow (1954) needs are classified (Figure 5–2) from lowest to highest in the following order:

1. Physiological—This classification refers to basic survival needs such as food, drink, clothing, shelter, and sex.
2. Safety—This refers to both physical safety and job safety (job security).
3. Belongingness and love—As lower needs are met, the worker expresses concern for social relationships with other employees.
4. Esteem—This classification refers to self-respect, recognition, prestige, and other measures of esteem in the work environment.
5. Self-actualization—This is the highest classification of needs and is considered general in that the need varies with different individuals. It refers to the desire to become what one is capable of becoming. The need is rarely met.

Maslow's theory can help managers to understand employee motives, both their complexity and their importance. Because each employee may be at a different level of need, the manager must get to know employees on an individual basis in an effort to meet both personal and organizational goals. It is important to know what satisfies a worker and also the sources of dissatisfaction.

Herzberg's Theory of Motivation

The two-factor model of motivation is based on motivators (satisfiers) and hygiene factors (dissatisfiers). According to

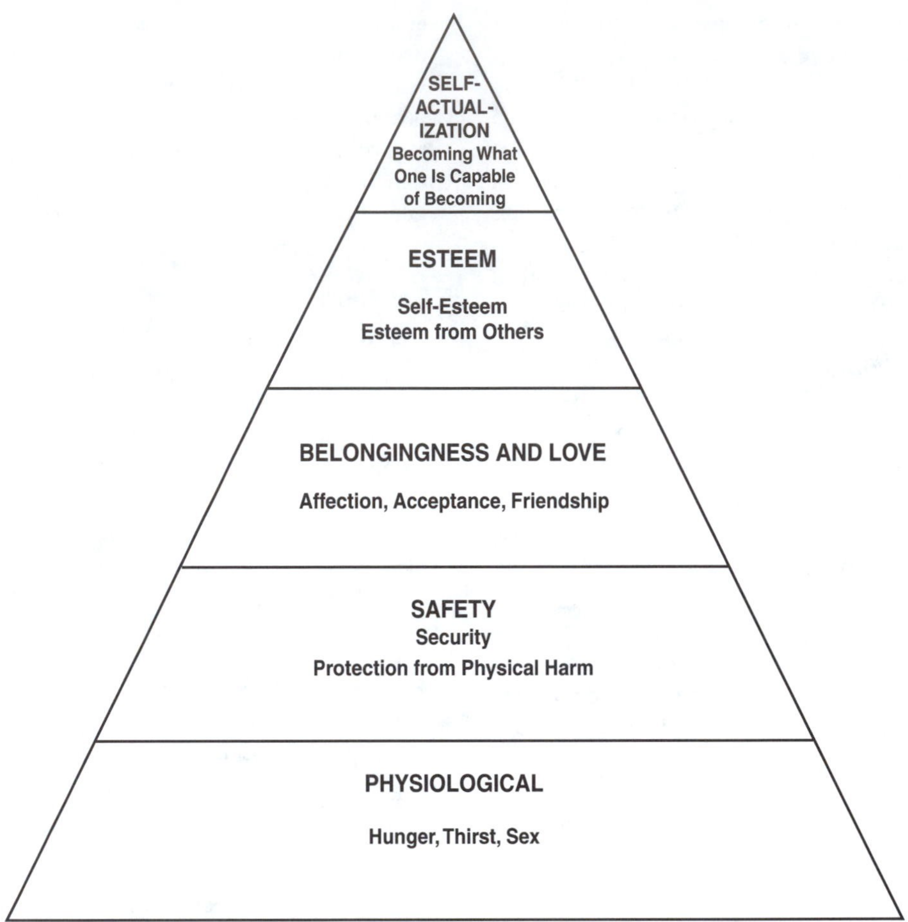

Figure 5–2 Hierarchy of Needs. *Source:* DATA (FOR DIAGRAM) BASED ON HIERARCHY OF NEEDS from MOTIVATION AND PERSONALITY, 3RD ED. by ABRAHAM H. MASLOW. Revised by Robert Frager, James Fadiman, Cynthia McReynolds, and Ruth Cox. Copyright 1954, © 1987 by Harper & Row, Publishers, Inc. Copyright © 1970 by Abraham H. Maslow. Reprinted by permission of HarperCollins Publishers, Inc.

Herzberg (1974), there are especially satisfying and therefore potentially motivating job situations that differ from especially dissatisfying job situations (Table 5–1). Satisfying situations include opportunities to experience achievement, responsibility, recognition, and advancement in types of work that are interesting to the individual. Dissatisfying work situations include incompetent supervision, inadequate salary, poor working conditions, unfair company policies, inadequate employee benefits, and other such negative work-related factors. If hygiene factors are missing, dissatisfaction may develop; however, the mere presence of hygiene factors will not guarantee satisfaction. It is not enough for the motivation factor to be fulfilled if the hygiene factor is lacking. Fulfillment of both factors is necessary for high employee job satisfaction.

Table 5–1 Herzberg's Two-Factor Model of Motivation

Hygiene Factors	*Motivators*
Incompetent supervision	Achievement
Inadequate salary	Responsibility
Poor work conditions	Recognition
Inadequate benefits	Advancement
Unfair company policies	Type of work

Source: Adapted from F. Herzberg, Motivation-Hygiene Profile: Pinpointing What Ails the Organization, *Organizational Dynamics*, Vol. 3, pp. 18–29, 1974.

Motivation and Work Values

Some of the traditional approaches, especially those relating to money or wage incentives, are no longer a major motivational factor. It requires more than the carrot-and-stick approach to motivate employees. The worker entering the work force today is seeking interesting, challenging work, with opportunities for advancement. The average worker seeks immediate gratification and is reluctant to work up the corporate ladder in the traditional manner.

Motivating the Contemporary Employee

One of the biggest managerial problems centers around contemporary employees and their differing work values. Motivating the employee to do more than put in eight hours on the job requires an understanding of people and the different values they hold regarding work. Equally important, managers must be aware of their own values. The questionnaire shown in (Exhibit 5–1) can be used to make a quick assessment of a manager's orientation toward employee motivation. According to Howe and

Exhibit 5–1 Instruction for Assessing Managerial Orientation Toward Employee Values

Assessing Your Orientation Toward Employee Values

1. Organizational success is usually due more to chance than systematic planning.
   Strongly disagree 1 2 3 4 5 6 7 Strongly agree
2. When people advance in the company, it is often because of "who they know" rather than how well they perform.
   Strongly disagree 1 2 3 4 5 6 7 Strongly agree
3. There is little luck involved in running a department effectively.
   Strongly disagree 1 2 3 4 5 6 7 Strongly agree
4. I exercise a great deal of self-control in my position.
   Strongly disagree 1 2 3 4 5 6 7 Strongly agree
5. It is important to provide frequent feedback to employees on how well they are performing.
   Strongly disagree 1 2 3 4 5 6 7 Strongly agree
6. My ideas are rarely well understood by others in the company.
   Strongly disagree 1 2 3 4 5 6 7 Strongly agree
7. There is no such thing as "one right way" of doing things.
   Strongly disagree 1 2 3 4 5 6 7 Strongly agree
8. I often make decisions based upon insufficient information.
   Strongly disagree 1 2 3 4 5 6 7 Strongly agree
9. As a manager, I enjoy working in unclear situations.
   Strongly disagree 1 2 3 4 5 6 7 Strongly agree
10. Most people in an organization work because they have to, not because they want to.
    Strongly disagree 1 2 3 4 5 6 7 Strongly agree
11. It is often necessary to "step on some toes" in order to get the job done.
    Strongly disagree 1 2 3 4 5 6 7 Strongly agree
12. I try not to let my feelings get in the way of business.
    Strongly disagree 1 2 3 4 5 6 7 Strongly agree
13. I often worry about what my job will be in five years.
    Strongly disagree 1 2 3 4 5 6 7 Strongly agree
14. I have a strong degree of loyalty to my company.
    Strongly disagree 1 2 3 4 5 6 7 Strongly agree
15. Job security is very important to me.
    Strongly disagree 1 2 3 4 5 6 7 Strongly agree

Source: Reprinted by permission of the publisher, from *Management Review,* September/1979 © 1979. American Management Association, New York. All rights reserved.

Mindell (1979), the instrument measures five major value dimensions:

1. Locus of control. Both traditional and contemporary managers believe that they have control over events through their decisions; that success cannot be left to chance, it must be planned; and that advancement of subordinates depends on achievement rather than politics, over which they have a great deal of control. Statements 1, 2, and 3 in Exhibit 5–1 represent three measures of locus of control. The ideal manager of either type of employee (contemporary or traditional) would strongly disagree with 1 and 2, and strongly agree with 3.
2. Self-esteem. The ideal manager should recognize employee accomplishments by providing feedback as a measure to preserve and enhance individual self-esteem. Managers who exercise self-control, who believe that their ideas are creative, understood, and accepted, and who believe that feedback is important tend to have high self-esteem. Managers who have a mistrust of employees and who appear critical, annoyed, or irritated with those with different ideas or values tend to score low in self-esteem. Items 3, 5, and 6 in Exhibit 5–1 are concerned with self-esteem. The ideal manager would score high and would strongly agree with 4 and 5 and would strongly disagree with 6.
3. Tolerance of ambiguity. Managers holding contemporary values can and often want to function in unstructured, ambiguous situations; believe that no problem is too complex to be solved; and strongly believe that there is more than one right way of doing things. Items 7, 8, and 9 relate to ambiguity. The ideal contemporary manager would strongly agree with each item. The ideal traditional manager would strongly disagree.
4. Social judgment. The contemporary manager is characterized by social perceptiveness, sensitivity, empathy, social intelligence, and social insight. Contemporary employees value good interpersonal relationships and personal recognition, and therefore work best for managers with these values. The contemporary manager believes that it is possible to create an environment where people work because they want to, rather than need to; where workers' feelings contribute to, rather than detract from, task accomplishment; and where rewards, rather than punishments, get the job done. Items 10, 11, and 12 refer to social judgment. The ideal contemporary manager would strongly disagree with each item. The more traditional manager would tend to agree with them, because he or she displays these characteristics only moderately.
5. Risk taking. Managers who seek excitement and changes and enjoy taking chances are more likely to have contemporary values than those who are cautious, consider matters very carefully, and are reluctant to take risks. The contemporary manager may be regarded by the traditional manager as impulsive and erratic. The contemporary manager has low dependency needs; is more concerned with the immediate future than with a long-term career; is loyal first to personal needs and desires over those of the organization; and is only moderately concerned with job security. Items 13, 14, and 15 measure risk taking. The ideal contemporary manager would generally disagree with all three. The converse is so for the ideal traditional manager.

As more and more contemporary employees enter the work force, there will be an increased demand for managers who understand their values.

REFERENCES

Albanese, R. 1975. *Management toward accountability for performance*. Homewood, IL: Richard D. Irwin.

Atlas, W. et al. 1996. Interview at Michigan Consolidated Gas Company, Detroit.

Carlisle, A.E. 1995. McGregor. *Organizational Dynamics* (autumn):68–78.

Herzberg, F. 1974. Motivation-hygiene profile: Pinpointing what ails the organization. *Organizational Dynamics* 3:18–29.

Howe, R.J., and M.G. Mindell. 1979. The challenge of changing work values: Motivating the contemporary employee. *Management Review* 68, no. 9:51–55.

Jick, T.D. 1995. Accelerating change for competitive advantage. *Organizational Dynamics* (summer):77–82.

Lester, R.I. 1981. Leadership: Some principles and concepts. *Personnel Journal* 60, no. 11:868–870.

Maslow, A.H. 1954. *Motivation and personality*. New York: Harper & Row.

McGregor, D. 1960. *The human side of enterprise*. New York: McGraw-Hill.

Tannenbaum, R., and W.H. Schmidt. 1973. How to choose a leadership pattern. *Harvard Business Review* 51 no. 3:162–175, 178–180.

Terry, G. 1978. *Principles of management*. Homewood, IL: Richard D. Irwin.

Zaleznik, A. 1977. Managers and leaders: Are they different? *Harvard Business Review* 55, no. 3:67–78.

Zoglio, S.W. 1994. *The participative leader*. Homewood, IL: Richard D. Irwin.

Chapter 6

Effective Communication

Communication is the flow of information from a sender to a receiver. The purpose of communication is to convey meaning and promote understanding; therefore, the message should be clearly expressed in the appropriate language. However, the message may encounter a number of interferences during its travel. To reduce the number of bottlenecks, a manager needs to understand possible causes and ways to overcome communication blocks.

COMMUNICATION CHANNELS

The three major channels used for communication are upward, downward, and horizontal.

Upward Communication

Upward communication is the flow of information from a subordinate to a superior. As a manager, you receive upward communication from your employees, and you communicate upward to an administrator. In some organizations, there is a free flow of information, whereas in other organizations blockage occurs. The difference is the organizational climate and how conducive it is to facilitating and encouraging the free exchange of ideas.

Based on past experience, employees may be reluctant to disclose information to superiors. This is especially true if employees fear that disclosure may lead to punishment or retaliation in some way. The withholding of information, the failure to provide feedback, or the provision of distorted information can be costly for superiors. How often has an employee been heard to remark, "I am not sure if I should tell you this"? Why do employees conceal their true feelings? Does the manager become angry, emotionally upset, or defensive? The attitude of the superior and the degree of openness exhibited with employees have a definite bearing on the amount of upward communication.

According to Gemmill (1970), if the superior's control over the personal goals of a subordinate were decreased, then their fear of receiving a penalty for disclosure would decrease. Given the organization structure as it exists today, the superior has a high degree of control over subordinates in the form of firing, laying off, blocking promotions and salary increases, and holding back developmental assignments if the superior does not like what he or she hears. One way to elicit disclosure is through rewards. The more a superior rewards disclosure of feelings, opinions, and difficulties by subordinates, the more likely they will be to disclose them. Merely stating that there will be no punishment and that they should feel free to express their opinions is not enough. Words must be followed by action. For full disclosure, subordinates must know that they can express themselves without fear of reprisal and that they can look upon the superior as a source of help, rather than a powerful judge.

Downward Communication

Downward communication refers to information flow from the superior to the subordinate. Employees at the lowest level want to know what is going on in the workplace. The manager should make use of all available techniques to keep employees informed, including written memos, face-to-face contact, and regularly scheduled group meetings. According to Chase (1970), an element of good downward communication is the content of the message to be transmitted, as follows:

- The message must be accurate and true, whether it is good or bad news concerning the organization. When employees realize that the information is only partly accurate, they will tend to ignore future messages.

- The message must be both definite and specific in meaning. The message should state clearly why a certain position was taken. It must define all actions taken and what effects it will have on members of the organization.
- The message must be forceful. A manager who does not agree with or believe in a decision that has been made cannot expect his or her employees to believe in it.
- The message must be receiver oriented. Subordinates should not have any difficulty understanding how the message directly affects them.
- The message should not contain complexities. It should be stated as simply as possible. An employee will spend two hours trying to compute the number of vacation days to which he or she is entitled, but will not spend five minutes trying to figure out a management directive on how to reduce waste.
- The message should not contain hidden meanings. To avoid misunderstanding, it is advisable to explain briefly the developments leading up to the message.

Employees can spend a great deal of nonproductive time discussing rumors that may or may not have any merit. Effective downward communication can reduce this waste of time and reduce any anxiety associated with distorted messages.

Horizontal Communication

Horizontal communication refers to information flow from one department to another. In complex, open organizations, direct horizontal communication is encouraged. Koontz and O'Donnell (1974) suggest that proper safeguards of horizontal communication rest in an understanding among superiors. Although interdepartmental relationships are encouraged, subordinates should refrain from making commitments beyond their authority and should keep their superiors informed of their activities.

In medical food service operations, upward, downward, and horizontal communication channels are necessary to coordinate patient care activities. For the food service director and other administrative personnel, information flow is most often between other department heads. For the clinical staff, information may flow to nurses, physicians, and other members of the health care team.

FEEDBACK

Positive feedback lets an individual know that he or she is doing well; negative feedback identifies areas where improvement is necessary. Feedback is most helpful when it is provided as soon after the given situation as possible. Negative feedback should not be given in public, however. In an organizational climate where feedback is encouraged, both the superior and the subordinate must be willing to accept criticism. It is up to the superior to convince subordinates that feedback is welcomed, and that management will not retaliate against an employee for the disclosure of information. Giving and receiving feedback is critical to effective communication because it lets individuals know how others view them.

THE JOHARI WINDOW

The process of giving and receiving information can be demonstrated by use of the Johari window (Fisher 1982). Looking at the four cells, as shown in Figure 6–1, the two vertical columns represent the self and the two horizontal rows represent others. Column one contains "things I know about myself"; column two contains "things I do not know about myself." Row one contains "things that others know about me"; row two contains "things that the others do not know about me." Cell information changes as the level of mutual trust and the exchange of feedback vary.

Information in the arena cell is public and is characterized by a free and open exchange of information. The blind spot contains information that a person does not know about himself or herself, but that others know. A person communicates all kinds of information of which he or she is not aware but is picked up by others. The information may be communicated by what is said, the way it is said, or by management style. In the facade or hidden area there are things about a person that he or she knows but of which others are unaware. For one reason or another, this information is kept silent. One reason information is hidden may be fear of rejection if real feelings are known. The unknown area contains things that neither a person nor others know about the person. This material is below the surface, and one may never become aware of it. However, the material can become public knowledge through an exchange of information. Internal boundaries in all cells can move backward and forward or up and down as a consequence of giving or receiving feedback.

Enlarging the Arena

To improve communication, the arena must be made as large as possible. This is done by reducing either the blind spot or the hidden area (Figure 6–2). The blind spot is reduced by accepting feedback. The more self-disclosure and feedback one gives, the farther down one pursues the horizontal line. The ideal window, in which there is a large arena, suggests that a person's behavior is aboveboard and open. Little questioning is needed to understand what the person is trying to do or say. A large facade or hidden area describes a person who asks for information but never volunteers any. Such a person eventually evokes feelings of distrust. When a

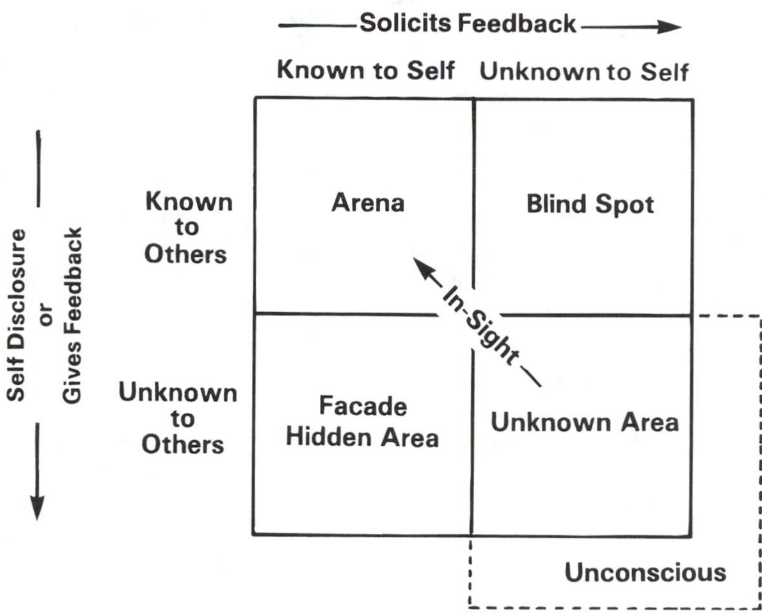

Figure 6–1 Johari Window. *Source:* Reprinted by permission of the publisher, from *Supervisory Management*, June/1982 © 1982. American Management Association, New York. All rights reserved.

person has a large blind spot, he or she gives feedback but cannot or will not accept it. A large unknown area represents a person who does not know much about herself or himself and about whom others do not know a great deal.

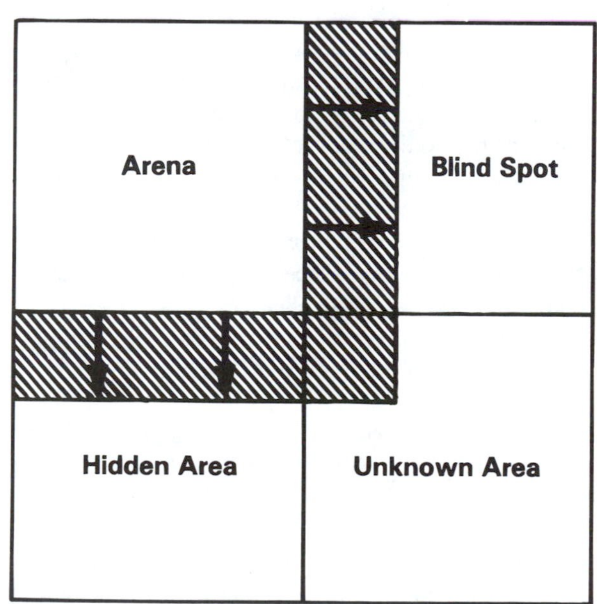

Figure 6–2 Johari Window: Enlarging the Arena. *Source:* Reprinted by permission of the publisher, from *Supervisory Management*, June/1982 © 1982. American Management Association, New York. All rights reserved.

Supervisory-Employee Relations

The goal of soliciting or giving feedback is to move information from the blind spot or facade into the arena, where it is available to everyone. As applied to relationships between a supervisor and an employee, the arena is composed of all activities performed by the employee and the supervisor (Figure 6–3). The blind spot holds those activities that the supervisor expects the employee to perform, but that the employee does not know he or she is expected to perform. The hidden area consists of activities performed by the employee. The supervisor does not know that the employee is performing these activities and does not expect them to be performed. The unknown area represents all activities that may be added or deleted from the employee's list of tasks and activities. Both the employee and the supervisor are unaware of the activities to be added or deleted. The goal of using this model is to increase the arena for both the supervisor and the employee.

A climate of mutual trust is conducive to feedback and results in effective communication. The Johari window, with the goal of increasing the size of the arena, is one way of promoting feedback that is objective and constructive.

BARRIERS TO COMMUNICATION

Effective communication is based on the free flow of information. An understanding of why a message does not get through should be a major concern. According to Strauss

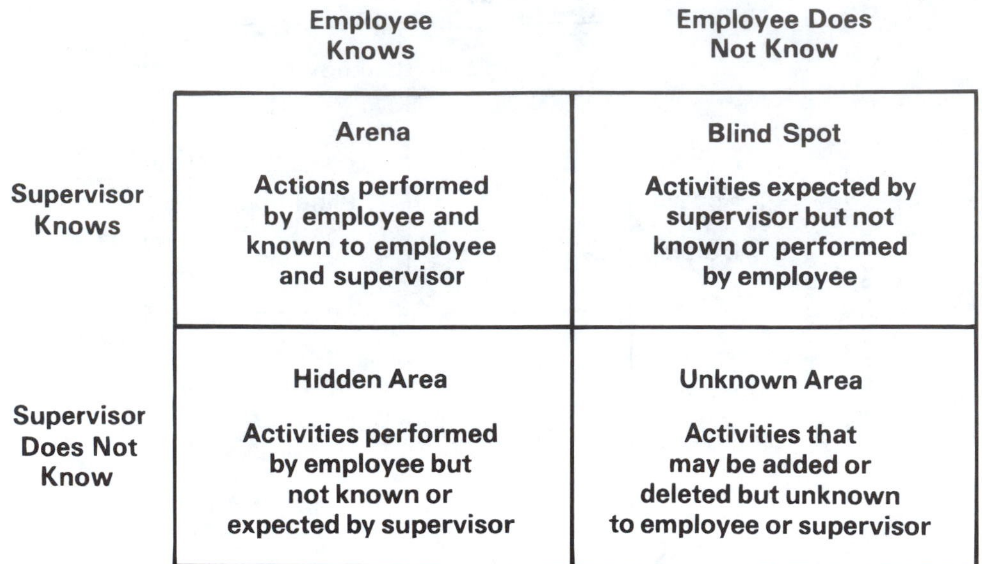

Employee Knows
Employee Does Not Know
Supervisor Knows
Supervisor Does Not Know
Arena
Actions performed by employee and known to employee and supervisor
Blind Spot
Activities expected by supervisor but not known or performed by employee
Hidden Area
Activities performed by employee but not known or expected by supervisor
Unknown Area
Activities that may be added or deleted but unknown to employee or supervisor

Figure 6–3 Johari Window: Supervisor-Employee Relations. *Source:* Reprinted by permission of the publisher, from *Supervisory Management* June/1982 © 1982. American Management Association, New York. All rights reserved.

and Sayles (1960), reasons for communication breakdowns are as follows:

- We hear what we expect to hear. What we hear is shaped by experience and background, and we reject messages that conflict.
- We have different perceptions. Our perceptions depend on previous experience.
- We evaluate the source. We evaluate the source not only in terms of our own background and experience, but also on how reliable we judge the source (sender) to be.
- Our emotional state conditions what we hear. When we are insecure, worried, or fearful, we hear and view messages as more threatening.
- We ignore information that conflicts with what we already know. Hearing that hard work leads to promotions conflicts with our knowledge that promotions are often based on favoritism.
- Words mean different things to different people. The use of words allows for discretion in interpretation.
- Words have symbolic meaning. For some employees a particular word may have a symbolic meaning that others overlook. For example, if the supervisor asks to see an employee in the office later in the day, one employee might feel important; another employee might feel threatened.

OVERCOMING BARRIERS TO COMMUNICATION

Perfect communication may not be attainable, but there are techniques that the manager can utilize in the day-to-day superior-subordinate relationship.

- Use feedback. Provide both positive and negative feedback when necessary. Observe nonverbal feedback, such as a nod of the head, puzzlement, anger, and body movement. Check on reception of messages with questions such as, "Do you understand?" "Is it clear?" and "Are there any questions?"
- Use face-to-face communication. This provides immediate feedback. Certain parts of the message can be emphasized, questions can be answered, and further explanation provided. For important messages, both the spoken word and the written word may be used.
- Be sensitive to the world of the receiver. Try to predict the impact of what is said on the receiver's feelings and attitudes.
- Be aware of symbolic meaning. If an employee resists or objects to a certain procedure, find out whether some symbolic meaning is attached.
- Time the deliverance of messages carefully. Employee conferences are often more effective at the end of the day.
- Reinforce words with action. Consistent reinforcement of words by action increases the likelihood that the message will be accepted.
- Use direct, simple language. Written communication should be as intelligible and readable as possible. In face-to-face communication, use words understood by the receiver. Avoid double talk and jargon that leaves the receiver with the feeling of "what did that mean?"

Developing good communication requires constant attention to channels of information flow, organizational climate, and day-to-day interpersonal behavior.

REFERENCES

Chase, A.B. 1970. How to make downward communication work. *Personnel Journal* (June):478–483.

Fisher, D.W. 1982. A model for better communication. *Supervisory Management* 27, no. 6:24–29.

Gemmill, G. 1970. Managing upward communication. *Personnel Journal* (February):107–110.

Koontz, H., and C. O'Donnell. 1974. *Essentials of management*. New York: McGraw-Hill.

Strauss, G., and L.R. Sayles. 1960. *Personnel: The human problems of management*. Englewood Cliffs, NJ: Prentice Hall.

CHAPTER 7

Decision Making

A decision is a choice among alternatives: to act or not to act in a given situation. The alternatives provided to the manager in a decision-making process may or may not be restrictive, depending on the nature aand the urgency of the decision. To illustrate, Braverman (1980) classifies decisions as programmable and unprogrammable.

TYPES OF DECISIONS

Programmable Decisions

Programmable decisions are decisions that occur with some frequency and are repetitive in nature. Programmable decisions, because they occur over and over again, can usually be solved without going through the decision-making process each time. As director of the food service operation, one is constantly faced with programmable decisions on a day-to-day basis. For example, when one decides to reduce the amount of food to prepare based on similar circumstances in the past, the decision maker is using past experience as the basis for decision making. However, as cautioned by Atchinson and Winston (1978), managers must take care to choose the appropriate programmed decision in situations that require new solutions. In the rush to make a decision, the situation confronted by a manager may resemble one for which there is an existing program. Other programmable decisions may be based on existing policies and procedures, requiring only minor changes based on environmental conditions.

Unprogrammable Decisions

Unprogrammable decisions are more complex and difficult to resolve. They are one-of-a-kind and will never recur in the same manner. No common solution can be applied to unprogrammable decision making because of the uniqueness of the situation. General procedures can be formulated and used, however. Some examples of unprogrammable decisions are those related to the present economic conditions, which may involve reorganization of the food service department as a result of reduced staffing, drastic changes in operating procedures, and embarking on a cooperative venture such as group food purchasing.

Decisions frequently result in a change of rules, policies, and procedures, or they may result in delay or inaction on the part of the decision maker. In both instances a decision has been made, because a decision to delay or not to act is as much a decision as the decision to act. Some managers use what is called snap decision making, based on judgment, intuition, and experience. Other managers make a choice among alternatives. One of the reasons for possible delay is a concern for the consequences of the decision. Some consequences are the acceptance or nonacceptance by those affected, the resulting social and psychological climate, and the profit or loss if the decision involves monetary values.

APPROACHES TO DECISION MAKING

The manager faced with a decision will have to decide on the most appropriate method to use. Although a number of approaches are available, the following discussion is limited to intuitive versus scientific, and individual versus group decision-making processes.

Intuitive Decision Making

When a manager uses intuition in decision making, the decision is based on past experience. The correctness of the decision will depend on whether the current situation is similar to one that has happened in the past. In medical food service, a manager is constantly involved in decision making. Most often, the decision must be made immediately, thus limiting the time for deliberation or the use of time-consuming analytical procedures. The amount of experience a manager has in certain situations, and the degree of learning from these experiences, will form a basis for the intuition used in making the decision. In other words, it can be stated that intuition comes from experience. Problems arise when the manager's experience is limited, when a current problem is misjudged to be similar to a situation in the past, when the situation is viewed as a new or unique problem with no immediate solution, and when the situation involves uncertainty and risk. Because a manager's reputation, prestige, and even job security may be affected by the number of correct decisions made, it is advisable for managers to seek and use additional methods for decision making.

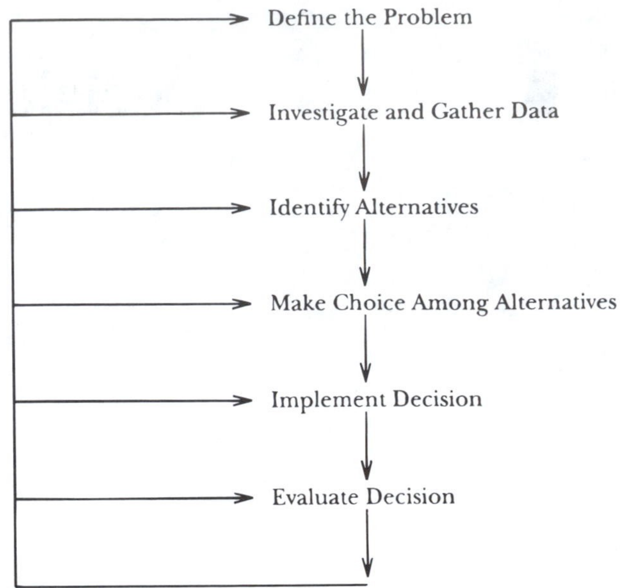

Figure 7–1 Steps in Problem Solving

Scientific Decision Making

The scientific approach forces the manager to analyze all viable alternatives to the problem prior to making a decision. An experimental research-type format is used involving statement of the problem, establishing hypotheses, experimentation, and results and conclusions. The procedure may prove to be too costly to the organization in terms of carrying out the experiment. Also, the use of a strictly scientific approach will depend on the ability and skill level of the manager. A more practical approach is the use of problem solving. The problem-solving approach permits the analysis required in arriving at a decision, yet does not involve the actual experimentation called for in the scientific approach.

Problem Solving

Problem solving and decision making are not the same. Problem solving is a part of the decision-making process and always leads to some decision (Braverman 1980). To solve a problem, one must realize that a problem exists. Problems are recognized in terms of the objectives and goals of the organization. When there is discrepancy between the current situation and the way it should be, a problem exists. Steps in problem solving (Figure 7–1) are as follows:

1. Define the problem. Determine the nature of the problem. Get a clear understanding of cause—why there is a discrepancy between the actual outcome and the expected outcome.
2. Investigate and gather data. Conduct a thorough investigation to obtain all relevant data. Observe and talk to those involved. Gather reports, records, and other written documents.
3. Identify alternatives. For each alternative, consider the impact on personnel in the involved department (i.e., determine the risks and benefits).
4. Make a choice among alternatives. Select the most appropriate solution with consideration to impact, consequences, and probability of the outcome.
5. Implement the decision. Avoid unnecessary delay in implementing the decision. Consider timing.
6. Evaluate the decision. Monitor and follow up on effects of implementation.

Individual versus Group Decision Making

A manager is oriented toward making decisions independently, but at times it may be advantageous to share decision making with others. In addition to required sharing of decisions, such as in union matters, the manager may have other reasons for delegating decision making to a group or ad hoc committee. According to Massie (1971), a critical factor in the use of committees is to state in explicit terms what function the group is to perform. Managers tend to appoint committees to share in the decision-making process under the following conditions:

- when there is a need for consensus among different individuals, groups, or departments

- when there is a need to gain acceptance by subordinates
- when there is a need to minimize conflict among subordinates
- when there is a need for creative ideas, suggestions, and alternatives
- when there is a need for expert opinions in different areas
- when there is a need to investigate and collect additional data
- when there is a need to train inexperienced personnel in decision making
- when there is a need to seek support for a decision that may prove unpopular
- when there is a need to make a final decision from among alternatives
- when there is a need to avoid the appearance of arbitrary decision making

Previous conditions can be considered as advantages to group decision making. There are certain disadvantages to committee appointments, however. Committee decisions may result in buck passing, in which no individual is held responsible for the decision. Further, committees are costly, considering the valuable time spent by individual members. Also, the group or committee decision-making process can become long and drawn out, resulting in compromise and indecision. Finally, committee decision making is not advisable if a decision must be made promptly.

PROBLEM-SOLVING TOOLS

A number of sophisticated analytical tools are available to the manager for problem solving that may result in decision making, but most require high levels of mathematical skills. According to Koontz and O'Donnell (1974), there is a gap between the manager, who is expected to use the models, and the operations researcher, who develops them. In essence, managers lack knowledge and appreciation of mathematics, and mathematicians lack an understanding of managerial problems. One technique using systematic analysis that has proven effective in the decision-making process is the decision tree.

The Decision Tree

The decision tree approach may be viewed as simple or complex, depending on the complexity of the decision to be made. The decision tree approach is most applicable when a decision must be made in an environment of uncertainty and in high-risk situations. A decision tree graphically illustrates all possible choices, risks, gains, and goals related to a decision. It also includes the likely payoff and the probability of success. Decision trees are normally drawn horizontally (Magee 1964), with the base at the left representing the current point. From the base, branches fork out to represent an alternate course of action. If the decision is a simple choice among alternatives, the decision tree is reduced to a single-stage analysis. For more complicated decisions, more stages are necessary to reflect all possible alternatives.

The methodology used in establishing a decision tree is as follows (Carlisle 1976):

1. A decision is recognized (decision point).
2. Alternatives are identified (possible actions).
3. Possible future conditions or situations are identified (states of nature).
4. The likelihood of each state of nature is determined (probabilities).
5. Results of alternatives are determined (payoffs).
6. Outcomes of payoffs are calculated by multiplying the probabilities of the different states of nature (expected value).
7. Follow-up on sequential decisions are evaluated in the same manner as the six previous steps.

The major advantage of using a decision tree is that it helps decision makers to identify alternatives and clarify the nature of risks involved.

Brainstorming

Brainstorming is a creative method used in a group setting for generating ideas or alternatives in a problem-solving process. As developed by Osborn (1963), group brainstorming is not meant to be used as a substitute for problem solving but as a supplement in these three ways:

1. as a supplement to individual ideation by generating a maximum number of potentially usable ideas in a minimum amount of time
2. as a supplement to conventional conferences if and when creative thinking is the primary purpose
3. as a supplement to creative thinking by including a more creative attitude and developing fluency of ideas

The group is formed by appointing a chairperson to present the problem and promote a free exchange of ideas, and appointing a recorder to write down all suggestions. The brainstorming environment encourages participants to talk freely by expressing any and all ideas, without criticism, judgment, or evaluation. The objective is to generate as many creative ideas as possible. At the end of the session, a compiled list is submitted to the decision maker for evaluation.

The ideas may or may not be useful in providing a solution to the problem.

Synectics

Synectics is a group-oriented process for generating creative solutions to problems. It is similar to brainstorming except for the following:

- The group is composed of a select group of experts on the particular problem.
- The quantity of solutions offered is not of essence.
- Criticism is allowed as new and different viewpoints are formed.
- The group is smaller.
- Before solutions are offered, analogies are developed for a better understanding of the problem.
- Every facet of the problem is analyzed in detail.

According to Braverman (1980), brainstorming attempts to promote new ideas by creating a climate conducive to generating a large quantity of suggestions. Synectics attempts to make the strange familiar and the familiar strange by looking at a problem in new and different ways.

The Delphi Method

The Delphi method is similar to brainstorming and synectics in that it is used to find solutions to problems. The method is used extensively by dietetic educators in arriving at competency statements for dietetic practitioners. Unlike other methods discussed, participants do not meet or communicate face to face. Generally, the procedure involves designing and sending a questionnaire to a large group of respondents, summarizing responses, analyzing results, and preparing and sending a new questionnaire based on results. The process is repeated, with feedback, to the respondents until an acceptable agreement is reached.

The use of problem-solving tools such as brainstorming, synectics, and the Delphi method can only assist the decision maker in making the best possible choice among alternatives; the tools cannot substitute for responsible judgment in making the final decision. An understanding of personal, organizational, and administrative factors that may affect decisions can be beneficial in the decision-making process.

PROBLEMS IN DECISION MAKING

There is a certain amount of risk involved in all decisions, in addition to other factors that have important bearings on the kind of decision made. The organization structure can be designed to facilitate and generate sound decisions and to minimize forces that inhibit good decision making. The following administrative problems affect decision making (McFarland 1966).

- Correctness of decisions. The probability that a particular decision will be correct depends on a number of factors, including the amount and accuracy of information gathered and the ability of the decision maker to analyze data correctly. Attempts are made to achieve the highest percentage of correct decisions possible and, if mistakes are made, to ensure that they are limited to minor decisions.
- The environment of decisions. A manager may be reluctant to make decisions because of the organizational climate. Decisiveness on the part of top administrators will help promote decisiveness throughout the organization. If a manager is unclear about the authority to decide or the responsibility to decide, however, decision making tends to be uncertain, erratic, or nonexistent. If decisions are rescinded over and over again, the manager will wait until he or she can clear decisions with higher administration and thus will become too cautious and slow to decide.
- Psychological elements in decision making. Decision making involves both personal and organizational factors. Personal factors that may influence an individual's organizational decision making include status, prestige, economic security, temperament, intelligence, energy, attitude, and emotions. The psychological view is that an individual's total personality must be considered in analyzing the decision-making process.
- Timing of decisions. Those affected by a decision, including superiors, need to be informed in a timely manner. Supervisors should always be informed ahead of their subordinates so that the decision can be effectively communicated downward.
- Communicating decisions. Timing is important in communicating a decision because undue delay may result in leaks through the grapevine. Leaks may be distorted, arousing antagonisms toward the decision before it is formally announced. Major decisions should be in writing. Those affected by the decision should understand its logic or relevance; therefore, both the written and oral versions of communication should be clear and simple.
- Participating in decision making. When individuals are allowed to participate in the decision-making process there is a sense of belongingness on the part of employees, improved work efficiency, a greater sense of responsibility, and a greater acceptance of change. To summarize, employees are more willing to carry out the demands of the decision if they had a part in the decision-making process.

REFERENCES

Atchinson, T.J., and W.H. Winston. 1978. *Management today*. New York: Harcourt, Brace.

Braverman, J.D. 1980. *Management decision making*. New York: AMACOM.

Carlisle, H.M. 1976. *Management concepts and situations*. Chicago: Science Research Associates.

Koontz, H., and C. O'Donnell. 1974. *Essentials of management*. New York: McGraw-Hill.

McFarland, D.E. 1966. *Management principles and practices*. New York: Macmillan Publishing.

Magee, J.F. 1964. Decision trees for decision making. *Harvard Business Review* 2, no. 4:126–138.

Massie, J.L. 1971. *Essentials of management*. Englewood Cliffs, NJ: Prentice Hall.

Osborn, A.F. 1963. *Applied imagination*. New York: Charles Scribner's Sons.

CHAPTER 8

Time Management

Managerial personnel must be able to manage their own personal and organizational time. As work-related tasks increase in quantity and complexity, placing greater demands on one's time, a carefully organized and coordinated approach must be given to all aspects of the job. Practices such as working long overtime hours or taking work home to be accomplished on off-duty time should be scrutinized in terms of long-term solutions. The quality of time is more important than the quantity of time involved in completing a task.

TIME CATEGORIES

According to a prescription for dynamic supervision in the hospital, published by the Bureau of Business Practice (1974), supervisors divide their time into four categories:

1. Hospital time. This is the time spent fulfilling obligations to other people in the organization. The time may include reports to higher management, meetings and discussions with associates and superiors, telephone calls, and progress reports.
2. Investment time. This is time spent directly on affairs that fall within the supervisor's immediate responsibility. Investment time means spending time now to make time in the future. An example of investment time is to train an employee who can eventually share the workload and help overcome the time pressure of the job. Other examples include time spent in planning the work of the department, making social contacts with people who may be able to help in some future activity, listening to complaints, and thinking creatively about the work.
3. Immediate reward time. This is time spent on activities that yield instant results. Delegation of activities fits into this category. When work is assigned to a subordinate, one can expect an immediate reward: one less thing to do. This category also includes helping an employee to solve on-the-job problems, dictating letters, writing interoffice memos, placing telephone calls, or any other activity that results in direct action or provides the information needed to take direct action.
4. Wasted time. This time represents work without beneficial results for the supervisor, the employees, or the department.

The first three categories may be classified as productive time; the fourth category may be classified as nonproductive time. It is important for managers to discuss the differences and make concerted efforts to reduce time wasters. It may involve changing or adjusting the daily routine, which may involve a break with tradition. Remember, it is necessary to invest time in order to save time.

SYSTEMS FOR ORGANIZING TIME

A systematic procedure for organizing and coordinating a time management program (Ashkenas and Schaffer 1982; Douglass and Douglass 1982; Ferderber 1981; Steffen 1982) is offered in the following sections.

Assessing Use of Time

The following analysis and questions are helpful when one needs to assess how one's time is spent:

- Analyze everything you do in terms of objectives. What needs to be done? When should it be done? Why should it be done? What are the consequences of not doing it? Maintain a time log of all activities on a daily, weekly, and monthly basis.

- Analyze objectives and goals. Are goals clearly defined and measurable? Are goals realistic? Are goals essential for meeting objectives?
- Analyze planned versus spontaneous or interrupted time. How much time is lost through interruptions either by telephone or office dropins?
- Analyze activities in terms of productivity. What activities that take more than 30 minutes per week can be eliminated? What activities taking an hour or more a week could be done in half the time? What activities taking more than 30 minutes could be delegated?
- Analyze the numbers and types of meetings attended. Rate the meetings according to effective use of time. Are meetings dull, unorganized, inefficient, and unproductive? Are meetings supportive of objectives and goals?

Planning Time

Objectives and goals must be considered when planning the use of time. The following should be considered:

- Plan objectives and goals, both personal and organizational. Be realistic in planning what can be accomplished in a given amount of time. Consider relevancy of goals to objectives.
- Plan ahead. Plan time on a daily basis to accomplish the most important tasks first. Plan for upcoming meetings, conferences, and appointments. Be prepared with necessary supportive documents and data.
- Plan to eliminate all nonessential, extraneous activities that are not supportive of objectives and goals.

Implementing Time Management

The use of time management practices can be very helpful and should include the following:

- Clarify objectives and goals in writing. Focus on objectives, not activities. Set at least one goal that can be reached on a daily basis.
- Set time limits for each task. Do not become a victim of Parkinson's Law, which says that work expands to fill the time available. Implement a "quiet time" for blocks of uninterrupted time to work on major projects. Be realistic. Avoid overcommitting yourself. Learn how to say no.
- Eliminate needless paperwork. Reduce the flow to your in-basket. Keep your desk clear of unnecessary paperwork by using the desk as a temporary stopover. Handle paperwork only once, and decide whether it should be filed or discarded.
- Reduce telephone time. Make notes of essentials to cover before placing the call. Have your secretary obtain information on the nature of the calls received while you are out of the office. When the call is returned, all files with necessary data can be available, thus eliminating additional calls.
- Reduce interruption time. Set a certain time for appointments. For walk-ins, confer standing up; sitting down invites extended conversations.
- Delegate. Give more of your own work to your secretary. Upgrade the job classification, if necessary. Assign tasks to subordinates with deadlines. Allow a subordinate freedom to complete the task independently without constant supervision. Make a note of the completion date on the calendar and follow up.
- Conquer procrastination. Concentrate on priorities. Finish what you start. It is better to complete one project than to work on three or four and not complete any of them.

Evaluating Effective Use of Time

The final step in organizing time is evaluation. The following processes are helpful in this phase.

- Reflect on time usage. Use the last 15 minutes of the day to determine whether objectives and goals were met.
- Update priorities continually. Review priorities at regular intervals, and readjust and make changes as necessary.

PROGRAM EVALUATION AND REVIEW TECHNIQUE

Time management is especially important in completing major projects that may appear difficult, complex, and ambiguous. The long-term effort required to complete such projects can be productive if it is organized, carefully planned, and well executed. One approach to time management that can be beneficial in completing major projects is the use of a program evaluation and review technique (PERT) network. PERT is a diagrammatic representation of a pattern of work assignments consisting of activities and events (Anderholm et al. 1981). The PERT network is designed to allow the planner to organize and arrange the sequences of the subtasks in such a way that the project's final time limitations and constraints are met. PERT is also known as critical path analysis (CPA), critical path method (CPM), and critical path planning (CPP). When time is chosen, the network analysis is referred to as PERT-time, and when cost is chosen, the network is referred to as PERT-cost (Taylor and Walting 1973).

The development of PERT is attributed to the Special Projects Office of the United States Navy, where it was successfully used to develop the Polaris missile system. It is widely used in business management and government today.

In the following example, PERT is used to indicate PERT-time in terms of weeks required to plan a dietetic internship program.

Minisystem Task Analysis and Flowchart

A task analysis is recommended for all activities involved in the project. The minisystem task analysis permits one to think through all possible functions, elements, and components required for getting the work done for a single activity. After all activities and events have been identified (Exhibit 8–1), it is necessary to establish a time sequence (Figure 8–1).

PERT has proven to be an invaluable tool in the analysis of time, one of our most critical resources.

PERT Network

The network diagram, as shown in Figure 8–2, represents the activities and events involved. An activity indicates work and is represented by an arrow. The length of the arrow has no significant meaning in the network; the main function is to indicate interrelationships and sequence of events. The events indicate accomplishments as a result of work or activity and are represented by a circle.

Exhibit 8–1 Task Analysis and Functions

Function

1. Determine type of input needed
2. Determine optimum number of advisors
3. Determine duties and responsibilities
4. List first and alternate choice of advisors
5. Submit invitations to first choice
6. Acknowledge positive responses
7. Formulate committee
8. Inform advisors of first meeting

Elements and Components Might Include

1. Division faculty
2. Place for meeting
3. Chairs
4. Desks, tables
5. Printed handouts
6. Chalkboard
7. Chalk
8. Overhead projector
9. Paper, pads
10. Pens, pencils

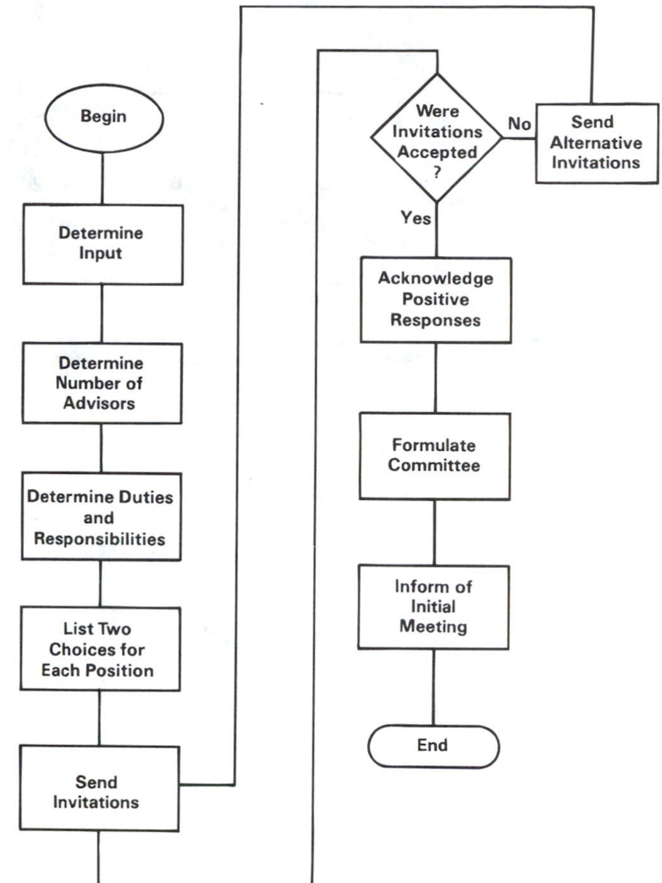

Figure 8–1 Flowchart for Activity

The critical path is the longest time path from the initial event and is determined by totaling the individual expected completion times (te). In the network, events 1–4–14–17–18–19 depict the critical path. T_E represents the earliest time for completion of an event; T_L represents the latest allowable completion time for an activity. To determine the amount of slack time for an event, subtract the event's earliest time from its latest time. In this PERT network, event 14 is a critical point because all preceding events must be completed before the project can continue.

Gantt Chart

The Gantt chart is used to supplement the PERT network because graphically it illustrates when to begin each activity. It reflects the time element depicted in the PERT network in such a manner that the overlapping of activities can be viewed readily. For example, in the PERT network, activity 1–3 has a te = 2, but it does not tell when to start work on the activity.

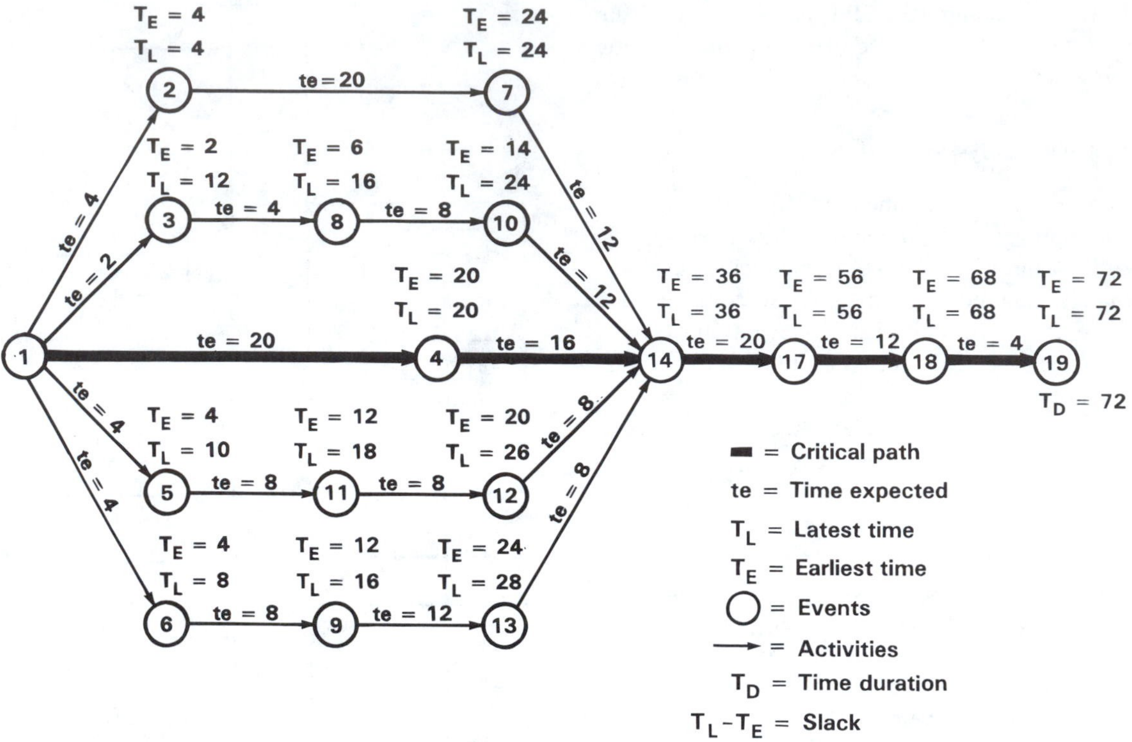

Figure 8–2 PERT Network for Planning a Dietetic Internship Program

---

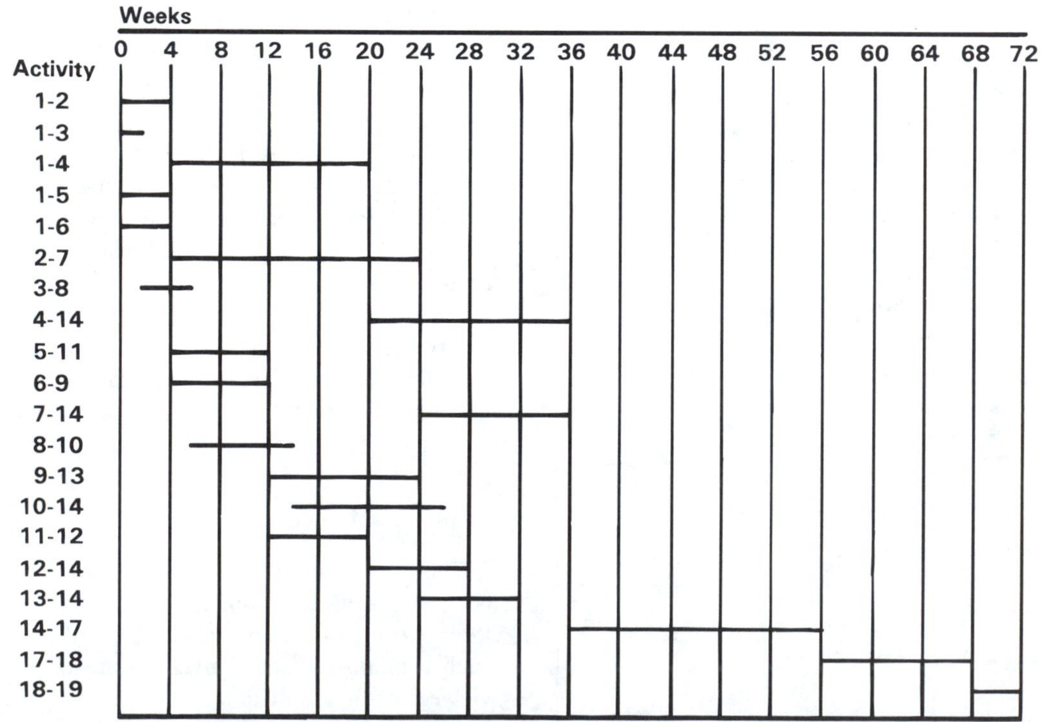

Figure 8–3 Gantt Chart Indicating Starting Time for Activities

Activities indicated on the Gantt chart (Figure 8–3) are as follows:

1-2	obtain program support (nonfinancial)
1-3	develop program philosophy, objectives, and goals
1-4	select internship program director
1-5	organize department to reflect internship program
1-6	formulate advisory committee
2-7	develop curriculum
3-8	designate clinical sites within the hospital; select outside clinical sites
4-14	conduct clinical staff development
5-11	recruit and select additional clinical staff, if necessary
6-9	recruit and select clerical staff
7-14	purchase equipment and supplies
8-10	evaluate on-site and outside clinical facilities
9-13	determine criteria for program evaluation
10-14	formulate contracts with outside clinical facilities
11-12	develop clinical components
12-14	develop course outlines
13-14	plan for student services
14-17	apply for accreditation
17-18	select students
18-19	implement program

PERT, used for planning comprehensive programs such as an internship program, offers the following advantages: (1) It permits participants to analyze all activities; (2) it serves to reduce the possibility of bottlenecks involved in massive organizational change; and (3) it expedites the expenditure of time and energy on the part of the planning team during implementation.

REFERENCES

Anderholm, F. et al. 1981. The utilization of PERT in the preparation of marketing budgets. *Managerial Planning* 30, no. 1:18–23.

Ashkenas, S.R.N., and R.H. Schaffer. 1982. Managers can avoid wasting time. *Harvard Business Review* 60:98–104.

Bureau of Business Practice. 1974. *Dynamic supervision in the hospital: Solving your time problems* (Pamphlet No. 244, April 25). Waterford, CT.

Douglass, M., and D. Douglass. 1982. It's about time: Successful time habits. *Personnel Administration* 27, no. 6:19.

Ferderber, C.J. 1981. 10 Techniques for managing your time more effectively. *Practical Accountant* 14, no. 8:67–69.

Steffen, R.J. 1982. How to stop wasting time. *Supervisory Management* 27, no. 5:22–25.

Taylor, W.J., and T.F. Walting. 1973. *Practical project management*. New York: John Wiley & Sons.

Chapter 9

Subsystem for Menu Planning

Menu planning is one of the most important parts of the food service system. The menu dictates the need for and the utilization of other resources within the system. When the menu is viewed as the hub of the system, the concepts of dependency and interdependency can be readily visualized. If this conceptual view is accepted, the menu should be planned first; then consideration should be given to other subsystems, based on menu requirements.

The menu should reflect the philosophy, objectives, and goals of the organization because the menu represents and serves as a communication link with the larger environment. By using this approach, it is expected that necessary resources (budget allocations for personnel, equipment, materials, and supplies) will be provided to meet stated objectives.

MENU CONSIDERATIONS

A basic objective of menu planning may be to serve nutritious, appetizing, and attractive food to meet the needs of patients and personnel. To meet this basic objective, the menu planner must have a knowledge of the population to be served, which includes eating habits and resulting food preferences; the nutritional needs of individuals and groups; and a wide variety of foods, acceptable combinations, preparation, and service techniques.

Food Preferences

Food preferences are based on long-standing and traditional eating habits. When patients enter the medical facility, they bring with them their traditional patterns of eating. Because food acceptance is important if the consumption of food is to meet therapeutic needs, an understanding of and a respect for diverse eating habits are major considerations. Traditional food preferences may be based on ethnic, cultural, regional, religious, and/or environmental factors. Therefore, the menu planner needs to be sensitive to the reality that humans are omnivorous, capable of eating everything from sheep's eyes to old eggs. This sensitivity will make individuals aware of their own taboos as related to food (Gibson 1981). Personal preferences should not be the criteria for menu planning, nor should one attempt to apply the melting pot theory, but it is important to be aware of the ethnic and culturally diverse eating habits of groups who may be part of the population served by a hospital food service.

Ethnic and cultural groups use a variety of ways to view foods in terms of what is appropriate to eat at mealtime, as between-meal snacks, on special occasions, and for various stages of growth, illness, and health.

In China food preferences vary, depending on the geographical location: northern and western regions, central region, and southern region. The styles of cooking are related to regional differences and are known as Mandarin (north), Shanghai (central), and Cantonese (south). Eating habits are influenced by two main principles, Fan-Ts'ai and Yin-Yang. The Fan-Ts'ai principle refers to the belief that the meal must be balanced with appropriate amounts of fan-ts'ai foods. *Fan* includes rice, wheat, millet, corn, flour, and noodles. *Ts'ai* includes any combination of meat and vegetables cooked in a variety of ways (boiled, steamed, stir-fried). The fan portion of the meal is considered indispensable; it is believed that one cannot be full without it. The Yin-Yang principle refers to the belief that there should be a balance of *yin* (hot) and *yang* (cold) foods. Fatty meats, fried, hot-flavored, and oily plant foods are classified as yin. Yang foods include most water plants, crustaceans, and certain beans (mung). The classification is unrelated to temperature; it is based on beliefs about how food reacts within the body, and the belief that an imbalance will result in improper bodily functions. This hot-cold dichotomy is widespread (Kirk and Eliason 1982). This principle is similar to practices observed by other Asian and Latin American groups.

The Jewish food pattern (Table 9–1) presents religious considerations. The practice of kashrut, the Jewish dietry laws, is oberved in varying degrees by members of the Jewish faith. The three major religious groups are Orthodox, Conservative, and Reform. Orthodox Jews strictly observe the dietary laws by observing the Sabbath as a complete day of rest, study, and prayer. Conservative Jews are less strict in their observance of the dietary laws and believe that the Bible may be interpreted in many ways. Reform Jews consider the teachings of Judaism more important than the ritual; however, they do celebrate holidays, as well as the Sabbath.

Milk and/or dairy products (milchig) and meat products (fleishig) may not be prepared, cooked, or eaten together. Pareve (neutral) foods include eggs, vegetables, fruits, grains, and fish with scales and fins. Pareve foods may be eaten with either milchig or fleishig products.

Another group, the Muslims, is also guided by religious considerations. The dietary pattern of the Muslims (Table 9–2) is based on the teachings of the Holy Koran. Strict guidelines on what to eat, as well as the number of meals per day, are practiced by those observing the Muslim faith.

Polish and Puerto Rican food patterns are also important for today's food service director. Regional differences occur within the United States as well. A "southern" meal pattern is found primarily among families in rural areas. (The meal pattern of urban southern families may be different, however, because of changes in socioeconomic status and acculturation to urban living.) A heavy meal (dinner) is usually served at midday, and a lighter meal (supper) in the evening.

Vegetarian diets are gaining popularity and may require special attention by the menu planner. Such diets can be divided into three categories (Endres and Rockwell 1980):

1. Pure or strict vegetarian diet. All foods of animal origin (meat, poultry, fish, eggs, and dairy products) are excluded from the diet. Vegans avoid one or more other food groups such as processed foods, cooked foods, legumes, cereals, grains, or fruits. Fruitarians limit food intake to raw and cooked fruits, nuts, honey, and oil.
2. Lactovegetarian. Meat, fish, and eggs are excluded; however, dairy products and plant foods are permitted.
3. Lacto-ovovegetarian. The diet includes eggs, dairy products, and plant foods; meat, poultry, and fish are excluded.

With careful planning, basic nutrients can be provided in all categories, except for those observing the vegan and fruitarian patterns.

In planning a vegetarian diet, one should choose a wide variety of food. The foods may include fresh fruits, vegetables, whole-grain breads and cereals, nuts and seeds, legumes, low-fat dairy products or fortified soy substitutes, and a limited number of eggs, if desired (American Dietetic Association 1987). Consumption of a good source of ascorbic acid with meals will further enhance absorption of available iron. It is the position of the American Dietetic Association that vegetarian diets are healthful and nutritionally adequate when appropriately planned.

Even though the health benefits of a vegetarian diet make it attractive from a nutrition standpoint, this does not preclude the possibility of obtaining similar health benefits from a prudent nonvegetarian diet if it can be planned in accordance with the dietary guidelines for Americans (American Dietetic Association 1988a). Well-planned vegetarian diets effectively meet the dietary guidelines for Americans, and the recommended dietary allowances (RDAs) and can be confidently embraced as a healthful dietary alternative.

Although the vegetarian diet pattern may meet the dietary guidelines for Americans and the RDAs, the new food guide pyramid is less effective in assessing the adequacy of a vegetarian diet (Mangels 1995). The food guide pyramid, according to Mangels, was designed for those eating typical American diets. A thorough diet history and an analysis for calories and key nutrients such as iron, calcium, and vitamin B_{12} provide a more reliable picture of a vegetarian diet. In general, intake and status of vegetarians using dairy products are similar to those of the general population. Vegans need to rely on nondairy sources such as low-oxalate leafy green vegetables, tofu processed with calcium sulfate, fortified juices and soy drinks, oranges, almonds, figs, and blackstrap molasses. Calcium supplements represent another alternative.

Vegetarians are not at greater risks for iron deficiency than nonvegetarians. Good sources of iron are available in the vegetarian diet. Vegetarians who do not use animal products need a reliable source of vitamin B_{12} because it is not synthesized by any plant. Reliable sources of vitamin B_{12} include B_{12}-fortified cereals and soy milks and fortified nutritional yeast. Vitamin B_{12} supplements are acceptable to some vegans. Lacto-ovo- and lactovegetarians will get adequate amounts of vitamin B_{12} from dairy products and eggs. Most vegetarian diets consisting of a variety of foods and containing sufficient calories to meet energy needs are adequate in protein. All too often vegetarians are told to combine proteins to meet protein requirements. This combining within a given meal is unnecessary and should not be stressed because it may make a vegetarian diet seem much more complicated than it needs to be. The most important factor is that dietary variety and adequacy should be stressed.

The effort expended to understand the patient profile can serve to maximize patient satisfaction. A knowledge of the inhabitants of the geographical location is important. For

Table 9–1 Jewish Food Pattern

Food Group	*Characteristics of Food Habits*
Milk	Six hours must elapse after a meal before dairy foods may be eaten; half an hour must elapse after eating a dairy food before food may be eaten. Consumption may be adequate if used at both the breakfast and dairy meal. Cheese, such as American, Muenster, and Swiss, is well-liked. Cottage cheese is eaten plain or in blintzes and noodle puddings.
	Low-sodium milk from L. K. Baker and Co., Columbus, Ohio, may be used. Featherweight low-sodium milk and Lonolac are also approved products.
Meat	Acceptable meat includes the flesh of all quadrupeds with a cloven hoof, that chew cud, such as cattle, sheep, goats, and deer. Orthodox Jews use only the forequarters (rib section forward).
	Meat of beef, lamb, goat, deer, chicken, turkey, goose, pheasant, and duck is allowed. Liver and tongue are used liberally.
	Fish with fins and scales (fresh and as gefilte fish); smoked; lox (salmon); and caviar are eaten. Shellfish and scavenger fish such as sturgeon and catfish are not allowed.
	Eggs are eaten in abundance. An egg with a clot of blood must be discarded.
	Dried beans, peas, and lentils are eaten, especially as soup.
Vegetables and fruits	All fruits and vegetables may be used. Popular greens include spinach or sorrell leaves (used for schav, a popular soup), broccoli, and chicory. Carrots, sweet potatoes, and green peppers are well liked. Green cabbage is often stuffed with a ground beef and raisin mixture with tomato sauce. Fresh and canned tomatoes are used extensively. Root vegetables and potatoes are liberally used. Potato pancakes (latkes) and potato pudding prepared with egg are popular, as well as noodle pudding. Beets are used in soup (borscht).
	Oranges or grapefruits or their juices are usually served for breakfast. Fresh or stewed fruits are often eaten as dessert with the meat meal.
Bread and cereal	Bagel, rye bread, and pumpernickel are often used, as these do not have milk or milk solids and therefore can be eaten with meat or dairy meals. They are considered pareve. Matzoth is also considered pareve and is the only bread product allowed during Passover. Whole grains such as oatmeal, brown rice, and buckwheat groats (kasha) are used.
	Ready-baked products must have U or K certification (see under miscellaneous). Cooked cereals must be instant packets.
Miscellaneous	Sweet (unsalted) butter, usually whipped, is preferred to salted butter. Vegetable oils and shortenings are considered pareve. Fat of chicken is used to brown meat and fry potato pancakes.
	Danish pastries, coffee cakes, homemade cakes, and cookies may be eaten in large quantities. Honey cakes are served for various holidays.
	Relishes such as pickled cucumbers and tomatoes, horseradish, and condiments are popular.
	Soup may be consumed at every meal. Chicken noodle and chicken rice soups are popular.
	Soft drinks are served with meat meals when milk beverages are forbidden.
	The following supplemental food products are approved for use: Sustagen, Sustacal, Ensure, Isomil, Vivonex 1000, Controlyte, Formula I, Meritene, Paygel–P, Nutramigen, Prosoybee, Isocal, and the fruit flavors of Precision LR, Flexical, and W–T Residue.
	Symbols used to indicate rabbinical supervision and certification are U — The Union of Orthodox Jewish Congregations of America. Used for canned, boxed, and bottled products VH or IVI — Vaad Harabonim of Boston K — Organized Kashrus Laboratories, not accepted by all observant Jews as rabbinical authority MK — Montreal Vaad Ha-ir C.O.R. — Council of Orthodox Rabbis of Toronto

Source: Data from *Standardized Recipes for Institutional Use,* © 1969, American Dietetic Association; A. B. Natow and J. Heslin, Understanding the Cultural Food Practices of Elderly Observant Jews, *Journal of Nutrition for the Elderly,* Vol. 2, No. 1, pp. 49–59, © 1982; and R. Meador and B. Montalbano, Practical Applications of Kosher Food Service in a Nonkosher Residential Health Care Facility, *Journal of Nutrition for the Elderly,* Vol. 2, No. 1, pp 61–69, © 1982.

Table 9–2 Muslim Food Pattern

Food Group	*Characteristics of Food Habits*
Milk	Milk is encouraged and used extensively. Cream cheese is recommended. Aged cheese is prohibited.
Meat	Beef and lamb are used in limited amounts. Lamb is preferred. Young pigeons are allowed. Do not eat birds that are permitted to fly around and search for their own food. No ground meat allowed unless the grinding process is observed. Chicken allowed if raised under controlled conditions. No wild game, except young pigeon. No pork or pork products allowed. Fish is allowed and should weigh less than 10 pounds. No halibut, carp, tuna, or scavenger seafood such as eel, catfish, oysters, crabs, clams, snails, and shrimp. No turtle or frog legs allowed. Portuguese sardines are recommended.
Vegetables and fruits	Most green leafy vegetables are encouraged, except collards, turnip greens, kale, and green leaves of cabbage. Turnip roots, cabbage (white head only), and cauliflower are preferred. Rutabaga and spinach should be eaten sparingly. White potatoes and rice are eaten only in cold climates. No sweet potatoes allowed. Fresh vegetables preferred to processed. Small navy beans allowed. Avoid use of all other types of beans, including soy or soy products. All fruits allowed and eaten extensively. Only sun-dried grapes allowed. Raw fruit is encouraged.
Bread and cereal	Rye and whole-wheat breads preferred (thoroughly cooked). Stale bread is better than fresh. No white flour or cornbread.
Miscellaneous	Butter is preferred to margarine. Vegetable oil is used (no soy). No fried foods. Brown sugar preferred. No white sugar. Bean pie (using navy beans) is a popular dessert. No nuts. Eat only one meal a day. No between-meal snacks.

Source: Data from E. Muhammad, *How to Live and Eat,* © 1967, Muhammad's Temple of Islam No. 2.

example, as reported in Abonyi et al. (1969), Detroit, Michigan has the largest Arabic-speaking population outside the Middle East; the largest concentration of Belgians, Chaldeans, and Maltese in the United States; and the second largest Polish population in the United States.

Nutritional Adequacy

The nutritional adequacy of the menu is based on the general requirements as reported in *Recommended Dietary Allowances* (Food and Nutrition Board—National Research Council 1989).

The RDA, based on current nutrition research, is designed to provide nutritional maintenance for healthy persons in the United States. The RDA is not designed to assess individual nutritional needs, nor is it designed to meet abnormalities associated with various disease entities. For individual diet planning requiring quantitative and qualitative nutrient modification, other tools are required. Because menu planning in an institutional setting is for a population group, the RDA serves as a frame of reference for meeting nutritional needs.

Nineteen nutrient allowances are presented in quantitative units for seventeen population groups based on age and sex; two groups (pregnancy and lactation) are based on conditions (see Appendix E).

Changes in the 10th edition include the following:

- *Age groupings.* Because peak bone mass is probably not attained before age 25 years, the age class of 19 to 22 years has been extended through age 24 for both sexes.
- *Reference individuals.* Heights and weights of reference adults in each age-sex class are the actual medians for the U.S. population of the designated age. In the previous edition, reference heights and weights were set at an arbitrary ideal.
- *Nutrients.* RDAs for women during pregnancy and lactation are tabulated as absolute figures rather than as additions to the basic allowances. RDAs during lactation are now provided for the first and second six-month periods to reflect the differences in the amount of milk produced (750 mL and 600 mL, respectively). In the ninth edition, a single allowance was provided throughout lactation based on secretion of 850 mL of milk.

RDAs for nutrients remain unchanged or were revised only slightly from the ninth edition. The following major changes were made:

- *Energy.* Energy allowances range from 2,300 to 2,900 kcal/day for adult men and 1,900 to 2,200 kcal/day for adult women.
- *Protein.* The allowance for adult men and women remains at 0.8 g/kg of body weight per day. The increment estimated for pregnancy is reduced from 30 to 10 g/per day; this revision is more heavily influenced by the theory of nitrogen gain and the efficiency with which dietary protein is converted to fetal, placental, and maternal tissues than by new evidence.
- *Vitamin K.* RDAs for vitamin K are established for the first time; they are based on recently published work. The RDA for adults and children is set at approximately 1 μg/kg of body weight. There is no recommended increment during pregnancy and lactation because the effects of pregnancy on vitamin K requirements are unknown and because lactation imposes little additional need for this nutrient.
- *Vitamin B_6.* An RDA of 0.016 mg of vitamin B_6 per gram of protein appears to ensure acceptable values for most indexes of nutritional status in adults of both sexes. The resulting vitamin B_6 allowances of 2.0 and 1.6 mg/day for adult men and women, respectively, are lower than those in the previous edition.
- *Folate.* Folate allowances in this edition are much lower (often by 50% or more) than those in the ninth edition for all the age-sex groups. The basis for lowering the RDA is the recognition that diets containing about half the previous RDA maintain adequate folate status and liver stores. The RDA for folate during pregnancy is 400 μg/day—half the RDA in the ninth edition. The subcommittee considers this amount sufficient to build or maintain maternal folate stores and to support rapidly growing tissue.
- *Vitamin B_{12}.* Vitamin B_{12} allowances are one third to one half lower than those in the ninth edition for all the age-sex groups. The change is based on recent data suggesting that the new allowances adequately sustain metabolic function and allow for biological variation, the maintenance of substantial body stores.
- *Calcium.* The calcium RDA for all adolescents was previously set at 1,200 mg/day to age 18. However, because peak bone mass is probably not attained before age 25 years, the allowance is extended through age 24 to promote full mineral deposition. For older ages, the allowance of 800 mg/day is maintained. RDAs for phosphorus parallel those for calcium except in infancy. In addition, the allowance for vitamin D, which promotes calcium absorption, is maintained at 10 μg/day throughout childhood to age 25 years.
- *Magnesium.* Increments of magnesium during pregnancy and lactation are far lower than in previous editions. The recommended amounts should be sufficient to meet the needs of the fetus and maternal tissue growth and to allow for individual variations. The lower allowance for children of both sexes between 1 and 15 years of age is 6.0 mg/kg, an amount above the levels found to be sufficient to support a positive magnesium balance in adolescent boys and girls.
- *Iron.* The recommended amount of 15 mg/day is lower than the previous allowance of 18 mg/day and should meet the needs of healthy adolescents and women. The allowance for adult men and postmenopausal women remains at 10 mg/day. No additional allowance of iron is recommended during pregnancy and/or lactation, because losses of iron in breast milk are less than losses in menstrual flow, which is often absent during lactation. People who eat little or no animal protein and whose diets are low in ascorbate may require higher amounts of food iron or vitamin C.
- *Zinc.* Currently, the RDA for adults remains at 15 mg/day for adult men, but is reduced to 12 mg/day for adult women on the basis of their lower body weight.
- *Selenium.* The RDA for selenium in adults is set at 70 μg/day for men and 55 μg/day for women. The RDAs for selenium, established for the first time, are based on studies of Chinese men.

Daily Food Guides

Daily food guides, as developed by the U.S. Department of Agriculture (1979, 1980), have been recommended for the practical application of the RDA in group menu planning for over 75 years. The food guides, first developed in the 1920s, have evolved from the basic four, the basic seven, the five food groups, the dietary guidelines for Americans, and currently to the food guide pyramid (U.S. Department of Agriculture 1995).

The Dietary Guidelines for Americans

The dietary guidelines for Americans (U.S. Department of Agriculture 1993a) were first introduced in 1980. Emphasis was placed on getting enough protein, starch, fiber, vitamins, and minerals, but not too much fat, sugar, and sodium. The basic messages of the first guidelines remain sound; however, some changes were made in later editions to reduce confusion on amounts to consume. Changes that appear in the 1993 edition are as follows:

- a daily food guide with suggested number of servings (food guide pyramid)
- more help for determining a "healthy" weight, including an easy way to check your body shape
- practical suggestions that focus on foods (such as vegetables and fruits) rather than food components (such as starch and fiber)

- more emphasis on physical activity, with an updated activity chart showing calories used per hour
- numeric goals for total fat and saturated fat intake
- a definition of "moderate" drinking for women and men

The dietary guidelines are seven recommendations about the foods you eat. They work together, emphasizing variety, balance, and moderation in the diet. The first two guidelines form the basis of a healthful diet. Two other guidelines stress the need for many Americans to consume less fat and cholesterol and more complex carbohydrates and fiber. Other guidelines suggest only moderate use of sugars, salt, and, if used at all, alcoholic beverages. The guidelines are as follows:

- Eat a variety of foods. Eating a variety of foods is the best way to get the energy, protein, carbohydrates, vitamins, minerals, and fiber you need for good health. No single food can supply all the nutrients in the amounts you need. For example, milk supplies calcium but little iron; meat supplies iron, but little calcium. Any food that supplies calories and nutrients can be part of a nutritious diet. It is the content of the total diet over a day or more that counts.
- Maintain healthy weight. Maintaining a healthy weight reduces your chances of developing high blood pressure, heart disease, stroke, certain cancers, and the most common type of diabetes. A healthy weight for adults means meeting these three conditions:
    1. Your weight falls within the range for your height and age.
    2. Your waist measure is smaller than your hip measure. Too much fat around the waist is believed to be of greater health risk than excess fat in the hips and thighs.
    3. Your doctor has advised you not to gain or lose weight because of a medical problem. If your weight is not healthy, set reasonable weight goals and try for long-term success through better eating habits and regular exercise.
- Choose a diet low in fat, saturated fat, and cholesterol. A diet low in fat (especially saturated fat) helps reduce your risk of heart attack and certain types of cancer. Because fat contains more than twice the calories of an equal amount of carbohydrates or protein, a diet low in fat can also help you maintain a healthy weight.
    1. *Total fat.* An amount that provides 30 percent or less of calories is suggested.
    2. *Saturated fat.* An amount that provides less than 10 percent of calories is suggested. All fats contain both saturated and unsaturated fat. The fats in animal products are the main source of saturated fat in the diet, with tropical oils (coconut, palm kernel, and palm oils) and hydrogenated fats providing smaller amounts.
    3. *Cholesterol.* Animal products are the sources of all dietary cholesterol. Eating less fat from animal sources will help lower cholesterol, total fat, and saturated fat in the diet. Remember that the suggested goals for fat apply to the diet over several days, not to a single meal or a single food.
- Choose a diet with plenty of vegetables, fruits, and grain products. These foods provide needed vitamins, minerals, complex carbohydrates, and fiber. They are generally low in fat. Eat more vegetables, including dry beans and peas; fruits; and breads, cereals, pasta, and rice. It is better to get fiber from foods that contain fiber naturally rather than from supplements. Some of the benefits from a high-fiber diet may be from the food that provides the fiber, not from the fiber alone.
- Use sugars only in moderation. Sugars and highly sweetened foods supply calories but are limited in vitamins and minerals. Sugars also contribute to tooth decay. Sugar comes in many forms, such as table sugar (sucrose), brown sugar, honey, syrup, corn sweetener, high-fructose corn sweetener, molasses, glucose (dextrose), fructose, maltose, and lactose. Use sparingly, if calorie needs are low.
- Use salt and sodium only in moderation. Eating less salt and foods containing salt and sodium will benefit those people whose blood pressure rises with higher sodium intake. Most Americans ingest more salt and sodium than they need. Use the following tips to reduce salt and sodium intake:
    1. Use salt sparingly, if at all, in cooking and at the table.
    2. Use in moderation foods high in sodium, such as cheeses, processed meats, most frozen dinners and entrees, most canned soups and vegetables, packaged mixes, salad dressings, and condiments.
    3. Use snacks, such as chips, crackers, pretzels, and nuts, sparingly.
    4. Check labels for the amount of sodium in food and choose those lower in sodium.
- If you drink alcoholic beverages, do so in moderation. Alcoholic beverages supply calories but few vitamins or minerals, and drinking is linked with many health problems. Nevertheless, many people consume alcohol. If you do, moderation is important—no more than one drink a day for women, two drinks a day for men.

Food Guide Pyramid

The food guide pyramid (U.S. Department of Agriculture 1993b) helps you to put the dietary guidelines into action by showing you the relative amounts of food to eat from each of the five major food groups. As shown in Figure 9–1, the pyramid shows a range of servings for each

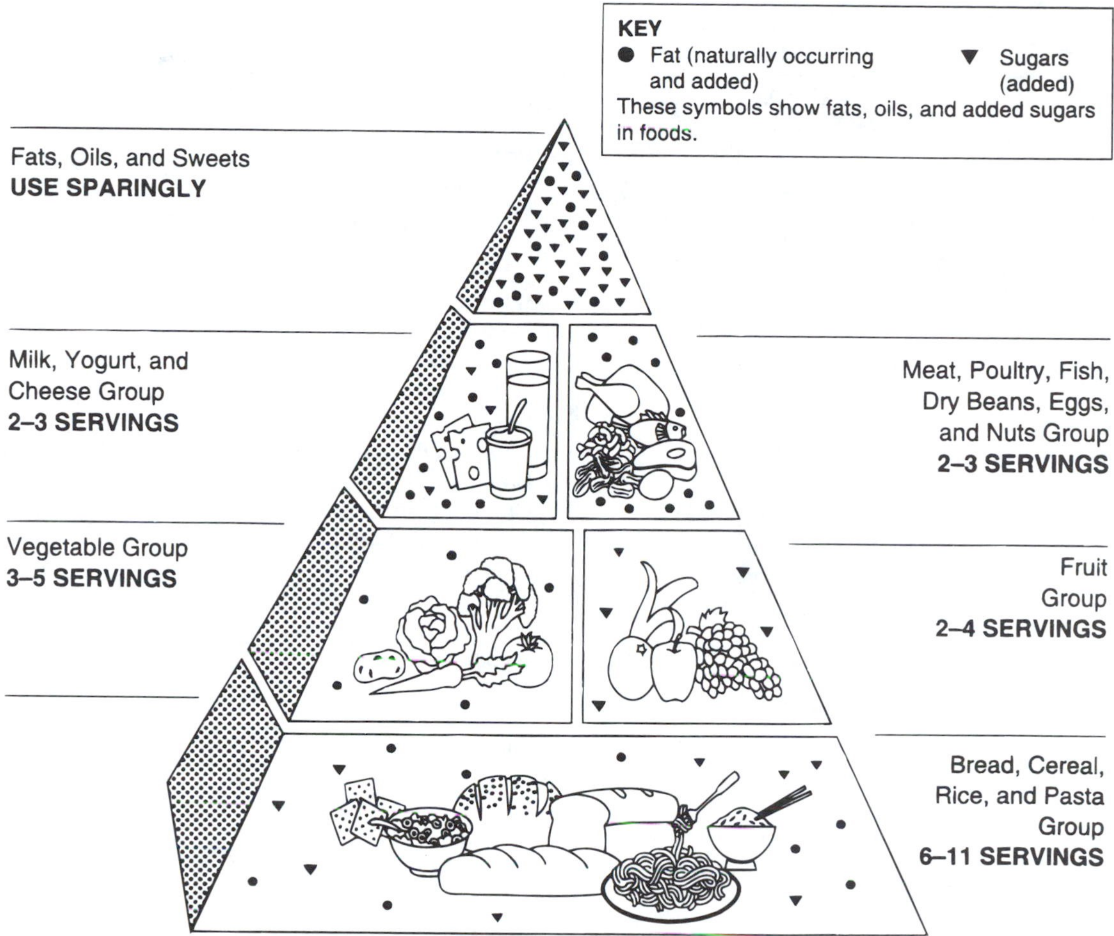

Figure 9–1 Food Guide Pyramid. *Source:* Reprinted from U.S. Department of Agriculture and U.S. Department of Health and Human Services.

major food group. Each of these food groups provides some, but not all, of the nutrients you need. The number of servings that are right for you depends on your age, sex, size, and activity level. Almost everyone should have at least the lowest number of servings from each food group daily. Many women, older children, and most teenagers and men need more.

Nutrition Analysis of Menu

After the menus are planned using the food guide pyramid, they should be analyzed for nutritional adequacy and compared with RDAs. The menu shown in Table 9–3 was analyzed and compared with RDAs for 25- to 50-year-old men. The caloric level is 3 percent below the recommended range. The percentages by calorie are protein, 16 percent; carbohydrate, 48 percent; and fat, 38 percent. All nutrients exceed the recommended dietary allowances.

The menu was also compared with dietary guidelines published by the American Heart Association (AHA). The AHA guidelines (1988) are as follows:

- Total fat should be less than 30 percent of calories.
- Saturated fat should be less than 10 percent of calories.
- Polyunsaturated fat should not exceed 10 percent of calories.
- Cholesterol should not exceed 300 mg/day.
- Carbohydrate should constitute 50 percent or more of calories with emphasis on complex carbohydrates.
- Protein should provide remainder of calories.
- Sodium should not exceed 3 mg/day.
- Total calories should maintain recommended body weight.
- Intake should include a wide variety of food.

The AHA comparison revealed that the menu is excessive in total fat by 8 percent, saturated fat by 4 percent,

Table 9–3 Sample Nutritional Analysis of One Day's Menu

Portion	*Weight*	*Menu Item*
½ cup	123 g	Chilled orange juice
½ cup	120 g	Oatmeal
1	50 g	Poached egg on
1 slice	25 g	whole-wheat toast
1 tsp	5 g	Margarine
1 cup	245 g	Low-fat milk
1 cup	240 g	Coffee
1 pkg	6 g	Sugar
1 Tbsp	15 g	Light cream
1 cup	250 g	Tomato soup
4	11 g	with crackers
¼	88 g	Baked chicken
½ cup	87 g	Steamed rice
½ cup	92 g	Broccoli
1 oz	33 g	Cranberry sauce
1 cup		Tossed salad, with
	34 g	Lettuce
	67 g	Tomato
	18 g	Green pepper
	20 g	Onion
1 tsp	5 g	Margarine
1	50 g	Hard roll
3-in square	63 g	Gingerbread
1 cup	245 g	Low-fat milk
1 cup	240 g	Coffee
1 pkg	6 g	Sugar
1 Tbsp	15 g	Light cream
1 Tbsp	15 g	Italian dressing
½ cup	124 g	Apple juice
3 oz	85 g	Braised beef cubes with
	8 g	mushrooms
½ cup	80 g	Noodles
½ cup	91 g	Mixed vegetables
⅛	17 g	Lettuce wedge
1 Tbsp	16 g	French dressing
1 slice	25 g	Whole-wheat bread
1 tsp	5 g	Margarine
1 cup	245 g	Low-fat milk
1 cup	240 g	Coffee
1 pkg	6 g	Sugar
1 Tbsp	15 g	Light cream
½ cup	128 g	Cling peaches

Nutritive components

Calories	2633 cal	(97%)	Cholesterol	520 mg
Protein	107.8 g	(192%)	Carbohydrate	313.1 g
Calcium	1498.5 mg	(187%)	Potassium	3961 mg
Phosphorus	1956.1 mg	(244%)	Sodium	3868.7 mg
Iron	15.8 mg	(158%)	Fat	111.6 g
Vitamin A	12434.7 IU	(248%)	Saturated fat	41.0 g
Thiamin	1.64 mg	(117%)	Oleic fat	36.4 g
Riboflavin	2.76 mg	(172%)	Linoleic fat	17.5 g
Niacin	22.4 mg	(124%)	Weight	3260 g
Vitamin C	185.5 mg	(309%)	Water	2243 g

Percentages by calories

Protein: 16% Carbohydrate: 48% Fat: 38%

cholesterol by 220 mg, and sodium by 0.89 g. Polyunsaturated fat, protein, and carbohydrate were below recommended guidelines. Suggestions to correct nutrient and calorie imbalance are as follows:

- To reduce saturated fat, change milk to ½% fat; use less milk in coffee and eliminate cream; remove skin from chicken before cooking; and check salad dressings to make sure polyunsaturated fats are used.
- To increase calories, carbohydrates, and protein, increase carboydrates such as grain and vegetables.
- To reduce sodium, reduce milk to two servings per day; eliminate cream; and use salt-free crackers.

Knowledge of Food

Menu planning need not be limited to the imagination of the menu planner. Suggestions from a number of sources can serve the planner in using a wide variety of food choices. It is important to keep in mind that the process of menu planning is more involved than merely listing food as if one were making out a food-purchasing list. The menu suggestions offered here reflect the distinction between the two processes. For example, in Table 9–3 "braised beef cubes with mushrooms" is a much more enticing menu item than simply "beef cubes." As presented in Table 9–4, different menu names are offered in six categories. For maximum use of the menu suggestions, one may add or delete food items depending on client preferences, budgetary allowances, or other pertinent factors of menu planning.

Budgetary Allowances

In most instances, the menu planner is given a prescribed budgetary allowance and must be able to provide nutritious, appetizing, and attractive meals within those allowances. To accomplish this task, the planner must know the cost of each food item placed on the menu, as well as the percentage of the food cost dollar allocated for each food category. (See Tables 15–1 and 15–2 for examples of meal cost allowances and food category cost allowances.) When using precosted menus, it is necessary to update cost figures as often as significant price changes occur.

Equipment Needs

Equipment is one of the resources that should be available according to the planned menu. Frequently, the menu is planned around equipment that has already been selected. In the latter instance, the menu planner must be aware of preparation techniques in order not to overload certain pieces of equipment. For example, the menu should not consist of all food items requiring the roast method of preparation if only one oven is available.

Table 9–4 Descriptive Menu Suggestions

Menu Item	*Description*
Entrees	
Beef stew	Savory beef stew with vegetables
Roast beef	Roast sirloin or beef au jus
Fried chicken	Country fried chicken with cream gravy
Broiled whitefish	Broiled whitefish with lemon-garlic butter
Pork chops	Stuffed pork chop au vin
Tenderloin of beef	Savory beef strips
Appetizers	
Fantail shrimp	Feathery shrimp cocktail
Apple juice	Chilled apple juice
Cantaloupe	Fresh melon balls
Orange juice	Tangy orange juice
Prunes	Sun-ripened prunes
Soups	
Mushroom soup	Fancy cream of mushroom soup
Pea soup	Zesty split pea soup
Vegetable soup	Home-style vegetable soup
Minestrone soup	Tasty minestrone soup
Broth	Golden chicken broth
Vegetables	
Cauliflower	Parslied crisp cauliflower
Carrots	Tangy glazed carrots
Broccoli	Chopped broccoli cuts
Mixed vegetables	Mixed vegetables medley
White potatoes	Boiled new potatoes
Green beans	Green bean almondine
Salads	
Lettuce or spinach	Fresh garden salad
Cranberry mold	Jellied cranberry salad
Lettuce heart	Crispy lettuce hearts
Coleslaw	Creamy coleslaw
Celery sticks	Crunchy celery sticks
Desserts	
Baked Alaska	Flaming baked Alaska
Brownies	Chewy fudge brownies
Applesauce cake	Spiced applesauce cake
Peach slices	Yellow cling peach slices
Lemon cake	Lemon icebox cake
Peach halves	Peaches en gelée

Personnel Needs

Personnel should be selected based on menu planning. When personnel are in place prior to menu planning, the planner must be aware of skills, employee limitations, and the number of employees available to produce planned-menu items. Although in-service training, with emphasis on work simplification and use of standardized recipes, can reduce the burden and frustrations of production workers, there are limits to the amount of quality food that can be produced in a specified time period.

Purchasing System

The menu planner will need to consider the form in which food is purchased, such as the amount of built-in convenience, the availability of certain food items, the frequency of deliveries, and the storage capacity.

Production System

The type of production system may pose limitations on the menu should menu planning take place after the system has been decided upon. For the total-convenience production system, menu planning may be limited because of the nonavailability of prepared food items. In the cook-chill and ready-serve systems there may be problems with certain food items not suitable for the required holding and rethermalizing processes. In the commissary system, problems may occur with attempts to maintain quality while transporting large quantities of prepared foods. Finally, the factor of time to meet culinary schedules may present problems in the conventional system, where all food for each meal is prepared as needed.

MEAL PATTERNS

Meal patterns vary from the most common type of three meals a day to four or five meals. Traditionally, patients receive three full meals daily with between-meal nourishments.

In the four-meal plan, patients receive three full meals daily with a substantial night nourishment. The five-meal pattern consists of two full meals and three small meals (Exhibit 9–1). Regardless of the meal pattern used, there should not be more than 14 hours between the serving of the evening meal and the next substantial meal for patients who are on oral intake and do not have specific dietary requirements.

The five-meal pattern gained popularity during the early 1960s. In this pattern, meals are usually scheduled to begin at about 6:00 AM, with three meals spaced between the first and the last meal, which is served about 8:00 PM. The nutritional composition of the five-meal pattern can be as adequate as the traditional three-meal pattern. However, considerably more thought in the planning process is required to ensure that nutrients are spread out over the total day's diet. The balancing of nutritional components is especially important in instances where the patient is a poor eater or simply refuses to eat all five meals. One should be careful to avoid the tendency to increase calories and neglect other nutrients, such as protein. The continental breakfast of sweet rolls and coffee or a small meal of juice and coffee is an example of an incomplete meal. It is believed that nutrients are utilized more efficiently by the body if each meal contains a balance of protein, fats, and carbohydrates.

MENU FORMAT

Establishing a menu format ensures that food from each of the five groups is included in the daily meal pattern. When the menu is planned, there must be at least one food item offered for each category specified. As shown in Table 9–5, the three-meal menu format may be simple or elaborate. Terminology used to designate the type of meal may be breakfast, dinner, and supper, or breakfast, lunch, and dinner. When the supper meal appears in the menu format, it is usually a lighter meal consisting of combination dishes, meat substitutes, or entrees with meat extenders. In the elaborate menu format, the lunch and dinner meals have the same number of food categories.

NONSELECTIVE VERSUS SELECTIVE MENUS

The nonselective menu offers only one food item in each category of the menu format, thereby offering no choice. In contrast, the selective menu offers at least two choices of food items for each category. A comparison of the two is given in Table 9–6. The nonselective menu is more often used in nursing homes and small acute care facilities. Arguments by those who continue to use the nonselective menu are as follows:

- The nonselective menu is less costly because fewer food items are offered.
- Additional personnel are not required for production of menu items.
- It is easier to control food intake with a nonselective menu.
- It is not left to chance that a patient will select a balanced diet.
- Purchasing is simplified.
- It is easier to control portions and service.

Although the list supporting a nonselective menu is impressive, it does not address issues of optimal patient care. Many of the arguments for a nonselective menu are related to employee convenience rather than patient satisfaction. Some of the advantages cited by those who have used the selective menu are as follows:

- The selective menu is often less expensive because the menu can be balanced with less expensive food choices (such as liver, as shown in Table 9–6) that may be desired by some individuals.
- There is increased food acceptance because patients are able to make their own selections.

Exhibit 9–1 Sample Selective Menu for Five-Meal Feeding Pattern

6:00 AM	*9:30* AM	*1:00* PM	*4:30* PM	*8:00* PM
Orange juice	Orange juice	*Vegetable soup*	*Beef noodle soup*	*Chicken broth*
Pineapple juice*	Apple juice	Tomato juice	Fresh fruit cup	Grapefruit juice
Fresh grapefruit†	*Fresh banana*			
Shredded wheat	Crisp bacon	Cottage cheese and fruit plate	Grilled cubed steak	*Submarine sandwich*
Cornflakes	Broiled sausage	Assorted cold cuts with potato salad	Baked pork chop	Corned beef on rye
Hot oatmeal	Grilled ham	*Tuna stuffed tomato* with chips and relishes	Roast chicken breast	Ham and Swiss cheese sandwich
	Corned beef hash	Maurice salad bowl	Broiled halibut steak	Assorted cheese and crackers
White toast	Eggs, any style		*Roast leg of lamb*	
Whole-wheat toast	Hotcakes with syrup	Fresh fruit in season	Buttered mashed potatoes	Fresh fruit in season
Raisin toast	French toast with honey	*Baked custard*	Baked potato	Assorted ice cream
Whole milk	*Blueberry muffin*	Assorted Jell-O	*Buttered rice*	*Sugar cookie*
Skim milk	White toast		Buttered green beans	
Chocolate milk	Whole-wheat toast		Buttered carrots	
Buttermilk			*Buttered broccoli*	
Coffee Tea			Tossed vegetable salad	
Sanka Cocoa			Creamy coleslaw	
			Lettuce and tomato salad	
Butter Cream			Cheesecake with strawberries	
Sugar Jelly			*Apple pie*	
Salt Pepper			*Chocolate fudge cake*	

* Condiments and beverages listed under 6:00 AM meal are available at other meals.
† Italicized words indicate specials of the day.
Source: Reprinted from C.F. Sullivan, *Proposal for Implementing Change in Hospital Feeding,* 1968.

- Selective menus can be used as a training tool to encourage proper eating habits.
- There are fewer leftovers because preparation is based on selections.
- There is less plate waste because patients will usually eat what they select.
- There is no increase in the quantity of portions produced, only in the variety of food items.

Use of the selective menu requires close monitoring to ensure that patients are receiving a balanced diet. After food selections are made by the patient, the individual menu should be checked by a qualified person to ensure that minimum daily requirements are met.

As a result of widespread employee layoff and efforts to reduce costs, food service departments are changing from selective to nonselective menus. As stated above, there is much controversy for and against selecting a style of menu in terms of cost savings. Although cost is a major factor to consider, the patient's or resident's food acceptance is equally important.

It would be prudent to answer the following questions prior to implementing the nonselective menu system:

- How will the change in menu system affect patient food acceptance?
- Will the less popular or less expensive food items, such as "broiled beef liver," appear on the menu?
- What accommodations will you give to patient food dislikes, allergies, vegetarians, non–pork or non–red meat eaters, and other food preferences?

Depending on the number of requests for substitute food items, it may be necessary to plan a quick and easy menu to offer those who do not prefer what is served on the nonselective menu.

STEPS IN MENU PLANNING

Menu planning, whether done on a weekly basis or for an extended period, is a time-consuming process. The individual responsible for this task must be skilled in both production and service, as well as have a knowledge of other menu

Table 9–5 Comparison of Simple and Elaborate Menu Formats

Simple Menu Format	*Elaborate Menu Format*
Breakfast	Breakfast
Fruit or juice	Fruit or juice
Cereal or egg	Cereal
Toast	Entree (egg, sausage, etc.)
Butter or margarine	Bread (pancakes, muffins, biscuits, toast, etc.)
Milk/beverage	Butter or margarine
	Milk/beverage
Dinner	Lunch
Entree (meat, fish, poultry)	Appetizer (soup, juice, etc.)
Potato or substitute	Entree
Vegetable	Potato or substitute
Salad	Vegetable
Bread	Salad
Butter or margarine	Bread
Dessert	Butter or margarine
Milk/beverage	Dessert
	Milk/beverage
Supper	Dinner
Appetizer (soup, juice, etc.)	Appetizer
Protein main dish	Entree
Vegetable or salad	Potato or substitute
Bread	Vegetable
Butter or margarine	Salad
Dessert	Bread
Milk/beverage	Butter or margarine
	Dessert
	Milk/beverage

factors, if a balanced menu is to be produced. Menu planning can be made easier when an established menu format is used along with a suggested list of food items that have proven to be acceptable to patients and personnel. The suggested steps in writing the menu are as follows:

1. Plan the lunch and dinner entrees for the entire week or for an extended period of time. When the entree is planned first, one is able to build the rest of the meal around the main dish by selecting foods that will enhance the appeal and attractiveness of the total meal.
2. Plan the vegetable and potato categories to accompany the entree. Give consideration to variety in color, texture, flavor, form or shape, and consistency.
3. Plan salads to accompany the rest of the meal. Use fruit or vegetables, rather than high-protein foods such as eggs, cheese, and seafood. Consider variety and avoid using foods that already appear on the menu.
4. Plan the bread category. The use of at least one hot bread a day will add variety and appeal.
5. Plan the appetizer. If soup is used, do not plan to serve, for example, chicken noodle soup when baked chicken is the entree. If fruit or juice is used, it should be different from the fruit in the salad or dessert category.
6. Plan a dessert to complement the meal. Do not repeat items in other categories. Seek variety in texture, temperature, and other factors that will add interest. Limit empty-calorie desserts as much as possible.
7. Plan the breakfast entree. Offer eggs at least four times during the week.
8. Plan the fruit or juice for the breakfast meal. Consider a good source of vitamin C.
9. Plan the cereal category. For a selective menu, plan one hot and one cold cereal.
10. Plan the breakfast bread. In addition to toast, plan for a hot bread, pancakes, or French toast for added interest.
11. Beverages such as coffee, tea, and milk are standard items, as well as condiments.
12. Plan a bedtime nourishment if it is served on a daily basis for all patients.

MODIFIED DIET MENU PLANNING

The menu for modified diets should be based on the regular menu. This practice should be used for a number of reasons:

- Patients on modified diets are more likely to eat their food if they receive the same food as that on regular diets. The primary differences may be modification of calories, nutrients, texture, seasoning, and method of preparation. For example, when fried chicken is planned for the regular diet, the preparation technique may be modified to baked chicken for patients on calorie-restricted diets.
- Frequently, patients in the same room may be on different diets. When patients realize that they are all eating the same basic foods, the meal is more acceptable.
- Modification of the menu in this manner serves as training for patients when they leave the medical facility. The patient is taught that emphasis is not on the purchasing of "special diet food," but merely on adjusting the preparation technique.
- Purchasing for the department is simplified when most patients can eat the same basic foods.
- Production is simplified. Cooks can simply subtract the number of modified servings from the regular menu and prepare according to respective diet modifications.

As shown in Table 9–7, this system results in minimizing the use of different foods. When planning the modified diet menu, the menu should not be cluttered with portions and

Table 9–6 Comparison of Nonselective and Selective Menus

Item	*Nonselective Menu*	*Selective Menu*
Soup or appetizer	Cream of asparagus soup	Cream of asparagus soup or Chilled tomato juice
Entree	Broiled beef liver with sautéed onions	Broiled beef liver with sautéed onions or Roast chicken with giblet gravy
Potato or substitute	Buttered mashed potatoes	Buttered mashed potatoes or Candied sweet potatoes
Vegetable	Buttered green peas	Buttered green peas or Steamed fresh cauliflower with almond butter
Salad	Crisp lettuce wedge	Crisp lettuce wedge or Molded cranberry relish salad
Bread	Hot bran muffin	Hot bran muffin or Hot cloverleaf roll
Dessert	Lemon meringue pie	Lemon meringue pie or Chilled watermelon

amounts for individual diets. The menu should be used as a guide for planning individual diets. When planned individually, each patient's diet can be adjusted for quantity, quality, and patient preferences as appropriate for the particular diet. Individual tray cards or individual menu selection sheets can be used to individualize the menu for each patient.

The use of arrows to indicate foods allowed on modified diets is not recommended. The procedure may be convenient for the data entry clerk, but it is too easy for cooks and others responsible for production and service to make errors when they must follow arrows across the page instead of reading the written word for each diet.

CYCLE MENUS

A cycle menu is one that is planned for a specified period of time such as three, four, five, or six weeks. The menus are used for the specified period of time, and then the cycle is repeated. The use of seasonal cycle menus is obsolete, for all practical purposes, because most foods are available throughout the year. The prohibitive use of certain foods may relate more to cost than availability.

The current trend in cycle menu planning is to plan the menu for a number of days that is not a multiple of 7, such as for 22 days, rather than for 21 days. By using this procedure, the same foods are not served on the same day of the week when the cycle is repeated. Therefore, when the menus are planned, they are not labeled as week one, but as day one, day two, and so forth. Another trend in cycle menu planning is to plan menus for special occasions to be inserted into the menu cycle as appropriate. Exhibit 9–2 presents a cycle menu rotation, using numbers instead of days of the week. The symbol H-4 represents the fourth holiday or special menu for the year.

Special menus are also planned for Friday (F) meals because most patients prefer some type of seafood on those days. For a 22-day menu cycle, four Friday menus are sufficient.

The length of the cycle depends on the type of facility. In nursing homes, the cycle may need to be planned for at least a four-week period because the stay for most patients is for an extended period of time. In acute care facilities, the cycle may be shorter because the average stay for patients is less than 10 days.

Cycle menus must be reviewed to take advantage of data collected during the previous cycle. The cycle also must be reviewed when new food items are added, old items are deleted, or substitutions are made. In the review of menus, it is important that food choices at the end of the cycle (menu No. 22) are different from choices at the beginning of the menu cycle (menu No. 1).

Advantages of planning and using a cycle menu are as follows:

- Reduces menu planning time. After the menus have been planned and evaluated, the amount of time spent in menu review is minimal.

Table 9–7 Modified Diet Menu

Regular	*Restricted Calorie*	*Restricted Fat*	*Restricted Fiber*	*Restricted Sodium*	*Full Liquid*
Orange juice	Unsweetened orange juice	Orange juice	Orange juice	Orange juice	Orange juice
Cream of wheat	Cream of wheat	Cream of wheat	Cream of wheat	SF* cream of wheat	Cream of wheat gruel
Scrambled eggs	FF† scrambled eggs	FF scrambled eggs	Scrambled eggs	SF scrambled eggs	
Buttered toast	Dry toast	Dry toast	Buttered toast	SF toast	
Whole milk	Skim milk	Skim milk	Whole milk	Whole milk	Whole milk
Coffee/tea	Coffee/tea	Coffee/tea	Coffee/tea	Coffee/tea	Coffee/tea
Vegetable soup	Vegetable soup	FF broth	Cream of tomato soup	SF vegetable soup	Cream of tomato soup
Baked honey chicken	FF baked chicken	Baked chicken (no skin)	Baked chicken	SF baked chicken	
Buttered noodles	FF noodles	FF noodles	Buttered noodles	SF buttered noodles	Vanilla pudding
Broccoli spears	FF broccoli spears	FF broccoli spears	Asparagus spears	SF broccoli spears	Grape juice
Cranberry-gelatin mold salad	Diet gelatin mold salad	Cranberry-gelatin mold salad	Cranberry-gelatin mold salad	SF cranberry-gelatin mold salad	
Chocolate fudge cake	Diet peaches	Cling peaches	Cling peaches	Cling peaches	
Whole milk	Skim milk	Skim milk	Whole milk	Whole milk	Whole milk
Coffee/tea	Coffee/tea	Coffee/tea	Coffee/tea	Coffee/tea	Coffee/tea
Chilled apple juice	Unsweetened apple juice	Chilled apple juice	Chilled apple juice	Chilled apple juice	Chilled apple juice
Tenderloin strips	Braised tenderloin strips	Braised tenderloin strips	Braised tenderloin strips	SF tenderloin strips	Cream of mushroom soup
Baked potato with sour cream	Baked potato	Baked potato	Baked potato (no skin)	Baked potato	
Green peas	Green peas	Green peas	Green beans	SF green peas	Baked custard
Fresh garden salad	Fresh garden salad	Fresh garden salad	Lettuce wedge	Fresh garden salad	
Creamy dressing	Lo-cal dressing	FF dressing	Salad dressing	SF dressing	
Cherry pie	Diet cherries	Bing cherries	Bing cherries	Bing cherries	
Whole milk	Skim milk	Skim milk	Whole milk	Whole milk	Whole milk
Coffee/tea	Coffee/tea	Coffee/tea	Coffee/tea	Coffee/tea	Coffee/tea

* SF indicates salt free.
† FF indicates fat free.

Exhibit 9–2 Rotation for 22–Day-Cycle Menu

MARCH 1997

Sunday	Monday	Tuesday	Wednesday	Thursday	Friday	Saturday
						1 No. 1
2 No. 2	3 No. 3	4 No. 4	5 No. 5	6 No. 6	7 F–1 Special	8 No. 7
9 No. 8	10 No. 9	11 No. 10	12 No. 11	13 No. 12	14 F–2 Special	15 No. 13
16 No. 14	17 H–4 Special	18 No. 15	19 No. 16	20 No. 17	21 F–3 Special	22 No. 18
23 No. 19	24 No. 20	25 No. 21	26 No. 22	27 No. 1	28 F–4 Special	29 No. 2
30 No. 3	31 No. 4					

- Streamlines purchasing procedures. Purchasing is somewhat repetitive, except for changes resulting from menu review.
- Aids in standardizing production. Employees become more proficient as they prepare the same menu items over and over again.
- Serves as a training tool. Repetitive production and service improve the ability of supervisors and others in organizing activities.
- Aids forecasting techniques. Data collected during previous menu cycle can be used to project future food needs.

The cycle menu planned for patients may also be used for employees. It may be necessary to supplement the number and variety of foods offered in order to avoid menu boredom. The availability of a "make your own" salad bar, items from the griddle or broiler, and "specials of the day" can add menu interest.

MENU REVIEW COMMITTEE

The review committee is responsible for analyzing data collected during the previous menu cycle in order to make intelligent decisions relative to menu changes. For adequate representation, the committee may include the chef or head cook, purchasing personnel, production and service supervisors, and the clinical dietitian, and be chaired by the food service director or a representative of administration.

Data collected may include census records, food acceptance results, plate waste studies, popular or unpopular food items, problems of quantity and/or quality control, and cost. The menu committee may recommend new recipes for testing or may add new items that have been tested with positive results. After all the changes have been made, the menu must be reevaluated. The following criteria are suggested for menu evaluation:

- Nutritional adequacy—Does the menu adhere to daily food guidelines as listed in the food groups?
- Food preferences—Do menu items reflect the ethnic, cultural, and regional food preferences of patients and employees?
- Personnel—Are employee skills adequate for preparation and service of planned menu items?
- Equipment—Is there an overload on any one piece of equipment that would interfere with quality preparation and service?
- Flavor—Is there a combination of mildly and strongly flavored foods?
- Consistency—Is there a combination of soft and crisp food items?
- Texture—Is there variety in ground and whole cuts of meat? Is there variation in texture?
- Color—Are contrasting color combinations used? Will food items appear attractive and appetizing when plated together?
- Variety—Is the same food item used more than once during the meal or during the day (e.g., tomato juice for breakfast, lettuce and tomato salad for lunch, and veal cutlet with tomato sauce for dinner)? Does the same food appear on the menu cycle for the previous day or the day after? Is the end of the menu cycle different from the beginning of the cycle?
- Cost—Is the daily menu within prescribed budgetary allowances?

Continuous quality improvement should begin with menu planning and prevail throughout the food service system. When effective menu evaluation techniques are used, one can be assured of quality control.

STANDARDIZED RECIPES

Standardized recipes are mandated for use in medical food service operations by outside accrediting agencies. The primary purpose for this requirement is to ensure that all meals served to patients meet quality and quantity standards. The term *standardized recipe* does not mean that recipes are developed by outside agencies and used by all food service facilities. Rather, a standardized recipe is defined as one that has been tested and adopted for use in a particular facility. In some respects, a standardized recipe is analogous to an organization chart; each must reflect the objectives and goals of the particular operation. A standardized recipe system involves recipe development and serves as a basis for menu pricing.

The development, maintenance, and use of a standardized recipe system require time, effort, and full cooperation of both management and employees. The task is compounded when there are a number of cooks on staff who prepare their own special dishes and are unwilling to share their secret recipes. The importance of seeking and gaining participation in all aspects of the developmental process cannot be overemphasized.

Recipe Development

Recipe development is not an easy task. The initial step is to decide on the format for the recipe card. As shown in Exhibit 9–3, the card should include information necessary for product uniformity in both quality and quantity. The recipe card should provide the user with the following:

- Recipe number
- Name of product
- Number of servings
- Size of servings

Exhibit 9–3 Sample Recipe Card

PLAIN MUFFIN
Total servings: 100
Serving size: 2 muffins each

Recipe No. ___________

	200 Muffins	Muffins	Muffins	
Ingredients	Weight	Weight	Weight	Procedure
Flour, all purpose	10 lb			1. Mix flour, baking powder, sugar, and salt.
Baking powder	9 oz			
Sugar, granulated	2 lb, 10 oz			
Salt	3½ oz			
Eggs, beaten	2 lb, 4 oz			2. Mix eggs, oil, and milk. Stir into flour mixture, stirring only until flour mixture is moistened (batter will be lumpy).
Oil	3 lb			
Milk, whole	10 lb			3. Using No. 20 scoop (3 1/5 Tbsp), portion into greased muffin tins. 4. Bake at 400°F for 20 minutes or until lightly browned.

Cost Data

	Cost per Recipe	*Cost per Serving*
Labor		
Food		
Energy		

- Ingredients (List in order of use, ingredient first and the form later—i.e., onions, chopped; fully described, i.e., flour, pastry or bread. Group ingredients that are to be combined or mixed together.)
- Measurements (List by weight, where possible.)
- Yield increments (Allow two or three columns for different yields on each card.)
- Procedure (List opposite ingredients.)
- Cooking temperature and time or cooling temperature and time
- Pan size and number of servings per pan or amount of mixture per pan
- Type and size of serving utensils (ladle, scoop, weight, volume)
- Potentially hazardous ingredients, indicated by an asterisk

The recipe card should be large enough for it to be read easily from a standing position with the card placed on a table top or clipped to a board; for example, the recipe might be written on a 5-by-8-inch index card or an 8½-by-11-inch sheet with bold, heavy type. For protection against soils as a result of employee handling, the card or sheet may be laminated or covered with plastic. A notebook with plastic liners can be used for each set of menus, i.e., soups, entrees, desserts. List the source of the original recipe for future reference. Additional information on the recipe card may include cost data for food, labor, and energy.

To minimize the possibility of errors, use standard terminology in describing ingredients, volumes, and weights. The employee responsible for preparation of a food product should not have to guess whether the ingredient amount is "as purchased" (AP) or "edible portion" (EP).

After the format has been established, start with some of the more popular food items currently prepared in the facility. Do not pressure the employees by attempting to standardize too many recipes at the very beginning. It may be advisable to gain the cooperation of the informal leader among the cooks and have this employee share and adjust the initial recipes. Other employees are more likely to cooperate when the project is approved by the informal leader. For recipes that have proved to be acceptable, the following steps are suggested:

1. Have the cook record the ingredients, amounts, and procedures, using the suggested recipe format. Convert all measurements to weights, if possible.
2. Observe preparation of the food item. Check to determine whether steps have been omitted in procedures or whether extra ingredients are added. Observe mixing or other manipulations and record the time required—for example, mix for 3 minutes at high speed.
3. Weigh and record weight of the raw product.
4. Observe cooking temperature and time, types and sizes of cooking utensils.

5. Weigh and record weight of the cooked product.
6. Determine net yield, number of servings, and serving size. Indicate serving utensils required.
7. If necessary, adjust the recipe as a result of observations.
8. Have another employee prepare the same food item, using the adjusted recipe.
9. Repeat steps 2 to 6.
10. If product quality and quantity are consistent, record the recipe in the permanent file.
11. Use safe food handling procedures during preparation.

Developing New Recipes

In standardizing new recipes, such as those found in newspapers, magazines, and food company brochures, it is suggested that the initial preparation should be in the smallest yield possible. Analyze the new recipe for answers to the following questions:

- Does the recipe contain foods that are acceptable to patients and personnel?
- Are ingredients readily available?
- Is the cost per serving within budgetary allowances?
- Is the preparation time reasonable for assigned personnel?
- Are personnel skills adequate for required preparation and service?
- Are utensils and equipment available for preparation and service in large quantity?

If answers to the above questions are positive, continue with the following steps:

1. Record all pertinent information from the new recipe on a recipe card. For accuracy, convert all measurements to weights. If procedures for preparation are incomplete or unclear, leave space on the recipe card so that information can be recorded during the trial preparation.
2. Discuss the original recipe with the cook responsible for preparation. Emphasize the importance of accuracy in recording information that will be helpful if a decision is made to adjust recipe to a larger quantity.
3. Develop a recipe evaluation sheet to assess quality and quantity (i.e., appearance, aroma, taste, tenderness, serving temperature, total yield, number of servings, and serving size).
4. Modify the recipe, if acceptable, for larger quantity. Calculate ingredients according to charts in Appendixes F and G, or use the factor method as illustrated in Exhibit 9–4. Adjust procedures to allow for additional mixing, cooking, or cooling time.
5. Conduct a second testing of the recipe. Follow steps 1 through 3 above. Evaluate the product.
6. Repeat testing of the recipe for the third and fourth trials, using different employees.
7. If product quality and quantity are acceptable, record the recipe in the permanent file.

Adjusting the Recipe

Errors in adjusting volume and weights in a recipe can be expensive in terms of both labor and food costs. Adjusting a recipe is a time-consuming task. One should be familiar with the procedures and allow ample time for the calculations. It is considered poor management to request a cook to double a recipe at the last minute. Frequently used methods for recipe adjustment include direct-reading weight tables, direct-reading measurement tables, and the factor method (Aldrich and Miller 1967).

The use of direct-reading tables requires a minimum amount of calculation (see Appendixes F and G). To obtain the desired yield in adjusting recipes, observe the following steps:

1. Locate the column that corresponds to the original yield of the recipe to be adjusted.
2. Move a ruler down the column until you find the ingredient amount you wish to adjust.
3. With the ruler in place, read across the line to the column that corresponds to the desired yield.
4. Record this figure as the amount of the ingredient required for the adjusted yield. Repeat steps 1, 2, and 3 for each ingredient in the original recipe to increase or decrease yield.
5. If it is necessary to combine two columns to obtain the desired yield, follow the above procedures and add together the amounts given in the two columns for the adjusted yield.
6. Amounts are given in exact weights, including fractional ounces. After yield adjustment has been made for each ingredient, refer to Appendix H for rounding off fractional amounts that are not of sufficient proportion to change product quality.

The values for rounding are within the limits of error normally introduced in the handling of ingredients. The primary purpose of Appendix H is to aid in rounding fractions and complex weights and measurements to ensure product quality control.

Because the original recipe may list ingredients in either weights or measures, it may be necessary to use both direct-reading tables together. To arrive at ingredient amounts, using measurement tables, follow the same procedures as outlined above for weights. The limiting factor in using direct-reading tables is that they can be used only when both the yield of the original recipe and the yield of the adjusted recipe can be divided by 25.

At times it may be necessary to adjust a recipe with an original yield of more or less than 25, especially when devel-

Exhibit 9–4 Illustration of the Factor Method for Recipe Adjustment

1 Original Recipe*		2 Change Measures to Weight	3 Change Weight to Ounces	4 Multiply by Factor	5 New Recipe (Ounces)	6 New Recipes† (Weight)
Flour	10 lb	Not	160	3.5	560	35 lb
Baking powder	9 oz	necessary for	9	3.5	31.50	1 lb, 15½ oz
Sugar, granulated	2 lb, 10 oz	this recipe	42	3.5	147	9 lb, 3 oz
Salt	3½ oz		3.50	3.5	12.25	12¼ oz
Egg, beaten	2 lb, 4 oz		36	3.5	126	7 lb, 14 oz
Oil	3 lb		48	3.5	168	10 lb, 8 oz
Milk, whole	10 lb		160	3.5	560	35 lb
Total			458.50 (28.656 or 28 lb, 10½ oz)		1,604.75 (100 lb, 4 oz)	100.29 (100 lb, 4 oz)

* Original recipe calls for 100 servings. Servings to be increased from 100 to 350. Factor is 350 ÷ 100 = 3.5.
† Check for calculation accuracy. Original recipe × factor = new recipe (28.656 × 3.5 = 100.29 or 100 lb, 4 oz).

oping recipes for modified diets and for special activities. In such cases, the use of the factor method is suggested. The factor method can be used to decrease or increase any recipe, regardless of the original yield. For example, to increase the original yield of the plain muffin recipe from 100 to 350 portions, one should follow the steps as follows:

1. Divide the desired yield by the known yield of the recipe (350 ÷ 100 = 3.5) to obtain the basic factor. When increasing a recipe yield, the factor will be greater than 1.0; when decreasing a recipe yield, the factor will be less than 1.0.
2. Convert to weights all amounts of ingredients given in measures (see Appendix I). Add weights of all ingredients to get the total weight of the original recipe. See Exhibit 9–4 for the factor method of recipe adjustment.
3. Change all weights to ounces. This makes the calculation easier. If you prefer to work with decimal parts of a pound instead of ounces for the multiplication, use Appendix J.
4. Multiply the amount of each ingredient in the original recipe by the factor.
5. Add together the new weights (ounces or decimals) of all ingredients for the adjusted recipe.
6. Convert ingredient weights back to pounds and ounces for ease of weighing by cooks. Use Appendix H for rounding off unnecessary fractions. The totals for steps 5 and 6 should be the same. If not, check calculations to determine whether mistakes were made in arithmetic.

Adapting Recipes to Metric System

In adapting recipes to the metric system, change all ingredient amounts in the original recipe to weights, then convert to metric. All recipes should be tested in the same manner as suggested for enlarging a recipe. For recipes such as stews and soups, a soft or approximate conversion is adequate. For cakes, pastries, and other baked products, where minor deviations may result in failure, exact conversions are suggested. (See Appendix K for soft and exact metric conversions.)

A recipe with both English and metric units may be confusing for employees responsible for preparation. In Exhibit 9–5, only metric units are used.

Recipe Costing

It is good management practice to know what is being served (standardized recipe), how much is being served (portion control), and how much each portion costs (recipe costing).

To determine recipe cost, add the cost of each ingredient in the recipe. Total all ingredient costs and divide by the number of servings or portions to find the portion cost.

$$\frac{\text{Total recipe cost}}{\text{No. of portions}} = \text{Cost per portion}$$

To determine the food cost percentage, divide the portion cost by the selling price. For example, if the portion cost is \$0.26 and the portion sells for \$0.55, then the food cost percentage is 0.47 or 47 percent.

Exhibit 9–5 Illustration of Adapting a Recipe Using the Metric System

1 Original Recipe*		2 Change Measures to Weight	3 Change Weight to Grams	4 Multiply by Factor	5 New Recipe (Grams)	6 New Recipe (Weight)
Flour	4.536 kg	Not	4,536	3.5	15,876	15.876 kg
Baking powder	255 g	necessary	225.15	3.5	788.02	788 g
Sugar, granulated	1.190 kg	for this	1,190.7	3.5	4,167.45	4.167 kg
Salt	99 g	recipe	99.22	3.5	347.27	347 g
Egg, beaten	1.020 kg		1,020.6	3.5	3,572.1	3.572 kg
Oil	1.360 kg		1,360.8	3.5	4,762.8	4.763 kg
Milk, whole	4.536 kg		4,536	3.5	15,876	15.876 kg
Total			12,968.47† (12.968 kg)		45,389.64† (45.389 kg)	(45.389 kg)

* Metric weights are conversions of weights in the original recipe (see Exhibit 9-4). Servings are to be increased from 100 to 350. Factor is 350 ÷ 100 = 3.5.
†Accuracy check: 45,389.64 ÷ 12,968.47 = 3.5.

$$\frac{\$0.26}{\$0.55} = 0.47 \text{ or } 47 \text{ percent}$$

If the objective is to maintain a minimum of 47 percent food cost, then divide the portion cost by the food cost percentage to obtain the selling price.

$$\frac{\$0.26}{\$0.47} = \$0.55$$

For more accuracy in computing the selling price of a food item, a prime cost method is used. The prime cost method includes both the food and labor costs, to which a percentage is added for profit and other costs. As shown in Exhibit 9–6, the selling price of each food item can be standardized if basic information, such as portion size, recipe cost, and labor computations, is provided. To determine the labor cost involved in the preparation of a food item, it is necessary to monitor the time it takes for an employee to prepare an item, and then multiply the time by the hourly rate paid to the employee. For example, if it takes one employee one hour to prepare 350 portions of blueberry muffins at a rate of pay of $5.75 per hour, the labor cost of each portion is $0.016 ($5.75 divided by 350 = $0.016). The labor cost includes only the preparation time. Cooking time is included in the labor cost only when attention is required during the cooking process, such as constant stirring, turning of foods, and other similar techniques.

The markup percentage is related to ingredient cost. In this example, the food cost of a blueberry muffin is calculated to be $0.213 and the labor cost is $0.016. Together these two costs represent the prime cost or 100 percent cost of the food item ($0.213 + $0.016 = $0.229). A markup percentage is established (in this example 225 percent) and the selling price is determined by multiplying the prime cost by the markup percentage ($0.229 × 225 percent = $0.5152). This figure is rounded to a selling price of $0.55 per muffin.

HAZARD ANALYSIS CRITICAL CONTROL POINT

The hazard analysis critical control point (HACCP) is a preventive food safety system, widely used throughout the food service industry. The system was initially used by the National Aeronautics and Space Administration to produce space food that was free of microbial contamination. It was later used successfully by commercial food processors as one of the best systems to prevent the deterioration of food quality.

Bobeng and David (1978) applied the HACCP system to the conventional, cook-chill, and cook-freeze hospital food service systems. Emphasis was on managerial awareness of microbiological hazards and on identifying the process stages at which loss of control could cause food safety risks. Each process stage of production was considered a control point. The system was further developed by the National Advisory Committee on Microbiological Criteria for Foods by establishing principles to follow in the HACCP process. The latest support for the HACCP system is from the Food and Drug Administration (FDA). Food Code 1993, designed around the HACCP principles, was released by the FDA (U.S. Department of Health and Human Services 1994). Although the code is not a law, it is expected that state, local, and other accrediting agencies

Exhibit 9–6 Illustration of Prime Cost Method for Determining Selling Price

Food Item	*Serving Size*	*Food Cost/Serving*	*Labor Cost/Serving*	*Prime Cost*	*Markup*	*Selling Price*
Blueberry muffin	1 (6 oz)	$0.213	$0.016	$0.229	225%	$0.55

will adopt the HACCP principles into their regulations for food service facilities.

The seven principles of the HACCP system are as follows (National Restaurant Association 1993):

1. Hazard analysis. Identify potentially hazardous foods in the food service operation. A hazard, as defined in Food Code 1993, means a biological, chemical, or physical property that may cause an unacceptable consumer health risk. Know what the risks are and how to control them, such as temperature for receiving, storage, preparation, holding, and serving.
2. Identify the critical control points (CCPs). A CCP is defined as any point or procedure in a food system where loss of control may result in an unacceptable health risk for consumers. For example, in cooking poultry the CCP is an internal temperature of 165°F prior to service.
3. Establish control limits for CCPs. Set control limits or procedures to ensure that CCPs are met. For example, leftover poultry must be heated to 165°F for at least 15 seconds prior to service as a criterion for time and end point heating temperature.
4. Establish procedures to monitor CCPs. Procedures should include time and temperature measurements, and criteria for visual evaluation of CCPs. For example, food-handling techniques used by personnel can be evaluated by observation.
5. Establish corrective action. Determine in advance what corrective action should be taken when the criteria for control have not been met. If the control point or critical limit has not been met, correct it immediately. For example, if poultry specifications indicate that poultry should be delivered in the frozen state, but upon delivery there is evidence of thawing, the product should be rejected.
6. Establish effective record-keeping systems. Use documents such as temperature charts, receiving records, recipes, and other management tools to document the HACCP system. Use a notebook to chart records such as time and temperature relating to the flow of food at CCPs. Record corrective actions when critical controls have not been met.
7. Establish procedures to verify that the system is working. This can be accomplished by visual observations to ensure that HACCP procedures are followed and by reviewing records to monitor accuracy in recording data. Microbiological tests can be made on food samples but may not be timely enough for corrective action. The old practice of saving a sample meal for testing is not an example of timeliness, because the meal has probably already been served to the consumer.

Critical control points are not indicated for all subsystems within the food service system. The HACCP system puts emphasis on time-temperature relationship as related to receiving, prepreparation, preparation, and service. Because all stages/processes dealing with food are not considered critical, noncritical control points are referred to simply as control points (CPs).

For purposes of this text, in promoting the systems approach to management of food service, all subsystems are classified as CPs. CPs for continuous quality improvement (CQI) are indicated for all subsystems as follows (see Figure 10–2 for a chart of food flow for various production systems):

- menu planning (recipe development)
- equipment (cleaning and sanitizing)
- purchasing (receiving, storing)
- food preparation (prepreparing, holding, portioning, assembling, transporting)
- food service (food handling and storing of leftovers)
- personnel (food handling, personal hygiene)
- financial (cost associated with loss of control)

CONTROL POINTS RELATED TO MENU PLANNING

Sound policies and procedures for food handling, with respect to prevention-based food safety problems, begin with menu planning. The use of standardized recipes is an important component of menu planning. CP measures include the following:

- Incorporate safe food handling of all potentially hazardous ingredients as one of the steps in designing the format for recipe cards. Use an asterisk to indicate any potentially hazardous food.

- For recipes that have proved to be acceptable, include safe food handling as one of the procedures to observe.
- Record safe handling of ingredients directly on the recipe card.

To assist management in complying with principles of the HACCP system, suggested forms are presented in Appendix L as follows:

- potentially hazardous foods
- HACCP refrigerator/freezer temperature log
- HACCP temperature for cooking and serving potentially hazardous foods
- HACCP temperature for cooling potentially hazardous leftover foods
- HACCP for reuse of leftover foods

COMPUTER APPLICATIONS

The use of computers in the management of medical food services has indeed expanded over the past decade. Software designed to process repetitive tasks; calculate vast numerical data; and store, retrieve, sort, and link information is widely used throughout the food service industry.

There are many software packages that enable the user to perform the menu-planning task. Some menu-planning software is specific to for-profit food service establishments whereas others focus on the menu-planning needs of nonprofit institutions. In institutional food service, the software available may offer menu planning as a part of a larger software package. Sophisticated and comprehensive computerized food service systems include menu design in addition to nutritional analysis, tray cards, production forms, cost accounting, and more. Less complex software may be limited to manipulating recipes and ingredients.

More advantageous is the use of software packages that offer components. The manager may choose to purchase only the components needed without being obligated to buy an entire software system.

Ascertaining whether a particular recipe program can be easily manipulated is a major purchase consideration. With user-friendly import/export access, the manager can modify the master recipe file to correspond to menu changes. Theoretical menus may be analyzed to determine the minimum cost combination of food items by integrating the menu-planning functions with cost-control functions.

The most common use of the computer in menu planning is the production of different menu and recipe modifications required for therapeutic diets. Menus for special occasions, special functions, and seasonal foods are easily generated via computer. Software for menu planning is a management tool to enhance efficiency and creativity.

For further discussion of computers and menu management see Chapters 12 and 13.

REFERENCES

Abonyi, D. et al. 1969. *Ethni-city: A guide to ethnic Detroit.* Detroit: Michigan Ethnic Heritage Studies Center and Center for Urban Studies, Wayne State University.

Aldrich, P.J., and Miller, G.A. 1967. *Standardized recipes for institutional use,* Chicago: American Dietetic Association.

American Dietetic Association. 1987. Position of the American Dietetic Association: Vegetarian diets. *Journal of the American Dietetic Association* 88, no. 3.

American Dietetic Association. 1988. *Handbook of clinical dietetics.* Chicago.

American Heart Association. 1988. Dietary guidelines for healthy American adults. Position statement. *Circulation* 70:1003.

Bobeng, B.J., and B.D. David. 1978. HACCP models for quality control of entree production in hospital food service systems. *Cornell HRA Quarterly 7,* no. 2: 84–87.

Endres, J.B., and R.E. Rockwell. 1980. *Food, nutrition, and the young child.* St. Louis, MO: CV Mosby.

Food and Nutrition Board—National Research Council. 1989. *Recommended dietary allowances.* 10th ed. Washington, DC: National Academy of Science.

Gibson, L.D. 1981. The psychology of food: Why we eat what we eat when we eat it. *Food Technology* 35, no. 2:54–56.

Kirk, D., and E.K. Eliason. 1982. *Food and people.* San Francisco: Boyd and Fraser Publishing.

Mangels, A.R. 1995. Working with vegetarian clients. *Vegetarian Dietetics* 5, no. 1.

National Restaurant Association. 1993. *HACCP reference book.* Chicago: Educational Foundation.

U.S. Department of Agriculture. 1980. *Food* (Science and Education Administration Home and Garden Bulletin No. 228). Washington, DC.

U.S. Department of Agriculture. 1993a. *Dietary guidelines and your diet: An overview* (Human Nutrition Information Service and Home and Garden Bulletin No. 253.1). Washington, DC: Superintendent of Documents, U.S. Government Printing Office.

U.S. Department of Agriculture. 1993b. *Eat a variety of foods* (Human Nutrition Information Service and Home and Garden Bulletin No. 253.2), 283. Washington, DC: Superintendent of Documents, U.S. Government Printing Office.

U.S. Department of Agriculture. 1995. *The food guide pyramid.* Washington, DC: Superintendent of Documents, U.S. Government Printing Office.

U.S. Department of Agriculture Food and Nutrition Service. 1979. *Building a better diet* (Program Aid No. 1241). Washington, DC.

U.S. Department of Health and Human Services. 1994. *Food and safety assurance program: Development of hazard analysis critical control points.* Proposed rule. Washington, DC: Food and Drug Administration. 21 CFR, Ch 1. August 4, 1994.

CHAPTER 10

Subsystem for Equipment Planning, Use, and Care

Most department heads have been involved in equipment selection, layout, and design. The involvement may have been the selection of a single piece of equipment or the complex responsibilities for planning a new or renovated facility. Food service directors are not expected to be experts in the area of equipment, but it is a costly resource that must be managed. Therefore, it is important to understand basic equipment principles and to possess knowledge sufficient to convey departmental needs to the appropriate authority.

MANAGERIAL RESPONSIBILITY

Because equipment does not last forever, one is expected to plan and submit an annual budget (capital expenditures) for the replacement of old or nonfunctioning equipment. To plan for capital expenditures with some degree of proficiency, one must be knowledgeable about the condition of the equipment in order to write a strong justification to the budget committee. As food service director, one should consider the following factors:

- Know equipment and keep appropriate records.
  1. Keep an up-to-date library of books (include expense in annual budget), and review current literature.
  2. Learn to read manufacturer's brochures for an understanding of terminology. This knowledge will aid in communicating departmental needs to equipment companies and to the internal budget review committee, and will assist in comparing features of different equipment models.
  3. Organize and maintain a working file of equipment catalogues and brochures.
  4. Keep in contact with equipment companies and their sales representatives. Make contacts at conventions and food shows. Know the latest equipment, whether or not you are currently in the market for new equipment.
- Analyze the food service department and set up a long-range equipment program.
  1. Take an inventory of all major equipment in the department. List age and condition of each piece of equipment, along with other pertinent data, as shown in Exhibit 15–18. The accumulated information can be used for justifying new equipment. It is not enough to say that you are tired of equipment breakdowns; you must have support in the form of records to justify the need.
  2. Determine replacement cost or time and new items needed. Life expectancy is approximately 10 years for most major equipment.
  3. Be aware of equipment costs and analyze each requirement with the view of saving money in the long run. The savings may be in repair costs or in food or labor costs. Good records will assist in figuring the pay-back period.
- Budget for equipment. Include equipment requirements in the annual budget. (See Exhibit 15–17, capital equipment budget request.)
- Establish priorities. List equipment as absolutely necessary or as desirable. This task is important in case it is necessary to eliminate certain equipment requests because of budget constraints.
- Coordinate requirements.
  1. Get to know the purchasing agent in the organization.
  2. Know the procedures and requirements for equipment requests.
  3. Be aware of budget meeting dates and deadlines for submitting requisitions. Know when requests should

be submitted and make sure that your requirements are included.

- Be knowledgeable of and prepared for equipment meetings. Know when the equipment review committee meets so that you are there to defend your request, if necessary. Be aware that food service will have competition from other departments within the facility for dollars spent on equipment.
- Write effective justifications.
  1. Provide a complete description, including manufacturer's name, model, type, size, shape, color, and electrical or plumbing characteristics. If required, list more than one source.
  2. If the request is for a replacement, state whether the present equipment is obsolete or is functionally inadequate.
  3. If the request is for an initial purchase, state how the function was performed in the past.
  4. If there has been a change in departmental function or its basic objective, refer to workload increase.
  5. State estimated initial cost, plus installation and maintenance costs.
  6. State how nonapproval of the request will affect departmental goals, employee morale, efficiency, or aesthetic value as related to patient care.

The above responsibilities should be performed whether the food service director is involved in selecting one piece of equipment, remodeling, or planning for a new facility.

FACILITY PLANNING

In planning for renovations or for a new facility, the food service director will or should be part of the planning team, along with the administrator, architect, contractor, and food service consultant. The food service director is sometimes not included as a member of the planning team for a number of reasons. It may be that the individual has not impressed administration with an interest in or knowledge of equipment selection, layout, and design. The contract for a food service consultant should be based on how much can be contributed by the food service director. For effective contributions, the food service director should be included as a member of the planning team during the very early stages. After plans have been finalized, little impact can be made.

Food Service Consultant

The food service consultant serves as the communicating link between the food service director and other members of the planning team. There are two organizations of food service consultants from which names of potential candidates may be obtained: the Food Facilities Consultant Society and the International Society of Food Service Consultants. Qualified consultants may or may not belong to one of the above organizations. One of the best methods to use in selecting a qualified consultant is through personal interview and information based on reputation. The food service consultant may be involved in the following duties (American Hospital Association 1977):

- Help to determine and select equipment.
- Prepare drawings of equipment layout.
- Prepare work flow for architect.
- Write specifications for specially fabricated equipment.
- Prepare equipment portfolio.
- Advise on ventilation, lighting, floors, walls, and other physical features.
- Check preliminary architectural drawings.
- Develop appropriate cost estimates.
- Advise on bids.
- Inspect fabricated equipment in plant before delivery.
- Assist in inspecting installation of equipment.
- Train personnel in use of equipment.
- Perform other services as required.

Factors for Preliminary Planning

The food service consultant works within limitations and guidelines established by the administrator and the food service director. For realistic planning, the consultant must know the objectives, goals, and basic functions of the department; menu and menu pattern; purchasing system; production and service systems; workload and personnel data; and quality standards. Answers to the following questions will assist the food service consultant in formulating layout and design concepts:

- What will be the bed capacity?
- What will be the patient profile? Adults only ______ Females only ______ Children only ______ Adults and children ______
- How many floors for patient care? ______ Number of patient care units on each floor ______ Number of beds on each patient care unit ______
- How many buildings will be served? Main building only ______ Satellite units ______ Estimated capacity of each satellite unit ______ Distance of satellite units from main building ______
- In addition to patient service, what other services will be provided? Employee cafeteria ______ Vending ______ Coffee shop ______ Executive dining ______ Catering ______ Restaurant ______
- What is the estimated number of meals to be served daily? Patients ______ Personnel ______ Guests/others ______

- What will be the operating hours? ______
- What will be the meal schedule? Patients ______ Personnel ______ Guests/others ______
- What type of menu system will be used? Selective ______ Nonselective ______ Cyclical (length) ______
- Will the same menu be used for patients and personnel?
- What will be the purchasing form for meat? Frozen ______ Chilled ______ Preportioned ______ Quarters ______ Wholesale ______
- What will be the purchasing form for fruits and vegetables? Frozen ______ Fresh ______ Canned ______ Dried ______
- What will be the purchasing form for baked products? Bread ______ Rolls, buns ______ Pies, cakes, cookies ______
- What will be the purchasing cycle?

	Daily	Weekly	Monthly
Meat	______	______	______
Poultry	______	______	______
Seafood	______	______	______
Produce	______	______	______
Groceries	______	______	______
Dairy products	______	______	______
Bread and baked products	______	______	______

- What type of production system will be used? Cook-serve ______ Cook-freeze ______ Cook-chill ______ Convenience ______
- What type of service system will be used for patient trays? Centralized ______ Decentralized ______
- What type of distribution will be used for patient service?
- What type of service ware will be used? China ______ Plastic ______ Disposables ______

All decisions related to planning must have administrative approval in order to receive adequate funding. This initial planning stage provides an excellent opportunity for input by the food service director. The initiative taken by the food service director at this time will have a tremendous effect on the outcome of the final plans.

SPACE ALLOCATION

The amount of space required by a food service department is directly related to the functions that must be performed and the various systems used to carry out those functions. For example, the dining space for a commercial restaurant may take priority over the production space because the operation is profit oriented, with emphasis placed on seat turnover for volume sales. The production system, for the most part, is designed for individual orders rather than for preparing food in quantity. In contrast, most medical food service operations are nonprofit, with cafeteria seating used by limited numbers of employees and guests. Furthermore, the production is designed to produce food for both employees and patients, with a large amount of space allotted to the patient tray setup.

Dining Space

Most authorities begin calculation of food service space with the dining area. The amount of space allotted is based on the following factors:

- Heaviest customer load at any one time. This factor is minimal for medical food service operations because most employees eat meals on a staggered basis in order to provide adequate coverage of patient units. Also, most employees are willing to adjust their meal hour to eat at a less busy time, if necessary.
- Speed of service. An average of five persons per minute can be served with a straight-line system. Less time per customer is involved with the scatter system, but a bottleneck may develop at the cash register unless adequate numbers of cashiers are scheduled for peak periods.
- Menu variety, preparation, and service techniques. A large number of food items from which to choose tends to slow the selection process. Most cafeteria menus include a mixture of ready-prepared food items and foods cooked to order, such as grilled sandwiches. The promptness of selection by the customer for self-serve items and the speed of the server for controlled items may speed or delay the rate of customer flow.
- Seat turnover. The term *seat turnover* refers to the number of customers occupying a seat during the hour. For example, if the seat is occupied an average of 20 minutes, the turnover rate is three (60 minutes ÷ 20 = 3). For employees in medical food service, the average time allotted for meals is 30 minutes; therefore, the turnover rate is two.
- Length of serving period. The longer the serving period, the fewer seats required to accommodate customers. The number of seats required for 1,000 customers, at a turnover rate of two, varies from 200 to 500.
- Space allocation per seat. Space allocation for one seat ranges from 12 to 15 sq ft (Kotschevar and Terrell 1977). Requirements vary from state to state; therefore, one should check local and state codes before a final decision is made on seat space allocations. To calculate the total cafeteria space required, multiply the space required for one seat by the number of seats required for one turnover. When using the above allowance for cafeteria space, additional space must be added to the total square footage for seating. The estimated width of the service area should be approximately 14 ft. This allows for 4 ft as customer line-up space, 1 ft tray slide, 2 ft

counter width, 4½ ft for workers behind the counter, and 2½ ft for the back bar (Kotschevar and Terrell 1977). The area allotted for the back bar may be reduced if reach-through refrigerators and warming units are used. The average length of a cafeteria counter in hospital food service operations is 30 to 32 ft.

Production and Service Space

Space allocations for production and service include prepreparation, cooking, baking, salad-sandwich, tray setup, and nourishment, as well as office space and dishwashing and potwashing space. During the planning stage, preliminary estimates of space needs for production and service can be based on the number of beds. Depending on the type of systems used, an allowance of 20 to 30 sq ft per bed is suggested (Kotschevar and Terrell 1977). More space is needed where full production is done, such as with the cook-serve system. Less space is required in production and service areas for a convenience system. The need for space per meal is reduced as the number of beds increases. The allowances do not include storage areas for dry, chilled, or frozen foods, nor do they include cafeteria, special dining rooms, employee facilities, or floor pantries.

A more precise calculation of space for production and service needs can be made later as consideration is given to planning factors related to menu, purchasing system, production, and service systems. It is suggested that space for each work center be calculated according to equipment needs, and then the space for all work centers totaled to provide space needs for the entire area (Avery 1979). See Table 10–1 for a guide to equipment selection based on menu.

Space required for patient service and setup, which is located in the production area, depends on the following:

- Type of tray service. A tray service system using carts to deliver trays to the patient units will require storage space for carts, plus space for cart cleaning.
- Number of patients served. For high-volume patient service, more carts are required for distribution, thus requiring more space.
- Menu variety for regular and modified diets. The number of different food items, each requiring serving space, will affect the amount of setup space needed.

The percentage of floor area required for production and service depends on the system used and the type of equipment associated with each system. According to Kotschevar and Terrell (1977), the space for equipment may comprise only 30 percent of the total space with 70 percent or more used for work areas, traffic aisles, and space around equipment for ease of operation and cleaning.

Space for storage includes dry storage, refrigerated, and low-temperature frozen food storage. Depending on the type of production system, there may exist a need for blast freezer space. In addition to the above, space must be provided for receiving and inspecting deliveries.

In the receiving area, space is required for scales and for some means for conveying goods received to their proper location, such as flatbed trucks, two-wheeled hand trucks, and conveyor belts, as well as space for the receiving office. Floor space required by the types of scales usually found in the receiving area varies from 30- to 300-lb capacity.

Provisions should be made for the storage and removal of trash near the receiving area. A separate room should be provided with enough space for a compactor and equipment for cleaning trash cans. Depending on how garbage is disposed of and the frequency of pickup, it may be necessary to provide for refrigerated storage in the trash area.

Space required for dry storage depends on the following:

- Menu—the variety and types of food items.
- Stock level required—the minimum and maximum amounts of food to keep on hand.
- Frequency of delivery—the size of deliveries is related to how often deliveries are made. Space is needed for the largest amount to be stored at one time.

Dry storage includes space for food items (canned, bottled, bagged), paper supplies and other disposables, and a separate area for cleaning supplies. According to Avery (1979), it is best to compute dry stores for one day, multiply this by the number of days food is to be stored plus 10 percent, and then double the amount to allow for aisles and waste space.

Space for refrigerated and low-temperature storage includes both the large walk-in refrigerators and freezers and the smaller units located throughout the production and service areas. Factors related to the amount of space needed for chilled and frozen food are the same as those associated with dry storage.

The importance given to space utilization cannot be overemphasized. Each square foot of space represents an enormous outlay of capital. The previous discussion on space allocation is considered preliminary. As work proceeds to equipment selection and layout, more exact calculations can be made with possible revisions in space allocation.

EQUIPMENT SELECTION

The menu is the basis for determining equipment needs. Based on menu items served, other factors such as the form of purchase, storage, preparation, and service techniques combine to indicate specific equipment needs. For example, the kitchen range, loaded with big pots and pans, is practically obsolete in medical food service operations. Most foods are prepared with the use of steam equipment and ovens. If the menu does not require certain kinds of equipment, then it is a waste to spend money to purchase them. In

Table 10–1 Menu Analysis for Equipment Needs

Menu Item	*Purchased Form, Preparation Technique*	*Major Equipment Needs*
Appetizers		
Chilled cranberry juice	Canned, bulk	Dry storage
Cream of celery soup	Fresh, scratch	Dry storage, refrigerator, kettle
Vegetable soup	Fresh, canned, scratch	Dry storage, refrigerator, kettle
Entrees (hot)		
Roast beef au jus	Fresh	Refrigerator, convection oven
Breaded veal cutlet with	Frozen	Freezer, fryer
mushroom sauce	Fresh	Refrigerator, tilting kettle
Grilled cheese sandwich	Scratch	Dry storage, refrigerator, slicer, griddle
Char-broiled hamburger on a bun	Fresh, scratch	Dry storage, refrigerator, broiler
Entrees (cold)		
Deluxe club sandwich	Scratch	Dry storage, refrigerator, slicer
Cottage cheese-fruit plate	Fresh, scratch	Refrigerator
Maurice salad	Fresh, scratch, precooked meat	Refrigerator, slicer, steamer
Vegetables		
Parslied potatoes	Fresh, prepeeled	Refrigerator, steamer
Baked potatoes	Fresh	Convection oven
Buttered broccoli	Frozen	Freezer, steamer
Green beans with pearl onions	Frozen	Freezer, steamer
Salads		
Tossed vegetable salad (VCM)	Fresh, scratch	Refrigerator, vertical cutter-mixer
Creamy coleslaw	Fresh, scratch	Dry storage, refrigerator, VCM
Molded peach on lettuce	Fresh, canned, scratch	Dry storage, refrigerator
Breads		
Hot rolls	Scratch	Dry storage, mixer, proofer, oven
White, wheat, rye	Commercial	Dry storage
Desserts		
Lemon cake with lemon icing	Scratch	Dry storage, refrigerator, mixer, oven
Cherry pie	Canned, scratch	Dry storage, kettle, mixer, oven
Chocolate chip cookies	Scratch	Dry storage, refrigerator, mixer, oven
Assorted ice cream	Commercial	
Beverages		
Coffee	Scratch, bulk	Dry storage, urn
Tea	Bag, individual	Hot water dispenser
Milk	Carton, individual	Refrigerator

addition, they use up valuable space. The complete menu cycle must be analyzed before decisions are made. An analysis of equipment needs based on one meal for one day is shown in Table 10–1.

The analysis listed in Table 10–1 provides only the type of equipment needed; it does not give information on the capacity needed or how many pieces of each type. To arrive at specifics in terms of size and number, one needs to calculate the portion size, total amount of food needed, batch size, and at what interval the food item is needed during the meal hour. For example, to cook 500 4-oz servings of roast beef (rolled and tied), one needs to know the following information to determine the number of deck ovens (32 × 42 in) required:

- number of servings—500
- size of roasting pan—16 × 20 in
- size of serving—4 oz
- number of roasts per pan—2
- size of roast—18-lb average
- number of pans per deck—4
- number of servings per roast—50
- number of decks needed—2
- number of pans needed—500 ÷ 100 = 5

In another example let us determine the amount of "reach-through" refrigerator space needed for salads, desserts, and other prepared cold food items. For the storage of 200 servings of tossed salad, one would need to know the following:

- serving size—1 cup
- dish used—salad bowl
- height of food and bowl—3½ in
- space between pans—3 in
- size of pan—18 × 26 in
- number of portions per pan—12
- number of pans for 100 servings—8⅓
- number of pans for 200 servings—17
- capacity per door opening (3-in spacing)—19
- total space required—one full height door opening

For food items that can be prepared in batches, equipment needs may be less than for foods prepared all at one time. For example, the operation may require 12 pans of baked macaroni and cheese, but this is a product that quickly deteriorates in quality if cooked too far in advance. Therefore, a large kettle is required for cooking and mixing, but less space is required for baking because only two or three pans are needed at a time. The use of menu analysis to determine equipment needs is a time-consuming task that is well worth the effort in ensuring adequacy in type and amount of equipment required for efficient and effective operation.

With equipment needs established, it is time to look at other factors involved in the selection process, such as performance, materials, construction and design, cost, safety, and sanitation features. The process may begin with a survey of equipment manufacturers to determine what is available.

Performance

In this context, performance refers to how well the equipment will function over a period of time to produce the volume needed for the operation. Research can be conducted by checking with other food service operations with the same equipment. Questions should be asked about the quality of products produced, ease of handling, number and types of repairs needed, availability of parts and promptness of repairs, and other pertinent information to assist in decision making.

Materials

The material used in the construction of the equipment should be suitable for the type of equipment, conforming to applicable standards as determined by the National Sanitation Foundation (NSF). Consider the gauge and finish of metals used for equipment. The gauge or thickness of sheet and plate metal is determined by the weight of metal per square foot. U.S. standard gauge numbers range from No. 000 with a 0.3750-in thickness to No. 24 with a 0.0239-in thickness (Kotschevar and Terrell 1977). The smaller numbers indicate a thicker metal. Numbers 10 to 14 gauge for galvanized steel and numbers 12 to 16 for noncorrosive metals are generally used for food service equipment (West et al. 1977). The lighter gauges, above No. 16, are generally used for sides of equipment or areas where the wear is light.

The finish refers to the degree of polish. For stainless steel, the degree of finish or polish is indicated by numbers 1 to 7. The smaller numbers indicate a dull finish; the larger numbers indicate a high-gloss polish. Finish No. 4 has a standard polish and is often used for equipment such as table tops, sinks, and counters. High-luster finishes cost more and should not be used unnecessarily, especially on surfaces not visible to customers. Most kitchen equipment is made of stainless steel because it is durable, easy to clean, resists corrosion, and has a good appearance. The type of stainless steel recommended for food service equipment is an alloy, commonly called 18-8 or No. 302. The 18-8 refers to the 18 percent chromium and 8 percent nickel it contains (West et al. 1977). Wood has limited use in food service operations because it is difficult to maintain proper sanitary conditions. Wood may be used only for single-service articles, such as chopsticks, stirrers, or ice cream spoons. The use of wood as a food contact surface under other circumstances is prohibited (U.S. Department of Health and Human Services 1976).

Sanitation and Safety

All multiuse equipment should have NSF and Underwriters Laboratory (UL) approval for maximum sanitation and safety. According to the U.S. Department of Health and Human Services (1976), "Multiuse equipment and utensils shall be constructed and repaired with safe materials, including finishing materials; shall be corrosion resistant and nonabsorbent; and shall be smooth, easily cleanable, and durable under conditions of normal use." To make sure that equipment meets required standards, one should check for NSF and UL seals of approval, which are prominently displayed on all approved equipment.

Prior to equipment selection, a comparison can be made for all major equipment. In making an equipment survey, list all desirable features and compare models. According to Hall (1982), the following recommendations should be considered during the selection process:

- Insulation should be maximum thickness for retention of cool air. Polyurethane insulation is recommended.
- Interior capacity should be visually evaluated for usable space. Placement of shelving and blower coils may take away valuable storage space. Top-mounted blower coils are suggested.
- Feet must be adjustable to allow for possible uneven flooring where equipment is to be installed.
- Door liners must be durable to withstand possible abuse from daily use.
- Warranties should be carefully evaluated. Seek the maximum warranty.

- Ask to see test results on temperature differentials throughout the cavity for uniformity of air flow.
- Consider pros and cons of a condensate evaporator system. Refrigerant is dispersed through the refrigerator condensate evaporator system by either capillary tubes, which provide an orifice of constant size, or an expansion valve, which has an orifice that changes in size to allow more or less refrigerant to evaporate as the temperature varies. Expansion valves can malfunction but can be repaired and do provide an efficient flow of refrigerant. Capillary tubes have no moving parts, thus providing a completely closed system; if malfunction occurs, however, the total system must be replaced.

General recommendations for the selection of freezers are as follows:

- polyurethane insulation, maximum thickness
- top-mounted blower coils
- adjustable feet
- exterior thermometer
- maximum warranty
- UL, NSF approval

SPECIFICATIONS

The writing of specifications was listed as one of the duties of the food service consultant, but this task should not be done in isolation. Input from the food service director and possibly from the employees who will have responsibility for the smooth functioning of equipment must be considered.

Specifications are written by the buyer and list in clear statements what is desired and under what conditions. The written statement, if accepted by a purveyor or manufacturer, represents a contract between the two parties. Unnecessary wording makes for a cumbersome specification and increases the possibility of error on the part of the writer. The responsibility for writing specifications is part of the food service consultant's duties, with input from management.

Types of Specifications

According to Harris (1981), specifications can be classified into four categories:

1. Closed specification—one in which the description is so detailed that only one product can qualify. The closed specification may be desirable when new materials or equipment must match existing equipment or decor, such as in renovation projects.
2. Open specification—one that allows a competitor to supply a number of products or materials that are considered equal or acceptable. If the "or equal" clause is used, it should be worded "or approved equal," meaning subject to administrative approval.
3. Manufacturer's specification—one that is written by manufacturers in such a way as to sell their particular product. The best qualifications are presented, and in most cases the specification fails to mention any deficiencies.
4. Performance specification—one that is written in a manner that stipulates all of the requirements that the installation or product must meet, but does not state how. It allows the methods and sometimes the materials to be selected by the contractor, who then assumes responsibility for desired results.

It may be necessary to combine one or more types of specifications to get the desired results.

Guidelines for Specification Writing

The most important aspect of specification writing is to explain exactly what is to be done in the most simple, clear, and concise manner. To assist the food service director in meeting responsibilities for specification writing, answers to the following questions should be beneficial (Avery 1978):

- Is the specification free of any possible misunderstanding? Is the language used to describe details similar to that used by manufacturers?
- Are all desired features included in the specification?
- Is the specification free of all frivolous requirements? Anything that is different from the standard manufacturer's specification sheet should be reviewed for absolute necessity. As a rule it will cost more and, in many cases, manufacturers of quality equipment are hesitant to bid on the equipment because they have not tested the modification and will not want their brand name on something they have not tested.
- Are gauges, finishes, and composition of materials described using standard terminology (such as No. 302 corrosion-resistant steel, 12-gauge metal thickness, and No. 4 finish)?
- Is the design well balanced? Is the frame adequate to support the top specified? Is the weight compatible with the floor on which the equipment will rest? Are hinges adequate for size and weight of the door? Will the drawer size carry the drawer weight plus contents? Has a table with an adequate gauge top been properly balanced with lightweight side panels?
- Are all construction details uniform so that several parts of similar purpose and design are described in identical terms?
- Are greater quality, more expensive metal, heavier gauge, or finer finish being used than is warranted based on anticipated equipment use?
- Does the specification indicate who will or will not provide associated equipment (faucets, valves and traps for

sinks, electrical connections for worktables, and similar equipment)?
- Who is responsible for installation? If the dealer is to install, does the responsibility include preparing the equipment location and bringing in utilities and drains?
- Is workmanship defined?
- If the successful bidder is to install equipment, is he or she required to submit proposed installation plans for approval?
- Is it specified that construction details, particularly those relating to water and drains, conform to local regulations? Does construction conform to Occupational Safety and Health Administration (OSHA) regulations?
- Has the terminology "good commercial practice" been used to cover any details of construction that may have been overlooked?
- Are provisions made in the equipment design for easy access to parts on which repair or adjustments will have to be made?
- If the intent is to encourage a number of bidders, has the specification been written loosely enough so that a number of manufacturers can comply with specification details? If the specification is written so that only one piece of equipment can comply with all of the details, the price may be high.

In addition to the above guidelines, the following particulars should be considered by the specification writer:

- State that all equipment shall be approved by the appropriate agency, such as NSF, UL, or the American Gas Association (AGA).
- Stipulate that bid prices should include taxes, shipping, and other related charges. If the facility has a tax-exempt status, it should be stated in the general information specification.
- Specify delivery and shipment conditions, dates for arrival, and method of shipping.
- Specify exact destination, such as that delivery is to be made to an off-site warehouse until ready for installation.
- State who is responsible for equipment assembly and training in use and care.
- Specify whether warranty is to be for both parts and labor, and length of warranty.
- Specify the length of time during which parts shall be available if the model is discontinued; it should be at least 10 years.
- Specify time span for service and repair of equipment, such as within 48 hours.

LAYOUT DESIGN

Having analyzed the menu to determine equipment needs, it is time to put the individual pieces of equipment into a layout design that will promote smooth, efficient operation. The complete layout is composed of work centers and sections (Kotschevar and Terrell 1977).

Work Centers

A work center is the smallest area, planned in the facility. It is an area where a group of related tasks are performed. Attention should be given to the following:

- Functions to be performed. The functions may include prepreparation, preparation, storage, setup, service, and clean-up. For example, in the salad-sandwich work center, the amount of prepreparation depends on whether all vegetables are cleaned and cut in the salad area or whether this work is accomplished in the ingredient room. If the functions are performed in the ingredient room, then there is no need for equipment such as a slicer or vegetable cutter. Space is required for mixing and dishing of salads and for assembling materials for sandwiches.
- Volume to be prepared. The largest amount of food required at any one time will affect layout design of the work center. It may be necessary to have all salads and sandwiches ready at the beginning of patient tray setup and enough portions ready for cafeteria service to get started with batch making throughout the service period.
- Number of employees. The number of employees is related to the functions and volume. Each employee requires a certain amount of space to perform tasks without bumping into another person and without excessive reaching and traveling.
- Kind and amount of equipment. The menu dictates the kind and amount of equipment needed. Equipment needs for the salad-sandwich area will include table-top space with sink and garbage disposal. Consider a U shape with the sink at the bottom of the U. Unless cooked foods are prepared in the main cook's area, a trunion-type kettle is required for foods such as cooked dressings, hard-cooked eggs, boiled shrimp, and hot water for jellied salads. Refrigerated space is required for holding salads and sandwiches.

The space allotted to a work center should be adjusted to take into account the above factors. For a medium-sized worker, the work center space should be approximately 15 sq ft, measuring about 2½ ft deep by 6 ft long (Kotschevar and Terrell 1977). Solicit the aid of workers to assist in designing work centers. Employees are more familiar with the work to be done and can offer useful suggestions on the placement of equipment that will reduce both time and energy in performing tasks. The use of paper, cardboard, or plastic templates, as shown in Figure 10–1, can be used to provide a visual presentation prior to final drawings.

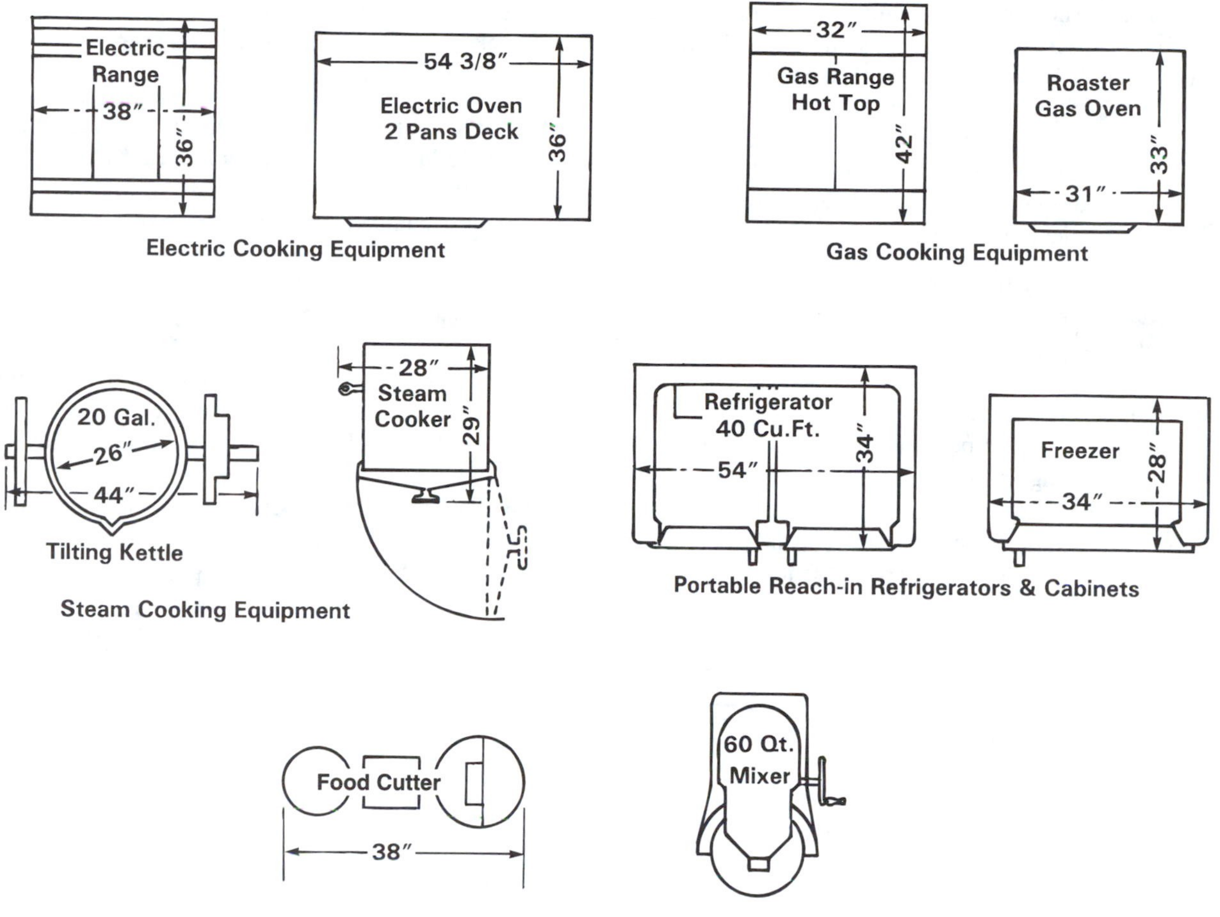

Figure 10–1 Equipment Templates for Layout Design

Templates are scaled representations of the actual size and shape of equipment. The standard scale is ¼ in equals 1 ft. If the template represents only the shape and size, allow space for workers and equipment clearances, such as bending and opening drawers and oven doors. With the use of templates, modifications can be made as work centers develop into sections, and sections develop into the complete layout.

Work Sections

A work section is composed of one or more work centers, such as vegetable and meat cookery, in the main cooking section. The sections are formed based on the interrelationships of work activity performed in the work centers. The sequence of work, used to plan work centers, applies to the joining of work centers into sections. Prime considerations are principles relating to travel time and energy expenditure on the part of employees; dual use of equipment, where possible; use of mobile equipment; and safety and sanitation standards.

The Layout

When planning is implemented into a complete layout, consideration must be given to the flow of materials, workers, and customers, and to the interrelationships of work activities within each section. Layout design is a compromise between a number of factors and is frequently complicated by the diversity and the number of functions, quality and cost control requirements, and the specific needs of the operation. The ideal layout cannot always be achieved, but certain principles and concepts should be considered. Major concerns relate to the flow of food products and the interrelationships of work sections.

Concept of Flow

The layout is guided by the basic concept of flow. Functions in proper sequence should follow the most direct and quickest route without crisscrossing, backtracking, interference, or delay. The arrows in Figure 10–2 indicate the flow of materials in a logical, efficient manner. Usually when the flow of materials is minimized, the flow of employees is also minimized. The planner of flow should have a knowledge of production and service functions in order to effectively plan the layout. As suggested by Kotschevar and Terrell (1977), there are eight principles to consider in establishing flow for efficient work accomplishment:

1. Make sure that functions proceed in a direct, straightforward sequence with a minimum of crisscrossing and backtracking.
2. Seek smooth, rapid production and service, with a minimum of time and energy expended by workers.
3. Eliminate, as much as possible, delay and storage of food in processing and serving.
4. Minimize travel distance for workers and materials.
5. Ensure minimum handling of materials and tools, and minimum worker attention for equipment.
6. Seek maximum utilization of space and equipment.
7. Seek quality control at all critical points.
8. Seek minimum cost of production.

It is important to keep in mind that even though the layout may include labor-saving equipment that is conveniently arranged, there can still be a waste of worker time and energy unless employee training is carried out.

Work-Activity-Section Relationship

It is important to seek a large number of interrelationships among sections to form the complete layout. Activities related to food materials, as they flow through the facility, are as follows: receiving, storing, preparing, cooking, distributing, and serving. To perform these activities in a safe and sanitary manner, other areas must be considered, such as dishwashing, pot and pan washing, and trash removal.

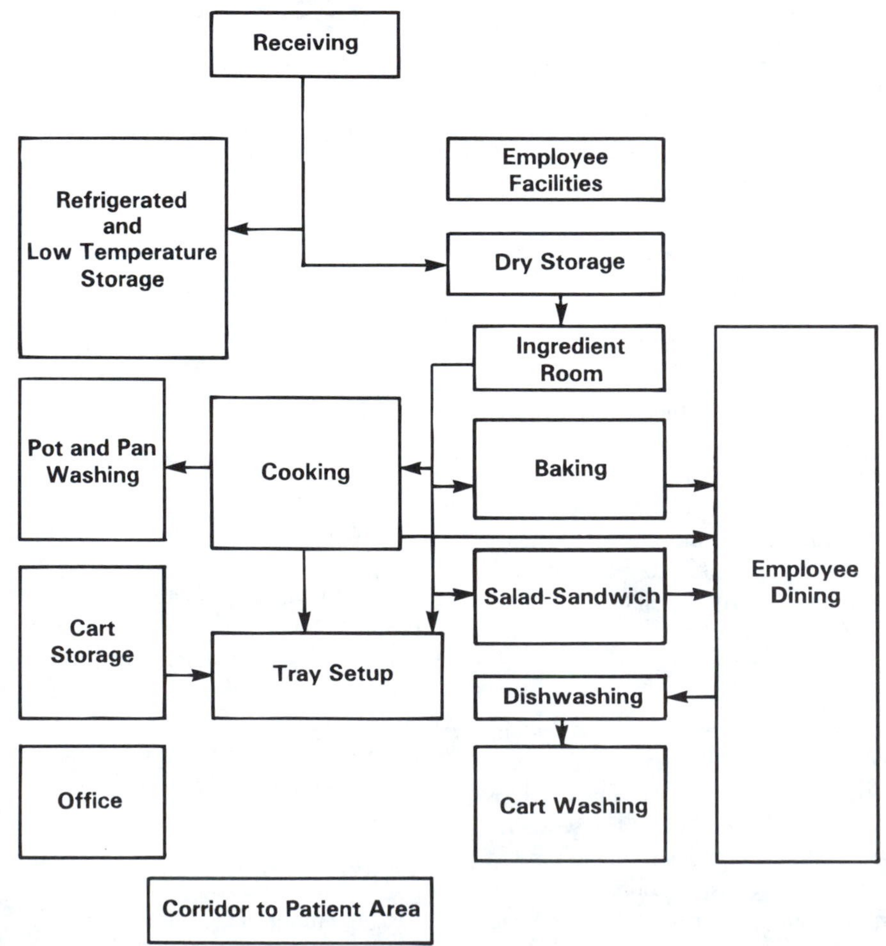

Figure 10–2 Food Product Flowchart

Receiving

The location of the receiving area should be convenient for the types of deliveries being made, whether by truck or car. The receiving platform should be at truck-bed height to avoid excessive lifting and handling of materials. In large facilities, nonperishable items may be stored in central stores with other hospital supplies or stored in a separate central storage area for food service items only. When a central storeroom is used, space for a daily storeroom must be provided near the production area. Doors for the receiving area must be large enough for bins, trucks, and other large equipment to pass through. Space for scales, receiving tables, trucks and carts used for transporting, desk, files, and tools for opening crates and cases must be provided. Adjacent to the receiving area should be space for the storage and disposal of trash and garbage. A separate outside entrance is suggested to avoid possibility of cross-contamination. A compactor and a can washer may be required in the garbage-trash area.

Storage Area

A dry storage area is required for staple food items, linen, paper supplies, and excess equipment (small utensils, dishes, silverware, silver service, glasses, banquet tables, folding chairs, floral arrangements, and other seasonal decorations). A separate storage area is required for cleaning supplies. Plan for small storage areas in each work section, unless an ingredient room is planned. With the use of an ingredient room, the need for individual storage areas is eliminated. Space utilization is increased with adjustable shelves. The use of mobile bins for dry products and drums with pumps or cradles for oils and other liquids is suggested. Space is needed for other equipment, such as a table, chair, and file cabinet, if an inventory system is maintained in this area. Consider ventilated storage space for items such as underripe fruits and vegetables.

Bulk refrigerated and low-temperature storage (walk-in types) should be located near the receiving area to eliminate distribution problems and to promote the forward flow of products. Other refrigerated and low-temperature storage may be located throughout the production and service areas. There may be a need for other types of refrigerated and low-temperature storage such as reach-in, pass-through, counter refrigeration, undercounter refrigeration and freezer, or portable ice cream freezers. Consider the pros and cons of combination coolers where the frozen food section opens into the refrigerated section instead of directly into the production area. If the production system is ready-serve, there will be a need for blast freezing with temperature range of –30°F instead of 0°F for low temperature. Thawing refrigerators are suggested for the safe thawing of frozen foods. During the thawing process, the food softens but the temperature of the food product never rises above a safe refrigerator temperature of 40°F. The food is thawed under controlled temperatures in approximately 12 hours, compared with 2 to 3 days for regular refrigerated thawing.

Prepreparation

Prepreparation tasks may take place at the individual work centers, or the activity may be accomplished in a separate work center such as a butcher shop or ingredient room. For operations using the carcass or wholesale cuts of meat, prepreparation is done in a butcher room. For operations using retail cuts and preportioned meat items, the prepreparation can be done in the ingredient room, along with other food items. One worktable with a sink should be used for meats, and another worktable with a sink should be used for fruits and vegetables. The two activities should be separated to avoid cross-contamination. The ingredient room is the area where all measuring, trimming, grinding, shaping, chopping, and similar activities take place. The location of the ingredient room should be convenient to dry, refrigerated, and low-temperature storage, and in direct flow to the production areas. Equipment required in the area may include scales, slicer, shredder, patty shaper, grinder, cuber, chopper, vegetable cutter, and reach-in and pass-through refrigerated space. The pass-through refrigerator, with roll-in racks, will be used for storage of portioned and measured food items. Portion scales (32-oz capacity with ½-oz gradations) are suggested for spices, and bench-type counter scales (30-lb capacity with 1-lb gradations) are required for weighing larger quantities. The number of each needed depends on the volume demand of the operation.

Cooking-Baking

The cooking and baking areas may be combined in small operations and in some large operations where a minimum amount of baked products are prepared from scratch. The major advantage in combining the two areas is the dual use of equipment such as mixers and ovens. Depending on the menu and volume, a separate bakery area will require much of the same equipment as the main cooking area, such as steam kettle, ovens, deep-fat fryer, mixer, and scales. In addition, specialized equipment such as yeast proofer and dough cutter will also be needed. Workers in the bakery area tend to work independently of other employees and prefer to have a separate pot and pan washing section to avoid mixing of equipment. Consider the flow of materials from dry and refrigerated storage to the work area and finally to the service area. When the bakery area is combined with the cooking of other foods, a separate table is required for panning and finishing of products. Mobile racks are required for storage and transport of finished products, such as a roll-in refrigerator type.

The most frequently used layout pattern for the cooking area is to have all dry heat and moisture-producing equipment grouped together under one ventilating hood. The parallel back-to-back arrangement is used with or without a wall separating the equipment. The arrangement is economical and may provide for good supervision of the work area if walls are eliminated. In the back-to-back arrangement, dry heat equipment such as ovens, fryers, broilers, and griddles are placed on one side, and steam equipment is placed on the other. Worktables are placed in front of equipment on both sides. The amount of prepreparation equipment required will depend on the use of an ingredient room. The use of partially or fully prepared foods will increase the need for refrigerated space. Efficient layout of this area is the key to the entire production and service areas. Consider the inflow of materials from storage or the ingredient room, and the outflow to serving areas and pot and pan washing.

Salad-Sandwich

The salad-sandwich section should be located near the serving areas with direct-flow from storage or the ingredient room. The amount of equipment required depends on the menu volume, and whether prepreparation is performed in the area. The flow of materials may be from storage or the ingredient room, to the cooking area (roast meat for sandwiches), or the vegetable cooking section (potatoes, hard-cooked eggs, and similar items). A table with sink and garbage disposal is required, along with other table-top equipment such as slicer, chopper, hot plate, and steam equipment—if the required food is not prepared in another section. Refrigerated space is required for bulk and portioned food items.

Patient Tray Setup

The tray line setup should have direct flow from the cooking, bakery, and salad-sandwich areas, as well as from storage for direct deliveries. Tray setup location should be near the dietitian's office for supervision, and near the dumb waiter, vertical conveyor, or exit to the elevator for distribution to the patient area. In addition to a horizontal conveyor for tray setup, mobile equipment is required for holding hot and cold foods. The type and amount of equipment needed depends on the menu variety, volume, and amount of preparation performed during serving, such as toast, eggs, and other foods that lose quality from extended holding. Space is required for storage of food carts, if used. To avoid cross-contamination, the return of soiled carts should proceed directly to dishroom and cart washing area without travel through the production and service areas.

Cafeteria Service

The cafeteria service area should be placed as close to production areas (main cooking, salad-sandwich, and bakery) as possible. The use of pass-through refrigeration and warming cabinets promotes efficiency for both kitchen and cafeteria personnel. Counter space is determined by menu variety, shape of the serving area, customer load, and anticipated traffic pattern. Counters may be arranged in a straight line, an L shape, a square, or a combination of the various types. The scatter or scramble arrangement is a popular system because it allows traffic to flow freely in a square area with various counters arranged around the perimeter. Space is provided in back of counters for workers and preparation equipment such as deep-fat fryers, broilers, and griddles. The arrangement chosen should prevent delays and bottlenecks at the cashier station, self-dispensing beverage area, salad bar, condiment station, and cook-to-order counters.

Dishroom

The dishroom should be conveniently located for the return of customer trays and the return of food carts from patient areas. Equipment should be arranged to avoid cross-contamination at the clean end of the dish machine. The use of self-leveling dispensers for dishes and glasses is encouraged.

Pot and Pan Washing

The area for pot washing should be located in an area convenient to all production areas. Space is required for storing clean equipment. A three-compartment sink is required for pot washing done by hand; a pot-washing machine may be considered, if volume justifies the use.

Employee Facilities

Locker rooms and toilets may be in the front or rear of the building. The important factor is that the location of these facilities should be near an entrance so that employees will not have to travel through the production and service areas in outside clothing.

Office Space

A number of sites throughout the facility are appropriate for office space, depending on the nature of activity. Office space for supervisors should be close to the area being supervised. The dietitian's office should be near an entrance, a location that is convenient for consultation with food service employees and personnel from other departments. Consider privacy and environmental factors, especially excessive noise.

Emphasis has been placed on flow, but other important factors of layout need to be considered:

- Efficient use of utilities. Group equipment according to type of utility as much as possible. All equipment requiring steam may be placed together, thereby reducing cost because fewer pipes are needed for installation.

- Efficient use of equipment. Promote dual use by placing equipment in a central location, if stationary, or use carts with wheel locks for moving equipment from one location to another.
- Efficient use of personnel. Arrange equipment for minimum movement and travel for skilled personnel. If a choice of travel is between two employees of different skills and pay levels, then the longer distance should be traveled by the less-skilled and lower-paid employee.
- Safety. Layout based only on flow may prove to be dangerous to workers in the area. For example, avoid placement of high-temperature equipment next to a traffic aisle, or doors opening to block the traffic aisle.
- Sanitation. An awareness of activities conducive to cross-contamination cannot be overlooked.
- Environmental factors. Lack of consideration may affect production, as discussed in the next section.

ENVIRONMENTAL FACTORS IN FACILITY DESIGN

Emphasis on environmental factors can have a positive impact on conditions under which employees must work. Although engineers must comply with established codes and regulations, there is a certain amount of flexibility in facility design. Poor working conditions contribute to decreased productivity, increased labor turnover, absenteeism, and employee fatigue. Employees do their best work in a comfortable work environment. Some factors that have a direct effect on worker efficiency are lighting, temperature, and noise.

Lighting

Consider lighting needs for specific work areas rather than having all ceiling lights with the same light intensity. Light intensity is measured in candlepower (cp), which indicates the strength or force of light going in any direction from the light source. Light meters are used to measure footcandles (fc), which indicate the amount of light concentrated on a surface area. Light quantity is measured in lumens (lm). Kotschevar and Terrell (1977) use the following calculation to derive the footcandle value: "If a lamp gives off 100 lm, 60 percent of which strikes a 10-sq ft surface (60 lm), the footcandles per square foot equals 6 fc." As a member of the planning team, the food service director needs to be somewhat familiar with light science technology in order to understand how engineers derive certain figures.

As reported by Myers (1979), the Illuminating Engineering Society suggests 30 fc throughout the kitchen, 70 fc at points where inspection and pricing are done, and 15 fc in storage areas. The food service director is familiar with activities to be performed in each work area, and is therefore in a position to offer suggestions on light intensity.

One of the problems associated with lighting is that of glare. The source of glare can be the color of walls, ceilings, or floor coverings, or reflections from bright stainless steel equipment. According to Avery's (n.d.) report on human engineering in kitchen design, the upper walls should be pale green, buff, light gray, or light blue and should reflect 50 percent to 60 percent of the light that strikes them. Ceilings may be white, off-white, yellow, ivory, or cream and should reflect 80 percent to 85 percent of the light. Lower walls should be darker shades of green, brown, gray, or blue. Floors should be light enough to reflect back 30 percent to 35 percent; equipment should reflect 30 percent to 50 percent.

Temperature

In many of the newer facilities, both the dining and production areas are air conditioned. The cost of air conditioning may be prohibitive for some operations; thus they compromise on a good ventilating system. The objective is to provide a comfortable work environment with temperatures ranging from 75° to 80°F, with a relative humidity of 50 percent. For proper ventilation, there needs to be a balance of air exhaust and air input. The two methods most frequently used to determine exhaust air flow requirements are the air change method and the fixed air velocity method (Myers 1979). The air change method is based on proper sizing of the exhaust system to provide a given number of air changes per hour. The theory is that if the air volume of a kitchen is exhausted every two or three minutes and replaced with fresh air, the kitchen temperature will be at a comfortable level and the air velocities will be high enough to remove cooking odors and vapors. The second method is based on maintaining a fixed air velocity across the entire area of the hood opening. Both methods require balancing the ventilation system so that fresh air is introduced proportionately to maintain a slightly negative pressure in the kitchen.

Noise

Careful attention should be given to possible noise that may be generated in work areas as the various activities are performed. In planning work sections, consider isolating high-noise-level areas, such as dishwashing, can crushing, and areas where noise is generated from power motors. An office where concentration is required should not be located near a high-noise-level activity such as dishwashing. High noise levels that are generated from improper handling of equipment (banging), improper equipment maintenance (squeaking), loud talking, and loud music can be controlled through proper and continuous employee training. According to West et al. (1977), noise over 40 decibels is considered a nuisance and disturbing.

EQUIPMENT USE AND CARE

Major equipment used for production and service of food may be classified as noncooking, cooking, storage, serving, and cleaning.

Noncooking Equipment

The food cutter is a common noncooking piece of equipment. One of the most popular types of cutters is the table model commonly known as the buffalo chopper (Figure 10–3). The equipment consists of a bowl that revolves rapidly around stationary blades. The blades and part of the bowl are covered with a hood for safety. The uncovered section of the bowl is used to add food, and continues to revolve until it is manually shut off. Limited amounts can be cut at one time in bowl sizes ranging in diameter from 8 to 14 in. The cutter may be purchased with added features for slicing, grinding, cubing, and shredding. For cleaning, the cover lifts up and the bowl can be removed. All electrical equipment should be disconnected before cleaning begins.

The vertical cutter-mixer (Figure 10–4) is larger, faster, and more versatile than the buffalo chopper. This cutter is capable of mixing and chopping large quantities of vegetables such as cabbage and lettuce in approximately 30 seconds. For example, to make coleslaw, the cleaned cabbage quarters, carrots, or other ingredients (including dressing) can all be put in at the same time. In less than a minute, the coleslaw is ready for portioning. The machine is also used for mixing doughs and batters, blending, emulsifying, and

Figure 10–3 Food Cutter. Courtesy of Hobart Corporation, Troy, Ohio.

Figure 10–4 Vertical Cutter-Mixer. Courtesy of Hobart Corporation, Troy, Ohio.

puréeing with similar speed. The equipment should be located near the water supply and drain. For cutting lettuce, water is added to prevent bruising. This equipment is often referred to as a cutter-mixer because of the many functions it can perform. The equipment is available in sizes ranging from 25 to 130 qt.

Food slicers are available in a variety of models from the conventional to the fully electronically controlled machines. For simple slicing tasks, a conventional type with a rotating blade is sufficient. For large-volume or more complicated tasks, the angular automatic slicer may be more suitable. Where portion control is stressed, a slicer with a scale attached is available. This slicer will automatically stop when the predetermined amount has been sliced. The machine is equipped with a graduated dial or lever that adjusts the thickness desired. To clean, the power source must be disconnected and the blade control set at zero. All removable parts should be washed, rinsed, and sanitized, and the clean knife guard should be replaced as quickly as possible to cover the exposed blade. Stationary parts may be cleaned with a long brush and wiped with a clean, thick cloth.

Mixers are available as table or floor models (Figure 10–5), with capacities ranging from 5 to 140 qt. Two agitators are considered standard: the beater, used for mashing, creaming, and blending, and the whip for egg form, whipped cream, and frosting. Other agitators are available such as the dough hook, pastry knife, and sweet dough arm. With the use of a universal hub, many attachments are available for chopping, grinding, and slicing. The equipment should be cleaned after each use by removing the bowl and attachments and washing with a mild detergent. If an egg mixture or flour ingredient was used, soak the bowl and attachments in cold water before washing.

Peelers are often referred to as potato peelers because potatoes are the main item prepared with this machine. The equipment is used to peel potatoes and other root vegetables with minimum waste by the action of a revolving abrasive

Figure 10–5 Floor Model Mixer. Courtesy of Hobart Corporation, Troy, Ohio.

disc. Potatoes and other vegetables should be loaded into the peeler according to size to avoid an uneven removal of peelings. Waste will result if the peeler continues to run until all eyes are removed. The machine should be located near a water source and sink so that vegetables can empty directly into the sink for further preparation. Vegetable peelers are available in table-top models and floor models, ranging in capacity from 15 to 50 lb. After each use, the inside of the peeler and disc should be flushed with water to remove all parings and sediment. Rinse and sanitize the peel tray and allow all parts to air dry.

Cooking Equipment

Most of the equipment found in the kitchen comes under this category.

Ovens

Ovens are one of the most useful pieces of equipment in a medical food service operation. Ovens are used to bake cakes and pastries, to roast meats, to oven-broil or oven-bake portion cuts of meat, and to rethermalize food items at the point of service. The conventional oven is available in single or deck variety. The single units are usually located under a range top, with a solid door and separate heat control. Deck ovens are stacked two to four decks high with separate heat controls for each oven. Compartment heights range from 8 in for baking to 15 in for roasting large cuts of meat. The convection oven (Figure 10–6) operates by forced air heating with a fan. Multiple racks are used in each deck to allow rapid circulation of air and even heat distribution to all food items. Convection ovens are designed to utilize fully all available space so that more food can be cooked in a shorter period of time. When conventional recipes are used, the temperature should be adjusted by reducing the thermostat by approximately 30 percent. The convection oven is available in a variety of sizes and styles. In one variety, the bottom rack can be removed as a rollout to allow full racks of food to be rolled in and out at one time. Smaller units are used to rethermalize food in the ward kitchen or floor pantry.

The convection combo (Figure 10–7) is a combination convection and steamer oven. Combo cooking means the controlled addition of moisture to the cavity while cooking. This combination of fan-forced air and steam is recommended for baking, roasting, oven braising, steaming, reconstituting, wet roasting, and crusty baking. Optional features include cook and hold and proofing capabilities. The unit is UL and NSF approved and listed.

The rotary and reel ovens operate on similar principles. In the rotary oven, the hearth rotates around a vertical axis like a merry-go-round; the reel oven rotates in a fashion similar to a ferris wheel. For both types, there is a single door opening where food is loaded on the revolving shelves as they appear opposite the opening. The ovens are suitable for large-quantity baking in a single facility or a commissary type operation.

Figure 10–6 Double-Deck Convection Oven. Courtesy of Southbend, Fuquay, North Carolina.

Microwave ovens are small units, used primarily to rethermalize food from both the chilled and frozen state. Food is cooked in microwave ovens by deep penetration of microwave energy into the food product. Heat is provided by magnetron tubes inserted in the ovens. The energy is similar to that used in television and radar. There are no thermostats, but heat level may be programmed for specific food applications. The degree of doneness is determined by the length of time food remains in the oven. When only one item is cooked in the oven, all of the microwave energy is concentrated on the one item, thus reducing the cooking time.

Ovens should be cleaned regularly to prevent buildup of charred food on interior surfaces. Conventional and convection ovens may be purchased with self-cleaning elements. The catalytic self-cleaning oven is continuous and operates

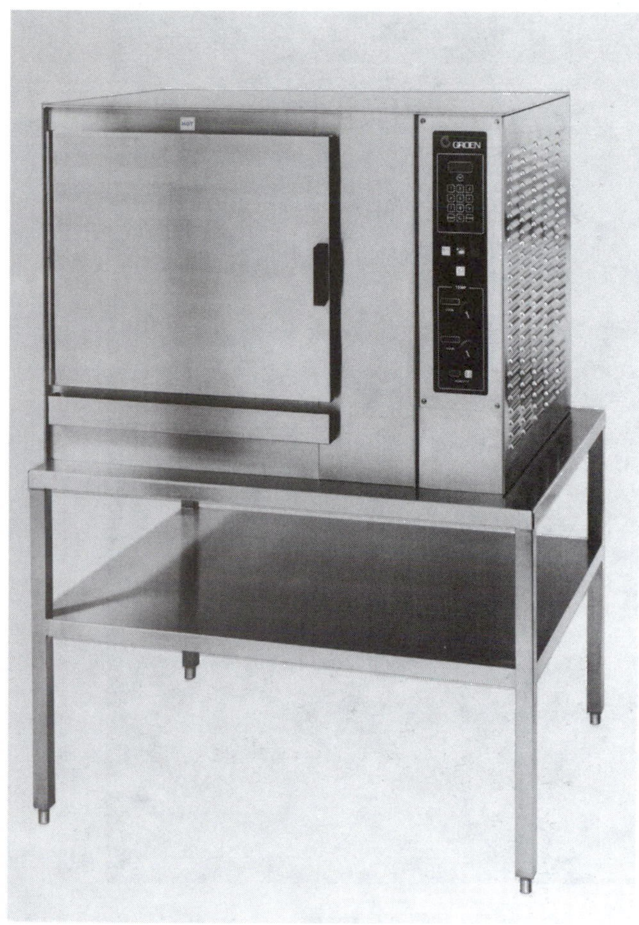

Figure 10–7 Convection Combo Oven Courtesy of Groen, A Dover Industries Company, Elk Grove Village, Illinois.

as the food is cooked. The catalytic coating of the oven interior prevents the buildup of grease and spilled food particles. The pyrolytic self-cleaning oven operates by setting a dial after all food is removed. When the dial is set, the doors are automatically locked and temperature of 1,000°F burns off all grease and food spills. The oven must be wiped clean after the self-cleaning process is completed. Microwave ovens should be wiped clean after each use with a cloth soaked in mild soapy water.

Steam Equipment

Steam equipment is clean, efficient, and fast. The use of steam equipment has practically eliminated the top-of-range cooking in medical food service operations. The steam-jacketed kettle is used for foods with a high liquid content or for food mixtures requiring a sauce or gravy. Models are available for mounting on a table, a wall, or the floor. The kettle may be full or two thirds jacketed, and powered with direct steam or self-generated steam.

The cooker-mixer models are equipped with an automatic stirrer, making it convenient to stir a large mass of food. Kettle sizes range from 10 qt to 150 gal. The cavity of the kettle may be shallow or deep. Cooking temperatures range from 215°F at 1 lb of pressure to 298°F at 50 lb of pressure. The trunion kettle is so called because it is mounted on trunions. The most popular model is the small, tilting type (1 qt to 10 gal) mounted on stainless steel tables with a drain. The hand tilting mechanism may be locked in several positions.

The compartment steamer is an upright type with one to four compartments. Food is placed in perforated or solid baskets, placed on compartment shelves, and cooked with 5 lb of pressure by direct contact of food with steam. The steamer is equipped with a safety valve for the manual release of pressure, if necessary. The equipment is used primarily for large-batch cookery. Power may be direct steam or self-generated.

High-compression steamers are smaller units, using at least 15 lb of pressure, and they cook food in a shorter period of time. The equipment is most suitable for small-batch cookery. A 2½- or 3-lb package of vegetables can be cooked in two or three minutes. Most units operate on self-generated steam.

Pressureless steamers cook food by steam that is not under pressure. The unique feature of the pressureless steamer is that the door can be opened at any time during the cooking process. The chambers are practically void of air because of the continuous and rapid venting of the steam. The steam transfers heat to the food product by convection. Pressureless steam cooking is faster than other types and produces food of good color and flavor, even when more than one type of food is cooked in the same chamber. Steam equipment should be cleaned on a daily basis. Water source and drains should be provided near all steam equipment for ease of cleaning all compartments, shelves, and gaskets.

Broilers

Broilers are available in a variety of designs. The fuel may be either gas or electric. The grid may be above or below the heat source, and can be adjusted to various positions. The char-broiler is designed with grids above the heat source. As fat drips from the meat, it burns and produces a smoked flavor in the meat. Counter broilers vary in grid sizes from 1.4 to 5.2 sq ft. An infrared broiler (salamander) is located above a cooking area, such as a range. As shown in Figure 10–8 the combined broiler, griddle, and open range top make a compact cooking section.

Griddles

Griddles are constructed of one-piece cast iron or polished steel, with raised edges and a grease trough. The equipment is frequently installed on a counter, back bar, or as part of a range top. Griddles are used for short-order cooking of indi-

Figure 10–8 Infrared Broiler (Salamander)-Griddle-Range Top Cooking Section. Courtesy of Southbend, Fuquay, North Carolina.

vidual portions of food. Griddles vary in thickness from ½ to 1 in. There is a minimum temperature drop when frozen foods are placed on the thicker griddles. There should be a separate thermostat for temperature control when different foods are cooked at the same time. Uniform heating surface and speed of temperature recovery are important features. It is necessary to season a new griddle prior to use and after each cleaning. To season, preheat the griddle to 400°F and spread with a thin film of fat. Wipe off excess fat and repeat the procedure again, allowing the fat to remain on the griddle for one or two minutes. Wipe off excess fat. To clean the griddle, use pumice or griddle stone and grease, and rub while the equipment is warm. Rub with the grain of the metal, then wipe clean with a damp cloth. Do not use steel wool. Remove grease trough and clean with detergent and water. Dry thoroughly.

Fryers

Fryers range from the small 11 × 11-in table model to the automatic continuous conveyor model. The conventional fryer may have single or multiple units, and is suitable for single operations such as cooking fried foods on an occasional basis. The ease of cleaning and safety of the equipment are key features to check. Most fryers are equipped with an automatic shut-off when the thermostat is not operating properly, or when the fat reaches a certain temperature. Other features include a cold zone for excess crumb accumulation, signal lights to indicate when heat is on, and controls to indicate when desired temperatures have been reached.

Single-unit pressure fryers are available with safety-lock covers. This equipment produces food that has a crisp outer surface, yet with the flesh retaining a desirable amount of moisture. The tightly sealed lid allows the moisture from the food to build up a steam pressure of 9 to 14 lb. Cooking time is considerably less than in conventional fryers. The entire cooking time for any food is within 10 minutes, as the temperature of the fat is held between 310°F and 325°F. An electronic computerized fryer is also available. Food is automatically lowered with a push of a button. When the cooking cycle is completed, the basket is automatically raised to a drain position.

The conveyor fryer is suitable for commissary or other systems where large quantities are produced at a given time.

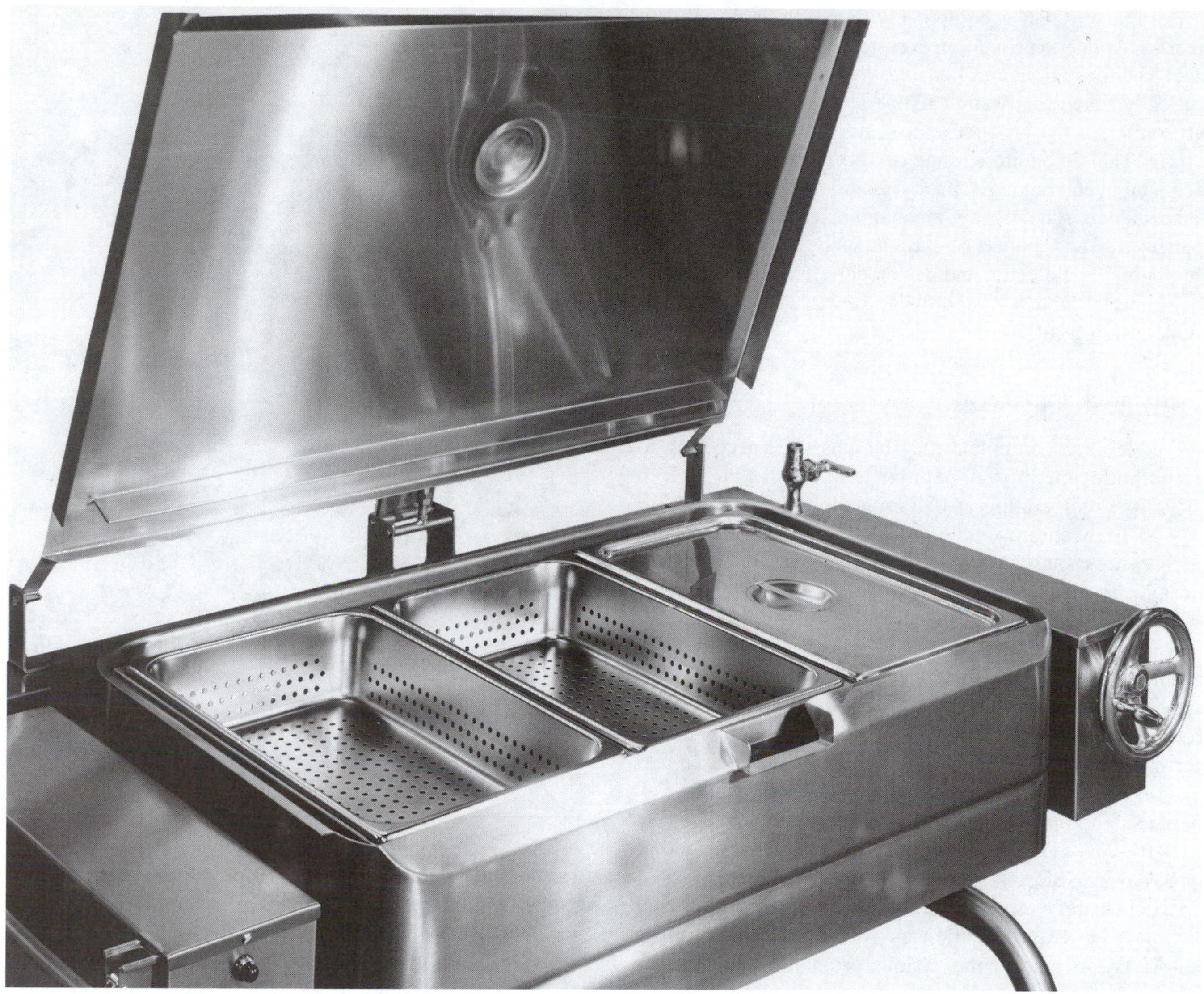

Figure 10–9 Tilting Braising Pan with Steamer Insert Assembly. Courtesy of Groen, A Dover Industries Company, Elk Grove Village, Illinois.

Automatic conveyor types are available in combination with a breading machine. The raw portions are put in at one end of the machine, the food is automatically breaded and fried, and the cooked portions are lowered into the serving pans.

For cleaning, fat should be filtered after each shift or at the end of the day, if the fryer is used continuously. Reusable fat should be refrigerated until ready for use. Commercial deep-fryer cleaning solutions can be used to remove carbon build-up.

Braising Pans

The braising pan is one of the most versatile pieces of equipment used in medical food service operations. The pan is used as follows:

- As a griddle to prepare foods such as eggs, French toast, pancakes, and hash-browned potatoes.
- As a fry pan to cook fish, chicken, doughnuts, and other foods requiring deep-fat cooking.
- As a kettle for stews, chili, chop suey, gravies, sauces, and most combination dishes.
- As a steamer for vegetables. As shown in Figure 10–9 the pan can be converted into a pressureless atmospheric steam cooker. The lightweight insert pans are easily removed for stacked storage. The complete unit includes pans, covers, and snap-on handles for removing pans.
- As an oven for roasting meat and poultry, by placing products on wire racks. With the cover closed, the cooking action is same as in a conventional oven.

The braising pan is equipped with a ⅜-in thick stainless steel–clad plate to provide an even-temperature cooking surface. Thermostatic control enables the pan to shut off automatically when the desired temperature is reached and to turn on when the product temperature falls below desired setting. The temperature range of 100°F to 425°F, flat surface, and even cooking capacity provide unlimited cooking performance. The tilting mechanism eliminates lifting, transferring, and the use of extra utensils. The unit is available in both the electric and gas models. The electric model should be UL and NSF approved; the gas model should be AGA design certified.

Cold-Storage Equipment

Cold-storage equipment may be classified according to temperature: medium or regular temperature at 35°F to 45°F; low temperature at 0°F; and rapid freeze at –20°F to –40°F. Medium-temperature cold storage includes refrigerators such as the large walk-in, reach-in, reach-through, under-the-counter, roll-in, refrigerated counters, and thaw refrigerators.

Walk-in refrigerators are used for bulk storage of food, usually in case lots. Separate walk-ins are used for produce, dairy foods, and prepared foods requiring no further heat treatment. Features should include a door latch with an interior safety release, an easy-to-read thermometer placed outside the door, and adequate insulation. Added features may include a glass-panelled door and an alarm to indicate when the refrigerator is malfunctioning. The equipment should be approved by NSF.

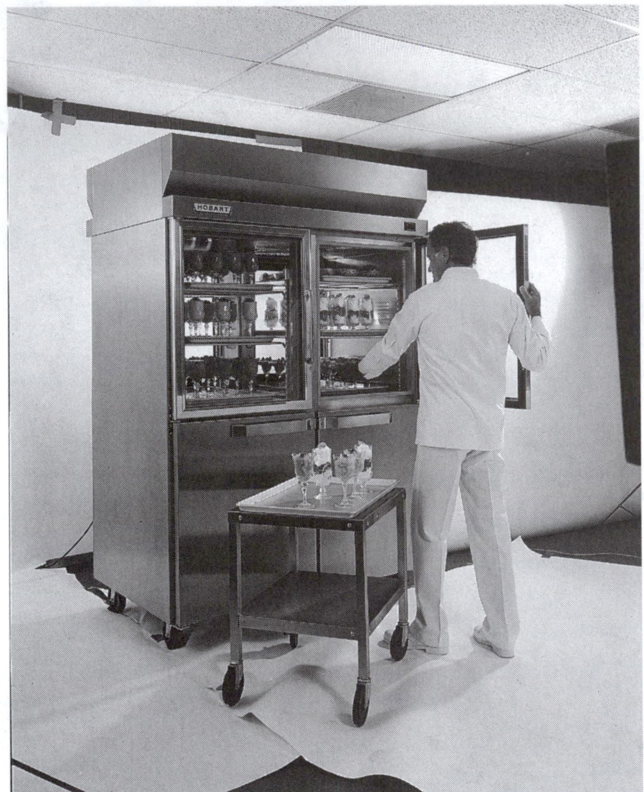

Figure 10–10 Reach-In Refrigerator. Courtesy of Hobart Corporation, Troy, Ohio.

Reach-in refrigerators (Figure 10–10) provide greater flexibility in terms of location and shelving. Reach-in refrigerators are located in the various production and service areas and in ward pantries. Adjustable shelving is available to allow for various heights of prepared food stored on trays. The reach-through refrigerator is located between production and service areas to allow prepared foods to be put in from one side and removed from the other side. The dual door openings prevent excessive walking by service personnel in replenishing the serving line. Under-the-counter refrigerators are convenient when located underneath a high-compression steamer, microwave oven, or service counter. These units are frequently referred to as refrigerated drawers. The major disadvantage of under-the-counter refrigeration is that the height is not convenient for cleaning. Roll-in refrigerators (Figure 10–11) are convenient for loading and transporting multiple trays of food at one time. The roll-in units may be purchased to fit into a convection oven or to roll into a refrigerator in another location. Refrigerated counters are used in the service areas for salads and desserts requiring refrigeration. The units are considered more sanitary than the use of crushed ice, which may come into contact with the food products. Thaw refrigerators operate under controlled humidity and temperature to protect food products from bacteria-conducing temperatures while thawing. The thaw refrigerators reduce thawing time from the two to three days it normally takes to approximately 12 hours. The controlled environment thaws without using temperatures over 45°F. When thawing is completed, the refrigeration system automatically changes over to standard refrigerator operation.

Low-temperature storage equipment is frequently referred to as freezers. The more appropriate label should be frozen-food holding cabinets, because freezers are not used to freeze food but to hold food that is already frozen. For institutional use, low-temperature equipment is available in walk-in and reach-in types. The walk-ins may be installed so that the frozen food unit opens into a medium-temperature section, instead of directly into the production area. Low-temperature walk-ins may also be installed outside the building.

Rapid-freeze equipment is used to freeze food quickly and efficiently. Although there are a number of freezing methods used by commercial manufacturers, blast freezing is most often associated with the freeze-serve production in

Figure 10–11 Reach-In Refrigerator with Roll-In Unit. Courtesy of Hobart Corporation, Troy, Ohio.

medical food service operations. Food is quickly frozen to temperatures of –40°F, which is an acceptable level for most food products. Quality loss can occur if food is overfrozen and becomes brittle. In blast freezing, food travels on a conveyor belt through a freezing chamber in which air circulates at high velocity by a mechanical unit. A Freon-type refrigerant is used. Other types of rapid-freeze equipment have not been used as extensively or with the efficiency that the blast-freeze type has. Nitrogen freezing was planned for the Walter Reed Army Medical Center in Washington, DC, but had to be canceled because of mechanical problems (Riggs 1981). Initially, a large-capacity cryogenic freezer was intended to handle rapid freezing for their ready-food production system. Problems arose when attempts were made to pipe liquid nitrogen, which was stored a considerable distance away, to the freezer. It was found that the temperature at the freezer was not low enough to meet freezing requirements. The operation was converted to blast freezing.

Cleaning and Sanitizing Equipment

Dishwashers are available in single- and multiple-tank varieties. The heat may be supplied by steam, gas, or electricity. The single-tank dishwasher is used in small operations serving 100 meals or less. Dishes are prerinsed, loaded into racks, and manually pushed through the machine. Only one tray of dishes is washed at a time, taking approximately 2 minutes for the complete wash and rinse cycle. The single-tank unit is also available with a conveyor belt that moves racks through the machine automatically. Doors are used on each end of the manually operated unit; curtains are used on the conveyor type, which makes for faster operation. Multiple-tank dishwashers are available in the rack or flight type. In the multiple-tank rack machine, dishes are prewashed by hand, or a prewash unit can be specified. Scraped dishes are arranged in racks and placed on a conveyor belt, which moves the trays through the wash, rinse, and final rinse cycle. With the increased length of the machine, there is less spillover of water from one tank to another. There should be a rack-return section so that racks are never placed on the floor. The flight dishwashing machine (Figure 10–12) is designed to be used with or without racks. The distinguishing feature of the flight-type machine is that dishes of various sizes can be placed directly on conveyor drive prongs. Because silverware, cups, and glasses must be racked for washing, it is both practical and economical to select a machine that can accommodate both operations. The rack-around dish machine, as shown in Figure 10–13, provides added versatility for dishwashing. The machine is a combination of rack and flight types, featuring continuous operation. Desirable features to specify with the dish machine include a soak or prewash sink with spray-rinse hose, a sorting table, a slanted shelf above the machine-loading section, and a booster heater to ensure 180°F water temperature for final rinse. All machines should be NSF approved. An automatic tray unloader is available and is considered practical for operations using disposable serviceware. The unit can be a separate tray-washing machine or can be furnished to wash dishes and other silverware and then convert to a tray-washing machine. To operate the automatic tray unloader, place the empty tray cart at the unloading end of the dishwasher. As trays are deposited from dishwasher onto the self-leveling tray cart, a tray carrier will descend and engage an actuating lever or limit switch that stops the conveyor when the cart is full. When the full cart is wheeled away, the conveyor is

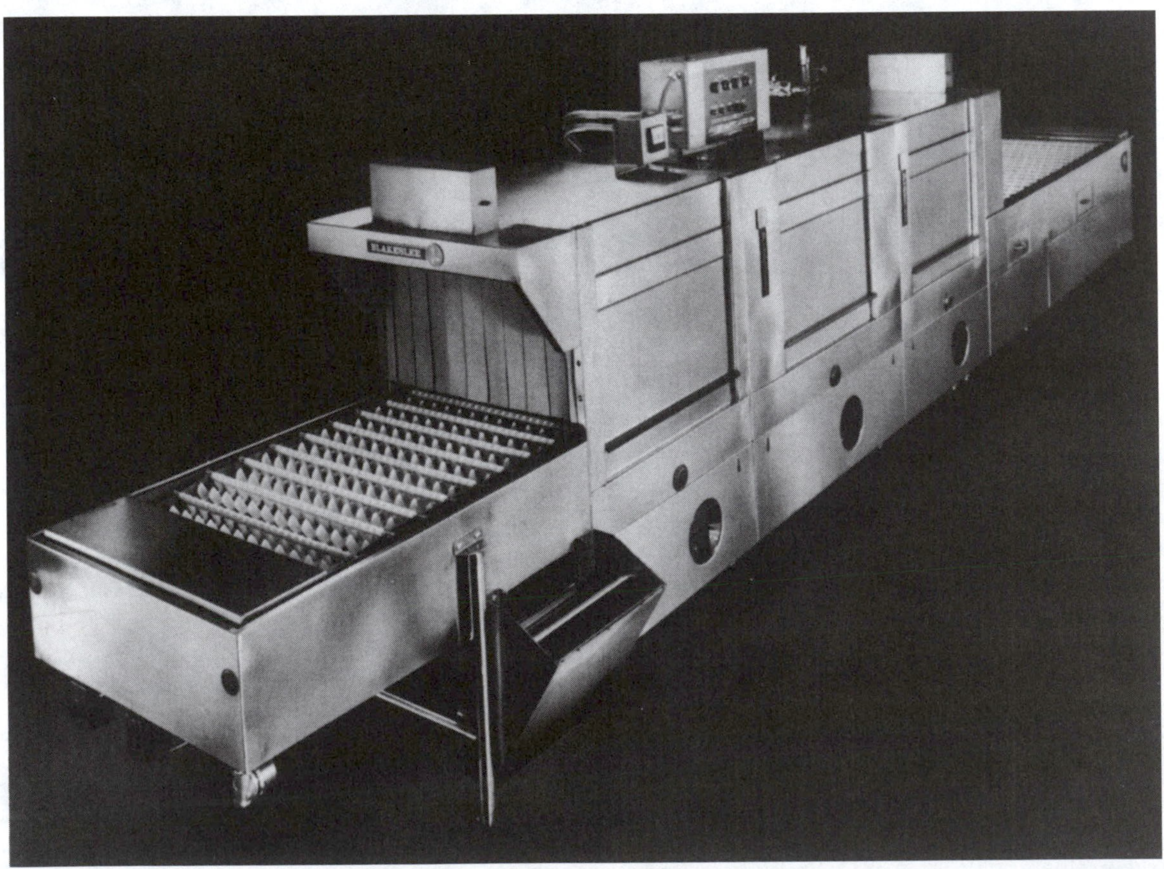

Figure 10–12 Flight Dishwashing Machine. Courtesy of G.S. Blakeslee and Company.

Figure 10–13 The Rack-a-Round Dishwashing Machine. Courtesy of G.S. Blakeslee and Company

automatically turned off, to be automatically turned on when the next tray cart is wheeled into position.

Low-temperature dishwashers are available with minimum temperature of 120°F for both wash and rinse. A chemical sanitizer, chlorine or iodine base, is used instead of the high temperature of 180°F for the final rinse. Federal sanitation guidelines require a wash temperature of 150°F to 165°F, and a final rinse temperature of 180°F. The low-temperature machines with sanitizers were introduced as energy savers. Food service directors should check state and local sanitation codes before purchasing this type of dishwashing machine. One manufacturer has developed dishwashing machines that can operate within a wide range of washing and rinsing temperatures, with or without chemical sanitizers. The ability to vary the wash and rinse temperatures from 120°F to 180°F provides flexibility for the operation. There is some concern that detergents are ineffective in removing animal fat from serviceware at temperatures below 130°F, and there may be problems with the use of chemical agents on silverware and pewter. Machines with dual operation provide flexibility for the food service director in deciding when to use a chemical or a 180°F hot-water rinse.

Dishwashing machines should be cleaned after each use. The strainer baskets should be carefully removed to avoid spills into the tank and cleaned of all food particles. Drain all water and rinse the interior with a hose. If the water is hard, a deliming agent may be required periodically. Rinse and air dry curtains. Remove washarms and flush out all sediments. Turn off the heat source and leave the side doors up so that the machine can air dry.

Pot, pan, and utensil washing is accomplished manually in small operations. A three-compartment sink is required for wash, rinse, and final rinse. A chemical sanitizer is used in the final-rinse sink with a minimum water temperature of 75°F. Drainboards are required and a garbage disposal is desirable. Pot and pan washing machines may be used for large facilities.

ENERGY MANAGEMENT RELATED TO EQUIPMENT PLANNING

Energy conservation should not compromise effective and efficient operation. Consider the following suggestions in terms of both energy savings and high quality standards:

- Avoid sliding glass doors in refrigeration equipment, if possible. The slide clearance does not allow a good, tight seal.
- Use full loads with dishwashers so that the machine can operate at full capacity. An automatic shut-off control that automatically turns the machine off when no dishes are being washed may be a sound investment.
- Use a rinse-saver device in the final rinse on flight-type machines to prevent the use of unnecessary 180°F water when there are no dishes to be rinsed.
- Locate refrigerators and freezers away from heat-producing appliances.
- On dish machines with gas heat, adjust the burners and gas pressure for maximum efficiency and install a gas pressure–reducing valve.
- Select correct size for all equipment, as much as possible. Unused space that must be heated is considered a waste.
- Specify see-through doors on refrigerators to prevent constant opening for inspection.
- Compare the use of gas versus electricity for cooking equipment. Gas is considered more efficient and less costly to operate.
- Consider a low-temperature dishwashing system, using sanitizing solution. The system reduces the amount of hot water required for the final rinse, but extra funds are spent for sanitizing solution. Check local codes on use of low-temperature systems.
- Specify electronic ignition on gas equipment instead of a pilot light.
- Energy demand is increased when all lights and all equipment are turned on at the same time. Stagger start-up times. Discourage cooks from turning on all equipment at the beginning of a shift.
- Use fluorescent lighting rather than incandescent. Avoid frequent turning on and off of incandescent lights. Leave fluorescent lights on unless they are off for at least 15 minutes.
- Install automatic light controls in walk-in refrigerators and freezers.
- Each compartment of a warming or serving table should be controlled by separate thermostats.
- Thick oven installation conserves energy. Specify 4 inches or more insulation.
- The deck oven with the bottom rack near the floor may constitute a waste of oven space, as employees will use the more convenient waist-high cavity.
- Convection ovens bake at temperatures 20°F to 50°F lower and are 10 percent to 15 percent faster than deck ovens.
- Establish an ongoing employee training program for proper use and care of equipment.

A gas convection oven introduced in the 1980s has a specially inserted tube that captures hot air that is normally vented immediately. These ovens are converted to direct-fired operations, eliminating the need for heavy, heat-absorbing parts used in direct-fired convection ovens. The new ovens use an input of only 60,000 British thermal units (BTU) and do the same job as gas convection ovens requiring 100,000 BTUs.

Manufacturers of deep-fat fryers offer the following developments in equipment design: (1) a built-in filter that enables the operator to strain the frying oil in a matter of seconds, at any time during the day; (2) an intermittent ignition device that eliminates the necessity for a standing gas pilot; (3) built-in computerized time and temperature controls that eliminate the guesswork, guarantee precise and consistent cooking of fried food, and minimize energy consumption; (4) fryers with a deep-cold zone that places food sediment out of the cooking temperature range to prolong fat life; and (5) a modified pressure fryer that increases efficiency by covering the heating well, thus retaining heat that might otherwise be lost.

New, more efficient gas griddles offer grooved surfaces for grid-marked meats, or the flexibility of a smooth surface when needed. Some new gas griddles are zoned to permit partial shutdown in slow periods and to provide for cooking more than one kind of food at a time.

The Gas Research Institute (Chicago, Illinois), formed in 1977, works with gas utility equipment manufacturers, the U.S. Department of Energy, and others to improve new gas equipment and to devise new concepts.

SAFETY FEATURES OF EQUIPMENT PLANNING

Safety is an important aspect of the manager's job. The following list will help ensure safety in the kitchen.

- Use mobile carts with wheel locks for equipment that must be moved to various locations within the department.
- Plan for adequate electrical outlets. Avoid use of extension cords that may result in accidents if people trip over them.
- Consider how equipment can be operated and cleaned in the same location, if stationary.
- Make sure all electrical equipment is grounded.
- Install plastic covers over light switches near walk-in refrigerators and freezers.
- Arrange equipment so that doors do not open into traffic aisles.
- If swinging doors are used, one should be clearly labeled "in" and the other labeled "out."
- Electrical equipment should have signal light to indicate whether electricity is on or off.

COMPUTERS IN FACILITY DESIGN

Computer-aided design (CAD) allows kitchen design consultants to develop their own libraries of food service floor plans and templates that can be conveniently modified. Using fiber optics, designers can begin with a plan from their existing library and adapt it to the needs of clients by rearranging equipment and structures. Walls can be moved and room dimensions changed. The computer automatically adjusts the layouts for plumbing and electrical specifications to match the new arrangement.

One of the most time-efficient advantages of CAD is its ability to do the tedious job of drawing and revising dimensions and specifications of equipment and floor plans. This allows the designer time to visualize alternatives, manipulate the design, and make appropriate decisions. A significant advance in CAD systems is the use of three-dimensional development and simulation, which allows the client to "walk through" a graphically simulated environment (Hysen 1996).

For today's food service manager, use of compact discs (CDs) to prepare equipment files is another valuable time-saving tool that may also be used for training. With CD-ROM, pictures of equipment, manufacturer's directions, and video clips are readily available for individual employee training sessions that do not require a facilitator.

Equipment data files may be compiled and cross-referenced to supply information as needed. Suggested data files should include the following information:

- manufacturer's name, address, phone and fax number
- model number
- serial number
- pertinent specifications
- local equipment brokers
- service representatives
- equipment demonstrations

In addition, programmed maintenence, sanitation, and operating procedures may be generated daily or periodically as employee task sheets. With a planned approach to equipment sanitation and maintenence, repairs are less frequent and therefore less costly. When repairs are needed a log that documents frequency and cost should be kept to provide justification for replacement equipment or related capital expenditures. Use of the computer to log, track, and merge data is a simple function that does not require sophisticated software.

In a broader application, major equipment such as freezers, refrigerators, and coolers may be linked to the facility's security system for monitoring overnight or during other down time.

AGENCIES RELATED TO EQUIPMENT MANAGEMENT

Familiarity with regulatory agencies and laws related to equipment management is a responsibility of the food service director. Basic knowledge of the following agencies and organizations can greatly enhance communications both internally and externally, throughout the planning stages.

National Sanitation Foundation

The NSF is an independent nonprofit organization dedicated to the improvement of public health and the environment. Activities of the foundation include providing liaison between industry, the public health professions, and the general public; conducting research and establishing standards on health-related equipment, processes, products, and services; disseminating research results; and issuing official NSF seals for display on equipment and products tested and found to meet NSF standards. Each standard is a detailed statement of what the equipment or product must be, or must do, in order to protect the public health. A booklet is published periodically that lists all manufacturers and their equipment having NSF approval.

Occupational Safety and Health Administration

The purpose of the Occupational Safety and Health Act of 1970 is to ensure safe and healthful working conditions. The law provides that each employer has the basic duty to furnish employees a place of employment that is free from recognized hazards that may cause death or serious physical harm (Michigan Department of Labor 1978). A specific standard relating to facility planning and use is that aisles and passageways must be kept clear and in good repair, with no obstruction across or in aisles that could create a hazard (U.S. Department of Labor 1972). The OSHA standards are carried out through the Department of Labor in each state. For compliance and other information, contact the OSHA division at the state level.

Underwriters Laboratories

Underwriters Laboratories, concerned with safety of electrical equipment, is operated similarly to NSF in that participation is on a voluntary basis. Products that have been tested and found to meet the rigid safety standards are authorized to use the UL seal. Each product is tested and approved for use and certified to be safe from electrical shock, hazard, and fire.

Other Professional Organizations and Agencies

In addition, the food service director should be familiar with federal, state, and local codes and ordinances for assistance in planning for a safe and sanitary workplace. Other helpful sources include professional organizations and utility companies such as the following:

- American Hospital Association
- American National Standards Institute (plumbing codes)
- American Society of Mechanical Engineers
- American National Safety Institute
- national and local restaurant associations
- National Fire Protection Association
- National Safety Council
- American Gas Association
- electric utility companies

CONTROL POINTS RELATED TO EQUIPMENT

Although not all control points (CPs) are classified as critical, they are considered control points because they relate directly to sanitation codes. CPs for equipment are as follows:

- A metal-stem product thermometer must be available and used to check internal food temperatures where it is impractical to install thermometers on equipment such as *bain-maries*, steam tables, steam kettles, heat lamps, or insulated food transport carriers.
- Equipment that comes in direct contact with food (choppers, mixers, slicers, and so forth) must be dismantled and cleaned after each use.
- Equipment used to store clean dishes, silverware, glasses, pots, and pans should be clean in order to avoid recontamination.
- Discard all chipped or cracked dishes and glasses. The cracks serve as hiding places for bacteria.
- Ice makers and ice storage equipment cannot be located under exposed or unprotected sewer lines or water lines, open stairwells, or other sources of contamination.
- Ice for consumer use shall be dispensed by an employee with an approved utensil or through an automatic self-serve dispensing machine. Do not use glass containers to scoop ice from the ice machine.
- Utility sinks should be available for used cleaning mops and disposal of mop water. Mops used in food service must not be used in other areas of the facility.

REFERENCES

American Hospital Association. 1977. *Guidelines for selecting a consultant in food service equipment and layout for hospitals and related health care institutions* (Pamphlet). Chicago.

Avery, A.C. 1978. Writing specifications. *Food Management* 13, no. 3:1–42, 66, 68.

Avery, A.C. 1979. Principles of kitchen design. In *Commercial kitchens*, ed. L.R. Myers. Arlington, VA: American Gas Association.

Avery, A.C. n.d. *Human engineering in kitchen design* (Pamphlet). Washington, DC: Department of the Navy, Bureau of Supplies and Accounts.

Hall, L.R. 1982. Equipment comparison. *Stokes Report* 2, no. 10. Atlanta: Judy Ford Stokes & Associates.

Hysen, P. 1996. Interview by Catherine Sullivan. The Hysen Group, Plymouth, MI, 13 February.

Harris, R.D. 1981. The how's and why's of preparing renovation specifications. *Hospital Topics* 59, no. 4.

Kotschevar, L.H., and M.E. Terrell. 1977. *Food service planning layout and equipment*. New York: John Wiley & Sons.

Michigan Department of Labor. 1978. *Employer and employee responsibilities and rights: Michigan Occupational Safety and Health Act 154 of P.A.* Lansing: Bureau of Safety and Regulations.

Myers, J.R. 1979. *Commercial kitchens*. Arlington, VA: American Gas Association.

Riggs, S. 1981. How well has Walter Reed's "revolutionary" food system worked? *Restaurants and Institutions* 88, no. 1:73–75.

U.S. Department of Health and Human Services. 1976. *Sanitation manual*. Washington, DC.

U.S. Department of Labor. 1972. *Recordkeeping requirements under the Williams-Steiger Occupational Safety and Health Act of 1970*. Washington, DC: Occupational Safety and Health Administration, U.S. Government Printing Office.

West, B.B. et al. 1977. *Food service in institutions*. New York: John Wiley & Sons.

Chapter 11

Subsystem for Food Purchasing

Food purchasing is based on the planned menu. The process is complex and diverse, requiring a high degree of proficiency on the part of the buyer. The most important factor is that the desired product be purchased at the right time, in the right amount, and at the level of quality specified.

ORGANIZATION OF THE PURCHASING UNIT

The actual purchasing functions may be performed inhouse by the food service director or a designated person, or the purchasing may be done by the purchasing agent, who is responsible not only for food and supplies required by the food service department, but also for purchasing needs of all other departments within the organization. Regardless of who is responsible for the actual purchasing, the food service director is responsible for the end product and therefore must be able to project the needs of the department in an organized, efficient, and effective manner. The food service director needs a basic knowledge of the following:

- food quality
- food processing
- food grades and yields
- food availability and marketing conditions
- purchasing systems
- product testing and evaluation
- specification writing
- ordering, receiving, and storing techniques
- production and service techniques

In addition to the required basic knowledge, the individual responsible for purchasing must have time available for researching new products, monitoring storeroom procedures, making visits to the marketplaces and food plants, conferring with salespersons and purveyors, and soliciting and analyzing bids. Considering the varied and complex duties, it may be advantageous to have this purchasing function performed by a central agent.

Food service directors have complained that central purchasing agents are not familiar with the uniqueness of medical food service operations and therefore are not sensitive to their needs. Establishing lines of authority and effective two-way communication can do much to minimize the problem. The amount of authority and how it is used by the purchasing agent affects the relationship with the using departments. Friction may develop when too much or too little authority is given or if the lines of authority are not clear to all concerned. Effective communication implies that the food service director will supply the necessary information to the purchasing agent so that intelligent purchasing decisions can be made and that the purchasing agent will provide prompt feedback to the food service director on decisions made. For both inhouse and central purchasing, all policies and procedures should have administrative approval as part of the internal communications network. The external communications network involves relationships with food purveyors and other food-related professional organizations and agencies. When the purchasing function is done by central purchasing, the entire purchasing process should be included, from ordering through inventory. The central storeroom may be in a remote area, with only a small daily storeroom in the food service department. Feedback from central stores on daily deliveries and issues should be prompt so that the food service director can be aware of food costs at all times.

QUALIFICATIONS OF THE PURCHASING AGENT

The individual responsible for purchasing wields a great deal of power because of the amount of money involved and the contacts made within and outside the organization. How the power and contacts are used to fulfill the responsibilities of the position will affect not only the food service department but the image of the entire organization. Qualifications of the purchasing agent should include, but not be limited to, the following: educational background, business background, and personal characteristics (Swindler 1978).

Educational Background

The educational background of purchasing agents may be as varied as the number of positions. There are few college or university programs that prepare students for the highly specialized and unique job of purchasing for a medical facility. The responsible individual should have general knowledge of medical terminology and specific knowledge about each of the departments within the medical facility with purchasing needs. Because of the accounting and other business activities associated with purchasing, students with a background in business administration are often appointed to the position. A program offered through a school of business administration may or may not offer any courses dealing with food purchasing and other related needs of a food service department. Faced with this situation, it is imperative that the food service director be able to communicate departmental needs in a clear and concise manner in order to obtain desired results.

The purchasing agent is responsible for the following:

- soliciting and awarding bids and contracts
- placing purchase orders
- supervising personnel in receiving, storing, and issuing food and other products
- establishing and maintaining inventory system
- training staff in accounting and cost procedures
- conducting research and testing of new products
- keeping up to date on changing economics and political conditions
- maintaining open lines of communication, both internal and external

The educational process is ongoing for the purchasing agent to acquire and maintain current information—essential for intelligent decision making.

Business Background

In addition to accounting and budgeting, any business experience relating to medical operations will be helpful to the purchasing agent. The individual must be thoroughly acquainted with the needs of the departments involved and the marketing conditions. In areas where the individual may be deficient, extra effort must be expended to learn as much about specific needs as possible whether through formal courses, on-the-job training, seminars, lectures, or other sources.

Personal Characteristics

The purchasing agent's personal characteristics are as important as technical knowledge and skills. The following traits are considered most important:

- *Cooperation*—The individual must be able to work in a cooperative manner with all department heads, higher administration, and subordinates.
- *Initiative*—The agent must display initiative and creativity in searching for new products and alternate supply sources.
- *Tact*—The person must be tactful in suggesting substitutes that will perform the same function without antagonizing the department involved or the relationship with the purveyor.
- *Dependability*—The departments must be able to rely on products or items being available at the time needed and in the correct quantity and quality.
- *Industriousness*—The agent must be able to seek out information that will assist him or her in doing a better job, whether the knowledge is acquired from purveyors, reading marketing newspapers and product brochures, attending conventions and seminars, or visiting manufacturing plants and purveyor sites.
- *Accuracy*—The purchasing agent must give attention to details of the job, such as reading and understanding all contracts and warranties. Neglect of such day-to-day routines can be costly.
- *Human relations*—The agent must be able to adjust to a wide variety of personalities both inside and outside the organization. The ability to establish close working relationships without being unduly influenced is an asset.
- *Ethical standards*—Exposure to opportunities for dishonest or unethical personal gain is prevalent. The individual must have a sense of what is right and wrong. He or she should resist gifts, kickbacks, or bribery, which may eventually affect the quality of products received, the cost of products, or the business relationship with purveyors due to obligations on the part of the buyer. The purchasing agent must avoid any appearances of unethical dealing, even refusing small gifts at Christmas or other times during the year. A common practice of asking purveyors to sponsor or contribute to various departmental activities may obligate the buyer to favor one purveyor over another. Gifts or discount coupons offered for doing business with the purveyor should be for departmental use only.

To summarize, the personal characteristics of the buyer should ensure that none of his or her actions tarnishes the reputation or image of the individual buyer or the organization.

PURCHASING SYSTEMS

The most common types of purchasing systems may be classified as either one-stop buying or competitive buying.

One-Stop Buying

In one-stop buying the purchaser orders all products or items from one purveyor. The one-step purveyor may handle products for more than 100 distributors. The combining of products results in a reduced number of orders to place, reduced number of deliveries, and reduced number of bills to pay by the purchasing department. One-stop companies spend an exorbitant amount of time and effort in marketing their services. For example, one such company provides menu planning, marketing data, financial planning, inventory control techniques, merchandising ideas, and technical problem solving.

The one-step buying system is frequently used by small operations to eliminate costs involved for small deliveries from several purveyors. The one big disadvantage to using this type of system is that the buyer has no control over the prices paid because there is no competition.

Competitive Buying

In competitive buying, more than one purveyor has an opportunity to bid on the desired products or items. The competition may be on an informal or formal basis. Informal bidding is less complicated than formal bidding and requires less time. Informal bidding may take place by telephone or be processed through the mail. In telephone bidding, the buyer lists all items on a sheet with space for item needed, item description, amount needed, delivery date, and price quotations from selected purveyors. As shown in Exhibit 11–1, emphasis is put on a full description of the item needed so that purveyors will know exactly what the buyer wants; it also ensures that all purveyors are bidding on the same item. The amount needed is important because it may affect the unit cost, depending on the size of the order. The delivery date will let the purveyor determine whether the time request can be met. The bid is awarded to the bidder with the lower price quote. To provide a written record of the transaction, a purchase order is mailed to the purveyor or is picked up by a sales representative. It is considered poor business practice to place the order by telephone, except in emergency situations.

For informal bidding by mail, specification sheets and a cover sheet of instructions are mailed to selected purveyors. The price quotations are returned by mail according to a prescribed time schedule. The bids are opened and evaluated, and items are assigned to the lowest bidder. Mail bidding is more time consuming than telephone bidding and can only be used if prices remain stable for the period of time required to complete the transaction.

Exhibit 11–1 Telephone Quotation Sheet

Quantity	Food Item Description	Delivery Date	Quotations		
			1	2	3
100 lb	Roast—ready rib no. 103	10-10-97	1.70	1.75	1.72

Formal bidding is more complex. An invitation to bid is mailed to selected purveyors. If completed and returned by the bidder, it is considered a legal, binding contract. All pertinent information relating to bid opening date, delivery date, payment terms, how bids are awarded, nonconformance, legal requirements, liability, and other general information are mailed to all bidders. Specifications, with detailed information on each item, are also mailed to the bidders. Bids are returned in sealed unmarked envelopes to protect the identity of the bidder until purchasing decisions are made. Formal bidding is usually reserved for stable items that can be stored over a period of time. If larger quantities are purchased and stored by the purveyor, the additional cost for storage must be considered. Because of current economic conditions and other factors that may affect cost (weather, union strikes, etc.), most long-term bids are set up on a fluctuating price basis.

Contract bidding is a formal competitive type of purchasing. In this system, the contract is frequently awarded for a period of 3 to 12 months for items such as bread, coffee, milk, ice cream, and similar foods that are used on a daily basis. The contract terms usually stipulate the purchasing of a minimum amount for a stated period. The daily or weekly orders may vary, but the total amount for a given period should equal the minimum bid.

Group Purchasing

More and more independent food service operations are participating in cooperative buying ventures as a means of reducing food costs. Many hospital administrators involved in group purchasing today would not have given the idea a serious thought several years ago. The fear of losing their autonomy and having to accept foods of a lower quality were the main reasons why some food service directors were reluctant to join purchasing groups. To combat such fears, most purchasing groups have formed committees with representatives from each participating facility. Committee members are responsible for research, testing, and evaluation of products prior to purchasing arrangements. When a consensus has been reached on a particular product or item, specifications are written and submitted to selected purveyors as part of the bidding process. Each participating facility is responsible for placing its own purchase order. The product or item is delivered directly to the individual facility or to central warehousing for storage. With central storage, there is a reduced delivery charge because the purveyor can make use of "drop shipments." Each participating facility orders and picks up from central storage as needed.

One of the problems associated with group purchasing is that a purveyor may be awarded a contract based on expected volume and later finds that the participating hospitals are not ordering in the amounts expected, possibly because of multiple memberships by some facilities. Instead of membership in only one group purchasing organization, the hospital may belong to several groups and utilize the service of the group offering the lowest price. As reported by Richards (1982), a recent trend in group purchasing is the change to committed-volume contracting, which provides a quantity guarantee for the purveyor. The price quotation is based on guaranteed volume.

The latest development in group purchasing is the banding together of purchasing groups into what is known as supergroups. Although the supergroups were formed primarily to establish a capital equipment purchasing program, food purchasing groups are expected to follow the trend. The rationale behind this trend is that the higher the volume, the more negotiating power is afforded the purchasing group.

The advantages of group purchasing far outweigh any disadvantages that may be associated with the purchasing system. In addition to the savings, there is the sharing of information on food quality, processing techniques, marketing conditions, and availability of new products. The disadvantage may be that of standardization. Hospitals can and do exert their individuality, however, by purchasing some items outside the group purchasing program. Items with the highest participation rate are canned fruits and vegetables, milk products, bread, paper supplies, and other disposables.

SPECIFICATIONS

Definition

A specification is a written statement in clear, concise terminology that states what is desired by the buyer. For a food product, the specification refers to the quality, size, and other factors needed to obtain the right item. The advantages of a well-written specification are as follows:

- Indicates that the buyer has given careful consideration to departmental needs.
- Ensures compliance with facility and departmental standards of quality.
- Eliminates misunderstandings between purveyor and purchasing agent on exactly what is required.
- Eliminates misunderstanding between the purchasing agent and the department making the request.
- Serves as a cross-check for the receiving clerk.
- Lowers bid prices because purveyors know exactly what is desired and what they are bidding on.

Specifications are not passed from one institution to another because they reflect the quality standards for a specific operation. The use of standards set by the federal government and other marketing agencies should be complied with, but they should be tailored to specific needs. Deviations from standard specifications can be costly and should not be practiced without valid justification. An exception to this is when specifications are written for convenience-modified diet foods to meet caloric, nutrient, or other restrictions.

Types of Specifications

Specifications may be classified as general or specific.

General specifications refer to arrangements with purveyors on factors such as method of payment, billing procedures, submission of samples for testing, failure to perform, rejection of products, delivery and receiving policies, and other pertinent information. General specifications are given to all purveyors doing business with the organization, including both food and supplies. The issues of billing and method of payment are crucial if the organization is to maintain a good credit rating with purveyors. Most purveyors will allow bills to be paid within 30 days. Even large accounts may be dropped if bills are not paid in a timely manner.

Specific specifications refer to one particular product or a group of related products. Exact descriptions are used to specify the desired product for factors such as grade, size, thickness, and count. Specifications are sent only to the purveyors providing a particular item. The following information should be included in a specific specification:

- the common, trade, standard of identity, or other name of the item
- the quality desired, using government, trade, or other grades, brands, or other standards
- the marketing form such as fresh, chilled, frozen, canned, or dried
- the weight, thickness, count, or size of the item, such as minimum and maximum weight range and number of units per case, crate, or carton
- the degree of ripeness
- the unit on which price is quoted, such as 50-lb sack, six no. 10 cans, and so forth
- additional statements needed for clarity of exact item desired such as Blue Lake, Michigan, or Midwest green beans

Specifications should be written for all food items purchased, but especially for items that comprise a large percentage of the food dollar. It is estimated that approximately 50 percent of the food dollar is spent on meat, seafood, and poultry. Fruits, vegetables, and dairy products are the next highest in cost. Therefore, the following discussion covers specification writing for meats, poultry, eggs, seafood, processed fruits and vegetables, and fresh fruits and vegetables.

Meat Specifications

The purchaser needs a knowledge of meat source and classification in order to determine the degree of tenderness, juiciness, flavor, yield, and other advantages or disadvantages of buying various cuts.

A knowledge of basic carcass structure is especially helpful when it is necessary to substitute one cut for another in the preparation of a food item. Knowing that the bottom round of beef (inside round) is less tender than the top round (outside round) may mean the difference between patient satisfaction and complaints. In reviewing the charts for beef (Figure 11–1), veal (Figure 11–2), lamb (Figure 11–3), and pork (Figure 11–4), it is well to remember that there is a difference in the color of the meat and the size of the cut, but the muscle and bone structures of the four meats are alike.

Many of the problems associated with meat specification have been eliminated with the development of national standards. Meat standardization began with the establishment of a voluntary "acceptance service" by the U.S. Department of Agriculture (USDA). The acceptance service, which certified meat grades and other characteristics, was paid for by the buyer. Each institution using the government service wrote its own specifications. During the mid-1950s a set of uniform specifications called Institutional Meat Purchasing Specifications (IMPS) was developed for use under the USDA acceptance service. The IMPS are published in a series of booklets for the following categories:

Title	Series (no)
General Requirements	
Fresh Beef	100
Fresh Lamb and Mutton	200
Fresh Veal and Calf	300
Fresh Pork	400
Cured, Cured and Smoked, and Fully Cooked Pork Products	500
Cured, Dried, and Smoked Beef Products	600
Edible Byproducts	700
Sausage Products	800
Portion-Cut Meat Products	1000

The National Association of Meat Purveyors (NAMP), in cooperation with the USDA, developed the *Meat Buyer's Guide to Standardized Meat Cuts* (National Association of Meat Purveyors 1960) and the *Meat Buyer's Guide to Portion Control Meat Cuts* during the late 1960s (National Association of Meat Purveyors 1967). In 1976, NAMP combined the two books into one entitled *Meat Buyer's Guide* (National Association of Meat Purveyors 1976). Both IMPS and NAMP use the same numbering system. For example, the IMPS standard specification number for a wholesale cut of beef short loin is no. 173—series 100; the standard NAMP number for a T-bone steak, prepared from a beef short loin, is no. 1173A. Each cut, both wholesale and portion cut, is fully described. In addition to the standardized

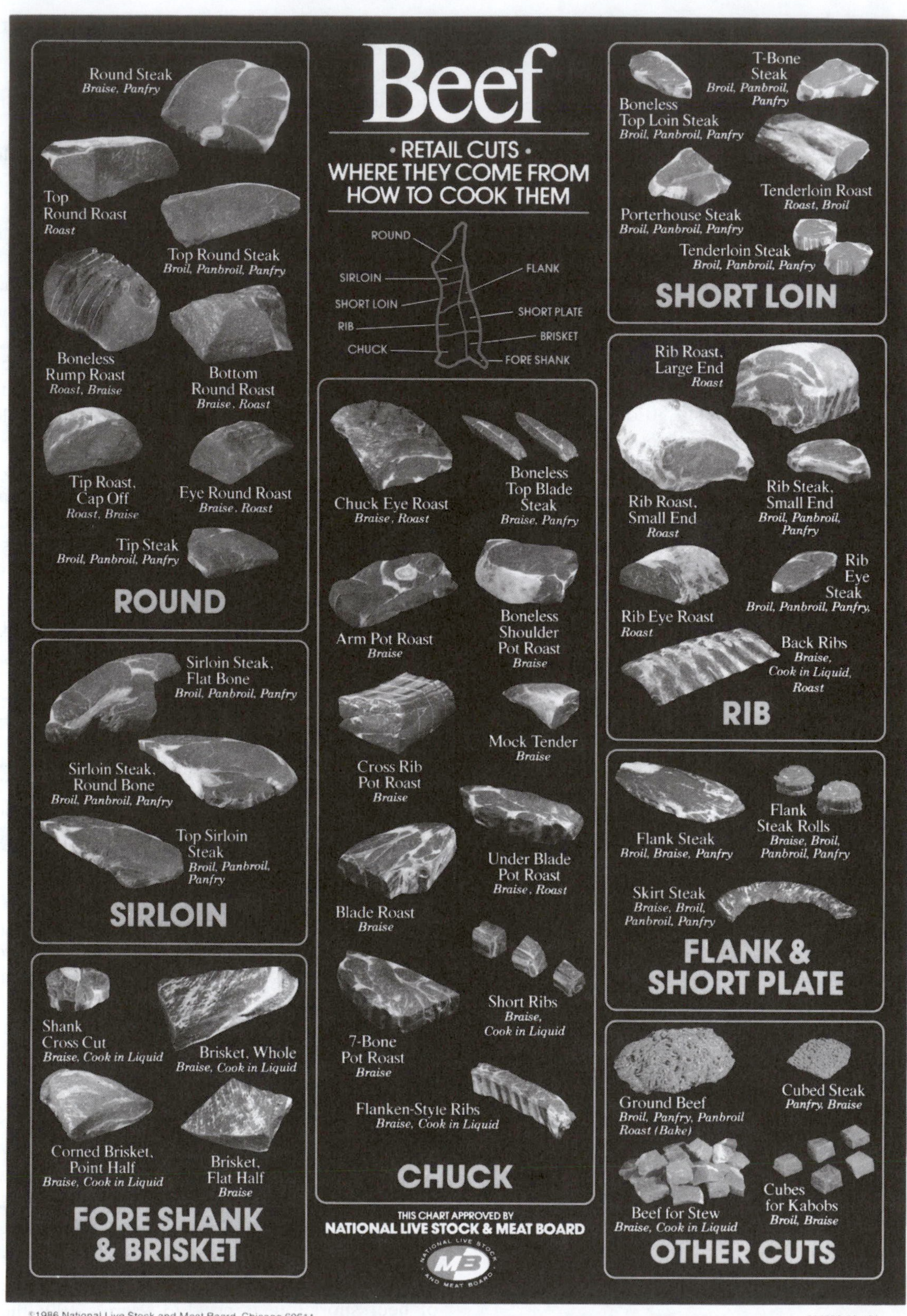

Figure 11–1 Retail Cuts of Beef. Reproduced courtesy of the National Cattlemen's Beef Association and the National Pork Producers Council. © 1986.

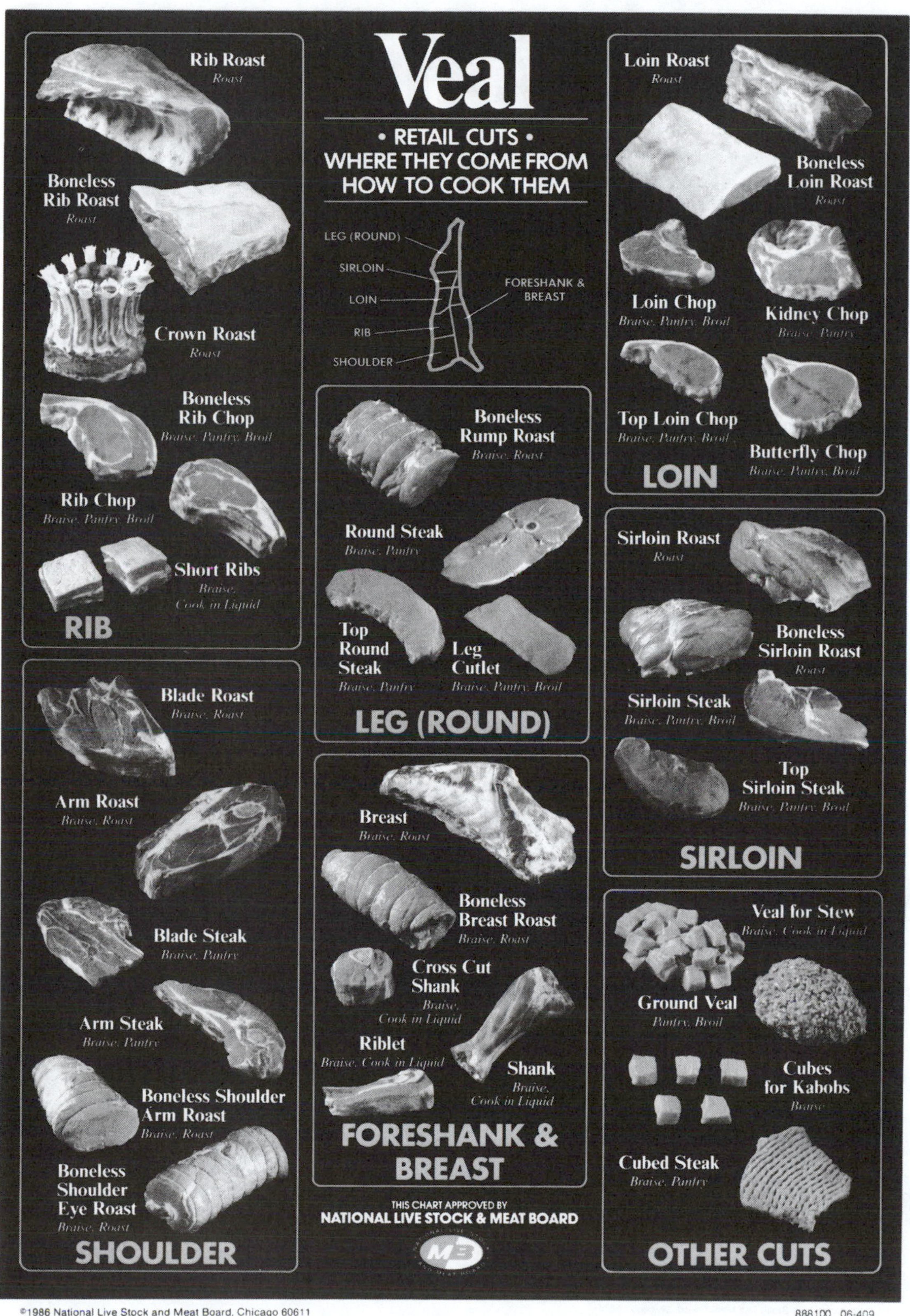

Figure 11–2 Retail Cuts of Veal. Reproduced courtesy of the National Cattlemen's Beef Association and the National Pork Producers Council. © 1986.

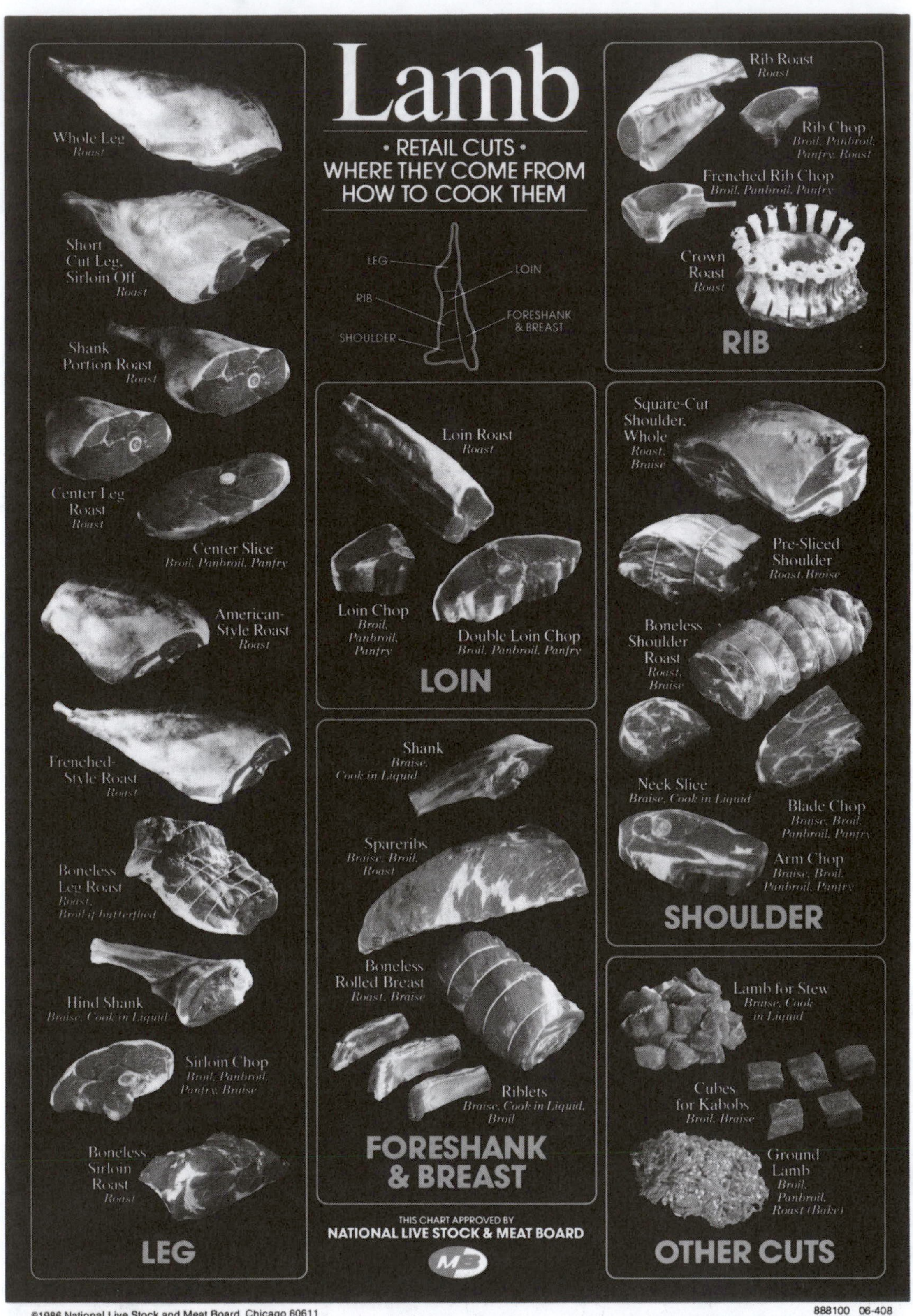

Figure 11–3 Retail Cuts of Lamb. Reproduced courtesy of the National Cattlemen's Beef Association and the National Pork Producers Council. © 1986.

Figure 11–4 Retail Cuts of Pork. Reproduced courtesy of the National Cattlemen's Beef Association and the National Pork Producers Council. © 1986.

number, the buyer must indicate specifics such as grade, thickness, and other factors relating to various classifications of meat.

Beef Cuts. For beef portion cuts and roasts, the buyer must specify the grade, thickness of portion weight for steaks or weight ranges in pounds for roasts, and state of refrigeration. A partial listing of roasts and suggested weight ranges is given in Table 11–1. For steaks, the buyer may specify the weight range of the trimmed meat cut from which the portions are to be produced. Common portion sizes for many beefsteaks are given in Table 11–2. A buyer may desire to purchase beef rib steak (bone-in), which may be cut from the chuck end of the rib or the loin end of the rib. If only steak from the loin end is desired, this must be specified.

The buyer must specify one of the quality grades as shown in Table 11–3. Meat inspection is mandatory, but federal meat grading is voluntary. The quality grade stamp (Figure 11–5) is routinely rolled on the top three grades; yield grades can be rolled on with the quality grade or stamped on each wholesale cut. All federally graded beef must be graded for both quality and yield; therefore, the buyer may also specify the yield. The yield grades, nos. 1 to 5, indicate the percentage of usable meat in a specific carcass. The lower grades have a higher percentage of available meat than carcasses graded no. 4 or no. 5. For example, a 600-lb USDA no. 1 beef carcass yields approximately 80 percent of its weight in trimmed cuts, compared with an approximate yield of 63 percent of its weight in trimmed cuts from a 600-lb USDA no. 5 carcass.

For portion weight items, the actual portion weight desired must be specified. Unless indicated by the buyer, depending on the portion weight specified, tolerances are permitted as follows: less than 6 oz, ± ¼ oz; 6 to 8 oz, ± ½ oz; 12 to 18 oz, ± ¾ oz; over 18 oz, ± 1 oz. The thickness of portion cuts may also be specified with tolerances: 1 in or less, ± 3⁄16 in; more than 1 in, ± ¼ in.

The surface fat limitations for steaks, chops, and roasts vary and should be indicated in the specifications. Generally recognized allowances are given in Table 11–4.

To indicate the state of refrigeration, the buyer should specify chilled or frozen. Portion cut meats to be delivered frozen may be produced from frozen cuts of meats that were previously accepted by federal meat graders. The meat must be maintained in excellent condition and be packaged, produced, and returned promptly to the frozen state.

The finest veal is milk fed, and the flesh has a pinkish hue. The buyer must specify the grade and class, thickness, and state of refrigeration. Suggested portion and weight ranges are shown in Table 11–5.

Lamb Cuts. Grading factors for lamb are similar to those for beef. Unlike beef, which must be federally graded for both quality and yield, federally graded lamb and mutton may be graded for either quality or yield, or both. Quality

Table 11–1 Sample Index of Beef Roasts and Stew and Suggested Weight Ranges

Item No.	*Item Names*	*Suggested Weight Ranges (lb)**				
1107R	Rib, bone-in, short cut	Under 20	20–23	24–26	27–30	31–up
1108R	Rib, boneless, tied, short cut	Under 17	17–19	20–22	23–25	26–up
1109R	Rib, bone-in, tied, roast ready	Under 17	17–19	20–22	23–25	26–up
1109AR	Rib, bone-in, tied, roast ready, special	Under 17	17–19	20–22	23–25	26–up
1110R	Rib, boneless, tied, roast ready	Under 14	14–16	17–19	20–22	23–up
1112R	Rib eye roll	Under 7	7–8	9–10	11–12	13–up
1114R	Shoulder clod, roast ready	Under 16	16–18	19–21	22–24	25–up
1116R	Chuck roll, boneless, tied	Under 15	15–17	18–21	22–25	26–up
1167R	Knuckle, boneless	Under 10	10–up			
1168R	Inside round	Under 18	18–20	21–23	24–26	27–up
1169R	Outside round	Under 11	11–13	14–16	17–19	20–up
1170R	Gooseneck round	Under 18	18–20	21–23	24–26	27–up
1180R	Strip loin, boneless, short cut	Under 8	9–10	11–12	13–14	15–up
1184R	Top sirloin butt, boneless	Under 8	8–10	11–13	14–up	
1186R	Bottom sirloin butt, boneless, trimmed	Under 4	4–6	7–up		
1189R	Full tenderloin, regular	Under 5	5–7	7–9	9–up	
1195	Beef for stewing		Amount specified			

*Because it is impractical to list all weights for roasts that purchasers may desire, those included in the index table are suggested only. Other weight ranges may be ordered if desired.

Source: Reprinted from *Institutional Meat Purchase Specifications for Portion-Cut Meat Products,* Series 1000, Consumer and Marketing Service, Livestock Division, U.S. Department of Agriculture, 1967.

Table 11–2 Sample Index of Beefsteaks and Patties and Suggested Portion Sizes

Item No.	*Item Names*	*Suggested Portion Sizes* (oz)*												
		3	*4*	*6*	*8*	*10*	*12*	*14*	*16*	*18*	*20*	*24*	*28*	*32*
1100	Cubed steaks, regular	×	×	×	×									
1101	Cubed steaks, special	×	×	×	×									
1102	Braising steaks, boneless (Swiss)		×	×	×									
1103	Rib steaks (bone-in)				×	×	×	×	×	×				
1103A	Rib steaks (boneless)		×	×	×	×	×							
1112	Rib eye roll steaks		×	×	×	×	×							
1136	Ground beef patties, regular	×	×	×	×									
1137	Ground beef patties, special	×	×	×	×									
1167	Knuckle steaks	×	×	×	×	×								
1169	Inside round steaks	×	×	×	×	×								
1170A	Bottom round steaks	×	×	×	×	×	×	×	×	×	×	×		
1173	Porterhouse steaks					×	×							
1174	T-Bone steaks				×	×	×	×	×	×	×			
1177	Strip loin steaks (bone-in), intermediate				×	×	×	×	×	×	×	×	×	
1178	Strip loin steaks (boneless), intermediate				×	×	×	×	×	×	×	×	×	
1179	Strip loin steaks (bone-in), short cut				×	×	×	×	×	×	×	×		
1179A	Strip loin steaks (bone-in), extra short cut				×	×	×	×	×	×	×	×		
1179B	Strip loin steaks (bone-in), special				×	×	×	×	×	×	×	×		
1180	Strip loin steaks (boneless), short cut			×	×	×	×	×	×	×	×			
1180A	Strip loin steaks (boneless), extra short cut			×	×	×	×	×	×	×	×			
1180B	Strip loin steaks (boneless), special			×	×	×	×	×	×	×	×			
1184	Top sirloin butt steaks (boneless)		×	×	×	×	×	×	×	×	×	×	×	
1184A	Top sirloin butt steaks (boneless), semi–center cut		×	×	×	×	×	×	×					
1184B	Top sirloin butt steaks (boneless), center cut		×	×	×	×	×	×	×					
1189	Tenderloin steaks, close trim		×	×	×	×	×	×						
1190	Tenderloin steaks, special trim	×	×	×	×	×	×	×						

*Because it is impractical to list all portion weights for steaks that purchasers may desire, those identified by × in the index table are suggested only. Other portion weights may be ordered if desired.

Source: Reprinted from *Institutional Meat Purchase Specifications for Portion-Cut Meat Products,* Series 100, Agricultural Marketing Service, Livestock and Seed Division, U.S. Department of Agriculture, 1996.

lamb is well fed, is finely grained, and has a pinkish red color. The purchaser must specify grade and class. Unless otherwise specified in the individual item specification, chops must be cut in full slices in a straight line, reasonably perpendicular to the other surface and at an approximate right angle to the length of the meat cut from which chops are produced. Suggested portion sizes and weight ranges for lamb chops and roasts are given in Table 11–6.

Pork Cuts. Grades for pork are based on a combination of quality and yield. The purchaser should specify U.S. No. 1 or U.S. No. 2. Unless otherwise specified in the individual

Table 11–3 Federal Classification, Grades, and Yields for Meats

Class		Grades	Yields
Beef	(steer, heifer, cow*)	Prime, Choice, Select, Standard, Commercial, Utility, Cutter, Canner	1,2,3,4,5
	(bullock)	Prime, Choice, Select, Standard, Utility	1,2,3,4,5
Veal		Prime, Choice, Good, Standard, Utility	1,2,3,4,5
Lamb†	(yearling mutton)	Prime, Choice, Good, Utility	1,2,3,4,5
	(mutton)	Choice, Good, Utility, Cull	1,2,3,4,5
Pork	(barrows and gilts)	U.S. No. 1, U.S. No. 2, U.S. No. 3, U.S. No. 4, U.S. Utility	
	(sows)	U.S. No. 1, U.S. No. 2, U.S. No. 3, Medium, Cull	

* Cows are not graded as prime.
† Federally graded lamb and mutton may be graded for either quality or yield, or both.

item specifications, filets, chops, and steaks must be cut in full slices in a straight line, reasonably perpendicular to the other surface and at an approximate right angle to the length of the meat cut from which the filets, chops, or steaks are produced. Suggested portion sizes and weight ranges for pork cuts are given in Table 11–7.

Poultry Specifications

Specifications for fresh poultry should include the grade, class, size, and state of refrigeration. They should also include the part, if cup-up poultry is specified. Poultry must be federally inspected for wholesomeness before it can be graded for quality. Often the grade shield and the inspection mark appear together (Figure 11–6). Both inspection and grading are mandatory.

The inspection mark on poultry and poultry products shows that they have been examined for wholesomeness under government supervision in an officially approved processing plant. Not all poultry that has been inspected carries the mark. The exception is that if chilled poultry is packed in large boxes, the box carries the seal.

The highest quality is U.S. Grade A. You may find the shield on any kind of chilled or frozen or ready-to-cook poultry or poultry parts. Grade A poultry is fully fleshed and meaty, well finished, and attractive in appearance (Figure 11–7). The U.S. grades apply to five kinds of poultry: chicken, turkey, duck, goose, and guinea. The grade does not indicate how tender the bird is; the age (class) is the determining factor. Poultry classifications are given in Table 11–8. Young birds are more tender than older ones. If the poultry is not young, the label will carry the words mature, old, or similar words to indicate the age.

Poultry Parts. The purchase of chicken parts is equivalent to purchasing portion cut meats such as steaks, chops, and cutlets. The USDA quality grades are the same as those for the whole bird, plus specific standards on how each part is to be cut. The USDA standards (U.S. Department of Agriculture 1972) exist for the following parts:

- Breast—may be split or in three pieces
- Breasts with ribs split or cut into three pieces with part of ribs attached
- Leg—includes whole leg (thigh and drumstick)
- Wings—include whole wing with all muscle and skin intact (wing tip may be removed)
- Drumsticks—separated from thigh by cut through knee joint
- Thigh—disjointed at hip joint; may include pelvic meat but not bone
- Halves—full-length back and breast split
- Quarters—split as for halves, then cut crosswise to form quarters

Figure 11–5 Quality and Yield Grades for Beef. *Source:* Reprinted from *How to Buy Meat*, Home and Garden Bulletin, No. 265, July 1995, U.S. Department of Agriculture.

Table 11–4 Allowable Surface Fat for Steaks, Chops, and Roasts

Item	*Allowable Surface Fat*
Steaks	Fat should not exceed an average of ¼ in. in thickness
Chops, cutlets, and filets	Surface fat, where present, should not exceed an average of ¼ in. in thickness
Roasts	Average surface fat should be ¼ in. in thickness

Source: Reprinted with permission from *Meat Buyers Guide*, © 1997, North American Meat Processors Association.

- Backs—include the pelvic bone and all vertebrae posterior to the shoulder joint
- Necks—separated from the carcass at the shoulder joint, with or without skin
- Giblets—approximately equal numbers of hearts, gizzards, and livers

Chicken parts are the most popular marketing form used in quantity food service. Breasts are especially well liked by patients and employees who prefer light meat; they can be prepared in a variety of ways and are easy to serve. The buyer should specify U.S. Grade A. To determine whether chicken parts are a good buy, the purchaser is referred to Table 11–9. For example, Table 11–9 shows that breast halves with ribs at $1.02 a pound, drumstick and thighs at $0.88 a pound, drumsticks at $0.86 a pound, thighs at $0.93 a pound, and wings at $0.50 a pound provide as much lean meat for the money as ready-to-cook whole chickens at $0.73. The purchaser pays for the convenience of having the parts of a chicken. A similar comparison can be made for turkey parts, as shown in Table 11–10.

Processed Chicken. Several varieties of processed poultry products are available, including canned, frozen, cooked, or partly cooked dishes. Many of these products are combination dishes, with vegetables, pasta, gravy, or other foods added. Federal standards exist for the minimum percentage of meat that manufacturers must include in combi-

Table 11–5 Sample Index of Veal and Calf Steaks, Chops, Cutlets, Roasts, and Stew and Suggested Portion Sizes and Weight Ranges

		*Suggested Portion Sizes and Weight Ranges**											
Item No.	*Item Names*	*3 oz*	*4 oz*	*5 oz*	*6 oz*	*8 oz*	*10 oz*	*12 oz*	*16 oz*	*lb*	*lb*	*lb*	*lb*
1300	Cubed steaks, regular	×	×	×	×	×							
1301	Cubed steaks, special	×	×	×	×	×							
1306	Rib chops		×	×	×	×							
1309	Shoulder chops		×	×	×	×							
1310	Shoulder clod steaks		×	×	×	×	×						
1332	Loin chops		×	×	×	×							
1336	Cutlet, regular	×	×	×	×	×							
1336A	Cutlet, special	×	×	×	×	×							
1309A	Chuck, shoulder blade chops		×	×	×	×							
310B	Shoulder clod, roast ready									Under 3	4–6	7–8	9–up
309	Chuck, square-cut, clod out, boneless, tied									Under 6	6–8	9–10	11–up
335	Leg, boneless, tied, roast ready									Under 10	10–15	16–22	23–up
395	Veal for stewing			Amount specified									

* Because it is impractical to list all portion weights for chops and all weight ranges for roasts that purchasers may desire, the portion weights identified by × and the weight ranges for roasts are suggested only. Other portion weights and weight ranges may be ordered if desired.

Source: Reprinted from *Institutional Meat Purchase Specifications for Portion-Cut Meat Products*, Series 300, Agricultural Marketing Service, Livestock and Seed Division, U.S. Department of Agriculture, 1995.

Table 11–6 Sample Index of Lamb, Yearling Mutton, and Mutton Chops, Roasts, and Stew and Suggested Portion Sizes and Weight Ranges

		*Suggested Portion Sizes and Weight Ranges**											
Item No.	*Item Names*	*3 oz*	*4 oz*	*5 oz*	*6 oz*	*7 oz*	*8 oz*	*9 oz*	*10 oz*	*lb*	*lb*	*lb*	*lb*
1204B	Rib chops	×	×	×	×	×	×						
1204C	Rib chops, frenched	×	×	×	×	×	×						
1207	Shoulder chops	×	×	×	×	×	×						
1232A	Loin chops	×	×	×	×	×	×						
1208R	Shoulder, boneless, tied									Under 4	4–6	7–8	9 and up
1234	Leg chops, boneless	×	×	×	×	×	×						
234	Leg, boneless, tied									5–8	8–11	11–13	13 and up
1295	Lamb for stewing	Amount specified											

*Because it is impractical to list all portion weights for chops and all weight ranges for roasts that purchasers may desire, the portion weights identified by × and the weight for roasts are suggested only. Other portion weights and weight ranges may be ordered if desired.

Source: Reprinted from *Institutional Meat Purchase Specifications for Portion-Cut Meat Products*, Series 200, Agricultural Marketing Service, Livestock and Seed Division, U.S. Department of Agriculture, 1996.

nation dishes, but the minimum may not be sufficient to meet the protein requirement for menus in a medical food service operation. (See Appendix M for combination foods containing poultry.) If used, the buyer will have to specify the ratio of poultry to the other ingredients of the combination dish. If the percentage of meat is inadequate, the product must be served with other protein foods such as cheese or eggs.

Egg Specifications

There are three consumer grades for eggs: U.S. Grade AA (or Fresh Fancy), U.S. Grade A, and U.S. Grade B. Graded

Table 11–7 Sample Index of Pork Filets, Steaks, Chops, and Roasts and Suggested Portion Sizes and Weight Ranges

		*Suggested Portion Sizes and Weight Ranges**									
Item No.	*Item Names*	*3 oz*	*4 oz*	*5 oz*	*6 oz*	*8 oz*	*10 oz*	*4–6 lb*	*6–8 lb*	*8–10 lb*	*10–12 lb*
1400	Steak, cubed	×	×	×	×	×					
1406	Boston butt steaks, bone-in		×	×	×	×					
1407	Shoulder butt steaks, boneless	×	×	×	×	×					
1410	Loin chops, regular	×	×	×	×	×					
1410A	Loin, rib chops		×	×	×	×					
1410B	Loin, end chops		×	×	×	×					
1411	Loin chops, bladeless	×	×	×	×	×					
1412	Loin chops, center cut	×	×	×	×	×					
1412A	Loin chops, center cut, special	×	×	×	×	×					
1412B	Loin chops, center cut, boneless	×	×	×	×	×					
1413	Loin chops, boneless	×	×	×	×	×					
402	Fresh ham, boneless, tied								×	×	×
1406	Boston butt, steaks		×	×	×	×					
413	Pork loin, boneless, tied								×	×	×

* Because it is impractical to list all portion weights for chops and all weight ranges for roasts that purchasers may desire, the portion weights and weight ranges identified by × are suggested only. Other portion weights and weight ranges may be ordered if desired.

Source: Reprinted from *Institutional Meat Purchase Specifications for Portion-Cut Meat Products*, Series 400, Agricultural Marketing Service, Livestock and Seed Division, U.S. Department of Agriculture, 1997.

Figure 11–6 Poultry Inspection Mark and Grade Shield. *Source:* Reprinted from How To Buy Poultry, *Home and Garden Bull.*, No. 157, U.S. Department of Agriculture, 1968.

eggs have been examined by an authorized grader to determine factors such as the condition of the white and yolk, and the cleanliness and soundness of the shell. Electronic equipment is used for flash scanning or flash candling, where eggs are placed on a continuous conveyor system and mechanically rotated over strong light. The egg size, which ranges from jumbo to peewee, is not related to egg quality (Table 11–11).

The U.S. Grade AA (or Fresh Fancy) is the top USDA consumer grade for shell eggs. The broken-out egg covers a small area. The white is thick and stands high, and the yolk is firm and high. Eggs with this grade are suitable for poaching, frying, or other uses where appearance is important.

The U.S. Grade A is the second highest USDA grade for shell eggs. The broken-out egg covers a moderate area. The white is reasonably thick and stands fairly high; the yolk is firm and high. Grade AA and A shields are shown in Figure 11–8.

The U.S. Grade B is the lowest consumer grade for eggs. The white is thinner than that of U.S. Grade AA and U.S. Grade A eggs, and the yolk is somewhat flattened. Grade B eggs are suitable for general cooking and baking where appearance is not important.

The buyer should specify both grade and size. Grade AA is used for poaching and frying and Grade A is used for hard-cooked, scrambled, and other cooking methods. Size depends on use. Compare price and size, as shown in Table 11–12.

Processed Eggs. All processed eggs must be pasteurized before processing. USDA inspection is mandatory. Processed eggs may be purchased in a variety of forms. The most popular types are the following:

- fresh liquid bulk—30-lb can
- frozen liquid eggs (whole, yolks, whites)—10-lb and 30-lb cans
- frozen hard-cooked eggs (chopped)—packed in plastic bags
- frozen egg rolls (yolk is centered, used for slicing or chopping)
- freeze-dried scrambled eggs—six 3-lb cans per case, 50-lb drums
- dried eggs—whole, yolks, or whites

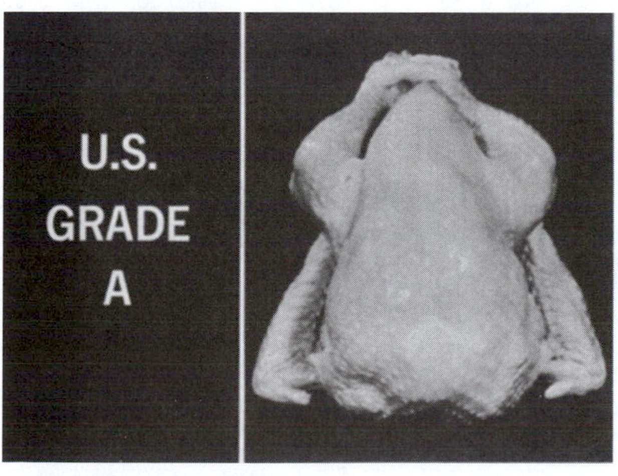

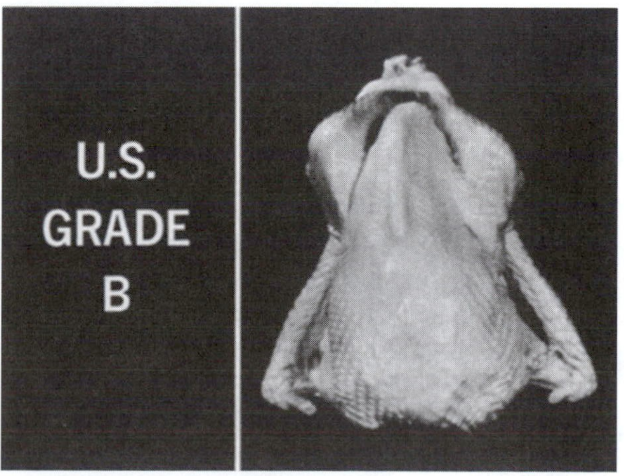

Figure 11–7 Comparison of Grade A and Grade B Poultry. *Source*: Reprinted from How To Buy Poultry, *Home and Garden Bull.*, No. 157, U.S. Department of Agriculture, 1968.

Table 11–8 Classification for Poultry

Class	*Description*
Young chickens	May be labeled young chicken, Rock Cornish hen, broiler, fryer roaster, or capon.
Young turkeys	May be labeled young turkey, fryer, roaster, young hen, or young tom.
Young ducks	May be labeled duckling, young duckling, broiler duckling, fryer duckling, or roaster duckling.
Mature chickens	May be labeled mature chicken, old chicken, stewing chicken, or fowl.
Mature turkeys	May be labeled mature turkey, yearling turkey, or old turkey.
Mature ducks, geese, or guineas	May be labeled as mature or old.

Source: Reprinted from How to Buy Poultry, *Home and Garden Bull.*, No. 157, U.S. Department of Agriculture, 1968.

Table 11–9 Cost of Chicken, Whole and Parts*

Price† per Pound (in Dollars) of Whole Fryers, Ready to Cook	*Chicken Parts Equally Good Buy at This Price per Pound (in Dollars)*						
	Breast Half (with Rib)	*Drumstick and Thigh*	*Drumstick*	*Thigh*	*Wing*	*Breast Quarter*	*Leg Quarter*
0.45	0.63	0.54	0.53	0.57	0.31	0.54	0.52
0.47	0.65	0.57	0.55	0.60	0.32	0.56	0.54
0.49	0.68	0.59	0.57	0.62	0.33	0.59	0.57
0.51	0.71	0.61	0.60	0.65	0.35	0.61	0.59
0.53	0.74	0.64	0.62	0.67	0.36	0.64	0.61
0.55	0.77	0.66	0.65	0.70	0.38	0.66	0.64
0.57	0.79	0.69	0.67	0.72	0.39	0.68	0.66
0.59	0.82	0.71	0.69	0.75	0.40	0.71	0.68
0.61	0.85	0.74	0.72	0.77	0.42	0.73	0.71
0.63	0.88	0.76	0.74	0.80	0.43	0.76	0.73
0.65	0.91	0.78	0.76	0.83	0.44	0.78	0.75
0.67	0.93	0.81	0.79	0.85	0.46	0.80	0.78
0.69	0.96	0.83	0.81	0.88	0.47	0.83	0.80
0.71	0.99	0.86	0.83	0.90	0.49	0.85	0.82
0.73	1.02	0.88	0.86	0.93	0.50	0.88	0.85
0.75	1.04	0.90	0.88	0.95	0.51	0.90	0.87
0.77	1.07	0.93	0.90	0.98	0.53	0.92	0.89
0.79	1.10	0.95	0.93	1.00	0.54	0.95	0.92
0.81	1.13	0.98	0.95	1.03	0.55	0.97	0.94
0.83	1.16	1.00	0.97	1.05	0.57	1.00	0.95
0.85	1.18	1.02	1.00	1.08	0.58	1.02	0.98
0.87	1.21	1.05	1.02	1.10	0.59	1.04	1.01
0.89	1.24	1.07	1.04	1.13	0.61	1.07	1.03
0.91	1.27	1.10	1.07	1.16	0.62	1.09	1.05
0.93	1.30	1.12	1.09	1.18	0.64	1.12	1.08
0.95	1.32	1.15	1.11	1.21	0.65	1.14	1.10
0.97	1.35	1.17	1.14	1.23	0.66	1.16	1.12
0.99	1.38	1.19	1.16	1.26	0.68	1.19	1.15

* Based on yields of cooked chicken meat without skin, from frying chickens that weighed about 3 lb.
† Price based on weight of chicken with neck and giblets.
Source: Reprinted from Your Money's Worth in Foods, *Home and Garden Bull.*, No. 183, Human Nutrition Information Service, U.S. Department of Agriculture, 1982.

Table 11–10 Comparative Costs of Turkey Parts*

Price per Pound (in Dollars) of Whole Turkey, Ready To Cook	*Turkey Parts and Products Equally Good Buy at This Price Per Pound (in Dollars)*										
							Turkey Roasts				
	Breast Quarter	*Leg Quarter*	*Breast, Whole or Half*	*Drum-stick*	*Thigh*	*Wing*	*Ready To Cook*†	*Cooked*‡	*Boned Turkey, Canned*	*Turkey with Gravy,*§ *Canned or Frozen*	*Gravy with Turkey,*‖ *Canned or Frozen*
0.51	0.57	0.55	0.65	0.52	0.62	0.47	0.87	1.17	1.15	0.45	0.19
0.53	0.60	0.57	0.68	0.54	0.65	0.49	0.93	1.22	1.19	0.46	0.20
0.55	0.62	0.59	0.70	0.56	0.67	0.51	0.96	1.26	1.24	0.48	0.21
0.57	0.64	0.61	0.73	0.58	0.70	0.53	1.00	1.31	1.28	0.50	0.21
0.59	0.66	0.63	0.75	0.60	0.72	0.55	1.03	1.36	1.33	0.52	0.22
0.61	0.69	0.66	0.78	0.63	0.75	0.56	1.07	1.40	1.37	0.53	0.23
0.63	0.71	0.68	0.80	0.65	0.77	0.58	1.10	1.45	1.42	0.55	0.24
0.65	0.73	0.70	0.83	0.67	0.80	0.60	1.14	1.50	1.46	0.57	0.24
0.67	0.75	0.72	0.85	0.69	0.82	0.62	1.17	1.54	1.51	0.59	0.25
0.69	0.78	0.74	0.88	0.71	0.85	0.64	1.21	1.59	1.55	0.60	0.26
0.71	0.80	0.76	0.91	0.73	0.87	0.66	1.24	1.63	1.60	0.62	0.27
0.73	0.82	0.78	0.93	0.75	0.89	0.68	1.28	1.68	1.64	0.64	0.27
0.75	0.84	0.81	0.96	0.77	0.92	0.69	1.31	1.72	1.69	0.66	0.28
0.77	0.87	0.83	0.98	0.79	0.94	0.71	1.35	1.77	1.73	0.67	0.29
0.79	0.89	0.85	1.01	0.81	0.97	0.73	1.38	1.82	1.78	0.69	0.30
0.81	0.91	0.87	1.03	0.83	0.99	0.75	1.42	1.86	1.82	0.71	0.30
0.83	0.93	0.89	1.06	0.85	1.02	0.77	1.45	1.91	1.87	0.73	0.31
0.85	0.96	0.91	1.08	0.87	1.04	0.79	1.49	1.96	1.91	0.74	0.32
0.87	0.98	0.94	1.11	0.89	1.07	0.80	1.52	2.00	1.96	0.76	0.33
0.89	1.00	0.96	1.13	0.91	1.09	0.82	1.56	2.05	2.00	0.78	0.33
0.91	1.02	0.98	1.16	0.93	1.11	0.84	1.59	2.09	2.05	0.80	0.34
0.93	1.05	1.00	1.19	0.95	1.14	0.86	1.63	2.14	2.09	0.81	0.35
0.95	1.07	1.02	1.21	0.97	1.15	0.88	1.66	2.18	2.14	0.83	0.36
0.97	1.09	1.04	1.24	0.99	1.19	0.90	1.70	2.23	2.18	0.85	0.36
0.99	1.11	1.06	1.26	1.01	1.21	0.92	1.73	2.28	2.23	0.87	0.37

* Based on yields of cooked turkey meat excluding skin, medium to large birds.
† Roast, as purchased, includes 15 percent skin or fat.
‡ Roast, as purchased, has no more than ¼-in skin and fat on any part of surface.
§ Assumes 35 percent cooked boned turkey, minimum required for product labeled "turkey with gravy."
‖ Assumes 15 percent cooked boned turkey, minimum required for product labeled "gravy with turkey."
Source: Reprinted from *How To Buy Food: Lesson Aids for Teachers*, No. 443, Agriculture Marketing Service, U.S. Department of Agriculture, 1975.

Processed eggs are primarily used for baking and other cooking needs. Fresh or frozen whole liquid eggs are convenient forms and are used for scrambled eggs.

Dairy Products Specifications

Butter and Margarine. Butter and margarine must meet minimum milk fat content of 80 percent. Butter is made from animal fat; margarine or oleomargarine is made from vegetable fat or a blend of both vegetable and animal fat. The grading standards range from U.S. Grade AA to U.S. Grade B, as shown in Figure 11–9. The products are sold in ¼-lb or 1-lb prints, 5-lb cartons with 72 to 90 pats per lb, and in 64-lb cubes.

Milk. Milk is marketed in a variety of forms. The more common types are fresh, canned, and dried. Standards for Grade A milk are established by state and local governments, as recommended in U.S. Public Health Service *Grade "A" Pasteurized Milk Ordinance* (U.S. Department of Health and Human Services 1965). The milk must come from healthy cows and be produced, pasteurized, and handled under strict sanitary conditions. The Grade A rating denotes wholesomeness rather than level of quality. Homogenized milk has been treated to reduce the size of the milk fat globules. This keeps the cream from separating. Fortified milk is milk with one or more nutrients added. Vitamin D milk is fortified with 400 international units (IU)

Table 11–11 Egg Size and Weight

Size (Name)	Per Dozen (oz)	Per 30-Dozen Case (lb)*
Jumbo	30	56
Extra Large	27	50½
Large	24	45
Medium	21	39½
Small	18	34
Peewee	15	28

*Weight includes approximately 4½ lb extra per case for corrugated fiber case and fillers between layers of eggs.

Table 11–12 Calculating the Cost of Eggs

Price per Dozen (in Cents) Large Eggs	Larger of Two Sizes Better Buy if Price Difference per Dozen (in Cents) Between One Size and Next Larger Size Less Than
41–48	6
49–56	7
57–64	8
65–72	9
73–80	10
81–88	11
89–96	12
97–104	13
105–112	14
113–120	15

Source: Reprinted from *How To Buy Food: Lesson Aids for Teachers,* No. 443, Agriculture Marketing Service, U.S. Department of Agriculture, 1975.

of vitamin D per quart. Fortified milk can be fortified with substances such as vitamins A and D, multivitamin preparations, minerals, lactose, and nonfat dry milk. Certified milk denotes that the milk was produced under sanitary conditions. Only certified milk that has been pasteurized should be used in food service operations. Pasteurized milk means that the product has been subjected to heat high enough to ensure pathogen destruction. The types of milk commonly used in food service operations are as follows:

- Whole milk contains a minimum of 3.25 percent milk fat with vitamin D added.
- Low-fat milk is partially skimmed milk that contains between 0.5 percent and 2 percent milk fat, depending on state regulations.
- Skim milk has less than 0.5 percent milk fat, the percentage allowed under federal regulations.
- Chocolate-flavored milk is made from pasteurized whole milk with sugar and chocolate syrup or cocoa added.
- Chocolate-flavored drink is similar to chocolate milk, except that the product does not have to conform to standards of identity established for milk. The product has a lower milk fat content than chocolate milk.

Figure 11–8 USDA Grade Shields for Fresh Eggs. *Source:* Reprinted from *How To Buy Food: Lesson Aids for Teachers,* No. 443, Agriculture Marketing Service, U.S. Department of Agriculture, 1975.

- Buttermilk is a cultured milk product made with skim milk fermented mainly by *Streptococcus lactis.*
- Two percent milk, as the name implies, contains 2 percent milk fat.
- Acidophilus milk is pasteurized skim milk, cultured with *Lactobacillus acidophilus*, and incubated at 100°F. This product is sometimes served to patients with a milk intolerance. It combats excessive intestinal putrefaction by changing the bacterial flora of the intestine.
- Yogurt has a consistency resembling custard and is made from fresh, partially skimmed milk and enriched and added milk solids. It is fermented by a mixed culture of one or more organisms as *Streptococcus thermophilus, Bacterium bulgaricus*, and *Plocamo-bacterium yoghourtii.*
- Evaporated milk is made by heating homogenized whole milk under a vacuum to remove half its water, then sealing it in cans and sterilizing it.
- Condensed milk is a concentrated milk with at least 40 percent sugar added to help preserve it. This canned milk is prepared by removing about half the water from whole milk. It contains at least 8.5 percent milk fat.
- Dry whole milk is pasteurized milk with water removed.
- Nonfat dry milk is processed to remove the fat and water and pasteurized to destroy microorganisms. It reconstitutes to fluid skim milk.
- Instant nonfat dry milk is processed to remove the fat and water from pasteurized fluid milk. It is made by a process that produces larger flakes than regular nonfat dry milk, and it dissolves instantly in water.

The buyer should purchase ready-to-drink milk in individual cartons as much as possible to prevent cross-contamination. Bulk milk for cooking may be purchased in

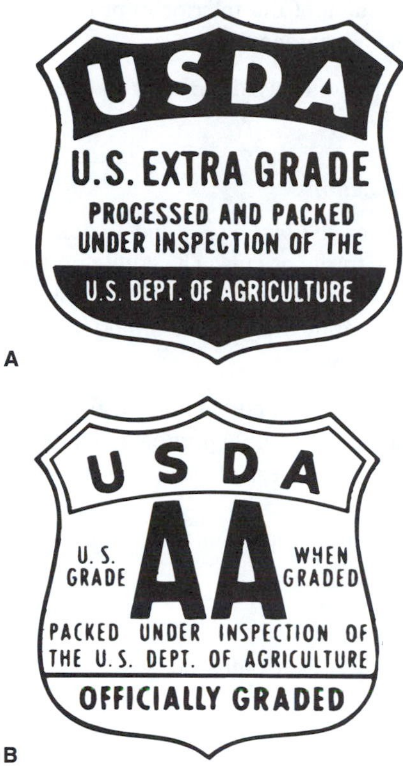

Figure 11–9 USDA Grades for Dairy Products. **A**, Used on instant nonfat dry milk. **B**, Highest quality grade for butter and cheddar cheese. **C**, Lowest quality grade for butter. **D**, Second highest grade for butter and cheddar cheese. *Source:* Reprinted from *How To Buy Food: Lesson Aids for Teachers*, No. 443, Agriculture Marketing Service, U.S. Department of Agriculture, 1975.

½-gal or 5-gal containers. Specify grade, type, and container size.

Standards of identity for cream have been established to indicate the minimum fat content. The product must be pasteurized, and if it contains less than 18 percent fat it cannot be called cream. Types available and used in food service operations are as follows:

- Light cream (also coffee or table cream) must have at least 18 percent milk fat.
- Light whipping cream must have a least 30 percent milk fat under federal standards of identity.
- Heavy whipping cream must have at least 36 percent milk fat.
- Half-and-half is a mixture of milk and cream that are homogenized. Under federal requirements, it must contain a minimum of 10.5 percent milk fat.
- Sour cream is made by adding lactic acid bacteria culture to light cream. It is smooth and thick and contains at least 18 percent milk fat.

Ice cream and other frozen dairy dessert-type products must be made from pasteurized milk. Standards of identity are as follows:

- Ice cream is made from cream, milk, sugar, flavoring, and stabilizers. It must contain at least 10 percent milk fat. Overrun (increase from whipping or freezing) is permitted up to 100 percent. The weight of a gallon of ice cream should not be less than 4½ lb.
- Ice milk is made from milk, stabilizers, sugar, and flavorings. It contains between 2 percent and 7 percent milk fat.
- Sherbet is made from milk, fruit or fruit juices, stabilizers, and sugar.
- Water ice is like sherbet except that it contains no milk.

Milk and milk-type products or imitation milks are available. They are difficult to define because of differing laws and regulations among the states. Two such products are identified as follows (U.S. Department of Health and Human Services 1969):

1. Filled milk is milk or cream (fluid, frozen, evaporated, condensed, concentrated, or dried) to which a fat other than butterfat has been added. The resulting product resembles milk or cream. A typical formulation consists of skim milk or nonfat dry milk and a vegetable fat. Artificial color or flavoring is frequently added.

Under the federal Filled Milk Act, filled milk may not be shipped in interstate or foreign commerce. Imitation milks, which may move in interstate commerce, are products resembling milk but containing no milk ingredients such as skim milk or nonfat dry milk. A typical formulation includes sodium caseinate, vegetable fat, corn syrup or dextrose, artificial color and flavor, and emulsifiers. The product must be labeled as imitation milk.

2. Coffee lighteners (or whiteners) are made in much the same manner as the imitation milk products, usually containing sodium caseinate, vegetable oil, and other ingredients.

Cheese. Cheese is available in a variety of different flavors and textures. Some types bear the "quality approved" shield, which ensures good quality and sanitary processing. USDA Grade AA cheddar cheese has been graded by a highly trained government grader and has been produced in a USDA-inspected and USDA-approved plant. The USDA Grade A cheese is also of good quality but not quite as good as Grade AA (see Figure 11–9 for USDA shields).

Natural cheese is manufactured directly from milk and includes cheddar, cottage, Parmesan, Swiss, blue, cream, Limburger, and hundreds of other varieties. Pasteurized process cheese is not a natural cheese; it is a blend of fresh and aged natural cheeses that are heated and mixed. Pasteurized process cheese spread is like cheese food, except that it has higher moisture and lower milk fat. Club cheese or cold pack cheese is a blend of natural cheeses, like process cheese, except that the cheese is blended without heat.

Natural cheeses are generally classified according to ripening time. There are six general classifications.

1. Unripened cheese includes both soft and firm. Soft unripened cheeses, such as cottage and cream cheese, have high moisture and undergo no ripening. Firm unripened cheeses such as mozzarella are not ripened but have very low moisture, so they may be stored longer.
2. Soft ripened cheeses are those such as Camembert. Curing progresses from the outside to the center.
3. Semisoft ripened cheeses, such as brick and Muenster, are less moist than soft-ripened cheeses. The cheeses ripen from the interior as well as the surface by using surface growth and bacterial culture.
4. Firm ripened cheeses, such as cheddar and Swiss, are ripened throughout the entire cheese. The cheese is lower in moisture, thus requiring a long curing time.
5. Very hard ripened cheeses, such as Parmesan and Romano, are cured very slowly because of their low moisture and high salt content.
6. Blue-vein mold ripened cheeses, such as blue cheese and Roquefort, are cured by using a mold culture that grows throughout the interior to produce the familiar flavor and appearance.

The more commonly used varieties of cheese are shown in Table 11–13.

Seafood Specifications

Fresh and Frozen Fish. Fresh and frozen fish are marketed in various forms or cuts. The edible portion will vary from 45 percent for whole fish to 100 percent for fillets. A knowledge of the following cuts is important in buying fish (Figure 11–10):

- Whole or round fish; edible portion about 45 percent.
- Drawn whole fish; edible portion about 48 percent.
- Dressed or pan-dressed fish; edible portion about 67 percent.
- Steaks. Usually about ¾-in thick; edible portion about 84 percent.
- Fillets.
- Butterfly fillet.
- Sticks. Each stick weighs not less than ¾ oz and not more than 1¼ oz.
- Portions—uniformly shaped pieces of boneless fish cut from blocks of frozen fillets. A portion cut is larger than a fish stick and has a thickness of ⅜ in.

Fish may be classified as freshwater or saltwater, fat or lean. The amount of fat is important, because it is related to the cooking method. To know the fat content is also important in purchasing fish for modified diets. Table 11–14 provides useful information for the buyer in purchasing the appropriate type of fish.

In determining quality characteristics of fresh whole and drawn fish, the buyer can expect high-quality fish to have firm flesh; fresh, mild odor; bright, clear, and full eyes; red gills; and shiny skin. Fresh fillets and steaks should have a freshly cut appearance and a firm texture, and should not show traces of browning or drying out. The odor should be fresh and mild.

Frozen fish of good quality should have no discoloration of flesh, have little or no odor, and be wrapped either individually or in packages of various weights in moisture- and vapor-proof materials with little or no air space between the fish and the wrapping.

The buyer should specify the type, size, and state of refrigeration. Fresh fish should be packed in ice for delivery and still be well iced when received. Frozen fish should be solidly frozen when bought and delivered. The most commonly used containers with net weights of packs are shown in Table 11–15.

A wide variety of canned fish and fish specialty items are available, including canned salmon, tuna, mackerel, cod, herring, shad, sardines, sturgeon, and others. Specialty

Table 11–13 Origin and Characteristics of Commonly Used Varieties of Natural Cheese*

Name	*Origin*	*Consistency and Texture*	*Color and Shape*
American pasteurized processed	United States	Semisoft to soft, smooth, plastic body	Light yellow to orange; square slices
Asiago, fresh, medium, old	Italy	Semisoft (fresh), medium, or hard (old); tiny gas holes or eyes	Light yellow; may be coated with paraffin, clear or colored black or brown; round and flat
Bel paese	Italy	Soft; smooth, waxy body	Slightly gray surface, creamy yellow interior; small wheels
Blue, Bleu	France	Semisoft; visible veins of mold on white cheese, pasty, sometimes crumbly	White, marbled with blue-green mold; cylindrical
Breakfast, Fruhstuck	Germany	Soft; smooth, waxy body	Cylindrical; 2½ to 3 in diameter
Brick	United States	Semisoft; smooth, open texture; numerous round and irregular-shaped eyes	Light yellow to orange; brick-shaped
Brie	France	Soft, thin edible crust, creamy interior	White crust, creamy yellow interior; large, medium, and small wheels
Caciocavallo	Italy	Hard, firm body; stringy texture	Light tan surface, interior; molded into distinctive shapes, typically spindle-shaped or oblong
Camembert	France	Soft, almost fluid in consistency; thin edible crust, creamy interior	Gray-white crust, creamy yellow interior; small wheels
Cheddar	England	Hard; smooth, firm body, can be crumbly	Nearly white to orange; varied shapes and styles
Colby	Unites States	Hard but softer and more open in texture than cheddar	White to light yellow, orange; cylindrical
Cottage, Dutch, Farmer's, Pot	Uncertain	Soft; moist, delicate, large or small curds	White; packaged in cuplike containers
Cream	United States	Soft; smooth, buttery	White; foil-wrapped in rectangular portions
Edam	Holland	Semisoft to hard; firm, crumbly body; small eyes	Creamy yellow with natural or red paraffin coat; flattened ball or loaf shape, about 4 lb
Feta	Greece	Soft, flaky, similar to very dry, high-acid cottage cheese	White
Gammelost	Norway	Semisoft	Brownish rind, brown-yellow interior with a blue-green tint; round and flat
Gjetost	Norway	Hard; buttery	Golden brown; cubical and rectangular
Gorgonzola	Italy	Semisoft; less moist than blue	Light tan surface, light yellow interior, marbled with blue-green mold; cylindrical and flat loaves
Gouda	Holland	Hard, but softer than cheddar; more open mealy body like Edam, small eyes	Creamy yellow with or without red wax coat; oval or flattened sphere of about 10 to 12 lb
Gruyere	Switzerland	Hard; tiny gas holes or eyes	Light yellow; flat wheels
Limburger	Belgium	Soft; smooth, waxy body	Creamy white interior, brownish exterior; rectangular
Monterey, Jack	United States	Semisoft (whole milk), hard (low-fat or skim milk); smooth texture with small openings throughout	Creamy white; round or rectangular
Mozzarella	Italy	Semisoft; plastic	Creamy white; rectangular and spherical, may be molded into various shapes

continues

Table 11–13 continued

Name	*Origin*	*Consistency and Texture*	*Color and Shape*
Muenster	Germany	Semisoft; smooth, waxy body, numerous small mechanical openings	Yellow, tan, or white surface, creamy white interior; cylindrical and flat or loaf shaped, small wheels and blocks
Neufchatel	France	Soft; smooth, creamy	White; foil-wrapped in rectangular retail portions
Parmesan, Reggiano	Italy	Very hard (grating), granular, hard brittle rind	Light yellow with brown or black coating, cylindrical
Port du salut, Oka	Trappist monasteries	Semisoft; smooth, buttery	Russet surface, creamy white interior; small wheels, cylindrical flat
Primost	Norway	Semisoft	Light brown; cubical and cylindrical
Provolone	Italy	Hard, stringy texture; cuts without crumbling, plastic	Light golden-yellow to golden-brown, shiny surface bound with cord; yellow-white interior. Made in various shapes (pear, sausage, salami) and sizes
Queso blanco, White Cheese	Latin America	Soft, dry and granular if not pressed; hard, open or crumbly if pressed	White; various shapes and sizes
Ricotta	Italy	Soft, moist and grainy, or dry	White; packaged fresh in paper, plastic, or metal containers, or dry for grating
Romano	Italy	Very hard, granular interior, hard brittle rind	Round with flat sides, various sizes
Roquefort	France	Semisoft, pasty and sometimes crumbly	White, marbled with blue-green mold; cylindrical
Sap Sago	Switzerland	Very hard (grating), granular, frequently dried	Light green; small, cone-shaped
Schloss, Castle cheese	Germany, Northern Austria	Soft; small, ripened	Molded in small rectangular blocks 1½ in square by 4 in long
Stilton	England	Semisoft-hard; open flaky texture, more crumbly than blue	White, marbled with blue-green mold; cylindrical
Swiss, Emmentaler	Switzerland	Hard; smooth with large gas holes or eyes	Pale yellow, shiny; rindless rectangular blocks and large wheels with rind

Flavor	*Basic Ingredient*	*Normal Ripening Period*	*Mode of Serving*
Mild	Cheddar, washed, Colby, or granulated (stirred curd) or mixture of two or more	Unripened after cheese(s) heated to blend	In sandwiches; on crackers
Piquant, sharp in aged cheese	Cow's milk, whole or low-fat	60 days minimum for fresh (semisoft), 6 months minimum for medium, 12 months minimum for old (grating)	Table cheese (slicing cheese) when not aged; as seasoning (grated) when aged
Mild to moderately robust	Cow's milk, whole	6–8 weeks	As such (dessert); on crackers; in sandwiches; with fruit
Piquant, tangy, spicy, peppery	Cow's milk, whole or goat's milk	60 days minimum; 3–4 months usually; 9 months for more flavor	As such (dessert); in dips, cooked foods; salads and dressings
Strong, aromatic	Cow's milk, whole or low-fat	Little or none (either)	As such (dessert); on crackers; in sandwiches
Mild but pungent and sweet	Cow's milk, whole	2–3 months	As such; in sandwiches, salads. Slices well without crumbling
Mild to pungent	Cow's milk, whole, low-fat, or skim	4–8 weeks	As such (dessert)

continues

Table 11–13 continued

Flavor	*Basic Ingredient*	*Normal Ripening Period*	*Mode of Serving*
Sharp, similar to provolone	Sheep's, goat's, or cow's milk (whole or low-fat) or mixtures of these	3 months minimum for table use, 12 months or longer for grating	As such; as seasoning (grated) when aged
Mild to pungent	Cow's milk, whole	4–5 weeks	As such (dessert)
Mild to sharp	Cow's milk, whole	60 days minimum; 3–6 months usually; 12 months or longer for sharp flavor	As such; in sandwiches, cooked foods
Mild to mellow	Cow's milk, whole	1–3 months	As such; in sandwiches, cooked foods
Mild, slightly acid, flavoring may be added	Cow's milk, skim; cream dressing may be added	Unripened	As such; in salads, dips, cooked foods
Mild, slightly acid, flavoring may be added	Cream and cow's milk, whole	Unripened	As such; in salads, in sandwiches, on crackers
Mild, sometimes salty	Cow's milk, low-fat	2 months or longer	As such; on crackers; with fresh fruit
Salty	Cow's, sheep's, or goat's milk	4–5 days to 1 month	As such; in cooked foods
Sharp, aromatic	Cow's milk, skim	4 weeks or longer	As such
Sweet, caramel	Whey from goat's milk	Unripened	As such; on crackers
Piquant, spicy, similar to blue	Cow's milk, whole or goat's milk, or mixtures of these	3 months minimum, frequently 6 months to 1 year	As such (dessert)
Mild, nutlike, similar to Edam	Cow's milk, low-fat but more milkfat than Edam	2–6 months	As such; on crackers, with fresh fruit; in cooked dishes
Mild, sweet	Cow's milk, whole	3 months minimum	As such (dessert); fondue
Strong, robust, highly aromatic	Cow's milk, whole or low-fat	1–2 months	In sandwiches; on crackers
Mild to mellow	Cow's milk, whole, low-fat, or skim	3–6 weeks for table use, 6 months minimum for grating	As such; in sandwiches; grating cheese if made from low-fat or skim milk
Mild, delicate	Cow's milk, whole or low-fat; may be acidified with vinegar	Unripened to 2 months	Generally used in cooking, pizza; as such
Mild to mellow, between brick and Limburger	Cow's milk, whole	2–8 weeks	As such; in sandwiches
Mild	Cow's milk, whole or skim, or a mixture of milk and cream	3–4 weeks or unripened	As such; in sandwiches, dips, salads
Sharp, piquant	Cow's milk, low-fat	10 months minimum	As such; as grated cheese on salads and soups
Mellow or mild to robust, similar to Gouda	Cow's milk, whole or low-fat	6–8 weeks	As such (dessert); with fresh fruit; on crackers
Mild, sweet, caramel	Whey with added buttermilk, whole milk, or cream	Unripened	As such; in cooked foods
Bland acid flavor to sharp and piquant, usually smoked	Cow's milk, whole	6–14 months	As such (dessert) after it has ripened for 6 to 9 months; grating cheese when aged
Salty, strong, may be smoked	Cow's milk, whole, low-fat, or skim or whole milk with cream or skim milk	Eaten within 2 days to 2 months or more; generally unripened if pressed	As such or later grated
Bland but semisweet	Whey and whole or skim milk or whole and low-fat milk	Unripened	As such; in cooked foods; as seasoning (grated) when dried

continues

Table 11–13 continued

Flavor	*Basic Ingredient*	*Normal Ripening Period*	*Mode of Serving*
Sharp, piquant if aged	Cow's milk (usually low-fat), goat's milk, or mixtures of these	5 months minimum; usually 5–8 months for table cheese; 12 months minimum for grating cheese	As such; grated and used as a seasoning
Sharp, spicy (pepper), piquant	Sheep's milk	2 months minimum; usually 2–5 months or longer	As such (dessert); in salads; on crackers
Sharp, pungent, flavored with leaves, sweet	Cow's milk, skim, slightly soured with buttermilk and whey	5 months minimum	As such; as seasoning (grated)
Similar to, but milder than Limburger	Cow's milk, whole or low-fat and/or casein	Less than 1 month; less intensively than Limburger	In sandwiches; on crackers
Piquant, spicy, but milder than Roquefort	Cow's milk, whole with added cream	4–6 months or longer	As such (dessert); in cooked foods
Mild, sweet, nutty	Cow's milk, low-fat	2 months minimum, 2–9 months usually	As such; in sandwiches; with salads; fondue

* Description of additional cheeses may be found in USDA (1978). *Cheese Varieties and Descriptions Agriculture Handbook No. 54.* U.S. Government Printing Office, Washington, D.C.

Newer Knowledge of Cheese, Courtesy of NATIONAL DAIRY COUNCIL®.

items include fish balls, chowders, cakes, and roe. The two most popular canned fish used in institutional food service operations are salmon and tuna.

Salmon canned on the Pacific Coast come from five distinct species and are usually sold by their names, which indicate differences in the type of meat. Salmon differs in color, texture, and flavor. The higher-priced varieties are deeper red and have a higher oil content. The five grades of salmon are

1. chinook or king salmon
2. red or sockeye salmon
3. medium red salmon
4. pink salmon
5. chum salmon

Salmon may be purchased in 3¾-, 7½-, 15½-, and 64-oz cans.

Tuna canned in the United States is produced from four species of the mackerel family—yellowfin, bluefin, skipjack, and albacore. Tuna is divided into grades, according to the type of meat used, as follows:

1. Fancy or fancy white meat tuna consists of choice cuts of cooked albacore tuna packed as large pieces of solid meat.
2. Standard tuna consists of cooked tuna meat packed in the approximate proportion of 75 percent large pieces and 25 percent flakes.
3. Grated or shredded tuna is cooked tuna packed in small uniform pieces.
4. Flaked tuna is cooked tuna packed in small pieces.

Tuna may be purchased in 3½-, 7-, and 13-oz cans. Tuna flakes and grated tuna are packed in 3-, 5-, 12-, and 64-oz cans (U.S. Department of the Interior 1964a).

Shellfish. Some of the more popular species of shellfish are shrimp, clams, oysters, crabs, lobsters, and scallops. Some shellfish are marketed alive. Other market forms (Figure 11–11), depending on the variety, include cooked whole in the shell, headless, fresh meat (shucked), and cooked meat.

The various kinds of shrimp range in color from greenish gray to brownish red when raw; they differ little in appearance and flavor when cooked. The market term *green shrimp* does not refer to color, but is the term used in the trade to describe shrimp that have not been cooked and have the head intact. Shrimp are sold on a size basis or by such terms as jumbo, large, medium, and small. The largest size or grade runs 15 or fewer shrimp to the pound. The smallest size runs 60 or more to the pound. The larger sizes are higher priced. Shrimp are sold as follows:

- fresh or frozen, headless, but with shells on
- fresh or frozen, cooked, generally peeled (shells removed and meat deveined)
- frozen, breaded (raw and cooked) after being peeled and deveined

The trade term for peeled, deveined, and quick-frozen is *PDQ*. Most shrimp marketed in the United States are sold as fresh or frozen; canned shrimp are available either packed in

Whole or round fish are those marketed just as they come from the water. Before cooking, they must be scaled and eviscerated (which means removing the entrails). The head, tail, and fins may be removed, if desired, and the fish either split or cut into serving-size portions, except in fish intended for baking. Some small fish, like smelt, are frequently cooked with only the entrails removed.

Drawn fish are marketed with only the entrails removed. In preparation for cooking, they generally are scaled. Head, tail, and fins are removed, if desired, and the fish split or cut into serving-size portions. Small drawn fish, or larger sizes intended for baking, may be cooked in the form purchased, after being scaled.

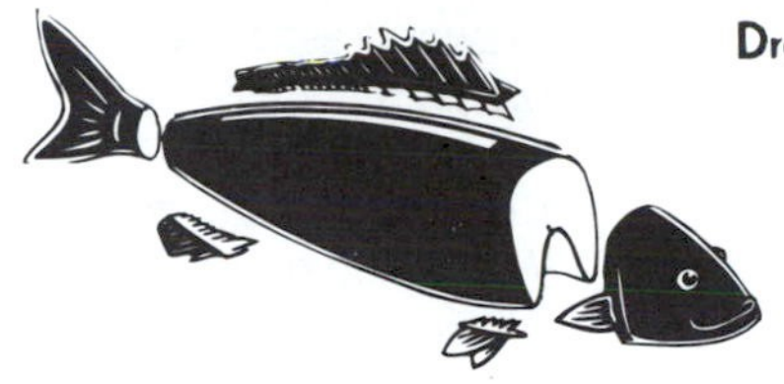

Dressed or pan-dressed fish are scaled and eviscerated, usually with the head, tail, and fins removed. The smaller sizes are ready for cooking as purchased (pan-dressed). The larger sizes of dressed fish may be baked as purchased but frequently are cut into steaks or serving-size portions.

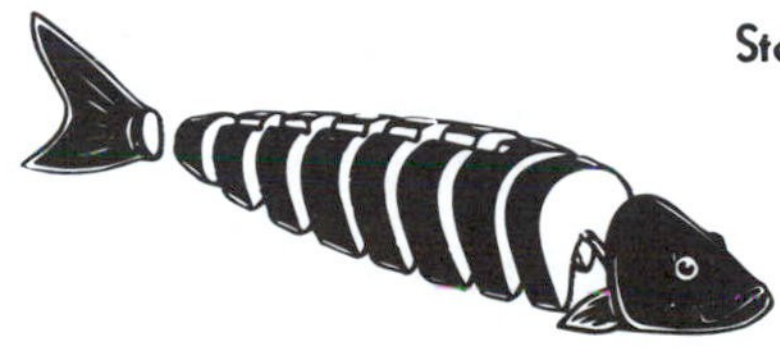

Steaks are cross-section slices of the larger sizes of dressed fish. They are ready to cook as purchased, except for dividing the very largest into serving-size portions. A cross-section of the backbone is usually the only bone in the steak.

Fillets are the sides of the fish, cut lengthwise away from the backbone. They are practically boneless and require no preparation for cooking. Sometimes the skin, with the scales removed, is left on the fillets; others are skinned. A fillet cut from one side of a fish is called a single fillet. This is the type of fillet most generally seen in the market.

Sticks are pieces of fish cut lengthwise or crosswise from fillets or steaks into portions of uniform width and length.

Butterfly fillets are the two sides of the fish corresponding to two single fillets held together by uncut flesh and the skin.

Figure 11–10 Market Forms of Fish. *Source:* Reprinted from *Fish Cookery for One Hundred*, Test Kitchen Series No. 1, U.S. Department of the Interior, 1964A.

Table 11–14 Classification of Seafood

Species	*Fat or Lean*	*Usual Range of Weight (lb)*	*Usual Market Forms*
Saltwater			
Bluefish	Lean	1–7	Whole and drawn
Butterfish	Fat	¼–1	Whole and dressed
Cod	Lean	3–20	Drawn, dressed, steaks, and fillets
Croaker	Lean	½–2½	Whole, dressed, and fillets
Flounder	Lean	¼–5	Whole, dressed, and fillets
Grouper	Lean	5–15	Whole, drawn, dressed, steaks, and fillets
Haddock	Lean	1½–7	Drawn and fillets
Hake	Lean	2–5	Whole, drawn, dressed, and fillets
Halibut	Lean	8–75	Dressed and steaks
Herring, sea	Fat	¼–1	Whole
Lingcod	Lean	5–20	Dressed, steaks, and fillets
Mackerel	Fat	¾–3	Whole, drawn, and fillets
Mullet	Lean	½–3	Whole
Pollock	Lean	3–14	Drawn, dressed, steaks, and fillets
Rockfish	Lean	2–5	Dressed and fillets
Rosefish	Lean	½–1¼	Fillets
Salmon	Fat	3–30	Drawn, dressed, steaks, and fillets
Scup (Porgy)	Lean	½–2	Whole and dressed
Sea bass	Lean	¼–4	Whole, dressed, and fillets
Sea trout	Lean	1–6	Whole, drawn, dressed, and fillets
Shad	Fat	1½–7	Whole, drawn, and fillets
Snapper, red	Lean	2–15	Drawn, dressed, steaks, and fillets
Spanish mackerel	Fat	1–4	Whole, drawn, dressed, and fillets
Spot	Lean	¼–1¼	Whole and dressed
Whiting	Lean	½–1½	Whole, drawn, dressed, and fillets
Freshwater			
Buffalo fish	Lean	5–15	Whole, drawn, dressed, and steaks
Carp	Lean	2–8	Whole and fillets
Catfish	Fat	1–10	Whole, dressed, and skinned
Lake herring	Lean	½–1	Whole, drawn, and fillets
Lake trout	Fat	1½–10	Drawn, dressed, and fillets
Sheepshead	Lean	½–3	Whole, drawn, dressed, and fillets
Suckers	Lean	½–4	Whole, drawn, dressed, and fillets
Whitefish	Fat	2–6	Whole, drawn, dressed, and fillets
Yellow perch	Lean	½–1	Whole and fillets
Yellow pike	Lean	1½–10	Whole, dressed, and fillets
Shellfish			
Clams	Lean		In the shell, shucked
Crabs	Lean		Live, cooked meat
Lobsters	Lean		Live, cooked meat
Oysters	Lean		In the shell, shucked
Shrimp	Lean		Headless, cooked meat

Source: Reprinted from *Basic Fish Cookery*, Test Kitchen Series No. 2, U.S. Department of the Interior, 1961.

brine or dry. The buyer should specify Grade A, count, class (headless, peeled, and deveined), and state of refrigeration (U.S. Department of the Interior 1964b).

Several species of clams are widely used for food. On the Atlantic Coast, the marketed species are the hard clams, the soft clams, and the surf clams. The hard-shell clam is commonly called quahog in New England, where the term *clam* generally means the soft-shell variety. In the Middle Atlantic states and southward, *clam* is the usual name for the hard clam.

Table 11–15 Commonly Used Containers for Seafood

Seafood	*Containers*	*Net Weights*
Fresh fish		
Whole, drawn, and dressed:		
Most varieties:		
Freshwater	Boxes	25, 40, 50, 60, 100 lb
Saltwater	Boxes	15, 100, 125, 150, 200 lb
	Barrels	125, 150, 250 lb
Some small fish:		
Freshwater	Boxes	10 to 20 lb
Saltwater	Boxes	10 to 30 lb
	Tight barrels	75 lb
Fillets and steaks:		
Freshwater	Tins	20, 25 lb
Saltwater	Tins	10, 15, 20, 25, 30 lb
Frozen fish		
Whole, drawn, and dressed:		
Most varieties:		
Freshwater	Boxes	60, 70, 100 lb
Saltwater	Boxes	50, 100, 150, 200 lb
Some small fish:		
Freshwater	Boxes	10, 20 lb
Saltwater	Boxes and packages	1, 5, 10, 15, 20, 25 lb
Fillets and steaks:		
Freshwater	Packages	1, 5, 10 lb
Saltwater	Packages	12 oz; 1, 5, 10, 15, 20, 25 lb
Fish portions:		
Unbreaded, breaded, and precooked	Packages	8, 10, 12, 14 oz; 1, 3, 4, 5, 6 lb
Fish sticks,		
Breaded and precooked	Packages	8, 10, 12, 14 oz; 1, 3, 4, 5, 6 lb
Shellfish		
Clams and oysters:		
In shell	Bags	100, 225, 250 lb
Shucked:		
Fresh	Tins	½ pt, 1 pt, 1 qt; ½, 1, 5 gal
Frozen	Tins and packages	12 oz, 5 lb
Crabs:		
Hard: Live	Bushel baskets; barrels	100 lb
Crabs:		
Soft:		
Live	Trunks	60, 80 lb
Frozen	Packages	Up to 1 lb
Dungeness eviscerated		
Frozen	Poly bags	1½–2½ lb
Crab meat, cooked:		
Blue	Tins	1 lb
Dungeness	Tins	1, 5 lb
King	Packages	6 oz, 3 lb
Lobsters, live	Barrels	50, 100 lb
	Boxes	25, 50 lb
Lobster meat, cooked, fresh, and frozen	Tins	6 oz, 14 oz; 1, 5 lb
Scallops, sea:		
Fresh meats	Tins	1 gal
	Bags	30, 40 lb

continues

Table 11–15 continued

Seafood	Containers	Net Weights
Frozen meats	Tins	1 gal
	Packages	10 oz; 1, 5, 10 lb
Frozen breaded and precooked	Packages	7 oz; 1, 2, 5 lb
Scallops, bay: Fresh meat	Tins	1 gal
Shrimp, headless:		
Fresh	Boxes	100 lb
Frozen	Tins and packages	6, 12 oz
	Packages	1, 2½, 5, 10 lb
Breaded, frozen	Packages	8, 10, 12 oz; 1, 5 lb
Shrimp meat, cooked, peeled, and deveined	Tins and packages	4, 8, 12 oz; 1, 5 lb

Source: Reprinted from *Guide for Buying Fresh and Frozen Fish and Shellfish*, U.S. Department of the Interior, 1959.

Littlenecks and cherrystones are dealers' names for the smaller-sized hard clams, generally served raw on the half shell. The larger sizes of hard clams are called chowders and are used mainly for chowders and soups. The larger sizes of soft clams are known as in-shells, and the smaller sizes as steamers.

On the Pacific Coast, the most common market species are the butter, littleneck, razor, and pismo clams. Clams in the shell should be alive and the shells should close tight when tapped lightly. Fresh clams are pale orange to deep orange and free of stale odor or taste. Clams are purchased by the dozen in the shell. If shucked, clams should be packed in little or no free liquid. Clams may be purchased in the frozen or canned state. Frozen clams are breaded and may be raw or cooked. Canned clams may be whole, minced, or in combination foods such as chowders and soups (U.S. Department of the Interior 1964c).

There are three major species of oysters available. The eastern oyster is found and cultivated from Massachusetts to Texas; the small Olympia oyster is found on the Pacific

Live

Shellfish, such as crabs, lobsters, clams, and oysters should be alive if purchased in the shell, except for boiled crabs and lobsters.

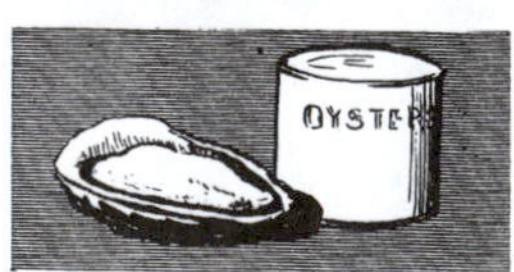

Shucked

Shucked shellfish are those which have been removed from their shells. Oysters, clams, and scallops are marketed in this manner.

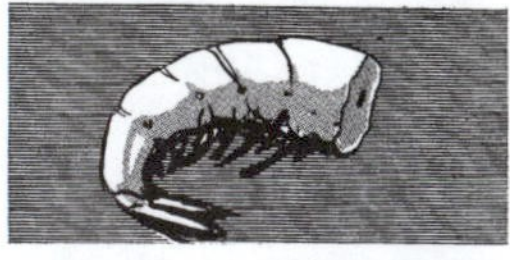

Headless

This term applies to shrimp, which are marketed in most areas with the head and thorax removed.

Cooked meat

The edible portion of shellfish is often sold cooked, ready to eat. Shrimp, crab, and lobster meat are marketed in this way.

Figure 11–11 Market Forms of Shellfish. *Source:* Reprinted from *Basic Fish Cookery*, Test Kitchen Series No. 2, U.S. Department of the Interior, 1961.

Coast from Washington to Mexico; and the larger Pacific or Japanese oyster is cultivated on the Pacific Coast. Oysters may be purchased in the following forms (U.S. Department of the Interior 1964d):

- Shell oysters. Oysters in the shell are sold by the dozen and must be alive when purchased. Gaping shells that do not close when tapped lightly indicate that the oysters are dead and therefore should not be used.
- Shucked oysters. These are oysters that have been removed from the shell and are usually sold by the pint or quart. Shucked oysters should be plump, have a natural creamy color with clear liquor, and be free from shell particles. Fresh shucked oysters are packed in metal containers or waxed cartons. The eastern oysters, comprising about 89 percent of the domestic oyster production, are packed in commercial grades as shown in Table 11–16.
- Frozen oysters. These are shucked oysters that have been quick-frozen. Frozen oysters should not be thawed until ready to use. Once thawed, they should never be refrozen. Frozen, raw, or cooked breaded oysters are also available.
- Canned oysters. Canned oysters packed on the Atlantic and Gulf Coasts are usually sold in No. 1 picnic cans containing 7½ oz drained weight of oysters. Oysters packed on the Pacific Coast are usually sold in cans containing 5 or 8 oz drained weight (U.S. Department of the Interior 1964d).

Crabs are one of the popular shellfish because of their tender meat and distinctive flavor. Blue crabs come from the Atlantic and Gulf coastal areas; Dungeness crabs are found on the Pacific Coast; king crabs come from the North Pacific off Alaska; and rock crabs are taken from the New England and California coasts. Blue crabs weigh ¼ to 1 lb. At different seasons, they are the eastern hard-shell crab and the soft-shell crab. Soft-shell crabs are molting blue crabs taken just after they have shed their hard shells and before new shells are formed. Dungeness crabs weigh 1¾ to 3½ lb, king crabs weigh 6 to 20 lb, and rock crabs weigh ⅓ to ½ lb (U.S. Department of the Interior 1964e).

Table 11–16 Grade and Count for Eastern Oysters

Grade	*Oysters per Gallon*
Counts or extra large	Not more than 160
Extra selects or large	161–210
Selects or medium	211–300
Standards or small	301–500
Standards or very small	Over 500

Source: Reprinted from *How to Cook Oysters*, Test Kitchen Series No. 3, U.S. Department of the Interior, 1964d.

Crabs are marketed as live, cooked in the shell, cooked and frozen, fresh cooked meat, and canned meat. Fresh hard-shell and soft-shell crabs should be alive at time of cooking. Cooked hard-shell crabs must be kept refrigerated, iced, or frozen from the time they are cooked until they are used. Frozen crab legs are cooked legs of the king crab. The large legs are either split or cut into sections. Canned crab meat may be from the blue, Dungeness, king, or rock crab. Fresh cooked meat is picked from the hard-shell crabs, packed, chilled, and sold by the pound. Fresh cooked meat from the blue crab is packed in four grades: (1) lump meat is the white meat from the body of the crab, (2) flake meat consists of small pieces of white meat from the rest of the body, (3) lump and flake meat is a combination of body and leg meat, and (4) claw meat is meat with a brownish tint from the claw. Fresh cooked meat from the Dungeness crab is picked from both body and claws, has a pinkish tinge, and is packed as one grade. Fresh cooked meat from the king crab is taken mostly from the legs. Fresh cooked meat from the rock crab is picked from both body and claws and is marketed as one grade.

Lobsters and spiny lobsters should show movement of legs when they are alive. The tail of the live lobster curls under the body and does not hang down when the lobster is picked up. The northern lobster, caught off the coasts of Maine and Massachusetts, is considered the true lobster. Another type, caught off the coasts of California and Florida, is known as the spiny or rock lobster. The difference is that the northern lobster has large, heavy claws; the spiny lobster has no claws. Frozen spiny or rock lobster tails should have clear white meat, be hard-frozen when bought, and have no odor. Whole lobsters are sold in the shell as fresh, frozen, or cooked and vary in size from ¾ to 4 lb. The buyer should specify lobster size as follows:

- chicken, ¾ to 1 lb
- quarters, 1¼ to 1½ lb
- large, 1½ to 2½ lb
- jumbo, over 3 lb

Cooked lobster meat is marketed as fresh pack, frozen, and canned. The meat should be white with deep pink covering and free of any disagreeable odors (U.S. Department of the Interior 1964f).

Scallops are a shellfish, a mollusk possessing two shells, similar to oysters and clams. Unlike other shellfish, scallops are marketed only as dressed meat. Because scallops are active swimmers, snapping their shells together to provide locomotion, an oversized muscle is developed, called the abductor muscle. This muscle is the only part of the scallop eaten by Americans (U.S. Department of the Interior 1964g).

There are two varieties of scallops, the large sea scallop and the smaller bay scallop. The sea scallop is taken from the waters of northern and middle Atlantic states and measures about ½ in across. The bay scallop is taken from inshore bays from New England to the Gulf of Mexico. Fresh scallops are a light cream color, sometimes varying to a delicate pink. Scallops are available fresh or frozen, but only in the form of dressed meat. The scallops are opened, packed, and iced at sea. Fresh and frozen scallops when thawed should have a sweetish odor and should be practically free of liquid.

Fresh Fruit and Vegetable Specifications

The produce market is one of the most difficult for the buyer because of variations in grading standards, methods of packaging, and the seasonableness of products.

In formulating standards for fruits and vegetables, the Department of Agriculture originally adopted the numerical system of nomenclature for grades, with some exceptions (U.S. Department of Agriculture 1956). The highest grade for a product is U.S. No. 1. Under normal conditions, more than half the crop usually will be U.S. No. 1 grade. The designation of U.S. No. 2 ordinarily represents the quality of the lowest grade that is deemed practical to pack under normal conditions. It was found that U.S. No. 1 and U.S. No. 2 designations were not sufficient to represent all the gradations of quality for a number of specialized products. Many shippers preferred to pack a top-grade product of high color and practically free from defects, for which they would receive premium prices. Thus it was necessary, in some sets of standards, to provide a grade designation for a product superior to that ordinarily termed U.S. No. 1. To meet this need the designation U.S. Fancy was chosen. In a few standards it was necessary to provide a grade designation for quality between U.S. Fancy and U.S. No. 1 as in standards for peaches and potatoes. The designation of U.S. Extra No. 1 is applied to this quality. It was also necessary to provide a grade designation between U.S. No. 1 and U.S. No. 2 for quality not up to U.S. No. 1, but superior to U.S. No. 2 grade. The terms U.S. Commercial and U.S. Combination were adopted. The grade designations prompted criticism that the system was misleading and confusing. In 1976, efforts to standardize grade designations resulted in the use of the following terms: U.S. Fancy, U.S. No. 1, U.S. No. 2, and U.S. No. 3. The U.S. No. 1 grade is generally recommended for institutional food service use.

The packaging or unit of purchasing ranges from loose pack by the pound to sacks, crates, cartons, boxes, baskets, lugs, gallons, and bunches (Table 11–17). Price quotations should be based on the pound, rather than the container. The buyer will need to study the specifications for each food item, and visually inspect fresh fruit and vegetables to recognize quality products.

Processed Fruit and Vegetable Specifications

With the use of processed foods, it is not necessary to have seasonal menus, except for economic reasons, because most foods are available year-round. Canned and frozen foods are types most often used in institutional food service. Other types of processed foods include vacuum-dried potatoes and onions, and freeze-dried fruits and vegetables.

The specification for canned fruits and vegetables should include the following:

- name of food item
- grade
- size of container
- style, type, or size
- other information to obtain desired product, such as variety, drained weight, syrup density, and harvest area

The USDA grades for fruits, vegetables, and juices are shown in Table 11–18. The factors used for scoring of products are color, absence of defects, and character. Absence of defects includes uniformity of product, whereas character refers to tenderness, texture, maturity, flavor, and odor. Some fruits and vegetables score at the bottom of the grade, as is frequently found in meat products. The buyer can request a grade certificate from the purveyor to determine the product score. The buyer can also conduct can-cutting experiments to compare quality. The general procedure is to remove all labels from the various brands and code each can prior to opening. Allow all products the same period of time for draining off liquid, usually two minutes. Compare products for color, texture, uniformity of products, count, size, and drained weight.

Processed fruits and vegetables must conform to labeling as established by the Food and Drug Administration (FDA; see Friedelson 1967). Basic information that must be on all food labels includes the following:

- The name of the product (common or usual).
- Form or style (whole, slices, or halves).
- The net contents or net weight. The net weight on canned food includes the liquid in which the product is packed, such as water in canned vegetables and syrup in canned fruit.
- The name and place of business of the manufacturer, packer, or distributor.

Other information, as required under certain conditions, must also be listed as follows:

- List of ingredients. On most foods, the ingredients must be listed in descending order, with the ingredients present in largest amount of weight first. Any additives used in the product must be listed, but colors and flavors do not have to be listed by name. If the flavors are artificial, this fact must be stated. The labels on butter, cheese, and ice cream do not need to include the listing of artificial color, because these foods have a standard

Table 11–17 Container Types and Approximate Weight for Fresh Fruits and Vegetables

Food Item	*Type of Container*	*Approximate Weight*	*Count*
Asparagus	Cartons	15–16 lb	
	Pyramid crates	30–32 lb	
Avocados	Cartons and flats	12–15 lb	
Beans, green or waxed	Basket	28–30 lb	
	Crates	28–30 lb	
	Cartons	28–30 lb	
Broccoli	Crates, wirebound	20 lb	
	Baskets	6 lb	
	Cartons, 14 bu	20–23 lb	
Brussels sprouts	Wooden drums	25 lb	
	Flats, 12 10-oz cups	7½–8 oz/cup	
Cabbage	Crates, 1⅜ bu	50–55 lb	
	Cartons	45–50 lb	
	Mesh sacks	50–60 lb	
Carrots (without tops)	Sacks	50 lb	
	Crates	50 lb	
	Baskets, bu	50 lb	
Cauliflower	Cartons	18–24 lb	12–16 heads
	Crates, wirebound	45–50 lb	
Celery	Crates, Florida, 16-in length	55–60 lb	
	Crates, California, 16-in length	60–65 lb	
Corn	Crates, wirebound	40–60 lb	4 doz ears
	Mesh bags	45–50 lb	
Cucumbers	Crates, 1⅛ bu	55 lb	
	Baskets, bu	47–55 lb	
	Cartons	26–30 lb	
	Lugs	26–30 lb	
Green, salad (chicory, endive, escarole)	Crates, 1⅛ bu	25–28 lb	
	1⅜ bu	33–40 lb	
	16-in crate	33–40 lb	
	Cartons	18–22 lb	
	Baskets, 24 qt	16 lb	
	Baskets, bu	25 lb	
Greens (collards, kale)	Baskets, bu	18–25 lb	
	Crates	18–25 lb	
Greens (spinach, turnip, mustard)	Baskets, bu	18–22 lb	
	Crates	18–22 lb	
	Crates, 1½ bu	30–32 lb	
	Cartons, 1⅛ bu	20–22 lb	
Lettuce (head)	Cartons	40–45 lb	2 doz heads
Lettuce (romaine)	Crates, wirebound, 1⅛ bu	28–32 lb	
	Cartons	34–36 lb	2 doz heads
Lettuce (leaf)	Baskets, 12 qt	7 lb	
	Other containers	5–10 lb	
		20–25 lb	
Okra	Baskets, bu	28–32 lb	
	Baskets, ½ bu	14–16 lb	
	Crates, bu	28–32 lb	
	Los Angeles (L.A.) lugs	17–19 lb	
Onions, mature	Mesh sacks	25 or 50 lb	
	Cartons	48–50 lb	

continues

Table 11–17 continued

Food Item	*Type of Container*	*Approximate Weight*	*Count*
Parsley	Crates, wirebound	20–22 lb	
	Cartons	20–22 lb	5 doz bunches
Peas, green (pods)	Baskets, bu	28–30 lb	
	Crates, western	28–30 lb	
Peppers	Crates, 1⅛ bu	28–33 lb	
	Baskets, bu	28–33 lb	
	Cartons, 1⅛ bu	28–34 lb	
	Lugs	18 lb	
Potatoes, white	Burlap sacks	50 or 100 lb	
	Paper cartons or paper bags	10, 15, 20, 25, or 50 lb	
Radishes (without tops)	Baskets	11¼ lb	
	Cartons	11¼ lb	
	Bags	25 or 40 lb	
Squash (summer)	Baskets, bu	40–45 lb	
	Baskets, ½ bu	20–22 lb	
	Crates, 1⅛ bu	42–45 lb	
	Crates, ⅝ bu	22–25 lb	
	Cartons	20–25 lb	
	Lugs	24 lb	
Squash (winter)	Baskets, bu	50 lb	
	Crates	40–50 lb	
	Cartons	20–25 lb	
Sweet potatoes	Baskets, bu	50 lb	
	Crates, bu	50 lb	
	Cartons	38–42 lb	
Tomatoes	Cartons	10, 20, 30, or 40 lb	
	Crates	40 lb	
	Lugs	30–34 lb	
	Flats	10–20 lb	
	Baskets (various)	9–20 lb	
Turnips (without tops)	Baskets, bu	50 lb	
	Sacks	50 lb	
	Cartons	40–50 lb	
Apples	Cartons, tray-pack 1 or 1⅛ bu	36–45 lb	113–138 (medium)
	Cartons, cell-pack 1 or 1⅛ bu	36–45 lb	100–140 (medium)
	Cartons, bulk (various)	20–46 lb	50–140 (medium)
	Cartons, boxes bu	36–44 lb	113–138 (medium)
	Cartons, baskets bu	36–44 lb	110–140 (medium)
Apricots	Lugs	25–30 lb	
	Cartons	12–25 lb	
	Cartons or crates, 4 baskets	20–26 lb	
Bananas	Cartons	40 lb	110–125 175–200 (petite)
Berries (blackberries, blueberries)	Trays, 12 pt	9–15 lb	
Cantaloupe	Crates	80–85 lb	27, 36, 45
	Cartons	38–41 lb	12, 18, 23
Cherries, sweet	Lugs or cartons	12, 14, 15, 18, or 20 lb	
	Crates, 8 qt	12 lb	

continues

Table 11–17 continued

Food Item	*Type of Container*	*Approximate Weight*	*Count*
Cranberries	Cartons, 24 packs	24 lb (1-lb packs)	
Grapefruit	Cartons, Texas, 7/10 bu	40 lb	
	Cartons, Florida, 4/5 bu	42 lb	
	Cartons, western half-box	34–36 lb	
Grapes	Lugs or cartons	17–28 lb	
Lemons	Cartons	37–39 lb	140–165 (medium)
Limes	Flats or cartons	10–11 lb	25–35 (medium)
	Boxes or cartons	40–41 lb	
Melons, honeydew	Crates	45–50 lb	6–8
	Cartons	29–32 lb	4–5
Nectarines	Sanger lugs or cartons	19–22 lb	64–82 (medium)
	L.A. lugs	22–29 lb	72–90
Oranges	Cartons, Florida and Texas	43–47 lb	100–125 (small)
	Cartons, California and Arizona, 4/5 lb	36–39 lb	88, 113, 138 (medium)
Peaches	Cartons, 3/4 bu	35–42 lb	100–125 (medium)
	Crates, 3/4 bu	35–42 lb	100–125
	Crates, 1/2 bu	22–28 lb	70–90
	Baskets, 3/4 bu	35–42 lb	100–125
	Baskets, 1/2 bu	22–28 lb	70–90
	Lugs	19–29 lb	60–70
Pears	Boxes	45–48 lb	110–150 (medium)
	Cartons	36–48 lb	60–150
	Lugs	21–26 lb	50–65
Pineapple	Cartons or crates	35 lb	9–12
Plums	Cartons, 4 baskets	26–30 lb	
	Crates	24–32 lb	
	Lugs	18–30 lb	
Raspberries	Trays, 12 pt	9–15 lb	
Strawberries	Trays, 12 pt	11–12 lb	
Tangerines	Crates, Florida	45 lb	210–294 (small)
	Cartons, Florida	30 lb	
	Cartons, California	23–30 lb	120–176 (medium)
Watermelon	Whole melon	15–18 lb	(small)
		19–28 lb	(medium)

Source: Reprinted from *Food Purchasing Pointers for School Food Service*, Program Aid No. 1160, Food and Nutrition Service, U.S. Department of Agriculture, 1977.

of identity. The only foods not required to list all ingredients are those that meet FDA standards of identity. These standards require that all foods called by a particular name (such as catsup and mayonnaise) contain certain mandatory ingredients. These standards of identity are published by the Office of the Federal Register (Code of Federal Register 1984).

- Nutrition labeling. Under FDA regulations, any food to which a nutrient has been added, or any food for which a nutritional claim is made, must have the nutritional content listed on the label.
- Common or usual name. For example, a noncarbonated beverage that appears to contain a fruit or vegetable juice but does not contain any juice must state on the label that it contains no fruit or vegetable juice. Another special label requirement concerns packaged foods in which the main ingredient or component of a recipe is not included. The regulation states that the picture must represent the product, such as cake with icing, chicken casserole, and so forth. A statement must be added such as "icing not included," or "you must add chicken to complete the recipe."

Table 11–18 USDA Grades for Canned Fruits, Vegetables, and Juice

Product	Grade	Score
Fruits	U.S. Grade A or U.S. Grade Fancy	90 and above
	U.S. Grade B or U.S. Choice	80–89
	U.S. Grade C or U.S. Standard	70–79
Vegetables	U.S. Grade A or U.S. Fancy	90 and above
	U.S. Grade B or U.S. Extra Standard	80–89
	U.S. Grade C or U.S. Standard	70–79
Fruit or vegetable juice	U.S. Grade A or U.S. Fancy	85–100
	U.S. Grade B, U.S. Choice, or U.S. Extra Standard	70–84

As a competitive edge, some manufacturers include voluntary statements such as the following:

- U.S. grade
- Size (extra large, small, midget, etc.)
- Descriptive terms (very young, young, mature)
- Serving suggestions (recipes, garnishes, and number of servings). If number of servings is given, the size of the serving must also be given.

Container sizes for canned fruits and vegetables are standardized throughout the industry. Except for small servings required for modified diets, the no. 10 can size is used for most fruits and vegetables in institutional food service. Other container sizes and their usual weight capacities are given in Table 11–19.

The style, type, or size should be specified in order to obtain the most appropriate food for a particular menu item. Some examples follow:

- peaches—halves, slices
- beets—whole, slices, julienne
- corn—whole kernel, cream style, yellow, white
- carrots—whole, slices, quarters, julienne, dices
- apples—slices, Northern Spy

The packing medium must be stated on the label and should be part of the specification to ensure appropriateness for the planned menu. The packing medium may be water, natural juice, slightly sweetened juice, light syrup, medium syrup, heavy syrup, or extra heavy syrup. Syrup density refers to the sweetness of the packing medium and is tested by using a Brix hydrometer. As measured one Brix equals 1 percent sugar. The syrup density at the time the can is opened, called "cut out," is lower than the syrup density at packing, which is called "put in." This is so because some of the sugar is absorbed by the fruit, making the syrup less concentrated.

Frozen Fruits, Vegetables, and Juices

Specification factors to consider are the same as those stated for canned products. The USDA grading system also applies to these foods. For frozen juice concentrates, the buyer should specify the water-juice ratio required for reconstitution. Frozen juice concentrate may be purchased in cans from 6 to 32 oz. Frozen fruits are packed in 1-, 2½-, and 5-lb packages and 6½- to 30-lb cans. Frozen vegetables may be purchased in 2-, 2½-, or 3-lb boxes and up to 20- or 30-lb bags. See Appendix M for purchase units and portion information for various frozen vegetables.

FOOD LABELING

The FDA implemented the Nutrition Labeling and Education Act of 1990 (NLEA), which requires nutrition labeling for most foods (except meat and poultry) and authorizes the use of nutrient content claims and appropriate FDA-approved health claims (Food and Drug Administration 1995).

The purposes of food label reform are to clear up confusion that has prevailed in supermarkets for years, to help consumers select more healthful diets, and to offer an incentive to food companies to improve the nutritional qualities of their products. Among key changes in the new regulations are the following:

- nutrition labeling for almost all foods
- a new easy-to-read format
- information on the amount per serving of saturated fat, cholesterol, dietary fiber, and other nutrients that are of major concern
- nutrient reference value expressed as percentages of daily values
- uniform definitions for terms that describe a food's nutrient content, such as "light," "low fat," and "high fiber"
- claims about the relationship between a nutrient or food and a disease or health-related condition, such as calcium and osteoporosis, and fat and cancer
- standardized serving sizes that make nutritional comparisons of similar products easier
- declaration of total percentage of juice in juice drinks

Table 11–19 Common Can and Jar Sizes

*Can Size (Industry Term)**	*Average Net Weight of Fluid Measure per Can†*		*Average Volume per Can*		*Cans per Case*	
	Customary	*Metric*	*Cups*	*Liters*	*(no.)*	*Principal Products*
No. 10	6 lb (96 oz) to 7 lb 5 oz (117 oz)	2.72 kg to 3.31 kg	12 to 13⅔	2.84 to 3.24	6	*Institutional size:* Fruits, vegetables, some other foods
No. 3 Cyl	51 oz (3 lb 3 oz) or 46 fl oz (1 qt 14 fl oz)	1.44 kg or 1.36 L	5¾	1.36	12	Condensed soups, some vegetables, meat and poultry products, fruit and vegetable juices
No. 2½	26 oz (1 lb 10 oz) to 30 oz (1 lb 14 oz)	737 g to 850 g	3½	0.83	24	*Family size:* Fruits, some vegetables
No. 2 Cyl	24 fl oz	709 mL	3	0.71	24	Juices, soups
No. 2	20 oz (1 lb 4 oz) or 18 fl oz (1 pt 2 fl oz)	567 g or 532 mL	2½	0.59	24	Juices, ready-to-serve soups, some fruits
No. 303	16 oz (1 lb) to 17 oz (1 lb 1 oz)	453 g to 481 g	2	0.47	24 or 36	*Small cans:* Fruits and vegetables, some meat and poultry products, ready-to-serve soups
No. 300	14 oz to 16 oz (1 lb)	396 g to 453 g	1¾	0.41	24	Some fruits and meat products
No. 2 (vacuum)	12 oz	340 g	1½	0.36	24	Principally vacuum-packed corn
No. 1 (picnic)	10½ oz to 12 oz	297 g to 340 g	1¼	0.30	48	Condensed soups, some fruits, vegetables, meat, fish
8 oz	8 oz	226 g	1	0.24	48 or 72	Ready-to-serve soups, fruits, vegetables

* Can sizes are industry terms and do not necessarily appear on the label.

† The net weight on can or jar labels differs according to the density of the contents. For example: A no. 10 can of sauerkraut weighs 6 lb 3 oz (2.81 kg); a no. 10 can of cranberry sauce weighs 7 lb 5 oz (3.32 kg). Meats, fish, and shellfish are known and sold by weight of contents.

Source: Reprinted from *Food Buying for School Food Service*, Program Aid No. 1257, U.S. Department of Agriculture, 1980.

- voluntary nutrition information for many raw foods: the 20 most frequently eaten raw fruits, vegetables, and fish, under FDA's voluntary point-of-purchase program, and the 45 best selling cuts of meat, under the USDA's program

Under the NLEA, some foods are exempt from nutrition labeling. These include the following:

- food served for immediate consumption, such as that served in hospital cafeterias and airplanes, and that sold by food service vendors
- ready-to-eat food that is for immediate consumption but is prepared primarily on-site, such as bakery and deli foods
- food shipped in bulk that is not for sale in that form
- medical foods, such as those used to address the nutritional needs of patients with certain diseases

- plain coffee and tea, some spices, and other foods that contain no significant amounts of any nutrients
- food produced by small businesses, based on the number of people a company employs and the number of units within a product line it makes yearly
- game meats, such as deer, bison, rabbit, quail, wild turkey, and ostrich, in individual packages

The new food label has a new title, "Nutrition Facts," which replaces "Nutrition Information per Serving." For the first time, there are requirements on type size, style, spacing, and contrast to ensure a more distinctive, easy-to-read label.

The serving size remains the basis for reporting each food's nutrient content. The serving size also must be expressed in both common household and metric measures. Ounces may be used, but only if a common household unit is not applicable and an appropriate visual unit is given, such as 1 oz (28 g or half a pickle). Grams and milliliters are the metric units that are used in serving size statements.

The NLEA defines serving size as the amount of food customarily eaten at one time. The serving size of products that come in discrete units, such as cookies, candy bars, and sliced products, is the number of whole units that most closely approximates the reference amount.

There is a new set of dietary components on the nutrition label. The mandatory and voluntary components and the order in which they must appear are as follows:

- total calories
- calories from fat
- calories from saturated fat
- total fat
- saturated fat
- polyunsaturated fat
- monounsaturated fat
- cholesterol
- sodium
- potassium
- total carbohydrate
- dietary fiber
- soluble fiber
- insoluble fiber
- sugars
- sugar alcohol (for example, the sugar substitute xylitol, mannitol, and sorbitol)
- other carbohydrates (the difference between total carbohydrate and the sum of dietary fiber, sugars, and sugar alcohol if declared)
- protein
- vitamin A
- percentage of vitamin A present as beta carotene
- vitamin C
- calcium
- iron
- other essential vitamins and minerals

These mandatory and volunteer components are the only ones allowed on the nutrition panel. The required nutrients were selected because they address today's health concerns. The order in which they must appear reflects the priority of current dietary recommendations.

The nutrition panel format also has been revised. Now, all nutrients must be declared as percentages of the daily value, the new label reference values. The amount, in grams, of macronutrients (such as fat, cholesterol, sodium, carbohydrates, and protein) still must be listed to the immediate right of the name of each of these nutrients. For the first time, a column headed "% Daily Value" appears. Requiring nutrients to be declared as a percentage of the daily value is intended to prevent misinterpretations that arise with quantitative values.

The daily value (DV) comprises two sets of dietary standards: daily reference value (DRV) and reference daily intakes (RDI). Only the daily value appears on the label to reduce confusion.

DRVs are being introduced for macronutrients that are sources of energy: fat, carbohydrate (including fiber), and protein; and for cholesterol, sodium, and potassium, which do not contribute calories. A daily intake of 2,000 calories has been established as the reference. DRVs for the energy-producing nutrients are calculated as follows:

- fat based on 30 percent of calories
- saturated fat based on 10 percent of calories
- carbohydrate based on 60 percent of calories
- protein based on 10 percent of calories (The DRVs for protein applies only to adults and children over age 4 years; DRVs for protein for special groups have been established.)
- fiber based on 11.5 g of fiber per 1,000 calories

Because of current public health recommendations, DRVs for some nutrients represent the uppermost limit that is considered desirable. The DRVs for fat, cholesterol, and sodium are as follows:

- total fat, less than 65 g
- saturated fat, less than 20 g
- cholesterol, less than 300 mg
- sodium, less than 2,400 mg

The RDI replaces the term "U.S. RDA," which was introduced in 1973 as a label reference value for vitamins, minerals, and protein in voluntary nutrition labeling. The name change was sought because of confusion that existed over "U.S. RDAs," the value determined by the FDA and used on food labels, and "RDAs" (recommended dietary allowances), the values determined by the National Academy of Sciences for various population groups and used by the FDA to figure the U.S. RDAs. (See Appendix E for a detailed review of the RDAs.)

The regulation also spells out what terms may be used to describe the level of a nutrient in a food and how they can be used. These are the core terms.

Descriptive Terms

- *Free.* This term means that a product contains no amount of, or only trivial amounts of, one or more of these components: fat, saturated fat, cholesterol, sodium, sugars, and calories. For example, "calorie free" means fewer than 5 calories per serving, and "sugar free" and "fat free" both mean less than 0.5 g per serving.
- *Low.* This term can be used for foods that may be eaten frequently without exceeding dietary guidelines for one or more of these components: fat, saturated fat, cholesterol, sodium, and calories. Thus, descriptors would be defined as follows:
  1. *low fat*, 3 g or less per serving
  2. *low saturated fat*, 1 g or less per serving
  3. *low sodium*, 140 mg or less per serving
  4. *very low sodium*, 35 mg or less per serving
  5. *low cholesterol*, 20 mg or less and 2 g or less of saturated fat per serving
  6. *low calorie (little, few, low source)*, 40 calories or less per serving
- *Lean and extra lean.* These terms can be used to describe the fat content of meat, poultry, seafood, and game meat:
  1. *lean*, less than 10 g of fat, 4.5 g or less of saturated fat, and less than 95 mg of cholesterol per serving and per 100 g
  2. *extra lean*, less than 5 g of fat, less than 2 g of saturated fat, and less than 95 mg of cholesterol per serving and per 100 g
- *High.* This term can be used if the food contains 20 percent or more of the daily value for a particular nutrient in a serving.
- *Good source.* This term means that one serving of a food contains 10 percent to 19 percent of the daily value for a particular nutrient.
- *Reduced.* This term means that a nutritionally altered product contains at least 25 percent less of a nutrient or of calories than the regular, or reference, product.
- *Less.* This term means that a food, whether or not altered, contains 25 percent less of a nutrient or of calories than the reference food. For example, pretzels that have 25 percent less fat than potato chips could carry a "less" claim. "Fewer" is an acceptable synonym.
- *Light.* This descriptor can mean two things: first, that a nutritionally altered product contains one third fewer calories or half the fat of the reference food. If the food derives 50 percent or more of its calories from fat, the reduction must be 50 percent of the fat. Second, that the sodium content of a low-calorie, low-fat food has been reduced by 50 percent. In addition, "light in sodium" may be used on food in which the sodium content has been reduced by at least 50 percent. The term *light* can still be used to describe such properties as texture and color, as long as the label explains the intent, for example, "light brown sugar" and "light and fluffy."
- *More.* This term means that a serving of food, whether or not altered, contains a nutrient that is at least 10 percent of the daily value more than the reference food. The 10 percent of the daily value also would apply to "fortified," "enriched," and "added" claims, but in those cases, the food must be altered. Alternative spellings of these descriptive terms and their synonyms are allowed, for example, "hi" and "lo," as long as the alternatives are not misleading.
- *Percent fat free.* A product bearing this claim must be a low-fat or a fat-free product. In addition, the claim must accurately reflect the amount of fat present in 100 g of the food. Thus, if a food contains 2.5 g of fat per 50 g, the claim must be "95 percent fat free."

Implied Claims

These types of claims are prohibited when they wrongly imply that a food contains or does not contain a meaningful level of a nutrient. For example, a product claiming to be made with an ingredient known to be a source of fiber (such as "made with oat bran") is not allowed unless the product contains enough of that ingredient to meet the definition for "good source."

Meals and Main Dishes

Claims that a meal or a main dish is "free" of a nutrient, such as sodium or cholesterol, must meet the same requirements as those for individual foods. Other claims can be used under special circumstances. For example, "low calorie" means that the meal or main dish contains 120 calories or less per 100 g. "Low sodium" means that the food has 140 mg or less per 100 g. "Low cholesterol" means that the food contains 20 mg of cholesterol or less per 100 g and no more than 2 g of saturated fat. "Light" means that the meal or main dish is low fat or low calorie.

Standardized Foods

Any nutrient content claims, such as "reduced fat," "low calorie," and "light," may be used in conjunction with a standardized term if the new product has been specifically formulated to meet the FDA's criteria for that claim, if the product is not nutritionally inferior to the traditional standardized food, and the new product complies with certain compositional requirements set by the FDA. A new product bearing a claim also must have performance characteristics similar to those of the referenced traditional standardized food. If the product does not and the differences limit the product's use, its label must state the differences (such as, "not recommended for baking") to inform consumers.

- *Healthy*. Under this proposal, the term *healthy* can be used to describe a food that is low in fat and saturated fat and contains no more than 480 mg of sodium and no more than 60 mg of cholesterol per serving.
- *Fresh*. Although not mandated by the NLEA, the FDA issued a regulation for the term *fresh*. The regulation defines "fresh" as pertaining to a food that is raw or unprocessed. In this context, "fresh" can be used only on a food that has never been frozen or heated and contains no preservatives. (Irradiation at low levels is allowed.) Other uses of "fresh," as in "fresh milk" or "freshly baked bread," are not affected.

Baby Foods

The FDA is not allowing the broad use of nutrient claims on infant and toddler foods. However, the agency may propose later claims specifically for these foods. The terms *unsweetened* and *unsalted* are allowed on these foods because they relate to taste and not nutrient content.

Health Claims

Claims for seven relationships between a nutrient or a food and the risk of a disease or health-related condition will be allowed for the first time. The allowed nutrient-disease relationship claims and rules for their use are as follows:

1. Calcium and osteoporosis. To carry this claim, a food must contain 20 percent or more of the daily value for calcium (200 mg) per serving, have a calcium content that equals or exceeds the food's content of phosphorus, and contain a form of calcium that can be readily absorbed and used by the body. The claim must name the target group most in need of adequate calcium intakes (that is, teens and young adult white and Asian women) and state the need for exercise and a healthy diet. A product that contains 40 percent or more of the daily value for calcium must state on the label that a total dietary intake greater than 200 percent of the daily value for calcium (that is, 2,000 mg or more) has no further known benefit.
2. Fat and cancer. To carry this claim, a food must meet the descriptor requirements for "low fat" or, if fish and game meats, for "extra lean."
3. Saturated fat, cholesterol, and coronary heart disease (CHD). This claim may be used if the food meets the definitions for the descriptors "low saturated fat," "low cholesterol," and "low fat," or, if fish and game meats, "extra lean." It may mention the link between reduced risk of CHD and lower saturated fat and cholesterol intakes to lower blood cholesterol levels.
4. Fiber-containing grain products, fruits, and vegetables, and cancer. To carry this claim, a food must be or must contain a grain product, fruit, or vegetable and meet the descriptor requirements for "low fat" and, without fortification, be a "good source" of dietary fiber.
5. Fruits, vegetables, and grain products that contain fiber and risk of CHD. To carry this claim, a food must be or must contain fruits, vegetables, and grain products. It also must meet the descriptor requirements for "low saturated fat," "low cholesterol," and "low fat" and, without fortification, must contain at least 0.6 g of soluble fiber per serving.
6. Sodium and hypertension (high blood pressure). To carry this claim, a food must meet the descriptor requirements for "low sodium."
7. Fruits and vegetables and cancer. This claim may be made for fruits and vegetables that meet the descriptor requirements for "low fat" and that, without fortification, for "good source" of at least one of the following: dietary fiber, vitamin A, or vitamin C. This claim relates to diets low in fat and rich in fruits and vegetables (and thus vitamins A and C and dietary fiber) to reduce cancer risk. The FDA authorized this claim in place of an antioxidant vitamin and cancer claim.

Folic Acid

On January 4, 1994, the FDA authorized the use of a health claim about the relationship between folic acid and the risk of neural tube birth defects for dietary supplements and for foods in conventional form that are naturally high in folic acid. (In 1992, the U.S. Public Health Service had recommended that all women of childbearing age consume 0.4 mg of folic acid daily to reduce their risk of giving birth to a child with a neural tube defect.) The FDA plans to issue a final rule to allow the folic acid–neural tube defect claim for fortified foods, too.

Ingredient Labeling

Chief among changes is a regulation that requires full ingredient labeling on "standardized foods," which previously were exempt. Ingredient declaration will now have to be on all foods that have more than one ingredient. The ingredient list will include the following, when appropriate:

- FDA-certified color additives, such as FD&C Blue No. 1, by name
- sources of protein hydrolysates, which are used in many foods as flavors and flavor enhancers

- declaration of caseinate as a milk derivative in the ingredient list of foods that claim to be nondairy, such as coffee whiteners
- in beverages that claim to contain juice, declaration of the total percentage of juice on the information panel

The regulations, most of which went into effect in 1994, call for mandatory nutrition labeling for most foods. In addition, they set up voluntary programs for nutrition education information for many raw foods, such as the 20 most frequently eaten raw fruits, vegetables, and fish, under the FDA's point-of-purchase nutrition information program, and the 45 best-selling cuts of meat, under the USDA's program.

DEALING WITH PURVEYORS

The selection of purveyors is not a simple task and should not be taken lightly. The buyer should conduct some investigation prior to contacting a particular purveyor. For example, a buyer can check on the reputation of a purveyor by talking with buyers at other food service facilities. Questions to ask should deal with company stability; reliability; honesty; ability to meet delivery schedules; product quality; ability to provide large quantities, if necessary; and competitive prices. After the list of prospects is narrowed down, the buyer should contact the purveyor for an interview. It is preferred that the interview take place at the company facilities so that observations can be made of processing sanitation, storage facilities, and other conditions.

Ordering

Before an order can be placed it is necessary to determine the item desired, its quality, and its quantity. The desired item is based on the planned menu; the quality is based on specification; and the quantity is based on the number of portions needed, through analytical forecasting.

Forecasting

Forecasting is a prediction of how much to buy based on previous records. In a medical food service operation, some of the managerial tools used in forecasting are the following:

- Production worksheet. At the end of each meal, the total amount of food used and the total number of persons served are entered on the production worksheet (see Chapter 12). The totals include food served to patients, personnel, and guests. This information, plus recording data on special events, weather conditions, and other significant factors, can be used as part of the forecasting process.
- Patient census. The average daily patient census for those requiring regular and modified-diet food must be calculated.
- Menu rotation. Check the day of the week that the menu item is to be served according to menu rotation. In some medical facilities, the patient census is lower on weekends and fewer employees are assigned for duty.
- Selective menu. Consider food preferences. How many patients selected a particular food item during the last menu cycle?
- Special activities. Check calendar for conferences, seminars, meetings, parties, and other activities.

Placing the Order

The actual ordering is a simple process, provided that the necessary groundwork has been done to make an intelligent purchasing decision. A written order form should be used as a matter of record keeping. Even when orders are placed by telephone, a written order should follow as a cross-check for receiving personnel. The order form should not be a duplication of the specification, assuming that copies of specifications have been distributed to all purveyors and purchasing personnel. A brief description of the item needed may be written on a form similar to Exhibit 11–2. The use of common language, such as USDA grades for fruits and vegetables and IMPS-NAMP numbers for meats, eliminates the need for full descriptions of each item, yet ensures that the order will be filled correctly.

A purchase order is written only after prices and other factors have been agreed upon between the buyer and the purveyor. The prices may be obtained by use of a telephone quotation sheet, such as Exhibit 11–1, or from long-term negotiated bids. Instructions for completing a purchase order such as Exhibit 11–2 are as follows:

1. List all items needed in column 1. If the facility is using the one-step buying system, there may be a mixture of staple foods, fresh foods, and frozen foods.
2. Briefly describe each item, based on specifications, in a clear and concise manner.
3. Specify amounts needed based on forecast.
4. Record the amount on hand (done by storeroom personnel from the perpetual inventory records).
5. Obtain the amount to order by subtracting the amount on hand from the amount needed. The amount to order may need adjusting if a minimum stock level has been established.
6. Record the purveyor quote based on prior agreement from telephone quotations or long-term negotiated or contract bids.
7. Calculate the delivery date based on the amount of lead time required for thawing, preparation, and other factors related to serving the menu item at the correct time.

Although the process is simple, it requires considerable thought and time. The buyer should never wait until the

Exhibit 11–2 Purchase Order Form

XYZ General Hospital
Purchase Order Form

Purveyor: ______________________ Date: ____________

(1) Item	(2) Description	(3) Amount Needed	(4) Amount on Hand	(5) Amount To Order	(6) Purveyor Quote	(7) Delivery Date

sales representative is in the office to complete the purchase order form. It should be filled out and ready to place, thus using the time with the salesperson to discuss new products. For daily deliveries of bread, ice cream, milk, and similar items, a standard preprinted order form with carbon copies may be used.

Receiving, Inspecting, and Storing

The receiving, inspecting, and storing of food are functions of the purchasing department. It is the responsibility of the purchasing director to establish controls to make sure that items received are in accord with items ordered. Receiving personnel should have copies of all specifications and be thoroughly familiar with quality standards. Receiving personnel also should have a copy of all orders placed. When food is delivered, the order form can be used to inspect for quantity. Procedures should be established to handle discrepancies such as shortages, poor quality, and general condition of food as delivered. It is important that only authorized personnel be allowed to receive food. The practice of allowing any food service or other employee sign for food is poor

Exhibit 11–3 Daily Receiving Record Form

Daily Receiving Record				
Date Received ______			Received by ______	
Vendor	Invoice		Description (Food, Paper, Cleaning, Office)	Cost
	Date	Number		

practice. These individuals cannot possibly check for quantity or quality with any degree of accuracy. Records of food received must be maintained by the purchasing department on forms such as Exhibits 11–3 and 11–4.

Adequate storage of food is essential in order to avoid a waste of time, energy, and funds expended during the purchasing process. Depending on the purchasing system, all food may be delivered to the food service department, all food may be delivered to central storage, or staples may be delivered to central storage while meats and fresh produce are delivered directly to the department involved.

There may be a loss of control when food is delivered to different areas unless trained personnel are available in the different areas to receive the food. The most efficient procedure is to have all deliveries made directly to one area, whether it is the using department or central storage. The food can be promptly and properly stored or distributed immediately to the department involved.

Proper storage of food, from the time it is delivered until it is consumed by the customer, is a managerial function that must be shared by the purchasing department and the food service director. When food is received, there should be adequate safe, clean, and sanitary space available for storage at the proper temperature. When personnel are aware of delivery schedules, food stores can be arranged to utilize the first-in-first-out (FIFO) system. With use of a marking pen, all food cartons can be dated upon arrival. A cleaning schedule should be provided for storeroom personnel so that the areas are clean and orderly at all times.

Food Requisition and Inventory

All food issued from stores should be accounted for by signed requisitions. It is management's responsibility to establish policies designating who is allowed to requisition food. The procedure varies, depending mainly on the size of the facility. In small operations, the food service supervisor or the head cook may be responsible for requisitioning all food for all work areas. In large operations, requisitions may be submitted by the various units, such as main production, salad, bakery, patient service, and cafeteria service. At no time should the storeroom be left unattended and unlocked. The practice of leaving the storeroom open and unattended or hanging the storeroom key in the production area, allowing employees to walk in and out all during the day, should be avoided. For security purposes, storeroom keys should be handled by storeroom personnel only and left at the facility when the shift is over. Many of the problems associated with requisitions and distribution of food are eliminated with the use of an ingredient room, as described in Chapter 12.

The requisition form (Exhibit 11–5) should indicate the item, unit, item description, and amount issued. At the end of the serving period, all items requisitioned and not used should be returned to storage and recorded by storeroom personnel. To determine the amount used, the amount returned is subtracted from the amount issued.

An effective system for recording the amount of food on hand is the use of both the perpetual and physical inventory. In the perpetual inventory method there is continuous or

Exhibit 11–4 Daily Receiving Record Form

Daily Receiving Record

Date Received ____________ Received by ____________

Vendor	Invoice		Fresh Meat, Fish, Poultry	Frozen Prepared Entrees	Canned Entrees	Frozen Fruits and Vegetables	Canned Fruits and Vegetables	Fresh Produce	Dairy	Bakery	Groceries	Other	Cost
	Date	Number											
Total													

Exhibit 11–5 Storeroom Requisition and Issue Form

Storeroom Requisition and Issue Form

Unit: ________________________ Date: ____________________

Requisitioned							
Amount	Unit	Description	Amount Issued	Amount Returned	Amount Used	Unit Cost (%)	Total Cost (%)

Requisitioned by: ________________________ Issued by: ________________________

daily posting of all food received and issued. There is a separate card (Exhibit 11–6) for each item with space for name of product, minimum stock levels, date, order numbers, amounts received, amounts issued, amounts returned, and amounts on hand. The daily invoices and requisition sheets are used for daily posting. The main advantage of the perpetual inventory is that it provides a running balance of food items, as needed by management.

The physical inventory system involves the actual counting of each item in storage at designated intervals, at least once a month. A sample form for taking physical inventory is shown in Exhibit 11–7. Sometimes a pretyped form may be used listing food items in alphabetical order or according to storeroom arrangement. The inventory is commonly taken by a storeroom employee and a disinterested party. The clerical task of costing may be accomplished by storeroom personnel or the accounting department. The perpetual inventory indicates the amount that should be on hand; the physical inventory gives an accurate record of what is actually on hand. If there is a discrepancy in the totals of the two inventories, management should investigate. The discrepancies may be due to pilferage or errors in recording data.

QUALITY CONTROL

Quality control should be checked at key points throughout the purchasing process: specification, system of purchasing, purveyor selection, ordering, receiving, and storing. When the stages of purchasing are considered as integral parts of the total purchasing system, quality can be controlled. Quality control points to remember include the following:

- Specify foods that have been federally inspected and graded.
- Agree on a purchasing system that will support specification standards.
- Do not compromise quality for price in awarding bids and contracts.
- Purchase only from reputable purveyors.
- Visit purveyor's company to check food handling and general sanitation.
- Buy from sources that comply with all laws relating to food and food labeling.
- Check trucks and other modes of transportation for cleanliness and adequate refrigeration.
- Buy only federally inspected meat and poultry.
- Buy only Grade A pasteurized milk and milk products.
- Buy seafood from approved sources.
- Upon delivery, check all food for signs of spoilage, filth, and damage.
- Accept only clean whole eggs with shells intact and without cracks.
- Reject bulging, leaking, and rusty canned foods.
- Check frozen foods for evidence of thawing.

Exhibit 11–6 Perpetual Inventory Form

Perpetual Inventory								
		Received			Issued			
Date	Order No.	Amount	Unit	Unit Cost	Amount	Unit	Amount Returned	Amount on Hand
1/14/97					4	no. 10	0	36
1/15/97	7214	6	Case	10.40				72
1/15/97					4	no. 10	1	69
1/18/97					4	no. 10	0	65
Stock Level: Minimum 5 cases (30 no. 10 cans)					Maximum 12 cases (72 no. 10 cans)			
Item: Peaches, halves, cling			Unit: no. 10		Style: Canned			

- Accept fresh and shucked shellfish only in nonreturnable containers.
- Store food separately from poisonous materials, such as insecticides, rodenticides, cleaning agents, acids, polishes, and other chemicals.
- Store food at least 6 inches off the floor and 2 inches from the wall.
- Keep storage area free from insects, rodents, dust, and leaky overhead pipes.
- Provide adequate storage space (dry and refrigerated) to allow for air circulation.
- Store frozen foods at 0°F or lower, refrigerated foods at 40°F or lower, and dry storage foods at 50° to 70°F.
- Use the FIFO system for rotating stored foods.
- Maintain storage areas in clean and sanitary condition.

LAWS RELATED TO FOOD PURCHASING

There are federal, state, and local laws relating to some aspect of food wholesomeness and quality. State and local laws must be as strict as federal laws, and in most instances the laws are much stricter. Agencies, as established by law, are responsible for ensuring that all food for human consumption is harvested, manufactured, processed, packaged, stored, and transported in a safe and sanitary manner. Reorganization of the various federal agencies is constantly under way in efforts to strengthen services for consumer protection. Major federal agencies responsible for food and quality are the USDA (Figure 11–12), U.S. Department of Health and Human Services, and the U.S. Department of Commerce. Other services are provided by the U.S. Department of Labor through the Occupational Safety and Health Administration and the U.S. Department of Public Health. Because of the constant reorganization of the various agencies, it is difficult to classify the duties assigned to each with complete accuracy.

U.S. government officials are making true the promise to downsize the federal government. This is apparent from the most recent reorganization of the Department of Agriculture (U.S. Department of Agriculture 1995–1996), shown in Figure 11–12. The three divisions that are more closely related to the management of food service are (1) marketing and regulatory programs, (2) food safety and inspection service, and (3) food, nutrition, and consumer services.

Marketing and Regulatory Programs

This area, formerly composed of the Agriculture Marketing Service (AMS), Animal and Plant Health Inspection Service (APHIS), Federal Grain Inspection Service (FGIS), Food Safety and Inspection Service (FSIS), and Packers and Stockyards Administration (P & SA), was divided into two areas. Food safety is now managed by the Under Secretary for Food Safety. Included in the 1994 re-

Exhibit 11–7 Physical Inventory Form

Physical Inventory

Location: ______________________ Date: ____________________
Value of Sheet: __________________ Page __________of ______

Unit	Food Item	Amount on Hand		Unit Cost	Total Cost	Remarks
		Physical	Perpetual			

Inventory Taken By:

_____________________ and _____________________
Name Name

_____________________ _____________________
Title Title

organization are the entire operational and support structure of FSIS, plus those units from AMS and APHIS with responsibility for ensuring the safety of food products.

The remaining units of AMS and APHIS report to the Assistant Secretary for Marketing and Regulatory Programs. In addition, two areas of responsibility delegated to FGIS and P & SA comprise the Grain Inspection, Packers and Stockyards Administration (GIPSAL). The service provides current, unbiased information to producers, processors, distributors, and others to assist them in the orderly marketing and distribution of farm commodities.

Food Safety and Inspection Service

This service was established in 1981, with delegated authority for regulating the meat and poultry industry to ensure that meat, poultry, and meat and poultry products moving in interstate and foreign commerce were safe. In the 1994 reorganization, the service's authority was extended to include the inspection of egg products. The FSIS conducts mandatory, continuous inspection of the production of liquid, dried, and frozen egg products to ensure that egg products are safe, wholesome, unadulterated, and accurately labeled. Facilities and equipment are approved by FSIS before inspection is granted. The agency monitors meat and poultry in storage, distribution, and retail channels; conducts state programs for the inspection of meat and poultry products sold in intrastate commerce; and monitors livestock upon arrival at federally inspected facilities to ensure compliance.

Food, Nutrition, and Consumer Services

This area of the USDA ensures access to nutritious, healthful diets for all Americans; coordinates the USDA's

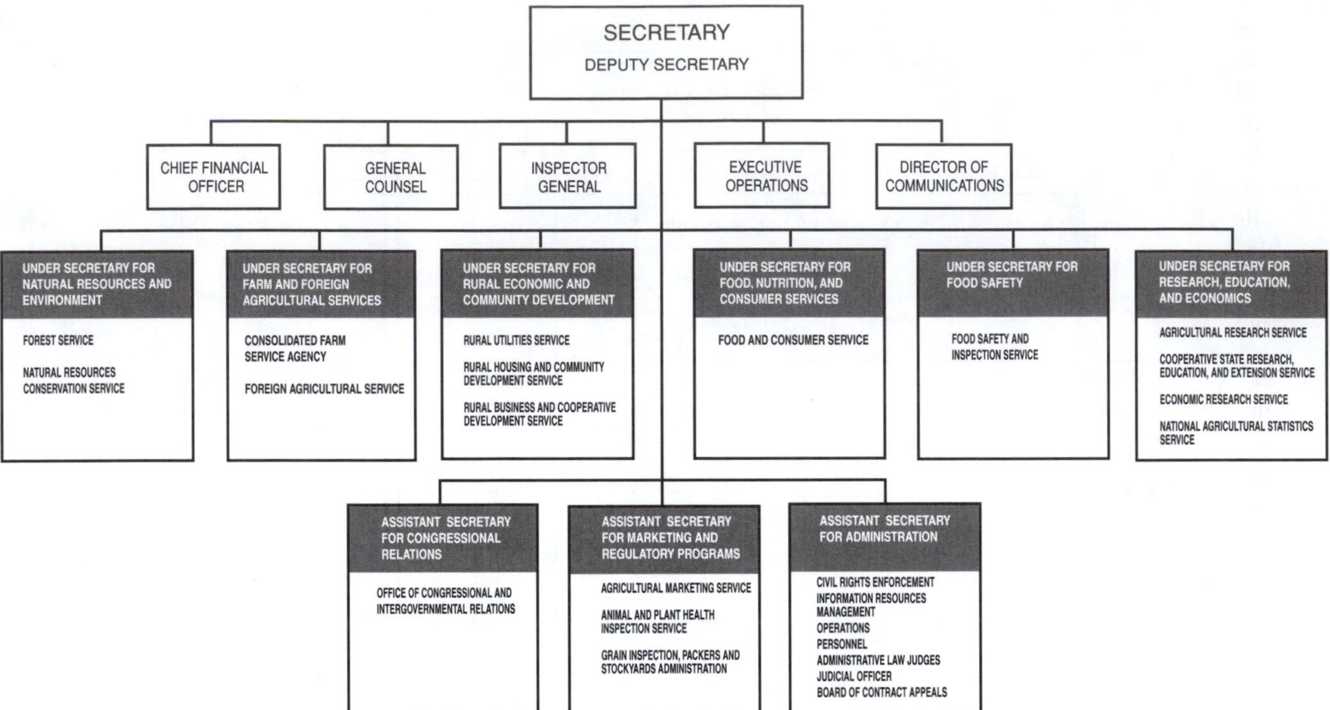

Figure 11–12 Organization of U.S. Department of Agriculture. Reprinted from U.S. Department of Agriculture, 1995–1996.

consumer education and outreach activities; encourages consumer involvement in USDA policy making; and ensures that the USDA adequately addresses consumer concerns and interests. The service concentrates on the electronic benefits transfer (EBT), eliminating the use of paper coupons while providing the recipient with a plastic card and personal identification number that functions like money. At the grocery checkout counter, no money and no food stamps change hands.

Under the USDA reorganization legislation, a center was created underscoring the department's commitment to nutrition and education.

The Food and Consumer Service is the agency that administers programs to make food assistance available to people who need it, such as the food stamp program, the national school lunch program, the school breakfast program, the summer food service program, the child and adult care food program, the special milk program for children, and the distribution program for commodity foods.

CONTROL POINTS RELATED TO FOOD PURCHASING

As with general quality control, quality should be checked at key points throughout the purchasing process: specification, system of purchasing, purveyor selection, food ordering, receiving, and storing. Control points to remember include those listed previously under quality control.

COMPUTER APPLICATIONS

Many food service departments now use some computer-assisted purchasing functions. The extent of use is usually a reflection of the size of the operation. Larger facilities and multiunit facilities are more likely to use fully integrated systems.

When purchasing is centralized for several operational units, the entire purchasing function—including recipes, menus, inventory, forecasting, and procurement—may be computerized. Vendor quotes may be completed using a modem; costs are entered and comparisons are computed automatically. The computer-generated purchase order, reflecting current prices, can then be electronically transfered to the purveyor. Contracted food service management companies and multiunit food service departments are examples of operations that use this technology extensively. Smaller facilities adapt available software or use spreadsheet and database software to provide many of the same results as their larger counterparts.

Previously, purchasing functions, especially cost and inventory, required numerous labor hours for data input to keep prices and usage current. The use of bar codes, scanners, and modems makes the use of computers feasible for cost and inventory control without a substantial increase in labor time. Another advantage of the prevailing use of technology in purchasing is the ready access to information regarding product availability. Being aware of product availability when an order is placed allows the purchaser to make proactive decisions about appropriate substitutions in advance of delivery.

The following subsections describe aspects of systems reported in the literature.

Inventory File

In order for the inventory function to be computerized, the department must be well organized. The database or file for a computerized inventory system contains information on all items ordered by the food service. This includes all food items on the menu and may include cleaning supplies, paper, and other miscellaneous items. Each item is coded to indicate food category, storage location, special use, or other categories that are necessary to the operation. Any information that supports the accuracy of the inventory may be included.

Census File

A census or forecast file can be created to store information regarding amounts of each item used, how many times the item appears on the menu, and the menu mix and usage according to the menu mix. For example, if baked chicken breast and tuna salad plate are the selections for a luncheon menu, the file may have stored information that the last time these two items were offered together the selection percentage was 90 percent for baked chicken breast and 10 percent for tuna salad plate. Therefore, if the projected census for this time estimates 500 servings total, then 450 servings (90 percent of 500) of baked chicken breast and 50 servings of tuna salad plate would be needed. This forecasting system requires daily updating with notes indicating unusual circumstances.

Recipe File

The recipe file consists of all standardized recipes needed for each item on the menu. Computer calculations adjust recipes for amounts and may convert these amounts to purchasing units. Recipe files that are used as a database for inventory should assign a special code number to items that may be purchased preprepared and items that are prepared on occasion and purchased ready to serve at other times.

As with any management information system, the quality and appropriateness of the output depends in great part on organizing and standardizing procedures during the planning stage.

REFERENCES

Code of Federal Register, Food and Drugs. 1984. *Standards of identity*. Title 21, Parts 130–169. Washington, DC: U.S. Government Printing Office.

Food and Drug Administration. 1995. The new food labels. *Buyers Guide* (April): 95–12.

Friedelson, I. 1967. *Fair packaging: Synopsis of food packaging and labeling regulations* (Reprint from FDA Papers). Washington, DC: U.S. Department of Health and Human Services, Food and Drug Administration.

National Association of Meat Purveyors. 1960. *Meat buyer's guide to standardized meat cuts*. Chicago.

National Association of Meat Purveyors. 1967. *Meat buyer's guide to portion control meat cuts*. Chicago.

National Association of Meat Purveyors. 1976. *Meat buyer's guide*. Chicago.

Office of the Federal Register. 1984. *U.S. government manual: 1984–1985*. National Archives and Records Service, General Service Administration, Superintendent of Documents. Washington, DC: U.S. Government Printing Office.

Richards, G. 1982. From light bulbs to CT scanners, group purchasing is filling the bill at a lower price. *Hospitals* 56, no 2:81–89.

Swindler, J.P. 1978. The future of the purchasing agent: Materials management as a profession. *Hospital Topics* 56, no. 4:22–26.

U.S. Department of Agriculture. 1956. *Standardization and inspection of fresh fruits and vegetables* (USDA Agriculture Marketing Service Publication No. 604). Washington, DC: U.S. Government Printing Office.

U.S. Department of Agriculture. 1972. *Regulations governing the grading and inspection of poultry and edible products thereof and U.S. classes, standards and grades with respect thereto* (7CFR, Pt. 70). Washington, DC.

U.S. Department of Agriculture. 1995–1996. *U.S. government manual*. Washington, DC: National Archives and Research Administration.

U.S. Department of Health and Human Services. 1965. *Grade "A" pasteurized milk ordinance: 1965 Recommendations of the U.S. Public Health Service* (Public Health Service Publication No. 229). Washington, DC.

U.S. Department of Health and Human Services. 1969. *FDA fact sheet: Milk and milk type products*. Public Health Service, Consumer Protection and Environmental Health Service, Food and Drug Administration. Washington, DC.

U.S. Department of the Interior. 1964a. *Fish cookery for one hundred* (Test Kitchen Series No. 1). Washington, DC.

U.S. Department of the Interior. 1964b. *How to cook shrimp* (Test Kitchen Series No. 7). Washington, DC.

U.S. Department of the Interior. 1964c. How to cook clams (Test Kitchen Series No. 8). Washington, DC.

U.S. Department of the Interior. 1964d. *How to cook oysters* (Test Kitchen Series No. 3). Washington, DC.

U.S. Department of the Interior. 1964e. *How to cook crabs* (Test Kitchen Series No. 10). Washington, DC.

U.S. Department of the Interior. 1964f. *How to cook lobsters* (Test Kitchen Series No. 11). Washington, DC.

U.S. Department of the Interior. 1964g. *How to cook scallops* (Test Kitchen Series No. 13). Washington, DC.

CHAPTER 12

Subsystem for Food Production

The planned menu precedes any decision relating to the type of production system to use in a food service operation. The decision should be based on an objective evaluation of menu requirements, with full consideration to other subsystems (food purchasing, equipment, distribution and service, personnel, and finances) required for a quality food service. Two menu factors that may affect the type of production system are the following:

1. Menu style or format. A nonselective menu or a selective menu with two or three choices could be used effectively by all production systems. A restaurant-type menu is more suitable for the cook-freeze-serve system if food items are individually packaged. The bulk packaging used for assembly-serve and for some freeze-serve systems may present problems in patient tray assembly because of the wide variety of menu items offered on a restaurant-type menu. The current trend in using restaurant-type menus is to preplate menu items prior to freezing. One of the problems associated with preplating menu items is that menu combinations may not be acceptable to patients. For example, if entree no. 1 (roast beef) is served with mashed potatoes and Brussels sprouts, the patient may not like the vegetable combination and ask for a substitute. If no substitutions are allowed the patient is unhappy, resulting in a lower rating for food acceptance.
2. Menu variety. Some questions need to be asked concerning system capability. Can the process method accommodate all planned menu items such as hard- and soft-cooked eggs, meats without sauce or gravy, flour- or cereal-based puddings, egg custards, and other similar foods? Can the system accommodate all food served to personnel and guests, for special activities, vending, and coffee shops, as well as patient food service? When a system is used for only part of the food service required, the use of the system may result in added labor, equipment, and food costs, as well as increased pressure on employees.

For a better understanding of how the menu is related to the production system, it is appropriate to discuss the various systems at this time.

PRODUCTION SYSTEMS

Food production systems currently used in medical food service operations can be classified into four categories: (1) cook-serve, (2) assembly-serve, (3) cook-freeze-serve, and (4) cook-chill-serve. The commissary or food factory is a method of producing food in large quantities and can be applied to all categories of food production systems.

Cook-Serve Production System

The cook-serve production system is sometimes referred to as conventional or conventional-convenience. The cook-serve system is characterized by on-premise preparation of food from the raw state (scratch cookery) on a daily basis for each meal. Food is assembled and served with a minimum holding period. Cook-serve is the system most often used in medical food service operations. Because of the lack of skilled employees and financial constraints, few cook-serve systems prepare all foods from scratch. Most operations use some form of commercially prepared convenience food. The use of a butcher shop for portioning, grinding, and cubing meat from carcass or wholesale cuts is practically extinct in medical food service. Meat is frequently purchased in portion-controlled units, either fresh or frozen. The large bake shops, where all types of bread, rolls, buns, cakes, and pastries were prepared, have practically disappeared. Today there is a dessert preparation area where mixes are used for cakes and cookies; frozen pies or frozen pie shells and canned or frozen fruit fillings are used; and bread, rolls, and buns are purchased from commercial bakeries.

Employees are assigned various duties to prepare all food for a particular meal just prior to serving time. Food is portioned, assembled, and transported to wards for patient service without additional heating. In most operations, employees prepare food for patients and personnel at the same time. After one meal is served and the preparation and service areas are cleaned, preparation begins for the next meal. Employees work overlapping shifts of eight hours each. For a three-meal feeding plan, employees may be scheduled to work from 6:00 AM to 2:00 PM for the first shift with responsibility for breakfast and lunch preparation. The second shift may be scheduled to work from 11:00 AM to 7:00 PM with responsibility to assist with lunch preparation and service, and to prepare and serve the dinner meal. The overlap time between 11:00 AM and 2:00 PM must be carefully planned and monitored for full utilization of employees.

Advantages of the cook-serve system are as follows:

- The system provides flexibility in menu planning for both regular and modified diets without dependence on outside preparation sources.
- Although some canned and frozen foods are used, patients and employees tend to equate the cook-serve system with the serving of fresh foods.
- With on-premise preparation, it is easier to cater to individual needs and preferences.
- Menu variety is not limited by any processing technique associated with the system.

The disadvantages of a cook-serve system are as follows:

- The rush periods associated with each meal hour may cause undue employee stress.
- Skilled employees must be scheduled for each shift, seven days a week.
- The overlap of work shifts may result in low productivity and high labor cost.

Assembly-Serve Production System

The assembly-serve production system is also referred to as total convenience and semiconvenience. In assembly-serve, all food is purchased in a prepared state from an outside source. The prepared frozen food is in bulk form, packaged in disposable pans. When ready for use, the food is thawed, plated, assembled, and distributed to wards for service to patients. For the employee cafeteria, food may be heated in disposable pans and served from a counter. Fresh produce is purchased in precut form, such as precut cabbage for coleslaw and precut mixed greens for tossed salad, and other forms requiring a minimum of preparation prior to service. Pies, cakes, and pastries are purchased in frozen state and require only thawing and portioning. For a limited number of assembly-serve operations, preplated entree-vegetable combination courses are purchased. In other operations, only the entree item is purchased from commercial sources and all other foods, such as vegetables, salads, and desserts, are prepared on premise. This arrangement is considered a semiconvenience system.

Managerial decisions to convert the operation to assembly-serve should be analyzed carefully in terms of not only cost but also menu variety, quality, and acceptability. With a full assembly-serve operation, equipment and labor costs are drastically reduced. When disposable serviceware is used, the cost is further reduced. Initial costs may involve additional freezer space, equipment on each ward for thermolizing plated food, purchasing of disposables, and equipment for disposing of disposables.

Menu variety may present a problem. A variety of convenience products is available, but the products are not consistent in terms of quality, size, and ingredients from one manufacturer to the other. It will be necessary to write specifications to accommodate the needs of the operation, such as the amount of protein per serving and the ratio of other ingredients in a particular product. Unless the amount ordered is large enough to justify a change in standard processing techniques, the cost may be prohibitive or the manufacturer may refuse to honor the specification. Most modified diets are multirestrictive, either in caloric or nutritive value. This requires careful planning in order to serve food as prescribed.

Consider food acceptance by patients and employees. Some individuals have a negative attitude toward convenience foods from early "TV dinner" experiences. Better appearance and greater acceptability are possible with the use of china or attractive plastic serviceware and garnishes.

Advantages of the assembly-serve production system are as follows:

- Labor costs are reduced. Skilled cooks are not required for production.
- The product is uniform. Food products are the same each time they are served.
- Waste resulting from excess trimming, overcooking, shrinkage, and spoilage is reduced.
- Portion control is assured. Pans are consistently filled with the same amount.
- Less equipment is required. Prepreparation and most cooking equipment can be eliminated. Dishwashers can be eliminated if disposables are used exclusively.
- Purchasing, inventory, and accounting procedures are easier.

Disadvantages of the assembly-serve production system are as follows:

- Food costs are increased. The price of the product includes the cost of food and the built-in labor costs.
- Food for modified diets may be limited. Acute care facilities may have problems meeting patient needs because of the complexity of diet prescriptions.
- Availability of the product is not assured. The manufacturer may decide to discontinue certain products or may go out of business.
- Satisfying individual food preferences is difficult.
- Patients may object to convenience foods, especially if food is served on disposables.
- Control over production is lost. Employees at the manufacturing company may go on strike.
- Initial equipment costs may be high. There will be a need for thermalizing equipment on each ward and possibly extra freezer space.

Cook-Freeze-Serve Production System

The cook-freeze-serve system is also referred to as ready-serve and ready-food. In medical food service operations, food is prepared on-premise, packaged in individual portions, blast frozen, freezer-stored, thawed, assembled, distributed cold to wards, rethermalized on wards, and served to patients. As conceptualized by researchers at Cornell's school of hotel administration (MacLennon 1968), the system is a ready-food production system and is distinguished from other ready-serve foods as follows:

- Food is prepared in large quantities. Master chefs and cooks work five days per week, preparing three or four different foods each day.
- The system returns to classic cooking methods. Because a single food item is prepared only about 5 or 10 times a year, extra time can be used to prepare classic foods.
- Single-portion packaging is used. Portions are rethermalized as needed, thus avoiding long periods on a steam table.
- Freezing is used as a means of preservation and storage. Food is blast-frozen and freezer stored.
- The system uses a simplified reheating process. Both "boil-in-a-bag" and microwave heating methods are used.
- The system operates on-premise. Because all foods are prepared on premise, quality standards are controlled.
- Ready-foods meet local tastes and portion sizes. Consumer preferences and portion sizes can be accommodated.
- Synthetics and food additives are not used. In this system, there is no need for preservatives, antioxidants, sequestrants, surfactants, stabilizers, thickeners, buffers, firming agents, tenderizers, or taste enhancers.

The system was developed for luxury hotel dining areas and included foods from appetizers and soups to desserts. Food is cooked, using conventional methods, to varying degrees of doneness. A modified starch is used for dishes that normally require tapioca starch. Single portions are packaged in plastic pouches or plastic airtight boxes, blast-frozen, and then held in frozen storage until ready for use. Special equipment was designed to complement the cook-in-a-bag process. Food is rethermalized from the frozen state.

For use in medical food service operations, the ready-food system was modified to accommodate the complexities of patient and cafeteria food service. In hospitals, the process is the same as originally designed through the blast-freezing stage. Instead of removing individual portions from the freezer as needed, all food required for a meal is removed at least one day in advance and placed in a thaw refrigerator. The thaw refrigerator is a special type that is capable of thawing food at a much faster rate than a regular refrigerator, which takes approximately three days. In this refrigerator, food is automatically thawed and maintained at a safe temperature, not exceeding 45°F. The thawed portions are cold-plated according to individual diet requirements or as indicated on the selective menu. Trays are transported to wards in refrigerated carts and remain under refrigeration until serving time. Prior to service, foods requiring heat are removed from the patient tray, rethermalized, returned to the tray along with other foods, and served immediately. In some operations, a tray cart is used with an electronic component beneath each tray for heating foods requiring heat and for supplying refrigerated air to keep cold food at the proper temperature.

Another variation of the hospital cook-freeze-serve production system is the Leeds cook-freeze system, developed by United Leeds Hospitals, Leeds, England (Rinke 1976). All foods, including entrees, soups, vegetables, starches, egg dishes, casseroles, and desserts, are prepared in the following manner:

1. Foods are slightly undercooked, to allow for further cooking during the rethermalizing process.
2. Foods are packed hot in polyethylene molds that hold six to eight portions.
3. Molds are blast-frozen.
4. Food is removed from molds in the form of frozen slabs.
5. The slabs are heat-sealed in polyethylene bags and packed in boxes for freeze storage.
6. Food is reconstituted by placing slabs in reusable metal pans that are heated on the wards in specially designed convection ovens.
7. Food is assembled and served from the ward pantry.

As noted, the multiportion frozen molds and the rethermalizing techniques are completely different from methods used in other freeze-serve production systems. The procedure of decentralized heating and plating of food may result in loss of managerial control over the finished product.

It is observed that the use of cook-freeze-serve for medical food service operations is designed only for patient service. Although patient food service should receive top priority, a dual production system of freeze-serve for patients and cook-serve for personnel is questionable. The dual production system negates most of the advantages normally expected from a freeze-serve system, such as reduced labor and food costs. For example, with a dual production system, only the cooks assigned to freeze-serve can be scheduled for a five-day Monday through Friday workweek. Other cooks responsible for the cook-serve system must be scheduled to work the three meals per day, seven days per week. MacLennan (1968) advised hotel food service operations either to go all the way with ready-food or not to use it at all. The advice can also apply to medical food service operations in the use of freeze-serve.

As reported by McIver (1970), bulk blast freezing has been used at the Brooklyn Hospital in New York since 1965. The procedure is as follows:

1. One cook is assigned to produce 1,600 portions of a given entree each day Monday through Friday, plus a variety of combination dishes for patient selective menu and personnel cafeteria.
2. Items are prepared in 200-portion units using both tilting skillets and steam kettles.
3. Completed items are portioned into 9½ × 12 × 1½-in foil pans with fold-over lids. Each pan is scaled to 5 lb and is considered a packed unit. Packages are labeled with date of preparation, contents, and reconstituting instructions.
4. Packages are quick-cooled by a cold water cooling jacket that causes the temperature to drop from 212°F to 150°F in 30 minutes, prior to blast freezing.
5. Packages are blast-frozen from two to three hours, depending on the product.
6. Convection ovens are used to reconstitute food, following time and temperature instructions given on the lid of each box.

The system used at Brooklyn Hospital appears to be a practical approach for serving both patients and personnel. When food is reconstituted in the main production area, it is hot-plated and served as described for the cook-serve system.

An interesting cook-freeze-serve system is the one designed and implemented for the 1,200-bed Walter Reed Army Medical Center in Washington, DC. Food is prepared for individual or bulk blast freezing. As designed, a monorail system is used to transport food deliveries to dry, refrigerated, or frozen storage, where movable shelving permits the first in, first out (FIFO) system of storage and issue. Food, as needed, is programmed to the ingredient room, preprepared, and delivered to the production area. In the production area, food preparation is monitored from the production manager's office, where computerized audiovisual panels are designed to control equipment, cooking cycle, speed of cooking conveyors, and temperature settings (Reed's semi-automatic food service 1977). Equipment features include the following:

- The system has a vegetable-fruit washer designed to raise the washed items out of the water.
- There are automatic breading machines for foods such as chops, fish, chicken, and some vegetables.
- Electrically heated braise and simmer kettles can cook up to 26 gallons of stews, sauces, and gravies. The equipment has an ingredient-dispensing unit with an instruction card reader to add ingredients automatically at the proper time.
- Double-jacketed steam kettles are equipped with self-contained stirrers, mashers, and purées.
- Two conveyorized fryer-griddles can produce over 2,200 portions of chops, sausage, or hamburger patties in one hour.
- Over 200 pounds of roast can be cooked in each of two rotating self-basting ovens. At the press of a button on the oven, natural juice is pumped from the bottom of the pan to baste the meat.

Most of the equipment was imported from European manufacturing companies (Simler 1978). The Tricalt revolving hot food tables were purchased in France; the Kuppersbusch models of continuous conveyor fryer-griddle, self-basting ovens, and semiautomated gravy and sauce makers were purchased from Germany. Blast freezers and the chill-therm food carts were manufactured by American companies.

Food is cooked, packaged in either individual portions or bulk containers, and rapidly frozen. Limited quantities of food are requisitioned from freeze-storage and thawed as needed. Patient trays are preplated manually (temporary procedure) and transported to patient wards in chill-therm carts, which are used to refrigerate and cook foods in dishes on fully assembled serving trays (see Chapter 13 for a description of the service system).

Advantages cited for use of cook-freeze-serve in medical food service operations are as follows:

- Employee scheduling is easier. Cooks and main production employees are scheduled for one eight-hour shift, Monday through Friday.
- Large-batch cooking reduces the number of times that a menu item must be prepared during a given period.
- Employees work in a more relaxed atmosphere without the pressure of meeting culinary schedules three times a day.
- Peak production workloads are eliminated; thus employees are utilized fully throughout the work shift.
- Labor costs may be reduced because large quantities are purchased at one time for bulk preparation.

Major disadvantages cited for use of the freeze-serve system are as follows:

- The system equipment entails an initial outlay of capital for added freezer space, packaging, and rethermalizing. There also may be a renovation cost if operation is converted from one type of system to another.
- A dual-system operation may be required. When freeze-serve is used for only part of the operation, there are added food and labor costs. Friction may develop between employees who are off on weekends and those who are not.

Cook-Chill-Serve Production System

The cook-chill-serve production system is characterized by the cooking of food in the conventional manner, quick-chilling, packaging, and chill-storing until ready for use (Figure 12–1). The first cook-chill-serve system to be designed was originated and implemented in the early 1960s at Nacka Hospital, Stockholm, Sweden.

As reported by Bjorkman and Delphin (1966), production of food at the Nacka Hospital took place under bacteriologically controlled conditions with food samples taken on the day of cooking and at the end of the storage period. Personnel, equipment, and materials were carefully checked. Food was prepared for the Nacka Hospital plus other facilities in the Stockholm area and for one facility over 220 miles away. Prepared food was transported in refrigerated vans to satellite units. The procedure at Nacka Hospital was as follows:

1. Food was conventionally cooked by frying, boiling, roasting, stewing, and other methods to a temperature of 176°F.
2. Hot food was transferred to plastic bags, five portions per bag.

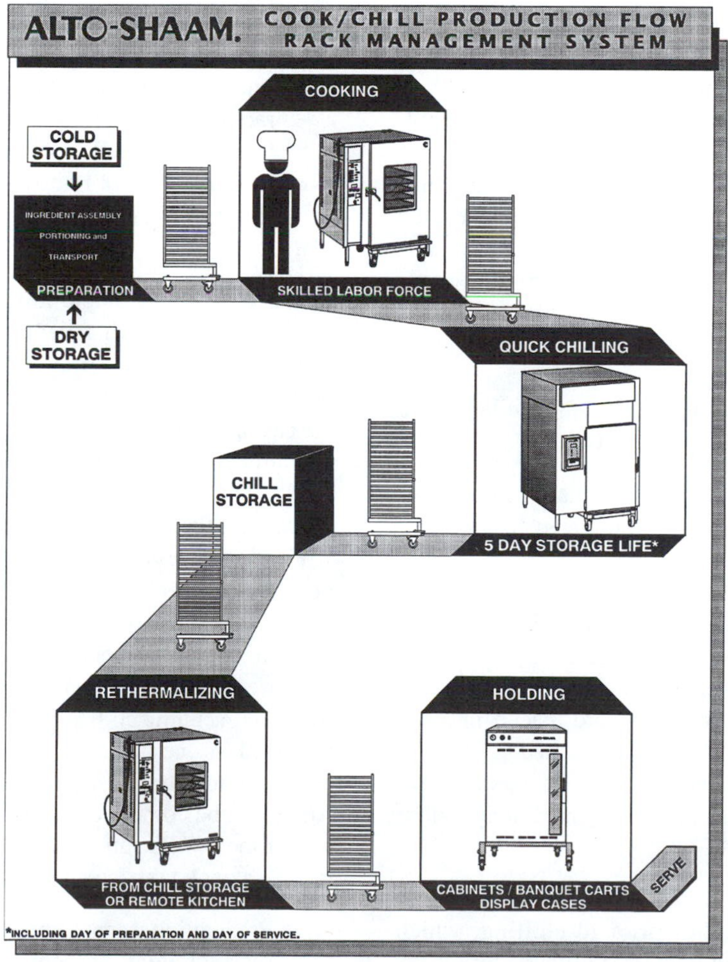

Figure 12–1 Cook–Chill Processing and Rack Management Food Production Flow. *Source:* Reprinted through the courtesy of Alto-Shaam, Inc., Menomonee Falls, Wisconsin.

3. Air was extracted from the bags and the food was sealed airtight by a Cryovac machine.
4. Bags were placed in boiling water (rectangular kettle for rapid heating) for three minutes.
5. Sealed bags passed through a tunnel with running water for one hour at a temperature of 50°F, then lowered to 37°F.
6. After quick-drying, packages were stored in a refrigerated room at 37°F or less.
7. At time of service, bags were placed in boiling water for 30 minutes.
8. Bags were cut open and contents served. Food could be emptied into a steam table pan and served from a counter.

The cook-chill-serve system is currently used by a number of facilities with slightly varied production procedures. Depending on the chilling procedures used, food is stored from one day to three weeks or more. In the United States, notable cook-chill systems were designed at the University of Wisconsin Hospitals and for a group of hospitals in South Carolina, known as the Anderson, Greenville, Spartanburg (AGS) food production system (McGuckian 1969).

At the University of Wisconsin, food was prepared one day in advance, chilled in bulk, portioned for tray assembly, and transported to patient areas in refrigerated carts (Kaud 1972). The unique feature of this system was the specially designed food carts, which contained refrigerated space for 30 trays, a microwave oven, coffee and hot water dispensers, and storage space for beverage servers and cups. There was a fold-up table attached to the side of the cart where a patient tray could be placed while food requiring heat could be thermalized.

The AGS system (McGuckian 1969) was similar to the Nacka system with the following exceptions:

1. Raw or partially cooked foods were placed in pouches and the cooking process was completed in temperature-controlled water baths.
2. After processing, products were chilled in ice water tanks, then chill-stored at 28° to 32°F.
3. Pouches were delivered to satellite units in covered plastic containers that were surrounded by ice.
4. Before serving, sealed pouches were placed in a hot water bath for 30 to 40 minutes and heated to 160°F.
5. When plated, entrees and other hot foods were microwaved for 10 to 20 seconds immediately before distribution to patients.

Both the Nacka and the AGS systems used the pasteurization process of heating pouches prior to chilling, which added an extra step in the food flow for chill-serve products. Each time food is handled represents a critical point for control of microbial, nutritional, and sensory qualities of the food. This is a major concern to researchers, managers, and consumers.

Another concern associated with the cook-chill-serve system is how to extend the shelf life of prepared food while maintaining high standards of quality. One system responding to this problem is the Groen Capkold system for kettle-cooked foods. With the specially designed equipment, food is produced for a cook-chill-serve system as follows:

1. Products to be prepared are cooked in a steam-jacketed kettle equipped with an agitator (see Figure 12–2).
2. Ingredients are added sequentially to ensure proper degree of doneness.
3. When the cooking process is completed, the product, at 180°F, is pumped into the Cryovac casing.
4. Packages of 1 gal, 5 qt, 1½ gal, or 2 gal are sealed with a positive clip closure and labeled.
5. The product is placed in a tumble chiller filled with cold water, 34° to 36°F, and gently agitated in constantly circulated cold water. In less than one hour, the product temperature is reduced to 40°F.
6. Cooled casings are immediately placed in the cooler for storage at 28° to 32°F until needed for distribution.
7. The finished product is stored in the casing on open racks or cartons for distribution to satellite units.
8. For serving, products can be heated in the casings in a hot water bath or removed from the casings and heated in any conventional manner.

The filling station (shown in Figure 12–3) is equipped with a very simple single-lobe pump that gently moves the food from the cooking vessel to the casing. Sanitation is assured because the product is transferred while hot, near pasteurization temperatures, from the cooking vessel into the casing, thus eliminating any chance for human or utensil contamination. The kettle-cooked Capkold system can be used for foods such as stews, casseroles, soups, gravies, and sauces and for uncooked products such as salad dressing.

For the processing of meat in quantity, including poultry, pork, corned beef, and spareribs, a stainless steel cook tank (Figure 12–4) can be used. The cook tank is a self-contained, automatic cooking system that incorporates controlled temperature water to automatically slow-cook meats and other foods in vacuumized bags. The bagged meat, or other food, is placed in one of five wire racks that stack into the tank, five bags to a tray. Large-batch cooking of up to 50 20-lb roasts can be completed in one cook tank. High quality and higher meat yields are produced. The procedure for cooking beef in a cook tank is as follows:

1. Preparation. Meat to be cooked is trimmed of excess or discolored fat. Seasonings are applied to the outer surface of the meat as a dry rub, or the meat may be injected up to 10 percent of its raw weight with a sea-

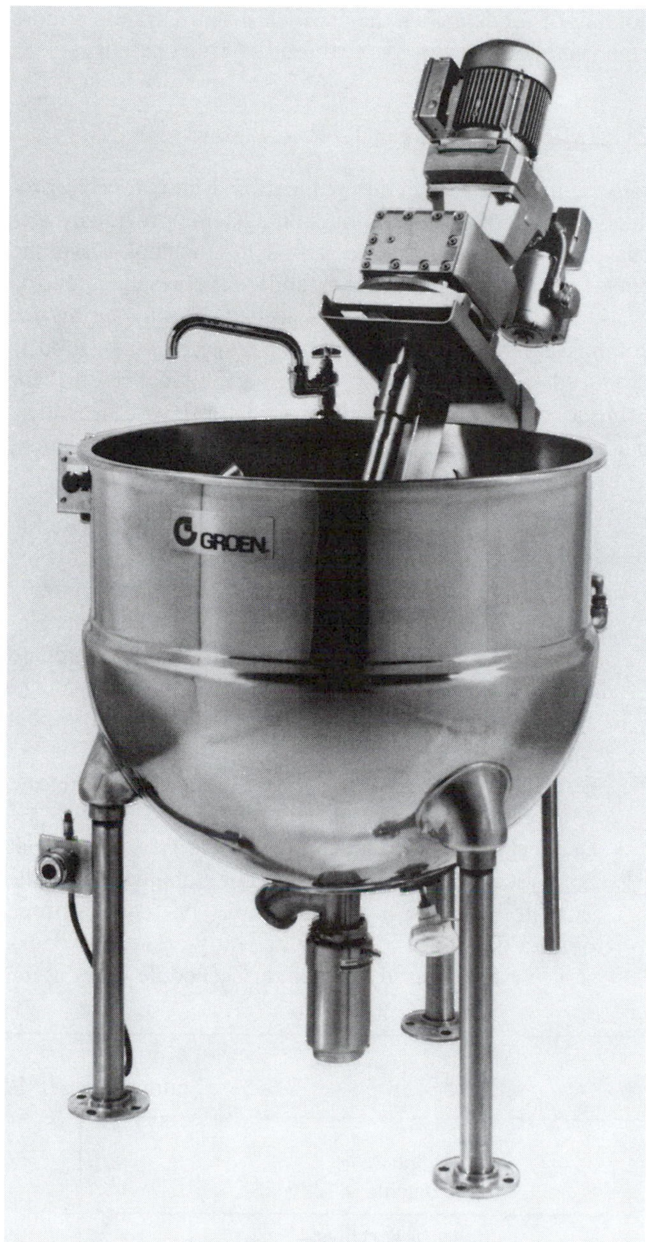

Figure 12–2 Agitator Kettle. Courtesy of Groen, A Dover Industries Company, Elk Grove Village, Illinois.

soning solution. Only spices or spice blends that carry a manufacturer's certification that they are free of pathogenic microorganisms should be used. Rubs give the meat the desired flavor and oven-roasted appearance.

2. Packaging. The trimmed product is placed in a polyolefin casing with one end preclipped. An air-powered heavy-duty vacuum system extracts the air from the bagged meat cut, gathers the neck of the bag, and applies a rugged clip. If natural meat juices are to be drained from the package after cooking, an additional 6-in tail is left to permit revacuumizing and reclipping the original casing.

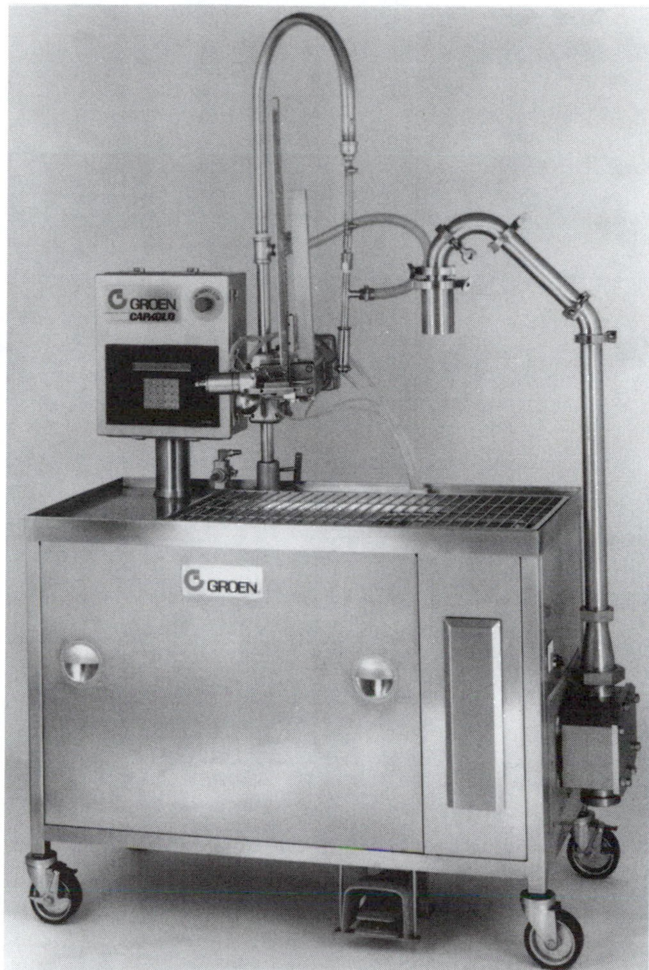

Figure 12–3 Filling Station. Courtesy of Groen, A Dover Industries Company, Elk Grove Village, Illinois.

3. Cooking. Meat in vacuum-sealed bags is cooked at controlled temperatures not exceeding 195°F. The cooking process meets U.S. Department of Agriculture guidelines for cooking requirements for cooked and roast beef (Federal Register 1978), which specify that all products must be cooked to an internal temperature of 145°F (63°C).
4. Chilling and storage. After cooking, the product is cooled to arrest any additional interior cooking of the meat. The hot water is drained from the tank, and city water or water from an ice builder is pumped through the tank to arrest the cooking process. Injected beef must be chilled below 40°F within a six-hour period. Cooked beef that has been injected with spices must be frozen at 0°F for storage and distribution. Beef that is

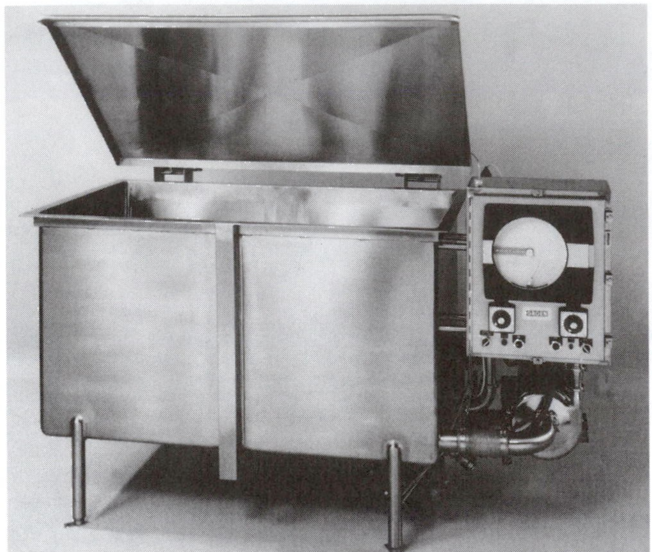

Figure 12–4 Stainless Steel Cook Tank. Courtesy of Groen, A Dover Industries Company, Elk Grove Village, Illinois.

not injected should be stored at 28° to 30°F for refrigerated storage of 6 to 12 weeks, or at 0°F for longer-term frozen storage.

The cook-chill tank is used for a number of products other than solid cuts of meat, such as liver and onions, meatloaf, salisbury steak, steamed rice, and other entree food items. The procedure for making liver and onions in the cook-chill tank is given in Exhibit 12–1. The extended time for chill-holding of foods makes the cook-chill-serve system a more practical alternative in medical food service operations.

COMMISSARY OR FOOD FACTORY

A commissary is a central location where food is produced using any of the production systems previously discussed. Food may be produced by using the cook-serve, the cook-freeze-serve, or the cook-chill-serve system. Food is transported to satellite units, as needed. The food flow for commissary food production is the same as when food is produced in a single facility. There are logical reasons for using a commissary to produce food for several facilities, but certain managerial decisions need careful consideration, as follows:

- Menu or type of food to be prepared. Will all satellite units use the same food items during a menu cycle? Will all units conform to standardized portion sizes? Will the commissary prepare food for patients, personnel, and special activities? Will the commissary prepare only hot foods, or both hot and cold?
- Type of production system. Which production system can best meet the needs of all satellite units? Consideration should be given to holding time and temperature in providing safe food.
- Delivery schedule. Depending on the type of production system used and the amount of storage space at the satellite units, food deliveries may be required three times a day, once a day, or once a week. If the cook-serve system is used, the delivery schedule is not at the

Exhibit 12–1 Recipe for Liver and Onions, Using Cook-Chill Tank

Name of Item: Liver and Onions	Date Prepared:		Batch Number: Size of Batch:
Type of Preparation: Cook in Casing	Serving Size:		Number of Servings: 36 portions (3½ oz slices)
	Measures		
Ingredients	Weight	Volume	Method of Preparation
Liver—3½-oz slices	8 lb		1. Dredge liver slices in seasoned flour; place 12 in each casing.
Browned flour (Mix)		2 cups	2. Fry bacon until crisp. Add 8-oz mixture of onions and bacon to each casing.
Salt (Mix)	1 oz		
Pepper (Mix)		1 Tbsp	
Bacon, sliced, diced	1 lb		
Onions, diced	1 lb		3. Vacuumize and cook in 180°F water for 50–55 minutes.
			4. Chill in ice.

Courtesy of Groen, A Dover Industries Company, Elk Grove Village, Illinois.

discretion of management; food must be delivered prior to each meal served with a minimum of holding.

- Packaging. The packaging depends on the state of readiness as food is delivered to the various units. For patient food service, food may be packaged as follows:
    1. bulk packaging with portioning and tray assembly at the satellite unit
    2. individual portions with tray assembly at the satellite unit
    3. individual portions with complete tray assembly at the commissary site
    4. bulk packaging for cafeteria service
- Processing equipment. Equipment should be appropriate for the type of system selected. Consider equipment that will reduce handling, thus minimizing contamination sources.
- Transporting equipment. For safe keeping of processed food, the temperature must be below 45°F or above 140°F. The type of equipment used to transport will depend on the preparation state, such as hot, cold, frozen, or chilled; holding time required; delays; and travel distance and time.

FOOD FLOW

Alternatives to the conventional cook-serve method of preparing food in quantity have reached major proportions since the early 1960s. Not only is the flow of food different, but there is an increase in the number of stages that must be completed before the food is served. Depending on the system, there may be 11 or more stages involved in food production and service. The various stages given for the four systems in Exhibit 12–2 are considered critical control points that may affect microbial, sensory, and nutritional quality of food.

Bobeng and David (1978) applied the hazard analysis critical control point (HACCP) model to the conventional, cook-

Exhibit 12–2 Food Flow for Various Production Systems

Cook-Serve	Assembly-Serve	Cook-Chill-Serve	Cook-Freeze-Serve
Purchasing	Purchasing	Purchasing	Purchasing
Receiving	Receiving	Receiving	Receiving
Storage (dry, refrigeration, and low temperature)	Storage (dry, refrigeration, and low temperature)	Storage (dry and refrigeration)	Storage (dry and refrigeration, and low temperature)
Prepreparation		Prepreparation	Prepreparation
Preparation		Preparation	Preparation
		Packaging	Packaging
Prepared holding (chill-hot)		Prepared holding (chill)	Prepared holding (low temperature)
	Thawing		Thawing
Portioning	Portioning (bulk)	Portioning	Portioning (bulk)
Assembly	Assembly	Assembly	Assembly
Transport/holding (chill-hot)	Transport/holding (chill)	Transport/holding (chill)	Transport/holding (chill)
	Rethermalize	Rethermalize	Rethermalize
Serve	Serve	Serve	Serve

chill, and cook-freeze hospital food service systems. HACCP is a system for preventing the deterioration of food quality that was successfully implemented by commercial food processors. Emphasis is on managerial awareness of microbiological hazards, and on identifying the process stages where loss of control could present food safety risks. Each process stage of production is considered a control point.

The study was limited to three on-premise food service systems. Control points were studied in relation to ingredient control and storage, equipment sanitation, personnel sanitation, and time-temperature relationships. It was determined that microbiological testing could be done but not in time to take corrective action for the current batch. Because of variations in types, sizes, equipment models, and kinds and numbers of employees for each food service operation, it was impossible to establish universal critical-control-point parameters for monitoring equipment and personnel sanitation. The most practical procedure, one that could be applied to all production systems, was the establishment of time-temperature standards. The time-temperature standards developed are similar to those specified by federal regulations for the holding of processed foods.

FOOD PRODUCTION

The daily production of food must be organized, regardless of the type of production system used. The most valuable tool for managerial control is the production worksheet (Exhibit 12–3). Depending on the size of the operation, a separate production worksheet may be used for each unit, such as cooking, baking, salad-sandwich, and others. In some operations, a separate area with diet cooks assigned is used for preparation of modified diet foods. The production worksheet is completed as follows:

1. Food item. The food items listed on the production worksheet are taken directly from the planned menu. Any deviations must have managerial approval.
2. Amount needed. The amount needed is based on the projected number of portions required. The amount may be adjusted on the day of service if an increase or decrease in patient census or some other special activity justifies the change. Space is provided for both regular and modified diets. Amounts in the regular column include amounts needed for patients on regular diets, amounts needed in the cafeteria, and amounts needed for special activities.
3. Prepared by. The chef or head cook responsible for completing the worksheet refers to the employee duty schedule and assigns work accordingly. When the production worksheet is posted one day in advance of preparation, employees know exactly what their duties will be and can plan work time efficiently.
4. Time of preparation. When food is prepared too early there may be a loss of quality in both taste and appearance. If food is not prepared on time, there may be undue pressure on employees and possibly chaotic situations in a rush to meet culinary schedules. Both situations can be eliminated by indicating the time to begin preparation.
5. Instructions. Information in this column may simply state, "Use recipe no. 42," or instructions may be given to serve larger portions of an entree item for a special activity.
6. Amount used. This column is to be completed at the end of the serving period. Information is obtained from the tray line, cafeteria, and special activities supervisors.
7. Amount left. The amount used is subtracted from the amount prepared to equal the amount left. The information is important for use in forecasting the amount to prepare during the next menu cycle.
8. Disposition. All leftover foods should be accounted for in some manner. The shift supervisor or person responsible for completing the form must indicate what disposition was made of leftover items, such as chill-stored, freezer-stored, or discarded.

At the end of service, additional information is recorded at the bottom of the worksheet by the shift supervisor, such as unexpected guests, weather conditions, or other significant events affecting the number of persons served. As a control tool, management can readily observe whether there were any irregularities during the preparation and service of the meal, and note the accuracy of forecasting. For example, if enough food were requisitioned and prepared for 500 portions, 450 portions were served, and no portions were left, management must find out what happened to 50 portions of food. The effectiveness of the production worksheet depends on managerial practices from menu planning and standardized recipes through food purchasing.

Food Production for Modified Diets

Food production for modified diets is often combined with the production of food for regular diets, personnel, and guests. The general practice is to omit seasoning and added fat for a given number of servings to be served to patients on modified diets. All patients are served plain, unseasoned food, regardless of type of diet modification. Cooks in the main production area often do not take the time to prepare tasty, attractive meals for modified diets. The primary purpose of a medical food service operation is to provide nutritious, appetizing, and attractive meals to patients; yet emphasis is often put on merchandising food served to physicians, administrators, employees, and others.

In some food service operations, there is a separate unit for the preparation of modified diet foods with specialty

Exhibit 12–3 Production Worksheet

UNIT ____________ MEAL ____________ DAY ____________ DATE ____________

(1)	(2) Amount Needed*						(3)	(4)	(5)	(6)	(7)	(8)
Food Item	Reg	Ca	Na	Fa	Fi	Li	Prepared by	Time of Preparation	Instructions	Amount Used	Amount Left	Disposition

Projected Number of Meals: Patients ____________ Cafeteria ____________ Other ____________

Actual Meals Served: Patients ____________ Cafeteria ____________ Other ____________

Comments: ____

____

Prepared by: ____________________ Shift Supervisor: ____________________

*Reg, regular; Ca, restricted calories; Na, restricted sodium; Fa, restricted fat; Fi, restricted fiber; Li, full liquid.

cooks assigned. Cooks assigned to this unit have a basic knowledge and understanding of diet modification and are trained in preparation techniques applicable to the various diets. The advantages of this type of production design are as follows:

- Assigned personnel will have the time to individualize the preparation of food for the various diets.
- Cooks can respond to special requests related to complicated or multirestricted diets.
- With a knowledge of diet modification, cooks can add allowed seasonings to make diets more appetizing.
- Cooks will have time to prepare combination dishes, as prescribed, such as beef cubes with vegetables, macaroni and cheese, tuna-noodle casserole, and other foods that normally are served only to patients on a regular diet.
- Cooks will be able to prepare specialty-type items for patients on restricted diets, for example, the preparation of bread using nonwheat flour for patients with wheat intolerance; pancakes with egg whites for restricted cholesterol diets, and other special considerations.
- Cooks will be able to prepare tasty cream soups, restricted calorie soups, and dressings for salads.

Patients will appreciate the attention given to preparation of food for modified diets, and employees will take pride in preparing food that patients will eat and enjoy.

Nourishments

Nourishments are foods served to patients, either as a supplement or as a part of the regular dietary regimen. Serving time is designated approximately two to three hours after the regular meal, such as 10:00 AM, 2:00 PM, and 8:00 PM. All patients normally receive the night nourishment; patients on modified diets, such as diets for diabetics, may receive nourishment three times a day. The nourishment menu should be planned on a rotation basis to ensure that a variety of food is served (Exhibit 12–4). For example, a patient on a clear liquid diet should not receive the same flavor for three consecutive times until the prepared batch is used. The employee assigned to nourishment preparation should have a basic knowledge of foods allowed on various diets and be able to measure and weigh prescribed amounts with accuracy. In a large facility, the preparation of nourishments is a full-time position. Because nourishments are an important part of the patient's total daily food intake, the task should not be assigned to any employee at random.

Special Activities

Medical food service operations should agree to provide food for special activities only after due consideration is given to the impact that the increased workload will have on patient food service. The handling of special activities for in-house and outside professional groups can enhance the image of the hospital and serve as good public relations, but such activities should not be promoted at the expense of patient care. To operate smoothly, special activities must be well planned.

Staffing, menus, and other arrangements require special attention. A special activities supervisor is needed for facilities catering to special activities on a daily basis. Other employees need to be assigned for table setup, arranging tables and chairs, and transporting food and other supplies to the service areas. Professional waiters and waitresses may work on an on-call basis. If elaborate or large catered functions are planned, it may be necessary to include a catering chef position as part of staffing.

A selection of precosted menus should be available to assist groups in making special requests. Groups can select preferred foods and know exactly how much they will cost. The cost per serving, whether it is for a coffee break or an elaborate dinner, should include all labor, food, and overhead costs. Additional charges may be assessed for alcoholic beverages, special floral arrangements, and other special requests. To allow the requesting party an opportunity to select preferred combinations, suggested menu items can be grouped as shown in Table 12–1, using the a la carte pricing method. Standardized recipes, indicating portion sizes, should be used for all catered food items. For example, a sandwich plate recipe may include both the ingredient amounts and a diagram showing how the ingredients should be arranged on the plate.

Record keeping is an important task associated with special activities. There should not be any mix-up concerning dates and times of planned activities. A reservation form such as Exhibit 12–5 can be used to document requests. Complete arrangements, including table and seating patterns, should be agreed upon so that correct charges can be made. All food requested, whether it is a pot of coffee or a gourmet dinner for a large party, should be charged to some account. Each request for special activity is charged to an account approved by administration, and processed for credit to the food service department. Copies of the approved reservation should be routed to the special activities supervisor, the requesting group, the accounting office, and the food service director's office.

VENDING SERVICE

Vending services are frequently offered in medical food service operations to accommodate employees and guests during hours when the cafeteria is closed. Services may be provided in-house or by outside vendors. Employees scheduled for night shifts often complain about the lack of variety

Exhibit 12–4 Sample Nourishment Menu

Day	Regular	Restricted Calories	Restricted Sodium	Restricted Fat	Restricted Fiber	Full Liquid	Clear Liquid
Sunday	Turkey Sandwich	FF Turkey Sandwich*	SF Turkey Sandwich†	FF Turkey Sandwich	Turkey Sandwich	Ice Cream	Apple Juice
	Pear Nectar	Pear Nectar	Pear Nectar	Pear Nectar	Pear Nectar		
Monday	Lime Sherbet	Diet Gelatin	Lime Sherbet	Lime Sherbet	Lime Sherbet	Lime Sherbet	Lime Gelatin
	Vanilla Wafers	Vanilla Wafers	Vanilla Wafers	Vanilla Wafers	Vanilla Wafers		
Tuesday	Cheese and Crackers	Cheese and Crackers	SF Cheese and SF Crackers	Low-fat Cheese and Crackers	Cheese and Crackers	Chocolate Milkshake	Cherry Popsicle
	Grape Juice	Grape Juice	Grape Juice	Grape Juice	Grape Juice		
Wednesday	Sugar Cookies	Vanilla Wafers	Sugar Cookies	Sugar Cookies	Sugar Cookies	Vanilla Yogurt	Orange Gelatin
	Whole Milk	Skim Milk	Whole Milk	Skim Milk	Whole Milk		
Thursday	Peanut Butter and Crackers	Peanut Butter and Crackers	SF Peanut Butter and SF Crackers	Canned Pears	Canned Pears	Orange Sherbet	Grape Popsicle
				Graham Crackers			
	Pineapple Juice	Pineapple Juice	Pineapple Juice	Pineapple Juice	Pineapple Juice		
Friday	Strawberry Gelatin	Diet Gelatin	SF Strawberry Gelatin	Strawberry Gelatin	Strawberry Gelatin	Strawberry Gelatin	Strawberry Gelatin
	Graham Crackers	Graham Crackers	Graham Crackers	Graham Crackers	Vanilla Wafers		
	Orange Juice	Orange Juice	Orange Juice	Orange Juice	Orange Juice	Whole Milk	
Saturday	Canned Peaches	Diet Peaches	Canned Peaches	Canned Peaches	Canned Peaches	Vanilla Milkshake	Ginger Ale
	Whole Milk	Skim Milk	Whole Milk	Skim Milk	Whole Milk		

*FF indicates fat-free.

†SF indicates salt-free.

Table 12–1 Suggested Menu for Special Activities

Food Category	*Suggested Menu Items*	*Cost*
Appetizers	Fresh Fruit Cup, Mint Garnish	________
	Grapefruit Juice, Lemon Twist	________
	Manhattan Clam Chowder	________
	French Onion Soup, Cheese Croutons	________
	Jumbo Shrimp Cocktail, Lemon Wedge	________
Entrees	Broiled Filet Mignon, Mushroom Cap	________
	Standing Rib Roast au Jus	________
	Breaded Center Cut Pork Chop	________
	Roast Pork Loin, Baked Apples	________
	Crusty Herb-Fried Chicken	________
	Baked Chicken Breast, Mushroom Sauce	________
	Roast Turkey, Cornbread Dressing	________
	Marinated Lamb Chops, Mint Jelly	________
	Stuffed Flounder	________
	Crispy Fried Farm-Raised Catfish	________
Potatoes or Substitutes	Baked Potato, Sour Cream	________
	Boiled Potatoes, Parsley Flakes	________
	Steamed Noodles, Alfredo Sauce	________
	Rice Pilaf	________
	Whole-Kernel Corn, Pimento	________
	Candied Sweet Potatoes	________
Vegetables	French Green Beans Amandine	________
	Broccoli Spears, Hollandaise Sauce	________
	Buttered Green Peas, Pearl Onions	________
	Baby Asparagus Spears	________
	Miniature Whole Carrots	________
Salads	Perfection Jell-O Mold	________
	Tossed Salad, Bleu Cheese Dressing	________
	Caesar Salad, Caesar Dressing	________
	Sliced Tomato & Cottage Cheese	________
	Lettuce, Cucumber, & Tomato, Ranch Dressing	________
Desserts	Lemon Sherbet or Peppermint Ice Cream	________
	Strawberry Shortcake, Whipped Cream	________
	Peach or Apple Cobbler	________
	Cheesecake, Strawberries/Cherries	________
Breads	Hard Wheat Roll	________
	Small Onion Roll	________
	Buttermilk Biscuit, Honey	________
Beverage	Coffee—Regular, Decaffeinated	________
	Tea—Iced, Hot	________
	Other	________

and quality of food available. To resolve the problem, some food service operations remain open for 24 hours; other operations prefer vending services. When the vending is in-house, the same high standards of quality should apply as for other services provided by the department. Advantages of in-house vending are the following:

- A variety of food items can be served, such as fresh fruits and salads. Complete meals can be cold-plated as in the procedure for patient service, using a microwave for reheating.
- Food quality can be controlled by removing unused items and replenishing with fresh food daily.

Exhibit 12–5 Special Activity Reservation Form

Name of Group: ______________________ Date of Activity: __________

Time of Activity: __________________ From: ________ To: __________

Type of Activity (Luncheon, Tea, Coffee Break, etc.): ______________________

____

Number expected: ____________Type of Service (Table, Buffet):____________

Type of Serviceware (Disposables, China, Silver Service): ________________

____

____

Menu:

Seating Arrangement:

Special Equipment Needs:______________________________________

____

____

____

Additional information (fresh floral arrangements, table arrangements, flowers at each table, small vase for each table, etc.):

____

____

____

Requested by: ________________ Acct. No.: __________ Date: __________

Approved by: ________________ Date: ____________

______________________ Date: ____________

Assistant Administrator

- Safety and sanitation is assured. Machines can be cleaned and checked for proper temperature on a daily basis. Preparation dates can be stamped on all perishables to ensure freshness.
- Foods provided by an outside vending company are limited to those with an extended shelf-life.
- With in-house repair staff, there is less waiting when machines malfunction.

Although there may be improved quality of food served when using in-house vending, there are also certain disadvantages:

- Additional staffing is required to prepare food items in an attractive and appetizing manner.
- Time is spent in training and supervising employees to load the machines properly and to rotate food items regularly to ensure freshness.
- Additional menu planning responsibilities are required. Vending menus must be an integral part of menu planning to avoid depending on the use of leftover foods.
- Increased supervision is necessary to ensure safety and sanitation. Food items must be dated, machines maintained in a clean and sanitary condition, and temperatures controlled.
- There is an increased cost for equipment and supplies. This cost includes the initial cost to purchase or rent machines, the maintenance and repairs, and the paper supplies designed especially for vending machines.

QUALITY CONTROL

The control of quality is a continuous process and should be closely monitored from menu planning until the food item is served to the consumer. Factors that affect the quality of food during the production stage are cooking time and temperature and the cooking method.

Time and Temperature

Control of these two variables is related to the type of product, size, thickness, degree of tenderness, composition of the food, temperature of the food, batch size, type of equipment, and degree of doneness desired. Depending on the qualities to be developed in the end product, some foods are cooked for a short period of time at high temperatures, whereas other foods are cooked at low temperatures for a long period of time.

Most roast meats are cooked at low temperatures to retain moisture and to improve flavor and texture. Thin cuts of meat, such as steaks, may be cooked at high temperatures for short periods of time to produce a brown attractive appearance but not long enough to burn or dry out the meat. Time and temperature charts have been developed as a guideline for meat cookery. As shown in Table 12–2, the cooking time is based on minutes per pound for each roast at refrigerated temperature. As noted, a longer time period is required for a boneless, rolled, and tied roast compared with a rib roast with bones included. The chart is based on meat that is cut according to Institutional Meat Purchasing (IMP)–National Association of Meat Purveyors (NAMP) standards. For other cuts of roast beef, such as a flat cut, which requires less cooking time, the chart may not be an accurate guide.

One of the best methods for determining the degree of doneness is with the use of a meat thermometer (Figure 12–5). According to standards published in the *Food Service Sanitation Manual* (U.S. Department of Health and Human Services 1976), "a metal-type numerically scaled indicating thermometer, accurate to ± 2°F, is the type approved for assuring proper internal cooking, holding, or refrigeration temperature of all potentially hazardous foods." An important aspect of meat cookery is that heat must be applied to all parts of the food to a temperature of at least 140°F. The exception is for rare roast beef, which may be cooked to a rare stage of 130°F. Pork and poultry require a much higher minimum temperature (Table 12–3).

Time and temperature are critical for seafood, because those products are frequently overcooked. Except for broiled shellfish and oven-fried breaded fish where a brown surface is desired, fish is cooked for a short period of time at moderate to high temperatures (Table 12–4).

Most vegetables can be cooked to a desirable state in a short period of time. Time and temperatures vary depending on the kind of vegetable and the type of equipment used. Vegetables cooked on the top of a stove in a pot of water take longer than those cooked in low- or high-pressure steamers. In medical food service operations, most vegetables are cooked in high-compression steamers for two to three minutes. The use of progressive cookery methods, whereby small batches are cooked throughout the serving period, is recommended for maximum retention of color, texture, flavor, and nutritive value. Consider the following measures in controlling nutrient losses:

- Purchase food of high quality. Wilted vegetables will have a lower nutritive value than crisp fresh vegetables because of evaporation of moisture.
- Store all foods at the proper temperature and humidity. Undue shrinkage results when the humidity is too low, causing nutrient and weight losses.
- Use the FIFO system for storing food to avoid excessive storage periods.
- Avoid excess trimming of vegetables and fruits, because some nutrients such as ascorbic acid are concentrated near the skin.
- Cook vegetables such as potatoes and carrots with skins on whenever possible.
- Outer leaves of green vegetables are often higher in vitamins and minerals than the center or the core. Avoid excess triming of vegetables such as cabbage and lettuce. The less tender leaves from cabbage can be cooked first, for a longer period of time, then crisp inner leaves may be added near the end of the cooking cycle.
- Avoid soaking of vegetables and fruits. Prolonged soaking periods cause loss of nutrients, especially ascorbic acid and thiamine.
- To prevent solubility of minerals and vitamins, cook vegetables in steamer without water; if water is added, use as little as possible.
- Do not add baking soda to green vegetables. The vegetables will retain a bright green color, but the soda will cause a loss of nutrients, such as ascorbic acid.
- Practice progressive cookery methods, whereby food is cooked in small batches, as needed.
- Cook vegetables and fruits whole, when possible. Dicing or cutting into small pieces reduces cooking time, but favors the loss of water-soluble nutrients as a result of greater surface exposure.

Method of Cooking

Food is cooked to make it more digestible, to destroy bacteria, and to increase palatability for some products. The cooking method is determined by a number of factors for different products (Table 12–5). Dry and moist heat methods of

Table 12–2 Timetable for Roasting Beef

Cut	Approximate Weight of Single Roast (lb)	No. of Roasts in Oven	Approximate Total Weight of Roasts (lb)	Oven Temperature (°F)	Interior Temperature of Roast when Removed from Oven (°F)	Minutes per Pound Based on One Roast	Minutes per Pound Based on Total Weight of Roast in Oven	Approximate Total Cooking Time
Rib, roast ready, no. 109	20–25			250	130	13–15		4½–5 hours
					140	15–17		5–6 hours
					150	17–19		6–6½ hours
Rib, roast ready, no. 109	20–25			300	130	10–12		4–4½ hours
					140	12–14		4½–5 hours
					150	14–16		5–5½ hours
Rib, roast ready, no. 109		2	56	300	130		5–6	5–5½ hours
					140		6	6 hours
					150		7–8	6–7 hours
Ribeye roll, no. 112 or no. 112A	4–6			350	140	18–20		1⅓–1⅔ hours
					160	20–22		1½–2 hours
					170	22–24		1⅔–2¼ hours
Full tenderloin, no. 189 or no. 190	4–6			425	140			45–60 minutes
Strip loin, boneless, no. 180	10–12			325	140	10		1½–2 hours
Top sirloin butt, no. 184	8			300	140	25		3½ hours
Top (inside) round, no. 168	10			300	140	18–19		3–3¼ hours
					150	22–23		3½–4 hours
Top (inside) round, no. 168	15			300	140	15		3½–4 hours
					150	17		4–4½ hours
Round, rump and shank off, boneless, tied, special, no. 165B	50			250	140	12		10 hours
					155	14		11–12 hours

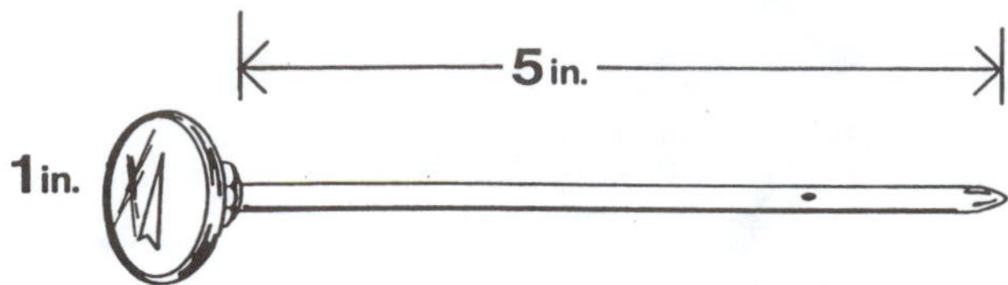

Figure 12–5 Dial Face Metal Probe Type Thermometer Has an Accuracy of ± 2°F (± 1°C) and a Temperature Range of 0° to 220°F(–18° to 110°C). *Source:* NSF International (formerly the National Sanitation Foundation) 1996.

cooking commonly used in medical food service operations are as follows:

- *Roasting* (dry) is to cook food uncovered in an oven without added liquids. The term is used interchangeably with *baking*. For example, ham appears on the menu as "baked ham," but it is really cooked by roasting. In addition to meats, poultry, and fish, some vegetables such as potatoes and squash may be roasted. Oven baking is a popular cooking method for fish fillets or steaks, either breaded or unbreaded. Dry heat methods are suitable for tender cuts of meat. Roasting is a popular method of cooking for poultry, with the exception of young chickens. Because of the lack of fat in young chickens, other methods such as frying may be more appropriate. In common usage, the term *baking* is reserved primarily for desserts, breads, and casseroles.
- *Pot roasting* (moist) is not a true roast method. Because liquid is added to the meat after it is browned and covered during the cooking process, the method is considered a form of braising. The method is popular for less tender cuts of beef.
- *Broiling* (dry) is to cook by direct heat. The heat source may be above or below the food to be cooked. The method is used for tender cuts of meat such as steaks and chops, fish with high fat content, young poultry, and vegetables and fruits, such as tomatoes, grapefruit, and bananas. Char broilers (electric or gas) are frequently used because of the distinctive charcoal flavor. When fish or chicken appears on the menu in a medical food service operation, the method of preparation is often oven broiled. Bacon is pan broiled in the oven by arranging strips of bacon on an 18 × 26-in sheet pan and baking at a temperature of 400°F for approximately 20 minutes.
- *Grilling* (dry) is to cook on a hot, solid surface with or without added fat. For most meats, it is not necessary to add fat because of the high fat content already in the meat. Fat is usually added for vegetables such as onions and mushrooms. When fat is added to the grill, the process is similar to sautéeing. The grill is frequently located near the service area so that progressive cookery can take place throughout the serving period. Foods that deteriorate in quality when held for long periods, such as eggs, pancakes, and hamburgers, are cooked in small batches on a grill.
- *Frying* (dry) is to cook food submerged in fat. The method is used less frequently in medical food service operations because of the emphasis on reduced fat intake. Frying is especially popular and suitable for breaded products such as fish, shrimp, young chicken, and chops.
- *Sautéeing* (dry) is to cook in a small amount of fat. In medical food service, sautéeing is a limited method of food preparation.
- *Steaming* (moist) is to cook in steam with or without pressure. Steaming is one of the most popular and versatile methods of preparing food in medical food service operations. The method is used for meats, vegetables, and other foods such as hard-cooked and scrambled eggs. Low- and high-pressure steam equipment, along with the tilting skillet, have practically eliminated the use of top-of-the stove cooking on a range.
- *Braising, Swissing*, and *fricasseeing* (moist) are methods used when meat is dredged in seasoned flour and browned in a small amount of fat; the cooking process completed by adding a small amount of liquid, covering, and cooking in the oven until tender. Popular menu items are braised short ribs of beef, Swiss steak, and chicken fricassee.

The use of standardized recipes and the production worksheet can resolve many of the problems associated with food quality. Both time and temperature can be controlled if these tools are used properly. When time, temperature, and method of cooking are adhered to, other desirable qualities such as flavor, color, texture, and nutrients are also controlled.

Table 12–3 Minimal Internal Temperature for Meat and Poultry Products

Food Item	*Temperature (°F)*
Beef	130–140
Poultry, poultry stuffing, and stuffed meats	165
Pork and any food containing pork	150

QUANTITY CONTROL

Quantity control in food production is concerned with minimizing food waste to maximize expected yield. When the menu is planned, a major factor used in the decision to put a food item on the menu is whether the portion size is within established monetary allowances. When the yield is less than expected because of controllable loss, there is a

Table 12–4 Temperatures for Seafood Cookery

Type of Seafood	*Recommended Cooking Temperature*	*Approximate Time (min)*
Lobster—broiled, split	Broil	10
Lobster and shrimp—steamed, whole	15-lb pressure	3
Fish—deep-fried	350°–375°F	4
Fish—oven-fried, breaded	450°–500°F	20–25
Fish—poached	185°F	4–5
Fish—oven-baked, unbreaded fillet	350°–400°F	15–20

waste of food and increased cost. Care must be taken to ensure that the portion planned is the amount produced and subsequently served. During the production stage, losses can occur as food is prepared, cooked, and portioned. Quantity losses can be minimized during prepreparation with the use of an ingredient room.

Ingredient Room

The ingredient room is an area where ingredients are measured or weighed and food is preprepared for the cooking or final stage of preparation. Prepreparation involves washing, peeling, cubing, slicing, and dicing of fruits and vegetables, and weighing, trimming, cubing, dicing, and portioning of meat. There should be a separate room for the prepreparation of meat or at least a separate area of the room with a sink and counter to be used only for raw meats. This measure is necessary to prevent cross-contamination of raw fruits and vegetables that require no further cooking.

To be effective, all food should flow directly from storage to the ingredient room, then to the various production areas. Exceptions may be for foods such as dry cereals, instant beverages, commercially baked products, ice cream, milk, and other such items requiring no additional preparation. Ingredient room procedures, in general, are as follows:

1. Using standardized recipes, food is requisitioned from storage for a given meal or for all meals to be served on a given day.
2. All ingredients are measured for each item on the menu. Seasonings are labeled so that cooks can accurately follow the recipe in adding ingredients. All food is washed or prepared in some other manner, as required, at least one day in advance.
3. Food for each menu item is placed on a separate tray and stored dry or refrigerated until ready for use by cooks.
4. On the day of use, trays are issued to cooks for final production.
5. All reusable leftover food is returned to the ingredient room. The food will be reissued as part of a new menu item. This practice prevents cooks from altering recipes by adding extra ingredients at their own discretion.

Cleaned fruits and vegetables may be stored in plastic bags or plastic containers with covers. Potatoes and carrots are usually peeled and stored in containers with enough water to cover the products. The use of sulfiting agents to prevent discoloration of fruits and vegetables is discouraged. The Michigan Department of Public Health, acting under Section 2-101 of the Food Sanitation Code, informed local health departments that fresh fruits, vegetables, and other products served in the raw state that have been treated with sulfiting agents may be served only if the customer is informed that such agents have been added. (A memorandum was sent to all local health departments on May 2, 1983.) The recommendation was in response to research indicating that certain individuals, primarily asthmatics, may suffer life-threatening respiratory distress when exposed to products treated with

Table 12–5 Factors Affecting Cooking Method for Different Foods

Meat	*Poultry*	*Fish*	*Fruits and Vegetables*
Marbling and fat content	Fat content	Fat content	Texture (cellulose)
Age	Age		Color (green, red, yellow, white)
Connective tissue	Size		Flavor (mild, strong)
Cut			Acidity
Kind of animal			Moisture

sulfites. Although cooking reduces the effects of sulfites, some residue may be left.

As of July 9, 1986, the Food and Drug Administration (FDA) has required the food industry to declare the presence of sulfites on product labels if the sulfite level in a finished food amounts to 10 or more parts per million (Lecos and Blumenthal 1990). The Food, Drug, and Cosmetic Act also requires that labels must so note when finished, packaged foods contain sulfites as preservatives. Products so labeled include lemon juice, maraschino cherries, grape juice, some packaged fresh mushrooms, dried fruits and vegetables, and some canned soups.

The second regulation, approved in August 1986, revokes the "generally recognized as safe" status of sulfites used on raw produce. This regulation primarily affects salads and salad bars in restaurants and other food service outlets, and also applies to raw produce sold in grocery stores and supermarkets. In March 1990, the FDA added fresh, peeled potatoes that are "served or sold unpackaged and unlabeled" to consumers to the list of products on which the use of sulfiting agents no longer will be allowed by the agency. The FDA advises consumers concerned about sulfites in food to ask restaurant personnel if they are used and to avoid restaurant foods in which sulfites may be used.

Sulfur dioxide and various forms of inorganic sulfites that release sulfur dioxide when used on food ingredients are known collectively as sulfiting agents. On food labels, their presence may be identified as sulfur dioxide, potassium bisulfite, potassium metabisulfite, sodium bisulfite, sodium metabisulfite, or sodium sulfite. Some of the major food categories in which they are used include the following:

- avocado dip and guacamole
- beer
- cider
- cod (dried)
- fruit (fresh peeled, dried, or maraschino type)
- fruit juices, purées, and fillings
- gelatin
- potatoes (fresh peeled, frozen, dried, or canned)
- salad dressing (dry mix) and relishes
- salads (particularly at salad bars)
- sauces and gravies (canned or dried)
- sauerkraut and coleslaw
- shellfish (fresh, frozen, canned, or dried), including clams, crabs, lobsters, scallops, and shrimp)
- soups (canned or dried)
- vegetables (fresh peeled, frozen, canned, or dried), including fresh mushrooms
- wine vinegar
- wine and wine coolers

The ingredient room system promotes quantity control and saves valuable time for highly paid, skilled employees. No time is wasted gathering supplies before production can begin. The emphasis on increased productivity and cost control is of concern to some researchers. According to Livingston and Chang (1979), the progress made in production control may well be a step backward in terms of nutrient retention. It is suggested that ingredient preparation should take place as close to the cooking and final preparation as possible. Adequate ingredient room facilities should be provided to reduce excessive advance preparation and extended holding of raw ingredients.

DISASTER FEEDING PLANS

As mandated by the Joint Commission on Accreditation of Healthcare Organizations (1988), "The dietetic department/service shall be able to meet the nutritional needs of patients and staff during a disaster, consistent with the capabilities of the hospital and community served." To fulfill this mandate, the food service department must have plans for emergency feeding in the "ready" state at all times.

Disasters may be classified as natural or man-made and may occur from both external and internal sources. Natural disasters include earthquake, fire, flood, hurricane, and tornado. Man-made disasters include chemical, nuclear, and atomic warfare and bomb and bomb threats. The disaster may be for a short or long period of time. The food service department must be able to respond with essential services as soon as possible. Local health authorities must be notified immediately when a disaster occurs that may possibly involve food contamination.

Emergency feeding plans must provide for a safe food and water supply. Menu planning should progress from simple, basic food to more complex meals. An initial feeding of a hot beverage and crackers or cookies will have a calming effect on both patient and personnel until food of a more substantial nature can be prepared. It may not be advisable initially to serve uncooked foods such as fruits and vegetables, depending on the amount of available safe water. The first hot food may consist of a single-dish type, such as stew. After full assessment of disaster conditions, available food, water, equipment, refrigeration, and utilities, a full meal can be prepared.

A supply of food and water should be available and stored off-site, in a location convenient to the facility. Depending on resulting conditions such as no refrigeration, no cooking facilities, and no safe water, it may be necessary to rely on canned and packaged foods that can be eaten cold. The suggested food list is as follows:

- ready-to-eat cereals
- evaporated milk
- canned fruits and fruit juice
- canned meat and beans

- processed cheese requiring no refrigeration
- crackers, cookies, and canned bread
- candy, jam, and jelly (individually wrapped)
- instant coffee and instant cocoa (if cooking facilities are available)
- canned soup and vegetables (if cooking facilities are available)

All bottled, potable water must be from a source that complies with all health laws and must be handled and stored in a way that protects it from contamination. Emergency foods must be inspected and rotated periodically. The emergency feeding plan should be checked and approved by local health authorities. In some communities, a cooperative emergency feeding plan is in effect. In this type of arrangement, the unaffected facility will prepare and transport food and beverages to the affected facility.

SAFETY AND SANITATION

Producing food under safe and sanitary conditions must be an integral part of the total systems approach. For medical food service operations, preventing food-borne illness is a critical task because of the nature of the clients. Patients enter the medical facility under varying physical conditions and are therefore more susceptible to adverse effects of food-borne illness than are clients served in other types of food service operations. The food service director must be aware of the source and cause of food-borne illness and take preventive measures to eliminate hazardous conditions.

Prevention of Food-Borne Illness

To prevent food-borne illness, food must be protected from filth, pathogenic microorganisms, and toxic chemicals. Bacteria cannot be seen with the naked eye; they are single-cell organisms that are visible with the aid of a microscope. "Sanitary" means that the product or article is free from pathogenic bacteria. It is possible for a product or article to be clean as inspected visually, yet it may not be sanitary. Microorganisms, especially pathogenic bacteria that are capable of causing food-borne illness, are of major concern in producing safe food. Other microorganisms that may cause illness are viruses and trichinae. Hundreds of kinds of germs can cause food poisoning. Most bacteria need warmth, moisture, and food to thrive. Some bacteria need air, whereas others thrive better without air. Bacteria thrive best in potentially hazardous foods at temperatures between 45°F and 145°F. A potentially hazardous food has been defined by the U.S. Department of Health and Human Services (1976) as "any food that consists in whole or in part of milk or milk products, eggs, meat, poultry, fish, shellfish, edible crustacea, or other ingredients in a form capable of supporting rapid and progressive growth of infectious or toxigenic microorganisms."

Salmonellae are bacteria occurring in the intestinal tracts of humans and animals. They can cause severe illness (salmonellosis) in humans which can result in death. One type of salmonella causes typhoid fever. Infected food animals can transmit the disease to humans through contaminated meat, fish, poultry, and other animal products such as eggs and milk. The usual symptoms are fever, diarrhea, and sometimes vomiting. The disease can be dangerous for the very young, very old, and persons already weakened by illness. Salmonella can be destroyed by heat. Pasteurization kills the organism in milk. Certain chemicals also can destroy the organism.

Preventive measures include observing the danger temperature zone for prepared foods by cooking and reheating foods to an internal temperature of 165°F, cleaning and sanitizing work surfaces and utensils used to prepare food of animal origin, establishing and enforcing proper hand-washing procedures for workers, and restricting work for employees suffering from diarrhea, fever, and vomiting.

Staphylococcus aureus is a bacterium that produces a toxin causing staphylococcus (staph) food poisoning. Humans carry these organisms on the hands and arms, in the nose and throat, on hairy regions of the body, and in infected boils and abscesses. The usual symptoms of vomiting, diarrhea, and abdominal cramps occur within three to eight hours after eating contaminated food. The toxin is very heat stable and is not destroyed by ordinary cooking methods. The illness is caused by unsanitary work habits in handling protein foods and by exposing such foods to warm temperatures for extended periods of time.

Preventive measures include making sure employees are free of infected lesions and respiratory illness, adhering to proper time-temperature procedures for holding food, and encouraging employees to practice good personal hygiene.

Clostridium botulinum produces a deadly toxin that causes a rare illness known as botulism. The main source of the bacteria is soil, and the organism may be found in almost any place. In food, the toxin is usually found in underprocessed, nonacid, home-canned products. The toxin can be destroyed by boiling food for 15 minutes. The symptoms are nausea, vomiting, dizziness, and breathing difficulties that may result in death.

Preventive measures include avoiding the use of home-canned foods (or boiling them for 15 minutes), and avoiding the use of commercially canned foods that show signs of spoilage such as bulging, rusting, and leaking.

Critical Control Points and Control Points as Related to Production

Both critical control points (CCPs) and control points (CPs) are intended to prevent contamination through mishandling and to prevent the rapid and progressive growth of disease-causing organisms that are naturally present in food. The following measures are recommended for preparing food in a sanitary and safe manner:

- Hot food should be served hot (140°F and above) and cold food should be served cold (45°F or below). Avoid hazardous food temperatures. The temperature between 45°F and 140°F is considered the danger zone for prepared food because bacterial growth is rapid if food remains in the danger zone for two hours or more.
- Prepare potentially hazardous food in small batches to avoid preparation time that requires raw food to be unrefrigerated for more than a one-hour period.
- Potentially hazardous foods requiring cooking should be cooked to heat all parts of the food to an internal temperature of at least 140°F, with the following exceptions:

  1. Poultry, poultry stuffing, stuffed meats, and stuffings containing meat must be cooked to heat all parts of the food to at least 165°F with no interruption in the cooking process.
  2. Pork and any food containing pork must be cooked to heat all parts of the food to at least 150°F.
  3. Rare roast beef must be cooked to an internal temperature of at least 130°F, unless otherwise ordered by the immediate consumer.

- Potentially hazardous foods requiring refrigeration after preparation must be cooled rapidly to an internal temperature of 45°F or below. Foods prepared in large quantities or of large volume must be cooled rapidly, utilizing shallow pans, agitation, quick chilling, or water circulation external to the food container.
- All fresh fruits and vegetables, dried fruits, raw poultry, fish, and variety meats must be washed prior to use.
- Liquid, frozen, and dry eggs and egg products are to be used only for cooking and baking purposes.
- Reconstituted dry milk products and dry milk products may be used in instant desserts, whipped potatoes, or for cooking and baking. The product should not be served as a beverage.
- Avoid the use of home-canned foods in quantity food service. Refuse all donations. Underprocessed home-canned food is a frequent source of the deadly toxin of *Clostridium botulinum*.
- Poultry stuffing should be cooked in a separate pan rather than in the cavity of the bird. Large turkeys that are stuffed are unsafe because of the possible lack of heat penetration in the center of the cavity.
- Defrost food requiring thawing under refrigeration, not to exceed 45°F, or by one of the following:

  1. under portable running water of a temperature of 70°F or below, with sufficient water velocity to agitate and float off loose particles into the overflow
  2. in a microwave oven only when the food will be transferred immediately to conventional cooking facilities as part of a continuous cooking process or when the entire, uninterrupted cooking process takes place in the microwave oven
  3. as part of a continuous cooking process

COMPUTER ASSISTANCE IN FOOD PRODUCTION

Food production has many important facets that can be made easier, more accurate, and less time consuming by use of a computer. Delegating, timing, assigning tasks, and supervising food preparation are all part of the process of preparing food for patients and personnel. These processes can be simplified and made more orderly by standardizing individual tasks with the use of a computer. Better working conditions can be realized when employees know what they are to do, when they are to do it, and how much time is allotted for the task.

Computer programs are available that allow the manager to create standardized procedures daily for each worker. The database program would contain the position titles and an identification number for titles that indicate more than one set of job responsibilities. For example, with cross-training there may be five or more variations assigned the job title "food service worker"; for each of the variations a number is assigned (e.g., food service worker 1a, 1b, 1c, etc.). A separate file would contain the task for each production function and a master file would have menu and recipe information with capabilities for forecasting and recipe conversions. Several programs are available that provide libraries of standardized recipes with the ability to convert recipe amounts and portion size, create lists of purchase requirements, and have editing functions. The ability of the program to edit, import, and export other recipes and information diminishes concern about the compatibility of formats and allows the manager to make adjustments necessary for menu production.

Creating the master file is key to a computer-assisted food production program. Depending on the requirements of the production staff, the master file should include the following data:

- master production summary forms
- unit production forms
- employee task forms
- storeroom requisition forms
- production records
- equipment load parameters
- capability to perform production analysis

Standardization and materials control are important components of computer-assisted food production. Utilizing an ingredient room helps to control materials and encourages the standardization of products. With an ingredient room, the computer uses the identified menu and recipes to generate a list of the amounts of each ingredient needed for production. This list becomes the stores requisition. The ingredient room employee weighs and assembles the ingredients according to the updated census and as specified for each recipe. This system of ingredient control is cost efficient. The computer combines the amounts of each ingredient needed from all recipes and presents the total amount required. The difference is returned to the storeroom rather than left in the preparation area to be added to a recipe or wasted. A food cost savings can be realized, and a better product is produced.

ENERGY CONSERVATION IN FOOD PRODUCTION

More energy is consumed in the production of food than in any other activity in the food service system. To comply with energy-conservation measures, the food service director needs the understanding and cooperation of all employees in the area. To reduce the amount of energy used, the following recommendations are offered:

- Refrain from turning on all equipment and lights at the beginning of the work shift. Enforce this practice. Most morning cooks will turn on all stoves, ovens, and other equipment requiring preheat time whether or not the equipment is to be used. Also, all cafeteria lights are turned on even though the service in the cafeteria may not begin for another hour. Do not tolerate these practices.
- Label all equipment with preheat time instructions. Preheat times vary, depending on the particular piece of equipment. For example, less time is required to preheat convection ovens than deck ovens. Setting the thermostat higher will not reduce preheat time; it will only waste energy.
- Remember that use of low temperatures for roasting meats results in reduced energy, higher yield, and a more tender and juicy product.
- Programmed use and care procedures reduce fuel cost. Load ovens to full capacity and take advantage of receding heat. Use correct size cooking utensils, as much as possible. Unused space that must be heated is a waste of fuel.
- Maintain equipment in good working order. Post cleaning instructions on all major equipment. Tag all equipment in need of repair.
- Clean equipment regularly. Establish a cleaning schedule indicating when the equipment is to be cleaned and who is responsible for the task.
- Avoid overloading fryers. Overloaded baskets increase cooking time, waste energy, and produce a less desirable product. Never use temperatures higher than 375°F.
- Conduct an ongoing employee training program on the following:

  1. how to use all major equipment
  2. how to clean all major equipment
  3. how to maintain equipment
  4. how to conserve energy (See Chapter 15 for information on establishing an energy management program.)

REFERENCES

Bjorkman, A., and K.A. Delphin. 1966. Sweden's Nacka Hospital food system centralizes preparation and distribution. *Cornell Hotel and Restaurant Administration Quarterly* 7, no. 3:84–87.

Bobeng, B.J., and B.D. David. 1978. HACCP models for quality control of entree production in hospital food service systems. *Journal of the American Dietetic Association* 73:524–529.

Federal Register. 1978. *Alternative processing procedures for preparing cooked beef.* 43(85), September 2, 18681–18682.

Joint Commission on Accreditation of Healthcare Organization. 1988. *Accreditation manual for hospitals*. Chicago.

Kaud, F.A. 1972. Implementing the chilled food concept. *Hospitals* 46, no. 15:97–100.

Lecos, C., and D. Blumenthal. 1990. *Reacting to sulfites*. Reprint from FDA Consumer Magazine, DHHS Publication No. (FDA) 90-2209. Rockville, MD.

Livingston, G.E., and C.M. Chang. 1979. Food service operation design for nutrient retention in foods. *Food Technology* 33, no. 3:32–37, 42.

MacLennan, H.A. 1968. Ready foods. *Cornell Hotel and Restaurant Administration Quarterly* 8, no. 4:56–58.

McGuckian, A.T. 1969. The A.G.S. food system: Chilled pasteurized foods. *Cornell Hotel and Restaurant Administration Quarterly* 10, no. 1:87–92.

McIver, C. 1970. Batch cooking. *Hospitals* 44, no. 20:84–85.

Reed's semi-automatic food service: Moving beyond the kitchen. 1977. *Stripe* 33, no. 38:16–17. (Special service edition of newspaper published for patients and staff at Walter Reed Medical Center.)

Rinke, W.J. 1976. Three major systems reviewed and evaluated. *Hospitals* 50, no. 4:73–78.

Simler, S. 1978. Walter Reed gears up fancy kitchen. *Modern Healthcare* 8, no. 10:32–33.

U.S. Department of Health and Human Services. 1976. *Food service sanitation manual.* Washington, DC: Public Health Service, Food and Drug Administration.

CHAPTER 13

Subsystem for Distribution and Service

Service of food is the stage in the food service system when the output (prepared food product) is evaluated by the consumer. As discussed in Chapter 1, if the outcome is unacceptable, mechanisms must be available for corrective actions. In most facilities both patients and personnel are serviced simultaneously, a situation that accounts for the peak periods of operation experienced in medical food service and the complexities involved in service.

PATIENT FOOD SERVICE

Food served to patients is based on the menu selections by individual patients or as prescribed by the physician, under the supervision of a registered dietitian. Standard operation procedures should be in effect for determining the type and amount of food served to patients. The procedure used for diet ordering and menu selection varies, depending on the type of facility.

Diet Ordering

Methods of diet ordering will vary, but most procedures will consist of the following:

1. Obtain the physician's diet order (usually given on a diet request sheet prepared by nursing personnel).
2. Interview all patients prior to diet preparation to ascertain preferences.
3. Record necessary information on the patient's chart and on the master diet card maintained in the food service department.
4. Plan the menu according to established patterns, taking into consideration patient preferences.
5. Translate the diet order for meal service (special preparation notes, etc.).
6. Serve meals to patients as needed.

There should be certain policies established within the department regarding diet orders, such as the following:

- effective time for order
- changes in diet order
- requests for special foods
- new admissions
- delayed trays
- orders for diets not listed in manual
- patient diet instructions for use after the patient leaves the hospital

In nursing homes, where the length of stay is for an extended period of time, the patient census sheet is changed less frequently than in acute care facilities. A new census sheet may be written once a week, with written instructions for additions or deletions as patients are admitted or discharged during the week. In hospitals, a new census sheet (Exhibit 13–1) is prepared by nursing personnel on a daily basis and is available to food service personnel prior to service of the breakfast meal. When tray setup is accomplished the day before service, the new census sheet is used to make any necessary changes. Prior to each meal, a diet change sheet (Exhibit 13–2) is prepared by nursing personnel and forwarded to the food service department. The practice of making diet changes by telephone should be discouraged because there is no authorized documentation of changes made. In addition, the possibility of error is increased when diet orders are issued verbally. The food service department should have a copy of diet changes at least half an hour prior to tray assembly. Timely communication is important in promoting patient satisfaction.

Menu Selection

Patients on regular and modified diets have an opportunity to choose their own food when selective menus are

Exhibit 13–1 Sample Patient Census Sheet

Ward ______________	Date ______________	
Room No.	Patient's Name	Type of Diet If diabetic, include insulin order. If restricted, indicate level.

used. All patients are encouraged to select foods that will provide a nutritionally balanced diet. The choices made by the patient are monitored by the dietitian for nutritional adequacy. (See Exhibit 13–3 for a sample menu.) The reverse side of the menu may provide general introductory remarks about the department and dietetic services, and information on the food guide pyramid.

The selective menus for patients on modified diets provide the same foods, to the extent possible, as those served on the regular diet. Patients are visited by the registered dietitian and instructed on the principles of the prescribed diet prior to menu selection. Sample menus for two modified diets are given in Exhibits 13–4 and 13–5. Follow-up diet instructions are given throughout the patient's stay in the hospital. The selective menus are distributed, collected, and tabulated by dietary aides or volunteer workers. The dietary aide or volunteer may also assist patients who need help in completing the selective menu.

When nonselective menus are used, the decision regarding food choices is made by food service personnel. The amount of input from patients varies from one facility to another. One method of promoting patient satisfaction is to conduct a survey of patients' food preferences. A food preference survey (Exhibit 13–6) may be used with both selective and nonselective menu systems, but it is especially helpful when patients have no choice in the type of food served. It is not enough to determine the likes and dislikes; there must be follow-through. For example, if a patient indicates a dislike for liver, there should be a mechanism established to ensure that the patient is not served that particular food item. The information should be recorded for use by dietary personnel responsible for tray assembly and also communicated to food preparation personnel so that an alternate food item is prepared and ready for service. The dietitian will lose credibility if the patient's food preferences are ignored. A cardex type card, as shown in Exhibit 13–7, can be used to record likes and dislikes and other patient-related information.

Tray Assembly

Tray assembly may be a continuous process, depending on the type of food production used. In facilities where food is prepared in advance (cook-freeze or cook-chill), there is no delay in tray assembly. As soon as one meal is assembled and served, the process begins for the next meal. Tray assembly may also depend on whether the tray service is centralized or decentralized. In a centralized tray service, all trays are assembled in one location near the production area. By following a patient menu selection sheet or a patient meal pattern card, individual trays are assembled, checked for accuracy, and loaded on food carts or other equipment used for distribution. In most operations, food serving tables for hot and cold foods and other equipment, such as toasters and coffee urns, are conveniently arranged alongside the tray line. Food items are dished, if not preplated, and

Exhibit 13–2 Sample Diet Change Sheet

Room and Bed	Patient's Name	N.P.O.	Delay Next Meal Only	Omit Next Meal Only	Special Meal (Test)	Change in Diet	Isolation—Protection	Admission	Discharge	Transfer to:	Ward ____ Date ____ Time ____ Type of Diet: If diabetic, include insulin order. If restricted, indicate level.

Signature of Charge Nurse Must Appear Below:

6:00 AM ____________ 10:00 AM ____________

2:00 PM ____________ 5:00 AM ____________

Exhibit 13–3 Selective Menu for Regular Diet

Lunch

Please (Circle) Desired Food Items

TO START YOUR MEAL
Cranberry Juice
Tomato Soup with Crackers

ENTREES (SELECT ONE)
Submarine Sandwich
—A tasty combination of deli meals and cheeses on a crusty roll with macaroni salad

Beef Stew
—A heavy mix of beef and vegetables in a brown gravy with a flaky biscuit

DESSERTS (SELECT ONE)
Chocolate Chip Cookies
Sliced Pears

BREADS AND SPREADS
Wheat Bread
White Bread
Margarine
Hot Sauce

BEVERAGES (LIMIT 2 SELECTIONS)
Coffee
Decaf Coffee
Tea
Decaf Tea
Skim Milk
2% Milk
Whole Milk
Lemon
Cream
Cola
Ginger Ale
Diet Cola
Diet Ginger Ale

THURSDAY **DIET: REGULAR**

Name ______________ Room ______

Dinner

Please (Circle) Desired Food Items

TO START YOUR MEAL
Cranberry Juice
Tomato Soup with Crackers
Tossed Salad
Ambrosia Salad

DRESSINGS
French
Italian
Buttermilk
Mayonnaise
Hot Sauce

ENTREES (SELECT ONE)
Roast Turkey and Gravy
—With cornbread dressing, accompanied with green beans and cranberry sauce

Swiss Steak
—Braised in a rich brown sauce with whipped potatoes and green peas

DESSERTS (SELECT ONE)
Rice Pudding
Sweet Potato Pie

BREADS AND SPREADS
Wheat Bread
White Bread
Margarine
Dinner Roll

BEVERAGES (LIMIT 2 SELECTIONS)
Coffee
Decaf Coffee
Tea
Decaf Tea
Skim Milk
2% Milk
Whole Milk
Lemon
Cream
Cola
Ginger Ale
Diet Cola
Diet Ginger Ale

THURSDAY **DIET: REGULAR**

Name ______________ Room ______

Breakfast

Please (Circle) Desired Food Items

❤ Items are reduced in Sodium and/or Fat Content

FRUITS AND JUICES (SELECT ONE)
Orange Juice
Grapefruit Juice
Apple Juice
Cranberry Juice
Prune Juice
Banana
Fruit Cup

CEREALS (SELECT ONE)
Corn Flakes
Frosted Flakes
Rice Krispies
Cheerios
Raisin Bran
Shredded Wheat
Oatmeal
Cream of Wheat
Grits

BREAKFAST ENTREES (LIMIT TWO SELECTIONS)
Scrambled Eggs
Omelet
❤ Egg Substitute
Waffle with Syrup
French Toast with Syrup
Sausage
Bacon
Hash Browns

BREAKFAST BREADS AND SPREADS
Biscuit
Bagel
Muffin
Danish Pastry
Margarine
Cream Cheese
Jelly
Catsup

BEVERAGES (LIMIT 2 SELECTIONS)
Coffee
Decaf Coffee
Tea
Decaf Tea
Skim Milk
2% Milk
Whole Milk
Cream
Lemon
Honey

FRIDAY **DIET:REGULAR**

Name ______________ Room ______

Courtesy of Detroit Receiving Hospital, Detroit, Michigan.

Exhibit 13–4 Selective Menu for Calorie-Controlled Diet

Lunch

Please (Circle) Desired Food Items

❤ Items are reduced in Sodium and/or Fat Content

ENTREES_____ounces
Hamburger Deluxe
(3 Meat + 2 Starch)

Vegetable Lasagna
(3 Meat + 2 Starch)

STARCHES SELECT_____
Chicken Noodle Soup with Crackers
Mashed Potatoes
Rice
❤ Chocolate Pudding
Crackers
Wheat Bread
White Bread

VEGETABLES SELECT_____
Broccoli
Sliced Tomato Salad

DESSERTS SELECT_____
Fruit Cocktail
Fresh Fruit

FATS SELECT_____
Margarine
Cream

BEVERAGES
Coffee
Decaf Coffee
Tea
Decaf Tea
Diet Pop

MILK SELECT_____
Skim Milk
2% Milk
Whole Milk

Lemon
Hot Sauce

WEDNESDAY **DIET: CALORIE CONTROLLED**

Name ______________ Room _____

Dinner

Please (Circle) Desired Food Items

❤ Items are reduced in Sodium and/or Fat Content

ENTREES_____ounces
❤ Pork Chop with Gravy

❤ Glazed Chicken Breast

STARCHES SELECT_____
Chicken Noodle Soup with Crackers
Mashed Potatoes
Rice
Mixed Vegetables
❤ Chocolate Pudding
Crackers
Wheat Bread
White Bread
Dinner Roll

VEGETABLES SELECT_____
Carrots
❤ Three Bean Salad

DESSERTS SELECT_____
Pineapple Chunks
Fresh Fruit

FATS SELECT_____
Margarine
Cream

BEVERAGES
Coffee
Decaf Coffee
Tea
Decaf Tea
Diet Pop

MILK SELECT_____
Skim Milk
2% Milk
Whole Milk

Lemon
Hot Sauce

WEDNESDAY **DIET: CALORIE CONTROLLED**

Name ______________ Room _____

Breakfast

Please (Circle) Desired Food Items

❤ Items are reduced in Sodium and/or Fat Content

FRUITS AND JUICES SELECT_____
Orange Juice
Grapefruit Juice
Apple Juice
Cranberry Juice
Prune Juice
Banana
Fruit Cup

CEREALS / BREAKFAST BREADS SELECT_____
Corn Flakes
Rice Krispies
Cheerios
Shredded Wheat
Oatmeal
Cream of Wheat
Grits
Bread
Biscuit (omit 1 fat)
Bagel
Waffle with Diet Syrup
❤ French Toast with Diet Syrup (omit 1 fat)

BREAKFAST ENTREES SELECT_____
Scrambled Eggs
❤ Egg Substitute
Sausage (omit 1 fat)

FATS SELECT_____
Margarine
Cream

BEVERAGES
Coffee
Decaf Coffee
Tea
Decaf Tea

MILK SELECT_____
Skim Milk
2% Milk
Whole Milk

Lemon
Diet Jelly
Catsup

THURSDAY **DIET: CALORIE CONTROLLED**

Name ______________ Room _____

Courtesy of Detroit Receiving Hospital, Detroit, Michigan.

Exhibit 13–5 Selective Menu for Sodium/Fat-Controlled Diet

Lunch

Please (Circle) Desired Food Items

❤ Items are reduced in Sodium and/or Fat Content

TO START YOUR MEAL
Grape Juice
❤ Chicken Noodle Soup with Crackers

ENTREES (SELECT ONE)
Hamburger Deluxe
—A quarter pound beef patty on a bun with lettuce and tomato

❤ Lasagna
—Layers of pasta and sauce served with broccoli

DESSERTS (SELECT ONE)
Vanilla Wafers
Fruit Cocktail

BREADS AND SPREADS
Wheat Bread
White Bread
Margarine

BEVERAGES (LIMIT 2 SELECTIONS)
Coffee
Decaf Coffee
Tea
Decaf Tea
Skim Milk
Lemon
❤ Creamer
Cola
Ginger Ale
Diet Cola
Diet Ginger Ale

WEDNESDAY DIET: SODIUM/FAT CONTROLLED

Name ______________ Room ______

Dinner

Please (Circle) Desired Food Items

❤ Items are reduced in Sodium and/or Fat Content

TO START YOUR MEAL (SELECT TWO)
Grape Juice
❤ Chicken Noodle Soup with Crackers
Tossed Salad
❤ Three Bean Salad

DRESSINGS
❤ French
❤ Italian
❤ Mayonnaise

ENTREES (SELECT ONE)
❤ Country Pork Chop
—Oven fried, served with carrots and homemade escalloped apples

❤ Glazed Chicken Breast
—In our own special sauce over rice with mixed vegetables

DESSERTS (SELECT ONE)
Pineapple Chunks
❤ Chocolate Pudding

BREADS AND SPREADS
Wheat Bread
White Bread
Margarine
Dinner Roll

BEVERAGES (LIMIT 2 SELECTIONS)
Coffee
Decaf Coffee
Tea
Decaf Tea
Skim Milk
Lemon
❤ Creamer
Cola
Ginger Ale
Diet Cola
Diet Ginger Ale

WEDNESDAY DIET: SODIUM/FAT CONTROLLED

Name ______________ Room ______

Breakfast

Please (Circle) Desired Food Items

❤ Items are reduced in Sodium and/or Fat Content

FRUITS AND JUICES (SELECT ONE)
Orange Juice
Grapefruit Juice
Apple Juice
Cranberry Juice
Prune Juice
Banana
Fruit Cup

CEREALS (SELECT ONE)
Corn Flakes
Frosted Flakes
Rice Krispies
Cheerios
Raisin Ban
Shredded Wheat
Oatmeal
Cream of Wheat
Grits

BREAKFAST ENTREES (LIMIT TWO SELECTIONS)
Scrambled Eggs
❤ Egg Substitute
Waffle with Syrup
French Toast with Syrup
❤ Sausage

BREAKFAST BREADS AND SPREADS
Bread
Bagel
Margarine
Jelly
❤ Catsup

BEVERAGES (LIMIT 2 SELECTIONS)
Coffee
Decaf Coffee
Tea
Decaf Tea
Skim Milk
❤ Creamer
Lemon
Honey

THURSDAY DIET: SODIUM/FAT CONTROLLED

Name ______________ Room ______

Courtesy of Detroit Receiving Hospital, Detroit, Michigan.

Exhibit 13–6 Food Preference Survey

Name ________________ Room & Bed No. ____ Date of Admission ____

( ) Check here if you have no food dislikes.
In Column I, check only your *likes* next to the food item.
In Column II, check only your *dislikes* next to the food item.

Foods	Column I Likes	Column II Dislikes
Juice		
Fruit		
White Bread		
Whole Wheat Bread		
Milk		
Macaroni		
Fresh Fish		
Canned Fish		
Shellfish		
Pork		
Beef		
Lamb		
Liver		
Turkey		
Chicken		
Cooked Vegetables		
Raw Vegetables		
Ice Cream		
Cheese		
Eggs		

placed on the trays, which are conveyed down the line. With the cook-serve production system, assembled trays are transported to the wards and served immediately. For other production systems, food is preplated in a cold state, assembled, transported to a floor pantry or galley, and rethermalized at time of service. Trays are assembled according to room numbers, as listed on patient census sheet, not according to type of diet.

When prepared food is transported to the floor pantry in bulk form, the system is known as a decentralized tray service. The pantry is equipped with hot and cold holding equipment, plus dishwashing facilities. Empty pans are returned to the kitchen for cleaning. The decentralized tray service is not used on a large scale in medical food service today because of technological advances in equipment, layout, and design of facilities. Major problems associated with this type of service are as follows:

- High labor costs. Employees must be assigned to each service area for tray assembly, distribution, and cleanup.
- Lack of adequate supervision. The manager loses control over the amount of food served, because a supervisor cannot be in all floor pantries at the same time to observe tray assembly.
- Excessive equipment costs. Duplication of equipment occurs because each pantry must be fully equipped.
- Undesirable environmental factors. Undesirable factors, such as excessive noise generated in pantries from dishwashing and other cleanup duties and food odors close to patient areas, are a problem.

In a centralized system a tray line is usually in operation. The following procedures should be followed for the tray assembly system:

1. Assembly should be standardized for speed and accuracy. A diagram of a completed tray should be available so that employees will know exactly where to place each food item on the tray. The diagram provides for ease of checking by the line supervisor prior to loading trays onto tray carts.
2. Modified diets should be included in the regular tray assembly so that all trays in a particular unit may be served at the same time.
3. In facilities where an automatic tray line is not used, it may be necessary to assemble trays in two phases. The cold food is put on the tray in advance of serving time, and the hot food is assembled just prior to service. This procedure results in double work because the trays are handled twice.
4. Each tray should be checked for accuracy before it leaves the assembly area.

Tray Identification

Tray identification is simply a method of designating the correct food tray for each patient. Color coding is often used to identify the various modified diets. For patients using selective menus to indicate desired foods, the same menu is used for tray identification. For nonselective menu systems, the individual diet pattern must be written on color-coded cards.

Food Transport

The assembled trays must be transported to the various units for either immediate service to patients or rethermalizing prior to patient service. Types of equipment used for transport are described below.

Exhibit 13–7 Patient Record (Cardex Type)

Meal Pattern				Date	Diet Prescription Changes
Bev: B_____ L_____ D_____					
AM	PM	HS			

Likes:			Patient Profile		
				Yes	No
			Difficulty chewing		
			Difficulty swallowing		
Dislikes:			Needs help eating		
			Needs help with menu selection		
Allergies:					

Room	Name	Nourishments	Current Diet Prescription

Match-a-Tray

This type of food cart is appropriate for a cook-serve production system. The cart has cold holding space for 20 trays and the hot section has space for 20 plates and 20 soup bowls. A coffee urn is built in on top of the hot food section, and freezer space for ice cream and other frozen dessert is on top of the cold section. For distribution and service, the hot food must be removed and placed on the tray with cold foods. Careful attention is required in matching the hot food plate to the proper tray.

Uni-Tray

This cart is used for the cook-serve production system. All menu selections are placed on a single tray that is divided by a hard rubber seal to separate the cold and hot foods. The advantage of using this equipment is that the tray assembly is complete when the cart leaves the production area. No further assembly or handling prior to service to the patient is needed.

Integral Heating System

This equipment is appropriate for assembly-serve, cook-freeze-serve, and cook-chill-serve production systems. Electrical energy is converted to heat through the use of resistors fused to the bottom of the dishes. The dishes used to heat the prepared frozen or chilled food are also used for service. Preplated trays are delivered to the floor pantry in refrigerated carts. The dishes requiring heat are placed in a heating cabinet that has an electronic memory unit designed for variable programming. A variety of food items requiring different heating times can be rethermalized in the same cabinet at the same time. Cabinets may be placed in the floor pantry or transported to any patient area for use and service.

Chill-Therm

This system is appropriate for assembly-serve, cook-freeze-serve, and cook-chill-serve production systems. The transport units are designed to refrigerate and cook foods alternately in dishes on fully assembled trays. The carts contain stainless steel shelves with five dish-sized heating elements on each shelf. All foods, including cold beverages, are placed on the patient tray. Trays are loaded on carts that are transported to the patient area by monorail, where they are attached to wall units that provide refrigerated air and electrical power for hot plates. The carts remain refrigerated until the heating cycle begins. Each of the five heating elements is separately controlled and timed. Instructions for each tray are electronically coded at the tray assembly line, allowing each heater to turn on and off during the heating cycle and ensuring that each food item reaches and remains at the desired temperature. Delayed meals are individually programmed and controlled to coincide with the patient's schedule (Riggs 1981).

AMSCAR

The AMSCAR transport system is appropriate for assembly-serve, cook-freeze-serve, and cook-chill-serve production systems. Chilled or frozen food, which has been preplated, is assembled on patient trays according to menu selection and loaded on refrigerated carts. Programmed for a specific destination, the battery-operated carts travel hospital corridors at a speed of 1 mile an hour. The carts follow electronic signals generated from wires located within the corridor floors. The units can be programmed to wait at hallway intersections for clearance before proceeding, enter and leave elevators, travel through tunnels, and stop upon contact with people and other machinery. As reported in *Hospitals* (Electric carts 1982), each cart is capable of reducing "portering" hours by 80 percent to 90 percent. When the AMSCAR reaches the floor pantry, the entire inside unit can be removed and transferred to a refrigerated unit until it is time to rethermalize food items requiring heat. The AMSCAR is programmed to return to the food service department, where it goes through an automatic cart wash, then to the tray assembly area for reloading. A microwave or some other type of oven is used in the floor pantry to rethermalize food prior to service.

Unitized Base

This unit is appropriate for the cook-serve production system. All food items are placed on one tray. The entree plate (either square or round) is placed on a preheated unitized base and covered with a domed cover. A suction lifter is used to remove the heated base from a lowerator (a container for clean dishes). Insulated soup and coffee mugs, with disposable lids, are filled and placed on the tray. Square dishes are used for salads and desserts and may be left uncovered if trays are transported in enclosed carts. Tray assembly is completed in the central area; therefore the tray is ready for service when it reaches the floor pantry or patient corridor area.

Pellet System

This system is similar to the unitized base except that a metal disc (pellet) is heated in a pellet machine designed to lower one pellet at a time onto a metal base. The plate, with hot foods, is placed directly onto the hot pellet and covered with a domed cover. Insulated servers are used for other hot foods. Cold foods may be left uncovered if trays are transported in closed carts.

Insulated Component

This type of service is appropriate for the cook-serve production system. The unit is composed of a bottom plastic tray with modular shaped grooves to accommodate specially designed disposable serviceware. After filled containers are placed on the tray in the proper section, the tray is covered with a tight-fitting plastic cover. The grooves in the top covers match the grooves in the bottom tray, providing the necessary insulation. Trays can be stacked one on top of another and transported to the patient on an open cart. Initial food temperatures are maintained for over a two-hour period. The completely assembled tray is removed from the cart and served to the patient.

Food Distribution and Service

The distribution and service of patient trays may be performed by food service or other personnel. The task is less difficult when the patient's tray is completely assembled in the central area, requiring no further handling by service personnel. When food requiring heat must be thermalized in the floor pantry, the task becomes more difficult. Considering the amount of time and effort expended in presenting an acceptable product to the patient, controls during the final process of service should not be left to untrained persons with little interest in how the task is to be performed. Food service personnel responsible for distribution and service have been oriented and trained regarding the objectives, policies and procedures, and standards related to patient food service. When the task is performed by other personnel, the food service director should require a similar orientation and training for nurse's aides or other persons assigned to distribute and serve food to patients. Because nurse's aides are not directly responsible to the food service director, the training program requires the cooperation and input of nursing personnel. The training may require instruction on how to rethermalize food items in facilities using the assembly-serve, cook-freeze-serve, and cook-chill-serve production systems. An overcooked or undercooked entree can ruin the entire meal.

Tray Presentation

In presenting the food tray to patients, the following recommendations are offered:

- Every effort should be made to make mealtime a pleasant experience for the patient. The patient should be prepared for meals with an adjustment of the bed and/or tray stand. An announcement should be made that the meal is about to be served.

- The tray must be attractive in appearance, with food items conveniently and neatly arranged. The tray cover should be clean and free of spills from soup, coffee, or other beverages.
- A final check of food trays for accuracy should be made.
- When the tray reaches the patient, hot foods should be hot and cold foods should be cold. If necessary, the patient should receive assistance with removing covers and lids from containers.

PERSONNEL AND GUEST SERVICE

In most medical food service operations, cafeteria service is provided for employees and guests. Additional services may include a physician's dining room, administrative dining room, coffee shop, and vending machines.

Cafeteria Service

The cafeteria should be a convenient, clean, comfortable place for employees to eat at reasonable cost. Most employees have only a half-hour meal period and would prefer to eat in the cafeteria rather than going to an outside food establishment. Serving appetizing, high-quality food will attract enough employees to the cafeteria that the food service operation can break even or even make a small profit.

Menus

The cafeteria menu should be an extension of the menu planned for patients, with additional food items added for variety. The practice of using the same menu for patients and personnel reduces materials handling for purchasing and production employees and eliminates the perception that more attention is given to the feeding of personnel than to the feeding of patients. A four-week menu cycle or a nine-day menu cycle, even for those persons who eat in the cafeteria on a regular basis, offers enough variety to prevent menu boredom. To increase variety in the cafeteria, rotate cold plates, cold sandwiches, grill items, and hot sandwiches. When merchandized properly these items increase customer satisfaction as well as bottom-line profits.

Service

The design of the service area should promote speed so that employees can make food selections, eat, and return to work in the time allowed for meals. The conventional design is a straight-line type of service. Customers enter at one end of the line and remain in line until all food is selected and paid for at the other end. The order of the line is cold entrees, salads, desserts, hot entrees, bread, and beverages. All self-serve foods, such as salads and desserts, should be clearly marked with the selling price to avoid return of a food item to the counter once it has been handled by the customer. Service may be slow, depending on the speed of the servers, the variety of food items, and the number and speed of cashiers. The straight-line service is frequently designed with space for a tray slide and space to bypass certain areas of service if no selection is desired. Yet most customers will stand in line just to purchase one or two food items, rather than cut in line in front of another person. In facilities where it is impossible to rearrange the service counters, there are some measures that management can take to reduce bottlenecks, such as the following:

- Remove from the counter all items that can be provided in a remote location, such as toaster, condiments, water dispenser and glasses, cutlery, and napkins.
- Provide a fan-type cashier area during peak periods. When customers reach a certain point in the serving line, they may form two or more lines to pay for selected items.
- Train employees to work efficiently. Avoid delays by keeping the service counters replenished at all times.

An alternate type of service is the scatter system, also referred to as scramble, freeflow, and hollow square. Instead of following a straight line, customers enter the service area and proceed to the service counter of their choice. Depending on the size of the area and the variety of menu offerings, there may be eight or ten different service stations. Each service station is clearly marked to indicate the types of foods available such as "Soups," "Hot Sandwiches," "Cold Sandwiches," "Hot Vegetables," and "Hot Entrees." The customers are free to leave the service area without delay by paying for selections as they exit. The scatter system provides flexibility for persons selecting a full course meal, and especially for those customers desiring only one or two food items.

Another type of cafeteria service system is the circular counter. This system, used primarily in commercial operations, eliminates all personal contacts between the customer and service employees. Food is arranged in serving dishes on a circular counter that revolves slowly through the production and service areas. Tiers are provided for the separation of hot and chilled food items. As the counter revolves through the production area, counters are replenished with fresh hot and chilled food items. Hot food temperatures are maintained with the use of infrared food warmers. Customers make their selections as the food counter slowly revolves from production to service. Labor cost is reduced, yet customers receive fast, efficient service.

Cashier's Station

Delays may occur at the cashier's station in both the straight-line and scatter systems. The cashier must be familiar with all food prices and be able to scan food selections on each tray quickly, read scales accurately, discern the portion size, and handle cash quickly and accurately. In medical food service operations, select groups of individuals are authorized to charge purchases; other individuals receive a free meal as part of fringe benefits. All food served must be accounted for either in cash or by signed receipts. The use of computerized cash registers at the point of sales can eliminate many of the problems associated with cash accountability by providing the following information:

- food item description
- quantity sold
- price of each food item
- employee sales
- nonemployee sales
- cash sales
- charge sales
- free employee meal
- total sales
- total tax collected
- total voids
- grand total

QUANTITY CONTROL

The number of portions available for service should be the same as the amount planned for the time of purchase. Assuming that quantity was controlled at all critical points, final control measures rest with the server. All employees responsible for dishing, cutting, weighing, and slicing of prepared food should be thoroughly trained in portion control.

Portions

Standardized portions should be established for all food items. The use of scoops, ladles, serving spoons, and certain dishes can serve as dependable measures for portioning (Table 13–1). Scoops may be used for portioning such foods as drop cookies, muffins, meatballs and patties, some vegetables such as mashed potatoes, and some salads such as coleslaw, potato salad, and other similar foods. The number of the scoop indicates the number of scoopfuls to make 1 qt. Ladles may be used to serve gravies, sauces, soups, stews, cream dishes, vegetables of thin consistency, and batters such as waffle and pancake. The ladles are labeled in ounces (Table 13–2); these are fluid ounces, which is a volume, not a weight measurement. Solid or perforated serving spoons may be used instead of a scoop or a ladle. Because these spoons are not identified by number, it is necessary to measure or weigh the quantity of food from the various sizes of spoons used to obtain the number of spoonfuls needed for the required serving size. Automatic slicers are available that can weigh slices of meat as sliced for service. The equipment aids portion control of sliced meat for sandwiches. Scales may be used at the cashier's stand for weighing food priced by weight, such as self-serve salads.

The shift supervisor or head cook must make sure that employees on each shift are familiar with portion sizes, proper utensils, and dishes to use for all food served. Information pertaining to portion sizes can be written on the production worksheet under instructions. The serving of carved meats, such as beef rounds and ham, should be performed by an individual who can make a fair estimate of weight by looking at the size and thickness of a cut or by using portion scales that are concealed from public view. The importance of portion control cannot be overemphasized, but it is not necessary to remind the customer constantly that every portion has been weighed or measured.

Table 13–1 Scoop Numbers and Approximate Measures

Scoop or Disher No.	*Level Measure*
6	⅔ cup
8	½ cup
10	⅜ cup
12	⅓ cup
16	¼ cup
20	3⅕ Tbsp
24	2⅔ Tbsp
30	2⅕ Tbsp
40	1⅗ Tbsp
50	3⅘ Tbsp
60	1 Tbsp

Source: Reprinted from *Food Buying Guide for School Food Service*, Food and Nutrition Service, U.S. Department of Agriculture, 1980.

Table 13–2 Ladle Numbers and Approximate Measures

No. on Ladle (oz)	*Approximate Measure (cup)*
1	⅛
2	¼
4	½
6	¾
8	1
12	1½

Source: Reprinted from *Food Buying Guide for School Food Service*, Food and Nutrition Service, U.S. Department of Agriculture, 1980.

Leftovers

With accurate forecasting, leftovers can be eliminated or at least reduced to a minimum. The disposition of leftovers should be recorded on the production worksheet at the end of service. If the leftover food is to be served at the next meal, it should be chill-stored until time for reheating. Leftover food should never be left in a food warmer or on the cook's table until the next meal, nor should it be served in the same form for the next meal. Normally, personnel will not complain about leftover food if is served as an added menu selection. The practice of using leftovers after the planned menu selections have been served should be discouraged.

QUALITY CONTROL

Standards of quality for prepared food are maintained when standardized recipes are used properly. Precautions must be taken to preserve food quality until it is consumed.

Temperature

The texture, flavor, and appearance of prepared food deteriorate quickly when improper temperatures are used for holding and serving. All hot food should be served hot, above 140°F; and all cold food should be served cold, below 45°F. Some prepared foods require a higher temperature than the minimum 140°F for improved palatability. The holding and serving temperatures of hot beverages, soups, and gravies should be at least 18°F; hot cereals and casseroles should be at least 150°F. A serving temperature should be established and maintained for all items served. Policies and procedures should require quality checks for temperature with a probe thermometer during assembly and prior to patient service. If temperatures fail to meet prescribed standards, corrective action should be taken.

Food Acceptance

It is important for management to know whether the food served to patients and personnel is of acceptable quality. Mechanisms should be established to provide both positive and negative feedback, with plans on how to take corrective action. For personnel and guests eating in the cafeteria, the placing of suggestion boxes in prominent places throughout the area may be sufficient to determine food acceptance. All food service personnel should have a general knowledge of menu items, such as major ingredients used in the preparation techniques. Informed employees can answer questions from customers immediately, thus reducing the number of written complaints. All comments should be brought to the attention of supervisory personnel. Supervisors should review, analyze, and act on written comments in a systematic manner, at regularly scheduled intervals.

To evaluate the level of patient satisfaction with food service and nutritional care, a survey (Exhibit 13–8) can be administered on a regular basis. The survey should be conducted by clinical dietitians and reviewed and analyzed by both administrative and clinical personnel. Results of the analysis will dictate the action plan to take. A more objective tool is a record of food acceptance. This is a record of the kind and amount of foods consumed by the patient, as observed by nursing or dietary personnel. Menus are carefully planned to meet the nutritional needs of patients. When food is not consumed, the objective is not met. As part of the nutritional care plan, the clinical dietitian must make notations in patients' records on the acceptance of food as prescribed. The charting of "appetite is good, fair, or poor" is meaningless; more concrete data are required. A record of food acceptance, as shown in Exhibit 13–9, can be used to collect data from patients on regular and modified diets. In most health care facilities, the majority of the nutritional care planning for patients is done on modified diets. However, teaching the protective value of following a nutritionally adequate, well-balanced diet can be beneficial for all patients and should be routinely practiced by the clinical dietitians. Monitoring of food choices and consumption can point out the need for individual counseling.

The clinical dietitian, with direct patient contact, represents the food service department. The individual must be knowledgeable of the administrative functions involved in providing nutritional care. In making patient care rounds, the dietitian should be able to answer general questions on major ingredients used in menu food items and the preparation procedure. A reply such as, "I do not have anything to do with the preparation of food," is inadequate. The dietitian should respond as intelligently as possible without shifting the blame to any individual or area within the department. All patients should be visited within 24 hours after admission, with follow-up visits on a daily basis.

CONTINUOUS QUALITY IMPROVEMENTS

Quality assurance, as related to dietetic services, can be defined as a systematic approach to verifying that optimal nutrition care is provided on a continuous basis. To assure quality, the food service director must first develop and implement quality control standards. In medical food service, acceptable criteria should be 100 percent for all patient-related tasks. Let's suppose that trays were set up and served to patients on 9 of the 10 patient care areas, thus the service was 90 percent correct. Is this acceptable quality? Suppose the dietitian conducts an initial assessment of 75 percent of patients admitted to the facility. Is this acceptable? The answer to both questions is no. When quality is

Exhibit 13–8 Sample Patient Food Questionnaire

Food Questionnaire

1. Name ________________ Room number ________ Date________
2. What type of diet?
   Regular ________________ Modified diet (type)________________
3. How long have you been in the hospital? ________________ days
4. Have you been visited by a dietitian to discuss your diet? Yes ________ No ________
5. Were there items missing from your tray that had been ordered? Yes ________
   No ________
   If *yes*, which item(s) ________________________________
   If *yes*, was it explained why these items were missing? Yes ________ No ________
6. How would you rate our food and service? Please check the appropriate box.

		Breakfast	Lunch	Supper
6a.	Appearance of food on tray			
	Excellent			
	Good			
	Satisfactory			
	Poor			
6b.	Taste of main course			
	Excellent			
	Good			
	Satisfactory			
	Poor			
6c.	Taste of other items			
	Excellent			
	Good			
	Satisfactory			
	Poor			
6d.	Size of portions			
	Excellent			
	Good			
	Satisfactory			
	Poor			
6e.	Menu variety			
	Excellent			
	Good			
	Satisfactory			
	Poor			
6f.	Temperature of food			
	Excellent			
	Good			
	Satisfactory			
	Poor			
6g.	Temperature of beverages			
	Excellent			
	Good			
	Satisfactory			
	Poor			
6h.	Coffee or tea			
	Excellent			
	Good			
	Satisfactory			
	Poor			
6i.	Courtesy of serving staff			
	Excellent			
	Good			
	Satisfactory			
	Poor			

Additional comments or suggestions:

Exhibit 13–9 Sample Record of Food Acceptance

Patient ______________________ Diet ______________________
Room no. ______________________ Diagnosis ______________________
Weight (lb) ______________________ ______________________
Height (in) ______________________ Age (yr) ______________________

Record of Food Acceptance

Date: ______________ To: ______________

	Meat/Egg			Cereal/Potato			Bread			Fruit			Vegetable			Milk			
Days	B	D	S	B	D	S	B	D	S	B	D	S	B	D	S	B	D	S	Initials
Monday																			
Tuesday																			
Wednesday																			
Thursday																			
Friday																			
Saturday																			
Sunday																			

Use the following symbols:

A All food eaten.
T Takes feeding given.
U Unable to eat.
R Refused to eat.

½, ¼, or ¾ Amount of food eaten.
S Substitution. (Record date, food substituted, and amounts on back of sheet.)

less than 100 percent, the impact on patient outcome has a negative effect (Joint Commission on Accreditation of Healthcare Organizations 1988).

According to the Joint Commission on Accreditation of Healthcare Organizations (Joint Commission; 1988), the dietetic department must have a planned and systematic process for monitoring and evaluating the quality and appropriateness of patient care. Although the process must be in writing, it need not involve excessive paperwork in order to be effecient and effective. After policies and procedures are established for the quality assurance committee, a one-sheet form can be used to doucment actions taken. The form should include space to document the following:

- date problem was identified
- date problem was resolved
- signature of person conducting quality assurance audit
- identified problem
- source of problem (patient/employee complaint, routine quality check)
- findings
- resolution of problem
- implementation of corrective action
- results of monitoring and evaluation
- impact on patient care

The program should be ongoing, with records maintained and filed for future reference. From a managerial perspective, problems should be resolved at the departmental level to the extent possible. Be prepared to report results at the hospital quality assurance committee meetings.

CRITICAL CONTROL POINTS AND CONTROL POINTS RELATED TO SERVICE OF FOOD

Policies and procedures on the display, service, transport, return of soiled dishes, and dishwashing should be an integral part of a program designed to protect food from external contamination and the rapid progressive growth of microorganisms.

Any lapse in control during the service of food can negate all the efforts of buying, storing, and preparing quality products that are safe for human consumption. Critical control points (CCPs) and control points (CPs) that should be observed are discussed below.

Food Display and Service

- Potentially hazardous foods should be kept at an internal temperature of 45°F or below, or at an internal temperature of 140°F or above during display and service, except that rare roast beef may be held for service at a temperature of at least 130°F.
- Milk and milk products for drinking should be served in an unopened, commercially filled package, or drawn from a commercially filled container stored in a mechanically refrigerated bulk milk dispenser. Where a bulk dispenser is not available and portions of less than ½ pint are required, milk products may be poured from a commercially filled container of not more than ½ gallon capacity.
- Cream, half-and-half, and nondairy cream should be served in individual containers, protected pour-type pitchers, or drawn from a refrigerated dispenser designed for such service.
- Condiments, seasonings, and dressings for self-service use should be provided in individual packages, from a dispenser or container, or from a serving line or a salad bar with protective devices.
- Condiments provided for table or counter use should be individually portioned except that catsup and other sauces may be served in the original container or pour-type dispenser. Sugar should be in individual packages or pour-type containers.
- Ice for consumer use should be dispensed only by employees with scoops, tongs, or other ice-dispensing utensils or through automatic self-service ice-dispensing equipment. Ice-dispensing utensils should be stored on a clean surface or in the ice with the utensil's handle extended out of the ice. Between use, ice-transfer receptacles should be stored to protect them from contamination.
- Disposable gloves may be used for food items that must be touched by the hands (check local sanitation codes). Discard gloves after each use. Do not use for more than one task.
- Wiping cloths used for wiping food spills on tableware, such as spills from plates or bowls being served to a customer, should be clean, dry, and used for no other purpose. Cloths used for wiping food spills on kitchenware and food-contact surfaces of equipment should be cleaned and rinsed frequently in a sanitizing solution and used for no other purpose. These cloths and sponges should be stored in a sanitizing solution between uses. Moist cloths and sponges used for cleaning non–food-contact surfaces of equipment such as counters and dining tabletops should be cleaned and rinsed in a sanitizing solution.

Food Transport

Protection from contamination and maintaining proper temperatures are critical for the safety and quality of transported food. During transportation, food and food utensils should be kept in covered containers or completely wrapped or packaged to be protected from contamination. Foods in original individual packages do not need to be overwrapped if the original package has not been torn or broken. During transportation, food should meet the requirements relating to food protection and food storage.

Return of Soiled Dishes

Trays should be collected from the patient areas and returned to the food service department approximately 45 minutes after trays have been served. Employees responsible for removing food trays from patient areas should be trained to look for and save all tray identification cards that may contain written comments from the patients. The comments should be given to supervisory personnel for analysis and corrective action, if necessary. Soiled disposable trays from isolated patient areas are double-bagged by nursing personnel and destroyed. Soiled isolated tray service should not be returned to the food service department. The food cart used to return soiled trays should be washed and sanitized prior to further use.

Dishwashing

To prevent cross-contamination, tableware and kitchenware should be washed, rinsed, and sanitized after each use and following any interruptions of operations during which contamination may have occurred. The following procedures are recommended:

- A three-compartment sink should be used for manual cleaning and sanitizing of utensils and equipment.
- For manual cleaning, all equipment and utensils should be sanitized by one of the following methods:
  1. immersion for at least 30 seconds in clean, hot water at a temperature of 170°F
  2. immersion for at least 1 minute in a clean solution containing at least 50 parts per million of available chlorine such as a hypochlorine and at a temperature of at least 75°F
  3. immersion for at least 1 minute in a clean solution containing at least 12.5 parts per million of available iodine and having a pH not higher than 5.0 and at a temperature of at least 75°F
- Temperatures for mechanical cleaning and sanitizing of equipment and utensils should be at least 140°F for wash, 160°F for rinse, and 180°F for final rinse.
- Clean and sanitized silverware should be touched only by the handles. This applies also to the practice of bagging or wrapping silverware for tray assembly.
- Clean and sanitized cups, glasses, bowls, plates, and similar items should be handled without contact with inside surfaces or surfaces that touch the user's mouth.
- Clean and sanitized utensils and equipment should be stored at least 6 inches above the floor in a clean, dry location, protected from contamination by splash, dust, or other contaminants.
- Utensils should be air dried before being stored or should be stored in a self-draining position.
- Glasses and cups should be stored inverted.
- Silverware in containers should be stored so that the handle is presented to the customer.

COMPUTER APPLICATIONS

Development of a computerized food service distribution system takes a great deal of time and effort. The goal of a computerized food service distribution system has to be compatible with that of the food service department, to distribute meals to patients that provide optimal nutrition. When this goal is central to the development of the system, it overrides the distraction of current trends in automated equipment and advanced technological systems.

The industries that provide food service management support have responded to the fact that there are fewer dollars available in medical facilities for major renovations. Companies that formerly designed only packaged systems have become innovative. Computer modules for diet office management, menu management, and nutritional analysis may be used independently or fully integrated.

Equipment manufacturers have responded accordingly. The major expense involved in purchasing the equipment necessary for a cook-chill system of production and distribution has often been prohibitive enough to overshadow the advantages of the system. Recently equipment models have been scaled down in size and cost, which makes them a feasible alternative.

Computer software for diet office management is also available in modular form. The diet office is often a place of much activity. Automated diet office tasks may include the following:

- continous electronic transfer of diet orders
- patient card files
- tray cards
- nourishment labels
- menu tallies
- printed menus
- standard menus for nonselective and new admissions

Each of the above computerized functions eliminates labor-intensive manual operations. More advanced systems provide the following support services:

- personalized messages on menus
- monitoring risk assessment
- restriction parameters for diet compliance
- Joint Commission and Omnibus Reconciliation Act audit features

- on-line patient menu selection
- interactive communication between departments
- nutrition screening that automatically prioritizes patient nutrition care

An increase in time and efficiency can be realized by automating many facets of the diet office with computer systems. The challenge is to be sure that the implementation of the system indeed results in a reduction in labor cost as well.

Computer systems designed to enhance the distribution of foods are usually an extension of the food production system. There are two categories of computer-driven equipment adaptable to distribution of foods prepared using cook-serve production: tray line equipment using light-emitting diodes (LEDs) and cathode ray tubes (CRTs) and robotic carts. As described by McLaren (1982), one hospital's system is designed with five modules that handle menu planning, purchasing, and production.

Distribution of food involves forecasting the amounts and destination of food requirements. Patient forecasts are automatically updated because the computer stores pertinent data from tray assembly at each meal. This information is then communicated to the forecast file for the next time the menu is used. Therefore, menu forecasts are based on usage information entered during each menu cycle.

Food distribution equipment to support cook-chill and cook-freeze food production may include computerized rethermalizing carts that transport food from the cook-chill storage to the point of service, then reheat the food.

REFERENCES

Electric carts—patient simulator: Robot slowly moving into hospitals. 1982. *Hospitals* 56, no. 13:36.

Joint Commission on Accreditation of Healthcare Organizations. 1988. *Accreditation manual for hospitals*. Chicago.

McLaren, A. 1982. High technology in Indianapolis. *Food Management* 17, no. 10:46–49.

Riggs, S. 1981. How well has Walter Reed's "revolutionary" food system worked? *Restaurants and Institutions* 88, no. 11:73–75.

CHAPTER 14

Subsystem for Personnel Management

Personnel is one of the more difficult resources to manage, primarily because of the human element involved and the constant changes taking place inside and outside the workplace. The food service director must have an understanding of human relations and how it relates to hiring, developing, maintaining, and utilizing an effective work force. In addition, changes in the work force, economic conditions, work environment, information technology, and outside regulatory agencies have an impact on the role a manager must play in supervising employees. The manager must be flexible and able to adapt to environmental changes. A systems approach for the management of personnel, which begins with preemployment and continues through the exit interview, eliminates many of the problems confronting a manager in a dynamic milieu.

DETERMINING STAFFING NEEDS

Staffing is the process of determining the need for hiring employees and the level of role occupancy required to carry out the functions of the organization. In medical food service, staffing levels are decided by each individual facility and may be based on one or a combination of the indexes used for determining staffing needs. One source recommends 1.5 full-time equivalents (FTEs) for each position, based on a 7-day operation (Stokes 1981). For example, the dishroom schedule should require a minimum of two employees per shift in order to prevent cross-contamination. Therefore, the minimum number of FTEs for dishroom duties should not be less than 3 in order to provide adequate coverage (1.5 × 2 = 3).

Another source (U.S. Department of Health and Human Services 1971) recommends three methods for determining dietary staffing needs.

Staffing Based on Number of Patients

Using one dietary employee for every eight patients, the following calculation is made:

Example. Given a 100-bed facility, this is explained as follows: 100-bed facility ÷ 8 patients = 12.5 employees per week, allowing for a 5-day workweek; 12.5 persons × 40-hour workweek = 500 man-hours needed per week. If it takes 1.4 persons to cover 7 days, this is equivalent to 56 hours per person: 1.4 persons × 40 hours (one position) = 56 hours or 7 days (one position) × 8 hours = 56 hours.

Now divide the number of man-hours needed per week (500) by the number of hours represented by one employee (56) to get the number for the day: 500 ÷ 56 = 8.93 employees. To convert this to number of man-hours multiply by 8 hours: 8.93 × 8 = 71.4 hours per day.

Per position, 1.6 rather than 1.4 persons are required to provide fringe benefits (e.g., sick leave, holidays, and vacations). The addition of 0.2 person at 8 hours is equivalent to 1.6 hours more per day.

These calculations were made on the basis of weekly work hours required, which remain the same. The number of persons needed varies with the actual number of work hours of each employee. If we assume that there are two 15-minute relief breaks, the following adjustment must be made based on actual work hours of 7.5 hours per day: 71.4 hours per day ÷ 7.5 = 9.52 employees per day.

If we assume a 30-minute meal break and two 15-minute relief breaks, this equals 7 working hours per day, and the following adjustment must be made: 71.4 hours per day ÷ 7 = 10.2 persons per day.

The use of part-time employees alters the number of bodies needed but does not alter the total daily hours or the FTE.

Staffing Based on Number of Positions

Count the number of positions that must be filled daily. It takes at least 1.4 persons working a 5-day week to fill each position, or 7 employees for five positions. Fringe benefits, relief workers for holidays, sick leave, and vacation must be included. To allow for benefits and vacation, management may wish to budget 1.6 employees for each position, or 8 employees to fill five positions.

Staffing Based on Labor Minutes per Meal

Use a figure of 14 minutes of labor required to serve one meal to one person:

Example. A 100-bed facility × 3 meals per day = 300 meals; 300 meals × 14 minutes = 4,200 minutes; 4,200 minutes ÷ 60 minutes = 70 hours per day; 70 hours per day × 7 days = 490 hours per week.

In some instances where there is a wide variety of diets and a limited use of convenience food, it has been estimated that it takes 17 minutes of employee time to prepare one meal. Using the preceding method, the result is 85 hours per day. This can be reduced further to number of employees required by using the procedure described under Staffing Based on Number of Patients.

Professional Staffing Based on Work Activity

In addition to staffing required in the kitchen for actual food preparation, professional staffing is needed to ensure quality nutritional care for the patients. A sample calculation of professional staffing requirements to achieve goals is based on the following two criteria (Brogan et al. 1981):

1. Meet the needs of 100 percent of patients on modified diets.
2. Conduct nutritional assessments on 25 percent of other patients at risk. (Assumption: 46 patients are on modified diets; 120 other patients are at risk; average hospital stay is seven days.)

The work activity is divided into five categories: (1) service time, (2) instruction time, (3) routine support service time, (4) nutritional assessment–special service time, and (5) available staff time.

Service Time

Compute figures by compiling time spent on the following activities.

Reviewing chart to determine nutritional risks and problems	20 min
Obtaining history from the patient (verbal interview or from a form completed by a technician)	15 min
Communicating with other team members (i.e., rounds, telephone, follow-up contacts)	20 min
Preparing and assembling materials for patient instruction	10 min
Developing a nutritional care plan	15 min
Recording in chart (i.e., diet given, recommendations, progress, implementation and evaluation of instruction, and follow-up)	20 min
Total	100 min

A = 100 min × 46 patients per week = 4,600 min per week

Instruction Time

Compute this figure from the client learning study (Callaghan et al. 1983), average time for each counseling session multiplied by the number of patients on each diet:

B = 574 min per day × 7 days = 4,018 min per week

Routine Support Service Time

Compute this figure by compiling time spent on all activities performed each day for all patients, such as checking menus:

C = 375 min per day × 7 days = 2,625 min per week

Nutritional Assessment–Special Service Time

Compute this figure by compiling time spent on only those activities not listed in A, B, or C above, such as anthropometric measuring or parenteral or enteral feeding formulation:

D = 80 min × 20 patients per week = 1,600 min per week

Available Staff Time

Number of hours available from a dietetic practitioner per year, allowing for personal time, administrative tasks, and vacation is 6.75 hours per day × 250 days = 1,687.5 hours per year. (The 6.75 hours per day allows for meal and break time. The 250 days per year is based on 5 days a week for 52 weeks, minus 10 days for leave time.) The calculation of time needed to meet the goal is as follows: $A + B + C + D$ = number of hours needed per year to meet the goal in this example.

4,600 min + 4,018 min + 2,625 min + 1,600 min
= 12,843 min per week
= 30.6 hours per day × 365 days per year
= 11,169 hours per year
= 11,169 staff hours needed/1,687.5 hours available per practitioner
= 6.6 FTE

Although the professional staffing requirements referred to here apply only to the clinical dietitian, similar data can be collected and analyzed for all professional activities. Staffing requirements are as important for professional employees as they are for nonprofessional employees. Staffing criteria should be established for both categories. It is difficult to state with any amount of specificity what the staffing requirements should be for a medical food service operation without consideration of the following factors:

- goals and objectives of the organization
- standards of performance
- efficiency of the work force
- type of production, distribution, and service system
- menu system (selective, nonselective, restaurant type)
- number of special activities
- kitchen layout and design
- location of kitchen from patient area
- number and type of diets (regular vs. modified)
- style of purchasing (convenience vs. scratch)
- sanitation and safety requirements (minimum shift requirements and amount of cleaning done by outside agencies)
- responsibility for distribution and service of trays to patients (dietary vs. nursing)
- hours of operation

WORK SCHEDULES

A work schedule is an organized procedure for ensuring staff utilization by indicating the hours of work per day, the time of work, and the number of days per week. Most workers in medical food service operations work a fixed shift of eight hours per day, five days per week. However, other types of work schedules are used, such as the compressed workweek and flextime.

A compressed workweek is used to schedule employees for a 40-hour week in less than the normal five days. For example, employees may be scheduled to work 10 hours per day, four days per week. The schedule permits more off-time for leisure and other personal activities and is favorably regarded by some workers. Where used, employees are scheduled for three days off at one time, such as Friday through Sunday. Because medical food service operations must provide three meals per day, seven days per week, the three-day-off schedule may not be feasible.

Flextime scheduling permits flexibility in the time an employee begins and ends the work shift. For example, an employee on the early shift may report for work at any time between the hours of 5:00 AM and 7:00 AM and remain on duty long enough to complete an eight-hour tour of duty. Flextime may be confined to flexible hours for lunch or break time, with the time of the activity left to the discretion of the employee. Flextime may be less than eight hours on some days and more than eight hours on other days, depending on peak periods of work. A number of problems may arise in the use of flextime in a medical food service operation, used as the following:

- Record keeping may be increased because the manager must check to make sure that each employee's work hours comply with provisions of the Fair Labor Standards Act.
- For employees requiring supervision, there may be excess time involved for supervisory personnel.
- It may be difficult to meet prescribed mealtimes in a timely manner.
- There may be delays in completing tasks, because most work activities in a medical food service operation are interdependent.
- Work activities cannot be delayed until the following day or later because meals must be served at least three times a day, seven days a week.

Both the compressed workweek and flextime need considerable study before they can be implemented effectively in a medical food service operation. The procedures are more applicable to industries that operate on a Monday-through-Friday workweek.

To eliminate problems associated with making out a fixed-hour work schedule, work criteria are recommended for use as a guide. The work criteria (see Exhibit 14–1) specify the number of workers needed for each shift, the level of workers required, the number of weekends off, maximum number of workers on leave at any one time, and necessary relief coverage. By using the criteria, the task of making out the work schedule can be a routine duty performed at the lowest supervisory level. Further, use of the criteria provides for uniformity, ensures fair and impartial treatment for all employees, conserves the supervisor's time, and makes for easy construction. There should be space on the work schedule sheet (Exhibit 14–2) for each assigned worker. The use of a clear, precise legend to indicate work and off-duty time eliminates confusion on the part of workers. In order to provide adequate coverage during employee vacation time, there should be a deadline for requesting vacation time. The policy will provide enough time for managerial decisions and approval. All off-time, including vacation, personal, and other requests, should be included in the work schedule prior to posting. A sample vacation request form is shown in Exhibit 14–3. The work schedule should be posted in a prominent place at least two weeks in advance of the work period. Work schedules should remain on file for three years.

VOLUNTEER WORKERS

The volunteer worker can be a valuable asset in extending the scope of services offered by a medical food service

Exhibit 14–1 Criteria for Work Schedule

Pertinent Information:

1. Three meals are served daily to patients and personnel eating in the cafeteria, plus night nourishment for patients.
2. Hours of operation for the department: 5:30 AM to 7:00 PM.
3. Meal hours are as follows:

	Cafeteria	*Ward*
Breakfast	6:30–8:00 AM	7:00 AM
Lunch	11:00 AM–1:00 PM	12:00 noon
Dinner	4:00–6:00 PM	5:00 PM
Nourishments		8:00 PM

4. Centralized meals on wheels, with eight food carts used for distribution.
5. Major clerical duties are performed by hospital secretarial staff; routine office work is performed by cashiers.
6. Patient food service prepares approximately 150 patient trays for each meal.
7. The cafeteria serves approximately 200 persons for breakfast, 300 for lunch, and 250 for dinner.

Instructions:

1. Schedule employees for 8 hours per day, 5 days per week. *No overtime.*
2. Schedule employees for no more than 5 consecutive days together.
3. Schedule should be balanced (approximately equal number of employees daily).
4. Include all "approved" off days, such as vacation, sick leave, or personal leave.
5. Use the following legend:

E = Early shift:	5:30 AM–2:00 PM
L = Late shift:	10:30 AM–7:00 PM
R = Regular shift:	8:00 AM–4:30 PM
O = Off duty	
V = Vacation	
S = Sick leave	
P = Personal leave	
A = Administrative leave (conferences, meetings, etc.)	

Employee Categories/Work Shift	Time Off
Director	
Regular shift, Monday–Friday	Every weekend
Administrative Dietitian	
Regular shift, Monday–Friday	Every weekend
Clinical Dietitian	
Regular shift, Monday–Friday	Every weekend
Patient Supervisor no. 1	
Early shift	Every other weekend (rotates weekend off days with Supervisor no. 2)
Patient Supervisor no. 2	
Late shift	Every other weekend (rotates with no. 1)
Production Supervisor no. 1	
Early shift	Every other weekend (rotates with no. 2)
Production Supervisor no. 2	
Late shift	Every other weekend (rotates with no. 1)
Head Cook no. 1	
Early shift	Every third weekend
Head Cook no. 2	
Late shift	Every third weekend
Head Cook no. 3	
Swing shift as relief for no. 1 and no. 2	Every third weekend

continues

Exhibit 14–1 continued

Employee Categories/Work Shift	Time Off
Assistant Cooks 1, 2, 3, 4	
Early shift	Every fourth weekend
Assistant Cooks 5, 6, 7, 8	
Late shift	Every fourth weekend
Dietary Aides 1, 2, 3, 4	
Early shift	One weekend per month
Dietary Aides 5, 6, 7, 8	
Late shift	One weekend per month
Baker	
Early shift Monday–Friday	Every weekend
Cashier no. 1	
Early shift	Every third weekend
Cashier no. 2	
Late shift	Every third weekend
Cashier no. 3	
Swing shift as relief for no. 1 and no. 2	Every third weekend
Storeroom Personnel no. 1	
Early shift	Every other weekend
Storeroom Personnel no. 2	
Late shift	Every other weekend
Food Service Workers 1, 2, 3, 4	
Early shift	One weekend per month
Food Service Workers 5, 6, 7, 8	
Late shift	One weekend per month

department. The volunteer program should not be set up in a haphazard manner. Volunteers assigned to the department must be carefully screened either by the director of volunteer services or by the food service director. The volunteer worker must be in good physical condition (as evidenced by a health card) and be willing to make a commitment for regular and continuous service. The worker must be provided with a job description and given an orientation to the department's objectives, functions, and health care standards.

According to guidelines published by the American Hospital Association (1974), volunteers may be involved in patient services, departmental activities, and community outreach programs as follows:

- Patient services
  1. distributing and collecting menus
  2. assisting patients with menu selections
  3. tabulating menu selections
  4. helping in preparation of materials to be used for patient instruction
  5. making favors and decorations for patients' trays
  6. distributing nourishments and other in-between feedings to patients
- Departmental activities
  1. serving as host or hostess in dining areas to assist patients or visitors
  2. acting as a guide for scheduled department tours
  3. arranging and preparing bulletin board displays
  4. assisting with clerical duties, such as supplementary typing
  5. hosting at special functions such as teas, parties, luncheons, and dinners for visitors, trustees, medical staff, and other groups
- Community outreach programs
  1. assisting with programs and activities such as satellite clinics, diet workshops, nutrition classes, continuing education for homebound patients, and feeding programs such as Meals on Wheels (For such program activity, adequate insurance coverage for the volunteers is essential.)

Volunteers should not be used to perform the work of paid employees, such as substituting for an employee who is absent from duty. The department should provide adequate training for all assigned tasks and take advantage of the special talents and attributes of the volunteers to enhance services to patients.

Exhibit 14–2 Sample Work Schedule

Work Schedule

Date:______________________________ to______________________________ Prepared by: ____________________________

Employees	S	M	T	W	T	F	S	S	M	T	W	T	F	S
Director														
Administrative Dietitian														
Clinical Dietitian														
Patient Supervisor no. 1														
Patient Supervisor no. 2														
Production Supervisor no. 1														
Production Supervisor no. 2														
Head Cook no. 1														
Head Cook no. 2														
Head Cook no. 3														
Assistant Cook no. 1														
2														
3														
4														
5														
6														
7														
8														
Dietary Aide no. 1														
2														
3														
4														
5														
6														
7														
8														
Baker														
Cashier no. 1														
Cashier no. 2														
Cashier no. 3														
Storeroom Personnel no. 1														
Storeroom Personnel no. 2														
Food Service Worker no. 1														
2														
3														
4														
5														
6														
7														
8														
Totals ________														

Exhibit 14–3 Vacation Request Form

Vacation Request

To be completed by the employee:

Name:____________________ ID#: ______________ Job Title: ____________________ Employment Date:______________

Anniversary Date:______________

Vacation Preference: **Note: A vacation week is from Monday through Sunday**

1st Choice: From:_______________ To:_______________

2nd Choice: From:_______________ To:_______________

3rd Choice: From:_______________ To:_______________

Vacation Days: With Pay:_________________ Without Pay:_________________

Remarks: ____

Date:_________________ Signature:____

To be completed by department head:

Approved:________________ Disapproved: _________________With Pay:________________ Without Pay:_______________

Return To Work: ____

Remarks: ____

Date:_____________________ Signature:________________________

Vacation Policy:

After 12 months from the date of employment and each anniversary year thereafter, each benefit status employee paid for at least 1000 hours in the 12-month period shall be entitled to vacation with pay. Full vacation benefits are as follows:

After completion of 1st through 4th year of employment—10 working days
After completion of 5 or more years of employment—15 working days
After completion of 18 or more years of employment—20 working days

Vacation benefits will be prorated for benefit status employees receiving less than 200 paid hours in the previous year.

Vacation schedules are made biannually by the departments and posted at least 1 week in advance of the effective beginning dates, October 1 and April 1. Vacations must be scheduled with and approved by the department head at least 1 month in advance of the desired vacation time. In the event that two or more employees doing similar work request vacations for the same period, the one with the most seniority will be given preference.

Vacation days cannot be accumulated from one year to the next. Vacations must be taken within 12 months of the benefits or anniversary date, or forfeited without pay. Vacations cannot be taken until they have been earned. If time off is desired prior to the time it has been earned, the employee may apply for an excused absence without pay on the proper form.

Deviations to this policy must be approved by the Vice President of Human Resources. This policy may be changed or altered at the discretion of the corporation with due notice of same.

THE HIRING PROCESS

Effective hiring procedures eliminate many of the problems related to work accomplishment. The individual should be suitable for the position for which he or she is hired. A well-planned process of ensuring that qualified persons are hired involves a series of steps, including recruitment, selection, personal interview, orientation, and performance evaluation.

Recruitment

Recruitment of personnel is most often a function of the personnel officer. Input from the food service director is necessary in order to seek applicants from the appropriate or most successful sources. Depending on the type of employee sought, such as professional or nonprofessional, sources of recruitment may be as follows:

- for professional personnel
  1. professional organizations
  2. professional journals
  3. private job placement agencies
  4. college and university placement services
  5. newspaper advertisements
  6. other professional employees on the job
- for nonprofessional personnel
  1. state and city employment agencies
  2. vocational educational schools
  3. newspaper advertisements
  4. radio and television announcements
  5. relatives, friends, and employees on the job

Internal vs. External Recruitment

To comply with equal opportunity hiring laws, all vacancies must be advertised in some form of public media. Federal civil rights laws prohibit any recruitment that indicates discrimination based on religion, race, color, national origin, age, sex, height, weight, or marital status. Most companies also have a policy that requires a notice of all vacant positions be posted on the bulletin board, in company newsletters, and in other public places to allow for recruitment from within the organization. The main advantage to recruitment from within is a promotion to a higher position for an employee. The practice may serve to bolster morale if employees know that they can progress from one position to another. On the other side, hiring from within may prevent bringing in employees with new and sometimes better ideas.

Selection

After prospective employees have been recruited, a process for screening out unacceptable applicants must be in effect. A wide variety of tools to aid the selection process are discussed below.

Application Form

The application form provides biographic data and specific information relating to the applicant's skills and abilities. All requested information should have a purpose, such as for research or for determining eligibility for the job. For example, more detailed information may be required from an applicant seeking a position as a dietitian than from an applicant seeking a position as a kitchen helper. In compliance with federal guidelines, each state government interprets and establishes basic rules and regulations. According to the Michigan Department of Civil Rights (1981), some informational items are considered unlawful preemployment inquiries (Exhibit 14–4). Additional information may be required for payroll and fringe benefit purposes but should not be included on the employment application. Data such as marital status, number of dependents, and other pertinent information can be lawfully secured subsequent to hiring and should have no bearing on the selection process. Sections of the Civil Rights Act provide for similar protection for the physically challenged if the information is unrelated to the individual's ability to perform the duties of a particular position. For example, dietitians are employable with the following physical impairments: amputated limb; medical disabilities, such as heart trouble, tuberculosis, diabetes, and loss of hearing; wheelchair bound; physically dwarfed; and paraplegia.

It is important for the employer to examine all job-related questions, keeping in mind that race, sex, and other stereotypical information may contribute to bias in the selection process.

Preemployment Tests

The use of preemployment tests will vary depending on the level of the position to be filled and the required skills of the applicant. Tests are frequently administered after the initial screening and prior to the personal interview. Commonly used tests include those discussed below.

Intelligence Tests. Intelligence tests measure the applicants' capacity for learning and indicate the level of their ability to problem solve. The test must be culture free to prevent bias in the selection process.

Aptitude Tests. Aptitude tests measure the probable success an applicant will achieve in a specific job classification. The test may be a combined aptitude-interest instrument designed to indicate both talent and preferences for certain jobs.

Achievement Tests. Achievement tests measure the degree of skill in a specific area such as typing, spelling, cooking, and diet modification. The test may be of the norm-referenced or criterion-referenced type. In the norm-referenced test, an applicant's score is compared with those of all other applicants. In the criterion-referenced test, an applicant's score is compared with an established standard and

Exhibit 14–4 Preemployment Inquiry Guide

SUBJECT	LAWFUL PREEMPLOYMENT INQUIRIES	UNLAWFUL PREEMPLOYMENT INQUIRIES
NAME:	Applicant's full name. Have you ever worked for this company under a different name? Is any additional information relative to a different name necessary to check your work record? If yes, explain.	Original name of an applicant whose name has been changed by court order or otherwise. Applicant's maiden name.
ADDRESS OR DURATION OF RESIDENCE:	How long a resident of this state or city?	
BIRTHPLACE:		Birthplace of applicant. Birthplace of applicant's parents, spouse, or other close relatives. Requirement that applicant submit birth certificate, naturalization, or baptismal record.
AGE:	Are you 18 years old or older?*	How old are you? What is your date of birth?
RELIGION OR CREED:		Inquiry into an applicant's religious denomination, religious affiliations, church, parish, pastor, or religious holidays observed. An applicant may not be told "This is a Catholic (Protestant or Jewish) organization."
RACE OR COLOR:		Complexion or color of skin.
PHOTOGRAPH:		Requirement that an applicant for employment affix a photograph to an employment application form. Request an applicant, at his or her option, to submit a photograph. Requirement for photograph after interview but before hiring.
HEIGHT:		Inquiry regarding applicant's height.
WEIGHT:		Inquiry regarding applicant's weight.
MARITAL STATUS:		Requirement that an applicant provide any information regarding marital status or children. Are you single or married? Do you have any children? Is your spouse employed? What is your spouse's name?
SEX:		Mr., Miss, or Mrs., or an inquiry regarding sex. Inquiry as to the ability to reproduce or advocacy of any form of birth control.
HEALTH:	Do you have any impairments, physical, mental, or medical, that would interfere with your ability to do the job for which you have applied?	

continues

Exhibit 14–4 continued

SUBJECT	LAWFUL PREEMPLOYMENT INQUIRIES	UNLAWFUL PREEMPLOYMENT INQUIRIES
	Inquiry into contagious or communicable diseases that may endanger others. If there are any positions for which you should not be considered or job duties you cannot perform because of a physical or mental impairment, please explain.	Requirement that women be given pelvic examinations.
CITIZENSHIP:	Are you a citizen of the United States? If not a citizen of the United States, do you intend to become a citizen of the United States? If you are not a United States citizen, have you the legal right to remain permanently in the United States? Do you intend to remain permanently in the United States?	Of what country are you a citizen? Whether an applicant is naturalized or a native-born citizen; the date when the applicant acquired citizenship. Requirement that an applicant produce naturalization papers or first papers. Whether applicant's parents or spouse are naturalized or native-born citizens of the United States; the date when such parent or spouse acquired citizenship.
NATIONAL ORIGIN:	Inquiry into languages applicant speaks and writes fluently.	Inquiry into applicant's (a) lineage; (b) ancestry; (c) national origin; (d) descent; (e) parentage or nationality. Nationality of applicant's parents or spouse. What is your mother tongue? Inquiry into how applicant acquired ability to read, write, or speak a foreign language.
EDUCATION:	Inquiry into the academic vocational or professional education of an applicant and the public and private schools attended.	
EXPERIENCE:	Inquiry into work experience. Inquiry into countries applicant has visited.	
ARRESTS:	Have you ever been convicted of a crime? If so, when, where, and nature of offense? Are there any felony charges pending against you?	Inquiry regarding arrests.
RELATIVES:	Names of applicant's relatives, other than a spouse, already employed by this company.	Address of any relative of applicant, other than address (within the United States) of applicant's father and mother, husband or wife and minor dependent children.
NOTICE IN CASE OF EMERGENCY:	Name and address of person to be notified in case of accident or emergency.	Name and address of nearest relative to be notified in case of accident or emergency.
MILITARY EXPERIENCE:	Inquiry into an applicant's military experience in the Armed Forces of the United States or in a state militia. Inquiry into applicant's service in a particular branch of United States Army, Navy, etc.	Inquiry into an applicant's general military experience.

continues

Exhibit 14–4 continued

SUBJECT	LAWFUL PREEMPLOYMENT INQUIRIES	UNLAWFUL PREEMPLOYMENT INQUIRIES
ORGANIZATION:	Inquiry into the organizations of which an applicant is a member excluding organizations the name or character of which indicates the race, color, religion, national origin or ancestry of its members.	List all clubs, societies, and lodges to which you belong.
REFERENCES:	Who suggested that you apply for a position here?	

*This question may be asked only for the purpose of determining whether applicants are of legal age for employment.

Source: Reprinted from *Pre-employment Inquiry Guide*, Michigan Civil Rights Commission, Michigan Department of Civil Rights, 1981.

the participant must score at a certain level in order to be considered for the position.

Personality Tests. Personality tests are used to measure an applicant's personal traits. The test may consist of a list of personal questions requiring a yes or no answer; or it may consist of projective techniques, requiring the applicant to tell what certain images mean to him or her. In a projective-type personality test, the applicant describes what he or she sees in a number of standardized inkblots. A trained psychologist analyzes the test results and often can recognize psychological tendencies that may enhance or hinder good work performance. Psychologists do not regard the results as conclusive evidence of an individual's personality.

The tests used for employee selection should be designed to predict which applicant will be the best worker for a particular job. Management must understand that test scores can provide only an estimate, rather than precise measurements, of an applicant's capabilities. If tests are used, it is recommended that more than one test be given, because several tests are considered more dependable than a single test.

According to Schmidt and Hunter (1981), many false beliefs about job aptitude tests are widely accepted by personnel psychologists, which may have serious consequences for productivity in the work force. The authors summarized research that contradicts the following myths:

- Employment aptitude tests' validities must be newly determined in each setting, company, or agency.
- An aptitude test may be valid for one job but invalid for another job.
- Tests that predict performance in training programs may not predict on-the-job performance, and vice versa.
- Selection procedures have very little impact on organizational productivity.
- A difference in average test scores between minority groups and majority groups shows that the test is unfair.

The interpretation of research data can be pro or con, and from different perspectives, as indicated by the position taken by enforcement agencies responsible for ensuring equality of employment opportunity. As reported by Schmidt and Hunter (1981), the American Psychological Association's Division of Industrial and Organizational Psychology revised its standards on employment testing and selection, based on their interpretation of findings in the late 1970s.

Screening for Substance Abuse

One of the problems facing management today is the widespread use of drugs and the resulting impact on productivity. Among the few drug addicts who are motivated to seek employment, most are discharged or dismissed within a short period of time because of absenteeism, poor performance, or theft to support their habit. Ideally, it would be better to screen prospective employees for substance abuse before they are hired. As reported by the Research Institute of America (1982), a system known as Emit is available for screening applicants. Applicants are screened for opiates, methadone, phencyclidine hydrochloride (PCP; "angel dust"), cocaine, cannabis (marijuana and hashish), barbituates, and amphetamines, as well as tranquilizers. When such a screening technique is used, management must take care in reducing the risk of discrimination charges by requiring all applicants to undergo the same screening process and by obtaining adequate legal counsel prior to administering the test.

From a legal perspective, preemployment testing or screening may be the safest option for management because the individual is not yet an employee vested with employment rights (Henry and Parrish 1988). Testing of current employees is riskier than preemployment testing for several reasons, as follows:

- constitutional right to privacy (Fourth Amendment of the United States Constitution)

- equal employment laws (Federal Rehabilitation Act of 1983)
- wrongful discharge litigation ("good" or "just" causes or implied contract with employee)
- civil tort liability (invasion of privacy, defamation, and intentional infliction of emotional distress)
- collective bargaining agreements (National Labor Relations Act [NLRA], unemployment compensation)

In making decisions related to drug use in the workplace, organizations often implement tough policies, such as mandatory testing. According to Schreier (1988), dealing with substance abuse is more than a policy and testing issue; it involves values, motivation, stress, communication, change, and conflict management. Companies that have avoided or decreased drug use in the workplace have done so through training supervisory and management personnel, creating employee assistance programs, and emphasizing both substance abuse and management issues. In a survey of training professionals, including health care, 65 of the respondents had formed employee assistance programs. Only 26.7 percent provide training, with most of the training focusing on policy and procedures and a lesser amount on confronting, counseling, and legal issues.

To assist the personnel officer in screening applications, other tools should be available, such as a job analysis, job description, and job specification.

Job Analysis

Job analysis is a detailed study of the job in terms of duties, tasks, procedures, and organizational aspects. It involves careful observation and investigation of all job essentials. The job analysis attempts to answer the following questions:

- What is the job?
- What kinds of tasks are involved and how do they cluster together?
- What are the features of the job?
- What employee behavior is required in the job?
- What personality characteristics may be required?
- How can the job analysis assist the selection process?

A number of techniques are used to obtain meaningful data about the job to be analyzed. The method used may or may not involve employee participation. Employees, as incumbents on the job, may provide information through a personal interview, recording in a daily diary, or completing a checklist or questionnaire about job content. A nonparticipative technique is the use of an expert job analyst to observe the incumbent as various activities are performed. When it is necessary to analyze a new position, occupational information may be obtained by means of a small survey of incumbents at other facilities, or the use of a technical conference in which experts write down activities based on recall. In addition to work activity, the method used must also provide an estimate of skills and knowledge, supervision, job and human interrelationships, and physical and mental requirements. The method used must be appropriate for the position to be analyzed. It is much easier to analyze a job composed of repetitive tasks than one that is supervisory. For supervisory or managerial positions, the analysis should cover the routine day-to-day tasks as well as the weekly, monthly, annual, and other organizational projects involved. Exhibit 14–5 shows a sample job analysis for the position of assistant director of food service in a 400-bed hospital. The sample job analysis is a summary of activities rather than a detailed breakdown of each task. Exhibit 14–6 depicts a sample job analysis for a kitchen helper. The analysis is job oriented and far less complicated than that for a higher-level position. Interpersonal skills are not considered high priority for this position.

The job analysis is basic to other tools used in the management of personnel, such as the job description, job specification, job standards, and job classifications. In addition, the job can serve the following purposes:

- planning work activity during nonpeak periods
- studying work methods as a basis for work simplification
- determining work methods and procedures
- preparing training needs and schedules
- improving recruitment and hiring procedures
- discovering job performance requirements as a basis for orientation and training
- proving job content to aid in better supervision
- providing facts for union negotiations and job classification
- discovering related and overlapping jobs that may be combined
- determining workload when new systems, new equipment, or new work methods are introduced
- providing data on safety precautions necessary to protect an employee's health
- providing data on time constraints in performing various tasks

Job Description

A job description is an organized list of general statements that reflect the duties and responsibilities of a job. The statements are compiled from the job analysis and should include all essential duties that are routinely performed. The job description should not be cluttered with occasional tasks that may be required of a worker in the position. For less frequently performed tasks, a statement at the end of the list of duties, such as "all related tasks," will suffice. A job description (Exhibit 14–7) must be precise enough to serve as a selection tool, yet flexible enough to serve functional purposes in

Exhibit 14–5 Job Analysis for Assistant Director

Assistant Director—Food Service Department

Daily (AM)

Review mail basket for notices concerning the department, bills, meetings, etc.
Consult with Chief of Clinical Services and Production Supervisor on menu, personnel, census, etc.
Consult with Cafeteria Service Supervisor on menu, personnel, etc.
Meet with director on agenda for the day, meetings, special assignments, etc.
Review lunch menu for the day and if necessary, give special instructions to Production Supervisor.
Review menu, production worksheet, and recipes for the following day, and check with storeroom personnel on availability of food items.
Order food items as needed.
Check with storeroom personnel on deliveries for accuracy and proper storage.
Inspect kitchen and dining area for cleanliness.
Check counter setup in dining room and on tray line. Make sure lines start on time.
Sample all lunch food items.

Daily (PM)

Work on special project or one of weekly duties.
Check work schedule for following day. Document any and all absences and tardiness, following standard procedures.
Check dinner menu with Late Supervisor.
Check counter setup in dining room and on tray line. Make sure lines start on time.
Sample dinner meal.

Weekly

Review cycle menus and make necessary changes relative to cost, availability of food items, acceptance, and manpower.
Make meal rounds.

Monthly

Attend staff meetings, assigned committee meetings, and employee meetings.
Write report on status of departmental goals and objectives.
Make out work schedule for all employees.
Monitor daily record of food cost and assist with monthly inventory.
Conduct and evaluate employer in-service program, and all other external training programs assigned.
Participate in departmental quality assurance program.

Annually

Assist in the development of the department's budget.
Write performance ratings on employees.
Review and evaluate policies, procedures, job descriptions, and standards of work. Update as necessary for compliance with accrediting agencies.
Develop goals and objectives for the smooth operation of the department. Review on a timely basis.

the organization. The job description may be written in narrative or outline form, to include identifying information, job summary, and duties and responsibilities. There should be a job description for each position shown on the organization chart. In the management of personnel, the job description can serve the following purposes:

- matching qualified applicants to the job
- establishing orientation and training programs
- establishing performance appraisal standards
- establishing job classification and rate of pay
- determining limits of authority and responsibility
- clarifying chain of command

Job Specification

A job specification is a written statement of the minimum requirements that must be met by an applicant for a particular job. The specification is based on the job analysis and is

Exhibit 14–6 Job Analysis for Kitchen Helper

Kitchen Helper

Prepare dish machine.
- Fill machine with water.
- Check temperatures.
- Check soap dispensing levels.

Operate dish machine.
Scrape, prewash, and stack soiled dishes.
Wash dishes, glasses, cups, and trays.
Wash silverware.
Soak cups for removal of stains.
Remove and store clean dishes, glasses, and cups.
Remove and stack clean trays.
Remove and store clean silverware.
Clean dish machine inside and outside.
Remove trash in dishroom area.
Clean floors in dishroom area.
Remove and dispose of old grease from kitchen areas.
Empty trash in production and service area.
Sweep floors in production and cafeteria areas.
Mop floors in production and service areas.
Change mop head.
Fill pot and pan sink with hot water.
Add sanitizing solution to final rinse sink.
Add soap to wash sink.
Scrape pots and pans of excess food.
Clean pots and pans.
Stack and store clean pots and pans.
Clean processing equipment.
Clean pot and pan washing area.
Assist in tray assembly.
Place food items on trays.
Load food trucks.
Deliver food trucks to patient areas.
Dismantle tray assembly line.
Pick up food trucks from patient areas.
Remove trays from food carts.
Wash and sanitize food carts.
Clean equipment in tray assembly area.
Sweep floor in tray assembly area.
Remove all trash from tray assembly area.
Mop floor in tray assembly area.
Change mop head.

used primarily by the personnel officer in screening job applicants. Typical information found in a job specification (see Exhibit 14–8) include experience required; education required; special training, knowledge, and skills needed; personal requirements; working conditions; hours of work; job classification, wage code, and grade; promotional opportunities; tests required; and professional or craft affiliation, license, and certification.

Personal Interview

The personal interview is usually the final step prior to making a decision on the hiring of an employee. The interview is an important part of the selection process and should receive adequate time and attention from the food service director or person conducting the interview.

Before the Interview

Some factors to consider before the interview begins are the following:

1. Determine the goal of the interview, such as to hire a cook in a full-time, part-time, or contingency position.
2. Prepare an outline as a guide during the interview. Study all information about the prospective employee, previously obtained from the application form, tests, and references.
3. Schedule the interview at a time convenient for both the interviewer and interviewee. Provide plenty of time to obtain adequate information for effective decision making.
4. Provide privacy. The interview should be conducted in a private office, without undue interruptions by telephone calls or by other employees entering the room.

During the Interview

The following guidelines will help the person conducting the interview:

- Permit the interviewee to settle down before beginning the interview.
- Make questions open ended to avoid yes or no answers. Seek information not included on the application form.
- Be a good listener. Let the interviewee finish one question before asking another, allowing the person time to think about the question before answering.
- When in doubt about what the interviewee is saying, summarize the statement. Make frequent use of "why" and "how." Do not hesitate to probe for a more complete answer.

Exhibit 14–7 Job Description for Kitchen Helper

Position Title: Kitchen Helper ______________________ Classification: ____________

I. *Introduction*

Position is located in production and service areas of food service department, under direct supervision of production supervisor. Works in dishroom, kitchen, and patient service area as assigned.

II. *Duties and Responsibilities*

1. Operates dish machine to wash dishes, glasses, cups, trays, and silverware.
2. Stores clean serviceware.
3. Cleans dish machine and dishroom area.
4. Washes pots, pans, and processing equipment.
5. Stores clean equipment and utensils.
6. Cleans pot and pan area.
7. Assists with tray assembly.
8. Delivers food carts to patient areas.
9. Picks up food carts from patient areas.
10. Cleans and sanitizes food carts.
11. Assists in maintaining preparation and service area in sanitary condition.
12. Performs other related duties as required.

____

Signature of Food Service Director   Date

Review Dates:

____

____

____

Exhibit 14–8 Job Specification for Kitchen Helper

Job Specification: Kitchen Helper ______________________ Date Reviewed: ________

Experience

None required.

Education

A minimum of eighth grade education.

Knowledge, Skills, Abilities

Able to read, write, and understand instructions.

Physical Demands

Must be able to remain standing for most of working hours.
Must be physically fit as determined by physical examination.
Must be nonallergic to a variety of soaps, detergents, and cleaning compounds.
Must be able to lift at least 35 pounds.

Working Conditions

Must be able to perform repetitive tasks.
Must be able to work flexible hours, either early or late shifts.
Must be able to work flexible days—weekdays and weekends.
May be exposed to sharp instruments and power-driven equipment.
May be exposed to hot, humid work areas.

- Use language appropriate to the skill level of the position to be filled.
- Do not let the interviewee know your sentiments. Avoid taking sides on issues.
- Be in control of the interview at all times. Follow the prepared outline to make sure all pertinent questions are asked.
- Avoid writing down answers to questions during the interview. This practice will inhibit the interviewee from talking freely.

After the Interview

The steps to follow after the interview include the following:

1. Inform the applicant when the final decision will be made on selection.
2. Review and reflect on information gained through the interview, and record pertinent data.
3. Compare personal interview notes with references, the application form, and other credentials for consistency.
4. Make your selection decision, based on objective data.
5. Inform the personnel office of your decision.
6. Inform the applicant of your decision.

Orientation

Orientation and training programs should be organized, consistent, and conducted by individuals knowledgeable of the job content. The practice of assigning a new employee to work with another employee until he or she gets the hang of it is one of the poorest methods of introducing a new employee to the job. The length of the orientation and training period is not as important as the thoroughness of information provided. A recommended program includes general orientation and specific orientation and training.

General Orientation

During this period, the trainer and the employee follow a checklist (Exhibit 14–9), prepared from the employee handbook, to cover all pertinent information of a general nature. The emphasis at this time is to develop an understanding of the organization structure and the interrelationships of systems and subsystems, and to familiarize the new employee with policies, procedures, and job responsibilities. Each employee receives a copy of the handbook to keep for future reference.

Orientation and Training Guidelines

Training is for a two-week period. During the first week, the employee has an opportunity to observe, demonstrate, and practice all functions listed in the job description (Exhibit 14–10). Performance standards are explained during the discussion and observation periods so that the employee is aware of the quality and quantity of work expected. During the second week, the employee has an opportunity to work independently, under supervision, in all assigned work areas (Exhibit 14–11).

At the end of the second week of training, the employee is either scheduled for a regular shift or referred for additional training, based on the performance rating (Exhibit 14–12). Factors used for rating training performance are the same as those used in the performance standards.

Performance Evaluation

The terms *performance evaluation, performance rating,* and *performance appraisal* are often used interchangeably to indicate a process of measuring work accomplishment. The evaluation of employee performance is a serious and important part of a manager's job and should not be looked upon as a dreaded activity to be accomplished at set intervals. Employee evaluation is an ongoing process, not a once-a-year task. Each time an employee is praised for doing a good job or criticized for a below-standard performance, evaluation is taking place on an informal basis. When such incidents are documented and used as a basis for evaluation, the formal evaluation process becomes less difficult.

Depending on the methods used for performance evaluation, there can be an enormous amount of fear, tension, and anxiety generated at the time of rating. After all, an employee's future may depend on or at least may be influenced by the rating. To alleviate the unpleasantness associated with employee evaluations, the following steps should be beneficial to both management and employees:

- Develop job standards. Job standards are predetermined criteria based on work samplings of duties and responsibilities as listed in the job description. For example, employees should not be told, "You are working too slow" or "Your work is not of good quality," unless standards have been developed. The terms *slow* and *good* are too ambiguous and subjective to be of any value in evaluating work performance. As shown in Exhibit 14–13, all standards should be stated in measurable terms. Employees know how much is to be done (quantity), how well it is to be done (quality), how quickly the job is to be done (time limitations), and how the job is to be done (policies or procedures).
- Determine the purpose of the evaluation. What is the evaluation used for? Is it routine paperwork that must be accomplished every six months or once a year? If the evaluation is used for a specific purpose such as promotion decisions, salary increases, or employee training and development, the employee should be so informed.
- Develop a performance evaluation tool. Performance evaluation is the appraisal of an employee's performance

Exhibit 14–9 General Orientation Checklist

Name:________________________________ Date of Hire: ____________________
Union:__________ Nonunion:__________ Orientation Date: From _______ To _______

All new employees must be given an orientation to the Dietary Services on the first and second days of employment, by the supervisor in charge of training. The intent of the orientation is to familiarize the new employee with various aspects of the Food Service Department and the hospital, and to prepare him or her for a thorough on-the-job training to be followed by in-service education.

Instructions for Preparing Checklist

1. This checklist must be prepared by the supervisor in charge of training. Check (✓) indicates that this area has been covered.
2. Employees must sign in the appropriate section of the checklist.
3. Additional orientation must be provided for employees with a less than satisfactory rating.

Comments | Date

_____1. The functions and purposes of a hospital have been explained.

_____2. The organization structure of Metropolitan Hospital has been explained.

_____3. Organization of Dietary Department—Show chart.
Lines of authority
Services provided by the department
—Inpatient meal service
—Cafeteria meal service
—Therapeutic diet counseling
—Goal/objectives
—Vision/mission

_____4. Was given a tour of the Food Service Department and introduced to staff members.

_____5. The following policies and procedures have been explained:

_____A. Wages and Payroll
—Rate of pay
—Pay day
—Overtime pay
—Payroll deductions

_____B. Hours of work
—Time schedule
—Mealtime, rest period
—Holidays
—Sick leave
—Vacation
—Punching of time clock
—Leave of absence with or without pay

_____C. Union affiliation

_____D. Personal health and appearance
—Physical examination
—Food handlers' card requirement
—Good hygiene
—Uniform regulations
—Identification nameplates

_____E. Sanitation and safety
—Disaster drill
—Fire regulations and drill
—Infection control
—Personal safety
—Accident procedure
—Safety equipment

Exhibit 14–10 Week 1 Orientation and Training Guidelines for Kitchen Helper

Monday:

Review General Orientation
- —Function and purpose
- —Organization structure
- —Job description
- —Performance standards
- —Reporting times/flextime
- —Logistics
- —Standards of behavior/disciplinary action policy
- —Safety standards/accident reporting

Discuss and observe dishwashing
- —Operation of dish machine
- —Tray conveyor
- —Prewashing and stacking soiled dishes
- —Washing silverware
- —Removing clean silverware

Tuesday:

Demonstrate and participate in dishwashing
- —Participate under supervision in operating dish machine according to procedures and standards
- —Stripping and stacking trays
- —Handling of clean dishes and trays, delivery to stations
- —Washing silverware, handling and storing clean silverware
- —Removing coffee stains from cups
- —Cleaning dish machine
- —Cleaning dishroom

Areas of Concern:

____

____

____

Corrective Action:

____

____

____

Wednesday:

Discuss and observe porter
- —Tour kitchen and cafeteria, pointing out areas to be swept and mopped
- —Observe preparation of cleaning solutions and equipment used
- —Observe time and frequency of cleaning
- —Observe collection of trash and grease and method for disposing

Practice porter functions
- —Participate under supervision in sweeping floors, mopping floors, removing trash, emptying old grease, etc .

Areas of Concern:

____

____

____

Corrective Action:

____

____

____

continues

Exhibit 14–10 continued

Thursday:

Discuss and observe pot and pan washing

—Tour pot-washing area, pointing out areas to be kept clean and sanitized

—Observe pot-washing procedure: filling sink with water, cleaning and sanitizing solutions, disposing of food waste, operation of garbage disposal, cleaning pots and pans, storing clean pots and pans, storing clean utensils, cleaning work area

Practice pot and pan washing

—Participate under supervision in washing pots, pans, and utensils

Areas of Concern:

____

____

____

Corrective Action:

____

____

____

Friday:

Discuss and observe tray assembly

—Observing tray assembly line

—Placing items on patient food tray

—Loading food trucks according to procedures

—Delivering and pickup of food trucks

—Cleaning tray carts

—Practicing tray assembly functions

Participate under supervision in assembling, loading, and transporting carts to patient area and cleanup

Areas of Concern:

____

____

____

Corrective Action:

____

____

____

against the job standards established for the position. It represents an objective review of how well the employee has performed and the possibilities for improvements and advancement. Factors included on the performance evaluation form should be identical to those listed on the job standards. A sample form is shown in Exhibit 14–14. Any factor can be used to evaluate employees if it is objective and easily understood by both the rater and the employee. For example, supervisory personnel may require expertise in leadership, labor relations, cost containment, resourcefulness, and interpersonal relationships.

- Communicate with employees. Each employee should have a copy of the job description and job standards for the job that he or she is hired to do. The manager should communicate throughout the appraisal period by letting the employee know when a job is well done or when improvements are needed. There should not be any shocking revelations during the performance appraisal conference.
- Encourage employee participation. One method of involvement is to inform the employee in advance that the evaluation will take place on a specified date. Ask the employee to prepare for the conference as follows:

1. Review your job description and job standards.
2. Compare your performance against the standards. Note areas where you have done well and areas where improvements are needed.
3. Make suggestions on how your work performance can be more effective. Suggestions may involve your section or the entire department.
4. For the conference, scheduled on _______, bring the assessment of your performance with you so that we can fully discuss your evaluation.

Exhibit 14–11 Week 2 Orientation and Training Guidelines for Kitchen Helper

Monday:
—Early dishroom
—Employee assigned to early dishroom shift with a trained employee and, under supervision, functions independently
—Evaluate and determine area for more practice
—Document areas of concern and actions to correct same
Tuesday:
—Late dishroom
—Same as early dishroom
Wednesday:
—Porter
—Employee assigned to porter schedule with a trained employee and, under supervision, functions independently
—Evaluate and determine areas for more practice
—Document areas of concern and actions to correct same
Thursday:
—Pot washer
—Employee assigned to pot washer schedule with a trained employee and, under supervision, functions independently
—Evaluate and determine areas for more practice
—Document areas of concern and actions to correct same
Friday:
—Tray assembly
—Employee assigned to assembly with a trained employee and, under supervision, functions independently
—Evaluate and determine areas for more practice
—Document areas of concern and action
—Decision point:
—Is more training necessary. If so, schedule same.
—Is employee ready for assignment to shift? If so, arrange same.

During the conference, there may be some disagreement on the final evaluation. The rater should be prepared to reach mutual agreement with documentation made throughout the appraisal period rather than depending on recall. The use of objective, factual documentation can remove the personal element from the discussion, and the time saved can be spent on corrective action, if necessary.

EDUCATION AND TRAINING PROGRAMS

Employee training begins as soon as the individual is hired. The training may be of an informal nature, such as learning from other workers how to perform certain tasks, or it can be more directed and controlled. The latter type of training is recommended for long-term operational efficiency. It is the food service director's responsibility to make sure that an effective education and training program is established and conducted on a continuous basis. In large- or medium-sized facilities, the education and training duties are performed by a qualified dietitian on a full-time basis. A variety of titles is used for the position, including in-service educator, dietetic educator, director of training and development, and others. The individual may be responsible for all training provided by the food service department.

The types of training programs may be classified as required, optional, or in-service.

Required Training

These programs consist of the following:

- orientation of new employees
- in-service training for all employees
- outside education for supervisory personnel

Optional Training

These programs include the following:

- outside education for all full-time employees
- field or work experience for high-school students

Exhibit 14–12 Performance Rating—Orientation and Training

Position Title: Kitchen Helper Department: Dietary
Prepared by:

Supervisor: ______________________ Department Head: ______________________
Name of Employee: ______________________
Training Period Date: ______________________ to ______________________

Objective: For the new food service employee to achieve and maintain high standards of efficiency and quality.

Dishroom	Excellent	Satisfactory	Unsatisfactory	Comments
1. Properly operates dish machine at designated temperatures using prescribed quantities of solution. a. Washing solution Guardian Esteem b. Prewash temperature 100°F–120°F c. Wash temperature 140°F–160°F d. Final rinse temperature 180°F–200°F				
2. Scrapes excessive food particles from patients' trays and dining room patrons' dishes. a. Food particles in garbage disposal b. Paper waste in trash receptacle				
3. Soiled dishes and trays stacked separately and uniformly in rack.				
4. Routinely stacks clean dishes in lowerators or appropriate containers according to description and delivers to proper kitchen areas.				
5. Soiled silverware presoaked in proper solution and cleaned according to standard procedure. a. Pre soak solution (Textrox) b. Separate silverware placed in cylinders, with handle up				
Porter				
1. Thoroughly cleans and sanitizes kitchen floors, dining area, offices, and rest rooms on daily basis. a. Cleaning solution: Conquest				
2. Routinely cleans and sanitizes refrigerators, freezers, and other equipment as needed.				
3. Collects trash and garbage from kitchen and dining room and disposes in dumpsters as needed.				
4. Frequently wipes up spillage on floors and work surfaces.				
Pot and Pan Washing				
1. Prepare pot washing sinks according to standard procedure. a. Washes sink with hot water solution Solution: Textrox, 2 Tbs to each gallon of water b. Rinses sink with clear hot water only c. Sanitizes sink with hot water and only sanitizing solution. Solution: 3 oz Wescodyne per 2½ gal of water. *Note*: Add Wescodyne after the water is in the sink to avoid foaming. d. Scrapes excessive food particles from pots and pans and utensils. e. Places discarded food items in garbage disposal. *Note:* Do not put bones or pour grease in disposal				

continues

Exhibit 14–12 continued

Pot and Pan Washing (continued)	Excellent	Satisfactory	Unsatisfactory	Comments
2. Maintains clean water.				
3. Allows pots, pans, and utensils to air dry.				
4. Safely cleans and sanitizes food processing equipment according to procedure.				
5. Cleans and sanitizes work area daily.				
Tray Assembly				
1. Loads patient trays in food carts in sequential order with proper tray identification.				
2. Prepares and sets up tray assembly work stations as assigned at each meal period.				
3. Checks trays for neatness.				
4. Accurately serves food items and/or accessories on patient trays according to menus.				
Transporting Food Carts				
1. Safely and promptly transports food carts to designated patient areas.				
2. Safely and promptly returns food carts complete with soiled trays to dishwashing area.				

- clinical experience for students in dietetic assistant and dietetic technician programs
- practicums and work experience for college students in dietetics and food systems management
- clinical experiences for students in coordinated undergraduate programs (CUPs)
- clinical experiences for students in dietetic internships sponsored by other hospitals, public schools, and public health departments
- six-month practical experience for graduate students in dietetics
- internship program for dietetic students

Written documentation is required for all training provided by the food service department. For orientation, a training schedule, such as the one used for the kitchen helper's position, should be established and used for each position in the department. Documentation of in-service training can be accomplished each time training is conducted by using a form such as the one depicted in Exhibit 14–15. Space is allotted for recording the names of those attending the training session, as well as space for the topic, summary, and evaluation. The form should be kept on file for future reference. All topics used for in-service training are derived from an assessment of needs and are scheduled for presentation so that employees from all work shifts can participate. Outside training for supervisory personnel may be in the form of workshops, seminars, conferences, formal classes, and other meaningful sources.

Optional education and training programs are provided by most medical food service operations. Contractual agreements are drawn up and signed by appropriate administrative personnel at both the requesting institution and the facility providing training. The contract is frequently referred to as a master agreement, with provisions for continuation or termination by either party. Thereafter, a one-page document, as shown in Exhibit 14–16, is normally sufficient to show that the food service department is in accord with accepting a student for training during a specified time period. A record of affiliation (Exhibit 14–17), maintained by the food service department, is required and should be kept on file. Training programs for students in CUP, internship, and graduate work experience must be approved and/or accredited by the American Dietetic Association. Qualified dietitians must be available for the supervision of students when they are directly engaged in patient care activities.

In-Service Training

There are four basic steps involved in establishing an in-service training program:

1. Assessing needs. Allow employee participation during this stage. Employees will suggest topics for which

Exhibit 14–13 Job Standard

Position: *Kitchen Helper*

1. *Quantity of work.* Acceptable standards are indicated when: *All dishes are washed and ready for meal service.*
2. *Quality of Work.* Acceptable standards are indicated when: *All dishes, glasses, and silverware are free from spots.*
3. *Job Knowledge.* Acceptable standards are indicated when: *Instructions are followed correctly in operating equipment.*
4. *Cooperation.* Acceptable standards are indicated when: *Employee willingly accepts related duties.*
5. *Display of Initiative.* Acceptable standards are indicated when: *Employee develops a better way to perform a job and reports it.*
6. *Reliability.* Acceptable standards are indicated when: *Employee reports for duty as scheduled.*
7. *Appearance.* Acceptable standards are indicated when: *Clean uniforms are worn daily.*

Exhibit 14–14 Performance Evaluation Form

XYZ GENERAL HOSPITAL
Employee Performance Evaluation Form

Anniversary ( ) Termination ( ) 90 Day ( ) Other ____________

Employee Name ____________ Position ____________
Department ____________ Date of Hire ____________

Factors	Rating Scale					Comments
	1	2	3	4	5	
1. Quantity of Work						
2. Quality of Work						
3. Job Knowledge						
4. Cooperation						
5. Display of Initiative						
6. Reliability						
7. Appearance						

GENERAL COMMENTS: ____________

EMPLOYEE COMMENTS: ____________

Employee Signature ____________ Date ____________
Evaluator Signature ____________ Date ____________
Department Head Signature ____________ Date ____________

Exhibit 14–15 Record of In-Service Training

Subject: ______________________ Date: ______________
Presenter-Trainer: ______________________
Attendance:

1. ____________	9. ____________
2. ____________	10. ____________
3. ____________	11. ____________
4. ____________	12. ____________
5. ____________	13. ____________
6. ____________	14. ____________
7. ____________	15. ____________
8. ____________	16. ____________

Summary of discussion:

Evaluation and follow-up:

they feel a need and that are of interest to them. This will serve to get the program off to a good start. Include areas where work improvement is needed by referring to previous evaluations or inspection reports. Topics such as safety, sanitation, infection control, proper production and service techniques, personal hygiene, and new policies and procedures are always important.

2. Planning. Compile all topics gathered during the assessment stage. Prioritize topics for presentation based on relevance and degree of urgency. Be prepared to answer the following questions:

   —Who will conduct the training sessions?
   —Who will attend the training sessions?
   —Where will the training sessions take place?
   —When will the training sessions take place?
   —Will the training schedule include convenient time periods for employees on all shifts?
   —How much advance time is required for posting notice of a training session so that supervisors can plan assignments?
   —How will employees be informed of the training sessions?
   —What methods of teaching will be used?
   —Where are resources located?
   —What form of evaluation will be used?

3. Implementation. Be prepared for each training session. Have all materials, supplies, and equipment ready before the session begins. Trial-test all equipment to make sure that it is working properly. Complete a written lesson plan for each scheduled session (Exhibit 14–18). Adjust the training method to meet the needs of the individual or group. This means that it is necessary to consider factors such as length of the session, learning speed, language barriers, attention span, state of learning readiness, motivation, nature of the material or task, and the amount of guidance needed. Provide an atmosphere that is conducive to learning. Allow trainees an opportunity to ask questions and take part in discussions and demonstrations. Provide feedback throughout the training session to promote the learning concept of reinforcement.
4. Evaluation. This final step actually begins with the assessment stage of training. When an employee is observed to be performing a task at less than the established proficiency rate, training is indicated. For corrective action to take place, a transfer of knowledge is required to improve the particular skills, knowledge, and/or attitudes. Assuming that appropriate training was used, the evaluation tool should measure any change in behavior that has taken place. Depending on training objectives, the evaluation may be in the form of written test questions, oral responses, or demonstrations (actual or simulated). The evaluation tool should be criterion referenced, based on performance standards. Training evaluations are confidential; therefore, precautions should be used

Exhibit 14–16 Agreement Form for Work Experience

Supervised Work Experience

Student's name ____________________ Date ____________________
I.D. number ____________________ Telephone number ____________________
Major __________ Course number __________ Credit hours __________
Location of training ____________________
Training period: ____________________ to ____________________

Description of study

Purpose: To gain practical experience in the operation and administration of a food service department.

Scope and limitation: Student will actively participate in all phases of the food service operation.

Procedure–activities:

1. Review the food service department organizational chart, policies, and procedures.
2. Study the administration of food production in the following areas: menu planning, purchasing, receiving, storing, prepreparation, salad units, sanitation, equipment maintenance, use, and care.
3. Work on special assignments, such as banquets and luncheons, at the discretion of the coordinator.
4. Turn in a written report of each assignment.
5. Use the attached assignment sheet as study guide.

Approved by:

____
Coordinator's signature

____
Academic advisor's signature

throughout the training process to protect employee rights.

One important in-service training topic is in the area of infection control—more specifically, human immunodeficiency virus (HIV) and acquired immunodeficiency syndrome (AIDS). Medical facilities are required to have infection control committees and established policies and procedures to protect employees and patients. Although medical facilities have always treated patients with infectious diseases, AIDS has generated a high degree of fear in that the disease is fatal with no cure. Another reason for the fear is that the general population is not convinced that transmission routes are limited to those identified at this time.

The Centers for Disease Control and Prevention (CDC) has recommended universal precautions for all patients, eliminating the need for the isolation category of blood and body fluid precautions (U.S. Department of Labor and U.S. Department of Health 1987). The recommendations have been endorsed by the American Hospital Association and by proposed guidelines of the National Committee for Clinical Laboratory Standards. A survey of the Society of Hospital Epidemiologists (SHEA) was conducted to determine their opinion on and their hospital's actual practice of universal precautions, HIV screening, and informed consent (Miller and Farr 1988). Fifty-seven percent of the respondents opposed the CDC recommendations to eliminate the category of blood and body fluid precautions, preferring to continue use of the category for patients with documented infections. This may explain why some medical facilities have discontinued use of isolation, whereas others continue to isolate patients with infectious diseases, including those with AIDS.

Food service employees do not have direct patient contact, but they must be aware of the potential for exposure. Training sessions to inform employees of known transmission routes will serve to dispel misinformation, and thus fear of casual contact. The trainer needs to be aware of facility policies on isolation and other procedures for infection control, present factual information, and document

Exhibit 14–17 Record of Affiliation Form

Record of Affiliation

Name of Trainee ______________________________

Trainee Experience Site ______________________________

Address ______________________________

City ____________ State ____________ Zip ____________

Area of learning experience ______________________________

Number of Weeks ____________ from ____________ to ____________

Signature of Trainee ____________ Date ____________

College ______________________________

Dates of attendance: From ____________ to ____________

Signature of On-site Advisor ____________ Date ____________

Signature of Department Director, Dietetics ____________ Date ____________

training to meet the standards of the Occupational Safety and Health Administration (OSHA) and those of the Joint Commission on Accreditation of Healthcare Organizations (Joint Commission). Consultant Dietitians in Health Care Facilities (1988) have developed an excellent training tool for in-service education on infection control and other food service–related topics. Food service directors in hospitals should collaborate with human resource development personnel to develop appropriate training tools.

UNION-MANAGEMENT RELATIONS

Unionization can be defined as a process whereby a group of employees, sharing similar interests, voluntarily agree to form an association for the purpose of maintaining or improving wages, hours of work, and working conditions. Although unions have been legally active since the mid-1930s, it was not until passage of the 1974 amendment to the National Labor Relations Act (Pub. L. No. 93-518, Ninety-

Exhibit 14–18 Lesson Plan for In-Service Training on Equipment

Lesson Plan

Instructional unit:

Method of presentation (lecture, film, demonstration, etc.):

Time required:

Lesson presented to (define audience, i.e., Cooks, Dietary Aides, Bakers, etc.):

Tools and equipment (tools needed for demonstration):

Instructional aids (brochures, handouts, etc.):

References (Operational Manual, Manufacturer's Guide, etc.):

Presentation:

- I. Introduction
  - A. Objectives
  - B. Standards of performance
- II. Explanation and demonstration
  - A. Mechanical features
  - B. Safety precautions
  - C. Maintenance
  - D. Cleaning
- III. Summary

third Congress, Second Session) that medical care facilities felt the impact of unionization.

Major Legislation

The legislation designed to ensure the rights of both labor and management includes the following:

- The Norris-LaGuardia Act (Anti-Injunction Act) of 1932 (U.S. Code Service, Title 18, Section 3692) was the first major federal legislation dealing with union activity. The intent of the law was to remove some of the hostility associated with employees' attempts to organize by placing restraints on employers and courts in dealing with union efforts and labor disputes. The act guaranteed the right to strike, to pay strike benefits, to picket, to ask other employees to strike, to assist financially in labor disputes, and to meet on strike strategy.
- The Wagner Act (National Labor Relations Act—NLRA) of 1935 (U.S. Code Service, Title 29, Section 151+) encouraged the growth and strength of unions by promoting practices and procedures of collective bargaining and the choosing of representation for negotiation purposes. The act made it legal for employees to organize and illegal for employers to interfere in such efforts. Unfair labor practices by an employer were specified as interference with an employee's right to join a union or with union activity, discrimination in hiring or discharging of employee based on union activity, and refusal to bargain in good faith.
- The Taft-Hartley Act (Labor Management Relations Act—LMRA) of 1947 (U.S. Code Service, Title 29, Section 141+) was passed to provide a balance of labor and management rights by amending the NLRA, providing additional facilities for mediation of labor disputes, and equalizing legal responsibilities of labor organizations and employers. The act specifically exempted health care facilities from union activity.
- The Landrum-Griffin Act (Labor Management Reporting and Disclosure Act—LMRDA) of 1959 (U.S. Code Service, Title 29, Sections 153, 158–160, 164, 186, 187, 401+) served to redefine and state unfair management-labor practices in more specific terms.
- The 1974 amendment to the NLRA and the LMRDA included nonprofit medical care facilities under the jurisdiction of the National Labor Relations Board (NLRB) for the first time. The amendment defined health care facilities to include any hospital, convalescent hospital, health maintenance organization, health clinic, nursing home, extended care facility, or any other institution devoted to the care of sick, infirm, or aged persons. Because of the nature of activities conducted in medical care facilities, special collective bargaining provisions were included in the amendment as follows:

  1. The employer or union must adhere to a 90-day notification period versus a 60-day period for other industries.
  2. For negotiation of contract renewal or modification, a 90-day notice by employer or union is required versus a 60-day notice period for other industries.
  3. Prior to the termination or expiration of a collective bargaining contract, the Federal Mediation and Conciliation Service (FMCS) must be given a 60-day notice versus a 30-day notice for other industries.
  4. The health care facility and the union may be required to participate in the mediation process for both renewal and initial contracts at the discretion of the FMCS versus no such provisions for other industries.
  5. The union must give the health care facility and the FMCS a 10-day notice prior to any picketing, strike, or other form of refusal to work versus no such provision for other industries.
  6. When there is a threatened or actual work stoppage that would impair health care delivery, the FMCS has the authority to establish an impartial board of inquiry to investigate the labor-management dispute and to make a written report of the findings.

Managerial Responsibilities

To carry out responsibilities related to union activity, a manager needs to understand the collective bargaining process and the strategy and tactics to use during organizing campaigns. Collective bargaining is a method of negotiation to resolve problems of employment. Employers must negotiate in good faith on wages, hours of work, fringe benefits, and conditions of work. Other items, such as grievance procedures, disciplinary actions, vacation times, holidays, leaves of absence, and seniority rights may also be part of the bargaining package. If a settlement is not agreed upon by the 90th day of collective bargaining, a mediator may be brought in to assist in reaching a decision. A mediator is an impartial third party whose primary purpose is to restate the positions of each side, to ensure harmonious agreement, and to encourage continuation of the collective bargaining process. Interventions by a mediator are not binding; the role is to assist or influence parties. Arbitration is also a process of involving a third party in the negotiation process. The difference between a mediator and an arbitrator is that the decision made by the arbitrator is binding for both parties. Unresolved controversies result in an impasse, culminating in a strike or a lockout by the party willing to impose the most pressure.

The union is authorized to strike if a majority of its members vote in favor of withdrawing services. The strike is normally called at a time when the most pressure can be exerted on management. When a strike is called, management may use its prerogative and hire replacements for the strikers. Striking employees who have been replaced by permanent new hires have no right to their job at the end of a strike. If the employer has not replaced the striking workers during the strike, the employer must take the strikers back at the end of the strike.

Managerial strategy and tactics used during an impending union election must be within guidelines established under fair labor practices (Azoff and Friedman 1982). Management can do the following:

- Restrict solicitation in immediate patient areas such as patient rooms, operating rooms, and places where patients receive treatment, including corridors adjacent to patient rooms, sitting rooms on patient floors adjacent to or used by patients, and elevators and stairs used primarily to transport patients.
- Prohibit solicitation and distribution during an employee's working time. Mealtimes and break times are considered nonwork time even when paid for by the health care facility.
- Prohibit outside organizers from entering the property.
- Include the following information in a letter to employees: (1) encouragement to vote, (2) cost of union dues, and (3) fringe benefits provided and how they compare with those of other health care facilities.

The laws also provide for protection against unfair employer practices as follows:

- Employers cannot interfere with the formation or administration of labor organizations. Do not make promises or threaten employees in any way that might influence voting outcome. Do not spy on union activities, ask employees about union activities, advise employees in their union activities, or make charges against unions during the union drive.
- Employers cannot discriminate against employees in hiring or tenure because of their union activity. Do not fire or threaten to fire an employee because of union activity, favor certain employees without merit consideration, discipline without sufficient warning, or transfer any employee in efforts to dilute union activity.
- Employers cannot discharge or discriminate against employees because they have filed charges against the company. Allow employees to file charges and testify to illegal employer actions without fear of reprisal from management.
- Employers cannot interfere with employees in their right to bargain collectively with their own representatives. Avoid any appearance of interference with union activities. Assure employees that they will not be discriminated against for union activities.
- Employers cannot refuse to bargain collectively with the employee representatives. Become thoroughly familiar with union proposals and counterproposals from management.

It may appear that management is confronted with undue restraints in the formation of administration of labor organizations, but unions also have legal responsibilities. The laws provide for six unfair union practices as follows (Azoff and Friedman 1982):

1. Unions cannot force employees to join a union unless a legal union shop exists. A union shop is a security provision in which all workers must join the union within a specified period of time after hiring. (Union shops are illegal in the public employment sector.) A closed shop is a union security provision whereby the employer is required to hire union members only. Membership in the union is also a condition of continued employment. (Closed shops are illegal in the public employment sector.) An agency shop is a union security provision that calls for nonunion employees in the bargaining unit either to join the union or to pay the union fee, usually equal to union dues. A conscientious clause allows individuals who oppose joining organizations for religious or deeply felt philosophical beliefs to be exempted from payment of union dues or fees. However, they may be required to contribute an amount equal to union dues to a tax-exempt charitable organization.
2. Unions cannot pressure employers to force employees to join a union or discriminate against employees who have denied union membership, unless they have failed to pay dues under union shop agreement.
3. Unions cannot refuse to bargain collectively with an employer if they are the legal representative of employees.
4. Unions cannot engage in secondary boycotts to force an employee not to do business with any other person or business. Unions cannot strike to force an employer to assign work to one union rather than another, or to force an employer to recognize a union that is not certified as the legal representative of the employees.
5. Unions cannot charge excessive or discriminatory fees.
6. Unions cannot cause an employer to pay for services that are not performed.

The negotiated contract is binding for both the employer and employees. It is a manager's responsibility to study the contract, to know the rights and power of management, to know the employees' rights, to know the duties and rights of the steward, and to understand procedures for settlement of grievances and disciplinary actions.

Grievances

A grievance is defined as any difference of opinion or any dissatisfaction arising between the health care facility and employee(s) in the interpretation or application of any provision of the contract agreement.

The grievance procedure is normally part of the negotiated contract. If no procedure exists, an employee has the right to file a grievance as outlined in Section 9 of the Taft-Hartley Act. Grievance procedures may vary from one facility to another, especially in the time involved for resolution. Depending on a grievance step, the time may vary from 2 to 30 days. A sample grievance procedure is outlined below.

Step One: The food service employee shall discuss the grievance with his or her immediate supervisor, with or without the steward, at the option of the employee. In the event the grievance is not satisfactorily settled within five working days, it shall be referred to step two.

Step Two: The food service employee and/or steward shall reduce the grievance to writing and submit it to the employee's department head with a copy to the personnel office. The department head shall meet with the employee, the steward, and the unit chairperson within two working days. The department head will give the steward his or her written answer, with a copy to the unit chairperson within three working days after the meeting. If a satisfactory settlement is not reached, the grievance shall be referred to step three within three working days after receipt of the written answer.

Step Three: The grievance committee, representative(s) from the union, the steward, and the food service employee shall take the grievance up with the executive administrator or his or her designee. A meeting with the executive administrator or designee will be held within three to ten working days. The executive administrator or designee shall give the union representative and the unit chairperson written answer within five working days after the meeting. If a satisfactory settlement is not reached, the grievance shall be referred to step four within five working days after receipt of the written answer.

Step Four: An impartial arbitrator shall be mutually agreed to within five working days between the union and the employer. In the event that mutual agreement on an arbitrator cannot be reached within the above period, either the union or the employer will submit the grievance to the American Arbitration Association. The employer and the union agree to follow the rules of the American Arbitration Association. The arbitrator shall be empowered to rule on all grievances within the established contract and wage structure. The cost of arbitration shall be shared equally by the employer and the union. No arbitration shall have any right to change, add to, subtract from, or modify any of the terms of any written agreement existing between the parties. The decision of the arbitrator shall be final and binding on both parties.

It is unrealistic to expect a food service department to operate without employee gripes, complaints, and grievances. A manager's responsibility is to resolve complaints as promptly and correctly as possible. Regardless of how minor or invalid a grievance appears to be, serious consideration must be given to all complaints. The objective is to handle gripes and complaints before they develop into a formal grievance.

Guides to Handling Grievances

The following five steps will help the manager in dealing with complaints.

1. Define the nature of the grievance. Pinpoint the main issues involved so that the reply can address each point. Determine whether the grievance refers to a provision of the contract agreement or other policies and procedures in the department or facility.
2. Gather all the facts. Answer questions of who, what, when, where, and how. Be precise in documenting day, month, year, and time of day the incident occurred. Check the files for a precedent. Review the employee's past record for pertinent facts that may have a bearing on the decision.
3. Assemble and verify the facts. Do not take anything for granted. Can the facts be substantiated by departmental or facility records? Can certain facts be supported by reliable witnesses? Do you have written statements for witnesses? If not, you may not be able to rely on a witness to testify, because many individuals are subjected to pressures from peers or other sources. Has the contract been violated? Has the employee been unfairly treated?
4. Make decisions. Be consistent with contract and facility policies. Make sure that the decision is based on facts that will be considered fair and just, should the grievance progress to the arbitration step. Check with higher administration in any areas of uncertainty.
5. Communicate the decision. The written reply should be well organized, arranged by subject or by order of events. Make sure the words used in denying a formal grievance state precisely your reason for denial. Cite the exact provisions of the contract or policies and procedures of the facility that give you the authority for your decision. Follow technical regulations, and comply with time limits as provided in the grievance procedure.

Disciplinary Action

The term *disciplinary action* refers to the steps taken to correct undesirable behavior. All managers must take disciplinary actions at one time or another because employees do not always follow policies and standard operating procedures. The word *discipline* denotes some form of punishment; thus careful attention is needed to make sure that the action taken does not result in negative attitudes toward work accomplishment. The aim of management should be to change behavior or attitude rather than just to invoke a punishment. Most union contracts include provisions for disciplinary actions similar to procedures for settling grievances.

Types of Disciplinary Actions

The type of disciplinary action taken depends on the nature of the offense. Normally, a progressive system is used, beginning with an oral warning and continuing, if necessary, to the final steps of discharge, as follows:

- Oral warning. An oral warning is a privately conducted interview between the supervisor and the employee to discuss the nature, cause, and corrective actions pertaining to the violation. The employee has an opportunity to explain fully the circumstances under which the violation occurred. Based on facts and the employee's explanation, the supervisor can either accept the explanation or explain to the employee why the explanation is not acceptable and how improvements can be made. A notation is made in the employee's record for follow-up action. The employee is informed of the written notation and subsequent notations on improvements. Oral warnings are considered temporary in the employee record.
- Written warning. A written warning is given for a repeat violation or as the first disciplinary action if the circumstance warrants. The employee is given an opportunity to explain and express his or her view of the circumstances. The employee is informed of the written warning by letter or by a standardized form, as shown in Exhibit 14–19. The employee may reply to the written warning. The disciplinary report and the employee's reply are forwarded to the personnel department and become a permanent part of the employee's record.
- Suspension. A suspension is a forced leave of absence, without pay. The length of time depends on the nature of the violation. The procedures for administration and reply by the employee are similar to those for a grievance with time allowed for reply. The disciplinary action becomes a permanent part of an employee's record.
- Dismissal. Dismissal is the most severe type of disciplinary action. In some instances, it may be used for the first offense, but normally a progression of actions has been taken prior to terminating an employee. This disciplinary action is used less frequently than oral and written warnings and suspension because of the cost of training a new employee. Procedures to follow should be provided in the contract agreement or in organizational policies and procedures.

The use of demotion as a disciplinary action is seldom used because of the effect it will have on the work environment. Transfers are considered more appropriate. Disciplinary actions can be abusive if left to the discretion of individual supervisors. Care must be taken to make sure that penalties are appropriate for the offenses and are applied in a consistent and fair manner. The guidelines shown in Table 14–1 can be helpful to both supervisors and employees in maintaining an atmosphere of good discipline in the workplace. The violations and penalties should be posted so that employees are aware of consequences.

Guides to Constructive Disciplinary Action

The purpose of disciplinary action should be to correct or change an employee's action or attitude before circumstances reach the dismissal stage. The following guidelines should be helpful:

- When it is necessary to discipline an employee, use the opportunity to train and control by making constructive criticism and following up with an explanation of how the incident should be handled.
- Refrain from reprimanding a worker at the height of an emotional state or in the presence of other employees.
- Practice fair and consistent treatment of all violations. A supervisor cannot afford to overlook incidents involving a certain employee because it will be difficult to replace that individual. Employees are constantly aware of what other employees are "getting away with."
- Handle the interview or counseling session so that the employee will realize the seriousness of the violation and will be open to future cooperation.
- Understand progressive discipline. Document efforts made to rehabilitate the employee prior to the suspension or dismissal stage.
- Investigate and review all facts prior to making a final decision on a penalty. If necessary, check with higher administration before informing the employee of your decision. A supervisor loses credibility when decisions are rescinded at a higher level.

EMPLOYEE TURNOVER

The rate of employee turnover in the medical care industry is high compared with that of other industries. A survey of nonbusiness groups, nonmanfacturing groups, and

Exhibit 14–19 Employee Disciplinary Report

To: Personnel Department

From: Food Service Department

Re: (Name of employee, position, or classification)

The following (warning or separation) was issued today, and it is to be made part of the official record.

1. ( ) Defective and improper work	9. ( ) Reporting under influence of drugs
2. ( ) Insubordination	10. ( ) Gambling
3. ( ) Carelessness	11. ( ) Firearms or other weapons
4. ( ) Unauthorized activities	12. ( ) Confidential information
5. ( ) Tardiness	13. ( ) Safety
6. ( ) Disorderly conduct	14. ( ) Destruction of property
7. ( ) Unauthorized absence	15. ( ) Other violations
8. ( ) Pilferage	

Remarks (Set forth all facts in detail, including time, date, and circumstances):

____

____

____

____

Signature of supervisor Date

I have read this report.

Signature of employee Date

Employee reply attached: yes ( ) no ( )

The above offense has been noted and is made a part of the above employee's record, as of this date.

Personnel Department Date

Offense no. 1 2 3 4

Name of Health Care Facility

financial organizations was conducted by the Bureau of National Affairs (Survey of industries 1982). Results indicated that the health care industry was tied with financial organizations for the highest turnover rate. A contributing factor for high turnover may be the low salary scale associated with the nonprofessional service-type jobs in hospitals and other health care facilities. The concern of management should be to determine the cause of the high turnover and take corrective action over areas of control. One method of determining the cause of turnover is the use of an exit interview.

The Exit Interview

The exit interview is as important as the hiring interview, and should be routine management practice whenever an employee leaves the organization. Management should be aware of reasons for turnover with detailed figures on causes of separation for reasons, such as death, retirement, accidents and illness, dismissals, layoffs, marriage, moving to another area, obtaining a better job, and attending school. It is less expensive to maintain a stable labor force than to hire and train new personnel.

Classifying departure, regardless of the reasons given by the employee, into specific categories can provide valuable information for use in recruitment, hiring, job design, and other areas of managerial control. Categories used for why individuals leave the work force may include the following:

- performance ratings—marginal, satisfactory, outstanding
- work shift—early, late
- length of time on job—0–1 year, 2–3 years, 4–5 years, 6–10 years, 10 years and longer
- rate of pay—step I, II, III, or IV

Table 14–1 Guidelines for Disciplinary Action

Offense	*First Occurrence*	*Second Occurrence*	*Third Occurrence*	*Fourth Occurrence*
Defective and improper work—work below standard in quality and quantity	Counseling	Written warning	Suspension	Dismissal
Insubordination—direct refusal or delay in carrying out instruction	Counseling	Suspension	Dismissal	
Carelessness—significant waste of food or supplies; attempt to cover up waste or destroy evidence of waste	Counseling	Written warning	Suspension	Dismissal
Unauthorized activities—significant participation in unauthorized activities during work hours; sleeping; leaving assigned work areas; promoting non–work-related activities	Counseling	Written warning	Suspension	Dismissal
Tardiness—reporting late for assigned work shift; returning late from authorized breaks	Counseling	Written warning	Suspension	Dismissal
Disorderly conduct—use of abusive language; quarreling; boisterous acts, causing disruption in production and service	Written warning	Suspension	Dismissal	
Unauthorized absence—				
Leaving work without permission	Written warning	Suspension	Dismissal	
Failure to report to work for one day except in case of emergency	Suspension			
Failure to report for work for three consecutive days, except in case of emergency	Dismissal			
Pilferage—theft or attempts to steal organizational property or the property of others	Suspension to dismissal	Dismissal		
Reporting under the influence of drugs—reporting to work under the influence of alcohol, drugs, or narcotics; drinking while on duty; use of drugs or narcotics	Written warning to suspension	Suspension	Dismissal	
Gambling—misuse of organization time for gambling	Suspension to dismissal	Dismissal		
Firearms or other weapons—concealing weapons, or the use of any weapon against another person on organization property	Dismissal			
Confidential information—revealing confidential information about patients and their families and/or co-workers	Dismissal			
Safety—acts considered dangerous to self and others				
Minor infraction	Written warning	Suspension	Dismissal	
Major infraction	Written warning to suspension	Suspension	Dismissal	
Threats of or acts of violence	Written warning to suspension	Suspension	Dismissal	
Destruction of property—intentional destruction of organization property or property of others				
Minor infraction	Written warning to suspension	Suspension	Dismissal	
Major infraction	Suspension to dismissal	Dismissal		
Other violations—other administrative policies, rules, and regulations not listed	Oral to written warning	Written warning	Suspension	Dismissal

Note: Above offenses are not all-inclusive. If other offenses not listed above are observed by management, corrective action will be taken.

- type of job—cashier, dishwasher, cook, etc.
- education level—K–8, 9–12, 1–2 years in college, 3–4 years in college
- previous work experience—0–1 year, 2–3 years, 4–5 years, 6–10 years, 10 years and longer
- previous job tenure—0–1 year, 2–3 years, 4–5 years

PERSONNEL RECORD KEEPING

Personnel records may be defined as records kept by an employer that may be used for employment, promotion, salary decision, or disciplinary action. A separate record is maintained for each employee assigned to the department. The manager must be aware of what can and cannot be included in an employee's file and the rights of employees to the information therein. Federal, state, and local laws have been passed to protect the privacy and confidentiality of records maintained on employees.

Employee Right To Know Act

In Michigan, the Bullard-Plawecki Employee Right to Know Act (1978, Michigan Compiled Law 423.501) established new restrictions on the manner in which Michigan employers may legally manage their work force. The law was based on the concept that individuals should have the right to know the nature of information being kept about them. The provisions of the act include employee access, disputes over accuracy of data, record-keeping restrictions, and release of information to a third party.

Employee Access

Upon written request, which describes the file in question, an employer must give an employee the opportunity to review that file. The review may be during working hours or at some other convenient time and place. If an on-site review is impossible, the employer must mail to the employee a written copy of the record specifically requested. Reviews may be limited to two times in a calendar year. Upon completion of a review, an employee so requesting must be given an opportunity to copy all or part of the information in the file.

Exemptions to Employee Access

The following parts of the file do not have to be released to the employee:

- letters of references, if identity of source is disclosed
- staff planning materials relating to compensation projections, promotions, and job assignments if materials relate to more than one person
- medical reports if the employee can secure access through the medical facility or doctor involved
- information that could infringe upon another individual's privacy
- separate files pertaining to grievance investigations if the grievance records are not used relative to an employee's qualification for employment, promotion, transfer, compensation, or discipline
- records kept by individual managers not shared with other persons (However, if employee access to such information is denied, the data may not be entered in a personnel file later than six months after the information was recorded.)

Disputes over Accuracy of Data

If agreement cannot be reached over the accuracy of information in the personnel file, the employee has the right to amend the file with a statement of his or her position, not to exceed five sheets of standard size paper. Either party can invoke legal action to remove false information knowingly put into the file by either party.

Record-Keeping Restrictions

Employers are barred from keeping a record of an employee's political activities, associations, publications, or communications relating to non–employment issues unless they occur on the employer's premises or during working hours, or written authorization is give by the employee.

Records of criminal investigators may be excluded from review only if they are kept separately from all other personnel record information. Upon completion of an investigation or after two years, whichever comes first, the employee must be notified of the investigation. If disciplinary action is not taken, the file must be destroyed.

Release of Information to a Third Party

Employers are required to notify employees by first-class mail if any information relative to discipline is divulged to a third party, unless one of the following occurs:

- The information is disseminated to the employee's labor organization.
- The disclosure is ordered in a legal action or arbitration.
- Dissemination is made to a government agent pursuant to a claim or complaint made by an employee.
- The employee has waived such requirements by signing a written statement to that effect on the employment application of another employer.

Managers should review record-keeping practices for assurance of compliance with applicable laws. Depending on how the open-file policy is approached and presented, it can serve to enhance employer-employee relations. In addition to the requirements and restrictions just stated, the Bureau of Employment Standards, Michigan Department of

Labor (1980) requires that an employer must keep employment records for each employee as follows:

- An employer shall keep employment records for each employee showing all of the following:
    1. name
    2. home address
    3. date of birth
    4. occupation in which employed
    5. total daily hours worked, computed to the nearest unit of 15 minutes
    6. total hours worked in each pay period
    7. total hours worked in each work period when the the work does not coincide with the pay period
    8. total hourly, daily, or weekly basic wage
    9. total wages paid each pay period
    10. itemization of all deductions made each pay period
    11. separate itemization of all credits for meals, tips, and lodging against the minimum wage taken for each pay period, if any
- If a credit is taken for meals and/or lodging provided to an employee, the employment records shall contain a statement signed by the employee that acknowledges that the meals and/or lodging were received.
- If employees of a hospital or an institution agree to have their overtime computed on the basis of a 14-day work period pursuant to Section 4a(3) of the act, the employment records shall contain the written agreement or written employment policy arrived at between the employer and the employee and shall be dated prior to the effective date of the agreement.
- Records required under this rule shall be preserved by the employer for three years after the date thereof.

EMPLOYEE SAFETY

An orientation on the hazards of safe practice related to specific job assignments should be incorporated into the orientation and training program recommended for each new employee. Management has a responsibility to train employees in safe work practices. Employees have a responsibility to cooperate by the application of safe work practices. Because work-related accidents and illnesses are costly for the employer, most organizations established and maintained effective safety programs before they were mandated by federal law.

Occupational Safety and Health Administration

According to Occupational Safety and Health Administration (OSHA) guidelines (U.S. Department of Labor 1972), a safety program depends on three essentials: (1) leadership by the employer, (2) safe and healthful working conditions, and (3) safe work practices by the employees. A safety and health committee, composed of top executives, supervision, and employees should be established.

The committee should hold regular monthly meetings to discuss recommendations, accidents, records, and program plans. Policies should include the following:

- establishing procedures for handling suggestions and recommendations
- inspecting an area of the establishment each month for the purpose of detecting hazards
- conducting regularly scheduled meetings to discuss accident and illness prevention methods, safety and health promotions, hazards noted on inspections, injury and illness records, and other pertinent subjects
- investigating accidents as a basis for recommending means to prevent recurrence
- providing information on safe and healthful working practices
- recommending changes or additions to improve protective clothing and equipment
- developing or revising rules to comply with current safety and health standards
- promoting safety and first-aid training for committee members and other employees
- promoting safety and health programs for all employees
- keeping records of minutes of meetings

In the event an accident does occur, the immediate supervisor on duty must assist the injured employee in obtaining medical attention. The employee may refuse medical treatment. Whether or not the employee receives medical treatment, the supervisor must complete a written report of the incident (Exhibit 14–20). The report must provide detailed information, including what happened and why, what could have been done to prevent the incident, and what can be done in the future. Documented in-service training records can be helpful in completing the investigation report (Exhibit 14–21).

Additional standards issued by OSHA (U.S. Department of Labor, OSHA 1983) require chemical manufacturers and importers to assess the hazards of chemicals that they produce or import and require all employers to provide information to their employees concerning hazardous chemicals by means of hazard communication programs. OSHA defines a hazardous chemical as "any chemical which is a physical hazard or a health hazard." Employers can reply on the information provided by the chemical's manufacturer or importer on the material safety data sheet (see Appendix N) to determine whether the chemical is hazardous. Employers are not required to test independently or otherwise evaluate the hazard potential of chemicals purchased and used in the workplace.

Exhibit 14–20 Employee Incident/Injury Report

Date of incident: ________________ Time: ______________ PM/AM ________________

Name of injured:____

last first middle initial

Description of incident:

What happened: ____

____

____

____

Where did it happen (i.e., foot of bed, hallway, etc.)? ____________________

____

Witnesses (Please attach signed statements describing incident):

Name(s)	Department	Employee No.
____________	____________	____________
____________	____________	____________

Cause of incident (if known): ________________________________

____

____

Name of employee reporting incident (if different from above): ________________

Department: ________________ Employee No.: ____________ Time: ________AM/PM

Name of person reporting incident: ________________________________

Date: __________ Time: __________AM/PM

Physician's statement of medical findings: ________________________

____

____

Medical treatment: ____

____

____

X-Rays: Yes: _____ No:_____ Results: ____________________________

____

Signature of Examining Physician:____________________ Date:______________

Important: Complete this form as soon as possible after the incident. Obtain required statements and signatures and forward to Administrator of Employee Safety. At no time shall it be submitted later than 5 working days after the incident.

All employees who are exposed or who may be accidentally exposed to hazardous chemicals must be trained. In addition, employees of contractors and subcontractors who are working at the facility and are exposed to hazardous chemicals must be trained, for example, employees of outside cleaning contractors, especially if the facility provides cleaning compounds. It is also important to know what chemicals are used by exterminators.

The food service director has the responsibility to do the following:

- Review and become familiar with the organization's written policies and procedures on the hazard communication program.
- Develop and maintain lists of each chemical used in the department. Keep the list current. Discontinued chemicals should be on file for 30 years with information on where and why they were used.
- Maintain on file all material safety data sheets, preferably in a loose-leaf notebook, arranged in alphabetical order. There should be no blank spaces on a sheet. If information requested is not applicable, then the designation "NA" should be entered.
- Develop safe use instructions from the material safety data sheets (MSDSs). Make these available in the workplace for employee review; update as necessary. If employees are interested in more detailed information, they must be shown the actual MSDS. If an employee

Exhibit 14–21 Supervisor's Investigation Report

Supervisor's Investigation Report

Use this form to record additional information in all cases of irregular activity, employee incidents, or incidents involving other persons.

Name ______________________ **Date of Occurrence** ________________

Location of Incident ______________ **Time of Occurrence** ________________

What Happened? Describe the incident that caused you to make this investigation.

____

____

____

____

Why did it happen? List why, what, when, where, and how.

____

____

____

____

What should be done? Determine which, if any, of the 12 items listed below require attention.

Equipment		Materials		People	
Select		Select		Select	
Arrange		Place		Place	
Use		Handle		Train	
Maintain		Process		Lead	

____

____

____

What have you done thus far? State actions taken. Was action effective? Recommend further action depending on your authority.

____

____

____

____

How will this improve operations? Be specific regarding performance, productivity, and job goals.

____

____

____

____

Investigated by ________________ **Date** ________________ **Reviewed by** ________________

requests copies of an MSDS, chemical materials list, or written program, the request must be in writing.

- Use the label format for all containers designated as hazardous (see Appendix O).
- Provide in-service training to all employees who are exposed or may be exposed to hazardous chemicals, and to employees of contractors who are working in the department. Train all new employees before they begin work. Provide additional training when a new chemical hazard is posed to chemicals already in use or when new information becomes available on a chemical currently in use.

Critical Control Points and Control Points Related to Personnel Management

The presence of infected employees who practice poor personal hygiene at work is one of the most common factors cited in food-borne outbreaks. Observation of effective food-handling procedures can serve as a preventive measure against bacterial contamination and cross-contamination. Employees therefore should be trained in food-handling techniques and the importance of good personal hygiene as follows:

- Wash hands with soap and warm water before beginning work; before hands touch any food; after using the toilet; after touching hair, face, telephone, money; after blowing nose, touching soiled dishes, smoking, or handling garbage and trash; and throughout tour of duty, as necessary.
- Keep fingernails clean and trimmed. Do not use nail polish.
- Take a bath daily. Shampoo hair regularly. Use deodorant. Wear a clean, washable uniform.
- Wear a hairnet or head cover to prevent hair from falling into food.
- Store all personal belongings, including purse, in lockers provided for employees.
- Wear well-fitting, low-heel, enclosed shoes in good repair and properly cleaned.
- Refrain from smoking in preparation, service, and food storage areas.
- Use combs and makeup only in restrooms.
- Treat all cuts and burns immediately to prevent infections.
- Do not taste food with the ladle or spoon used in food preparation or service. Utensils used for tasting should be washed between tastes.
- Keep hands away from face and hair while handling food.
- Avoid washing hands in sink where dishes are washed or where food is prepared.
- Do not lick fingers to pick up menus, diet cards, or napkins.
- Do not chew gum in preparation and service area.
- Do not eat or drink in the preparation and service areas.
- Refrain from sitting or leaning on work surfaces.
- Keep work areas, surfaces, and utensils clean and orderly.

LAWS RELATING TO PERSONNEL

In addition to the OSHA provisions and laws covered under the broad title of Management-Union Relations, other major laws having direct impact on personnel management are Fair Labor Standards Act, Civil Rights Act, Workers' Compensation, Unemployment Compensation, Family and Medical Leave Act, and Americans with Disabilities Act.

Fair Labor Standards Act

This law, enacted in 1938 and commonly known as the wage-hour law (U.S. Code Service, Title 29, Section 210) was instrumental in establishing the 40-hour five-day workweek and uniform minimum wage.

Minimum Wage

The minimum wage established by the wage-hour law did not include food service workers until 1966. The minimum wage of $0.25 hour in 1938 had been increased over the years to a minimum of $3.35 in 1983. Recently, Congress increased the minimum wage in two increments. On July 1, 1996, the minimum wage increased from $4.25 to $4.75, and beginning July 1, 1997, the minimum wage increased from $4.75 to $5.15 (U.S. Code 1996). There are exemptions to the minimum wage law. Employers granted wage exemption certificates from the U.S. Department of Labor can pay less than the minimum wage to the following worker categories:

- Co-op students. Students 16 years of age, enrolled in a state-approved technical education program, and employed in a job directly related to the course of study, may receive no less than 75 percent of the minimum wage.
- Full-time students. Students at least 14 years of age, enrolled in a bona fide education institution, may be employed in retail, service, or agriculture-related work for no less than 85 percent of the minimum wage.
- Handicapped workers. The individual must be mentally or physically handicapped. Employers may pay no less than 50 percent of the minimum wage without approval of the state vocational rehabilitation agency, as low as 25 percent with prior agency approval.

Work Hours and Duties

Child labor laws regulate the work hours of duties of employees. Employees 16 and 17 years old may work in any occupation that is not classified as hazardous by the U.S. Department of Labor. In food service operations, power-driven equipment such as slicers, cutters, and mixers are declared hazardous and can only be operated or cleaned by students enrolled in food-related programs. All persons under age 18 years must have a work permit from school, except as follows: (1) 16- or 17-year-old high-school graduates, (2) 17-year-olds who have passed the general education development (GED) test, and (3) minors who are married or have court order of emancipation. The employer must have proof of exemption on file. The act has been amended to include these additional provisions.

Overtime Pay

Overtime pay to equal one and one-half the base pay and bonuses must be paid for all hours worked in excess of 40 hours for a one-week period. Salaried employees in executive, administrative, or professional classifications are exempted for overtime pay if no more than 40 percent of their time is spent in managerial-type duties and they earn a salary of at least $150 per week.

Donated Time

If an employee donates time to an employer, it is compensable time and must be paid accordingly. According to Stokes (1981), if a food service worker reports for work 30 minutes early every day because that is when the bus arrives or if an employee is willing to work on his or her own time to learn skills necessary to advance, both are interpreted as compensable time.

Meal Credit

An employer is allowed a meal credit, as part of the minimum wage, for the cost of providing meals for employees. The federal wage-hour law does not stipulate the amount of credit allowed. However, some state laws limit the amount of deductions for meals and housing. In Michigan, restrictions and deductions allowed from the minimum wage rate for meals and lodging are as follows (Michigan Department of Labor 1980):

- An amount not to exceed 25 percent of the state minimum wage rate may be credited as minimum wages paid for lodging provided to an employee if the employee is informed of the cost of the lodging that will be deducted from wages paid and if the employee signs a statement that acknowledges that the lodging was received.
- An amount not to exceed 25 percent of the state minimum wage rate may be credited as minimum wages paid for meals provided to an employee if the employee is informed of the cost of the meals that will be deducted from wages paid and if the employee signs a statement that acknowledges that the meals were received.
- Meals shall consist of adequate portions of a variety of wholesome and nutritious foods provided by the employer to the employee at the usual mealtime or as nearly as possible thereto. A wholesome meal shall include a selection of an entree of eggs, meat, fish, or poultry, two vegetables, salad, beverage, and bread and butter.

The regulation is interpreted to mean that under no circumstance can combined total deductions for lodging and meals exceed 25 percent of the minimum wage. However, under the new regulation, if no other credit is taken an employer may credit the cost provided up to 25 percent of the minimum wage, provided the employee is notified of the cost amount and acknowledges that the meals were served.

Equal Pay

The equal pay law of 1963, as part of the Wage-Hour Act, prohibits wage discrimination based on sex. All persons performing similar work and having similar qualifications must receive the same rate of pay.

Civil Rights Act

The Civil Rights Act of 1964 was amended by the Equal Employment Act of 1972. The act prohibits discrimination in employment based on race, sex, color, religion, and national origin. The Equal Opportunity Commission is responsible for administering all federal laws relating to the Equal Employment Act, including the uniform guidelines on employment selection and promotion, guidelines on sexual harassment, and guidelines on discrimination because of national origin. The Equal Employment Act has an impact on all areas of personnel management from recruitment, selection, and hiring to performance evaluation for the designated protected groups. The protected groups include blacks, Hispanics, American Indians, Pacific Islanders, women, disabled persons, veterans, and older persons (40 to 70 years old).

Workers' Compensation

Workers' compensation insurance is paid for by the employer. The program is designed to compensate employees for disability or death resulting from accidental injury or disease related to employment, regardless of who may be at fault. Employees are entitled to weekly compensation based on a formula established by the individual state's department of labor.

Unemployment Compensation

Unemployment compensation, as a part of the Social Security Act of 1935, provides for payments to an employee between jobs. Eligibility requires that an individual has worked a specified number of weeks prior to unemployment and is willing to accept a suitable position offered through a state's employment office. The program is funded by federal and state governments from taxes paid by the employer and calculated according to total wages paid. The employee receives approximately 50 percent or more of his or her wages for a period of 26 weeks. The compensation may be extended for a longer period of time by acts of Congress. When an employee voluntarily quits or is fired for theft, misconduct, or destruction of property, a penalty is imposed that disqualifies the individual for a number of weeks before payment can be made.

Laws relating to human resource management are constantly changing. An alert personnel officer will keep managers informed of changes, but the ultimate responsibility rests with the individual manager.

Family and Medical Leave Act

The Family and Medical Leave Act (FMLA) went into effect for covered employees in August 1993 (U.S. Department of Labor 1993). The FMLA provides eligible employees the right to take an unpaid leave of absence for a period of up to 12 weeks for birth of a newborn; placement of an adopted or foster child; the care of a seriously ill child, spouse, or parent; or their own serious illness. The FMLA applies to private employers with 50 or more employees and to public agencies regardless of the number of employees. The act provides for the following:

- Unpaid leave must be granted for any of the reasons stated above. At the employee's or employer's option, certain kinds of paid leave may be substituted for unpaid leave.
- The employee ordinarily must provide 30 days' advance notice when the leave is "foreseeable."
- An employer may require medical certification to support a request for leave because of a serious health condition, and may require second or third opinions (at the employer's expense) and a fitness for duty report to return to work.
- For the duration of FMLA leave, the employer must maintain the employee's coverage under any "group health plan."
- Upon return from FMLA leave, most employees must be restored to their original or equivalent positions with equivalent pay, benefits, and other employment terms.
- The use of FMLA leave cannot result in the loss of any employment benefit that accrued prior to the start of an employee's leave.
- It is unlawful for any employer to interfere with, restrain, or deny the exercise of any right provided under FMLA.
- The U.S. Department of Labor is authorized to investigate and resolve complaints of violations.

Americans with Disabilities Act

The provisions of the Americans with Disabilities Act (ADA) apply to private employers, state and local government agencies, and labor unions. Employers with 25 or more employees were covered in July 1992, when the employment provisions went into effect. Employers with 15 or more employees were covered two years later, in July 1994.

The ADA, enforced by the U.S. Department of Justice (1991), prohibits discrimination in all employment practices, including job application procedures, hiring, firing, advancements, compensation, training, and other terms, conditions, and privileges of employment. It applies to recruitment, advertising, tenure, layoff, leave, fringe benefits, and all other employment-related activities.

The employment provisions of the ADA will be enforced under the same procedures now applicable to race, sex, national origin, and religious discrimination under Title VII of the Civil Rights Act of 1964. Complaints regarding actions that occur after July 1992 may be filed with the Equal Employment Opportunity Commission or designated state human rights agencies. Available remedies include hiring, reinstatement, back pay, and court orders to stop discrimination.

COMPUTER APPLICATIONS

Consider the management functions discussed in previous chapters—planning, organizing, controlling; there are repetitive tasks inherent in each of those functions. These tasks, such as creating work schedules, are easily adapted to computer-generated forms. Management may choose to use software as a simple tool or as a means to effect employee needs that go beyond salary and benefits. In addition to templates that give up-to-the minute schedule and production changes, a template can also be created to announce birthdays, employee achievements, and other significant accomplishments.

Another management tool is the use of software that links data files. Role delineation could be linked to job descriptions. Accrediting regulations could be linked to department goals and objectives. Hazard analysis control point guidelines could be linked to policies and procedures and linked again to job task forms. Committee and team reports could be linked for documentation purposes.

Technology has had a tremendous effect on how we communicate in our personal lives and in the workplace. Popular examples of applications that enhance communication are Email, the Internet, fax, interactive video, and teleconferencing. Interactive computer programs designed for training purposes support individual employee training and reinforcement of new procedures.

A review of software literature suggests that integrated software packages are available that perform many personnel functions. The features of a comprehensive human resources package can be evaluated through a software checklist for personnel management (Technological Horizons in Education Journal 1995), as follows:

- Provides tools necessary to effectively manage employee record keeping.
- Monitors benefit qualifications, certification, and expiration.
- Links with human resources and payroll applications. Notes performance appraisals.
- Applies corporate policies on attendance, tardiness, vacations, work force.
- Consolidates data from multiple locations and features.
- Automates the functions associated with writing, revising, and conducting performance appraisals.
- Utilizes performance elements such as job knowledge, attendance, and punctuality as key factors.
- Rates employees on a predetermined scale.
- Offers clear and complete job descriptions.

- Generates clear, natural text that recognizes employee strong points and targets areas for improvement.
- Generates job duties for interviewing.
- Complies with the Americans with Disabilities Act and other employment laws.
- Automates personnel policy writing.
- Covers various workplace situations that might need a policy.
- Probes, using key questions in subject areas, then uses the answers to write policies.
- Dates policies for archiving and review.
- Creates a table of contents.

REFERENCES

American Hospital Association. 1974. *Volunteers in the food service department of health care institutions*. Chicago.

Azoff, E.S., and P.L. Friedman. 1982. Solicitation-distribution rules: A developing doctrine. *Hospital Progress* 63, no. 2:44–48, 54.

Brogan, S. et al. 1981. *Guidelines for clinical dietetics time study: A collection of data on efficiency*. Nutritional Care Practices Committee, Michigan Dietetic Association, Lansing, MI.

Callaghan, C. et al. 1983. *Guidelines for client-learning time study: A collection of data on effectiveness*. Nutrition Care Practices Committee, Michigan Dietetic Association, Lansing, MI.

Consultant Dietitians in Health Care Facilities: An ADA practice group. 1988. Columbus, OH: Ross Laboratories.

Henry, K.H., and S.W. Parrish. 1988. Substance abuse in the workplace: Drug testing and the health care industry. *Health Care Supervisor* 7, no. 1:1–10.

Michigan Department of Civil Rights. 1981. *Pre-employment inquiry guide*. Michigan Civil Rights Commission, Detroit.

Michigan Department of Labor, Bureau of Employment Standards. 1980. *1981 Annual Supplement*, pp. 546–549. Michigan Administrative Code 1979. Legislative Service Bureau, Department of Management and Budget, Lansing, MI.

Miller, P.J., and B.M. Farr. 1988. A survey of SHEA members on universal precautions and HIV screening. *Infection Control and Hospital Epidemiology* 9, no. 4:163–165.

Research Institute of America. 1982. *Personal Report for the Executive—Special Report*. New York.

Schmidt, F.L., and J.E. Hunter. 1981. Myths meet realities in the 1980s. *Management* 2, no. 3:23–27.

Schreier, J.W. 1988. Combatting drugs at work. *Training and Development Journal* 42, no. 10:56–60.

Stokes, J.F. 1981. Beware of wage and hour violations. *Food Service Marketing* 43, no. 70:13.

Survey of industries find hospitals 1st in turnovers, 3rd in absenteeism. 1982. *Hospitals* 56, no. 9:39.

Technological Horizons in Education Journal. September 1995. 23, no. 2.

U.S. Code. 1996. *Minimum wage increase. Congressional and administrative news*. 104th Congress. No. 8, October. St. Paul, MN: West Publishing Co.

U.S. Department of Health and Human Services. 1971. *A guide to nutrition and food service*. Public Health Service Publication No. (HSM) 71-6701. Washington, DC: U.S. Government Printing Office.

U.S. Department of Justice, Civil Rights Division. 1991. *The Americans with Disabilities Act*. Washington, DC.

U.S. Department of Labor. 1993. *Your rights under the Family and Medical Leave Act of 1993*. Publication 1420. Washington, DC.

U.S. Department of Labor. 1972. *Guidelines for setting up job safety and health programs*. Stock No. 8501-17. Washington, DC.

U.S. Department of Labor and Department of Health and Human Services. 1987. Joint advisory notice: Protection against occupational exposure to hepatitis B virus (HBV) and human immunodeficiency virus (HIV). *Federal Register* 52(210): 41818-41823.

U.S. Department of Labor, Occupational Safety and Health Administration. 1983. Hazard communication. *Federal Register* 48(228): 53280-53348.

Chapter 15

Subsystem for Financial Management

Medical food service operations have undergone major changes during the last decade in terms of managing available resources. As a result of escalating costs of medical services, all aspects of the medical organization have become more accountable for managerial action. No longer are directors of medical food service operations permitted to operate with unlimited budgets. Today, the emphasis is on setting goals to meet quality standards within prescribed budgetary allowances. This approach requires strict internal controls in an effort to remain solvent in view of external economic cutbacks and inflation.

FOOD COST CONTROL

Food cost is a major component of financial management, and the challenge to management is to control costs while maintaining high standards of quality. Therefore, management should strive for a balance between qualitative and quantitative controls. When food costs become excessive, the easiest form of control is to raise menu prices rather than to practice effective food cost controls. Because there is an upper limit to raising menu prices, management must seek other alternatives. Cost containment begins with effective menu planning and flows through to other subsystems.

Menu Planning

The use of cyclical menus, whether they are selective or nonselective, can serve as a reliable tool for determining budgetary allowances for food. Management can readily observe changes in food prices when the same menus are used over a set period of time. To arrive at the amount of money needed for the daily meal allowance, it is necessary to precost each item on the menu. Thus, the average daily cost of foods served will be used as the daily meal allowance. The precosting can be accomplished with the use of standardized recipes.

Daily Meal Allowance

Assuming that menus have been planned in accordance with the goals and objectives of the organization and have top administrative approval, the meal allowance will be an average cost of menu items served to patients and employees. In order to calculate the average cost of menu items, the facility must use standardized recipes and must know the daily cost of all food used. For example, if the daily meal allowance is $6.75 per person per day, then each meal and each food category should receive a certain percentage of the food dollar. A typical breakdown by meal is shown in Table 15–1.

The meal breakdown is not enough to determine whether certain food items, as listed on the menu, fall within the cost allowance. To assist further in the decision-making process, food categories for each meal may be designated as a percentage of the food dollar. Table 15–2 provides a breakdown for the dinner meal.

The use of precosted standardized recipes and strict portion controls will ensure that costs remain within the budgetary allowance. As the price of food escalates, management is in a position to make decisions based on sound financial management practices.

Employee Meals

The price of menu items served to employees and guests in the cafeteria and the price of menu items for special activities depend on administrative policies and procedures. In some operations, the food budget is partially subsidized by

Table 15–1 Meal Cost Allowances

Meal	*Percentage*	*Cost*
Breakfast	20	$1.35
Lunch	35	2.36
Dinner	39	2.63
Nourishment	6	0.41
Total	100	$6.75

the medical organization, resulting in lower menu prices for employees and guests. In such cases, the food cost percentage may be as high as 70 percent of the total price, depending on whether the food is a convenience item or one made from scratch. In other operations, the cost of employees' meals is considered a fringe benefit. In this case, the cost of meals is charged to labor costs. Regardless of the system used, the food service department should get credit for all food served.

Food Specifications

Specifications are directly related to food cost controls and should be used for all purchases to ensure quality. Well-written specifications contribute to lower bid prices because vendors know precisely what the buyer expects and know what they are bidding on. Specifications not only should be well written but also should be communicated to all vendors as well as to all persons responsible for purchasing and receiving food. The most effective specifications are those that indicate different levels of quality, depending on the intended use for the food item. For example, tomatoes used in soups and stews need not be perfectly shaped, and fruit used in gelatin molds need not be perfectly cut.

Table 15–2 Food Category Cost Allowance—Dinner

Food Category	*Percentage*	*Cost*
Appetizer	6	$0.158
Entree	51	1.340
Potato or substitute	5	0.132
Cooked vegetable	10	0.263
Salad and dressing	9	0.237
Bread	4	0.105
Dessert	8	0.210
Beverage	5	0.132
Miscellaneous	2	0.051
Total	100	$2.628

Forecasting

Forecasting, as related to food, can be defined as a method of using available data to project the amount of food required for a meal, a day, or a longer period of time. Forecasting is used to determine the amounts to purchase, the amounts to requisition from storage, and the amounts to prepare. All phases of forecasting are critical in efforts to contain food costs.

Forecasting the Amounts To Purchase

The first phase begins with the standardized recipe. If properly formulated, as shown on the recipe card (Exhibit 15–1), information pertaining to portion size can be used to project the total amount needed by multiplying each portion by the projected number of servings needed.

Another tool useful in forecasting the amount to purchase is the production worksheet. The production worksheet provides information such as the amount of food requisitioned, the amount used, the projected number of meals, and the actual number of meals served.

Space is provided for comments by the shift supervisor that may explain discrepancies, if any, between the projected number of meals and the actual number served. Comments may refer to weather conditions, employee payday, special activities, and so forth. For example, during inclement weather conditions, more employees tend to eat in the cafeteria than on fair, sunny days when they prefer to leave the facility for meals elsewhere. Also, employees tend to go out for lunch on paydays in order to cash checks. Special activities may include scheduled conferences at the facility, patient tours or outings as practiced in many nursing homes, and holidays when guests often eat with patients. The day of the week is an important variable because the census is usually lower on weekends than during the week.

At the end of each meal, data should be recorded on the number of meals served in various categories to provide a cumulative daily total. As shown in Exhibit 15–2, information helpful to management is the number of meals served to patients, employees, and others. This information is necessary in computing daily food costs.

The record of meals served may vary from data on patient census sheets for several reasons. First, the official patient census may include patients who did not consume a meal because of an NPO notation (instructions not to feed by mouth), leave of absence during mealtime, or other reasons. Second, meals are frequently delivered to patient care areas for patients who have been discharged. Third, all patients are counted on the official census—even newborn babies who receive commercial-type formulas provided by the pharmacy. Although records maintained in the dietary department may not be totally accurate, the data do provide general guidelines for cost control.

Exhibit 15–1 Standardized Recipe Card

Plain Muffins

Total Servings: 100
Serving size: 2 Muffins Each

	200 Portions		Cost		Portions		Cost		
Ingredients	Volume	Weight	Per Pound	Total	Volume	Weight	Per Pound	Total	Directions

Cost Data

	Cost per Recipe	Cost per Serving
Labor		
Food		
Energy (Conventional)		
(Convection)		
Total cost		

Comments (Type of energy used, seasonableness of food items, etc.) ____________________

Determining the Amounts To Requisition

This second phase is based on the type of menu item and the state of purchase (frozen, fresh, etc.). It may be necessary to requisition certain food items from storage several days in advance. For example, frozen meats that are scheduled for service on Friday should be requisitioned on Wednesday to allow time for thawing. Although management is still relying on past records, a more accurate prediction can be made at this time than at the time of purchase.

Determining the Amounts To Prepare

The third phase is the final phase of forecasting, and projections are made on the day of preparation. At this time, a more accurate projection can be made because of the current information available to management, such as the selective menu tally and the daily patient census. As one progresses through the forecasting stages, the amount of food needed may be more or less than the amount originally projected. For example, based on data at the time of purchase, it was determined that 200 lb of beef was needed for 500 servings of roast beef. At the time of requisition, the weather forecast indicated a warm, sunny day. With the realization that some employees would leave the building during the meal hour, the amount of food requisitioned was reduced by 20 lb, or 50 servings less than the amount purchased. Finally, on the day of preparation, it was determined that the beef order should be reduced further because more patients selected the alternate entree than was anticipated. Because the daily food costs reflect the amount of food actually used, rather than the amount purchased, management can effect a savings by observing the steps outlined above in forecasting amounts of food.

Receiving Food

Errors in delivery can be costly. Individuals responsible for accepting food delivered to the facility should be designated in writing by management. A copy of the policy should be communicated to all vendors. The practice of allowing anyone in the work area to sign for deliveries is not in the best interest of management for several reasons. First,

Exhibit 15–2 Record of Meals Served

_____________19_____ Month																	
	Patients						Personnel						Guests			Total Meals Served	
	Regular			Modified			Food Service			Other			Guests			Total Meals Served	
Day	B	L	D	B	L	D	B	L	D	B	L	D	B	L	D	Today	To Date
1																	
2																	
3																	
4																	
5																	
6																	
7																	
8																	
9																	
10																	
11																	
12																	
13																	
14																	
15																	
16																	
17																	
18																	
19																	
20																	
21																	
22																	
23																	
24																	
25																	
26																	
27																	
28																	
29																	
30																	
31																	
Total																	

unless receiving is an assigned duty, the employee may not take the time necessary to check for quantity or quality. Second, the employee will not be familiar with amounts ordered or the quoted price. An example of the type of form that may be used to designate responsible individuals is shown in Exhibit 15–3.

Records of all food received should be compiled by receiving personnel in order to provide data for managerial control. Depending on the degree of detail, a variety of forms may be used. For example, if data are needed only on the total amount of food and other items received, a form such as Exhibit 15–4 may be used.

The advantage of using a more detailed form such as Exhibit 15–5 is that management can readily detect when there is an increase in food costs for a particular category. With the use of cycle menus, the increase in food cost should correspond to the inflation rate. When sharp increases occur in food costs, management should investigate immediately.

In addition to the preceding policies, management can observe the following practices in efforts to control costs related to the receiving of food:

- Use an invoice stamp to indicate date received, quantity check, quality check, unit price check, and signature of receiver.
- Provide receiving personnel with copies of specifications, purchase orders, and price quotations.
- Give receiving personnel the authority to reject unsatisfactory products.
- Provide personnel with the tools necessary to weigh, count, and check for quality (i.e., scales and thermometers).
- Question deliveries made to the facility either before or after scheduled hours.

Food Storage

Spoiled or deteriorated food is a waste of money. When foods are stored at the correct temperature and humidity, they are less likely to spoil or deteriorate. To ensure freshness, date all perishables and follow the first-in-first-out (FIFO) system for storing and issuing food. Finally, to prevent contamination, store all food items at least 6 in off the floor in a storage area that is tightly sealed to keep out insects and rodents.

Requisitions and Issues

Only authorized personnel should be allowed to requisition from storage. Depending on the size of the operation, one person may be responsible for requisitioning food for all units. An example is the supervisor in a nursing home or

Exhibit 15–3 Authorized Receiving Signatures

Memorandum

From: Jane Doe, Food Service Director
To: Food Service Employees, Vendors, and Accounting Department
Re: Authorized Receiving Signatures
Date: January 1, 1997

The following food service personnel are authorized to sign for food and supplies delivered to the food service department. Nonauthorized signatures may result in nonpayment of bill

____
James M. Brown, Purchasing Manager

____
Vernon Case, Storeroom Supervisor

____
Andre Fisk, Storeroom Clerk

____
Angela Evans, Storeroom Clerk

____
Mark Rice, Storeroom Clerk

Exhibit 15–4 Receiving Record

Daily Receiving Record

Date received ______________________ Received by ______________________

Vendor	Invoice		Description (Food, Paper, Cleaning, Office)	Cost
	Date	Number		

small hospital. In large operations, storeroom personnel may receive requisitions from each unit, such as cook, salad, bakery, tray setup, and nourishment. Control forms should provide information as shown in Exhibit 15–6.

At the end of the serving period, all unopened or unused food items should be returned to storage. After returns, storeroom personnel can compile total amounts of food used, thus giving management a daily food cost record on a form such as Exhibit 15–7. The amount of food used, not the amount requisitioned, is used to compute daily food costs.

For operations with an ingredient room, the requisitioning and issuing procedures are simplified. All foods are requisitioned by personnel assigned to the ingredient room and all issues are delivered to one unit (ingredient room), thus adding controls in the use of food items.

Inventory

All foods purchased by the department should be accounted for. The use of both perpetual and physical inventory systems can aid in the accountability process. To maintain a perpetual inventory, the use of a 5 × 7-in cardex system is suggested. With this procedure, each food item is listed on a separate card, as shown in Exhibit 11–6. When a cardex folder is used to hold the cards, the information on the bottom of each card is readily visible. The policy of returning unused and unopened foods to storage will prevent undue accumulation of food in the preparation and service areas.

A physical inventory is obtained by actually counting each item in the storeroom. It should be taken at least once a month or more often, if warranted. The monetary value of the physical inventory should equal the value of the perpetual inventory. When discrepancies occur, they should be thoroughly investigated and corrected immediately. Exhibit 11–7 shows information needed on a physical inventory.

In the use of physical inventory forms, the column for perpetual inventory should not be completed until after the physical inventory is taken. Any discrepancies between the two should appear in the remarks column.

The cost of food used for a one-month or longer period is based on the physical inventory. To compute the cost of food for a given period, the following formula is used:

$$B + P - E = C$$

where
B = beginning inventory,
P = purchases,
E = ending inventory, and
C = food cost.

Exhibit 15–5 Receiving Record (More Detailed)

Daily Receiving Record

Date received ____________________ Received by ________________

Vendor	Invoice Date	Invoice Number	Fresh meat, fish, poultry	Fresh prepared entrees	Canned entrees	Frozen fruits and vegetables	Canned fruits and vegetables	Fresh produce	Dairy	Bakery	Groceries	Other	Cost
Total													

Pilferage

To secure food is to save money. The following precautions are suggested to provide adequate security:

- Secure storage areas during nonoperating hours.
- Permit storeroom keys to be used only by storeroom personnel.
- Require storeroom personnel to sign for and turn in keys at the beginning and at the end of the shift. (The key may be left at the front desk of the facility.)
- Establish policies on package takeout by employees.
- Secure preparation and service refrigerators during nonoperating hours.
- Control trash and other pickup operations from the department.

Prepreparation

Use of an ingredient room where prepreparation is centralized is the best form of control. For departments without ingredient rooms, each employee must be instructed in techniques of prepreparation in order to minimize waste. Some forms of waste are considered unavoidable, such as bones, fat, certain fruit and vegetable peelings and cores, and some outside leaves. Special attention should be given to the amount of outside leaves trimmed from vegetables, the amount of skin peeled from fruit and vegetables, and the amount of usable meat left on bones after the boning process. Even techniques that may appear minor can add up to big savings over time.

Preparation of Food

The most important tool to consider in the preparation of food is the use of standardized recipes that have been tested for yield. If instructions are followed from the recipes, along with information from the production worksheet on the time to begin preparation, management need not be concerned about shrinkage, overcooking, or other wasteful practices. These instructions set limits on time and temperature, which are important factors in quality control. Food of poor quality may not be consumed and therefore will constitute waste.

Exhibit 15–6 Requisition and Issue Form

Storeroom Requisition and Issue Form

Unit ____________________ Date ____________________

Requisitioned							
Amount	Unit	Description	Amount Issued	Amount Returned	Amount Used	Unit Cost	Total Cost

Requisitioned by ____________________ Issued by ____________________

Service of Food

Whether from a tray line or from a cafeteria counter, employees must be instructed to practice prescribed portion control in the service of food. Much of the portioning can be done at the time of purchase, during prepreparation, or, for prepared foods, prior to service. For bulk foods that must be portioned as served, proper utensils should be provided, such as ladles, scoops, and scales. (Refer to portion control as presented in Chapters 12 and 13.)

When patients select double portions, the menu tally should reflect two servings instead of one. Employees may request double servings from cafeteria lines; cashiers therefore should be alerted so that charges can be made accordingly. Also, tapes from computerized cash registers, as discussed in Chapter 13, will serve as a control in the handling of cash. Cost of condiments can be controlled to some extent for patient service by limiting food items only to those selected. The practice of serving dressings with salads, or routinely serving salt, pepper, and sugar should not be allowed because all items returned on trays must be discarded.

Employee Meals

The cost of meals served to employees should receive careful scrutiny. Several practices are followed in terms of employees' meals:

- Employees pay full menu price for all food consumed.
- Employees pay a reduced price for all food consumed.
- Employees receive meals (one or more) as part of wages.
- Employees receive meals as a fringe benefit.

If meals are served as a fringe benefit, they should be charged to the cost of labor. In efforts to control costs in this area, management should review policies on the following:

- Are employees allowed to eat as much as desired?
- Are employees limited on the more expensive menu items?
- How many meals are employees entitled to eat during a regular eight-hour shift?
- Are part-time employees entitled to eat a meal?
- Are employees entitled to eat during scheduled rest periods?
- Is coffee or another beverage (such as pop) available to employees throughout the scheduled shift?

Exhibit 15–7 Daily Food Cost Record

Date_______________

Day	Total Food Costs		Total Meals		Cost per Meal		Budgeted Food Cost
	Today	To Date	Today	To Date	Today	To Date	To Date
1							
2							
3							
4							
5							
6							
7							
8							
9							
10							
11							
12							
13							
14							
15							
16							
17							
18							
19							
20							
21							
22							
23							
24							
25							
26							
27							
28							
29							
30							
31							
Total							

Special Activities

All food prepared and served in the department should be charged to some account. This includes coffee breaks, special luncheons, teas, banquets, coffee served at committee meetings, and others. Forms that may be useful in controlling costs of special activities are shown in Exhibits 15–8 and 15–9.

Exhibit 15–8 provides a listing of organizations and committees that frequently request food and/or services from the department. Because account numbers are assigned by the accounting department, it is easier to maintain records and control.

Menus for special luncheons and other activities are precosted and updated as often as necessary. The menus and instructions for making selections are given to groups requesting service. After the selection has been made, the menu is typed on a meeting reservation form and submitted to administration for approval, as shown in Exhibit 15–9.

Leftovers

The optimal form of operation is to eliminate leftovers completely. Because this is not always possible, management should provide for the economic use of leftover foods. A review of the production worksheet (Exhibit 12–3) will show a column for disposition of foods left after the serving period. This column should be used to indicate how the food will be used. Most foods can be used again in a different form. A list of suggested ways to use leftovers can be compiled and available for cooks or personnel in the ingredient room.

Frequently overlooked in the control of leftovers is a check of unused trays delivered to patients in the patient care areas. At one hospital, a daily check of unused trays revealed a startling number of 240 unused trays for a one-month period. Management used a form to keep records of unused trays, as depicted in Exhibit 15–10.

The number of unused trays, multiplied by the average cost per meal, equals the dollar amount lost. Because all food returned to the dietary department must be discarded, control in this area alone could amount to savings in the thousands of dollars over a one-year period.

Nourishments

Standard operating procedures should indicate what foods are stocked on the patient care areas routinely and what foods should be delivered by request only. Because nourishments make up part of the cost per meal served to patients, management must make sure that nourishments are being consumed by patients and not by personnel on the wards. All requests in excessive amounts and all unusual requests should be investigated. A form such as Exhibit 15–11 can serve as a control tool.

It is important that all requisitions be approved by supervisory staff, rather than by the dietary clerk responsible for nourishment preparation. Special attention should be given to the amount left over from the previous day and whether ward personnel are using the FIFO system in distributing nourishments to patients. Cost records should be maintained for both bulk nourishments and individual between-meal feeding for patients.

LABOR COST CONTROL

Labor costs are directly related to the number of full-time equivalents (FTEs) employed by the facility and the amount of salary paid, including wages and benefits. When the labor cost percentage is higher than established limits for staffing, management must increase the number of meals served, reduce the number of employees, or develop and maintain effective labor cost controls. The latter alternative is suggested.

Direct and Indirect Labor Costs

Labor costs can be classified as direct or indirect. Direct costs are those related to wages paid for productive work hours or actual hours on the job. Indirect costs refer to activities and benefits such as vacation, sick leave, holidays, personal leave, employee meals, life-health accident insurance, Federal Insurance Contributions Act (FICA) payments, workers' compensation, unemployment compensation, pension, retirement, and other benefits that may be part of the labor agreement. Indirect labor costs, frequently referred to as nonproductive labor costs, equal as much as 50 percent of the total labor costs (Rose 1980).

Labor costs can be broken down further into noncontrollable and controllable costs. Wages and benefits that have been negotiated and agreed upon, as well as costs established by external agencies (i.e., FICA, workers' compensation) may be classified as noncontrollable costs. The following discussion concentrates on labor costs that can be controlled, in varying degrees, by the food service department. These are some areas in which management can exert some control in reducing labor costs.

Menu Planning

Consider changing labor-intensive menu items, such as complex, gourmet-type foods that require highly skilled chefs to prepare. Because highly skilled chefs expect and get higher wages, the labor cost per FTE will be higher.

The coordination of menu items served to patients on regular and modified diets and employees in the cafeteria is another factor to consider. A menu policy that requires the use of the same food item for all areas of service when feasi-

Exhibit 15–8 Special Activity Cost Record Form

Special Activity Cost Record

To: Accounting Office
From: Director of Dietetics
Subject: Monthly Charges
Month: ________________

Date	Group	Account No.	Charges

Exhibit 15–9 Special Activity Approval Form

Meeting Reservations

Group ______________________ Phone ______________________

Chairperson ______________________ Dept. ______________________

Date ____________ Time ____________ No. Attending ____________

Today's Date ______________ Contact Person ______________________

Type of Event ______________________

Location of Event:
Atrium ____________ Main Lobby ____________ Auditorium ____________
Cafeteria ____________
Conf. Room A ____________ Conf. Room B ____________ Conf. Room C ____________

Type of Service:
Cafe. Line ____________ Cafe. Table ____________ Buffet ____________ Waitress ____________

Charge to (Account No.) ____________

Remarks:

Administrator's Approval ______________________ Date ____________

Menu

ble reduces the handling, preparation, and service required of employees.

Equipment

Purchasing mechanical equipment and requiring employees to use such equipment possibly can save a fraction of an FTE. When FTE savings are used to justify the investment of funds for equipment, the total FTE should be reduced and not absorbed within the department.

Purchasing and Issuing of Food

The form in which food is purchased affects labor costs. The use of convenience foods will decrease labor costs but will increase food costs. Investigate the degree of convenience in relation to labor cost savings.

The use of an ingredient room for centralized issuing, measuring, portioning, and manipulating food saves time in the production area. An excessive amount of time can be wasted by highly paid employees in the aforementioned activities.

Production

Full utilization of scheduled employees will reduce the amount of money paid for idle time. Higher labor cost is associated with the conventional food production system because of uneven work distribution. The peak periods of operation are at mealtimes, which take up four to six hours

Exhibit 15–10 Records of Trays Returned

Record of Tray Return													
	Ward												
Date	ICU	1-1	2-1	2-2	2-3	2-4	3-1	3-2	3-3	4-1	4-2	4-3	Total
													Breakfast ______ Lunch ______ Dinner ______ Total ______
													Breakfast ______ Lunch ______ Dinner ______ Total ______
													Breakfast ______ Lunch ______ Dinner ______ Total ______

Abbreviations: NPO—nothing by mouth, D—discharged, DC—diet change, T—transferred.

Collected data are used to improve cost savings through employee in-service, better communication with nursing staff, and close monitoring of patient census.

of an eight-hour shift. Decreased activity, which occurs between meals, accounts for two to four hours of the regular shift. Management needs to monitor this period to determine exactly what employees are doing. For managers involved in planning a new facility or renovation, consideration should be given to other types of production systems that have proved to be more labor efficient.

Service

Decentralized service is more costly in terms of labor than centralized service because of the amount of supervision required. Each patient care area pantry requires adequate supervision for assurance of quality and quantity standards. Although there is a decrease in labor costs when the task of patient food service is performed by nursing personnel, the food service department loses control of the finished product. Depending on the location of the dietary department in relation to the patient care area, ambulatory patients may be permitted to consume meals in the cafeteria. This practice is particularly applicable to small hospitals and nursing homes.

Consider the use of disposable serviceware. The use of disposables will reduce labor costs (dishwashing) but may increase costs in other areas such as trash removal, storage, and cost of disposable serviceware.

Investigate alternative production and service patterns. The traditional three-meals-a-day plan may be substituted with a four- or five-meal plan. The major advantage of alternate patterns is that peaks and valleys are practically eliminated.

For cafeteria service, consider the use of more self-service. Quantities can be controlled for self-service food items with the size of the serving dish and the use of scales and selected serving utensils. Also, the self-busing of trays, the removal of disposables such as paper napkins, and the sorting of silverware by those eating in the cafeteria will reduce labor costs.

Personnel

This is the area where the most dramatic labor cost savings can be realized without increasing other costs. The factors discussed below may contribute to labor costs. (See Chapter 14 for full discussion of each entity.)

Job Analysis, Description, and Specification

Has each position undergone analysis for job content, been well defined in the job description, and been specified in writing for use by personnel responsible for hiring? The hiring practice has a direct bearing on tardiness, absenteeism, productivity, and turnover.

Job Standard

Decreased employee activity can be measured by using standards of performance. For labor cost savings, standards

Exhibit 15–11 Nourishment Ordering Form

Nourishment Order Sheet

Ward ____________________ Date ____________________

Unit	Food Item	Quantity on Hand	Quantity Ordered	Quantity Delivered	Total Cost ($)	Cost ($)

Ordered by: __________ Approved by: __________ Filled by: __________

refer to the quantity of work performed. For each position, employees need to know what and how much is required for full productivity. Accumulated data based on job standards can serve as counseling tools to rehabilitate the nonproductive employee or can provide objective measures for termination.

Work Methods

All supervisory personnel should be trained in the fundamentals of work simplification. With this knowledge, supervisors can use concepts of motion economy to analyze how tasks are performed, develop improved methods, and train employees in new procedures.

Work Schedules

Establish criteria for employee work schedules based on service required and not for the convenience of the employee. The traditional method of scheduling employees with overlapping early and late shifts over a seven-day period is costly. The practice is primarily associated with conventional production systems. It is easier to change the method of scheduling than the type of production system. For cost savings, consider alternate scheduling systems such as flextime, compressed or four-day workweek, or permanent part-time. It has been reported at one facility that a schedule change to four days on and three days off for cooks resulted in lower labor costs plus other favorable side effects (Longrigg 1981).

Absenteeism and Turnover

Absenteeism and turnover are grouped together because chronic absenteeism frequently results in employee turnover, and also because both are classified as nonproductive labor costs (paid days off and workers' compensation). The traditional use of strong disciplinary measures to curb absenteeism is not effective (Taylor 1981). For any meaningful cost reduction in this area, management will need to determine the underlying factors contributing to high absenteeism and turnover. Maintaining records, as described in Chapter 14, and careful scrutiny of managerial practices will supply adequate data for corrective action.

Employee Training

Effective training can serve to correct undesirable employee practices that contribute to labor costs. Tools available in a well-organized department that can be used for training are policies, procedures, job analysis, job descriptions, job specifications, job standards, performance evaluation, accumulated work records, and safety and sanitation reports. The overall objective of training is to produce an efficient, cost-effective work force.

ENERGY COST CONTROL

Medical food service operations must become actively involved in energy conservation not only because energy is a scarce resource but also because of the steady increase in energy costs. Food service directors in medical facilities encounter problems in dealing with energy control that are not found in single or independent food service operations. The facility is complex and composed of many departments, all of which are energy intensive to provide required services. In most medical facilities, energy used for heat, light, ventilation, refrigeration, and hot water are not measured and charged to individual departments. Therefore, it is difficult for the food service director to determine whether the department is energy efficient. Despite these problems, there is much that can be done to conserve energy and thus reduce cost in this area.

Establishing an Energy Program

The control of energy, as in the control of food and labor costs, begins with the menu system and continues as an integral part of all basic resources that must be controlled. Specific techniques for energy cost controls, as discussed in Chapters 9 through 15, should become part of a long-range plan for energy conservation. The major stages to consider in establishing a long-range energy program are the same as those required in other systematic processes. As shown in Figure 15–1, management must assess, plan, implement, and evaluate.

Assessment

Begin the assessment by stating why an energy program is needed. As part of the statement of need, include documentation on existing energy costs. The accounting department in the facility should be of help in supplying information on the amount of energy used for a given period. The data can be compared with those for future increases or decreases. Another concern during this stage is to determine whether major changes have occurred in the operation that may have contributed to increased use of energy, such as an expansion of the facility, a change in the production system, or the purchase of additional equipment. It is important that the complete energy program be in writing for two reasons. First, when ideas are on paper, efforts can be more effectively directed toward improved energy control. Second, the written version can serve as a guide for all employees involved in the program.

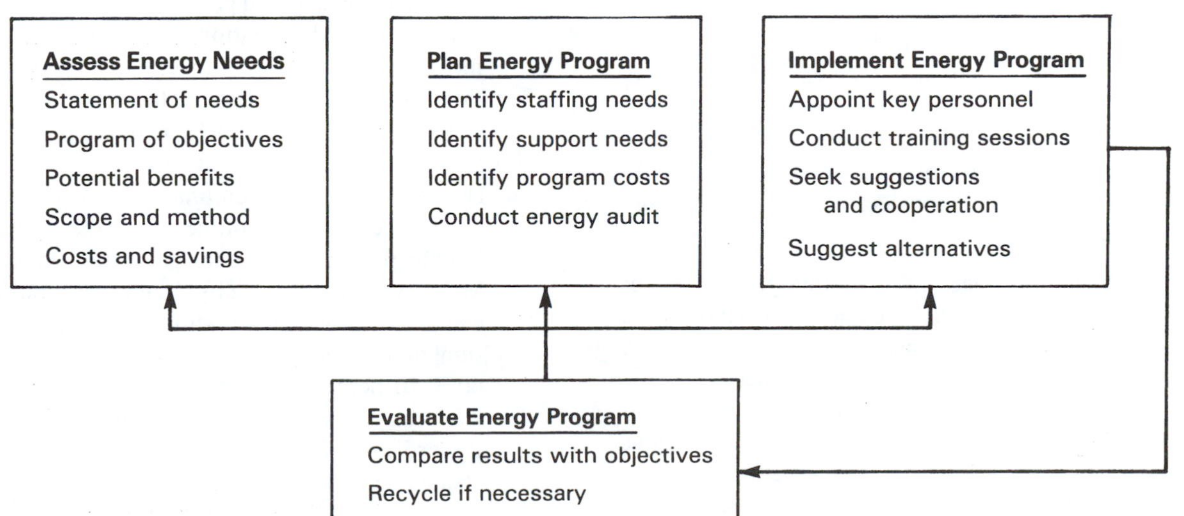

Figure 15–1 Energy Management System

Program objectives should be written in broad statements, which are then further defined in measurable terms. This procedure will prove to be an important step during the evaluation, when one must determine whether objectives have been met. Make objectives and goals both realistic and attainable.

In addition to cost savings, which is the primary interest of top administrators, list other potential benefits that may occur as a result of an energy control program. For example, how will the program affect the management of other resources such as personnel? Will employee morale improve as a result of active participation? Will the program foster cohesiveness among employees because it is a group project?

To indicate the scope and method to be used, consideration should be given to the following questions:

- Will the plan cover the whole department or will it be limited to specific areas such as production and service?
- What are the tasks to be accomplished?
- Will all employees become involved?
- Will written reports be required by key personnel on a daily, weekly, or monthly basis?
- Who will run the program?
- How much support is needed from higher administration?
- Will outside consultants be necessary?
- Will technical assistance from other departments within the medical facility be needed?

Finally, during the assessment stage an estimate of the annual costs and savings should be made. Estimates should include the cost to implement the program, as well as the savings-to-cost ratio or payback period. It should be remembered that the plan will be more acceptable to higher management if both energy and money can be saved.

Planning

During the planning stage, decisions should be made in reference to questions raised during the assessment period. For example, will staffing availability permit the use of a manager, a first-line supervisor, or the head cook to run the program, or will the department head take on this task? As part of the plan, one should consider the use of an energy audit, as follows:

- Document energy usage and operating procedures for major pieces of equipment, using Forms 1 and 2 (Exhibits 15–12 and 15–13). The findings can be used for reference during the implementation and evaluation stages.
- Formulate a checklist to identify opportunities for cost savings. Group energy usage according to sections within the department and list this information on the left side of the checklist. Opposite each section, list suggested cost savings obtained from the remarks section of Forms 1 and 2. In addition to techniques for energy control, as discussed in Chapters 9 through 14, employees should be encouraged to make additional suggestions.

Implementation

The key to effective implementation is to seek and gain the full cooperation of all employees. It may be necessary to provide some kind of incentive for employee participation based on the degree of goal fulfillment. Employees should be involved as early as possible and to the greatest extent possible. Training sessions should be initiated for one section at a time with emphasis on temperature, time, and proper use and care of equipment in order to document energy usage accurately.

To determine the amount of energy used in the preparation of a food item, management may use meters that can be attached to individual pieces of equipment or conduct studies of time and temperature. The use of meters to measure the cubic feet of gas or the kilowatt hours of electricity expended is the most reliable method, but it may partially defeat the purpose of cost savings, because an outlay of funds is required for purchasing and installing the instruments. A less costly method, and the one recommended, is calculation of time and temperature multiplied by the energy ratings for individual pieces of equipment. A study using this method of estimating energy consumption was conducted to determine which of four types of electrical equipment was least energy intensive and produced the most acceptable product (Romanelli 1979). The technique, which requires only the use of a stopwatch and a record of dates, involves the following steps:

1. Measure the on-time of the thermostat signal light immediately after placing the food item into the equipment.
2. Record the total on-time of the signal light immediately after removing the food product from the equipment.
3. Conduct five duplications, using identical equipment, cooking temperatures, and food products. Food products should have the same size, weight, initial temperature, and final internal temperature for each replication.
4. Determine the average on-time for the five replications.
5. Divide the average on-time of the thermostat signal light by 60 to determine the percentage for one hour.
6. Multiply the percentage by the electrical rating of the equipment to obtain the estimated kilowatt-hour consumption. (Example: 30 minutes average on-time ÷ 60 = 50 percent, and 50 percent × an equipment kWh rating of 12 = 6 kWh consumed.)
7. Record kilowatt-hour (kWh) consumption on the standardized recipe card.

When this type of information is recorded on each standardized recipe in a cycle menu system, management can

Exhibit 15–12 Form Detailing Usage and Cost of Electricity

Form 1—Use and Cost of Electricity

Equipment (type and location) ____________ Date ____________ to ____________

Electrical use per device (kW)	Number of devices	Total electrical use (kW) [(1) × (2)]	Operating hours per week	Operating weeks per year	Estimated kWh per year [(3) × (4) × (5)]
(1)	(2)	(3)	(4)	(5)	(6)

Prepared by: ______________________________

Comments/remarks (operating procedures, temperature, time, etc.) ____________________

make accurate decisions in efforts to reduce energy costs. The recording of these data also provides tangible evidence that an energy control program is in effect. The cost of energy, as well as labor and food costs, should become a permanent part of each standardized recipe as a basis for establishing the selling price of a food item.

Evaluation

Results should be measured against the stated objectives. It is possible that expectations have been exceeded. Should results fail to measure up to objectives, it will be necessary to reexamine the various stages to determine where difficulties exist.

BUDGET SYSTEMS

A budget is defined as a written financial statement, expressed in numerical terms, for a specified period of time. A budgeting system is more comprehensive and is defined as a process of planning, coordinating, and controlling financial resources in order to meet the objectives and goals of the organization. In medical operations, the objective has been one of mission or service, with minimal attention to the budgetary process as practiced by profit-oriented businesses. Recently, however, because of escalating costs of medical care, medical operations have been faced with the challenge of seeking congruence between service and fiscal responsibility.

Traditional Budgeting System

The most widely used method of allocating funds is the use of the traditional budgeting system. In this system, use of funds is not always questioned unless there is an excessive overrun. Each year, based on last year's budgetary allowance, additional funds are added to the operating budget. The amount of increased funding is usually associated with the inflation rate. This type of budgeting may well perpetuate inefficiency because objectives are not redefined to reflect

Exhibit 15–13 Form Detailing Usage and Cost of Natural Gas

Form 2—Use and Cost of Natural Gas

Equipment (type and location) ____________ Date ____________ to ____________

Fuel use per device	Number of devices	Total gas use (cu ft/hr) [(1) × (2)]	Operating hours per week	Operating weeks per year	Estimated cubic feet per year [(3) × (4) × (5)]
(1)	(2)	(3)	(4)	(5)	(6)

Prepared by: ____________________

Comments/remarks (operating procedures, temperature, time, etc.) ____________________

changes that may have occurred. In addition, when funds are limited, cuts in the operating budget are made across the board, regardless of departmental objectives and goals.

Although medical organizations may be reluctant to do so, they must look beyond the traditional budgeting system. The reluctance to use what has been described as more complex systems for financial control in medical organizations may stem from the nonfinancial background of most professionals who head various departments. According to Deters (1980), employees in nonfinancial areas are sometimes intimidated by financial jargon and should be taught basic concepts through well-developed educational programs.

Some of the more widely used systems for planning, coordinating, and controlling financial resources today are management by objectives (see Chapter 2 for a full discussion); planning, programming, and budgeting systems; and zero-base budgeting. Zero-base budgeting is the latest to receive widespread managerial support and therefore is described in more detail.

Planning, Programming, and Budgeting System

The planning, programming, and budgeting system (PPBS) is an integrated, analytical approach used to allocate resources in the most effective manner to meet goals of the operation. Emphasis is on planning to achieve stated goals; consideration is then given to resources necessary to obtain the desired results. In this system, budgeting plays a secondary role to setting goals and establishing plans.

Concepts of PPBS were first used in private industry by companies such as the Rand Corporation, General Motors, and DuPont (Novick 1969). As early as 1940, principles of PPBS were used for World War II production controls. The system received national attention in 1961 when it was introduced by Secretary of Defense Robert McNamara. As used in the Defense Department, it served to improve management decision making in the federal government and was mandated for use by all federal agencies in 1965 by President Lyndon Johnson. The system provided a uniform language to be used by all agencies requesting funding over a multiyear period.

Pyhrr (1973) cites the following major components of PPBS as used in the Defense Department:

1. Program structures are the groupings of activities (intra- and interagencywide) that have the same common goal. The basic unit of the program structure is the program element. The charting or breaking down of elements within a program structure is analogous to an organization chart, with elements defined at different organizational levels. The purpose of this phase is to analyze all relevant activities by different agencies relating to a given objective, to eliminate overlap, and to identify gaps in the services provided.
2. Issue letters, formulated through consensus of the agencies involved, concentrate on major issues that need in-depth analysis. Issue letters are used early in the cycle so that agreement can be reached on the nature of the problem and alternatives formulated for evaluation.
3. Special analytical studies relate to issues identified in the issue letters. Support documents used to analyze issues may include statistical models, surveys, and other data needed to support issues.
4. Program memoranda relate to analysis of issues as identified in and among agencies and the alternatives considered. Program memoranda are used to summarize agency decisions.
5. Program and financial plans include the actual data for the two preceding years, plus the projected funds for the next five years. Because the time plan for spending was increased to five years or more, the plans attempted to bridge the gap between long-range objectives and the current year's budget allocation; to identify future commitment based on past decisions; and to identify consequences of current decisions.

Because PPBS is more complex than this simplistic description portrays, some federal and private organizations fail to utilize all components of the system fully.

Zero-Base Budgeting

Zero-base budgeting (ZBB) is a managerial technique developed by Peter A. Pyhrr. The budgeting system was first applied at the Texas Instrument Company in Dallas for its staff and research budget for 1970 (Pyhrr 1970). It quickly became a well-known concept in the business world, with more than 300 businesses and a dozen state governments using the technique within a few years of its introduction (Carter 1977).

The budgeting process received its widest application when Governor Carter of Georgia decided to use it for the 1973 state budget. He was convinced at that time that ZBB was a most effective method for analyzing and evaluating all activities, both current and new, before allocating funds. As president, Mr. Carter was also convinced that the same general principles of budgeting could be successfully applied to most federal funding.

To clarify and provide mutual understanding, it may be necessary to define briefly certain terms related to the discussion of ZBB.

Activity is the basic work or action of an individual or group in the accomplishment of objectives established for a program.

Alternative is the comparison of two or more methods of accomplishing or performing the operation or activity and choosing the one that is considered best.

Cost-benefit is an analytical approach to solving problems of choice. It involves alternative ways of achieving objectives that yield the greatest benefit for the least cost.

Decision package is a document that identifies and describes a specific activity so that management can evaluate and rank it against other activities competing for funds in terms of approval or disapproval.

Incremental packages reflect different levels of effort that may be expended on a specific function.

Issue identification results in the review of decision packages and the ranking process in which additional issues, alternatives, and policy questions may arise as analysts evaluate the impact of the operations on program objectives.

Mutually exclusive packages identify alternative means for performing the same function. The best alternative is chosen, and the other packages are discarded.

Program structure is a clear identification of the interaction of operations in the program.

Special analysis is a method of offering a ready-made data source as a result of the mass of information and analysis provided.

Zero-base budgeting is a technique of starting from scratch in identifying, analyzing, and evaluating all activities (current and new) before funds are allocated. Each manager evaluates and considers the need for each function, different levels of effort, and alternative ways of performing different functions.

Implementation of ZBB involves two major or basic steps: (1) describing each decision unit as a *decision package* and (2) evaluating and ranking all decision packages by cost-benefit analysis to develop the budget request and the profit-and-loss statements.

In defining decision units, ZBB attempts to focus management's attention on evaluating activities and making decisions related to their continuation. Each organization must determine for itself what is meaningful in terms of the decision units. In practice, the organization or program level at which decision units are defined is usually determined by top management.

After the decision units have been identified, top management must then explain the decision package concept to all levels of management and present guidelines for individual managers to use in breaking down their areas into workable packages. The decision package is the building block of the ZBB process and is designed to identify activity, function, or operation in a definitive manner for management evaluation and comparison with other activities. The decision package should include the purpose, consequences of not performing the activity, measures of performance, alternative courses of action, and cost-benefit ratio.

The ranking process is accomplished by managers in the various departments as they identify all packages in order of decreasing benefit to the organization. The process then pinpoints the benefits to be gained at each level of expenditure and considers the consequences of not approving additional decision packages ranked below a certain expenditure level. This process allows upper management an opportunity to trade off expenditures among cost centers and other larger divisions of the organization.

The initial implementation of ZBB is often done by a task force of operating and financial managers who are responsible for the design and administration of the process throughout the organization. Each organization must decide whether to install ZBB throughout the organization or only within special departments first. Duties of the task force in managing the process involve the following steps:

1. Design the process to fit the needs of the organization.
2. Prepare a simplified budget manual that illustrates examples of analyses required and explains the decision package and ranking concepts.
3. Present the process to management, and train operating managers in the application of the technique.
4. Work with division unit managers to improve and expedite the analysis.
5. Work with middle management to review and rank decision packages.
6. Evaluate the process and revise it accordingly.

There are distinct problems associated with ZBB. The major causes of problems in implementation stem from lack of support from top management, ineffective design of the system to meet the needs of the user organization, and ineffective management of the system. Administrative problems may arise if operating managers are apprehensive of the process because their functions are being scrutinized; if there is a lack of communication of goals, objectives, and purpose; if there is a lack of planning assumptions; and because extra time is required during the first year.

The benefits of ZBB far outweigh the possible problems that may be encountered. One of the unique features of ZBB is that it requires the participation of all managers at all levels of the organization, whereas in many organizations the planning and budgeting process is done by financial and fiscal people with participation of only top management. The benefits that each organization can derive from ZBB can be divided into three general categories:

1. improved plans and budgets
2. residual benefits, realized during the operating years
3. a skilled management team

The improved plans and budgets offer the most immediate benefits because of the identification, evaluation, and justification of all activities proposed rather than just the increase or decrease from current operating levels. Great flexibility is also provided to top management in reallocating resources. Zero-base budgeting combines planning, goal setting, budgeting, and operational decision making and results in an integrated approach. Duplication of efforts among organizational units will be identified and can be eliminated with this system.

A major follow-up benefit is that managers' effectiveness can be measured against the goals, performance, and benefits to which they commit themselves, as indicated in the decision packages and in their budgets. In addition, ZBB trains managers to think continually along the analytical lines that the process requires.

In developing the managerial team, ZBB can be considered an educational process. The identification and evaluation required in ranking decision packages can become an ingrained thought process, whereby managers evaluate their planning, operations, efficiency, and cost effectiveness on a continuous basis.

In the sample *decision package* format (Exhibit 15–14), the problem relates to eliminating an unfilled position in the storeroom section in order to effect a cost-benefit result. It is clearly up to the manager of that section to identify and evaluate alternatives. This process need not be accomplished by the manager alone; all employees in the section may assist in reaching a decision. Note that the sample format is the first of three decision packages and concentrates on the minimum level of performance required to deliver services. It reflects the loss of one technical assistant and the savings of $18,000 while at the same time letting management know the consequences of this change.

The alternatives suggested in section 10 of Exhibit 15–14 offer two levels of effort with recommendations for adoption of package 2 of 3 packages. In section 11, different ways of performing the same activity are suggested with resulting consequences. Management may require a detailed explanation relating to the poor logistic setup alluded to in that section. In section 12, management can readily review and analyze the resources required, which will be important in the ranking process. Formulating alter-

Exhibit 15–14 Zero-Base Budgeting Decision Package

(1) *Package Name*	(2) *Division*	(3) *Department*	(4) *Cost Center*	(5) *Rank*
Basic Plan (1 of 3)	Storeroom	Food Service	56	3

(6) *Statement of Purpose*
To provide minimum level of storeroom operation in terms of receiving, storing, and issuing of food, and maintenance of records.

(7) *Description of Actions (Operations)*
Receive food and check for quantity according to purchase order.
Verify all items listed for quality as stated in food specifications.
Store foods according to safety and sanitation codes, using FIFO.
Issue foods as requisitioned by production and service units.
Maintain perpetual and physical inventory records.
I Professional, I Technical Assistant

(8) *Benefits*
This is a minimum level of planning required to deliver services.
Personnel: 2 Cost: $36,000

(9) *Consequences of Not Approving Package*
Elimination of technical assistant position results in zero incremental costs, but a breakdown in control standards plus excessive delays in receiving and issuing would develop.

(10) *Alternatives (Different Levels of Effort) and Cost*
Package 2 of 3 (cost $47, 960): Provides the storeroom section with more manpower during its heaviest work period (early AM) by hiring two part-time assistants at lower rates (20 hours per week @ $5.75 per hour). *Recommended Package.*
Package 3 of 3 (cost $56,610): retain technical assistant position @ $18,000.

(11) *Alternatives (Different Ways of Performing the Same Activity)*
Combine storeroom and production sections (rotate assistant cooks to storeroom duties).
Shift other production and service personnel to storeroom duties on a short-term basis.
NOTE: Both alternatives would result in poor logistic setup—in addition to possible lowering of control standards.

(12) *Resources Required*

1996	$56,610	Personnel: 3	(1 Professional + 2 Technical Assistants)
1997	$47,960	Personnel: 4	(1 Professional + Technical Assistant and 2 Part-Time Assistants)
	8,650	+1	

Manager J.P. Doe Prepared by J.P. Doe Date 10-10-96 Page 1

Source: Data from *Zero-Base Budgeting,* ©1973, John Wiley & Sons.

natives in terms of effort and identifying different ways of performing the same task are the most important aspects of the decision package.

Implications for medical food service management are apparent. Because ZBB is becoming more and more popular in business, industry, and government, the food service director should be aware of its implications for food service management. Also, because most medical organizations receive some type of state or federal funding it is advantageous for the food service director to understand how these funds are allocated.

The food service director has the major responsibility for exerting leadership in developing financial plans; therefore it is imperative that the managerial staff remain alert to new and innovative techniques. Current economic conditions dictate that one means of accountability will surely be in the form of finance. Funds are no longer handed out based on status quo but require detailed scrutiny at all levels.

UNIFORM SYSTEM OF ACCOUNTING

There are similarities among various types of food service operations, yet each is uniquely different. One difference is in the accounting procedures. Because of this difference, each major segment of the food service industry (hotels, restaurants, school lunch program, hospitals) has developed a uniform system for reporting costs. For hospitals, the uniform system of accounting is performed by Hospital Administrative Services (HAS).

Hospital Administrative Services

The primary function of HAS is to provide comparative cost data to hospital administrators. Statistical indicators are used to compare hospitals according to size, type, and geographical location. To obtain cost data, based on group mediums, hospitals must pay a fee and submit data on income and expenses, using uniform accounting procedures. HAS has developed specific guidelines (HAS 1973) for determining the number of patient meals served; equivalent number of cafeteria meals served; where and how to report personnel salaries and man-hours; food and other direct expenses; and procedures for reporting all revenue (cafeteria, vending, coffee shop, etc.).

A confidential monthly report is sent to each participating hospital so that the administrator can compare his or her operation to a group medium in eight categories. The HAS indicators and possible reasons for deviation from the group medium are shown in each report. It should be pointed out that although resolution of problem areas is not the responsibility of HAS, it does suggest possible causes for extreme deviations. Hospitals may use the information in a number of ways to evaluate the effectiveness of the department. Should it become necessary to investigate significant differences, management can begin with a check on accuracy of data as reported by the department head. If data are reported accurately, management might refer to factors of food and labor cost controls as discussed earlier in this chapter.

BUDGET PREPARATION

The degree to which department heads are involved in budget preparation varies from one institution to another, based on administrative policies and procedures, the degree of accountability for cost controls, the amount of budget information communicated from top management, and the level of budgeting knowledge possessed by the food service director.

The following questions help discern the administrative policies that may affect department head involvement. Are the policies of the organization based on participatory budget preparation or are all budget estimates made by the accounting department? On what basis are budget estimates approved or disapproved before they become effective or a part of the general budget? What is the procedure for making changes in the budget?

The amount of information communicated to the food service director has the most direct bearing on his or her involvement. In addition to accurate records of prior costs, the food service director needs information on both short- and long-range goals of the organization. For example, major policy changes, significant increases in patient census, major renovations, or plans for a new facility could have direct effects on the food service budget.

One method of communication is through the use of a budget questionnaire. This procedure requires more than just a listing of items and dollar amounts; it also requires the individual to state departmental objectives and justifications for expenditures. Sample questions asked by one organization are shown in Exhibit 15–15.

In addition to the questionnaire, department heads are required to complete another form that lists departmental objectives, how objectives will be accomplished, and the time frame for completion. This method of budget preparation is not as complex as the budget systems discussed earlier, but it does require more than the superficial planning associated with the traditional method.

The food service director is probably more prepared to participate in budget preparation than most department heads in a medical operation, because accounting and cost control courses are included in the curriculum for food service management. Department heads in other areas are professionally competent in their specialty areas but may have little interest in or knowledge of financial management. Therefore, participative financial management practices are not fully utilized in some medical organizations.

The food service budget, in numerical terms, should include the following costs (Exhibit 15–16): raw food, labor, supply, equipment, and other.

Food Costs

The budget amount for food will depend on the projected number of meals multiplied by the projected cost per meal. Unless there has been a change in menu offerings, a good estimate can be made from current food costs. A review of current food costs compared with costs during the previous year will give the rate of increase in cost. The

Exhibit 15–15 Sample Budget Questionnaire

Budget Questionnaire
Fiscal year _____

DEPARTMENT ______________________________ DATE ______________________________

1. List all changes in departmental responsibilities, functions, or other factors during the present year that have caused an increase/decrease in the department's volume of work.

____
____
____
____
____
____
____
____
____
____
____
____
____
____

2. What functions are you and your department performing that should be eliminated, transferred, or curtailed? What cost savings will result?
3. What paperwork does your department perform or receive that should be simplified, eliminated, or computerized?
4. What services did/will you perform this year that will not be an expense factor next year?
5. What deficiencies of other departments, or lack of coordination, made work for your department?
6. In the event of reduced income below current level, what changes could you make and still maintain patient outcome at an acceptable level?
7. How does the ratio of personnel to departmental activity compare with last year, current year, and proposed for next year? Explain any differences.

projection is only as accurate as the records that have been maintained.

Labor Costs

Labor costs include wages, FICA, and fringe benefits. To arrive at a projected cost figure for nonmanagement employees, multiply the number of man-hours required by the hourly wage for each worker classification. The amount to add for fringe benefits can be obtained from the accounting office. In some cases, this is done by adding a certain percentage to the base salary. Fringe benefits and other employee costs may include holiday pay, vacation pay, sick leave, funeral leave, personal days, group hospital insurance, group life, pension, workers' compensation, and unemployment compensation. In addition to FICA and fringe benefits, consider wage increases that have been negotiated, promotions, minimum wage increases as a result of federal regulations, projected overtime, and differential pay. Management-level employees are not subject to overtime or differential pay, but consideration must be given to costs of annual increases and promotions. It is estimated that from 6 percent to 20 percent of total labor costs can be paid for management and still maintain an efficient operation (Kotschevar 1973).

Exhibit 15–16 Monthly Expense Report Form

Monthly Expense Report

Department ________________ Date________________

Expense Item	Account No.	Total Amount Spent: Month ($)	Total Amount Spent: YTD (Year to Date)	Total Amount Budgeted ($)
Food (costs based on amounts purchased minus inventory)				
Meat, fish, poultry				
Groceries				
Fruits and vegetables				
Dairy products				
Bakery				
Total		$	$	$
Labor				
Wages				
FICA				
Overtime premium				
Differential pay				
Vacation pay				
Holiday pay				
Sick leave				
Funeral				
Personal time				
Group hospital insurance				
Group life				
Workers' compensation				
Unemployment compensation				
Pension				
Total		$	$	$
Supply				
Cleaning materials				
Disposables				
China				
Glassware				
Silverware				
Office supplies				
Small equipment				
Total		$	$	$
Equipment				
Total		$	$	$
Other costs				
Laundry				
Uniforms				
Utilities				
Education				
Administrative overhead				
Printing				
Contractual services				
Contingency				
Total		$	$	$

Supply Costs

In this category, funds should be allocated for cleaning materials, disposables, china, glassware, flatware, office supplies, and small equipment. Here again, usage records can be used to project funds needed for optimal operation. The amount needed for cleaning supplies (detergent, soap, sanitizers, dishwashing compounds, mop heads, etc.) will depend on who is responsible for cleaning. If housekeeping or outside contractors are used, the supply costs will be less, but the contractual fee will be higher. Cleaning supplies should be securely stored and issued in the same manner as food supplies. Employees responsible for cleaning duty should be fully informed on the use of all cleaning compounds, including amounts for different types such as "full strength" or "diluted." The use of automatic dispensers in areas such as dish machines, kitchen hand sinks, and employee facilities can result in savings.

Disposables include all paper and plastic supplies needed, such as napkins, plates, cups, trays for isolated patients, straws, sandwich wrap, and aluminum foil. To reduce costs of paper supplies, consider group purchasing or purchasing in bulk, if storage space is available. The use of dispensers for paper supplies such as napkins, straws, and cups tends to discourage taking more than one at a time. The amount of office supplies needed will depend on the form, type, and amount of paperwork generated in the food service department.

Small equipment costs refer to costs of pots and pans, trays, serving utensils, knives, and so forth. Pilferage and improper handling by employees are major causes of cost escalation in this category; therefore, replacement is warranted on an annual basis. Make employees aware of the cost of each piece of small equipment, china, and silverware. Take pre- and post-inventories for a period of time and share information on shortages with employees. Post the price of each item on the bulletin boards in the work areas so that employees will know the monetary loss to the department caused by improper handling and breakage. Check trash for silverware thrown away as dishes and trays are scraped. Savings from the above practices can outweigh the cost of time involved.

Equipment Costs

Funding for large equipment (new, replacement, repair, and maintenance) is included in the capital budget. The need for effective capital budgeting is emphasized not only because of the increasing costs of capital items but also because the failure to make timely replacement of inefficient equipment can impair the quantity and quality of food production and service. Capital budgeting practices require long-range planning consistent with the needs of the organization. Because the medical organization may not have enough funds to meet all budgeted requests, careful consideration is given to approval. In most instances, a separate request form is used for each piece of equipment or project, such as the example shown in Exhibit 15–17.

Justifications are required for each request and should be submitted with the budget. Records of repair and maintenance, as shown in Exhibit 15–18, can serve as part of the justification. If your records show that the amount of down time for a piece of equipment or the cost of repairs results in inefficiency, you are more likely to get the budget request approved. Keep in mind that the food service budget is in competition with the budgets of other departments of the facility, which may (in the eyes of the equipment committee) have a higher priority for funds.

Other Costs

In addition to food, labor, supply, and equipment costs, consideration should be given to the following: laundry, uniforms, utilities, continuing education, administrative overhead, printing, contractual services, and contingency. In most organizations, laundry is a contractual service. Whether this service is contracted or accomplished in-house, the cost will be minimal because most uniforms are the non-cotton, permanent press type. Dish towels are not permitted for drying dishes or utensils, but clean, sanitized cloths are needed for cleaning tabletops and other areas of food preparation and service. If disposable cleaning cloths are used, the cost should be included in the supply category. The costs associated with uniform purchase, if paid for by the organization, should be part of the fringe benefits. Some organizations prefer to provide both the uniform and the upkeep in order to ensure that employees are neat and clean for duty.

Utility costs are those such as heat, light, power, and water. Because the food service department is unlikely to have separate meters for these costs, they are usually prorated. Check with the accounting department to determine the percentage of utility costs charged to food service.

Continuing education is an ongoing cost and should receive adequate attention to provide for in-service training of employees; attendance at conventions, workshops, and seminars; formal courses taken by employees; and books and other reference materials. To make sure that an adequate amount of funds is allotted for travel to out-of-town educational meetings, determine the number of employees attending, the mode of travel, and the cost of lodging and meals. For most annual meetings, the location is determined at least one year in advance. If formal courses taken by employees are counted as fringe benefits, the cost should be reflected in the labor category.

Exhibit 15–17 Capital Equipment Budget Request Form

Capital Equipment Budget Request
Fiscal Year 19____

Department: ______________________ Date Submitted: ______________________
Capital Expenditure No.: ______________ Date Approved: ______________________

Directions: Complete *one* form for each item requested.

1. Item (equipment) ____
2. Description (manufacturer, model, serial no., etc.) ______________________
____

3. *Classification*
   _____Initial
   _____Replacement
   _____Expansion

4. *Priority*
   _____Absolutely Essential
   _____Necessary
   _____Desirable

5. What is the anticipated cost (include expenses below) $______________________
   Basic Equipment $__________ Auxiliary Cost $______________________
   Freight $__________________ Installation $______________________

Other Expenses (explain) $ ____

6. Warranty Period _________ months/years 7. Estimated Useful Life ___________
8. If maintenance contract is required, what is monthly cost? $__________________
9. If replacement item, state plans for disposition of replaced item.
   ____
10. Briefly justify the expenditure (cost savings, quality control, revenue generated, new service, etc.) ____
   ____
   ____

Requested by ______________________

Administrative Action:

Approved _________ Disapproved _________ Date __________

Comments: ____
____

Administrative overhead may include occupancy space, interest, mortgage depreciation, and salaries for staff and functional employees. All these are costs prorated. Most organizations have calculations for operational cost based on square footage and may charge a percentage of that cost to food service or make the charges to the general fund.

Printing costs refer to expenses incurred for the printing of standardized forms. Color-coded "front-of-the-house" menus are a major part of this cost, in addition to other forms used on a regular basis.

Contractual services may include garbage and trash removal, housekeeping duties, exterminating services, and cleaning of vents, hoods, and windows. Consider reducing the amount of garbage and trash by using heavy-duty disposals and compactors. Investigate the sale of discarded fat and compacted or compressed paper waste, especially corrugated boxes. Compare the cost and quality of outside housekeeping with cost and quality of in-house housekeeping. Exterminating services are essential for high standards of sanitation and safety, but cost and effectiveness of these services should be scrutinized. For all contractual services, know what you are being charged for by keeping records of services rendered. Compare services with bills submitted by contractors, especially the number of hours spent in the department.

Contingency funds may be allowed, depending on the policies of the organization. Some organizations permit the

Exhibit 15–18 Equipment Record Form

Equipment Record

Equipment ______________________ Purchase date ______________________

Cost ______________________ Full depreciation date ______________________

Location ____

Motor serial no. ______________________ Model ______________________

Motor specifications: (W) __________ (V) __________ (amp) __________ (hp) __________

Description: (type) ______________________ (size) ______________________

(capacity) ______________________ (design) ______________________

Repair Maintenance and Replacement

Date	Nature	By Whom	Cost	Remarks

inclusion of a certain percentage of the total budget for unexpected financial outlay.

OPERATING REPORTS AND ANALYSIS

Operating reports are provided at designated intervals as feedback for the department head. The most useful report is a comparison of costs on a monthly basis. As shown in Exhibit 15–16, the food service director can readily determine whether costs are out of line by comparing cost to date with budgeted amount. The analysis of costs on a monthly basis will provide enough time to investigate significant deviations from the budgeted amount and thus take corrective action.

COMPUTER APPLICATIONS FOR FINANCIAL MANAGEMENT

Traditionally, food services in health care facilities have been managed on a nonprofit basis. This has often meant that food services were subsidized by the health care facility, at best breaking even. However, this situation is no longer acceptable. Every department within a health care facility has to be cost-effective and create ways to generate income. Astute managers realize that they must set financial goals for their departments to make a profit.

Electronic data processing (EDP), including computer systems, is used for control purposes in food service operations. Five categories of software are commonly used in business: accounting, inventory, word processing, spreadsheets, and databases.

Inventory and word processing with computer tools have been discussed. Modular computer programs for business accounting include purchase journals, accounts receivable, and accounts payable computer modules. Spreadsheet applications have replaced calculators for most routine calculations. A spreadsheet has cells, arranged in numbered vertical columns and horizontal rows, that contain data to be used in calculations. Spreadsheets are commonly used to compute cost percentages, utilize costing formulas to isolate fixed, variable, semivariable, controllable; and noncontrollable cost; track sales history; and develop budgets. Menu engineering and recipe and portion cost analysis are also considerably less tedious when done by computer.

In menu engineering, the manager can establish cost goals, as well as other goals, and utilize the computer to generate menu item combinations that meet them. Computer applications based upon menu engineering theories use data on menu mix percentage and contribution margin to clarify the profit performance and popularity of menu items (Sackler and Trapani 1995). With the use of this tool managers are better able to react to current market prices and thereby exercise tighter budgetary controls.

A budget is a realistic expression of management's goals and objectives expressed in financial terms. "The budget for the foodservice department is often the second highest cost center in the hospital" (Stokes 1989). With spreadsheet applications the data needed to develop an operating budget can be transferred from other data files such as the monthly expense report. Published industry standards and departmental cost allocations may be incorporated and used as yardsticks by which to monitor and evaluate achievement of financial goals and objectives.

Daniels and Gregoire (1993) state that "many directors use some form of capital budgeting techniques." Four recognized techniques are payback period, average accounting rate of return, net profitability index, and internal rate of return. Many software programs have been designed specifically for institutional and hospitality food services. These programs range from simple budget applications to more sophisticated, decision-making expert systems, the branch of artificial intelligence research that uses specialized knowledge to emulate the decision-making ability of a human expert to reason and explain (Gregoire and Nettles 1994). Expert systems consist of a knowledge base and an inference engine used to process information, draw conclusions, and give advice, based upon a set of rules established by the human expert.

Ideally, managers should use some form of historical and current data analysis as a basis for decision making in food services. Microcomputer software applications and systems are readily available to transform data about food census counts, food cost percentages, raw food cost, menu mix, and so forth into meaningful information that can be manipulated and analyzed to present realistic scenarios for cost-effective operations.

CRITICAL CONTROL POINTS AND CONTROL POINTS RELATED TO FINANCIAL MANAGEMENT

Management must be committed to the hazard analysis critical control point (HACCP) system by providing support for its continued implementation. Financial costs may be incurred in steps to ensure observation of the HACCP system, as follows:

- Train staff on hazards, critical points, and monitoring procedures.
- Provide employees with the proper equipment and materials to do their jobs well.
- Take corrective actions, which may involve the discarding of food products (a costly loss to the operation).

REFERENCES

Carter, J.E. 1977. Jimmy Carter tells why he will use zero-base budgeting. *Nation's Business* 65, no 1:24–26.

Daniels, R.D., and M.F. Gregoire. 1993. Use of capital budgeting techniques by foodservice directors in for-profit and not-for-profit hospitals. *Journal of the American Dietetic Association* 93:63–69.

Deters, J.R. 1980. Teaching finance to the non-financial manager. *Financial Executive* 48, no. 1:28–34.

Gregoire, M., and M. F. Nettles. 1994. Is it time for computer-assisted decision making to improve the quality of food and nutrition services? *Journal of the American Dietetic Association* 94, no. 12:1371–1374.

Hospital Administrative Services. 1973. *Uniform system of accounts*. Chicago: American Hospital Association.

Kotschevar, L. H. 1973. *Foodservice for the extended care facility*. Boston: Cahners Books.

Longrigg, J. 1981. Casebook no. 165: How to reduce staff turnover. *Hospital-Nursing Homes* 16, no. 10:98.

Novick, D. 1969. The origin and history of program budgeting. *California Management Review* 11, no. 1:7–12.

Pyhrr, P. 1970. Zero-base budgeting. *Harvard Business Review* 48: 111–121.

Pyhrr, P. 1973. *Zero-base budgeting*. New York: John Wiley & Sons.

Romanelli, F. 1979. Study shows how to measure energy use, costs, in food service. *Hospitals* 53, no. 3:77–78, 91.

Rose, J.C. 1980. Containing the labor cost of foodservice. *Hospitals* 54, no. 6:93–98.

Sackler, W., and S.R. Trapani. 1995. *Foodservice cost control using Lotus 1-2-3*. New York: John Wiley & Sons.

Stokes, J.K. 1989. Effective quality food service: An institutional guide. Gaithersburg, MD: Aspen Publishers, Inc.

Taylor, W.C. 1981. Absenteeism in health care food service. *Journal of the American Dietetic Association* 79, no. 6:699–701.

Appendix Table of Contents

APPENDIX A

Long-Term Care Standards for Dietary Survey (Management Component)

Tag Number	*Regulation*	*Guidance to Surveyors*
F360	§483.35 Dietary Services. The facility must provide each resident with a nourishing, palatable, well-balanced diet that meets the daily nutritional and special dietary needs of each resident.	
F361	(a) Staffing. The facility must employ a qualified dietitian either full-time, part-time, or on a consultant basis. (1) If a qualified dietitian is not employed full-time, the facility must designate a person to serve as the director of food service who receives frequently scheduled consultation from a qualified dietitian. (2) A qualified dietitian is one who is qualified based upon either registration by the Commission on Dietetic Registration of the American Dietetic Association, or on the basis of education, training, or experience in identification of dietary needs, planning, and implementation of dietary programs.	Intent: §483.35(a) The intent of this regulation is to ensure that a qualified dietitian is utilized in planning, managing and implementing dietary service activities in order to assure that the residents receive adequate nutrition. A director of food services has no required minimum qualifications, but must be able to function collaboratively with a qualified dietitian in meeting the nutritional needs of the residents. Guidelines: §483.35(a) A dietitian qualified on the basis of education, training, or experience in identification of dietary needs, planning and implementation of dietary programs has experience or training which includes: • Assessing special nutritional needs of geriatric and physically impaired persons; • Developing therapeutic diets; • Developing "regular diets" to meet the specialized needs of geriatric and physically impaired persons; • Developing and implementing continuing education programs for dietary services and nursing personnel; • Participating in interdisciplinary care planning; • Budgeting and purchasing food and supplies; and • Supervising institutional food preparation, service and storage.

Source: Reprinted from *Long Term Care Survey Protocol and Interpretive Guidelines,* 1995, Health Care Financing Administration.

Tag Number	*Regulation*	*Guidance to Surveyors*
		Procedures: §483.35(a) If resident reviews determine that residents have nutritional problems, determine if these nutritional problems relate to inadequate or inappropriate diet nutrition/assessment and monitoring. Determine if these are related to dietitian qualifications. Probes: §483.35(a) If the survey team finds problems in resident nutritional status: • Do practices of the dietitian or food services director contribute to the identified problems in residents' nutritional status? If yes, what are they? • What are the educational, training, and experience qualifications of the facility's dietitian?
F362	(b) Sufficient staff. The facility must employ sufficient support personnel competent to carry out the functions of the dietary service.	Guidelines: §483.35(b) "Sufficient support personnel" is defined as enough staff to prepare and serve palatable, attractive, nutritionally adequate meals at proper temperatures and appropriate times and support proper sanitary techniques being utilized. Procedures: §483.35(b) For residents who have been triggered for a dining review, do they report that meals are palatable, attractive, served at the proper temperatures and at appropriate times? Probes: §483.35(b) (Sufficient staff preparation) Is food prepared in scheduled time-frames in accordance with established professional practices? Observe food service: Does food leave kitchen in scheduled time-frames? Is food served to residents in scheduled time-frames?
F563	(c) Menus and nutritional adequacy. Menus must	
	(1) Meet the nutritional needs of residents in accordance with the recommended dietary allowances of the Food and Nutrition Board of the National Research Council, National Academy of Sciences;	Intent: §483.35(c)(1)(2)(3) The intent of this regulation is to assure that the meals served meet the nutritional needs of the resident in accordance with the recommended dietary allowances (RDAs) of the Food and Nutrition Board of the National Research Council, of the National Academy of Sciences. This regulation also assures that there is a prepared menu by which nutritionally adequate meals have been planned for the resident and followed. Procedures: §483.35(c)(1) • For sampled residents who have a comprehensive review or a focused review, as appropriate, observe if meals served are consistent with the planned menu and care plan in the amounts, types and consistency of foods served. If the survey team observes deviation from the planned menu, review appropriate documentation from diet card, record review, and interviews with food service manager or dietitian to support reason(s) for deviation from the written menu.

Tag Number	*Regulation*	*Guidance to Surveyors*
		Probes: §483.35(c)(1) • Are residents receiving food in the amount, type, consistency and frequency to maintain normal body weight and acceptable nutritional values? • If food intake appears inadequate based on meal observations, or resident's nutritional status is poor based on resident review, determine if menus have been adjusted to meet the caloric and nutrient-intake needs of each resident. • If a food group is missing from the resident's daily diet, does the facility have an alternative means of satisfying the resident's nutrient needs? If so, does the facility perform a follow-up? (Menu adequately provides the daily basic food groups) Does the menu meet basic nutritional needs by providing daily food in the groups of the food pyramid system and based on individual nutritional assessment taking into account current nutritional recommendations? Note: A standard meal planning guide (e.g., food pyramid) is used primarily for menu planning and food purchasing. It is not intended to meet the nutritional needs of all residents. This guide must be adjusted to consider individual differences. Some residents will need more due to age, size, gender, physical activity, and state of health. There are many meal planning guides from reputable sources, i.e., American Diabetes Association, American Dietetic Association, American Medical Association, or U.S. Department of Agriculture, that are available and appropriate for use when adjusted to meet each resident's needs.
	(2) Be prepared in advance; and	Probes: §483.35(c)(2) (Menu prepared in advance) Are there preplanned menus for both regular and therapeutic diets?
	(3) Be followed.	Probes: §483.35(c)(3) (Menu followed) Is food served as planned? If not, why? There may be legitimate and extenuating circumstances why food may not be available on the day of the survey and must be considered before a concern is noted.
F364	(d) Food. Each resident receives and the facility provides (1) Food prepared by methods that conserve nutritive value, flavor, and appearance; (2) Food that is palatable, attractive, and at the proper temperature;	Intent: §483.35(d)(1)(2) The intent of this regulation is to assure that the nutritive value of food is not compromised and destroyed because of prolonged food storage, light, and air exposure; prolonged cooking of foods in a large volume of water and prolonged holding on steam table; and the addition of baking soda. Food should be palatable, attractive, and at the proper temperature as determined by the type of food to ensure resident's satisfaction. Refer to §483.15(e) and/or §483.15(a). Guidelines: §483.35(d)(1) "Food palatability" refers to the taste and/or flavor of the food. "Food attractiveness" refers to the appearance of the food when *served* to residents. Procedures: §483.35(d)(1) Evidence for palatability and attractiveness of food, from day to day and meal to meal, may be strengthened through sources such as: additional

Tag Number	*Regulation*	*Guidance to Surveyors*
		observation, resident and staff interviews, and review of resident council minutes. Review nutritional adequacy in §483.25(i)(1). Probes: §483.35(d)(1)(2) Does food have a distinctly appetizing aroma *and* appearance, which is varied in color and texture? Is food generally well seasoned (use of spices, herbs, etc.) *and* acceptable to residents? (Conserves nutritive value) Is food prepared in a way to preserve vitamins? Method of storage and preparation should cause minimum loss of nutrients. (Food—temperature) Is food served at preferable temperature (hot foods are served hot and cold foods are served cold) as discerned by the resident *and* customary practice? Not to be confused with the proper holding temperature.
F365	(3) Food prepared in a form designed to meet individual needs; and	Intent: §483.35(d)(3)(4) The intent of this regulation is to assure that food is served in a form that meets the resident's needs and satisfaction; and that the resident receives appropriate nutrition when a substitute is offered.
F366	(4) Substitutes offered of similar nutritive value to residents who refuse food served.	Procedures: §483.35(d)(3)(4) Observe trays to assure that food is appropriate to resident according to assessment and care plan. Ask the residents how well the food meets their taste needs. Ask if residents are offered or are given the opportunity to receive substitutes when refusing food on the original menu. Probes: §483.35(d)(3)(4) Is food cut, chopped, or ground for individual resident's needs? Are residents who refuse food offered substitutes of similar nutritive value? Guidelines: §483.35(d)(4) A food substitute should be consistent with the usual and ordinary food items provided by the facility. For example, if a facility never serves smoked salmon, they would not be required to serve this as a food substitute; or the facility may, instead of grapefruit juice, substitute another citrus juice or vitamin C rich juice that the resident likes.
F367	(e) Therapeutic diets. Therapeutic diets must be prescribed by the attending physician.	Intent: §483.35(e) The intent of this regulation is to assure that the resident receives and consumes foods in the appropriate form and/or the appropriate nutritive content as prescribed by a physician and/or assessed by the interdisciplinary team to support the treatment and plan of care. Guidelines: §483.35(e) "Therapeutic diet" is defined as a diet ordered by a physician as part of treatment for a disease or clinical condition, or to eliminate or decrease specific nutrients in the diet (e.g., sodium), or to increase specific nutrients in the diet (e.g., potassium), or to provide food the resident is able to eat (e.g., a mechanically altered diet).

Tag Number	*Regulation*	*Guidance to Surveyors*
		"Mechanically altered diet" is one in which the texture of a diet is altered. When the texture is modified, the type of texture modification must be specific and part of the physicians' order. Procedures: §483.35(e) If the resident has inadequate nutrition or nutritional deficits that manifest into and/or are a product of weight loss or other medical problems, determine if there is a therapeutic diet that is medically prescribed. Probes: §483.35(e) Is the therapeutic diet that the resident receives prescribed by the physician? Also, see §483.25(i), Nutritional Status.
F368	(f) Frequency of meals. (1) Each resident receives and the facility provides at least three meals daily, at regular times comparable to normal mealtimes in the community. (2) There must be no more than 14 hours between a substantial evening meal and breakfast the following day, except as provided in (4) below. (3) The facility must offer snacks at bedtime daily. (4) When a nourishing snack is provided at bedtime, up to 16 hours may elapse between a substantial evening meal and breakfast the following day if a resident group agrees to this meal span, and a nourishing snack is served.	Intent: §483.35(f)(1)(2)(3)(4) The intent of this regulation is to assure that the resident receives his/her meals at times most accepted by the community and that there are not extensive time lapses between meals. This assures that the resident receives adequate and frequent meals. Guidelines: §483.35(f)(1)(2)(3)(4) A "substantial evening meal" is defined as an offering of three or more menu items at one time, one of which includes a high-quality protein such as meat, fish, eggs, or cheese. The meal should represent no less than 20 percent of the day's total nutritional requirements. "Nourishing snack" is defined as a verbal offering of items, single or in combination, from the basic food groups. Adequacy of the "nourishing snack" will be determined both by resident interviews and by evaluation of the overall nutritional status of residents in the facility (e.g., is the offered snack usually satisfying?). Procedures: §483.35(f)(1)(2)(3)(4) Observe meal times and schedules and determine if there is a lapse in time between meals. Ask for resident input on meal service schedules, to verify if there are extensive lapses in time between meals.
F369	(g) Assistive devices. The facility must provide special eating equipment and utensils for residents who need them.	Intent: §483.35(g) The intent of this regulation is to provide residents with assistive devices to maintain or improve their ability to eat independently. For example, improving poor grasp by enlarging silverware handles with foam padding, aiding residents with impaired coordination or tremor by installing plate guards, or providing postural supports for head, trunk, and arms. Procedures: §483.35(g) Review sampled residents comprehensive assessment for eating ability. Determine if recommendations were made for adaptive utensils and if they were, determine if these utensils are available and utilized by resident. If recommended but not used, determine if this is by resident's choice. If utensils are not being utilized, determine when these were recommended and how their use is being monitored by the facility and if the staff is developing alternative recommendations.

Tag Number	*Regulation*	*Guidance to Surveyors*
	(h) Sanitary conditions. The facility must	
F370	(1) Produce food from sources approved or considered satisfactory by federal, state or local authorities;	Intent: §483.35(h)(2) The intent of this regulation is to prevent the spread of food-borne illness and reduce those practices which result in food contamination and compromised food safety in nursing homes. Since food-borne illness is often fatal to nursing home residents, it can and must be avoided.
F371	(2) Store, prepare, distribute, and serve food under sanitary conditions; and	Guidelines: §483.35(h)(2) "Sanitary conditions" is defined as storing, preparing, distributing, and serving food properly to prevent food-borne illness. Potentially hazardous foods must be subject to continuous time/temperature controls in order to prevent either the rapid and progressive growth of infectious or toxigenic microorganisms such as *Salmonella* or the slower growth of *Clostridium botulinum.* In addition, foods of plant origin become potentially hazardous when the skin, husk, peel, or rind is breached, thereby possibly contaminating the fruit or vegetable with disease-causing microorganisms. Potentially hazardous food tends to focus on animal products, including but not limited to milk, eggs, and poultry. Improper holding temperature is a common contributing factor of food-borne illness. The facility must follow proper procedures in cooking, cooling, and storing food according to time, temperatures, and sanitary guidelines. Improper handling of food can cause *Salmonella* and *Escherichia coli* contamination. The 1993 FDA Food Code advises the following precautions: Note: The 1993 FDA Food Code is not regulation and cannot be enforced as such. The food temperatures cited that are recommended in the 1993 FDA Food Code are target temperatures and give a margin of safety in temperature ranges and to avoid known harmful temperatures. Refrigerator storage of food to prevent food-borne illness includes storing raw meat away from vegetables and other foods. Raw meat should be separated from cooked foods and other foods and refrigerated on its own tray on a bottom shelf so meat juices do not drip on other foods. Foods of both plant and animal origin must be cooked, maintained and stored at appropriate temperatures. • Foods of both plant and animal origin must be cooked, and maintained, and stored at appropriate temperatures. These temperatures are better utilized as food hold temperatures rather than the food temperatures as residents receive the food. • Hot foods which are potentially hazardous should leave the kitchen (or steam table) above 140°F, and cold foods at or below 41°F and freezer temperatures should be at 0°F or below. Refrigerator temperatures should be maintained at 41°F or below. The 1993 FDA Food Code can be used as an authoritative guide to clarify regulatory requirements on how to prepare and serve food to prevent food-borne illness. As the public becomes more informed and educated on how to prevent food-borne illness, this code will become the standard of practice the same as the 1976 Food Service Sanitation Manual did prior to 1993.

Tag Number	*Regulation*	*Guidance to Surveyors*

Procedures: §483.35(h)(2)
Observe storage, cooling, and cooking of food. Record the time and date of all observations. If a problem is noted, conduct additional observations to verify findings.

Observe that employees are effectively cleaning their hands prior to preparing, serving and distributing food. Observe that food is covered to maintain temperature and protect from other contaminants when transporting meals to residents.

Refrigerated storage: Check all refrigerators and freezers for temperatures. Use the facility's or the surveyor's own properly sanitized thermometer to evaluate the internal temperatures of potentially hazardous foods with a focus on the quantity of leftovers and the container sizes in which bulk leftovers are stored.

Food preparation: Use a sanitized thermometer to evaluate food temperatures. In addition, how do kitchen staff process leftovers? Are they heated to the appropriate temperatures? How is frozen food thawed? How is potentially hazardous food handled during multistep food preparation (e.g., chicken salad, egg salad)? Is hand contact with food minimized?

Food service: Using a properly sanitized thermometer, check the temperatures of hot and cold food prior to serving. How long is milk held without refrigeration prior to distribution?

Food distribution: Is the food protected from contamination as it is transported to the dining rooms and residents' rooms?

Pest free: Is the area pest free? (See §483.70(h)(4).) Look for signs of pests such as mice, roaches, rats, flies.

(Preventing contamination)
Are handwashing facilities convenient and properly equipped for dietary services staff use? (Staff uses good hygienic practices and staff with communicable diseases or infected skin lesions do not have contact with food if that contact will transmit the disease.)

(Hazard free)
Are toxic items (such as insecticides, detergent, polishes) properly stored, labeled, and used separate from the food?

Probes: §483.35(h)(2)
Observe food storage rooms and food storage in the kitchen. Are containers of food stored off the floor and on clean surfaces in a manner that protects it from contamination? Are other areas under storage shelves monitored for cleanliness to reduce attraction of pests?

Are potentially hazardous foods stored at 41°F or below and frozen foods kept at 0°F or below?

Do staff handle and cook potentially hazardous foods properly?

Are potentially hazardous foods kept at an internal temperature of 41°F or below in cold food storage unit, or at an internal temperature of 140°F or above in a hot food storage unit during display and service?

Tag Number	Regulation	Guidance to Surveyors
		Is food transported in a way that protects against contamination (i.e., covered containers, wrapped, or packaged)? Is there any sign of rodent or insect infestation? (Dishwashing) The current 1993 Food Code, DHHS, FDA, PHS recommends the following water temperatures and manual washing instructions: MACHINE: 1. Hot Water: a. 140°F Wash (or according to the manufacturer's specifications or instructions). b. 180°F Rinse (180°, 160° or greater at the rack and dish/utensils surfaces). 2. Low Temperature: a. 120°F + 25 ppm (parts per million) hypochlorite (household bleach) on dish surface. MANUAL: 1. 3 Compartment Sink (wash, rinse and sanitize): Sanitizing solution used according to manufacturer's instructions. a. 75°F—50 ppm hypochlorite (household bleach) or equivalent, or 12.5 ppm of iodine. b. Hot Water Immersion at 170°F for at least 30 seconds. (Dishwashing) Are food preparation equipment, dishes, and utensils effectively sanitized and cleaned to destroy potential disease carrying organisms and stored in a protected manner?
F372	(3) Dispose of garbage and refuse properly.	Guidelines: §483.35(h)(3) The intent of this regulation is to assure that garbage and refuse be properly disposed. Procedures: §483.35(h)(3) (Garbage/refuse) Observe garbage and refuse container construction, and outside storage receptacles. Probes: §483.35(h)(3) Are garbage and refuse containers in good condition (no leaks) and is waste properly contained in dumpsters or compactors with lids or otherwise covered? Are areas such as loading docks, hallways, and elevators used for both garbage disposal and clean food transport kept clean, free of debris and free of foul odors and waste fat? Is the garbage storage area maintained in a sanitary condition to prevent the harborage and feeding of pests? Are garbage receptacles covered when being removed from the kitchen area to the dumpster?

APPENDIX B

Long-Term Care Standards for Dietary Survey (Clinical Standards)

Federal and state surveys of nursing homes are conducted differently since implementation of OBRA. Three major components are reviewed during surveys of dietary departments:

1. Quality of care
2. Quality of life
3. Dietary services

QUALITY OF CARE

Surveyors may spend half of their time on quality of care issues. They gather information through chart reviews by looking at assessments and care plans. Residents who receive tube feedings or have pressure sores, weight loss, protein malnutrition, or dehydration receive an in-depth review. Residents are observed for their nutritional appearance, and they are interviewed to identify if they are receiving the care that is written in the care plan.

To prepare for the surveyors' chart review, ask yourself the following questions concerning quality of care issues:

- Has a complete nutritional assessment been performed on each resident?
- Are the MDS, RAP Summary form, and ICP completed and accurate?
- Do the last two assessments, quarterly reviews, and progress notes accurately portray the resident's current status and recent history?
- Is the care plan being implemented as written?

OBRA does not require that nursing homes employ a registered or licensed dietitian although state laws may make the requirement. OBRA does require, however, that the facility employ a qualified dietitian full-time, part-time, or on a consulting basis. A dietetic technician or certified dietary manager may have the skills to fulfill this requirement. But this person should be able to conduct nutritional assessments, assess nutritional needs of geriatric and physically impaired persons, participate in interdisciplinary care planning, develop "regular diets" and therapeutic diets to meet the specialized needs of geriatric and physically impaired persons, supervise food preparation and service, oversee budgeting and purchasing of food and supplies, and develop and implement continuing education programs for dietary and nursing personnel. In concert, the nurse, dietitian, and pharmacist are responsible for nutrient-drug interactions.

QUALITY OF LIFE

Surveyors will spend less but equally important time on the quality of life component of the survey. Quality of life issues include dignity, self-determination, and participation.

Self-determination questions that a surveyor may ask a resident include the following:

- Do you like the time for dining and snacks?
- Are you offered a bedtime snack?
- Do you like (agree with) your diet order?
- Do you know you can refuse to eat your meals?
- Can you eat where you desire?
- Can you eat with whom you desire?
- Do you receive the foods you enjoy?
- Have you made any special food requests? Were they considered?
- Is the consistency of foods you receive appropriate for your ability to chew and swallow?

Source: Used with permission of Ross Products Division, Abbott Laboratories, Columbus, Ohio, from *OBRA: A Challenge and an Opportunity for Nutrition Care* by Charlotte R. Gallagher-Allred.

- Do you receive foods consistent with your ethnic background?
- Are the portion sizes appropriate?

Participation questions may include the following:

- Do you feed yourself?
- Are there appropriate tools for self-feeding?
- Can you participate in Resident Council and provide ideas regarding meals, meal timing, snacks, special meals, menu items, etc., without fear of reprisal?
- Are your suggestions implemented?
- Is there a feeding program available for those who can be retrained to self-feed?

The menus must meet the Recommended Dietary Allowances for nutrients as set by the Food and Nutrition Board of the National Research Council, National Academy of Sciences. The menu does not have to be selective, but a substitute entree at every meal is required if the resident desires. Surveyors will want to see a facility's menus so they can evaluate residents' comments if residents say they get too much food, too little variety, etc.

An assessment of food service will include evaluating the preparation and distribution of food. The adage "it is impossible to provide high-quality nutritional care without high-quality food service" is important to remember.

Surveyors will be in the dietary department at least four times, not only to observe preparation and distribution of food but also to evaluate the department for safety and sanitation. Generally, surveyors will be in the department as follows:

- Two times to observe meals, including food portioning, temperature, and delivery
- One time to observe food production and dish washing
- One time to meet with the food service director or dietitian and review the dietary cardex/file by comparing diet orders written in residents' medical records with the diet order written on the diet card on the meal trays of several residents

Adherence to infection control procedures is especially important when residents have enteral feeding tubes, IV fluids, ostomies, or skin problems. Although an infection control committee is no longer required by OBRA, some state laws still require such a committee. Under OBRA, overall infection control is part of the umbrella Quality Assessment and Assurance Committee.

The quality of life component of OBRA may result in significant conflict between resident and facility. For example, the facility's obligation to meet the resident's nutritional needs is long-term. Yet the resident has the right to refuse a nutritionally adequate diet and may request substitutes daily.

When a resident's rights conflict with the best possible medical care, the question, "What should the facility do?" is a poignant one. This question requires the staff to ask another question, "Is there a negative outcome to the resident's behavior?" If the answer to the second question is no, then it is wise to clearly and objectively document what is happening in the plan of care and appropriate progress notes. If the answer to the question is yes, then the staff must act professionally and ethically and seek assistance in overcoming the problem as needed.

It is important to remember that the mentally competent resident has the right to refuse treatment (e.g., eating, tube, or parenteral feedings) if expressed consistently with state laws. If a resident refuses appropriate treatment, then such refusal should be consistent, frequent, and well-documented.

A psychological consultation is appropriate if the resident is confused and refuses treatment but has provided no advanced directive. An ombudsman and family consultation may also be appropriate. In order to act professionally and ethically, a facility may need to discharge a noncompliant resident to another facility that will provide essential care and/or obtain a guardian for the resident if needed.

APPENDIX C

Long-Term Care Standards for Patient Rights

Tag Number	*Regulation*	*Guidance to Surveyors*
	§483.10 Resident rights. The resident has a right to a dignified existence, self-determination, and communication with and access to persons and services inside and outside the facility. A facility must protect and promote the rights of each resident, including each of the following rights:	Guidelines: §483.10 All residents in long-term care facilities have rights guaranteed to them under federal and state law. Requirements concerning resident rights are specified in §483.10, 483.12, 483.13, and 483.15. Section 483.10 is intended to lay the foundation for the remaining resident's rights requirements which cover more specific areas. These rights include the resident's right to: • Exercise his or her rights (§483.10(a)); • Be informed about what rights and responsibilities he or she has (§483.10(b)); • If he or she wishes, have the facility manage personal funds (§483.10(c)); • Choose a physician and treatment and participate in decisions and care planning (§483.10(d)); • Privacy and confidentiality (§483.10(e)); • Voice grievances and have the facility respond to those grievances (§483.10(f)); • Examine survey results (§483.10(g)); • Work or not work (§483.10(h)); • Privacy in sending and receiving mail (§483.10(i)); • Visit and be visited by others from outside the facility (§483.10(j)); • Use a telephone in privacy (§483.10(k)); • Retain and use personal possessions (§483.10(l)) to the maximum extent that space and safety permit; • Share a room with a spouse, if that is mutually agreeable (§483.10(m)); • Self-administer medication, if the interdisciplinary care planning team determines it is safe (§483.10(n)); and • Refuse a transfer from a distinct part, within the institution (§483.10(o)). A facility must promote the exercise of rights for each resident, including any who face barriers (such as communication problems, hearing problems and cognition limits) in the exercise of these rights. A resident, even though determined to be incompetent, should be able to assert these rights based on his or her degree of capability.

Source: Reprinted from *Long Term Care Survey Protocol and Interpretive Guidelines,* 1995, Health Care Financing Administration.

Tag Number	*Regulation*	*Guidance to Surveyors*
F151	(a) Exercise of rights. (1) The resident has the right to exercise his or her rights as a resident of the facility and as a citizen or resident of the United States. (2) The resident has the right to be free of interference, coercion, discrimination, and reprisal from the facility in exercising his or her rights.	Guidelines: §483.10(a)(1) Exercising rights means that residents have autonomy and choice, to the maximum extent possible, about how they wish to live their everyday lives and receive care, subject to the facility's rules, as long as those rules do not violate a regulatory requirement. Intent: §483.10(a)(2) This regulation is intended to protect each resident in the exercise of his or her rights. Guidelines: §483.10(a)(2) The facility must not hamper, compel, treat differentially, or retaliate against a resident for exercising his/her rights. Facility behaviors designed to support and encourage resident participation in meeting care planning goals as documented in the resident assessment and care plan are not interference or coercion. Examples of facility practices that may limit autonomy or choice in exercising rights include reducing the group activity time of a resident trying to organize a residents' group; requiring residents to seek prior approval to distribute information about the facility; discouraging a resident from hanging a religious ornament above his or her bed; singling out residents for prejudicial treatment such as isolating residents in activities; or purposefully assigning inexperienced aides to a resident with heavy care needs because the resident and/or his/her representative, exercised his/her rights. Procedures: §483.10(a)(2) Pay close attention to resident or staff remarks and staff behavior that may represent deliberate actions to promote or to limit a resident's autonomy or choice, particularly in ways that affect independent functioning. Because reprisals may indicate abuse, if the team determines that a facility has violated this requirement through reprisals taken against residents, then further determine if the facility has an effective system to prevent the neglect and abuse of residents. (§483.13(c), F224–F225.)
F152	(3) In the case of a resident adjudged incompetent under the laws of a state by a court of competent jurisdiction, the rights of the resident are exercised by the person appointed under state law to act on the resident's behalf. (4) In the case of a resident who has not been adjudged incompetent by the state court, any legal-surrogate designated in accordance with state law may exercise the resident's rights to the extent provided by state law.	Guidelines: §483.10(a)(3) and (4) When reference is made to "resident" in the Guidelines, it also refers to any person who may, under state law, act on the resident's behalf when the resident is unable to act for himself or herself. That person is referred to as the resident's surrogate or representative. If the resident has been formally declared incompetent by a court, the surrogate or representative is whoever was appointed by the court—a guardian, conservator, or committee. The facility should verify that a surrogate or representative has the necessary authority. For example, a court-appointed conservator might have the power to make financial decisions, but not health care decisions. A resident may wish to delegate decision making to specific persons, or the resident and family may have agreed among themselves on a decision-making process. To the degree permitted by state law, and to the maximum extent practicable, the facility must respect the resident's wishes and follow that process.

Tag Number	*Regulation*	*Guidance to Surveyors*
		The rights of the resident that may be exercised by the surrogate or representative include the right to make health care decisions. However, the facility may seek a health care decision (or any other decision or authorization) from a surrogate or representative only when the resident is unable to make the decision. If there is a question as to whether the resident is able to make a health care decision, staff should discuss the matter with the resident at a suitable time and judge how well the resident understands the information. In the case of a resident who has been formally declared incompetent by a court, lack of capacity is presumed. Notwithstanding the above, if such a resident can understand the situation and express a preference, the resident should be informed and his/her wishes respected to the degree practicable. Any violations with respect to the resident's exercise of rights should be cited under the applicable tag number. The involvement of a surrogate or representative does not automatically relieve a facility of its duty to protect and promote the resident's interests. For example, a surrogate or representative does not have the right to insist that a treatment be performed that is not medically appropriate, and the right of a surrogate or representative to reject treatment may be subject to state law limits. <u>Procedures: §483.10(a)(3) and (4)</u> Determine as appropriate if the rights of a resident who has been adjudged incompetent or who has a representative acting on his/her behalf to help exercise his/her rights are exercised by the legally appointed individual.
Refer to F156	<u>(b) Notice of rights and services.</u> (1) The facility must inform the resident both orally and in writing in a language that the resident understands of his or her rights and all rules and regulations governing resident conduct and responsibilities during the stay in the facility. The facility must also provide the resident with the notice (if any) of the state developed under §1919(a)(6) of the Act. Such notification must be made prior to or upon admission and during the resident's stay. Receipt of such information, and any amendments to it, must be acknowledged in writing;	<u>Intent: §483.10(b)(1)</u> This requirement is intended to assure that each resident knows his or her rights and responsibilities and that the facility communicates this information prior to or upon admission, as appropriate during the resident's stay, and when the facility's rules change. <u>Guidelines: §483.10(b)(1)</u> "In a language that the resident understands" is defined as communication of information concerning rights and responsibilities that is clear and understandable to each resident, to the extent possible considering impediments which may be created by the resident's health and mental status. If the resident's knowledge of English or the predominant language of the facility is inadequate for comprehension, a means to communicate the information concerning rights and responsibilities in a language familiar to the resident must be available and implemented. For foreign languages commonly encountered in the facility locale, the facility should have written translations of its statement of rights and responsibilities, and should make the services of an interpreter available. In the case of less commonly encountered foreign languages, however, a representative of the resident may sign that he or she has explained the statement of rights to the resident prior to his/her acknowledgement of receipt. For hearing impaired residents who communicate by signing, the facility is expected to provide an interpreter. Large print texts of the facility's statement of resident rights and responsibilities should also be available.

Tag Number	*Regulation*	*Guidance to Surveyors*
		"Both orally and in writing" means if a resident can read and understand written materials without assistance, an oral summary, along with the written document, is acceptable. Any time state or federal laws relating to resident rights or facility rules change during the resident's stay in the facility, he/she must promptly be informed of these changes. "All rules and regulations" relates to facility policies governing resident conduct. A facility cannot reasonably expect a resident to abide by rules he or she has never been told about. Whatever rules the facility has formalized, and by which it expects residents to abide, should be included in the statement of rights and responsibilities.
F153	(2) The resident or his or her legal representative has the right (i) Upon an oral or written request, to access all records pertaining to himself or herself including current clinical records within 24 hours (excluding weekends and holidays); and (ii) After receipt of his or her records for inspection, to purchase at a cost not to exceed the community standard photocopies of the records or any portions of them upon request and 2 working days advance notice to the facility.	Guidelines: §483.10(b)(2) An oral request is sufficient to produce the current record for review. In addition to clinical records, the term "records" includes all records pertaining to the resident, such as trust fund ledgers pertinent to the resident and contracts between the resident and the facility. "Purchase" is defined as a charge to the resident for photocopying. If state statute has defined the "community standard" rates, facilities should follow that rate. In the absence of state statute, the "cost not to exceed the community standard" is that rate charged per copy by organizations such as the public library, the Post Office or a commercial copy center, which would be selected by a prudent buyer in addition to the cost of the clerical time needed to photocopy the records. Additional fees for locating the records or typing forms/envelopes may not be assessed.
F154	(3) The resident has the right to be fully informed in language that he or she can understand of his or her total health status, including, but not limited to, his or her medical condition;	Guidelines: §483.10(b)(3) "Total health status" includes functional status, medical care, nursing care, nutritional status, rehabilitation and restorative potential, activities potential, cognitive status, oral health status, psychosocial status, and sensory and physical impairments. Information on health status must be presented in language that the resident can understand. This includes minimizing use of technical jargon in communicating with the resident, having the ability to communicate in a foreign language and the use of sign language or other aids, as necessary. (See §483.10(d)(3), F175 for the right of the resident to plan care and treatment.) Procedures: §483.10(b)(3) Look, particularly during observations and record reviews, for ongoing efforts on the part of facility staff to keep residents informed. Look for evidence that information is communicated in a manner that is understandable to residents and communicated at times it could be most useful to residents, such as when they are expressing concerns, or raising questions, as well as on an ongoing basis.

Tag Number	*Regulation*	*Guidance to Surveyors*
F155	(4) The resident has the right to refuse treatment, to refuse to participate in experimental research, and to formulate an advance directive as specified in paragraph (8) of this section	Guidelines: §483.10(b)(4) "Treatment" is defined as care provided for purposes of maintaining/restoring health, improving functional level, or relieving symptoms. "Experimental research" is defined as development and testing of clinical treatments, such as an investigational drug or therapy, that involve treatment and/or control groups. For example, a clinical trial of an investigational drug would be experimental research. "Advance directive" means a written instruction, such as a living will or durable power of attorney for health care, recognized under state law relating to the provision of health care when the individual is incapacitated. As provided under state law, a resident who has the capacity to make a health care decision and who withholds consent to treatment or makes an explicit refusal of treatment either directly or through an advance directive, may not be treated against his/her wishes. A facility may not transfer or discharge a resident for refusing treatment unless the criteria for transfer or discharge are met. (See §483.12(a)(1) and (2).)

Appendix D

OBRA Assessment Forms

Numeric Identifier______________________

MINIMUM DATA SET (MDS) — *VERSION 2.0*

FOR NURSING HOME RESIDENT ASSESSMENT AND CARE SCREENING

BASIC ASSESSMENT TRACKING FORM

SECTION AA. IDENTIFICATION INFORMATION

1.	RESIDENT NAME ⊛	a. (First) b. (Middle Initial) c. (Last) d. (Jr./Sr.)
2.	GENDER ⊛	1. Male 2. Female
3.	BIRTHDATE ⊛	Month – Day – Year
4.	RACE/ ⊛ ETHNICITY	1. American Indian/Alaskan Native 2. Asian/Pacific Islander 3. Black, not of Hispanic origin 4. Hispanic 5. White, not of Hispanic origin
5.	SOCIAL ⊛ SECURITY AND ⊛ MEDICARE NUMBERS [C in 1st box if non Med. no.]	a. Social Security Number — — b. Medicare number (or comparable railroad insurance number)
6.	FACILITY PROVIDER NO. ⊛	a. State No. b. Federal No.
7.	MEDICAID NO. *["+" if pending, "N" if not a Medicaid recipient]* ⊛	
8.	REASONS FOR ASSESS-MENT	[Note—Other codes do not apply to this form] a. Primary reason for assessment 1. Admission assessment (required by day 14) 2. Annual assessment 3. Significant change in status assessment 4. Significant correction of prior assessment 5. Quarterly review assessment 0. *NONE OF ABOVE* b. ***Special codes for use with supplemental assessment types in Case Mix demonstration states or other states where required*** *1. 5 day assessment* *2. 30 day assessment* *3. 60 day assessment* *4. Quarterly assessment using full MDS form* *5. Readmission/return assessment* *6. Other state required assessment*
9.	SIGNATURES OF PERSONS COMPLETING THESE ITEMS:	

a. Signatures	Title	Date
b.		Date

GENERAL INSTRUCTIONS

Complete this information for submission with all full and quarterly assessments (Admission, Annual, Significant Change, State or Medicare required assessments, or Quarterly Reviews, etc.).

⊛ = Key items for computerized resident tracking

[shaded box] = When box blank, must enter number or letter

[a.] = When letter in box, check if condition applies

Source: Reprinted from Health Care Financing Administration.

Resident ______ Numeric Identifier ______

MINIMUM DATA SET (MDS) — *VERSION 2.0*

FOR NURSING HOME RESIDENT ASSESSMENT AND CARE SCREENING

BACKGROUND (FACE SHEET) INFORMATION AT ADMISSION

SECTION AB. DEMOGRAPHIC INFORMATION

1.	DATE OF ENTRY	*Date the stay began. Note — Does not include readmission if record was closed at time of temporary discharge to hospital, etc. In such cases, use prior admission date.* Month — Day — Year	
2.	ADMITTED FROM (AT ENTRY)	1. Private home/apt. with no home health services 2. Private home/apt. with home health services 3. Board and care/assisted living/group home 4. Nursing home 5. Acute care hospital 6. Psychiatric hospital, MR/DD facility 7. Rehabilitation hospital 8. Other	
3.	LIVED ALONE (PRIOR TO ENTRY)	0. No 1. Yes 2. In other facility	
4.	ZIP CODE OF PRIOR PRIMARY RESIDENCE		
5.	RESIDENTIAL HISTORY 5 YEARS PRIOR TO ENTRY	***(Check all settings** resident **lived in** during 5 years prior to date of entry given in item AB1 above.)*	
		Prior stay at this nursing home	a.
		Stay in other nursing home	b.
		Other residential facility — board and care home, assisted living, group home	c.
		MH/psychiatric setting	d.
		MR/DD setting	e.
		NONE OF ABOVE	f.
6.	LIFETIME OCCUPATION(S) (Put "/" between two occupations)		
7.	EDUCATION *(Highest level completed)*	1. No schooling 5. Technical or trade school 2. 8th grade/less 6. Some college 3. 9-11 grades 7. Bachelor's degree 4. High school 8. Graduate degree	
8.	LANGUAGE	*(Code for correct response)* a. Primary Language 0. English 1. Spanish 2. French 3. Other	
		b. If other, specify	
9.	MENTAL HEALTH HISTORY	Does resident's RECORD indicate any history of mental retardation, mental illness, or developmental disability problem? 0. No 1. Yes	
10.	CONDITIONS RELATED TO MR/DD STATUS	***(Check all conditions** that are related to MR/DD status that were manifested before age 22, and are likely to continue indefinitely)*	
		Not applicable — no MR/DD (Skip to AB11)	a.
		MR/DD with organic condition	
		Down's syndrome	b.
		Autism	c.
		Epilepsy	d.
		Other organic condition related to MR/DD	e.
		MR/DD with no organic condition	f.
11.	DATE BACKGROUND INFORMATION COMPLETED	Month — Day — Year	

[shaded box] = When box blank, must enter number or letter

[a.] = When letter in box, check if condition applies

SECTION AC. CUSTOMARY ROUTINE

1.	CUSTOMARY ROUTINE *(In year prior to DATE OF ENTRY to this nursing home, or year last in community if now being admitted from another nursing home)*	***(Check all that apply.** If all information UNKNOWN, check last box only.)*	
		CYCLE OF DAILY EVENTS	
		Stays up late at night (e.g., after 9 pm)	a.
		Naps regularly during day (at least 1 hour)	b.
		Goes out 1+ days a week	c.
		Stays busy with hobbies, reading, or fixed daily routine	d.
		Spends most of time alone or watching TV	e.
		Moves independently indoors (with appliances, if used)	f.
		Use of tobacco products at least daily	g.
		NONE OF ABOVE	h.
		EATING PATTERNS	
		Distinct food preferences	i.
		Eats between meals all or most days	j.
		Use of alcoholic beverage(s) at least weekly	k.
		NONE OF ABOVE	l.
		ADL PATTERNS	
		In bedclothes much of day	m.
		Wakens to toilet all or most nights	n.
		Has irregular bowel movement pattern	o.
		Showers for bathing	p.
		Bathing in PM	q.
		NONE OF ABOVE	r.
		INVOLVEMENT PATTERNS	
		Daily contact with relatives/close friends	s.
		Usually attends church, temple, synagogue (etc.)	t.
		Finds strength in faith	u.
		Daily animal companion/presence	v.
		Involved in group activities	w.
		NONE OF ABOVE	x.
		UNKNOWN — Resident/family unable to provide information	y.

END

SECTION AD. FACE SHEET SIGNATURES

SIGNATURES OF PERSONS COMPLETING FACE SHEET:

a. Signature of RN Assessment Coordinator			Date
b. Signatures	Title	Sections	Date
c.			Date
d.			Date
e.			Date
f.			Date
g.			Date

Resident ______________ Numeric Identifier ______________

MINIMUM DATA SET (MDS) — *VERSION 2.0*

FOR NURSING HOME RESIDENT ASSESSMENT AND CARE SCREENING

FULL ASSESSMENT FORM

(Status in last 7 days, unless other time frame indicated)

SECTION A. IDENTIFICATION AND BACKGROUND INFORMATION

1.	RESIDENT NAME	a. (First) b. (Middle Initial) c. (Last) d. (Jr./Sr.)
2.	ROOM NUMBER	
3.	ASSESSMENT REFERENCE DATE	a. *Last day of MDS observation period* Month — Day — Year b. Original (0) or corrected copy of form (enter number of correction)
4a.	DATE OF REENTRY	Date of reentry from most recent temporary discharge to a hospital in last 90 days (or since last assessment or admission if less than 90 days) Month — Day — Year
5.	MARITAL STATUS	1. Never married 2. Married 3. Widowed 4. Separated 5. Divorced
6.	MEDICAL RECORD NO.	
7.	CURRENT PAYMENT SOURCES FOR N.H. STAY	*(Billing Office to indicate;* ***check all that apply in last 30 days)*** Medicaid per diem a. Medicare per diem b. Medicare ancillary part A c. Medicare ancillary part B d. CHAMPUS per diem e. VA per diem f. Self or family pays for full per diem g. Medicaid resident liability or Medicare co-payment h. Private insurance per diem (including co-payment) i. Other per diem j.
8.	REASONS FOR ASSESSMENT *[Note—If this is a discharge or reentry assessment, only a limited subset of MDS items need be completed]*	a. Primary reason for assessment 1. Admission assessment (required by day 14) 2. Annual assessment 3. Significant change in status assessment 4. Significant correction of prior assessment 5. Quarterly review assessment 6. Discharged—return not anticipated 7. Discharged—return anticipated 8. Discharged prior to completing initial assessment 9. Reentry 0. *NONE OF ABOVE* b. ***Special codes for use with supplemental assessment types in Case Mix demonstration states or other states where required*** 1. 5 day assessment 2. 30 day assessment 3. 60 day assessment 4. Quarterly assessment using full MDS form 5. Readmission/return assessment 6. Other state required assessment
9.	RESPONSIBILITY/ LEGAL GUARDIAN	*(Check all that apply)* Legal guardian a. Other legal oversight b. Durable power of attorney/health care c. Durable power of attorney/financial d. Family member responsible e. Patient responsible for self f. *NONE OF ABOVE* g.
10.	ADVANCED DIRECTIVES	*(For those items with supporting documentation in the medical record,* ***check all that apply)*** Living will a. Do not resuscitate b. Do not hospitalize c. Organ donation d. Autopsy request e. Feeding restrictions f. Medication restrictions g. Other treatment restrictions h. *NONE OF ABOVE* i.

SECTION B. COGNITIVE PATTERNS

1.	COMATOSE	*(Persistent vegetative state/no discernible consciousness)* 0. No 1. Yes ***(If yes, skip to Section G)***
2.	MEMORY	*(Recall of what was learned or known)* a. Short-term memory OK—seems/appears to recall after 5 minutes 0. Memory OK 1. Memory problem b. Long-term memory OK—seems/appears to recall long past 0. Memory OK 1. Memory problem
3.	MEMORY/ RECALL ABILITY	***(Check all*** *that resident was* ***normally able to recall during last 7 days)*** Current season a. Location of own room b. Staff names/faces c. That he/she is in a nursing home d. *NONE OF ABOVE* are recalled e.
4.	COGNITIVE SKILLS FOR DAILY DECISION-MAKING	*(Made decisions regarding tasks of daily life)* 0. *INDEPENDENT*—decisions consistent/reasonable 1. *MODIFIED INDEPENDENCE*—some difficulty in new situations only 2. *MODERATELY IMPAIRED*—decisions poor; cues/ supervision required 3. *SEVERELY IMPAIRED*—never/rarely made decisions
5.	INDICATORS OF DELIRIUM—PERIODIC DISORDERED THINKING/ AWARENESS	*(Code for behavior in the* ***last 7 days.)*** **[*Note: Accurate assessment requires conversations with staff and family who have direct knowledge of resident's behavior over this time.*]** 0. Behavior not present 1. Behavior present, not of recent onset 2. Behavior present, over last 7 days appears different from resident's usual functioning (e.g., new onset or worsening) a. EASILY DISTRACTED—(e.g., difficulty paying attention; gets sidetracked) b. PERIODS OF ALTERED PERCEPTION OR AWARENESS OF SURROUNDINGS—(e.g., moves lips or talks to someone not present; believes he/she is somewhere else; confuses night and day) c. EPISODES OF DISORGANIZED SPEECH—(e.g., speech is incoherent, nonsensical, irrelevant, or rambling from subject to subject; loses train of thought) d. PERIODS OF RESTLESSNESS—(e.g., fidgeting or picking at skin, clothing, napkins, etc.; frequent position changes; repetitive physical movements or calling out) e. PERIODS OF LETHARGY—(e.g., sluggishness; staring into space; difficult to arouse; little body movement) f. MENTAL FUNCTION VARIES OVER THE COURSE OF THE DAY—(e.g., sometimes better, sometimes worse; behaviors sometimes present, sometimes not)
6.	CHANGE IN COGNITIVE STATUS	Resident's cognitive status, skills, or abilities have changed as compared to status of **90 days ago** (or since last assessment if less than 90 days) 0. No change 1. Improved 2. Deteriorated

SECTION C. COMMUNICATION/HEARING PATTERNS

1.	HEARING	*(With hearing appliance, if used)* 0. *HEARS ADEQUATELY*—normal talk, TV, phone 1. *MINIMAL DIFFICULTY* when not in quiet setting 2. *HEARS IN SPECIAL SITUATIONS ONLY*—speaker has to adjust tonal quality and speak distinctly 3. *HIGHLY IMPAIRED*/absence of useful hearing
2.	COMMUNICATION DEVICES/ TECHNIQUES	***(Check all that apply*** *during last 7 days)* Hearing aid, present and used a. Hearing aid, present and not used regularly b. Other receptive comm. techniques used (e.g., lip reading) c. *NONE OF ABOVE* d.
3.	MODES OF EXPRESSION	***(Check all used by*** *resident to make needs known)* Speech a. Writing messages to express or clarify needs b. American sign language or Braille c. Signs/gestures/sounds d. Communication board e. Other f. *NONE OF ABOVE* g.
4.	MAKING SELF UNDERSTOOD	*(Expressing information content—however able)* 0. *UNDERSTOOD* 1. *USUALLY UNDERSTOOD*—difficulty finding words or finishing thoughts 2. *SOMETIMES UNDERSTOOD*—ability is limited to making concrete requests 3. *RARELY/NEVER UNDERSTOOD*
5.	SPEECH CLARITY	*(Code for speech in the* ***last 7 days)*** 0. *CLEAR SPEECH*—distinct, intelligible words 1. *UNCLEAR SPEECH*—slurred, mumbled words 2. *NO SPEECH*—absence of spoken words
6.	ABILITY TO UNDERSTAND OTHERS	*(Understanding verbal information content—however able)* 0. *UNDERSTANDS* 1. *USUALLY UNDERSTANDS*—may miss some part/ intent of message 2. *SOMETIMES UNDERSTANDS*—responds adequately to simple, direct communication 3. *RARELY/NEVER UNDERSTANDS*
7.	CHANGE IN COMMUNICATION/ HEARING	Resident's ability to express, understand, or hear information has changed as compared to status of ***90 days ago*** *(or since last assessment if less than 90 days)* 0. No change 1. Improved 2. Deteriorated

[ ] = When box blank, must enter number or letter.

[a.] = When letter in box, check if condition applies

Resident ________

SECTION D. VISION PATTERNS

1.	VISION	*(Ability to see in adequate light and with glasses if used)* 0. *ADEQUATE*—sees fine detail, including regular print in newspapers/books 1. *IMPAIRED*—sees large print, but not regular print in newspapers/books 2. *MODERATELY IMPAIRED*—limited vision; not able to see newspaper headlines, but can identify objects 3. *HIGHLY IMPAIRED*—object identification in question, but eyes appear to follow objects 4. *SEVERELY IMPAIRED*—no vision or sees only light, colors, or shapes; eyes do not appear to follow objects	
2.	VISUAL LIMITATIONS/ DIFFICULTIES	Side vision problems—decreased peripheral vision (e.g., leaves food on one side of tray, difficulty traveling, bumps into people and objects, misjudges placement of chair when seating self)	a.
		Experiences any of following: sees halos or rings around lights; sees flashes of light; sees "curtains" over eyes	b.
		NONE OF ABOVE	c.
3.	VISUAL APPLIANCES	Glasses; contact lenses; magnifying glass 0. No 1. Yes	

SECTION E. MOOD AND BEHAVIOR PATTERNS

1.	INDICATORS OF DEPRESSION, ANXIETY, SAD MOOD	***(Code for indicators observed in last 30 days, irrespective of the assumed cause)*** 0. Indicator not exhibited in last 30 days 1. Indicator of this type exhibited up to five days a week 2. Indicator of this type exhibited daily or almost daily (6, 7 days a week)

VERBAL EXPRESSIONS OF DISTRESS

a. Resident made negative statements—e.g., *"Nothing matters; Would rather be dead; What's the use; Regrets having lived so long; Let me die"*

b. Repetitive questions—e.g., *"Where do I go; What do I do?"*

c. Repetitive verbalizations— e.g., calling out for help *("God help me")*

d. Persistent anger with self or others—e.g., easily annoyed, anger at placement in nursing home; anger at care received

e. Self deprecation—e.g., *"I am nothing; I am of no use to anyone"*

f. Expressions of what appear to be unrealistic fears—e.g., fear of being abandoned, left alone, being with others

g. Recurrent statements that something terrible is about to happen—e.g., believes he or she is about to die, have a heart attack

h. Repetitive health complaints—e.g., persistently seeks medical attention, obsessive concern with body functions

i. Repetitive anxious complaints/concerns (non-health related) e.g., persistently seeks attention/reassurance regarding schedules, meals, laundry/clothing, relationship issues

SLEEP-CYCLE ISSUES

j. Unpleasant mood in morning

k. Insomnia/change in usual sleep pattern

SAD, APATHETIC, ANXIOUS APPEARANCE

l. Sad, pained, worried facial expressions—e.g., furrowed brows

m. Crying, tearfulness

n. Repetitive physical movements—e.g., pacing, hand wringing, restlessness, fidgeting, picking

LOSS OF INTEREST

o. Withdrawal from activities of interest—e.g., no interest in longstanding activities or being with family/friends

p. Reduced social interaction

2.	MOOD PERSISTENCE	**One or more indicators of depressed, sad or anxious mood were not easily altered by attempts to "cheer up", console, or reassure the resident over last 7 days** 0. No mood indicators 1. Indicators present, easily altered 2. Indicators present, not easily altered
3.	CHANGE IN MOOD	Resident's mood status has changed as compared to status of **90 days ago** (or since last assessment if **less than 90 days**) 0. No change 1. Improved 2. Deteriorated
4.	BEHAVIORAL SYMPTOMS	*(A)* ***Behavioral*** *symptom* ***frequency*** *in* ***last 7 days*** 0. Behavior not exhibited in last 7 days 1. Behavior of this type occurred 1 to 3 days in last 7 days 2. Behavior of this type occurred 4 to 6 days, but less than daily 3. Behavior of this type occurred daily *(B)* ***Behavioral*** *symptom* ***alterability*** *in* ***last 7 days*** 0. Behavior not present OR behavior was easily altered 1. Behavior was not easily altered

	(A)	(B)
a. WANDERING (moved with no rational purpose, seemingly oblivious to needs or safety)		
b. VERBALLY ABUSIVE BEHAVIORAL SYMPTOMS (others were threatened, screamed at, cursed at)		
c. PHYSICALLY ABUSIVE BEHAVIORAL SYMPTOMS (others were hit, shoved, scratched, sexually abused)		
d. SOCIALLY INAPPROPRIATE/DISRUPTIVE BEHAVIORAL SYMPTOMS (made disruptive sounds, noisiness, screaming, self-abusive acts, sexual behavior or disrobing in public, smeared/threw food/feces, hoarding, rummaged through others' belongings)		
e. RESISTS CARE (resisted taking medications/injections, ADL assistance, or eating)		

Numeric Identifier ________

5.	CHANGE IN BEHAVIORAL SYMPTOMS	Resident's behavior status has changed as compared to **status of 90 days ago** (or since last assessment if less than 90 days) 0. No change 1. Improved 2. Deteriorated

SECTION F. PSYCHOSOCIAL WELL-BEING

1.	SENSE OF INITIATIVE/ INVOLVEMENT	At ease interacting with others	a.
		At ease doing planned or structured activities	b.
		At ease doing self-initiated activities	c.
		Establishes own goals	d.
		Pursues involvement in life of facility (e.g., makes/keeps friends; involved in group activities; responds positively to new activities; assists at religious services)	e.
		Accepts invitations into most group activities	f.
		NONE OF ABOVE	g.
2.	UNSETTLED RELATIONSHIPS	Covert/open conflict with or repeated criticism of staff	a.
		Unhappy with roommate	b.
		Unhappy with residents other than roommate	c.
		Openly expresses conflict/anger with family/friends	d.
		Absence of personal contact with family/friends	e.
		Recent loss of close family member/friend	f.
		Does not adjust easily to change in routines	g.
		NONE OF ABOVE	h.
3.	PAST ROLES	Strong identification with past roles and life status	a.
		Expresses sadness/anger/empty feeling over lost roles/status	b.
		Resident perceives that daily routine (customary routine, activities) is very different from prior pattern in the community	c.
		NONE OF ABOVE	d.

SECTION G. PHYSICAL FUNCTIONING AND STRUCTURAL PROBLEMS

1. (A) ADL SELF-PERFORMANCE—***(Code for resident's PERFORMANCE OVER ALL SHIFTS during last 7 days—****Not including setup)*

0. *INDEPENDENT*—No help or oversight—OR—Help/oversight provided only 1 or 2 times during last 7 days
1. *SUPERVISION*—Oversight, encouragement or cueing provided 3 or more times during last 7 days—OR—Supervision (3 or more times) plus physical assistance provided only 1 or 2 times during last 7 days
2. *LIMITED ASSISTANCE*—Resident highly involved in activity; received physical help in guided maneuvering of limbs or other nonweight bearing assistance 3 or more times—OR—More help provided only 1 or 2 times during last 7 days
3. *EXTENSIVE ASSISTANCE*—While resident performed part of activity, over last 7-day period, help of following type(s) provided 3 or more times:
   —Weight-bearing support
   —Full staff performance during part (but not all) of last 7 days
4. *TOTAL DEPENDENCE*—Full staff performance of activity during entire 7 days
8. *ACTIVITY DID NOT OCCUR* during entire 7 days

(B) ADL SUPPORT PROVIDED—***(Code for MOST SUPPORT PROVIDED OVER ALL SHIFTS during last 7 days; code regardless of*** *resident's self-performance classification)*

0. No setup or physical help from staff
1. Setup help only
2. One person physical assist
3. Two+ persons physical assist
8. ADL activity itself did not occur during entire 7 days

			(A) SELF-PERF	(B) SUPPORT
a.	BED MOBILITY	How resident moves to and from lying position, turns side to side, and positions body while in bed		
b.	TRANSFER	How resident moves between surfaces—to/from: bed, chair, wheelchair, standing position (EXCLUDE to/from bath/toilet)		
c.	WALK IN ROOM	How resident walks between locations in his/her room		
d.	WALK IN CORRIDOR	How resident walks in corridor on unit		
e.	LOCOMOTION ON UNIT	How resident moves between locations in his/her room and adjacent corridor on same floor. If in wheelchair, self-sufficiency once in chair		
f.	LOCOMOTION OFF UNIT	How resident moves to and returns from off unit locations (e.g., areas set aside for dining, activities, or treatments). **If facility has only one floor,** how resident moves to and from distant areas on the floor. If in wheelchair, self-sufficiency once in chair		
g.	DRESSING	How resident puts on, fastens, and takes off all items of **street clothing**, including donning/removing prosthesis		
h.	EATING	How resident eats and drinks (regardless of skill). Includes intake of nourishment by other means (e.g., tube feeding, total parenteral nutrition)		
i.	TOILET USE	How resident uses the toilet room (or commode, bedpan, urinal); transfers on/off toilet, cleanses, changes pad, manages ostomy or catheter, adjusts clothes		
j.	PERSONAL HYGIENE	How resident maintains personal hygiene, including combing hair, brushing teeth, shaving, applying makeup, washing/drying face, hands, and perineum (EXCLUDE baths and showers)		

Resident ____________________

2.	BATHING	How resident takes full-body bath/shower, sponge bath, and transfers in/out of tub/shower (EXCLUDE washing of back and hair). *Code for most dependent* in self-performance and support. (A) BATHING SELF-PERFORMANCE codes appear below. (A) (B) 0. Independent—No help provided 1. Supervision—Oversight help only 2. Physical help limited to transfer only 3. Physical help in part of bathing activity 4. Total dependence 8. Activity itself did not occur during entire 7 days *(Bathing support codes are as defined in Item 1, code B above)*
3.	TEST FOR BALANCE (See training manual)	*(Code for ability during test in the last 7 days)* 0. Maintained position as required in test 1. Unsteady, but able to rebalance self without physical support 2. Partial physical support during test; or stands (sits) but does not follow directions for test 3. Not able to attempt test without physical help a. Balance while standing b. Balance while sitting—position, trunk control
4.	FUNCTIONAL LIMITATION IN RANGE OF MOTION (see training manual)	*(Code for limitations during last 7 days that interfered with daily functions or placed resident at risk of injury)* **(A) *RANGE OF MOTION*** — 0. No limitation; 1. Limitation on one side; 2. Limitation on both sides **(B) *VOLUNTARY MOVEMENT*** — 0. No loss; 1. Partial loss; 2. Full loss (A) (B) a. Neck b. Arm—Including shoulder or elbow c. Hand—Including wrist or fingers d. Leg—Including hip or knee e. Foot—Including ankle or toes f. Other limitation or loss
5.	MODES OF LOCOMOTION	***(Check all that apply during last 7 days)*** Cane/walker/crutch a. Wheeled self b. Other person wheeled c. Wheelchair primary mode of locomotion d. *NONE OF ABOVE* e.
6.	MODES OF TRANSFER	***(Check all that apply during last 7 days)*** Bedfast all or most of time a. Bed rails used for bed mobility or transfer b. Lifted manually c. Lifted mechanically d. Transfer aid (e.g., slide board, trapeze, cane, walker, brace) e. *NONE OF ABOVE* f.
7.	TASK SEGMENTATION	Some or all of ADL activities were broken into subtasks during **last 7 days** so that resident could perform them 0. No 1. Yes
8.	ADL FUNCTIONAL REHABILITATION POTENTIAL	Resident believes he/she is capable of increased independence in at least some ADLs a. Direct care staff believe resident is capable of increased independence in at least some ADLs b. Resident able to perform tasks/activity but is very slow c. Difference in ADL Self-Performance or ADL Support, comparing mornings to evenings d. *NONE OF ABOVE* e.
9.	CHANGE IN ADL FUNCTION	Resident's ADL self-performance status has changed as compared to status of **90 days ago** (or since last assessment if less than 90 days) 0. No change 1. Improved 2. Deteriorated

SECTION H. CONTINENCE IN LAST 14 DAYS

1.		CONTINENCE SELF-CONTROL CATEGORIES ***(Code for resident's PERFORMANCE OVER ALL SHIFTS)*** 0. ***CONTINENT***—Complete control *(includes use of indwelling urinary catheter or ostomy device that does not leak urine or stool)* 1. ***USUALLY CONTINENT***—BLADDER, incontinent episodes once a week or less; BOWEL, less than weekly 2. ***OCCASIONALLY INCONTINENT***—BLADDER, 2 or more times a week but not daily; BOWEL, once a week 3. ***FREQUENTLY INCONTINENT***—BLADDER, tended to be incontinent daily, but some control present (e.g., on day shift); BOWEL, 2-3 times a week 4. ***INCONTINENT***—Had inadequate control. BLADDER, multiple daily episodes; BOWEL, all (or almost all) of the time
a.	BOWEL CONTINENCE	Control of bowel movement, with appliance or bowel continence programs, if employed
b.	BLADDER CONTINENCE	Control of urinary bladder function (if dribbles, volume insufficient to soak through underpants), with appliances (e.g., foley) or continence programs, if employed
2.	BOWEL ELIMINATION PATTERN	Bowel elimination pattern regular—at least one movement every three days a. Constipation b. Diarrhea c. Fecal impaction d. *NONE OF ABOVE* e.

Numeric Identifier ____________________

3.	APPLIANCES AND PROGRAMS	Any scheduled toileting plan a. Bladder retraining program b. External (condom) catheter c. Indwelling catheter d. Intermittent catheter e. Did not use toilet room/commode/urinal f. Pads/briefs used g. Enemas/irrigation h. Ostomy present i. *NONE OF ABOVE* j.
4.	CHANGE IN URINARY CONTINENCE	Resident's urinary continence has changed as compared to status of **90 days ago** (or since last assessment if less than 90 days) 0. No change 1. Improved 2. Deteriorated

SECTION I. DISEASE DIAGNOSES

Check only **those diseases that have a relationship** to current ADL status, cognitive status, mood and behavior status, medical treatments, nursing monitoring, or risk of death. (Do not list inactive diagnoses)

1.	DISEASES	***(If none apply, CHECK the NONE OF ABOVE box)*** **ENDOCRINE/METABOLIC/NUTRITIONAL** Diabetes mellitus a. Hyperthyroidism b. Hypothyroidism c. **HEART/CIRCULATION** Arteriosclerotic heart disease (ASHD) d. Cardiac dysrhythmias e. Congestive heart failure f. Deep vein thrombosis g. Hypertension h. Hypotension i. Peripheral vascular disease j. Other cardiovascular disease k. **MUSCULOSKELETAL** Arthritis l. Hip fracture m. Missing limb (e.g., amputation) n. Osteoporosis o. Pathological bone fracture p. **NEUROLOGICAL** Alzheimer's disease q. Aphasia r. Cerebral palsy s. Cerebrovascular accident (stroke) t. Dementia other than Alzheimer's disease u. Hemiplegia/Hemiparesis v. Multiple sclerosis w. Paraplegia x. Parkinson's disease y. Quadriplegia z. Seizure disorder aa. Transient ischemic attack (TIA) bb. Traumatic brain injury cc. **PSYCHIATRIC/MOOD** Anxiety disorder dd. Depression ee. Manic depression (bipolar disease) ff. Schizophrenia gg. **PULMONARY** Asthma hh. Emphysema/COPD ii. **SENSORY** Cataracts jj. Diabetic retinopathy kk. Glaucoma ll. Macular degeneration mm. **OTHER** Allergies nn. Anemia oo. Cancer pp. Renal failure qq. *NONE OF ABOVE* rr.
2.	INFECTIONS	***(If none apply, CHECK the NONE OF ABOVE box)*** Antibiotic resistant infection (e.g., Methicillin resistant staph) a. Clostridium difficile (c. diff.) b. Conjunctivitis c. HIV infection d. Pneumonia e. Respiratory infection f. Septicemia g. Sexually transmitted diseases h. Tuberculosis i. Urinary tract infection **in last 30 days** j. Viral hepatitis k. Wound infection l. *NONE OF ABOVE* m.
3.	OTHER CURRENT OR MORE DETAILED DIAGNOSES AND ICD-9 CODES	a. ____________ _ _ _ . _ _ b. ____________ _ _ _ . _ _ c. ____________ _ _ _ . _ _ d. ____________ _ _ _ . _ _ e. ____________ _ _ _ . _ _

SECTION J. HEALTH CONDITIONS

1.	PROBLEM CONDITIONS	***(Check all problems present in last 7 days*** *unless other time frame is indicated)* **INDICATORS OF FLUID STATUS** Weight gain or loss of 3 or more pounds within a 7 day period a. Inability to lie flat due to shortness of breath b. Dehydrated; output exceeds input c. Insufficient fluid; did **NOT** consume all/almost all liquids provided during **last 3 days** d. **OTHER** Delusions e. Dizziness/Vertigo f. Edema g. Fever h. Hallucinations i. Internal bleeding j. Recurrent lung aspirations **in last 90 days** k. Shortness of breath l. Syncope (fainting) m. Unsteady gait n. Vomiting o. *NONE OF ABOVE* p.

Resident ______ Numeric Identifier ______

2.	PAIN SYMPTOMS	*(Code the **highest level of pain** present in **the last 7 days**)* a. **FREQUENCY** with which resident complains or shows evidence of pain 0. No pain ***(skip to J4)*** 1. Pain less than daily 2. Pain daily	b. **INTENSITY** of pain 1. Mild pain 2. Moderate pain 3. Times when pain is horrible or excruciating	
3.	PAIN SITE	*(If pain present, **check all sites** that apply in **last 7 days**)*		
		Back pain	a.	Incisional pain f.
		Bone pain	b.	Joint pain (other than hip) g.
		Chest pain while doing usual activities	c.	Soft tissue pain (e.g., lesion, muscle) h.
		Headache	d.	Stomach pain i.
		Hip pain	e.	Other j.
4.	ACCIDENTS	*(Check all that apply)* Fell in **past 30 days** a. Fell in **past 31-180 days** b.		Hip fracture in **last 180 days** c. Other fracture in **last 180 days** d. *NONE OF ABOVE* e.
5.	STABILITY OF CONDITIONS	Conditions/diseases make resident's cognitive, ADL, mood or behavior patterns unstable—(fluctuating, precarious, or deteriorating)		a.
		Resident experiencing an acute episode or a flare-up of a recurrent or chronic problem		b.
		End-stage disease, 6 or fewer months to live		c.
		NONE OF ABOVE		d.

SECTION K. ORAL/NUTRITIONAL STATUS

1.	ORAL PROBLEMS	Chewing problem	a.
		Swallowing problem	b.
		Mouth pain	c.
		NONE OF ABOVE	d.
2.	HEIGHT AND WEIGHT	*Record **(a.)** height in inches and **(b.)** weight in pounds. Base weight on most recent measure in **last 30 days;** measure weight consistently in accord with standard facility practice—e.g., in a.m. after voiding, before meal, with shoes off, and in nightclothes.* a. HT (in.) b. WT (lb.)	
3.	WEIGHT CHANGE	**a. Weight loss**—5% or more in **last 30 days**; or 10% or more in **last 180 days** 0. No 1. Yes	
		b. Weight gain—5% or more in **last 30 days**; or 10% or more in **last 180 days** 0. No 1. Yes	
4.	NUTRITIONAL PROBLEMS	Complains about the taste of many foods a. Regular or repetitive complaints of hunger b.	Leaves 25% or more of food uneaten at most meals c. *NONE OF ABOVE* d.
5.	NUTRITIONAL APPROACHES	*(Check all that apply in last 7 days)* Parenteral/IV a. Feeding tube b. Mechanically altered diet c. Syringe (oral feeding) d. Therapeutic diet e.	Dietary supplement between meals f. Plate guard, stabilized built-up utensil, etc. g. On a planned weight change program h. *NONE OF ABOVE* i.
6.	PARENTERAL OR ENTERAL INTAKE	***(Skip to Section L if neither 5a nor 5b is checked)*** a. Code the proportion of **total calories** the resident received through parenteral or tube feedings in the **last 7 days** 0. None 3. 51% to 75% 1. 1% to 25% 4. 76% to 100% 2. 26% to 50%	
		b. Code the average **fluid intake** per day by IV or tube in **last 7 days** 0. None 3. 1001 to 1500 cc/day 1. 1 to 500 cc/day 4. 1501 to 2000 cc/day 2. 501 to 1000 cc/day 5. 2001 or more cc/day	

SECTION L. ORAL/DENTAL STATUS

1.	ORAL STATUS AND DISEASE PREVENTION	Debris (soft, easily movable substances) present in mouth prior to going to bed at night	a.
		Has dentures or removable bridge	b.
		Some/all natural teeth lost—does not have or does not use dentures (or partial plates)	c.
		Broken, loose, or carious teeth	d.
		Inflamed gums (gingiva); swollen or bleeding gums; oral abscesses; ulcers or rashes	e.
		Daily cleaning of teeth/dentures or daily mouth care—by resident or staff	f.
		NONE OF ABOVE	g.

SECTION M. SKIN CONDITION

1.	ULCERS (Due to any cause)	*(Record the number of ulcers at each ulcer stage—regardless of cause. If none present at a stage, record "0" (zero). Code all that apply during* ***last 7 days.*** *Code 9 = 9 or more.)* ***[Requires full body exam.]***	Number at Stage
		a. Stage 1. A persistent area of skin redness (without a break in the skin) that does not disappear when pressure is relieved.	
		b. Stage 2. A partial thickness loss of skin layers that presents clinically as an abrasion, blister, or shallow crater.	
		c. Stage 3. A full thickness of skin is lost, exposing the subcutaneous tissues—presents as a deep crater with or without undermining adjacent tissue.	
		d. Stage 4. A full thickness of skin and subcutaneous tissue is lost, exposing muscle or bone.	
2.	TYPE OF ULCER	*(For each type of ulcer,* ***code for the highest stage in the last 7 days*** *using scale in item M1—i.e., 0=none; stages 1, 2, 3, 4)*	
		a. Pressure ulcer—any lesion caused by pressure resulting in damage of underlying tissue	
		b. Stasis ulcer—open lesion caused by poor circulation in the lower extremities	
3.	HISTORY OF RESOLVED ULCERS	Resident had an ulcer that was resolved or cured in **LAST 90 DAYS** 0. No 1. Yes	
4.	OTHER SKIN PROBLEMS OR LESIONS PRESENT	*(Check all that apply during* ***last 7 days)***	
		Abrasions, bruises	a.
		Burns (second or third degree)	b.
		Open lesions other than ulcers, rashes, cuts (e.g., cancer lesions)	c.
		Rashes—e.g., intertrigo, eczema, drug rash, heat rash, herpes zoster	d.
		Skin desensitized to pain or pressure	e.
		Skin tears or cuts (other than surgery)	f.
		Surgical wounds	g.
		NONE OF ABOVE	h.
5.	SKIN TREATMENTS	*(Check all that apply during* ***last 7 days)***	
		Pressure relieving device(s) for chair	a.
		Pressure relieving device(s) for bed	b.
		Turning/repositioning program	c.
		Nutrition or hydration intervention to manage skin problems	d.
		Ulcer care	e.
		Surgical wound care	f.
		Application of dressings (with or without topical medications) other than to feet	g.
		Application of ointments/medications (other than to feet)	h.
		Other preventative or protective skin care (other than to feet)	i.
		NONE OF ABOVE	j.
6.	FOOT PROBLEMS AND CARE	*(Check all that apply during* ***last 7 days)***	
		Resident has one or more foot problems—e.g., corns, calluses, bunions, hammer toes, overlapping toes, pain, structural problems	a.
		Infection of the foot—e.g., cellulitis, purulent drainage	b.
		Open lesions on the foot	c.
		Nails/calluses trimmed during **last 90 days**	d.
		Received preventative or protective foot care (e.g., used special shoes, inserts, pads, toe separators)	e.
		Application of dressings (with or without topical medications)	f.
		NONE OF ABOVE	g.

SECTION N. ACTIVITY PURSUIT PATTERNS

1.	TIME AWAKE	***(Check appropriate time periods over last 7 days)*** Resident awake all or most of time (i.e., naps no more than one hour per time period) in the: Morning a. Evening c. Afternoon b. *NONE OF ABOVE* d.	

(IF RESIDENT IS COMATOSE, SKIP TO SECTION O)

2.	AVERAGE TIME INVOLVED IN ACTIVITIES	**(When awake and not receiving treatments or ADL care)** 0. Most—more than 2/3 of time 1. Some—from 1/3 to 2/3 of time 2. Little—less than 1/3 of time 3. None	
3.	PREFERRED ACTIVITY SETTINGS	***(Check all settings*** *in which activities are* ***preferred)*** Own room a. Day/activity room b. Inside NH/off unit c. Outside facility d. *NONE OF ABOVE* e.	
4.	GENERAL ACTIVITY PREFERENCES (Adapted to resident's current abilities)	***(Check all PREFERENCES*** *whether or not activity is currently available to resident)* Cards/other games a. Crafts/arts b. Exercise/sports c. Music d. Reading/writing e. Spiritual/religious activities f.	Trips/shopping g. Walking/wheeling outdoors h. Watching TV i. Gardening or plants j. Talking or conversing k. Helping others l. *NONE OF ABOVE* m.

Resident ______ Numeric Identifier ______

5.	PREFERS CHANGE IN DAILY ROUTINE	*Code for resident preferences in daily routines* 0. No change 1. Slight change 2. Major change a. Type of activities in which resident is currently involved b. Extent of resident involvement in activity

SECTION O. MEDICATIONS

1.	NUMBER OF MEDICATIONS	***(Record the number of different** medications used in the **last 7 days;** enter "0" if none used)*
2.	NEW MEDICATIONS	*(Resident currently receiving medications that were initiated during the **last 90 days)*** 0. No 1. Yes
3.	INJECTIONS	***(Record the number of DAYS** injections of any type received during the **last 7 days;** enter "0" if none used)*
4.	DAYS RECEIVED THE FOLLOWING MEDICATION	***(Record the number of DAYS** during **last 7 days;** enter "0" if not used. Note—enter "1" for long acting meds used less than weekly)* a. Antipsychotic d. Hypnotic b. Antianxiety e. Diuretic c. Antidepressant

SECTION P. SPECIAL TREATMENTS AND PROCEDURES

1.	SPECIAL TREATMENTS, PROCEDURES, AND PROGRAMS	**a. SPECIAL CARE—***Check treatments or programs received during the **last 14 days***

TREATMENTS			
Chemotherapy	a.	Ventilator or respirator	l.
		PROGRAMS	
Dialysis	b.	Alcohol/drug treatment program	m.
IV medication	c.	Alzheimer's/dementia special care unit	n.
Intake/output	d.	Hospice care	o.
Monitoring acute medical condition	e.	Pediatric unit	p.
Ostomy care	f.	Respite care	q.
Oxygen therapy	g.	Training in skills required to return to the community (e.g., taking medications, house work, shopping, transportation, ADLs)	r.
Radiation	h.		
Suctioning	i.		
Tracheostomy care	j.		
Transfusions	k.	*NONE OF ABOVE*	s.

b. THERAPIES—*Record the number of days and total minutes each of the following therapies was administered (for at least 15 minutes a day) in the **last 7 calendar days** (Enter 0 if none or less than 15 min. daily)* **[Note—count only post admission therapies]**

(A) = # of days administered for **15 minutes or more**
(B) = **total # of minutes** provided in **last 7 days**

	DAYS (A)	MINUTES (B)
a. Speech-language pathology and audiology services		
b. Occupational therapy		
c. Physical therapy		
d. Respiratory therapy		
e. Psychological therapy (by any licensed mental health professional)		

2.	INTERVENTION PROGRAMS FOR MOOD, BEHAVIOR, COGNITIVE LOSS	(Check all interventions or strategies used in **last 7 days**—no matter where received)	
		Special behavior symptom evaluation program	a.
		Evaluation by a licensed mental health specialist in **last 90 days**	b.
		Group therapy	c.
		Resident-specific deliberate changes in the environment to address mood/behavior patterns—e.g., providing bureau in which to rummage	d.
		Reorientation—e.g., cueing	e.
		NONE OF ABOVE	f.

3.	NURSING REHABILITATION/ RESTORATIVE CARE	*Record the NUMBER OF DAYS each of the following rehabilitation or restorative techniques or practices was **provided to the resident for more than or equal to 15 minutes** per day in the **last 7 days** (Enter 0 if none or less than 15 min. daily.)*

a. Range of motion (passive)	f. Walking
b. Range of motion (active)	g. Dressing or grooming
c. Splint or brace assistance	h. Eating or swallowing
TRAINING AND SKILL PRACTICE IN:	i. Amputation/ prosthesis care
	j. Communication
d. Bed mobility	k. Other
e. Transfer	

4.	DEVICES AND RESTRAINTS	*(Use the following codes for **last 7 days:)*** 0. Not used 1. Used less than daily 2. Used daily Bed rails a. —Full bed rails on all open sides of bed b. —Other types of side rails used (e.g., half rail, one side) c. Trunk restraint d. Limb restraint e. Chair prevents rising
5.	HOSPITAL STAY(S)	Record number of times resident was admitted to hospital with an overnight stay in **last 90 days** (or since last assessment if less than 90 days). *(Enter 0 if no hospital admissions)*
6.	EMERGENCY ROOM (ER) VISIT(S)	Record number of times resident visited ER without an overnight stay in **last 90 days** (or since last assessment if less than 90 days). *(Enter 0 if no ER visits)*
7.	PHYSICIAN VISITS	In the **LAST 14 DAYS** (or since admission if less than 14 days in facility) how many days has the physician (or authorized assistant or practitioner) examined the resident? *(Enter 0 if none)*
8.	PHYSICIAN ORDERS	In the **LAST 14 DAYS** (or since admission if less than 14 days in facility) how many days has the physician (or authorized assistant or practitioner) changed the resident's orders? *Do not include order renewals without change. (Enter 0 if none)*
9.	ABNORMAL LAB VALUES	Has the resident had any abnormal lab values during the **last 90 days** (or since admission)? 0. No 1. Yes

SECTION Q. DISCHARGE POTENTIAL AND OVERALL STATUS

1.	DISCHARGE POTENTIAL	a. Resident expresses/indicates preference to return to the community 0. No 1. Yes b. Resident has a support person who is positive toward discharge 0. No 1. Yes c. Stay projected to be of a short duration—discharge projected **within 90 days** (do not include expected discharge due to death) 0. No 2. Within 31-90 days 1. Within 30 days 3. Discharge status uncertain
2.	OVERALL CHANGE IN CARE NEEDS	Resident's overall self sufficiency has changed significantly as compared to status of **90 days ago** (or since last assessment if less than 90 days) 0. No change 1. Improved—receives fewer supports, needs less restrictive level of care 2. Deteriorated—receives more support

SECTION R. ASSESSMENT INFORMATION

1.	PARTICIPATION IN ASSESSMENT	a. Resident:	0. No	1. Yes	
		b. Family:	0. No	1. Yes	2. No family
		c. Significant other:	0. No	1. Yes	2. None

2. SIGNATURES OF PERSONS COMPLETING THE ASSESSMENT:

a. Signature of RN Assessment Coordinator (sign on above line)

b. Date RN Assessment Coordinator signed as complete ___ – ___ – ___
Month Day Year

	Title	Sections	Date
c. Other Signatures			Date
d.			Date
e.			Date
f.			Date
g.			Date
h.			Date

MDS QUARTERLY ASSESSMENT FORM

A1.	RESIDENT NAME	a. (First) b. (Middle Initial) c. (Last) d. (Jr/Sr)
A2.	ROOM NUMBER	
A3.	ASSESS-MENT REFERENCE DATE	A. Last day of MDS observation period Month – Day – Year b. Original (0) or corrected copy of form (enter number of correction)
A4a.	DATE OF REENTRY	**Date of reentry from most recent temporary discharge to a hospital in last 90 days (or since last assessment or admission if less than 90 days)** Month – Day – Year
A6.	MEDICAL RECORD NO.	
B1.	COMATOSE	*(Persistent vegetative state/no discernible consciousness)* 0. No 1. Yes ***(Skip to Section G)***
B2.	MEMORY	*(Recall of what was learned or known)* a. Short-term memory OK—seems/appears to recall after 5 minutes 0. Memory OK 1. Memory problem b. Long-term memory OK—seems/appears to recall long past 0. Memory OK 1. Memory problem
B4.	COGNITIVE SKILLS FOR DAILY DECISION-MAKING	*(Made decisions regarding tasks of daily life)* 0. *INDEPENDENT*—decisions consistent/reasonable 1. *MODIFIED INDEPENDENCE*—some difficulty in new situations only 2. *MODERATELY IMPAIRED*—decisions poor; cues/supervision required 3. *SEVERELY IMPAIRED*—never/rarely made decisions
B5.	INDICATORS OF DELIRIUM—PERIODIC DISOR-DERED THINKING/AWARENESS	*(Code for behavior in the* ***last 7 days.)*** ***[Note: Accurate assessment requires conversations with staff and family who have direct knowledge of resident's behavior over this time.]*** 0. Behavior not present 1. Behavior present, not of recent onset 2. Behavior present, over last 7 days appears different from resident's usual functioning (e.g., new onset or worsening) a. EASILY DISTRACTED—(e.g., difficulty paying attention; gets sidetracked) b. PERIODS OF ALTERED PERCEPTION OR AWARENESS OF SURROUNDINGS—(e.g., moves lips or talks to someone not present; believes he/she is somewhere else; confuses night and day) c. EPISODES OF DISORGANIZED SPEECH—(e.g., speech is incoherent, nonsensical, irrelevant, or rambling from subject to subject; loses train of thought) d. PERIODS OF RESTLESSNESS—(e.g., fidgeting or picking at skin, clothing, napkins, etc; frequent position changes; repetitive physical movements or calling out) e. PERIODS OF LETHARGY—(e.g., sluggishness; staring into space; difficult to arouse; little body movement) f. MENTAL FUNCTION VARIES OVER THE COURSE OF THE DAY—(e.g., sometimes better, sometimes worse; behaviors sometimes present, sometimes not)
C4.	MAKING SELF UNDER-STOOD	*(Expressing information content—however able)* 0. *UNDERSTOOD* 1. *USUALLY UNDERSTOOD*—difficulty finding words or finishing thoughts 2. *SOMETIMES UNDERSTOOD*—ability is limited to making concrete requests 3. *RARELY/NEVER UNDERSTOOD*
C6.	ABILITY TO UNDER-STAND OTHERS	*(Understanding verbal information content—however able)* 0. *UNDERSTANDS* 1. *USUALLY UNDERSTANDS*—may miss some part/intent of message 2. *SOMETIMES UNDERSTANDS*—responds adequately to simple, direct communication 3. *RARELY/NEVER UNDERSTANDS*
E1.	INDICATORS OF DEPRES-SION, ANXIETY, SAD MOOD	***(Code for indicators observed in last 30 days, irrespective of the assumed cause)*** 0. Indicator not exhibited in last 30 days 1. Indicator of this type exhibited up to five days a week 2. Indicator of this type exhibited daily or almost daily (6, 7 days a week) **VERBAL EXPRESSIONS OF DISTRESS** a. Resident made negative statements—e.g.,*"Nothing matters; Would rather be dead; What's the use; Regrets having lived so long; Let me die"* b. Repetitive questions—e.g., *"Where do I go; What do I do?"* c. Repetitive verbalizations—e.g., calling out for help, *("God help me")* d. Persistent anger with self or others—e.g., easily annoyed, anger at placement in nursing home; anger at care received e. Self deprecation—e.g., *"I am nothing; I am of no use to anyone"*

Numeric Identifier ____________

E1.	INDICATORS OF DEPRES-SION, ANXIETY, SAD MOOD (cont.)	**VERBAL EXPRESSIONS OF DISTRESS** f. Expressions of what appear to be unrealistic fears—e.g., fear of being abandoned, left alone, being with others g. Recurrent statements that something terrible is about to happen—e.g., believes he or she is about to die, have a heart attack h. Repetitive health complaints—e.g., persistently seeks medical attention, obsessive concern with body functions i. Repetitive anxious complaints/concerns (non-health related) e.g., persistently seeks attention/reassurance regarding schedules, meals, laundry, clothing, relationship issues **SLEEP-CYCLE ISSUES** j. Unpleasant mood in morning k. Insomnia/change in usual sleep pattern **SAD, APATHETIC, ANXIOUS APPEARANCE** l. Sad, pained, worried facial expressions—e.g., furrowed brows m. Crying, tearfulness n. Repetitive physical movements—e.g., pacing, hand wringing, restlessness, fidgeting, picking **LOSS OF INTEREST** o. Withdrawal from activities of interest—e.g., no interest in long standing activities or being with family/friends p. Reduced social interaction
E2.	MOOD PERSIS-TENCE	**One or more indicators** of depressed, sad or anxious mood **were not easily altered by attempts to "cheer up", console, or reassure the resident over last 7 days** 0. No mood indicators 1. Indicators present, easily altered 2. Indicators present, not easily altered
E4.	BEHAVIORAL SYMPTOMS	(A) ***Behavioral** symptom **frequency in last 7 days*** 0. Behavior not exhibited in last 7 days 1. Behavior of this type occurred 1 to 3 days in last 7 days 2. Behavior of this type occurred 4 to 6 days, but less than daily 3. Behavior of this type occurred daily (B) ***Behavioral** symptom **alterability in last 7 days*** 0. Behavior not present OR behavior was easily altered 1. Behavior was not easily altered **(A) (B)** a. WANDERING (moving with no rational purpose, seemingly oblivious to needs or safety) b. VERBALLY ABUSIVE BEHAVIORAL SYMPTOMS (others were threatened, screamed at, cursed at) c. PHYSICALLY ABUSIVE BEHAVIORAL SYMPTOMS (others were hit, shoved, scratched, sexually abused) d. SOCIALLY INAPPROPRIATE/DISRUPTIVE BEHAVIORAL SYMPTOMS (made disruptive sounds, noisiness, screaming, self-abusive acts, sexual behavior or disrobing in public, smeared/threw food/ hoarding, rummaged through others' belongings) e. RESISTS CARE (resisted taking medications/ injections, ADL assistance, or eating)
G1.		(A) ADL SELF-PERFORMANCE—***(Code for resident's PERFORMANCE OVER ALL SHIFTS during last 7 days—*** *Not including setup)* 0. *INDEPENDENT*—No help or oversight—OR—Help/oversignt provided only 1 or 2 times during last 7 days 1. *SUPERVISION*—Oversight, encouragement or cueing provided 3 or more times during last 7 days—OR—Supervision (3 or more times) plus physical assistance provided only 1 or 2 times during last 7 days 2. *LIMITED ASSISTANCE*—Resident highly involved in activity; received physical help in guided maneuvering of limbs or other nonweight bearing assistance 3 or more times—OR—More help provided only 1 or 2 times during last 7 days 3. *EXTENSIVE ASSISTANCE*—While resident performed part of activity, over last 7-day period, help of the following type(s) provided 3 or more times: – Weight-bearing support – Full staff performance during part (but not all) of last 7 days 4. *TOTAL DEPENDENCE*—Full staff performance of activity during entire 7 days 8. *ACTIVITY DID NOT OCCUR* during entire 7 days **(A)**
a.	BED MOBILITY	How resident moves to and from lying position, turns side to side, and positions body while in bed.
b.	TRANSFER	How resident moves between surfaces—to/from: bed, chair, wheelchair, standing position (EXCLUDE to/from bath/toilet).
c.	WALK IN ROOM	How resident walks between locations in his/her room.
d.	WALK IN CORRIDOR	How resident walks in corridor on unit.
e.	LOCOMO-TION ON UNIT	How resident moves between locations in his/her room and adjacent corridor on same floor. If in wheelchair, self-sufficiency once in chair.
f.	LOCOMO-TION OFF UNIT	How resident moves to and returns from off unit locations (e.g., areas set aside for dining, activities, or treatments). **If facility has only one floor**, how resident moves to and from distant areas on the floor. If in wheelchair, self-sufficiency once in chair.
g.	DRESSING	How resident puts on, fastens, and takes off all items of **street clothing**, including donning/removing prosthesis.
h.	EATING	How resident eats and drinks (regardless of skill). Includes intake of nourishment by other means (e.g., tube feeding, total parenteral nutrition).

Resident ______________________

i.	TOILET USE	How resident uses the toilet room (or commode, bedpan, urinal); transfers on/off toilet, cleanses, changes pad, manages ostomy or catheter, adjusts clothes
j.	PERSONAL HYGIENE	How resident maintains personal hygiene, including combing hair, brushing teeth, shaving, applying makeup, washing/drying face, hands, and perineum (EXCLUDE baths and showers)
G2.	BATHING	How resident takes full-body bath/shower, sponge bath, and transfers in/out of tub/shower (EXCLUDE washing of back and hair.) ***Code for most dependent** in self-performance.* (A) BATHING SELF-PERFORMANCE codes appear below 0. Independent—No help provided 1. Supervision—Oversight help only 2. Physical help limited to transfer only 3. Physical help in part of bathing activity 4. Total dependence 8. Activity itself did not occur during entire 7 days (A)
G4.	FUNCTIONAL LIMITATION IN RANGE OF MOTION	*(Code for limitations during **last 7 days** that interfered with daily functions or placed residents at risk of injury)* (A) *RANGE OF MOTION* — 0. No limitation; 1. Limitation on one side; 2. Limitation on both sides (B) *VOLUNTARY MOVEMENT* — 0. No loss; 1. Partial loss; 2. Full loss (A) (B) a. Neck b. Arm—Including shoulder or elbow c. Hand—Including wrist or fingers d. Leg—Including hip or knee e. Foot—Including ankle or toes f. Other limitation or loss
G6.	MODES OF TRANSFER	***(Check all that apply** during **last 7 days)*** Bedfast all or most of time a. Bed rails used for bed mobility or transfer b. *NONE OF ABOVE* f.
H1.		CONTINENCE SELF-CONTROL CATEGORIES ***(Code for resident's PERFORMANCE OVER ALL SHIFTS)*** 0. *CONTINENT*—Complete control [*includes use of indwelling urinary catheter or ostomy device that does not leak urine or stool*] 1. *USUALLY CONTINENT*—BLADDER, incontinent episodes once a week or less; BOWEL, less than weekly 2. *OCCASIONALLY INCONTINENT*—BLADDER, 2 or more times a week but not daily; BOWEL, once a week 3. *FREQUENTLY INCONTINENT*—BLADDER, tended to be incontinent daily, but some control present (e.g., on day shift); BOWEL, 2-3 times a week 4. *INCONTINENT*—Had inadequate control. BLADDER, multiple daily episodes; BOWEL, all (or almost all) of the time
a.	BOWEL CONTI-NENCE	Control of bowel movement, with appliance or bowel continence programs, if employed
b.	BLADDER CONTI-NENCE	Control of urinary bladder function (if dribbles, volume insufficient to soak through underpants), with appliances (e.g., foley) or continence programs, if employed
H2.	BOWEL ELIMINATION PATTERN	Fecal impaction d. *NONE OF ABOVE* e.
H3.	APPLIANCES AND PROGRAMS	Any scheduled toileting plan a. Bladder retraining program b. External (condom) catheter c. Indwelling catheter d. Ostomy present i. *NONE OF ABOVE* j.
I2.	INFECTIONS	Urinary tract infection **in last 30 days** j. *NONE OF ABOVE* m.
I3.	OTHER CURRENT DIAGNOSES AND ICD-9 CODES	*(Include **only those diseases diagnosed in the last 90 days that have a relationship** to current ADL status, behavior status, medical treatments, nursing monitoring, or risk of death)* a. ___ ___ ___ ___ . ___ b. ___ ___ ___ ___ . ___
J1.	PROBLEM CONDITIONS	***(Check all problems present** in **last 7 days)*** Dehydrated; output exceeds input c. Hallucinations i. *NONE OF ABOVE* p.
J2.	PAIN SYMPTOMS	*(Code the **highest level of pain** present in the **last 7 days**)* a. **FREQUENCY** with which resident complains or shows evidence of pain 0. No pain ***(skip to J4)*** 1. Pain less than daily 2. Pain daily b. **INTENSITY** of pain 1. Mild pain 2. Moderate pain 3. Times when pain is horrible or excruciating
J4.	ACCIDENTS	***(Check all that apply)*** Fell in **past 30 days** a. Fell in **past 31-180 days** b. Hip fracture in **last 180 days** c. Other fracture in **last 180 days** d. *NONE OF ABOVE* e.

Numeric Identifier ______________________

J5.	STABILITY OF CONDITIONS	Conditions/diseases make resident's cognitive, ADL, mood or behavior status unstable—(fluctuating, precarious, or deteriorating) a. Resident experiencing an acute episode or a flare-up of a recurrent or chronic problem b. End-stage disease, 6 or fewer months to live c. *NONE OF ABOVE* d.
K3.	WEIGHT CHANGE	a. **Weight loss**—5% or more in **last 30 days**; or 10% or more in **last 180 days** 0. No 1. Yes b. **Weight gain**—5% or more in **last 30 days**; or 10% or more in **last 180 days** 0. No 1. Yes
K5.	NUTRITIONAL APPROACHES	Feeding tube b. On a planned weight change program h. *NONE OF ABOVE* i.
M1.	ULCERS (Due to any cause)	*(Record the number of ulcers at each ulcer stage—regardless of cause. If none present at a stage, record "0" (zero). Code all that apply during **last 7 days.** Code 9 = 9 or more.)* **[Requires full body exam.]** — Number at Stage a. Stage 1. A persistent area of skin redness (without a break in the skin) that does not disappear when pressure is relieved. b. Stage 2. A partial thickness loss of skin layers that presents clinically as an abrasion, blister, or shallow crater. c. Stage 3. A full thickness of skin is lost, exposing the subcutaneous tissues-presents as a deep crater with or without undermining adjacent tissue. d. Stage 4. A full thickness of skin and subcutaneous tissue is lost, exposing muscle or bone.
M2.	TYPE OF ULCER	*(For each type of ulcer, **code for the highest stage in the last 7 days** using scale in item M1—i.e., 0=none; stages 1, 2, 3, 4)* a. Pressure ulcer—any lesion caused by pressure resulting in damage of underlying tissue b. Stasis ulcer—open lesion caused by poor circulation in the lower extremities
N1.	TIME AWAKE	***(Check appropriate time periods over last 7 days)*** Resident awake all or most of time (i.e., naps no more than one hour per time period) in the: Morning a. Afternoon b. Evening c. *NONE OF ABOVE* d.

(If resident comatose, skip to Section O)

N2.	AVERAGE TIME INVOLVED IN ACTIVITIES	**(When awake and not receiving treatments or ADL care)** 0. Most—more than 2/3 of time 1. Some—from 1/3 to 2/3 of time 2. Little—less than 1/3 of time 3. None
O1.	NUMBER OF MEDICATIONS	*(Record the number of **different** medications used in the **last 7 days;** enter "0" if none used)*
O4.	DAYS RECEIVED THE FOLLOWING MEDICATION	*(**Record the number of DAYS** during **last 7 days;** enter "0" if not used. Note—enter "1" for long-acting meds used less than weekly)* a. Antipsychotic b. Antianxiety c. Antidepressant d. Hypnotic e. Diuretic
P4.	DEVICES AND RESTRAINTS	*Use the following codes for **last 7 days:*** 0. Not used 1. Used less than daily 2. Used daily Bed rails a. — Full bed rails on all open sides of bed b. — Other types of side rails used (e.g., half rail, one side) c. Trunk restraint d. Limb restraint e. Chair prevents rising
Q2.	OVERALL CHANGE IN CARE NEEDS	Resident's overall level of self sufficiency has changed significantly as compared to status of **90 days ago** (or since last assessment if less than 90 days) 0. No change 1. Improved—receives fewer supports, needs less restrictive level of care 2. Deteriorated—receives more support

R2. SIGNATURES OF PERSONS COMPLETING THE ASSESSMENT:

a. Signature of RN Assessment Coordinator (sign on above line)

b. Date RN Assessment Coordinator signed as complete ___ ___ — ___ ___ — ___ ___ ___ ___
Month Day Year

	Title	Sections	Date
c. Other Signatures			Date
d.			Date
e.			Date
f.			Date
g.			Date

NUTRITIONAL ASSESSMENT FORM

Diagnosis ______________________________
Sex: __________ Age: ________ yrs Admission Date: ______________
Diet order (date): ______________________________
Perceived Rationale for Diet Order: ______________________________
Route: Oral: ☐ Feeding tube: ☐ Parenteral/IV: ☐ Combinations: ______________
Oral supplementation: ☐ Describe: ______________________________
Height: ______________ Weight: ______________ Ideal body weight: ______________
Resident's desired body weight: ______________ Interdisciplinary team goal weight: ______________
Percent weight change since last assessment: Intentional change? Yes ☐ No ☐
New assessment: ☐ Explain change: ______________________________

ABILITY TO PROVIDE FOOD PREFERENCE/OPINIONS ABOUT MEALS/MEAL TIMES/DIET

Method of Communication:
☐ Oral ☐ Writing
☐ Communication board ☐ Signs/gestures/sounds
☐ Unable to communicate and make self understood
☐ Information from family/others (Name): ______________________________

Ability to understand others:	Adequate ☐	Inadequate ☐	Variable ☐
Visual ability to see tray food:	Adequate ☐	Inadequate ☐	Variable ☐
Visual ability to see written menu:	Adequate ☐	Inadequate ☐	Variable ☐

Food preferences: ______________________________
Food allergies/sensitivities: ______________________________
Food dislikes: ______________________________

Likes diet order:	Yes ☐	No ☐	Unable to determine ☐
Understands reason for diet order:	Yes ☐	No ☐	Unable to determine ☐
Likes foods offered on menu:	Yes ☐	No ☐	Unable to determine ☐
Has difficulty choosing what to eat:	Yes ☐	No ☐	Unable to determine ☐
Likes foods received at snacks:	Yes ☐	No ☐	Unable to determine ☐
Receives food preferences:	Yes ☐	No ☐	Unable to determine ☐
Likes time of meals/snacks:	Yes ☐	No ☐	Unable to determine ☐
Chooses (or likes) meal partners:	Yes ☐	No ☐	Unable to determine ☐
Presence of advanced directives including feeding restrictions:		Yes ☐	No ☐

Signed by: ______________________________ Date: ______________

Change since last assessment:	Yes ☐	No ☐	New assessment ☐

Explain: ______________________________

ABILITY TO SELF-FEED

Route of feeding: Self-feed ☐ Self-feed with assistance ☐ Unable to self-feed ☐
Feeding devices: ______________________________

Able to use feeding devices:	Yes ☐	No ☐	Devices not needed ☐
Difference in feeding self in mornings and evenings:	Yes ☐	No ☐	Does not self-feed ☐

Physical functioning disabilities affecting ability to self-feed:

Bedfast all or most of the time:	Yes ☐	On dominate side ☐	No ☐
Hemiplegia/hemiparesis/quadriplegia:	Yes ☐	On dominate side ☐	No ☐
Arm: partial or total loss of voluntary movement:	Yes ☐	On dominate side ☐	No ☐
Hand: lack of dexterity or presence of contractures:	Yes ☐	On dominate side ☐	No ☐
Trunk: partial or total loss of ability to position:	Yes ☐	On dominate side ☐	No ☐

Amputee (explain): ______________________________
Other: ______________________________

Observation of ability to self-feed:
Resident desires to increase self-feeding: Yes ☐ No ☐ Unknown ☐ N/A ☐
Resident believes is capable of increased independence in self-feeding: Yes ☐ No ☐
Direct care staff believe resident is capabale of increased independence in self-feeding: Yes ☐ No ☐ N/A ☐
Change since last assessment: Yes ☐ No ☐ New assessment ☐
Explain: ______________________________

NAME ______________________________ PHYSICIAN ______________ ROOM NUMBER ________
Last First Middle

**Source:* Used with permission of Ross Products Division, Abbott Laboratories, Columbus, Ohio, from *OBRA: A Challenge and an Opportunity for Nutrition Care*, December 1992, pp. 52–55.

ABILITY TO EAT AS DESIRED

Forgets meals: Yes ☐ No ☐

Eats at desired place: Yes ☐ No ☐ Unable to determine desired place ☐ Usual place for meals ________

Eats away from facility on occasion: Yes ☐ No ☐ How often ________

Factors affecting ability to eat meals in desired place: None ☐

☐ Behavioral problems (e.g., throws/steals food, verbally disruptive)

☐ Mobility limitations ☐ Psychosocial problems (e.g., fear)

☐ Facility limitations ☐ Wanders

☐ Resident's safety ☐ Other ________

Change since last assessment: Yes ☐ No ☐ New assessment ☐

Explain: ________

USUAL FOOD INTAKE

Food intake prior to admission: Good ☐ Fair ☐ Poor ☐ Unknown ☐

Resists assistance with feeding: Yes ☐ No ☐ N/A ☐

Consumes adequate fluid to prevent dehydration: Yes ☐ No ☐

Order to force or limit fluids: Yes to force ☐ No ☐ Yes to limit ☐

Regularly complains of hunger: Yes ☐ No ☐ If yes, when ________

Complains about taste of many foods: Yes ☐ No ☐

Leaves 25+% food uneaten at most meals: Yes ☐ No ☐

Refuses meals/substitutes/supplements: Yes ☐ No ☐ How often ________

Consumes varied well-balanced diet daily: Yes ☐ No ☐

______ % time eats 4–6 oz meat/fish/poultry/meat substitute

______ % time eats/drinks 2 servings dairy products

______ % time eats 2 vegetables (1 deep-yellow or leafy-green)

______ % time eats 2 fruits (1 citrus)

______ % time eats substitute if less than 75% of meal eaten; takes oral supplement as ordered

______ % time eats evening snack

Consumes foods other than at mealtimes: Yes ☐ No ☐ Sometimes ☐

Eats or drinks at activities: Yes ☐ No ☐ Sometimes ☐

Has food at bedside: Yes ☐ No ☐ Sometimes ☐

Food brought in from outside facility: Yes ☐ No ☐ Sometimes ☐

Uses vending machine: Yes ☐ No ☐ Sometimes ☐

Receives foods consistent with cultural/ethnic/religious background: Yes ☐ No ☐

Enjoys relationships with staff/family who feed: Yes ☐ No ☐ Unknown ☐ N/A ☐

Food becomes unpalatable or staff removes tray before resident has finished eating: Yes ☐ No ☐

Change since last assessment: Yes ☐ No ☐ New assessment ☐

Explain: ________

DISEASES/CONDITIONS THAT DECREASE NUTRIENT INTAKE: None ☐

______ Alzheimer's disease or other dementias

______ Anorexia

______ Complaint about taste/variety of foods

______ Depression/anxiety

______ Food preferences idiosyncrasies

______ Frequent refusal to eat

______ Impaired mentation

______ Inadequate environment/staff at facility

______ Lethargy-tiredness

______ Nausea

______ Pain

______ Possible food-drug interaction

______ Shortness of breath

______ Unrealistic fear of food or eating

Change since last assessment: Yes ☐ No ☐ New assessment ☐

Explain: ________

DISEASES/CONDITIONS THAT INCREASE NUTRIENT REQUIREMENTS: None ☐

______ Burns

______ Cancer

______ Emphysema/asthma/COPD

______ Fractures (date/location ________)

______ Hyperthyroidism

______ Malabsorption/diarrhea/ostomy losses

______ Motor agitation (pacing, wandering, tremors)

______ Pneumonia

______ Pressure ulcers/stasis ulcers

______ Septicemia/infection/fever

______ Surgical wounds (date ________)

______ Vomiting

Increased requirements for which nutrients? ________

Change since last assessment: Yes ☐ No ☐ New assessment ☐

Explain: ________

DISEASES/CONDITIONS THAT MAY SUGGEST NEED FOR THERAPEUTIC DIET OR FOOD TEXTURE MODIFICATION: None ☐

_____ Cardiovascular disease/stroke
_____ Chewing problems
  _____ facial paralysis
  _____ broken, loose, decayed, or missing teeth
  _____ presence of ill-fitting dentures
  _____ refusal to chew
  _____ other _____
_____ Congestive heart failure
_____ Dehydration
_____ Diabetes mellitus/gastroparesis
_____ Edema/ascites
_____ Gastrointestinal surgery/food intolerances (explain) _____
_____ Hypertension
_____ Immune disorders/immunosuppression/AIDS
_____ Liver failure/alcoholic liver disease
_____ Other _____
_____ Mouth problems
  _____ inability to suck through a straw
  _____ oral abscess
  _____ swollen or bleeding gums
  _____ toothache
  _____ other _____
_____ Renal failure
_____ Swallowing problems
  _____ fear of choking
  _____ history/potential for choking or aspiration
  _____ refusal to swallow
  _____ inability to or difficulty in swallowing
  _____ pain on swallowing
  _____ pockets food in cheeks
  _____ cannot swallow thick liquids
  _____ cannot swallow thin liquids

Change since last assessment: Yes ☐ No ☐ New assessment ☐
Explain: _____

DISEASES/CONDITIONS THAT MAY SUGGEST NEED FOR SUPPLEMENTATION: None ☐

_____ Alcohol/drug abuse
_____ Anemia/internal bleeding
_____ Constipation/fecal impaction (chronic)
_____ Erratic food consumption
_____ Malabsorption/diarrhea (chronic)
_____ Malnutrition (ICD Code # _____)
_____ Osteoporosis/fractures
_____ Polypharmacy
_____ Pressure ulcers/stasis ulcers (number _____ stage_____)
_____ Urinary tract infections (chronic)
_____ Other _____

Which nutrients may need to be supplemented? _____
Change since last assessment: Yes ☐ No ☐ New assessment ☐
Explain: _____

MEDICATIONS AND TREATMENTS/PROCEDURES THAT AFFECT NUTRITIONAL STATUS OR DIET ORDER
(Identify name, dose, frequency)

Medications None ☐
_____ Analgesics _____
_____ Antacids _____
_____ Antibiotics _____
_____ Anticoagulants _____
_____ Anticonvulsants _____
_____
_____ Antihypertensives _____
_____
_____ Anti-Parkinsonian _____
_____ Cardiac glycosides _____
_____ Diuretics _____
_____ Insulin/hypoglycemic agents _____
_____
_____ Laxatives _____
_____ Lipid lowering _____
_____ Non-steroidals _____
_____ Psychotherapeutic drugs _____
_____
_____ Steroids _____
_____ Vitamin/mineral supplements _____
_____

Treatments/procedures None ☐
_____ Catheter (indwelling urinary) _____
_____ Chemotherapy _____
_____ Dialysis _____
_____ Enema _____
_____ Isolation _____
_____ Ostomy (type) _____
_____ Oxygen _____
_____ Prosthesis (type) _____
_____ Radiation _____
_____ Speech therapy _____
_____ Suctioning (oral) _____
_____ Suctioning (gastric) _____
_____ Other _____

_____ Other _____
_____ Possible food-drug interactions (identify) _____
_____

LABORATORY DATA INDICATIVE OF NUTRITIONAL STATUS Date(s) ______

	High	Low	WNL		High	Low	WNL
Hgb (g/dL)				Serum Na+(mEq/L)			
Hct (%)				Serum K+ (mEq/L)			
MCV/MCH (m^3/μμg)				BUN (mg/dL)			
Total Lymph Count				Creatinine (mg/dL)			
Glucose (mg/dL)				Osmolality (mosm/kg)			
Albumin (g/dL)				Blood pressure			
Cholesterol (mg/dL)				Thyroid (T3/T4/FTI)			

Other: ______

Change since last assessment: Yes ☐ No ☐ New assessment ☐

Explain: ______

PRESENCE OF SYMPTOMS POTENTIALLY INDICATIVE OF POOR NUTRITIONAL STATUS

______ Cachexia, loss of body fat/muscle
______ Edema, bilateral, generalized
______ Eyes, dull, pale, xerosis
______ Hair, dry, dull, thin, easily plucked
______ Irritability
______ Lips/gums, swollen, pale, angular fissures
______ Muscles, wasted, weak, calf pain
______ Nails, clubbed, pale nailbeds
______ Pressure ulcers/open wounds
______ Skin, poor turgor, pale, petechiae, dermatosis
______ Tongue, swollen, dry, scarlet, magenta
______ Other ______

Change since last assessment: Yes ☐ No ☐ New assessment ☐

Explain: ______

SUMMARY: LEVEL OF NUTRITIONAL CARE

______ Basic: Weight within normal/desirec/stable range. Lab data essentially within normal range. Medical condition stable. Food intake well-balanced and varied.

______ Moderate: Weight fluctuates. Lab data consistent with potential for malnutrition. Medical condition unstable. Food intake fluctuates.

______ Intensive: Excessive weight loss or gain. Lab data/diagnosis consistent with potential for or presence of malnutrition. Food intake poor. Resident receives tube feeding, has pressure sores, or is in critical medical condition.

Change since last assessment: Yes ☐ No ☐ New assessment ☐

Summary Rationale or Explanation of Change Since Last Assessment: ______

______

______

______

ESTIMATED DAILY NUTRIENT NEEDS

REE: ______ kcal Total energy: ______ kcal Protein: ______ g Fluid: ______ mL

GOALS: ______

______

______

SUMMARY OF RESIDENT AND FAMILY INPUT INTO NUTRITIONAL CARE: ______

______

______

DISCHARGE POTENTIAL Good ☐ Fair ☐ Poor ☐

Need for Nutrition Education for Home Care: Yes ☐ No ☐ Unknown ☐

PLAN OF CARE, consistent with assessment and goals, developed/revised on (date): ______

Signature: ______ Date: ______

FEEDING TUBES
MDS 2.0 RAP MODULE

INSTRUCTIONS: Identify the MDS 2.0 items that specifically triggered this RAP in the space provided and review the RAP Guidelines. Working one section of this RAP Module at a time, check Yes, No, or Not Applicable (N/A) for each question asked. Use space available to expand, as appropriate, on any/all of your responses. At the end of each section, summarize and document your findings in the Summary of Findings section located on the reverse. Proceed to the next section. Once this has been done for all sections, review and analyze the *entire* Summary section and formulate your care planning decision.

What MDS 2.0 item(s) triggered this RAP? ____

MEDICAL FACTORS FOR CONSIDERATION	YES	NO	N/A
1. Feeding tube has been in use since (date) ____			
2. Has resident had abnormal lab values within the last 90 days? *(P9)* ____			
3. Is tube feeding use expected to be long term? ____			
4. Would removal of feeding tube cause nutrition/dehydration problems? ____			
5. Is resident comatose? *(B1)* ____			
If No, does resident have:			
a. Chewing problem? *(K1a)* ____			
b. Swallowing problem? *(K1b)* ____			
c. Mouth pain? *(K1c)* ____			
6. Does resident have a diagnosis or diagnostic condition of:			
a. CVA? *(I1t)* ____			
b. Gastric ulcers? *(I3)* ____			
c. Repetitive physical movement? *(E1n)* ____			
d. Lung aspirations? *(J1k)* ____			
7. Does Resident have gastric bleeding? *(From record)* ____			
8. Has resident exhibited signs/symptoms of infection in lung/trachea? If Yes, identify: Pneumonia *(I2c)*; Fever *(J1h)*; Shortness of breath *(J1l)*; Signs/Symptoms of respiratory problems (e.g., pneumothorax, hydrothorax, airway obstruction, acute respiratory distress) *(I3, From observation, Record)* Other (specify) ____			
9. Has resident exhibited signs/symptoms of cardiac problems? If yes, identify: Cardiac distress/ arrest; Loss of heartbeat; Loss of consciousness; Breathing distress; Chest pain *(J3c)*; Other (specify) ____			
10. Has resident had side effects of enteral feeding solutions? If yes, identify: Constipation *(H2b)*; Diarrhea *(H2c)*; Fecal impaction *(H2d)*; Dehydration *(J1c)*; Abdominal distention/pain; Other (specify) ____			
11. Based on the above review, does resident have medical conditions that impede removal of feeding tube or places him/her at risk for complications of tube feeding usage? Indicate Yes or No and specifically document your findings in the Summary of Findings section.			

COGNITIVE FACTORS FOR CONSIDERATION	YES	NO	N/A
1. Has the resident been diagnosed and/or exhibited symptoms of:			
a. Delirium (acute confusional state)? *(B5)* ____			
b. Anxiety (fearful, nervous)? *(I1dd)* ____			
c. Depression (crying, non-communicative, no motivation? *(I1ee)* ____			
2. Based on the above review, does resident have cognitive deficit(s) which place him/her at risk for complications for tube feeding usage? Indicate Yes or No and specifically document your findings in the Summary of Findings section.			

Name—Last	First	Middle	Attending Physician	I.D. No.

FEEDING TUBES

Source: Reprinted with permission of Briggs Health Care Products, Des Moines, Iowa 50306* (800) 247–2343.

FEEDING TUBES
MDS 2.0 RAP MODULE

FUNCTIONAL FACTORS FOR CONSIDERATION	YES	NO	N/A
1. Does resident consume adequate nutritional intake? *(K4c)*			
2. Does resident resist assistance in eating? *(E4e)*			
3. Has resident removed feeding tube (self-extubation)? *(See Medical Record)*			
4. Are limb restraints or other devices required to prevent self-extubation? *(P4d)*			
If Yes, specify:			
5. Based on the above review, does resident have functional deficit(s) which impede removal of feeding tube or places him/her at risk for complications for tube feeding? Indicate Yes or No and specifically document your findings in the Summary of Findings section.			

SUMMARY OF FINDINGS

NOTE: This documentation must support the criteria outlined in instruction #2 on the Resident Assessment Protocol Summary (MDS 2.0, Section V.). In short, you must describe the nature of the problem; causes, complications and risk factors (including impact on health and well-being); and provide justification for proceeding or not proceeding to care planning.

CARE PLAN DECISION BASED ON SUMMARY ABOVE: ☐ **Proceed with care planning** ☐ **Not proceed with care planning**

Signature, Title & Dates of Staff Who Completed RAP

Name—Last	First	Middle	Attending Physician	I.D. No.

FEEDING TUBES

RESIDENT ASSESSMENT PROTOCOL SUMMARY

Resident's Name:	Medical Record No.:

1. Check if RAP is triggered.
2. For each triggered RAP, use the RAP guidelines to identify areas needing further assessment. Document relevant assessment information regarding the resident's status.
   - Describe:
     —Nature of the condition (may include presence or lack of objective data and subjective complaints).
     —Complications and risk factors that affect your decision to proceed to care planning.
     —Factors that must be considered in developing individualized care plan interventions.
     —Need for referrals/further evaluation by appropriate health professionals.
   - Documentation should support your decision-making regarding whether to proceed with a care plan for a triggered RAP and the type(s) of care plan interventions that are appropriate for a particular resident.
   - Documentation may appear anywhere in the clinical record (e.g., progress notes, consults, flowsheets, etc.).
3. Indicate under the Location of RAP Assessment Documentation column where information related to the RAP assessment can be found.
4. For each triggered RAP, indicate whether a new care plan, care plan revision, or continuation of current care plan is necessary to address the problem(s) identified in your assessment. The Care Planning Decision column must be completed within 7 days of completing the RAI (MDS and RAPs).

A. RAP Problem Area	(a) Check if Triggered	Location and Date of RAP Assessment Documentation	(b) Care Planning Decision—check if addressed in care plan
1. DELIRIUM	☐		☐
2. COGNITIVE LOSS	☐		☐
3. VISUAL FUNCTION	☐		☐
4. COMMUNICATION	☐		☐
5. ADL FUNCTIONAL/ REHABILITATION POTENTIAL	☐		☐
6. URINARY INCONTINENCE AND INDWELLING CATHETER	☐		☐
7. PSYCHOSOCIAL WELL-BEING	☐		☐
8. MOOD STATE	☐		☐
9. BEHAVIORAL SYMPTOMS	☐		☐
10. ACTIVITIES	☐		☐
11. FALLS	☐		☐
12. NUTRITIONAL STATUS	☐		☐
13. FEEDING TUBES	☐		☐
14. DEHYDRATION/FLUID MAINTENANCE	☐		☐
15. ORAL/DENTAL CARE	☐		☐
16. PRESSURE ULCERS	☐		☐
17. PSYCHOTROPIC DRUG USE	☐		☐
18. PHYSICAL RESTRAINTS	☐		☐

B. ______________________________ 2. ☐☐ – ☐☐ – ☐☐☐☐
1. Signature of RN Coordinator for RAP Assessment Process — Month Day Year

______________________________ 4. ☐☐ – ☐☐ – ☐☐☐☐
3. Signature of Person Completing Care Planning Decision — Month Day Year

Source: Reprinted from Health Care Financing Administration.

APPENDIX E

Dietary Information

RECOMMENDED DIETARY ALLOWANCES OF SELECTED VITAMINS AND MINERALS*

							Fat-Soluble Vitamins				Water-Soluble Vitamins							Minerals						
Category	Age (years) or Condition	Weight† (kg)	Weight† (lb)	Height† (cm)	Height† (in)	Protein (g)	Vitamin A (μg REM)‡	Vitamin D (μg)§	Vitamin E (mg α-TE)‖	Vitamin K (μg)	Vitamin C (mg)	Thiamine (mg)	Riboflavin (mg)	Niacin (mg NE)#	Vitamin B_6 (mg)	Folate (μg)	Vitamin B_{12} (μg)	Calcium (mg)	Phosphorus (mg)	Magnesium (mg)	Iron (mg)	Zinc (mg)	Iodine (μg)	Selenium (μg)
Infants	0.0–0.5	6	13	60	24	13	375	7.5	3	5	30	0.3	0.4	5	0.3	25	0.3	400	300	40	6	5	40	10
	0.5–1.0	9	20	71	28	14	375	10	4	10	35	0.4	0.5	6	0.6	35	0.5	600	500	60	10	5	50	15
Children	1–3	13	29	90	35	16	400	10	6	15	40	0.7	0.8	9	1.0	50	0.7	800	800	80	10	10	70	20
	4–6	20	44	112	44	24	500	10	7	20	45	0.9	1.1	12	1.1	75	1.0	800	800	120	10	10	90	20
	7–10	28	62	132	52	28	700	10	7	30	45	1.0	1.2	13	1.4	100	1.4	800	800	170	10	10	120	30
Males	11–14	45	99	157	62	45	1,000	10	10	45	50	1.3	1.5	17	1.7	150	2.0	1,200	1,200	270	12	15	150	40
	15–18	66	145	176	69	59	1,000	10	10	65	60	1.5	1.8	20	2.0	200	2.0	1,200	1,200	400	12	15	150	50
	19–24	72	160	177	70	58	1,000	10	10	70	60	1.5	1.7	19	2.0	200	2.0	1,200	1,200	350	10	15	150	70
	25–50	79	174	176	70	63	1,000	5	10	80	60	1.5	1.7	19	2.0	200	2.0	800	800	350	10	15	150	70
	51+	77	170	173	68	63	1,000	5	10	80	60	1.2	1.4	15	2.0	200	2.0	800	800	350	10	15	150	70
Females	11–14	46	101	157	62	46	800	10	8	45	50	1.1	1.3	15	1.4	150	2.0	1,200	1,200	280	15	12	150	45
	15–18	55	120	163	64	44	800	10	8	55	60	1.1	1.3	15	1.5	180	2.0	1,200	1,200	300	15	12	150	50
	19–24	58	128	164	65	46	800	10	8	60	60	1.1	1.3	15	1.6	180	2.0	1,200	1,200	280	15	12	150	55
	25–50	63	138	163	64	50	800	5	8	65	60	1.1	1.3	15	1.6	180	2.0	800	800	280	15	12	150	55
	51+	65	143	160	63	50	800	5	8	65	60	1.0	1.2	13	1.6	180	2.0	800	800	280	10	12	150	55
Pregnant						60	800	10	10	65	70	1.5	1.6	17	2.2	400	2.2	1,200	1,200	320	30	15	175	65
Lactating	1st 6 months					65	1,300	10	12	65	95	1.6	1.8	20	2.1	280	2.6	1,200	1,200	355	15	19	200	75
	2nd 6 months					62	1,200	10	11	65	90	1.6	1.7	20	2.1	260	2.6	1,200	1,200	340	15	16	200	75

* Revised 1989. The allowances, expressed as average daily intakes over time, are intended to provide for individual variations among most normal persons as they live in the United States under usual environmental stresses. Dets should be based on a variety of common foods in order to provide other nutrients for which human requirements have been less well defined.

† Weights and heights of Reference Adults are actual medians for the U.S. population of the designated age, as reported by NHANES II. The use of these figures does not imply that the height-to-weight ratios are ideal.

‡ Retinol equivalents. 1 retinol equivalent = 1 μg retinol of 6 μg β-carotene.

§ As cholecalciferol. 10 μg cholecalciferol = 400 IU of vitamin D.

‖ α-Tocopherol equivalents. 1 mg d-α tocopherol = 1 α-TE.

\# 1 NE (niacin equivalent) is equal to 1 mg of niacin or 60 mg of dietary tryptophan.

Source: Reprinted with permission from *Recommended Dietary Allowances: 10th Edition.* Copyright 1989 by the National Academy of Sciences. Courtesy of the National Academy Press, Washington, D.C.

MEDIAN HEIGHTS AND WEIGHTS AND RECOMMENDED ENERGY INTAKE

Category	Age (years) or Condition	Weight (kg)	Weight (lb)	Height (cm)	Height (in)	REE* (kcal/day)	Average Energy Allowance (kcal)†		
							Multiples of REE	Per kg	Per day‡
Infants	0.0–0.5	6	13	60	24	320		108	650
	0.5–1.0	9	20	71	28	500		98	850
Children	1–3	13	29	90	35	740		102	1,300
	4–6	20	44	112	44	950		90	1,800
	7–10	28	62	132	52	1,130		70	2,000
Males	11–14	45	99	157	62	1,440	1.70	55	2,500
	15–18	66	145	176	69	1,760	1.67	45	3,000
	19–24	72	160	177	70	1,780	1.67	40	2,900
	25–50	79	174	176	70	1,800	1.60	37	2,900
	51+	77	170	173	68	1,530	1.50	30	2,300
Females	11–14	46	101	157	62	1,310	1.67	47	2,200
	15–18	55	120	163	64	1,370	1.60	40	2,200
	19–24	58	128	164	65	1,350	1.60	38	2,200
	25–50	63	138	163	64	1,380	1.55	36	2,200
	51+	65	143	160	63	1,280	1.50	30	1,900
Pregnant	1st trimester								+0
	2nd trimester								+300
	3rd trimester								+300
Lactating	1st 6 months								+500
	2nd 6 months								+500

* Calculation of REE (resting energy expenditure) based on FAO equations, then rounded.
† In the range of light to moderate activity, the coefficient of variations is ± 20%.
‡ Figure is rounded.

Source: Reprinted with permission from *Recommended Dietary Allowances: 10th Edition.* Copyright 1989 by the National Academy of Sciences. Courtesy of the National Academy Press, Washington, D.C.

ESTIMATED SAFE AND ADEQUATE DAILY DIETARY INTAKES OF SELECTED VITAMINS AND MINERALS*

Category	Age (years)	Vitamins		Trace Elements†				
		Biotin (μg)	Pantothenic Acid (mg)	Copper (mg)	Manganese (mg)	Fluoride (mg)	Chromium (μg)	Molybdenum (μg)
Infants	0–0.5	10	2	0.4–0.6	0.3–0.6	0.1–0.5	10–40	15–30
	0.5–1	15	3	0.6–0.7	0.6–1.0	0.2–1.0	20–60	20–40
Children and adolescents	1–3	20	3	0.7–1.0	1.0–1.5	0.5–1.5	20–80	25–50
	4–6	25	3–4	1.0–1.5	1.5–2.0	1.0–2.5	30–120	30–75
	7–10	30	4–5	1.0–2.0	2.0–3.0	1.5–2.5	50–200	50–150
	11+	30–100	4–7	1.5–2.5	2.0–5.0	1.5–2.5	50–200	75–250
Adults		30–100	4–7	1.5–3.0	2.0–5.0	1.5–4.0	50–200	75–250

* Because there is less information on which to base allowances, these figures are not given in the main table of RDA and are provided here in the form of ranges of recommended intakes.

† Since the toxic levels for many trace elements may be only several times usual intakes, the upper levels for the trace elements given in this table should not be habitually exceeded.

Source: Reprinted with permission from *Recommended Dietary Allowances: 10th Edition.* Copyright 1989 by the National Academy of Sciences. Courtesy of the National Academy Press, Washington, D.C.

ESTIMATED SODIUM, CHLORIDE, AND POTASSIUM MINIMUM REQUIREMENTS OF HEALTHY PERSONS*

Age	*Weight (kg)**	*Sodium (mg)**†	*Chloride (mg)**†	*Potassium (mg)*‡
Months				
0–5	4.5	120	180	500
6–11	8.9	200	300	700
Years				
1	11.0	225	350	1,000
2–5	16.0	300	500	1,400
6–9	25.0	400	600	1,600
10–18	50.0	500	750	2,000
<18§	70.0	500	750	2,000

* No allowance has been included for large, prolonged losses from the skin through sweat.

† There is no evidence that higher intakes confer any health benefit.

‡ Desirable intakes of potassium may considerably exceed these values (~3,500 mg for adults).

§ No allowance induced for growth. Values for those below 18 years assume a growth rate at the 50th percentile reported by the National Center for Health Statistics and averaged for males and females.

Source: Reprinted with permission from *Recommended Dietary Allowances: 10th Edition.* Copyright 1989 by the National Academy of Sciences. Courtesy of the National Academy Press, Washington, D.C.

APPENDIX F

Adjusting Yield of Weight Amounts

The following instructions explain the use of Appendix F.

1. Locate the column that corresponds to the original yield of the recipe you wish to adjust. For example, assume that your original recipe for meat loaf yields 100 portions. Locate the 100 column.
2. Run your finger down this column until you come to the amount of the ingredient required (or closest to this figure) in the recipe you wish to adjust. Say that your original recipe for 100 portions of meat loaf requires 21 lb of ground beef. Run your finger down the column headed 100 until you come to 21 lb.
3. Next, run your finger across the page, in line with that amount, until you come to the column which is headed to correspond with the yield you desire. Suppose you want to make 75 portions of meat loaf. Starting with your finger under the 21 lb (in the 100 column), slide it across to the column headed 75 and read the figure. You see you need 15 lb 12 oz ground beef to make 75 portions with your recipe.
4. Record this figure as the amount of the ingredient required for the new yield of your recipe. Repeat steps 1, 2, and 3 for each ingredient in your original recipe to obtain the adjusted ingredient weight needed of each for your new yield. You can increase or decrease yield in this manner.
5. If you need to combine two columns to obtain your desired yield, follow the above procedure and add together the amounts given in the two columns to get the amount required for your adjusted yield. For example, to find the amount of ground beef for 225 portions of meat loaf (using the same recipe for 100 used above) locate the figures in columns headed 200 and 25 and add them. In this case they would be: 42 lb + 5 lb 4 oz, and the required total would be 47 lb 4 oz.
6. The figures in Appendix F are given in exact weights including fractional ounces. After you have made yield adjustments for every ingredient, refer to Appendix H for "rounding-off" fractional amounts which are not of sufficient proportion to change product quality. No rounding-off is required for amounts needed for adjusted ingredients in the examples we have used here.

Source: Reprinted with permission from *Standardizing Recipes for Institutional Use*, © 1967, American Dietetic Association.

DIRECT-READING TABLE FOR ADJUSTING YIELD OF RECIPES WITH INGREDIENT AMOUNTS GIVEN IN WEIGHTS*

25 Portions		*50 Portions*		*75 Portions*		*100 Portions*		*200 Portions*		*300 Portions*		*400 Portions*		*500 Portions*	
lb	*oz*	*lb*	*oz*	*lb*	*oz*	*lb*	*oz*	*lb*	*oz*	*lb*	*oz*	*lb*	*oz*	*lb*	*oz*
	2		4		6		8	1		1	8	2		2	8
	2¼		4¼		6½		8½	1	1	1	9½	2	2	2	10½
	2¼		4½		6¾		9	1	2	1	11	2	4	2	13
	2½		4¾		7¼		9½	1	3	1	12½	2	6	2	15½
	2½		5		7½		10	1	4	1	14	2	8	3	2
	2¾		5½		8½		11	1	6	2	1	2	12	3	7
	3		6		9		12	1	8	2	4	3		3	12
	3¼		6½		9¾		13	1	10	2	7	3	4	4	1
	3½		7		10½		14	1	12	2	10	3	8	4	6
	3¾		7½		11¼		15	1	14	2	13	3	12	4	11
	4		8		12	1		2		3		4		5	
	4½		9		13½	1	2	2	4	3	6	4	8	5	10
	5		10		15	1	4	2	8	3	12	5		6	4
	5½		11	1	½	1	6	2	12	4	2	5	8	6	14
	6		12	1	2	1	8	3		4	8	6		7	8
	6½		13	1	3½	1	10	3	4	4	14	6	8	8	2
	7		14	1	5	1	12	3	8	5	4	7		8	12
	7½		15	1	6½	1	14	3	12	5	10	7	8	9	6
	8	1		1	8	2		4		6		8		10	
	8½	1	1	1	9½	2	2	4	4	6	6	8	8	10	10
	9	1	2	1	11	2	4	4	8	6	12	9		11	4
	9½	1	3	1	12½	2	6	4	12	7	2	9	8	11	14
	10	1	4	1	14	2	8	5		7	8	10		12	8
	11	1	6	2	1	2	12	5	8	8	4	11		13	12
	12	1	8	2	4	3		6		9		12		15	
	13	1	10	2	7	3	4	6	8	9	12	13		16	4
	14	1	12	2	10	3	8	7		10	8	14		17	8
	15	1	14	2	13	3	12	7	8	11	4	15		18	12
1		2		3		4		8		12		16		20	
1	1	2	2	3	3	4	4	8	8	12	12	17		21	4
1	2	2	4	3	6	4	8	9		13	8	18		22	8
1	3	2	6	3	9	4	12	9	8	14	4	19		23	12
1	4	2	8	3	12	5		10		15		20		25	
1	5	2	10	3	15	5	4	10	8	15	12	21		26	4
1	6	2	12	4	2	5	8	11		16	8	22		27	8
1	7	2	14	4	5	5	12	11	8	17	4	23		28	12
1	8	3		4	8	6		12		18		24		30	
1	10	3	4	4	14	6	8	13		19	8	26		32	8
1	12	3	8	5	4	7		14		21		28		35	
1	14	3	12	5	10	7	8	15		22	8	30		37	8
2		4		6		8		16		24		32		40	
2	2	4	4	6	6	8	8	17		25	8	34		42	8
2	4	4	8	6	12	9		18		27		36		45	
2	6	4	12	7	2	9	8	19		28	8	38		47	8
2	8	5		7	8	10		20		30		40		50	
2	12	5	8	8	4	11		22		33		44		55	
3		6		9		12		24		36		48		60	
3	4	6	8	9	12	13		26		39		52		65	
3	8	7		10	8	14		28		42		56		70	
3	12	7	8	11	4	15		30		45		60		75	
4		8		12		16		32		48		64		80	

25 Portions		50 Portions		75 Portions		100 Portions		200 Portions		300 Portions		400 Portions		500 Portions	
lb	*oz*	*lb*	*oz*	*lb*	*oz*	*lb*	*oz*	*lb*	*oz*	*lb*	*oz*	*lb*	*oz*	*lb*	*oz*
4	4	8	8	12	12	17		34		51		68		85	
4	8	9		13	8	18		36		54		72		90	
4	12	9	8	14	2	19		38		57		76		95	
5		10		15		20		40		60		80		100	
5	4	10	8	15	12	21		42		63		84		105	
5	8	11		16	8	22		44		66		88		110	
5	12	11	8	17	4	23		46		69		92		115	
6		12		18		24		48		72		96		120	
6	4	12	8	18	12	25		50		75		100		125	
7	8	15		22	8	30		60		90		120		150	
8	12	17	8	26	4	35		70		105		140		175	
10		20		30		40		80		120		160		200	
11	4	22	8	33	12	45		90		135		180		225	
12	8	25		37	8	50		100		150		200		250	

*This table is primarily for adjusting recipes with original and desired portion yields which can be divided by 25.

APPENDIX G

Adjusting Yield of Measurement Amounts

The following instructions explain the use of Appendix G.

1. Locate the column that corresponds to the original yield of the recipe you wish to adjust. For example, let us assume that your original sour cream cookie recipe yields 300 cookies. Locate the 300 column.
2. Run your finger down this column until you come to the amount of the ingredient required (or closest to this figure) in the recipe you wish to adjust. Say that your original recipe for 300 cookies required 2¼ cups fat. Run your finger down the column headed 300 until you come to 2¼ cup.
3. Next, run your finger across the page, in line with that amount, until you come to the column which is headed to correspond with the yield you desire. Suppose you want to make 75 cookies. Starting with your finger under the 2¼ cup (in the 300 column), slide it across to the column headed 75 and read the figure. You see you need ½ cup + 1 Tbsp fat to make 75 cookies from your recipe.
4. Record this figure as the amount of the ingredient required for the new yield of your recipe. Repeat steps 1, 2, 3 for each ingredient in your original recipe to obtain the adjusted measure needed of each for your new yield. You can increase or decrease yield in this manner.
5. If you need to combine two columns to obtain your desired yield, follow the above procedure and add together the amounts given in the two columns to get the amount required by your adjusted yield. For example, to find the amount of fat needed to make 550 cookies (using the same basic recipe as above) locate the figures in column headed 500 and 50 and add them. In this case they would be 3¾ cup + 6 Tbsp and the required total would be 1 qt + 2 Tbsp fat.
6. The figures in Appendix G are given in measurements which provide absolute accuracy. After you have made yield adjustments for each ingredient, refer to Appendix H for rounding off odd fractions and complicated measurements. You can safely round off to 1 qt as shown in Appendix H, for the amount of fat needed in the recipe for 550 cookies.

Source: Reprinted with permission from *Standardizing Recipes for Institutional Use,* © 1967, American Dietetic Association.

DIRECT-READING TABLE FOR ADJUSTING YIELD OF RECIPES WITH INGREDIENT AMOUNTS GIVEN IN MEASUREMENT*

25 Portions	*50 Portions*	*75 Portions*	*100 Portions*	*200 Portions*	*300 Portions*	*400 Portions*	*500 Portions*
1 Tbsp	2 Tbsp	3 Tbsp	¼ cup	½ cup	¾ cup	1 cup	1¼ cup
1 Tbsp + 1 tsp	2 Tbsp + 2 tsp	¼ cup	⅓ cup	⅔ cup	1 cup	1⅓ cup	1⅔ cup
2 Tbsp	¼ cup	¼ cup + 2 Tbsp	½ cup	1 cup	1½ cup	2 cup	2½ cup
2 Tbsp + 2 tsp	⅓ cup	½ cup	⅔ cup	1⅓ cup	2 cup	2⅔ cup	3⅓ cup
3 Tbsp	6 Tbsp	½ cup + 1 Tbsp	¾ cup	1½ cup	2¼ cup	3 cup	3¾ cup
¼ cup	½ cup	¾ cup	1 cup	2 cup	3 cup	1 qt	1¼ qt
¼ cup + 1 Tbsp	½ cup + 2 Tbsp	¾ cup + 3 Tbsp	1¼ cup	2½ cup	3¾ cup	1¼ qt	1½ qt + ¼ cup
⅓ cup	⅔ cup	1 cup	1⅓ cup	2⅔ cup	1 qt	1¼ qt + ⅓ cup	1½ qt + ⅔ cup
⅓ cup + 2 Tbsp	¾ cup	1 cup + 2 Tbsp	1½ cup	3 cup	1 qt + ½ cup	1½ qt	1¾ qt + ½ cup
6 Tbsp + 2 tsp	¼ cup + 4 Tbsp	1¼ cup	1⅔ cup	3⅓ cup	1¼ qt	1½ qt + ⅔ cup	2 qt + ⅓ cup
¼ cup + 3 Tbsp	¾ cup + 2 Tbsp	1¼ cup + 1 Tbsp	1¾ cup	3½ cup	1¼ qt + ¼ cup	1¾ qt	2 qt + ¾ cup
½ cup	1 cup	1½ cup	2 cup	1 qt	1½ qt	2 qt	2½ qt
½ cup + 1 Tbsp	1 cup + 2 Tbsp	1½ cup + 3 Tbsp	2¼ cup	1 qt + ½ cup	1½ qt + ¾ cup	2¼ qt	2¾ qt + ¼ cup
½ cup + 4 tsp	1 cup + 2 Tbsp	1¾ cup	2⅓ cup	1 qt + ⅔ cup	1¾ qt	2¼ qt + ⅓ cup	2¾ qt + ⅔ cup
½ cup + 2 Tbsp	1¼ cup	1¾ cup + 2 Tbsp	2½ cup	1¼ qt	1¾ qt + ½ cup	2½ qt	3 qt + ½ cup
⅔ cup	1⅓ cup	2 cup	2⅔ cup	1 ¼ qt + ⅓ cup	2 qt	2½ qt + ⅔ cup	3 qt + ⅓ cup
¾ cup	1½ cup	2¼ cup	3 cup	1½ qt	2¼ qt	3 qt	3¾ qt
¾ cup + 1 Tbsp	1½ cup + 2 Tbsp	2¼ cup + 3 Tbsp	3¼ cup	1½ qt + ½ cup	2¼ qt + ¾ cup	3¼ qt	1 gal + ¼ cup
¾ cup + 4 Tbsp	1⅔ cup	2½ cup	3⅓ cup	1½ qt + ⅔ cup	2½ qt	3¼ qt + ⅓ cup	1 gal + ⅔ cup
¾ cup + 2 Tbsp + 2½ tsp	1¾ cup + 4 Tbsp	2¾ cup + ½ tsp	3⅔ cup	1¾ qt + ⅓ cup	2¾ qt	3½ qt + ⅔ cup	1 gal + 1⅔ cup
¾ cup + 3 Tbsp	1¾ cup + 2 Tbsp	2¾ cup + 1 Tbsp	3¾ cup	1¾ qt + ½ cup	3 qt + ¼ cup	1 gal	1 gal + 3¾ cup
1 cup	2 cup	3 cup	1 qt	2 qt	3 qt	1 gal	1¼ gal
1½ cup	3 cup	1 qt	1½ qt	3 qt	1 gal + 2 cup	1½ gal	1¾ gal + 2 cup
1¾ cup	3½ cup	1¼ qt + ¼ cup	1¾ qt	3½ qt	1¼ gal + 1 cup	1¾ gal	2 gal + 3 cup
2 cup	1 qt	1½ qt	2 qt	1 gal	1½ gal	2 gal	2½ gal
2¼ cup	1 qt + ½ cup	1½ qt + ¾ cup	2¼ qt	1 gal + 2 cup	1½ gal + 3 cup	2¼ gal	2¾ gal + 1 cup
2½ cup	1¼ qt	1¾ qt + ½ cup	2½ qt	1¼ gal	1¾ gal + 2 cup	2½ gal	3 gal + 2 cup
2¾ cup	1¼ qt + ½ cup	2 qt + ¼ cup	2¾ qt	1¼ gal + 2 cup	2 gal + 1 cup	2¾ gal	3¼ gal + 3 cup
3 cup	1½ qt	2¼ qt	3 qt	1½ gal	2¼ gal	3 gal	3¾ gal

25 Portions	*50 Portions*	*75 Portions*	*100 Portions*	*200 Portions*	*300 Portions*	*400 Portions*	*500 Portions*
3¼ cup	1½ qt + ½ cup	2¼ qt + ¾ cup	3¼ qt	1½ gal + 2 cup	2¼ gal + 3 cup	3¼ gal	4 gal + 1 cup
3½ cup	1¾ qt	2½ qt + ½ cup	3½ qt	1¾ gal	2½ gal + 2 cup	3½ gal	4¼ gal + 2 cup
3¾ cup	1¾ qt + ½ cup	2¾ qt + ¼ cup	3¾ qt	1¾ gal + 2 cup	2¾ gal + 1 cup	3¾ gal	4½ gal + 3 cup
1 qt	2 qt	3 qt	1 gal	2 gal	3 gal	4 gal	5 gal
1¼ qt	2½ qt	3¾ qt	1¼ gal	2½ gal	3¾ gal	5 gal	6¼ gal
1½ qt	3 qt	1 gal + 2 cup	1½ gal	3 gal	4½ gal	6 gal	7½ gal
1¾ qt	3½ qt	1¼ gal + 1 cup	1¾ gal	3½ gal	5¼ gal	7 gal	8¼ gal
2 qt	1 gal	1½ gal	2 gal	4 gal	6 gal	8 gal	10 gal
2¼ qt	1 gal + 2 cup	1½ gal + 3 cup	2¼ gal	4½ gal	6¾ gal	9 gal	11¼ gal
2½ qt	1¼ gal	1¾ gal + 2 cup	2½ gal	5 gal	7½ gal	10 gal	12½ gal
2¾ qt	1¼ gal + 2 cup	2 gal + 1 cup	2¾ gal	5½ gal	8¼ gal	11 gal	13¾ gal
3 qt	1½ gal	2¼ gal	3 gal	6 gal	9 gal	12 gal	15 gal
3 qt + 1 cup	1½ gal + 2 cup	2¼ gal + 3 cup	3¼ gal	6½ gal	9¾ gal	13 gal	16¼ gal
3½ qt	1¾ gal	2½ gal + 2 cup	3½ gal	7 gal	10½ gal	14 gal	17½ gal
3½ qt + 1 cup	1¾ gal + 2 cup	2¾ gal + 1 cup	3¾ gal	7½ gal	11¼ gal	15 gal	18¾ gal
1 gal	2 gal	3 gal	4 gal	8 gal	12 gal	16 gal	20 gal

*This table is primarily for adjusting recipes with original and desired portion yields which can be divided by 25. *Abbreviations in table*: tsp is teaspoon; Tbsp, tablespoon; qt, quart; and gal, gallon. *Basic information*: For ¾ tsp, combine ½ tsp + ¼ tsp; for ⅛ tsp use half of the ¼ tsp. Equivalents are: 3 tsp, 1 Tbsp; 4 Tbsp, ¼ cup; 5 Tbsp + 1 tsp, ⅓ cup; 8 Tbsp, ½ cup; 10 Tbsp + 2 tsp, ⅔ cup; 12 Tbsp, ¾ cup; 16 Tbsp, 1 cup; 4 cups, 1 qt; and 4 qt, 1 gal.

Appendix H

Rounding Off Weights and Measures

Item	If Total Amount of an Ingredient Is	Round It To
Weights	less than 2 oz	measure unless wt is in ¼, ½, or ¾ oz amounts
Various miscellaneous ingredients	2–10 oz	closest ¼ oz or convert to measure
	more than 10 oz, but less than 2 lb 8 oz	closest ½ oz
	2 lb 8 oz to 5 lb	closest full oz
	more than 5 lb	closest ¼ lb
Measures		
Primarily spices, seasonings, flavorings, condiments, leavenings, and similar items	less than 1 Tbsp	closest ⅛ tsp
	more than 1 Tbsp but less than 3 Tbsp	closest ¼ tsp
	3 Tbsp to ½ cup	closest ½ tsp or convert to weight
	more than ½ cup but less than ¾ cup	closest full tsp or convert to weight
	more than ¾ cup but less than 2 cups	closest full Tbsp or convert to weight
	2 cup to 2 qt	nearest ¼ cup
Primarily milk, water, eggs, juice, oil, syrup, molasses, etc.	more than 2 qt but less than 4 qt	nearest ½ cup
	1 gal to 2 gal	nearest full cup or ¼ qt
	more than 2 gal but less than 10 gal	nearest full qt
	more than 10 gal but less than 20 gal	closest ½ gal
	over 20 gal	closest full gal

Source: Reprinted with permission from *Standardizing Recipes for Institutional Use*, © 1967, American Dietetic Association.

APPENDIX I

Equivalent Measures and Weights of Commonly Used Foods

Food Item and Form	Approximate Weight per Cup (g)	(oz)
Dairy products		
Butter	224	7.9
whipped	152	5.4
Cheese		
cheddar (natural or processed), grated or chopped	113	4.0
cottage	236	8.3
cream	230	8.1
Parmesan	92	3.3
Cream		
light (table)	240	8.5
heavy (whipping), whipped	236	8.3
sour	241	8.5
half-and-half (cream, milk), sweet	242	8.5
half-and-half, sour	242	8.5
Milk		
whole or skim	242	8.5
buttermilk	242	8.5
sweetened condensed	306	10.8
evaporated, whole or skim, reconstituted	252	8.9
dry, whole, reconstituted	121	4.3
dry, nonfat		
instant, reconstituted	75	2.6
noninstant, reconstituted	131	4.6
Milk desserts		
ice cream	142	5.0
ice milk	187	6.6
sherbet	193	6.8
Yogurt	246	8.7
Eggs		
whole	248	8.8
frozen	248	8.8

Source: Reprinted with permission from *Handbook of Food Preparation*, © 1975, American Association of Family and Consumer Sciences.

Food Item and Form	Approximate Weight per Cup (g)	(oz)
dried, sifted	86	3.0
whites		
fresh	246	8.7
frozen	246	8.7
dried, sifted	89	3.1
yolks		
fresh	233	8.2
frozen	233	8.2
dried, sifted	80	2.8
Fats and oils		
oils: corn, cottonseed, olive, peanut, and safflower	210	7.4
margarine	224	7.9
whipped	149	5.3
hydrogenated fat	188	6.6
lard and rendered fat	220	7.8
Fruits		
Apples		
pared and sliced	122	4.3
sauce, sweetened (not canned)	252	8.9
frozen, sliced, sweetened	205	7.2
canned, sliced	204	7.5
juice	249	8.8
sauce	259	9.1
dried	104	3.7
cooked	244	8.6
Apricots		
fresh, whole	115	4.1
sliced or halved	156	5.5
canned whole (medium)	225	7.9
halved (medium)	217	7.7
dried	150	5.3
cooked	249	8.8
Avocado		
sliced, diced, wedges	142	5.0
Banana		
fresh, sliced	142	5.0
mashed	232	8.2
dried	100	3.5
Blueberries		
fresh	146	5.2
frozen	161	5.7
canned	170	6.0
Cherries		
fresh, red, pitted	154	5.4
frozen	210	7.4
canned	177	6.2
Cranberries		
fresh	114	4.0
sauce	215	7.6
canned		
sauce	278	9.8
juice	250	8.8

Food Item and Form	Approximate Weight per Cup (g)	(oz)
Currants, dried	140	4.9
Dates, pitted, cut	178	6.3
Figs		
canned	230	4.9
dried, cut fine	168	5.9
Fruit juice		
canned	247	8.7
Fruits		
canned, cocktail or salad	229	8.1
Grapefruit		
fresh sections	194	6.8
frozen sections	219	7.7
canned, sections	241	8.5
Grapes, fresh		
seeded	184	6.5
seedless	169	6.0
Lemons		
fresh, juice	247	8.7
frozen, juice	283	10.0
canned, juice	245	8.6
Melon		
frozen	231	8.2
Oranges		
fresh, diced or sectioned	214	7.5
juice	247	8.7
frozen, juice, concentrated	268	9.5
canned, juice	247	8.7
Peaches		
fresh, sliced	177	6.2
frozen, halves	220	7.8
canned		
halves	224	7.9
slices	218	7.7
dried	160	5.6
cooked	224	8.6
Pears		
fresh, sliced	158	5.6
canned, halves	227	8.0
Pineapples		
fresh, cubed	146	5.2
frozen, chunks	204	7.2
canned, chunks, tidbits	198	7.0
crushed	260	9.2
sliced	208	7.3
Plums		
fresh, halved	185	6.5
canned, whole	223	7.9
Prunes		
canned	196	6.9
dried, whole	176	6.2
cooked	229	8.1
pitted	162	5.7
cooked	210	7.4

Food Item and Form	*Approximate Weight per Cup (g)*	*(oz)*
Raisins		
seeded		
whole	142	5.0
chopped	182	6.4
seedless		
whole	146	5.2
cooked	183	6.5
chopped	189	6.7
Rhubarb		
fresh		
cut	122	4.3
cooked	242	8.5
frozen, sliced	168	5.9
Strawberries		
fresh		
whole	144	5.1
sliced	148	5.2
frozen		
whole	204	7.2
sliced or halved	235	8.3
Cereals		
Bulgur		
uncooked	162	5.7
cooked	230	8.1
Cornmeal		
white, uncooked	129	4.6
yellow		
uncooked	152	5.4
cooked	238	8.4
Farina		
cooked	238	8.4
Hominy, whole		
cooked	182	6.4
Grits		
uncooked	154	5.4
cooked	236	8.3
Oats, rolled		
uncooked	72	2.5
cooked	240	8.5
Ready-to-eat		
flaked	32	1.1
granulated	87	3.1
puffed	23	0.8
shredded	37	1.3
Flours		
corn	116	4.1
gluten, sifted	142	5.0
rice		
sifted	126	4.4
stirred, spooned	158	5.6
rye		
light, sifted	88	3.1
dark, sifted	127	4.5

Food Item and Form	Approximate Weight per Cup (g)	(oz)
soy		
full-fat, sifted	60	2.1
lowfat	83	2.9
wheat, all-purpose		
sifted	115	4.1
unsifted, spooned	125	4.4
instant	129	4.6
bread, sifted	112	4.0
cake		
sifted	96	3.4
spooned	111	3.9
pastry, sifted	100	3.5
self-rising, sifted	106	3.7
whole-wheat, stirred	132	4.7
Starch		
corn, stirred	128	4.5
potato, stirred	142	5.0
Sweetening Agents		
Sugar		
brown, light	200	7.1
dark, packed	212	7.5
cane or beet granulated	200	7.1
superfine	196	6.9
confectioner's unsifted	123	4.3
confectioner's sifted	95	3.4
Corn syrup, light and dark	328	11.6
Honey	332	11.7
Maple syrup	312	11.0
Molasses, cane	309	10.9
Sorghum	330	11.6
Vegetables		
Asparagus, spears		
fresh, cooked	181	6.4
canned	195	6.9
frozen spears, cuts, and tips	181	6.4
Beans, green		
fresh	114	4.0
cooked	125	4.4
frozen	161	5.7
canned	135	4.8
Beans, kidney, canned	187	6.6
dried		
uncooked	184	6.5
cooked	185	6.5
Beans, lima, shelled		
fresh		
raw	155	5.5
cooked	166	5.9
frozen	173	6.1
canned	170	6.0
dried		
uncooked	180	6.3
cooked	186	6.6

Food Item and Form	*Approximate Weight per Cup* (g)	(oz)
Beans, navy		
dried	190	6.7
cooked	191	6.7
Beans, soybeans, dried	210	7.4
Beets, without tops		
fresh		
uncooked	145	5.1
cooked	180	6.3
canned	167	5.9
Broccoli		
fresh, cooked	164	5.8
spears, chopped, frozen	188	6.6
Brussels sprouts		
fresh		
uncooked	102	3.6
cooked	180	6.4
Cabbage		
fresh, shredded	80	2.8
cooked	146	5.2
Carrots, without tops		
fresh	112	4.0
shredded	137	4.8
diced	160	5.6
cooked		
frozen, cooked	165	5.8
canned	159	5.6
Cauliflower, fresh		
raw	104	3.7
cooked	125	4.4
frozen		
uncooked	152	5.4
cooked	179	6.3
Celery, fresh		
raw	121	4.3
cooked	153	5.4
Corn, fresh ears		
cooked	165	5.8
frozen		
uncooked	135	4.8
cooked	182	6.4
canned, cream style	249	8.8
whole kernel	169	6.0
Eggplant, fresh		
diced		
uncooked	99	3.5
cooked	213	7.5
Greens, fresh		
raw	77	2.7
cooked	190	6.7
frozen	187	6.6
Lentils		
dried	191	6.7
cooked	202	7.1

Food Item and Form	Approximate Weight per Cup (g)	(oz)
Mixed vegetables		
frozen	182	6.4
canned	179	6.3
Mushrooms, fresh, sliced		
raw	68	2.4
canned	161	7.4
Okra, fresh		
cooked	177	6.2
frozen	209	7.4
canned	171	6.0
Onions, fresh		
chopped, uncooked	135	4.8
cooked	197	6.9
dried	64	2.3
Parsnips, fresh		
cooked	211	7.4
Peas, green, fresh, in pod		
shelled		
raw	138	4.9
cooked	163	5.7
frozen		
raw	156	5.5
cooked	167	5.9
canned	168	5.9
dried, split		
uncooked	200	7.1
cooked	194	6.8
Peas, black-eyed, fresh		
raw	144	5.1
cooked	162	5.7
frozen, cooked	171	6.0
canned	205	7.2
dried, split		
uncooked	200	7.1
cooked	248	8.7
Potatoes, white, fresh		
raw	164	5.8
cooked	163	5.7
mashed	207	7.3
canned, whole	179	6.3
dried flakes	36	1.3
reconstituted	212	7.5
dried granules	201	7.1
reconstituted	212	7.5
Pumpkin, fresh		
cooked, mashed	247	8.7
canned	244	8.6
Rutabaga, fresh, cubed		
raw	139	4.9
cooked	163	5.7
Sauerkraut, canned	188	6.6
Spinach, fresh		
raw	54	1.9

Food Item and Form	*Approximate Weight per Cup* (g)	(oz)
cooked	200	7.1
frozen	190	6.7
canned	221	7.8
Squash, winter, fresh		
cooked, mashed	244	8.6
frozen	242	8.5
Squash, summer, fresh		
raw	136	4.8
cooked, mashed	238	8.4
frozen, sliced	221	7.4
Sweet potatoes, fresh		
cooked, sliced	232	8.2
frozen	200	7.1
canned	220	7.8
dried, flakes	115	4.1
reconstituted	255	9.0
Tomatoes		
fresh	162	5.7
canned, whole	238	8.4
sauce	258	9.1
Turnips, fresh		
raw	134	4.7
cooked	196	6.9
Miscellaneous		
Bread, sliced		
crumbs, soft	46	1.6
dry	113	3.6
Catsup, tomato	273	9.6
Chocolate, bitter or semisweet	225	7.9
Cocoa		
prepared drink	112	4.0
instant, prepared drink	139	4.9
Coconut, long thread	80	2.8
canned	85	3.0
Coffee		
brewed	85	3.0
instant	38	1.4
Crackers		
graham, crumbs	86	3.0
soda, crumbs		
soda, crumbs, fine	70	2.5
Gelatin		
unflavored, granulated, unprepared	150	5.3
flavored, unprepared	179	6.3
prepared	557	19.5
Mayonnaise	243	8.6
Nuts, shelled		
almonds, blanched	152	5.4
filberts, whole	134	4.7
peanuts	144	5.1
pecans		
halved	108	3.8
chopped	118	4.2
pistachio	125	4.4

Food Item and Form	*Approximate Weight per Cup* (g)	(oz)
walnuts, Persian, English		
halved	100	3.5
chopped	119	4.2
Pasta		
macaroni, 1-in. pieces		
raw	123	4.3
cooked	140	4.9
macaroni, shell, raw	115	4.1
noodles, 1-in. pieces	73	2.6
spaghetti, 2-in. pieces		
raw	94	3.3
cooked	160	5.6
Peanut butter	251	8.9
Salad dressing, French	248	8.8
Salt, free-running	288	10.2
Soups		
canned, ready-to-serve	227	8.0
dried, reconstituted	231	8.2
Tapioca, quick-cooking	152	5.4
Tea, leaves		
brewed	72	2.5
instant	34	1.2
Water	237	8.4

	Approximate Weight (g) (per tsp)	(per Tbsp)
Leavening agents		
Baking powder		
phosphate	4.1	12.7
SAS—phosphate	3.2	10.2
tartrate	2.9	9.2
Baking soda	4.0	12.2
Cream of tartar	3.1	9.4
Yeast		
active dry	2.5	7.5
compressed	4.2	12.8

APPENDIX J

Decimal Parts of a Pound

Ounces	Decimal Part of a Pound	Ounces	Decimal Part of a Pound
¼	0.016	8¼	0.516
½	0.031	8½	0.531
¾	0.047	8¾	0.547
1	0.063	9	0.563
1¼	0.078	9¼	0.578
1½	0.094	9½	0.594
1¾	0.109	9¾	0.609
2	0.125	10	0.625
2¼	0.141	10¼	0.641
2½	0.156	10½	0.656
2¾	0.172	10¾	0.672
3	0.188	11	0.688
3¼	0.203	11¼	0.703
3½	0.219	11½	0.719
3¾	0.234	11¾	0.734
4	0.250	12	0.750
4¼	0.266	12¼	0.766
4½	0.281	12½	0.781
4¾	0.297	12¾	0.797
5	0.313	13	0.813
5¼	0.328	13¼	0.828
5½	0.344	13½	0.844
5¾	0.359	13¾	0.859
6	0.375	14	0.875
6¼	0.391	14¼	0.891
6½	0.406	14½	0.906
6¾	0.422	14¾	0.922
7	0.438	15	0.938
7¼	0.453	15¼	0.953
7½	0.469	15½	0.969
7¾	0.484	15¾	0.984
8	0.500	16	1.000

Source: Reprinted with permission from *Standardizing Recipes for Institutional Use*, © 1967, American Dietetic Association.

APPENDIX K

Factors for Metric Conversion

English Unit		Multiply by Exact	Soft		Metric Unit
Weight					
ounces (oz)	×	28.35	or 28.00	=	grams (g)
pounds (lb or #)	×	0.453	or 0.45	=	kilograms (kg)
Volume					
teaspoons (tsp)	×	4.97	or 5.00	=	milliliters (ml)
tablespoons (Tbsp)	×	14.8	or 15.00	=	ml
fluid ounces (fl oz)	×	29.575	or 30.00	=	ml
cups (C)	×	.2366	or 0.240	=	ml
pints (pt)	×	0.473	or 0.47	=	liters (L)
quarts (qt)	×	0.946	or 0.95	=	L
gallons (gal)	×	3.786	or 3.80	=	L
Pressure					
pounds per square inch (psi)	×		6.90	=	kilopascals (kPa)
Temperature					
degrees Fahrenheit (°F)	× 5/9 (after subtracting 32)			=	degrees Celsius (°C)

Source: Reprinted with permission from *Standardizing Recipes for Institutional Use*, © 1967, American Dietetic Association.

Appendix L

HACCP Forms

POTENTIALLY HAZARDOUS FOODS

Foods or products containing these foods are considered potentially hazardous. They are especially vulnerable to microorganisms that are the major cause of foodborne illness:

- Meats (beef, pork, lamb, veal, and other red meat)
- Poultry (chicken, turkey, duck, goose, squab, Rock Cornish hen, pheasant)
- Shellfish (oysters, scallops, mussels, clams, frog legs)
- Edible crustacea (such as crabs, crayfish, shrimp, lobster)
- Milk and milk products (such as cheese, yogurt, ice cream)
- Eggs and egg products (shell eggs, liquid pasteurized eggs)
- Cooked vegetable products (such as potato salad)
- Tofu or other soy-protein foods (such as textured soy protein used as hamburger supplement)
- Plant foods that have been heat-treated (such as beans, rice, and pasta)
- Raw seed sprouts (such as alfalfa, beans, and others)
- Sliced melons (all varieties)
- Fresh garlic in oil

Source: Reprinted from Food and Safety Assurance Program: Development of Hazard Analysis Critical Control Points; Proposed Rule. 21 CFR, Ch. 1, 1994. Food and Drug Administration.

HACCP REFRIGERATOR/FREEZER TEMPERATURE LOG

For Month of __________, 19______

Type of Equipment ____ Location_____________________

- Record temperature two different times during a 24-hour period.
- Record unit temperature as indicated by thermometer on outside of door.
- Compare recorded temperature with HACCP standards: refrigerator 37°F (2.8°C) or lower; freezer 0°F (–17.7°C) or lower.
- Complete Corrective Action column if temperatures are not in proper range.

	Date	Time	Unit Temperature	Time	Unit Temperature	Corrective Action
1						
2						
3						
4						
5						
6						
7						
8						
9						
10						
11						
12						
13						
14						
15						
16						
17						
18						
19						
20						
21						
22						
23						
24						
25						
26						
27						
28						
29						
30						
31						

HACCP TEMPERATURE FOR COOKING AND SERVING POTENTIALLY HAZARDOUS FOODS

Date:_____________

Product	Time End of Prep	Temperature	Time Holding	Temperature	Time Serving	Temperature	Corrective Action

Critical Control Points

1. Raw food cooked to minimal internal temperature:
   Poultry, stuffed meats, stuffed poultry, wild game animals, stuffed pasta, and stuffed fish, 165°F (74°C); pork, ground beef, and ground pork, 155°F (68°C); fish and eggs, 145°F (63°C); beef, veal, lamb, and other red meats, 145°F (63°C).
2. During holding period food must be at minimal temperature of 140°F (60°C).
3. During service food must remain at a minimal temperature of 140°F (60°C).
4. Record corrective action if temperature is lower than minimum for HACCP.

HACCP TEMPERATURE FOR COOLING POTENTIALLY HAZARDOUS FOODS

Date:_____________

Product	Quantity	Cooling Procedure			Corrective Action
		Start Time	Temp after two hours	Temp after six hours	

Critical Control Points

1. Leftover food is cooled to 70°F (21°C) within two hours and from 70°F (21°C) to 40°F (4°C) within four hours for a total of six hours to reach standard.
2. Reheat leftover food to 165°F (74°C) within two hours.
3. Serve at temperature not less than internal temperature of 140°F (60°C).
4. Record corrective action if standards are not met.

HACCP FOR REUSE OF LEFTOVER FOODS

Date:_____________

Product	Meal Product Reused	Reheating Procedure			Corrective Action
		Start Time	Final Time	Internal Temp	

Critical Control Points

1. Reheat leftover food to 165°F (74°C) within two hours.
2. Reheated products that remain below 165°F (74°C) after two hours of initial reheating must be discarded.
3. Record corrective action, if standards are not met.

APPENDIX M

Purchase Units for Commonly Used Foods

MEATS

Meat as Purchased; Unit of Purchase, lb	Yield, Cooked: As Served (%)	Yield, Cooked: Lean Only (%)	Description of Portion as Served	Size of Portion: As Served (oz)	Size of Portion: Lean Only (oz)	Portions per Purchase Unit (no.)	Approximate Purchase Units for 25 Portions (no.)	Approximate Purchase Units for 100 Portions (no.)
Beef, fresh or frozen								
Brisket:								
corned, bone out	60	41	Simmered	4	2.8	2.40	10½	41¾
				3	2.1	3.20	8	31¼
fresh:								
bone in	52	36	Simmered, bone out	4	2.8	2.08	12¼	48¼
				3	2.1	2.77	9¼	36¼
bone out	67	46	Simmered	4	2.8	2.68	9½	37½
				3	2.1	3.57	7¼	28¼
Ground beef:								
lean	75	75	Broiled	3	3.0	4.00	6¼	25
				2	2.0	6.00	4¼	16¾
regular	72	72	Pan-fried	3	3.0	3.84	6¾	26¼
				2	2.0	5.76	4½	17½
Heart	39	39		2	2.0	3.12	8¼	32¼
Kidney	39	39		2	2.0	3.12	8¼	32¼
Liver	69	69	Braised	3	3.0	3.68	7	27¼
				2	2.0	5.52	4¾	18¼
Oxtails	29	29		—*	—*	—*	—*	—*
Roasts:								
chuck:								
bone in	52	42	Roasted, moist heat, bone out	4	3.2	2.08	12¼	48¼
				3	2.4	2.77	9¼	36¼
bone out	67	54	Roasted, moist heat	4	3.2	2.68	9½	37½
				3	2.4	3.57	7¼	28¼
7-rib (shortribs removed):								
bone in	65	42	Roasted, dry heat, bone out	4	2.6	2.60	9¾	38½
				3	1.9	3.47	7¼	29

Source: Reprinted from *Food Purchasing Guide for Group Feeding*, No. 284, U.S. Department of Agriculture, 1976.

Meat as Purchased; Unit of Purchase, lb	Yield, Cooked: As Served (%)	Yield, Cooked: Lean Only (%)	Description of Portion as Served	Size of Portion: As Served (oz)	Size of Portion: Lean Only (oz)	Portions per Purchase Unit (no.)	Approximate Purchase Units for 25 Portions (no.)	Approximate Purchase Units for 100 Portions (no.)
bone out	73	47	Roasted, dry heat	4	2.6	2.92	8¾	34¼
				3	1.9	3.89	6½	25¾
round:								
bone in	69	56	Roasted, dry heat,	4	3.3	2.76	9¼	36¼
			medium, bone out	3	2.5	3.68	7	27¼
bone out	73	60	Roasted, dry heat,	4	3.3	2.92	8¾	34¼
			medium	3	2.5	3.89	6½	25¼
rump:								
bone in	58	43	Roasted, dry heat,	4	3.0	2.32	11	43¼
			bone out	3	2.2	3.09	8¼	32½
bone out	73	55	Roasted, dry heat	4	3.0	2.92	8¾	34¼
				3	2.2	3.89	6½	25¾
shortribs	67	32	Braised, bone in	6	2.9	1.79	14	56
				4	1.9	2.68	9½	37½
Steaks:								
club:								
bone in	73	33	Broiled, bone in	6	2.7	1.95	13	51½
				4	1.8	2.92	8¾	34¼
bone out	73	42	Broiled	4	2.3	2.92	8¾	34¼
				3	1.7	3.89	6½	25¾
flank	67	67	Braised	3	3.0	3.57	7¼	28¼
				2	2.0	5.36	4¾	18¾
hip:								
bone in	73	32	Broiled, bone in	6	2.6	1.95	13	51½
				4	1.8	2.92	8¾	34¼
bone out	73	40	Broiled	4	2.2	2.92	8¾	34¼
				3	1.6	3.89	6½	25¾
minute, cubed	75	75	Pan-fried	3	3.0	4.00	6¼	25
				2	2.0	6.00	4¼	16¾
porterhouse:								
bone in	73	36	Broiled, bone in	8	4.0	1.46	17¼	68½
				6	3.0	1.95	13	51½
				4	2.0	2.92	8¾	34¼
bone out	73	42	Broiled	4	2.3	2.92	8¾	34½
				3	1.7	3.89	6½	25¾
round:								
bone in	73	56	Broiled, bone in	4	3.1	2.92	8¾	34¼
				3	2.3	3.89	6½	25¾
bone out	73	60	Broiled	4	3.3	2.92	8¾	34½
				3	2.5	3.89	6½	25¾
sirloin (wedge and round):								
bone in	73	44	Broiled, bone in	6	3.6	1.95	13	51½
				4	2.4	2.92	8¾	31¼
bone out	73	48	Broiled	4	2.6	2.92	8¾	31¼
				3	2.0	3.89	6½	25¾
T-bone:								
bone in	73	34	Broiled, bone in	8	3.8	1.46	17¼	68½
				6	2.8	1.95	13	51½
				4	1.9	2.92	8¾	34¼
bone out	73	41	Broiled	4	2.2	2.92	8¾	34¼
				3	1.7	3.89	6½	25¾
Stew meat (chuck), bone out	67	54	Cooked, moist heat	3	2.4	3.57	7¼	28¼
				2	1.6	5.36	4¾	18¾

Meat as Purchased; Unit of Purchase, lb	Yield, Cooked: As Served (%)	Yield, Cooked: Lean Only (%)	Description of Portion as Served	Size of Portion: As Served (oz)	Size of Portion: Lean Only (oz)	Portions per Purchase Unit (no.)	Approximate Purchase Units for 25 Portions (no.)	Approximate Purchase Units for 100 Portions (no.)
Tongue:								
fresh	59	59	Cooked, moist heat	3	3.0	3.15	8	31¾
				2	2.0	4.72	5½	21¼
smoked	51	51	Cooked, moist heat	3	3.0	2.72	9¼	37
				2	2.0	4.08	6¼	24¾
Beef canned								
Beef, corned	100	100	Heated	3	3.0	5.33	4¾	19
6-lb can	100	100	Heated	2	2.0	8.00	3¼	12½
				3	3.0	32.00	1	3¼
Beef, dried								
Beef, chipped	125	125	Cooked, moist heat	3	3.0	6.67	3¾	15
				2	2.0	10.00	2⅓	10
Lamb, fresh or frozen								
Chops:								
loin	76	41	Broiled, bone in	5.0	2.7	2.43	10½	41¼
rib	76	34	Broiled, bone in	5.0	2.2	2.43	10½	41¼
shoulder	70	41	Broiled, bone in	5.0	2.9	2.24	11¼	44¾
Ground lamb	68	68	Broiled patties	3.0	3.0	3.63	7	27¾
				2.0	2.0	5.44	4¾	18½
Roasts:								
leg								
bone in	54	45	Roasted, bone out	4.0	3.3	2.16	11¾	46½
				3.0	2.5	2.88	8¾	34¾
bone out	70	58	Roasted	4.0	3.3	2.80	9	35¾
				3.0	2.5	3.73	6¾	27
shoulder								
bone in	55	41	Roasted, bone out	4.0	3.0	2.20	11½	45½
				3.0	2.2	2.93	8¾	34¼
bone out	70	52	Roasted	4.0	3.0	2.80	9	35¾
				3.0	2.2	3.73	6¾	27
Stew, meat,† bone out	66	—	Simmered	3.0	—	3.52	7¼	28½
				2.0	—	5.28	4¾	19
Pork, cured (mild)								
Bacon (2–4 slices per pound)	32	—	Fried or broiled	2 Slices	—	12.00	2¼	8½
Canadian bacon	63	63	Broiled, sliced	2	2.0	5.04	5	20
				1	1.0	10.08	2½	10
Ham:								
bone in	67	54	Roasted, slices and pieces	4	2.9	2.68	9½	37½
				3	2.2	3.57	7¼	28¼
	56	44	Roasted, slices	4	2.4	2.24	11¼	44¾
				3	1.8	2.99	8½	33½
bone out	77	72	Roasted, slices and pieces	4	2.9	3.08	8¼	32½
				3	2.2	4.11	6¼	24½
	64	60	Roasted, slices	4	2.4	2.56	10	39¼
				3	1.8	3.41	7½	29½
ground	77	77	Patties	3	3.0	4.11	6¼	24½
				2	2.0	6.16	4¼	16¼
Shoulder, Boston butt:								
bone in	67	52	Roasted, bone out	4	3.1	2.68	9½	37½
				3	2.3	3.57	7¼	28¼

Meat as Purchased; Unit of Purchase, lb	Yield, Cooked		Description of Portion as Served	Size of Portion		Portions per Purchase Unit (no.)	Approximate Purchase Units for	
	As Served (%)	Lean Only (%)		As Served (oz)	Lean Only (oz)		25 Portions (no.)	100 Portions (no.)
bone out	74	58	Roasted	4	3.1	2.96	8½	34
				3	2.3	3.95	6½	25½
Shoulder, picnic:								
bone in	56	41	Roasted, bone out	4	3.9	2.24	11¼	44¾
				3	2.2	2.99	8½	33½
bone out	74	53	Roasted	4	3.9	2.96	8½	34
				3	2.2	3.95	6½	25½
Pork, fresh								
Chops:								
loin	69	42	Broiled, bone in	5	3.0	2.21	11½	45¼
				3	1.8	3.68	7	27¼
rib	70	37	Broiled, bone in	5	2.6	2.24	11¼	44¼
				3	1.6	3.73	6¾	27
Cutlet, tenderloin	75	75	Broiled	3	3.0	4.00	6¼	25
				2	2.0	6.00	4¼	16¾
Ground pork	57	57	Broiled, bone in	3	3.0	3.04	8¼	33
				2	2.0	4.56	5½	22
Liver	60	60	Pan- or oven-fried	3	3.0	3.20	8	31¼
				2	2.0	4.80	5¼	21
Roasts:								
ham:								
bone in	54	40	Roasted, bone out	4	3.0	2.16	11¾	46⅓
				3	2.2	2.88	8¾	34¾
bone out	68	50	Roasted	4	3.0	2.72	9¼	37
				3	2.2	3.63	7	27¾
loin:								
bone in	68	37	Roasted, bone in	5	2.8	2.18	11⅓	46
				4	2.2	2.72	9¼	37
	47	37	Roasted, bone out	4	3.2	1.88	13½	53¼
				3	2.4	2.51	10	40
bone out	68	54	Roasted	4	3.2	2.72	9¼	37
				3	2.4	3.63	7	27¾
Shoulder, Boston butt:								
bone in	62	49	Roasted, bone out	4	3.2	2.48	10¼	40½
				3	2.4	3.31	7¾	30¼
bone out	68	54	Roasted	4	3.2	2.72	9¼	37
				3	2.4	3.63	7	27¾
Shoulder, picnic:								
bone in	47	35	Simmered, bone out	4	3.0	1.88	13½	53¾
				3	2.2	2.51	10	40
bone out	64	47	Simmered	4	3.0	2.56	10	39¼
				3	2.2	3.41	7½	29½
Sausage:								
brown and serve	81	81	Heated	3	3.0	4.32	6	23¼
				2	2.0	6.48	4	15½
bulk or link	48	48	Oven-fried	3	3.0	2.56	10	39¼
				2	2.0	3.84	6¾	26¼
Spareribs	66	26	Braised, bone in	6	2.3‡	1.76	14¼	57
				4	1.6‡	2.64	9½	38
Pork canned								
Ham, chopped	100	100	Sliced	3	3.0	5.33	4¾	19
				2	2.0	8.00	3¼	12½

Meat as Purchased; Unit of Purchase, lb	Yield, Cooked: As Served (%)	Yield, Cooked: Lean Only (%)	Description of Portion as Served	Size of Portion: As Served (oz)	Size of Portion: Lean Only (oz)	Portions per Purchase Unit (no.)	Approximate Purchase Units for 25 Portions (no.)	Approximate Purchase Units for 100 Portions (no.)
Ham, smoked	77	75	Slices and pieces	3	2.9	4.11	6¼	24½
				2	1.9	6.16	4¼	16¼
	73	71	Slices	3	2.9	3.89	6½	25¾
				2	1.9	5.84	4½	17¼
Pork luncheon meat (with natural juices)	89	89	Unheated	3	3.0	4.75	5½	21¼
				2	2.0	7.12	3¾	14¼
Sausages								
Frankfurters:								
8/lb	98	—	2 Frankfurters	—	—	4.00	6¼	25
			1 Frankfurter	—	—	8.00	3¼	12½
10/lb	98	—	2 Frankfurters	—	—	5.00	5	20
			1 Frankfurter	—	—	10.00	2½	10
Luncheon meats (all meat varieties)	100	100	—	3	3.0	5.33	4¾	19
				2	2.0	8.00	3¼	12½
Vienna sausage (all meat) (drained weight)	100	100	About 4 sausages	2	2.0	8.00	3¼	12½
			About 2 sausages	1	1.0	16.00	1¾	6¼
Veal, fresh or frozen								
Chops:								
loin	78	47	Broiled, bone in	5	3.0	2.50	10	40
				3	1.8	4.16	6	24¼
rib	69	38	Broiled, bone in	5	2.8	2.21	11½	45¼
				3	1.6	3.68	7	27¼
shoulder	66	40	Broiled, bone in	5	3.0	2.11	12	47½
				3	1.8	3.52	7¼	28½
Cutlet, bone out	75	75	Broiled	4	3.0	3.00	8½	33½
				3	2.2	4.00	6¼	25
Ground	64	64	Oven- or pan-fried	3	3.0	3.41	7½	29½
				2	2.0	5.12	5	19¾
Heart	35	35	Braised	2	2.0	2.80	9	35¾
Liver, calf	58	58	Fried or braised	3	3.0	3.09	8¼	32½
				2	2.0	4.64	5½	21¾
Roasts:								
chuck (shoulder):								
bone in	46	40	Braised, bone out	4	3.4	1.84	13¾	54½
				3	2.6	2.45	10¼	41
bone out	66	56	Braised	4	3.4	2.64	9½	38
				3	2.6	3.52	7¼	28½
leg:								
bone in	44	36	Roasted, bone out	4	3.3	1.76	14¼	57
				3	2.5	2.35	10¾	42¼
bone out	66	54	Roasted	4	3.3	2.64	9½	38
				3	2.5	3.20	7¼	28½
plate (breast):								
bone in	45	33	Stewed, bone out	4	2.9	1.80	14	55¾
				3	2.2	2.40	10½	41¾
bone out	66	48	Stewed	4	2.9	2.64	9½	38
				3	2.2	3.52	7¼	28½
Stew meat	66	48	Stewed	4	2.9	2.64	9½	38
				3	2.2	3.52	7¼	28½

* Size of portion and number of portions per purchase unit are determined by use.
† Breast, flank.
‡ Fat and lean.

COMBINATION FOODS CONTAINING MEAT

Meat Combinations, Canned or Frozen, as Purchased	Unit of Purchase	Weight per Unit* (lb)	Cooked Meat (%)	Size of Portion (oz)	Meat in Portion (oz)	Portions per Purchase Unit (no.)	Approximate Purchase Units for 25 Portions (no.)	Approximate Purchase Units for 100 Portions (no.)
Beans with frank-furters in sauce	Pound	1.00	20	8	1.6	2.00	12½	50
	No. 3 cylinder	3.12	20	8	1.6	6.24	4¼	16¼
	No. 10 can	6.75	20	8	1.6	13.50	2	7½
Beans with ham in sauce	Pound	1.00	12	8	1.0	2.00	12¼	50
	No. 3 cylinder	3.19	12	8	1.0	6.38	4	15¾
Beans with meat in chili sauce	Pound	1.00	8	8	0.6	2.00	12½	50
	No. 10 can	6.50	8	8	0.6	13.00	2	7¼
Beef goulash:								
canned	Pound	1.00	18	8	1.4	2.00	12½	50
	No. 3 cylinder	3.12	18	8	1.4	6.24	4¼	16¼
frozen	Carton	5.00	18	8	1.4	10.00	2½	10
	Carton	6.75	18	9	1.6	12.00	2¼	8½
	Carton	8.25	18	11	2.0	12.00	2¼	8½
Beef stew	Pound	1.00	18	8	1.4	2.00	12½	50
	No. 3 cylinder	3.12	18	8	1.4	6.24	4¼	16¼
	No. 10 can	6.62	18	8	1.4	13.24	2	7¾
Beef with barbecue sauce	Pound	1.00	50	6	3.0	2.67	9½	37½
	No. 3 cylinder	3.25	50	6	3.0	8.67	3	11¾
	No. 10 can	6.50	50	6	3.0	17.33	1½	6
Beef with gravy	Pound	1.00	50	6	3.0	2.67	9½	37½
	No. 3 cylinder	3.00	50	6	3.0	8.00	3¼	12¾
	No. 10 can	6.50	50	6	3.0	17.33	1½	6
Brunswick stew	Pound	1.00	18	8	1.4	2.00	12½	50
	No. 10 can	6.62	18	8	1.4	13.24	2	7¾
Chili con carne	Pound	1.00	28	8	2.2	2.00	12½	50
	No. 3 cylinder	3.19	28	8	2.2	6.38	4	15¾
	No. 10 can	6.75	28	8	2.2	13.50	2	7½
Chili con carne with beans	Pound	1.00	18	8	1.4	2.00	12½	50
	No. 3 cylinder	3.19	18	8	1.4	6.38	4	15¾
	No. 10 can	6.75	18	8	1.4	13.50	2	7½
Chili mac	Pound	1.00	18	8	1.4	2.00	12½	50
	No. 3 cylinder	3.19	18	8	1.4	6.38	4	15¼
	No. 10 can	6.50	18	8	1.4	13.00	2	7¾
Chop suey or chow mein vegetables with meat:								
canned	Pound	1.00	8	8	0.6	2.00	12½	50
	No. 3 cylinder	3.06	8	8	0.6	6.12	4¼	16½
frozen	Carton	5.00	8	8	0.6	10.00	2½	10
Hash, corn beef, roast beef, beef	Pound	1.00	35	7	2.4	2.29	11¼	44¼
	No. 3 cylinder	3.19	35	7	2.4	7.29	3½	14
	No. 10 can	6.50	35	7	2.4	14.86	1¾	7
Lamb stew	Pound	1.00	18	8	1.4	2.00	12½	50
	No. 3 cylinder	3.19	18	8	1.4	6.38	4	15¾
	No. 10 can	6.62	18	8	1.4	13.24	2	7¾
Macaroni and beef in tomato sauce	Pound	1.00	8	8	0.6	2.00	12½	50
	No. 10 can	6.50	8	8	0.6	13.00	2	7¾
Meatballs with gravy:								
canned	Pound	1.00 (10 count)	38	6	2.3 (4 count)	2.67	9½	37½

Meat Combinations, Canned or Frozen, as Purchased	*Unit of Purchase*	*Weight per Unit* (lb)*	*Cooked Meat (%)*	*Size of Portion (oz)*	*Meat in Portion (oz)*	*Portions per Purchase Unit (no.)*	*Approximate Purchase Units for 25 Portions (no.)*	*Approximate Purchase Units for 100 Portions (no.)*
	No. 10 can	6.50 (70 count)	38	6	2.3 (4 count)	17.33	1½	6
frozen	Carton	8.00 (160 count)	38	6	2.3 (7½ count)	21.33	1¼	5
	Carton	10.00 (100 count)	38	6	2.3 (4 count)	26.67	1	4
Pork with barbecue sauce:								
canned	Pound	1.00	50	6	3.0	2.67	9½	37½
	No. 3 cylinder	3.19	50	6	3.0	8.51	3	12
	No. 10 can	6.62	50	6	3.0	17.65	1½	5¾
in waxed tub	4-pound tub	4.00	50	6	3.0	10.67	2½	9½
(perishable)	5-pound tub	5.00	50	6	3.0	13.33	2	7¾
Pork with gravy	Pound	1.00	50	6	3.0	2.67	9½	37½
	No. 3 cylinder	3.12	50	6	3.0	8.32	3¼	12¼
	No. 10 can	6.50	50	6	3.0	17.33	1½	6
Ravioli with meat	Pound	1.00	7	8	0.6	2.00	12½	50
in sauce	No. 3 cylinder	3.19	7	8	0.6	6.38	4	15¾
		3.62	7	8	0.6	7.24	3½	14
Spaghetti with meat-	Pound	1.00	8	8	0.6	2.00	12½	50
balls and sauce	No. 3 cylinder	3.19	8	8	0.6	6.38	4	15¾
	No. 10 can	6.62	8	8	0.6	13.24	2	7¾
Tamales, frozen	Pound	1.00 (4 tamales)	18	8 (2 tamales)	1.4	2.00	12½	50
	Carton	6.00 (24 tamales)	18	8 (2 tamales)	1.4	12.00	2¼	8½
	Carton	18.00	18	8	1.4	36.00	—[†]	3
Tamales with gravy or	Pound	1.00	14	8	1.1	2.00	12½	50
sauce (packed in sizes from 1½–6 oz per tamale)	No. 10 can	6.50	14	8	1.1	13.00	2	7¾

* Net weights of containers are not standardized and may vary depending on establishment preparing the product.

† Number of purchase units needed is less than one.

POULTRY

Poultry as Purchased: Unit of Purchase, lb	Yield, as Served (%)	Description of Portion as Served	Size of Portion: As Served (oz)	Size of Portion: Edible Portion* (oz)	Portions per Purchase Unit (no.)	Approximate Purchase Units for: 25 Portions (no.)	Approximate Purchase Units for: 100 Portions (no.)
Chicken, fresh or frozen							
Live:							
roasters	30	Boned, excludes neck	3.0	3.0	1.60	15¾	62½
		and giblets	2.0	2.0	2.40	10½	41¾
stewers	34	Boned, includes neck	3.0	3.0	1.81	14	55¼
		and giblets	2.0	2.0	2.72	9¼	37
Ready-to-cook:							
broilers, ½-lb bird	70	½ bird	8.3	5.4	2.00	12½	50
fryers, 2½-lb bird	43	Boned	3.0	3.0	2.29	11	43¾
			2.0	2.0	3.44	7½	29¼
		¼ bird	5.8	3.9	4.00	6¼	25
	65	⅙ bird	3.9	2.6	6.00	4¼	16¾
		⅛ bird	2.9	1.9	8.00	3¼	12½
parts (from 2½-lb bird):							
breast half	67	With bone	3.2	2.6	3.35	7½	30
drumstick	72	With bone	2.1	1.4	5.49	4¾	18¼
thigh	68	With bone	2.2	1.6	4.95	5¼	20¼
drumstick and thigh	70	With bone	4.3	3.1	2.60	9¾	38½
wing	64	With bone	1.6	0.8	6.40	4	15¾
back	49	With bone	2.5	1.3	3.14	8	32
rib	65	With bone	2.5	1.3	4.16	6¼	24¼
giblets							
gizzards	26	—	2	2	2.08	12¼	48¼
hearts	38	—	2	2	3.04	8¼	33
livers	65	—	2	2	5.20	5	19¼
roasters	42	Boned, excludes neck	3	3	2.24	11¼	44¾
		and giblets	2	2	3.36	7½	30
stewers	47	Boned, includes neck	3	3	2.51	10	40
		and giblets	2	2	3.76	6¾	26¾
Chicken, canned							
Boned	90	Meat	3	3	4.80	5¼	21
			2	2	7.20	3½	14
Can (35 oz)	90	Meat	3	3	10.50	2½	9¾
			2	2	15.75	1¾	6½
Boned, solid pack	95	Meat	3	3	5.07	5	19¼
			2	2	7.60	3½	13¼
Boned, with broth	80	Meat	3	3	4.27	6	23½
			2	2	6.40	4	15¾
Whole	32	Meat	3	3	1.71	14¾	58½
			2	2	2.56	10	39¼
Turkey, fresh or frozen							
Live	36	Excludes neck and	3	3	1.92	13¼	52¼
		giblets	2	2	2.88	8¾	34¾
Ready-to-cook:							
roasters	47	Excludes neck and	3	3	2.51	10	40
		giblets	2	2	3.76	6¾	26¾
parts:							
breasts, whole	60	—	3	3	3.20	8	31¼
			2	2	4.80	5¼	21

Poultry as Purchased: Unit of Purchase, lb	Yield, as Served (%)	Description of Portion as Served	Size of Portion: As Served (oz)	Size of Portion: Edible Portion* (oz)	Portions per Purchase Unit (no.)	Approximate Purchase Units for 25 Portions (no.)	Approximate Purchase Units for 100 Portions (no.)
legs (thigh and	48	—	3	3	2.56	10	39¼
drumstick)			2	2	3.84	6¾	26¼
giblets							
gizzards	34	—	2	2	2.72	9¼	37
hearts	38	—	2	2	3.04	8¼	33
livers	67	—	2	2	5.36	4¾	18¾
Turkey, frozen only							
Stuffed, whole	33	Boned meat	3	3	1.76	14¼	57
			2	2	2.64	9½	38
Rolls, precooked	92	Meat	3	3	4.91	5¼	20½
			2	2	7.36	3½	13¾
Rolls, ready-to-cook	61	Meat	3	3	3.25	7¼	31
			2	2	4.88	5¼	20½
Turkey, canned							
Boned	90	Meat	3	3	4.80	5¼	21
			2	2	7.20	3½	14
can (35 oz)	90	Meat	3	3	10.50	2½	9¼
			2	2	15.75	1¾	6½
Boned, solid pack	95	Meat	3	3	5.07	5	19¾
			2	2	7.60	3½	13¼
Boned, with broth	80	Meat	3	3	4.27	6	23⅓
			2	2	6.40	4	15¾
Other poultry, fresh or frozen							
Duck, ready-to-cook	38	Boned, excludes neck	3	3	2.03	12½	49½
		and giblets	2	2	3.04	8¼	33
Goose, ready-to-cook	39	Boned, excludes neck	3	3	2.08	12¼	48¼
		and giblets	2	2	3.12	8¼	32¼

* Includes edible skin.

COMBINATION FOODS CONTAINING POULTRY

Poultry Combinations, Canned or Frozen, as Purchased, Unit of Purchase, lb; Weight per Unit, 1 lb*	*Cooked Meat (%)*	*Size of Portion (oz)*	*Meat in Portion (oz)*	*Portions per Purchase Unit (no.)*	*Approximate Purchase Units for 25 Portions (no.)*	*Approximate Purchase Units for 100 Portions (no.)*
Chicken a la king	20	8	1.60	2.00	12½	50
Chickenburgers	100	3	3.00	5.33	4¾	19
Chicken cacciatore	20	8	1.60	2.00	12½	50
Chicken chop suey	4	8	0.32	2.00	12½	50
Chicken chow mein	4	8	0.32	2.00	12½	50
Chicken fricassee	20	8	1.60	2.00	12½	50
Chicken noodles or dumplings	15	8	1.20	2.00	12½	50
Chicken potpie	14	8	1.12	2.00	12½	50
Chicken stew	12	8	0.96	2.00	12½	50
Chicken tamales	6	8	0.48	2.00	12½	50
Creamed chicken	20	8	1.60	2.00	12½	50
Creamed turkey	20	8	1.60	2.00	12½	50
Minced chicken barbecue	40	3	1.20	5.33	4¾	19
Noodles or dumplings with chicken	6	8	0.48	2.00	12½	50
Sliced chicken with gravy	35	6	2.10	2.67	9½	37½
Sliced turkey with gravy	35	6	2.10	2.67	9½	37½
Turkey a la king	20	8	1.60	2.00	12½	50
Turkey fricassee	20	8	1.60	2.00	12½	50
Turkey potpie	14	8	1.12	2.00	12½	50

* There is no standardization of can or carton sizes for canned and frozen poultry products. Information given for a pound may be related to the weight of the contents of the can or carton.

FISH AND SHELLFISH

Fish and Shellfish as Purchased	*Unit of Purchase*	*Weight per Unit (lb)*	*Yield, as Served (%)*	*Portions as Served*	*Portions per Purchase Unit (no.)*	*Approximate Purchase Units for 25 Portions (no.)*	*Approximate Purchase Units for 100 Portions (no.)*
Fish, canned							
Gefiltefish	16-oz can (9¼ oz drained)	1.00	58	3 oz drained	3.08	8¼	32½
				2 oz drained	4.62	5½	21¾
	32-oz can (20½ oz drained)	2.00	64	3 oz drained	6.83	3¾	14¾
				2 oz drained	10.25	2½	10
	51-oz can (39 oz drained)	3.19	76	3 oz drained	13.00	2	7¾
				2 oz drained	19.50	1½	5¼
Mackerel	15-oz can (12½ oz drained)	0.94	83	3 oz drained	4.17	6	24
				2 oz drained	6.25	4	16
Salmon	3¾-oz can (2¼ oz drained)	0.23	60	2¼ oz drained	1.00	25	100
	16-oz can (13 oz drained)	1.00	81	3 oz drained	4.33	6	23¼
				2 oz drained	6.50	4	15½
	64-oz can (50 oz drained)	4.00	78	3 oz drained	16.67	1½	6
				2 oz drained	25.00	1	4
Sardines:							
Maine	3¾- to 4-oz can (3¾ oz drained)	0.23–0.25	100	3 oz drained	1.25	20	80
				2 oz drained	1.87	13½	53½
	12-oz can (10¾ oz drained)	0.75	90	3 oz drained	3.58	7	28
				2 oz drained	5.38	4¾	18¾
Pacific:							
in brine	15-oz can (11½ oz drained)	0.94	77	3 oz drained	3.83	6¾	26¼
				2 oz drained	5.75	4½	17½
in mustard or tomato sauce	15-oz can	0.94	100	3 oz drained	5.00	5	20
				2 oz drained	7.50	3½	13½
Tuna	3½- to 4-oz can (3¼ oz drained)	0.22–0.25	93	3¼ oz drained	1.00	25	100
	6- to 7-oz can (6 oz drained)	0.38–0.44	100	3 oz drained	2.00	12½	50
				2 oz drained	3.00	8½	33½
	60- to 66½-oz can (58 oz drained)	3.75–4.16	97	3 oz drained	19.33	1½	5½
				2 oz drained	29.00	—*	3½
Fish, dried							
Salt cod	Pound	1.00	72	3 oz	3.84	6¾	26¼
				2 oz	5.76	4½	17½
Fish, fresh or frozen							
Fillets	Pound	1.00	64	3 oz	3.41	7½	29½
				2 oz	5.12	5	19¾
Steaks (backbone in)	Pound	1.00	58†	3 oz	3.09	8¼	32¼
				2 oz	4.64	5½	21¾
Dressed (scaled and eviscerated, usually head, tail, and fins removed)	Pound	1.00	45†	3 oz	2.40	10½	41¾
				2 oz	3.60	7	28
Drawn (entrails removed)	Pound	1.00	32†	3 oz	1.71	14¾	58½
				2 oz	2.56	10	39¼
Whole, or round (as caught)	Pound	1.00	27†	3 oz	1.44	17½	69½
				2 oz	2.16	11¾	46½

Fish and Shellfish as Purchased	*Unit of Purchase*	*Weight per Unit (lb)*	*Yield, as Served (%)*	*Portions as Served*	*Portions per Purchase Unit (no.)*	*Approximate Purchase Units for 25 Portions (no.)*	*Approximate Purchase Units for 100 Portions (no.)*
Fish, frozen							
Portions							
breaded, fried or raw:							
5½-oz	Pound	1.00	95	1 portion	3.00	8½	33½
4-oz	Pound	1.00	95	1 portion	4.00	6¼	25
3-oz	Pound	1.00	95	1 portion	5.33	4¾	18¾
2-oz	Pound	1.00	95	1 portion	8.00	3¼	12½
unbreaded:							
4-oz	Pound	1.00	69	1 portion	4.00	6¼	25
3-oz	Pound	1.00	69	1 portion	5.33	4¾	18¾
2-oz	Pound	1.00	68	1 portion	8.00	3¼	12½
Sticks, breaded, fried or raw, 1-oz	Pound	1.00	85	4 sticks	4.00	6¼	25
				3 sticks	5.33	4¾	18¾
				2 sticks	8.00	3¼	12½
Shellfish, canned							
Clam chowder	8-oz can, ready-to-serve	0.50	100	8 oz	1.00	25	100
	10½-oz can, condensed	0.66	200	8 oz	2.62	9¾	38¼
	15-oz can, condensed	0.94	200	8 oz	3.75	6¾	26¾
	50- to 51-oz can, condensed	3.12–3.19	200	8 oz	12.50	2	8
Clam juice	8-fluid-oz can	—	100	3 fl oz	2.67	9½	37½
	12-fluid-oz can	—	100	3 fl oz	4.00	6¼	25
Clams, minced	7½-oz can	0.47	100	3 oz	2.50	10	40
				2 oz	3.75	6¾	26¾
	51-oz can	3.19	100	3 oz	17.00	1½	6
				2 oz	25.50	1	4
Crabmeat	6½-oz can (5½ oz drained)	0.41	85	3 oz drained	1.83	13¾	54¾
				2 oz drained	2.75	9¼	36½
Oysters, whole	5-oz can (5 oz drained)	0.31	100	3 oz drained	1.67	15	60
				2 oz drained	2.50	10	40
Oyster stew	10½-oz can, ready-to-serve	0.66	100	8 oz	1.31	19¼	76½
Shrimp	4½-oz can (4½ oz drained)	0.28	100	3 oz drained	1.50	16¾	66¾
				2 oz drained	2.25	11¼	44½
Shellfish, fresh, live in shell							
Clams:							
hard	Dozen	—	14†	6 clams on half shell	2.00	12½	50
soft	Dozen	—	29†	12 clams in the shell	1.00	25	100
Crabs:							
blue	Pound	1.00	14	3 oz cooked	0.75	33½	133½
				2 oz cooked	1.12	22½	89½
Dungeness	Pound	1.00	24	3 oz cooked	1.28	19¾	78¼
				2 oz cooked	1.92	13¼	52¼
Oysters	Dozen	—	12†	6 oysters on half shell	2.00	12½	50

Fish and Shellfish as Purchased	*Unit of Purchase*	*Weight per Unit (lb)*	*Yield, as Served (%)*	*Portions as Served*	*Portions per Purchase Unit (no.)*	*Approximate Purchase Units for 25 Portions (no.)*	*Approximate Purchase Units for 100 Portions (no.)*
Shellfish, fresh or frozen							
Clams, shucked	Pound	1.00	48	3 oz meat	2.56	10	39¼
				2 oz meat	3.82	6¾	26
Crabs, cooked in shell:							
blue	Pound	1.00	14	3 oz meat	0.75	33½	133½
				2 oz meat	1.12	22½	89½
Dungeness	Pound	1.00	24	3 oz meat	1.28	19¾	78¼
				2 oz meat	1.92	13¼	52¼
Crabmeat	Pound	1.00	97	3 oz	5.17	5	19½
				2 oz	7.76	3¼	13
Lobster, cooked in shell	Pound	1.00	25†	1 lobster	1.00	25	100
				1½ lobster	2.00	12½	50
Lobster meat	Pound	1.00	91	3 oz	4.85	5¼	20¼
				2 oz	7.28	3½	13 ¾
Oysters, shucked	Pound	1.00	40	3 oz	2.13	11¾	47
				2 oz	3.20	8	31¼
Scallops, shucked	Pound	1.00	63	3 oz	3.36	7½	30
				2 oz	5.04	5	20
Shrimp cooked, peeled, cleaned	Pound	1.00	100	3 oz	5.33	4¾	19
				2 oz	8.00	3¼	12½
raw, in shell	Pound	1.00	50	3 oz meat	2.67	9½	37½
				2 oz meat	4.00	6¼	25
raw, peeled	Pound	1.00	62	3 oz meat	3.30	7¾	30½
				2 oz meat	4.96	5¼	20¼
Shellfish, frozen							
Clams, breaded:							
fried	Pound	1.00	85	3 oz	4.53	5¾	22½
				2 oz	6.80	3¾	14¼
raw	Pound	1.00	83	3 oz	4.43	5¾	22¾
				2 oz	6.64	4	15¼
Crabcakes, fried	Pound	1.00	95	3 oz	5.07	5	19¼
				2 oz	7.60	3½	13¾
Lobster, spiny tails							
8 oz	Pound	1.00	51†	1 tail	2.00	12½	50
6 oz	Pound	1.00	51†	1 tail	2.67	9½	37½
4 oz	Pound	1.00	51†	1 tail	4.00	6¼	25
Oysters, breaded, raw	Pound	1.00	88	3 oz	4.69	5½	21½
				2 oz	7.04	3¾	14¼
Scallops, breaded							
fried	Pound	1.00	93	3 oz	4.96	5¼	20¼
				2 oz	7.44	3½	13½
raw	Pound	1.00	81	3 oz	4.32	6	23¼
				2 oz	6.48	4	15½
Shrimp, breaded							
fried	Pound	1.00	88	3 oz	4.69	5½	21½
				2 oz	7.04	3¾	14¼
raw	Pound	1.00	85	3 oz	4.53	5¾	22¼
				2 oz	6.80	3¾	14¾

* Number of purchase units needed is less than one.
† Yield, edible portion.

EGGS

Eggs, In Shell, Frozen, and Dried, as Purchased	*Unit of Purchase*	*Weight per Unit (lb)*	*Portions as Served or Used*	*Portions per Purchase Unit (no.)*	*Approximate Purchase Units for 25 Portions (no.)*	*Approximate Purchase Units for 100 Portions (no.)*
In shell						
large	Dozen	1.50	1 egg	12.00	2¼	8½
	Case	45.00	1 egg	360.00	—*	—*
medium	Dozen	1.31	1 egg	12.00	2¼	8½
	Case	39.50	1 egg	360.00	—*	—*
small	Dozen	1.12	1 egg	12.00	2¼	8½
	Case	34.00	1 egg	360.00	—*	—*
Frozen						
whole eggs	Pound	1.00	1 egg (3 Tbsp thawed)	10.00	—†	—†
			12 eggs (2¼ cup thawed)	0.83	—†	—†
	Can	10.00	1 egg	100.00	—†	—†
	Can	30.00	1 egg	300.00	—†	—†
egg yolks	Pound	1.00	1 yolk (1⅓ Tbsp thawed)	26.00	—†	—†
			12 yolks (1 cup thawed)	2.16	—†	—†
egg whites	Pound	1.00	1 white (2 Tbsp thawed)	16.00	—†	—†
			12 whites (1½ cup thawed)	1.33	—†	—†
Dried						
whole eggs	Pound	1.00	1 large egg (½ oz or 2½ Tbsp dried + 2½ Tbsp water)	32.00	—†	—†
			12 large eggs (6 oz or 2 cups dried + 2 cups water)	2.67	—†	—†
	13-oz package	0.81	1 large egg	26.00	—†	—†
	No. 10 can	3.00	1 large egg	96.00	—†	—†
	Package	25.00	1 large egg	800.00	—†	—†
	Package	50.00	1 large egg	1600.00	—†	—†
egg yolks	Pound	1.00	1 large yolk (2 Tbsp dried + 2 tsp water)	51.00	—†	—†
			12 large yolks (1½ cup dried + 1½ cup water)	4.50	—†	—†
	Package	3.00	1 large yolk	162.00	—†	—†
egg white, spray-dried	Pound	1.00	1 large white (2 tsp dried + 2 Tbsp water)	100.00	—†	—†
			12 large whites (½ cup dried + 1½ cups water)	8.33	—†	—†
	Package	3.00	1 large white	300.00	—†	—†

* Number of purchase units needed is less than one.
† Number of purchase units needed is determined by use.

NUTS

Nuts in Shell and Peanut Butter as Purchased; Unit of Purchase, lb	*Weight per Unit (lb)*	*Yield, as Served (%)*	*Portion as Used*	*Portions per Purchase Unit (no.)*	*Approximate Purchase Units for*	
					25 Portions (no.)	*100 Portions (no.)*
Almonds						
nonpareil (softshell)	1.00	60	1 cup (0.31 lb)	1.94	—*	—*
peerless (hardshell)	1.00	35	1 cup (0.31 lb)	1.13	—*	—*
Brazil nuts	1.00	48	1 cup (0.31 lb)	1.55	—*	—*
Cashew nuts	1.00	22	1 cup (0.30 lb)	0.73	—*	—*
Chestnuts	1.00	84	8 large nuts (0.11 lb)	7.64	—*	—*
Coconut						
dried	1.00	100	1 cup (0.14 lb)	7.14	—*	—*
fresh, in shell	1.00	52	1 cup (0.21 lb)	2.48	—*	—*
Filberts	1.00	39	1 cup (0.30 lb)	1.50	—*	—*
Peanuts, roasted	1.00	68	1 cup (0.32 lb)	2.12	—*	—*
Peanut butter	1.00	100	2 Tbsp (0.07 lb)	14.29	1¾	7
no. 10 can	6.75	100	2 Tbsp (0.07 lb)	96.43	—†	1¼
Pecans	1.00	52	1 cup halves (0.24 lb)	2.17	—*	—*
Walnuts						
black	1.00	22	1 cup (0.28 lb)	0.79	—*	—*
English	1.00	45	1 cup (0.22 lb)	2.05	—*	—*

* Number of purchase units needed is determined by use.
† Number of purchase units needed is less than one.

DAIRY PRODUCTS

Dairy Products as Purchased	Unit of Purchase	Weight per Unit (lb)	Yield, as Served (%)	Portions as Served or Used	Portions per Purchase Unit (no.)	Approximate Purchase Units for 25 Portions (no.)	Approximate Purchase Units for 100 Portions (no.)
Cheese:							
cheddar	Pound	1.00	100	4 oz, grated, 1 cup	4.00	6¼	25
	Pound	1.00	100	2 oz	8.00	3¼	12½
	Pound	1.00	100	1 oz	16.00	1¾	6¼
	Longhorn	11–13	100	2 oz	88–104	—*	1¼
	Daisies	20–25	100	2 oz	160–200	—*	—*
	Flats	32–37	100	2 oz	256–296	—*	—*
	Cheddars	70–78	100	2 oz	560–624	—*	—*
	Block	20	100	2 oz	160.00	—*	—*
	Block	40	100	2 oz	320.00	—*	—*
cottage, small or large curd, with pineapple or chive	Pound	1.00	100	4 oz	4.00	6¼	25
				2 oz	8.00	3¼	12½
	23-oz carton	2.00	100	4 oz	8.00	3¼	12½
	Tin	30.00	100	4 oz	120.00	—*	—*
cream	8-oz package	0.50	100	1 oz	8.00	3¼	12½
	12-oz package	0.75	100	1 oz	12.00	2¼	8½
	16-oz package	1.00	100	1 oz	16.00	1¾	6¼
processed, cheese food	Pound	1.00	100	2 oz	8.00	3¼	12½
				1 oz, 1 slice	16.00	1¾	6¼
	Package	2.00	100	2 oz	16.00	1¾	6¼
	Package	5.00	100	2 oz	40.00	—*	2½
Cream:							
half-and-half	Pint	1.07	100	1½ Tbsp	21.33	1¼	4¾
	Quart	2.14	100	1½ Tbsp	42.67	—*	2½
light	Pint	1.06	100	1½ Tbsp	21.33	1½	4¾
	Quart	2.13	100	1½ Tbsp	42.67	—*	2½
sour	½ pint	0.53	100	1 Tbsp	16.00	1¾	6¼
	¾ pint	0.80	100	1 Tbsp	24.00	1¼	4¼
whipping (volume doubles when whipped)	Pint	1.05	100	1¼ Tbsp	25.60	1	4
	Quart	2.10	100	1¼ Tbsp	51.20	—*	2
Ice cream:							
brick	Quart	1.25	100	1 slice (½ cup)	8.00	3¼	12½
bulk	Gallon	4.50	100	No. 12 scoop (sundae)	22–26	1	4
				No. 16 scoop	31–35	—*	3
				No. 20 scoop (a la mode)	38–42	—*	2½
				No. 24 scoop	47–51	—*	2
cups	3-oz	0.19	100	1 cup	1.00	25	100
	5-oz	0.31	100	1 cup	1.00	25	100
Sherbet	Gallon	6.00	100	No. 12 scoop	25.00	1	4
				No. 16 scoop	35.00	—*	3
				No. 20 scoop	42.00	—*	2½
				No. 24 scoop	50.00	—*	2
Milk:							
fluid†	Quart	2.15	100	1 cup	4.00	6¼	25
	Gallon	8.60	100	1 cup	16.00	1¾	6¼
	5-gal	43.00	100	1 cup	80.00	—*	1¼
condensed	14-oz can	0.88	100	1 cup	1.24	—‡	—‡
	15-oz can	0.94	100	1 cup	1.33	—‡	—‡

Dairy Products as Purchased	*Unit of Purchase*	*Weight per Unit (lb)*	*Yield, as Served (%)*	*Portions as Served or Used*	*Portions per Purchase Unit (no.)*	*Approximate Purchase Units for 25 Portions (no.)*	*Approximate Purchase Units for 100 Portions (no.)*
evaporated	14½-oz can	0.91	100	1 cup as is	1.67	—‡	—‡
		0.91	200	1 cup reconstituted	3.33	—‡	—‡
	No. 10 can	8.00	100	1 cup as is	14.00	—‡	—‡
		8.00	200 (measure)	1 cup reconstituted	28.00	—‡	—‡
dry:							
nonfat instant	Pound (about 6½ cups)	1.00	100	1 cup as is	6.50	—‡	—‡
		1.00	267 (measure)	1 cup reconstituted	17.06	—‡	—‡
regular (USDA)	Pound (about 3¼ cups)	1.00	100	1 cup as is	3.25	—‡	—‡
		1.00	533 (measure)	1 cup reconstituted	17.06	—‡	—‡
whole	Pound (about 3½ cups)	1.00	100	1 cup as is	3.50	—‡	—‡
		1.00	400 (measure)	1 cup reconstituted	14.22	—‡	—‡

* Number of purchase units needed is less than one.
† Skim milk and buttermilk weigh slightly more than whole fluid milk.
‡ Number of purchase units needed is determined by use.

VEGETABLES—FRESH

Fresh Vegetables as Purchased	Unit of Purchase	Weight per Unit* (lb)	Yield, as Served (%)	Portions as Served	Portions per Purchase Unit (no.)	Approximate Purchase Units for 25 Portions (no.)	Approximate Purchase Units for 100 Portions (no.)
Asparagus	Pound	1.00	—	4 medium spears, cooked	3.38	7½	29¾
	Pound	1.00	49	3 oz cut spears, cooked	2.61	9¾	38½
	Crate	28.00	49	3 oz cut spears, cooked	73.17	—†	1½
Beans, lima, green in pod	Pound	1.00	40	3 oz cooked	2.13	11¾	47
	Bushel	32.00	40	3 oz cooked	68.27	—†	1½
shelled	Pound	1.00	102	3 oz cooked	5.44	4¾	18½
Beans, snap,	Pound	1.00	84	3 oz cooked	4.48	5¾	22½
green or wax	Bushel	30.00	84	3 oz cooked	134.40	—†	—†
Beet greens,	Pound	1.00	44	3 oz cooked	2.35	10¾	42¾
untrimmed	Bushel	20.00	44	3 oz cooked	46.93	—†	2¼
Beets with tops	Pound	1.00	43	3 oz sliced or diced, cooked	2.29	11	43¾
without tops	Pound	1.00	76	3 oz sliced or diced, cooked	4.05	6¼	24¾
	Burlap bag	50.00	76	3 oz sliced or diced, cooked	202.67	—†	—†
Black-eyed peas, shelled	Pound	1.00	93	3 oz cooked	4.96	5¼	20¼
Broccoli	Pound	1.00	—	2 medium spears, cooked	4.57	5½	22
	Pound	1.00	62	3 oz cut spears, cooked	3.31	7¾	30¼
	Crate	40.00	62	3 oz cut spears, cooked	132.27	—†	—†
Brussels sprouts	Pound	1.00	77	3 oz cooked	4.11	6¼	24½
Cabbage	Bulk	1.00	79	2 oz coleslaw	6.32	4	16
	Bulk	1.00	75	3 oz sliced, cooked	4.00	6¼	25
	Bulk	1.00	80	3-oz wedge, cooked	4.27	6	23½
	Crate or sack	50.00	80	3-oz wedge, cooked	213.33	—†	—†
Cabbage, Chinese	Pound	1.00	88	2 oz raw	7.04	3¾	14¼
Carrots, without tops	Pound	1.00	82	2 oz shredded or grated, strips or diced, raw	6.56	4	15¼
	Pound	1.00	75	3 oz sliced or diced, cooked	4.00	6¼	25
	Bushel	50.00	75	3 oz sliced or diced, cooked	200.00	—†	—†
Cauliflower	Pound	1.00	45	2 oz sliced, raw	3.60	7	28
	Pound	1.00	44	3 oz cooked	2.35	10¾	42¾
	Crate	37.00	44	3 oz cooked	86.83	—†	1¼
	Crate, large	50.00	44	3 oz cooked	117.33	—†	—†
Celery	Pound	1.00	70	3 oz chopped, cooked	3.73	6¾	27
	Pound	1.00	75	3 oz sliced, raw	4.00	6¼	25

Fresh Vegetables as Purchased	Unit of Purchase	Weight per Unit* (lb)	Yield, as Served (%)	Portions as Served	Portions per Purchase Unit (no.)	Approximate Purchase Units for 25 Portions (no.)	Approximate Purchase Units for 100 Portions (no.)
	Pound	1.00	75	2 oz strips, raw	6.00	4¼	16¾
	Crate	60.00	75	3 oz chopped, raw	240.00	—†	—†
Celery hearts (24 pack)	Crate or box	30.00	95	2 oz strips, raw	228.00	—†	—†
Chard, untrimmed	Pound	1.00	56	3 oz	2.99	8½	33½
Collards	Pound	1.00	81	3 oz cooked	4.32	6	23¼
	Bushel	20.00	81	3 oz cooked	86.40	—†	1¼
Corn, in husks	Dozen	8.00	37	3 oz cooked kernels	15.79	1¾	6½
	Dozen	8.00	—	1 ear, cooked	12.00	2¼	8½
	5-dozen crate or bag	40.00	—	1 ear, cooked	60.00	—†	1¾
Cucumber	Pound	1.00	73	3 oz sliced, peeled, raw	3.89	6½	25¾
	Pound	1.00	95	3 oz sliced, unpeeled, raw	5.07	5	19¾
	Bushel	48.00	95	3 oz sliced, unpeeled, raw	243.20	—†	—†
Eggplant	Pound	1.00	75	4 oz cooked	3.00	8½	33½
	Bushel	33.00	75	4 oz cooked	100.00	—†	1
Endive, escarole, chicory	Pound	1.00	75	1 oz raw	12.00	2¼	8½
	Bushel	25.00	75	1 oz raw	300.00	—†	—†
Kale, untrimmed	Pound	1.00	81	3 oz cooked	4.32	6	23¼
	Bushel	18.00	81	3 oz cooked	77.76	—†	1½
Kohlrabi	Pound	1.00	50	3 oz cooked	2.67	9½	37½
Lettuce							
head	Pound	1.00	74	2 oz raw	5.92	4¼	17
iceberg	Carton	2 doz heads	—	⅙ head, raw	144.00	4¼ heads	17 heads
Romaine	Pound	1.00	64	1 oz raw	10.24	2½	10
Mushrooms	Pound	1.00	67	1 oz sliced, cooked	10.72	2½	9½
	Basket	3.00	67	3 oz sliced, cooked	10.72	2½	9½
	Basket	9.00	67	3 oz sliced, cooked	32.16	—†	3¼
Mustard greens	Pound	1.00	59	3 oz cooked	3.15	8	31¾
	Bushel	20.00	59	3 oz cooked	62.93	—†	1¾
Okra	Pound	1.00	96	3 oz cooked	5.12	5	19¾
	Bushel	30.00	96	3 oz cooked	153.60	—†	—†
Onions							
green, partly topped	Pound	1.00	60	3 oz raw	3.20	8	31¼
	Wirebound crate	50.00	60	3 oz raw	160.00	—†	—†
mature	Pound	1.00	89	1 oz chopped or grated, raw	14.24	2	7¼
	Pound	1.00	76	3 oz small whole or pieces, cooked	4.05	6¼	24¾
	Sack	50.00	76	3 oz small whole or pieces, cooked	202.67	—†	—†
Parsley	Pound	1.00	—	½ cup	16.00	—‡	—‡
	Crate	19.00	—	½ cup	304.00	—‡	—‡
Parsnips	Pound	1.00	84	3 oz cooked	4.48	5¾	22½
	Bushel	50.00	84	3 oz cooked	224.00	—†	—†

Fresh Vegetables as Purchased	*Unit of Purchase*	*Weight per Unit** *(lb)*	*Yield, as Served (%)*	*Portions as Served*	*Portions per Purchase Unit (no.)*	*Approximate Purchase Units for 25 Portions (no.)*	*Approximate Purchase Units for 100 Portions (no.)*
Peas, green							
in pod	Pound	1.00	36	3 oz cooked	1.92	13¼	52¼
	Basket	15.00	36	3 oz cooked	28.80	—†	3½
	Bushel	28.00	36	3 oz cooked	53.76	—†	2
shelled	Pound	1.00	96	3 oz cooked	5.12	5	19¾
Peppers, green	Pound	1.00	82	1 oz diced or strips, raw	13.12	2	7¼
	Bushel	25.00	82	1 oz diced or strips, raw	328.00	—†	—†
	Carton	30.00	82	1 oz diced or strips, raw	393.60	—†	—†
	Pound	1.00	75	2 oz strips, cooked	6.00	4¼	16¾
Potatoes							
to be pared by hand	Pound	1.00	—	1 medium boiled	3.00	8½	33½
	Pound	1.00	54	2 oz french fried	4.32	6	23¼
	Pound	1.00	80	3 oz cubed and diced, cooked	4.27	6	23½
	Pound	1.00	95	4 oz mashed	3.80	6¾	26½
to be pared by machine	Pound	1.00	—	1 medium, boiled	3.00	8½	33½
	Pound	1.00	52	2 oz french fried	4.16	6¼	24¼
	Pound	1.00	76	3 oz cubed and diced, cooked	4.05	6¼	24¾
	Pound	1.00	90	4 oz mashed	3.60	7	28
ready-to-cook	Pound	1.00	—	1 medium, boiled	3.00	8½	33½
	Pound	1.00	68	2 oz french fried	5.44	4¾	18½
	Pound	1.00	119	4 oz mashed	4.76	5¼	21¼
to be cooked in jacket	Pound	1.00	—	1 medium, baked in jacket	3.00	8½	33½
	Pound	1.00	—	1 medium, boiled	3.00	8½	33½
	Pound	1.00	87	3 oz cubed and diced	4.64	5½	21¾
	Pound	1.00	104	4 oz mashed	4.16	6¼	24¼
Pumpkin	Pound	1.00	63	4 oz mashed, cooked	2.52	10	39¾
Radishes							
with tops	Pound	1.00	63	1 oz sliced, raw	10.08	2½	10
	Pound	1.00	—	4 small	11.34	2½	9
without tops	Pound	1.00	90	1 oz sliced, raw	14.40	1¾	7
Rutabagas	Pound	1.00	79	3 oz cubed, cooked	4.21	6	24
	Pound	1.00	77	4 oz mashed	3.08	8¼	32½
	Bushel	56.00	77	4 oz mashed	172.48	—†	—†
Spinach							
partly trimmed	Pound	1.00	92	1 oz raw for salad	14.72	1¾	7
untrimmed	Pound	1.00	72	1 oz raw for salad	11.52	2¼	8¾
	Pound	1.00	67	3 oz cooked	3.57	7¼	28¼
	Bushel	20.00	67	3 oz cooked	71.47	—†	1½
Squash, summer	Pound	1.00	83	3 oz diced or sliced, cooked	4.43	5¾	22¾
	Bushel	35.00	83	3 oz diced or sliced, cooked	154.93	—†	—†
	Pound	1.00	83	4 oz mashed	3.32	7¾	30¼
Squash, winter							
acorn	Pound	1.00	—	½ medium, baked	2.00	12½	50

Fresh Vegetables as Purchased	Unit of Purchase	Weight per Unit* (lb)	Yield, as Served (%)	Portions as Served	Portions per Purchase Unit (no.)	Approximate Purchase Units for 25 Portions (no.)	Approximate Purchase Units for 100 Portions (no.)
hubbard	Pound	1.00	58	4 oz cubed, cooked	2.32	11	43¼
	Pound	1.00	57	4 oz mashed	2.28	11	44
Sweet potatoes	Pound	1.00	—	1 medium, cooked in jacket	2.00	12½	50
	Pound	1.00	83	3 oz sliced	4.43	5¾	22¾
	Pound	1.00	81	4 oz mashed	3.24	7¼	31
	Bushel	50.00	—	1 medium, cooked in jacket	100.00	—†	1
Tomatoes (medium)	Pound	1.00	91	2 slices	7.50	3½	13½
	Pound	1.00	—	1 wedge	12.00	2¼	8½
	Lug	32.00	—	1 wedge	384.00	—†	—†
	Bushel	53.00	—	1 wedge	636.00	—†	—†
Turnip greens, untrimmed	Pound	1.00	48	3 oz cooked	2.56	10	39¼
	Bushel	20.00	48	3 oz cooked	51.20	—†	—†
Turnips, without tops	Pound	1.00	74	3 oz cubed, cooked	3.95	6½	25½
	Pound	1.00	73	4 oz mashed	2.92	8¾	34¼
	Bushel	50.00	73	4 oz mashed	146.00	—†	—†
Watercress	Bunch	1.00	92	½ cup	27.77	—‡	—‡

* Legal weights for contents of bushels, lugs, crates, and boxes vary among states
† Number of purchase units needed is less than one
‡ Number of purchase units needed is determined by use

VEGETABLES—CANNED

Canned Vegetables as Purchased	*Unit of Purchase*	*Weight per Unit (lb)*	*Yield, as Served (%)*	*Portions as Served*	*Portions per Purchase Unit (no.)*	*Approximate Purchase Units for 25 Portions (no.)*	*Approximate Purchase Units for 100 Portions (no.)*
Asparagus							
cuts and tips	No. 300 can	0.88	61	3 oz	2.86	8¾	35
	No. 10 can	6.31	60	3 oz	20.19	1¼	5
spears	No. 300 can	0.91	—	6 medium	2.57	9¾	39
	No. 10 can	6.44	—	6 medium	18.53	1½	5½
Beans, lima,	No. 303 can	1.00	69	3 oz	3.68	7	27¼
green	No. 10 can	6.56	69	3 oz	24.14	1¼	4¼
Beans, snap,	No. 303 can	0.97	59	3 oz	3.05	8¼	33
green or wax	No. 2½ can	1.75	59	3 oz	5.51	4¾	18¼
	No. 10 can	6.31	62	3 oz	20.87	1¼	5
Beans, dry—kidney,	No. 303 can	1.00	80	6 oz	2.13	11¾	47
lima, or navy	No. 10 can	6.75	80	6 oz	14.40	1¾	6¾
Bean sprouts	No. 10 can	6.62	52	3 oz	18.37	1½	5½
Beets							
diced	No. 303 can	1.00	66	3 oz	3.52	7¼	28¼
	No. 10 can	6.50	69	3 oz	23.92	1¼	4¼
sliced	No. 303 can	1.00	61	3 oz	3.25	7¾	31
	No. 10 can	6.50	65	3 oz	22.53	1¼	4½
whole baby	No. 303 can	1.00	62	3 oz	3.31	7¾	30¼
beets	No. 10 can	6.50	66	3 oz	22.88	1¼	4½
Carrots							
diced	No. 303 can	1.00	62	3 oz	3.31	7¾	30¼
	No. 10 can	6.50	69	3 oz	23.92	1¼	4¼
sliced	No. 303 can	1.00	62	3 oz	3.31	7¾	30¼
	No. 10 can	6.50	66	3 oz	22.88	1¼	4½
Chop suey vegetables	No. 10 can	6.38	100	3 oz	34.00	—*	3
Collards	No. 303 can	0.94	72	4 oz	2.71	9¼	37
	No. 2½ can	1.69	70	4 oz	4.73	5½	21¼
	No. 10 can	6.12	61	4 oz	14.93	1¾	6¾
Corn							
cream style	No. 303 can	1.00	100	4 oz	4.00	6¼	25
	No. 10 can	6.62	100	4 oz	26.48	1	4
whole kernel	No. 303 can	1.00	66	3 oz	3.52	7¼	28½
	No. 10 can	6.62	66	3 oz	23.30	1¼	4½
Kale	No. 303 can	0.94	72	4 oz	2.71	9¼	37
	No. 2½ can	1.69	70	4 oz	4.73	5½	21¼
	No. 10 can	6.12	61	4 oz	14.93	1¼	6¾
Mushrooms	8 oz	0.78	64	3 oz	2.66	9½	37¼
	No. 10 can	0.44	66	3 oz	22.67	1¼	4½
Mustard greens	No. 303 can	0.94	72	4 oz	2.71	9¼	37
	No. 2½ can	1.69	70	4 oz	4.73	5½	21¼
	No. 10 can	0.12	61	4 oz	14.93	1¾	6¾
Okra	No. 303 can	0.97	68	3 oz	3.51	7¼	28½
	No. 10 can	6.19	61	3 oz	20.14	1¼	5
Okra and tomatoes	No. 303 can	0.94	100	3 oz	5.01	5	20
	No. 10 can	6.31	100	3 oz	33.65	—*	3

Canned Vegetables as Purchased	Unit of Purchase	Weight per Unit (lb)	Yield, as Served (%)	Portions as Served	Portions per Purchase Unit (no.)	Approximate Purchase Units for 25 Portions (no.)	Approximate Purchase Units for 100 Portions (no.)
Olives, large							
ripe							
pitted	No. 1 tall	0.47†	—	2 olives	21.33	1¼	4¾
whole	No. 1 tall	0.56†	—	2 olives	25.60	1	4
	No. 10	4.12†	—	2 olives	187.69	—*	—*
green, whole	Gallon	5.50†	—	2 olives	250.25	—*	—*
Onions, small,	No. 303 can	1.00	56	3 oz	2.99	8½	33½
whole	No. 10 can	6.31	59	3 oz	19.86	1½	5¼
Peas, green	No. 303 can	1.00	64	3 oz	3.41	7½	29½
	No. 10 can	6.56	64	3 oz	22.39	1¼	4½
Peas and carrots	No. 303 can	1.00	69	3 oz	3.68	7	27¼
	No. 10 can	6.56	69	3 oz	24.14	1¼	4¼
Pickles							
dill or sour							
sliced or cut	Quart jar	1.38†	100	1 oz	22.00	1¼	4¼
	No. 10 jar	4.50†	100	1 oz	72.00	—*	1½
	Gallon jar	5.62†	100	1 oz	90.00	—*	1¼
whole	No. 2½ jar	1.19†	100	1 oz	19.00	1½	5½
	Quart jar	1.31†	100	1 oz	21.00	1¼	5
sweet							
sliced or cut	Quart jar	1.50†	100	1 oz	24.00	1¼	4¼
	No. 10 jar	4.88†	100	1 oz	78.00	—*	1½
	Gallon jar	5.94†	100	1 oz	95.00	—*	1¼
whole	No. 2½ jar	1.28†	100	1 oz	20.50	1¼	5
	Quart jar	1.38†	100	1 oz	22.00	1¼	4¾
Pickle relish							
sour	Quart	1.61†	100	1 oz	25.75	1	4
	No. 10 jar	5.73†	100	1 oz	91.75	—*	1¼
	Gallon jar	7.16†	100	1 oz	114.50	—*	—*
sweet	Quart	1.75†	100	1 oz	28.00	1	3¼
	No. 10 jar	6.25†	100	1 oz	100.00	—*	1
	Gallon jar	7.81†	100	1 oz	125.00	—*	—*
Pimientos,	No. 2½ can	1.75	73	½ cup	4.80	—‡	—‡
chopped	No. 10 can	6.81	68	½ cup	17.39	—‡	—‡
Potatoes, small	No. 2 can	1.25	—	2–3 cups	4.00	6¼	25
whole	No. 10 can	6.38	—	2–3 cups	25.00	1	4
Pumpkin, mashed	No. 300 can	0.91	100	4 oz	3.64	7	27½
	No. 2½ can	1.81	100	4 oz	7.24	3½	14
	No. 10 can	6.62	100	4 oz	26.50	1	4
Sauerkraut	No. 303 can	1.00	82	3 oz	4.37	5¾	23
	No. 2½ can	1.69	85	3 oz	7.66	3½	13¼
	No. 10 can	6.19	81	3 oz	26.74	1	3¾
Soups							
condensed	No. 1 picnic	0.66–0.75	200	1 cup diluted	2.50	10	40
	No. 3 cylinder	3.12	200	1 cup diluted	11.50	2¼	8¾
ready-to-serve	12-fl oz can	—	100	1 cup	1.50	16¾	66¾
	25-fl oz can (No. 2½)	—	100	1 cup	3.12	8¼	32¼
Spinach	No. 303 can	0.94	72	4 oz	2.71	9¼	37
	No. 2½ can	1.69	70	4 oz	4.73	5½	21¼
	No. 10 can	6.12	61	4 oz	14.93	1¾	6¾

Canned Vegetables as Purchased	Unit of Purchase	Weight per Unit (lb)	Yield, as Served (%)	Portions as Served	Portions per Purchase Unit (no.)	Approximate Purchase Units for 25 Portions (no.)	Approximate Purchase Units for 100 Portions (no.)
Squash, summer	No. 303 can	1.00	69	4 oz	2.75	9¼	36½
	No. 10 can	6.62	69	4 oz	17.50	1½	5¼
Squash, winter	No. 300 can	0.91	100	4 oz	3.64	7	27½
	No. 2½ can	1.81	100	4 oz	7.24	3½	14
	No. 10 can	6.62	100	4 oz	26.48	1	4
Succotash	No. 303 can	1.00	65	3 oz	3.47	7¼	29
	No. 10 can	6.75	65	3 oz	23.40	1¼	4½
Sweet potatoes	No. 3 vacuum or squat	1.44	65	4 oz	3.74	6¾	26¾
	No. 2½ can, with syrup	1.81	66	4 oz	4.78	5¼	21
	No. 10 can, with syrup	6.38	71	4 oz	18.00	1½	5¾
Tomatoes	No. 303 can	1.00	100	4 oz	4.00	6¼	25
	No. 2½ can	1.75	100	4 oz	7.00	3¾	14½
	No. 10 can	6.38	100	4 oz	25.52	1	4
Tomato products							
catsup	14-oz bottle	0.88	100	1 oz	14.00	2	7¼
	No. 10 can	6.94	100	1 oz	111.00	—*	1
chili sauce	12-oz jar	0.75	100	1 Tbsp	20.27	1¼	5
	No. 10 can	6.56	100	1 Tbsp	177.30	—*	—*
juice, concentrate§	6-fl oz can	0.43	400	4 fl oz	6.00	4¼	16¾
Turnip greens	No. 303 can	0.94	72	4 oz	2.71	9¼	37
	No. 2½ can	1.69	70	4 oz	4.73	5½	21¼
	No. 10 can	6.12	61	4 oz	14.93	1¾	6¾
Vegetable juices	23-fl oz can	1.54	100	4 fl oz	5.75	4½	17½
	46-fl oz can	3.07	100	4 fl oz	11.50	2¼	8¾
	96-fl oz can	6.41	100	4 fl oz	24.00	1¼	4¼
Vegetables, mixed	No. 303 can	1.00	68	3 oz	3.63	7	27¾
	No. 10 can	6.50	68	3 oz	23.57	1¼	4¼

* Number of purchase units needed is less than one.
† Drained weight.
‡ Number or purchase units needed is determined by use.
§ See vegetable juices for canned tomato juice.

VEGETABLES—FROZEN

Frozen Vegetables as Purchased	*Unit of Purchase*	*Weight per Unit (lb)*	*Yield, as Served (%)*	*Portions as Served*	*Portions per Purchase Unit (no.)*	*Approximate Purchase Units for*	
						25 Portions (no.)	*100 Portions (no.)*
Asparagus							
spears	Pound	1.00	—	4 medium, cooked	3.38	7½	29¾
	Package	2.50	—	4 medium, cooked	8.44	3	12
cuts and tips	Pound	1.00	80	3 oz cooked	4.27	6	23½
	Package	2.50	80	3 oz cooked	10.67	2½	9½
Beans, butter (lima)	Pound	1.00	100	3 oz cooked	5.33	4¾	19
	Package	2.50	100	3 oz cooked	13.33	2	7½
	Package	3.00	100	3 oz cooked	16.00	1¾	6¼
Beans, lima, green	Pound	1.00	100	3 oz cooked	5.33	4¾	19
	Package	2.50	100	3 oz cooked	13.33	2	7½
Beans, snap,	Pound	1.00	91	3 oz cooked	4.85	5¼	20¾
green, or wax	Package	2.50	91	3 oz cooked	12.13	2¼	8¼
Blackeyed peas	Pound	1.00	111	3 oz cooked	5.92	4¼	17
	Package	2.50	111	3 oz cooked	14.80	1¾	7
	Package	3.00	111	3 oz cooked	17.76	1½	5¾
Broccoli							
spears	Pound	1.00	—	2 medium	4.57	5½	22
	Package	2.50	—	2 medium	11.43	2¼	8¾
cut or chopped	Pound	1.00	85	3 oz cooked	4.53	5¾	22¼
	Package	2.50	85	3 oz cooked	11.33	2¼	9
Brussels sprouts	Pound	1.00	96	3 oz cooked	5.12	5	19¾
	Package	2.50	96	3 oz cooked	12.80	2	8
Carrots, sliced or	Pound	1.00	96	3 oz cooked	5.12	5	19¾
diced	Package	2.50	96	3 oz cooked	12.80	2	8
Cauliflower	Pound	1.00	90	3 oz cooked	4.80	5¼	21
	Package	2.50	90	3 oz cooked	12.00	2¼	8½
Collards	Pound	1.00	89	3 oz cooked	4.75	5½	21¼
	Package	2.50	89	3 oz cooked	11.87	2¼	8½
Corn							
on cob	Pound (about three 5-in ears)	1.00	—	1 ear, cooked	3.00	8½	33½
whole kernel	Pound	1.00	97	3 oz cooked	5.17	5	19½
	Package	2.50	97	3 oz cooked	12.93	2	7¾
Kale	Pound	1.00	77	3 oz cooked	4.11	6¼	24½
	Package	2.50	77	3 oz cooked	10.27	2½	9¾
	Package	3.00	77	3 oz cooked	12.32	2¼	8¼
Mustard greens,	Pound	1.00	80	3 oz cooked	4.27	6	23½
leaf or chopped	Package	2.50	80	3 oz cooked	10.67	2½	9½
	Package	3.00	80	3 oz cooked	12.80	2	8
Okra, whole	Pound	1.00	82	3 oz cooked	4.37	5¾	23
	Package	2.50	82	3 oz cooked	10.93	2½	9¼
	Package	3.00	82	3 oz cooked	13.12	2	7¾
Peas, green	Pound	1.00	96	3 oz cooked	5.12	5	19¾
	Package	2.50	96	3 oz cooked	12.80	2	8
	Package	3.00	96	3 oz cooked	15.36	1¾	6¾
Peas and carrots	Pound	1.00	98	3 oz cooked	5.23	5	19¼
	Package	2.50	98	3 oz cooked	13.07	2	7¾

Frozen Vegetables as Purchased	*Unit of Purchase*	*Weight per Unit (lb)*	*Yield, as Served (%)*	*Portions as Served*	*Portions per Purchase Unit (no.)*	*Approximate Purchase Units for 25 Portions (no.)*	*Approximate Purchase Units for 100 Portions (no.)*
Peppers, green whole	Package	1.00	—	½ pepper, cooked	12.00	2¼	8½
	Package	2.50	—	½ pepper, cooked	30.00	—*	3½
diced or sliced	Pound	1.00	97	1 oz cooked	15.52	1¾	6½
	Package	2.50	97	1 oz cooked	38.80	—*	2¾
Potatoes french fried	Package	1.00	—	10 pieces	8.00	3¼	12½
	Package	5.00	—	10 pieces	40.00	—*	2½
small whole	Container	5.00	—	3 cooked	16.67	1½	6
Spinach	Pound	1.00	80	3 oz cooked	4.27	6	23½
	Package	2.50	80	3 oz cooked	10.67	2½	9½
	Package	3.00	80	3 oz cooked	12.80	2	8
Squash, summer,	Pound	1.00	87	3 oz cooked	4.64	5½	21¾
sliced	Package	2.50	87	3 oz cooked	11.60	2¼	8¾
	Package	3.00	87	3 oz cooked	13.92	2	7¼
Squash, winter,	Pound	1.00	92	4 oz cooked	3.68	7	27¼
mashed	Package	2.50	92	4 oz cooked	9.20	2¾	11
Sweet potatoes whole	Pound	1.00	—	1 whole, cooked	2.63	9¾	38¼
	Pound	1.00	98	4 oz cooked	3.92	6½	25¾
sliced	Package	2.50	98	4 oz cooked	9.80	2¾	10¼
	Package	3.00	98	4 oz cooked	11.76	2¼	8¾
Succotash	Pound	1.00	106	3 oz cooked	5.65	4½	17¾
	Package	2.50	106	3 oz cooked	14.13	2	7¼
Turnip greens,	Pound	1.00	80	3 oz cooked	4.27	6	23½
leaf or chopped	Package	2.50	80	3 oz cooked	10.67	2½	9½
	Package	3.00	80	3 oz cooked	12.80	2	8
Turnip greens with	Pound	1.00	89	3 oz cooked	4.75	5½	21¼
turnips	Package	3.00	89	3 oz cooked	14.24	2	7¼
Vegetables, mixed	Pound	1.00	95	3 oz cooked	5.07	5	19¾
	Package	2.50	95	3 oz cooked	12.67	2	8

* Number of purchase units needed is less than one.

VEGETABLES—DRIED

Vegetables, Dried, Regular and Low-Moisture, as Purchased	*Unit of Purchase*	*Weight per Unit (lb)*	*Yield, as Served (%)*	*Portion as Served*	*Portions per Purchase Unit (no.)*	*Approximate Purchase Units for 25 Portions (no.)*	*Approximate Purchase Units for 100 Portions (no.)*
Regular							
Beans (includes white beans, lima beans, kidney beans, black-eyed beans or peas)	Pound	1.00	232	3 oz cooked	12.37	2¼	8¼
Peas (includes any type, whole peas, split peas, or lentils)	Pound	1.00	223	3 oz cooked	11.89	2¼	8½
	Bushel	60.00	223	3 oz cooked	713.60	—*	—*
Low moisture							
Onions, sliced	Pound	1.00	417	3 oz cooked	22.24	1¼	4½
Potatoes, white flakes	Pound	1.00	521	4 oz cooked	20.84	1¼	5
	Package	2.50	521	4 oz cooked	52.10	—*	2
granules	Pound	1.00	506	4 oz cooked	20.24	1¼	5
	Package	2.50	506	4 oz cooked	50.60	—*	2
Sweet potatoes, flakes	Pound	1.00	294	4 oz cooked	11.76	2¼	8¾

* Number of purchase units needed is less than one.

FRUITS—FRESH

Fresh Fruits as Purchased	*Unit of Purchase*	*Weight per Unit* (lb)*	*Yield, as Served (%)*	*Portion as Served*	*Portions per Purchase Unit (no.)*	*Approximate Purchase Units for 25 Portions (no.)*	*Approximate Purchase Units for 100 Portions (no.)*
Apples	Pound	1.00	—	1 medium, baked or raw	3.00	8½	33½
	Bushel	40.00	—	1 medium, baked or or raw	120.00	—†	—†
	Pound	1.00	76	2 oz raw, chopped or raw	6.08	4½	16½
	Pound	1.00	87	4 oz applesauce	3.48	7¼	28¾
	Pound	1.00	63	4 oz cooked, sliced or diced	2.52	10	39¼
	Pound	1.00	—	⅙ 9-in pie (2.12 lb apples per pie)	2.83	9	35½
	Pound	1.00	—	⅛ 9-in pie	3.77	6¾	26¾
Apricots	Pound	1.00	—	2 medium	6.00	4¼	16¾
	Lug	24.00	—	2 medium	144.00	—†	—†
Avocados	Pound	1.00	75	2 oz sliced, diced, or wedges	6.00	4¼	16¾
	Lug	12.00	75	2 oz sliced, diced, or wedges	72.00	—†	1½
	Box (⅘ bushel)	36.00	75	2 oz sliced, diced, or wedges	216.00	—†	—†
Bananas	Pound	1.00	—	1 medium	3.00	8½	33½
	Box	25.00	—	1 medium	75.00	—†	1½
	Pound	1.00	68	2 oz sliced for fruit cup	5.44	4¾	18½
	Pound	1.00	68	3 oz sliced for dessert	3.63	7	27¾
	Pound	1.00	68	4 oz mashed	2.72	9¼	37
Blackberries	Quart	1.42	95	1 oz salad garnish	21.53	1¼	4¾
	Quart	1.42	95	3 oz	7.18	3½	14
	Crate (24 quarts)	34.00	95	3 oz	172.22	—†	—†
	Quart	1.42	—	⅙ 9-in pie (0.92 quart per pie)	6.54	4	15½
	Quart	1.42	—	⅛ 9-in pie	8.70	3	11½
Blueberries	Quart	1.97	92	1 oz salad garnish	28.98	—†	3½
	Quart	1.97	92	3 oz	9.66	2¾	10½
	Crate (24 quarts)	47.25	92	3 oz	231.84	—†	—†
	Quart	1.97	—	⅙ 9-in pie (0.59 quart per pie)	10.20	2½	10
	Quart	1.97	—	⅛ 9-in pie	13.51	2	7½
Cantaloupe	Pound	1.00	50	3 oz sliced or diced	2.67	9½	37½
	1 (No. 36)	2.50	—	½ medium	2.00	12½	50
	Crate (No. 36)	80.00	—	½ medium	64.00	—†	1¾
Cherries	Pound	1.00	89	3 oz pitted, raw	4.75	5½	21¼
	Lug	16.00	89	3 oz pitted, raw	75.95	—†	1½
	Pound	1.00	—	⅙ 9-in pie (1.60 lb per pie)	3.75	6¾	26¾
	Pound	1.00	—	⅛ 9-in pie	5.00	5	20

Fresh Fruits as Purchased	Unit of Purchase	Weight per Unit* (lb)	Yield, as Served (%)	Portion as Served	Portions per Purchase Unit (no.)	Approximate Purchase Units for 25 Portions (no.)	Approximate Purchase Units for 100 Portions (no.)
Cranberries	Pound	1.00	96	1 oz raw, chopped, for relish	15.36	1¾	6¾
	Pound	1.00	182	2 oz sauce, strained	14.56	1¾	7
	Pound	1.00	239	2 oz cooked, whole	19.12	1½	5¼
	Box	25.00	239	2 oz cooked, whole	478.00	—†	—†
Figs	Pound	1.00	—	3 medium	4.00	6¼	25
	Box	6.00	—	3 medium	24.00	1¼	4¼
Grapefruit	Pound	1.00	44	4 fl oz juice	1.61	15¾	62¼
	Dozen (No. 64)	15.00	44	4 fl oz juice	24.22	1¼	4¼
	Pound	1.00	47	4 oz segments	1.88	13½	53¼
	Dozen	15.00	47	4 oz segments	28.20	—†	3¾
	Dozen	15.00	—	½ medium	24.00	1¼	4¼
Grapefruit segments	½-gal jar	4.22	100	4 oz	16.88	1½	6
Grapes							
with seeds	Pound	1.00	89	4 oz, seed removed	3.56	7¼	28¼
seedless	Pound	1.00	94	4 oz	3.76	6¾	26¾
	Lug	24.00	94	4 oz	90.24	—†	1¼
Honeydew melon	Pound	1.00	60	3 oz sliced or diced	3.20	8	31¼
	1 melon	4.00	—	Wedge, ⅛ melon	8.00	3¼	12½
	1 melon	4.00	60	3 oz sliced or diced	12.80	2	8
Lemons	1 lemon (medium)	0.23	—	1 slice	8.00	3¼	12½
	1 lemon (medium)	0.23	—	1 wedge	6.00	4¼	16¾
	Pound (about 4 lemons)	1.00	43	2 fl oz juice	3.16	8	31¾
	Carton	36.00	43	2 fl oz juice	113.76	—†	—†
Limes	1 lime (medium)	0.15	—	Wedge, ¼ lime	4.00	6¼	25
	Pound	1.00	48	2 fl oz juice	3.52	7¼	28½
	Box (⅘ bushel)	40.00	48	2 fl oz juice	140.80	—†	—†
Mangoes	Pound	1.00	67	3 oz sliced or diced	3.57	7¼	28¼
	Lug	24.00	67	3 oz sliced or diced	85.76	—†	1¼
Oranges	Pound	1.00	50	4 fl oz juice	1.83	13¾	54¾
	Pound	1.00	56	4-oz sections (no membrane)	2.24	11¼	44¾
	Pound	1.00	70	4-oz sections (with membrane)	2.80	9	35¾
California	Carton	38.00	70	4-oz sections (with membrane)	106.40	—†	—†
Florida	Box	85.00	50	4 fl oz juice	155.55	—†	—†
medium	Pound	1.00	—	1 whole	2.00	12½	50
no. 176	Dozen	6.00	50	4 fl oz juice	11.01	2½	9¼
	Dozen	6.00	56	4-oz sections (no membrane)	13.44	2	7½
small no.	Pound	1.00	—	1 whole	3.00	8½	33½
250	Dozen	4.00	50	4 fl oz juice	7.34	3½	13¾
	Dozen	4.00	56	4 oz sections (no membrane)	8.96	3	11¼
Orange segments	½-gal jar	4.28	100	4 oz	17.12	1½	6
Peaches	Pound	1.00	—	1 medium	4.00	6¼	25
	Pound	1.00	76	3 oz sliced or diced	4.05	6¼	24¾

Fresh Fruits as Purchased	Unit of Purchase	Weight per Unit* (lb)	Yield, as Served (%)	Portion as Served	Portions per Purchase Unit (no.)	Approximate Purchase Units for 25 Portions (no.)	Approximate Purchase Units for 100 Portions (no.)
	Bushel	48.00	76	3 oz sliced or diced	194.56	—†	—†
	Pound	1.00	—	⅙ 9-in pie (1.88 lb per pie)	3.19	8	31½
	Pound	1.00	—	⅛ 9-in pie	4.26	6	23½
Pears	Pound	1.00	—	1 medium	3.00	8½	33½
	Pound	1.00	78	3 oz sliced or diced	4.16	6¼	24¼
	Bushel	46.00	78	3 oz or sliced or diced	191.36	—†	—†
Pineapples	Pound	1.00	52	3 oz cubed	2.77	9¼	36¼
	½ crate	35.00	52	3 oz cubed	97.07	—†	1¼
Pineapple chunks	½-gal jar	4.36	100	4 oz	17.44	1½	5¾
Plums	Pound	1.00	—	3 medium	2.67	9½	37½
	Pound	1.00	94	3 oz halves pitted	5.01	5	20
	4-basket crate	28.00	94	3 oz halves pitted	140.37	—†	—†
Raspberries	Quart	1.47	97	1 oz salad garnish	22.87	1¼	4½
	Quart	1.47	97	3 oz	7.62	3½	13¼
	Crate (24 quarts)	35.00	97	3 oz	181.07	—†	—†
	Quart	1.46	—	⅙ 9-in pie (0.68 quart per pie)	8.85	3	11½
	Quart	1.46	—	⅛ 9-in pie	11.76	2¼	8¾
Rhubarb, trimmed	Pound	1.00	103	3 oz cooked	5.49	4¾	18¼
	Pound	1.00	—	⅙ 9-in pie (1.44 lb per pie)	4.17	6	24
	Pound	1.00	—	⅛ 9-in pie	5.56	4½	18
Strawberries	Quart	1.48	87	1 oz salad garnish	20.53	1¼	5
	Quart	1.48	87	3 oz	6.84	3¾	14¾
	Crate (24 quarts)	35.00	87	3 oz	162.40	—†	—†
	Quart	1.46	—	⅙ 9-in pie (1 quart per pie)	6.00	4¼	16¾
	Quart	1.46	—	⅛ 9-in pie	8.00	3¼	12½
Tangerines	Pound	1.00	—	1 medium	4.00	6¼	25
	Box	45.00	—	1 medium	180.00	—†	—†
	Pound	1.00	74	3 oz sections	3.95	6½	25½
Watermelon	Pound	1.00	46	3 oz	2.45	10¼	41
	1 melon	18 to 30	—	¹⁄₁₆ melon	16.00	1¾	6¼

* Legal weights for contents of bushels, lugs, crates, and boxes vary among states.
† Number of purchase units needed is less than one.

FRUITS—CANNED

Canned Fruits as Purchased	Unit of Purchase	Weight per Unit (lb)	Yield, as Served (%)	Portion as Served	Portions per Purchase Unit (no.)	Approximate Purchase Units for 25 Portions (no.)	Approximate Purchase Units for 100 Portions (no.)
Apples, solid pack	No. 2 can	1.12	100	4 oz	4.48	5¾	22½
	No. 2½ can	1.62	100	4 oz	6.48	4	15½
	No. 10 can	6.00	100	4 oz	24.00	1¼	4¼
				⅙ 9-in pie	24.00	1¼	4¼
Apple juice	23-fl oz can	1.57	100	4 fl oz	5.75	4½	17½
	46-fl oz can	3.14	100	4 fl oz	11.50	2¼	8¾
	96-fl oz can	6.56	100	4 fl oz	24.00	1¼	4¼
Applesauce	No. 303 can	1.00	100	4 oz	4.00	6¼	25
	No. 2½ can	1.81	100	4 oz	7.24	3½	14
	No. 10 can	6.75	100	4 oz	27.00	1	3¾
Apricots, halves	No. 303 can	1.00	—	3–5 medium	4.00	6¼	25
	No. 2½ can	1.88	—	3–5 medium	7.00	3¾	14½
	No. 10 can	6.62	—	3–5 medium	25.00	1	4
Blackberries	No. 303 can	1.00	100	4 oz	4.00	6¼	25
	No. 10 can	6.62	100	4 oz	26.48	1	4
Blueberries	No. 300 can	0.91	199	4 oz	3.64	7	27½
	No. 10 can	6.56	199	4 oz	26.24	1	4
Boysenberries	No. 303 can	0.94	100	4 oz	3.76	6¾	26¾
	No. 10 can	6.62	100	4 oz	26.48	1	4
Cherries	No. 303 can	1.00	100	4 oz	4.00	6¼	25
red, sour, pitted	No. 10 can	6.56	100	4 oz	26.24	1	4
				⅙ 9-in pie	24.00	1¼	4¼
sweet	No. 303 can	1.00	100	4 oz	4.00	6¼	25
	No. 2½ can	1.81	100	4 oz	7.24	3½	14
	No. 10 can	6.75	100	4 oz	27.00	1	3¾
Cranberries,	No. 300 can	1.00	100	2 oz	8.00	3¼	12½
strained or whole	No. 10 can	7.31	100	2 oz	58.50	—*	1¾
Cranberry juice	1 pint	1.11	100	4 fl oz	4.00	6¼	25
	1 quart	2.23	100	4 fl oz	8.00	3¼	12½
	1 gallon	8.92	100	4 fl oz	32.00	—*	3¼
Figs	No. 303 can	1.06		3–4 figs	4.00	6¼	25
				3–4 figs	7.00	3¾	14½
	No. 2½ can	1.88		3–4 figs	25.00	1	4
	No. 10 can	7.00					
Fruit cocktail or	No. 303 can	1.06	100	4 oz	4.24	6	23¾
salad	No. 2½ can	1.88	100	4 oz	7.52	3½	13½
	No. 10 can	6.75	100	4 oz	27.00	1	3¾
Grapefruit juice	18-fl oz can	1.24	100	4 fl oz	4.50	5¾	22¼
	46-fl oz can	3.14	100	4 fl oz	11.50	2¼	8¾
	96-fl oz can	6.57	100	4 fl oz	24.00	1¼	4¼
Grapefruit sections	No. 303 can	1.00	100	4 oz	4.00	6¼	25
	No. 3 cylinder	3.12	100	4 oz	12.48	2¼	8¼
Lemon juice	32-fl oz can	2.16	100	2 fl oz	16.00	1¾	6¼
Lime juice	32-fl oz can	2.17	100	2 fl oz	16.00	1¾	6½
Orange juice	18-fl oz can	1.24	100	4 fl oz	4.50	5¾	22¼
	46-fl oz can	3.16	100	4 fl oz	11.50	2¼	8¾
	96-fl oz can	6.59	100	4 fl oz	24.00	1¼	4¼
Oranges, mandarin	No. 10 can	6.38	100	4 oz	25.50	1	4

Canned Fruits as Purchased	Unit of Purchase	Weight per Unit (lb)	Yield, as Served (%)	Portion as Served	Portions per Purchase Unit (no.)	Approximate Purchase Units for 25 Portions (no.)	Approximate Purchase Units for 100 Portions (no.)
Peaches	No. 303 can	1.00	—	2 medium	3.00	8½	33½
halves or slices	No. 2½ can	1.81	—	2 medium	7.00	3¾	14½
	No. 10 can	6.75	—	2 medium	25.00	1	4
				⅙ 9-in pie	24.00	1¼	4¼
whole, spiced	No. 10 can	6.88	—	1 each	25.00	1	4
Pears, halves	No. 303 can	1.00	—	2 medium	3.00	8½	33½
	No. 2½ can	1.81	—	2 medium	7.00	3¾	14½
	No. 10 can	6.62	—	2 medium	25.00	1	4
Pineapple	No. 2½ can	1.88	100	4 oz	7.52	3½	13½
chunks and cubes	No. 10 can	6.75	100	4 oz	27.00	1	3¾
crushed	No. 2½ can	1.88	100	4 oz	7.52	3½	13½
	No. 10 can	6.81	100	4 oz	27.24	1	3¾
sliced	No. 2½ can	1.88	—	1 large	8.00	3¼	12½
	No. 10 can	6.81	—	1 large or 2 small	25.00	1	4
Pineapple juice	18-fl oz can	1.24	100	4 fl oz	4.50	5¾	22¼
	46-fl oz can	3.17	100	4 fl oz	11.50	2¼	8¾
	96-fl oz can	6.62	100	4 fl oz	24.00	1¼	4¼
Plums	No. 2½ can	1.88	—	2–3 plums	7.00	3¾	14½
	No. 10 can	6.75	—	2–3 plums	25.00	1	4
Prunes	No. 2½ can	1.88	100	4 oz	7.52	3½	13½
	No. 10 can	6.88	100	4 oz	27.52	1	3¾
Raspberries	No. 303 can	1.00	100	4 oz	4.00	6¼	25
	No. 10 can	6.75	100	4 oz	27.00	1	3¾
Strawberries	No. 303 can	1.00	100	4 oz	4.00	6¼	25
	No. 10 can	6.75	100	4 oz	27.00	1	3¾

*Number of purchase units needed is less than one.

FRUITS—FROZEN

Frozen Fruits as Purchased	Unit of Purchase	Weight per Unit (lb)	Yield, as Served (%)	Portion as Served	Portions per Purchase Unit (no.)	Approximate Purchase Units for 25 Portions (no.)	Approximate Purchase Units for 100 Portions (no.)
Apples, sliced	Pound	1.00	106	4 oz	4.24	6	23¾
				⅙ 9-in pie (1.50 lb per pie)	4.00	6¼	25
	Package	2.50	106	4 oz	10.60	2½	9½
	Package	5.00	106	4 oz	21.20	1¼	4¾
	Can	30.00	106	4 oz	127.20	—*	—*
Apricots	Pound	1.00	95	4 oz	3.80	6¾	26½
	Can	25.00	95	4 oz	95.00	—*	1¼
	Can	30.00	95	4 oz	114.00	—*	—*
Blackberries	Pound	1.00	103	4 oz	4.12	6¼	24½
	Can	30.00	103	4 oz	123.60	—*	—*
Blueberries	Pound	1.00	108	4 oz	4.32	6	23½
	Package	2.50	108	4 oz	10.80	2½	9½
	Can	25.00	108	4 oz	108.00	—*	1
	Can	30.00	108	4 oz	129.60	—*	—*
Cherries, red, sour, pitted	Pound	1.00	100	4 oz	4.00	6¼	25
				⅙ 9-in pie (1.50 lb per pie)	4.00	6¼	25
	Can	30.00	100	4 oz	120.00	—*	—*
Grapefruit sections	Pound	1.00	100	4 oz	4.00	6¼	25
	Package	3.00	100	4 oz	12.00	2¼	8½
Grapefruit juice, concentrate	6-fl oz can	0.46	400	4 fl oz	6.00	4¼	16¾
	32-fl oz can	2.46	400	4 fl oz	32.00	—*	3¼
Grape juice, concentrate	6-fl oz can	0.48	400	4 fl oz	6.00	4¼	16¾
	32-fl oz can	2.54	400	4 fl oz	32.00	—*	3¼
Lemon juice, concentrate	4-fl oz can	0.31	500	2 fl oz	10.00	2½	10
	6-fl oz can	0.47	500	2 fl oz	15.00	1¾	6¾
Lemonade, concentrate	6-fl oz can	0.49	700	2 fl oz	21.00	1¼	5
	18-fl oz can	1.46	700	2 fl oz	63.00	—*	1¾
Melon scoops	Pound	1.00	100	3 oz	5.33	4¾	19
	Package	6.50	100	3 oz	34.67	—*	3
Orange juice, concentrate	6-fl oz can	0.46	400	4 fl oz	6.00	4¼	16¾
	12-fl oz can	0.93	400	4 fl oz	12.00	2¼	8½
	32-fl oz can	2.48	400	4 fl oz	32.00	—*	3¼
Peaches, sliced	Pound	1.00	95	4 oz	3.80	6¾	26½
				⅙ 9-in pie (1.33 lb per pie)	4.50	5¾	22¼
	Can	6.50	95	4 oz	24.70	1¼	4¼
	Can	10.00	95	4 oz	38.00	—*	2¾
	Can	30.00	95	4 oz	114.00	—*	—*
Pineapple chunks crushed	Pound	1.00	100	4 oz	4.00	6¼	25
	Can	10.00	100	4 oz	40.00	—*	2½
	Can	30.00	100	4 oz	120.00	—*	—*
Pineapple juice, concentrate	6-fl oz can	0.47	400	4 fl oz	6.00	4¼	16¾
	32-fl oz can	2.53	400	4 fl oz	32.00	—*	3¼
Raspberries	Pound	1.00	100	4 oz	4.00	6¼	25
	Can	6.50	100	4 oz	26.00	1	4
	Can	10.00	100	4 oz	40.00	—*	2½
	Can	30.00	100	4 oz	120.00	—*	—*

Frozen Fruits as Purchased	*Unit of Purchase*	*Weight per Unit (lb)*	*Yield, as Served (%)*	*Portion as Served*	*Portions per Purchase Unit (no.)*	*Approximate Purchase Units for 25 Portions (no.)*	*Approximate Purchase Units for 100 Portions (no.)*
Rhubarb	Pound	1.00	106	4 oz	4.24	6	23¾
				⅙ 9-in pie (1.50 lb per pie)	4.00	6¼	25
	Package	2.50	106	4 oz	10.60	2½	9½
	Can	10.00	106	4 oz	42.40	—*	2½
	Can	25.00	106	4 oz	106.00	—*	1
	Can	30.00	106	4 oz	127.20	—*	—*
Strawberries	Pound	1.00	100	4 oz	4.00	6¼	25
	Can	6.50	100	4 oz	26.00	1	4
	Can	10.00	100	4 oz	40.00	—*	2½
	Can	30.00	100	4 oz	120.00	—*	—*
Tangerine juice, concentrate	6-fl oz can	0.47	400	4 fl oz	6.00	4¼	16¾
	32-fl oz can	2.48	400	4 fl oz	32.00	—*	3¼

* Number of purchase units needed is less than one.

FRUITS—DRIED

Fruits, Dried, Regular and Low-Moisture, as Purchased	Unit of Purchase	Weight per Unit (lb)	Yield, as Served (%)	Portion as Served	Portions per Purchase Unit (no.)	Approximate Purchase Units for 25 Portions (no.)	Approximate Purchase Units for 100 Portions (no.)
Regular							
Apple slices	Pound	1.00	412	4 oz	16.48	1¾	6¼
				⅙ 9-in pie (½ lb per pie)	18.00	1½	5¼
	Carton	5.00	412	4 oz	82.40	—*	1¼
Apricots	11-oz package	0.69	344	4 oz	9.46	2¾	10¾
	Pound	1.00	344	4 oz	13.76	2	7½
	Carton	30.00	344	4 oz	412.80	—*	—*
Dates	12-oz package	0.75	100	3 oz	4.00	6¼	25
	Pound	1.00	100	3 oz	5.33	4¾	19
	Carton	15.00	100	3 oz	80.00	—*	1¼
Peaches	11-oz package	0.69	422	4 oz	11.60	2¼	8¾
	Pound	1.00	422	4 oz	16.88	1½	6
				⅙ 9-in pie (⅓ lb per pie)	18.00	1½	5¾
	Carton	30.00	422	4 oz	506.40	—*	—*
Prunes	Pound	1.00	253	4 oz	10.12	2½	10
	2-lb package	2.00	253	4 oz	20.24	1¼	5
	Carton	30.00	253	4 oz	303.60	—*	—*
Raisins	Pound	1.00	100	½ cup	6.00	4¼	16¾
Low moisture							
Apples	Pound	1.00	584	4 oz	23.36	1¼	4½
				⅙ 9-in pie (¼ lb per pie)	24.00	1¼	4¼
	No. 10 can	1.50	584	4 oz	35.04	—*	3
Applesauce	Pound	1.00	911	4 oz	36.44	—*	2¾
	No. 10 can	2.50	911	4 oz	91.10	—*	1¼
Apricots	Pound	1.00	505	4 oz	20.20	1¼	5
	No. 10 can	3.50	505	4 oz	70.70	—*	1½
Fruit cocktail	Pound	1.00	558	4 oz	22.32	1¼	4½
	No. 10 can	2.75	558	4 oz	61.38	—*	1¾
Peaches	Pound	1.00	534	4 oz	21.36	1¼	4¾
				⅙ 9-in pie (¼ lb per pie)	24.00	1¼	4¾
	No. 10 can	3.00	534	4 oz	64.08	—*	1¾
Prunes, whole, pitted	Pound	1.00	462	4 oz	18.48	1½	5½
	No. 10 can	3.00	462	4 oz	55.44	—*	2

* Number of purchase units needed is less than one.

FLOUR, CEREALS, AND MIXES

Flour, Cereals, and Mixes, as Purchased	*Unit of Purchase*	*Weight per Unit (lb)*	*Yield, as Served (%)*	*Portion as Served or Used*	*Portions per Purchase Unit (no.)*	*Approximate Purchase Units for*	
						25 Portions (no.)	*100 Portions (no.)*
Flour	5-lb bag	5.00	—	1 cup	20.00	—*	—*
	25-lb bag	25.00	—	1 cup	100.00	—*	—*
	100-lb sack	100.00	—	1 cup	400.00	—	—
Cereals, uncooked							
bulgur, cracked wheat (USDA)	Pound	1.00	401	¾ cup cooked	10.67	2½	9½
				1 cup uncooked	2.67	—*	—*
cornmeal	1-lb box	1.00	628	¾ cup cooked	15.33	1¾	6¾
	5-lb bag	5.00	628	¾ cup cooked	76.65	—†	1½
	10-lb bag	10.00	628	¾ cup cooked	153.30	—†	—†
	1-lb box	1.00	100	1 cup uncooked	3.00	—*	—*
corn grits	1-lb box	1.00	628	¾ cup cooked	16.43	1¾	6¼
	1-lb box	1.00	100	1 cup uncooked	2.75	—*	—*
farina	1-lb box	1.00	855	¾ cup cooked	21.92	1¼	4¾
	5-lb bag	5.00	855	¾ cup cooked	109.60	—†	1
macaroni	1-lb box	1.00	311	¾ cup cooked	12.00	2¼	8½
	20-lb box	20.00	311	¾ cup cooked	240.00	—†	—†
	1-lb box	1.00	100	1 cup uncooked	3.75	—*	—*
noodles	1-lb box	1.00	329	¾ cup cooked	10.67	2½	9½
	20-lb box	20.00	329	¾ cup cooked	213.40	—†	—†
	1-lb box	1.00	100	1 cup uncooked	7.25	—*	—*
rice	1-lb box	1.00	320	¾ cup cooked	11.27	2¼	9
	10-lb box	10.00	320	¾ cup cooked	112.70	—†	—†
	100-lb sack	100.00	320	¾ cup cooked	1,127.00	—†	—†
	1-lb box	1.00	100	1 cup uncooked	2.75	—*	—*
rolled oats	1-lb box	1.00	610	¾ cup cooked	15.33	1¾	6¾
	3-lb box	3.00	610	¾ cup cooked	46.00	—†	2¼
	50-lb sack	50.00	610	¾ cup cooked	766.50	—†	—†
	1-lb box	1.00	100	1 cup uncooked	4.50	—*	—*
rolled wheat (USDA)	1-lb box	1.00	375	¾ cup cooked	8.89	3	11¼
	3-lb box	3.00	375	¾ cup cooked	26.67	—†	3¾
spaghetti	1-lb box	1.00	359	¾ cup cooked	12.12	2¼	8¼
	20-lb box	20.00	359	¾ cup cooked	242.40	—†	—†
	1-lb box	1.00	100	1 cup uncooked	6.06	—*	—*
whole wheat	1-lb box	1.00	608	¾ cup cooked	15.20	1¾	6¾
	4½-lb box	4.50	608	¾ cup cooked	68.40	—†	1½
	50-lb sack	50.00	608	¾ cup cooked	760.00	—†	—†
Cereals, ready-to-eat							
bran flakes (25% to 40%)	Pound	1.00	100	1 oz	16.00	1¾	6¼
	14½-oz package	0.91	100	1 oz	14.50	1¾	7
	10-lb package	10.00	100	1 oz	160.00	—†	—†
bran flakes with raisins	Pound	1.00	100	1¼ oz	12.80	2	8
	14-oz package	0.88	100	1¼ oz	11.20	2¼	9
	200 individuals	15.62	100	1¼ oz	200.00	—†	—†
corn flakes	Pound	1.00	100	1 oz	16.00	1¾	6¼
	12-oz package	0.75	100	1 oz	12.00	2¼	8½
	10-lb package	10.00	100	1 oz	160.00	—†	—†
puffed rice	Pound	1.00	100	⅝ oz	25.60	1	4
	8-oz package	0.50	100	⅝ oz	12.80	2	8
	10-oz package	10.00	100	⅝ oz	256.00	—†	—†

Flour, Cereals and Mixes, as Purchased	Unit of Purchase	Weight per Unit (lb)	Yield, as Served (%)	Portion as Served or Used	Portions per Purchase Unit (no.)	Approximate Purchase Units for 25 Portions (no.)	Approximate Purchase Units for 100 Portions (no.)
puffed wheat	Pound	1.00	100	½ oz	32.00	—†	3¼
	8-oz package	0.50	100	½ oz	16.00	1¾	6¼
	10-lb package	10.00	100	½ oz	320.00	—†	—†
puffed wheat, pre-sweetened	Pound	1.00	100	⅞ oz	18.29	1½	5½
	9-oz package	0.56	100	⅞ oz	10.29	2½	9¾
	200 individuals	10.94	100	⅞ oz	200.00	—†	—†
rice flakes	Pound	1.00	100	⅞ oz	18.29	1½	5½
	9½-oz package	0.59	100	⅞ oz	10.86	2½	9¼
	10-lb package	10.00	100	⅞ oz	182.86	—†	—†
shredded wheat	Pound	1.00	100	1⅗ oz	10.00	2½	10
	12-oz package	0.75	100	1⅗ oz (2 small)	7.50	3½	13½
	200 individuals	20.00	100	1⅗ oz	200.00	—†	—†
wheat flakes	Pound	1.00	100	1 oz	16.00	1¾	6¼
	10-oz package	0.62	100	1 oz	10.00	2½	10
	10-lb package	10.00	100	1 oz	160.00	—†	—†
Mixes‡							
cake							
angel food	Pound	1.00	—	1/12 10-in cake	12.00	2¼	8½
	12-cake case	12.00	—	1/12 10-in cake	144.00	—†	—†
other	Pound	1.00	—	2 in × 3 in cut	15.20	1¾	6¾
				Cupcake	20.00	1¼	5
	5-lb box	5.00	—	2 in × 3 in cut	75.10	—†	1½
				Cupcake	100.00	—†	1
frosting	Pound	1.00	—	2 in × 2 in	38–39	—†	2¾
				Cupcake	36–37	—†	3
	5-lb box	5.00	—	2 in × 2 in	190–195	—†	—†
				Cupcake	180–185	—†	—†
Cookie							
basic sugar	Pound	1.00	—	2½-oz cookies	17–20	1½	6
	5-lb box	5.00	—	2½-oz cookies	85–100	—†	1¼
brownie	Pound	1.00	—	2 in × 2 in	20–30	1¼	5
	5-lb box	5.00	—	2 in × 2 in	100–150	—†	1
Hot bread	Pound	1.00	—	2-in biscuit	20.00	1¼	5
biscuit	5-lb box	5.00	—	2-in biscuit	100.00	—†	1
muffins	Pound	1.00	—	1½-oz muffin	14–16	2	7¼
	5-lb box	5.00	—	1½-oz muffin	70–80	—†	1½
rolls							
sweet	Pound	1.00	—	1¼-oz roll	18–19	1½	5¾
	5-lb box	5.00	—	1¼-oz roll	90–95	—†	1¼
yeast	Pound	1.00	—	1-oz roll	23–25	1¼	4½
	5-lb box	5.00	—	1-oz roll	115–120	—†	—†
Piecrust	Pound	1.00	—	9-in shell	3.00	8	33½
	5-lb box	5.00	—	9-in shell	16.00	1¾	6¼

* Number of purchase units needed is determined by use.
† Number of purchase units needed is less than one.
‡ Yields of mixes vary widely, depending on manufacturer, size of pan, and baking time and temperature. See instructions on package or box.

BAKERY FOODS

Bakery Foods as Purchased	Unit of Purchase	Weight per Unit (lb)	Portion as Served	Portions per Purchase Unit (no.)	Approximate Purchase Units for 25 Portions (no.)	Approximate Purchase Units for 100 Portions (no.)
Breads*						
raisin	1-lb loaf	1.00	1 slice	18.00	1½	5¾
	2-lb loaf	2.00	1 slice	36.00	—†	3
rye	1-lb loaf	1.00	1 slice	23.00	1¼	4½
	1½-lb loaf	1.50	1 slice	28.00	1	3¾
	2-lb loaf	2.00	1 slice	33.00	—†	3¼
white and whole wheat	1-lb loaf	1.00	⅝-in. slice	16.00	1¾	6¼
			1 cup soft cubes or crumbs	18.00	1½	5¾
			1 cup toasted cubes	13.50	2	7½
			1 cup dry crumbs	6.00	4¼	16¾
	1¼-lb loaf	1.25	⅝-in slice	19.00	1½	5½
	1½-lb loaf	1.50	⅝-in slice	24.00	1¼	4¼
	2-lb loaf	2.00	½-in slice	28.00	1	4
			⅜-in slice	36.00	—†	3
	3-lb loaf	3.00	½-in slice	44.00	—†	2½
			⅜-in slice	56.00	—†	2
Cake						
layer	8-in	—	1/12 cake	12.00	2¼	8½
	9-in	—	1/16 cake	16.00	1¾	6¼
	12-in	—	1/30 cake	30.00	—†	3½
	14-in	—	1/40 cake	40.00	—†	2½
loaf	Pound	1.00	⅛ cake	8.00	3¼	12½
sheet	8-in square	—	2 in × 2 in (small)	16.00	1¾	6¼
	9 in × 13 in	—	3 in × 3 in (regular)	12.00	2¼	8½
	12 in × 18 in	—	2 in × 2 in	54.00	—†	2
			3 in × 3 in	24.00	1¼	4¼
	16 in × 24 in	—	2 in × 2 in	96.00	—†	1¼
			3 in × 3 in	40.00	—†	2½
Cookies						
brownies	Pound	1.00	2 cookies	18.00	1½	5¾
butter	Pound	1.00	2 cookies	46.50	—†	2¼
chocolate chip	Pound	1.00	2 cookies	21.50	1¼	4¾
cream filled	Pound	1.00	2 cookies	19.50	1½	5¼
fig bars	Pound	1.00	2 cookies	15.50	1¾	6½
gingersnaps	Pound	1.00	2 cookies	30.00	—†	3½
shortbread	Pound	1.00	2 cookies	29.00	—†	3½
sugar	Pound	1.00	2 cookies	10.50	2 ½	9¾
vanilla	Pound	1.00	2 cookies	46.50	—†	2¼
Crackers						
graham	Pound	1.00	2 crackers	32.50	—†	3¼
saltines	Pound	1.00	2 crackers	65–70	—†	1¾
soda	Pound	1.00	2 crackers	30–35	—†	3½
Rolls						
frankfurter	Pound	1.00	1 roll (1⅓ oz)	12.03	2¼	8½
hamburger	Pound	1.00	1 roll (1¾ oz)	9.14	2¾	11
hard, round	Pound	1.00	1 roll (1⅝ oz)	8.74	3	11½
plain, pan	Pound	1.00	1 roll (1⅓ oz)	12.03	2¼	8½
sweet, pan	Pound	1.00	1 roll (1½ oz)	10.67	2½	9½
Pie	8-in	—	⅙ pie	6.00	4¼	16¾
	9-in	—	½ pie	7.00	3¾	14½
	10-in	—	⅛ pie	8.00	3¼	12½

* End crusts of bread were excluded in determining portions per purchase unit.

† Number of purchase units needed is less than one.

FATS AND OILS

Fats and Oils as Purchased	*Unit of Purchase*	*Weight per Unit (lb)*	*Portion as Served or Used*	*Portions per Purchase Unit (no.)*	*Approximate Purchase Units for 25 Portions (no.)*	*Approximate Purchase Units for 100 Portions (no.)*
Butter or margarine pound print	Carton	1.00	1 cup	2.00	—*	—*
			1 pat	72.00	—†	1½
¼-lb print	Carton	1.00	1 pat	72.00	—†	1¼
chips	Case	5.00	1 pat	360.00	—†	—†
Lard	Carton	1.00	1 cup	2.00	—*	—*
	Can	50.00	1 cup	100.00	—*	—*
Salad dressing (oil or mayonnaise type)	Pint	1.00	1 Tbsp	32.00	—†	3¼
	Quart	2.00	1 Tbsp	64.00	—†	1¾
	Gallon	8.00	1 Tbsp	256.00	—†	—†
Salad oil	Pint	0.97	1 cup	2.00	—*	—*
	Quart	1.94	1 cup	4.00	—*	—*
	Gallon	7.76	1 cup	16.00	—*	—*
Shortening (hydrogenated)	Can	1.00	1 cup	2.50	—*	—*
	Can	3.00	1 cup	7.50	—*	—*
	Can	50.00	1 cup	125.00	—*	—*

* Number of purchase units needed is determined by use.
† Number of purchase units needed is less than one.

SUGAR AND SWEETS

Sugar and Sweets as Purchased	*Unit of Purchase*	*Weight per Unit (lb)*	*Portion as Served or Used*	*Portions per Purchase Unit (no.)*	*Approximate Purchase Units for 25 Portions (no.)*	*Approximate Purchase Units for 100 Portions (no.)*
Sugar						
brown, dark or light	Carton	1.00	1 cup	2.00	—*	—*
		25.00	1 cup	50.00	—*	—*
cubes	Carton	1.00	2 cubes	40.00	—†	2½
	Bulk	25.00	2 cubes	1,000.00	—†	—†
granulated						
bulk	Carton	1.00	2 level or 1 rounded tsp	54.00	—†	2
			1 cup	2.25	—*	—*
	Bag	5.00	1 cup	11.25	—*	—*
	Bag	25.00	1 cup	56.25	—*	—*
	Sack	100.00	1 cup	225.00	—*	—*
individuals	Package	1.50	1 packet	100.00	—†	1
	Carton	45.00	1 packet	3,000.00	—†	—†
powdered	Carton	1.00	1 cup	3.50	—*	—*
(confectioners)	Sack	25.00	1 cup	87.50	—*	—*
Syrup						
blends	12-fl-oz bottle	1.03	2 Tbsp	12.00	2¼	8½
	Quart	2.83	2 Tbsp	32.00	—†	3¼
	No. 10 can	8.50	2 Tbsp	96.00	—†	1¼
	Gallon	11.00	2 Tbsp	128.00	—†	—†
corn	Pint	1.50	2 Tbsp	16.00	1¾	6¼
	5-lb can	5.00	2 Tbsp	53.33	—†	2
	No. 10 can	8.79	2 Tbsp	93.76	—†	1¼
			1 cup	11.72	—*	—*
maple	Pint	1.38	2 Tbsp	16.00	1¾	6¼
	Gallon	11.00	2 Tbsp	128.00	—†	—†
molasses	Pint	1.50	2 Tbsp	16.00	1¾	6¼
	Jar	2.00	2 Tbsp	21.00	1¼	5
	No. 10 can	9.31	2 Tbsp	99.00	—†	1
Jam, jelly, marmalade						
bulk	Jar	1.00	1 Tbsp	23.00	1¼	4½
	No. 10 can	8.38	1 Tbsp	192.00	—†	—†
individuals	Carton	—	1 packet	200.00	—†	—†
Other sweets						
apple butter	Jar	1.00	1 packet	11.00	2½	9¼
	No. 10 can	7.50	1 packet	81.00	—†	1¼
honey	Jar	1.00	1 packet	11.00	2½	9¼
	2-lb can	2.00	1 packet	22.00	1¼	4 ¾
	5-lb can	5.00	1 packet	54.00	— †	2
Desserts, dry						
gelatin, flavored	3-oz package	0.19	½ cup	4.00	6¼	25
	6-oz package	0.38	½ cup	8.00	3¾	12½
	Pound	1.00	½ cup	21.33	1¼	4¾
Pudding, pie filling						
chocolate	4-oz package	0.25	½ cup	4.00	6¼	25
	Pound	1.00	4 oz	20.00	1¼	5
			Fill for ⅙ 9-in pie	18.67	1½	5½
lemon chiffon	Pound	1.00	Fill for ⅙ 9-in pie	32.00	—†	3¼
vanilla	3-oz package	0.19	½ cup	4.00	6¼	25

Sugar and Sweets as Purchased	Unit of Purchase	Weight per Unit (lb)	Portion as Served or Used	Portions per Purchase Unit (no.)	Approximate Purchase Units for 25 Portions (no.)	Approximate Purchase Units for 100 Portions (no.)
	Pound	1.00	4 oz	25.60	1	4
			Fill for ⅙ 9-in pie	24.00	1¼	4¼
Pudding, instant						
chocolate	4½-oz package	0.28	½ cup	4.00	6¼	25
	Pound	1.00	½ cup	14.29	1¾	7
vanilla	3¾-oz package	0.23	½ cup	4.00	6¼	25
	Pound	1.00	½ cup	17.39	1½	5¾

* Number of purchase units needed is determined by use.

† Number of purchase units needed is less than one.

BEVERAGES

Beverages as Purchased	*Unit of Purchase*	*Weight per Unit (lb)*	*Portion as Served*	*Portions per Purchase Unit (no.)*	*Approximate Purchase Units* for 25 Portions (no.)*	*Approximate Purchase Units* for 100 Portions (no.)*
Carbonated drinks						
6-oz bottles	Case (24)	—	6 fl oz	24.00	—	—
12-oz bottles	Case (24)	—	6 fl oz	48.00	—	—
16-oz bottles	Case (24)	—	6 fl oz	64.00	—	—
Cocoa						
regular, unsweetened	Pound	1.00	1 measuring cup, prepared	50.00	½	2
instant, sweetened						
bulk	8-oz carton	0.50	1 cup	28.00	(1½ cup)	(6 cup)
	38-oz carton	2.38	1 cup	133.00	(1½ cup)	(6 cup)
individuals	Carton (50)	—	1 packet	50.00	½	2
syrup, sweetened	16-oz can	1.00	1 cup	29.00	1	3½
Coffee						
ground	Pound	1.00	1 measuring cup, prepared	37.00†	—	—
instant						
bulk	6-oz jar	0.38	1 level tsp	180.00	(½ cup + 1 tsp)	(2 cup + 4 tsp)
			1 rounded tsp	90.00	(½ cup + 1 tsp)	(2 cup + 4 tsp)
	10-oz jar	0.62	1 level tsp	300.00	(½ cup + 1 tsp)	(2 cup + 4 tsp)
individuals	Carton (72)	—	1 packet	72.00	—	—
Tea						
bulk	Pound	1.00	1 measuring cup, prepared	256.00	—	(6¼ oz)
bags	Package (48)	0.24	1 measuring cup or more	48.00	—	—
	Carton (100)	0.50	1 measuring cup or more	100.00	¼	1
instant	1½-oz jar	0.09	1 cup hot tea	96.00	(½ cup + 1 cup)	(2 cup + 4 tsp)
			1 cup iced tea	64.00	(¾ cup)	(3 cup)

* Numbers in parentheses refer to approximate measure to serve 25 and 100 portions.
† Varies depending on brand of coffee used and method of preparation.

APPENDIX N

Material Safety Data Sheet

Section I.	
Manufacturer's Name	Emergency Telephone Number
Address (Number, City, State, and Zip Code)	
Chemical Name and Synonyms	Trade Name and Synonyms
Chemical Family	Formula

Section II. Hazardous Ingredients			
Carcinogen	Material	Percent	TLV (units)

Section III. Physical Data			
Boiling Point		Specific Gravity (water = 1)	
Vapor Pressure (mm Hg)		Percent Volatile by Volume	
Vapor Density (air = 1)		Evaporation Rate	
Solubility in Water			
Appearance and Odor			

Section IV. Fire and Explosion Hazards			
Flash Point	Flammable Limits	LE	LE
Extinguishing Media			
Special Fire-Fighting Procedures			
Unusual Fire and Explosion Hazards			

Section V. Health Hazard Data
Threshold Limit Value
Effects of Overexposure
Emergency and First Aid Procedures

Section VI. Reactivity Data			
Stability	Stable		Conditions To Avoid
	Unstable		
Incompatibility (materials to avoid)			
Hazardous Decomposition Products			
Hazardous Polymerization	May Occur		Conditions To Avoid
	Will Not Occur		

Section VII. Spill or Leak Procedures
Steps To Be Taken if Material Is Released or Spilled
Waste Disposal Method

<table>
<tr><th colspan="4">Section VIII. Special Protection Information</th></tr>
<tr><td colspan="4">Respiratory Protection</td></tr>
<tr><td rowspan="2">Ventilation</td><td colspan="2">Local Exhaust</td><td>Special</td></tr>
<tr><td colspan="2">Mechanical (General)</td><td>Other</td></tr>
<tr><td colspan="2">Protective Gloves</td><td colspan="2">Eye Protection</td></tr>
<tr><td colspan="4">Other Protective Equipment</td></tr>
</table>

<table>
<tr><th>Section IX. Special Precautions</th></tr>
<tr><td>Precautions To Be Taken Handling and Storing</td></tr>
<tr><td></td></tr>
<tr><td>Other Precautions</td></tr>
<tr><td></td></tr>
</table>

Appendix O

Label Format for Containers

Product Name or Material Identity

Safe Use Category*____

W A R N I N G !

Overexposure may result in respiratory, skin, or eye irritation.

Check Appropriate Box(es):

- ☐ Do Not Use in Confined Space Without Appropriate Protective Equipment
- ☐ Flammable

Health Hazards:

- ☐ Harmful if Inhaled or Swallowed
- ☐ Harmful if Absorbed Through Skin
- ☐ Cancer-Suspect Agent (C)

____

Specific Chemicals with Additional Health Hazards—See Safe Use Instructions:

____

____

____

____

* Employees have the right and are encouraged to review the MSDS and Safe Use Instructions for additional chemical and health hazard information.

Index

A

B

C

D

L

M

N

O

Q

U

V

W

Y

Z